MEMBERS OF THE UNITED STATES SUPREME COURT 1789–1982

JOHN BLAIR
1789-1796

JAMES IREDELL
1790-1799

ALFRED MOORE
1799-1804

AMUEL CHASE
1796-1811

WILLIAM JOHNSON
1804-1834

THOMAS TODD
1807-1826

BRIEL DUVAL
1811-1835

ROBERT TRIMBLE
1826-1828

LIP P. BARBOUR
1836-1841

JOHN McLEAN
1829-1861

JOHN McKINLEY
1837-1852

ER V. DANIEL
1841-1860

JAMES M. WAYNE
1835-1867

JOHN CATRON
1837-1865

JOHN A. CAMPBELL
1853-1861

CHART CONTINUED

ON BACK ENDPAPER

DAVID DAVIS
1862-1877

UEL F. MILLER
1862-1890

NOAH H. SWAYNE
1862-1881

STEPHEN J. FIELD
1863-1897

JOSEPH P. BRADLEY
1870-1892

JOHN MARSHALL
HARLAN
1877-1911

STANLEY MATTHEWS
1881-1889

THE AMERICAN CONSTITUTION
ITS ORIGINS AND DEVELOPMENT

THE AMERICAN CONSTITUTION ITS ORIGINS AND DEVELOPMENT

by
Alfred H. Kelly, Winfred A. Harbison,
and
Herman Belz

SIXTH EDITION

W · W · NORTON & COMPANY · INC ·

NEW YORK · LONDON

SIXTH EDITION

Library of Congress Cataloging in Publication Data
Kelly, Alfred Hinsey
    The American Constitution.
    Bibliography: p.
    Includes index.
    1. United States—Constitutional history.
I. Harbison, Winfred Audif. II. Belz, Herman. III. Title.
JK31.K4 1983.   342.73′029   82–6339
ISBN 0-393-95204-5   347.30229   AACR2

W. W. Norton & Company, Inc. 500 Fifth Avenue, New York, N. Y. 10110
W. W. Norton & Company Ltd. 37 Great Russell Street, London WC1B 3NU

1 2 3 4 5 6 7 8 9 0

ISBN 0-393-95204-5

FOR KRISTIN AND AARON

Contents

＋＋＋

TRIAL OF ENEMY WAR CRIMINALS • THE CRAMER AND HAUPT TREASON CASES:
WHAT IS AN OVERT ACT? • OTHER WARTIME CIVIL LIBERTIES ISSUES:
DENATURALIZATION AND ESPIONAGE CASES • THE SIGNIFICANCE OF WORLD
WAR II FOR CONSTITUTIONAL GOVERNMENT

PRESIDENCY • THE WATERGATE AFFAIR • THE SIGNIFICANCE OF WATERGATE • THE POST-WATERGATE PRESIDENCY

Preface

——————————————— ✦ ✦ ✦ ———————————————

IN THE YEARS SINCE its original publication Alfred H. Kelly and Winfred A. Harbison's *The American Constitution* has become recognized as the standard work in the field of American constitutional history. Valuable as a reference work, textbook, and single-volume account of the American constitutional experience, it was distinguished by a judicious blend of specialized constitutional knowledge and perceptive understanding of the broad political and social forces that have shaped constitutional institutions in the United States. In recent years, however, widespread interest in and willingness to reconsider basic constitutional issues—stimulated by the constitutional crisis through which the nation passed a decade and more ago—have produced important new findings in history, law, and political science dealing with the subject of constitutional change. In significant ways these findings have altered the contour and content of American constitutional history. Accordingly, in preparing this edition of *The American Constitution* I have undertaken a thorough and comprehensive revision of both narrative and interpretation. The result is a substantially new book based on the extensive body of scholarship that in the past generation has altered our understanding of virtually every aspect of the American constitutional experience.

Written from the perspective of progressive historiography and the liberal nationalist reform tradition, Kelly and Harbison's work reflected the acceptance of and confidence in federal centralization and activist, interventionist government that achieved political and intellectual ascendancy in the New Deal era. That era has come to an end, however, and events in the 1960s and 1970s have revealed a deep-seated and continuing skepticism about whether centralized bureaucratic institutions can fulfill the ideals of liberty, equality, and democratic self-government that historically have defined American nationality. We have been forcefully reminded—by movements on both the left and the right—of the strength and persistence of decentralist, democratic-participatory, and antigovernmental values in the

American constitutional order. Without rejecting the valuable insights offered by the liberal nationalist perspective, I have perforce recognized the enduring legitimacy and influence of the alternative decentralist, individualist, laissez-faire tradition in American constitutionalism. Furthermore, I have tried to incorporate in this book an awareness, greater perhaps than was available in the scholarship of a generation ago, of the centrality in American thought of constitutionalism as a basic ideology and approach to political life, rather than, as the progressive generation of historians was wont to regard it, as an expedient method of promoting class and economic interests.

Numerous colleagues and friends have helped me in writing this book. I owe special thanks to Professors Maxwell Bloomfield of the Catholic University of America, George M. Dennison of Colorado State University, Phillip S. Paludan of the University of Kansas, Stanley I. Kutler of the University of Wisconsin, R. T. Miller of Baylor University, Michael Les Benedict of Ohio State University, and Harold M. Hyman of Rice University, all of whom offered perceptive and extremely helpful criticism at various stages of the preparation of the manuscript.

HERMAN BELZ

Introduction

————————— ✦✦✦ —————————

IN BROADEST PERSPECTIVE, American constitutional history is concerned with the interaction between law and politics in American government. Its most obvious focus is the federal Constitution of 1787, which marked the founding of the nation's principal governing institutions and after almost two hundred years continues to serve as its pre-eminent symbol and source of legitimate governmental authority. Yet American constitutional history is more than an account of the written Constitution, important as that instrument has been in the nation's political life. Constitutional history goes beyond the history of constitutional law because the actual constitution of government has consisted in practices and understandings shaped as much by political exigency and constitutional theory as by the prescriptions of the documentary text.

As in physiology the word *constitution* refers to the make-up of the human body, so in politics it describes the framework and parts of government or the overall composition of the polity. In ancient Greek political thought a constitution was the principles, institutions, laws, practices, and traditions by which a people carried on their political and governmental life. The term carries the same broad meaning today. From one standpoint it is descriptive, referring to existing governmental arrangements. In this descriptive sense it may be said that every country has a constitution. But like law itself, a constitution also has a normative content which is intended to guide and control political and governmental action—to state what ought to be rather than what is. In this sense a constitution prescribes official conduct and provides a standard of legitimacy for assessing the validity of governmental action. In the ancient and medieval world this normative function derived from the belief that the way a people traditionally organized and managed their political life, in accordance with human nature and their distinctive character, was the most reliable indication of what was reasonable and just. In the modern era, beginning with the American Revolution, nations have adopted the practice of fixing in a written constitution the basic values and procedures that express their sense of political right and legitimacy.

The purpose of a constitution, then, is not merely to create, organize, and distribute governmental power, but also to assure that governmental power is exercised legitimately. Inherent in the concept of legitimacy is the idea of imposing restraints on government, lest it degenerate into tyranny. Indeed, the very notion of defining institutions of government implies placing limits on them. Accordingly, constitutional government has usually been described as limited government. Constitutionalism, in turn, is the theory and practice of conducting politics in accordance with a constitution.

An essential component of constitutionalism is legalism, the belief that right conduct consists in following rules. This is especially so in the United States, where the Constitution is expressly declared to be "the supreme Law of the Land." Yet constitutionalism cannot be exclusively or excessively legalistic. Lest it become arid formalism, divorced from the forces of social change which it is intended to modulate and channel, constitutionalism must accommodate—without being overwhelmed by—purposive political action.

Without diminishing the importance, especially in modern society, of mobilizing governmental power for the accomplishment of positive social goals, it would be accurate to say that the major challenge to constitutionalism throughout history has been to make constitutional limitations effective against rulers to whom they have theoretically applied. In general there have been two basic approaches to this problem. One is the rule-of-law tradition, in which judges test the legitimacy of governmental action by holding it against the standard of a higher or fundamental law. The second basic technique of constitutionalism is to so structure and balance the institutions of government that power is limited as a result.

The rule-of-law tradition derives from ancient Rome and medieval England. In the writings of the Roman jurists the law of nature provided a standard of justice and equity whereby the validity of the positive laws enacted by government could be judged. Roman constitutionalism, however, was unable to evolve effective sanctions for holding government to account under natural law norms. In medieval England, by contrast, the rule of law acquired a greater degree of practical effectiveness as a restraint on royal power. Like other feudal lords, the king was bound by a web of contractual rights and obligations under the common law deriving from ownership of the land. These mutual obligations created a sphere of personal liberty and individual right protected by the courts, which placed the king under the law. On the other hand, in matters of war, diplomacy, and commerce the king had unlimited power.

The immediate origins of American constitutionalism lay in the English Civil War and the Glorious Revolution of the seventeenth century. Parliament, supported by the common law courts, significantly strength-

ened the rule of law by extending legal limitations into the sphere of government previously under the exclusive control of the royal prerogative. A
struggle for sovereignty occurred between the king and Parliament in which
the latter prevailed. The power of Parliament, however, though supreme in
relation to the crown, was not unlimited. It was considered to be subject to
the basic principles of the common law, or what was also referred to as
fundamental law. Moreover, Parliament identified itself with the people as
the source of legimate authority, and this identification imposed a further
restraint on its sovereignty. In constitutional theory, then, English government after the Glorious Revolution was subject to fundamental law and
was accountable to the people. The first essential of constitutional government was in place.

In their struggle against the crown seventeenth-century Englishmen
also employed the second basic method of constitutionalism. They attempted to devise an institutional structure to balance and correlate the
major forces in society and government. Ancient political thought, going
back to Aristotle, had taught that there were three elements in society which
had to be recognized in the structure of government: monarchy, aristocracy,
and democracy. If any one of these elements controlled the government, the
result would be despotism, oligarchy, or mobocracy. But if they were all
balanced in some way, tyranny and corruption would be prevented.

English constitutionalism in the late medieval and early modern period
adhered to this theory of mixed government. As the royal prerogative was
steadily circumscribed, king, lords, and commons shared in the tasks of
government. During the Civil War, however, Parliament claimed exclusive
sovereignty under the new theory of the separation of powers. Instead of
combining the social orders in a system of fused or mixed powers, this
theory sharply differentiated between government and society. Whereas in
mixed government king, lords, and commons were seen as jointly engaged
in one essential activity—to declare through legislation what the law was—
the separation-of-powers theory held that government consisted of two
basic functions: making law and enforcing or applying it. The new theory
further provided that the law-making power, tantamount to sovereignty,
belonged exclusively to Parliament. The king was to be confined to a strictly
administrative function. Although with the restoration of the monarchy the
forms of mixed government were revived, the essential feature of the separation-of-powers theory persisted—namely, Parliamentary control over lawmaking.

These constitutional changes of the seventeenth century, illustrating
both the rule-of-law or juridical approach to constitutionalism and the institutional balance or forms-of-government technique, occurred during the
time of the founding of the American colonies. English government itself
was to develop along the lines of the second of these two constitutional
methods, with the rise of cabinet government in the eighteenth century. In

the American colonies, however, both techniques of enforcing limitations on government took root. Out of them a distinctive American theory of constitutionalism would evolve.

As even this brief survey suggests, the legal and governmental substance of constitutional history cannot be understood apart from a broad knowledge of political and social history. In a sense constitutional history may be thought of as an extension of social history, inasmuch as constitutional problems originate in and reflect substantive conflicts in the society. Yet the relationship between a constitution and the society in which it exists is reciprocal. If social change affects the constitution, the constitution has an equally important impact on political and social events. The very structure of politics and the course that political events take depend on the shaping power of constitutional principles, rules, and understandings.

A constitution shapes political reality in a variety of ways. Constitutional principles, like political ideas in general, can become matters of belief and commitment providing an ideological orientation and focus of loyalty. Constitutions may thus motivate political action. Moreover when citizens and governing officials internalize constitutional values and rules, acting out of fidelity to law rather than political expediency, the values and rules give direction to political action. The constitution thus has a configurative effect.

The constitution has yet a further configurative influence insofar as it provides the institutional forms, rhetoric, and symbols by which politics is carried on in the United States. Groups and individuals choose courses of action that are consistent with or sanctioned by the Constitution. They do so not because they are in each instance irrevocably committed to the constitutional rule or principle at issue; on the contrary, in different circumstances they may employ a conflicting principle or rule. Rather, political actors adhere to constitutional principles and doctrines because they know that the public takes the Constitution seriously. The American people believe that it embodies fundamental values and prescribes procedures that are the touchstone of governmental legitimacy. The French observer Alexis de Tocqueville long ago noted the tendency of Americans to transform political issues into judicial controversies. This was not because of any inherent national character trait, but because of the peculiar facts of American history which made the Constitution an object of public veneration. The Constitution, as many have remarked, became America's "uncrowned king."

Although modern constitutional politics dates from the adoption of the federal Constitution in 1789, the founding of the colonies in the seventeenth century marks the proximate beginning of American constitutional history. For a century and a half the American colonists exercised broad powers of self-government within the British Empire. From diverse origins they evolved similar institutional structures, legal doctrines, and political assumptions which in effect formed a colonial constitution. The Declaration of Independence transformed the colonies into independent states, and these states created republican governments based on written constitutions of liberty. At the same time the states were loosely organized into a continental union under the Articles of Confederation, a constitutional framework intended to secure cooperation for diplomatic and military purposes which expressed a nascent sense of American nationality. Subsequently, the necessity of strengthening the Confederation and reforming the state governments led to the Constitutional Convention of 1787 and the formation of a republican government for the entire nation. The successful establishment of this new republican regime by 1801 closed the first period of American constitutional development.

Between 1800 and 1877 the central constitutional issue facing the American people concerned the nature of the Union. At the outset the federal government was intended to combine features both of a unitary state and a confederation. Sovereign in the authority it derived directly from the people as constituent power, it was nevertheless limited in the range of its powers by the existence of the states. As American culture and society became more nationally uniform in the first half of the nineteenth century, the constitutional system paradoxically became more decentralized. The westward movement had centrifugal consequences as the number of states increased. Jacksonian democracy, based on the constitutional philosophy of dual federalism, was even more important in causing a shift of power from the national government to the states. After 1840 the struggle over slavery between North and South exacerbated these decentralizing tendencies.

In order to defend slavery, southerners used the doctrine of state sovereignty to deny any degree of sovereign authority to the federal government. When this constitutional theory failed to give the slaveholding states the security they desired within the Union, they seceded and formed the Confederate States of America. The Civil War ensued, a crisis of constitutionalism and the rule of law as well as of national unity. The outcome of the war vindicated the Union government's claim to sovereignty as a legitimate nation-state without denying a legitimate, albeit reduced, sphere of states' rights. The reconstruction period ended with the authority of the federal government greatly expanded in consequence of the Thirteenth, Fourteenth, and Fifteenth Amendments, but with the states still exercising preponderant power in the regulation of civil society.

In the third phase of constitutional development, from 1877 to 1933, the social transformations wrought by industrialization and urbanization imposed severe strains on the political order. Principles of limited government and entrepreneurial liberty which in the preindustrial era had encouraged broadly democratic economic progress now contributed to disparities of wealth and power that challenged republican liberty and equality. Reformers began to demand that government not merely allocate economic resources as it had traditionally done, but also regulate the economic market with a view toward restricting the power of private corporations and redistributing social goods. Considering the powerful appeal of localism, minimal government, and laissez-faire economic theory, public policy in the late nineteenth and early twentieth centuries to a surprising extent adjusted to the requirements of the new age. Yet classical liberal constitutionalism remained dominant on the whole.

The New Deal of the 1930s marked the fourth major phase of American constitutional development. In a governmental system that was designed to give wide scope to executive leadership, Franklin D. Roosevelt went further than any previous chief executive in making the presidency constitutionally dominant. Almost irrespective of the personal inclinations of the incumbent of the office, even when political circumstances have weakened executive influence, presidential government has remained the American norm. Furthermore, as entrepreneurial capitalism evolved into the mixed economy of interest-group liberalism, blurring the distinction between public authority and private power, the New Deal inaugurated an American version of bureaucratic centralization. To be sure, elements of continuity persisted between the new constitutional order and the old. Most conspicuous was the power of the federal judiciary, which after 1937 was used to uphold the civil liberties and civil rights of liberal constituencies in the New Deal political coalition, rather than as previously to protect conservative property interests. Nevertheless, half a century after the "Roosevelt revolution," it was clear that the New Deal, by creating a sovereign central authority within the federal system, had profoundly altered the constitutional order.

THE AMERICAN
CONSTITUTION
ITS ORIGINS AND
DEVELOPMENT

ONE

The Founding of English Colonies in North America

——————————— ✦ ✦ ✦ ———————————

IN CONTRAST TO the governments of most European countries, American government began at an identifiable historical moment as an instrument for accomplishing specific and limited purposes. Its character was, therefore, in a sense artificial rather than natural and organic in the manner of governments rooted in the immemorial past. Government in the United States has, moreover, rested on a broadly popular base. Because the ruling authorities have been limited in their powers, ordinary citizens have borne a larger share of the responsibility of government than have their counterparts in European nations. These defining characteristics of American constitutionalism derived from the circumstances of English colonization in North America in the early seventeenth century.

The English colonies in the New World gave broader scope to private initiative than did the colonies of European states such as France or Spain. Nevertheless, English colonization was not the almost exclusively private enterprise sometimes described. Although the English government did not aggressively initiate and control settlement like the Spanish crown, English colonization had a distinctive public and national character. At the start of the seventeenth century the English monarchy was immeasurably stronger than it had been a hundred years earlier; the existence of a powerful centralized government was indeed a precondition of the overseas expansion of which colonization was an integral part. Yet in comparison with the monarchies of Spain and France, the English crown was weak and its financial resources limited. Accordingly, although the English government was vitally interested in competition for trade and overseas dominion, it was forced to rely on private adventurers, merchants, and members of the aristocracy to carry out English ambitions in the world. For their part, the sponsors of overseas settlement had personal reasons for undertaking colonization, but they were also conscious of extending English influence, including the religious purpose of promoting the Protestant faith against Roman Catholics.

The specific constitutional problem presented by the settlements of the early seventeenth century was the founding of government in new territory. It would be a recurrent one in American constitutional history for over two centuries. After the nation gained its independence, Americans typically sent a governor and council to organize unsettled lands. But while the Spanish and French employed this method in their seventeenth-century colonizing efforts, the English government, unable to commit the resources required by this approach, did not. Instead it used two governmental instruments that had been historically relevant to the problems posed by colonization. These were the feudal proprietary grant and the corporation charter. A third method of organizing government in unsettled territory derived from the religious principle of the covenant.

The Corporation Colonies: Virginia and Massachusetts Bay

Virginia and Massachusetts Bay were founded on the joint-stock principle, an instrument of early English commercial expansion that lay ready to hand as a means of overseas settlement at the start of the seventeenth century. We tend to regard the joint-stock company as an economic institution, for it was only through this form of associated endeavor that the capital needed to initiate English colonization could be raised. For present purposes, however, the political and governmental aspect of the joint-stock company commands our attention.

The joint-stock company was a type of corporation, and corporations in an important sense had been used in England since the fourteenth century as an instrument of government. A corporation was a body or association of persons upon whom the crown conferred rights and powers appropriate for the carrying out of specific public purposes or functions. Guilds, boroughs, ecclesiastical bodies, and educational institutions, for example, benefited from the privilege of incorporation. Through the grant of corporate status, expressed in a legal charter which imposed duties and responsibilities as well as bestowing powers, the crown could adjust relations among and within social groups and exercise greater control over the internal affairs of the realm. In this sense incorporation served the purpose of centralized royal administration. On the other hand, incorporated groups received the power to regulate their own affairs—that is, to govern themselves. Incorporation thus extended governmental powers to private groups that in consequence assumed the character of public, or quasi-public, organizations. According to the understanding of the time, the idea of a private corporation was a contradiction in terms.

The joint-stock company, the form of incorporation that was used in planting colonies in English North America, had its origins in the Middle Ages. The merchants of fifteenth-century Italy developed the business technique of pooling capital resources to expand operations and distribute risk, and English merchants no doubt borrowed from the Italian idea. The English joint-stock companies, however, also evolved directly out of the medieval guild merchant. Since the twelfth century it had been customary for the merchants of a community to organize guilds merchant for the purpose of carrying on trade. The guild often became a kind of closed corporation—that is, one to which admission was necessary if a merchant wished to trade within the area over which the guild had control. Very often it sought and obtained from the crown a charter giving legal recognition to the trade rights it claimed, a step particularly important to the guild when it had secured a monopoly over some segment of foreign trade.

Organizations of "merchant-adventurers," as this type of guild was sometimes called, were fairly common in fifteenth-century England. They were not joint-stock companies in the later sense of the term, for they seldom undertook any common group venture. The membership simply carried on individual operations under the protection of the privileges assured by membership in the guild.

In the great commercial development of the sixteenth century, the principle of the "company of merchant-adventurers," a corporate entity licensed by the crown and having certain trade privileges, was combined with the continental device of pooling the capital of investors to share both risk and profits in a common enterprise. The result was the emergence of the great English trading companies of the late sixteenth and early seventeenth centuries as the principal media of English commercial and colonial expansion.

It became the practice for various groups of traders to petition the crown for charters affording commercial favors, prescribing their form of organization, and granting the right to raise money by selling stock. A typical joint-stock charter of this time gave the company a name and a formally recognized legal position, and specified the terms of organization. The charter usually vested control in a council, the original members of which were customarily named in the document. Generally, the membership of this body varied from six to more than twenty, and the direction of the affairs of the company was in its hands. Sometimes the charter provided for a governor as the head of the company, in which case he was chosen by the council, usually from its own membership. Membership in the company was secured through stock ownership. The smaller stockholders had little to say about general policy; however, they met periodically in a general court to elect members to vacancies in the council and occasionally to express their opinion upon some major question of policy.

The typical charter also granted a number of privileges thought to be of some financial advantage. These might include a grant of land, the right to convey title to any portion of its domains, and the title to all precious metals discovered within the specified region. A monopoly of trade within the area was an almost invariable provision.

Finally, the charter sometimes conferred upon the company extensive governing powers. This was necessary either because the contemplated region to be exploited was unsettled wilderness, as in America, or because the company was to be the actual instrument of English conquest in an already civilized region, as in India. In either case the company needed authority to establish law and order within its domains, and, therefore, the charter commonly bestowed the right to set up some local governing body, to maintain defense, to coin money, to establish courts, and to enact ordinances for local government. Thus certain of the companies took on a quasi-sovereign character.

Virginia, the earliest successful English colony, was founded in 1607 by the Virginia Company of London under a grant from the crown which gave it the right to found a colony anywhere between the 34th and 41st parallels on the North American continent. The company's charter provided for a governor, who with an advisory council of thirteen was empowered to direct the general affairs of the organization. The stockholders were also instructed to assemble from time to time in a general court. Concurrently, a second group of merchants from Plymouth were authorized by the crown to form the Virginia Company of Plymouth and to settle in the area between the 38th and 45th parallels. Taking a strong interest in the overseas venture, the crown also established a Royal Council in London, separate from the company's council, with power to supervise matters that affected the government's interests. The original plan for Virginia thus provided for dual control by royal and company authority in England. Local matters within the colony would be in the hands of a governor and council appointed from London. Ordinary settlers were given no part in the government.

The Plymouth group failed in its efforts to establish a colony in Maine, and economic and political difficulties led the London Company to secure a new charter in 1609. The company now became a regular joint-stock concern, with some seven hundred permanent stockholders. The separate royal council in London was abolished, control now being vested in the company's treasurer and the London council. The crown also extended the company's lands to include all the lands from sea to sea for two hundred miles on either side of its settlement. A supplementary charter of 1612 strengthened the stockholders' control of company affairs by providing for four "great courts" or stockholders' meetings each year to dispose of matters of great importance. The 1612 charter also extended the company's boundaries three hundred leagues seaward to include Bermuda.

In 1610 the reorganized company resorted to outright military rule in Virginia. The treasurer and council revoked the authority of the local governor and council and vested absolute authority in a "lord-governor and captain-general" who was given full military, executive, and lawmaking power. By this experiment in autocracy the company hoped to end the indolence and petty wrangling which had so far crippled the colony's life.

The enterprise nonetheless did not prosper, mainly because it lacked an adequate economic base. The settlers had attempted more or less unsuccessfully to raise corn, produce wine and silk, and mine gold. Although the cultivation of tobacco, begun in 1612, brought some prosperity, the significance of the new crop was not appreciated, and the company still failed to pay dividends. Furthermore, the despotic local government gave the settlement a bad name and discouraged immigration.

In 1618 the company, in an effort to encourage immigration and to promote a better spirit among the colonists, attempted a general reorganization of local government in Virginia. The governor's instructions for 1619 contained an order for the establishment of a local representative assembly. This body, patterned after the company's general court or stockholders' meeting in London, was the beginning of the Virginia colonial legislature. The local council, which at first sat with the assembly to compose one chamber, was a counterpart of the company's council in London.

Thus, through the establishment of a local governor, a council, and a representative assembly, the Virginia Company of London evolved a colonial government for Virginia modeled upon its own charter provisions. Substantially the same pattern of government eventually appeared in all the English colonies.

The Virginia Company of London, beset by financial failure and internal dissension, lost its charter in 1624. The king now named a royal governor and, the following year, formally incorporated Virginia in the royal domain. Virginia thereby became the first royal colony in America. The assembly, a mere creature of the company, might well have expired at this time, and in fact no regular assemblies met in Virginia from 1623 to 1628. Thereafter the legislature met annually, although it was not until 1639 that the king recognized the right of the assembly to permanent existence. By that time the future of Virginia as a royal colony was assured, but the frame of government of the Old Dominion, both as colony and as state, continued to be that imposed by the joint-stock company.

The alteration of government that occurred in Virginia in 1619 was constitutionally significant as the first instance in which the corporation principle provided the basis for a self-governing polity. Nor was the governmental change merely formal. Before 1618 Virginia had been, in a strict sense, a business enterprise in which governmental and political considerations were subordinate. The abandonment of military government and the adaptation of the corporation for the purposes of local self-government signified the transformation of the business into a political society. It was constitutionally appropriate, therefore, that the joint-stock company should be dissolved a few years later. The formation of a representative assembly by the company in 1619 is significant also for what it was *not*—namely, a conscious borrowing of English political institutions. The Virginia House of Burgesses, of course, resembled Parliament insofar as it embodied the principle of representation, and in later years local lawmakers argued the comparability of their assembly with the House of Commons. But the impetus for creating a body of elected representatives came from no innate spirit of liberty or self-government, but rather from practical necessities that stimulated the adaptation of a business instrument to the purpose of organizing political relationships.

Like Virginia, Massachusetts Bay was founded by a trading company, but in its case the company's charter straightaway became the actual constitution of the colony. The company's founders were for the most part middle-class Puritans who desired to found a Calvinist religious refuge in the wilderness. Many of the stockholders had mercantile backgrounds, however, and some were interested primarily in the venture's commercial possibilities. Hence it was not unnatural for the interested parties to organize as a joint-stock company.

The charter of the Massachusetts Bay Company, secured in 1629, provided for a governor, a deputy governor, and eighteen assistants, who together were to constitute the council. Provision was made for four "great and general courts" each year, to be attended by the freemen of the company. The power to make laws and ordinances not contrary to the laws of England was bestowed in a somewhat ambiguous fashion upon the governor, the deputy governor, the assistants, and the general court. The charter granted also the right to establish all necessary offices and to appoint appropriate magistrates. Included also was a grant of all the land lying between a point three miles south of the Charles River and three miles north of the Merrimac River, extending to the "Westerne Sea."

While the foregoing provisions were not unusual, the charter in one important respect differed vitally from others of the period in that it failed to specify where the seat of government was to be located. The omission may have been an inadvertent one, for it was only reasonable to assume that the governor and assistants would normally reside in London; or it may have been intentional, at least on the part of some of the grantees. In either case, the absence of any such stipulation opened the way for the eventual transfer, in 1630, of the seat of government of the colony from London to Massachusetts.

At this time most of the influential members of the Massachusetts Bay Company belonged to the faction interested in a religious colony rather than a commercial enterprise. Many of them preferred to migrate to Massachusetts along with other religious dissidents and direct company affairs on the scene rather than stay in England. The mercantile group still had some influence, however, and they would not concur in a move which might foreclose the possibility of future profits from the venture. The result was a compromise, arrived at in the famous Cambridge Agreement of 1629. The mercantile group assented to the removal of the company to Massachusetts Bay, and in return the merchants were given certain exclusive trading concessions with the colony. This made possible the transfer of the seat of government to Massachusetts Bay, a move that was symbolized by the actual transfer of the charter to the new colony. The company's connection with any superior governing body in England within the corporation forthwith ceased.

Although Massachusetts Bay provides the clearest illustration of the adaptation of the corporation charter to the purposes of a political constitution, it is impossible to understand the distinctive character of this most important colony without taking into account its religious dimension. Central to the Puritan world view was the idea of the covenant. Puritans believed that God had formed a covenant or contract with them which, though not dictating a particular form of government, made them a distinct people. Belief in the covenant held the community together and was a source of energy for political action that was given shape and direction by the use of the corporate form. Within the body of the Puritan community another kind of agreement or contract existed between the rulers and the ruled. Believing themselves blessed by God and commanded to rule, leaders such as Governor John Winthrop espoused the aristocratic view that the people should unquestioningly obey them.

As designated officers of the trading company, Winthrop and the few corporation members who came to New England could have governed entirely by themselves in the General Court. They chose to broaden the base of their new political society, however, by admitting 116 men to freemanship status in 1631. These freemen, who became members of the General Court, agreed to confine their role to that of electing the assistants (called magistrates) in the government; the magistrates would elect the governor and deputy governor, who together with the magistrates would make the laws, levy taxes, and run things generally. To assure that the proper religious perspective would be maintained, freemanship was restricted to church members.

The same political logic that led to the transformation of Virginia government produced in 1634 a significant broadening of the base of Massachusetts government. Dissatisfied with the tax levies imposed by Winthrop and the magistrates, a number of freemen protested and were allowed to consult with the governor about taxation. Encouraged, they next made their famous demand to see the charter, with a view toward exercising the rights that were legally theirs as members of the General Court. With some reluctance, the governor and his assistants produced the charter, and by it, the freeholders were able to demonstrate that the lawmaking powers of the corporation were vested in the General Court. The governor and assistants were forced to consent to the calling of the General Court at regular intervals to function as a legislature, and from that time on, the supremacy of the General Court was never questioned.

The metamorphosis of a trading-company charter into the constitution of an English colony thus determined the outlines of the government of Massachusetts. The governor, the deputy governor, and the eighteen assistants, who together had constituted the board of directors of the trading corporation, functioned almost from the start as the executive council which handled day-to-day affairs of the colony. The "Great and General Court," formerly the quarterly meeting of the stockholders, now became the legislature, and each town was authorized to send two representatives to its annual meetings. The only important subsequent change in the structure of the General Court was the introduction of bicameralism in 1644.

In Virginia the dissolution of the joint-stock company was followed by the imposition of royal-colony status. In Massachusetts Bay the business corporation that founded the colony also ceased to exist in a political and constitutional sense, but the Puritan leaders successfully resisted English attempts to bring them under royal administration. The rights of self-government which the charter granted the company, symbolized in the physical transfer of the charter itself, enabled Massachusetts Bay to flourish for fifty years as a virtually autonomous commonwealth only nominally accountable to English authority.

Government by Compact: Plymouth, Rhode Island, Connecticut, and New Haven

Just as voluntary association for business purposes became the basis for political society in the corporate colonies, so association for religious reasons formed the foundation for self-governing polities in Plymouth, Rhode Island, Connecticut, and New Haven. These colonies never acquired the political importance that Massachusetts Bay did, and they were constitutionally derivative insofar as they borrowed the governmental forms of their larger New England neighbor. Nevertheless, they were constitutionally significant because they illustrated the idea of government based on a social compact.

In Protestant theory every man was ultimately his own source of authority in religious matters, and it followed logically from this that mere agreement among individuals was all that was necessary for church organization. Applying this idea, a Calvinist sect known as separatists in the late sixteenth century advocated separation from the Church of England and the formation of churches by covenant or compact among the body of believers. Rejecting any connection with the Church of England, the separatists came into direct conflict with established Anglican authorities and with the English government itself. Since the church was still regarded as an arm of the state and the king the personal head of the church, to deny the authority of the church government was to attack the authority of the state itself. Mild persecution under the reign of Elizabeth became more serious under James I, with the result that various separatist groups in search of greater religious freedom migrated shortly after 1600 to the Netherlands, a country already practicing almost complete religious toleration.

Intent upon creating a wilderness Zion, a number of separatist families resident in Holland decided to migrate to America. After some negotiation they secured consent from the Virginia Company of London to settle within its domain. There followed the voyage on the *Mayflower* and the founding of Plymouth Colony in November 1620.

The Plymouth colonists thus found themselves presented with a unique opportunity to apply the compact doctrine, hitherto used by the separatists only for church organization, to the organization of a body politic. In the Mayflower Compact, they translated abstract theory into practice. Their grant from the Virginia Company of London proved meaningless, since the portion of the New England coast upon which they were to settle lay entirely outside the company's domains, and hence they were without any recognized political authority. Before landing, therefore, the adult males of the little body of separatists gathered in the cabin of the *Mayflower,* and there set their hands to a covenant intended to provide the basis for civil government:

We whose names are underwritten . . . Do by these Presents, solemnly and mutually in the Presence of God and one another, covenant and combine ourselves together into a civil Body Politick . . .

Here for the first time the compact theory of the state found expression in America. Plymouth Colony, in fact, had no other formal basis for its political order throughout its seventy-one years of existence.

The Mayflower Compact was only the first of many such covenants by which civil authority was established within the various New England settlements. When Roger Williams and his followers fled from Massachusetts to Rhode Island in the winter of 1636 and founded the town of Providence, they also found themselves outside all organized government. They solved their problem as the settlers at Plymouth had, binding themselves by a compact very similar to that executed aboard the *Mayflower.* The other principal Rhode Island towns founded within the next few years, notably Newport and Portsmouth, established governments in the same fashion.

The Puritan followers of John Davenport and Theophilus Eaton, who founded New Haven Colony, likewise organized their body politic through compact. They first met at New Haven in 1639, and with the declaration that the Bible offered perfect guidance for establishing government, they covenanted together in a body politic to enforce the laws of God. Seven men, known as the "seven Pillars," were chosen to constitute the government; and to them was granted virtual dictatorial power to make laws, administer affairs, and admit new freemen to the colony.

Eventually, a number of towns grew up around New Haven, and in 1643 they united to form the colony of New Haven. Under this compact the freemen of the colony elected a governor, deputy governor, and magistrates, while the several towns each sent two delegates to a General Court. The governor, deputy governor, and magistrates sat with the delegates to compose a one-house legislature with general lawmaking and taxing powers and supreme judicial authority.

The most famous of all early covenants after the Mayflower Compact was the Fundamental Orders of Connecticut, executed in 1639 among the settlers in the Connecticut River towns of Hartford, Windsor, and Wethersfield. The covenant created a government patterned after the joint-stock company organization. Once a year all freemen in the colony were to assemble in a "Courte of Election" to choose a governor and a board of magistrates. In addition, each of the three towns elected four deputies to meet with the governor and magistrates in a General Court or legislature. The General Court possessed all lawmaking authority for the colony, including the power to raise taxes, admit freemen, make grants of undisposed lands, and call the magistrates to account for misconduct. The General Court was more powerful than the governor; it could meet and adjourn without the consent of the governor and magistrates, while the governor possessed no veto but only a casting vote in case of a tie.

The Fundamental Orders of Connecticut have been described as the first modern written constitution because they were a written compact of the people by which a fundamental frame of government was erected. This is an exaggeration which gives Connecticut more credit than it deserves and unfairly diminishes the significance of the other early colonies. Although the Connecticut scheme was more elaborate, it was not essentially different from the formal written compacts that provided the basis of government in Plymouth, Rhode Island, and New Haven. Moreover, if one is concerned with the functional equivalent of a modern written constitution, one finds it more conspicuously in the corporation charters, which, though granted by the crown rather than invented by the people, supplied frames of government. In point here is the evident copying in the Fundamental Orders of Connecticut from the Massachusetts Bay charter. The Fundamental Orders of Connecticut furthermore differed from a modern constitution in failing to make a distinction between organic supreme law and ordinary enactments of the legislature; that distinction, unknown also to the corporation charters, would not appear until the late eighteenth century. Nevertheless, compacts such as the Fundamental Orders, like the corporation charters, were enormously important in the development of American constitutionalism because they expressed the idea that government could be created in a self-conscious and purposeful way, with definite, circumscribed powers.

The Proprietary Principle

A third method of establishing overseas settlement in the seventeenth century employed the feudal proprietary principle. It consisted in the grant of a feudal patent which gave the recipient vast land holdings and endowed him virtually with the powers of a king to rule new territory. Initially used to settle parts of northern England in the Middle Ages, the feudal patent legitimized the abortive colonization efforts of Sir Humphrey Gilbert and Sir Walter Raleigh in the late sixteenth century. The proprietary principle continued to have political and social relevance in the seventeenth century. Despite the growing power of the English mercantile classes, the landed aristocracy retained its influence at court, and many nobles looked on overseas settlement, carried out under a feudal patent, as a way of acquiring wealth and power. For this reason the proprietary principle became the favored means of promoting English colonization in the latter part of the seventeenth century. It also formed the basis of the colony founded by George Calvert, the first Lord Baltimore, in the 1630s.

The proprietary grant for Maryland came close to erecting an autonomous feudal principality in America. In the patent issued in 1632, Charles I as overlord granted Lord Baltimore all the rights, privileges, and immunities possessed then or in the past by the bishop of Durham. Between the years 1300 and 1500 the palatinate of Durham in England had been little less than an independent feudal state, and thus by implication reference to Durham's past status made Baltimore a virtually independent feudal lord, with but very slight obligation to the crown. The Maryland charter also gave the proprietor complete control over local administration, lawmaking, and military matters in his province. He could establish an assembly, but was not required to do so. All writs ran in his name, and no appeals could be taken to England from his courts. He possessed the right of subinfeudation, and the charter provided further that grantees owed allegiance only to Baltimore and not directly to the king. In short, Baltimore enjoyed a status not unlike that of a king except that he had no crown.

Nevertheless, political institutions developed in Maryland along the lines already marked out in Virginia, albeit more slowly. Cecilius Calvert, the second Lord Baltimore, in 1638 called an assembly of freemen to consult with the proprietary governor, and within a few years the assembly became an established body which began to demand a share of the legislative power. Indeed, as the proprietor was in effect a king in the new territory, the assembly soon identified itself as a little Parliament. In that sense

Maryland and the later proprietary colonies offer an example of the transfer of English political institutions. In a more practical political sense, however, the model for Maryland's constitutional development was neighboring Virginia, with its elected assembly. Experience there, as well as in Massachusetts Bay, made it clear that successful colonization required giving to those whose labor was essential to the prosperity of the community a share in its government.

By 1640 the first wave of colonization to North America had ended, with settlements established in Virginia, Massachusetts Bay, Plymouth, New Haven, the Rhode Island and Connecticut River towns, and Maryland. The corporation, the covenant, and the feudal patent provided the means of founding governments in the new territory, and of these the corporate principle was the most important. Virginia and Massachusetts Bay were politically dominant in their regions and served as a model for governmental development in nearby colonies. To be sure, the covenant colonies were significant for the social-compact theory of government that became so influential during the American Revolution. Yet governments founded as corporations also expressed the idea of creating political authority out of voluntary association, or social compact. Moreover, the corporation was most important in supplying a structure of governmental authority to colonies founded on covenant or feudal patent. Although power relationships differed in the several colonies, in each a governor, council, and assembly shared the functions of government. Having their origin in written charters that served as a source of authority and prescribed an institutional structure, the corporate colonies foreshadowed the central theme in American constitutional history: the idea of limited government under a positive fundamental law.

TWO

The Formation of the Colonial Constitution: 1640–1700

—————————————— ✦ ✦ ✦ ——————————————

Two FUNDAMENTAL ISSUES have given shape and direction to American constitutional history. The first has concerned the structure of government, the distribution of power among its parts, the relationship of individual citizens to the government. Although the colonists differed in their approach to these matters, by 1700 a general pattern of institutional practice had taken shape which in effect created a colonial constitution. The second fundamental issue in American constitutional development has been the relationship of several smaller governments to a central authority. In the seventeenth and eighteenth centuries this issue took the form of the imperial question. Because of domestic political turmoil and limited resources, the earliest English colonization efforts lacked coherent overall direction. The relationship of the parts to the whole was implicit in the founding of the colonies, however, and in the middle of the seventeenth century it became a matter of conscious concern. By the end of the century attempts to coordinate colonial affairs had evolved into an imperial constitutional system. As far as Americans were concerned, the critical question that was resolved in the sixty years after the initial period of settlement was whether they would achieve a distinct constitutional order of their own or remain entirely subservient to English governmental control.

Events favored the first of these alternatives. From 1640 to 1700 the central theme in constitutional development was the extension and confirmation of local self-government through the instrumentality of elected assemblies. In some colonies the assemblies achieved considerble powers, especially in the period of the English Civil War and Interregnum. Indeed, while the English were preoccupied with internal politics, the assemblies in Massachusetts Bay, Virginia, and Maryland aggrandized power to such an extent that these colonies for a time enjoyed virtual autonomy. After 1660 the idea of self-governing representative institutions found expression in the founding of several new colonies, all but one of which from the outset had elected assemblies that struggled with the executive for a greater share of governmental power.

In imperial affairs the chief development in the latter half of the seventeenth century was the formation of a coherent policy drawing the colonies more closely into the orbit of English government and asserting greater control over them. Heightened consciousness of imperial administration was evident in the period 1640 to 1660, even though little was accomplished in the way of structural reform because of internal political upheaval. In the Restoration era after 1660 the English purposefully set about extending their overseas influence through the founding of several additional colonies and the adoption of systematic policies not only for commercial regulation, but also for the internal political administration of the colonies.

Because the American Revolution in the most general sense resulted from the conflict between the American desire for self-government and the English insistence on imperial control, it appears paradoxical to say that events of the seventeenth century advanced both of these themes simultaneously. As yet, however, the contradiction between these ideas was not apparent. The interests of Englishmen in North America and Englishmen at home could be compatibly pursued within evolving constitutional arrangements that recognized the legitimacy both of the power of the colonial assemblies and the imperial authority.

Colonial Autonomy during the English Civil War

In the period of the Civil War and Interregnum the General Court of Massachusetts Bay became the dominant political institution in a virtually independent state. Internally a key structural development in this period was the division of the General Court into two distinct bodies. This change resulted from political conflict between the wealthier and more socially prominent men who served as magistrates on the governor's council, and the men of lesser property who asserted their interests as elected delegates in the General Court.

The governor and magistrates at first held preponderant power and were fearful that too large a role for the elected members of the General Court would jeopardize authority and order. Accordingly, the magistrates reserved to themselves the right to approve any action taken by the General Court. Moreover, they constituted a standing council which exercised executive powers when the legislature was not in session. For their part the elected delegates expressed fear of arbitrary government and tried to curb the magistrates' power. In 1644 the two groups resolved the conflict by agreeing to an institutional separation. Henceforth the magistrates and the elected delegates, though together continuing to form the General Court, would sit separately and each would possess a veto over legislation. This change marked an apparent victory for the deputies, since they acquired a power that had not previously been theirs. In a more significant sense it was a victory for the magistrates, who retained a power that had been under attack for several years. This bicameral legislative structure reflected the differentiation of interests in the new society, and in the eyes of both deputies and magistrates kept a proper balance between stability and order on the one hand and the rights and liberties of the people on the other.

More constitutionally significant than this internal development was the fact that Massachusetts Bay gained an autonomous position in imperial affairs in the troubled decades from 1640 to 1660. As early as 1637 royal authorities, mainly out of hostility to Puritanism, had tried to invalidate the Massachusetts charter. As the power of English Puritanism rose and became ascendant in the 1640s and 1650s, the English government persisted in the endeavor to subject Massachusetts Bay to English authority. But continued political unrest at home prevented the Commonwealth government from doing more than sending a commission to secure the subordination of the remote settlement on Massachusetts Bay (as well as of the other colonies in North America). Though religiously sympathetic to the Cromwellian regime, the Puritans of New England were uncompromising in their insistence on maintaining their independence. In 1645 the General Court denied any subordination to the English government and declared that the laws of Parliament and the king's writ did not affect them. As though to express this autonomy, the General Court adopted a code of laws in 1648 (the *Laws and Liberties of Massachusetts*), and in 1652 required all inhabitants to subscribe an oath of loyalty to the laws of the colony. In the same year Massachusetts took control of settlements that had been undertaken under proprietary grants in Maine and New Hampshire. These were acts of sovereignty that for all practical purposes identified Massachusetts Bay as an independent state. The General Court at no point disavowed allegiance to England, but this loyalty was merely an empty formality.

In these same years Virginia, though continuing to be a royal colony, acquired a more substantial measure of autonomy under an increasingly assertive elected assembly. A creature of the joint-stock company, the House of Burgesses met only intermittently after the crown took control of the colony in 1625. In 1639, however, on royal instructions, the elected assembly achieved a fixed position in the constitution of the colony. This was principally because it had become an essential means of securing the support and cooperation of the varied political and economic interests that appeared as settlement spread. In the 1640s the House of Burgesses professed loyalty to the crown, and after the abolition of the monarchy in 1649, it resisted the demand of the Commonwealth government for subordination to English authority.

Virginia eventually yielded where the Bay colony did not, the fact of twenty-five years of royal rule and the absence of a charter having an evident effect. But the outcome of negotiations between Virginia's political leaders and the commissioners whom the Commonwealth government sent to the colony in 1652 was a significant shift in constitutional power from the governor and council, previously the main source of law and policy, to the House of Burgesses. The elected deputies now chose the governor and council, appointed justices of the peace (the chief officers in the politically and administratively important county courts), and in general controlled the government in the 1650s. After the restoration of the Stuart monarchy, William Berkeley returned to power as governor, the choice both of imperial authorities and local political leaders. But the House of Burgesses, though it ceased to be the dominant force in the government, occupied a stronger position than it had prior to the Commonwealth period. Having made Berkeley's appointment contingent on its approval, the Burgesses successfully insisted on their right to meet regularly in biennial session, to be dissolved by the governor only with their consent, and to approve appointments to the governor's council. In 1663, as a sign of its institutional maturity and political influence, the House of Burgesses began to sit separately. Virginia, of course, never ceased to be a royal colony, but in the mid-seventeenth century it attained, and under the locally popular Governor Berkeley continued to enjoy, a considerable autonomy.

In still a third colony, proprietary Maryland, the assembly played a more conspicuous governmental role in the Interregnum period. In Maryland the proprietor permitted an assembly to be formed in 1637, but was for all intents and purposes the government. Small in number (about twenty members) and serving strictly as a consultative body, the assembly throughout the 1640s sought the right to initiate legislation and sit separately. Aided by the fact that they comprised a large Protestant interest and that the proprietor, a Catholic, was the object of antiproprietary pressure from the Puritan Commonwealth government in England, the assembly in 1650 secured these goals. Through the ensuing decade the government of Maryland was in turmoil as Catholics and Protestants, looking to the powers of the proprietor and the assembly respectively, tried to establish control. From 1655 to 1658 the Puritan-dominated assembly repudiated the proprietor and governed the colony. In 1660 the proprietor regained political control and relegated the assembly again to a subordinate role. Retaining its legislative initiative and bicameral status, however, the assembly adopted an opposition stance and attacked the exercise of power by the proprietary governor and council for the next thirty years.

Massachusetts Bay, Virginia, and Maryland thus secured a broad degree of assembly-based autonomy, despite the imperial ambitions of both royalist and parliamentary English authorities. Because of their necessary preoccupation with domestic politics, neither crown nor Commonwealth officials could do much to promote imperial control. The restoration of the monarchy in 1660, however, provided that opportunity. For the next thirty years the founding of additional colonies and the formulation of a commercial policy for the overseas settlements gave substance to the imperial vision.

The Second Wave of Colonization in English North America

From 1607 to 1641 about 70,000 English men and women migrated to the colonies in New England and the Chesapeake region. From 1664 to 1681 a second wave of emigration produced colonies in New York, New Jersey, Carolina, and Pennsylvania. All of these colonies were founded on the proprietary principle. Nevertheless, despite the theoretically autocratic nature of this governing instrument, their constitutional development, with one exception, reinforced the tradition of local self-government under an elected assembly.

The revival of aristocratic influence under Charles II made the feudal patent an appropriate means of colonization in the Restoration era. The crown had political obligations that could be repaid with land grants in North America, and ambitious members of the nobility were eager to seek power and wealth as feudal lords in the New World. At the same time the joint-stock corporation no longer appealed as a colonizing device since settlements based on this approach had not rewarded their investors, however successful they had become as political communities. Accordingly, in 1662 Charles II granted extensive lands along the Atlantic coast south of Virginia to eight court favorites who were empowered to rule, as Maryland's proprietor had been, with all the rights and privileges of the bishop of Durham. Named Carolina after the king, the colony consisted of three widely scattered settlements. When the English conquered New Netherlands in 1664, Charles II granted it to his brother James, duke of York, through a proprietary charter that gave him absolute power; James in turn made a grant of part of the land to John Berkeley and George Carteret as proprietors of New Jersey. Finally, in 1681 the Quaker gentleman William Penn secured a proprietary grant to found a colony to the west of New Jersey, along the Delaware River.

What was constitutionally significant about these colonies, with the exception of New York, was that their original design provided for an elected assembly. Earlier in the seventeenth century the assembly was a political expedient needed to make settlement more attractive, as in Virginia. Later, in Massachusetts Bay, Maryland, and the New England covenant colonies, the assembly served the constitutional purpose of coordinating and achieving a proper balance between the interests of rulers and ruled. By the 1660s the planners of new settlements saw the assembly as a necessary part of a colony's political institutions. Along with the promise of religious toleration and the availability of cheap land, the promise of political participation through an elected assembly was an important inducement for settlers.

In order to appeal especially to New England Puritans accustomed to representation in an assembly, the proprietors of Carolina and New Jersey, in the Concessions and Agreement of 1665, provided for elected assemblies in the two colonies. Together with a governor and council, these bodies would possess the lawmaking power. In Carolina each of the three dispersed settlements (Charlestown, Albemarle, and Port Royal) was to have an assembly. Subsequently, the Fundamental Constitutions of Carolina, an elaborate governmental plan drawn up in 1669 to regulate the aristocratic and democratic elements of society, proposed to create a parliament in which elected freeholders would share legislative power with a governor and deputies of the proprietors and the nobility. Farther north the Quakers who bought part of the New Jersey grant and founded the colony of West Jersey, in their Concessions and Agreement of 1677 projected a representative body having exclusive lawmaking power. And in 1682 William Penn included an assembly in the first of several frames of government designed to serve as the constitutional foundation for Pennsylvania.

From the proprietors' standpoint the promise of representative institutions was a promotional device more than an expression of philosophical or ideological commitment. It was only with difficulty that settlers succeeded in translating the promise into institutional reality. Expecting deference, the sponsors of the later proprietary colonies assumed that government would remain the exclusive affair of the landed elite. The freeholder-dominated assemblies did constant battle, however, seeking to go beyond a merely consultative role and win the right to initiate legislation. In 1671, for example, the Carolina assembly at Charlestown refused to accept the Fundamental Constitutions of Carolina because that document did not concede such a right. The assembly in West Jersey gained the right to initiate legislation and other powers in relation to the colony executive in 1681. And in 1682 the Pennsylvania assembly, protesting William Penn's paternalistic, council-dominated scheme of government, began a fourteen-year struggle to attain genuine legislative power. New York had no assembly, but it too witnessed a drive for popular participation in government, led by Puritan settlers from New England who agitated for the creation of an elective lawmaking body. In 1683 the duke of York, proprietor of the colony, relented and allowed an elected assembly to convene. Subsequent political changes in the colony and the empire, however, prevented it from continuing. Nevertheless, throughout the colonies people were coming to regard the existence of an assembly as a matter of right and a necessary part of the colonial constitution.

By achieving self-government through representative institutions despite their proprietors' reluctance, the restoration colonies gave promise of becoming practically autonomous, like the earlier corporate colonies. This autonomy was in large part based on the fact that they were the personal property of recipients of feudal patents. Yet colonial independence conflicted with the desire of many of the king's advisers for more systematic imperial control. By 1680, when William Penn sought his charter, the inconsistency inherent in trying to create a centralized empire while giving away vast territories to men with virtually independent powers of government led imperial officials to impose limitations on the Pennsylvania charter. Penn had to agree to send the colony's laws to England for acceptance or disallowance, allow appeals from the colony's courts, and recognize the king's reserved right to levy taxes on the colony. Furthermore he must promise to obey the series of laws governing imperial trade enacted by Parliament over the previous two decades as an expression of the new quest for empire.

Imperial Centralization

International rivalry with the Netherlands, Spain, and France led English statesmen to seek a more centralized administration of the colonies and to coordinate colonial economic affairs with those of England. Between 1661 and 1675 Parliament passed a series of Navigation Acts, embodying the fundamental principles of mercantilism. All trade with the colonies was required to be carried in English or colonial ships, and the colonies were to have a monopoly in the English market for their leading products, the so-called enumerated commodities including tobacco, sugar, indigo, rice, cotton, ginger, and naval stores. These could be sent only to England, and except for a few products such as wine and salt, the colonies were obliged in turn to get all their imports from England. The colonies also had to pay duties on their products, meaning that trade within the empire was not free but preferential.

The acts implementing this commercial design not only affected the American colonists in an obvious economic sense, but also politically and constitutionally. In this respect the Plantation Duties Act of 1673 was the most important of the new measures. Obliged to carry their enumerated products to English or other colonial ports, American merchants at first evaded the rule by landing their cargo in a colonial port before reshipping it outside the empire. The act of 1673 stopped this practice by requiring merchants to pay export duties on enumerated products at the point of departure, and it provided for the appointment of customs collectors assigned from London. Previously, customs collection had been a responsibility of the colonial governors, only one of whom—in Virginia—was a royal officer. Now English customs officials might be placed in North America and expected to assume a role in the administration of a colony's internal affairs. Although historians have traditionally drawn a sharp distinction between the British commercial system of the seventeenth century and the internal colonial administration undertaken after 1763, there was both a logical and historical connection between the two phases of imperial control which began to appear at this time.

Indeed, after 1660 crown officials set in motion a process of systematizing and tightening the relationship of the colonies to England which, in conjunction with the requirements of the Navigation Acts, in the 1680s culminated in the establishment of centralized imperial rule over most of the American colonies. Imperial power expanded in the 1660s and 1670s through the imposition of royal governments, under the command of military officers, in Jamaica (formerly a Spanish colony) and Barbados and the Leeward Islands (formerly proprietaries); the conquest of New Netherlands from the Dutch; and the reassertion of royal influence in Virginia. In 1662 and 1663 the crown granted charters to Connecticut and Rhode Island, covenant colonies which feared that Charles II might refuse to recognize their existing governments. Except for a parliamentary grant to Rhode Island in 1644, these colonies possessed no official sanction or legitimacy. Their new charters in effect confirmed the existing governments in each colony, which in Connecticut was enlarged by the absorption of New Haven. But the charters also required that Rhode Island and Connecticut submit to royal customs control and agree not to enact laws contrary to the laws of England. Connecticut and Rhode Island welcomed the protection of royal charters because they feared being taken over by Massachusetts, a not unreasonable apprehension considering the Bay colony's willingness to challenge even the authority of England.

On several counts Massachusetts Bay stood as an affront to the emerging imperial policy. Controlled by an entrenched Puritan oligarchy, Massachusetts refused to permit Anglican or other kinds of worship outside the state-established Congregational church. It also restricted suffrage to church members. To complaints about the colony's long-standing religious intolerance was added growing impatience with its equally long-standing insistence on its constitutional autonomy. Only in the most general sense did Massachusetts profess allegiance to Charles II in 1662, when the crown demanded expressions of subordination from the colonies. Most of the time, as when it was charged with violating the Navigation Acts, the Bay colony declared itself beyond the scope of parliamentary law. In the late 1670s English authorities began a concerted effort to bring Massachusetts into line by appointing Edward Randolph collector of customs, the first royal official resident in the colonies charged with enforcing the trade acts. Massachusetts' leaders remained obdurate, however. They declared the Navigation Acts in force by the authority of the General Court and appointed the colony's own customs collectors. Supremely uncompromising, the colony kept the customs revenues for itself. These actions presented the English government with a challenge to its sovereignty that it could not avoid. Accordingly, imperial officials inaugurated legal proceedings against Massachusetts Bay in the royal courts and in 1684 secured the desired result: revocation of the colony's charter.

This momentous step prepared the way for the creation of centralized imperial control over the northern colonies. Concurrently with the campaign against Massachusetts, crown officials in the early 1680s tightened the administration of the Navigation Acts and initiated legal action against the proprietary grants in Maryland, New Jersey, and Carolina, with a view toward making them royal colonies. The death of Charles II in 1685 and the accession of James II, a Catholic with even more pronounced imperial ambitions, brought plans for the subordination of the colonies rapidly to fruition.

To begin with, James was the proprietor of New York, which meant that upon his accession it became a royal colony. Politically and strategically, however, Massachusetts was the critical problem. In place of the deposed charter-based Puritan oligarchy, James and his advisers decided that an English governor-general should rule, assisted by a council but without a locally elected assembly. Instead of governing themselves, the colonists should pay taxes and obediently accept the laws given to them by the governor-general, on the theory that the colonies were the personal possession of the king.[1] In the view of imperial officials, the very existence of the colonies and whatever representative institutions they possessed depended on royal grace and favor, not on any right of political participation or self-government that the colonists might claim.

To carry out this conception of empire, as well as to enforce England's commercial policy and strengthen English military power against the Indians and the French in North America, James II appointed Edmund Andros governor-general of a new imperial administrative structure, the Dominion of New England. In 1687 Andros went to Boston as a military officer charged with the conduct of government and civil administration.[2] Aided by internal opposition to the Puritan establishment, Andros took control of Massachusetts Bay, appointed a council from among the anti-Puritan element, and in due course forced the submission of Plymouth, New Hampshire, Maine, Rhode Island, and Connecticut to imperial rule. In 1688 the

1. In technical legal terms the colonies were *dominions* of the king, subject to his personal rule, as distinguished from the *realm* of England where the king's rule was limited by the common law.

2. Reliance on military officers in politico-administrative positions was characteristic of the British Empire from the outset. Approximately 90 percent of the 206 commanders in chief of royal colonies who were appointed between 1660 and 1727 were English army officers. This fact is evidence that imperial officials sought to promote the traditional social values of order, obedience, and military security, all of which at times conflicted with the more modern commercial values that overseas trade encouraged.

crown added New York and East and West Jersey to the Dominion's jurisdiction.

In destroying the elected assemblies in eight colonies the Dominion of New England had a profound constitutional impact. Indeed, the new imperial structure denied the very idea of a colonial constitution, resting instead on the theory that there was only an imperial constitution in which the colonies were utter dependencies of the crown. In Massachusetts the consequences of imperial reorganization transcended the governmental sphere and affected the religio-social order that had existed for fifty years. It was bad enough to legislate and levy taxes without the consent of the inhabitants in the General Court. What was even more objectionable, Andros insisted on religious toleration, introduced Anglican worship, and prohibited the government from paying ministers' salaries. The consequence was the disestablishment of the Congregational church. Furthermore, on the theory that all land should be held from the king, Andros negated land titles, required owners of real property to petition for royal patents, and forced them to pay a quitrent to the crown. When people used town meetings (the basic form of local government) to protest the collection of taxes without their consent, Andros restricted the towns to one meeting a year. He also changed the judicial system by permitting nonchurch members to sit on juries. The other colonies that came under Dominion rule suffered the loss of their assemblies, but they were not subjected to the same treatment as Massachusetts because they were less important. They were also far enough away from Boston to make direct imperial control impractical.

The Glorious Revolution in America

The Dominion of New England lasted only as long as the government that had created it. The Revolution of 1688, which deposed James II and brought William of Orange to the throne, had an American phase that overthrew the Dominion government in Boston and New York. The Glorious Revolution in America also included the removal of the proprietary government in Maryland. These colonial uprisings expressed Americans' opposition to imperial centralization, led to a redefinition of the status of the colonies in the empire, and in effect revised both the colonial and imperial constitutions. But the rebellions of 1689 also reflected internal political and social pressures within the colonies that had developed in the context of the new imperial order. For this reason it is necessary to consider briefly the nature of American politics in the late seventeenth century.

In most colonies politics consisted of a struggle between an established oligarchy that was secure in the governor's council, and new groups of ambitious men who used the assembly to seek political power appropriate to their economic position. Turbulent without outside influences, political conflict became even more intense and destabilizing when imperial policy intruded into the local situation. The uprising in Virginia in the 1670s known as Bacon's Rebellion provides apt illustration.

Impatient with the governor's lenient Indian policy as well as frustrated by a declining tobacco market for which the Navigation Acts were partly responsible, lesser landowners and gentry in 1676 rebelled against Governor William Berkeley. Their rebellion mainly took the form of a vigilante expedition, led by Nathaniel Bacon, against neighboring Indians. Bacon's followers showed no inclination to repudiate their English allegiance; their grievances were directed at specific policies and at the council-dominated political establishment rather than at royal authority as such. Nevertheless, the uprising was regarded in England as a challenge to imperial authority, and it was met by a show of imperial strength. The crown dispatched 1,100 troops to maintain the government, thus for the first time establishing a military garrison in North America. As it happened, the troops were not needed, for the rebellion quickly collapsed when Bacon died in late 1676. In the aftermath of the uprising a series of laws was adopted limiting the privileges of the council, extending the suffrage, and broadening opportunities for participation in local government. But these reforms were soon repealed. The local elite maintained its hold on politics and society, and imperial control was strengthened, although the garrison was disbanded. With the appointment of a new royal governor, the House of Burgesses agreed to grant the crown a permanent revenue and to surrender its right to sit as the highest court of appeals in the colony.

In other colonies internal political tensions, exacerbated by the imperial policy of the 1680s, erupted in the rebellions of 1689. In Massachusetts and Connecticut merchants hostile to the Puritan ruling group at first supported the Dominion of New England with a view toward advancing their own political and economic interests. Opposition to the Andros regime became so widespread, however, that when news of the English Revolution reached Massachusetts Bay in 1689 it touched off an armed uprising that immediately destroyed the authority of the Dominion government. Local leaders formed a provisional government and, significantly deciding against restoration of the old charter government, began negotiations with the new monarch, William III, to determine the nature of the colony's government and its constitutional status in the empire.

In the other New England colonies the fall of the Dominion government was quietly followed by the resumption of the old governments, but in New York political upheaval ensued and important changes took place. Local merchants and gentry, many of them Puritan immigrants from New England who had long criticized the concentration of power in the governor's council and demanded an assembly, seized on the news of Andros's fall to overthrow the lieutenant governor of the Dominion, stationed in

New York. Claiming authority under the neglected Charter of Liberties of 1683, they organized a provisional government under the leadership of Captain Jacob Leisler, held elections for an assembly, and proclaimed the new king.

In Maryland imperial authority was not involved in the political struggle, but word of the Glorious Revolution was a signal for the Protestant-dominated assembly, after years of contesting the special privilege and power belonging to the governor and council, to cast off proprietary rule itself. Seizing control of the government, the assembly proclaimed William and Mary the new sovereigns and sent delegates to England requesting that the colony be made a royal province. There was governmental turmoil also at this time in Carolina and Pennsylvania. A revolt in Albemarle County, in northern Carolina, resulted in the dispatch of an agent to England seeking aid in resolving the local conflict, and Pennsylvania continued to witness conflict between the council and the assembly. Meanwhile in England William Penn tried to keep hold of his colony against strong antiproprietary sentiment in imperial circles.

The extent to which political and constitutional instability was a general characteristic of the colonies at this time can be seen in the fact that in 1689 ten colonies—Massachusetts, New Hampshire, Rhode Island, Connecticut, East and West Jersey, North and South Carolina,[3] Maryland, and New York—had agents in England negotiating the status if not the very existence of their local governments in the empire. Conditions were more unsettled in some of these colonies than in others, but all of them sought a sanction—in the form of a charter from the English government—that would guarantee their right to exist as something more than mere dependencies of the crown. In the most literal sense they were going through a crisis of legitimacy as self-governing polities. For their part the officials and advisers under William III, though seeking to avoid the excesses of the imperial system of James II, were little inclined to yield where questions of English sovereignty were involved. Both colonists and imperialists, however, had learned something from the disastrous experiment in centralized imperial administration. The constitutional settlement that was worked out in the decade following the Glorious Revolution secured the basic goals of each group.

Significance of the Revolutionary Settlement

The most conspicuous feature of the constitutional settlement was the extension of royal authority into new spheres. Massachusetts was the prize

---

3. Carolina had in reality become two colonies by this time. In 1691 this distinction was formally recognized by the proprietors.

example in this respect: the only colony able to secure a charter, nevertheless it now became a royal colony. Its governor was to be appointed by the crown, and it was required to send its laws to England for approval. The autonomy of the old Puritan Commonwealth was plainly ended. In neighboring New Hampshire, which the crown had removed from the jurisdiction of Massachusetts Bay in 1679 only to lose it again in the aftermath of the rebellion in 1689, royal authority was restored. Elsewhere, in a significant change, Maryland became a royal colony, although the proprietor was permitted to keep the land and the revenues from it. New York had been a royal colony since 1685, but it now received a typical royal government for the first time. Pennsylvania and the Carolinas remained proprietaries, though from 1692 to 1694 the former came under the jurisdiction of the royal government in New York, and as of 1696 the governors of both proprietary colonies had to be approved by the crown. An antiproprietary drive continued to characterize imperial policy, and East Jersey and West Jersey maintained separate existences only until 1702, when they were united as a single royal colony. Connecticut and Rhode Island, regarded as politically insignificant, resumed their charter governments in 1689 and were pretty much left alone. Finally Plymouth Plantation was absorbed into Massachusetts.

Accompanying the increase in the number of royal colonies was the extension and strengthening of the imperial commercial system. In the Navigation Act of 1696 Parliament placed the customs service on a more solid legal basis, enlarged the collection bureaucracy, and authorized the creation of twelve vice-admiralty courts for enforcing the Navigation Acts. Vice-admiralty courts operated directly under crown authority and, unlike common law courts, lacked juries. Colonial common law courts in the colonies, which had previously tried violations of the trade acts, were permitted under the act of 1696 to have concurrent jurisdiction with the new courts. But the royal governor had the power to determine which tribunal would be used to enforce the commercial regulations. The crown also expressed its seriousness of imperial purpose by creating in 1696 the Board of Trade. A body of salaried officials, many of them merchants, the board replaced the subcommittee of the Privy Council known as the Lords of Trade that had existed since 1675. The Board of Trade prepared instructions for colonial governors, reviewed colonial legislation, and in general advised the crown and Parliament on colonial matters.

If the settlement achieved at the end of the seventeenth century strengthened the authority of the English government in North America, it also underscored the importance of the assembly in the colonial constitution and confirmed it as an element in the imperial constitution. Continuous as the growth of representative institutions had been since the original settlements, the Dominion of New England showed how vulnerable the assemblies were. In the Glorious Revolution and its aftermath the colonists restored the assemblies and extended their powers. Connecticut and Rhode Island revived their assemblies without incident. In Massachusetts the new charter of 1691 provided for a General Court. Although its powers were more circumscribed than they had been in the period of independence, it enjoyed a privileged position relative to the governor unlike that found in any other royal colony. The elected deputies in the General Court chose the governor's council, created new courts, and held annual sessions under a guarantee contained in the charter.

In Maryland the assembly gained control over taxation, the judicial system, and the determination of its membership and internal organization, issues over which it had struggled for decades with the proprietary council. Especially notable was the establishment of a representative assembly in New York. Promised in the Charter of Liberties of 1683 but never realized, the creation of an assembly was the first work of the Leisler rebels in 1689. The New York assembly straightaway assumed an important governmental role as it settled land titles, passed tax measures, and reorganized the judicial system.

With the exception of New England, the role of the assembly in the seventeenth century had been more consultative than decisive or determinative. By 1700, however, each colony had an assembly, and everywhere, with the ironic exception of Massachusetts, it played a more forceful and significant role than it had previously. All the assemblies had won the right to initiate legislation, to sit separately, and to participate in the shaping of fiscal policy. Increasingly, the assemblies gave up the judicial functions that they had shared with the council and the courts, and confined themselves to legislation (which function they continued to share with the governor and council). Assemblies at this time also cultivated the habit of referring to Parliament as a legislative model, as they tried to wrest from the governor privileges which the House of Commons had won against the crown throughout the seventeenth century.

The clearest expression of the enhanced position of the lower houses of assembly appeared in the Pennsylvania Charter of Privileges of 1701. The last in a series of constitutional instruments in Pennsylvania's founding period, this frame of government ended two decades of struggle between council and assembly by excluding the former from lawmaking and placing the legislative function entirely in the latter's hands. Possessing the power to choose its own speaker and to pass on the qualifications of its members, as well as to hold fixed meetings and control its adjournment, the Pennsylvania deputies asserted their right to "all other powers and privileges of an assembly, according to the rights of the free born subjects of England." More successful than their counterparts in other colonies, the Pennsylvania assembly pointed out the direction of constitutional change in the eighteenth century.

The assembly was the key institution in the colonial constitution, and by 1700 it had become in practice and experience a fixed part of the constitution of the empire. English officials, however, held theories about the imperial constitution which clashed with colonial reality. They regarded the colonies as dominions of the king, subject to his personal rule and outside the scope of the common law except insofar as he might choose to apply it there. In 1689–91 many colonists disputed this view, arguing that they possessed all the rights of English subjects under the common law, such as the right to representation and the guarantee of protection against arbitrary deprivation of their liberty and property. Pursuing this constitutional position, the assemblies in New York and Maryland in the 1690s passed resolutions stating that representation in an elected assembly was a right based on Magna Charta or the fundamental laws of England. English officials rejected these declarations, insisting on the contrary that such representative institutions as existed in the colonies flowed from royal favor rather than constitutional right. Yet the more important fact was that, despite its own theories, the English government after 1690 acted as though representation in an assembly, and a substantial degree of assembly self-government in local affairs, existed by right. Never thereafter did the English found a colony without an elected assembly. In American eyes the perpetuation of this political practice created a constitutional right of representation and local self-government.

Nowhere in the colonies did political leaders in the late seventeenth century seek or even contemplate an independent existence for their provincial governments outside the empire and completely detached from the English nation. For that reason, despite some similarity in the arguments presented, the historical situation that the colonists faced in the 1680s differed fundamentally from that which existed on the eve of the Revolution in the eighteenth century. Indeed, as a result of the changes in the late seventeenth century the colonists became more self-consciously English in their constitutional outlook. This tendency was evident in Massachusetts. In the long dispute over the status of Massachusetts Bay that lasted from 1660 to 1684, the colony's spokesmen had relied on the charter and the covenant to defend their position. Once the charter was abrogated, however, they turned elsewhere. In resisting the Dominion of New England and in demanding the restoration of local liberties after the Glorious Revolution, the representatives of Massachusetts argued from the constitution and laws of England. These instruments, they contended, guaranteed them fundamental rights of representation, consent to taxation, and protection to their person and property. In other colonies, especially New York and Maryland, where rebellions took place, colonists made the same argument.

The English denied that the principles of the Glorious Revolution applied to the colonies. The colonists insisted that they did, and in the course of the eighteenth century they built a constitutional tradition of resistance to arbitrary executive power on this foundation. Though at the end of the seventeenth century they were hardly equals within the empire—that is, possessed of the same liberties as subjects of the king within the realm of England—the logic of their rights-of-Englishmen argument suggested that equality was the goal toward which they were moving. Whether it was a feasible objective events would reveal.

THREE

The Colonial Constitution in the Eighteenth Century

—————————————— ✦✦✦ ——————————————

IN THE FIRST HALF OF THE EIGHTEENTH CENTURY the American colonies evolved constitutionally along the paths marked out in the aftermath of the Glorious Revolution of 1689. It is clear in retrospect that the colonists continued to prepare the institutional and ideological foundations on which republican government was later established. The steady increase in colonial population, wealth, and prosperity suggests a growing organism whose differentiation and eventual separation from England were natural and irresistible. Yet in this period Americans consciously tried to emulate their English superiors, like any intelligent colonial people. This was true in society and culture, where increasing stratification and concentration of wealth made the colonies more nearly resemble England in the eighteenth century than they had in the seventeenth. It was true also in government and politics, where, employing the concepts and practices of English constitutionalism, the American colonists extended the powers of their provincial assemblies and achieved a broader degree of autonomy within the empire.

The expansion of colonial political power in the eighteenth century took place within the framework of—indeed, it was encouraged by—the British imperial system. From 1700 to about 1720 military-executive control of imperial affairs in London operated in effective balance with the management of local affairs in America by the several provincial assemblies. As a practical arrangement rather than a formal legal enactment, a division of power and responsibility existed which adumbrated the division of sovereignty later provided for in American federalism. During Queen Anne's War (1702–13) the crown made territorial gains in French Canada, while the colonial assemblies played a pivotal role in shaping local defense and finance policies. As a matter of conscious policy, England assigned the task of raising and equipping a fighting force to the colonies, who in the process were able to expand the powers of the assembly vis-à-vis the governor.

In England after 1720 Whig views of empire favoring commercial interests and tolerant of local assembly autonomy prevailed over the more centralized, land-oriented and military-dominated approach to imperial administration urged by the Tories. A period of "salutary neglect" ensued during which the assemblies strengthened their position in relation to the royal governor, the influence of the Board of Trade declined, and imperial affairs lacked systematic direction and control. Responsibility for the government of the empire was shared among the Privy Council, Secretary of State, Treasury, Admiralty, and Parliament, along with the Board of Trade; the result was often confusion and mismanagement. In order to keep abreast of imperial politics and defend colonial interests, the colonies were authorized to send agents to England in a kind of diplomatic capacity. Although imperial officials approved of this practice, by 1750 the assemblies had gained the power to appoint the colonial agents, another step in their assumption of a larger governmental role.

The Theory of Mixed Government

Within this loose imperial framework the American colonists managed local affairs according to English precepts. As they looked to the common law for guidance in settling private disputes, so they regarded the English constitution as their model in public law and governance. What distinguished the English constitution as the colonists considered it was the balance that existed among the component parts of the government, a balance intended to preserve liberty while providing the necessary degree of authority to maintain social order. This concern with balance, which was to remain a central theme in American constitutionalism, is usually associated with the separation of powers and checks and balances. In the eighteenth century, however, the separation of powers was a new doctrine not widely accepted. A different and much older concept—the theory of mixed government—served as the principal means of reconciling liberty and authority. This doctrine provided the intellectual framework for Anglo-American thinking about government.

The basic point of mixed-government theory was to give a distinct role in the governmental structure to the constituent elements of society. Modern constitutional theory, since the ascendancy of the rival doctrine of separation of powers, is premised on the division of government into three essential functions—the legislative, executive, and judicial. In the theory of mixed government, however, no such functional distinction existed. Rather, government power was conceived of as generalized, undifferentiated, unspecialized. Writers on government referred mainly to the tasks of government, such as levying and collecting taxes, regulating trade, controlling the militia, conducting diplomacy, and so on—matters that we would regard as policy questions. Insofar as the making and executing of law were discussed, people thought these powers were shared by all the parts of a government. The key distinction was not between separate governmental functions, but rather, as in medieval theory, between the sphere of government power (or *gubernaculum*) on the one hand and the rights and liberties of subjects (or *jurisdictio*) on the other.

Focusing on the estates or orders of society, the theory of mixed government was intended to maintain equilibrium among them, lest government come under the exclusive control of any single social class. This theory was rooted in the ancient notion, central to classical political thought, that if not checked, the monarchical element in society would degenerate into tyranny, the aristocratic element into oligarchy, and the democratic element into mob rule. Mixed-government theory in England tried to accomplish this purpose by bringing King, Lords, and Commons together in Parliament, where each body, representing a distinct social order, would share in the exercise of governmental power. Mixed together in the structure of government, each order would balance and restrain the others by assuming particular tasks of government, as in the practice by which money bills originated in the House of Commons. Finally, mixed-government doctrine identified basic political values with the different social orders. The king was thought to provide energy and dispatch in government; the House of Lords, wisdom; the House of Commons, a special concern for liberty and virtue.

Despite the assertion of parliamentary sovereignty in the seventeenth century, English government in the eighteenth century conformed to mixed-government theory. In the aftermath of the Glorious Revolution, English politics became stabilized under the rule of a Whig oligarchy. Parliament was theoretically supreme as the lawmaking power and the king a mere executive, but in practice a strong executive institution emerged. This occurred through the development of cabinet government under a prime minister. During the administration of Robert Walpole (1721–42), usually regarded as the first prime minister, Parliament was effectively controlled by the king's officers, through methods of patronage disposition and electoral manipulation that came under the heading of "influence." The key to the system was the actual presence in Parliament of the cabinet ministers, including the prime minister, which represented an adaptation of the older mixed-government idea that English government consisted of the king in Parliament.

American colonial government as it had evolved by the eighteenth century adhered to the theory of mixed government. Its chief structural characteristic was that the governor, council, and elected deputies together formed the legislature and shared many governmental tasks. The governor performed what we would consider to be executive functions, but he was not confined to an executive role; sitting with the council, he possessed lawmaking power as a member of the upper house of the legislature. In the proprietary colonies the proprietor or his appointed governor initially controlled lawmaking, but in time came to share this power with the deputies in the lower house. In the royal colonies that began as corporations, elected representatives earlier acquired lawmaking power which they shared with the governor and council. By the same token the lower houses of assembly joined in what we would define as executive functions, such as the appointment of administrative officers. Frequently, the deputies in the lower house acted in a judicial capacity, settling disputes, punishing offenders, and hearing cases on appeal from the colony's common law courts, although it was more usual for the governor and council to serve in an appellate judicial capacity.

The Growth of Assembly Power

Despite a superficial resemblance based on common acceptance of the theory of mixed government, American constitutionalism in the eighteenth century differed significantly from the English pattern. The chief difference appeared in the imbalance that arose between the assembly and the royal governor. The lower houses of assembly steadily gained power, until on the eve of the American Revolution they formed not merely a counterweight to the executive, but a preponderant force that signaled a shift in the center of constitutional gravity from the executive to the popular element in government. Socially, this expansion of authority reflected the emergence in the colonies of a prosperous class of merchants, lawyers, and planters ambitious for a political role. In the seventeenth century elected deputies had typically come from the ranks of smaller property owners, while the governor's council comprised men of greater wealth. Social and economic change in the eighteenth century, however, produced elite groups too numerous to be accommodated in the council, which ordinarily numbered only about a dozen men. The lower houses of assembly, whose membership ranged from fifty to one hundred, offered opportunities for political careers congruent with the aspirations of emergent elites.

The rise of the assembly in part resulted from the colonists' application of English constitutional principles—in particular those identified with the Glorious Revolution—to problems in their local communities. Underlying it was the colonists' belief that they were entitled to the same rights enjoyed by Englishmen at home, under the protection of the common law and the English constitution. Moreover, the view sometimes expressed by royal officials—that the assembly existed only at the sufferance of the crown and possessed the powers merely of a local corporation—stimulated colonial self-consciousness about the colonies' constitutional status. But often what appears in retrospect as the assemblies' quest for power proceeded on an expedient basis, from one pedestrian issue to another without regard to or seeming awareness of constitutional theory. The building of roads, ferries, and wharves; the formulation of land policy; the issuance of paper currency; defense against Indians and promotion of the Indian trade; the regulation of immigration into the colony; boundary disputes between colonies—all of these matters supplied the content of everyday politics. And most of the time in dealing with them, assembly delegates were primarily concerned with achieving a particular result. Nevertheless, whether by forcing concessions from the governor or by cooperating with him, the lower houses enhanced their institutional stature and established precedents that in time assumed constitutional significance.

Having acquired the right to sit separately, elect a speaker, and initiate legislation, the assemblies in the first half of the eighteenth century further defined their identity and maintained their integrity as a legislative body. Consciously imitating Parliament, they requested and secured freedom of speech on the floor of the assembly; immunity from arrest and molestation; access to the governor; the right to fix the qualifications for membership and to judge the elections and returns of deputies in the lower house; the right to try and punish outsiders who abused, insulted, or committed violence against a member; and the right to organize internal proceedings and discipline members who violated the rules of procedure. Together these rights were known as parliamentary privilege, and although certain privileges that Parliament enjoyed remained beyond the grasp of the assemblies—for example, the right to hold regular meetings irrespective of the will of the governor—the elected deputies in the colonies were highly successful in establishing the analogy between themselves and the House of Commons in relation to the executive power.

To these legislative attainments the lower houses of assembly added substantial powers over administration and policy making. Gaining control over finance was the single most important step in the process. Drawing on the parliamentary tradition by which elected representatives consented to and later came to control taxation, the lower houses acquired exclusive power to initiate all revenue and appropriations measures and to exercise administrative oversight concerning the expenditures of funds. In most colonies the assembly appointed the treasurer, or finance minister. Equipped with these powers, the deputies were able to resist the repeated demands of royal governors, acting on instructions from London, for permanent revenue acts that would make annual appropriations unnecessary. Victory in the struggle for the purse strings was of tremendous importance in the growth of colonial internal autonomy. Governors could not very well maintain royal or proprietary prerogative against assemblies which could specify the expenditure of every penny and withhold money from any governmental function, however vital. Hardly less important was the power the assemblies gained in the years before 1756 in regard to Indian policy, defense, and intercolonial relations, matters that in theory belonged to imperial authorities but that in practice were left to local governments. In establishing policy in these spheres the lower houses of assembly appointed subordinate officials and created committees to supervise their administrative performance.

The Governor and Council

The lower houses of assembly gained power at the expense of the colonial governor, who, with the exception of proprietary Maryland, Pennsylvania, and Delaware and the covenant-charter colonies of Connecticut and Rhode Island, was appointed by the crown. As the king's representative in lands deemed his personal dominions, the governor in legal theory exercised virtually all the traditional prerogatives of the English monarchy. He was empowered to summon the assembly; make laws with the assent of the elected deputies; exercise an absolute veto over legislation and nominal control over appropriations and expenditures; administer and enforce laws; appoint subordinate officers; command military and naval forces; act as head of the established church; create courts and appoint judges; and serve in a judicial capacity as a chancery court (with equity powers) and, with the council, as a court of appeals.

Great as these powers were in theory, they amounted to something less in practice because of the tenuous position the governor occupied in the structure of colonial politics. Often caught in a cross fire between imperial authorities and provincial leaders, royal governors lacked political experience—or at least the kind of experience needed in the more democratic politics that colonial conditions encouraged. At the same time royal instructions restricted the governors' political latitude. Uncertain of the discretion available to them, they might be recalled if they showed too much flexibility in responding to local pressures. But the governors' principal weakness stemmed from their inability to control finance and administration. A governor who tried to execute locally disagreeable instructions from London was likely to become embroiled in a long struggle with the assembly, which he would probably lose. For effective political power lay in the hands of those who controlled taxes and expenditures. Although the lower houses of assembly did so infrequently, the fact that they could withhold the governor's salary dramatically illustrates the weakness of his position. Far more common, however, and more effective in demonstrating executive weakness, were the deputies' threats to withhold appropriations for the implementation of imperial policies. The Board of Trade's failure to obtain a permanent civil list—that is, a budgetary supply line for the support of royal officers independent of assembly appropriations—was a continuing reminder of the political disadvantage under which the governor labored.

Nevertheless, the royal governor was hardly an abject prisoner or mere puppet of the assembly. In an age when deference to established rulers and elites was still the norm and democratic sentiments sparked fear, the governor's office carried great prestige and authority. The rise of the assembly notwithstanding, the governor remained a formidable constitutional force. Try as they might, the elected deputies could not wrest from him a number of key powers, especially those that permitted him to veto legislation, prorogue and dissolve the assembly, create new electoral districts, and appoint judges. The assemblies were also unable to secure the right to hold guaranteed regular meetings and to have their choice of a speaker automatically accepted by the governor.

The colonial council, supposedly the voice of the aristocratic element in society, was an anomalous institution that failed to give the governor the support that theoretically he was entitled to. Appointed by the crown, the council was chiefly an advisory body to the governor. In conjunction with him, it also formed the upper house of the assembly and sat as an appellate court. Intended to balance the democratic element represented by the elected deputies, the council was unsuccessful in fulfilling its role of buttressing royal authority because it did not in fact represent interests basically different from those found in the lower house. American society lacked a hereditary aristocracy on the English model, which meant that the council could hardly become the analogue of the English House of Lords. Drawn from the same planter-merchant-lawyer elite that populated the lower houses of assembly, the council usually sided with the deputies in their struggles with the governor.

Political Instability in America

Although in formal terms the structure of colonial government was similar to that of the mother country, it failed to produce the political stability that characterized English constitutionalism in the age of Walpole. American politics was volatile, disputatious, and kinetic, in part because no settled and cooperative relationship between governor and assembly existed. Political instability was rooted also in anxieties provoked by perceived discrepancies between the colonial and the English constitution. These anxieties were in turn shaped and reinforced by the writings of critics of the ruling Whig oligarchy in England, which found a ready audience in the colonies. Directed against schemes of executive influence which were thought to corrupt the legislature, their main effect was to stimulate Americans' fear of a loss of local liberty through the undermining of assembly power. American politics furthermore reflected the democratizing tendencies released by the Great Awakening of the 1740s. Sensitive to conflict, the colonial constitution thus provided a milieu in which the changes that took place in imperial policy after 1763 assumed alarming and portentous meaning in American eyes.

Beyond the inability of the governor to control the assembly, an important cause of political instability in the colonies was the openness and expandibility of the electoral system. It contrasted markedly with the closed system controlled by the executive in England. Property ownership was a prerequisite for colonial voting, but the typical qualifications—possession of land returning an income of 40 shillings per year or land or other property valued at 50 to 300 pounds—were easy to meet. As population increased, the franchise was broadened until about three-fourths of adult white males could vote. The result was the continual expansion of the assembly's political base and the source of its power.

The colonial system of representation further limited executive influence. With population growth new towns and counties were created. As these were the constituent units in the assembly, the size of that institution—and its political power—accordingly increased. Although newly settled areas were sometimes underrepresented, representation, on the whole, was equitably apportioned. Moreover, seats in the colonial assembly were not regarded as the personal property of the incumbent, nor were there "rotten boroughs"—that is, districts without population that were nevertheless entitled to representation, as in England—which the royal executive could control to his advantage. The decentralized and localist nature of representation in the colonies also helped to curb executive influence. Members of the assembly usually lived in the town or county that they represented, giving rise to a residency requirement that still exists. They were viewed as attorneys for the people who elected them rather than as independent-minded statesmen representing some broader interest or concern. Frequently, voters bound their deputies' actions in the assembly by express instructions. Because more people in the colonies, in comparison to England, actually voted for deputies, and because the deputies tended to represent the views actually held by the local electorate, American representation was *actual* representation. In England, by contrast, *virtual* representation existed. Subjects were said to be virtually represented, regardless of whether they had actually voted for a member of Parliament, so long as there were members whose interests were similar to theirs.

The chronic instability of American politics in the eighteenth century was an expression not only of differences between English and colonial constitutionalism, but also of the character of American society. As the medieval world gave way to the modern, economic interests replaced religious passion and the quest for glory as the principal motivating force in politics. In England this historical transformation was modulated by established institutions and social orders. By the middle of the eighteenth century the interests that dominated English politics were few in number, clearly defined in identity, and relatively stable in their functional relationships. Land, commerce, the church, the army, and the professions were represented in the mixed and balanced constitution. In the fragment of English society that had been flung off into North America, however, no such historical stabilization or rationalization had taken place. Consequently, the interests that entered the arena of colonial politics, interests that more often than not were motivated by bourgeois economic aspirations, produced an often turbulent factionalism.

Although immigration from non-English countries gave rise to ethnic, cultural, and religious factionalism, the major source of interest-conflict was the economic rewards that control of government offered in a rapidly expanding society. Wealth and power inevitably attach to political office, but the American environment gave a special urgency to the struggle for power because government necessarily had a more active role to play than it did in the more settled society of England. Moreover, the mercantilist assumptions of the age called for government promotion and regulation of economic activity. Accordingly, questions concerning land distribution, paper money, the Indian trade, and internal improvements lay at the heart of colonial political factionalism. In a constitutional order that encouraged institutional conflict between governor and assembly, and that lacked the mediating influence of an established class structure, the development of an interest-group mentality contributed to political and constitutional instability.

Pre-Revolutionary Political Thought

As Americans considered their constitutional arrangements in the light of mixed government theory and the tenets of English constitutionalism, they found perplexing and disturbing discrepancies. Unable to appreciate the advantage the assembly enjoyed in its dealings with the royal governor, they focused attention on the extensive powers that the colonial executive retained—powers greater indeed than those possessed by the monarchy in the English constitution. Believing their assemblies stood in a direct line of descent from Parliament's triumph over executive tyranny in the Revolution of 1689, the colonials formed a body of principles and ideas that shaped not only their struggles against the governor, but also their actions in controversies over imperial policy from 1765 to 1776.

Colonial political thought in general was concerned with the origins and nature of government, and the proper combination of the parts of government in a sound constitution. In addressing the former issue Americans drew on the tradition of natural law and natural rights that derived from antiquity through the medieval era to early modern times. In their quest for a proper governmental balance they turned to eighteenth-century English political writers who criticized the British system of mixed government.

Natural law theory held that certain eternal principles were inherent in the very structure of the universe which the positive law of a state, in order to be regarded as true law worthy of being obeyed, must embody or affirm. Perhaps the greatest classical advocate of this point of view was the Roman legist Cicero, who argued that the binding quality of civil law depended on its being in harmony with the principles of right and justice found in the law of nature. Important in the medieval period, this theory became even more prominent in the seventeenth century, when it was joined with the idea of the social compact as expressed in Calvinist covenantal theology. In this form it provided sanction and legitimacy for the modern nation-state.

Natural law theory, as Americans received it from seventeenth-century English writers such as John Locke, James Harrington, and Algernon Sidney, posited a state of nature which preceded the creation of society and government. According to Locke's second *Treatise on Civil Government,* the most famous explication of the theory, human nature was essentially good. For the better protection of the principles of right and justice inherent in the natural order, however, men and women, through a social compact, formed a government and agreed on rules for its operation. Government created in this manner rested on the consent of the governed: the people surrendered the unfettered liberty of the state of nature and gave allegiance to government in return for protection of their natural rights. The most important of these rights were life, liberty, and property, which were to be given broad application so long as their exercise did not threaten the common good or bring injury to others. Indeed, the purpose of government was to preserve the natural law, including fundamental natural rights, and to promote peace, security, and the public good. In pursuing these ends rulers were granted powers which they were to exercise as a public trust. But the whole emphasis of natural law theory was on limiting governmental power. If government violated the purposes and rules contained in the social compact, if it denied natural rights and abused public trust, the people were justified in resisting and overthrowing it.

In America natural law ideas figured prominently in the writings of John Winthrop, Thomas Hooker, and Roger Williams, theorists and architects of covenant communities in the founding period. In the eighteenth century outstanding clerical exponents of natural law were John Wise, who argued that the people had a right to determine their own form of ecclesiastical and civil government, and Jonathan Mayhew, who counseled resistance to tyranny in church and state. Natural law reasoning and rhetoric appeared in the opposition to the Dominion of New England in the 1680s, and even more conspicuously in the resistance to British imperialism in the 1760s and 1770s. The natural law tradition thus lay at the foundation of American political thought.

In the eighteenth century, however, until the eve of the Revolution, Americans were chiefly concerned with maintaining a proper relationship between the parts of government in order to preserve local autonomy and individual liberty. For instruction in these matters they consulted English critics of the ruling Whig oligarchy such as Viscount Bolingbroke, and John Trenchard and Thomas Gordon, authors of the widely circulated *Cato's Letters* (1720–23). These men, who have been labeled opposition writers, provided a body of ideas that appealed to Americans in their conflicts with the royal governors and that influenced their perceptions of British imperial policy after 1763.

The English opposition writers and the colonial pamphleteers and essayists who applied their teachings regarded the preservation of liberty through a properly mixed and balanced constitution as the basic purpose of political life. Unlike modern constitutional critics, they did not seek to *change* the constitution, but rather to *prevent* change from occurring. For it was axiomatic that constitutional change meant degeneration and decline, resulting in the destruction of liberty. Especially to be feared was the consolidation of power by a single part of the government representing only one of the component elements of society. Of course, considered abstractly, social order and the active exercise of governmental power were as important to a sound constitutional structure as was liberty. Opposition writers and their American adherents believed, however, that in actuality government power constantly threatened to undermine liberty.

The preservation of liberty depended not only on a properly balanced constitution, but also on civic and personal virtue. As conceived of in eighteenth-century opposition ideology, virtue had its foundation in the social independence that resulted from the ownership of property. Only a person who was independent in this sense, who could transcend selfish considerations and resist manipulation by men ambitious for power, was truly free politically to act for the good of the commonwealth. The great enemy of virtue was corruption. This term carried the ordinary meaning of immoral conduct based on dishonesty, profligacy, luxury, and other forms of vice. But it also possessed a technical constitutional meaning. It referred to the subversion of civic virtue through the ability of the executive to influence the elected representatives of the people.

In England the crown and the ministries, in the colonies the royal or proprietary governor, were believed to threaten the proper balance of the constitution by controlling the assembly, thus undermining civic virtue and liberty. An aggrandizing executive could work corruption by placing office holders in the legislature, as was the practice in England; by creating a numerous and supine bureaucracy to carry the government's point of view to the public; by buying votes and otherwise trying to rig the outcome of elections; by incurring large debts and then levying taxes requiring the appointment of still more officials; and by encouraging luxury, wealth, credit, and speculation at the expense of habits of frugality and honest labor that were the basis of civic and personal virtue.

To preserve liberty, believed to be the special interest of the people's elected representatives, opposition writers argued for the complete exclusion of executive officials from the legislature. Instead of a *sharing* of power, there should be a *separation* of powers. The lawmaking power ought to be given to the people's deputies; the executive power, for strictly administrative, nondiscretionary tasks, assigned to the king's ministers or the royal governor. The separation of powers had first been advanced by parliamentary opponents of the crown in the seventeenth-century Civil War. The opposition writers of the eighteenth century popularized the theory as a means of achieving the desired balance between liberty and power.

Americans found the idea of a separation of powers suitable to their needs. The reason was not, as has sometimes been suggested, that it confirmed already existing institutional practice; on the contrary, in their actual constitutional arrangements they followed conventional mixed-government theory. Since the establishment of the imperial system in the late seventeenth century, however, the colonists had often acted from a point of view so different from that of the colonial governor as to constitute a separate interest or outlook. In this sense their political experience disposed them toward the separation of powers as an alternative to mixed government. Accordingly, departing from mixed-government theory, they tried to make the assembly more independent of the governor. This could be achieved by securing a guarantee of regular elections and meetings of the assembly; by denying the governor the right to reject the speaker and prorogue the assembly; and by passing laws, known as place acts, which prohibited executive and administrative officials from sitting in the assembly. Only in regard to the last issue were the assembly leaders successful; on the other two counts the governors retained their accustomed powers. Despite their effectiveness in dealing with the governor, therefore, colonial political leaders continued to fear the broad legal powers of the royal governor. Their familiarity with the opposition literature sharpened their sensitivity to questions of authority and inclined them, when changes in imperial policy in the 1760s gave royal officials new powers, to suspect the worst: a conspiracy to destroy their rights and liberties. When American interests eventually demanded independence from England, the doctrine of the separation of powers, which had become intellectually popular in the colonies through the dissemination of Montesquieu's *The Spirit of the Laws* (1748), stood ready to hand as a basis for constitutional organization in a time of revolutionary crisis.

Colonial Courts

In their concern for constitutional balance and the preservation of liberty, Americans relied principally on the assembly rather than courts of law. Nevertheless, colonial courts formed an important if subordinate part of the structure of local government that had evolved by the middle of the eighteenth century.

In understanding the place of courts and the legal system in the colonial constitution it is necessary to keep in mind that judicial tasks were not confined to a segregated corps of judges, as under the modern theory of the separation of powers. Mixed government, of course, provided for judicial officers, but they frequently exercised nonjuridical powers. By the same token, executive and legislative officers often performed judicial tasks. This sharing of power, as we have seen, was characteristic of mixed government. Conceptually, it was rooted in the medieval belief that the purpose of government was essentially judicial—to declare and carry out the word of God. Thus law was not made by human agency, but was discovered. Before Parliament acquired supreme lawmaking power in the seventeenth century, it was viewed as a court; in the traditional expression, it was "the High Court of Parliament." During the Civil War the common law courts sided with Parliament in resisting royal power. Moreover, in establishing its supremacy over the crown Parliament removed the courts from royal influence (though not from parliamentary oversight). This was accomplished by the Act of Settlement of 1701, which provided that judges should serve during good behavior rather than at the pleasure of the crown. In the colonies, however, no such condition of judicial independence existed.

In creating their legal institutions the colonists understandably relied from the beginning on their experience with English law. There was, however, no unified system of English law to be appropriated, but rather several different systems of law, including the common law, admiralty, equity, ecclesiastical and mercantile law, and the local and customary law of towns, boroughs, and counties. In addition to fashioning entirely new law to deal with their special circumstances, the colonists in the earlier phases of settlement borrowed most heavily from English local law and from what they knew of the common law doctrines formulated by the king's courts at Westminster. The presence of English judges and lawyers in the colonies after 1660 facilitated the reception of the common law as the most important source of colonial law. What the common law provided was not so much a body of technical legal precedents as a set of fundamental principles of public law that placed limitations on government and hence were constitutional in nature. In the eighteenth century the common law became more widely accepted in the colonies, although imperial authorities never officially conceded its rightful application in America since to do so would imply restrictions on royal power.

A variety of officials carried on judicial business. In most of the colonies in the founding period the governor and council settled disputes at law. The assembly also took part in the administration of justice, although by the end of the seventeenth century the deputies confined themselves more exclusively to legislative and administrative matters. As population spread, a more highly articulated judicial system came into existence. Local courts of original jurisdiction were created, usually at the county level by executive order. County courts had jurisdiction of most civil and criminal matters; the individual magistrates or justices of the peace who sat on the county court in turn resolved petty legal conflicts in the towns where they lived. From the county courts cases were taken on appeal to the governor and council, who in most colonies sat as a kind of supreme court. The Privy Council in England could also act as an appeals or reviewing court, although it in fact did little in this regard. In comparison to England's courts, the rudimentary judicial systems in the colonies were fairly unified and hierarchical because the appellate principle received more recognition than it did in the home country.

Courts became the object of struggle between the governor and assembly in the eighteenth century. One source of conflict was the creation of new courts. The governor's commission charged him with this responsibility, but assemblies asserted their power in the matter. By about 1760 it was generally accepted that the governor would not create new tribunals without the approval of the assembly. On the other hand, the governor controlled judicial tenure, another contentious issue in several colonies. Assemblies wanted judges to serve during good behavior, as provided in the Act of Settlement of 1701, rather than at the pleasure of the crown. Because this arrangement would place judges beyond the influence of the executive, however, imperial officers regarded it as subversive of royal authority. Hence they refused to permit "good behavior" appointments.

Disputes over admiralty and chancery courts also assumed political importance. Introduced into the colonies by the Navigation Act of 1696, nine vice-admiralty courts dealt with enforcement of trade acts and other maritime matters. These courts aroused opposition because, lacking juries, they operated beyond the reach of public opinion. Chancery courts, which also lacked juries, dealt with special or emergency situations by the application of equity principles and rules. They provided remedies that were not available in common law courts. Chancery courts were unpopular among the colonists not on principle, but as a vehicle of executive power. In some colonies the county courts possessed both common law and equity powers. In others, however, the chancery courts were composed of the governor alone, or the governor and council. It was the latter situation that provoked opposition. Fearful of executive power, the colonists objected to royal authority as the source of equity jurisdiction. They looked instead to the assembly, and ultimately to the people, as the source of this special branch of law, which they would assign to the local courts in addition to their common law jurisdiction.

Local Government

The interest in colonial autonomy evinced at the provincial level in matters such as judicial tenure and chancery courts was evident also in the development of governmental institutions at the local level. In founding local institutions the colonists adopted the forms they had known in England—namely, county, church parish, and municipal corporation. In the southern and middle colonies the county was the basic governmental unit as well as the constituent unit in the assembly (i.e., representation was apportioned by counties as corporate entities rather than according to the population of the county). In New England, counties and townships were the relevant form of government, the towns being the constituent element in the assembly, and in all the colonies a number of municipal corporations governed themselves under charters granted by the provincial assembly.

If mixed government characterized constitutional arrangements at the provincial level, it was all the more evident at the local level, where a single agency performed a wide variety of governmental tasks embracing what we now describe as executive, legislative, and judicial functions. The county court provides the clearest illustration. Composed of justices of the peace nominally appointed by the governor but actually self-selected by the magistrates themselves, the county court exercised judicial responsibilities, as previously noted. But it also wielded a wide array of executive, administrative, and legislative powers in dispatching the numerous duties it acquired over the course of a century. The county court supervised the construction and maintenance of roads, bridges, docks, ferries; levied taxes; adopted local ordinances concerning trade and industry; issued licenses to inns and taverns; cared for the indigent (in conjunction with the parish vestry); acted as a probate court and orphan's court; enforced the laws of the assembly; and in general managed local affairs.

In New England the township, formed in conjunction with the creation of Congregational churches, was the principal unit that attended to the general range of executive and administrative tasks. The town assembly, or meeting, which by about 1700 permitted all adult male residents to vote, was the local legislative authority. A popularly elected body of selectmen carried out executive and administrative duties between town meetings. County courts in New England confined themselves more to judicial matters than elsewhere, though they too had some administrative duties. By 1750, moreover, the chartered municipal corporation, under the direction of a mayor and council, provided local government in fourteen cities scattered along the Atlantic coast. Unlike the towns and counties of New England

and elsewhere, the main purpose of local government in these municipalities, as specified in their charters, was to promote and regulate commercial and industrial development.

Local government early assumed an importance in American political culture that in modified form it retains to the present day. In studying it historians have analyzed the political sociology of the county courts, the degree of popular participation in the New England town meeting, and the nature and extent of the social control wielded by that institution. These studies, conducted with a view toward determining whether democracy existed in early America, show that local government provided significant opportunities for political activity and experience. Under the hierarchical and deferential attitudes of the day, however, local office holding was largely confined to a narrow segment of colonial society.

Though hardly democratic in a modern sense, local institutions were important in the development of republican government in America because they reinforced the decentralist tendencies in colonial government. In England local government, like the common law linked to the national monarchy, promoted the centralization of power. In the colonies local government was connected to provincial authority rather than to the empire. As a result it strengthened the movement toward autonomy that flourished in the assembly. When this concern for local autonomy eventuated in the American Revolution, institutions of local government served as focal points for organizing resistance to English rule. They also acted as a stabilizing force and provided a constitutional basis for the creation of new state governments.

FOUR

The American Revolution

—————————————— ✦✦✦ ——————————————

REVOLUTIONS BY DEFINITION HAVE CONSTITUTIONAL SIGNIFICANCE, for if they accomplish nothing else they remove the existing regime and install another one—in theory different—in its place. This fact notwithstanding, modern revolutions are usually thought of as social and economic rather than constitutional in nature, their purpose being to overthrow an oppressive ruling class and create a new order of society. The American Revolution differed from the stereotype of modern revolution. It produced significant constitutional change—the creation of thirteen republican state governments organized in a continental union—and the issues that provoked it were pre-eminently constitutional. It was not the purpose of the Revolution, moreover, to construct a new social order. Furthermore, while the American Revolution led to the creation of an independent people and a new nation, it differed from twentieth-century colonial uprisings and national liberation movements by virtue of the fact that the American colonists living under English rule had long enjoyed substantial political autonomy. They rebelled against England in order to preserve their local governing establishments rather than to acquire political liberty after decades of acute subordination.

Two fundamental constitutional issues lay at the heart of the imperial conflict that led to the American Revolution. The first and more conspicuous, a source of contention as early as the seventeenth century, concerned the place of the colonies in the British empire. What powers did the colonies possess in relation to the English government, and what was the status of the American colonists under the laws and constitution of England? These were esssentially questions of intergovernmental or interstate relations. They led to a series of attempts to formulate theories of imperial organization, which, though unsuccessful in resolving Americans' conflict with Britain, significantly foreshadowed the development of American federalism. The rights of individual subjects or citizens were also involved in the imperial controversy, giving rise to the second major constitutional issue of the

Revolution: the proper organization and distribution of governmental power in the polity. More so than the matter of relations among states, this question raised the basic problem of constitutionalism—namely, how to create a structure of authority and rules of public law that gave government sufficient power to maintain order while limiting that power in the interest of individual liberty and political and social freedom.

In struggling with this issue in the revolutionary era, Americans embarked on a reconsideration of the very nature of constitutionalism and fundamental law as the English had understood them. In England the constitution was the general structure of principles, laws, and institutions by which government was carried on. Government was not separate from the constitution, so that Parliament, for example, could change the constitution through its legislation. The Americans, in contrast, conceived of a constitution as anterior to and separate from government. For them a constitution was a written instrument that fixed in unalterable form the principles necessary for achieving a proper balance between power and liberty.

Imperial Reorganization

Constitutional controversy erupted when England introduced major changes in imperial policy following the Seven Years' War (1756–63). To deal with the territorial gains and financial burden that resulted from the war, the ministry determined to tighten the administration of the now sprawling British Empire. Accordingly, the loosely fitting commercial, civilian-legislative rule that prevailed after 1720 gave way to a more highly centralized military-executive style of government that looked to closer supervision of colonial affairs, including for the first time direct taxation of the colonists. Although this policy plainly differed from the casually enforced mercantilism that preceded it, it would be a mistake to regard it wholly as innovation. A degree of internal administrative control had always been implicit in the Navigation Acts, and for a brief period under the Dominion of New England had become oppressively explicit. One reason Americans reacted so swiftly to the imposition of political controls after 1763 is that their earlier experience had alerted them to its dangers.

The immediate crisis in imperial affairs was precipitated by the attempt of the ministry of George Grenville to impose certain reforms upon the administration of the colonies. Colonial military cooperation with Britain, based upon voluntary appropriations by the colonial assemblies, had all but collapsed in the Seven Years' War. Grenville and his associates therefore concluded, with much justice, that since the colonies would not voluntarily defend either themselves or the empire, regular British troops must be sent to the colonies. As Britain had already incurred a heavy indebtedness in defense of the empire, and since her tax burden was considered already too heavy, the ministry determined to levy taxes on the colonies to pay for the new army. In addition, Grenville decided to tighten enforcement of the custom laws, a step that might be made to yield still further revenue.

The ministry was also concerned with the problem of the trans-Allegheny West. Extensive colonial migration into this region appeared to be imminent, and such a development might injure British speculative landholdings on the seaboard, prejudice imperial relations with the Indian tribes controlling the valuable fur trade, and ultimately build a new colonial world too remote for effective British control. Grenville, therefore, determined to check western settlement for the moment.

The ministry resorted to three principal measures to accomplish these ends: the Proclamation of 1763, the Sugar Act of 1764, and the Stamp Act of 1765. The Proclamation of 1763 closed the frontier west of the Alleghenies to further settlement and forbade further land purchases or patents in the region. Although the decree was of slight constitutional significance, it greatly annoyed colonial land speculators and western settlers.

The Sugar Act, however, provoked powerful constitutional objections in the colonies. The statute levied a duty of threepence per gallon on molasses imported into the colonies, and it also levied small duties on a variety of other imports, among them sugar, indigo, coffee, wines, calicoes, and linens. On the surface there was nothing revolutionary in the character of these duties, for England had long imposed small tariffs upon the colonies for the regulation of trade, and under the Molasses Act of 1733 Britain had levied a duty of sixpence per gallon on molasses imported into the colonies from other than the British West Indies.

What was revolutionary in the Sugar Act was the statement in the preamble of the statute that the proceeds were to be applied toward "defraying the expenses of defending, protecting, and securing the colonies." In other words, the Sugar Act was a revenue measure, not a regulation of trade, and thus it raised the whole question of the power of Britain to tax the colonies.

In February 1765 Parliament passed the Stamp Act, the second revenue measure in Grenville's series of imperial reforms. This law provided for excise duties, to be paid by affixing revenue stamps upon a variety of legal documents, bills of sale, liquor licenses, playing cards, newspapers, and so on. The duties, which ranged from one halfpenny to six pounds and were required to be paid in specie, touched nearly every aspect of commercial and industrial life in the colonies. The power of Parliament to lay taxes of this sort immediately became of vital concern.

At the suggestion of Massachusetts, delegates from nine colonies gathered in New York in October 1765 to protest against the law. The Stamp Act Congress objected to the parliamentary measure on the ground that it violated the rights of the colonists as Englishmen under the constitution and laws of England, and the rights of the colonies as member states in the empire. The former of these positions provided the first line of protest against the act. Resolutions emanating from the Stamp Act Congress stated: "It is inseparably essential to the freedom of a people, and the undoubted right of Englishmen, that no taxes be imposed on them, but with their own consent, given personally or by their representatives." In the Virginia House of Burgesses Patrick Henry advanced the same view. By the original corporate charter, he declared, Virginians possessed all the rights, privileges, and immunities of Englishmen. He reasoned that "taxation of the people by themselves" was "the distinguishing characteristic of British freedom, without which the ancient Constitution cannot exist." The colonists furthermore made clear their belief that local circumstances prevented their ever being represented in the House of Commons. Asserting the need for actual representation, they rejected the idea that they were virtually represented in the English legislature.

Almost imperceptibly the rights-of-Englishmen argument passed into the very different theoretical proposition that the Stamp Act was unconstitutional because it violated the rights of the colonies in the empire. After denying the validity of virtual representation, the Stamp Act Congress declared that "the only Representatives of the people of these Colonies are people chosen therein by themselves, and that no taxes ever have been, or can be constitutionally imposed on them, but by their respective Legislature." As Patrick Henry expressed it: "the General Assembly of this Colony have the only and sole exclusive right and power to lay taxes and impositions upon the inhabitants of this Colony." But while insisting that the whole subject of taxation belonged to the colonial assembly, the colonists agreed that other matters came under the purview of Parliament. It was not simply a desire to be diplomatic that led the Stamp Act Congress to profess "the same Allegiance to the Crown of Great Britain, that is owing from his Subjects born within the Realm, and all due Subordination to that August Body the Parliament of Great Britain." As numerous contemporary documents make clear, the colonists regarded the power of Parliament as controlling in trade and other matters of general concern throughout the empire.

The Federal Theory of Empire

Implicit in the protest against the Stamp Act was a conception of the relationship between the colonies and England that can be described as a federal theory of empire. The essence of federalism is the division of sovereignty, or governmental authority, among several states. For over a century this circumstance had characterized the actual operation of the empire. Through their assemblies the colonists had managed their own internal affairs, including taxation, trade, and the administration of justice; had paid for the support of civil administration; and had even shared responsibility in matters reaching beyond strictly local concern such as Indian affairs and the currency. On the other hand the king and Parliament governed in matters of interest to the empire as a whole, viz., commerce, foreign affairs including war and peace, the control of military and naval forces, the post office, and the money supply. To these responsibilities imperial officials, after the Seven Years' War, added territorial administration of the western lands and defense against the Indians. Occasionally, parliamentary legislation bore directly on internal affairs in the colonies, as in the Woolen Act (1699), the Hat Act (1733), the Iron Act (1750), the act fixing the value of foreign coins in the colonies (1708), and the act forbidding the issuance of paper money in New England (1751). These measures were concerned with policy for the entire empire, however, rather than with strictly local concerns. Finally, although the crown was the more heavily involved in imperial government, Parliament had plainly legislated in matters of import to the empire as a whole, and the colonies had just as plainly accepted this legislation as legitimate.

In the years immediately after the Stamp Act several American political leaders propounded a federal theory of empire. Governor Stephen Hopkins of Rhode Island wrote that "each of the colonies hath a legislature within itself, to take care of its Interests ... yet there are things of a more general nature, quite out of reach of these particular legislatures, which it is necessary should be regulated, ordered, and governed." These general concerns, including commerce, money, and credit, were properly in the keeping of Parliament. Daniel Dulany of Maryland acknowledged the dependence of the colonies on England and their subordination to Parliament in matters of general significance for the empire. But though subordinate, the colonies had the rightful power to deal with local subjects not pertinent to the empire as a whole. Dulany alluded to the division of power that was taking shape in American minds when he distinguished between legislation that imposed a tax for the purpose of revenue and legislation to regulate trade that might incidentally produce revenue. The former was properly within the power of the colonial assembly, the latter within the power of Parliament.

The clearest exposition of federal imperial theory came from John Dickinson in *The Letters from a Pennsylvania Farmer* (1768). Dickinson began with an attack on the supposed distinction between internal and external taxes which Benjamin Franklin had conspicuously referred to in his famous examination before the House of Commons in 1766, but which had almost no standing in America. No such difference could be admitted, Dickinson reasoned; Parliament in fact had no authority "to lay upon these colonies any tax whatever." He admitted that Parliament had in the past levied certain charges incident to the regulation of trade. These were in no way taxes, however, for their main purpose was the regulation of commerce, and the duties were purely incidental to that end. To Dickinson, there was a profound difference between the power to regulate commerce and the power to tax. That Parliament properly could regulate the trade of the colonies no one denied; that it could tax the colonies in any guise, Dickinson utterly denied.

This statement clearly implied that two types of governmental powers were exercised within the empire, those properly exercised by Parliament, and those properly exercised by the local or colonial governments. Here was plainly a federal conception of the British Empire. Dickinson went on to describe the empire as it had in fact existed for a century—a great federal state with a practical distribution of authority between local and central governments.

Protest against the Stamp Act proceeded on the level of direct political action as well as constitutional theory. Popular mobbing, which sometimes ran to excess but was on the whole kept under restraint, intimidated appointed stamp collectors into resigning and effectively nullified the act. Concurrently, American leaders organized nonimportation agreements directed against English products. London merchants, their trade badly injured, clamored for repeal. All this had its effect upon the government in London. The ministry of the Marquis of Rockingham, which succeeded that of Grenville in 1766, determined upon repeal of the law.

Before the act was repealed, however, an extensive debate in both houses of Parliament revealed how profoundly English thinking differed from American on the question of imperial relations. Almost without exception English leaders insisted that sovereignty was unitary and indivisible, that it lay in Parliament, and that Parliament was the supreme legislative body not only for the realm of England but also for the empire as a whole, including the colonies. This conclusion was the result of periodic attempts since the late seventeenth century to rationalize the relationship of the colonies to the mother country and their place in the empire.

Initially the colonies had been regarded as vacant, discovered territories rather than as conquered kingdoms to be ruled by force rather than law.[1] According to this discovery theory of imperial expansion, the American emigrant-settlers were English subjects, entitled to claim the protection of the common law and so much of parliamentary statute as was applicable to their local situation. The American colonists thus enjoyed a privileged

---

1. English constitutional theory at the end of the seventeenth century distinguished between infidel and Christian conquered territory. In the former, all law and governmental authority ceased to exist upon conquest, the land being subject to the will of the king. In Christian territory existing law continued until the king chose to alter it or create new law. In either case, however, the rule of the king was subject to the ultimate supervisory authority of Parliament, in accordance with the theory of parliamentary sovereignty.

status. But the corollary of the status was an obligation to accept the ultimate authority of Parliament. Later, in the mid-eighteenth century, imperial officials justified parliamentary control over the colonies by reference to orthodox Lockean social compact theory. They held that the colonists, like all English subjects, had entered into the original compact that formed the basis of legitimate governmental authority. Having given their consent, the colonists received the protection of government and law. In return, as natural-born subjects, they owed perpetual allegiance to the English nation. The American colonists thus were seen as members of a unified political community—the empire—governed by a single sovereign, Parliament, in which they like all English subjects were represented.

Accordingly, the English rejected the American contention that there were limits to the authority of Parliament over the colonies, that the colonists' right of representation could be exercised only in their provincial assemblies, and that these assemblies had exclusive power over legislation in local affairs. Lord Mansfield, for example, held that the British legislature "represents the whole British Empire, and has authority to bind every part and every subject without the least distinction." Lord Lyttleton stated the case for the unlimited authority of Parliament with the remark that "in all states . . . the government must rest somewhere, and that must be fixed, or otherwise there is an end of all government. . . . The only question before your lordships is, whether the American colonies are a part of the dominions or the crown of Great Britain? If not, Parliament has no jurisdiction, if they are, as many statutes have declared them to be, they must be proper subjects of our legislation."

The English rejection of federalism as incomprehensible was eminently reasonable from the standpoint of conventional political science, for no doctrine seemed more certain than that within the state there must be one supreme authority. If sovereignty was supreme authority, it was by definition destroyed when divided. It was illogical and irrational to contemplate a government within a government—an *imperium in imperio*—as Americans did in suggesting that within the empire, side by side with Parliament's power over commerce and other general matters, the colonial assemblies possessed sovereignty in local affairs. The English had for so long clung to the idea of the colonies as local corporations, dependent on royal grace and favor for their very existence, that they were unable to grasp the historical reality that the empire had become a federal state.

In the debate in Commons, most members were also unwilling to accept the American doctrine of actual representation. George Grenville, author of the Stamp Act, declared for the complete sovereignty of Parliament and added that "taxation is a part of the sovereign power." Another member stated that "enacting laws and laying taxes so intirely go together that if we surrender the one we lose the others." With reference to the claim that taxation and representation were inseparable, a third member said: "I thought that argument had been beat out of the House. There never was a time when that Idea was true."

However, America was not without friends in Parliament. In the Commons the great William Pitt lent the weight of his immense prestige to the American cause. He upheld the supremacy of Parliament, but almost alone among Englishmen he insisted at the same time that "taxation is no part of the governing or legislating power." He followed this assertion with a direct attack upon the whole theory of virtual representation, which he called "the most contemptible idea that ever entered the head of man." In the House of Lords, Lord Camden put forth the same idea with the statement that "taxation and representation are inseparable;—this position is founded on the laws of nature."

A shrewd commentary upon the conflict was made by Edmund Burke, in afteryears to become known as the great English champion of American rights. On parliamentary taxation he pointed out that "some of the Charters declare the Right, others suppose it, none deny it." But he saw "a real Distinction in every Country between the speculative and practical constitution of that country. . . . The British empire must be governed on a plan of freedom, for it will be governed by no other." The colonies, he continued, "were mere Corporations, Fishermen and Furriers, they are now commonwealths. Give them an interest in his [the king's] Allegiance, give them some Resemblance to the British Constitution . . . ," and American loyalty would then follow as a matter of course.

Burke was issuing a warning that if archaic constitutional theories were allowed to blind Parliament to the fact that the colonies were rapidly becoming great and powerful states, then the empire was headed for disaster. The colonies were not corporations, but great states whose population, commerce, and industry were thriving and whose economic and social order was now powerful enough to stand alone, even if British politicians were unaware of it. American requests for freedom from taxation and for internal autonomy were demands that this situation be recognized.

Parliament at length repealed the Stamp Act, but not before asserting the very principle of parliamentary supremacy and unitary sovereignty that Americans had called into question. It affirmed this constitutional position, at least to its own satisfaction, in the Declaratory Act of 1766, which stated simply that Parliament had full power to make laws and statutes binding the colonies "in all cases whatsoever." Although the act carefully avoided any reference to taxation, debate in Parliament made it clear that it was intended to comprehend that issue, the main source of conflict. But Americans, not knowing the legislative history of the measure and observing its omission of any mention of taxation, could plausibly regard it as not inconsistent with their federal conception of empire.

The Formation of an American Resistance Movement

England persisted in its determination to tax the colonies in 1767 under Pitt as prime minister and Charles Townshend as Chancellor of the Exchequer. Acting on the distinction between internal and external taxes misleadingly laid down by Benjamin Franklin, Townshend proposed a revenue act in June 1767 that levied a series of duties upon glass, red and white lead, painters' colors, tea, and paper imported into the colonies. While the manner of collection was not different from those older duties incident to the enforcement of the Navigation Laws, the law's preamble specifically stated that it was a revenue measure for "the support of civil government, in such provinces as it shall be found necessary." The law was an undisguised tax measure, not a commercial regulation.

The Americans were particularly alarmed by Townshend's proposal to use the proceeds of the law to create a colonial civil list, from which colonial governors and judges would receive their salaries. This struck directly at the hard-won control that the assemblies had come to exercise over the colonial governors. If the governors were given independent salaries and a civil list independent of assembly control, much of colonial autonomy would be destroyed. The colonists also objected to another statute of Townshend's which created a separate board of customs commissioners for the American colonies. They viewed the board as merely another instrument of sharpened British control and unconstitutional taxation. Still another Townshend statute created new admiralty courts and specifically authorized the hated writs of assistance permitting open-ended searches in customs cases.

The direct political action that had met the Stamp Act resumed in response to the Townshend Acts. Nonimportation associations, backed by petition campaigns and Sons of Liberty organizations, applied economic pressure. Again Parliament undertook a tactical retreat. In 1769 it repealed all the duties except the tax on tea, with the result that colonial boycotts for the most part collapsed. By 1770 the crisis precipitated by the Townshend measures was at an end.

The years 1770–73 were superficially a period of quiescence. But the suspicion of the English government that Americans harbored and their heightened political awareness made further conflict highly probable, if not inevitable, so long as England insisted on a unitary theory of sovereignty in its imperial policy. Now the years of exposure to the opposition ideology, with its stress on the continual struggle between power and liberty, had a telling effect on the colonists. Matters which when considered in isolation would seem of minor importance, took on ominous significance as part of an apparent attack on American liberty. In addition to their protest against taxation without actual representation, Americans criticized British reliance on juryless vice-admiralty courts for enforcement of the Navigation Acts, and prosecution in common law courts by the use of informations rather than through grand-jury proceedings. Both practices eliminated the influence of public opinion in the administration of justice and added to Americans' fear of executive control of the government. A threat to liberty also appeared in the Quartering Act of 1765, which required any colony in which English troops were stationed to supply them with provisions. Regarded as tantamount to a tax, the act in colonial minds augured the imposition of a standing army, one of the most persistent themes in the opposition literature. Another provocative measure emanating from Parliament was the Restraining Act of 1767. Less well known than the revenue laws but pehaps even more threatening, it suspended the power of the New York assembly until it should comply with the Quartering Act. But even without such bluntly repressive legislation the power of the assemblies seemed in jeopardy, and with it the colonists' treasured local autonomy.

John Dickinson's *Letters of a Pennsylvania Farmer* captured the sense of apprehension that eroded American trust in British intentions even before critical events in the mid-1770s precipitated armed struggle. Describing the substance of local sovereignty, Dickinson observed that the assembly had been responsible for the defense of society, the administration of justice, and the support of civil government in general. But the expected consequence of the Townshend revenue act, with its establishment of a colonial civil list, would be the superseding of the assembly in its governing function. "Why should these trusts be wrested out of their hands?" Dickinson asked. "Why should they not be permitted to enjoy the authority, which they have exercised from the first settlement of these colonies?" To conduct government at the expense of the people, Dickinson averred, but independently of their opinions and judgment, was slavery. The reaction to imperial centralization also had a personal, psychological dimension. Assemblymen whose authority had been comparable to Roman senators, Dickinson wrote, would have no more importance than local constables making rules for the yoking of hogs or the impounding of stray cattle! In the very terms employed in the opposition writings which Americans had read for decades, Dickinson warned against the extension of ministerial influence through the appointment of revenue collectors, customs officers, postal agents, and sundry government officials. He reminded his readers that perpetual vigilance about liberty was essential in all free states, especially in a mixed constitution where domination by any single part of the government forecast tyranny.

In an atmosphere tense not only with the resentment at specific imperial policies but also with pervasive distrust of British authority in general, the Tea Act of 1773 triggered a series of events that swiftly transformed colonial resistance into incipient revolution. The act granted a bounty to the East India Company on its tea exports to America, thereby enabling it to undersell all other competitors, including colonial merchants. In response to the act Massachusetts patriots destroyed 20,000 pounds worth of tea in the famous Boston Tea Party. The English government retaliated with the so-called Intolerable Acts, which in colonial eyes conclusively demonstrated the English intention to subject the colonists to political slavery.

The Boston Port Act, March 31, 1774, closed the port of Boston until the town should make restitution to the East India Company. The Massachusetts Government Act, May 20, 1774, altered the charter of Massachusetts in an attempt to bring the colony more directly under the control of the English government. The assistants were no longer to be elected by the General Court but appointed by the crown. The governor was also given the power to appoint, without consent of the council, all judges of inferior courts, and to nominate all judges of superior courts. In the future, also, no town was to call any meeting of its selectmen other than the annual meeting without the consent of the governor.

The Administration of Justice Act, May 20, 1774, provided that in case of alleged felonies committed by crown officers, magistrates, and so on, in pursuit of their duties in Massachusetts Bay, trial was, upon order of the governor, to be moved to some other colony or to Great Britain. The act was intended to protect officials in the discharge of their duties by guaranteeing them against the wrath of colonial juries. The Quartering Act, June 2, 1774, permitted officials in any colony to quarter royal troops upon the inhabitants of a town when necessary. This law was intended to force the colonists to make adequate provision for housing soldiers wherever they might be needed; yet clearly it violated one of the traditional guarantees of the Petition of Right.

The Quebec Act, passed June 22, 1774, although not intended as a punitive measure, was so regarded in America. The law extended the boundaries of the Province of Quebec to include the area north of the Ohio and west of the Proclamation Line of 1763, and it thus appeared to violate several colonial charters by stripping the colonies of their trans-Allegheny possessions. The law also extended religious liberty to the Catholics of Quebec. While this provision was of no constitutional or social significance to the seaboard colonies, it was nonetheless represented as an attempt to impose the hated Church of Rome upon Protestant America.

The Dominion Theory of Empire

As the rift between the colonies and the mother country grew wider and the possibility of independence was bruited about, colonial leaders altered their conception of empire accordingly. They now brought forward a commonwealth or dominion theory of empire, holding that each colony, like England itself, had a sovereign and independent legislature and was connected to Great Britain only through the king. English history and law—as Americans interpreted it—offered solid support for such a view. The relevant historical example was Scotland. An independent kingdom before the accession of James VI to the English throne, Scotland afterward remained a separate political jurisdiction, not subject to parliamentary rule. Yet, as laid down in Calvin's case (1608), the historic decision that defined the nature of the union between Scotland and England, the Scots were English subjects, loyal to the king.[2] This was precisely the situation that the American colonists desired: political autonomy within a single community of allegiance to the English crown. Accordingly, the colonists made frequent reference to Calvin's case in their arguments of the 1770s.

The dominion theory of empire aptly served American purposes. It preserved internal autonomy while enabling the colonists to maintain their loyalty to the king and their connection to the empire. The constitutional significance of the theory was its categorical denial of parliamentary authority over the colonies, including commercial regulation. The original domain of North America, wrote Samuel Adams in 1773, was not part of the realm of England but adhered to the crown alone, as the king's personal property. Through the prerogative, the king could dispose of his domains as he wished. Adams and others contended that royal grants, in the form of seventeenth-century corporate and proprietary charters, established a direct link between the colonies and the crown which lay outside the sphere of parliamentary competence.

The dominion theory reflected the colonists' seemingly paradoxical desire to assume a position of equality with England, while remaining within the empire and hence in some sense in a dependent status. Like the thesis of imperial centralization and parliamentary supremacy maintained by the English, the dominion theory was doctrinaire in its failure to recognize the actual division of sovereignty that existed in the empire. Aside from the psychological benefit of enabling the colonists still to profess loyalty to Great Britain, it was hard to see the practical significance of the imperial tie in the theory as formally presented; apparently there was none, the king as the common sovereign of the colonies possessing merely a nominal authority. Yet even as they denied any legitimate parliamentary power in the dominion theory, Americans were in fact prepared to ac-

2. A contrived suit brought for the purpose of settling the constitutional dispute over the relationship between Scotland and England caused by the accession of James VI, Calvin's case concerned the right of Robert Calvin, a Scots infant born in 1606 after the accession, to inherit property in England. If, in addition to being a subject of Scotland, Robert Calvin was in the eyes of English law also an English subject, he could inherit property. If not, he was an alien and could not own property in England. Edward Coke, chief justice of common pleas, whose opinion of the several rendered was accepted as authoritative, held that Calvin was a subject of the king of England and, therefore, eligible to inherit property. Insofar as Scots and English subjects were bound in a common allegiance to the king, the two countries were united. Yet the union was a limited one, for Coke declared Scotland and England to be separate jurisdictions, with distinct legal systems and political institutions.

knowledge parliamentary legislation for imperial purposes on a pragmatic basis. In the words of John Adams: "Parliament has no authority over the colonies, except to regulate their trade, and this not by any principle of common law, but merely by the consent of the colonies, founded on the obvious necessities of the case." James Madison said that commercial regulation by Parliament was "a practice without a right, and contrary to the true theory of the constitution." But it was nevertheless convenient and necessary, and hence permissible as a measure that might preserve imperial unity.

While the colonists clung, albeit in attenuated fashion, to the imperial tie, their protest against taxation and other imperial innovations by 1774 directly challenged English authority and led to the formation of a revolutionary governing apparatus. Rioting in response to the Stamp Act, though controlled and discriminating in its application, forced many English officers to resign and encouraged more systematic American efforts at political organization. One result was the spread of nonimportation associations that made and enforced rules of economic boycott. Acting like authentic governments, they inspected merchants' activities, judged persons accused of violating the agreements, and imposed sanctions on the guilty. The nonimportation associations also received reinforcement from established local institutions like the town meeting. Further significant steps toward revolutionary government came with the formation of committees of correspondence in New England and Virginia in 1772–73, and throughout the rest of the colonies in 1774 in reaction to the Intolerable Acts. Like the economic boycott groups, the committees assumed duties commonly vested only in sovereign political bodies. Most important was their attempt to give colonial boycott agreements the force of law by means of publicity, intimidation, and resolutions against offenders. In reality the committees were revolutionary bodies, taking the lead in concerted resistance to British authority.

These committees soon gave rise to colony-wide revolutionary governments. Thus in Massachusetts, General Thomas Gage, now governor of the colony, dissolved the regularly constituted General Court in June, and the Boston committee of correspondence thereupon demanded the election of a provincial congress to take charge of the government of Massachusetts until Parliament and the crown should accept their constitutional functions. The provincial congress met in October 1774, and henceforth the effective government of Massachusetts Bay was no longer in the hands of the governor and the other regularly constituted crown officers, but in the hands of the provincial congress.

Events took a similar turn in the other colonies. In Virginia, the royal governor dissolved the assembly in May because of its rebellious temper. Thereupon a portion of the House of Burgesses under the leadership of Patrick Henry, Thomas Jefferson, and others, issued a call for an election of

members of a provincial congress to meet in Williamsburg on August 1. By
the close of 1774, all the royal and proprietary colonies except New York,
Pennsylvania, and Georgia had established provincial congresses, and these
three colonies took this step the following year. In the two charter colonies
of Connecticut and Rhode Island, the legal governments were so nearly
autonomous that no such move was necessary. The existing governments
simply accepted the patriot cause.

In most of the colonies the governor's dissolution of the regularly constituted legislature or his refusal to call it into session was the immediate
occasion for the erection of the provincial congress. In some cases, a congress was a rump of the regular assembly, composed of delegates in sympathy with the popular cause. This was true in Massachusetts, New
Hampshire, Delaware, Virginia, and North Carolina. In New Jersey, Maryland, and South Carolina, delegates to the congresses were chosen by means
of elections held at popular meetings throughout the colonies.

As noted, the provincial congresses were in fact revolutionary state
governments. Although the members protested their loyalty to the crown,
they engaged in steady suppression of the remnants of royal authority in the
colonies. Thus the Massachusetts congress, late in 1774, took over the tax
machinery and the operation of the courts, and began raising an army for
the field. Much the same seizure of power occurred in all the colonies. The
American colonies were now in the process of becoming the American
states, a metamorphosis completed by 1776, some time before the Declaration of Independence was signed.

The First Continental Congress

While this revolution was going on within the various colonies, the
pyramid of revolutionary government was completed by the establishment
of an intercolonial congress. In September 1774 the First Continental Con-
gress, called at the suggestion of several of the provincial congresses, met in
Philadelphia. All the colonies except Georgia were represented, and
some of the most distinguished men in America were present, among them
Samuel and John Adams of Massachusetts, Stephen Hopkins of Rhode
Island, Roger Sherman of Connecticut, John Jay and Philip Livingston of
New York, John Dickinson and Joseph Galloway of Pennsylvania, George
Washington, Richard Henry Lee, and Patrick Henry of Virginia, and John
Rutledge of South Carolina.

Although the delegations varied in size and represented colonies of
different territorial extent and population, it was nevertheless shortly decided that the vote would be taken by states, each state present having one
vote. Thus the principle of state equality was established, a principle soon to
be incorporated in the Articles of Confederation and later to gain limited
recognition in the Constitution of the United States.

The temper of the congress, despite its revolutionary status, was at first somewhat conservative. The delegates were inclined to listen to men of caution in the persons of Dickinson, Jay, Galloway, and Rutledge. These men advocated a constructive solution of the imperial problem rather than a break with England. The more radical and revolutionary views of the two Adamses, Hopkins, Lee, and Henry were thrust temporarily into the background.

For a time the delegates considered a plan of union submitted by Joseph Galloway of Pennsylvania. This plan proposed the establishment of an intercolonial legislature or "grand council" composed of delegates chosen for three years by the respective colonial assemblies. A president-general appointed by the king would preside. The grand council would be "an inferior and distinct branch of the British Legislature," and would have authority over the general affairs of the colonies. Either the British Parliament or the grand council would enact legislation for intercolonial matters, but the assent of both legislatures would be necessary before any statute became valid.

In a calmer day the plan might have been adopted and might have paved the way for dominion status for America, but the trend was against conciliatory measures. After some indecision the plan was tabled by a majority of one vote, and the congress turned toward more radical proposals.

The first evidence that the extremist faction was obtaining the upper hand came with the introduction of the Suffolk Resolves, a series of resolutions of a popular convention in Suffolk County, Massachusetts. The resolves asserted that no obedience was due the Intolerable Acts and that no taxes should be paid into the provincial treasury until constitutional government was restored in the colony. Their introduction was in reality a successful stratagem to force the congress toward a more radical position. Although the congress took no positive action upon the resolves, the reaction toward the measures nonetheless indicated the steady growth of radical opinion among the delegates.

The Declaration and Resolves of the First Continental Congress, a series of resolutions adopted by the congress on October 14, showed how far radical sentiment had progressed in the gathering. This document, though conciliatory in tone, virtually reiterated the dominion conception of colonial status, which had become extremely popular among the colonial radicals. The Declaration and Resolves held the colonists to be "entitled to a free and exclusive power of legislation in their several provincial legislatures ... in all cases of taxation and internal polity, subject only to the negative of their sovereign." The only concession to parliamentary authority was a provision that "from the necessity of the case, and a regard to the mutual interest of both countries, we cheerfully consent to the operation of such acts of the British parliament, as are bona fide restrained to the regulation of our external commerce." This expressed not only a desire to win moderate support, but also the continuing appeal of a federal division of sovereignty.

Other provisions of the resolutions amounted essentially to an assertion of a colonial bill of rights as against even royal authority. The colonists were declared entitled to "life, liberty, and property," and to "all the rights, liberties, and immunities of free and natural-born subjects within the realm of England." They were further declared entitled to the common law of England, to the benefits of such English statutes as had existed at the time of their colonization and that had been found applicable to American circumstances, and to all the privileges and immunities granted by the several royal charters or secured by their own legal systems. The resolutions affirmed further the colonists' right to assemble peaceably, consider their grievances, and petition the king. They denounced as "against law" the maintenance of a standing army in any colony in time of peace without the consent of the legislature of that colony. Finally, they condemned appointment of colonial councils by the crown as "unconstitutional, dangerous, and destructive to the freedom of American legislation."

Six days after the adoption of the Declaration and Resolves came the formation of the Continental Association, the first positive measure of resistance to British authority taken by the colonies acting in their united capacity. Through this organization the congress laid down an intercolonial nonimportation agreement against all British goods, effective December 1, 1774. The slave trade as well was banned as of the same date. The congress also threatened to invoke nonexportation to Britain, to be effective September 1, 1775, unless the obnoxious acts of Parliament were repealed. The boycott was given sanctions by recommending the formation of local committees "whose business it shall be attentively to observe the conduct of all persons touching this association."

With the creation of the Continental Congress, the pyramid of local, state, and federal revolutionary governments was complete. However, neither the local committes of correspondence, the provincial assemblies, nor the Continental Congress before January 1776 laid claim to any regular sovereign political authority. Nor, at first, was it their overt intention to engage in armed rebellion against England. Actually, however, they not only steadily carried out the seizure of authority from agents of the crown, but in April 1775 they began an armed rebellion against British troops.

The Coming of Independence

When the Second Continental Congress met in May 1775, the battle of Lexington and Concord had been fought, armed clashes had occurred in Virginia, and the major battle of Bunker Hill was in the offing. The congress responded to the challenge by raising and appointing an army and naming Washington to command it. In July, the congress issued a Declaration of the Causes and Necessity of Taking Up Arms, a document prepared by Dickinson and Jefferson. It disavowed any intention of seeking independence, but pledged resistance until Parliament abandoned its unconstitutional rule in America. The estrangement between England and America was now complete, though there was a general reluctance in the colonies to admit the fact. The king's Proclamation of Rebellion in August 1775, the Prohibitory Act of December 1775, by which Parliament declared the colonies outside Britain's protection and proclaimed a blockade of all colonial ports, and the steady extension of military engagements, made reconciliation impossible. Throughout 1775 most colonials denounced the idea of independence, but early in 1776 there developed a marked increase in the sentiment for formal separation from the mother country.

In January 1776 Thomas Paine's pamphlet *Common Sense* gave a powerful impetus both to the movement for independence and the idea of republican government as an alternative to monarchy. After nine months of actual warfare, Paine's tract answered Americans' need for convincing reasons for complete separation. In a vivid and emotional style that made the work immediately accessible and popular (it sold 120,000 copies in three months), Paine said that further dependence on England would be ruinous for it would mean involvement in European wars and the destruction of American commerce. It was politically absurd moreover, he observed, for a continent to be governed by an island. More significant in a constitutional sense and equally important in stimulating sentiment for independence was Paine's attack on monarchy and the English mixed constitution. This was truly radical and outrageous. Employing the analysis made familiar in the opposition literature of the eighteenth century, Paine condemned the corruption and despotism inherent in a government that gave special powers, transmitted by hereditary right, to monarchy and aristocracy. It was farcical, he charged, to suppose that the different parts of the English constitution checked and balanced each other when the same people—the king's ministers and appointees—both advised and carried out as the executive part of the government what they enacted as law in Parliament. Arguing for the abolition of crown and nobility, Paine urged a republican conception of the state that would derive government exclusively from the people. Having in a symbolic sense killed the king, *Common Sense* transferred the sovereignty once possessed by the crown to the people of America.

Powerful as it was, Paine's pamphlet did no more than hasten an already inevitable separation. By 1776 the rebellious colonists had carried their movement too far to turn back without abandoning the whole cause and placing their very lives in danger. They had organized *de facto* state and national governments and had shot the king's troops, ousted his officials, and destroyed his trade. Conciliation was impossible. Independence was already a fact, and it remained only to make it true in theory and law as well.

In the spring of 1776 events moved swiftly toward the establishment of formal independence. On April 6 the congress declared all colonial ports open to foreign trade, thus repudiating imperial trade laws. On May 10 it adopted a resolution calling upon the several colonies to create regular state governments. A preamble to this resolution, adopted on May 15, went even further; it stated that since Great Britain had placed the colonies outside her protection and made war upon them, it was now necessary that every kind of authority under the crown be totally suppressed and all governmental powers transferred to the people of the several colonies.

On June 7, Richard Henry Lee, acting in accordance with instructions from the state of Virginia, laid the following resolution before the congress:

Resolved, that these United Colonies are, and of right ought to be, free and independent States, and that they are absolved from all allegiance to the British Crown, and that all connection between them and the State of Great Britain is, and ought to be, totally dissolved.

On June 11, the congress referred Lee's resolution to a committee of five men, Thomas Jefferson, John Adams, Benjamin Franklin, Roger Sherman, and Robert Livingston, who were assigned the task of drafting a "declaration to the effect of the said resolution." The result was the Declaration of Independence.

Although Americans frequently appealed to natural law in their protest against British policies, their chief reliance had been on the rights of Englishmen under the constitution and laws of England, and on the federal and dominion theories of empire. In throwing off English authority, however, they appealed primarily to the law of nature. Jefferson's opening paragraph in the Declaration of Independence signaled the necessary shift in perspective:

When in the course of human events, it becomes necessary for one people to dissolve the political bands which have connected them with another, and to assume among the powers of the earth the separate and equal station to which the Laws of Nature and of Nature's God entitle them, a decent respect to the opinions of mankind requires that they should declare the causes which impel them to the separation.

Jefferson next proposed a condensed statement of the natural law–compact philosophy then prevalent in America:

We hold these truths to be self-evident, that all men are created equal, that they are endowed by their Creator with certain unalienable rights, that among these are life, liberty, and the pursuit of happiness. That to secure these rights, governments are instituted among men, deriving their just powers from the consent of the governed. That whenever any form of government becomes destructive of these ends, it is the right of the people to alter or to abolish it, and to institute new government. . . . Prudence, indeed, will dictate that governments long established should not be changed for light and transient causes; . . . But when a long train of abuses and usurpations, pursuing invariably the same object, evinces a design to reduce them under absolute despotism, it is their right, it is their duty, to throw off such government, and to provide new guards for their future security.

There are four fundamental political ideas here: the doctrine of natural law and natural rights, the compact theory of the state, the doctrine of popular sovereignty, and the right of revolution. These conceptions were common to nearly all seventeenth- and eighteenth-century natural law theorists, but Jefferson's phraseology was closely modeled on John Locke's *Second Treatise.*

Jefferson's declaration that "all men are created equal" was to become a political credo that had a profound effect upon the political life of the new nation. In the revolutionary era, it served at a minimum to condemn hereditary legal and political privilege. This tendency reached fruition in the concept of careers open to talent in the Jacksonian period. In the Civil War era controversy focused on whether Jefferson's appeal to equality was intended to apply universally—that is, to slaves—or whether it encompassed only those who were already members of the political community. In the twentieth century the Declaration's language of equality has taken on even broader import as American society has become increasingly sensitive to inequality in all its forms. Jefferson did not, however, intend to lay down any broad premise of extreme democratic equality. He did not mean that all people were equal in moral, spiritual, or intellectual ability, or that government should try to create equality of condition for all people. Natural law theory held that in a state of nature all men were equal in the possession of certain inalienable rights—"life, liberty, and the pursuit of happiness," in Jefferson's words. Government was instituted to protect those rights and could not impair them; it must, in other words, regard all men as equal in the eyes of the law. It was in this sense that Jefferson believed all men were created equal.

Twentieth-century liberals favoring a bureaucratic and socially responsive government have made much of Jefferson's substitution of "happiness" for "property" in his description of natural, inalienable rights. In conventional natural law theory the happiness of society, or public happiness, was the first end of government. This was not understood in contradistinction to property, however, but as complementary to and even contingent upon it. Property meant pre-eminently land or access to land, ownership of which enabled a person to become truly independent. It was the basis of civic virtue on which republican government depended. Property and liberty were thus inextricably related, and were considered necessary for the attainment of happiness. It is inaccurate, therefore, to see in the Declaration of Independence a distinction between property rights and human rights.

Jefferson presented an indictment of George III to illustrate "the long train of abuses" that had spurred the colonies to revolt. Most of the alleged offenses had grown out of issues that had arisen since 1763, involving acts of Parliament asserting authority over the colonies. Yet the Declaration attacked the crown and said virtually nothing of Parliament. This rhetorical strategy was necessary because Jefferson and the congress accepted the dominion theory of empire, which presented the colonies as united to England only through the person of the king and denied all parliamentary authority over the colonies.

The American Conception of Constitutionalism

Although the colonists objected to imperial policy as a violation of their rights under the constitution and laws of England, their protest led them to question not only the authority of the English government, but also the English conception of constitutionalism. In the prerevolutionary era they began to formulate a new approach to constitutionalism that ultimately caused American political development to differ basically from that of England.

In England the constitution was the complex of institutions, laws, customs, practices, and principles by which the people conducted their political and governmental life. In theory the constitution derived from established principles of reason and justice, its purpose being to promote the common good and achieve a proper balance between liberty and order. Although certain historic documents such as Magna Charta possessed special significance, the constitution was not a written instrument but an organically evolving assemblage of statute, belief, and institutional practice.

The ability of the constitution to limit governmental power came from three sources: common-law guarantees of private rights and individual liberty (*jurisdictio*) enforced by the courts against government (*gubernaculum*); balanced institutional arrangements according to the theory of mixed government; and fundamental law. Although usually equated with natural law, fundamental law had a more explicit content in the principles of reason used in interpreting and applying the common law. It was in this sense that Sir Edward Coke, the great seventeenth-century jurist, had pursued the idea of constitutional limitations on government in the famous case of Dr. Bonham in 1610. Dr. Bonham was charged with violating an act of Parliament that authorized the London College of Physicians to license the practice of medicine in the city, and that empowered the college to punish physicians practicing without the required license. Coke found Dr. Bonham innocent on the ground that the law in question was void. The common law, Coke said, will control acts of Parliament and sometimes adjudge them to be void when an act is against common right or reason, repugnant, or impossible to be performed.

Coke did not mean that English courts could declare acts of Parliament unconstitutional, as American courts were to do under the doctrine of judicial review. The separation of powers did not yet exist; Parliament was a court as well as a legislative body and formed part of the constitution. Nor did Coke mean that the entire body of the common law stood as a restraint on Parliament's lawmaking power. The London College of Physicians, however, by charging Dr. Bonham, by finding him guilty, and by collecting half the fine he was assessed as punishment, had in effect decided a matter in which it had an interest. And this violated the common-law principle that no man should be a judge in his own case. Coke's opinion nevertheless contained the idea of a fundamental or higher law restraining governmental acts.

In the seventeenth century Parliament established its legislative supremacy. By the mid-eighteenth century the doctrine of fundamental law had lost much of its intellectual appeal and delimiting force in English political life. Considering Parliament's claim to sovereignty, and the fact that its enactments were by definition part of the constitution, how could there be any limits on its power? Although theorists might say that Parliament was obliged to follow principles of right reason and natural justice in its actions, it was difficult to see how the English constitution restrained government in the interest of liberty.

This at any rate was the way it appeared to Americans as they contemplated imperial affairs. If Parliament was sovereign, then the constitution was not really a constitution at all. In protesting parliamentary statutes Americans argued that a constitution, in order to accomplish its purpose of controlling the government, must be fixed. Moreover, it must be separate from and antecedent to government so as to be unalterable by the legislature or other agencies. Americans reasoned that the essential principles of reason and justice, and the rules for the proper arrangement and distribution of governmental power, must be abstracted from actual institutions and given fixed form. Eventually, after the blow for independence was struck, they concluded that these principles and rules must be given positive, written, documentary expression as a fixed standard—a higher law— against which to hold the government accountable.

In 1761 James Otis pointed toward the new American conception of constitutionalism in his attack on parliamentary authorized writs of assistance, recently employed in Massachusetts to enforce the Navigation Laws. Citing Coke's opinion in Dr. Bonham's case, Otis said the writs violated fundamental principles of law which guaranteed a man security in his own home. An act of Parliament against natural equity was void, Otis reasoned, and so too was an act against the constitution. In 1768 the *Circular Letter* of the Massachusetts General Court to the assemblies of the other colonies argued that the constitution consisted in fundamental rules which neither the legislature nor executive could alter. "In all free states," the Massachusetts deputies declared in protest against the Townshend Acts, "the constitution is fixed, and the supreme legislative power of the nation, from thence derives its authority." The *Circular Letter* stated that the constitution ascertains and limits sovereignty, and that the legislature could not "overleap the bounds of the constitution without subverting its own foundation." John Dickinson apprehended the new conception of constitutionalism when he wrote, in *Letters from a Pennsylvania Farmer,* that a free people are "Not those over whom government is reasonably and equitably exercised, but those, who live under a government so constitutionally checked and controlled, that proper provision is made against its being otherwise exercised."

The idea of a fixed, normative constitution existing outside of and superior to government represented a significant theoretical innovation. Yet in the American context it was not altogether unfamiliar. On the contrary, the seventeenth-century experience in founding new governments had prepared the way for this conceptual development. The joint-stock corporation charters, proprietary concessions and agreements, and fundamental orders of the covenant-compact colonies resembled fixed constitutional instruments. Although they never assumed the extrainstitutional status that constitutions in the revolutionary era did, they were antecedent to government and were later appealed to as a restraint on imperial authority. In Bernard Bailyn's apt expression, the new American conception of constitutionalism represented experience elevated to principle.

Revolutionary constitutionalism also drew upon the Western tradition of natural law and English notions of fundamental law, both of which contained the idea of protecting legal rights by placing limitations on legislative power. But, though occasionally invoked by common law courts, these traditions suffered distinct institutional weakness because their implementation essentially depended on their being internalized by governing officials. Americans tried to remedy this defect by giving fundamental law positive expression in written constitutions. At the same time they regarded written constitutions as embodying moral values derived from natural law.

There were philosophical difficulties inherent in this attempt to combine positive law and natural law. Legal positivism, the belief that authoritative and effective law must be expressed in formal, positive terms, separates law from morality and encourages legalism. It stands at the opposite pole from natural law, which insists on an identification between law and morality and encourages a peculiar kind of moralism. The new American conception of constitutionalism was intended not only to use natural law as a standard for judging the wisdom and morality of government actions, but also to give it a fixed, definite form as a standard for assessing the legality of government actions as well. American constitutionalism thus contained within it a theoretical tension, which began to manifest itself as Americans constructed revolutionary state governments following the break from England.

FIVE

Revolutionary Constitutionalism: The States and the Articles of Confederation

—— ✦✦✦ ——

IN ITS INITIAL PHASE the American Revolution was an attempt to protect the rights and liberties of the colonists as individual subjects and of the colonies as states or units in the empire under the laws and constitution of England. When Americans realized the impossibility of this task and forcibly rejected English authority, however, they were concerned with achieving not only home rule as a separate people, but also a particular kind of home rule. English imperial policy had threatened to impose what Americans regarded as an outside or alien presence. It also threatened to destroy institutions of local liberty, rooted in the very founding of the colonies, which to a significant extent were based on the democratic element in society. With the collapse of English authority, Americans of necessity organized new governments. But in restoring law and order they did not simply maintain their old political establishments. They seized the opportunity which the struggle for national liberation presented to create constitutions of liberty that expressed even more cogently than the Declaration of Independence the "spirit of '76."

The essence of that spirit was republican constitutionalism. The governments that Americans now projected for their independent states rested on the new conception of constitutionalism and fundamental law formulated during the imperial controversy. Equally significant was the assertion of republicanism as the philosophical foundation of the new American political order. Until the eve of the Revolution most colonists could scarcely conceive of a political framework other than mixed government and constitutional monarchy. The English constitution and their own provincial constitutions contained a democratic component, but a government based entirely on the popular element was practically unthinkable. In the received wisdom of the day republics were disdained as small, weak, and ineffective; the word *republican* was derisive, a term of opprobrium. With the abolition of monarchy in America, however, the perception of republican government changed.

Americans espoused the idea of republicanism with conviction, even fervor. In a sense it was familiar to them from their history, for colonial government manifested many of the characteristics of local liberty and responsiveness to public opinion identified with republican government. And considering the absence in America of a titled aristocracy, the elimination of the crown left the popular element as the only basis of government. Yet if republican constitutionalism was the product of history, and even in some sense historically necessary, the fact is incontrovertible that in making republicanism the foundation of their polity Americans acted with a self-conscious sense of purpose, choice, and commitment. Furthermore, for all the practical anticipation of republican politics evident in the colonial period, Americans made significant constitutional innovations in creating state governments. Rejecting mixed government as an organizing principle, they structured their republican state constitutions on the doctrine of the separation of powers.

Republicanism As a Revolutionary Philosophy

Republican theory dealt mainly with the nature and sources of political and legal authority rather than with the internal constitutional structure of the polity. Derived from the Latin *res publica,* or "public thing," republicanism defined government as a public matter, the people's affair conducted for their interest and well-being rather than for the benefit of the ruler. Accordingly, republican government had its origin in and derived its authority from the people. The precise forms that popular action might take in creating government could, of course, vary, although the theory of the social contract supplied the intellectual rationale of the process. Eventually, the constitutional convention, superseding *ad hoc* interventions of state legislatures, became the accepted mode by which the people as constituent power formed their government.

Americans' rapid conversion to republicanism after the Declaration of Independence so thoroughly established it as the theoretical basis of the new order that it is difficult to grasp the radicalism of the undertaking as it appeared to contemporaries. It was radical chiefly because it abolished monarchy and aristocracy, two of the three components of mixed government, and proposed to base government exclusively on the democratic element in society. Yet at the same time republicanism was a traditional, even conservative doctrine insofar as, in the manner of premodern political philosophy in general, it emphasized pursuit of the common good over and against individualism.

In the writings of Harrington, Sidney, and other seventeenth-century theorists of republicanism, the interest and welfare of society as a whole transcended the interests of particular groups or individuals. Corporatist in outlook, republicanism held that the purpose of political action and of government was to transcend individual interests and promote the common good. A corporatist or commonwealth spirit was expressed in the revolutionary period in America in the strict control of markets, price fixing, restriction of consumption by sumptuary legislation, and general economic regulation undertaken by the state governments. These policies were consistent moreover with contemporary doctrines of mercantilism, which assigned government broad responsibility for the promotion and regulation of economic life. Economic individualism and free trade stood at the opposite pole from mercantilism.

Alongside the corporatist tendency in revolutionary republicanism, however, powerful individualistic strains were apparent. Until recently historians treated the Revolution as a vindication of life, liberty, and the pursuit of happiness understood in the classic laissez-faire sense of property accumulation by self-seeking individuals. The discovery of a corporatist dimension to revolutionary thought has provided an important corrective to the earlier view of a primeval Lockean liberalism dominating American politics and society. Yet individualism, which was supported for civic and moral as well as economic reasons, was a potent force in revolutionary politics. At the height of the revolutionary crisis the corporatist outlook was stronger, especially in areas touched by the war; otherwise, it was on the wane. Colonial politics was interest- and faction-dominated, and despite the appeal of revolutionary leaders to patriotism and the common good, the individualism that stimulated interest-group politics was widely evident in state politics during and after the Revolution.

This tension within republicanism may also be considered in terms of positive and negative conceptions of liberty. Central to the opposition ideology that influenced American thinking in the prerevolutionary period was the idea that true liberty consisted in political action. Liberty as political participation was thought to be the key to personal and civic virtue, the essence of which was to act for the good of the whole rather than for individual ends. Derived from Aristotle by way of Florentine civic humanism of the fifteenth century and the English republican theorists of the seventeenth century, this positive conception of liberty offered one approach to revolutionary republicanism. Looked at in this light, the pursuit of happiness referred to in the Declaration of Independence meant *public* happiness, in which individuals devoted themselves to the commonwealth rather than to narrow personal ends.

The alternative conception of liberty and republican government emphasized limitations on government in the interest of individual freedom. Negative in the sense that it sought to curtail government, this conception of liberty depended on common law property rights, privileges and immunities, guarantees of due process, and fundamental law. Rooted in ancient and medieval natural law doctrines, it lay at the heart of English constitutionalism and was conspicuous in the seventeenth-century struggle against the monarchy. The animus of negative liberty also played a central part in the American struggle against British imperialism.

In the American Revolution these two traditions of liberty fused in republican constitutionalism. The exigencies of the revolutionary crisis required decisive political action, which usually was justified under the ideal of positive liberty and civic virtue. At the same time, a sober regard for the propensities of ordinary human nature, in the context of the natural rights, social contract, and fundamental law traditions, led Americans to base their constitutions more on the negative than the positive conception of liberty. Liberty as participation and political action was by no means foreclosed; on the contrary, it remained a fundamental requirement of American constitutionalism. But guarantees of property rights and protection of individual liberty against arbitrary power acquired precedence in constitution writing and in the conduct of American politics.

The State Constitutions

Whatever the exact relationship between negative and positive liberty in revolutionary constitutionalism, it was axiomatic in the 1770s that republican government could exist only in small geographical areas. This belief, which reflected and confirmed the historical development of the colonies as autonomous units of government, caused the spirit of '76 to be expressed principally in the formation of constitutions and codes of law in the states.

It was of the utmost importance for American constitutional development that the political events by which Americans first defined themselves as a national people occurred at the state level. The Continental Congress, first convened in 1774, was a kind of continuing emergency meeting of representatives from the states. Its very name signified an assembly of ambassadors from independent states, which was precisely what the Declaration of Independence proclaimed the former colonies to be ("these United Colonies are, and of Right ought to be Free and Independent States"). The common cause was to secure the independence of thirteen separate states. No one doubted that the work of forming governments and establishing civil order—work that would determine the nature of the new nation's political institutions—would take place in the states. For that reason many revolutionary leaders spent most of the war years engaged in state constitution making. Americans were aware, moreover, of having a decisive opportunity to act as lawgivers and founders of new commonwealths. "In no age did man ever possess an election of the kind of government under which he would choose to live," observed the physician-historian David Ramsay of South Carolina. "In America alone," he wrote, "reason and liberty concurred in the formation of constitutions."

After the break from England—and in a few colonies even before then—constitution writing was the first objective of revolutionary political action. The purpose of the Revolution became the founding of constitutions of liberty. Revolutionary councils and committees of public safety governed from October 1774 through 1775, following the collapse of British authority. All things considered, the period of emergency government was of short duration because many colonial leaders feared that protest against authority might get out of hand. In fact, as early as six months before the Declaration of Independence, the process of regularizing and legitimizing revolutionary government by making constitutions had begun. In January 1776 New Hampshire adopted a brief, temporary constitution; South Carolina did the same in March. In June a convention of members of the Virginia House of Burgesses wrote a constitution for that state, and after the Declaration seven other states placed their government on a new foundation by approving constitutions. New York and Georgia wrote charters of fundamental law in 1777, and Massachusetts, after one unsuccessful attempt, adopted a constitution in 1780. Rhode Island and Connecticut retained their corporate charters from colonial days as state constitutions.

Although Americans had begun to think of a constitution as a higher law separate from legislative institutions, the first state constitutions reflected this view in an imperfect way. For the most part they were written and adopted by provincial congresses or state legislatures that also dealt with routine legislative matters and thus were not truly distinctive in function. In New Jersey, Virginia, and South Carolina the revolutionary provincial congresses drafted permanent constitutions without seeking any new authority from the people. New Hampshire, New York, Pennsylvania, Delaware, Maryland, North Carolina, and Georgia all held special elections for new congresses to write constitutions, but these bodies also legislated. In none of the states acting in 1776–77 did the constitution-writing assemblies submit their work to the people for popular approval; they merely proclaimed the new constitution to be in effect.

In the early period of constitution making there was confusion concerning the source of constitutional enactments. The constitution must derive from the people, but the state legislatures might be considered as fulfilling this requirement. As a result of factional struggles provoked by constitution making in the legislature, however, the practice arose of holding popular conventions to draft constitutions, which were subsequently submitted to the people for ratification. The Massachusetts constitution of

1780, drafted by a special convention after the constitution written by the state legislature was rejected in part because it emanated from the General Court, illustrated what soon became orthodox constitutional procedure.

Constitution making proceeded under the moral sanction provided by social contract theory—the first principle of republican philosophy. Indeed, it was by considering the framing of the first constitutions in light of the requirement of popular consent that critics were able to gain acceptance for the convention-and-ratification method of adopting or changing the fundamental law. In this sense social contract theory stimulated change. In other respects, however, the use of social contract theory reflected the limits of revolutionary constitutional change.

A key result of the galvanizing of political awareness that the Revolution produced was the emergence of new men in local politics. Frequently critical of the colonial political establishment, these men sought to extend the principle of self-government to its logical conclusion by making town and county government more independent of state authority. Leaders at the state level, however, successfully resisted these efforts. Denying that all the bonds of government had been dissolved in the movement for independence, they rejected the application of social contract theory to justify changes in local government. Throughout the revolutionary era, accordingly, institutions of local government tended to serve as a stabilizing force. They were able to do so in part because state constitution making absorbed the potential for disruption that the struggle for independence released.

The new state constitutions offer a body of evidence for addressing the time-honored but still important question of the radicalism of the American Revolution. Did the Revolution promote radical change, or did it merely consummate and confirm tendencies long evident in the colonial period? Two basic responses to this question have usually been given, one progressive or radical, the other conservative. The former holds that the Revolution, though initiated by the merchant-lawyer-planter elite that controlled colonial politics, became a truly radical movement of the middle and lower classes for political, social, and economic democracy. According to the progressive interpretation, this democratization can be seen in the assertion of legislative supremacy in the state constitutions and Articles of Confederation. The conservative interpretation contends that in a society that was already in social and economic terms broadly democratic, the purpose of the Revolution was to preserve the institutions of political democracy that imperial policy threatened. In separating from England, historians of this persuasion argue, the most radical change was the founding of a new nation and eventually a strong central government expressing the sense of American nationality.

The evidence of the state constitutions suggests that although there was little authentic class conflict in the sense of pitched battle between distinctly higher and lower social groups, republican principles had a potentially radical effect on American politics. State politics showed that the language of equality, consent, and individual liberty quickly acquired a persuasiveness and legitimacy that conferred an advantage on those who could employ it most effectively. At best, republican principles became ideals guiding political action by groups seeking to eliminate injustice and improve society. At worst they became shibboleths that obscured self-seeking political expediency and the quest for power.

In any event, it was not simply a nation, but a *republican* nation that the Revolution created. This republican identity was at once old and new. Historically, it rested on what were in effect republican tendencies in colonial politics, even though they were not so regarded at the time. The elevation of these tendencies and practices to the level of republican theory and ideological commitment, however, was new. A pattern of institutional continuity and theoretical innovation thus stands out as characteristic of revolutionary constitutionalism.

The Separation of Powers and the State Constitutions

Continuity and change are evident in the most important result of state constitution making, the ascendancy of the legislative and the reduction of the executive power. This dual development culminated trends of long duration in the colonial period, yet it occurred within a new constitutional framework. This framework was the doctrine of the separation of powers.

In repudiating English authority Americans also repudiated the organizing principle of English constitutionalism, the theory of mixed government. In its place they substituted the theory of the separation of powers. Because both of these doctrines aimed at achieving balance in government, they are often seen as similar, if not interchangeable. In fact they differed profoundly. Mixed government, as noted previously, recognized and gave a place in the structure of government to the several orders of society. In the hierarchical, feudal society in which it developed it expressed the assumption that social and political authority were identical, that government and society were organically linked and overlapping. The separation of powers, by contrast, rested on recognition of distinct and clearly differentiated functions of government. It held that governmental powers, not social classes, must be kept in balance in order to preserve liberty. Separation theory was not in a formal sense concerned with sociology or class structure, although historically it developed in the distinctive social setting created by the rise of the bourgeoisie. The first to argue for the separation of powers, the leaders of Parliament in their struggle against the crown in the seventeenth century, professed to speak for the entire people, whom they regarded as the basis of each distinct branch or function of government. As mixed government was appropriate in hierarchical premodern society, separation of powers was appropriate in America—a society so thoroughly middle class and open that compared to England it was a classless society.

The constitutions adopted in 1776 showed the swift conversion of Americans to the separation of powers as an organizing principle of government. Republican teaching did not logically require the separation-of-powers structure. Yet given the abolition of monarchy and the absence of aristocracy and inherited legal privilege, the theory of separation was the only available doctrine on which to base constitutions of liberty. Thus the Virginia constitution of 1776 stated that "The legislative, executive and judiciary departments shall be separate and distinct, so that neither exercises the powers properly belonging to the other: nor shall any person exercise the powers of more than one of them at the same time." Five other states established governments on this basis, all of them for the most part rejecting the idea of checks and balances, or *sharing of power,* required by the theory of mixed government. In its theoretically pure or radical form the separation principle placed all legislative power in a single body—a unicameral legislature. (Bicameralism, characteristic of mixed government, provided for sharing of the lawmaking power by two legislative houses, each drawn from a distinct social order.) In its pure form, too, the separation doctrine denied any lawmaking power to the executive, who was simply to enforce and administer the law. In revolutionary America actual experience with the separation of powers ranged from radical or pure application with a unicameral legislature and plural executive (Pennsylvania) to substantial though not complete acceptance in most of the states that employed the principle (Virginia, North Carolina, Georgia, Maryland, New York, Massachusetts, New Hampshire, South Carolina, Delaware) to no acceptance at all (Rhode Island, Connecticut, and New Jersey, which retained their colonial constitutional structures).

The separation-of-powers principle served much the same purpose in revolutionary America as it had in the English Civil War: to assert the supremacy of the people's representatives in lawmaking and, by denying the executive any share in this highest and most important power of government, to confine him to a merely administrative function. Republican government was to be grounded in the action and consent of the people, and the separation theory was a means of establishing this popular control. It was a democratizing instrument which carried to completion the drive of the colonial assembly for legislative hegemony. Moreover, in conjunction with the fear of executive power inculcated by the eighteenth-century opposition writers, it resulted in the transformation of the executive office.

Instead of possessing a wide range of prerogative powers that placed him at the very center of the government, as in the colonial mixed constitution, the governor (or president or executive council) under the separation of powers merely enforced the rules made by the legislature. Accordingly, the state constitutions either denied the executive a veto power outright (eleven states) or permitted him to exercise it in restricted form; where the veto was provided for, it was reversible by a simple majority of the legislature. The method of appointing the governor was a second key issue in defining the executive office. Where the separation principle was more thoroughly applied, the executive was chosen by the people, with a view toward making the office independent of the legislature. In some states, however, fear that the executive office might become more than merely administrative caused constitution makers to entrust election of the governor to the legislature. The same fear led to either a categorical denial or severe restriction of the governor's appointive power. In accordance with the long-standing belief that the greatest danger to liberty lay in executive corruption—that is, the undermining of civic virtue and the independence of the people's deputies through the distribution of patronage, emoluments, bribes, etc.—many state constitutions gave the power of appointment to the legislature exclusively. In some states the governor had limited appointment powers, but in none did he possess the power exclusively. The state constitutions also made provision for impeachment of the governor, although this was a checks-and-balances device not strictly consistent with the separation principle. Its inclusion further expressed fear of a strong executive, as did the provision for short terms in office and restrictions on the re-election of the executive. The only element of the prerogative substantially retained by the governor was the power of pardon and reprieve.

Related to the transformation of the governor's office was the abolition of the governor's council. Its lawmaking powers were assumed by the upper house of the legislature, leaving it a strictly advisory body in the executive branch. So diminished was the role of the governor that he was viewed essentially as first among equals on the executive council. The council, moreover, was elected by the people or the legislature rather than appointed by the governor, as in the colonial constitution.

The redistribution of power resulting from the transformation of the governor's office located the constitutional center of gravity in the new state governments in the legislative branch. After decades of struggle against the royal governor, the colonial assemblies, like Parliament in the seventeenth century, seized the opportunity that a revolutionary situation presented to assert their supremacy in lawmaking. This highest power in government now belonged exclusively, or nearly so, to the people's representatives. Along with it went technical parliamentary powers that the colonial assemblies had long struggled to acquire, such as the right to establish regular meetings, determine their own membership by judging the elections and qualifications of members, and control their own internal organization. Under the separation of powers the executive was denied the power to prorogue and dissolve the legislature and to reject the speaker, important prerogatives of the colonial governor.

In the first few years of government based on the separation of powers, it was not clear what the limits of legislative authority were. The purpose of the separation theory was to prevent any single branch of government from controlling the other two. Legislative supremacy in lawmaking was not to be a warrant for supremacy over government in general. Yet in practice, under the pressure of political events, there proved to be few effective limitations on the state legislatures. In the volatile setting of interest-group and factional politics, legislative power was used in ways that many people considered improper—for example, to set aside judicial decisions in disputes over property. It soon became apparent that a proper separation of powers required certain institutional checks and balances, and this need to curtail state legislative power became a central issue of constitutional reform in the 1780s. These facts do not justify the conclusion, however, that the separation of powers was not taken seriously in the first state constitutions. In fact the state legislatures' bold exercise of power and their eclipse of the executive was evidence of the impact the separation-of-powers theory had on revolutionary constitutionalism.

The Problem of Representation

In addition to the distribution of power between the legislature and executive, the traditional colonial system of representation underwent change during the Revolution. In the colonial period towns and counties were the constituent units in the assembly. Population did not affect the apportionment of deputies, since representation was conceived of in corporate rather than individualistic terms. In a few states after 1776, however, the constituent basis of representation shifted to population and property. In Massachusetts, for example, commercial interests from coastal Essex County resented their lack of political power relative to the agrarian counties in the western part of the state. The proportion of taxes the county paid was greater than the share of power it enjoyed in the General Court under the system of equal town representation. Accordingly, in the Massachusetts constitution of 1780, Essex County delegates obtained the representation of numbers and property. Each town would still receive a minimal number of deputies, but more populous towns would have more representatives in the lower house. In the state senate, on the other hand, property was recognized. Counties were the basic unit of representation here, but they were awarded representatives according to the taxes paid. These changes expressed the idea that the constituent elements of government were people and property.

This conjunction of values reflected the connection that existed in republican philosophy between liberty and property: the latter was the necessary basis of the former. Population was a rational basis for representation because it was considered an accurate indication of the wealth and economic power of an area. If property interests were to be recognized in the structure of government, it made sense to give a more prominent place to the principle of the numerical majority.

American representation also changed during the Revolution as a result of suffrage reform. As noted previously, because of the broad-based character of the electorate, actual rather than virtual representation tended to exist in the colonies. Yet as long as suffrage was restricted, an element of virtual representation persisted. Only persons with a sufficient property interest were permitted to vote, on the theory that only in this way could there be assurance of the personal and civic virtue needed to sustain political independence and concern for the common good. Yet such an arrangement resembled English representation: those who did not vote were thought to be virtually represented by those who did. Once the principle of no taxation without actual representation gained currency in the prerevolutionary years, however, it was inevitable—given the factional nature of American politics—that it should be introduced into local politics.

Accordingly, in several states the process of constitution making included attempts to extend actual representation by broadening the suffrage. If all men were created equal, and if government rested on public opinion and the consent of the governed, then it followed that the implicit consent of virtual representation was inadequate. Reformers argued that all men, or at least more than were presently permitted to do so, ought actually to vote. Under this natural-rights rationale, reinforced by political pressure to extend rights to men being called on to fight a war, suffrage reform proceeded in Pennsylvania, New Hampshire, New Jersey, Georgia, and Maryland. In general the change consisted in substituting a taxpayer qualification for the freehold qualification of colonial times. Although liberalization of the suffrage resulted in only a modest increase in the number of voters (because widespread distribution of property already created a broad electorate), and although property was not altogether rejected as a relevant consideration, the reforms that took place were a significant step toward universal manhood suffrage.

The changes that occurred in American representation make it clear that republican constitutionalism had genuine, if limited, democratizing effects. The struggle against imperial policy, carried on in the pluralistic arena of colonial politics, stimulated political awareness and drew new men into public life who challenged the traditional colonial elite. The protest against England also provoked a degree of hostility toward authority in general, which to some extent undermined the spirit of deference that prevailed in colonial politics. Furthermore, the principles of equality and natural rights employed in the struggle against England could be and were used to seek changes in American society. Yet this is not to say, as some historians have argued, that deep-seated class conflict characterized the American Revolution.

Interest groups—merchants, lawyers, planters, farmers, artisans, and others—disagreed in their views of sound public policy and, in their disagreement, hurled charges of "aristocracy" and "democracy" against each other with deceptive certainty. In fact, however, no objective social and economic reality, such as would warrant describing the struggle as a class conflict, divided them. On the contrary, once the restraining influence of British authority was removed, there occurred a proliferation and intensification of group conflict. Intended to influence public opinion, it not only drew new men into politics, but also spread throughout the society ideas such as equality, natural rights, and popular sovereignty that appealed to a large and continually expanding electorate. Conflict there undeniably was in American politics, but it occurred in an open and materially abundant social order. Moreover—and this is the point of significance for constitutional history—conflict ran in channels marked out by agreed-upon principles of government. Republicanism based on the natural rights philosophy and the separation of powers were the central ideas, and despite disagreement about their application, almost all Americans supported them as the basis of the new political order.

The chief significance of revolutionary constitutionalism, then, was to create limited governments that would safeguard individual liberty and property as well as promote the common good. Particularly expressive of this purpose were the bills of rights that revolutionary leaders included in most of the state constitutions. Drawn from English history and the colonial experience, the bills of rights guaranteed jury trial, moderate bail, fair procedure in criminal cases, freedom of speech, press, and religious worship; prohibited unreasonable searches and seizures; forbade taxation without the consent and representation of the people; espoused the principle of a free militia; and upheld the right of resistance to arbitrary rule and oppression. Of special interest in the bills of rights was the assertion of the doctrine of natural rights and the social-contract origins of the state, in contrast to the customary basis of rights in English law. Consistent with the opposition ideology that shaped their political outlook, revolutionary constitution writers regarded bills of rights as a necessary means of defending liberty against relentlessly aggressive governmental—especially executive—power.

The Articles of Confederation

While revolutionary leaders dealt with the problems of constitutionalism in the states, the necessity of conducting the war against England led them to create a continental union that received definite form in the Articles of Confederation. The Articles reflected the idea that in joining together for the purpose of achieving their independence as individual sovereignties the states created a new political unit which expressed a nascent sense of American nationality. It is also true that the Confederation in many respects acted like a government in coordinating the states' united effort against England. Nevertheless, the Confederation was not in any systematic or comprehensive sense an authentic government possessing the sanction of law and the power of command; it was at best a quasi-government. Moreover, the spirit of nationality it embodied was expressed constitutionally in the dispersal of power that the establishment of state governments signified, rather than in any provision for unitary sovereignty such as is usually identified with the modern nation-state.

The Articles of Confederation are often described as the first constitution of the United States. Insofar as they set forth a plan of federal organization that divided sovereignty between the states and a central authority, thus anticipating the Constitution of 1787, the description is apt. Yet, recalling the republican spirit of '76, it cannot be said that the Articles were truly or primarily an attempt to implement revolutionary constitutionalism. In a broad political sense the United States may have been a republic from 1776 to 1787, considering that public opinion and sectional and interest-group pressures influenced the actions of Congress. In a legal and constitutional sense, however, the Confederation did not possess a republican form of government—that is, a government based on the people as constituent power and organized and conducted according to the principles of revolutionary constitutionalism. The Articles were concerned with relations among states rather than with the proper balance between power and liberty in the constitutional structure.

The proximate origins of the Confederation lay in the formation of the First Continental Congress in 1774. The ambivalence concerning the true nature of the Confederation that characterized it throughout its fifteen-year history—its status as a quasi-government—was evident at the outset of the revolutionary crisis. Congress exercised real political power but, carefully respecting the fact that it represented autonomous colonies or states, it left to them the performance of authentic acts of sovereignty in relation to individual citizens. Congress clearly directed military and diplomatic efforts pointing to independence, for example, and in May 1776, declaring British authority at an end, instructed the colonies to form regular constitutional governments. But it did all of this as a kind of superintending advisory body communicating the consensus of patriotic opinion and recommending governmental action. It was for the states to enact laws punishing treason, exacting loyalty oaths, levying taxes, regulating trade, and so on.

Pertinent in this connection is the question of citizenship. If we regard determination of the qualifications and admission to citizenship as a test of governmental sovereignty, it is apparent that Congress was not sovereign.

The Confederation did not naturalize aliens, nor was it the object of loyalty oaths and affirmations. In June 1776 Congress adopted a resolution providing a general definition of citizenship, but that definition specified only state citizenship. It proposed that all free persons residing in a state be regarded as citizens of that state. The states accordingly naturalized aliens, and it was to the states that allegiance was due. An idea of national citizenship existed, but it was shadowy and amorphous at best.[1]

The nature of the Confederation was established in 1774, when the First Continental Congress decided that each colony would have one vote in the conduct of congressional affairs. This action resolved the question of how the Confederation should be constituted; and although the matter was raised again in subsequent years, no different approach was ever agreed on. In 1774 delegates from some of the larger states proposed to base representation on the population, wealth, and general weight or importance of the several states as measured by various economic criteria. That this approach would have placed the Confederation on a direct popular basis—that is, the people of the United States considered as a single national entity—cannot be assumed, for the people represented in Congress could be merely the people of the several states. Congress rejected this method of representation, however, principally because in the crisis that existed in 1774 it was not feasible to determine the relative weight of each state before taking action. Moreover, the data for making this kind of determination were not available. Needless to say, the decision for state equality, which made it difficult to ratify the Articles and impossible to amend them, was profoundly important.

At the same time that it issued the Declaration of Independence, the congress began to draft Articles of Confederation, a set of rules for the cooperation of the states in matters of common concern. A proposed version of the Articles was debated in July 1776, in the spring of 1777, and still further in November 1777, when, amid pressing war matters, it was adopted by Congress and sent to the states for approval. In March 1781 endorsement of the Articles by the Maryland legislature fulfilled the requirement of unanimity in the ratification process and enabled the Articles formally to go into effect.

Congress early acquired certain functions and responsibilities in rela-

---

1. The comity clause of the Articles of Confederation (Article IV, Section 1) expressed the idea of national citizenship. It stated that "the free inhabitants of each of these states . . . shall be entitled to all privileges and immunities of free citizens in the several states; and the people of each state shall have free ingress and regress to and from any other state, and shall enjoy therein all the privileges of trade and commerce, subject to the same duties, impositions, and restrictions, as the inhabitants thereof respectively." However, the precise legal effect of this language was highly uncertain. It appeared to provide that a noncitizen (inhabitant) in a state could acquire in another state rights of citizenship not available to him in his state of residence.

tion to the states. In the opening months of 1776, for example, it seized the political initiative in urging the colonial assemblies to repudiate British authority and organize state governments. Subsequently, it defined treason and citizenship, and supervised the military and diplomatic phases of the war for independence. So far from projecting a new relationship between Congress and the states, the Articles of Confederation confirmed the existing *ad hoc* pattern and translated the political power of Congress into formal terms. By the time the Articles assumed final form, however, Congress possessed less influence than during the crisis of 1776.

The first version of the Articles of Confederation, known as the Dickinson draft, reflected the stronger political position Congress enjoyed at the moment of separation from England. It gave the Confederation exclusive power to settle disputes concerning boundaries, jurisdictions, and other matters between the states, and said the states could retain their local laws and regulate internal police in all matters that did not interfere with the Articles. This language suggested that the Articles might become a standard against which the exercise of state powers would be measured, and implied the existence of an undefined, residual sphere of power in Congress that could be used to encroach on state jurisdiction. Nevertheless, because the Dickinson draft fully recognized state equality in representation and voting, and because it denied Congress taxing and commerce powers, it can hardly be regarded as a centralizing instrument. So widespread and pronounced was the belief in state sovereignty, however, and so keen the apprehension that one section would use a stronger Confederation to impose its own political and social views on the others, that a reaction set in against the modestly integrating tendency of the Dickinson draft. The provisions alluded to were struck out and a ringing assertion of state sovereignty added. Article II now announced: "Each state retains its sovereignty, freedom and independence, and every Power, Jurisdiction, and right, which is not by this confederation expressly delegated to the United States, in Congress assembled."

The inclusion of this language in the Articles of Confederation did not guarantee that the states would actually qualify as fully sovereign and independent governments in the sense of international law. In fact they did not, despite an inclination in this direction based on the assumption that the collapse of British authority had resulted in a transfer of sovereignty to them. Yet if the sovereign power of the states was incomplete, that of Congress was far more so. If not entirely chimerical, its formal sovereignty was insufficiently developed to permit it effectively to fulfill the responsibilities assigned to it by events themselves or by the formal plan of union. The central fact of constitutional history in this period, accordingly, is a division of sovereignty between the states and the Confederation, according to an as yet imperfectly realized federal principle. This division of power can be seen in express provisions of the Articles and in the actions of Congress during and after the war.

The distribution of specific powers between the states and the Confederation presented little difficulty. Since the Confederation was to be a league or alliance rather than a government, there was no thought of giving it powers of taxation and commercial regulation, except in relation to Indian tribes. It is often said that Americans denied these critical powers to the Confederation in a fit of irrational pique that reflected their hostility to England rather than sober judgment. Certainly, anti-English sentiment abounded, but the point is that with the British presence removed Americans could organize the empire as all along they thought it should be. And their preference clearly excluded the exercise of taxing and local commercial regulation bearing on individual citizens. More than that, the American conception of imperial organization categorically denied the central authority any legislative power. Here language is revealing. Congress, according to the Articles, could make resolutions, determinations, and regulations, but not laws. Only the states, in which the people as constituent power were represented, had legislatures—and executive and judicial establishments as well.

As a superintending authority in matters that concerned all the states, Congress had an array of powers similar to those of Parliament and the crown under the old empire. Thus it was given authority to make war and peace, send and receive ambassadors, enter into treaties and alliances, coin money, fix the standard of weights and measures throughout the United States, establish a post office, regulate Indian affairs, and appoint officers and make rules for military forces in the service of the United States. Congress could also establish rules for captures on land or water, grant letters of marque and reprisal, appoint courts for the trial of piracies, and settle on appeal disputes between the states. On the other hand, despite the affirmation of state sovereignty, the states were expressly prohibited from declaring war, making treaties, and so on. And they were enjoined to abide by the determinations of Congress and observe the Articles of Confederation.

The division of authority and responsibility evident in the Articles can be seen also in the political history of the Confederation. It is apparent that in many respects the states shaped policy as sovereign governments, though not in a comprehensive way. By the same token, for all its institutional weaknesses, the Confederation in some respects acted like a real government. Most conspicuous was its conduct of the war and diplomacy. But it also vindicated its authority in a keenly disputed nonmilitary sphere—the problem of the western lands. This question was of great importance because it involved fixing the boundaries of states with claims to the west, forming a policy of land distribution, and determining the principles of settlement that would shape the future of civil society in a large part of the country. In a larger political sense the West had a potentially nationalizing influence that could hold the Confederation together.

The Dickinson draft of the Articles gave Congress power to settle the states' conflicting western claims, dispose of lands not held by any state or purchased from the Indians, and create territories for the formation of new states. The objections of states with land claims—Virginia, Pennsylvania, Massachusetts, New York, Connecticut—caused the elimination of these provisions, however, and the Articles as approved by Congress in 1777 merely stated that no state shall be deprived of territory for the benefit of the United States. Yet this stipulation proved unacceptable to states without land claims, and eventually they were able to force a change. In 1779 Congress passed a resolution asking states with western claims to suspend land sales and transfer title to all trans-Allegheny lands to the Confederation. A more far-reaching resolution was adopted in 1780, which proposed that all lands that were ceded to Congress should be disposed of for the common benefit of the United States and settled and formed into republican states and admitted to the Union. Opinion having shifted against them, the landed states ceded their claims, and Maryland, which had withheld its approval of the Articles over this issue, finally ratified the plan of confederation in March 1781. Subsequently, Congress adopted the Ordinance of 1785 and the Northwest Ordinance of 1787, establishing a territorial policy based on the principle of national supervision of state making with guaranteed admission to the Union.

Congress not only acted in some matters like a real government, but it also served as a forum for the expression of opinions and interests that to some extent achieved the effect of a republican government. With the New England, middle, and southern states voting in blocs, the clearest source of political identity in Congress was sectionalism. Economic interests that were dependent on geographical as well as social and demographic differences gave specific content to sectionalism, as did variations in the way puritanical New Englanders, commercial-minded middle-states men, and slavery-protecting southerners viewed republicanism. States also acted on the basis of their size, population, and wealth—that is, as large or small states.

Yet if republican tendencies found expression in congressional politics, the organization of the Confederation on the principle of state equality ignored the forms and procedures of republicanism in a way that presented insuperable obstacles to the successful conduct of continental affairs. It may be conceded that the Articles were adequate as a framework for cooperation among the states. They even contained provisions of a genuinely nationalizing, integrating tendency, such as the comity clause guaranteeing the inhabitants of each state all privileges and immunities of citizens in the several states, and the provision requiring each state to give full faith and credit to the judicial proceedings of the other states. But the Confederation did not—and probably could not—overcome the structural defects that denied it the formal attributes of a republican government. Constituted as it was, it could not transcend its nature as an alliance.

James Madison accurately summarized the difficulty when he observed that the Confederation suffered not from a want of specific powers, but of power in general. Congress lacked power—the legal sanction of command—because it did not rest on the people as constituent power. Nor did its organization conform to the separation of powers, the new structural principle of American constitutionalism. Embodying the separation-of-powers doctrine and based on direct popular consent, the state governments were both republican in their political character and legally authoritative. The problem with the Confederation thus was not an insufficiently national outlook where its responsibilities were concerned, but a lack of republican power and authority in its formal constitution.

SIX

Constitutional Reform and the Federal Convention of 1787

♦ ♦ ♦

THE WEAKNESS OF THE CONFEDERATION stimulated numerous reform efforts in the 1780s. That it might more effectively discharge its responsibilities, it seemed necessary, at a minimum, to strengthen Congress by giving it a source of revenue independent of the states. Continental-minded statesmen with an interest in commercial development, such as Alexander Hamilton and Robert Morris, led the way in proposing such reforms, but most state-based politicians agreed that reinforcement of Confederate authority was imperative. Nevertheless, by itself the problem of a weak central authority could not command the attention and support needed to bring about change. Only when the prospect of a stronger Union served the additional purpose of improving, if not actually preserving, republican government in the states did national constitutional reform succeed. In an atmosphere marked by apprehension over the instability of the state governments, as well as by discouragement at the commercial, diplomatic, and military weakness of the Confederation, the Constitutional Convention met at Philadelphia in May 1787.

There was no denying that Congress was embarrassingly weak. Most of Congress's difficulties between 1776 and 1787 were connected in some degree with its financial incompetence, in turn ascribable to its lack of taxing power and the habitual failure of the states to meet their assessments promptly. During the Revolutionary War, the army went chronically unpaid, while in 1783 the officers encamped at Newburg, New York, threatened mutiny in attempt to recover back salaries. In despair the Continental Congress resorted to the printing presses to finance itself, issuing, by 1780, some $40,000,000 in paper money, the entire issue ultimately being virtually repudiated. Also Congress borrowed several million between 1778 and 1783 from the French and Dutch governments; during the Confederation period it was unable even to meet the interest on these loans, and interest and principal accumulated until the national debt was refunded under the Constitution. Financial weakness after 1783 also made it difficult to protect the great trans-Allegheny wilderness region acquired in the Peace of 1783, for Congress was utterly without the resources to garrison the West properly in order to protect settlers, keep out British and Spanish intruders, and control the Indian tribes. As a result, Britain, contrary to the provisions of peace, retained her forts in the Northwest Territory, both Spain and England intrigued to separate the West from the new republic, and Indians ravaged the settlements in Kentucky and Tennessee.

Another important series of difficulties arose out of congressional impotence in the field of foreign and interstate commerce. It was almost impossible for Congress to negotiate commercial treaties with foreign states, in part because they realized that Congress could not guarantee compliance by the states with any commercial policy agreed to. When John Adams, American minister to England, sought a commercial treaty with Britain, Foreign Secretary Charles James Fox contemptuously suggested that ambassadors from the thirteen states ought to be present, since Congress had no authority over the subject. Recognizing that Congress was impotent to impose a retaliatory commercial policy, Britain closed the West Indies to American trade, and discriminated against Yankee merchantmen in her own ports. Within the Confederation, the various states carried on retaliatory trade wars against one another, Congress being powerless to interfere. New York, for example, profiting by her port of entry, laid duties upon incoming commerce destined for New Jersey and Connecticut, while these states in return taxed interstate commerce with New York.

Further numerous difficulties arose out of the inability of Congress to compel obedience by the states and individuals to acts of Congress and treaties. The weakness of Confederation foreign policy was in part due to this fact. Congress was unable to compel the states to execute the provisions in the treaty of peace with respect to the return of Tory property and the payment of merchant debts, and Britain used this as an excuse to retain control of the Northwest forts. France and Holland also hesitated to negotiate treaties with a nation that could not meet its commitments.

The Problem of Excessive State Power

While Congress conducted continental affairs in a fitful manner, the actions of the state legislatures raised doubts in the minds of many about the future of republican government in America. In the flush of revolutionary enthusiasm Americans gave their elected deputies virtually exclusive control over lawmaking under the separation-of-powers doctrine. In effect they regarded the state legislatures as inheritors of the sovereignty that Parliament had attempted to exercise. At the same time, however, the potentially conflicting idea of popular sovereignty took hold. This was derived from belief in the people as constituent power not only capable of creating government *de novo,* but also justified in acting outside of established institutions should government prove repressive or irresponsible. From both sources came political tensions and anxieties that spurred the movement for constitutional reform in the 1780s.

On the eve of the Federal Convention a popular uprising in Massachusetts known as Shays' Rebellion caused alarm that unruly mobs, falsely acting in the name of popular sovereignty, might bring republican government to ruin. Demanding inflationary legislation, armed bands of farmers closed the courts in western Massachusetts and even threatened to lay siege to Boston to force the General Court to grant credit relief. State officials dealt with the crisis without Confederation assistance, but not because they did not desire it; Congress simply lacked the ability to respond to a crisis of this sort. The event made many people aware of the need for a stronger central authority to support state governments against internal subversion, and was directly responsible for the inclusion in the Constitution of a guarantee of republican government to each state in the Union. More vexing than the people acting "out of doors" in defiance of established authority, however, was the tendency toward unlimited legislative power in the states.

Although at first the scope of legislative power was understandably imprecise under the separation-of-powers doctrine, by the mid-1780s much of this uncertainty was gone. Men professed to know the limits of legislative power, and concluded with equal certainty that those limits had been breached. In several states lawmakers usurped power thought properly to belong to the executive or judicial branch of the government. Legislatures vacated judicial proceedings, modified court judgments, authorized appeals, reopened controversies, expounded the law, and granted exemptions from the standing law. They also passed legislation authorizing the emission of paper money, suspending actions on debts or permitting them to be paid in kind, and declaring paper money a legal tender. Supported by agrarian majorities, these measures reflected the vigorous factionalism of American political life. To unsympathetic contemporaries, however, they threatened individual property rights and public virtue. Troublesome, too, was the variability of state legislation. State legislatures passed laws one year which they repealed the next, thereby producing political instability and undermining public confidence in republican government. Added to more familiar grievances such as the failure of the states to meet their financial quotas, their mutual hostility in matters of trade and taxation, and their encroachment on congressional authority, state legislative excesses gave Confederation reform the practical significance it needed to enable it to succeed.

The movement for constitutional reform that culminated in the Philadelphia Convention in 1787 began with changes in state government during the later stages of the Revolution. Experience showed that the separation of powers in its pure or radical form did not effectively limit legislative power. The solution to this problem was to give the executive and judicial branches greater leverage vis-à-vis the legislature by instituting checks and balances derived from the older theory of mixed government. Most apparent was the need to strengthen the executive by giving him a share of the lawmaking power in the form of a qualified veto; by placing his election directly in the hands of the people so as to make him independent of the legislature; and by restoring the power to appoint subordinate administrators which had belonged to the royal governor. The New York constitution of 1777 and the Massachusetts constitution of 1780 contained these provisions for checks and balances. *The Essex Result,* a political pamphlet written in support of the Massachusetts constitution, expressed the rationale of the separation of powers, modified by the addition of checks and balances: "Each branch is to be independent, and further, to be so balanced, and be able to exert such check upon the others, as will preserve it from a dependence on, or a union with them." By the time of the Philadelphia convention widespread agreement existed on the need for checks and balances within the framework of the separation of powers.

Bicameralism, in most states a relic of mixed government that reflected the force of institutional habit more than rational design, assumed new importance in the 1780s as a further restraint on legislative power. In the radical version of the separation of powers a single-chamber legislature was seen as the appropriate forum for the expression of the homogeneous public opinion that republican theory posited. Although only Pennsylvania had a unicameral assembly, republican theory in the early stages of the Revolution offered no rationale for the two-chamber arrangement that the other states retained from their colonial constitution. As the pressure of factional politics grew more intense, however, and legislatures aggrandized power, bicameralism recommended itself as a barrier to precipitate action.

An additional reason for bicameralism lay in the distinction between property and numbers that was coming to characterize American representation. No one doubted that in a republican society it was essential for the people to express their views in the legislature. But given the danger of popular majorities overriding minority rights, there was reason to give property interests representation also. A solution lay in representing population in the lower chamber and property in the upper, as in the Massachusetts constitution of 1780. As checks and balances were derived from the theory of mixed government, so the introduction of property and numbers as constitutional considerations represented an adaptation in the American setting of the older mixed-government idea that the distinct orders of society ought to have formal recognition in the structure of government.

Still another change in state constitutionalism that anticipated reform at the continental level concerned the judiciary. At the height of the Revolution the chief constitutional difficulty lay in redefining the relationship between the executive and legislature. Beyond the settlement of private disputes, the role of the judiciary under the separation of powers was as yet unclear. As legislatures extended their power, however, their political opponents turned to the courts as a means of restricting them. The basic purpose of the new American conception of constitutionalism was to limit legislative power. Given a written constitution as supreme law, an independent judiciary as posited in the separation of powers, and the traditional assumption that courts had a responsibility to declare the law, a rational basis existed for judicial review. It was plausible to argue, in other words, that courts ought to declare the meaning of the constitution and determine when legislation transgressed constitutional limits.

Although the earliest state cases involving judicial review contained technical ambiguities, they reflected a tendency to seek limits on legislative power by holding lawmakers accountable to the fundamental law. *Holmes* v. *Walton,* a New Jersey case of 1780, involved an appeal to the Supreme Court from a trial under a state law of 1778 for forfeiture of property taken in trade with the enemy. The law in question provided for trial of small causes (those involving less than £10) by six-man juries in apparent violation of the guarantee of twelve-man jury trial in the Constitution of 1776. The difficulty with the precedent was that the *Walton* case itself was not a "small cause," and the Court apparently reversed the trial court because the latter had violated the law itself as much as because six-man juries violated the constitution. The New Jersey assembly, however, in a strenuous protest indicated that it considered the court actually to have declared the law void.

In the more famous case of *Trevett* v. *Weeden* (1786), the Rhode Island Superior Court went to the verge of specifically declaring unconstitutional the state's recently enacted paper-money force act. Technically, however, the judges merely refused to entertain an action for damages under the law on the ground that the act was "internally repugnant," in that it contradicted itself in providing for trials without jury "according to the law of the land." It is quite clear, nonetheless, that they took this position because they thought the law violated the property guarantees of the old charter.

Bayard v. *Singleton,* a North Carolina case of 1787, was an even clearer instance of judicial review. Here the Supreme Court held unconstitutional a law of 1785 requiring a trial court to dismiss forthwith any action for the recovery of property under an earlier Tory confiscation law, on the ground that the statute in question violated the constitutional guarantee that "every citizen had undoubtedly a right to a decision of his property by trial by jury."

Republicanism and the Constitution

Like constitutional reformers in the states, the members of the Constitutional Convention sought to limit state legislative power. It is often said that the framers' great achievement was to create a truly national government in place of the decentralized Confederation. Clearly, the Constitution adjusted and improved the relationship between the states and the central government, creating "a more perfect Union." The more significant change, however, concerned not the scope of the new government—on that score the Confederation was satisfactorily national—but rather the legal sanction and power of command that it acquired as an authentic sovereign government. This sovereign capability depended on the fact that the federal government derived its authority from the people as constituent power. It was, in short, a genuine republican government. And although the political values of the Revolution may seem to have precluded any other outcome, the creation of an effective republican system depended heavily on constitutional changes that had taken place in the states.

The framers of the Constitution resolved the crisis of republicanism which had its source in state legislative excesses by erecting a new layer of republican government at the continental level. This new government formed a counterweight to and in a relative sense restricted the power of the states. The framers accomplished this end by denying certain powers to the states and by giving the federal government broad powers to encourage national economic unity and integration. The guiding principle of the convention, in Madison's words, was to provide a republican remedy for the diseases most incident to republican government.

Proximate steps leading to the Federal Convention began in 1785, when Virginia and Maryland signed an agreement settling a long-standing dispute over commercial regulation of the Potomac. The Maryland legislature subsequently proposed a general commercial convention to include Delaware and Pennsylvania, and Virginia suggested that the invitation be extended to all the states for the purpose of considering a common interstate policy. The convention met at Annapolis, Maryland, in September 1786. Although delegates from only fives states were present, Alexander Hamilton and James Madison used the occasion to call for a new convention to be held at Philadelphia in May of the following year. Congress was initially too jealous of its power to endorse the call, but eventually did so after every state except Rhode Island approved it.

The convention met at Philadelphia in May 1787 with fifty-five delegates from seven states in attendance. (By July twelve states were represented.) It was decided at the outset that voting would be by states, and that a majority of the states present must decide any question. The Virginia delegation had prepared a plan of government that served as the starting point for the convention's deliberations. Referred to the committee of the whole in order to permit informal discussion of its provisions, the plan was debated from May 31 to June 19, during which time the committee examined it point by point, voting to accept, reject, or modify each item it contained. From June 19 to July 26 the full convention debated the report of the committee of the whole, and then gave twenty-three resolutions on which agreement had been reached to a five-man committee on detail. This committee on August 6 reported a draft constitution of twenty-three articles, which was the subject of discussion for several weeks. Early in August a committee on unfinished business settled certain matters, including the method of choosing the president, and on September 8 a committee of style was named to prepare the final draft of the Constitution.

The Virginia Plan provided for a legislative body of two chambers, the lower house to be elected by the people of the respective states, and the upper house to be chosen by the lower house from nominations submitted by the state legislatures. The powers of Congress were to be those enjoyed under the Articles of Confederation, with the important addition of the right "to legislate in all cases in which the separate States are incompetent." The executive was to be chosen by the legislature for an unspecified term and was to be ineligible for re-election. The executive, together with a portion of the national judiciary, was to constitute a Council of Revision, with an absolute veto over acts of the legislature. A national judiciary was to be established, consisting of one or more supreme courts and such inferior tribunals as the legislature might determine upon. Federal judicial authority was to extend to all cases involving piracies and felonies on the high seas, captures from an enemy, foreigners or citizens of different states, collection of the national revenue, impeachment of national officers, and questions involving national peace and harmony.

The Virginia Plan offered a plainly centralist solution to the problem of federalism created under the Articles of Confederation. What was needed was some arrangement by which the central and state governments would each exercise effective jurisdiction unhampered within their respective spheres without intruding upon the functions entrusted to the other, and which would settle any disputes that might arise as to the extent of state or national power.

The Virginia Plan principally attempted to solve this problem by giving Congress a negative over state legislation. In language drafted and supported by Madison in particular, the plan empowered Congress "to negative all laws passed by the several States, contravening in the opinion of the National Legislature the articles of Union." To reinforce the authority of the central government, the succeeding clause contemplated the coercion of a state, by force if necessary. Congress was authorized "to call forth the force of the Union against any member of the Union failing to fulfill its duty under the articles thereof." The negative over state legislation was similar to the power exercised by the Board of Trade over the colonial assemblies before the Revolution. But whereas the latter had operated as a subsequent check, Madison's negative was to occur previous to the legislation's taking effect. Its purpose was to make the national legislature in effect a supervisory branch of the state legislatures.

The Virginia Plan also gave Congress a broad and indefinite grant of legislative authority in all cases where the states were "incompetent." It is not clear from the phraseology whether the plan intended to give Congress the power to alter at will the extent of its authority and that of the states; at the very least, however, the plan would solve the problem of federalism by giving Congress the power to define the extent of its own authority and that of the states. There was to be but one check upon this power: the Council of Revision was authorized to examine "every act of a particular legislature before a negative thereon shall be final."

With the Virginia Plan before it, the convention went into a committee of the whole house. Immediately thereafter, the centralizers scored an important victory when, at the suggestion of Gouverneur Morris, Edmund Randolph moved the postponement of the first point in his plan in order to present a new resolution. This asserted that no "Union of the States merely federal" nor any "treaty or treaties among the whole or part of the States" would be sufficient. It concluded:

That a *national* government ought to be established consisting of a *supreme* Legislative, Executive and Judiciary.

The meaning of this resolution was clear. It went beyond any proposal to establish a federal state with limited powers in the central government. In the discussion that followed, Morris contended "that in all Communities there must be one supreme power, and one only," and proposed that this supreme power be lodged unequivocally in the national government. Several delegates objected to the proposal as meaning that state sovereignty was to be obliterated and replaced by a powerful national government. The resolution was nevertheless adopted, only Connecticut voting in the negative.

This was an astounding victory for centralization in a convention that had been commissioned merely to modify the Articles of Confederation. It put to rout at the very beginning proponents of state sovereignty and those who wished merely to patch up the Articles. Later the localists were to rally sufficiently to secure the formation of a government based upon the principles of divided sovereignty. But for the moment it appeared that the proponents of national sovereignty were in complete control and that any suggestions for preserving state autonomy would be swept aside.

With this crucial problem disposed of, the committee of the whole now took up the provisions of the Virginia Plan point by point. The composition of the legislature involved the most fundamental question the convention faced—namely, the basis on which the new government would be constituted. Would the constituent units be the states, represented equally by delegates chosen by the state legislatures, as the small-state group desired? Or would the constituent element be the people of the United States, choosing the members of both houses of the legislature through direct election and with representation in both chambers apportioned according to population, as the large-state group wished? The former method would retain the essential plan of the Confederation and imply state sovereignty; the latter would signify that the central government rested directly upon individuals rather than states and was truly sovereign in character.

The mode of election of national lawmakers was a subordinate issue in the composition of the legislature on which both sides showed a willingness to compromise. The small states accepted the proposal in the Virginia Plan for direct popular election of the lower house. But almost no one thought that the lower house should elect members of the upper, and a resolution to that effect was voted down 7 to 3 when it was first considered. John Dickinson of Delaware then moved on June 7 that the Senate be elected by the various state legislatures. In the debate that followed, Madison and James Wilson contended that authority in a truly national government ought to flow directly from the people, while Roger Sherman, speaking for the small-state faction, argued that representation of the states as such would maintain balance and harmony between the states and the national government. It was clear that the small states were prepared to insist upon representation of the states as such in at least one chamber, and at the end of the discussion, the convention adopted Dickinson's resolution unanimously.

Meanwhile, the convention attacked the more vital issue of whether representation in the two houses should be apportioned according to population or based upon state equality. Debate continued for some days, and at times became very heated. Madison and Wilson repeatedly insisted that in a proportional system, the people as such, rather than states, would be represented, and that on this basis the people of Delaware would have the same representation in Congress as would those of Pennsylvania or Virginia. They were nonetheless unable to quiet the apprehensions of the small-state faction that proportional representation would swallow up the existence of the small states, and Paterson proclaimed that his state would "rather submit to a monarch, to a despot, than to such a fate." Wilson impatiently struck back with the warning that "if New Jersey will not part with her Sovereignty, it is in vain to talk of government."

Many moderates in the small-state faction were in reality prepared to compromise on the issue of proportional versus equal representation, and to concede proportional representation in the lower house, insisting only upon state equality in the Senate. Sherman suggested this solution on June 11, at the opening of an important debate on the question.

However, the centralizers were at the moment in control of affairs, and they carried the day without compromise. Sherman's proposal was silently rejected, and immediately thereafter Rufus King moved that suffrage in the lower house ought to be "according to some equitable ratio of representation." After some debate, the resolution was carried, 7 to 3, only New

York, New Jersey, and Delaware opposing, with Maryland divided. Sherman thereupon moved that each state have one vote in the upper house. "Everything," he said, "depended upon this," since "the smaller states would never agree to the plan on any other principle than an equality of suffrage in this branch." In spite of this warning, the convention rejected his motion, 6 to 5, and then adopted by the same vote a resolution of Wilson and Hamilton that representation in the upper house be apportioned "according to the same rule as in the 1st branch."

Thus as the committee of the whole neared completion of its work, the centralizers had scored victories on three out of four points. They had won proportional representation in both chambers and popular election in the lower house, and had conceded only that state legislatures might still elect the Senate. Whether they could retain their gains, however, remained to be seen.

The New Jersey Plan

On June 15, the committee of the whole finished its discussion of the Virginia Plan and prepared to report the revised draft out upon the floor of the convention; but at this point the small-state party counterattacked powerfully. Their ranks had been augmented by the arrival of additional delegates from the small states, among them Luther Martin of Maryland, Gunning Bedford of Delaware, and John Lansing of New York, and they evidently felt that if the drift toward complete centralization was to be checked at all, it must be done then and there. Accordingly, William Paterson of New Jersey now asked permission to introduce an alternate plan, of which the small states approved and which was "purely federal" in principle as opposed to the centralizing Randolph Plan.

The New Jersey Plan was a modification of the Articles of Confederation. It would have expanded the powers of Congress by adding the right to tax and to regulate commerce. Curiously, the Virginia Plan failed to make specific provision for these two critically important powers, and their inclusion in the small-state proposal indicates that the key issue was not how strong the general government ought to be, but who would control it. Ultimately, the question was whether the existence of an authentic government at the continental level would jeopardize the continued vitality of the states. The small-state or states'-rights delegates clearly supported a stronger central authority, but they insisted that institutional changes resulting in a stronger Union should rest on an affirmation of states' rights. Unless protected against congressional encroachment, the powers of the states, they believed, would be eroded and superseded through a consolidation of power in the central authority. To provide the necessary guarantee against this eventuality, the New Jersey Plan retained state equality in the legislature and created an executive directly subject to state control. It also granted the federal government the right to coerce recalcitrant states, a further indication of the small-state interest in creating a more potent central authority.

The New Jersey Plan showed that the basic division in the convention was not between centralizers and localists, but between centralizers like Madison, who at best thought the states might be retained merely as subordinate administrative units, and states'-rights men, who supported both state sovereignty and a stronger central government. The supremacy clause in the New Jersey Plan, which has often seemed a curious if not paradoxical part of the states'-rights counteroffensive, further illustrates the dual emphasis of the small-state outlook. The clause declared that all acts of Congress and treaties made under the authority of the United States "shall be the Supreme law of the respective States," so far as they relate to the states or their citizens. It also said that the state courts shall be bound by acts of Congress and U.S. treaties in their decisions. This provision subsequently proved to be the solution to the problem of federalism, an ironic outcome if one sees the small-states men merely as localists, yet appropriate if one considers their desire both to strengthen national authority and guarantee the integrity of the states.

After sharp debate in the committee of the whole, the New Jersey Plan was voted down 7 to 3. Again the proponents of centralization had triumphed. Yet the small states, realizing that no plan could succeed without their support, were now determined to force a compromise between centralization and state sovereignty.

The modified Virginia Plan was reported from the committee of the whole on June 19. By large majorities the convention accepted popular election of the lower house and election of the upper chamber by state legislatures. But when on June 27 the convention touched upon the question of proportional representation versus state equality in the two chambers, all the differences between the large-state and small-state factions flared up again. Two days later the convention once again voted, six states to four, for proportional representation in the lower house. The moderates on both sides at once saw in this vote the possibility of compromise: the small-state faction would accept proportional representation in the lower house in return for state equality in the upper. Arguing for this solution, Oliver Ellsworth pointed out that "we were partly federal, partly national." The compromise would recognize both the unitary and federal elements and would mutually protect the large and small states against one another. The convention was not yet ready to accept this solution, however, but neither was it prepared to adopt the large-state view. On July 2 the question of proportional representation in the upper house was put, and the small-state faction deadlocked the vote, 5 to 5.

The Great Compromise

At this point the convention appointed a committee of eleven, one man from each state, to devise a compromise. The committee consisted entirely of moderates or defenders of state sovereignty, and their report on July 5 was regarded by the centralizers as a setback. The committee recommended that in the lower house each state be allowed one member for every 40,000 inhabitants; that all bills for raising or appropriating money originate in the lower house without amendment by the upper; and that each state have an equal vote in the upper house. (It had already been decided that the Senate was to be elected by the legislatures of the several states.)

Up to this time the principal line of division in the convention was between large-state and small-state blocs, or centralizers and defenders of state sovereignty. Now, however, the politics of the convention became sectional, and it was sectional interests that led the delegates finally to accept the compromise recommended by the committee of eleven.

Important as the perception of large-state and small-state differences was with respect to population and area, the distinction also contained a sectional coloration. Although the large-state bloc included Massachusetts and Pennsylvania, four states in this group were southern: Virginia, North Carolina, South Carolina, and Georgia. The small-state group on the other hand was principally northern: Maryland, Delaware, New Jersey, New York, Connecticut, and New Hampshire. Furthermore the average population of the large states, exclusive of heavily populated Virginia, was 307,000; of the small states, excluding tiny Delaware, it was 278,000, a relatively small difference. That sectional interests should lie barely below the surface of the large- versus small-state distinction is hardly surprising, moreover, when one considers that Confederation politics usually rested on conflicting regional interests.

In the convention debate over representation in the upper house of the national legislature, the large-state delegates had rested their case on the correctness of the republican principle of representation of individual citizens rather than states. Toward the end of June, however, sectional considerations emerged as a crucial factor in the delegates' thinking. The disposition and development of the western lands as part of the Union provided the focal point for this sectional concern.

Southerners looked to the West in an expansionist way. Led by Virginia, which had a long history of involvement in the Northwest and claimed large land holdings in what later became Kentucky, southerners anticipated migration across the Appalachians and north of the Ohio, where they would build a society based on agrarian republican principles and preserving slavery. Delegates from the mid-Atlantic and New England states, however, representing commercial and professional interests, were hostile toward the prospect of western development, especially under southern auspices. They opposed the creation of new states in the West and the admission of these states to the Union on an equal basis with the original ones. Gouverneur Morris of Pennsylvania and Elbridge Gerry of Massachusetts, for example, argued that the Atlantic states ought to maintain control over the interior of the continent lest populous new western states undermine their power. Evidence of sectional thinking was apparent, too, in the delegates' reaction to a report in early July assigning representatives in the lower house on the basis of population. Suddenly, instead of seeing their states as large or small, members of the convention saw them as belonging to regional blocs.

The emergence of sectional attitudes did not by itself resolve the deadlock over representation in the upper legislative house. What assisted in preparing the way for the Great Compromise was action taken by the Confederation Congress, which was simultaneously in session in New York. Addressing itself to the issue that had provoked sectional deadlock at the convention—the disposition of the western lands—Congress effected a sectional compromise that pointed the way toward a solution of the problem in Philadelphia. It did so by adopting the Northwest Ordinance.

Although the Northwest Ordinance contained an antislavery provision that later figured prominently in abolitionist rhetoric and strategy, it represented a southern policy-making initiative. Its main effect was to integrate the West into the Union on terms beneficial to the South. Expansionist in outlook, southerners hoped to people the West rapidly, create a number of states, and secure their admission to the Union on terms of equality with the original states. Southerners also desired to organize territorial government in the West to assist diplomatically in gaining access to the Ohio and Mississippi Rivers as an outlet for commercial agriculture. In order to secure these objectives they were willing to permit the prohibition of slavery in territory north of the Ohio River, provided that a fugitive slave law operated in the area and provided further that slavery be permitted to expand into unorganized territory lying south of the Ohio. Southerners gave up their hope of creating ten new states in the Northwest, but they succeeded in reducing the length of the territorial period preceding statehood. The required population for statehood was set at 60,000, rather than one-thirteenth of the population of the original states, as previously agreed. For their part, northerners gave up the idea of retaining permanent control over the West, which would have been difficult to do in any case, given the national commitment to republicanism. What the North got out of the compromise, besides the prohibition of slavery, was a limit on the number of states that could be formed in the Northwest (no fewer than three nor more than five). And although southerners were regarded as more expansionist, northerners, too, could set their sights on the West and send emigrants there to reproduce their own social institutions.

The accomplishment chiefly of southern delegates (with northern land speculators outside Congress also supplying much impetus), the Northwest Ordinance was a sectional compromise that went far toward resolving the thorny question of the disposition of the western lands that had emerged as a source of contention in Philadelphia. Given final form in Congress on July 11, with the help of four southern delegates who left the convention and traveled to New York so Congress would have a quorum, the ordinance was at once reported to the Philadelphia assemblage, where it appears to have assisted in settling the North-South conflict over the composition of the legislature. On July 16 the convention approved the Connecticut or Great Compromise by a 5-4-1 vote. Two states that had previously supported proportional representation in the Senate now did not. North Carolina voted for the compromise and for state equality in the Senate, while Massachusetts, some of whose delegates feared western influence, split its vote and hence was counted as an abstention.

The Great Compromise was acceptable because it met the needs of both sections. Although at the time the North had a larger population, it expected in the future to be outnumbered by the South and it, therefore, looked on equal state representation in the Senate as providing needed long-range protection. In the meantime, proportional representation in the House of Representatives would register its existing population superiority. The South, on the other hand, for the time being had protection against northern numbers in the Senate and could look forward to proportional representation in the lower house as a guarantee of its interests.

A series of other North-South compromises, based on the views and votes of mid-Atlantic states which held the balance of power, followed the critical mid-July accommodation over the composition of the legislature. Fearful that northerners would use a centralized commerce power against them, southerners had initially demanded a two-thirds majority for the enactment of commerce or navigation laws. Eventually, they accepted simple majority approval of exercises of the commerce power, however, in return for a constitutional prohibition of taxes on exports. Three provisions concerning slavery also reflected sectional adjustment: the fugitive slave clause, declaring that persons held to service or labor under the laws of a state shall be returned to the person claiming service; the denial of congressional power to prohibit the slave trade for a twenty-year period; and the three-fifths clause, which included slaves in the reckoning of population for the purposes of representation and direct taxation. The third of these measures further illustrated the sectional conflict between North and South that had the West as its focal point.

The idea of counting five slaves as three free persons was first suggested in Congress in 1783 as part of a plan for basing taxation on population. Although the plan was not adopted, the three-fifths ratio aroused no sectional antagonism, and it was introduced without incident in the Constitutional Convention and approved as part of a plan for proportional representation in the early stages of proceedings. When sectional hostility crystallized in early July, however, the three-fifths clause was identified as a sectional issue. It was connected with another sectional problem—whether the apportionment of representatives in the national legislature should be determined by Congress or by a constitutionally required decennial census. Several northern delegates, fearing the rapid development of the West, sought to keep control over apportionment in the national legislature. Although they did not repudiate the three-fifths clause, they now labeled it a prosouthern instrument and opposed its adoption either as a constitutional provision or subsequently in the form of a national statute. Southerners protested that if Congress controlled representation, it might reject the three-fifths idea. Accordingly, with the help of a few strongly committed ideological republicans like James Wilson of Pennsylvania, who saw the three-fifths clause as a means of gaining southern support for the principle of representation of persons rather than property, they succeeded in writing both the requirement of a decennial census and the three-fifths clause into the Constitution. Two key issues of interest to the proslavery South were thus removed from a potentially hostile national legislature.

The Executive

Throughout the convention, as different issues were dealt with, coalitions formed on the basis of sectional division or large-state versus small-state identification. The latter was especially prominent in discussions of the executive. Fearful of being overwhelmed by the large states, the small states insisted that the election of the president—the major point of contention in shaping the executive branch—should in certain crucial respects be on their terms.

Two schools of thought existed concerning the executive. The first, represented by Sherman of Connecticut, Dickinson of Delaware, and Martin of Maryland, argued for a weak executive, chosen by and responsible to the legislature. The second point of view, represented by James Wilson, James Madison, Gouverneur Morris, and Alexander Hamilton, proposed a strong, independent executive, preferably chosen by direct popular election. These two conceptions of the presidency came into conflict the moment the committee of the whole took up the matter. The strong-executive men attacked the Virginia Plan provision for an executive elected by Congress, and Wilson suggested direct popular election as an alternative. This idea received little favor with most of the delegates, in part because it was too democratic, in part because the idea of a popularly elected executive was as yet largely foreign to American experience. Wilson then offered as a compromise that the people of the states should choose presidential electors, who should meet and choose the executive. This was defeated, eight states to two. The convention proceeded to ratify the plan for the election of the president by Congress, and there matters stood when the committee of the whole reported on June 15.

Proponents of a strong executive in debates throughout July hammered away at the idea that an executive chosen by the legislature would be corrupt and incompetent. They scored a temporary success when on July 19 the convention voted 6 to 3 to accept the electoral college idea. But on July 26 the delegates reversed themselves by adopting legislative election once again. A month later, on August 31, the convention appointed a committee of eleven to consider parts of the Constitution that had been postponed.

Comprising one delegate from each state, the committee on postponed parts was dominated by a group of small northern and middle states—New Hampshire, Connecticut, New Jersey, Delaware, and Maryland—who together with Massachusetts and Georgia formed a controlling coalition. The committee recommended the electoral college method of choosing the president. Each state was to choose its own electors in a manner prescribed by its legislature. This provision recognized the states, yet allowed for the possibility of popular choice of the electors. The electors were to vote by ballot for two persons, the one receiving the greatest number of votes to be president, providing that the number of votes cast for him was a majority of all the electors. If no candidate won a majority, the Senate was to elect the president, providing that the number of votes cast for him was a majority of electoral votes.

Debate revealed, however, a widely shared belief that in most elections no candidate would receive a majority in the electoral college for want of systematic coordination of the voting process from state to state. Yet the committee's proposal in that circumstance to shift the election of the president to the Senate was opposed by a minority of large and southern states—Virginia, Pennsylvania, North Carolina, and South Carolina—who feared that the Senate as a bastion of aristocracy would become too powerful. The solution offered by the committee was to place the choice in the House of Representatives, with voting by the states equally. The convention accepted this proposal. The small states thus gained satisfaction in the thought that they would have final control over the selection of the president most of the time, while the large-state minority kept the choice out of the Senate. The convention also followed the recommendations of the committee on unfinished parts by giving the treaty-making power and the power to appoint ambassadors and public ministers to the president with the advice and consent of the Senate, and by giving the Senate the power of trial in impeachment. Like the method of electing the president, these decisions were intended to satisfy the small-state point of view in particular.

On balance the convention created a strong, unitary executive, rejecting both the plural executive found at the time in most of the states and the

British concept of a ministerial executive responsible to the legislature. In transforming the Confederation into a genuine government it was necessary to give it not only legislative power, but also executive power capable of acting directly upon individual citizens to enforce or give sanction to the laws. Although republican theory up to this time preferred a weak executive out of fear that a strong one would undermine liberty, in the reassessment of republicanism that took place in the 1780s an executive possessed of energy, dispatch, and responsibility came to be seen as necessary. Accordingly, the convention gave the president the power to act as commander in chief of the army and navy, to make treaties and conduct foreign relations, and to appoint judges and subordinate officers for the internal administration of the government. The executive was authorized to recommend measures to Congress and was given an express role in the legislative process in the form of a veto. The president was also eligible for re-election. Finally, the language of Article II of the Constitution creating the executive suggested an undefined, residual authority in stating that "The executive Power shall be vested in a President of the United States." The powers of Congress, by contrast, were carefully enumerated.

Federal Supremacy and the Judiciary

Intermittently, the convention returned to the two related problems that had plagued the Confederation in the 1780s: the use of the states as agencies of the central government, and the demarcation of the spheres of state and federal power. As it became clear that the federal government would act directly on individuals rather than states, the proposal in the Virginia Plan for coercion of states deficient in their obligations to the Union came to appear irrelevant. The central government would possess its own agents—executive officers, courts, attorneys, marshals, revenue officers, and the like—to carry out its functions and impose its will. Viewed in this light, the idea of coercing states implied that the Union was still a league or confederation dependent on the will of the various sovereign states. Coercion of a state would then, as Madison observed, "look more like a declaration of war, than an infliction of punishment, and would probably be considered by the party attacked as a dissolution of the union."

Coercion was dropped, but the problem of safeguarding and defining the spheres of state and central governments—the problem of federalism—remained. Madison's congressional negative in the Virginia Plan, in conjunction with the grant of power in Congress to legislate in all cases to which the states were incompetent or in which individual state legislation might be disruptive of unity, offered a highly centralist solution. At first the negative found favor, but by mid-July its weaknesses stood out. Because it would in effect have made Congress an integral part of the state legislatures, many delegates saw it as a genuine menace to the states and thought the people would never accept it. The congressional negative also presented grave practical difficulties. In order to review all state legislation Congress would have to be in session continuously and would have little time for anything else. Moreover if Congress did not veto a law that was unconstitutional (the negative had been amended to apply only to unconstitutional state acts), it would by implication remain operative even though contrary to the fundamental law. Such a circumstance, as Sherman of Connecticut said, involved a "wrong principle." Whatever the force of these difficulties, the decision in mid-July to create a partly confederate and partly unitary government eliminated the negative from serious consideration. Intended to consolidate a confederate system, it was out of place in the mixed regime that the Great Compromise produced.

Having rejected the congressional negative, the convention accepted a judicial veto as the solution to the federal problem. The key maneuver here was Luther Martin's introduction of a provision from the New Jersey Plan declaring federal law supreme and making state courts the agency by which the states and the federal government would be kept within their respective spheres. Martin's resolution stated that national legislation and treaties were to be the supreme law of the states, with state courts bound thereby, anything in their state laws to the contrary notwithstanding. Subsequent changes made judges "in the states," rather than "of the states," the enforcing authority; announced "This Constitution," as well as laws and treaties, as the supreme law of the land; and declared all of these instruments superior to state constitutions as well as state laws. The result was the all-important supremacy clause (Article VI, Section 2), which in express terms gave the Constitution the force of law. As Edward S. Corwin observed many years ago, it was not the aspect of supremacy that was so critical or distinctive in the new Constitution, but rather its character as law, enforceable in ordinary courts throughout the land. The Constitution was not, in other words, mere political exhortation.

Although the supremacy clause seems plainly to imply judicial review, it does not specifically provide for appeals from state to federal courts. Nevertheless, there is evidence that many delegates assumed the existence of such a power. The original Virginia Plan, for example, provided for one or more supreme and lower federal tribunals. States'-rights men, believing lower federal courts would undercut the state courts, objected and argued that the latter could act as courts of first instance for federal cases. They also said that uniformity of decision could be secured by granting a right of appeal to the supreme national tribunal. Although the convention rejected the proposal for establishing inferior national courts, preferring to leave that issue for Congress, it is clear that the delegates contemplated the possibility of appeals from state courts to the Supreme Court. Yet it is equally true that the convention did not regard the right of appeal as involving or creating a general power in the federal judiciary to interpret in a comprehensive way the extent of state authority under the Constitution.

Similarly, many delegates seem to have thought that the federal judiciary would have the right to refuse to recognize an unconstitutional federal law without attributing to it an ultimate power to fix the meaning of the Constitution. Probably most members of the convention would have agreed with Gouverneur Morris that the judiciary should not be bound "to say that a direct violation of the constitution was law." Yet this did not mean that the Supreme Court had a general power to interpret the Constitution. In point here was debate over extending the jurisdiction of the Supreme Court to "all cases arising under this Constitution" and the laws passed by Congress. According to Madison:

[there was doubt] whether it was not going too far to extend the jurisdiction of the Court generally to cases arising under the Constitution & whether it ought not to be limited to cases of a Judiciary Nature. The right of expounding the Constitution in cases not of this nature ought not to be given to that Department ... it being generally supposed that the jurisdiction given was constructively limited to cases of a Judiciary nature.

If the import of this passage is correct, the delegates were generally agreed that the federal judiciary was not to possess the general power of expounding the Constitution.

Regardless of where the final power to interpret the Constitution was to be lodged, there is no doubt that the convention intended the federal sphere of sovereignty to be a limited one. As previously noted, in the Virginia Plan the scope of federal power was defined in broad and general terms to include power over all matters in which the states were incompetent, as well as those over which power was exercised by the Confederation Congress. This proposal would have given Congress vast authority of a vague and undefined character, inconsistent with the nature of a federal state. Although two or three delegates expressed alarm at the sweeping grant of power it implied, the convention took no positive action until the committee on detail produced a draft constitution early in August.

In this draft the committee had abandoned the original vague statement of congressional authority, and incorporated a series of specific delegated powers. This was done partly out of fear of an indefinite grant of legislative authority to the general government. Another reason lay in the necessity of separating and assigning to different branches of the new government powers that had been exercised by Congress under the Confederation. By the same token, some powers that were traditionally executive, such as the power to declare war or to create government offices, were to be given to Congress. In order to make clear this reassignment of powers, enumeration was necessary. Although there is little documentary evidence explaining enumeration, its constitutional significance proved to be profound. For it expressed in unmistakable terms the central theme of American constitutionalism: the limitation of legislative power by fundamental law. That the new government had only the powers assigned to it meant that other powers were kept by the states or the people, the constituent elements of the new government.

The Locus of Sovereignty

The enumeration of congressional powers throws light on the founding fathers' disposition of the question that lay at the root of the imperial controversy—the problem of sovereignty. In English and European constitutional theory sovereignty was unitary and indivisible. In the dispute over the imperial constitution, Americans rejected this notion and argued for divided sovereignty. Subsequently, however, they embraced the orthodox theory themselves in their assertions of state sovereignty during the Revolution. Yet this situation proved unsatisfactory, not only because it encouraged legislative excesses in the states, but also because it contradicted the republican principle of the people as constituent power possessing ultimate authority. The solution was to transfer sovereignty to the people, who could then allocate it in appropriate measure to the central and state governments. The first phase of this process took place in state constitution making during the Revolution. The second phase occurred at the Constitutional Convention and in the campaign for ratification that followed it.

Regarding the people as sovereign, the convention denied sovereignty to both state and federal governments. This denial of sovereignty was implicit in the very act of framing a government of defined and hence limited powers, and it was expressed documentarily—albeit in a negative way—by the omission from the Constitution of any reference to sovereignty. It proved virtually impossible in the future to conduct government without reference to the language of sovereignty. Hence in the debates over ratification and in the political struggles of the 1790s, and indeed throughout the nineteenth century, the locus of sovereignty in the states or the federal government formed a major theme of constitutional discourse. Yet the division of power between the states and the federal government had changed the meaning of sovereignty in the American constitutional order.

That two authentic governments could exist in the same geographic area, resting on the same constituent basis, was impossible to conceive of under the older theory of sovereignty. Critics dismissed it as illogical, an *imperium in imperio* (a government within a government) which denied all reason. But this was precisely what American federalism provided for, and the doctrine of popular sovereignty made it possible. Created by the people, state and federal governments could legislate and govern concurrently over the same population in the same territory. The difference between the two kinds of government, the one general, the other local, lay in the purposes assigned to each. Thus a federal republic—a compound scheme embodying the characteristics both of a confederation and a unitary government—was the American answer to the problem of sovereignty.

The Constitution Completed

In early September, with substantive matters disposed of, the convention appointed a committee of style to produce a finished document. The actual task of drafting the final version was performed by Gouverneur Morris, assisted by Alexander Hamilton, William Samuel Johnson, and Rufus King. The committee's draft was accepted almost as it stood, the only substantial change being a reduction of the ratio of representation for members of the House of Representatives from 40,000 to 30,000.

The convention had previously decided upon ratification by state conventions, favorable action by any nine states to be sufficient to establish the Constitution among those states so acting. This plan violated the method of amendment in the Articles of Confederation, which stipulated that proposed amendments must be submitted by Congress and ratified by all the states before becoming effective. But an alternative suggestion that the Constitution be submitted and approved in this manner was rejected on the ground that it would endanger the chances of adoption. Forty-two of the fifty-five delegates were still present, and on September 17, 1787, thirty-nine of them signed the new instrument of government. The convention then adjourned. Ten days later Congress submitted the Constitution to the states, which proceeded to set convention dates and issue calls for the election of delegates. The Rhode Island legislature refused to cooperate, but in the other states attempts to block the calling of conventions were defeated. Accordingly, starting in late 1787 delegates met in twelve states to consider the question of entry into the new union.

SEVEN

Ratification of the Constitution

$\bullet \bullet \bullet$

RATIFICATION OF THE CONSTITUTION, decided by popularly elected state conventions, provided the occasion for the new nation's first organized political struggle. Characterized both by legalistic debate and the rhetoric of social conflict, ratification inaugurated a new style of constitutional politics. Interest groups played a major role in the ratification contest, and their involvement foreshadowed a key feature of the developing American political system. Of increasing importance in the late colonial period, interest groups now began to assume a legitimate place in the constitutional order. In still another way the ratification struggle anticipated modern American politics. Federalists and Antifederalists fought bitterly over the Constitution, but once the issue was resolved, they cooperated in implementing the new system of government. Shared political values permitted this cooperation. Yet in 1787–88 the most important principles on which the American national consensus was based—unionism and republicanism—received sharply conflicting interpretations from the opposing sides in the ratification fight.

In discussing ratification a word on nomenclature is necessary at the outset. In the late eighteenth century federalism referred to a confederation, league, or alliance—the opposite of a unitary sovereign government. Although the critics of the Constitution desired a stronger central government, in arguing to retain the Articles of Confederation they were closer to this position than were the advocates of the new government. Yet the latter appropriated the term "federalism" for themselves and pinned the label "Antifederalist" on their opponents. This gave them an important tactical advantage. Proposing a formidable new central authority that was sure to arouse fear of consolidation, they sought to disarm their adversary and allay states'-rights apprehension by identifying their cause—through their choice of rhetoric in calling themselves "Federalists"—with the values of decentralization which had a presumptive legitimacy in American political culture.

The Antifederalist leader Abraham Yates believed a more accurate description of the division over ratification would have been "republican" versus "antirepublican." This would have been misleading in implying that the supporters of the Constitution were not republican in outlook. Nevertheless, their republicanism differed considerably from that of their opponents. Yates's suggestion would have appealed to many contemporaries who saw the Antifederalist position as being more consistent with the spirit of revolutionary republicanism than was the Federalist position.

Antifederalist Principles

The geographical area appropriate to republican government was the most obvious problem in republican theory on which Antifederalists based their opposition to the Constitution. In accordance with conventional political science, Antifederalists insisted that republican government could succeed only in smaller nations possessing a high degree of social harmony and homogeneity. This proposition rested more on history than on logic: large republics had failed, and the American colonies, considered to be relatively small, had flourished as the embryo of republican self-government. Small as they were, it was difficult in the states to transcend conflicting interests and legislate for the common good. Antifederalists argued that in the geographically extensive government projected in the Constitution it would be impossible to do so. The result would be the disintegration of republicanism into warring factions.

Antifederalists further objected that only in a small republic could full and equal representation be achieved. Republican government required close contact between electors and deputies. In order to represent their interests effectively, elected delegates must be familiar with their constituents' opinions and outlook. This familiarity was possible only in compact jurisdictions. It followed that full and equal representation required numerous representatives. Inasmuch as there were 200 state senators in the thirteen states, reasoned Antifederalist leader Richard Henry Lee of Virginia, to have fewer than that number in the national legislature would be inadequate. Yet the framers of the Constitution had provided for only 65 members in the House of Representatives—one for every 30,000 people. It was inconceivable to the Antifederalists that this arrangement could satisfactorily represent the people or create in them the reciprocal interest in supporting the new government that its success required. Noting the differences that separated the states, critics of the Constitution denied that a single national policy could or should be applied to such a variety of interests and conditions. Antifederalists warned that the new government, distant from the people because of its vast size, would maintain itself by standing armies and military coercion rather than by winning the affection and consent of its constituents.

Antifederalists further contended that the government envisioned in the Constitution would centralize and consolidate power, thus destroying republican government in the states. Behind this fear of consolidation lay the Antifederalists' adherence to the orthodox view of sovereignty as unitary and indivisible. Seeing only the alternatives of autonomous states joined in a confederation or a unitary government, they placed the new government in the latter category. Although Richard Henry Lee and other Antifederalist leaders professed to desire a plan of union that would create a unitary power for certain general purposes while leaving local matters to the states, they rejected the Federalist contention that the new government, by combining confederate and unitary features, satisfied this criterion. Guided by the unitary theory of sovereignty, the Antifederalists said it was impossible to have two governments exercising sovereign power within the same territory over the same population. To suggest such a scheme was a contradiction in terms—an *imperium in imperio*—which would result in the larger and stronger government aggrandizing power at the expense of the smaller and weaker. In short, the very existence of a central government with legislative, executive, and judicial powers threatened the states, and hence American republicanism.

Among the powers conferred by the Constitution Antifederalists especially objected to those assigned to the executive. In this they expressed the traditional republican fear of corruption or executive influence in the form of patronage distribution and electoral manipulation which undermined the independence of the legislature. The relationship between the executive and the Senate, whose members enjoyed six-year terms and who possessed special powers in treaty making and administrative appointments, was a particular source of apprehension. Fearing that the president and the Senate would form a conspiracy of power, many critics called for a more complete separation of powers.

But it was not simply the specter of executive corruption that stirred Antifederalist suspicion toward the new Constitution. Their ingrained republican hostility to government in general was reflected in opposition to national legislative powers as a threat to republican liberty. The power to tax and appropriate money; to declare war, raise armies, and command the state militia; to make laws necessary and proper for carrying into execution the enumerated powers of Congress and "all other powers vested . . . in the Government of the United States, or in any Department or Officer thereof"—all seemed to augur consolidation of legislative power in derogation of the states. Finally, the supremacy clause, declaring the Constitution and laws and treaties passed in pursuance of it superior to state constitutions and laws, expressed in Antifederalist eyes a centralizing purpose.

Still another Antifederalist objection to the Constitution concerned the absence of a bill of rights. The convention had briefly considered a proposal for a bill of rights, but decided against it on the ground that if the general government had only the powers delegated to it, a bill of rights reserving powers to the people was superfluous. The state constitutions, which did contain bills of rights, were thought to be a sufficient protection of individual liberty. In the state ratifying conventions, however, the Antifederalists seized on the absence of a bill of rights with telling effect. Reflecting orthodox republican theory, they viewed politics as a struggle between power and liberty, and the Constitution as a contract between rulers and ruled. Hence they insisted on a bill of rights as an additional guarantee of individual liberty. The argument was effective. Unwilling to appear less solicitous of liberty than their opponents, Federalists in several states informally agreed to accept subsequent inclusion of a bill of rights as a condition of ratification.

Federalist Constitutional Theory

As advocates of a stronger Union, the Federalists have gone down in history pre-eminently as nationalists. It would be a mistake to place too much emphasis on this fact, however, first, because it implies that opponents of the Constitution did not care about strengthening the Union—a point that is manifestly untrue—and second, because it obscures the significant contribution the Federalists made to the theory and practice of republicanism. The founding of republican governments in the states was the quintessential expression of the spirit of '76, and the Federalist authors of the Constitution brought the Revolution to completion by establishing a republican government for the Union as a whole. In doing so they modified republican theory and infused federalism with a republican content that enabled the new central government, in consequence of the identification that it now enjoyed with the sovereign people, to become a national government.

Federalists modified republican theory most significantly by asserting the idea of an extended sphere of government. According to the conventional teaching, as noted previously, republican principles were considered appropriate in a circumscribed territory with basically homogeneous interests. The experience of the states since the Revolution, however, showed the impossibility of subordinating interest-group conflict to the general good. Accordingly, the Federalists proposed an extended sphere of government that would be large enough to accommodate interest-group conflict, while preventing any single interest from gaining control of the government.

The best exposition of Federalist ideas appeared in *The Federalist,* a series of eighty-five newspaper essays written by James Madison, Alexander

Hamilton, and John Jay to support ratification in New York and published in 1787–88 under the pseudonym of Publius. The most famous of the essays, which subsequently were accepted as an authoritative treatise on the meaning of the Constitution, was Madison's No. 10, setting forth the classic exposition of the doctrine of the extended republic.

In *The Federalist* No. 10 Madison lamented the frequent conflict that existed between the factions into which American society was divided and the public good. Nevertheless, he regarded landed, mercantile, manufacturing, creditor, and monied interests as necessarily involved in the operations of government. Ordinarily, he explained, legislation could control the spirit of faction through the operation of majority rule. Where the controlling faction was a majority, however, the rights and interests of minorities had no protection. In this situation, which Madison said existed in several states, constitutional forms concealed the fact that the actions of the majority were based on narrow factional concerns rather than on the general welfare. The proper remedy—a republican remedy, Madison pointedly observed—was to enlarge the sphere of government in which factions might compete. Coming together in the legislature of the new federal republic, interest groups would seek to influence the government, but they would be too numerous and varied to allow any one faction to gain control of the government.

Instead of arguing that the purpose of politics was to deny or transcend the differences between interest groups, as conventional republican theory held, Madison reasoned that republican government should give expression to the various interests in society. Abandoning the traditional republican belief in the necessity of social homogeneity, Madison and his Federalist colleagues adopted a positive, though not uncritical, view of interest groups which went far toward establishing pluralistic conflict as the norm in American politics. Madison did not entirely reject the notion of a general good existing apart from competing groups. But he suggested that most of the time, for most purposes, factional struggle would *ipso facto* promote the good of the whole.

In the Federalists' extended republic representation served a modulating, restraining purpose that set it apart from the more populistic view of attorneyship representation favored by the Antifederalists. The extensive public space created by the Constitution would impede but could not by itself provide an absolute guarantee against factional domination of the government. Wisdom and virtue were also needed, and these qualities would be supplied by the men of learning, ability, and standing in the community whom Madison and his fellow Federalists counted on to support the new Constitution. Aware of the social dimension of politics, Federalists entered the ratification debate with the expectation that men of distinction would be chosen as representatives in the new government. Larger electoral districts—one representative for every 30,000 people—

would place elected lawmakers at a certain remove from the people and enable them to refine, filter, and enlarge public opinion while discouraging demogoguery. Originating in discussions of the House of Representatives, this argument applied with special force to the Senate, elected as it was by the state legislatures, and to the president, chosen by the electoral college. It is pertinent to note also that although the framers of the Constitution did not in express terms require a property qualification to vote in elections for U.S. representatives, in effect they did so by accepting as criteria in national elections state qualifications for electors of the more numerous branch of the state legislature. Representation in the Federalist view would thus be republican, but it would be modified in ways that would restrain the tendency in the states toward a more volatile and potentially despotic populist rule.

The Federalists' appeal for moderation and stability in state affairs could be appreciated by many Antifederalist leaders, who also opposed paper money and other economic measures that in effect threatened to alter property values. What was more difficult for the Federalists to deal with, what they had especially to overcome, was the charge that the new Constitution would consolidate power in the general government. To counter this charge they offered the theory of federalism as divided sovereignty.

Once again it was Madison, in *The Federalist* No. 39, who provided the most cogent argument in behalf of the proposed Constitution. A few specific powers were to be withdrawn from the states, he explained, but in general they would retain their sovereign authority. On the other hand, the central government would blend characteristics of a unitary national government with those of a confederation so as to give the states as distinct role in the new constitutional order. Seeking to allay the apprehensions of state-minded men, Madison said the new government would be a confederation as far as the source of its power was concerned. The act establishing it—ratification of the Constitution—would rest on "the people of America," which Madison said meant the people as citizens of separate states rather than of a unitary nation. With respect to enumerated powers, those possessed by the House of Representatives rested directly on popular election and derived their legitimacy from the unitary model, while those of the Senate derived authority from the confederation model. In view of the electoral college method of choosing a president, executive powers derived from both sources. In the scope of its powers, too, the new government would be both unitary and confederate. Insofar as its powers were enumerated and restricted to certain spheres it was a confederation, all other powers by implication being reserved for the states or the people. Insofar as its powers were supreme, as stated in the supremacy clause of the Constitution, it was a unitary nation.

Conventional political science classified governments as either unitary or federal (i.e., a confederation). The proposed new government combined the characteristics of both types, yet its supporters called it a federal plan. They thus gave a new meaning to the term *federal*. Because of the novelty of the plan no one knew the effect it would have on the states, or how conflicts between the states and the federal government would be resolved. All that was certain was that within a single constitutional system both central and state governments would act directly on individuals, exercising a dual, and hence qualified, sovereignty. The Federalists' outstanding achievement, necessitated by the existence of the states as powerful sovereignties, was to employ the principle of duality and the language of coordinate or co-equal status to define federalism as divided sovereignty and to project it as the political organization of the new nation.

The third major element in Federalist ratification strategy was popular sovereignty. Like the doctrine of divided sovereignty, this, too, had a lasting effect on American constitutionalism. Although the Antifederalists saw themselves as closer to the people and more sympathetic with democratic tendencies than their opponents, it was the Federalists who seized the initiative on this score and emphasized popular sovereignty as the distinguishing feature of the new government. In Federalist theory the sovereign people, standing outside the government, expressed their will in the form of a written Constitution which placed absolute limits on elected officials. Furthermore, it was the people who divided governmental power between the states and the central government. Indeed, popular sovereignty rendered intelligible the definition of federalism as divided sovereignty and enabled the Federalists to answer the Antifederalist charge that the Constitution created an *imperium in imperio*. For if the people possessed and were the source of power to begin with, they could give some of it to the central government and some of it to the states without any sense of internal contradiction. Assigning sovereignty to the people thus meant the rejection of sovereignty in anything like its traditional sense. This relocation of sovereignty also underscored the limited nature of federal authority as a delegated, enumerated power and explained the absence of a bill of rights in the Constitution. If the new government had only the powers given to it and the people retained all the rest, reasoned the Federalists, a bill of rights, denying the government powers that no one pretended it had, was superfluous.

That stability-seeking Federalists should appeal to popular sovereignty in the ratification debates has seemed to some historians a disingenuous tactic aimed at reversing the democratic course of the Revolution. According to this point of view, the Constitution was a conservative, centralizing reaction to the states'-rights democracy sanctioned by the Declaration of Independence and the Articles of Confederation. This argument is unconvincing, however, because there is no warrant for concluding either that the essence of the Revolution was a spirit of radical populistic democracy or that the Antifederalists represented more genuinely popular tendencies than the Federalists. Although the Federalists were critical of the popularly elected state legislatures in the 1780s, their commitment to republican self-government was no less sincere than that of their opponents. The support that the Constitution received from a majority of the electorate in the ratification elections and conventions is evidence of its democratic character.

The Triumph of the Federalists

Ratification occurred over a ten-month period in eleven states. In smaller states which were less capable of maintaining an independent sovereign existence or which stood in special need of a strong central government, the Constitution received rapid and broad popular endorsement. Delaware, New Jersey, Connecticut, and Maryland were in the former category, while Georgia, with her fear of Indian attacks, was in the latter. States that had been more successful, but in which factionalism had been a disruptive element, ratified with greater difficulty and by smaller margins. These states were Pennsylvania, South Carolina, New Hampshire, and Massachusetts. In Virginia and New York, the largest and most powerful states, ratification succeeded by very slim margins, and two states that thought they could go it alone, North Carolina and Rhode Island, at first rejected the Constitution and then adopted it in 1789 and 1790 respectively. Where the struggle was close, the Federalists won decisive votes by promising to add amendments to the Constitution incorporating Antifederalist demands for a bill of rights.

Inequalities in the apportionment of delegates to the state ratifying conventions, which was based on the system employed in the state legislatures, gave an advantage to the Antifederalists in six states that approved the Constitution by wide margins, and to the Federalists in two states of strategic importance, where the contest was close. To this limited extent ratification was influenced by less than fully democratic procedures. In South Carolina, the eighth state to ratify, delegates voting for the Constitution represented only 39 percent of the population; in New York, whose ratification as the eleventh state was politically though not legally necessary to launch the new government, pro-Constitution delegates represented 33 percent of the population. Nevertheless, in the first nine states that ratified, delegates representing 65 percent of the population voted for the Constitution. By July 1788, after eleven states had given their approval, pro-Constitution delegates represented a majority of the total United States population. When the process of ratification was completed in 1790, the proportion of the entire population represented by pro-Constitution delegates stood at 59 percent. Thus in actual practice as well as in republican theory, the Constitution expressed the people's will. Nor does the disfranchisement of landless and propertyless persons gainsay the accuracy of this conclusion. Certainly, in formal terms the Constitution rested on a more complete expression of public opinion than either the Declaration of Independence or the Articles of Confederation.

It is possible to analyze the controversy over ratification along socioeconomic lines, following Charles A. Beard's famous work, *An Economic Interpretation of the Constitution of the United States* (1913). Beard argued that the framers of the Constitution, through their possession of public securities and paper assets, had a personal economic interest in the establishment of a strong central government that would aid the mercantile and creditor classes. The opponents of the Constitution, he contended, were agrarian and debtor classes whose economic interest lay in land. Although more numerous than their rival, the Antifederalists were politically outmaneuvered by the Federalists. Beard's thesis in its original formulation has long since been disproved. But in attenuated form it persists in studies that show that the Constitution was supported by occupational groups—in rural as well as urban areas—which were involved in the market economy, and that it was opposed by groups whose economic outlook and needs were oriented toward subsistence and hence were strictly local. In other words, commercial-cosmopolitan interests struggled against agrarian-localist interests.

If one assumes that decisions on political questions follow an underlying and often obscure economic calculus, then the market-orientation analysis of ratification is convincing. But to reach this conclusion requires ignoring or discounting a vast body of evidence that on its face suggests that constitutional concerns—especially Unionism and republicanism—disposed people for and against the Constitution. This is not to deny that economic issues were related to political-constitutional considerations or that governmental decisions had economic consequences. It is to deny that constitutional choices can be reduced to economic interest as the chief motivating element.

It is true that some on the pro-Constitution side started from the premise that the country's most pressing need was economic reforms— funding of the national debt, establishment of a sound currency, the creation of a national bank and a free market for internal commerce—and that constitutional reform was necessary to achieve these results. The more common perception, however, was that the Union needed to be strengthened and republicanism improved, and that as a corollary of these changes certain economic consequences would follow. After the new government came into existence, Hamilton's policies as secretary of the Treasury introduced changes in public finance and taxation, but these consequencs prove nothing about the intention of the framers and ratifiers of the Constitution. The Constitution, in other words, was pre-eminently a political, not an economic, document.

Even when we consider ratification from an economic perspective, it is attitudes toward the constitutional issue of centralization that stand out as decisive. It is obvious that economic problems such as tariffs, currency, and regulation of markets commanded the attention of political leaders and that governmental control in this sphere appealed widely to Americans. Most people were mercantilist rather than laissez faire in outlook. Yet though the Constitution addressed many of these issues by direct and indirect means, the participants in the ratification debate showed no inclination to seek support on this basis. The Antifederalists criticized the Constitution out of opposition to centralized control of economic life; the Federalists denied that ratification would lead to any such centralized result. Both sides thus respected the value of decentralization or state control of economic affairs. They differed principally in their views of the kind or degree of Union needed to promote what Hamilton, in *The Federalist* No. 1, called the "political prosperity" of the nation and in their understanding of the effect of the Constitution on republican government.

If the ratification debates provide little support for an economic interpretation of the Constitution, they nevertheless contain much extreme language that appears to express class hostility. Antifederalists charged their opponents with an aristocratic ambition to control the new government in the interest of the wealthy few, while Federalists attacked critics of the Constitution as irresponsible and unprincipled demagogues, preoccupied with the pursuit of selfish local interests. Rhetoric of this sort obviously has significance, but that it can be taken as evidence of deep-seated class conflict is doubtful. Although some Antifederalist leaders were of socially modest background and means, too many of them possessed generally the same educational, cultural, and social qualifications as their opponents to permit the conclusion that ratification was at bottom a question of class struggle.

Rather than taken literally, the rhetoric of aristocracy versus democracy ought to be seen as an expression of a struggle between competing groups who were trying to appeal to fundamental values in the political order. The republican spirit of equality stimulated by the Revolution condemned aristocratic special privilege, and Antifederalists traded on this theme heavily—and with exaggeration—in their campaign against the Constitution. It is important to note, however, that the Antifederalists did not seek to promote political democracy by extending the franchise to the propertyless classes. Popular sovereignty notwithstanding, the spirit of the Revolution also condemned excessive reliance on the popular element in the actual conduct of government. On the other hand, the Federalists were reckless in accusing their opponents of desiring a mobocracy. What the ratification struggle reveals, then, is differently situated but not basically dissimilar social groups seeking to influence public opinion by appealing to different strands in the doctrine of revolutionary republicanism.

The Constitution and the Revolution

If republicanism were a static system of ideas and institutional practices with a fixed content, it would perhaps be possible to say that one side or the other in the ratification debate was more faithful to the essential meaning of the Revolution. The spirit of '76 was not a rigid theoretical construct, however, but a dynamic ideology that changed in response to actual events. If the Antifederalists had reason to be apprehensive about their opponents' high-toned style, the Federalists spoke truly when they identified their cause with the constitutional limitations that lay at the heart of the Revolution. When the actions of the state legislatures in the 1780s forced a greater appreciation of this aspect of republicanism, those who prescribed remedies in the new Constitution were completing the Revolution, not diverting it from its true course. Madison was not being disingenuous when he said that the objective of the framers was to preserve the public good and private rights while retaining the form and spirit of popular government. If local self-government was the goal of the Revolution, and if Union among the states was a means of establishing republican rule, then to strengthen the Union in order to improve republicanism in the states, as the Federalists did, was a proper culmination of the Revolution.

To call attention to the narrow range of disagreement in this first organized national political controversy does not rob the conflict of its essential meaning. On the contrary, it enables us to understand how the Federalists were able to present their plan for a centralized government—something that most Americans opposed when considered in the abstract—as a *national* government endorsed by the people of the states. Republican values characterized American society, but the Confederation did not reflect or embody republican values in ways that would lead the people to develop a sustained interest in or attachment to it. Hence its weakness and ineptness. Recognizing and appealing to interests in an essentially modern way, yet at the same time trying to restrain them out of concern for the general good, the Federalists used the idea of popular sovereignty and republican representation and citizenship to legitimize the central government that they believed necessary to limit state power.

At bottom the dispute between the Federalists and Antifederalists was over the nature of the Union, not over whether there ought to be a union or whether republican government ought to be the political system of America. As the Civil War would show, in other historical circumstances controversy over the nature of the Union was capable of generating the most profound and rending conflict. But in this formative era of nation- and constitution-making, union was a means of achieving republican self-government rather than an end in itself. Federalists and Antifederalists disagreed about the kind of union that should be created to give expression to American nationality. But their commitment to republicanism, despite different emphases in their approach to it, explains how the new central government acquired legitimacy as a popular national government.

As the creation of republican governments in the states gave rise to national consciousness at the start of the Revolution, so the Constitution identified American nationality with republican forms and values. American nationality derived from practical, utilitarian considerations, rather than from religion, race, culture, and an immemorial past as in Europe. What Americans had in common was citizenship in republican state governments; it was this that gave them a distinct national character. By providing for republican government at the continental level, the Constitution strengthened American nationality. Accordingly, the national idea in America was defined not simply by identifying it with sovereign governmental powers—the taxing and commerce powers, for example, or the power of legal sanction and command—but by establishing a *republican* government. In this sense the Constitution pointed ahead to the correlation between nationalism and liberalism that existed in the nineteenth century and that characterized the defense of the Union during the Civil War.

In other respects the Constitution summarized eighteenth-century political ideas. In a general sense the Constitutional Convention was an expression of the Enlightenment's abiding faith in the supremacy of reason. Man was a rational being. It was, therefore, possible for men of various and conflicting interests to meet together and by discussion, by argument, by the application of reason solve the problems of the state in a rational manner. This solution could then be embodied in a compact based upon the reign of law, simply because it was to the mutual interest of all rational men to accept the most intelligent solution of the problem of government that human reason could devise. The convention inaugurated an era of formal constitution making; the French revolutionists and early nineteenth-century European liberals were also to engage in the same practice with the same implicit faith in the supremacy of reason.

The Constitution gave recognition to several ideas of colonial and Revolutionary political philosophy: the compact theory of the state, the notion of a written constitution, the conception of constitutional supremacy and limited legislative capacity, the doctrine of natural rights, and the separation of powers. As a formal compact setting up government, the Constitution's antecedents ran back to the Mayflower Compact, the Fundamental Orders of Connecticut, the great natural law philosophers, and the state constitutions of the Revolutionary era. As a written document, the Constitution reflected the late colonial and Revolutionary belief that the compact ought to be a written one. The notion of constitutional supremacy was also recognized; the Constitution was made supreme law, controlling state law and by implication federal law as well. Federal legislative capacity was strictly defined and enumerated; by implication it was limited to the express terms of the grant. Although the Constitution contained no separate bill of rights, certain natural rights were specifically guaranteed against invasion in the clauses prohibiting ex post facto laws and bills of attainder and guaranteeing the writ of habeas corpus. The doctrine of the separation of powers was implied in the Constitution's organization and content, legislative, executive, and judicial powers being granted separately in three different articles.

The powers granted the new government reflected in part American experience with federalism under the British Empire and the Articles of Confederation. The scope of federal authority was essentially the same as that of the central governments under the old British Empire and under the Articles of Confederation. Experience had taught the statesmen of the Revolutionary era that a central government could not function effectively without the right to tax and to regulate commerce, and they now added these items to the grant of federal authority. Yet the federal government was still conceived of as having few other functions than the maintenance of peace against external and internal disturbance, though for this purpose it was thought that it must also be financially sound and efficient. Even the power over interstate commerce, eventually to become so potent an arm of federal authority, was apparently granted for negative rather than positive reasons—to protect trade from the manifold abuses of state control rather than to make possible extensive regulation by the central government.

As America's middle-class social order was basically similar to English society yet different in the emphasis it placed on individualism, competition, and mobility, so government and politics in the United States shared the general purposes and aspirations of English constitutionalism while employing different institutional means. Like the English, Americans sought to create and maintain balanced and limited government in the interest of individual and local liberty. But whereas English constitutionalism developed for the most part incrementally and organically by essentially political means, Americans dealt with constitutional change in a more rationally deliberative, positivistic, and legalistic way. The adoption of a written constitution as the fundamental law and framework of government, while it brought to completion tendencies deeply rooted in the colonial experience, signified the beginning of a distinctive method and style of constitutional politics which carried American constitutionalism in the future ever further from the English model.

EIGHT

Establishing the New Government: Federalist Constitutionalism

——————————— ✦✦✦ ———————————

ATHOUGH THE CONSTITUTIONAL CONVENTION determined the basic character of the new government, ratification by no means completed the task of constitutional formation. Defining the nature of the executive, legislative, and judicial branches through institutional practice was the most important, if also the most perduring, of the problems facing American political leaders. Other issues dealt with in the 1790s included the place of an organized political opposition in the constitutional system, the manner of settling disputes about the meaning of the Constitution, and the proper relationship between the states and the federal government. Yet preceding all of these questions was the problem of establishing the legitimacy of the new central government.

Legitimacy in the sense in which it is used here meant political acceptance of the new government by the states and the people—the constituent elements in the new order. Because the political culture of America was republican, the popular base on which the government rested was an asset. Yet the value of this asset was limited by the fact that conflicting approaches to republicanism were possible that were capable of provoking potentially disruptive opposition threatening to the government. Unionism was another source of legitimacy, for all Americans believed that some degree of cooperation among the states was necessary. This was an even more tenuous source of legitimacy, however, inasmuch as the Antifederalists saw the new government as tending toward a centralized unitary state. Needless to say, no government in America could claim legitimacy if perceived in that light. Thus, although in a general sense the new government was consistent with American political values, that fact alone would not win it acceptance. Legitimacy would depend more on specific policies adopted by the government than on what it represented in an abstract or theoretical sense.

An important source of legitimacy on which the new government drew was the character and personality of George Washington, the first president. Handsome in appearance, renowned for his military accomplishments, possessing a reputation for integrity, dignity, and republican virtue that made him trusted and revered among all segments of the population, Washington was a charismatic figure to Americans of the Revolutionary generation. More to the point, he was a symbol of Unionism and republicanism without whom it is possible that the presidential office as conceived by the Constitutional Convention would never have been agreed on. Unquestionably, Washington's presence imparted to the new regime a firm presumption of legitimacy.

The Bill of Rights

The recommendation by the first Congress of a bill of rights was an important step in winning acceptance for the general government. It will be recalled that during the contest over ratification, Federalists had won in several states by promising a series of constitutional amendments embodying a bill of rights. Many members of the first Congress now felt a moral obligation to fulfill these promises. They believed moreover that persons lukewarm or unfriendly to the new government could be enlisted in support of it should such amendments be adopted. Accordingly, James Madison, now a representative from Virginia, took the initiative in coordinating the suggestions of the state ratifying conventions, formulating amendments, and introducing them into the House.

A few Federalists continued to oppose a bill of rights on the ground that since the government possessed only delegated powers, it was superfluous to enumerate the things it could not do. Opponents of the Constitution, however, had announced their intention to seek a second constitutional convention for the ostensible purpose of adding a bill of rights, but actually with a view toward undoing the work of the convention. Politically, therefore, it was of the utmost importance to carry through the project for a bill of rights.

As prepared by Madison and approved by the House of Representatives, the Bill of Rights restricted both the federal and state governments. In the Senate, however, the states'-rights point of view prevailed, and the seventeen amendments under consideration were altered to apply only to the federal government. This was, of course, a momentous change which showed that federalism—rather than a desire to protect individual liberty against government encroachment from whatever source—was the chief

concern of Congress in approving the Bill of Rights. Madison and his colleagues had sought to appease states'-rights sentiment by offering general
guarantees of individual liberty, but the states'-rights men exacted a higher
price by turning the amendments exclusively into restrictions on the federal
government.

By the proposed amendments, Congress was to be prohibited from
abridging the freedom of religion, speech, the press, assembly, petition, or
the right to bear arms; federal authority was closely restricted in quartering
troops, prosecuting citizens for crimes, and inflicting punishments. Out of
these proposals grew the first five amendments and the Eighth Amendment.
Extensive changes designed to guarantee the citizen a fair trial by a jury in his
own district as well as the benefits of the common law were also proposed;
these eventually became the Sixth and Seventh Amendments. The Ninth
Amendment, stating that "The enumeration in the Constitution, of certain
rights, shall not be construed to deny or disparage others retained by the
people," responded to the contention that it might be dangerous to make
only a partial listing of the basic rights guaranteed in the Constitution.

One of the most significant events in framing the Bill of Rights was the
failure of states'-rights advocates, in what became the Tenth Amendment,
to limit the federal government to those powers "expressly" enumerated in
the Constitution. This move was blocked by Madison and others, who believed that in any effective government some powers "must necessarily be
admitted by implication." In its final form the Tenth Amendment stated
that "The powers not delegated to the United States by the Constitution,
nor prohibited by it to the States, are reserved to the States respectively, or
to the people." Even without restrictive language negating the possibility of
implied federal powers, however, the Tenth Amendment provided a textual
basis for striking down federal legislation as an encroachment on states'
rights. It proved to be a kind of supremacy clause for the states.

In September 1789 Congress submitted twelve proposed amendments
to the states. Two proposals, one providing that there should be not less
than one representative in the lower house for every 50,000 persons and
another postponing the effect of any alteration in the compensation of
senators and representatives until an election had intervened, failed to secure acceptance. The ten amendments, which were approved by the requisite number of states in November 1791, worked no real alteration in
federal power and thus may be described as declaratory of the existing
Constitution. They gave formal recognition to certain traditionally accepted
natural rights, hitherto incorporated in the English charters, colonial grants,
and state bills of rights. They took no substantive powers from Congress
that could reasonably have been implied before the amendments had been
passed, and most of the procedural limitations probably would have been
taken for granted in any event.

Organization of the Executive Department

In September 1788, after eleven states had ratified the Constitution, the Confederation Congress designated the first Wednesday of the following January for the selection of presidential electors, the first Wednesday in February for the casting of the electoral vote, and the first Wednesday in March (March 4) for the inauguration of the new government. The Constitution had left the method of selecting presidential electors to the state legislatures. In the first election the states accordingly chose their electors in a variety of ways, some by popular election on a general ticket, some by popular district election, and some by legislative vote. This lack of uniform electoral procedure was to continue for several elections, and it was not until after 1860 that the choice of electors on a general ticket became universal.

When the electoral vote was counted, George Washington was found to have received one of the two votes cast by every elector. John Adams received the second highest number of electoral votes and thereby became vice-president. Meanwhile the various states held elections for members of the House of Representatives, and the state legislatures chose their senators. A large majority of the successful candidates for both houses had actively supported ratification of the new Constitution, although a few opponents of ratification won seats. The success of the Federalists was due in part to the prestige these men had gained through sponsorship of the Constitution and to the discomfiture of the Constitution's opponents, and in part to the fact that the Constitution's champions were vitally interested in the successful operation of the new government and hence sought office in greater numbers than did the Antifederalists.

Congress, meeting in New York by direction of the Confederation Congress, obtained a quorum and began to do business in April 1789. Among the first statutes it enacted were laws providing for the establishment of three executive departments—the State, Treasury, and War Departments. The Constitution made no direct provision for administrative departments. Congress thus had a large measure of discretion in the matter, though the system of administrative departments evolved in the later Confederation period was available as a precedent.

Madison's proposal of May 1789 to create a Department of Foreign Affairs precipitated a prolonged debate on the president's removal power. The bill expressly granted the president the right to remove the head of the prospective department. The Constitution was silent on the removal power, an omission which was to open the way for a century and a half of intermittent controversy on the question. Some congressmen now opposed the provision in Madison's bill on the grounds that the Senate, being associated with the president in appointments, was by implication properly associated with him in removals as well. Others contended that the removal power was an inherent part of the executive prerogative and a proper means of implementing the president's duty to take care that the laws be faithfully executed; hence, they held, the president could properly make removals without the Senate's consent. Still others argued that the Constitution permitted Congress to locate the removal power according to its judgment. The bill in question was finally phrased so as to imply that the power of removal had already been lodged in the president by the convention. While this precedent was for a time generally followed in subsequent legislation, the question of the removal power arose again during the administrations of Jackson and Johnson in the nineteenth century.

In creating a Treasury Department Congress took deliberate steps to make the secretary of the Treasury responsible to Congress as well as to the president. The secretary was required from time to time to make reports and "give information to either branch of the legislature, in person or in writing (as may be required), respecting all matters referred to him by the Senate or the House of Representatives, or which shall appertain to his office; and generally shall perform all such services relative to the finances, as he shall be directed to perform." Thus, while Congress made the heads of other departments subordinates of the president, it made the secretary of the Treasury, primarily at least, its own agent to execute its constitutional powers in the field of finance.

Here was an important move toward ministerial responsibility and parliamentary government. The basic proposition implied in the Treasury Act was that Congress could constitutionally make an executive department responsible to itself rather than to the president. Subsequent developments, however, were to arrest the trend toward ministerial responsibility.

The creation of other departments involved no major controversies. The War Department received supervision over both military and naval affairs, an arrangement continued until 1798, when the quasi-war with France led to the establishment of a separate Navy Department. The Judiciary Act of 1789 provided for an attorney general, whose chief duties were to prosecute cases for the United States before the Supreme Court and to give legal advice to the president and the heads of departments. Although he did not become the official head of a department until 1870, he became immediately a principal executive officer and presidential adviser. The post office was organized on an annual basis until 1794, when it was given permanent standing; not until 1829, however, did the postmaster general become a regular cabinet member.

A proposal of August 1789 to create a Home Department failed because of the implied invasion of state authority; instead, Congress altered the name of the Department of Foreign Affairs to the Department of State, a title general enough to cover a variety of small additional duties then assigned to the department—among them the custody of public records and correspondence with the states.

The Constitutional Convention had contemplated a strong executive, who would not only execute federal laws but would also take a prominent part in the formulation of legislation. The Constitution provided several possible instruments for executive leadership in Congress, among them the president's duty to advise Congress on the state of the Union and to "recommend to their Consideration such Measures as he shall judge necessary and expedient," and his veto power. Eventually, also, the appointive power was to become an important device for the control of policy, although it did not develop as such during Washington's time.

In advising Congress on the state of the Union, Washington early adopted the practice of appearing in person before Congress at the opening of each session to review the developments of the preceding year and to recommend matters for congressional consideration. During sessions also he sent special messages, chiefly to provide Congress with information as occasion arose. Although early Congresses followed an elaborate ceremonial in making formal response to the president's annual messages, they did not always accept his recommendations. The annual message was in fact not destined to become a major instrument of executive leadership in Congress.

The veto was also potentially an important instrument for the control of legislative policy, but it, too, did not become significant in the early national period. Federalist leaders favored the exercise of the veto power as a part of a desirable strong executive. Their opponents, on the other hand, conscious of the unpopularity of the governor's veto power in the colonial era and aware of the weak veto given most state governors, believed that the power should be used very sparingly.

Washington first used the veto in 1791, when he refused his assent to a bill apportioning representation in the House in such a manner that some states would have more than the one representative for every 30,000 inhabitants permissible under the Constitution. The president sympathized with Jefferson's argument that he ought not to refuse his assent to any bill unless he was certain that it was unauthorized by the Constitution. However, in his opinion the bill under consideration was unquestionably unconstitutional, and he finally vetoed it on that ground. While use of the veto in this case aroused little opposition, the veto power was to be used very rarely for a long time. Neither Adams nor Jefferson vetoed a single law, and not until Jackson's time was the veto used to defeat any measure that the president considered objectionable for reasons of policy.

During Washington's first administration, department heads took an active part in advising Congress upon legislative policy, even to the extent of drafting legislation. Alexander Hamilton, secretary of the Treasury, in particular considered himself to be a kind of prime minister, a coordinator between Congress and the president. Washington, other department heads, and many members of Congress were at first inclined to accept him as such. The House refused to allow Hamilton to appear before it in person; but by means of written reports, the domination of party caucuses, and the control of congressional committee personnel, the secretary of the Treasury became for a time the most important person in the government in the determination of legislative policy.

This trend toward executive leadership in Congress was sharply checked during Washington's second term and the Adams administration. The change was due not to an altered conception of the presidency by either incumbent, but to a less favorable response to such leadership from Congress. With the rapid growth and crystallization of the Republican opposition in Congress, Hamilton and his colleagues were faced by 1793 with a hostile majority in the House. Not only did Hamilton's hopes for a premiership disappear but also he was subjected to various attacks in both houses, charging him with intruding upon congressional authority and with certain improprieties and actual violations of law.

Through the rest of the decade, under the impetus provided by the nascent Republican party, Congress asserted its institutional autonomy and resisted executive domination. A principal reason for this development was the fear, central to the Anglo-American republican tradition, of undue executive influence or corruption. Insisting on the importance of the separation of powers, Republicans held that reliance on the executive departments for proposals and advice allowed those officers to usurp the lawmaking function of Congress. In accordance with this view, they formed standing committees that could gather information and expertise needed for legislation. Ways and Means, Manufactures, and Commerce were among the earliest important committees by which Congress avoided dependence on the executive departments. Republicans did not, however, aim at a complete or extreme separation of powers. Rather they looked on standing committees as a way of maintaining the necessary degree of legislative autonomy, while making it possible occasionally to call on the executive branch for guidance.

Although the Constitutional Convention had made no specific provision for an advisory council to the president, to some extent the finished Constitution implied that the Senate was to serve in this capacity. It was given two specific advisory functions: treaty making, and the appointment of diplomatic, judicial, and administrative officers. The Senate's small size and the fact that since colonial times the upper house had constituted an executive council strengthened the concept of the Senate as a presidential advisory body. The upper house did not, however, fulfill this expectation. Washington's initial request for senatorial advice led to misunderstanding and irritation, and caused the president subsequently to submit finished treaties to the Senate merely for their acceptance or rejection.

The development of a cabinet of department heads was both a cause and a result of the failure of the Senate to become an advisory body. Washington early requested written opinions from department heads, and by 1793 regular meetings of these officers as an executive cabinet were taking place. Soon, too, the cabinet came to be made up exclusively of men who were personally loyal to the president and in agreement with him on policies of the administration. Washington's attempt to draw on men of differing outlook, as when Hamilton and Jefferson were in the cabinet, proved unsatisfactory. The president's power to remove principal policy-making subordinates, first confirmed by Congress in 1789, became an additional factor in establishing cabinet unity. Under President John Adams a partial and temporary disintegration of executive unity occurred, largely because Adams retained Washington's cabinet, several members of which were loyal to Hamilton. But when Jefferson became president, he formed a cabinet of men who accepted his leadership and strove to carry out his program. Only rarely thereafter were cabinet officers to be much more than the president's subordinates and agents.

Foreign Policy and Executive Prerogative

The idea of the president as a powerful independent executive capable of initiating policy and controlling events on his own responsibility was strongly reinforced by the exercise of executive policy in foreign affairs during Washington's administration.

At the outbreak of war between France and Britain in 1793, France sent a new minister to the United States, one Edmond Genêt, to obtain this country's cooperation with the French war effort. Genêt came as emissary from the new French republic, the monarchy having been overturned in 1792 by revolution. His reception by the United States would under international law constitute formal recognition of the new French government, and the question, therefore, arose as to whether under the Constitution the president was authorized to take this step. The cabinet nonetheless agreed that Washington should receive Genêt, an action which set a precedent for the absorption by the executive of the right to extend recognition to a foreign government.

Though the United States had signed a treaty of alliance with monarchist France in 1778, Washington's cabinet was unanimously of the opinion that the nation ought to remain neutral in the current war. It was accordingly agreed that Washington should issue a proclamation of neutrality, a step shortly taken.

The administration's opponents immediately charged that Washington's proclamation of neutrality had infringed upon the province of Congress, to which the Constitution had assigned the authority to declare war. Hamilton replied by publishing in the press, under the pseudonym of "Pacificus," an elaborate statement of his theory of the strong executive. "If, on the one hand," he concluded, "the Legislature have a right to declare war, it is on the other, the duty of the executive to preserve peace till the declaration is made."

Hamilton then advanced the startling contention that the president possessed an inherent body of executive prerogative, above and beyond those rights and duties specifically mentioned in the Constitution. "The general doctrine of our Constitution, then, is," he asserted, "that the *executive power* of the nation is vested in the President; subject only to the *exceptions* and *qualifications* which are expressed in the instrument." To put it differently, the clause in the Constitution vesting executive authority in the president was itself a general grant of executive power, and the subsequent enumeration of functions was not in any sense all-inclusive. Part of the inherent executive prerogative, Hamilton added, was the general authority to conduct foreign relations and to interpret treaties in their nonjudicial aspects.

This broad claim of inherent executive prerogative caused Jefferson and Madison to believe with some reason that Hamilton was contriving to attach to the president powers approximating the royal prerogatives of the British crown. To Jefferson and his colleagues the executive authority was limited by the specific grants of the Constitution and of laws, and in domestic affairs this concept has since largely prevailed. The Hamiltonian doctrine, however, strongly supported by the hard fact that the executive department is always available and has superior sources of information regarding foreign affairs, has succeeded in giving the president very broad powers in the conduct of foreign relations.

The phase of the foreign policy of the Washington administration that aroused the bitterest opposition was the treaty drawn up by John Jay with Great Britain in 1794. It provided for the clarification of commercial relationships as well as for an amicable settlement of outstanding differences growing out of the misunderstanding and nonfulfillment of the Treaty of Peace of 1783. Since Britain now occupied an advantageous diplomatic position, most of the terms of the Jay Treaty were more favorable to her than to the United States. The treaty was, therefore, unpopular in many parts of the country, but the Federalist-dominated Senate in 1795 agreed to all of it except one clause.

Certain provisions in the treaty required appropriations of money before they could be put into effect. This necessitated action by the House of Representatives, where the opponents of the treaty were especially strong. By a considerable majority the House requested the president to furnish that body with a copy of the instructions to Jay and of other documents relative to the treaty.

Washington, with the approval of his cabinet, refused to comply with this request on the ground that the papers demanded had no relation to the functions of the House. He also reminded the representatives that the Constitutional Convention had very deliberately assigned the power of making treaties to the president and the Senate, and he insisted that "the boundaries fixed by the Constitution between the different departments should be preserved." The House then disclaimed any part in the treaty-making power but insisted upon its rights to originate all appropriations, even those for treaties, and, therefore, upon its inherent right to deliberate upon the expediency of carrying the treaty into effect. Washington held to his position and finally, by a very narrow margin, the House acquiesced and voted the necessary appropriation.

Hamiltonian Broad Construction

Simultaneous with these institutional developments, Alexander Hamilton, the first secretary of the Treasury, formulated an economic program aimed at building up the political support needed to assure the legitimacy of the new government. In a series of reports to Congress in 1790–91 dealing with the public credit, Hamilton proposed to fund the outstanding Confederation debt at face value, assume the unpaid debts of the states contracted during the Revolutionary War, and charter a national bank to assist in handling the government's monetary and financial problems. He intended thereby to create a network of influence connecting creditors, men of property, and the commercial classes in general with the federal government. Appealing to motives of economic self-interest, which he believed could be made to serve the public good, Hamilton hoped to draw mercantile groups away from a primary attachment to the state governments and link their interest to that of the general government. The result would be a mutually beneficial relationship that would at once promote commercial growth and assure the stability and success of the new republic.

There was comparatively little opposition to the refunding of the national debt, which was guaranteed by the Constitution itself. However, certain congressmen did object to paying the old obligations off at face value, a step which they argued would redound to the advantage of the speculator class. And the states'-rights faction attacked the assumption of state debts by the federal government as a scheme to consolidate national authority at the expense of the states. The Virginia legislature adopted a resolution declaring assumption to be both dangerous to the states and repugnant to the Constitution. Representatives from states that had already paid off a large part of their debts also objected to assumption as inequitable. Hamilton nonetheless carried his proposal through Congress with the aid of a political bargain by which certain southern members voted for assumption in return for some northern support for a bill to locate the future national capital on the Potomac River.

Hamilton's proposal to charter a national bank was severely attacked in Congress on constitutional grounds. The opposition was led by Madison, who was becoming increasingly hostile to Hamilton's program. Although the two men had supported strong national government in the convention and had worked together to secure ratification of the Constitution, neither their constitutional philosophies nor their economic interests were harmonious. Hamilton wished to push still further in the direction of a powerful central government, while Madison, now conscious of the economic implications of Hamilton's program and aware of the hostility which the drift toward nationalism had aroused in his own section of the country, favored a middle course between centralization and states' rights.

In the Constitutional Convention Madison had proposed that Congress be empowered to "grant charters of incorporation," but the delegates had rejected his suggestion. In view of this action, he now believed that to assume that the power of incorporation could rightfully be implied either from the power to borrow money or from the "necessary and proper" clause in Article I, Section 8, would be an unwarranted and dangerous precedent.

In February 1791, the bank bill was passed by Congress, but President Washington, who still considered himself a sort of mediator between conflicting factions, wished to be certain of its constitutionality before signing it. Among others, Jefferson was asked for his view, which in turn was submitted to Hamilton for rebuttal.

In a strong argument Jefferson advocated the doctrine of strict construction and maintained that the bank bill was unconstitutional. Taking as his premise the Tenth Amendment (which had not yet become a part of the Constitution), he contended that the incorporation of a bank was neither an enumerated power of Congress nor a part of any granted power and that implied powers were inadmissible.

He further denied that authority to establish a bank could be derived either from the "general welfare" or the "necessary and proper" clause. The constitutional clause granting Congress power to impose taxes for the "general welfare" was not of all-inclusive scope, he said, but was merely a general statement to indicate the sum of the enumerated powers of Congress. In short, the "general welfare" clause did not even convey the power to appropriate for the general welfare but merely the right to appropriate pursuant to the enumerated powers of Congress.

With reference to the clause empowering Congress to make all laws necessary and proper for carrying into execution the enumerated powers, Jefferson emphasized the word "necessary," and argued that the means employed to carry out the delegated powers must be indispensable and not merely "convenient." Consequently, the Constitution, he said, restrained Congress "to those means without which the grant of power would be nugatory."

In rebuttal Hamilton presented what was to become the classic exposition of the doctrine of the broad construction of federal powers under the Constitution. He claimed for Congress, in addition to expressly enumerated powers, resultant and implied powers. Resultant powers were those resulting from the powers that had been granted to the government, such as the right of the United States to possess sovereign jurisdiction over conquered territory. Implied powers, upon which Hamilton placed his chief reliance, were those derived from the "necessary and proper" clause. He rejected the doctrine that the Constitution restricted Congress to those means that are absolutely indispensable. According to his interpretation, "necessary often means no more than needful, requisite, incidental, useful, or conducive to. . . . The degree in which a measure is necessary, can never be a test of the legal right to adopt it; that must be a matter of opinion, and can only be a test of expediency."

Then followed Hamilton's famous test for determining the constitutionality of a proposed act of Congress: "This criterion is the *end,* to which the measure relates as a *mean.* If the *end* be clearly comprehended within any of the specified powers, and if the measure have an obvious relation to that *end,* and is not forbidden by any particular provision of the Constitution, it may safely be deemed to come within the compass of the national authority." This conception of implied powers was later to be adopted by John Marshall and incorporated in the Supreme Court's opinion in *McCulloch* v. *Maryland* on the constitutionality of the second national bank.

In his report on manufactures, Hamilton presented a powerful argument for a protective tariff for certain industries as a means of attaining a proper balance between agriculture, commerce, and manufacturing, and a prosperous and expanding economy. Since the protection of industry was not an enumerated power of Congress, the authority for such action had to rest again upon the doctrine of implied powers. Although Hamilton's recommendation to Congress was adopted in only a modified form, the opposition to the protective tariff was based more upon policy than upon alleged unconstitutionality.

Distinctly unsympathetic to the states, Hamilton used the doctrine of implied powers to advance a centralizing conception of federalism. At the Constitutional Convention Hamilton had supported a general legislative power for Congress; in interpreting the Constitution in the 1790s he fashioned virtually a plenary power out of the taxing, spending, and commerce powers of Congress. The taxing power, he held, was limited only by the restrictions contained in the Constitution that duties be uniform throughout the United States and that direct taxes be levied in proportion to population. The power to promote the general welfare through appropriations was limited only by the requirement that the objects sought be general rather than local. And the commerce power in Hamilton's view extended to all commercial activity in the United States, whether crossing state lines or confined within the borders of a single state. Although never formally disavowing the divided sovereignty of federalist theory, Hamilton came close to asserting exclusive sovereignty in the general government.

Hamilton's constitutional program secured for the federal government the support it needed to achieve legitimacy in the public mind. Confirmation of this fact came in the Whisky Rebellion of 1794, when farmers in Pennsylvania protested and threatened to block execution of the excise tax on whisky contained in Hamilton's fiscal program. Alarmed by frontier unrest and eager to assert national authority, Congress in May 1792 enacted a law authorizing the president to call out the militia in case an insurrection occurred against federal authority or in case a state, threatened by internal disorder beyond its control, called for federal aid. Based on the idea that the employment of military power should be unequivocally subordinated to the processes of civil government, the act provided that the militia was to be employed only when "the laws of the United States shall be opposed, or the execution thereof obstructed, in any state, by combinations too powerful to be suppressed by the ordinary course of judicial proceedings, or by the powers vested in the marshals." Even then the president was required first to issue a proclamation warning the insurrectionists to disperse peaceably.

In 1794 resistance to the whisky tax in western Pennsylvania took on an organized character and threatened to result in a serious breakdown of the federal revenue laws. In August 1794, therefore, Washington issued a proclamation in accordance with the Act of 1792, commanding all insurgents to submit to federal authority within three weeks. When they failed to do so, he proceeded to call out 13,000 militiamen from Pennsylvania and nearby states to suppress the insurrection. The uprising quickly disintegrated, a few of the leading rebels being arrested and tried for treason. The episode demonstrated conclusively that the new federal government possessed ample power to enforce its authority over individuals, even recalcitrant ones.

The Rise of Political Parties

Hamilton's program depended for its success on systematic political support in the national legislature. This, in turn, provoked a rival constellation of interests and ideas that led to a major and entirely unforeseen constitutional development: the formation of political parties. Previously in the states a system of factional politics had existed in which alignments changed from one issue to the next in a fitful and episodic way. Within a few years of the launching of the new government, however, something very like modern political parties—voluntary associations identified by a distinctive ideology and possessing a permanent organization that extended from the general government to the local level—became a principal force in American political life.

The requirements of organizing public opinion and directing the activity of the new continental government provided the occasion for organizing political parties. The starting point was Congress. Supporters of Hamilton's mercantilist program, most of whom had been Federalists in the ratification campaign, coordinated their votes in adopting his recommendations. Led by the Virginians James Madison and Thomas Jefferson, the latter the secretary of state in Washington's administration, critics of Hamilton's policies reacted by forming a southern-oriented and agrarian-based opposition—the Republican party. Foreign policy questions, especially those arising out of the necessity of adopting a position on the French Revolution, presented additional issues in relation to which the nascent party groups formed distinct identities.

Sympathetic to the French republic, the party of Madison and Jefferson adhered to classical agrarian republicanism. In the political context of the 1790s the chief tenets of Republican ideology were the moral and social necessity of a virtuous and economically independent yeomanry; fear of mercantilist-designed schemes of executive influence or corruption; resistance to centralizing broad construction of federal legislative power; and support of state powers and local sovereignty. The Federalist party, in contrast, was less confident of the collective wisdom of the people and hence more elitist in its political style. Federalists promoted mercantile capitalist economic development through a broad construction of federal power, a strong and unitary executive branch, subordination of state powers to a centralizing federalism, and a foreign policy openly oriented toward British interests.

From a constitutional perspective the formation of political parties was a surprising innovation, for the framers of the Constitution had anticipated no such development. Even as political leaders conformed to the dictates of party behavior and constructed a party system in the 1790s, they persisted in the ancient belief that a permanent organized opposition was a danger to the body politic and inherently seditious. Yet ancient beliefs notwithstanding, in the expanded republic it was necessary to organize and transmit public opinion to elected officials as a guide to policy making. It was further necessary to combine, coordinate, and mobilize the welter of competing interests that characterized American society. And it was necessary also to bring together in some manner the branches of government that were disjoined under the doctrine of the separation of powers. All of these constitutional purposes were served by political parties, which accordingly may be described as having a constituent or constitutional function. In the broadest sense, then, parties were an extension and refinement of republican representation, a manifestation of popular sovereignty that transformed the idea of government by consent into a dynamic and continuing institutional process.

Constitution Worship

The emergence of political parties had still further significance related to the concern for constitutional fidelity that early came to characterize American politics. The rapid acceptance of the Constitution as a test of political legitimacy, despite conflicting interpretations of the basic document, has often been noted. In a general way the practice can be explained as a consequence of the new theory of constitutionalism which Americans adopted during the Revolution. Political circumstances in the 1790s, however, supplied the decisive impetus that committed Americans to Constitution worship as a political method and style.

Ironically, principal credit for insisting on literal fidelity to the Constitution as a test of political action belongs to Antifederalist critics of the Constitution, many of whom formed the Republican party in the early 1790s. Imbued with eighteenth-century republican opposition ideas, the party of Madison and Jefferson feared arbitrary executive power, broad construction leading to consolidation of legislative power in the federal government, and corruption in the form of "government by debt" as in Hamilton's fiscal policies. More to the point, these several threats stimulated a general fear of constitutional degeneration and decline that was an essential element in classical republican thought. Indeed, it was axiomatic in the republican tradition that the tendency of any constitution was toward degeneration. Vigilance in its defense was necessary, therefore, lest liberty be destroyed. Accordingly, although many Republicans had opposed ratification, once the Constitution was adopted, they insisted in a highly literal way that its provisions be maintained. As classical eighteenth-century republicans had venerated the ancient constitution of England, so Republicans worshiped America's new Constitution as though it were old. Functionally and effectively, the Constitution became the ancient constitution, to be venerated for the sake of preserving republican liberty. The movement toward party identification in the early 1790s thus stimulated Constitution worship, which in turn provided a further rationale for promoting party organization.

The Sedition Act Crisis

At the end of the decade, deteriorating relations between the United States and France resulted in an undeclared naval war which provided the occasion for the new nation's first constitutional crisis. In 1798 the Federalist majority in Congress, responding to the intense excitement generated by the war, enacted the Alien and Sedition Acts. Based generally on the conventional view that equated organized political opposition with treason, these measures, of which there were four, were intended to suppress the partisan activities of the Republican opposition.

Least open to constitutional attack was a new Naturalization Act, which stipulated that an alien, to be eligible for citizenship, must prove fourteen years of residence within the United States. Far more controversial were the Alien Act, the Alien Enemies Act, and the Sedition Act. The Alien Act authorized the president to order the deportation of an alien whom he deemed dangerous to the peace and safety of the United States. The Alien Enemies Act empowered the president in case of war to deport aliens of an enemy country or to subject them to important restraints if they were permitted to remain in this country. The Sedition Act not only made it a high misdemeanor for any person to conspire to oppose any measure or to impede the operation of any law of the United States but also made it illegal for any person to write, print, or publish "any false, scandalous and malicious writing ... against the government of the United States, or either house of the Congress ... , or the President ... , with intent to defame ... , or to bring them, or either of them, into contempt or disrepute; or to excite against them, or either or any of them, the hatred of the good people of the United States."

The two Alien Acts were aimed at French and pro-French foreigners in the United States, who were virtually unanimous in their support of the Republican party. Jefferson's followers at once attacked the laws as grossly unconstitutional. They argued, first, that the acts would deprive persons of their liberty without due process of law in violation of the Fifth Amendment and, second, that they contemplated the imposition of penalties without judicial process upon persons not convicted of any offense.

The Sedition Act posed a far more difficult constitutional problem. The sponsors of the law admittedly had intended virtually to re-enact the English common law of seditious libel as a congressional statute. The First Amendment, the Federalists contended, had merely incorporated the English common-law guarantee of "no prior restraint," which prohibited censorship before publication but which permitted very broad prosecution for seditious libel subsequent to the publication of anything unfriendly to the government. The truth of the published matter at issue did not constitute a defense, and the judge had sole power to decide whether or not it was libelous. English freedom of the press thus meant little more than a prior right to publish, or a prohibition of prior censorship. The present law softened the traditional law of seditious libel, for it permitted truth as a defense and allowed the jury to decide whether an utterance was libelous—two reforms for which the champions of free speech had long contended.

Federalists held to the existence of a federal criminal common law, received into American law from the English courts and enforceable by the federal judiciary. Under this law Federalists reasoned that it would be constitutional to institute prosecutions in the federal courts for seditious libel without benefit of any statute, and in 1797 they began two common-law prosecutions of Republican newspaper editors for seditious libel in lower federal courts. To provide a more secure political basis for dealing with the opposition, however, and because there was doubt in some circles about the existence of federal criminal common law, the Federalists enacted antisedition legislation. Their constitutional argument was that the First Amendment accepted and was compatible with the English view of freedom of speech as no prior restraint. The Sedition Act imposed no prior restraint, and thus in no way interfered with freedom of the press. The act did interfere with the licentiousness of the press, but Federalists believed that this merely maintained true liberty of the press.

The Adams administration enforced the Sedition Act with vigor, securing some fifteen indictments and ten convictions. The hope entertained by some Republicans that the federal courts might declare the law unconstitutional proved false; Federalist judges refused to allow counsel to challenge its constitutionality. Technically, most presiding judges allowed defense counsel to plead the truth of alleged libel, but in their charges to the jury refused to admit proof of libel, so this defense invariably failed. In addition, Federalist judges conducted Sedition Act trials in a partisan manner, browbeating counsel and witnesses and delivering partisan harangues to the jury.

The Virginia and Kentucky Resolutions

Republicans strenuously protested the Sedition Act. Given the risks that now attended published criticism of the government, and the refusal of the Federalist-dominated judiciary to permit the constitutionality of the measure to be tested in court, the Republicans' immediate problem was to find an appropriate forum in which to argue for repeal of the act. Their choice was the state legislatures. Accordingly, Thomas Jefferson and James Madison anonymously prepared resolutions denouncing the Sedition Act and its companion measures, which they caused to be introduced into the legislatures of Kentucky and Virginia. Framed for the practical purpose of removing what Republicans considered obnoxious legislation, the Kentucky and Virginia Resolutions also were documents of seminal importance in the development of American constitutional theory.

The Virginia legislature expressed "a warm attachment to the union of the states" and a firm resolve to support the government of the United States in all of its legitimate powers. But it viewed "the powers of the

Federal Government as resulting from the compact to which the states are parties, as limited by the plain sense and intention of the instrument constituting that compact; as no further valid than they are authorized by the grants enumerated in that compact." The Kentucky legislature also subscribed to the idea of the Constitution as a compact, and both states condemned the Sedition Act as unconstitutional. Each also appealed to the other states for support in sustaining this judgment and in bringing about the repeal of the measure.

In the Kentucky and Virginia Resolutions and in related protest writings, Republicans raised four fundamental constitutional issues: the scope of federal legislative power; the settlement of constitutional disputes and the role of the states therein; the nature of the Union; and the meaning of freedom of speech and of the press and its bearing on the question of legitimate political opposition.

Republicans held the Sedition Act to be a violation of the First Amendment prohibition against congressional legislation abridging freedom of speech and of the press. But this transgression of constitutional limitations was objectionable, according to Jefferson's Kentucky Resolutions, not because it was wrong for government in general to restrict the freedom of the press, but because regulation of the press lay in the sphere of state power. "No power over the freedom of religion, speech, press being delegated to the United States by the Constitution, nor prohibited by it to the states," Jefferson wrote, "all lawful powers respecting the same did of right remain, and were reserved to the states, or to the people." The states and the people thus retained "the right of judging how far the licentiousness of speech and of the press may be abridged without lessening their useful freedom." Deference to state power—or a concern for federalism—was thus the principal reason for limiting the scope of federal legislative authority.

A related consideration, pertinent to limiting not only federal legislative but also judicial power, was the Republican rejection of a federal common law of crimes. According to the Republican view, Congress could punish as crimes only those matters enumerated as such in the Constitution; seditious libel not having been so enumerated, Congress lacked the power to enact a sedition law. Repudiation of the idea of a federal common law of crimes, and by extension a general common law, was important for the implications it contained for the scope of federal legislative power. In England, a common-law country, Parliament was empowered to legislate on any subject dealt with in the common law. If the common law were regarded as federal law and liable to revision and alteration by Congress, Madison wrote in 1800,

it then follows that the authority of Congress is coextensive with the objects of common law; that is to say, with every object of legislation; for to every such object does some branch or other of the common law extend. The authority of Congress would, therefore, be no longer under the limitations marked out by the Constitution. They would be authorized to legislate in all cases whatever.

Congress would in effect have a general legislative power, as in a unitary state, contrary to the federal requirement of divided sovereignty.

Federal judicial authority would, of course, also expand enormously if a federal common law were recognized. Jefferson warned against this danger in attacking as most "novel" and "formidable" the Federalist argument for "a system of law for the United States without the adoption of their legislature [i.e., the common law]." "If this assumption be yielded to," Jefferson predicted, "the state courts may be shut up, as there will be nothing to hinder citizens of the same state suing each other in the federal courts in every case."

A second issue in the Sedition Act crisis concerned the settlement of constitutional disputes in general, and those involving the exercise of federal powers in particular. Eventually the Supreme Court was to assume the power to resolve questions about the meaning of the Constitution, but in the early years of the republic the federal judiciary played no such role. Either the separate branches of the government presumed to exercise this power or, as in the Sedition Act episode, the states tried to determine the meaning of the Constitution and keep the federal government from transgressing constitutional limitations. Denying that the federal government had the exclusive power to judge the extent of its own powers, the legislatures of Kentucky and Virginia declared that "in case of a deliberate, palpable, and dangerous exercise of other powers not granted by the said compact, the states, who are parties thereto, have the right and are in duty bound to interpose for arresting the progress of the evil, and for maintaining within their respective limits the authorities, rights, and liberties appertaining to them." Kentucky and Virginia also expressed confidence that the other states would join in declaring the Sedition Act and the other Federalist measures unconstitutional.

Reliance on the states to decide constitutional controversies grew out of the Republican theory of the Union, the third major constitutional issue in the Sedition Act crisis. Seizing on the confederation aspect of the mixed system created by the Constitutional Convention, Jefferson and Madison declared the Union to be a compact among sovereign states, rather than the constituent act of the people of the United States considered as a single polity. In the language of the Kentucky Resolutions, the Constitution was a compact to which "each State acceded as a State, and is an integral party, its co-States forming, as to itself, the other party."

The precise meaning of the compact theory as presented in the Virginia and Kentucky Resolutions was and remains problematic even today. It may have been nothing more than a self-evident statement of political philosophy derived from the Revolution and asserting the compact theory of the state and the limited character of federal sovereignty. Probably it did not signify rejection of the divided sovereignty of federalism. Nevertheless, as John C. Calhoun and a later generation of southern political leaders showed, the language of the Kentucky and Virginia Resolutions lent itself to an interpretation denying federal sovereignty altogether. Although Madison in his last years disavowed any legitimate connection between the Virginia Resolutions and Calhoun's doctrine of state sovereignty, nullification, and secession, the conclusion is inescapable that Madison and Jefferson prepared the way for, if they did not fully anticipate, the South Carolina theory.

More pertinent perhaps than the subsequent application of Madison and Jefferson's theory of the Union are the questions of what the Republican leaders hoped to achieve in 1798 and how they expected to accomplish their goal. The Kentucky Resolves declared that the Alien and Sedition laws exceeded the constitutional power of Congress and hence were "not law" but were "altogether void and of no force." The legislature said further that the states would not tamely submit to such extension of congressional authority beyond the constitutional limits, and it added ominously that "these and successive acts of the same character, unless arrested on the threshold, may tend to drive these States into revolution and blood."

Jefferson's original draft had declared that "where powers are assumed which have not been delegated, a nullification of the act is the right remedy," and had expressed hope that the "co-States . . . will concur in declaring these [Alien and Sedition] acts void and of no force, and will each take measures of its own for providing that neither of these acts . . . shall be exercised within their respective territories." For expediency or other reasons this section was replaced by an appeal to the other states and by instructions to Kentucky's congressional representatives "to use their best endeavors to procure, at the next session of Congress, a repeal of the . . . unconstitutional and obnoxious acts."

In 1799 Kentucky issued a second set of resolves reasserting the view that if the general government was the exclusive judge of its own delegated powers, the result would be despotism. Now Jefferson stated "That the several States who formed that instrument [the Constitution] being sovereign and independent, have the unquestionable right to judge of the infraction; and, that a nullification of those sovereignties, of all unauthorized acts done under color of that instrument is the rightful remedy."

In the antebellum period "interposition" and "nullification" became terms to conjure with, and it is an intriguing question to ask what Madison and Jefferson meant in using this language in 1798. These were strong words which conceivably implied the use of force. At a time when the Revolution was vividly etched in recent memory, this eventuality would not have been farfetched or illegitimate. Yet it is likely that Madison and Jefferson had something else in mind—a coordinated and peaceful state re-

sponse, employing the convention method of political action in preference
to state legislative decision. Their purpose, it should be recalled, was to get
the Sedition Act and the other Federalist measures repealed.

Madison and Jefferson's success in protesting the Sedition Act depended on the cooperation of the other states. On this score the results were
not encouraging. The other southern states made no official response, sentiment being fairly evenly divided in their legislatures, and the northern
states, controlled by Federalists, endorsed the Alien and Sedition measures.
The northern states also held that the federal courts, not the state legislatures, were the proper tribunal for settling constitutional disputes. The Sedition Act was thus not repealed, but expired according to its original terms
at the end of the Adams administration in March 1801.

Behind the controversy over state interposition and the settlement of
constitutional disputes lay the fact that there was no general agreement on
the precise nature of the Union. Everybody agreed that the powers of the
government were divided between the states and the central government. It
was also evident that the Constitution had made no explicit provision for
the settlement of disputes over power between the two units of government.
Article VI, which provides for the supremacy of the Constitution and federal laws, might be balanced against the Tenth Amendment, which provides for the reservation of undelegated powers to the states, without
producing a conclusive answer. The government established under the
Constitution was essentially a compromise between a confederation and a
unitary state. In limited and varying degrees the political leaders realized
that in the long run such a compromise might prove unworkable and that
the federal system might evolve either into modified confederation or into a
strongly centralized national government. The Republicans were essentially
right in claiming that if a branch of the federal government had the final
power to judge of the extent of federal authority, the states would ultimately and inevitably be reduced to a subordinate position. On the other
hand, the Federalists were correct in asserting that the recognition of the
right of each state to act as final judge in case of vital disputes would lead to
utter confusion and probably to "an interruption of the peace of the states
by civil discord." No decision on this all-important issue was reached in
1799, and in one form or another the question was to crop up almost
continuously through the years until it was finally settled on the battlefield.

The Sedition Act gave rise to a fourth constitutional issue: the meaning
of freedom of speech and of the press and the relevance of these First
Amendment freedoms to the legitimacy of an organized political opposition. From the Republican standpoint the reforms that the Federalists had
put into the Sedition Act were inconsequential: the very idea that freedom
of the press existed so long as there was no prior restraint of publication
suddenly appeared inadequate. Punishment after publication, Republicans
argued, was every bit as inhibiting as prior censorship. Accordingly, they

repudiated the whole idea of seditious libel and drew a modern libertarian distinction between critical, even inflammatory words, which they believed should be permitted, and overt actions injurious to the state, which they believed government could properly prevent. Republicans furthermore rejected the notion that political opinions could be subjected to tests of truth and falsehood, as the existing law on seditious libel assumed. On the contrary, it now began to appear that political opinions were subjective and relative, and thus not capable of evaluation according to objective criteria. Moreover, Republicans turned their new libertarian view of the First Amendment to the legitimation of party activity. In a republican constitutional order, they reasoned, a free press was an essential means of shaping the public opinion needed to control and direct government. An organized political opposition was but a refinement of this process of forming and expressing the public opinion on which republican government rested.

The Republican argument for a modern view of freedom of the press and a legitimate opposition was by no means conclusive or decisive. For one thing, despite the existence of the rule that defined freedom of the press as no prior restraint, in the American colonies there had been relatively little punishment after publication and hence much that we would recognize as freedom of the press in a modern sense. Second, when the Republicans came to power after 1800 they violated the standards of free speech and a free press which they had invoked against the Federalists in 1798. On several occasions they prosecuted Federalist editors in the state courts for seditious libel against state governments. Nor did the Republican justification of an organized political opposition compel an abandonment of earlier views denying the legitimacy of party. Nevertheless, despite the persistence of rhetoric suggesting otherwise, political opposition in the United States was not subsequently to be treated as subversive. Nor had it been so regarded in actual practice. The Sedition Act, although understandable under the circumstances, was an aberration.

Although constitutional theory lagged behind events, in a practical sense political parties were recognized as legitimate in the election of 1800. With Jefferson's election as president, power was transferred peacefully from the party that had written and implemented the Constitution to the organized opposition, whose protests of government policy only a few months earlier had been branded seditious. The "Revolution of 1800" ended the period of constitutional formation and inaugurated an era of Republican constitutionalism.

NINE

Republican Constitutionalism: 1801–1828

◆ ◆ ◆

THE ELECTION OF 1800 brought to power a party whose character and identity were shaped by eighteenth-century English opposition thought, and whose constitutional principles were set forth in the Virginia and Kentucky Resolutions. At the core of Republican ideology lay a cluster of constitutional ideas: the separation of powers and legislative independence, resistance to executive influence, strict construction of federal powers, and states' rights and the compact theory of the Union. In the first Jefferson administration Republicans adopted policies that were both consistent with these constitutional precepts and politically effective. Starting with the Embargo of 1807, however, Republican constitutionalism underwent profound change, until by the 1820s it evinced the same centralizing, consolidating tendency that it had originally opposed.

The causes of this transformation were diplomatic and military events beyond the power of Americans to control, and the inevitable requirement that theory yield to practice in the actual conduct of government. The changes in Republican constitutionalism also reflected the irresistible tendency in modernizing countries, of which the United States was an early example, toward integration and centralization in government, law, and administration. Yet because decentralist, antigovernmental values were deeply embedded in the political culture, the trend toward constitutional centralization was soon arrested. Although largely abandoned by the Republican party after the War of 1812, classical agrarian republican ideology embodying these values reappeared as the constitutional basis of a new opposition party in the 1820s, the Jacksonian Democrats.

Republican Constitutional Ideas

Both Federalists and Republicans referred to the election of 1800 as a revolution because it portended the introduction of political and constitutional values entirely different from those that prevailed in the first decade of the new government. Instead of anticipating a new order in the manner of modern revolution, however, the Republicans saw their victory as signaling a return to an earlier condition of liberty and civic virtue. Regarding Federalist rule as a threat to republicanism, the triumphant Jeffersonian party proposed to restore the true principles of the American Revolution.

Republicans took as their point of departure the familiar eighteenth-century opposition ideology, which regarded land as the source of all political, social, and economic values. Ownership of land enabled men to become personally and politically independent and hence capable of civic virtue and patriotism. In the Republican theory of society, therefore, agriculture was the pre-eminent concern; commerce was a useful and necessary adjunct to it. This was not true, however, of banks, credit, paper money, and the related instruments of capitalist expansion that had developed in England and, under the auspices of the Federalist party, were spreading with dangerous effect in the United States. These mercantilist devices, seen in Hamilton's funding, assumption, national bank, and protective tariff schemes, not only lacked the moral sanction bestowed by productive enterprise on the soil, but they also created social and political distinctions and privileges that threatened the liberty and equality of republican self-government. This agrarian philosophy naturally appealed to the principal constituent elements in the Jeffersonian party—southern planters and yeoman farmers, both North and South. But its vision of a natural social order in which individual liberty was reconciled with social justice, and in which a general equality of condition could result from the rule of equal opportunity and individual initiative in a materially abundant environment, held attraction also for urban merchants, artisans, and craftsmen whose original loyalty to the Federalist party was eroded by Hamilton's high-toned and elitist policies. When Jefferson in his inaugural address said "We are all Republicans, we are all Federalists," he was expressing his belief that his election demonstrated the appeal of his party's ideals to all groups in the society.

Legislative independence based on the separation of powers provided the foundation principle of Republican constitutionalism. The separation of powers was important chiefly as a means of resisting British-style ministerial government, emanating from the executive branch and undermining legislative autonomy through patronage, a national bank and national debt, a standing army and navy, and monopolistic corporate privileges. This, of course, was what Hamilton's policies represented in the eyes of Republicans, and, as noted previously, it was to prevent this kind of ministerial manipulation that Republicans formed standing committees in Congress in the later 1790s. Recalling parliamentary spokesmen in the seventeenth century and American revolutionary leaders in 1776, Republicans appealed to the separation-of-powers theory in its radical form in an attempt to make the lawmaking branch paramount. In contrast to the Federalists, the Republicans came to power as the party of the legislature and hence of the people.

This legislative identification notwithstanding, Republicans also endorsed strict construction of congressional power and—its logical corollary under federal theory—states' rights. The strict-construction–states'-rights equation was not basic to Republican ideology in the same way that the separation of powers or opposition to executive influence were. This was because the problem of federal-state relations was not part of the body of classical republican thought transmitted by the opposition writers of the eighteenth century. Republican theory was concerned with the essential problems of constitutionalism: the relationship between citizens and the government, the distribution of powers among the parts of government, the proper limits on governmental power in the interest of individual liberty. By contrast, federalism, rooted in the peculiar history of the American colonies and intended to satisfy conflicting tendencies toward centralization and local autonomy in American society, was a deliberately ambiguous institutional arrangement which invited a tactical, expedient response.

This is not to say that the Republican party did not embrace federalism as a principle of union expressing the American people's sense of nationality. Within the framework of federal theory, however, a number of approaches were possible, one of which was summed up in the strict-construction–states'-rights formula. As an opposition party challenging Federalist rule, the Republicans necessarily were attracted to and employed theories that would deny the constitutional basis of Federalist policies. When under the pressure of subsequent events they adopted a more centralizing stance and favored the exercise of national power, they were not being cynical and opportunistic, but rather were obeying the imperative of constitutional politics within a federal framework. Groups or parties involved in public policy making could be expected to shift their position on the grid of federal-state relations as their needs and circumstances altered. More important than consistency in adhering to a particular view of the federal-state balance was the commitment to Unionism that was implied in the different approaches to federalism adopted in the nineteenth century.

The compact theory of the Union, the third major element of Republican constitutionalism, was, of course, the foundation of the strict-construction–states'-rights idea. Here, too, however, it would be a mistake to exaggerate the importance of this doctrine in the Jeffersonian outlook or to read back into the period of Federalist-Republican struggle theories about the nature of the Union that were not developed in a systematic way until the 1820s and 1830s. When Virginia and Kentucky protested the Sedition Act, no other state supported them. But all the states except one accepted the compact theory; only Vermont argued in contrast that the Union was formed by the people of the United States. The compact theory was thus not specially identified with the Republican party, despite its conspicuous recognition in the events of 1798. Its widespread acceptance was perhaps a further reason why upon taking office Jefferson felt able to emphasize the elements of consensus between Republicans and Federalists.

Jefferson's inaugural address pronounced good government to be "a wise and frugal Government, which shall restrain men from injuring one another [and] shall leave them otherwise free to regulate their own pursuits of industry and improvement." To a considerable extent Republican policies during Jefferson's first term were able to implement this laissez-faire, republican ideal. The Hamilton national bank and funding system was left in place, but internal excise taxes were repealed, government expenditures were reduced by the elimination of certain civil offices, and the regular army and navy were drastically cut back. Using revenues from customs duties and public land sales, Republicans also went far toward retiring the public debt, the hated engine of corruption according to their opposition republican philosophy.

The Jeffersonian Executive

Successful as these reform efforts were in fulfilling the promise of the Revolution of 1800, in several respects Republicans departed from the constitutional position they professed in their opposition period. Despite their earlier appeal to the strict separation of powers, for example, Republican practice rapidly evolved a system of coordination between the executive and legislative branches that depended heavily on presidential leadership and influence. Like their Federalist predecessors, the Jeffersonians had to figure out a way to make Congress an effective policy-making body. Hamilton had tried to do so by creating a ministerial system on the British model. Without formally abjuring the separation of powers, the Republicans fashioned their own system of executive influence.

Jefferson solved the problem of coordinating the political branches within the separation-of-powers framework through the great prestige and unquestioned ascendancy he possessed as party leader. Nominally, he accepted the theory of congressional ascendancy in legislation. Unlike Washington and Adams, he sent his messages to Congress by a clerk rather than reading them in person, and he was uniformly deferential in his messages and in his other relationships with Congress. He did not veto a single bill.

At the same time, Jefferson used a variety of methods to assert a strong executive leadership in Congress. Although his practice varied, depending upon conditions, he often had his political lieutenants placed in key legislative and political positions and worked through them to effect his legislative program. Also, Treasury Secretary Gallatin served as an effective and valuable liaison officer between the president and Congress. Although the

Republicans had earlier condemned the Federalist practice of referring legislative matters to Hamilton as secretary of the Treasury, they now revived the practice by asking Gallatin to make reports and proposals to the House. He attended committee meetings and assisted in the preparation of reports to be presented to the House. In general he became a sort of executive manager who cooperated with the congressional leaders in steering measures through Congress.

This unofficial fusion of the executive and legislative departments would have been very difficult if not impossible without the employment of another extraconstitutional device, the party caucus. From time to time the president, cabinet officers, and party members in Congress met in caucus and discussed proposed legislation fully and came to a conclusion upon policy before specific measures reached the floor of either house. It was alleged that Jefferson himself upon occasion presided at these secret meetings. By holding doubtful members in line, the caucus increased party solidarity in Congress and facilitated enactment of important measures.

Before Jefferson became president, Hamilton said of him that he would be no enemy to executive power, while John Marshall, in a contrary estimate, predicted that Jefferson would weaken the presidency by embodying himself in the legislature. In different ways both of these judgments proved accurate. To be sure, Jefferson vigorously employed—or created—executive power, in particular by relying on skills of persuasion but also occasionally by using the power of legal compulsion and even military coercion. At the same time, however, Jefferson's exercise of power caused no immediate or permanent alteration in the contours of the office. Rather the result was, as Marshall had feared, the cultivation of lines of influence into Congress through which power could and did run in the opposite direction when presidents lacking Jefferson's enormous prestige and instinct for power occupied the White House. Such was the case with the successor Republican presidents James Madison, James Monroe, and John Quincy Adams. Indeed, their tenure in office can be described as a period of congressional government, when Congress formulated policy, involved itself deeply in the administration of the government, and, through a system of standing committees, used the power of investigation to hold the executive closely accountable for the conduct of public business. Further evidence of a decline in executive power was the fact that cabinet offices were frequently continuous from one administration to the next, with the president acting as head of a directory or first among equals.

Nevertheless, Jefferson changed the presidential office, or showed a previously unrealized dimension, by making it a popular institution. The founding fathers, and Washington and Adams as the first chief executives, viewed the presidency as a counterweight to the popularly elected legislature, and thus in some sense as an anti- or a nonrepublican institution.

Jefferson, however, as head of government and head of state who was also the leader of a political party, politicized the office in an unprecedented way. Under the separation-of-powers doctrine the legislative branch could always claim to be in a special sense the voice of the people, but starting with Jefferson, presidents could make the same claim by virtue of their identification with a political party. Although the personality and political standing of the incumbent would always do much to determine the actual power of the executive office at any given time, Jefferson made American government in some permanent sense presidential government.

Finally, the republicanization of the executive office associated with the rise of political parties was related to a formal constitutional change in the method of electing the president. Under the framers' plan for filtering and refining public opinion, the Constitution required electors in the states to vote for two persons, the one with the most votes to become president, the runner-up vice-president. The emergence of political parties in the 1790s politicized the operation of the electoral college, however, and in 1796 resulted in the election of a president, Adams, and vice-president, Jefferson, who belonged to different parties. Further difficulty occurred in 1800 when a tie vote between Jefferson and Aaron Burr threw the election into the House of Representatives. To avoid a repetition of this situation and to assure a unified executive, and fearing machinations between Burr and the Federalists that might enable the latter to win the vice-presidency,[1] the Republicans proposed a constitutional amendment providing for separate ballots for president and vice-president. Ratified in September 1804, the Twelfth Amendment reflected the politicization of the presidency and Republican determination to unify the executive branch under their control.

The Louisiana Purchase

Paralleling the spread of republican influence in the constitutional order was the expansion of the republic itself through territorial annexation. The acquisition of Louisiana from France provided the occasion for this constitutional development.

Expansion was inherent in the very founding of the colonies in the seventeenth century. After more than a century and a half of social and demographic growth, the founding fathers transposed this expansionist tendency into a constitutional key in the expanded republic of 1787. The Constitution left territorial matters rather vague, principally because of

1. Republicans feared that Federalist votes would be cast for Burr, forcing them to scatter their second votes to ensure the election of Jefferson as president and allowing their opponents to secure the vice-presidency.

sectional disagreement over the character and disposition of the western lands as a national resource. With the launching of the new government, however, expansion became a more urgent issue as southern and western landed and commercial interests pressed the federal government to take control of the Mississippi River from Spain and later France. In 1803 the Jefferson administration, seeking to satisfy the land hunger of its agrarian constituents, purchased and proposed to annex to the Union the vast area of Louisiana. This bold step promised to secure far into the future a seemingly endless supply of land for territorial expansion.

The Louisiana Purchase raised two important constitutional questions: Did the United States have the power to acquire foreign territory, and, if so, could territory such as Louisiana be governed and admitted to the Union as a state on the basis of equality with the original states? Republicans were proponents of the theory of strict construction, which limited federal authority to specifically enumerated powers. Yet the Constitution said nothing of a right to acquire territory. If so sweeping a power were considered to be implied, it would discredit the doctrine of strict construction and go far toward legitimizing the Hamilton theory of implied powers.

Jefferson at first proposed to resolve the dilemma by amending the Constitution to grant the federal government the requisite authority to purchase territory. His advisers argued, however, that it might be dangerous to allow the purchase treaty to be delayed while waiting for a constitutional amendment to be ratified. Napoleon might change his mind and the opportunity be lost. The president's advisers also argued that the power to acquire territory was inherent in the very existence of the United States as a sovereign nation—a proposition that challenged the Republican theory of the Union as a compact among states. Jefferson reluctantly but prudently accepted this view.

Concerning the government and disposition of the Louisiana lands, sharp controversy arose when the president asked Congress to approve and implement the purchase treaty. The focal point of dispute was a provision in the treaty stating that "The inhabitants of the ceded territory shall be incorporated in the Union of the United States, and admitted as soon as possible, according to the principles of the Federal Constitution, to the enjoyment of all the rights, advantages, and immunities of citizens of the United States; and in the mean time they shall be maintained and protected in the free enjoyment of their liberty, property, and the Religion which they profess." This provision was essentially a promise of eventual statehood for the people of Louisiana, and Federalists strongly objected to it on the ground that under the Constitution the admission of new states was left to the discretion of Congress. Fearful that the creation of new southern and western states would further weaken their already declining political position, Federalists held that territory could be acquired by conquest or purchase, but must be governed as a colony. Republicans answered that the treaty did not positively guarantee statehood, inasmuch as territorial status would satisfy the requirements set forth therein. Whether states should be admitted from the Louisiana Territory would be left to the future discretion of Congress.

The Senate ratified the treaty in October 1803, 26 to 5, and both houses then appropriated the money and made temporary provisions for the government of the new territory. Since a majority of Congress did not believe that the people of the acquired territory were yet ready for a large amount of self-government, the first governing act provided that all military, civil, and judicial authority in Louisiana should be vested in appointees of the president. Since the Constitution explicitly gave Congress the power to "make all needful Rules and Regulations" respecting the territory of the United States, there was inherent in this measure no serious question of congressional authority. However, objection was raised to the autocratic nature of the territorial government, and soon the administration sponsored another measure providing for a gradual preparation of the French and Spanish inhabitants of Louisiana for self-government. This second law provided for government by a powerful governor and a weak council to be appointed by the president from the property-holding residents of the territory.

American immigrants were soon settling in Louisiana and demanding greater participation in the government. Consequently, in 1805 a third act gave the Territory of Orleans, as the lower part of the Louisiana purchase was termed, a territorial government very similar to that outlined in the Northwest Ordinance of 1787. The vast area north of the present state of Louisiana contained few white people and was temporarily attached to Indiana Territory for purposes of administration. Thus did the territory acquired from France rapidly come to have a constitutional status practically identical with that of the original territory of the United States.

It is customary to say that the significance of the Louisiana episode was to weaken the strict-construction–states'-rights mode of constitutionalism. Certainly the Republicans departed from their avowed principles of '98, in part because of the exigencies of practical statemanship. In a deeper sense, however, the reversal of roles between Republicans and Federalists on strict versus broad construction and the compact theory of the Union was testimony to the strength and appeal of these constitutional principles. In order for constitutional rhetoric to have effect it need not be applied with consistency. Indeed, when groups or parties shift constitutional positions, as Federalists and Republicans started to do in these years, they do so because they believe the new theories and principles they espouse embody values in the political culture on the basis of which they can appeal to public opinion in the altered circumstances in which they find themselves. The significance of the Louisiana controversy, therefore, lies not in some supposed cynicism about constitutional principles that political expediency inspires, nor even in the cautionary reminder that practice must temper theory. Rather it lies in the insight it offers into the development of a distinctively American form of constitutional politics, based on rhetoric and principles that have the power to influence public opinion because they express fundamental values.

The Embargo

If the annexation of Louisiana created a new and expanded Union which in Republican eyes was merely an expansion of the republican empire of liberty, the major event in Jefferson's second term—the embargo—transformed Republican constitutionalism in a more questionable way by interjecting federal executive authority deeply into the commercial life of the society. Professing the enlightened purpose of avoiding war, Jefferson imposed on the country an apparatus of coercion that seriously threatened republican liberty.

Caught between warring France and England, Jefferson hoped to be able to force the depradating European powers to respect American neutrality and maritime rights by denying them the benefits of American trade. Accordingly, in December 1807 he proposed to Congress an embargo on all foreign commerce. After only four days of debate Congress adopted the measure by large majorities. The act placed a ban on all U.S. ships bound to any foreign port and required ships in the coastal trade to post bond double the value of the cargo as a guarantee that the goods would be relanded in the United States. The embargo did not close American ports to European imported goods carried in the ships of other nations. In 1808 three supplementary measures were passed tightening the shutdown of American shipping. Their principal effect was to prohibit exports by land as well as by sea and to strengthen executive enforcement of the embargo. Conceived as a defensive measure intended to buy time and preserve American maritime resources against the eventuality of a war with Great Britain, the embargo by the end of 1808 became in Jefferson's view an offensive weapon of economic coercion by which to purify the republic by ridding it of corrupt commercial interests.

The first of several constitutional issues raised by the embargo concerned the nature and scope of the commerce power, the main constitutional basis of the law. According to Republicans, the commerce power was complete and could be extended to include outright prohibitions upon all commercial activity. Some administration supporters drew a distinction between federal power over interstate commerce and federal power over foreign commerce. They admitted that Congress could not constitutionally lay any outright prohibitions upon commerce between the states, but they insisted that federal power over commerce with foreign nations was of a more complete character, since the commerce clause was reinforced in that field by the government's control over foreign affairs. The Federalist opposition, on the other hand, insisted upon an extremely narrow definition of the commerce power. The right to regulate, they said, implied only the right to protect in order to extend benefits thereto. The power was not restrictive, and certainly was not prohibitive. Neither, they said, could the commerce power be used for any ulterior purpose—that is, any purpose other than the protection of commerce itself. Here was the question of the motive behind the exercise of federal power, an issue of substantial consequence in later constitutional law.

Under the circumstances, the action of Congress in passing the embargo went far toward settling the question of its constitutionality. Confirmation of the congressional judgment came from the federal judiciary and, ironically, from a Federalist judge. In October 1808, in the federal district court for Massachusetts, Judge John Davis upheld the embargo in very broad terms in the case of *U.S.* v. *The William.* "The degree or extent of the prohibition" imposed on foreign commerce, Davis said, must properly be left to "the discretion of the national government, to whom the subject appears to be committed." Davis rejected the contention that the commerce power could be used only for the protection of commerce itself: "the power to regulate commerce is not confined to the adoption of measures exclusively beneficial to commerce itself, or tending to its advancement; but in our national system, as in all modern sovereignties, it is also to be considered as an instrument for other purposes of general policy and interest." He also sustained the embargo under the war power as a preparation for war, and under the necessary and proper clause as appropriate for the protection of the nation's inherent sovereignty. Davis pointed out finally that although under the Confederation states had an express power to prohibit commerce, since the adoption of the Constitution no one had ever claimed this power on behalf of the states. Therefore, unless the power had ceased to exist, it was given to Congress by the Constitution.

The scope of executive authority was a second constitutional issue raised by the embargo. The several acts of Congress gave the president sweeping authority to enforce the ban on trade as he saw fit through military and revenue officers, and even required his special permission before any ship could depart for an American port adjacent to foreign territory. Subordinate enforcement officers operated without benefit of search warrants or court process, giving rise to questions of unreasonable search and seizure in possible violation of the Fourth Amendment. No search-and-seizure issue was ever presented in litigation, but the scope of executive authority was nevertheless questioned in an important lower federal court decision handed down by a Republican Supreme Court justice, William Johnson.

The collector of the port of Charleston, South Carolina, acting under discretionary authority given by Congress in the fourth Embargo Act, gave clearance to a ship bound for Baltimore, but then detained it on subsequent orders from Jefferson implementing the statute. The owner of the ship petitioned the federal circuit court for a writ of mandamus directing the collector to clear the vessel; Justice Johnson, sitting on circuit, decided for the shipowner. Johnson held that the collector had discretionary authority from Congress that the president could not override. More broadly and provocatively, Johnson declared: "The officers of our government, from the highest to the lowest, are equally subjected to legal restraint; and it is confidently believed that all of them feel themselves equally incapable, as well from law as from inclination, to attempt an unsanctioned encroachment on individual liberty." Through the attorney general, Jefferson denied the court's authority to issue a writ of mandamus, and his lieutenants in Congress introduced a bill making customs collectors expressly subject to executive direction. To combat the growing public disregard of the embargo, the bill authorized the president to use military force—without the requirement of a proclamation—to compel obedience to the policy. In January 1809 Congress passed this extraordinary enforcement act.

It would have been difficult to enforce the embargo even in a centralized unitary state. In the decentralized federal republic the task was extremely difficult. Jefferson devoted nearly all his energies to supervising enforcement of the embargo, becoming, in the words of a recent biographer, "commissar of the nation's economy." Normally a skilled and persuasive political tactician, Jefferson in this instance failed to prepare the public for the sacrifices demanded of it, and strangely refrained from presenting a justification of the policy when dissatisfaction with it spread. Enforcement of the embargo was carried out for the most part under federal admiralty jurisdiction, under *in rem* proceedings which did not require juries. It was possible, however, for defendants charged with violating the embargo laws to seek trial by jury at common law. In New England especially jury trials provided a forum for protesting the administration policy and usually ended in acquittal.

Enforcement of the embargo has been estimated as being 95 percent effective—astonishing evidence of the extent to which federal authority had been accepted as legitimate in the space of a generation. Yet incidents of illegal trade and militant opposition to the series of laws became increasingly conspicuous—and politically costly. In New York, for example, along the Canadian border where resistance was particularly intense, Jefferson proclaimed an insurrection and ordered several persons prosecuted for treason. The suit was unsuccessful. Republican Supreme Court Justice Brockholst Livingston held on circuit, in the case of *U.S.* v. *Hoxie,* that no matter how violent, refusal to obey a law in time of peace could not be construed as levying war against the United States.[1]

---

1. Article III, Section 3 of the Constitution defines treason as levying war against the United States or adhering to their enemies, giving them aid and comfort.

Laudable as Jefferson's intentions were, the embargo proved to be, in the eyes of an increasing number of citizens, destructive of republican liberty. The economic distress it caused, added to the political and constitutional costs it exacted, marked it an egregious failure. In March 1809, as Jefferson left office, Congress repealed the embargo.

The War of 1812 and National Republican Mercantilism

If in his first term Jefferson was on the whole successful in governing according to his party's original tenets, his doctrinaire adherence to peaceful coercion in his second term served to discredit both executive authority and agrarian republicanism. During the successor administrations of James Madison and James Monroe the party's identification with the principles of the Virginia and Kentucky Resolutions became increasingly tenuous as the need to generate and exercise power—required by the War of 1812 and then by the task of internal economic development—became more compelling. In the postwar period Republicans combined centralizing elements of Hamiltonian political economy with the expansionist and populistic republicanism of their original outlook. The result was a policy of national mercantilism. Meanwhile, the Federalist party, where it continued to exist, had recourse to the opposition philosophy of strict construction and states' rights set forth by the Republicans in 1798.

Bitterly opposed to the War of 1812, Federalists seized on the issue of federal control of the state militia to challenge the authority of the general government. The Constitution dealt with the problem in a seemingly clear way by giving Congress the power "To provide for calling forth the Militia to execute the Laws of the Union, suppress Insurrections, and repel Invasions." Congress was also authorized "To provide for organizing, arming, and disciplining the Militia, and for governing such Part of them as may be employed in the Service of the United States." Against the manifest intention of these provisions, several New England states under Federalist control refused to permit their militia to be commanded by federal officers or to become an integral part of the army of the United States. Furthermore, all of the New England states attempted to ban service of their militia outside their borders and in effect built up separate state armies for their own defense against British attack.

Federalist discontent came to a head in the Hartford Convention, called by Massachusetts in December 1814. Although the idea of secession had been urged by extremist Federalists, moderates who controlled the convention proposed state interposition and amendment of the Constitution as milder alternatives to disunion. The states were urged to protect their citizens against unconstitutional federal militia and conscription legislation, and to request the federal government to permit the separate states to defend themselves and receive federal tax credits for such action. The Hartford Convention also proposed seven amendments to the federal constitution. One proposal would eliminate the three-fifths clause in the Constitution and base representation in the House of Representatives solely upon free population. Embargoes were to be limited to sixty days. A two-thirds vote of both houses of Congress would be required to admit a new state, to interdict commerce with foreign nations, or to declare war except in case of actual invasion. Naturalized citizens were to be disqualified from federal elective or appointive office. No president was to serve two terms, and no two successive presidents were to come from the same state. The final resolution proposed the calling of another convention if the war continued and the federal government failed to respond favorably to the recommendations of the convention.

Federalist sponsors of states'-rights–based constitutional reform fared no better than the Republicans had in 1798–99. Only Connecticut and Massachusetts approved the Hartford proposals, while nine states disapproved or dissented. From a practical standpoint the chief consequence of the proceedings was further to discredit the Federalist party in the arena of national politics. Constitutionally, the convention was significant because it endorsed—and thus nationalized—the state's-rights-strict-construction idea as a basic axiom of American politics. Useful especially for opposing the policies of the federal government, this constitutional method had first been asserted by southern agrarians in the Sedition Act crisis. Now it was taken up by New England merchants and shown to have national appeal, even though, as before, the interest it served was narrowly sectional. In adopting the stance they did, the Federalists were on the opposite side of the constitutional fence. This shift signified the emergence of a structure of politics based on constitutional principles and rhetoric—such as states' rights and strict construction—which embodied basic American political values. Carried to the extreme of state sovereignty, as it eventually would be in the antebellum period, the states'-rights idea had disunionist consequences. But used as it was in the Hartford Convention to repudiate secession and support the moderate alternatives of state interposition and constitutional amendment, the states'-rights idea helped to strengthen the emerging system of constitutional politics within the federal framework.

After 1815, with the threat to national independence removed in foreign affairs and the Federalist challenge eliminated at home, the Republican party turned its attention to the country's internal economic development. In dealing with this issue Republicans employed centralizing constitutional instruments in a context of mercantilism that carried the party further from the principles of '98.

Despite the emphasis in the American constitutional tradition on governmental limitations and guarantees of individual liberty, the mercantilist conception of positive government actively promoting and regulating economic affairs continued to have appeal during the revolutionary and early national periods. In this pre–laissez-faire era the question was not whether government would intervene, but how it would do so and to what extent. In the 1790s Hamilton's policies intruded federal authority into the commercial life of the nation, and Republican administrations, notwithstanding Jefferson's frequent paeans to frugal and minimal government, early showed themselves willing to use power for what they regarded as suitably republican purposes, as in the Louisiana Purchase. From 1815 to 1825 Republicans employed broad construction to fashion a democratized, westward-looking mercantilism—the famous American System of Clay, Calhoun, and Webster.

Republican mercantilism resembled Federalist policy in certain respects, but was notably different in others. It comprehended a national bank, but not a national debt intended to connect the most powerful commercial groups with the government, as in Federalist political economy. The Republican outlook was also distinguished from Hamiltonianism by its commitment to territorial and political expansion and by its concern for both agrarian and commercial development. Furthermore, although Republican mercantilists exercised federal power vigorously, they took a more favorable view of states' rights than the Federalists. Centralizing though it was in comparison to the localist tendency of the party's opposition phase, Republican mercantilism nevertheless looked to a balance between the states and the federal government. Republicans expressed this balanced conception of Union in legislative programs in which, to a limited extent, federal and state governments shared power and responsibility in banking, internal improvements, and land distribution.

As with the Federalists twenty years earlier, the first step in creating a Republican system of mercantilism was to establish a national bank. In 1811 Congress, dominated by Republicans, had refused to grant a new charter to the Bank of the United States. Since that time, however, many strict-constructionist Republicans had changed their mind about the wisdom and constitutionality of a national bank. The demise of the first bank in 1811 had caused the states to charter a number of state banking institutions, many of which failed to observe the elementary rules of sound banking practice. They had issued large quantities of paper money, much of it of little or no value, which circulated as part of the nation's monetary system and often caused great confusion in commerical and industrial circles. The Constitution specifically forbade the states to coin money and emit bills of credit, but as John C. Calhoun pointed out, the chartering of state banks had enabled the states to elude this restriction and usurp control of the monetary system. The absence of a national bank also proved a serious handicap to federal fiscal policy and financial activities during the War of

1812, for the government not only lacked any adequate agency of deposit, but it also missed the financial assistance such a bank might have been able to extend.

The Republican nationalists accordingly brought about the passage of a national bank bill in January 1815. Madison vetoed the measure as inadequate, but at the same time indicated his belief that the bank was constitutional, and in his annual message of December 1815 he again recommended passage of a national bank law. In January 1816, accordingly, Calhoun, as chairman of the special committee on uniform national currency, introduced a bill to incorporate a new bank of the United States for twenty years with a capital of $35,000,000, one-fifth of which was to be subscribed by the federal government.

Calhoun defended this measure's constitutionality by holding that it was a necessary and proper means to the establishment of a uniform national currency. The main object of the framers of the Constitution in giving Congress the power to coin money and regulate its value, he thought, must have been to give steadiness and fixed value to the currency of the United States. The various states, through their banking activities, had recently worked the defeat of this end and had actually taken over control of the nation's monetary system. Consequently, he concluded, it was the duty of Congress to recover control over the monetary system, and this could best be done through the medium of a national bank.

Congress passed the bill creating the second Bank of the United States (BUS) in 1816. The measure was centralizing to the extent that it created a federal agency where none existed before, or rather for five years previous, but it also recognized the rights and powers of the states by giving state banks a role in the national fiscal system. In contrast to 1791, when the first Bank of the United States was chartered, numerous state banks were now in existence (most of them created by Republicans under state law after 1800), and these banks constituted an interest powerful enough to prevent establishment of a federal bank had they been so disposed. Most state banks recognized the need for national coordination, however, and supported the act of 1816. In 1817 the BUS and the state banks agreed to resume redemption of their notes in specie and thereafter created forms of cooperation in the management of the banking business that resulted in a national fiscal system.

Internal improvements was a more contentious constitutional problem, the resolution of which passed through a series of stages. Expansionist in outlook, Republicans early supported the construction or improvement of roads, canals, waterways, and harbors in order to promote commerce and internal communications. The act admitting Ohio to the Union in 1802, for example, provided that 5 percent of the revenue from public land sales be directed toward the building of roads. In 1806 Jefferson recommended to Congress the application of surplus federal revenue to public education and internal improvements, to be undertaken after the adoption of a constitutional amendment authorizing legislation for this purpose. Congress ignored the suggestion of a constitutional amendment and authorized construction of the National Road, from Cumberland, Maryland, to the Mississippi River. Only a few miles of the road were constructed before foreign-policy problems caused the temporary abandonment of internal improvement projects, including a ten-year plan prepared by Secretary of the Treasury Albert Gallatin in 1808.

The War of 1812 having demonstrated the need for more effective internal transportation and communication, Madison in 1815 and 1816 advocated a federal program. Like Jefferson, he regarded a constitutional amendment as necessary to give Congress the power to carry out such a program. Republicans in Congress thought otherwise, however, and, employing broad construction, passed the so-called Bonus Bill, setting aside the $1,500,000 bonus paid by the national bank for its charter and the United States government's bank dividends as a permanent fund for internal improvements. John C. Calhoun of South Carolina cited the general-welfare clause as a constitutional basis for the bill, arguing on the example of the Louisiana Purchase and the National Road, that federal appropriations need not be confined to enumerated powers. Others cited the commerce power as constitutional justification, insisting that Congress could authorize projects crossing state lines or confined to single states.

Having accepted broad construction on the bank question, Madison rejected it with respect to internal improvements. He vetoed the Bonus Bill on the ground that, no power for this purpose having been enumerated in the Constitution, approval would have the effect of acknowledging or creating a general legislative power in the federal government. In particular the general-welfare clause should not be interpreted or employed as Congress proposed, Madison reasoned, lest the whole scheme of enumeration and limitation of powers be abandoned. Nor in Madison's view did the general-welfare clause authorize appropriations of money beyond the enumerated powers of Congress.

A kind of constitutional dialogue now ensued between Republican president and Congress that resulted in a compromise on the internal-improvements question. President James Monroe in 1817 advocated a constitutional amendment authorizing federal legislation in this sphere, and an amendment was brought in giving Congress power to appropriate money accordingly. The House believed it already possessed this power, however, and passed a resolution in 1818 stating that Congress could appropriate money for post roads, military highways, and canals. On the other hand it rejected a resolution stating that the federal government had the power to construct internal improvements. In 1819 Secretary of War John C. Calhoun submitted plans for a comprehensive system of internal improvements that called for both direct federal construction on a military basis and federal-state cooperation in the form of federal appropriations and state construction.

Monroe accepted federal-state cooperation in his Cumberland Road Veto of 1822, and it subsequently became the basis for a federally sponsored program of internal improvements. The bill that Monroe vetoed provided for federal toll gates and maintenance, and gave the federal government certain jurisdictional rights over the road within the various states. Monroe rejected it on the ground that collecting tolls was an exercise of local sovereignty and thus an invasion of the state police power. But he said Congress could appropriate money for internal improvements with the consent of the states affected. It was this approach that was adopted in the General Survey Act of 1824.

The act of 1824 authorized comprehensive surveys by army engineers of routes for roads and canals judged by the president to be in the national interest. It took the view that actual construction and operation of internal improvements lay within state jurisdiction. In the next several years Congress appropriated money to several interstate canal projects that were constructed by private corporations incorporated under state law, or by the states themselves. By the mid-1830s, too, Congress ceded the Cumberland National Road to the states through which it passed. This resolution of the question and the consistent rejection of exclusively federal projects may be said to have vindicated the states'-rights–strict-construction point of view. But the more important point is that a national policy took shape under federal sponsorship in a way that respected the sensibilities of states'-rights advocates.

Republican Constitutional Method

Republican national mercantilism encouraged a dynamic method of constitutional interpretation that regarded the Constitution more as an instrument of power than as a source of limitations. Republican constitutionalism also looked to the legislature and ultimately the people as authoritative expositors of the Constitution. Madison subscribed to this view when he said, in his bank bill veto message of 1815, that all question of the bank's constitutionality had been precluded by "repeated recognition under varied circumstances of the validity of such an institution in acts of the legislative, executive, and judicial branches of the Government, accompanied by indications, in different modes, of a concurrence of the general will of the nation." Calhoun said the same thing in defending the Bonus Bill in 1816. He admitted that the Constitution was founded on positive and written principles rather than precedents, but he insisted that continuous popular approval of internal improvements was "better evidence of the true interpretation of the constitution, than the most refined and subtle arguments."

Henry Clay went further in holding that changes in circumstances created or led to the discovery of new constitutional powers. Clay reasoned that whereas in 1811 the Bank of the United States recharter bill was unconstitutional, in 1816 it was constitutional because conditions had changed and a national bank was now necessary to give effect to the enumerated powers of the Constitution. Carried to its logical extreme this method of interpretation would eliminate all fixed limitations on the federal government and create an utterly elastic fundamental law that could be changed by the legislature itself. The result would negate the very premise of American constitutionalism that governmental and especially legislative power must be kept subordinate to the organic law of the Constitution. A few states'-rights critics attacked the idea that federal legislation could settle constitutional questions on the ground that it would make the Constitution a dead letter, but these fears were exaggerated. Nevertheless, Republicans showed the potential for expansion of government power inherent in a pragmatic, instrumental conception of the Constitution in a way that was prophetic of government in the twentieth century.

The mercantilist phase of Republican constitutionalism came to a culmination—and produced a strong strict-construction–states'-rights reaction—in the administration of John Quincy Adams (1825–29). Stating that the purpose of civil government was to improve the condition of its constituents, Adams in his annual message to Congress in 1825 asserted that the exercise of delegated powers under the Constitution was "a duty as sacred and indispensable as the usurpation of powers not granted is criminal and odious." Adams acknowledged that the Constitution was a charter of limited powers, but, citing the enumerated powers of Congress and also the general-welfare and necessary-and-proper clauses, he said that to refrain from exercising these powers "would be treachery to the most sacred of trusts." The limiting Constitution thus became an authorizing and empowering instrument. Arguing that "liberty is power," Adams urged upon Congress a multitude of governmental projects, from the founding of a national university to the construction of roads and canals on a vast scale. Pointing to recent state accomplishments in the internal-improvements field that he offered as motivation for more extensive federal efforts, he admonished Congress not "to slumber in indolence" or be "palsied by the will of our constituents."

Adams's appeal to positive government and broad construction aroused vigorous opposition. For nearly two decades, since Jefferson's departure from the principles of '98, an Old Republican faction centering on the agrarians John Randolph and John Taylor of Virginia had steadily criticized the centralizing trend in Republican constitutionalism. By the mid-1820s this link with the opposition Jeffersonian tradition had, through the political enterprise of Martin Van Buren of New York, developed into a coalition of southern planters, northern farmers, and small entrepreneurs that appealed to the principles of states' rights and strict construction. President Adams, meanwhile, lacking a broad political base to begin with since he owed his election to the House of Representatives, lost what little political capital he had through his high-toned appeal to public improvement under federal auspices. Committed to a kind of commonwealth vision of the national interest, Adams appeared as a defender of a narrow northeastern commercial and industrial interest. Thus the stage was set for yet another "revolution"—the triumph of Jacksonian Democracy—which its supporters hoped would arrest the trend toward centralization and restore states' rights to a more prominent position.

TEN

The Place of the Judiciary in the Constitutional System and the Origins of Judicial Review

———————————— ✦✦✦ ————————————

THE DECISIVE ROLE acquired by the judiciary in interpreting and applying the written Constitution has caused American constitutionalism to be highly legalistic and juridical compared to the constitutional systems of England and European nations. The primary basis of judicial power has been judicial review, the practice by which courts determine the legitimacy of legislative acts by considering them against the requirements of a written constitution. Moreover, judicial review has given rise to the judicial monopoly theory of constitutional interpretation—the belief that final authority to state the meaning of the Constitution and to settle constitutional controversies belongs exclusively to the courts. This outlook differs greatly from that which prevailed in the early years of the new government. The "least dangerous branch," as Hamilton described it, the judiciary occupied an uncertain position in relation to the other branches of government. Courts struggled to defend their independence against legislatures and executives, and to vindicate their authority to settle constitutional disputes over individual rights. Problematic also was the structure of the American judicial system. The organization of federal courts, their relationship to the state courts, and the place, if any, of the English common law in national law were all highly controversial matters.

The Judiciary Act of 1789

During the American Revolution legislatures dominated constitutional change, expanding their power and frequently interfering in disputes over private rights. Although the judiciary was recognized as a coordinate branch of government under the separation-of-powers theory, its power was tenuous and uncertain. Controversy at the state level centered on whether judges would be appointed or elected, and whether they should enjoy tenure during good behavior or serve a limited term. The underlying issue was the responsibility or political accountability of the judiciary to the community, and until it was settled the administration of justice was uneven, if not capricious, in many states. Dissatisfaction with this situation became widespread in the 1780s and contributed to the demand for constitutional reform at the continental level. A major concern of the Constitutional Convention, therefore, was to create a national judicial system that would provide a more uniform administration of justice than the courts of the states were able to provide.

In accordance with the separation-of-powers doctrine, the Constitutional Convention created a judicial department and vested in it "the judicial Power of the United States." The judicial power extended "to all cases, in law and equity, arising under this constitution, the laws of the United States, and treaties made ... under their authority," and to cases involving ambassadors, public ministers, admiralty jurisdiction, controversies between states and between citizens of different states. Desiring a uniform judicial system for the nation, the framers differed over how best to establish it. All agreed that a single tribunal—the Supreme Court—ought to stand at the apex of the system. But it was not at all clear whether the national judicial system below the Supreme Court ought to consist in state courts, acting in a dual state and federal capacity, or lower federal courts. Unable to decide the question, the convention chose neither alternative, but rather authorized Congress to create inferior federal courts at its discretion. It also stipulated tenure during good behavior, placed appointment in the hands of the executive, and endorsed a limited form of judicial review as part of the system of checks and balances.

The first Congress promptly enacted legislation creating a system of inferior federal courts. The work principally of centralist-minded Federalists, especially Oliver Ellsworth of Connecticut, the Judiciary Act of September 24, 1789, incorporated the principle of federal supremacy into the national judicial system. It provided for a Supreme Court consisting of a chief justice and five associate justices; thirteen federal district courts of one judge each—one district for each of the eleven existing states and two additional districts, in Virginia and Massachusetts, for Kentucky and Maine; three circuit courts, each composed of two justices of the Supreme Court sitting in conjunction with one district court judge. The jurisdiction of the various courts was stated in great detail, and, to a lesser degree, their organization and procedure.

Although the Judiciary Act upheld the principle of federal supremacy, it was in essence a compromise between states' rights and centralization.

The centralizers' chief accomplishment was Section 25 of the act, which brought the state courts directly under federal appellate jurisdiction by providing for appeals from state courts to the federal judiciary. Under this section, appeals could be taken to the United States Supreme Court whenever the highest state court having jurisdiction of a case (1) ruled against the constitutionality of a federal treaty or law; (2) ruled in favor of the validity of a state act which had been challenged as contrary to the Constitution, treaties, or laws of the United States; or (3) ruled against a right or privilege claimed under the Constitution or federal law. In effect, this meant that appeals would be taken in all instances where the state judiciary assertedly failed to give full recognition to the supremacy of the Constitution or to the treaties and laws of the United States, as provided by Article VI of the Constitution.

This provision, which solved the problem of conflicts between state and national spheres of authority, was to become the very crux of American federalism. If the Constitution and federal laws and treaties were to be "the supreme Law of the Land," it was vital that they be interpreted with reasonable uniformity. Unless the Supreme Court were given authority to review the decisions of state courts in disputes between the states and the federal government over their respective powers, it would be possible for state courts practically to nullify federal authority, just as state legislatures had virtually nullified the authority of Congress under the Confederation. Therefore, the nationalists insisted that the Supreme Court must be the final interpreter of the Constitution and as such must have the right to receive appeals from state courts.

The Constitutional Convention had not specifically provided for appeals from state to federal courts, but Ellsworth and the other centralizers in Congress assumed the right to be implied in the Constitution. In 1789 and for many years afterward, the critics of Section 25 of the Judiciary Act claimed that the Constitution specifically placed the responsibility for upholding federal supremacy upon the state courts and that Congress had no authority to subject their decisions to review by the Supreme Court of the United States. This opposition was motivated by the fear that the state judiciaries and state powers would be gradually absorbed by federal authority, a fear that made it almost impossible for this group to see the necessity for the uniform upholding of federal supremacy throughout the Union.

Although the creation of inferior federal courts was a centralist victory, it was balanced by the granting of a significant amount of jurisdiction to the state courts. Some Federalists thought that the inferior federal courts should have all the judicial authority that the Constitution made available—that is, in "all cases in law and equity" arising under the Constitution, laws, and treaties. In the opinion of these lawmakers Congress had no discretion in the matter, but must vest in the lower courts the entire judicial power allowed by the Constitution. This centralizing effort failed, however, with the result that the federal courts had limited exclusive original jurisdiction and much concurrent original jurisdiction with the state courts.

Federal district courts received exclusive original jurisdiction in admiralty and maritime cases and in cases involving crimes and offenses cognizable under the authority of the United States. At the least, this meant crimes specified by act of Congress; whether it also referred to crimes at common law was a disputed issue. Unlike the situation today, federal circuit courts were to be the main courts of general original jurisdiction in the federal system and could hear suits of a civil nature at common law or in equity where the matter in dispute exceeded the sum of $500. But the state courts were given concurrent original jurisdiction in civil suits at common law or equity; and because they were more numerous, they could be expected to be the principal courts of first instance in the national judicial system. The influence of the states was further apparent in the decision to have the federal courts adopt the methods and procedures of the state courts. Section 34 of the Judiciary Act stated that "The laws of the several States, except where the Constitution, treaties, or statutes of the United States shall otherwise require or provide, shall be regarded as rules of decision in trials at common law in the courts of the United States in cases where they apply."

The Federal Judiciary in the 1790s

The federal judiciary was slow to acquire a position of prestige and importance. During the first three years of its existence the Supreme Court had no cases to decide. Most legal matters were handled through the state courts, and many people were jealous of the potential power of the new federal judicial system. Only gradually did the Supreme Court's work grow in volume and importance; it was the federal circuit courts, where Supreme Court justices presided, that first brought federal judicial authority home to the people. Through the charges to grand juries by judges of these courts, the public was informed regarding the basic principles of the new government and the provisions of important federal statutes. And although the state courts predominated, the volume of business in the federal courts was more considerable than historians have usually assumed.

The basic question concerning the judiciary in the 1790s was its relationship to the political branches of government. The courts were subjected to much political pressure. At both the state and federal level judges tried to deal with this situation by drawing a distinction between law and politics that would reserve the former sphere—especially matters of individual right—to courts, while allowing legislatures and executives to prevail in the latter. Federal courts sought to establish this distinction by restricting their decisions and opinions to the adjudication of specific cases duly brought before them. Thus in 1792, in the so-called *Hayburn's* case, certain circuit court judges expressed their disagreement with a recent act of Congress which provided that the circuit courts should pass upon certain claims of disabled veterans of the Revolutionary War. "Neither the Legislative nor the Executive branches," said the judges, "can constitutionally assign to the judicial any duties but such as are properly judicial and to be performed in a judicial manner."

The following year President Washington, desiring legal advice on the questions of neutrality, had his secretary of state address a letter to Chief Justice John Jay asking the justices of the Supreme Court whether the chief executive might seek their advice on questions of law. The judges were also presented with a list of specific questions on international law and neutrality. After due consideration the judges declined to give their opinion on the questions of law on the grounds that the constitutional separation of the three departments prevented them from deciding extrajudicial questions.

The function of the federal judiciary that was of the greatest public concern during its first decade, and by and large until 1861, was its determination of the compatibility of state constitutions, statutes, and court decisions with "the supreme Law of the Land." This function was of the utmost importance in the operation of the federal system of government, for it not only tended to establish the Court as the final interpreter of the Constitution, but it also emphasized the supremacy of the national government. The guardianship of the distribution of powers between the states and the central government was not explicitly assigned by the Constitution to the federal courts, but the Judiciary Act of 1789 had taken a long step in that direction by providing for appeals from state to federal courts on constitutional questions.

In May 1791 the United States Circuit Court for Connecticut took the lead in asserting federal judicial authority over state law when it held an act of that state unconstitutional as an infringement of the treaty of peace with Great Britain. The following year the Circuit Court for Rhode Island, in *Champion* v. *Casey,* declared void a state law giving a debtor citizen an extension of three years in which to pay this debts. "The Legislature of a State," the court said, "have no right to make a law ... impairing the obligation of contracts, and therefore contrary to the Constitution of the United States," It will be remembered that many laws similar to this one had been enacted by various states during the period of the Articles of Confederation, and that the creditor element had been influenced by the resulting apprehension to strive for a stronger central government to check such measures. However, the return of prosperity and the popular acceptance of the new federal government obviated any widespread opposition to this decision. In subsequent years various laws of other states were invalidated by the federal circuit courts without any serious challenge by states'-rights advocates to the exercise of such power.

Considerable popular dissatisfaction, however, was aroused by the Supreme Court in 1796 in the case of *Ware* v. *Hylton,* which declared invalid a Virginia statute of 1777 sequestering pre-Revolutionary debts of British creditors. The treaty of peace had provided that no impediment was to be placed on the recovery by British subjects of debts due to them from Americans. Under the Articles of Confederation this provision had been of little practical value to British creditors. The Court now held that the treaty nullified the earlier law of Virginia, destroyed the payment made under it, revived the debt, and gave a right of recovery against the debtor, notwithstanding the payment made under the authority of the state law. Such a sweeping and retroactive interpretation of the supremacy of treaties over state law on the sensitive issue of Revolutionary debts led to Republican criticism of the judges as pro-British Federalists.

Even more serious opposition to federal judicial authority was excited by the decision in *Chisholm* v. *Georgia* (1793), a case involving the right of the federal judiciary to summon a state as defendant and to adjudicate its rights and liabilities. The Constitution expressly gave the federal courts jurisdiction over "controversies between a state and citizens of another state." In the campaign for the ratification of the Constitution in the various states prominent Federalists had assured their apprehensive opponents that this provision would not encompass suits against states without their consent. Almost from the establishment of the federal judiciary, however, suits were instituted against states by citizens of other states. In *Chisholm* v. *Georgia,* two citizens of South Carolina, executors of a British creditor, brought suit in the Supreme Court against the state of Georgia for recovery of confiscated property. The state refused to appear and presented a written protest denying the jurisdiction of the Court. Meanwhile the Georgia legislature considered a resolution declaring that the exercise of such authority by the federal judiciary "would effectually destroy the retained sovereignty of the States."

The Supreme Court rendered its decision in favor of Chisholm, and the individual justices presented elaborate opinions explaining the nature of the federal union and the extent of federal judicial authority. The majority of justices, especially John Jay and James Wilson, discussed at length the nature of sovereignty and maintained that under the Constitution sovereignty was vested in the people of the United States for "purposes of Union" and in the people of the several states for "more domestic concerns." In ordaining and establishing the Constitution the people acted "as sovereigns of the whole country." They established, said Chief Justice Jay, "a constitution by which it was their will, that the state governments should be bound, and to which the state constitutions should be made to conform."

Consequently, the state of Georgia, "by being a party to the national compact," in order "to establish justice," consented to be suable by individual citizens of another state. In dissenting from the decision Justice James Iredell, while admitting that sovereignty under the Constitution was divided between the United States and the individual states, denied that the English common law, under which a sovereignty could not be sued without its consent, had been superseded either by constitutional provision or by statute law.

In this case, however, the Supreme Court did not have the final word. The old Antifederalist hostility to a consolidated government flared up, especially in those states where suits similar to Chisholm's were pending or were instituted against the state. Georgia refused to permit the *Chisholm* verdict to be executed. The day following the decision there was initiated congressional action, which a year later resulted in the submission of the Eleventh Amendment to the states for ratification. It provided: "The Judicial power of the United States shall not be construed to extend to any suit in law or equity, commenced or prosecuted against one of the United States by Citizens of another State, or by Citizens or Subjects of any Foreign State." Because of indifference or Federalist opposition the amendment was not ratified by the requisite number of states until January 1798. Thus for the only time in its history the federal judiciary had its jurisdiction directly curtailed by constitutional amendment.

Judicial Reform: The Judiciary Act of 1801

The controversy in which the federal judiciary found itself as a result of *Chisholm* v. *Georgia* was exceptional, for more often than not the federal courts labored in obscurity. Technical or professional problems afflicted the national court system from the outset, however, and when political and economic circumstances in the late 1790s caused the federal judiciary to become strategically important, reforms affecting the organization and jurisdiction of the national courts gained support in Congress. The result of this heightened interest in judicial power was the Judiciary Act of 1801.

From the beginning of the national court system in 1789 dissatisfaction arose with the organization of the circuit courts. Supreme Court justices did not like riding circuit nine months out of the year, as they were required to do. More important, they did not like acting in an appellate capacity in the Supreme Court on matters that they had already decided as circuit court judges. As early as 1790, therefore, proposals were introduced into Congress for removing Supreme Court justices from circuit duty and creating a separate circuit court judiciary. Nothing came of these measures, however, because the federal judiciary lacked the political significance needed to achieve such a reform.

This situation began to change in the late 1790s as a result of economic controversies involving Federalist land speculators and Republican-controlled state courts. In several states large land companies became embroiled in disputes arising out of the interpretation and application of state land laws. Under the Judiciary Act of 1789 these matters lay within the jurisdiction of state courts; accordingly, in Georgia, Kentucky, Pennsylvania, and Virginia, where major disputes existed and Republicans were in control, Federalist speculators faced the prospect of litigation in unfriendly courts that tended to favor settlers. Under these circumstances land companies took an interest in judicial reorganization since it offered the possibility, through a change in the jurisdiction of federal courts, of gaining access to a more sympathetic forum than the states would provide.

The Sedition Act crisis further stimulated political interest in the federal judiciary. Even before the act was passed, suits were brought in federal courts under the common law of seditious libel. More suits were initiated after adoption of the measure, and as tension mounted in 1799, Federalists who heretofore had ignored the judiciary began to see expansion of federal court jurisdiction as a means of containing the Republican insurgency. Suddenly, the technical problems of judicial organization and jurisdiction acquired large importance. Regarded in 1799 as a defense against potential Republican subversion, judicial reform after the election of 1800 seemed necessary to combat the decline of public order that Federalists feared would result from Jefferson's triumph. In this situation they adopted the Judiciary Act of 1801.

The act established six new circuit courts with their own judiciary, thereby requiring the appointment of sixteen circuit judges. It also provided for several new district courts. This increase in judicial personnel—the appointment of the famous "midnight judges" by outgoing president John Adams—was the most obvious and politically conspicuous result of the act. The Federalists' partisan purpose was plain enough. Losing power and fearing revolution, they wanted reliable conservatives on the federal bench to maintain the status quo. An additional provision of the act, reducing the size of the Supreme Court from six justices to five effective with the next vacancy, eliminated tie votes, but also deprived the incoming president of his first appointment. It further emphasized the law's partisan aim.

But more important constitutionally than the appointment of Federalist judges was the expansion of federal jurisdiction authorized by the act of 1801. Here the major change concerned the circuit courts. Previously, their role as courts of first instance in private law matters was circumscribed by the requirement that the amount of money involved in a controversy had to be more than $500, and by the extension of concurrent jurisdiction to state courts. By contrast, under the act of 1801 circuit courts were given trial jurisdiction in all cases in law and equity arising under the Constitution and under laws and treaties passed in pursuance of it. In other words, the act gave circuit courts the full measure of judicial power authorized by the

Constitution, thus going far toward creating the uniform judicial system envisioned by the framers of the Judiciary Act of 1789. The act of 1801 also removed the $500 requirement in civil litigation, and expressly gave circuit court jurisdiction over cases involving disputed land titles without regard to the amount involved. Finally, the act made it easier to remove from state to federal courts without regard to jurisdictional amount, and enlarged the jurisdiction of federal courts in diversity cases (i.e., between citizens of different states). Previously, diversity jurisdiction arose only between a citizen of the state in which a suit was brought and a citizen of another state. Now any suit between citizens of different states was triable in any federal circuit court.

The immediate purpose of these provisions was to protect Federalist political and economic interests threatened by the Republican party's rise to power. But this political motivation should not obscure the corollary aim of reforming the circuit court system, nor the effect the law had in promoting a more uniform administration of justice and bringing the federal judiciary closer to the people. If the state judiciary served as the people's courts in the first decade of the government, it was by no means certain that they alone were capable of fulfilling this function. Had the act of 1801 remained in effect, it might have popularized federal authority and detracted from the influence of the state courts. Indeed, it was this fear that caused Republicans to repeal the judicial legislation of 1801.

Federal Common Law

An additional reason why the Judiciary Act of 1801 was controversial concerned the question of a federal common law of crimes. The English common law, modified for local circumstances, was adopted or received by the American colonies throughout the eighteenth century as the basis of separate systems of private law. After the Revolution the states continued to adapt English rules and decisions, and around 1800 began to keep records of their own courts' proceedings. They thus created an indigenous body of common law on the English basis. The question necessarily arose, however, as to whether the English common law had also entered into national as well as state law. Federalists argued in the affirmative. Their theory was that the common law had been law for the empire as a whole and at the time of the Revolution was received into a general body of national law. Republicans held in contrast that the state courts alone had common law jurisdiction. For federal courts to entertain suits at common law, they contended, was a usurpation of states' rights.

There is evidence to suggest that the framers of the Constitution and the members of the first Congress regarded the common law as part of federal law. In drafting the judiciary article of the Constitution, the convention rejected language that would have confined the jurisdiction of the

Supreme Court to all cases arising under the laws of the national legislature. Similarly, Congress in the Judiciary Act of 1789 rejected a limitation of lower federal court jurisdiction to crimes defined by United States statute. In each instance the purpose appears to have been to allow federal courts to assume common law jurisdiction as well as jurisdiction in pursuance of acts of Congress. Furthermore, there are references in the Constitution to elements of the common law, such as the writ of habeas corpus, which seem to rest on the assumption that the common law was an available source of national law.

At any rate, it is clear that many federal judges and other officers in the first few years of the government acted on the theory that the criminal common law was part of United States law. This was reflected in the government's decision to proseute in the lower federal courts offenses that were not declared to be crimes under any act of Congress, and also in the instructions which judges gave to juries. Moreover, several cases at common law were successfully prosecuted in jury trials, which suggests that public opinion did not oppose the idea that the criminal common law had been received into federal jurisdiction. Yet the question of a federal common law had by no means been resolved, nor was it perceived as having any special political significance.

Toward the end of the 1790s, however, as the ideological differences between Federalists and Republicans crystallized, the issue of federal common law became politically controversial. *United States* v. *Worrall,* a circuit court case of 1798, illustrates this transition. Worrall was indicted at common law for attempting to bribe the United States commissioner of revenue, despite the fact that no congressional statute designated this act a federal crime. The jury found Worrall guilty, and he was convicted. Attention in the case focused, however, on the argument of defense counsel Alexander James Dallas, a Republican, who attacked the notion of a federal common law jurisdiction. The very idea of federal common law, he argued, was contrary to the nature of the Union. Citing the Tenth Amendment, Dallas said the powers of the federal government were delegated and strictly limited. The federal judiciary, accordingly, derived its authority solely from the Constitution and acts of Congress; the common law was not available as a source of jurisdiction. Dallas insisted that to allow the national courts to assume a common law jurisdiction would undermine state judicial authority and consolidate power in the federal government.

During the foreign policy crisis of 1798, Federalists relied on the criminal common law to deal with the threat to national security which they perceived in Republican criticism of the government. Hence they initiated prosecution of Republican editors in the lower federal courts under the common law of seditious libel. The passage of the Sedition Act provided a statutory basis for prosecuting for seditious libel in place of or in addition to the common law. Yet Republicans remained keenly aware of the threat to state power implicit in the assumption of federal common law jurisdiction. They were justifiably alarmed when Congress, in the Judiciary Act of 1801, extended the jurisdiction of the federal circuit courts to all cases in law or equity arising under the Constitution and laws of the United States. For under this sweeping authorization it was likely that the doctrine of a national common law, already supported by a majority of the Supreme Court, would gain acceptance throughout the federal judiciary.

Republicans not only feared that federal courts would supersede state courts in the administration of justice, but they also saw in the idea of federal common law the danger of centralized legislative power. This apprehension was based on the fact that the common law dealt with virtually every aspect of social life and that it was subject to legislative revision. If the United States had a common law, Republicans reasoned, Congress would be able to legislate on anything the common law touched, which meant in effect a general legislative power. In 1800 Thomas Jefferson stated: "If the principle were to prevail of a common law being in force in the U.S.," it would "possess the general government at once of all the powers of the state governments and reduce [the country] to a single consolidated government." In the opinion of the Republican *Virginia Argus,* the doctrine of a national common law "gives the Federal Government and its Courts jurisdiction over every subject that has hitherto been supposed to belong to the States; instead of the General Government being instituted for particular purposes, it embraces every subject to which government can apply."

After 1800 Republicans were in a position to resolve the question of federal common law on their own terms. Eventually, they did so in the Supreme Court case of *U.S.* v. *Hudson and Goodwin* in 1812. Ironically, the case began with Republican efforts to bring federal common law indictments against Federalist editors for libeling President Thomas Jefferson. Jefferson ordered the indictments dropped when he learned of them, but one case made its way to the Supreme Court. In *U.S.* v. *Hudson and Goodwin,* Republican justice William Johnson held the indictment invalid on the ground that federal courts had no common law criminal jurisdiction. In orthodox Jeffersonian fashion, Johnson argued that the powers of the federal government were strictly enumerated, including the powers of the judiciary. Federal courts, other than the Supreme Court, were created by Congress and possessed only the jurisdiction that Congress gave them. Accordingly, criminal indictments could not be based on the common law, but must depend on statutes of Congress defining particular acts as federal crimes.

The Revolution of 1800 and the Judiciary

Rejection of a federal common law formed part of a more general strategy toward the judiciary that the Republican party pursued during the first Jefferson administration. Upon assuming power the party was hostile to Federalist interpretations of the Constitution, but owing to the internal division between radicals and moderates it lacked a clearly defined policy toward the judiciary. The radicals expressed a democratic tendency in republican thought dating from the Revolution which sought to make the judiciary directly responsive to the political will of the community. This view argued that federal and state judges should be popularly elected, should hold limited tenure, and should be accountable to the political branches. Furthermore, radicals insisted that justice be dispensed at the most local level, and not necessarily by persons trained in the law. Moderates, on the other hand, preferred a strong and independent judiciary, appointed during good behavior and recruited from professionally trained lawyers. Instead of demanding judicial deference to legislatures, moderates desired the separation of law and politics.

From their criticism of the "midnight judges," the Republicans could be expected to repeal the Judiciary Act of 1801. In actuality their decision to do so did not take shape until the Federalists provoked it by trying to force the administration to deliver the commission of one William Marbury as justice of the peace for the District of Columbia. Initially, pursuing his conciliatory strategy toward the Federalists, Jefferson had been content simply to call attention to the recently enacted judicial law and to submit a summary of the business of the federal courts intended to show that the new circuit courts were not needed. In January 1802, however, after the Supreme Court agreed to receive Marbury's request for a preliminary writ that would lead to his getting his commission, Jefferson agreed to seek repeal.

In the congressional debate over repeal of the 1801 statute, a controversy developed concerning the constitutional authority of Congress to deprive the judges appointed under the act of their offices by abolishing the positions they held. Federalist spokesmen answered the question emphatically in the negative by maintaining that repeal would violate the provision of the Constitution which guaranteed tenure during good behavior to federal judges. Republicans replied that the creation and abolition of inferior courts were left by the Constitution to the discretion of Congress, and that the offices did not become the vested property of the judges. Senators and congressmen from Kentucky and Virginia in particular were well aware of the widespread sentiment among their constituents for the complete abolition of the inferior federal courts lest the decisions of those courts jeopardize existing land titles in those states. To the Federalist charge that the repeal bill was a partisan attempt to control what the Constitution had placed above partisanship, the Republicans retorted that the Judiciary Act of 1801 was the original sin in that respect.

The Republicans had their way, and on March 31, 1802, the repeal bill became law. The immediate effect was to revive the judicial system based on the Judiciary Act of 1789. Promptly, the Republicans enacted another law providing for annual instead of semiannual sessions of the Supreme Court, the effect being to postpone the Court's next session until February 1803. The law's sponsors evidently hoped thereby to discourage any of the displaced circuit judges from attacking the validity of the Repeal Act before the Court.

In April 1802 the Republican-dominated Congress passed a new Circuit Court Act by which the country was divided into six instead of three circuits, to each of which was assigned a separate justice of the Supreme Court, who, together with a district judge, should compose the circuit court. As new states were later admitted into the Union, this federal judicial system was extended, with no basic change being made until after the Civil War.

Impeachment of Federal Judges

If the repeal of the Judiciary Act was more a vindication of congressional power over inferior federal courts than an attack on the judiciary, the impeachment of federal judges in 1804–5 reflected the desire of the radical faction of the Republican party to subordinate the judiciary to the political branches of the government.

Under the Constitution impeachment is the only legal method of removing federal executive and judicial officers. The House of Representatives is authorized to impeach "all civil Officers of the United States" for "Treason, Bribery, or other high Crimes and Misdemeanors," whereupon they are to be tried before the Senate. As in many other provisions of the Constitution, the real scope and meaning of impeachment could be determined only by practical application and experiment.

Although the Constitution prescribed the impeachment of federal judges only for high crimes and misdemeanors, Jefferson's supporters were inclined to take an extremely broad view of the impeachment power. By the more partisan Republicans impeachment was considered a proper instrument for removing from office judges who had fallen too far out of step with public opinion. This conception made impeachment largely a political proceeding in which any judge could be removed from office should both the House and the Senate think it expedient to do so.

To the Federalist argument that the judiciary should be above political considerations, Jefferson's supporters replied that the federal judiciary had already entered the political arena and that it must abide by the consequences. More moderate Republicans were not willing to go this far, but they held that "high crimes and misdemeanors" might be construed broadly, so that bad judicial ethics or misconduct on the bench would become impeachable offenses. Some judges had taken advantage of their responsibility in charging grand juries to make political speeches from the bench; others had left their work to participate in political campaigns; still others had interpreted and applied the Sedition Law with gross partisanship. Many moderate Republicans thought these offenses properly impeachable.

The Republicans first tested the impeachment process against Judge John Pickering of the District Court of New Hampshire. In February 1803, while the *Marbury* case was pending, Jefferson sent to the House of Representatives a message accompanied by documentary evidence showing that Pickering was guilty of intoxication and profanity on the bench. The House later impeached the judge on charges of malfeasance and general unfitness for office because of his loose morals and intemperate habits. In March 1804 Pickering was tried before the Senate, where it became obvious that he was insane.

This raised the question of the extent of the impeachment power in a most embarrassing form. It could hardly be argued plausibly that an insane man's conduct constituted either high crime or misdemeanor, since such offenses implied "a vicious will" on the part of the person involved. Yet unless the impeachment power was to be construed broadly enough to remove Pickering, the precedent would be established that there was actually no method of removing an incompetent or incapacitated judge from office.

A majority even of the Republican senators were apparently persuaded that Pickering, being insane, could not properly be convicted on any of the specific counts in the House impeachment. Nonetheless, they believed Pickering unfit for office and either abstained from voting or joined their colleagues in voting that the accused was "guilty as charged." He was convicted by a 19-to-7 vote and removed from office. The Pickering impeachment was so confused and contradictory, however, that it was not thereafter treated as having established the general power of impeachment for mere incompetence or incapacity in office.

Following Pickering's conviction, the Republicans moved to impeach Justice Samuel Chase of the Supreme Court. Republican leaders were generally agreed that Chase's conduct on the bench in the sedition cases had been inexcusable; moreover, they felt that he had forfeited any claim to judicial impartiality by actively campaigning for Adams in 1800. In 1803 he provided additional grounds for impeachment, when in a long charge to a Baltimore grand jury he severely criticized Congress for abolishing the circuit judges and jeopardizing the "independence" of the judiciary. He also attacked the Jefferson administration and its doctrine "that all men, in a state of society, are entitled to enjoy equal liberty and equal rights," a doctrine which he said had "brought this mighty mischief upon us," a mischief that would "rapidly progress, until peace and order, freedom and property, shall be destroyed." Universal suffrage, he contended, would cause "our republican Constitution" to "sink into a mobocracy."

Led by John Randolph of Virginia, a radical Republican strongly committed to the twin doctrines of states' rights and agrarianism, the House of Representatives in January 1804 appointed a committee to inquire into Chase's conduct. This resulted in the House's impeachment of Chase on March 12 by a strictly partisan vote of 73 to 32. To prosecute the case against Chase the House appointed a committee of managers, headed by Randolph, who presented eight articles of impeachment. No infraction of law was alleged. The first seven articles concerned Chase's "oppressive conduct" as a presiding judge in several criminal trials of 1800 which had arisen under the Sedition Act. The final article related to the Baltimore address, which was characterized as "an intemperate and inflammatory political harangue," designed "to excite the fears and resentment . . . of the good people of Maryland against their State government . . . [and] against the Government of the United States."

In February 1805 the trial got under way before the Senate. It was evident to observers that although the fate of the federal judiciary might hinge on the verdict, the trial was to be a heroic partisan contest. The vital issue concerned the proper scope of impeachment under the Constitution. The counsel for the defense did not claim that Chase was above reproach, but they consistently maintained that an offense to be impeachable must be indictable in law. On the other hand, certain members of the impeachment committee, notably Randolph, took the extreme view that impeachment was not necessarily a criminal proceeding at all, but rather that on occasion it could be resorted to as a constitutional means of keeping the courts in reasonable harmony with the will of the nation, as expressed through politically responsible departments. The weight of this argument was increased by the fact that President Jefferson had just been re-elected in the presidential campaign of 1804 by an overwhelming electoral vote, with increased Republican majorities in Congress.

The other House managers did not adhere to such a broad interpretation of impeachment. They merely argued logically that, since impeachment was the only constitutionally recognized method of removing federal judges, the terms "high Crimes and Misdemeanors" must necessarily include all cases of willful misconduct in office, whether indictable in law or not.

The Senate was composed of thirty-four members, twenty-five Republicans and nine Federalists. With twenty-three votes necessary for conviction, the Republicans clearly had the requisite two-thirds majority, provided balloting on the articles of impeachment followed strict party lines. But several moderate Republicans remained unconvinced of Chase's guilt, being persuaded neither by the evidence nor by the prosecution's arguments. Several Republican senators also had been antagonized either by Randolph's extreme position or by his opposition to certain legislative measures sponsored by party moderates. Moreover, the president himself maintained a hands-off policy. The prosecution's efforts to enlist Vice-President Aaron Burr's influence with northern Republican senators also proved futile.

As a consequence, the Republican leadership failed to obtain the necessary two-thirds majority for conviction on each article of impeachment. On three articles there was a simple majority to convict, but even on the last article, where the prosecution had its strongest case, the vote fell four short of the necessary twenty-three. Immediately, Republican leaders introduced into both houses of Congress resolutions to amend the Constitution so as to provide for the removal of federal judges "by the President on joint address of both Houses of Congress." Although this action was in part a gesture—since the Republicans could hardly have expected to secure the adoption of such an amendment at that time—they repeatedly used the threat of an amendment of this kind in their struggles with the Federalist judges.

The failure to impeach Chase ended the Republicans' antijudiciary campaign at the national level and left the federal court system pretty much as it was in 1800. In the next several years moderate and radical Republicans further contested issues of judicial reform in the states, and there, too, the moderates generally succeeded in establishing a systematic and uniform administration of justice free from political control. Although the removal of Chase would not necessarily have led to action against other Supreme Court justices or to the destruction of judicial independence, his successful defense signified the abandonment of impeachment as a political device. This outcome, in the opinion of most students of constitutional history, has been salutary because it has furnished protection against a potential instrument of legislative hegemony.

Meanwhile, on another front the Supreme Court had taken steps to achieve an accommodation with the political branches of the government that was also intended to guard judicial independence. This additional means of defense was the doctrine of judicial review, announced in the famous case of *Marbury* v. *Madison* in 1803.

Judicial Review

In a general sense the practice by which courts pass on the constitutionality of acts of the legislature was an outgrowth of the English idea of fundamental law. Given the history of English courts' involvement in political matters, it appears to have been almost inevitable that the American judiciary, after the adoption of written constitutions, should assume to preserve the fundamental law through judicial review. Whether or not judicial review was the logical culmination of Anglo-American constitutional development, however, the fact is that it began to emerge in recognizable form in the 1780s as a means of restraining state legislatures. The founding fathers accepted judicial review, and in the first decade after ratification the federal judiciary acted on the assumption that it could declare acts of Congress unconstitutional. Pathbreaking as it was in the development of modern judicial power, therefore, John Marshall's assertion of judicial review in *Marbury* v. *Madison* rested on intellectual and institutional tendencies that began at least during the Revolution.

Judicial review involves more than a simple declaration that an act of a legislature is invalid. A crucial question concerns the scope and effect of the judicial ruling. Does it, of its own force, eliminate the unconstitutional law from the statute book and fix the meaning of the Constitution for the executive and legislative branches? Or does it simply resolve the instant case? Furthermore, can the judiciary, under the power of judicial review, consider and decide any conceivable question that might arise in the constitutional system? Different answers have been given to these questions.

The basic task that Marshall was to describe as the essence of judicial review—the assessment of the compatibility of a questioned statute with a written constitutional requirement—continues to characterize orthodox judicial review theory. This similarity notwithstanding, it is the differences between judicial review in the early national period and the modern era that stand out as more important. In the twentieth century the judiciary has monopolized constitutional interpretation, and judicial review has become a powerful instrument of policy making. By contrast, in the early years of the republic it was principally a means of holding the legislature in check and protecting courts against legislative encroachment. Similarly, where we now take it for granted that Supreme Court decision making is political, in the early nineteenth century defenders of judicial review drew a distinction between law and politics, reserving the former sphere to the judiciary and the latter to the political branches. However political early instances of judicial review may appear in retrospect, jurists in Marshall's era *thought* that their office obligated them to eschew politics and confine themselves to legal considerations. It was in this intellectual context, and in the hostile climate produced by Republican efforts to make the judiciary more politically accountable, that judicial review emerged.

Although the Constitution did not in express terms give courts the power to pass on the constitutionality of legislative acts, most members of the Constitutional Convention regarded this power—narrowly conceived—as legitimate. Its textual basis was the supremacy clause and Article III, Section 2 of the Constitution, which states that the judicial power shall extend to all cases in law and equity arising under the Constitution. The purpose of judicial review was to keep the legislature within proper limits. The framers, therefore, believed the judiciary might declare unconstitu-

tional acts of Congress that plainly contradicted specific provisions of the
Constitution. Realizing that much of the Constitution was concerned with
political matters beyond the competence of the courts, they did not intend
the judiciary to have a general power to interpret every conceivable constitutional issue that might arise. In addition to limiting the legislature, judicial review furnished the courts with a means of self-protection against
legislative encroachment. Most members of the convention believed the
courts would have a special warrant to interpret the Constitution in cases
that raised questions about the exercise of judicial power. In contrast to the
modern era, then, judicial review in the early national period was not seen
as having a policy-making or legislative purpose.

Occasionally in the 1790s the Supreme Court acted as though it could
pass on the constitutionality of acts of Congress. In *Hylton* v. *United States*
(1796), for example, the question of the constitutionality of legislation levying a tax on carriages came before the Court. The specific issue was whether
the levy in question was a direct tax or an excise. If the former, it would
conflict with the constitutional provision requiring all direct taxes to be
apportioned among the states according to population. The Court held that
only land taxes and capitations or head taxes were direct taxes, and that the
carriage tax was an indirect tax and, therefore, constitutional. But the opinion openly assumed that the Court had the right to declare an act of Congress void should the justices find that the law conflicted with the
Constitution. By 1800 nearly all federal justices, as well as a majority of the
legal profession, had accepted the principle that the Supreme Court could
declare acts of Congress unconstitutional.

The narrow conception of judicial review that found favor among the
judiciary was compatible with the departmental theory of constitutional
interpretation endorsed by most lawmakers and executives at the time.
According to the departmental theory, the Constitution was the fundamental political law of the nation which combined matters of strictly legal import, such as habeas corpus and trial by jury, with matters of broad political
import, such as the distribution of power among the parts of government.
The Constitution was both ordinary law, enforceable in the courts, and a set
of political rules for the conduct of government by the executive and legislative branches. Distinguishing between law and politics, the departmental
theory held that politico-constitutional questions were for the political
branches to decide, and legal-juridical questions for the judiciary. The theory thus avoided the dangers of legislative control of constitutional interpretation, as in England.

The departmental theory of interpretation first appeared in the debate
over the removal power, in the first Congress, where many members asserted their right and duty to settle the meaning of the Constitution. Formulated initially by Federalists, the theory was endorsed also by the
Republicans. Thus Jefferson wrote in 1801 that each of the three equal and

independent branches of government "must have a right in cases which arise within the line of its proper functions, where, equally with the others, it acts in the last resort and without appeal, to decide on the validity of an act according to its own judgment, and uncontrolled by the opinions of any other department." Madison similarly acknowledged the responsibility of the judiciary to expound the meaning of the Constitution and the laws "in the ordinary course of government," especially with regard to property and other individual rights and the administration of justice. He denied, however, that any one department had greater power than any other to mark out the limits of the powers of the other departments.

Marbury v. Madison

The theory of judicial review advanced by John Marshall in *Marbury v. Madison* was congruent with this approach to constitutional interpretation. The case arose out of Marbury's attempt, already noted, to assume his position as justice of the peace for the District of Columbia. His commission had been signed and sealed but not delivered when Jefferson took office. Believing the appointment had not been consummated, Jefferson ordered James Madison, his secretary of state, to withhold the commission. Thereupon Marbury, acting under Section 13 of the Judiciary Act of 1789, applied to the Supreme Court for a rule or preliminary writ to Madison to show cause why a mandamus should not be issued directing the secretary of state to deliver the commission. When the preliminary writ was issued, Madison ignored it as a judicial interference with the executive department.

At the Supreme Court's next session in February 1803, Marshall handed down an opinion on Marbury's application for a mandamus. Addressing the logically necessary first phase of the jurisdiction question—whether the issue raised by Marbury was justiciable—Marshall asked: "Has the applicant a right to the commission he demands?" His answer was in the affirmative. When a commission has been signed and sealed, Marshall said, the appointment is legally complete. "To withhold his commission," he added, "is an act deemed by the court not warranted by law, but violative of a vested legal right." The chief justice next asked if the applicant's rights have been violated, "do the laws of his country afford him a remedy?" Again Marshall answered yes: "Having this legal title to the office, he [the applicant] has a consequent right to the commission; a refusal to deliver which is a plain violation of that right, for which the laws of his country afford him a remedy."

Having found the issue justiciable, Marshall at this point properly considered whether the Supreme Court had jurisdiction over it. Was the proper remedy for the applicant "a mandamus issuing from this Court"? Under the Judiciary Act of 1789, Section 13, the Supreme Court had been

authorized "to issue . . . writs of *mandamus* . . . to . . . persons holding office
under the authority of the United States." Since the secretary of state definitely came within that description, "if this court is not authorized to issue a
writ of mandamus to such an officer, it must be because the law is unconstitutional." Marshall then argued that the Constitution prescribed specifically the Supreme Court's original jurisdiction, that this jurisdiction did not
include the power to issue writs of mandamus to federal officials, and that
Congress had no power to alter this jurisdiction. Therefore, the attempt of
Congress in the Judiciary Act of 1789 to give the Supreme Court authority
to issue writs of mandamus to public officers "appears not to be warranted
by the constitution." Consequently, Marbury's application for a mandamus
was denied.

Having declared void a section of the Judiciary Act of 1789, Marshall
then passed to his now famous argument defending the Court's power to
hold acts of Congress unconstitutional. His argument rested more upon certain general principles of constitutional government than upon specific
provisions in the Constitution itself. First, he observed that the Constitution
was the "fundamental and paramount law of the nation." Second, it was the
particular duty of the Courts to interpret the law—that is, "to say what the
law is." "Thus," the chief justice concluded, "the particular phraseology of
the constitution of the United States confirms and strengthens the principle,
supposed to be essential to all written constitutions, that a law repugnant to
the constitution is void, and that the courts, as well as other departments,
are bound by that instrument." Therefore, in conflicts between the Constitution and acts of Congress, it is the Court's duty to enforce the Constitution
and to ignore the statute—that is, to refuse to enforce the unconstitutional
law.

Taken out of context, Marshall's statement of the doctrine of judicial
review can be read as a defense of the modern judicial monopoly theory of
constitutional interpretation. In fact, however, it was not, for early in the
opinion Marshall acknowledged a sphere of political questions arising
under the Constitution exclusively reserved for executive determination.
"By the constitution," Marshall observed, "the President is invested with
certain important political powers, in the exercise of which he is to use his
own discretion, and is accountable only to his country in his political character and to his own conscience." Matters entrusted to the president under
his constitutional powers were political because they concerned "the nation,
not individual rights," Marshall said. The decision of the executive was
conclusive concerning the propriety of actions taken in this sphere.

The scope of Marshall's theory of judicial review was further qualified
by the fact that the law declared unconstitutional in *Marbury* v. *Madison*
specifically dealt with the judiciary. Marshall made no general assertion
that a judicial decision regarding the constitutionality of an act of Congress
was binding on the political branches. Nor did he contend that the inter-

pretation of the judiciary was superior to or entitled to precedence over that of Congress or the executive. He claimed no more than that each department should have final authority to pass on constitutional questions affecting its own duties and responsibilities. This was the essence of the departmental theory of constitutional interpretation. Marshall's version of the theory gave the judiciary an advantage over the political branches, since most legislation potentially involved questions of individual legal right that could be construed as appropriate for judicial determination. But the judicial interpretation of the Constitution would have only such force as its logic and persuasiveness might give it.

In the political context created by the Republican assault on the judiciary, Marshall's opinion necessarily carried political overtones. The chief justice had pointedly yet shrewdly lectured Jefferson on the legal rights of persons appointed to office and claimed for the judiciary authority to settle constitutional controversies involving individual rights. In a larger and more important sense, however, Marshall's opinion signified prudent retreat in the face of a threat to judicial independence. Though critical of the executive, Marshall refused to issue the mandamus, thus letting the administration win the battle. He recognized, moreover, a sphere of discretionary political action in which the judiciary lacked competence to judge of constitutionality or determine the meaning of the Constitution. Acquiescing to this extent in the political power that Jefferson represented, Marshall nevertheless established a limit beyond which the political branches could not go. This was the sphere of law, or individual legal right, which belonged to the judiciary and upon which the political departments could not encroach. In this sphere lay protection against undue political influence. Bold as Marshall's strategy was in *Marbury* v. *Madison,* his assertion of judicial review was thus basically defensive in nature.

The Supreme Court's accomodationist outlook was evident a few days later in the case of *Stuart* v. *Laird* (1803) where the constitutionality of the Judicial Repeal Act of 1802 was at issue. As noted, Federalists regarded the repeal of the 1801 law as unconstitutional because it deprived judges of good behavior tenure as guaranteed by the Constitution. They also argued—and it is known that Marshall agreed—that the Constitution did not authorize Congress to require Supreme Court justices to sit on circuit courts because that entailed the exercise of original jurisdiction, which only the Constitution could confer. Yet in *Stuart* v. *Laird* Marshall accepted the Circuit Court Act of 1802 as constitutional on the ground that "practice and acquiescence" in the assignment of circuit court duty to Supreme Court justices dating from the Judiciary Act of 1789 had fixed the meaning of the Constitution on this point. Significantly, the question of depriving judges of good behavior lifetime tenure did not arise, because Stuart was merely a litigant protesting the transfer of his case from a court constituted under the act of 1801 to one organized under the act of 1802. The power of Congress to organize the lower federal courts was thus the issue, and Marshall upheld it.

The political drama surrounding *Marbury* v. *Madison* notwithstanding, Marshall's decision signaled a desire to stay out of partisan controversy and defer to the political branches, provided the latter respected the independence of the judiciary and its authority to settle constitutional disputes involving individual rights. This position was agreeable to moderate Republicans, who desired an independent and strong judiciary and did not deny the right of the judiciary to decide questions of constitutionality in matters that specifically concerned it. The Federalists' decision to bring the *Marbury* case forward had in part provoked Republicans into repealing the Judiciary Act of 1801, but Marshall's accommodation of political majoritarianism in his *Marbury* opinion strengthened the Republican moderates in their ensuring struggle with the radicals over impeachment. The radicals' failure at impeachment left the moderates in control of the party and the independence of the judiciary assured.

The Burr Trial and Judicial Independence

Political controversies threatening to the courts would recur, but the foundation of judicial independence had been laid. Chief Justice Marshall's handling of the celebrated trial of Aaron Burr for treason in 1807, in the face of tremendous political pressure from the Jefferson administration, demonstrated the point.

In 1806, his political career in ruins after the tragic duel with Alexander Hamilton, Burr formed a scheme either to seize Mexico for the United States or, as many Republicans believed, to detach the southwestern states and territory from the rest of the Union. Whatever his ultimate objective, Burr procured—although he did not attend—the assemblage of a small armed force on Blennerhassett's Island in the Ohio River and conducted it down the river toward New Orleans. Subsequently, the conspiracy collapsed, and Burr was captured and brought for trial in Richmond. Jefferson, who even before Burr's arrest publicly pronounced him guilty of treason, personally directed the prosecution and worked fervently to secure his conviction. Marshall, however, presiding over the United States Circuit Court for Virginia, successfully resisted the administration's attempt to use prosecution for treason as a political instrument.

The main issue in the trial was whether Burr's actions constituted treason as defined in the Constitution. Article III, Section 3 states: "Treason against the United States, shall consist only in levying War against them, or in adhering to their Enemies, giving them Aid and Comfort. No Person shall be convicted of Treason unless on the Testimony of two Witnesses to the same overt Act, or on Confession in open Court." The defense contended that Burr could have had no part in any overt act of levying war against the United States since he was not present during the assemblage on Blennerhassett's Island. The defense thus drew a distinction between the real act of levying war, which was treason, and the act of advising such action, which was only "constructive treason." The prosecution argued the English common law doctrine that "in treason all are principals," and that Burr as procurer of the unlawful gathering was as guilty as any of the men who attended it.

The framers of the Constitution had deliberately defined treason narrowly, in reaction against the practice in Britain and in many European countries, where the offense had been loosely defined to include a variety of political acts against the state. In the Burr trial Marshall adhered to the framers' narrow conception of treason. He first declared that the element of force was essential to any attempt to prove that the act of levying war had occurred. Yet the government had not proved this fact in relation to the motley assemblage in question. Marshall further distinguished between the act of levying war, which was treason, and the act of advising such action, which was not. More difficult was the question of whether the abettor or procurer of a treasonable assemblage, as the Republicans regarded Burr, could be charged with treason.

Six months earlier in another case arising out of Burr's military adventure, *Ex parte Bollman and Swartwout,* the Jefferson administration had tried to indict two of Burr's assistants for treason. The Supreme Court ordered the two prisoners released on a writ of habeas corpus because of insufficient evidence. But Chief Justice Marshall, making a bow toward the Jeffersonian point of view, had stated that if an assemblage was gathered to effect a treasonable purpose by force, all who performed a part in it, however minute or remote, were also traitors. In the Burr trial Marshall in a similar vein raised the question of whether one who procured a treason could be said to have taken part in levying war. He refused to answer it, however, on the ground that it was not essential to a decision in the case. It was sufficient to point out merely that the government's indictment of Burr was faulty.

Burr was indicted on a general charge of levying war on Blennerhassett's Island. Yet he had not been present on the island, and Marshall rejected the government's argument that he had been "constructively present." Even if the government had indicted Burr for procuring treason, Marshall reasoned, which it had not, the specific overt act must be attested by two witnesses, in accordance with the Constitution. On this statement of the law the Republican jury found Burr not guilty. Marshall has been accused of allowing his dislike of Jefferson to politicize his decision, but in fact he courageously resisted Jefferson's attempt to write constructive treason into constitutional law. Marshall thus vindicated the integrity of the judiciary on behalf of individual rights and fair criminal procedure.

Between 1804 and 1807 three Republican justices—William Johnson, H. Brockholst Livingston, and Thomas Todd—were appointed to the Supreme Court. But they were moderates sympathetic to a strong and independent judiciary and thus acceptable to Federalists like Marshall. The subsequent appointment of Joseph Story and Gabriel Duval placed on the Court two additional Republicans who differed little from Marshall on the role of the judiciary and the importance of upholding national power. Federalists and Republicans thus reached a consensus on the place of the federal judiciary in the constitutional system which prepared the way for a series of major Supreme Court decisions in the next two decades. These decisions established the basic principles of American constitutional law.

ELEVEN

John Marshall and Constitutional Nationalism

—————————————— ✦ ✦ ✦ ——————————————

AS CHIEF JUSTICE OF THE SUPREME COURT from 1801 until his death in 1835, John Marshall was a staunch nationalist and upholder of property rights. He was not, however, as the folklore of American politics would have it, the lonely and embattled Federalist defending these values against the hostile forces of Jeffersonian democracy. On the contrary, Marshall's opinions dealing with federalism, property rights, and national economic development were consistent with the policies of the Republican party in its mercantilist phase from 1815 to 1828. Never an extreme Federalist, Marshall opposed his party's reactionary wing in the crisis of 1798–1800. Like almost all Americans of his day, Marshall was a Lockean republican who valued property not as an economic end in itself, but rather as the foundation of civil liberty and a free society. Property was the source both of individual happiness and social stability and progress.

Marshall evinced strong centralizing tendencies in his theory of federalism and completely rejected the compact theory of the Union expressed in the Virginia and Kentucky Resolutions. Yet his outlook was compatible with the Unionism that formed the basis of the post-1815 American System of the Republican party. Not that Marshall shared the democratic sensibilities of the Republicans; like his fellow Federalists, he tended to distrust the common people and saw in legislative majoritarianism a force that was potentially hostile to constitutionalism and the rule of law. But aversion to democracy was not the hallmark of Marshall's constitutional jurisprudence. Its central features rather were a commitment to federal authority versus states' rights and a socially productive and economically dynamic conception of property rights. Marshall's support of these principles placed him near the mainstream of American politics in the years between the War of 1812 and the conquest of Jacksonian Democracy.

Judicial Nationalism

In the long run, the most important decisions of the Marshall Court were those upholding the authority of the federal government against the states. *Marbury* v. *Madison* provided a jurisprudential basis for this undertaking, but the practical significance of judicial review in the Marshall era concerned the state legislatures rather than Congress. The most serious challenge to national authority resulted from state attempts to administer their judicial systems independent of the Supreme Court's appellate supervision as directed by the Judiciary Act of 1789. In successfully resisting this challenge, the Marshall Court not only averted a practical disruption of the federal system, but it also evolved doctrines of national supremacy which helped preserve the Union during the Civil War.

Marshall's first major defense of federal judicial authority came in *U.S.* v. *Peters* in 1809. The case arose out of litigation in which one Gideon Olmstead sought to recover from the state of Pennsylvania certain proceeds from the sale of a prize ship captured and sold during the Revolution. In 1803, after several years, Olmstead's title was affirmed by Judge Richard Peters in the U.S. District Court for Pennsylvania. The state legislature thereupon passed a law defying the federal court decree and authorizing the governor to use the state militia to protect the rights of the state against any process that might issue from federal authority. This action, plus Republican threats to impeach him, so intimidated Judge Peters that he refused to sign his own court order disposing of the case. Olmstead then appealed to the United States Supreme Court and obtained a writ of mandamus directing Judge Peters to issue the writ of execution.

Chief Justice Marshall's opinion in *U.S.* v. *Peters* was a strong defense of federal authority. "If the legislatures of the several states," he said, "may, at will, annul the judgments of the courts of the United States, and destroy the rights acquired under those judgments, the constitution itself becomes a solemn mockery, and the nation is deprived of the means of enforcing its laws by the instrumentality of its own tribunals." Marshall also denied that the suit was either commenced or prosecuted against the state in violation of the Eleventh Amendment. The Pennsylvania legislature ultimately yielded, but not before it protested the Supreme Court action and recommended a constitutional amendment creating an impartial tribunal to settle constitutional disputes.

A second assertion of federal judicial authority against state power came in *Fletcher* v. *Peck* in 1810. This case arose out of the famous Yazoo land fraud, in which the Georgia legislature rescinded earlier land-grant legislation passed by lawmakers who had been bribed. For reasons to be discussed below in connection with the contract clause, the Supreme Court held the rescinding measure to be unconstitutional. This was the first time the high court invalidated a state law as contrary to the Constitution, previous state laws having been negated because of conflict with federal laws and treaties.

The most important vindication of federal judicial authority against state power occurred in the controversy over the appellate jurisdiction of the Supreme Court. It will be recalled that Section 25 of the Judiciary Act of 1789 provided that whenever the highest state court rendered a decision against a person who claimed rights under the federal Constitution, laws, or treaties, the judgment could be reviewed, and possibly reversed, by the Supreme Court. At the time some of the states'-rights advocates approved this arrangement because it gave the state courts a share in a jurisdiction which might otherwise have been assigned exclusively to federal courts. Others saw only the danger to the sovereignty of the states if their highest courts could be overruled by the federal judiciary.

The first important controversy over the question of the Supreme Court's appellate jurisdiction from state courts grew out of an old case involving the vast lands of Lord Fairfax, a Virginia loyalist. During the Revolution, Virginia confiscated his estate and also enacted a law denying the right of an alien to inherit real property. After the Revolution, Virginia according to this law refused to allow Fairfax's English heir to inherit the estate, despite his rights under treaties with Great Britain. The Virginia Court of Appeals eventually upheld the state laws, but the case was taken on writ of error to the United States Supreme Court, where the Virginia decision was reversed. Since Marshall had earlier participated in the litigation, he absented himself, and the Court's decision was rendered by Justice Story. The decision practically emasculated the state's alien-inheritance and confiscation laws, which had been enforced by the state judiciary for a generation. The Virginia judges, headed by Spencer Roane, responded by declaring unconstitutional Section 25 of the Judiciary Act and by refusing to carry into effect the Supreme Court's mandate.

This refusal caused the case to be taken again to the Supreme Court as *Martin* v. *Hunter's Lessee* (1816). Story again rendered the opinion and presented a powerful argument in support of the Court's right to review decisions of state courts. He maintained that, since Congress constitutionally could have vested all federal jurisdiction in the federal courts, the voluntary granting of concurrent jurisdiction in certain cases to the state courts did not divest the Supreme Court of its appellate jurisdiction. In other words, the concurrent jurisdiction clauses of the Judiciary Act had incorporated the state courts, for certain cases, into the federal judicial system. Story declared, moreover, that the Constitution, laws, and treaties of the United States could be maintained uniformly as the supreme law of the land only if the Supreme Court had the right to review and to harmonize the decisions of all inferior courts applying that supreme law. Story thus appealed to the structure of the federal system and the logic of federal supremacy and national uniformity as the basis of his decision, rather than to a specific constitutional text.

The Court's stand was repeatedly attacked by the states'-rights Virginians. Judge Spencer Roane presented their ablest argument. He maintained not only that the Constitution established a federal rather than a consolidated union, but also that it contained no provision that authorized the central government to be the final judge of the extent of its own power, legislative or judicial. Nor, he argued, was there any clause in the Constitution that expressly denied the power of state courts to pass with finality upon the validity of their own legislation. To be sure, he said, the judges in every state were bound by the Constitution to uphold "the supreme law of the land," even when it was in conflict with the constitution and laws of any state; but they were bound as state judges only, and, therefore, their decisions were not subject to review or correction by the courts of another jurisdiction. Hence, he contended, Section 25 of the Judiciary Act was unconstitutional. In fact, Roane concluded, the state's sovereignty could not be protected against federal encroachment if the final decision on the constitutionality of both federal and state acts rested with the Supreme Court.

The Court's opportunity to answer Roane came in *Cohens* v. *Virginia* (1821). The Cohens were convicted by a Virginia court of selling lottery tickets in violation of a state statute, although they claimed the protection of an act of Congress authorizing a lottery for the District of Columbia. When the Cohens appealed to the Supreme Court under Section 25 of the Judiciary Act, counsel for Virginia denied the Court's right of review and insisted that a state could never be subjected to any private individual's suit before any judicial tribunal without the state's own consent. This immunity resulted, the state claimed, in part from the sovereign nature of the states, "as properly sovereign now as they were under the confederacy," and in part from the Eleventh Amendment, which prohibited the federal judiciary from taking jurisdiction of a suit prosecuted against a state.

Marshall began his opinion by defining the extent of federal judicial power. The jurisdiction of the federal courts under the Constitution, he observed, extended to two general classes of cases. In the first class, jurisdiction depended upon the "character of the cause," and included "all cases in law and equity arising under this constitution, the laws of the United States, and treaties made, or which shall be made, under their authority." In the second class, jurisdiction depended on the character of the parties, and included controversies between two or more states, between a state and citizens of another state, and between a state and foreign states' citizens or subjects. Any case falling within either of these clases, Marshall said, came within the jurisdiction of the federal courts, even though one of the parties might be a state of the Union.

Marshall then examined Virginia's contention that because of the sovereign, independent character of the states they could not be sued without their consent. The chief justice replied that for some purposes the states were no longer soverign—they had surrendered some of their sovereignty into the keeping of a national government. Maintenance of national supremacy, he continued, made it necessary for the states to submit to federal jurisdiction; the contrary situation would prostrate the government "at the feet of every state in the Union."

Nor did the Eleventh Amendment, which protected the states against suits by private individuals, exempt the state of Virginia from federal jurisdiction in the present instance. The present action, Marshall said, was not commenced or prosecuted by an individual against a state; rather the appeal was merely part of an action begun by the state against the Cohens, and thus the state could not claim immunity from the appeal by virtue of the Eleventh Amendment.

Finally, Marshall turned to Virginia's argument that in any event there existed no right of appeal from the state courts to the United States Supreme Court, because the state and federal judicial systems were entirely distinct and the Constitution did not provide for such appeals. Marshall's reply again was to cite the doctrine of national supremacy and to argue that the maintenance of that supremacy made such appeals necessary. "America has chosen to be, in many respects, and to many purposes, a nation; and for all these purposes, her government is complete; to all these objects, it is competent. The people have declared, that in the exercise of all powers given for these objects it is supreme. It can, then, in effecting these objects, legitimately control all individuals or governments within the American territory." In a government so constituted, Marshall continued, the national judiciary must be able to decide whether or not the constitution and laws of any state are conformable to the federal Constitution and laws, and for this purpose the Supreme Court's right to hear appeals from the state courts was a necessity.

The Court then decided the specific question at issue in favor of Virginia, holding that the congressional lottery ordinance was limited to the city of Washington and that the Cohens, therefore, had no legal right to sell tickets in Virginia.

Virginia's nominal victory brought the state little satisfaction. It was overshadowed by the Court's sweeping and definitive interpretation of its right of appellate jurisdiction over decisions of the highest state courts in all questions involving national powers. Accordingly, Virginia states' rightists, led by Judge Roane, attacked the Court's assertion of authority over the states. Roane tried to persuade ex-President Madison to join the attack, but the latter refused. Thomas Jefferson, however, ever hostile toward Marshall and doctrinaire in his states'-rights agrarianism, denounced the decision as another step in the scheme of the Supreme Court to consolidate power in the federal government.

Marshall's Theory of Federalism

Scarcely less important than the Supreme Court's defense of federal judicial authority was its refutation of the Jeffersonian strict-construction-compact theory of the Union. Although Marshall expounded his alternative theory of national supremacy in many opinions, in none did he give it more forceful expression than in *McCulloch* v. *Maryland* (1819).

The famous bank case arose out of state efforts to tax the second Bank of the United States. The bank had been created with little controversy in 1816, but within a few years it became the object of widespread hostility because of its speculative operations and occasionally fraudulent financial practices. Several southern and western states took action to prevent the bank from operating within their borders, either prohibiting it directly in the state constitution or indirectly by heavy taxation. The state of Maryland chose the latter course, levying a tax in 1818 on the bank's Baltimore branch. The validity of the law was upheld in the state courts, whereupon the bank appealed the case to the federal Supreme Court.

The case was elaborately argued by six of the greatest lawyers in the country, including Daniel Webster and William Pinckney for the bank, and Luther Martin and Joseph Hopkinson for Maryland. Three days after the close of the argument, on March 6, 1819, the chief justice handed down the unanimous judgment of the Court, upholding the constitutional power of Congress to charter the bank and to have exclusive control over it, denying the right of Maryland to interfere with the federal government by taxing its agencies, and declaring the state law unconstitutional.

The first important question involved in the case was: Has Congress power to incorporate a bank? In answering this question in the affirmative Marshall proceed to analyze at some length the nature of the Constitution and the American Union. His argument was directed mainly to upholding the doctrines of national sovereignty and broad construction. National sovereignty he upheld by emphasizing that the federal government rested directly upon a popular base, having derived its authority from the people of the states rather than from the states as sovereign entities. Marshall admitted that sovereignty was divided between the states and national government and that the states retained a sphere of sovereign authority. But the national government, he said, "though limited in its powers, is supreme within its sphere of action." This argument that national sovereignty was derived from the direct popular base of the Constitution was later to be eloquently reasserted by Webster and Lincoln and was to become one of the main tenets of American nationalism.

Marshall then set forth what was essentially the same doctrine of broad construction and implied powers that Hamilton had advanced in his bank message of 1791. He admitted that the right to establish a bank was not among the enumerated powers of Congress, but he held that the national government also possessed implied powers as well as those enumerated in the Constitution. Implied powers, he said, could be drawn from two sources. First, every legislature must by its very nature have the right to select appropriate means to carry out its powers. Second, he pointed to the necessary and proper clause, which he construed as broadly as Hamilton had previously done. "Necessary and proper," he said, did not mean "absolutely indispensable," for there were various degrees of necessity. Then followed the test for determining the constitutionality of an implied power, stated almost in the words of Hamilton's original formula: "Let the end be legitimate, let it be within the scope of the constitution, and all means which are appropriate, which are plainly adapted to that end, which are not prohibited, but consist with the letter and spirit of the constitution, are constitutional."

The second question involved in the case was whether the state of Maryland could constitutionally tax a branch of the national bank. In defending Maryland's right to tax the bank, counsel for the state had resorted to the states'-rights argument of dual federalism. The states and the federal government, according to this view, constituted two mutually exclusive fields of power, the sphere of authority of each being an absolute barrier to the encroachment of the other. The right to charter corporations was a state power, and the state, therefore, had a right to regulate or exclude from its limits corporations not chartered by itself.

In refuting this argument Marshall again invoked the principle of national supremacy. He cited the supremacy clause of the Constitution and observed that when state law conflicted with national law, the latter must prevail. Since the bank was a lawful instrument of federal authority, the congressional statute establishing it overcame any state attempt to limit or control the bank's functions. The very structure and logic of the constitutional system demanded this result. In no state, Marshall reasoned, would the people trust the legislature of another state to exercise power over them since they would have no control over it. By the same token it was impermissible for a state to tax the operations of the federal government, because it would be acting "on institutions created, not by their own constituents, but by people over whom they claim no control." Thus a state legislature might tax banks and other institutions of its constituents who had leverage over the lawmakers at the polls. The federal government might tax state-chartered institutions, since the people of the states were represented in Congress. But the state of Maryland could not tax an agency of the federal government because the people of the United States had no means of controlling or removing the legislators of Maryland.

Marshall recognized the divided sovereignty of American federalism and acknowledgd a sphere in which the states were supreme. At no time did he hold the United States to be a unitary nation or espouse an unqualified centralization. Nevertheless, Marshall's theory of Unionism unequivocally insisted on federal supremacy in cases where an apparently legitimate state power conflicted with a properly exercised federal power. Marshall rejected the view that some state powers when properly exercised were exlusive—that is, capable of excluding a constitutional exercise of federal power. He declared in *McCulloch* v. *Maryland:* "Such is the paramount character of the constitution, that its capacity to withdraw any subject from the action of even this power [i.e., the state taxing power], is admitted." The practical consequence, as Marshall stated in *Cohens* v. *Virginia,* was that in exercising its powers over the objects assigned it by the Constitution, the federal government "can . . . legitimately control all individuals or governments within the American territory."

Marshall's opinion in *McCulloch* v. *Maryland* aroused immediate interest because of its impact on the bank question. Provoked by the simultaneously occurring Missouri Compromise debate on slavery, however, a few perceptive states'-rights critics grasped its long-range theoretical significance. In a series of essays the ever-vigilant Judge Spencer Roane and his colleague Judge William Brockenbrough of Virginia attacked Marshall's opinion as a prescription for consolidation. In their view Marshall's profession of federal constitutional limitations was negated by the doctrine of implied powers and broad construction. Marshall replied in a series of anonymous essays in which he denied the charge of consolidation and insisted that the McCulloch opinion dealt strictly with the problem of the means to be used in executing the specified powers of Congress. He did not, however, retract his argument that state powers, though otherwise legitimate, could not displace federal authority. In effect, Marshall held that conflicts between state and federal exercises of power must be resolved in favor of the federal government.

The Supreme Court withstood a second states'-rights challenge to federal authority in *Osborn* v. *The Bank of the United States* (1824). The case arose when Ohio disregarded the *McCulloch* decision and persisted in its attempt to levy a $50,000 tax on the bank. To prevent collection of the tax, the bank obtained an injunction against Osborn, the state auditor, and subsequently instituted a suit for damages against him. The Supreme Court dismissed the state's contention that the tax was constitutional. The crucial question, therefore, was whether the bank's suit was a suit against a state in violation of the Eleventh Amendment. On the flimsy ground that the state was not the actual party on record, the Court held that it was not. When acting under authority of an unconstitutional statute, the Court declared, an agent of a state is personally responsible for any injury inflicted in his attempt to execute an act. This involved a transfer to constitutional law of the principle of private law that every man is responsible for the wrongs he inflicts—an important means of protecting personal liberty in view of the fact that governments could not be sued for torts. Nevertheless, the decision further negated the purpose of the Eleventh Amendment by reducing the scope of state immunity to litigation.

Vested Rights and the Contract Clause

In defending the Bank of the United States against state attack the Supreme Court protected a key feature of the Republican party's policy of national mercantilism. In a series of other cases dealing with the contract and commerce clauses of the Constitution, the Marshall Court similarly encouraged mercantilist policy.

Marshall's decisions in this sphere have usually been described as conservative because they upheld private property rights. The description is misleading if it is taken to imply that Marshall's critics and opponents in the states repudiated private property as a basic social value. On the contrary, as constitutional historian Edward S. Corwin has written, capitalist expansion, private property, and vested rights were the prepossession of the entire nation. There was, however, conflict, but it arose between groups seeking economic benefits and advantages at the state level and those seeking benefits at the national level. It is important to note also that Marshall's defense of vested rights and contracts, instead of protecting established, passive wealth, encouraged economic growth that altered the status quo. Only if one assumes that state policies were always democratic in serving the interest of the people, can one regard Marshall's anti–states'–rights economic decisions as a conservative defense of the status quo.

The contract clause of the Constitution (Article I, Section 10) was intended to safeguard property rights against state paper-money laws, debtor relief measures, and acts setting aside court decisions. It forbade the states to emit bills of credit, make anything but gold and silver legal tender in payment of debts, or enact any law impairing the obligation of contracts. These provisions gave expression to one of the basic principles of American constitutionalism—the doctrine of vested rights.

A direct outgrowth of the natural rights philosophy of the Revolutionary period, the doctrine of vested rights held that certain rights were so fundamental to an individual as to be beyond governmental control. Constitutional government existed for the protection of these natural rights, which were derived from the very nature of justice. Some of these rights were specified in the bills of rights to state constitutions, but these lists were not to be considered exclusive. Among the most important of these rights was the individual's right to be secure in his possession of private property. Therefore, the legislature of a state did not have an unlimited right to interfere in an arbitrary manner with private property. According to the doctrine of vested rights, it was the duty of the courts to declare invalid statutes considered violative of existing property rights, not necessarily by virtue of any specific provision in the federal or state constitution but rather on the grounds that such statutes violated the fundamental nature of all constitutional government.

In 1795, Justice William Paterson in the Circuit Court for Pennsylvania stated this doctrine of vested rights in guarded terms in the case of *Van-horne's Lessee* v. *Dorrance*. The decision turned upon the invalidity of an act of the Pennsylvania legislature which attempted to vest the ownership of some disputed land in one party after the land had been originally granted to another party. Paterson asserted that "the right of acquiring and possessing property and having it protected, is one of the natural inherent and unalienable rights of man. . . . The legislature, therefore, had no authority to make an act divesting one citizen of his freehold, and vesting it in another, without a just compensation. It is inconsistent with the principles of reason, justice, and moral rectitude; it is incompatible with the comfort, peace, and happiness of mankind; it is contrary to the principles of social alliance in every free government." Paterson also declared the Pennsylvania act unconstitutional because it impaired the obligation of a contract and thus was prohibited by Article I, Section 10 of the Constitution.

This doctrine of vested rights was refined and restricted somewhat by the Supreme Court in *Calder* v. *Bull* (1798). The decision in this case hinged upon whether the provision in Article I, Section 10 of the federal Constitution forbidding states to enact ex post facto laws encompassed a prohibition upon state laws which interfered with the decisions of the state courts affecting property and contractual rights. The justices hesitated to interfere with a legislative practice that had been employed extensively in certain states and decided that "ex post facto laws extend to criminal, and not to civil cases." As Justice Iredell expressed it, "Some of the most necessary and important acts of legislation are . . . founded upon the principle, that private rights must yield to public exigencies."

In another opinion Justice Samuel Chase nonetheless found occasion to pay homage to the doctrine of vested rights. "There are certain vital principles in our free Republican governments," he said, "which will determine and overrule an apparent and flagrant abuse of legislative powers; as to authorize manifest injustice by positive law; or to take away that security for personal liberty, or private property, for the protection whereof the government was established. An act of the Legislature (for I cannot call it a law) contrary to the great first principles of the social compact, cannot be considered a rightful exercise of legislative authority."

In the next three decades the doctrine of vested rights was frequently invoked by state courts as a means of restricting state legislative power. These decisions did not establish an absolute guarantee against state interference with property holdings, but they did require convincing justification in public policy before a state could legislate in this sphere. In a series of obscure and generally nonpolitical cases state courts applied vested rights ideas to impose limitations on states' powers of taxation, eminent domain, and local sovereignty. In the process they frequently for the first time exercised the power of judicial review.

Instinctive as the doctrine of vested rights was in America, it proved less effective as a means of negating legislative acts than specific constitutional provisions. Its chief political drawback was that it could mean anything the judiciary wanted it to mean—a possibility that was bound to arouse opposition among supporters of popular sovereignty and legislative ascendancy. Increasingly, therefore, courts substituted documentary guarantees of property rights for the vested-rights doctrine. During the Marshall era the contract clause of the Constitution, infused with vested-rights meaning, served as the main instrument for protecting private property against legislative interference.

The first case involving the contract clause was *Fletcher* v. *Peck* (1810), the Yazoo land fraud case. In 1795 the Georgia legislature, influenced in part by bribery of many of its members, had granted millions of acres of land along the Yazoo River to certain land companies. At its next session the legislature rescinded the grant, but not before some of the land had been sold to innocent third parties. The status of the Yazoo lands was debated repeatedly in Congress and dragged through the courts until it finally reached the Supreme Court in 1810.

Chief Justice Marshall, speaking for the Court, upheld the original grant made by the Georgia legislature on the ground that the courts could not inquire into the motives of legislators no matter how corrupt those motives might be. Marshall's intent was not to uphold fraudulent transactions, which could be corrected by courts at common law, but rather to establish as a matter of general jurisprudence that courts could not lightly second-guess legislatures. More important, legislatures could not simply invalidate contracts. Thus Marshall challenged the validity of the rescinding act on the ground that it was a fundamental interference with private rights and hence beyond the constitutional authority of any legislative body—an allusion to the doctrine of vested rights.

Marshall was not willing to rest the decision entirely on such general principles, however, and he next held that the Georgia rescinding act came within the constitutional provision forbidding any state to impair the obligation of contracts. A contract he defined as "a compact between two or more parties," and as "either executory or executed." Either kind of contract contained obligations binding on the parties. A grant made by a state and accepted by the grantee, he added, is in substance an executed contract, the obligation of which still continues. The constitutional provision, he observed, made no distinction between public and private contracts. The rescinding act was, therefore, invalid.

In holding that the obligation-of-contracts clause applied to public grants as well as to private contracts, Marshall in all probability misconstrued the intent of the Constitution's framers. The preponderant evidence indicates that the convention had intended merely to prohibit the states from interfering with the contractual relations of two or more private persons. By holding that contracts entered into by the state also came under the contract clause, Marshall gave the provision a far broader meaning than the convention had intended.

Two years later, in *New Jersey* v. *Wilson* (1812), the Court extended the contract clause to protect and perpetuate a state grant of exemption from taxation. Some years before the Revolution, New Jersey had granted the Delaware Indians exemption from taxation on certain lands held by them. After the Revolution the lands in question were sold to white men, and when New Jersey attempted to tax them, the owners appealed to the courts, claiming that the original grant of tax exemption had passed to the new owners. When the case reached the Supreme Court, Marshall wrote an opinion holding that New Jersey's attempt to tax the lands involved constituted an impairment of New Jersey's obligation of contract.

The decision not only lacked adequate precedent but also had the effect of impairing New Jersey's indispensable power of taxation. Nevertheless, Marshall's opinion was accepted by the entire Court and has never been repudiated by that body. As a consequence many later state constitutions either prohibited or sharply limited legislative grants of tax immunity.

Green v. *Biddle* (1823), a case involving the relationship between the contract clause and political agreements between states, provided yet another example of the Supreme Court's willingness to promote land speculation in the face of state regulation. At the time of Kentucky's separation from Virginia, the two states had entered into an agreement by which Kentucky recognized the validity of land titles issued under Virginia law. Land titles in Kentucky were nonetheless extremely confused because of the large number of overlapping and conflicting claims, and for many years after 1792 they gave rise to a constant procession of lawsuits in the state's courts. In order to remedy this situation, the Kentucky legislature enacted a series of laws providing that no claimant should be awarded possession of land to which he proved title without compensating the occupant for the latter's improvement; in default thereof, the disputed title was to rest in the occupant upon payment of the value of the land without improvements. By implication at least, these laws impaired the full validity of land titles secured under the Kentucky-Virginia agreement, and the acts in question were, therefore, attacked in the federal courts.

The Supreme Court, speaking through Justice Bushrod Washington, held that the contract clause in the Constitution applied to contracts between two states as well as those between private persons or between a state and a private individual. The Court also denied Kentucky's claim that the agreement in question was invalid because Congress had not given its assent to the agreement as required by the Constitution. The Constitution, Justice Washington observed, required no particular mode of consent by

Congress, and he held that Congress had implicitly assented to the compact when it admitted Kentucky to the Union.

The opinion provoked widespread criticism, for the prevailing opinion was that the Convention of 1787 had never intended to include interstate political agreements within the contract clause. In Congress there arose a renewed demand for reform and restriction of the federal judiciary. Kentucky, embittered because the Court's decision benefited numerous absentee landowners, continued for the most part to enforce its own laws, thereby virtually ignoring the Court's ruling. Moreover, later cases involving interstate issues were usually decided under the interstate compact clause.

The Corporation in Constitutional Law

In expanding the contract clause to protect vested rights the Supreme Court defended not static, entrenched wealth, but rather an expansive, dynamic agrarian capitalism that supplied venture capital for more general economic development. The growth of the corporation, which the Supreme Court also promoted through its interpretation of the contract clause, was the chief manifestation of this wider economic purpose.

In the colonial period, as we have seen, the corporation was principally a method of political organization, although occasionally it served as the means by which government accomplished broad social purposes such as providing transportation facilities for the public. In the early nineteenth century the corporation became an instrument of general economic development. Legally, a corporation was a voluntary association of individuals who upon application to the legislature received specific and exclusive powers and privileges for carrying on a particular enterprise or activity. Though consisting of private persons, the legal character of the corporation was that of a public institution created by legislative authority and subject to governmental regulation and control. Nevertheless, the fact that private individuals actually managed them made corporations also in some sense private as well as public institutions.

In the period 1800 to 1820, as corporations came to serve a wider variety of productive purposes going well beyond their traditional use in building transportation facilities, hospitals, and the like, the *de facto* private character of the corporation was elevated into constitutional principle. In the case of *Terrett* v. *Taylor* in 1815, the Supreme Court took this step by announcing a distinction between public and private corporations and the degree of government control to which they were subject. Justice Joseph Story explained for the Court that public corporations, by which he meant counties, townships, and cities, could be modified by the legislature. Private corporations, however, which presumably meant all other kinds of incorporated bodies, enjoyed more substantial protection against legislative interference under "the principles of natural justice" and "the fundamental laws of every free government." Story did not say how much protection private corporations were entitled to, and he probably did not intend businesses incorporated under state law to be completely beyond the scope of subsequent legislative regulation. But by recognizing what had previously been thought a contradiction in terms—that is, a private corporation—Story enabled an increasingly large segment of business enterprise to receive the protection that the vested-rights doctrine and its documentary constitutional equivalent, the contract clause, gave to individual citizens.

Building on Story's distinction between public and private corporations but eschewing his natural law orientation, the Supreme Court in *Dartmouth College* v. *Woodward* (1819) brought private corporations under the protection of the contract clause. In doing so Chief Justice Marshall further expanded the contract clause by ruling that a charter of incorporation was a private contract protected against legislative infringement by the Constitution.

The case grew out of the efforts of the New Hampshire legislature to alter the charter granted by George III in 1769 to the trustees of Dartmouth College, conveying to them "forever" the right to govern the institution and to fill vacancies in their own body. The charter continued unchanged throughout the Revolutionary period, but in 1816 the Republican governor and legislature, believing that the old charter was based upon principles more congenial to monarchy than to "a free government," attempted to bring the college under public control. Accordingly, they passed laws that virtually took the control of the institution from the hands of the Federalist-dominated trustees and placed it under a board of overseers appointed by the governor. The trustees thereupon turned for relief to the state judiciary, but the New Hampshire Superior Court upheld the legislature's acts, chiefly on the ground that the college was essentially a public corporation whose powers and franchises were exercised for public purposes and were, therefore, subject to public control. The trustees of the college then appealed the case upon writ of error to the Supreme Court.

By a vote of 5 to 1, the Court decided that the New Hampshire laws in question were unconstitutional as impairment of the obligation of contract. The chief justice, in giving the opinion of the Court, admitted an important constitutional argument of the state: that "the framers of the constitution did not intend to restrain the states in the regulation of their civil institutions, adopted for internal government." He went to great length, however, to demonstrate that Dartmouth College was not a public institution subject to state control but instead was a "private eleemosynary institution." Although he cited no authorities, Marshall declared that the charter granted by the British crown to the trustees was a contract within the meaning of the Constitution. By virtue of the Revolution, he said, the powers and duties of government had devolved upon the people of New Hampshire. At any time prior to the adoption of the Constitution the power of the state to repeal or alter the charter was restricted only by the state constitution, but after 1789 that power was further restrained by the obligation-of-contract clause.

The *Dartmouth College* decision aided business interests at a time when privately funded internal-improvement companies, including some in Virginia in which Marshall had an interest, were vulnerable to legislative attack. Marshall's purpose, however, was not to place private corporations beyond public control, but rather to assure capitalists the expectation of a reasonable return on their investment in return for providing public improvements and services useful to the community at large. The legislative charter was an instrument both of promotion and regulation, for the mutual benefit of both private entrepreneur and the society. Accordingly, Marshall's *Dartmouth College* opinion made it clear that state legislatures might reserve the right to repeal or to modify the charters that they granted, and in the future most legislatures took advantage of this right. In the coming decades the number and importance of private corporations in the fields of transportation, finance, and industry rapidly expanded, but this expansion was due less to their legally protected position than to the economic advantages they offered.

The Contract Clause and Bankruptcy Laws

In the context of the panic of 1819, state bankruptcy laws raised further constitutional questions about the scope of the contract clause as a limitation on state legislative power. The Supreme Court insisted on the applicability of the clause in bankruptcy matters, but, responding to changing political circumstances in the 1820s, it eventually permitted the states a degree of latitude in this field.

Sturges v. *Crowninshield* (1819) involved the constitutionality of a New York law for the relief of insolvent debtors from debts contracted before the law was enacted. Two related issues were involved: first, whether the state had the right to enact any bankruptcy legislation in the light of the provision in the Constitution specifically delegating to Congress the power to make uniform laws on bankruptcy; and second, whether the New York act violated the contract clause. Marshall held that state bankruptcy legislation was permissible in the absence of any federal statute, provided the act in question did not violate other constitutional requirements. However, he also held that the New York law impaired the obligation of contracts. Any law, said Marshall, that released a man in whole or in part from his agreement to pay another man a sum of money at a certain time impaired the obligation of contracts and could not be reconciled with the Constitution.

Sturges v. *Crowninshield* resulted in a general limitation of state authority over bankruptcy matters. The economic depression caused by the panic of 1819, however, led several states to seek a loophole in the decision by enacting bankruptcy laws applying solely to debts contracted after the statute's passage. Reflecting a shift toward the states'-rights point of view, the Supreme Court approved this type of legislation.

In *Ogden* v. *Saunders* (1827) the Court decided, 4 to 3, that a state bankruptcy law discharging both the person of the debtor and his future acquisition of property did not impair the obligation of contracts entered into after the passage of the law. Six justices offered opinions, which revealed that the Court was not only badly divided on the present question but had also been divided in *Sturges* v. *Crowninshield.* Justice Johnson now admitted that the earlier decision had been arrived at as a compromise among the justices rather than as an act of "legal adjudication." Johnson and other states'-rights–minded justices, it appeared, had acquiesced in the invalidation of state laws regulating anterior contracts only with the proviso that the opinion be so guarded as to secure the states' power over posterior contracts. It was this latter point that the present majority now insisted upon.

Among the majority justices Johnson offered a neo-Jeffersonian defense of state authority to regulate contractual dealings and relationships. In his view, "all the contracts of men receive a relative, and not a positive interpretation: for the rights of all must be held and enjoyed in subserviency to the good of the whole. The state construes them, the state applies them, and the state decides how far the social exercise of the rights they give us over each other can be justly asserted." This was substantially an anticipation of the later doctrine of the state's police power.

Marshall vigorously dissented, the first and only time he did so on an important question of constitutional law. Arguing that the Constitution protected all contract, past or future, from state legislation that in any manner impaired their obligation, he maintained that the position of the majority would virtually destroy the contract clause. He admitted, however, that the constitutional prohibition of the impairment of the obligation of contracts did not prohibit a state legislature from changing the remedies for the enforcement of contracts.

On another issue raised in *Ogden* v. *Saunders* Johnson joined Marshall in a majority opinion. They both declared that a state's insolvency law could not discharge a contract owed to a citizen of another state, since such action would produce "a conflict of sovereign power, and a collision with the judicial powers granted to the United States." In sum, the Court's position was that state bankruptcy and insolvency laws were unconstitutional when they operated on contracts entered into before their passage, but were constitutional with respect to contracts entered into after their passage. Second, they were unconstitutional if they invalidated a contract owed to a citizen of another state. Thus the Court took the first important step in restricting the scope of the contract clause as it had been interpreted between 1810 and 1819.

The Commerce Clause

If the contract clause protected corporate development against undue state interference, the commerce clause provided a means of creating a national free trade area as an encouragement to economic expansion. In a series of commerce power cases the Supreme Court in the 1820s pursued this nationalistic economic purpose, although here, too, it made concessions to the states'-rights point of view.

One of the chief objectives of the framers of the Constitution had been to replace the confused condition of foreign and interstate commercial relations prevailing in 1787 with an orderly and uniform system. Consequently, the Constitution empowered Congress "to regulate Commerce with foreign Nations, and among the several States, and with the Indian Tribes." After the adoption of the Constitution the volume of both foreign and interstate commerce increased rapidly. Congress early made legal provision for the regulation of ships and cargoes from foreign countries and passed a law providing for the licensing of vessels engaged in the important coastal trade. On the other hand, Congress took virtually no positive action for the control of interstate commerce, but such commerce flourished without much federal aid or regulation, since the states abandoned their former discriminations against vessels and products from other states.

The constitutional definition of commerce and the power of Congress over it meanwhile were subjects of intermittent controversy. By 1820 two theories existed. The first, deriving from the view that seems generally to have prevailed in the eighteenth century and that Alexander Hamilton supported, interpreted commerce "among the states" to mean all commercial activity in the United States, irrespective of state lines. The power of Congress in this view was a plenary legislative power, the same as it would be if the United States were a unitary government. The second theory, advanced originally by Jefferson in his bank opinion of 1791, held that the language of Article I, Section 8 referred to commerce *between* two or more states—that is, interstate commerce. In this territorially rather than functionally defined conception, commerce was either confined to a single state, in which case it was beyond the scope of federal legislative power, or it crossed from one state into another, in which case Congress could legislate concerning it. In 1824, when the Supreme Court first addressed the question, neither of these theories was written into constitutional law, although the evidence of congressional debate on internal-improvements legislation suggests that the interstate view was gaining favor.

The Marshall Court's first venture into commerce clause interpretation dealt with the strategically important steamboat business. During the first quarter of the nineteenth century the steamboat was developed into an important means of transportation in the coastal trade and especially on the rivers and lakes of the interior of the country. By the 1820s the free development of interstate trade by this new means of transportation was being threatened by attempts of various states to grant exclusive privileges to various interests over the steam navigation of "state waters." This policy led to retaliation of state against state. Thus monopoly and localism were joining hands in a movement of state restriction upon interstate commerce that was reminiscent of the days of the Confederation.

In 1808 Robert Fulton and Robert Livingston, pioneers in the development of a practical steamboat, secured from the New York legislature a grant of the exclusive right to operate steamboats on the state's waters. From this monopoly Aaron Ogden secured the exclusive right to certain steam navigation across the Hudson River between New York and New Jersey. Thomas Gibbons, however, proceeded to engage in competition with Ogden, claiming the right under a license granted under the federal coasting act. Ogden's suit to restrain Gibbons from engaging in this interstate navigation was sustained by the New York courts in 1819 and 1820, with Chancellor James Kent, perhaps the most learned jurist in America, upholding Ogden and the steamboat monopoly act. Gibbons appealed to the United States Supreme Court, where the case of *Gibbons* v. *Ogden* was finally heard in 1824.

Although the argument of the case took a wide range, Chief Justice Marshall, in handing down the unanimous decision of the Court, devoted himself to four main points or questions. First, what does commerce comprehend? Second, to what extent may Congress exercise its commercial regulatory power within the separate states? Third, is congressional power to regulate interstate commerce exclusive, or does a state have concurrent power in this field? Fourth, should the commerce power of Congress (and inferentially other powers, too) be construed broadly for the national welfare or be construed strictly in order to protect the reserved police powers of the states?

In discussing the first question, Marshall rejected the argument of Ogden's counsel that commerce should be narrowly defined as "traffic" or the mere buying or selling of goods, including only such transportation as was purely auxiliary thereto. "Commerce, undoubtedly, is traffic," he said, "but it is something more; it is intercourse." It encompasses navigation and general commercial relations. The meaning of the word, he added, is just as comprehensive when applied to "commerce among the several states" as when applied to foreign commerce, where it admittedly comprehends "every species of commercial intercourse."

Turning to the second and vital question of the power to regulate commerce, Marshall accepted the more confining interstate view, although, perhaps significantly, he did not use that term. "Comprehensive as the word 'among' is," he wrote in explication of the language of the commerce clause, "it may very properly be restricted to that commerce which concerns more states than one." The corollary was that congressional power did not extend to "that commerce, which is completely internal, which is carried on between man and man in a state, or between different parts of the same state, and which does not extend to or affect other states." Although this language can be interpreted as permitting federal regulation of intrastate commerce if it can be shown to have an effect on business in another state, its clearer import was to endorse the states'-rights or *interstate* restriction on the commerce power of the federal government.

As Marshall adopted the more limited view of congressional power, so he in effect conceded a concurrent state power to regulate commerce in the absence of federal legislation. Counsel for Gibbons had argued that the constitutional grant of power to Congress was exclusive, meaning that whether or not Congress legislated, the states had no concurrent power over interstate commerce. Justice Johnson endorsed this more centralizing view, but Chief Justice Marshall did not. Instead, he struck down the New York monopoly grant on the ground that it conflicted with the federal Coasting Act of 1793. He went on to explain that the states could pass inspection laws and other health and safety measures which might have a remote effect on commerce. Formally, Marshall held such laws to be an exercise of the states' reserved powers—what would later be called the police power—rather than the commerce power. Nevertheless, in a practical sense Marshall recognized a concurrent state commerce power and thus acknowledged the heightened concern for states' rights in the mid-1820s.

Although conceding more scope to the states'-rights point of view than he ordinarily did, Marshall's opinion was strongly centralizing in answering the fourth question of whether the enumerated powers of Congress should be construed narrowly or broadly. At the outset, in the most emphatic terms, he rejected strict construction, arguing that it "would cripple the government, and render it unequal to the objects for which it is declared to be instituted." In closing he reiterated his criticism of those who, by narrowly contracting federal power, would "explain away the constitution of our country, and leave it a magnificent structure indeed, to look at, but totally unfit for use." And in asserting congressional power over commerce he described it as plenary, limited only by the "wisdom and discretion of congress, their identity with the people, and the influence which their constituents possess at elections." Regarding the matter thus as a political question, Marshall in effect denied the judiciary any role in restraining congressional exercise of the commerce power.

Because monopolies were unpopular, the Gibbons decision, unlike most of Marshall's centralizing opinions, received wide popular approval. It

had the useful effect, moreover, of keeping steamboat navigation and subsequently railroad transportation free of the impediment of state monopolies and competitive on a national scale. At the same time, however, the
decision failed to prevent the states from regulating interstate commerce in
other respects. In subsequent years states legislated on pilotage, turnpikes,
ferries, canal boats, railroads, and the immigrant passenger trade in ways
that clearly had interstate effect. Thus *Gibbons* v. *Ogden* did not thwart the
powerful current of state mercantilism and economic policy making that
characterized Jacksonian Democracy.

Before these results became clear, however, the Marshall Court handed
down two further opinions drawing a line between state powers and constitutionally protected commerce. In the first of these cases, *Brown* v. *Maryland* (1827), Marshall formulated the "original package" doctrine. The
question at issue was whether a Maryland statute requiring wholesalers of
imported goods to take out a special license came within the state's taxing
power or infringed upon the federal commerce power. The chief justice
declared that whenever imported goods became "mixed up with the mass of
property in the country," they became subject to the state's taxing power,
but that as long as the goods remained the property of the importer and in
the original form or package, any state tax upon them constituted an unconstitutional interference with the regulation of commerce. The principle
was stated so broadly that it would apply to interstate as well as foreign
commerce and to any degree of state taxation.

Two years later, however, in *Willson* v. *Black Bird Creek Marsh Company* (1829), Marshall upheld a Delaware law authorizing the damming of a
creek to exclude water from a marsh, even though the stream was navigable
and had occasionally been used in the coasting trade. Willson's vessel was
licensed under the same coasting act as that cited in *Gibbons* v. *Ogden,* and
Marshall, therefore, might have held that the state statute infringed upon
the federal commerce power. Instead, however, he held that the federal
government had not yet acted, and that the state's regulation was, therefore,
valid in the absence of any federal statute. Thus Marshall and the Court
anticipated an important doctrinal trend that would become the central
theme in commerce-clause interpretation under Marshall's successor,
Roger B. Taney.

Marshall's Contribution to American Constitutionalism

John Marshall's signal achievement was to vindicate federal authority
against state attempts to deny the supervisory power of the federal government which would have made the federal union in effect a confederation of
sovereign states. Marshall accomplished this purpose by writing into constitutional law the theory of national-supremacy federalism. Its central

principle was that the federal government, founded by the constituent act of the people of the United States, possessed sovereign power in relation to the objects or purposes assigned to it by the Constitution. In the proper exercise of its constitutional powers, this government could control any person or other government within the territorial United States.

Under Marshall's leadership the Supreme Court blocked state efforts to repudiate the appellate power of the federal judiciary and declared unconstitutional acts of more than half of the state legislatures. By invalidating state laws the Court prevented the states from becoming the final arbiter in disputes between themselves and the federal government. Opponents of the Supreme Court tried to curb its power through congressional action, especially between 1819 and 1827, when state laws were being set aside at almost every session of the Court. The most drastic attempt to restrict the Court was initiated by Senator Richard Johnson of Kentucky, who proposed to constitute the Senate a court of last resort in all cases involving the constitutionality of state laws or to which a state should be a party. Bills were also introduced to increase the size of the Supreme Court and to require more than a bare majority decision to invalidate a state law. None of these measures was adopted. In 1831 the House Judiciary Committee reported a bill repealing Section 25 of the Judiciary Act of 1789, under which the Supreme Court heard cases on appeal from the state courts, but this proposal was also defeated.

Reflecting the growing reaction against Republican national mercantilism, the Supreme Court in the last decade of the Marshall era gave broader scope to state powers and less consistent protection to property rights. The state of Georgia defied judgments of the Supreme Court in cases concerning the rights of Indian tribes, and in 1833 the Court handed down an exceedingly important states'-rights decision in holding, in *Barron* v. *Baltimore,* that the Fifth Amendment and the Bill of Rights limited only the federal government and not the states. Nevertheless, when John Marshall died in 1835 constitutional law firmly and unequivocally recognized the sovereignty of the federal government and its supremacy over the states. Moreover, the Court had acquired sufficient influence and institutional autonomy to enable it to act most of the time as the nation's pre-eminent arbiter of constitutional controversy. Despite its expansion of judicial authority and prestige, however, the Marshall Court rarely challenged the political branches of the government. For the most part, its policies complemented those of the national legislature.

The use of Marshall's nationalist doctrines to support federal regulatory legislation in the twentieth century has led many scholars to regard his constitutional outlook as anticipating modern judicial liberalism, with its emphasis on the creation of new governmental powers to meet new social conditions and needs. To be sure, Marshall's doctrine of implied powers emphasized the exercise of federal power rather than its limitation. Moreover, in *McCulloch* v. *Maryland,* in language that has often been taken as foreshadowing modern judicial activism, Marshall declared: "We must never forget that it is a *constitution* we are expounding ... intended to endure for ages to come, and consequently, to be adapted to the various *crises* of human affairs." Yet Marshall did not mean that new powers could be fashioned out of whole cloth by judicial or legislative interpretation for purposes or objects not encompassed by the Constitution.

Answering the confining literalism of the Virginia strict constructionists, who attacked the theory of implied powers as a prescription for centralization, Marshall denied any intention of augmenting the powers of Congress or engaging in "latitudinous" or "liberal" construction of the Constitution in this regard. Defending his opinion in *McCulloch* v. *Maryland* in a series of anonymous newspaper essays in 1819, Marshall stated that the Court's chief concern in that case was with the means by which delegated powers were employed and the purposes of federal authority carried out. He reiterated what he had written in the *McCulloch* opinion: that if Congress, "under the pretext of executing its powers," should "pass laws for the accomplishment of objects not intrusted to the government," the judiciary would declare them unconstitutional. Marshall, of course, recognized the fact of social change, but he denied that social change, except as it was translated into proposals for constitutional amendments, changed the Constitution. In the fundamental purposes it defined and in the powers it assigned to the federal government, the Constitution was in Marshall's view a fixed, objective structure, not a growing, living organism as later generations—seeking to escape the restrictions of the written Constitution—would conceive of it. Finally, though emphasizing implied powers, Marshall never disavowed the jurisprudential theory of *Marbury* v. *Madison.* This theory enjoined courts impartially to declare the law, rather than in legislative fashion to make law and apply it on grounds of expediency as an instrument of policy.

Although not a forerunner of modern liberal jurisprudence, Marshall's refutation of the crabbed legalisms of his states'-rights adversaries was of the greatest constitutional significance. The distinctive mark of Marshall's constitutional jurisprudence was his willingness to base decisions on broadly political considerations of structure and relationship in the constitutional order, rather than on specific constitutional texts. Denying that the Constitution was a mere legal code, he regarded the basic principles on which the government was founded as the ultimate guide to decision making. Of these principles, the most important was the sovereignty of the federal government in the exercise of its constitutional powers.

TWELVE

Jacksonian Democracy and Dual Federalism

◆ ◆ ◆

THE ELECTION OF ANDREW JACKSON as a states'-rights candidate in 1828 effected a political realignment which established the basic direction of constitutional change for the next generation. Intended to restore the decentralized constitutionalism of Jeffersonian republicanism, the movement over which Jackson presided was the catalyst in creating the American two-party system essentially in its modern form. As a direct corollary of that development, Jackson as chief executive strengthened and democratized presidential power beyond anything Jefferson had contemplated. Consciously identifying himself with the people, Jackson stimulated reforms through methods of direct political action which often disregarded established institutions and constitutional procedures.

In an age of intense nationalism and increasing nationalization of social and cultural life, Jacksonian Democracy paradoxically resulted in a shift of power from the federal government to the states. This shift was a response to the localism of American politics and to the need of an increasingly apprehensive class of southern slaveholders to protect their peculiar institution against political attack. Based in a constitutional sense on the evolution of strict construction and states' rights into the theory of dual federalism, Jacksonian Democracy was committed to the restoration of republicanism, the defense of slavery, and the preservation of the Union. When changes in public attitudes toward slavery subsequently caused these purposes to become contradictory, Democratic dual federalism was transformed into the militantly proslavery doctrine of state sovereignty under which the South moved resolutely toward secession and civil war.

Jacksonian Ideology

Joined loosely under the Jacksonian banner were three distinct sectional groups: plain republicans of the North; western farmers, frontiersmen, and entrepreneurs; and southern planters. Old Republicans in New York and Virginia, led by Martin Van Buren and Thomas Ritchie, respectively, in the early 1820s began to organize a party to oppose the centralizing policies of the Adams administration. Critical of the speculative tendencies encouraged by the American System, as manifested in the Panic of 1819, Van Buren spoke for northern farmers, artisans, and working men in arguing for a return to the laissez-faire, strict construction, and states'-rights outlook of agrarian republican theory. Van Buren found a ready ally in the Virginia states'-rights critics of federal supremacy, who saw an ominous threat to the South in the recently concluded Missouri crisis.

In 1819 a united front of Federalist and northern Republican antislavery representatives denied Missouri, a slave territory, admission to the Union. A compromise was eventually reached that permitted Missouri to enter the Union as a slave state, but that prohibited slavery in Louisiana Purchase territory north of 36° 30′ latitude. Perceiving a threat to the southern social order, Virginia Republicans looked for protection to a national political organization based on states' rights and strict construction which could prevent federal power from being used against slavery. Accordingly, they agreed to cooperate with Van Buren, who subsequently brought into the emerging coalition a western element. Though more for entrepreneurial than ideological reasons, the original Jackson men from Tennessee, Kentucky, and Ohio shared the antibanking, laissez-faire views of the Old Republicans. They contributed to the party furthermore an antieastern bias and democratic resentment against the special privilege on which the American System depended. Finally, for political as well as proslavery ideological reasons, a contingent of South Carolina politicians led by John C. Calhoun joined the Jackson movement in protest against the national mercantilism of the Adams administration.

Placed in office under a popular mandate that rejected centralization and promised to restore government to the people, but was agreeably vague on specific questions of policy, the Jackson administration defined its Old Republican and dual-federalist character in dismantling the American System. In pursuing this negative task Jackson made vigorous use of federal executive power. He was also aided by a highly disciplined national party organization that introduced into political life an aggressively egalitarian outlook. Yet the essence of the old Republican spirit was local and individual liberty. And while this liberty was threatened by mercantilist centralization, it was also threatened by the opposite doctrine of state sovereignty and nullification. From the Jacksonian standpoint, Union was essential for republican liberty not so much as a source of power for the attainment of social purposes, but rather as a territorially expanding framework within which the states and the people could pursue their interests and govern themselves. The theory of dual federalism expressed this balanced conception of the Union and the heightened importance of the states in Democratic constitutionalism.

Taking as its point of departure the orthodox notion of federalism as divided sovereignty, dual federalism posited the existence of mutually exclusive and reciprocally limiting spheres of state and federal power, neither of which was superior to the other in a categorical sense. Dual-federalist theory attached as much importance to the Tenth Amendment, reserving to the states or the people powers not delegated to the general government, as John Marshall did to the supremacy clause. But Jacksonians by no means abandoned the idea of federal sovereignty. The nullification crisis of 1832–33, which saw Jackson repudiate South Carolina's assertion of state sovereignty, demonstrated the dual-federalist commitment to Union and federal sovereignty. As an alternative to centralizing mercantilism, however, the historical and political logic of dual federalism was to enlarge the power of the states. Accordingly, its chief practical significance consisted in self-denying actions by the federal government which allowed national economic policy making to be determined by the states.

The Jackson administration first clarified its Old Republican–dual-federalist identity in relation to the internal-improvements question. By 1828 a substantial program of federally supported internal improvements existed, which many western Democrats, despite their dissatisfaction with the American System in general, favored. In 1830, however, in order to reassure northern and southern Old Republicans of the party's commitment to strict construction, Jackson vetoed four internal-improvement bills, including one for twenty miles of turnpike in Kentucky called the Maysville Road.

Jackson rejected the narrowest states'-rights view of the internal-improvements question—viz., Madison's argument that the federal government could take no action in this field without a constitutional amendment. He accepted as constitutional the practice of appropriating federal money for state or privately constructed improvements. But he held that a genuine national purpose must justify such expenditures, and he concluded that no such purpose was present in the Maysville appropriation, a purely local project lying entirely within the state of Kentucky. To disregard this requirement, reasoned Jackson, "would of necessity lead to the subversion of the federal system." Because western demands persisted, the Maysville veto did not lead to the discontinuation of federal support for internal improvements. In fact the Jackson administration approved other measures scarcely more national or less local than the Kentucky road. In doing so, however, the administration did not formulate a coherent national policy but rather acquiesced in state demands. And as the Democratic party became more ideologically consistent in the late 1830s, the national government withdrew entirely from the internal-improvements field and left it to the states. The culmination of this approach was President James K. Polk's veto in 1846 of a bill appropriating federal money for river and harbor improvements on the narrow states'-rights ground that Congress possessed no power whatsoever in this sphere.

On other issues the Jackson administration deferred to the states, in accordance with Old Republican–dual-federalist ideology. A problem that arose in the mid-1830s was how to dispose of a surplus in the federal Treasury caused by the imminent extinguishment of the national debt and continued high revenues from government land sales. The Whig party, successor to the Adams-Clay National Republicans of 1832, in orthodox mercantilist fashion proposed to distribute the proceeds of land sales to the states, with the proviso that the money be applied to education, internal improvements, or the reduction of state taxes. In support of the proposal Henry Clay argued that the public domain was a great national heritage which should be used by the federal government for the benefit of all the people. Democrats, on the other hand, proposed to reduce the price of public lands and ultimately dispose of the federal surplus by ceding all public lands to the states in which they lay. They thus sought to appeal both to western land hunger and to the Old Republican fear of federal power and prestige, which they believed derived in part from the national government's control of the public domain. Jackson vetoed a distribution bill in 1833, but in 1836 Democrats passed a measure that satisfied the states'-rights point of view by depositing the federal surplus (about $30 million) on account with the states. Constitutionally, Democrats distinguished between depositing money, which was acceptable, and making an outright gift, which was not. It was understood, however, that the deposits would never be recalled, so in effect the act of 1836 gave money to the states with no strings attached.

Georgia and Federal Indian Policy

In Indian affairs the Jackson administration also acquiesced to the states, allowing them to determine national policy for all practical purposes. Denied citizenship, exempted from taxation, and not counted in the apportionment of representation and direct taxes, Indians within the territorial limits of the United States occupied an indefinite status under the Constitution. From the start of the government, however, following the British example, federal officials employed the constitutionally prescribed power to regulate commerce with the Indian tribes, and the treaty-making and war powers to license and regulate trade with the Indians and to sign treaties with them for the acquisition of Indian lands. The government's purpose was to remove the Indians so white settlement could proceed, while protecting them in unceded lands. Unable to carry out this purpose, the government in the 1820s urged the removal of the Indian tribes to the West. Several southern states within whose limits the tribes resided expedited the process by taking independent action against the Indians, and the Jackson administration supported these efforts by securing the adoption of the Indian

Removal Act of 1830. The measure appropriated $500,000 for treaties that would remove the southeastern tribes west of the Mississippi.

In the early 1830s matters came to a head in a conflict between the state of Georgia, backed by the Jackson administration, and the Cherokee Indians. In 1802 Georgia ceded her western lands to the United States in return for a promise to secure for the state at federal expense all Indian lands lying within the state "as early as the same can possibly be obtained on reasonable terms." The Indians in Georgia were the Creeks and Cherokees, tribes that had adopted an agricultural way of life and were determined not to give up their lands. Federal evacuation proceeded very slowly, therefore, and the Georgia government, dissatisfied with federal inaction, in 1826 ordered state surveys of lands that the Creeks had been "persuaded" to cede. President Adams threatened to use the army to restrain Georgia's surveyors, and an open conflict between federal and state authority was averted only by the capitulation of the Creeks and their removal west. The conflict continued, however, when the Cherokees in 1827 adopted a written constitution and proclaimed themselves an independent state. In response to this action the Georgia legislature extended state law over Indian territory, annulled all Indian law, and directed the seizure of all Indian lands.

In accordance with the newly asserted jurisdiction, the state presently tried and convicted a Cherokee Indian, one Corn Tassel, for murder. The United States Supreme Court shortly granted Corn Tassel a writ of error, but the state refused to honor it. The Governor, with the support of the legislature, declared that he would resist all interference from whatever quarter with the state's courts. Suiting actions to words, the state promptly executed the Indian.

Consistent with his states'-rights outlook, President Jackson denied that Indians could become an independent nation within sovereign states, and said it was absurd to make treaties with Indian tribes as though they were sovereign nations. He, therefore, refused to take any action in defense of Indians rights secured by earlier treaties. Friends of the Cherokees, however, sought an injunction in the Supreme Court to restrain Georgia from seizing the Indian lands. In *Cherokee Nation* v. *Georgia* (1831) the Court held in an opinion of Chief Justice Marshall that an Indian tribe was neither a state in the Union nor a foreign nation within the meaning of the Constitution and, therefore, could not maintain an action in the federal courts. But Marshall added that the Indians were "domestic dependent nations" under the sovereignty and dominion of the United States, who had an unquestionable right to the lands they occupied until title should be extinguished by voluntary cession to the United States. This equivocal decision left Georgia defiant and the Cherokees unprotected.

In *Worcester* v. *Georgia* (1832), a case involving the conviction by the state of two Protestant missionaries for residence on Indian lands without a license from the state, Marshall went further and held that the Cherokee nation was a distinct political community. It had territorial boundaries, he said, within which "the laws of Georgia can have no force, and which the citizens of Georgia have no right to enter but with the assent of the Cherokees themselves or in conformity with treaties and with the acts of Congress." Georgia openly flouted this decision, however, refusing either to appear at the bar of the Court or to order the release of the missionaries.

President Jackson took no steps to implement the Supreme Court's decision, but he was under no legal obligation to do so. The Supreme Court remanded the case to the Superior Court of Georgia, and under the Judiciary Act of 1789 the Court could issue a final order disposing of the case only after it had been remanded once without effect. Plainly, the Georgia court would ignore the decision, but it was up to Samuel Worcester and his fellow missionary to continue the litigation by appealing again to the federal judiciary, at which time the Supreme Court might have issued a final order possibly placing the executive under an obligation to act. This next step was never taken, however, because the concurrently unfolding South Carolina nullification crisis in December 1832 gave the administration, the state, and the missionaries reason to compose the conflict.

Seeking to isolate South Carolina politically by avoiding any provocation of Georgia that might drive her into the arms of the nullifiers, the Jackson administration applied pressure on Governor Lumpkin of Georgia to pardon the missionaries without conceding the correctness of the Supreme Court decision. This would eliminate any possibility of federal authority being arrayed against the state as a final outcome of the case. For their part the missionaries and their sponsors were now convinced that Cherokee removal was inevitable, the Supreme Court notwithstanding. They were also fearful that continued legal resistance, possibly requiring the federal executive to oppose the state, would drive Georgia into alliance with South Carolina. They, therefore, dropped the case, whereupon the governor of Georgia pardoned them. Jackson went on to face down the South Carolina nullifiers, and federal Indian removal policy proceeded in accordance with the southern states' demands.

The Bank War

The principal event that established the Old Republican–dual-federalist identity of the Democratic party was the bank war of 1832. The pivotal institution in Republican national mercantilism, the second Bank of the United States came under attack in the 1820s as an agency of corrupt financial speculation and aristocratic privilege that undermined republican virtue, liberty, and states' rights. In 1832, long before its charter was to expire, the bank's supporters pushed a recharter bill through Congress. Jackson vetoed the measure as a violation of the republican equal-rights idea and the principle of dual federalism.

Although the constitutionality of the bank seemed to have been long since settled so that even its opponents did not object to it as unconstitutional in the congressional debate of 1832, Jackson reopened the question by noting the numerous opinions that had been expressed over the years against the bank's constitutionality, especially in the states. Acknowledging the Supreme Court's affirmation of the bank in *McCulloch* v. *Maryland,* he discounted the significance of this decision by arguing that the political branches were not bound by the judiciary's reading of the Constitution, but rather were obliged to interpret the fundamental law for themselves. Jackson pointed out, moreover, that in the McCulloch case the Court said the degree of necessity of a legislative act, under the necessary-and-proper clause, was a matter of political discretion. Permitted thus to examine the bill on its merits, Jackson described the bank as a potentially "self-elected directory" possessing monopolistic power that was capable of influencing elections and controlling the affairs of the nation. Especially insofar as it was connected with foreign capital, reasoned Jackson, the bank was a "danger to our liberty and independence."

Examining the matter in a more technical and specific constitutional sense, Jackson condemned the bank as a violation of dual-federalist principles. The recharter bill restricted Congress in various particulars concerning the capital of existing or future banks in the District of Columbia, and Jackson seized on this provision as an unconstitutional attempt by Congress to limit its own sovereign power. The argument was strained, as though Jackson included it out of a theoretical requirement to acknowledge federal sovereignty. More convincingly, and to the point of the dual-federalist enlargement of state powers, Jackson then argued that by exempting the private business of the bank from state taxation, the recharter bill, "as a means of executing the powers delegated to the General Government," attacked "the substantive and most essential powers reserved by the States." The framers of the Constitution, Jackson declared, never imagined "that any portion of the taxing power of the States not prohibited to them nor delegated to Congress was to be swept away and annihilated as a means of executing certain powers delegated to Congress." The contrast with John Marshall's doctrine of national-supremacy federalism was profound: whereas Marshall held that federal power properly exercised could stop the state taxing power, Democratic dual federalism permitted the states to exclude the exercise of a constitutional federal power.

The bank veto was the first in a series of steps that ultimately committed the federal government to a radical hard-money policy and drove many entrepreneurial-minded Democrats into the National Republican and later the Whig party. In 1833 Jackson withdrew federal deposits from the Bank of the United States and placed them in twenty-three state banks, thereby encouraging speculative tendencies. After the charter of the BUS expired, Congress in 1840 enacted a subtreasury system for receiving, transferring, and paying out federal funds. The constitutional theory behind this scheme, according to President Martin Van Buren, was that the federal government had no authority to associate itself in any way with private banking activities or business pursuits and was, therefore, obliged to manage its money without the assistance of private institutions. The Whigs in 1841 repealed the subtreasury legislation, but were twice prevented from creating another national bank by President John Tyler, successor to William Henry Harrison. Tyler, a states'-rights, strict constructionist from Virginia, held that Congress had no constitutional power "to create a national bank to operate *per se* over the Union." He would accept a national bank only if the establishment of the bank's branches was made dependent on the positive consent of the states in which the bank would operate. Finally, when the Democrats returned to power under President James K. Polk, they reestablished the independent treasury system in 1846, leaving control of the nation's banking system to the states.

Nullification: Calhoun's Theory

If the bank war revealed the states'-rights side of Democratic dual federalism, Jackson's response to the nullification crisis in South Carolina showed his commitment to the federal-supremacy side. The crisis that came to a head in South Carolina in the winter of 1832–33 had its origins in economic difficulties caused by the spread of cotton cultivation to the Southwest and by a decline in the agricultural export trade that was attributable to the contraction of credit in the international market but that South Carolinians blamed on the protective tariff. They despised the tariff not only for economic reasons, but also because it represented an external authority that was capable of disrupting, if not destroying, the state's distinctive slave-based social order. Provoked by the "Tariff of Abominations," the most highly protective impost law ever adopted by Congress, as well as by recent slave uprisings and abolitionist attacks, the South Carolina legislature in 1830 issued the South Carolina Exposition. Secretly written by Vice-President John C. Calhoun, the Exposition condemned the tariff as unconstitutional and asserted the power of the state to nullify federal legislation. Suddenly, nullification became the central issue in South Carolina politics, a States Rights party forming in its defense and a Unionist party in opposition. Matters assumed an even more serious aspect in 1831 when Vice-President Calhoun publicly endorsed nullification and advanced a constitutional argument to defend it.

Although its association with secession and hence its disunionist connotation have cast the doctrine as a constitutional perversity, nullification dealt with and depended on well-recognized problems and features in the constitutional order. This fact gave it more than a degree of plausibility. The general problem Calhoun faced was that of protecting minorities against the tyranny of the majority. Madison had proposed to deal with this fundamental issue by expanding the size of the republic, and from time to time the institutions of the Senate, the executive veto, and judicial review offered constitutional means of safeguarding minority interests. These instruments not being politically available to South Carolina in the late 1820s, however, Calhoun feared that the power of the numerical majority acting in the national legislature would overwhelm the interests of his state and region. To guard against this eventuality, he proposed that the states judge the constitutionality of federal legislation and nullify federal acts that contradicted their interests or encroached on their reserved rights.

Calhoun derived the power of nullification in the first place from his general theory of sovereignty. Since the time of the Revolution, Americans had posited divided sovereignty as the basis of American federalism. Calhoun rejected this approach, however, and returned to the older European and English idea of sovereignty as unitary and indivisible. He was consistent with the American constitutional tradition in speaking of the people as the ultimate sovereign, but he identified the people exclusively with the states in declaring that sovereignty was "an entire thing" and that "to divide is to destroy it." Drawing on Madison and Jefferson's Old Republican principles of '98, Calhoun invoked the familiar compact theory of the Union as the immediate source of the power of nullification. Independent sovereign communities after the separation from Great Britain, the states in this view created the Articles of Confederation and were the constituent power in forming the federal union in 1787. The Constitution was a compact, in the nature of a treaty, between equal sovereign states. Delegating certain powers to the general government as their agent, the states did not surrender their sovereignty, something by nature indivisible. Accordingly, the federal government possessed no sovereignty, but merely such limited powers as the states chose to give it in order to carry out their purposes.

In positing nullification on these foundations, Calhoun employed another well-established feature of American constitutionalism—the popularly elected convention. Should the people of a state object to a law or action of the federal government, they could, acting outside their legislature in a state convention, judge it unconstitutional and declare it null and void within the limits of the state. This negation would be but a suspensory veto, however; to settle the controversy finally Calhoun invoked yet another familiar constitutional device, the amending power. A convention of all the states would consider the nullified federal act, and if three-fourths of them approved, nullification would be confirmed. Finally, if the nullifying state was overruled and it persisted in regarding the terms of the compact violated, it could secede from the Union.

It is easy to point out historical weaknesses in Calhoun's theory, ignoring as it did the seemingly clear intention of the framers to divide sovereignty and make the federal government supreme over the states. Every theory of the union in the nineteenth century can be critized on historical grounds, however, and Calhoun's doctrine, for all its flaws, was supported

by the incontestable fact that during the Revolution state sovereignty was
more apparent than Confederation sovereignty. Because secession eventually occurred, moreover, Calhoun's theory appears inherently disunionist.
But in conception and intention it was not a disunionist doctrine. Eschewing
a national-party organization to protect the South and prevent sectional
division, such as the Jacksonian Democrats employed, Calhoun used the
doctrinaire and seemingly impractical legal instrument of nullification. His
purpose, however, was not simply to protect South Carolina, but to protect
South Carolina *in the Union.* Nullification was a way of maintaining the
Union. Calhoun did not abandon the national sentiment that had earlier
led him to support a centralizing conception of federalism. In the altered
circumstances of the 1830s, he expressed his love of the Union in the theory
of state sovereignty and nullification. So far from being the purpose or end
of nullification, secession was a desperate final alternative that signified its
failure as an instrument of constitutional politics.

Nevertheless, Calhoun's argument for nullification marked a significant turning point in nineteenth-century constitutionalism. Up to this time
debate over federalism had tended to focus on the division and allocation of
powers between the federal government and the states. People could argue
about the locus of specific powers without having to challenge the Union.
But Calhoun's insistence on a unitary conception of sovereignty had the
effect of forcing a more precise definition of the federal-state relationship.
The result was the introduction of an element of ideological or doctrinal
rigidity which caused people to differ over the principle of union itself.

The Nullification Crisis: Federal Sovereignty Vindicated

In the winter of 1832–33 South Carolina employed the doctrine of
nullification to challenge the authority of the federal government. In November 1832 a state convention, called by State Rights party legislators who
had been elected on an antitariff, pronullification platform, adopted an
ordinance declaring the federal Tariff Acts of 1828 and 1832 null and void
and instructing the state legislature to pass all legislation necessary to give it
full effect. The convention decreed that the ordinance could not be questioned in any case in law or equity in the state courts; prohibited an appeal
of any case in which it might be involved to the Supreme Court; required
state officers and jurors in cases involving the ordinance to swear an oath to
obey and enforce it; and stated that any federal effort to enforce the tariff
acts or coerce the state would cause South Carolina to secede from the
Union. The nullifying convention also announced that the people of South
Carolina owed allegiance to the state alone, not to the federal government,
and it issued an appeal for a general convention of the states to consider the
tariff problem. Meeting a few days later, the state legislature adopted a test
oath act for judges and jurors and a replevin act authorizing the owner of

imported goods seized for nonpayment of duties to recover them or twice their value from custom officials. The legislature also authorized the governor to call out the militia to enforce the laws of the state.

President Jackson had long-standing personal reasons for disliking Calhoun. These, combined with his love of the Union and belief in federal sovereignty, led him to condemn the nullification ordinance in a proclamation to the people of South Carolina in December 1832. Jackson started with the Jeffersonian compact theory of the Union, noting that the states gave up certain powers in the process of constituting the general government. He relied on Federalist theory, however, in stating that the Union formed by the Constitution was not a league, but a government in which all the people of the nation were represented and which operated directly upon them. Moreover the Constitution as a compact created a "binding obligation" and was backed by an explicit sanction that made an attempt to destroy the government by force an offense punishable under the public law of self-defense. The states had no power to annul a law of the United States; the very idea, said Jackson, was incompatible with the existence of the Union. And the states had no right to secede. "To say that any State may at pleasure secede from the Union," Jackson explained, "is to say that the United States are not a nation." Asserting that disunion by armed force was treason, he urged the citizens of South Carolina to uphold the Constitution and laws and announced his intention to enforce the tariff laws.

On January 16, 1833, after potential conflict with the state of Georgia had been averted by the settlement of the controversy over Indian removal, Jackson requested that Congress take steps that would "solemnly proclaim that the Constitution and the laws are supreme and the Union indissoluble." He asked Congress not for new authority to use against the nullifiers—legislation of 1795 and 1807 authorized the executive to use force to uphold federal laws—but rather for means that would facilitate the exercise of power already possessed and enable the government to thwart the nullifiers without actually using military power. Congress complied by adopting the act of March 2, 1833, for enforcing the tariff—known as the Force Act. The legislation authorized the president to employ his authority in support of federal law against any obstruction, civil or military, even if the obstruction be made by authority of a state. The statute provided judicial protection for federal officers enforcing national law, including for the first time a provision permitting federal courts to issue a writ of habeas corpus against a state officer.[1] And it authorized the president to close ports of entry or alter collection districts, were such steps necessary to collect customs duties. The bill thus asserted the sovereignty of the federal govern-

1. The writ of habeas corpus, in Anglo-American law the traditional means of maintaining personal liberty against wrongful detention, was mainly important in state law. Under the Judiciary Act of 1789, federal courts could issue a writ of habeas corpus against officers of the national government. Persons wrongfully detained by state officers thus had no means of securing release by turning to federal authority.

ment and its authority to enforce its statutes directly upon individuals by force if necessary.

Although Jackson unhesitatingly defended federal authority, he regarded the protective tariff as an instrument of antirepublican privilege. Even before the nullification ordinance, therefore, he favored its downward revision. Jackson's outlook made possible a compromise which enabled South Carolina partially to secure its objective. While the Force Act defended federal sovereignty, a tariff law announced a gradual reduction in duties to a 20-percent maximum in 1842. Meanwhile strong displays of Unionist sentiment in other southern states left South Carolina politically isolated and helped weaken the nullifiers' resolve. In January a States Rights party convention recommended virtual suspension of nullification until Congress acted on the compromise tariff bill, a step that effectively ended the crisis. After Congress lowered the tariff the South Carolina convention reassembled and rescinded the ordinance of nullification against the tariff, though in a final and futile attempt to save face it adopted another ordinance nullifying the Force Act.

If South Carolina primarily sought a change in federal tariff policy, its resort to nullification was partially successful. Clearly, however, the nullifiers were trying to fashion a new constitutional instrument for defending southern interests, and on this score they suffered a crushing defeat.

While based on the states'-rights–compact theory of the Virginia and Kentucky Resolutions, Calhoun's doctrine of nullification went beyond the principles asserted by Jefferson and Madison. Indeed, Calhoun transformed states' rights into a doctrine of state sovereignty with profound implications for the federal system. Believing that the South would ultimately fight to defend slavery against abolitionist attack, he concluded that the only way to preserve the Union was to give the southern minority a constitutional means of protecting itself. Calhoun continued to support nullification even after it failed to gain acceptance as a legitimate constitutional instrument, but most South Carolinians abandoned it. With most southerners, they became convinced that if a "sovereign" state's remonstrances against objectionable federal policy proved unavailing, the only alternatives were to submit or secede.

If the nullification crisis was a crucial turning point in the transformation of states' rights into state sovereignty, it was equally significant in the development of Unionism. Prior to this time union was a rationally and deliberately chosen instrument for the promotion of republican values. It was an artifice, utilitarian device, and experiment. And implicit in its experimental nature was the possibility—which was occasionally made explicit—that rational, pragmatic reasons might require the abandonment of union. On more than a few occasions states'-rights men talked of secession, while defenders of the Union spoke of the practical value of federalism as a framework of liberty. Unionists did not insist on the permanence or indissolubility of the Union. But they did when Calhoun broached his doctrine of nullification. Now for the first time defenders of federal authority asserted that the Union was permanent. Andrew Jackson offered the most famous statement of the theory of perpetual union, but Daniel Webster and Henry Clay among the National Republicans (later Whigs) were equally firm in their support of the idea. After fifty years, union was becoming an end in itself, a political absolute rooted in history, geography, and sentiment. Not that it ceased to function as a means of securing republican liberty, but the traditional utilitarian basis of Unionism gradually evolved into a transcendent, organic rationale appropriate to the age of romanticism.

Jackson expressed both the older instrumental conception of union and the newer organic, absolute approach. His famous Jefferson Day exclamation of 1830—"our Federal Union—It must be preserved"—as well as his proclamation of 1833 asserting the indissolubility of the Union rested ultimately on the idea that the United States had a right, as a living organism, to defend its existence. However, Jackson also saw Calhoun and the nullifiers as ambitious men bent on undermining republican government. Therefore, he also defended the Union as a means of maintaining republican liberty. Jacksonian adviser Amos Kendall expressed this in 1832. "With us," he said, "the Union is *sacred.* Its preservation is the only *means* of preserving our civil liberty." In his proclamation to South Carolina, Jackson similarly reasoned that the crisis of the Union involved the future of "all free governments" and concluded that its successful defense would "inspire new confidence in republican institutions."

Dual federalism thus blended the potentially contradictory elements of states' rights and federal sovereignty. It struck a compromise between Calhoun's doctrine of state sovereignty and the National Republican or Whig preference for centralization. Whigs held that the Constitution was a completed or executed contract, made by the people of the United States, which created a permanent sovereign government. In this view the Union was older than the states. Calhoun's theory was precisely the opposite: sovereign states, antedating the Union, entered into a contractual agreement or constitutional compact which required their continuing consent to make it effective and from which they could withdraw if the terms of the contract were violated. Democratic dual federalism regarded the Union as a continuing contract, but also as a binding agreement that imposed a perpetual obligation on the states. In the Jacksonian view, Whig centralization threatened liberty, while Calhoun's state sovereignty and nullification threatened union. Dual federalism was intended to promote republican liberty in a permanent, indissoluble, and expanding Union.

The Modern Two-Party System

The bank war and the nullification crisis served further to catalyze the Jacksonian political realignment in ways that permanently altered the constitutional system. Banking- and business-minded Democrats on the one hand, and Calhoun's South Carolina followers on the other, left the party and joined the National Republicans in the aftermath of these events. By 1834 this anti-Jackson coalition called itself the Whig party. The constitutional significance of these changes lay in the fact that by 1840 they produced the second American party system.

The first party system, lasting from 1794 to about 1815, performed a representative, constitutional function by providing mechanisms for choosing officials, shaping public opinion, and mediating generally between the people and the government. Despite the more democratic style of the Republicans in contrast to the Federalists, however, the system was closer to the deferential, leader-oriented factional conflict of colonial politics than to the modern, mass-based party struggles of the nineteenth century. The parties of the early national period lacked comprehensive, articulated organization reaching to the local level and mobilizing voter participation. Moreover, party leaders persisted in seeing organized partisan opposition as dangerous to the government; the idea of a legitimate opposition, and hence of parties themselves, was not yet accepted. Federalists and Republicans were elite-led groups who assumed that the people would recognize their virtue and entrust them with the management of public affairs. Once the people made the correct choice, the defeated party would disappear.

The political realignment that occurred from 1828 to 1840 changed all of this. Disciplined, mass-based, permanent organizations emerged as characteristic of American politics as partisan activity was democratized and institutionalized. The process of political democratization had begun in the colonial period and had received a tremendous impetus with the forming of republican governments and the expansion of the suffrage during the Revolution. It continued in the early nineteenth century as both Federalists and Republicans competed in efforts to broaden the suffrage. Property and taxpayer qualifications for voting and office holding were removed in most states, with liberalizing changes in Connecticut, Massachusetts, and New York from 1818 to 1821 forming a decisive turning point in the movement for democracy. Only in Rhode Island, Virginia, and Louisiana did serious suffrage restrictions remain. Meanwhile several new states—Indiana, Illinois, Alabama, Mississippi, and Missouri—entered the Union between 1816 and 1821 with constitutions providing for universal white manhood suffrage. Voter participation was high, moreover, especially in state and local elections where a genuine party conflict existed.

The Jackson men built on these institutional changes in the late 1820s as they formed a national party organization with a self-consciously democratic ethos and a high degree of discipline and structure. By the mid-1830s the elements of a modern party were present: leaders, cadre, constituents; a party press; effective use of patronage to hold the party together; a set of principles or an ideology to identify the party and maintain voters' loyalty and commitment; reliance on popular conventions from the local to the national level to choose party candidates (replacing the elite-dominated legislative caucus); and a uniform outlook on specific policy questions that required subordination of sectional views to a national party perspective. Attacking the older deferential politics, the Jacksonian party also argued for rotation in office on the democratic principle that the intelligence and virtue of the common man qualified him for the duty of public services.

The Democrats as the first modern party did not serve simply a constituent or constitutional function; they had a programmatic purpose as well, expressed in their Old Republican ideology. Nevertheless, in a very real sense the party organization existed to gain power as an end in itself. This is not to say that partisan activity could be reduced merely to the cynical pursuit of office, although there was a good deal of that involved. But parties existed for their own sake in the sense that they were now looked on as permanent organizations. And almost irrespective of the motivation of party leaders, the party system had a democratizing effect on political life.

Although Jacksonians appealed to the common man in 1828, the Democratic party was a coalition of diverse interests until the events of 1832 led it to seek a mass-voter orientation based on the Old Republican ideology. The Whig party, in contrast, at first rejected the populistic approach to politics. Calling Jackson a tyrant for his use of presidential power, Whigs assumed the banner of resistance to executive usurpation and persisted in the older leader-oriented, local-based, deferential style of politics. They attacked Jackson as a demagogue and objected to his reliance on a "kitchen cabinet" outside the established leadership structure. In 1836 the Whigs ran four regional or favorite-son presidential candidates, a strategy aimed at preventing Van Buren from getting a majority of votes in the electoral college and throwing the election into the House of Representatives. But the strategy also reflected their "local notable" outlook and their lack of a broadly based constituency. Soundly defeated, the Whigs took a lesson in the new democratic style of politics and won the election of 1840 with their famous "log cabin" campaign that put William Henry Harrison in the White House. Thereafter, accepting each other as a legitimate opposition and organized party conflict as healthy for republican government, Whigs and Democrats competed as mass-based national organizations until the issue of slavery caused a sectional political realignment in the 1850s.

Jackson and Executive Power

In his inaugural address in 1840 President William Henry Harrison, promising to arrest what he called a trend toward monarchy, warned against the danger of excessive concentration of power in the federal government. Exaggerated as this view of recent presidential history was, it suggests something of the impact that Jackson's actions had on the development of the executive branch. Mainly concerned with expanding the power of the states where questions of federalism arose, Jackson nevertheless used executive power vigorously in his dealings with Congress in a conscious effort to democratize the presidential office.

Perceiving himself the champion of the people, Jackson was determined to play an independent role in the formation of national policy. To this end he willingly defied both Congress and the Supreme Court when it became necessary for him to do so. Nor were instruments of presidential power wanting, even though they had long lain dormant. Jackson ultimately made use of three of these instruments of power—the veto power, his power over appointments and removals, and his position as a party leader.

It was Jackson's bank veto that first led him to assert comprehensively his ideas on executive independence. His veto message set forth two fairly distinct constitutional concepts, both of which infuriated the Whigs—that the Supreme Court was not the final arbiter of all constitutional questions, and that the president could exercise a judgment independent of Congress upon matters of policy, presumably even where constitutional issues were not involved.

Constitutional questions, Jackson said, could not be regarded as settled merely because the Supreme Court had passed upon them. "The Congress, the Executive, and the Court," he asserted, "must each of itself be guided by its own opinion of the Constitution. Each public officer who takes an oath to support the Constitution swears that he will support it as he understands it, and not as it is understood by others. It is as much the duty of the House of Representatives, of the Senate, and of the President to decide upon the constitutionality of any bill or resolution which may be presented to them for passage of approval as it is of the supreme judges when it may be brought before them for judicial decision. The opinion of the judges has no more authority over Congress than the opinion of Congress has over the judges, and on that point the President is independent of both."

Although Jackson's position contradicted a developing tendency to regard the judiciary as the final authority on constitutional questions, it possessed a reliable basis in the departmental theory of review established in the Jeffersonian era. More important was Jackson's objection to the bank not only on the basis of constitutionality strictly considered, but also for reasons of policy. Ten previous exercises of the executive veto power had rested mainly on constitutional grounds, although occasionally expediency was the justification. Jackson's bank veto and his six internal-improvement vetoes changed this pattern. In addition to the dual-federalist objections already discussed, Jackson opposed the bank as an unwise and inexpedient interference with republican liberty. The Whigs argued from a strict separation-of-powers theory that the executive was not part of the legislature and hence could not use the veto out of policy considerations such as lawmakers might entertain; the veto could be employed only when Congress had clearly overstepped its constitutional authority. There was no compelling reason, however, to regard the president as other than a genuine participant in the legislative process and thus entitled to consider the substantive policy as well as the constitutional form of legislation. Presidents after Jackson accepted his broad conception of the executive veto, which anticipated later nineteenth-century checks on legislative power in the form of constitutional revision by popularly elected conventions and judicial review.

Having decided to remove government deposits from the Bank of the United States, Jackson continued the struggle with Congress over currency policy in yet another constitutional controversy concerning the removal power. In accordance with the bank's charter, the president ordered the secretary of the Treasury, Louis McLane, to remove the deposits. McLane refused to do so, however, whereupon Jackson replaced him with William Duane, who also refused on the ground that as secretary of the Treasury he had discretionary authority from Congress to decide the matter. Jackson then read to the cabinet a paper, written by Attorney General Roger B. Taney, asserting the president's power to impose his will on his subordinates. When Duane continued recalcitrant, Jackson replaced him with Taney, who promptly removed the deposits. The Senate proceeded to request a copy of Jackson's cabinet paper, and when Jackson denied the request, the Senate censured him for assuming unconstitutional powers. Jackson replied with a "Protest" in which he argued, on the theory of a unitary executive, that the entire executive power was vested in the president; that the power to remove officers charged with assisting in executing the law belonged to the president as well; and that the secretary of the Treasury was a subordinate officer who in managing the public money was subject to the supervision and control of the president.

The basic issue was whether the president, through his constitutionally implied power of dismissal, could dictate to the secretary of the Treasury how he should exercise the discretionary power vested exclusively in him by Congress. The Whigs argued that the Constitution specifically granted Congress control over public funds, and that Congress in 1789 had purposely placed the Treasury Department under congressional rather than executive control. Therefore, the president had no constitutional right either to dismiss the secretary or to force removal of the public deposits under presidential authority. Certainly, there was something to this argument, but if the issue had to be decided one way or the other, Jackson was on solid ground in insisting on executive unity and responsibility. This had been the accepted theory and practice of the government from its inception, although Congress in creating the Treasury Department departed from it by making the secretary accountable to itself as well as to the president. Jackson's actions, based on the well-established belief that the power of removal, like that of appointment, was inherent in executive power and subject only to specific constitutional limitations, ended the ambiguity.

Jackson had the last word in his struggle to remove the deposits, but an extreme assertion of executive power by the Jackson administration was rebuffed by the Supreme Court in the case of *Kendall* v. *U.S. ex rel. Stokes* in 1838. Amos Kendall, postmaster general, refused to enforce government contracts with a fraud-tainted mail transport firm, Stockton and Stokes. Stokes got Congress to pass a law giving the solicitor in the Treasury Department power to settle the dispute; the solicitor decided for Stokes; Stokes then filed suit for a writ of mandamus compelling Kendall to pay the firm. Kendall refused, arguing that he was subject only to the direction of the president and that even in applying an act of Congress the judiciary could not control his actions. The Supreme Court viewed this argument as a denial of congressional power to impose duties it thought proper on an executive officer and rejected it. The position of the administration, said the Court, would give the president power to control the legislation of Congress. Describing the action of the postmaster general as merely ministerial, the Court held that Kendall must pay Stokes, in accordance with the act of Congress. The decision placed a modest restraint on the executive without interfering with his determination of discretionary political matters.

State Constitutional Change

Numerous changes in state government, usually the result of state constitutional conventions, had a democratizing effect on the constitutional order. One manifestation of this trend, as noted previously, was the extension of the franchise and the increased electoral participation that resulted from the formation of disciplined, mass political parties. Democratization also occurred in the reapportionment of state legislatures, demanded in the name of political equality by western or up-country groups who were underrepresented in relation to eastern mercantile interests and tidewater planters. In Virginia a notable struggle over reapportionment took place in 1829–30, in which entrenched eastern interests retained political control in a new constitution. About 1850, however, most of the southeastern states granted representation to western regions.

In the interest of establishing more direct popular control of government, the new constitutions drafted between 1820 and 1850 increased restrictions on the power and discretion of state legislatures. Earlier constitutions embodied the assumption that the legislature was the sovereign voice of the free people, and they had placed but few constitutional checks upon legislature authority. The extravagant state banking laws and internal improvement schemes of the generation after 1815 led to a growing popular distrust of the integrity and capacity of state legislators, a distrust that greatly increased after the financial collapse of many of the states following the Panic of 1837.

As a result, the constitutions drafted in the 1840s imposed substantial limitations upon legislative discretion. Generally, they placed limitations upon the time, frequency, and expense of legislative sessions; abolished the legislature's right to enact special legislation benefiting individuals or corporations; required a two-thirds vote or popular approval for the creation of state banks or public-works projects; and limited the amount of the state debt and the objects for which it could be contracted. Many of the constitutions contained lengthy provisions which were legislative in character rather than organic, an additional indication of unwillingness to trust legislative discretion completely.

While legislative authority declined, the power of the governor was increased. The earlier constitutions had in general given the governor no veto or had permitted the legislature to override a veto by a majority vote, while the new documents usually granted the executive a more effective veto power. The new constitutions also granted the governor much of the appointive power hitherto lodged in the legislature. These provisions reflected growing recognition of the governor as an influential political and executive leader and a valuable constitutional check upon the legislature rather than as a mere ceremonial head of the state.

The new constitutions also generally provided for the popular election of nearly all state and county administrative officers, including even minor officials. The responsibilities of the electorate were thus multiplied in a sometimes bewildering fashion that increased the need of party functionaries to oversee the electoral process. At some point the theoretically democratic character of mass political parties might be contradicted by their perhaps necessarily manipulative tactics, but for the time being the belief prevailed that the party was the embodiment of the people. What disturbed many conservatives was the fear that popular power, organized in mass parties and exercised through executive and legislative institutions, would weaken traditional constitutional restraints on governmental power.

Highly controversial were the provisions in several state constitutions for popular election of the judiciary. A few of the constitutions adopted in the 1820s provided for the popular election of judges of inferior courts, and the Mississippi Constitution of 1832 carried a far more radical provision that called for the choice of supreme court judges by the electorate. For a time no other state followed Mississippi in this procedure, but in 1846 New York wrote a similar provision into its new constitution. Conservatives and even many moderates fought hard against such radicalism, but they were unable to stem the tide. Within a few years nearly all the western states framed constitutions incorporating the principle of an elective judiciary, and many of the eastern states did likewise. To guarantee popular control of the judiciary still further, many of the new constitutions empowered the legislature to remove any judge simply by a majority vote.

Popular Sovereignty

After the establishment of republican governments during the Revolution Americans generally assumed that popular sovereignty was properly manifested in prescribed constitutional forms and procedures. Nevertheless, the revolutionary tradition of direct political action in the name of the sovereign people, carried on "out of doors" or outside established institutions and procedures, continued to have influence and was vigorously asserted by many reform-minded groups in the 1830s and 1840s.

The settlement of the western territories provided a continuing opportunity for the implementation of a more immediate and spontaneous conception of republican self-government and popular sovereignty. Congress had formal power to create territories and supervise their transformation into states, but settlers often impatiently took matters into their own hands by creating governments without congressional authorization and seeking admission to the Union. Considering the undeveloped nature and scope of federal administrative authority and the fact that the Constitution nowhere refers to a *congressional* power to make or create states, there was warrant in this popular response. Manifest from the beginning of the government, it was illustrated in 1836 when settlers in Michigan territory grew tired of waiting for Congress to grant permission to form a state government. Without federal approval they drafted a constitution, elected state officers, and sent representatives to Washington to demand recognition as a state. Congress acceded to the popular demand by agreeing to a compromise that acknowledged both the right of the people in the territory to create a state and of Congress to control the process.

The tendency to take direct political action in the name of the people was not confined to the territories. In Maryland in 1836, for example, Democratic state senators seeking reapportionment of the legislature threatened to boycott the deliberations of that body in an attempt to force the Whig majority to reform the state constitution. They were prepared by this action to destroy the government and, in the words of a contemporary, to throw the state government into a state of nature in which the people could write a new constitution. To that end, acting without formal authority, they elected delegates to a constitutional convention. The Whigs yielded, agreeing to accept constitutional reforms providing for greater popular participation in government. At about the same time in Pennsylvania the "Buckshot War" also evinced the power of aroused citizens acting in defiance of established authority. After a bitterly contested election, crowds of Democratic partisans fell on the capital at Harrisburg to force

Whig officials in the state senate to acknowledge their party's apparent victory at the polls. The popular protest, carried directly to the state house, prevented Whigs from organizing the house of representatives, whereupon the governor called out the state militia to secure order. In the face of this popular demonstration, Whig officials acknowledged Democratic control of the state assembly.

The largest and most significant expression of direct-action popular sovereignty in the Jacksonian era was the Dorr Rebellion in Rhode Island in 1842. Rhode Island was still governed under the colonial charter granted in 1662, and although changes had occurred, an exclusive oligarchy, protected by a stiff property requirement for voting and office holding, controlled the state government. After reformers unsuccessfully sought in the 1830s to broaden the suffrage through established constitutional methods, they held a convention without the authorization of the charter government. Professing popular sovereignty and allegiance to the true principles of republican government, they wrote a constitution and formed a parallel state government. In the face of this challenge, the charter government passed a treason law directed at the irregular action, invoked martial law, and appealed to the president of the United States to assist in putting down the insurrection. The Dorr Rebellion, so named for its leader, Democrat Thomas Wilson Dorr, failed when the majority of the people in the state continued to support the charter government. They did so in large part because state officials, provoked into action by the Dorrites, drafted a new constitution embodying the reformers' demands. Dorr and his fellow defenders of popular sovereignty refused to acquiesce in this result, however, and persisted in their attempt to vindicate what they termed "peaceable revolution": the right of the people to alter their government whenever they pleased without regard to existing authority.

Long after the desired democratic reforms had been introduced into the state government, the Dorrites' defense of popular sovereignty eventuated in the Supreme Court decision in *Luther* v. *Borden* (1849). Not surprisingly, the Court rejected the popular-sovereignty argument. Asked to decide which of the competing governments in Rhode Island in 1842 had been the legitimate republican state government, the Court formally disavowed an answer on the ground that it was a political question beyond the competence of the judiciary to decide. In effect, however, the Supreme Court acknowledged the charter government as legitimate and repudiated the Dorrites by holding, in an interpretation of the guarantee-of-republican-government clause, that the action of Congress in seating representatives stamped the seal of republican legitimacy on the government that sent them. In the case of Rhode Island in 1842, of course, this meant the charter government. The Supreme Court thus defended stability and order, and gave broad latitude to states to regulate civil and political liberty within their boundaries. In the context of increasing sectional hostility and southern fear of abolitionist-inspired attacks on slavery as a state institution, this defense of existing state authority was politically significant.

Related to these specifically governmental applications of direct-action popular sovereignty was an outburst of rioting throughout the country in the 1830s aimed at a variety of social problems and grievances. Mobs formed with alarming frequency—there were fifty-three in 1834–35—to protest any number of things from banking policy to blacks' civil rights. Riots were not directed against the existing order, however, but rather, in the eyes of participants, were exercises of the people's right to correct abuses that could not be rectified through established legal channels. They were a form of popular sovereignty, collective expressions of the power of individuals to govern themselves. To some degree local officials seem to have accepted this view of rioting, for they usually refrained from vigorous and heavy applications of force to control the mobs. In some sense officials regarded popular riots as compatible with the existing political order, as had been the case in the colonies in the eighteenth century, when rioting was often accepted as an instrument of political protest.

Nevertheless, despite the rioters' acceptance of the existing order, their actions challenged the rule of law and inspired conservative apprehension over the future of republican constitutionalism. It is significant that Abraham Lincoln's first important political act—his Springfield Lyceum address of 1838—condemned the recent wave of riots as a threat to American institutions. Warning that rioting would destroy the people's attachment to the government, Lincoln insisted on respect for law as a safeguard for republican liberty. He urged that reverence for the Constitution and the law become "the *political religion* of the nation."

Confidence in the virtue, wisdom, and ability of the people thus had important consequences for American constitutionalism, not all of them unambiguously beneficial or positive. Carried to an extreme, popular sovereignty contained tendencies inimical to limited government and the rule of law. Similarly ambiguous was Andrew Jackson's constitutional role and legacy. As the tribune of the people, his bold exercise of presidental power changed the contours of the executive office but perhaps weakened the spirit of constitutional restraint that existed in the early national period. In any event, the states eagerly grasped the power that devolved upon them as a result of dual-federalist theory and practice, frequently facilitated by Jackson's executive actions. They were aided, moreover, by Supreme Court decisions, under Jacksonian Chief Justice Roger B. Taney, which wrote dual federalism into constitutional law.

THIRTEEN

Jacksonian Jurisprudence: The Taney Court and Constitutional Law

————————————— ◆ ◆ ◆ —————————————

SEVERAL YEARS ELAPSED before the Democratic party, having gained control of the presidency, acquired dominant influence on the Supreme Court. At the start of his administration President Jackson appointed John McLean of Ohio to the Court; in 1835 he named three more justices, James Wayne of Georgia, Philip Barbour of Virginia, and, as chief justice, Roger B. Taney of Maryland. Then, after Congress increased the size of the Supreme Court to nine members in 1837, President Martin Van Buren appointed two more Democrats, John McKinley of Alabama and John Catron of Tennessee. These changes in the membership of the high bench were, of course, intended to shape the development of public law in accordance with the principles of the Democratic party. The Taney Court, therefore, lost little time confirming and extending the acquisition of power by the states under the theory of dual federalism.

The shift in the Court's political complexion raised in a particularly acute form the problem of accommodating social and political change while maintaining continuity in the law. Political folklore long attributed to the Taney Court a revolutionary impact, positing a fundamental conflict between its constitutional outlook and that of the Marshall Court. Modern scholarship has corrected this overdrawn judgment. It is clear, for example, that in the last years of Marshall's tenure the Supreme Court to some extent reflected the rising states'-rights sentiment. In effect it permitted states to exercise a concurrent power to regulate interstate commerce (*Willson* v. *Blackbird Creek Marsh Co.,* 1829); upheld the state taxing power against a corporation's claim of implied immunity under a charter grant (*Providence Bank* v. *Billings,* 1830); and refused to apply the Fifth Amendment as a restriction on the states (*Barron* v. *Baltimore,* 1833). By the same token, the new Democratic justices by no means abandoned or overturned the leading constitutional doctrines laid down in the Marshall era. In economic matters especially, they followed the example of the Marshall Court in protecting property rights and facilitating capitalist expansion, although they tended to favor the states rather than the national government for this purpose. Sanctity of contract, interpreted to include legislative charter grants, remained a basic premise of constitutional law. The Taney Court also demonstrated continuity of outlook with its predecessor in enlarging the jurisdiction of the federal judiciary. Nevertheless, the Marshall and Taney Courts differed in significant respects.

The most important change in constitutional law that occurred in the Jacksonian era concerned the nature of the Union and federal-state relations. Rejecting the Marshall Court's bias toward national supremacy, the Taney justices acknowledged the exclusive power of the states in relation to the federal government. The theory of dual federalism, as Jackson's policies showed, did not formally deny federal sovereignty. Nevertheless, its historic purpose was to expand the power of the states relative to the federal government, and after it was transformed into the doctrine of state sovereignty it denied federal sovereignty entirely. The relative decline in national power resulting from dual federalism was not necessarily fatal to the Union. Yet, subordinated as it was to the ambitions of the slave power in the 1850s, dual federalism failed to restrain—if it did not positively encourage—southern disunionism. To be sure, Roger B. Taney was never so inflexible in his conception of state sovereignty as John C. Calhoun or even some of his southern colleagues on the Court. His interest in capitalist expansion, inherently centralizing in its effect, kept him from agrarian localist extremes. In the final analysis, however, Taney's commitment to slavery, like that of the party whose views he represented, caused him to reject the idea of authentic federal legislative sovereignty, thus facilitating the disintegration of the Union.

The New Era in Constitutional Law

The 1837 term of the Supreme Court revealed the new emphases and interests of the Democratic majority. The Court decided three cases carried over from earlier years dealing with paper money and state banking, state regulation of interstate commerce, and state encouragement of economic development through corporation charters. These were all key issues in Jacksonian politics, and in each instance the Supreme Court, ignoring or reinterpreting precedents from the Marshall era, endorsed the exercise of state power. The results delighted Democrats and appalled Whigs, who read them as evidence of a dangerous expansion in governmental power, politicization of the rule of law, and general decline in constitutional morality. *Briscoe* v. *The Bank of Kentucky* (1837), the paper money–state banking case, illustrates the conflicting attitudes and aspirations provoked by the emergence of a distinctive Jacksonian jurisprudence.

The *Briscoe* case involved the constitutional status of state bills of credit. In *Craig* v. *Missouri* (1830) the Marshall Court had held that interest-bearing notes issued by the state of Missouri were bills of credit and thus prohibited by the Constitution. The Bank of the Commonwealth of Kentucky was created and owned by the state, which authorized it to issue notes for public circulation as legal tender, chose its officers, and was heavily involved in its management. Although there were differences between the situations in Missouri and Kentucky, chiefly in the fact that acts of the Kentucky bank were taken in its own name rather than the state's, for all practical purposes they were the same. The Supreme Court, however, sensitive to states' rights and the need for a circulating medium to fill the void left by the demise of the Bank of the United States, professed to see a difference. John McLean for the Court held that the bank notes in question were not constitutionally prohibited bills of credit because they were not issued by a state and were not designated to circulate as money on the faith and credit of the state. Justice Story dissented, arguing that the state and the bank were in effect the same and that the notes were state bills of credit. As a Whig, Story appreciated the need for a circulating medium, but believed private banks chartered by states could supply this want. In his view the Constitution plainly prohibited states from issuing paper money, and he thought the Court was engaging in a subterfuge by regarding the Kentucky bank as private. Exaggerated as Story's lamentation on the passing of the old order may have been, his dissent underscored the expedient nature of the decision.

The Charles River Bridge Case

The most important case in the early years of the Taney era, from the standpoint of constitutional ideology, was the famous controversy in Massachusetts over the Charles River Bridge. In the *Dartmouth College* case the Marshall Court had held that state-issued charters of incorporation were contracts in the sense of the Constitution and could not be abrogated or impaired. Under that ruling states could reserve the right to modify corporation charters. But many states failed to do so, and disputes arose over the precise nature of privileges bestowed on corporations by legislative charters. Treating the charter as a contract was a useful means of guaranteeing entrepreneurs the security they seemed to deserve for making public improvements. It was also true, however, that corporations could act in ways injurious to the public, and this fact stimulated anticorporation sentiment among both Old Republican and entrepreneurial-minded Jacksonians. Not the fundamentally contractual nature of state-granted charters, therefore, but rather the scope of corporate privilege under them was the issue in the Massachusetts bridge case.

As well as the increased economic importance of the corporation, developments in the field of transportation formed the context for the bridge controversy. A transportation revolution was occurring. Turnpike travel in the early nineteenth century was superseded by canal and river transport, which in turn were challenged by the railroad. At each stage the existing mode of commerce and transportation, protected by legal franchises awarded by the state, fought the superior competitive advantage possessed by the newer mode. Sound public policy suggested the wisdom of encouraging new forms of transportation and enterprise in general. Yet it seemed equally important, in order to assure technological progress in the future, to protect those willing to venture their capital in risky public improvement projects. Although new modes of transportation were not involved in the bridge case, the legal principles that resolved it had application in this dynamic sector of the nineteenth-century economy.

In 1785 the Massachusetts legislature had incorporated the Charles River Bridge Company for a period of forty years, and had empowered it to erect a bridge over the Charles River and to collect tolls for passage over the bridge. In 1792 the life of the original charter was extended to seventy years. Before the expiration of the charter, however, the legislature authorized another corporation, the Warren Bridge Company, to erect another bridge over the Charles River at a point less than three hundred yards from the earlier bridge. By the terms of its charter, the new corporation was to turn its bridge over to the state as soon as its expenses of construction were paid; it was, therefore, potentially toll-free and threatened to destroy almost entirely the value of the earlier bridge. Accordingly, in 1829 the Charles River Bridge Company sought an injunction against the construction of the new bridge, on the grounds that the older charter by implication gave it sole and exclusive right to operate a bridge at the point in question during the life of its charter, and that the second charter, therefore, constituted an impairment of the obligation of contracts.

The Supreme Court denied that the state had violated the contractual rights of the Charles River Bridge Company in chartering the new bridge. Chief Justice Taney in his majority opinion disarmed his critics by citing at the outset an opinion of John Marshall, in *Providence Bank* v. *Billings* (1830), rejecting the idea that a state bank charter by implication gave exemption from state taxation. Marshall had said the taxing power was too important to be relinquished by presumption; Taney extended the idea to all the powers of state government as he described the central tenet of Jacksonian dual federalism—the doctrine of the police power. "The object and end of all government," Taney declared, "is to promote the happiness and prosperity of the community by which it is established; and it can never be assumed, that the government intended to diminish its power of accomplishing the end for which it was created." Rejecting the argument for an implied corporate privilege, he added: "We cannot deal thus with the rights reserved to the States, and by legal intendments and mere technical reasoning, take away from them any portion of that power over their own internal police and improvement, which is so necessary to their well being and prosperity."

Taney argued further that to allow the old bridge to block the construction of the new one would jeopardize progress in internal improvements. The old turnpike companies, he warned, would claim in their charters "unknown and undefined property in a line of travelling" and would ask courts to keep canals and railroads from being built. Millions of dollars of investments would be threatened, and the country would stand still until the claims of obsolete enterprises were satisfied. Only then, said Taney, would these companies permit the states "to avail themselves of the lights of modern science, and to partake of the benefit of those improvements which are now adding to the wealth and prosperity, and the convenience and comfort of every other part of the civilized world." In other words, creative destruction of existing property rights was occasionally necessary to achieve economic progress.

To be sure, Taney did not disavow the rule of the *Darmouth College* case that a state charter of incorporation was a contract. He held that charter grants must be interpreted strictly, that corporation privileges could not be created by implication, and that ambiguities must be resolved in favor of the state. Modern commentators have concluded, therefore, that he merely refrained from extending the principle of the *Dartmouth College* decision. Yet in reality the difference between Marshall and Taney was much greater than this formal analysis suggests, for Taney abandoned the entire conceptual approach employed in the *Dartmouth College* case. This becomes apparent when one considers Justice Story's dissenting opinion.

As Story saw it, the state wanted a bridge built and the proprietors sought a profit; the two parties, therefore, reached an understanding and entered into a contract in the form of the charter of incorporation. The Charles River Bridge Company got the right to collect tolls and in return built and operated a bridge which it promised to give to the state after a period of years. According to Story, the bridge company never would have agreed to the contract if the investors had thought the legislature was reserving the right to destroy the enterprise by chartering a free bridge right next to it. This elementary perception was common sense and common law, said Story, and it must control the disposition of the matter. The charter must be interpreted, in other words, as a contract in private law.

It was this private-law contractual character of the transaction that Taney denied. Instead he argued that the charter was like a royal grant. Plausible as this analogy may appear, it contained revealing—and for Story disturbing—implications about Jacksonian constitutional philosophy. For it amounted to the substitution of a ruler-subject relationship for the relationship between equals that was implicit in the private-law contract theory. If the charter was like a royal grant, then the state legislature was like a king. Possessing sovereign power, it had the right to determine the public good and override the rights of individuals in order to obtain it. Story contended on the contrary that legislatures were not like kings; they were not sovereign. Rather, the people were sovereign, and legislative power was limited.

Story desired to encourage venture capital and economic progress, as did the majority of the Court. He did not defend static, unproductive vested rights. In his view, however, economic development required predictability and certainty of legal outcomes that would guarantee investors a return on their investment. Moreover, he believed the means chosen by Taney to promote economic progress threatened basic principles of republican constitutionalism. Taney would lodge sovereign power in the state government, backed by the will of the majority. The result would be the triumph of political expediency over the rule of law. In reaching this conclusion Story, whose emotional involvement in the case was considerable, perhaps exaggerated. Yet historians generally agree that Taney's opinion, for all its legalistic cleverness and plausibility, was heavily instrumental and pragmatic, a response to the social and economic demands of the Jacksonian majority. Story's dissent reflected an older conception of republican constitutional morality, Taney's a newer approach that emphasized the creation and exercise of power in the name of state legislative sovereignty, guided by political expediency rather than fixed constitutional principle. Whether the active government posited in Taney's politicized constitutional vision would be limited and responsible government, and thus consistent with the American constitutional tradition, remained to be seen. In any event, more was at stake in the bridge case than simply the question of interpreting corporation charters.

The Taney Court consistently adhered to the rule of strict construction of charter grants, and in an important related development held that state exercises of the power of eminent domain that abrogated charters were not violations of the contract clause. This point was settled in *West River Bridge Company* v. *Dix* (1848). The state of Vermont had granted a franchise to a bridge company to collect tolls, but subsequently took it away with a view toward constructing a free public highway. Although the bridge company got compensation, it argued that the taking impaired the obligation of the contract. It also condemned the theory of an eminent-domain power as a new and despotic doctrine that would enable states to take property unrestrainedly. The Supreme Court upheld the taking as constitutional. For the Court, Justice Peter V. Daniel asserted that every sovereign political community had the right and duty, under the power of eminent domain, to protect its interests and welfare, both in external relations and in its interior polity and social life. Paramount to all private rights vested under the government, said Daniel, the eminent-domain power was retained by the states when they entered the Union and could be used to promote the public good.

The Sanctity of Contract

Despite the anticorporation overtones emanating from decisions based on the rule of strict interpretation of charter grants, the Taney Court more than adequately protected property rights and encouraged corporation growth. It scrupulously guarded corporate privileges that were specifically identified in charters. In the notable case of *Gelpcke* v. *Dubuque* (1864), it went so far as to hold that a state supreme court decision interpreting the state constitution to permit repudiation of a bond issue violated the contract clause.

The *Gelpcke* case involved a provision in the Iowa state constitution limiting state indebtedness to $100,000. The legislature circumvented the restriction by authorizing municipalities to issue bonds, and the city of Dubuque did so in order to get a railroad. The road was never built, however, and taxpayers filed suit against payment of the bonds. They were upheld by the state supreme court, which declared the bond issue in violation of the state constitution. The United States Supreme Court, for the first time overruling a state court decision interpreting the state's own constitution, reversed the decision. It held the bond issue valid as a contract which at the time it was made was sanctioned by state law. At stake were millions of dollars worth of bond issues all over the country, and even though there seemed to be justice in the complaint of communities that had to pay for railroads that were never built, the Court insisted on the sanctity of contractual obligations.

In cases involving state debtor-relief laws and private contractual rights between individuals, the Court also enforced the contract clause. In part this was because much current legislation of this kind, especially the debtor-relief legislation arising out of the long depression following the Panic of 1837, concerned property rights in land and mortgages, toward which most of the justices were more sympathetic than they were toward corporate property. In the outstanding case of this kind, *Bronson* v. *Kinzie* (1843), the Court declared invalid as an impairment of the obligation of contracts two Illinois laws restricting foreclosure sales and giving debtors certain broad rights to repurchase foreclosed property. Most state bankruptcy statutes of the day were not as radical as these, however; they seldom attempted to reduce or modify the debt, but instead contented themselves with softening the methods of execution by permitting installment payments, extending redemption dates, and the like. The Court customarily upheld this type of law under the doctrine advanced by Marshall in *Sturges* v. *Crowninshield* that the state could rightfully modify the legal "remedy" or method of enforcing a contract as long as it did not impair the terms of the contract itself.

The Supreme Court's application of the contract clause reflected the social approval of contract at this time as an instrument of economic growth. Under the supervision of the state courts, contract law was one of the most dynamic areas of private law. Used to extend market operations and introduce greater stability and predictability into economic exchange, it had major consequences for public policy. Philosophically contract-law interpretation shifted from a precommercial point of view which had allowed courts to judge the essential fairness of business dealings. The new basis of contract-law adjudication was the laissez-faire belief that individuals should be free to bargain as they saw fit in order to promote their own interests. The corollary was that courts would enforce contracts without regard to their moral content. In any event, as American political practice had drawn heavily on contract theory, so the burgeoning commercial capitalism of the antebellum era utilized the legal instrument of contract.

The Legal Status of Corporations

Closely related to the use of contract was reliance on the corporation as a means of economic expansion. Corporations were increasingly popular for their economic usefulness. Yet they were also objects of hostility because of the exclusive legal privileges they enjoyed, such as the power of eminent domain and freedom from competition. These privileges were obtained by special acts of the state legislatures. One response to the problem of the corporation, therefore, was to adopt general incorporation laws permitting anyone to secure the benefits that corporate status provided. The alternative was to prohibit corporations or strictly to regulate them through legislation. States that pursued the latter course frequently attempted to restrict corporations created in other states. Accordingly, cases came before the Supreme Court questioning the status of corporations under the rules of interstate relations, or comity, and also under the diversity of citizenship clause of the Constitution. In both situations the Taney Court acted favorably toward corporations, and extended legal protection to them.

Bank of Augusta v. *Earle* was the most important of three cases in 1839 dealing with the power of a state to exclude foreign (i.e., out of state) corporations. An Alabama citizen refused to pay the bills of exchange of a Georgia bank on the ground that a foreign corporation had no legal right to make a contract within a sovereign state. Counsel for the bank argued that a corporation, like a citizen, could enter another state and engage in business under the protection of the privileges-and-immunities clause of the federal Constitution.

The Court's decision, rendered by Chief Justice Taney, recognized the general right of a corporation to do business under interstate comity within other states. But it also recognized the right of the states to exclude foreign corporations by positive action if they so desired. Taney also refused to recognize corporations as possessing all the legal rights guaranteed to natural persons under the Constitution. Accordingly, he held that a corporation could have legal existence only in the state creating it, and that it could not migrate to another state by virtue of any right bestowed in the privileges-and-immunities clause, though it might do business in other states if they consented. The immediate question was whether this consent must be expressed or merely implied. Taney maintained that "the silence of the state authorities" in face of extensive activities by outside corporations gave presumption of the state's acquiescence. Alabama law prohibited out-of-state banking but was ambiguous as to whether selling bills of exchange was included in banking. Disavowing any intention of determining state policy, Taney nevertheless did precisely that by adopting the rule of comity and interpreting Alabama law so as to allow the bills in question. His carefully constructed opinion plainly upheld the power of states to prohibit or regulate foreign corporations, and states subsequently enacted much legislation of this sort. On balance, however, the decision was more favorable to corporations than to their critics.

Although the Court continued to deny corporations citizenship status under the privileges-and-immunities clause (a question of great complexity and uncertainty because of the problem of defining the status of free Negroes), it recognized corporations as citizens under the clause giving federal courts jurisdiction in controversies between citizens of different states. The Marshall Court had held that only if all members of a corporation were residents of another state could a citizen bring suit against it in federal court under the diversity clause. As corporations grew more numerous there was dissatisfaction with this rule, which made it practically impossible for them to go into the national courts. In *Louisville, Cincinnati and Charleston Railroad Company* v. *Letson* (1844) the Taney Court opened the federal courts to the new business associations by holding that a corporation was a citizen of the state in which it was chartered, irrespective of where its members resided. States'-rights judges, such as Peter V. Daniel and John A. Campbell, objected to this change, but the Court affirmed it in *Marshall* v. *Baltimore and Ohio Railroad Company* (1854). Although corporations did not at this time uniformly seek access to the federal courts, and continued to be denied the more comprehensive citizenship that potentially lay in the privileges-and-immunities clause, the Letson rule proved beneficial to them because it led to the creation by the federal courts of a more uniform body of commercial law beyond the reach of state power. Thus in a field where slavery was not involved, the Taney Court tended toward centralization, albeit of a judicial rather than a legislative kind.

The Commerce Power and Dual Federalism

In questions of economic policy the Court tried to balance the need for nationally protected commercial development against promotional and occasional regulatory tendencies in the states. But in a variety of controversial internal social matters that came to it through commerce-clause litigation it conspicuously deferred to the states under the theory of dual federalism. From the 1820s, when John Marshall broadly expounded the federal commerce power, southerners were keenly aware of the potential harm that could come to slavery from this source. By 1837 an abolition movement existed in the northern states; southerners were defending slavery as a positive good; and Democratic politicians had difficulty keeping the slavery question out of national politics. Under the circumstances the Supreme Court, with five southerners forming a majority, was acutely sensitive to the danger to slavery inherent in a broad definition of commerce that would regard slaves as articles of commerce and in an expansive conception of congressional power to regulate interstate commerce. Accordingly, in contrast to the Marshall Court, the Taney Court defined commerce narrowly and allowed the states to exercise the police power in ways that affected interstate commerce. Eventually, the Court recognized a concurrent state power to regulate interstate commerce in the absence of congressional legislation.

New York v. *Miln,* one of the three major cases of the 1837 term carried over from the Marshall era, revealed the dual-federalist approach the Court would take in commerce-power controversies. The case involved the validity of a New York law requiring masters of ships arriving in New York to report certain data on all passengers brought into port. The law had been attacked as an interference with congressional authority over foreign commerce, but Justice Barbour, speaking for five of the seven justices, held the law valid as a legitimate exercise of the state's police power, since the state's internal welfare was the obvious purpose of the statute. Unlike the act in *Gibbons* v. *Ogden,* he said, the New York law did not conflict with any act of Congress so as to raise a question about the scope of the state police power in relation to the federal commerce power. Barbour said further that the act was legitimate even if considered as a commercial regulation because Congress had not acted. He thus suggested that the states possessed a concurrent commerce power. In good dual-federalist fashion, however, Barbour based his decision on what he called the "impregnable" doctrine of the police power: that a state has the same unlimited jurisdiction over persons and things within its territorial limits as a foreign nation, except as restrained by the Constitution. The authority of a state in exercising the police power to promote the well-being of the community, said Barbour, "is complete, unqualified, and exclusive." Nevertheless, Barbour took the opportunity to state that goods were articles of commerce, but persons were not. This dictum was immediately relevant to the slavery issue, and it provoked objections from northern justices.

The relation between slavery and the commerce power came under discussion in *Groves* v. *Slaughter* (1841). The case involved a provision of the Mississippi constitution intended to prohibit the introduction of slaves into the state for the purpose of selling them. The specific question was whether the constitutional provision operated of its own force, in which case the sale of slaves after its adoption would be illegal, or whether it needed to be implemented by legislation, in which case the sale of slaves would not be illegal. The Court approved the sale in question, reasoning that the constitution was not effective until implemented by legislation.

The relationship between the Mississippi prohibition of slaves and the federal commerce power was not at issue in *Groves* v. *Slaughter* and did not need to be resolved, but Justice McLean of Ohio addressed it in a separate opinion. Rejecting the conclusion of the *Miln* case, he asserted that slaves *were* articles of commerce, and indeed were persons under the Constitution. He also said that Congress had exclusive power over interstate commerce. Nevertheless, he retreated from this bold position in saying, contradictorily, that the states had exclusive power over slavery. Thinking no doubt of his own state, Ohio, McLean declared that each state had a right to protect itself against "the inconveniences and danger of a slave population." This right, he added, was "higher and deeper than the Constitution." In one of the many ironies that characterized the sectional struggle over slavery, Chief Justice Taney accepted this conclusion, but for entirely different reasons. State regulation of the introduction or control of slaves within their territorial limits, said Taney, could not be controlled by Congress under the commerce power or any other power.

In the *License Cases* (1847) the Court upheld state power, although the justices were unable to agree on a single rationale for the decision. The cases concerned the validity of three statutes of Massachusetts, Rhode Island, and New Hampshire regulating and taxing the sale of alcoholic liquors. The laws were attacked on the ground that in taxing liquor imported from outside the state they in effect imposed unconstitutional regulations upon interstate commerce and so were void. The New Hampshire case was of particular interest, for here the tax had been levied upon liquor still in the "original package," in apparent violation of the dictum in *Brown* v. *Maryland*. There was considerable difference among the justices about certain legal details—the six justices wrote nine different opinions. But certain propositions stood out clearly amid the welter of legal reasoning. The justices were in general agreement that the fact that a state tax law levied for internal police purposes has an incidental effect upon interstate commerce did not thereby make it invalid.

Four justices—Taney, John Catron, Samuel Nelson, and Levi Woodbury—also thought the states had a concurrent right to regulate interstate commerce in the absence of federal action; and it was on this basis that the first three sustained the New Hampshire law. The federal commerce power, Taney maintained, was not exclusive. "It appears to me to be very clear," he said, "that the mere grant of power to the general government cannot, upon any just principles of construction, be construed to be an absolute prohibition to the exercise of any power over the same subject by the States.... In my judgment, the State may nevertheless, for the safety or convenience of trade, or for the protection of the health of its citizens, make regulations of commerce for its own ports and harbors, and for its own territory; and such regulations are valid unless they come in conflict with a law of Congress." The basis of this power in Taney's view, however, was not a concurrent commerce power, but rather "the powers of government inherent in every sovereignty . . . the power to govern men and things within the limits of its dominion." Leaving northerners like McLean to use the language of the police power, Taney took the high road of state sovereignty.

In the *Passenger Cases* (1849) it became clear, however, that the various justices were still far from agreement upon the precise line between the states' internal police power and the commerce power and upon the question of whether the commerce power was exclusive or concurrent. The cases involved the validity of New York and Massachusetts statutes imposing head taxes upon alien passengers arriving in the states' ports. Five justices thought the acts a direct regulation of interstate commerce and so void, McLean flatly declaring that the federal commerce power was lodged exclusively in the federal government and could not be exercised by the states even in the absence of congressional action. Amid the confusion of eight separate opinions, the Court at least seemed to have decided that persons were articles of commerce. This perception and the vindication of federal authority in the absence of congressional legislation caused many southerners to fear that state inspection laws aimed at preventing the abduction of slaves and laws barring entry of free Negro seamen in southern ports would be held unconstitutional. Justice Wayne of Georgia made it clear, however, that in his view states could separate slaves and free Negroes from commerce and protect their institutions against federal encroachment by means of the commerce power. For the minority, Chief Justice Taney argued that the state laws in question were specifically aimed at the prevention of disease and pauperism and hence were valid exercises of state sovereignty. States could not, Taney insisted, be forced to admit persons whom the federal government might choose to admit. They could remove or prohibit any one they chose, employing their reserved power of "self-preservation" as independent sovereignties. This was not a concurrent power, said Taney, and any act of the federal government in conflict with it was void.

Disagreement among the justices over the nature of the commerce power was largely reconciled in *Cooley* v. *Board of Wardens* (1851), a case in which the Court upheld a Pennsylvania statute regulating pilotage in the port of Philadelphia. Justice Benjamin Curtis, a Boston Whig lawyer recently appointed to the Court, speaking for six justices, said that the power to regulate commerce involved a vast field, some phases of which were national in character and so demanded congressional action. Here federal power was properly exclusive. Other aspects of commerce were local in character and demanded a diversity of local regulations. Here the states properly had a concurrent power to legislate in the absence of federal action. There was thus a limited concurrent state power over interstate commerce, exercisable only where Congress had not yet acted. Pennsylvania's regulation of pilotage came within this power.

This doctrine of "selective exclusiveness" took a more restrained view of state authority over commerce than Taney previously had. The important point for the advocates of dual federalism, however, was the concurrent power of the states or the nonexclusiveness of federal power, and since Curtis's opinion embodied this idea, Taney silently agreed with it. Justice Daniel alone protested that state power over local commerce was original and inherent in the states and not subject to federal control. McLean and Wayne dissented outright from the majority decision, insisting on the exclusive character of the federal commerce power. The Cooley rule expressed in a formal way the pragmatic approach that had characterized the Court's disposition of commerce power cases. Although it focused attention on the nature of commerce rather than on the nature of congressional power, it provided no guidelines for distinguishing between national and local commerce. The rule was an eloquent statement of indefiniteness. Yet, as Professor Swisher has observed, with the statement, the indefiniteness seemed more manageable.[1]

At the same session at which the *Cooley* case was decided, the Court in *Pennsylvania* v. *Wheeling Bridge Company* (1851) showed its willingness to respect federal authority over commerce when the exercise of that power came into conflict with that of the states. The state of Pennsylvania had attacked the bridge company's right to construct a bridge over the Ohio River under the supposed authority of Virginia statutes, claiming that the prospective bridge would interrupt interstate river navigation. The case attracted great popular interest because it involved a conflict between rival transportation systems—rivers and railroads—which was an important economic issue at the time. The Court held, with Justice McLean delivering the

---

1. Carl B. Swisher, *History of the Supreme Court of the United States,* Vol. V: *The Taney Period 1836-64* (1974), p. 407.

opinion, that the bridge was an interference with the federal commerce power as exercised by Congress in the coasting license acts. Its construction was, therefore, unlawful. Subsequently, however, Congress declared the bridge not to be an obstruction to navigation, and in a second case in 1856 the Supreme Court acquiesced in this view.

The Taney Court's commerce decisions expressed its dual-federalist conception of the Union. Without disavowing federal supremacy, the Court treated the existence of the states with their reserved powers as a limitation on federal authority. The state police power, or as Taney preferred to call it, state sovereignty, marked out certain subjects as exclusively within the jurisdiction of the states and beyond the reach of the national government. This feature of dual federalism subsequently enabled it to serve the South's need for an instrument of constitutional power with which to protect slavery against federal intervention.

The Taney Court and Judicial Nationalism

Although unsympathetic to a broad construction of national legislative power, the Taney Court significantly expanded federal judicial power. One aspect of this expansion, in response especially to the growth of the market economy, was the enlargement of federal court jurisdiction. Another aspect, the practical upshot of many of the rules of interpretation evolved in contract and commerce-clause cases, was an expansion of the federal courts' discretionary policy-making authority. Occasionally, the Taney justices made deferential gestures toward legislative authority, but these were more apparent than real. Eventually, the *Dred Scott* decision, in which the Court tried to settle the most explosive political issue of the day, gave the lie to the idea that the Taney justices were guided by a philosophy of judicial restraint. In fact, under pressure to defend slavery the Court regarded itself as uniquely qualified to umpire conflicts within the federal system. This attitude can be seen as continuous with the judicial nationalism of the Marshall era, but its subordination to proslavery state sovereignty caused it to be a distorted expression of the Marshall legacy.

Ironically, the Taney Court's concern for economic expansion led it to acquire a common-law jurisdiction denied to the Marshall Court. In 1812, it will be recalled, the Supreme Court held in *United States* v. *Hudson and Goodwin* that the federal courts possessed no common law criminal jurisdiction. In another case, *Wheaton* v. *Peters* (1834), it reiterated that there was no federal common law. In exercising jurisdiction in diversity-of-citizenship cases, moreover, the federal courts were required, under Section 34 of the Judiciary Act of 1789, to use the laws of the several states as rules of decision in trials at common law where the federal Constitution, statutes, or treaties were not controlling. Although in 1789 Congress seemingly intended to include state court decisions in the state law which the federal judiciary was instructed to apply, several judges in the Jacksonian era sought to escape this restriction. One means of doing so was to employ equity jurisprudence—a body of rules distinct from the common law—in diversity cases, in disregard of state court equity rulings. Justice Joseph Story, fearful of growing state power and the decline of federal authority, pursued this objective in his circuit court opinions. In *United States* v. *King* (1849), the Supreme Court, after Story's death, accepted the argument for federal equity jurisprudence.

More important was the attempt to fashion a federal common law jurisdiction. Despite repeated denials by the Supreme Court that a federal common law existed, compelling economic reasons urged federal judges in the 1830s to expand their power in this direction. Left to their own devices, states discriminated against out-of-state businesses and generally created conditions of legal uncertainty and instability that discouraged national economic development. Occasionally, in diversity litigation the Supreme Court under John Marshall had refused to be guided by state laws that were flagrantly hostile to interstate commercial interests. But the accepted interpretation of Section 34 of the Judiciary Act, which made state court decisions the rule of decision in interstate controversies, apparently blocked any serious attempt to counteract the particularity of state legislation by establishing a uniform commercial law.

Economic pressures following the Panic of 1837, however, led the Supreme Court to attempt to rectify this situation. In *Swift* v. *Tyson* (1842), it held that federal courts need not be bound by state court decisions in settling conflicts between citizens of different states that did not involve the federal Constitution, laws, or treaties. The case arose when one Tyson purchased land with a bill of exchange which through a separate transaction ended up in the possession of Swift. The original transaction turned out to be fraudulent, and Tyson argued that under New York law, including state court decisions that the federal courts were required to follow according to Section 34, the bill of exchange was invalid because corrupted by the original fraud. For a unanimous Court Justice Story held that the bill must be paid. In matters of a general nature not conditioned by local circumstances or governed by local statute, he reasoned, as in the construction of contracts and questions of general commercial law, the federal courts in diversity cases were not bound by state statutes or court rulings. Interpreting Section 34, Story said that state court decisions were not part of the "laws of the states" which federal courts were obliged to follow in diversity suits. Court decisions, he explained, were not laws; at most they were evidence of what the law was. Section 34, according to Story, thus referred to state statute law only. Moreover, it applied only to strictly local matters, not to questions of general commercial law. These broader questions, Story concluded, the federal courts were free to resolve according to their own interpretation of "the general principles and doctrines of commercial jurisprudence."

The Supreme Court subsequently affirmed *Swift* v. *Tyson* with a view toward creating a uniform body of national commercial law. This law would be functionally the same as the common law in its nonstatutory origins and judicial means of development, although historically it derived from the international law merchant rather than from the common law of England. At any rate the decision promised significantly to expand the sphere of federal judicial authority. Nationalists like Story assumed that the state courts would seek to apply the same principles of general commercial law in matters of general or extraterritorial import, and hence would be guided by federal court decisions explicating and developing this law. In practice, however, the state courts paid small regard to the federal judiciary's attempts to shape a national commercial common law. The consequence, by the late nineteenth century, was the existence of separate bodies of state and federal commercial common law which were the source of much confusion.

The Taney Court achieved greater success in extending the admiralty jurisdiction of the federal courts. In England admiralty jurisdiction applied only in tidal waters, and in 1825, in *The Thomas Jefferson,* the Supreme Court adopted this rule as a limitation on the admiralty and maritime jurisdiction of the federal judiciary. Subsequently the expansion of river and lake navigation and commerce led business interests to seek the extension of admiralty law to inland lakes, rivers, and waterways. Accordingly in 1845, for the benefit of businessmen in the interior of the country, Congress passed a law providing for the use of the forms and remedies of admiralty law in matters of tort and contract involving navigation and commerce on lakes and navigable waters between states and territories. In *Propeller Genesee Chief* v. *Fitzhugh* (1851) the Supreme Court upheld the broadened federal jurisdiction. Chief Justice Taney overruled the earlier Marshall decision, pointing out the inappropriateness of the tidal-waters limitation in light of the development of navigation in the interior of the nation. Resolving a matter that Congress had left ambiguous, Taney based the expanded federal jurisdiction on the admiralty power rather than the commerce clause. To make the commerce power the basis of the new jurisdiction, he said, would unduly extend federal legislative power into land commerce.

Expansion of judicial discretion in decision making, in contrast to formal jurisdiction, also occurred under Taney. An example was the invitation issued in the *Letson* case for corporations to enter the forum of the federal courts. The Court's pragmatic, case-by-case interpretation of the contract and commerce clauses further reflected the willingness of Jacksonian judges to assume a larger policy-making role. And when rules for deciding future conflicts were announced, as in the *Cooley* case, their practical import often was to enlarge the scope of judicial discretion. The *Cooley* rule of selective exclusiveness, for example, really meant that the Court would decide what was national commerce and what local.

These facts offer a corrective to the view sometimes advanced that the Taney Court rejected the political activism of the Marshall Court in favor of judicial restraint. Taney's defenders point to his dissent in the *Wheeling Bridge* case, for example. There he announced that as the Supreme Court had never exercised jurisdiction over the construction of bridges over navigable streams, and as Congress had power over the entire subject, it would be "too near the confines of legislation" for the Court to determine the question. The outstanding illustration of Taney's judicial restraint, however, is usually considered to be his opinion in *Luther* v. *Borden* (1849), announcing the doctrine of political questions.

As noted previously, the Court in this case formally refused to decide which of two competing governments in Rhode Island during the Dorr War was the legitimate state government. The question was political, declared Taney, and thus beyond the proper scope of judicial power. Yet Taney in effect did decide the question, in his interpretation of the guarantee-of-republican-government clause. He gratuitously defined the duties of the political branches under the guarantee clause and for all practical purposes acknowledged the existing charter government of Rhode Island as the legitimate state government. In actuality, *Luther* v. *Borden* expressed more of judicial assertiveness than restraint.

Unlike John Marshall, whose exercise of judicial power basically complemented the political branches of the national government, Taney conceived of the Supreme Court as a supranational and suprapolitical guardian of the Constitution. He saw the Court as the umpire of the federal system, charged with the responsibility of preventing the competing sovereignties—the states and the federal government—from invading each other's sphere of authority. Discussing the difficulty of drawing a line between federal and state power over commerce, Taney in the *License Cases* reasoned that as the Constitution did not attempt to fix the line of demarcation, and as neither Congress nor the states could enlarge their powers by legislation, "the question is necessarily one for judicial discretion."

Taney's strongest assertion of the role of the Supreme Court appeared in *Ableman* v. *Booth,* the famous fugitive slave case on the eve of the Civil War. Using ostensibly centralizing rhetoric, Taney spoke of the need to uphold national law, in this instance the Fugitive Slave Act of 1850. It was equally necessary, however, to protect the states against federal encroachment. The Supreme Court, said Taney, was created in order to provide this reciprocal protection, but it was not created by the federal government, "but by the people of the States." The judicial power was intended to maintain the supremacy of United States laws, and to guard the states against any invasion of their reserved rights by the federal government. "So long, therefore, as this Constitution shall endure," Taney declared, "this tribunal must exist with it, deciding the angry and irritating controversies between sovereignties, which in other countries have been determined by the arbitrament of force."

Even-handed as this dual-federalist, judicial supremacist doctrine appears to be, its application was guided by a commitment to the defense of slavery that invariably led the Taney Court to uphold state power. When the sectional struggle over slavery reached a climax in the late 1850s, Taney's dual federalism was ultimately subordinated to or became indistinguishable from a theory of state sovereignty that categorically denied national legislative sovereignty. In practical effect dual federalism was a doctrine of state power that encouraged the disunionist tendencies of the slave power. To give Taney his due it must be said that, like Calhoun, he was motivated also by a genuine desire to preserve the Union. Yet in Taney's view the fundamental purpose of the Union was to protect state interests and institutions, and pre-eminently the institution of slavery. This became the ultimate test of constitutional and political legitimacy under the doctrine of dual federalism.

State Mercantilism

In matters distinct from slavery the chief significance of dual federalism was to release state power for economic and social purposes. It remains briefly to consider the use that the states made of the power that devolved upon them during the era of dual federalism.

The formal division of sovereignty in American federalism notwithstanding, the states exercised most of the real power of government in the period before the Civil War. The distribution of economic resources was the major public policy issue, and although prior to Jackson's administration the federal government adopted policies on the tariff, land, money and banking, immigration, and patents for inventions, after 1832 it withdrew from much of this activity. The states meanwhile formulated mercantilist policies under the police power, the concurrent power over interstate commerce, and the power of eminent domain. They chartered corporations, including banks; built or funded internal improvements; allocated land and other natural resources; and distributed legal privileges and immunities that enabled entrepreneurial activitiy to flourish. Frequently, states expropriated property to promote economic development. State legislatures could take property under the law of eminent domain on condition that there be a legitimate public purpose and that the owner be given just compensation. Moreover, states sometimes delegated the power of eminent domain to turnpike, canal, bridge, railroad, and manufacturing companies.

State courts played an especially key role in state mercantilism by reshaping the common law into an instrument of economic progress. Perhaps the most fundamental change effected by the state judiciary was to redefine the legal conception of property in a manner appropriate to an expanding capitalist economy. In the eighteenth century the basic tenet of property law was the absolute right of a landowner to undisturbed enjoyment of his property. This was a static conception consistent with the outlook of an agrarian society. In the nineteenth century, by contrast, state common law courts sanctioned uses of property that were injurious to adjacent landowners. Damage to another's property was considered justified if it was economically and socially beneficial, as in the construction of dams and mills.

State courts in effect subsidized the development of the economy by fashioning legal doctrines and rules that shifted the cost of economic and technological change from the entrepreneur to the community. In tort law, for example, courts rejected the eighteenth-century standard of strict liability under which damages could be recovered for an injury regardless of its cause or the intention of the injuring party. Instead they formulated the negligence doctrine. This doctrine stated that damages for injuries occurring as a result of industrial or commercial activity (such as the operation of a railroad) could be recovered only on a showing of carelessness by the operating company or corporation. Furthermore, by redefining the legal meaning of injury, state courts were able to limit the effect of the just-compensation doctrine in situations where the power of eminent domain was exercised by transportation companies. Similarly, the law of nuisance, which in the eighteenth century protected landowners against interference with their property, was narrowly interpreted to prevent the award of damages for encroachment on property rights resulting from productive economic activity. Courts thus expressed the judgment of society that a certain amount of injury to person and property was a reasonable price to pay for economic progress.

State mercantilist policies in effect determined national economic policy, with results that were often haphazard, prodigal, and corrupt. Competition among groups for distributionist advantages from government was keen and figured largely in party battles between Whigs and Democrats. Nevertheless, a strong social consensus supported economic growth, and, because of the nature of distributionist policy, it was possible for government to satisfy competing interest-group demands by giving something to each. By the 1850s, moreover, the Old Republican animus against commercial development had disappeared from Democratic rhetoric, and Jacksonians as well as Whigs promoted internal improvements.

Central as it was, however, economic development was not the only concern of the states in the era of dual federalism. Suffrage, representation, and other political and constitutional problems, as we have seen, were important and contentious issues. Much as Americans might agree on the necessity of private property, government by consent, constitutional limitations, and national Union, the application of these fundamental principles stirred deep controversy. The organization and distribution of power were at issue here, and while economic policy sometimes provided the occasion for conflict in this sphere, by the 1850s a more difficult problem—one that was not amenable to solution in the piecemeal, decentralist way that characterized distribution policy—had emerged to dominate American politics. That problem, which concerned not only the distribution of power but the very nature of the Union and the future of the republic, was the problem of slavery.

FOURTEEN

Slavery and the Constitution

——————————— ✦ ✦ ✦ ———————————

THE COEXISTENCE OF NEGRO SLAVERY and republican liberty created an internal contradiction in American politics that eventually threatened not only the existence of the Union, but also constitutionalism and the rule of law. Slavery's flagrant violation of republican liberty and equality made it the object of abolitionist legislation in the northern states during and after the Revolution. Yet slavery was sanctioned by the Constitutional Convention, and throughout the early national period it remained a quiescent issue. In the Missouri crisis of 1820 diverging sectional attitudes and interests briefly though with alarming intensity made slavery a divisive national problem. Tensions eased with the formation of the Jacksonian coalition in the 1820s. By combining northern republicanism and southern defense of slavery the Jacksonians generally succeeded in keeping the slavery question out of national politics. With the rise of an organized abolition movement in the 1830s, however, this task became increasingly difficult. By the 1840s the nation's irresistible impulse toward territorial expansion caused the abandonment of the agreements and understandings which for a generation had assigned slavery a subordinate place in American politics.

Territorial expansion and the westward movement pre-eminently involved the founding of new communities and social institutions which could decisively influence the future development of the nation. In this context the possibility of slavery expansion into the interior of the continent was fraught with enormous consequences. It forced Americans to resolve fundamental ambiguities about the nature of the Union and the meaning of American nationality.

In the first half of the nineteenth century changes in culture, society, and economy produced an increasing degree of national uniformity and integration. At the same time geographical and territorial expansion enlarged the size of the nation. This process of nationalization, whether considered from a social-cultural or a geographical perspective, required coming to grips with the question of slavery. Would slavery, which by the end of the Revolutionary era had been placed outside the mainstream of American values as the South's "peculiar" institution, assume a central position in American politics and society? In constitutional terms the question was whether the law of slavery would become nationalized and be given ascendancy over the institutions of republican liberty that existed in the northern states.

Slavery and Republican Government

If slavery became the overriding issue in American politics only in the mid-nineteenth century, it had a long legal and constitutional history that placed limits on the way in which it could be dealt with politically. Although slavery had existed throughout human history, in Western societies it was never regarded as part of the natural order, but was seen as requiring the sanction and justification of positive law. In the American colonies in the seventeenth century local labor needs, economic exigency, racial prejudice, and the impulse toward European commercial expansion combined to transform the indentured servitude of black Africans into lifetime bondage. In the formative stages of this transformation positive law as adopted by colonial legislatures performed an important legitimizing function. By the time of the American Revolution slavery was legally recognized in all of the American colonies. Starting during the Revolution, however, the marginal economic value of slavery in the northern states permitted its gradual abolition, in accordance with the ideal of republican liberty. Although given prospective rather than immediate effect, gradual emancipation rendered slavery a local rather than a national institution.

The Constitutional Convention confirmed the character of slavery as a local institution. Although it might be argued that the sanction given slavery in the Constitution made it in some sense a national institution, the framers' chief purpose in this regard was to affirm state rather than federal power over the institution. Indeed, one of the fundamental ideas on which the Union may be said to have rested was that only the states could abolish or regulate slavery in the states where it existed. The corollary was that the federal government should remain divorced from the institution. Nevertheless, this separation was not to be absolute. Congress was authorized to abolish the international slave trade after twenty years; fugitive slaves (less offensively referred to in the language of the Constitution as persons "held to service or labor") could arguably become the subject of congressional legislation; and the federal promise to protect the states against insurrection, expressed in the guarantee-of-republican-government clause, could require the federal government to suppress slave rebellions.

Unquestionably, the founding fathers, although eschewing the word "slavery," gave positive recognition to the institution. In addition to the provisions already noted, they permitted the states to count three-fifths of their slave population (described as "other than free" persons) in the basis for apportionment of representatives. Yet while protecting slavery in the short run, the framers also took antislavery steps that pointed in the direction of the possible abolition of slavery. The provision for ending the slave trade after twenty years, despite the discretionary nature of the grant of power to Congress, was one such indication. Another was the exclusion of slavery from the Northwest Territory, an action of the Confederation Congress that was confirmed by the new federal legislature. To be sure, southerners approved the Northwest Ordinance, evidence that it was not uniformly perceived as auguring the eventual abolition of slavery. But the Ordinace expressed a resolve to stop the spread of slavery, and in practical effect it proved an essential barrier to the expansion of slavery into the states formed in the Northwest Territory in the next fifty years. If the revolutionary generation legitimized slavery in the nation's fundamental law, its actions also marked the beginning of an antislavery political tradition.

Allowed to remain more or less implicit at the Constitutional Convention, an attitude of neutrality toward slavery on the part of the federal government was expressly declared in the first Congress. At the urging of Quaker abolitionists, the House of Representatives created a special committee to consider the powers of Congress in relation to slavery. Although stopping well short of any finding of a general power of emancipation in the federal government, the committee took the position that Congress could indirectly regulate conditions in which slaves were held. But this was objectionable to the South. At the instance of James Madison, a substitute resolution was approved stating that Congress had no authority to interfere in slave emancipation or in the treatment of slaves. Madison's resolution concluded that the states alone possessed authority to regulate slavery. This change was acquiesced in by many northern representatives who were previously inclined toward an antislavery position, but who in order to win southern support for the assumption of state debts now refrained from backing any measures hostile to slavery.

Slavery was thus officially pronounced to be a local or municipal institution. South of the Mason-Dixon line it became the subject of separate systems of state law intended to protect it.[1] More slowly and intermittently it became the object of legislative and judicial action in the northern states aimed at excluding it in any form through guarantees of personal liberty. Because of the federal government's posture of neutrality, constitutional

1. As an aspect of state private law, slavery gave rise to numerous conflicts, which generally resulted from the contradiction between the status of the slave as property and the fact of his humanity. A similar contradiction existed between the rule of law and the personal dominion exercised by the master over his slave. As the need to defend slavery increased in the antebellum period, the law of slavery in the southern states evolved into a separate set of rules under the supervision of special courts, distinct from the regular legal system.

problems concerning slavery usually took the form of conflicts between states over the law to be applied in resolving disputes over personal liberty. One of the most important sources of antislavery jurisprudence relied on in these conflicts was the famous English case of *Somerset* v. *Stewart* (1772).

James Somerset was a slave brought to England from Jamaica in 1769, who was captured after escaping and held in detention for subsequent sale. Through the intervention of British abolitionists, Somerset obtained a writ of habeas corpus from Lord Mansfield, chief justice of King's Bench, who ruled that he was free by virtue of having lived in England, where slavery was not recognized. In words that had a profound influence on the American antislavery movement in the nineteenth century, Mansfield said that seizing a slave was "so high an act of dominion" that it "must be recognized by the law of the country where it is used." Mansfield stated further: "The state of slavery is of such a nature, that it is incapable of being introduced on any reasons, moral or political; but only [by] positive law. . . . It's so odious, that nothing can be suffered to support it but positive law." Narrowly construed, the decision meant that an escaped slave could not be captured and sold in England, or, by analogy, in any free state. Interpreted more broadly it meant that the law of slavery under which a slave was held did not by implication or presumption extend into a free polity. For slavery to exist, it must be recognized in positive law. Most broadly, Mansfield's opinion could be transformed into the doctrine that slavery was illegal because it violated natural law.

Slavery may have been a violation of natural law, but as long as only the tiniest part of the population felt that way the institution retained its legitimacy in the constitutional order. The *Somerset* case initially, therefore, had little influence outside abolitionist circles. Nevertheless, it was potentially of great importance because the conflict-of-laws situation that it presented offered a parallel to the way slavery questions might be raised in the United States. Given the legal status of slavery as a municipal institution and the presumption against federal involvement, constitutional problems concerning slavery arose most frequently in the context of interstate relations.

In essence the slavery controversy in the United States involved a fundamental conflict between opposing legal systems. Law in the southern states gave positive recognition to slavery, and generally assumed further that persons of color were slaves until they could prove themselves free. Because *Negro* slavery existed in the South, to assume otherwise would create serious difficulties in maintaining the basic principle of southern law—the right of the master to his property. An essential buttress to this principle was the right of recaption, a common law right that permitted the owner of property—in this instance slave property—to recapture it without judicial or other legal process, provided only that he do so in a manner consistent with public peace and order.

In the free states on the other hand the law presumed the freedom of all persons and provided legal means for guaranteeing personal liberty irrespective of color. The privilege of the writ of habeas corpus, by which courts could inquire into the causes of a person's detention and secure his release, and the right of personal replevin, a common law process for dealing with property that could also be used to win freedom for slaves, were the principal legal instruments employed to uphold the presumption of freedom. Trial by jury, a requirement under the process of personal replevin and occasionally in habeas corpus proceedings, was a third instrument for the protection of liberty. Under the constitutional dispensation that gave states virtually complete power to regulate personal liberty and civil rights, the presumption was strong that states could maintain the freedom of all persons within their jurisdiction.

The fundamental question in interstate controversies over slavery was whether the law of slavery of a southern state was valid and effective outside the state. Did, for example, a slave who entered a free state acquire personal liberty, or did his or her slave status continue in the free state? Five situations presented this conflict of laws: slaves brought for permanent residence in a free state; sojourning slaves brought for a limited period into a free state; *in transitu* slaves being taken from one slave jurisdiction to another; and fugitive slaves entering a free state. A fifth situation occurred when a slave who was emancipated in a free state returned to the slave state of origin, and the question arose whether his or her slave status resumed.

From 1790 to about 1830 free and slave states accommodated each other on questions concerning the extraterritorial or extrajurisdictional effect of their laws. Employing the rules of comity, by which sovereign states as a matter of discretion and convenience choose to recognize the laws of another jurisdiction, northern states permitted sojourning and *in transitu* slaves to reside temporarily on free soil and cooperated in the return of fugitive slaves. On the other hand, southern states acknowledged that indefinite or permanent residence in a free state resulted in emancipation, and southern courts recognized this condition of freedom in controversies caused by the return of former slaves to the South.

In the 1830s, however, after Nat Turner's Rebellion and with the emergence of abolitionism at the North and proslavery apologetics at the South, the period of accommodation ended. Now the *Somerset* doctrine, asserting the incompatibility of slavery and natural law and insisting on positive law as the only basis for slavery, became directly relevant. In 1836, for example, the Massachusetts Supreme Court incorporated *Somerset* doctrine in *Commonwealth* v. *Aves,* a case involving the personal liberty of a sojourner slave from Louisiana. Chief Justice Lemuel Shaw held the slave free on the ground that Louisiana slave law had no application in Massachusetts. Slavery was contrary to the constitution and laws of Massachusetts, said Shaw, and any attempt to bring a slave into the state

automatically resulted in emancipation. Furthermore, slavery was so repugnant to natural law that it had to be established by positive law. Similar
rulings against sojourner slave status were forthcoming in other northern
states. Southern states for their part reciprocated by refusing to recognize
the personal liberty acquired by blacks from residence in free states or
territories.

The Problem of Fugitive Slaves

The most contentious issue in relations between free and slave states
concerned the return of fugitive slaves. Yet since the rendition of fugitives
was dealt with in the federal Constitution, it was arguably a subject over
which the national government had power to act. Indeed, it was pressure for
national action on the fugitive slave question that first significantly weakened the rule of federal nonintervention with regard to slavery.

Article IV, Section 2 of the Constitution provided that persons "held to
Service or Labour" in one state who escaped into another state were not
thereby to be "discharged from Service" but were to be "delivered up on
Claim of the Party to whom such Service or Labour shall be due." The
precise meaning of this section was vague in that it did not make clear what
agency, state or federal, was charged with its execution. Article IV of the
Constitution dealt with various matters of interstate comity, and from this it
might have been assumed that the mutual return of fugitive slaves was an
obligation imposed upon the states rather than the federal government.
This supposition was strengthened by the fact that power to enact a fugitive
slave law was not among the enumerated powers of Congress.

In spite of this ambiguity, Congress in 1793 enacted a fugitive slave
law. This statute provided that fugitives escaping from one state into another might be seized by the master or his agent, brought before any federal
or state court within the state, and returned under warrant upon proof of
identity. The act thus put the responsibility for the return of fugitives upon
both federal and state courts, and so made state officials agents for the
enforcement of a federal constitutional provision. Various states, North and
South, also enacted fugitive slave laws which provided legal processes for
the seizure, detention, and return of fugitives through state police officers
and courts. This system of joint federal-state responsibility worked well
enough for a long time, and no one thought to challenge its constitutionality.

The fugitive slave law of 1793 gave a significant advantage to the
southern states, for it meant that the law of slavery would, or at least ought
to, prevail over the law of freedom in the event of conflict over runaway
slaves. It gave extraterritorial effect to the municipal law of slavery. The
corollary was that the free states were constitutionally prevented from ex-

ercising plenary power over the personal liberty and civil rights of all persons within their territorial limits.

As antislavery sentiment spread, dissatisfaction with this constitutional limitation increased and led to the adoption of personal liberty laws. The object of these laws was to throw legal safeguards around alleged fugitives and protect free Negroes from kidnaping. The Pennsylvania personal liberty law of 1826, for example, ostensibly intended to enforce the federal fugitive slave act, imposed stringent requirements on persons claiming alleged fugitives, provided for jury trial and Negro testimony, and prohibited lower state magistrates from taking cognizance of fugitive slave cases under the federal law. Connecticut also imposed the latter restriction and, together with Illinois, New York, and Vermont, guaranteed fugitives a jury trial.

The constitutionality of the Pennsylvania personal liberty law and the federal fugitive slave act of 1793 came before the Supreme Court in the case of *Prigg* v. *Pennsylvania* (1842). Edward Prigg, a slaveholders' agent from Maryland, had seized a runaway in Pennsylvania. Upon being denied a warrant in the state courts he had forcibly carried the slave back to Maryland without benefit of further legal proceedings. Returning to Pennsylvania, he was indicted and convicted of violating the kidnaping clause in the act of 1826. This verdict was sustained by the Pennsylvania Supreme Court, and an appeal was thereupon taken to the United States Supreme Court.

Justice Story, giving the opinion of the Court, held the Pennsylvania law to be in conflict with the federal law and thus unconstitutional. Story began by positing the right to recapture fugitive slaves as a self-executing, fundamental constitutional right, available to the master without the aid of federal legislation or judicial process in any state. But, he reasoned, since the right of recaption was confined to no territorial limits, and since the subject demanded uniform national treatment to prevent states from adopting conflicting measures upholding the right, the power over fugitive slaves belonged exclusively to Congress. Rejecting the antislavery argument that Congress lacked power to enact fugitive slave legislation and that the entire subject lay within state jurisdiction, Story pronounced the 1793 act constitutional. Because the Pennsylvania law conflicted with it by denying the right to recapture fugitive slaves, it must be struck down.

The *Prigg* decision constituted a major victory for the slave interest. In the most unequivocal terms Story wrote into constitutional law the southern states' right of recaption. He described this as "an absolute and positive right ... pervading the whole Union with an equal and supreme force, uncontrolled and uncontrollable by State sovereignty or State legislation." On the surface the decision was highly centralizing in its effect. Yet in reality it endorsed state sovereignty by upholding the slave states' right of recaption, which was now imposed on the free states in derogation of their desire to protect personal liberty. With reason abolitionists promptly condemned the result. Yet Story's opinion also contained a dissonant note that proved to have antislavery potential.

The discordant note appeared in Story's interpretation of the exclusive nature of federal power over fugitive slaves. His opinion was unclear as to whether states could, if they wished, assist in enforcing the federal fugitive slave law and, if they did not so wish, whether they could be compelled to do so. Story said yes on the first count and no on the second. The act of 1793 plainly conferred authority on the states, and as Story regarded this meaure as constitutional, he obviously was prepared to accept reliance on state officers as constitutionally permissible. Undoubtedly, state magistrates "may, if they choose," Story noted, exercise the authority over fugitive slaves conferred on them by the federal statute. States could also use the police power to arrest, restrain, and remove fugitive slaves from their borders. What they could not do was adopt additional regulations inhibiting the exercise of the right to recapture runaway slaves. Nevertheless, Story refrained from saying that states had a duty or obligation to assist in the rendition of fugitives. On the contrary, he declared that states could not be compelled to enforce provisions of the Constitution entrusting duties to the federal government. Thus if state officers might choose to cooperate in returning fugitives, the states could also prohibit such cooperation.

These utterances offered a degree of solace to antislavery men and provided northern states with an instrument with which to protect personal liberty in controversies over alleged fugitives. In a concurring opinion Chief Justice Taney attacked Story's emphasis on federal exclusivity on the ground that it would encourage state noncooperation; the states had a duty to assist in enforcing the fugitive slave law, Taney argued. And in fact a majority of the justices believed that states could legislate in support of the federal rendition process, as they held in *Moore* v. *Illinois* in 1852. However, antislavery lawyers, judges, and legislators put Story's dictum to precisely the opposite use. They cited it as authority for denying jurisdiction over fugitive cases, thus freeing alleged runaways. They also used it to justify legislation prohibiting state officials from enforcing the federal fugitive slave law and denying the use of state facilities for that purpose.

The Supreme Court was thus widely if inaccurately perceived as having prohibited state action to assist in the return of fugitives. One direct consequence was the enactment in several northern states of personal liberty laws aiming at noncooperation. A second consequence was a determined effort by southerners, in part provoked by the new personal liberty laws, to adopt a more stringent fugitive slave law based exclusively on federal power. A few years later, as part of the Compromise of 1850, Congress adopted such a measure.

The Fugitive Slave Act of 1850 provided for the appointment, by federal circuit courts, of federal commissioners who were given concurrent jurisdiction with federal district courts over fugitive slave questions. Upon presentation of satisfactory proof of ownership, the federal commissioner was authorized to permit the claimant to remove the fugitive slave or, if circumstances warranted, to entrust the rendition to a federal marshal. The act provided no jury trial, nor did it permit the alleged fugitive slave to testify. Moreover, the decision of the federal commissioner was declared conclusive as against the issuance of a state writ of habeas corpus.

Antislavery men regarded these provisions as a gross violation of rights guaranteed in the Fifth and Sixth Amendments. They contended that Congress had no power over fugitive slaves, and that since the decision-making process envisioned in the law was essentially judicial, reliance on federal commissioners violated the requirements of the Constitution concerning the exercise of judicial power. Defenders of the fugitive slave act cited Story's *Prigg* opinion as authority. They held further that the rendition of fugitives was a ministerial rather than a judicial process, and hence not subject to the procedural guarantees appropriate to a court of law.

The Nationalization of the Slavery Question

If the fugitive slave problem involved both state and federal governments, other aspects of the slavery question mainly concerned the federal government. A consensus on the wisdom and desirability of federal neutrality toward slavery had long served to keep the issue subordinated and out of the mainstream of political controversy. As the fugitive slave question showed, however, public opinion in the 1840s increasingly demanded that slavery be dealt with as a national issue. The Compromise of 1850, followed by the formation of the Republican party as an exclusively sectional antislavery organization in 1854, signified the abandonment of the idea of federal neutrality and the nationalization of the slavery problem. When that happened the Union itself was placed in jeopardy.

The Constitutional Convention made an exception to the rule of federal neutrality by confining the subject of the slave trade to Congress. Article I, Section 9 of the Constitution stated: "The migration or importation of such persons as any of the States now existing shall think proper to admit, shall not be prohibited by the congress prior to the year one thousand eight hundred and eight." This language undoubtedly empowered Congress to ban the international slave trade, and possibly also the domestic or interstate traffic in slaves. Whether it did depended on the meaning of "such persons." Obviously, the term referred to slaves, whom the founding fathers once again refused to name out of deference to moral sensibility. But if it referred only to slaves, as everyone assumed when the Constitution was written and ratified, then the clause could be construed as giving Congress the power, after 1808, to prohibit the migration of slaves, as opposed to their importation; in other words, as prohibiting the interstate slave trade. By the early nineteenth century, however, this interpretation was obviously unacceptable to southerners because of its antislavery potential. They insisted that the clause, and the words "such persons," referred to white aliens as well as Negroes. The term "importation," they reasoned, described Negro slaves, and "migration" white foreigners. Southerners thus tried to restrict the migration and importation clause—and hence congressional power over commerce—to matters pertaining to entry into the United States from abroad. Under this interpretation Congress in 1808 legislated against the international slave trade.

The southern view of the importation and migration clause and also of the commerce power, earnestly supported by Madison and Jefferson, eventually prevailed. In the wake of the Missouri crisis southerners feared in the 1820s that the federal commerce power would be employed against the domestic slave trade, even as it had been used against the international slave trade. From a constitutional standpoint the fear was not unfounded, for in 1804 Congress had legislated against the internal slave trade. The Orleans (Louisiana) territorial act of that year forbade the importation of slaves from abroad, and also "from any port or place within the limits of the United States." Although the act was not enforced, and a year later the domestic slave trade ban was dropped from further territorial legislation in Louisiana, it showed the possibility of an antislavery interpretation of the commerce power.

Controversies over southern states' black seamen's laws in the 1820s raised further questions about the federal commerce power and slavery. In 1822 South Carolina, reacting to an alleged slave uprising, passed a law providing that all free Negroes who came as sailors into the ports of the state should be arrested by the local sheriff and held in jail until their ship was ready to sail. In the case of *Elkinson* v. *Deliesseline* (1823) in federal circuit court, Justice William Johnson held the South Carolina law unconstitutional as an encroachment on the exclusive power of Congress over foreign and interstate commerce. South Carolina ceased to enforce the statute against British Negroes after the English government protested that it violated a commercial treaty with the United States. But, disregarding the federal court ruling, South Carolina applied the law against Negroes from northern states.

In the 1830s, as we have seen, the scope of the commerce power and its relation to slavery came before the Supreme Court. Despite some vacillation, the Taney Court held generally that persons—and most importantly slaves—were not articles of commerce. Rather, the entire subject of slavery was subject to the police power under the doctrine of state sovereignty. Even an antislavery-tending justice such as McLean of Ohio, who regarded the federal commerce power as exclusive, agreed that slaves were beyond the scope of the federal commercial authority. The Court thus gave no encouragement to the possible use of the commerce power to prohibit or regulate the interstate slave trade.

Other questions concerning slavery obtruded on national politics in the 1830s, despite Jacksonian efforts to keep the issue muted. One controversy concerned federal and state powers in relation to the delivery of mail. The abolitionists early adopted the device of flooding the mails with quantities of pamphlets, newspapers, and circulars addressed to southerners and in some instances to slaves themselves. Southerners, not unnaturally, hotly resented this practice as an attempt to stir up servile insurrection, and postmasters in the South often took it upon themselves, without formal legal sanction, to destroy such material. President Jackson sympathized with the southern attitude in this matter, and in December 1835 he recommended the passage of a federal censorship law.

Calhoun and other southerners, however, feared the centralizing effects of federal postal censorship, and they, therefore, opposed Jackson's suggestion. Instead, in February 1836, a Senate committee under Calhoun's chairmanship reported a bill providing that it should be unlawful for any deputy postmaster knowingly to receive and mail any matter "touching the subject of slavery, directed to any person or post-office in any state where by the laws thereof their circulation is prohibited." Calhoun recognized congressional power to regulate the mail, but saw this as a mere delegated power subordinate to the states' power and right to enforce laws necessary for their peace and security. The southern states' laws recognizing and protecting slavery, an expression of state sovereignty, had primacy, and the federal government as agent of the states was obligated to uphold them.

The Senate rejected Calhoun's bill, whereupon Congress passed a law prohibiting federal postmasters from refusing to deliver mail to its proper address. Apparently a blow for liberty and antislavery, the law was never enforced at the South. Nonenforcement was premised on the theory that federal power over the mail ceased upon reception in the state, at which point state power became exclusive and state laws governing the circulation of incendiary material took effect. Consistent with its policy of subordinating slavery while accommodating southern interests, the Jackson administration acquiesced in this solution to the problem.

Controversy also developed over abolitionist petitions and memorials asking Congress to abolish slavery in the District of Columbia. Since the federal government presumably had full police power in the District, the petitions had a plausible constitutional foundation, but they infuriated southern congressmen, who not without reason regarded them as attempts to drive a wedge into the institution of slavery. In any event, they said, Congress had no lawful authority to interfere with slavery in the District, for the institution was protected by a federal contract with the states of Virginia and Maryland. This contract had been incorporated in the Act of

1802, which organized government in the District and by which Congress had promised not to interfere with the domestic institutions and property rights of residents in the ceded areas.

The debate over slavery in the District was notable for the reliance of both pro- and antislavery men on the due process clause of the Fifth Amendment. Drawing on traditional vested-rights doctrine, defenders of slavery held that the Fifth Amendment guarantee against deprivation of life, liberty, and property without due process of law prevented any federal interference with slave property in the District of Columbia. Antislavery reformers used the amendment to condemn the deprivation of slaves' liberty without due process of law (as well as without jury trial and judicial process). Moreover, both groups advanced a substantive interpretation of the Fifth Amendment due process clause. Regardless of the procedure or forms employed, they reasoned, no act of Congress was legitimate or constitutional which, depending on one's point of view, in substance or effect destroyed property in slaves or deprived black persons of their liberty.

The right to petition Congress was seemingly protected by the First Amendment, but the steady flow of abolitionist petitions in Congress nevertheless inspired southern congressmen to find some means of banning them. Southerners contended that the First Amendment guaranteed the right of petition only upon subjects within the constitutional competence of Congress, and that Congress was under no obligation to receive petitions upon matters beyond its lawful concern. Slavery, they pointed out, was a domestic institution of the states over which Congress had no authority; hence petitions on slavery could be lawfully rejected. Many northern delegates in Congress, anxious to suppress antislavery agitation, were sympathetic with this attitude, although others thought that any house rule barring petitions would violate the Constitution.

After some months of intermittent debate, the House of Representatives in May 1836 adopted a "gag rule" intended to bar abolitionist petitions entirely. The rule, drawn by Representative Henry Pinckney of South Carolina, stated that "all petitions, memorials, resolutions, propositions, or papers relating in any way, or to any extent whatsoever, to the subject of slavery, or the abolition of slavery, shall, without being either printed or referred, be laid upon the table, and no further action whatever shall be had thereon." The resolution passed, 117 to 68, over the bitter protests of John Quincy Adams of Massachusetts, who denounced the proposal as "a direct violation of the constitution of the United States, the rules of this House, and the rights of my constituents." In spite of Adams's continued opposition, the House strengthened the rule in 1840 to ban outright any attempt to introduce petitions on slavery. This was a more extreme prohibition than that of 1836, which had merely established a uniform rule for disposing of memorials.

Adams made the repeal of the House gag rule a *cause célèbre,* which he carried on for years, much to the displeasure of his colleagues. He was finally successful in obtaining repeal in 1844, largely because the growth of northern antislavery sentiment had convinced most northern congressmen that it would be politically unwise to support the rule longer.

Protective of slavery as the gag rule was, it failed to satisfy Calhoun and the South Carolinians, who wanted Congress categorically to reject antislavery petitions without even receiving them. In order to bind congressional opinion more firmly to the southern point of view, Calhoun in December 1837 introduced state-sovereignty resolutions into the Senate. The resolutions held that the several states had voluntarily entered the Union as independent and sovereign states, retaining "sole and exclusive" control of their domestic institutions, and that the federal government was a common agent of the several states and, therefore, "bound so to exercise its powers as to give ... increased stability and security to the domestic institutions of the states that compose the union." It was, therefore, "the solemn duty of the government to resist all attempts by one portion of the Union to use it as an instrument to attack the domestic institutions of the other states." The resolutions added that "domestic slavery, as it exists in the Southern and Western states of this Union composes an important part of their domestic institutions," and warned that all attacks against it on the part of other states of the Union, including even attempts to abolish slavery in the District of Columbia or the territories, were "a violation of the mutual and solemn pledge given to protect and defend each other" when the states adopted the Constitution. The resolutions ended with an implied threat of secession were southern rights denied and the equality of the Union thereby destroyed. All but the last of these resolutions passed the Senate by large majorities, partly because they involved no specific political interest of the moment and partly because certain senators found it expedient to conciliate Calhoun. However, Calhoun's main argument on the nature of the Union went unchallenged in debate, so far had the conception of national sovereignty evidently disintegrated since 1789.

Calhoun's resolutions marked the firm union of the proslavery and state-sovereignty arguments. As Calhoun put it in debate, the resolutions were aimed directly at the proposition that the United States was "one great Republic." Such a doctrine, he said, would strengthen the abolitionists and prepare the ground for an attack on slavery in the southern states through the medium of the national government. From this time onward, Calhoun invariably called forth the logic of his resolutions in support of southern interests in the slavery debate, and other southern statesmen were quick to see the advantage and do the same. The resolutions thus became the basis of the main southern argument concerning slavery in the territories as developed in the debate preceding the Compromise of 1850.

Slavery in the Territories

The issue that forced final abandonment of federal neutrality toward slavery concerned the expansion of slavery into the territories. The movement for continental expansion in the 1840s carried American settlement to the Pacific coast, demanded the annexation of Texas, and provoked the Mexican War. In this new political situation the Democratic party could no longer subordinate the slavery question. Bitter political controversy ensued which called into question the long-settled congressional policy dealing with slavery in the territories. This issue lay at the heart of the conflict between North and South that brought the nation to the brink of war in 1850.

At the beginning of the government congressional power to legislate on slavery in the territories was unquestioned, despite the somewhat anomalous position territories occupied in the constitutional system. The Union consisted of organized states in which federal and state authority coexisted. States possessed the power of local self-government, but in unorganized national territory they had no such authority. Indeed, in the Confederation period the creation of a national territory was contingent on the denial of state claims to the area. Congress could, therefore, govern unorganized national territory, regulating property, personal liberty, civil rights, and social and political organization, even as the states did within their borders. Congressional authority was described in Article IV, Section 3 of the Constitution, which declared: "The Congress shall have power to dispose of and make all needful Rules and Regulations respecting the Territory or other Property belonging to the United States."

Whatever qualifications on congressional power this language later seemed to imply, for more than fifty years it provided ample authority for federal legislation against slavery in the national domain. The first and perhaps most important exercise of the power occurred in 1789, when Congress confirmed by legislation the prohibition of slavery adopted by the Confederation Congress in the Northwest Ordinance of 1787. Other antislavery measures followed: in 1798 Congress prohibited slave importation from abroad in the Mississippi territorial act; in 1804 it excluded both the domestic and foreign slave trade from Louisiana Territory; in 1805 it created Michigan Territory and in 1809 Illinois Territory with slavery excluded. Meanwhile, in legislation creating territories south of the Ohio River Congress refrained from prohibiting slavery, permitting local settlers to introduce, establish, or recognize it if they chose. This dual approach—prohibition of slavery north and toleration of it south of a sectional dividing line—was challenged but eventually reaffirmed in the Missouri crisis of 1819–20.

Constitutionally, the Missouri crisis involved the questions of whether Congress could prohibit slavery in the territories, and whether in admitting new states it could impose conditions affecting their internal organization.

The controversy began when Missouri, a slave territory, applied for admission to the Union. Led by antislavery Federalists, the House passed an enabling bill that admitted Missouri, but required it gradually to abolish slavery. The Senate rejected this proposal, recommending instead a compromise by which Missouri would be brought into the Union as a slave state balanced by the admission of Maine as a free state. Slavery would also be prohibited in Louisiana Purchase Territory north of 36°30′, a line extending Missouri's southern border.

In debate, antislavery men argued that Congress could govern the territories as it saw fit and impose restrictions on them in the nature of a contract enforceable after the territory became a state. They also held that Congress could set conditions on statehood, as it had done in relation to several states, including the prohibition of slavery in the constitutions of Ohio, Indiana, and Illinois. Southerners contended that Congress could not impose terms on statehood lest it impair the equal sovereignty to which the states were entitled. Significantly, southerners acknowledged that Congress could legislate against slavery in the territories, although they said such restrictions would cease to apply after the attainment of statehood. The first stage of the crisis ended when Congress admitted Missouri as a slave state and prohibited slavery in the Louisiana Purchase Territory north of 36°30′.[2]

As noted previously, the Missouri Compromise provoked southern apprehension about possible antislavery uses of federal legislative power and led northern republicans and southern planters to form an alliance aimed at protecting slavery through a national political party. When in the 1840s territorial expansion again dominated national politics, this apprehension grew into open repudiation of the constitutional theory and practice concerning slavery in the territories that had prevailed for several decades.

The annexation of Texas in 1845, which many northerners saw as a form of proslavery aggression, severely tested the long-standing Democratic policy of keeping slavery out of national politics. Antislavery men denounced as grossly unconstitutional the annexation of Texas by joint resolution of Congress, a device resorted to when ratification by the required two-thirds majority of the Senate appeared to be impossible of attainment. Texas, they said, was a foreign state and could be dealt with only by treaty. They denounced as mere sophistry the administration argument that since Texas was admitted as a state, Congress possessed the requisite power to act.

Northern resentment increased when the expansionist Polk administration declared war against Mexico in 1846. A large minority in the North regarded the war as one of conquest waged for the purpose of gaining more slave territory. Accordingly, northern Democrats, in order to allay northern

2. The second phase of the Missouri crisis concerned the attempt by Missouri to exclude free Negroes from the state and the question of Negro citizenship. See below, pp. 279–80.

apprehensions, maintain party unity in support of the war, and relegate slavery to the subordinate place it had occupied for over two decades, introduced the Wilmot Proviso into Congress in August 1846. The strategy backfired, however. Within a few months the proviso became a symbol of northern resolve to keep the slave power from dominating the government, and a practical instrument for protecting new national territory—and, by implication, the nation—against the blight of slavery.

Introduced by Representative David Wilmot of Pennsylvania, an anti-abolitionist, anti-Negro Democrat in the Van Buren wing of the party, the proviso stated that as an express and fundamental condition to the acquisition of any territory from Mexico, "neither slavery nor involuntary servitude shall ever exist in any part of said territory." Constitutionally, the measure was thoroughly orthodox, since Congress on numerous occasions had legislated to prohibit slavery in territories. In a sense it was politically orthodox, too, in its intention to bank the fires of pro- and antislavery agitation in national politics. Yet in a more profound sense the proviso was politically radical, for it proposed to abrogate the dividing-line approach to territorial policy that had existed implicitly since 1789 and explicitly since the Missouri crisis. Indeed, in the southern view the policy of dividing national territory and new states evenly between slavery and freedom was so solidly established that it was to be regarded as having the force of constitutional law. From this perspective the proviso was unconstitutional.

The Wilmot Proviso initiated a fourteen-year controversy over the power of Congress over slavery in the territories. Four distinct positions on the question emerged. The proviso itself from 1846 to 1850 represented the views of dissident Democrats, antislavery-minded Whigs, and moderate political abolitionists in the Liberty party—the diverse groups that converged in the Free-Soil party of 1848. Constitutionally, this position held that Congress had full sovereignty over the territories by virtue of the territorial clause and the federal treaty and war powers. Existing constitutional law as seen in congressional legislation affirmed plenary federal legislative power, and the Supreme Court in *American Insurance Co.* v. *Canter* (1828) had declared that Congress in legislating for the territories exercised the powers both of the general government and the states. A more radical version of the free soil position held that the Fifth Amendment guarantee against federal deprivation of liberty without due process of law prohibited slavery in the territories and prevented Congress from recognizing the institution there. Still another variation applied the Somerset doctrine, insisting that the natural condition of all territory was freedom and that slavery could exist only by virtue of positive municipal legislation. The lands acquired from Mexico had been free under Mexican law; therefore, their normal condition was freedom, which Congress was powerless to change by introducing slavery.

A second position recognized congressional power over slavery in the territories, but advocated discretionary use of the power in extending the Missouri line to the Pacific coast. Because this position acknowledged federal authority over slavery, most southerners rejected it. Yet a surprising number did not, even though the dividing line extended would not positively, but only by implication, establish slavery south of 36°30'. Actually extension of the Missouri line would have guaranteed a larger area for free soil than was secured by the territorial legislation that eventually was adopted in the Compromise of 1850. However, when the idea of extending the dividing line was broached in 1846, northern free-soilers categorically rejected it, probably because it implied equal moral and political standing for slavery and freedom.

A third position on the territorial question, supported by many if not yet a majority of southerners in the period 1846 to 1850, denied congressional power to interfere with slavery and insisted on the right of slave-owners to take their property into the territories under the doctrine of state sovereignty and the protection of the Fifth Amendment. This position, identified most clearly with Calhoun, was subsequently expressed by Chief Justice Taney in the *Dred Scott* decision. It held that Congress could not exercise local police power such as was required to legislate concerning municipal institutions. It also denied that the people of a territory, not yet having attained statehood, possessed sovereignty. The conclusion that followed was that only the states were sovereign and capable of legislating on slavery as a municipal institution. Accordingly, the states were the source of police-power legislation for the territories.

Calhoun's theory of federal agency provided the means by which the states could exercise this power. The agent or trustee of the sovereign states, the federal government in this view was charged with protecting their interests, but was denied sovereign legislative authority for dealing with slavery. Federal power rather was limited, ministerial, nondiscretionary. Moreover, the recognition of slavery in the Constitution—as in the fugitive slave clause—was taken as a recognition of slave state law and as indicating a commitment to give the law of slavery priority over the law of freedom in the event of conflict, such as might occur in the territories. In other words, under the theory of state sovereignty and federal agency the slave states were regarded as the only authoritative source of law and policy for dealing with questions of slavery outside the states that had abolished it. In relation to slavery in the territories, as in the matter of fugitive slaves, the laws of the southern states would have extrajurisdictional effect and determine policy for the nation.

The common property doctrine was a corollary of the state sovereignty theory of congressional nonintervention. The doctrine asserted that the territories were the common property of the states, held in trust for them by their agent, the federal government. The agent had no right to act against the property interests of any of the sovereign principals and hence could not ban slavery in the territories, an act construed as against slave-state rights in the common property.

From still another angle—that of individual property rights—southerners argued against congressional interference with slavery in the territories. The idea here was that slave property was entitled to no less protection against legislative interference than any other property under the doctrine of vested rights and the guarantees of the Constitution. Slaveholders were citizens who had a right under the Fifth Amendment to take their property into national territory. This did not mean, argued defenders of southern rights such as Calhoun and Jefferson Davis, that Congress should establish slavery in the territories by legislative act; on the contrary, all that was sought was protection of the same rights of national citizenship that non-slaveholders enjoyed in entering the national domain.

The property rights strategy contained a further implication about the enforcement of constitutional rights that encouraged reliance on judicial power to resolve the controversy over slavery in the territories. Disavowing protection of slavery by act of Congress, southerners also rejected the idea of territorial sovereignty and the notion of vigilante-style, self-help protection by private individuals. The alternative, consistent with time-honored tenets of American constitutionalism, was to seek protection in a court of law. Accordingly, as part of their strategy for dealing with the territorial question, southerners after 1846 included recourse to the federal judiciary for the protection of slave property rights.

The fourth position on slavery in the territories that emerged in the period 1846 to 1850 was popular sovereignty. Advanced as a compromise solution by the party of proslavery accommodation and national unity, Democratic popular sovereignty located the all-important police power not in Congress or in the states, but in the people of the territory. Theorists of this doctrine seized on the language of the territorial clause, which authorized Congress to dispose of and make rules for national territory in the same terms as ordinary property. They concluded that it did not give Congress plenary, discretionary, sovereign power to govern. At most Congress could draw territorial boundaries and provide forms of government; the substance of sovereignty lay in the people of the territory.

The historic role that local self-government or "squatter sovereignty" played in the development of American territorial policy, far more than this labored interpretation of the Constitution, provided the basis for the widespread appeal of popular sovereignty in the 1840s. Congress had passed territorial acts establishing forms of government and enabling legislation that permitted or recognized the attainment of statehood. But for all practical purposes the people of the territories had governed themselves, adopting local laws and police regulations, founding municipal institutions, and creating new states for admission into the Union. Popular sovereignty was thus not an instrument of recent invention when Lewis Cass, Stephen A.

Douglas, and other Democrats proposed it as a solution to the question of slavery in the territories in 1847. Instead of the dividing line that had served since 1820 as the organizing principle of territorial policy on slavery, and in preference to the extremist alternatives of free soil restriction or categorical support of slavery under the state sovereignty doctrine, Democrats insisted that people at the local level should decide whether slavery should enter the newly acquired western territories.

The Compromise of 1850

The territorial question was one of several North-South issues that produced a crisis of the Union in 1850. California, seized from Mexico and settled rapidly, had skipped the territorial stage of organization and sought admission to the Union as a free state. The border between Texas and New Mexico, a source of bitter contention, needed to be drawn, and the lands of the Mexican cession outside of California had to be organized into territories and the status of slavery therein resolved. Finally, the abolitionist demand for the abolition of the slave trade in the District of Columbia and the southern demand for a stronger fugitive slave law were highly charged issues on which action seemed long past due.

The Wilmot Proviso forms the proximate starting point for a narrative of the events culminating in the Compromise of 1850. Twice the proviso was passed by the House of Representatives but defeated in the Senate. In 1848 two attempts were made to resolve the dispute over slavery in the new territories. A Senate committee headed by John Clayton of Delaware proposed to organize California and New Mexico as separate territories with the status of slavery therein to be determined by the territorial court, with a right of appeal to the Supreme Court. As a concession to the North, Oregon, which because of southern opposition had for years gone without a territorial government, would be organized as a free territory. The Clayton compromise passed the Senate, but failed in the House. A second compromise was offered by Stephen A. Douglas, who proposed to extend the Missouri Compromise line through the new territories to the Pacific Ocean. Douglas's proposal also passed the Senate, but died in the House as northern members stood by the Wilmot Proviso.

In 1848 Oregon was organized as a free territory. In approving the Oregon bill President Polk observed that as the territory lay north of the 36°30′ Missouri line, it could be regarded as a continuation of the traditional dividing-line approach to slavery in the territories. This view had little appeal for most northerners, however, who insisted on admitting California as a free state without regard to the Missouri line. As pressure to admit California mounted in 1849, southerners, facing the prospect of free state superiority in the Senate, dug in their heels and demanded satisfaction of some sort in the organization of the former Mexican lands. Their demand made Utah and New Mexico territorial legislation the central focus of compromise strategy in Congress in 1850.

In February 1850, after months of bitter debate and amid serious talk of secession in South Carolina, Georgia, and Mississippi, Henry Clay offered an elaborate eight-point plan for the Senate's consideration. By the first resolution, California was to be admitted to the Union at once without any restrictions upon its right to exclude or include slaves. In effect this meant California's admission as a free state. Second, the New Mexico Territory was to be organized without any restrictions or limitations upon the status of slavery. Clay's third and fourth resolutions fixed the western Texan boundary so as to deprive the state of the disputed region between the Del Norte and the Rio Grande rivers but proposed to compensate Texas by the assumption by the federal government of the state's preannexation public debt. The fifth resolution submitted that it was "inexpedient" to abolish slavery in the District of Columbia, but the sixth proposed that the trade in imported and exported slaves be banned in the District. The seventh resolution asked for a more effective fugitive slave law, while the eighth stated merely that Congress had no authority over the interstate slave trade.

When it proved impossible to get even a scaled-down version of this compromise plan through the Senate (i.e., the so-called Omnibus bill linking California, New Mexico, and Utah), Douglas broke Clay's original proposal into separate pieces of legislation. Aided by the death of anticompromise-minded President Zachary Taylor, in September 1850 he guided the separate bills through the Senate principally with the support of northern Democratic votes. A few days later Douglas Democrats secured passage of the several measures in the House of Representatives. The first and decisive bill dealt with New Mexico Territory and also included the Texas boundary and debt. Most important for purposes of sectional compromise, it embodied the doctrine of popular sovereignty.

In its original formulation the New Mexico bill prohibited the territorial legislature from legislating on slavery. Although some northerners, on the theory that Mexican antislavery law had made the territory free, could support this provision, southerners who believed that Mexican law had lapsed and that slaveholders could take their property there under constitutional protection, provided most of the backing for this restriction on the territorial legislature. But to deny the territorial legislature power to act on slavery contradicted too bluntly Douglas's conception of popular sovereignty and seemed to threaten passage of the bill. Accordingly, the ban on legislation concerning slavery was dropped, and the power of the territorial legislature was described as "extending to all rightful subjects of legislation consistent with the Constitution of the United States." Another section stated that the territory, when admitted as a state, was to be received with or without slavery as its constitution provided. Still another provision, in the manner of the Clayton compromise, permitted judicial determination of questions concerning title to slaves or personal liberty, with appeal to the Supreme Court.

Popular sovereignty as incorporated in the New Mexico and Utah territorial bills served principally as a means of uniting the Democratic party; only indirectly, through the instrumentality of the party, was it the basis of North-South compromise. The special virtue of popular sovereignty was its ambiguity about *when* the people in a territory could take action for or against slavery. Douglas and the northern Democrats interpreted the removal of the ban on legislation dealing with slavery as authorizing the territorial legislature to act on slavery from the moment it was created. Southerners, however, believed that only when the people of a territory wrote a state constitution and applied for admission to the Union could they take action on slavery. They reasoned that until statehood was attained, slaveholders as United States citizens had a constitutional right to take their property into the territory—a right that could presumably be upheld in the territorial court and the Supreme Court. The New Mexico and Utah territorial bills did not expressly endorse either of these points of view. Accordingly, interpreting the legislation in their different ways, enough southern and northern Democrats were able to support the measures to assure their passage.

The abandonment of the Wilmot Proviso in favor of popular sovereignty was the critical step in achieving the Compromise of 1850. Democrats acted mainly to preserve party unity. Equally decisive, however, was the willingness of northern representatives, some of free soil inclination, to accept popular sovereignty after standing firmly behind the Wilmot Proviso. Their reasons for doing so remain unclear, but the most important factors seem to have been their belief that climate and geography would keep slavery out of the Southwest, their lack of legislative organization, and their responsiveness to public fear of disunion and desire for compromise. The result was a significant concession to the South—regardless of whether the northern or southern view of popular sovereignty would prevail.

After passage of the New Mexico bill, the other Compromise measures were rapidly adopted. Utah Territory was organized on the same basis as New Mexico; California was admitted as a free state; a new fugitive slave law was enacted; and the slave trade in the District of Columbia was abolished. Although Douglas's legislative strategy made it possible for members of Congress to vote only for the particular measures they favored, avoiding compromise in the more important sense of voting for measures that conflicted with their sectional interest, the country welcomed the acts of 1850 as a deliverance from a genuine crisis that threatened to disrupt the Union. Surely, this perception was justified. Yet a decade later it was less clear that northern willingness to treat the combination of issues as a true crisis, requiring accommodation to southern threats of secession and demands for concessions on the slavery question, had been the wisest course.

It is, of course, impossible to say whether the South would have seceded in 1850 if northern support for the Wilmot Proviso had persisted or President Taylor had lived to insist solely on the admission of California as a free state. What is clear is that the South, gaining confidence in its ability to use the threat of secession as an effective political instrument, secured a stronger fugitive slave law and legislation denying congressional power to legislate on slavery in the territory acquired from Mexico. Moreover, the new territorial policy of popular sovereignty, unlike the Wilmot Proviso and in contrast even to the dividing-line approach of the Missouri Compromise, contained no hint of moral condemnation of slavery.

It was not exactly clear what the term meant, but both North and South agreed that popular sovereignty opened the possibility of "nationalizing" slavery. Federal law had never recognized or established slavery in a positive sense; at most, south of 36°30', it had remained silent on the matter. Slavery was, therefore, viewed as a local institution, and freedom as national. Although popular sovereignty in a technical sense continued the posture of congressional silence toward slavery, in effect it would allow slavery to enter lands from which it had been previously excluded by law (i.e., Mexican law). Theoretically neutral, popular sovereignty in the territorial legislation of 1850 signified a subtle shift toward a proslavery territorial policy, no matter how much Douglas might protest that it would also permit the prohibition of slavery. Conceivably, the adoption of popular sovereignty in 1850 might even imply the substitution of a policy of toleration toward slavery in other national territory, as yet unorganized, where the dividing line of the Missouri Compromise had been projected but not actually applied. As the movement for territorial expansion proceeded in the 1850s, this question became the focal point of sectional conflict over the place of slavery in the American republic.

FIFTEEN

Slavery and the Crisis of the American Republic

————————— ✦ ✦ ✦ —————————

IN A POLITICAL SYSTEM that had accommodated the fact of Negro slavery for seventy-five years, there was ample reason to think that the Compromise of 1850, intended to end sectional agitation of the slavery question, would accomplish its purpose. The two major parties agreed on the wisdom of the Compromise measures. These measures settled the constitutional status of slavery in the former Mexican territory, while the Missouri Compromise Act remained in effect in the lands of the Louisiana Purchase. Slavery in the territories was thus a closed issue, should the status quo be accepted as permanent. The parties could persist in their rivalry as national organizations, moreover, and the Union, threatened by sectional polarization in the recent crisis, would endure. Nor would it be necessary to resolve the fundamental ambiguity that had existed from the beginning of the government about the nature of the Union. The federal republic could be at once a confederation of equal sovereign states, expressing the diversity and particularity of American politics, and also a unitary sovereign government expressing the sense of nationality that Americans shared.

It proved impossible, however, to subordinate the slavery issue politically, to prolong the existence of the national party system on which the existence of the Union depended, or to persist in the flexible and politically useful ambiguity about the nature of the Union that had helped sustain the parties as legitimate representative institutions. Ironically, the decision of both Whigs and Democrats to support the Compromise of 1850 had the indirect consequence of permitting slavery once again to dominate politics, revealing the weakness of the party system. It was not the moral and political force of the slavery question per se that undermined the parties. Not even anxiety about the nature of the Union and its survival could do that. These factors could, of course, add momentum to any attack on the party system, but problems arising out of the social and economic issues of the age were more immediate, concrete, and threatening to political stability. This was true even though these issues had provided the rationale for party conflict since the 1830s.

The Political Realignment of the 1850s

By 1854, when the slavery question again challenged the integrity of national parties by attracting people to sectional loyalties, party bonds were weakened by changing attitudes toward socioeconomic issues. Whigs had stood for a national bank, the protective tariff, internal improvements, a restrictive public land policy, and, in general, federal government promotion of economic development. Democrats were antibank and pro-hard money, favored a liberal land distribution policy, opposed the protective tariff and internal improvements, and generally demanded federal nonintervention in the economy. By 1850, however, many western Democrats had shifted to support of banks, internal improvements, and homestead legislation requiring positive government action, thus blurring the lines between the parties. Moreover, conflicts between Democrats who supported and Whigs who opposed democratizing state constitutional reform had largely been resolved by 1852, so this issue, too, was removed from the field of electoral competition. The effect of these changes was to diminish the legitimacy of the parties in the eyes of voters, who saw fewer real differences between them. Increasingly, the parties seemed concerned solely with privilege and power, rather than with the genuine interests of their constituents.

As these older issues were composed, new ones took shape as a result of commercial expansion, the growth of cities, and the great influx of immigrants that came to the United States principally from Ireland and Germany between 1846 and 1854. The existing parties might have dealt with the social dislocation and resentment caused by these developments within the traditional framework of electoral conflict, but, often for very good reasons, they did not. The Whigs, for example, were responsive in the 1840s to native Americans' criticism of immigrant groups. In the early 1850s, however, trying to compete with the Democrats, they sought to attract the immigrant vote. Unsuccessful against the Democrats, who were the traditional party of the immigrant, they managed only to eliminate another difference between the parties. Nativist and temperance groups, fearful of the effect of immigration on American society, therefore pursued their reform purposes in new parties, which began to appear at the state level in 1851. These developments weakened the major parties by causing them to appear useless and hence illegitimate in the eyes of voters. And when both parties agreed to submerge differences over slavery and accept the Compromise of 1850, the effect was similar.

To large numbers of people, therefore, the national parties in the early 1850s seemed corrupt and irrelevant, if not dangerous to republican values. The moribund state of the parties, however, which allowed voters to embrace exclusively sectional alignments, only became apparent after slavery was reintroduced into national politics. This fateful step was taken by Stephen A. Douglas, the chief architect of the Compromise of 1850, acting in response to pressures within the Democratic party arising out of the ambiguous meaning of popular sovereignty.

The Kansas-Nebraska Bill

In the Kansas-Nebraska bill Douglas pushed through Congress a popular sovereignty proposal that almost immediately caused the formation of an exclusively sectional free soil party. Besides being ideologically committed to popular sovereignty, Douglas was under tremendous pressure from southern Democrats who, fearful that their "peculiar" institution would be "de-nationalized," insisted on concessions to slavery that decisively affected the legislative history of the measure. These concessions were to be used to impose discipline on a party that, though officially committed to the Compromise of 1850, remained seriously divided internally.

Many northern Democrats of free soil proclivity who had left the party in 1850 returned to it during the election of 1852, in which Franklin Pierce of New Hampshire defeated the Whig candidate, General Winfield Scott. Typified by the Barnburners of New York, these apostates were welcomed back by moderate supporters of the administration, but were strongly opposed by hard-line, proslavery administration men. In the South similar conflict existed between those who had called for a southern-rights party in 1850 and those who had stood by the Union irrespective of party lines. In this confused situation Pierce tried to alleviate internal strife by distributing the patronage to all factions. His policy was notably unsuccessful, however, and when Congress met at the end of 1853, it was left for the ambitious Douglas of Illinois to try to unify the party through a vigorous program of western expansion.

Since 1845 Douglas had been trying to organize Nebraska Territory, the remaining unorganized portion of the Louisiana Purchase lands lying north of the Indian territory. A major reason for wanting to do so was to facilitate the construction of a transcontinental railroad from Illinois to the Pacific coast. Douglas believed an aggressive western policy based on Nebraska would provide the Democratic party with an important national issue, enhance his stature as a national figure, and even make him a logical choice for the presidency. Yet a major obstacle stood in Douglas's way: a group of southern senators who were prepared to oppose the organization of Nebraska Territory unless the legislation benefited the South. This meant, in particular, concessions on the slavery question that could be forced on free soil northern Democrats.

In December 1853, Senator Augustus C. Dodge of Iowa introduced a bill to organize the Nebraska Territory. The bill was referred to the Senate committee on territories, of which Douglas was chairman. Douglas added provisions borrowed from the New Mexico and Utah territorial acts of 1850 stipulating that Nebraska Territory, when admitted into the Union as a state or states, "shall be received . . . with or without slavery as their constitution may prescribe at the time of their admission." Another section provided that all questions involving title to slaves in the territory should be tried in the territorial courts, with appeal to the Supreme Court.

This bill technically did not repeal the Missouri Compromise restriction on slavery, for Douglas realized that to do so would excite free soil opinion. Nevertheless, because of southern demands for concessions on slavery, and because he was genuinely committed to the approach, Douglas argued that popular sovereignty should be made the basis of settlement in Nebraska. He would accomplish this, however, not by repealing the Missouri Compromise restriction on slavery, but by ignoring it. He believed popular sovereignty was sufficiently expressed in the provisions already mentioned and in an accompanying committee report which asserted that the bill embodied the principles of the Compromise of 1850. These principles, the report explained, were intended to apply to all national territories, not simply the former Mexican lands, and were meant to avoid future agitation of the slavery issue by reserving to local settlers the right to decide questions concerning slavery. Douglas drew a parallel between the situation in 1850 and the present one. As the status of slavery in the Mexican Cession was uncertain because of doubts about the effect of the Mexican law abolishing slavery, he explained, so there were doubts, based on the theory of congressional nonintervention in the territories, about the constitutionality of the Missouri Compromise restriction on slavery. As in 1850, Douglas said the sound course was to rely on the right of local self-determination.

The committee report notwithstanding, southerners rejected Douglas's proposal because it permitted the Missouri restriction on slavery to remain in effect in the decisive period of settlement before the territory might form a constitution and seek statehood. A right to choose slavery at that point was no right at all. Acknowledging the fact, and the impossibility of reconciling popular sovereignty with the Missouri restriction, Douglas now began the process of accommodation to the slave interest that reopened the sectional struggle at a new level of intensity. The reluctance with which he proceeded in his unpleasant yet politically necessary task, as though aware of the momentous consequences his actions would produce, can be seen in the successive formulations of the Nebraska bill that he offered in the hope of avoiding outright repeal of the thirty-four-year-old Missouri law.

First, to the original bill Douglas added a section, which he later said had been omitted through a "clerical error," stating that to avoid any misunderstanding about the purpose of the legislation, its true intent was to apply the principles of the Compromise of 1850 and to leave all questions pertaining to slavery in the territories to the decision of the people therein, through their appropriate representatives. This was characteristically ambiguous in its refusal to say which territorial representatives were to act on slavery and when they should do so, but it implied that the Missouri restriction would cease to have effect. Not satisfied with this formulation, James Dixon of Maryland, a southern Whig trying to restore his party's credentials as a defender of southern rights, proposed outright repeal of the Missouri Compromise. Alarmed by this proposal, which swiftly found favor among southerners of *both* parties, Douglas tried to keep control of the situation by bringing in a second Nebraska bill that moved closer toward repeal. It stated that the Missouri Compromise restriction on slavery was "superseded by the principles of the legislation of 1850" and accordingly was "inoperative." The bill also divided the area into two territories: Kansas, directly west of a slave state (Missouri), and Nebraska, directly west of a free state (Iowa). Sensing the gravity of the situation, Douglas took the extraordinary step of getting President Pierce's personal written endorsement of the bill as an administration measure.

Still it was not enough. Coincidental with the introduction of Douglas's second bill, free soil members of Congress published the Appeal of Independent Democrats, a vigorous denunciation of the *original* Nebraska bill as tantamount to a repeal of the Missouri Compromise. If that was to be the northern reaction, southerners were determined to have outright repeal, and Douglas was in no position to deny them. Accordingly, in February 1854 he brought in yet a third Nebraska bill. This one stated that the Missouri Compromise, "being inconsistent with the principles of non-intervention by Congress with slavery in the States and territories, as recognized by the legislation of 1850, is hereby declared inoperative and void." The word "repeal" was not used, but it was a distinction without a difference. The bill also stated that its true intent was not to legislate slavery into or exclude it from any territory or state, but "to leave the people thereof free to form and regulate their own domestic institutions in their own way, subject only to the Constitution of the United States."

Having condemned Douglas's first attempt to shift the basis of Nebraska territorial organization from slavery restriction to popular sovereignty, antislavery men were relentless in attacking subsequent versions of the bill. In their view Douglas had violated a national commitment, expressed in the Missouri Compromise, to keep lands north of 36°30' free, when it was too late to reclaim the territory lying south of the dividing line from the rule of slavery. Free-soilers also denied that anyone in 1850 thought popular sovereignty as applied to Utah and New Mexico extended as well to all unorganized national territory.

For their part, Democrats adhered to the principle of popular sovereignty, which through artful ambiguity was still able to provide a common ground on which the northern and southern wings of the party could stand. Both groups agreed on congressional nonintervention. Beyond that they disagreed over *when* popular sovereignty became effective in relation to slavery: at the outset of the territorial period, as Douglas believed, or only upon admission to the Union, with the right of slave property constitutionally protected up to that time, as southerners contended. Each side could read into the Kansas-Nebraska bill its own conception of popular sovereignty. But in the final analysis the "true" meaning of popular sovereignty would depend on the interpretation given the provision in the Nebraska bill stating that the people of the territories and the states could shape and regulate their own local institutions, "subject to the Constitution of the United States." And to explain what these words meant it was likely that the Supreme Court, already invited by another section of the Kansas-Nebraska bill to settle disputes over slavery in the territory, would be consulted.

The Kansas-Nebraska Act, approved by Congress in March 1854, immediately provoked a political upheaval. Anti-Nebraska and antiadministration coalitions quickly formed, and within a few months there existed an exclusively sectional antislavery organization—the Republican party. Alongside it appeared another new political grouping, the Native American or Know Nothing party, which expressed the social and cultural pressures that eroded traditional party loyalties in the early 1850s. For a while the two new parties competed on equal terms, but by 1856 the Republicans achieved major party status while the Native American party was virtually extinct. Meanwhile the Democratic party experienced internal realignment as former southern Whigs joined its ranks. From 1856 to 1860 the Democrats continued to be a national party, but their outlook and policies became increasingly proslavery.

The Dred Scott *Case*

Revived with a vengeance in the debate over the Kansas-Nebraska Act, agitation of the slavery question grew more fierce in the attempt to implement popular sovereignty in Kansas between 1855 and 1858. Proslavery and antislavery groups erected territorial governments, and in June 1856 hostilities broke out between them. Although the Pierce administration recognized the proslavery government, Congress became deadlocked on the issue when the House of Representatives approved, but the Senate rejected, a bill to make Kansas a free state. In these highly charged circumstances, amounting virtually to civil war in the territory, the Supreme Court attempted to settle the question of the status of slavery in the territories.

Dred Scott was a Negro slave, formerly the property of one Dr. Emerson, a surgeon in the United States Army. In 1834, Emerson took Scott to the free state of Illinois, and thence in 1836 to Fort Snelling, in what was then the Wisconsin Territory, free soil under the Missouri Compromise and the act of 1836 organizing Wisconsin's territorial government. Eventually, Emerson returned to Missouri, taking Scott with him. The surgeon died shortly thereafter, and title to Scott eventually passed to John F. A. Sanford, a citizen of New York.

In 1846 Scott brought suit in the Missouri state courts for his freedom. At the time this action apparently had no political import. Though Scott won a favorable decision in the lower courts, the Missouri Supreme Court eventually rejected his plea, on the grounds that the laws of Illinois and of free territory did not have extraterritorial status in Missouri and could not affect his status as a slave after his return. Scott's attorney then began, in 1854, a new suit against Sanford in the United States Circuit Court for Missouri. The case was now frankly political in character, and both sides pressed it through to a conclusion in order to obtain a judicial opinion upon slavery in the territories.

Scott's right to sue Sanford in a federal court rested upon his contention that he was a citizen of the state of Missouri, and that the case involved a suit between citizens of different states. Sanford replied to Scott's suit with a plea in abatement—that is, a demand that the court dismiss the case for want of jurisdiction, on the ground that since Scott was a Negro he was not a citizen of Missouri. To this plea, Scott demurred. The circuit court sustained the demurrer (thereby implying that Scott might be a citizen), but it then returned a verdict in favor of Sanford. Scott now appealed to the Supreme Court of the United States on a writ of error.

The Court first heard argument on the case in February 1856, at the height of the Kansas furor. Opinion was divided on the question of jurisdiction, however, and this division, combined with a reluctance to take up politically controversial issues in an election year, led the justices to order the case reargued at its next term, in December 1857. In contrast to its first appearance on the docket, the case now aroused enormous interest, and the arguments of counsel, which went heavily into the question of congressional power over slavery in the territories, were closely attended. Nevertheless, the Court's initial response was to dismiss the case for want of jurisdiction. A clear and recent precedent for such a decision was available. In 1850, in *Strader* v. *Graham,* the Court without dissent had refused to consider the argument that a slave automatically became free through residence in a free state, and had held instead that the decision of the state courts was final in determining the slave status of a Negro. A majority of seven justices apparently now believed this precedent to be a decisive one, and in accordance with their wishes Justice Samuel Nelson actually prepared an opinion for the Court based on *Strader* v. *Graham,* a course avoiding all discussion of slavery in the territories.

It proved impossible, however, because of the tremendous interest the case had generated and because of the strength of the proslavery point of view on the Court, to maintain this attitude of restraint. In fact the decision to use the *Strader* precedent and avoid the explosive territorial question was not as settled as it appeared; at least two and perhaps four justices—all southerners—were preparing concurring opinions in which they would deal with it. Accordingly, a few days after agreeing to an opinion from Justice Nelson, the Court, at the urging of Justice Wayne of Georgia, voted to take up all of the controversial issues raised in the reargument and entrust the writing of a new opinion to Chief Justice Taney. Undoubtedly, the by now habitual tendency of politicians to refer to the territorial issue as a "judicial question," a tendency expressed in the provision for judicial determination of all questions concerning slavery in the territories in legislation of 1848, 1850, and 1854, had its effect as the Court now changed its mind. It seems equally clear, however, that the desire of proslavery justices to settle the territorial question and remove it from politics influenced the decision to take up the disputed matters.

One further step was necessary. That was to enlist at least one northern justice on the majority side to avoid the appearance of a strictly sectional decision. To this end Justice Catron of Tennessee asked the help of President-elect James Buchanan in persuading Justice Grier of Pennsylvania to join the majority. Buchanan did so, and in turn was permitted to learn that the Court's imminent decision in the *Dred Scott* case would dispose of the territorial question. Buchanan, who had hoped for judicial assistance in quieting the struggle in Kansas, now made bold to say in his inaugural address on March 4, 1857, that the point of time when the people of a territory could decide the question of slavery was "a judicial question, which legitimately belongs to the Supreme Court of the United States, before whom it is now pending, and will, it is understood, be speedily and finally settled." "In common with all good citizens," Buchanan added, he would "cheerfully submit" to the Court's decision, whatever this may be."[1]

On March 6, 1857, by a 7 to 2 vote, the Supreme Court decided that Scott could not sue, and that he was still a slave. In his opinion for the Court, Chief Justice Taney explained that Scott could not sue because he was not a citizen of the United States. And he was not a citizen because he was a Negro and a slave.

1. Buchanan evidently thought the Court would deal with the problem of resolving the ambiguity in popular sovereignty; hence his reference to the power of the people in a territory over slavery. The Court, however, was interested in settling the larger and more fundamental issue of congressional power over slavery in the territories.

At the time the Constitution was written, Taney said, Negroes were not citizens of any states; therefore, none became a citizen of the United States. After the start of the government Negroes might become state citizens, for the states could make any one they pleased a citizen. But this was state citizenship for strictly local purposes and it did not make a person a citizen of the United States. In contradiction to accepted doctrines of constitutional law, Taney thus asserted that state and national citizenship were absolutely separate. More precisely, he held that two kinds of state citizenship existed: one for national purposes, as expressed in the diversity-of-citizenship and privileges-and-immunities clauses of the Constitution, and one for exclusively state purposes. Because they were excluded from state citizenship in 1789—the only time, in Taney's view, when state-created citizenship conferred national citizenship—Negroes could never thereafter, except presumably by constitutional amendment, become state citizens in the sense of the Constitution and entitled to sue in federal courts as citizens of the United States.

Taney's opinion on citizenship resolved a long-standing controversy over the status of free Negroes in the United States. American law since the Revolution recognized no gradations of citizenship: persons were either citizens or aliens. Public law also adhered to the traditional doctrine that place of birth determined citizenship. By these standards blacks born free in the United States were citizens, and some states, though discriminating against them in respect of political rights, so recognized them and protected them in the rights of personal liberty, property, access to courts, domestic relations, and the like—the rights that legally appertained to citizenship. Southerners, however, guided by the widespread discrimination against blacks that everywhere existed in the United States, denied that Negroes were citizens. In the southern view, at least as far as Negroes were concerned, citizenship did not confer the minimal rights of civil liberty, but rather was a condition to be deduced from the possession of all the civil rights of every other person in the community under like circumstances. Although as late as the 1830s some southern courts held to traditional birthright citizenship and recognized free Negroes as citizens, by the time of the *Dred Scott* case the weight of southern legal opinion was against Negro citizenship.

Taney's opinion resolved the question by denying that blacks were U.S. citizens or state citizens under the Constitution. Yet they were not aliens. Indeed, Taney said, born in the United States, whether slave or free, blacks owed allegiance to the government. In effect, Taney placed Negroes in a third category between citizenship and alienage, as subject-nationals or quasi-citizens. This determination was nowhere recognized in the American law of citizenship, but it was not greatly at variance with the actual conditions of Negro life in the antebellum period.

An important feature of Taney's opinion was his discussion of national citizenship based on the privileges-and-immunities clause of the Constitution. This was another question in antebellum constitutional law that was rendered problematic by the presence of large numbers of free Negroes in the United States. Whether Negroes as state citizens enjoyed national protection under the privileges-and-immunities clause had been an issue since the Missouri crisis of 1820. At that time Missouri sought admission to the Union under a constitution that excluded free Negroes from the state. Northerners argued that this restriction violated the privileges-and-immunities clause by denying rights to Negroes who were state citizens under the Constitution, and thus entitled to national protection. Congress failed to resolve the issue, and in succeeding years antislavery constitutionalists fashioned a doctrine of national citizenship under the privileges-and-immunities clause for the protection of blacks.[2]

In the *Dred Scott* case Chief Justice Taney accepted a broad, nationalistic view of the privileges-and-immunities clause. He was at pains, however, precisely because of the apparent protective force of this constitutional provision, to refute the idea of Negro citizenship and exclude blacks from the political community of the nation. If Negroes were regarded as state citizens under the Constitution, he observed, other states would have to receive them and acknowledge their right to paramount federal protection of the privileges and immunities of citizens. Negroes would be exempt from the operation of special laws and police regulations essential to public safety in the slave states, and would be entitled to freedom of speech, the right to keep and bear arms, the right of assembly, and so on. The effect, Taney predicted, would be to produce discontent and insubordination in slave society.

Taney had given as a second reason why Scott was not a citizen the fact that he was a slave. The chief justice might have made this point simply by citing the opinion of the lower Missouri courts, with a reference to *Strader* v. *Graham* as precedent. Instead he proceeded to consider the effect of Scott's residence on free soil, a matter enabling him to discuss the constitutional status of slavery in the territories. Republican critics at once pronounced Taney's subsequent denial of congressional power over slavery in the territories obiter dictum. In a legal sense the charge was mistaken, for the case was before the Court on a writ of error, and contemporary practice permitted the Court to consider all phases of an opinion taken from the lower courts on a writ of error, even though a decision on any one point might be sufficient to dispose of the case. Nevertheless, though Taney's course was not inconsistent with accepted procedure, he acted as he did not

---

2. Congress admitted Missouri on condition that its constitution not be interpreted as authorizing the passage of any law excluding the citizens of any state from enjoying the privileges and immunities guaranteed by the Constitution of the United States. The requirement was a dead letter from the outset.

strictly out of legal obligation. He also wished to demolish the idea of congressional power to restrict slavery in the territories—the central tenet of antislavery constitutionalism since the introduction of the Wilmot Proviso.

Taney began his argument on the effects of Scott's residence on free soil with the novel contention that federal authority over the territories was derived from the power to acquire territory by treaty and to create new states, not from the clause empowering Congress to make necessary rules and regulations for governing the territories. The latter clause, he said, was a mere emergency provision applying only to lands ceded by the original states to the Confederation; it did not validate federal authority in territories acquired after 1789. That authority, Taney went on to explain, was not a general, discretionary, sovereign legislative power, but rather a limited, protective power appropriate to the trusteeship or agency function that properly belonged to the federal government. Whatever the government acquired, Taney said, it acquired "for the benefit of the people of the several States who created it. It is their trustee acting for them, and charged with protecting the interests of the whole people of the Union." Moreover, congressional power over the person and property of a citizen "can never be a mere discretionary power." Citizens of the United States who migrate to the territories, Taney admonished, "cannot be ruled as mere colonists, dependent on the will of the General Government, to be governed by any laws it may think proper." The federal government could thus exercise no power of internal police, nor infringe any property right enjoyed by a citizen under the laws of his own state.

Additional strictures on congressional power derived from the Fifth Amendment. Federal authority in the territories, Taney observed, was limited by the various provisions in the federal Bill of Rights, including the Fifth Amendment guarantee of due process of law. "And an act of Congress," said the chief justice, "which deprives a citizen of the United States of his liberty or property, merely because he came himself or brought his property into a particular Territory of the United States, and who had committed no offence against the laws, could hardly be dignified with the name of due process of law." Taney thus invoked the doctrine of vested interests, tied it to the due process clause in the Fifth Amendment, and applied it to property in slaves.

Taney then concluded that the Missouri Compromise Act prohibiting slavery north of the 36°30′ line was "not warranted by the Constitution" and was, therefore, void. Dred Scott's residence on free soil had not made him a free man, since slavery had not lawfully been excluded from the Wisconsin Territory. The federal government, in short, could not lawfully exclude slavery from any of the territories. And for good measure, although it was not an issue in the case, Taney announced that a territorial legislature lacked power to prohibit slavery under the doctrine of popular sovereignty. If Congress could not interfere with property rights, he said, it could not authorize a territorial government to do so. Congress "could confer no power on any local government established by its authority, to violate the provisions of the Constitution."

Thus, on the one hand, Taney discovered in the Constitution restrictions on federal and territorial legislative power and, on the other hand, positive protection of slave property going far beyond the right of recaption in fugitive slave cases that marked the most aggressive grasp of proslavery constitutionalism to this time. In describing limits on legislative power and the sanctity of property rights, Taney invoked fundamental principles of American constitutionalism. But in employing them for the defense of slavery he transmuted them in ways that, in the eyes of an ever larger segment of the public, contradicted the very purpose of republican constitutionalism. The febrile state of Taney's mind as he attempted, more openly than ever before, to destroy antislavery constitutionalism was evident in his assertion that "the right of property in a slave is distinctly and expressly affirmed in the Constitution." This was manifestly untrue. With equal license and imagination he concluded: "No word can be found in the Constitution which gives Congress a greater power over slave property, or which entitles property of that kind to less protection than property of any other description. The only power conferred is the power coupled with the duty of guarding and protecting the owner in his rights."

Justices Nelson, Daniel, Campbell, Catron, Wayne, and Grier all concurred in Taney's conclusion that Scott was a slave, although they arrived at this finding by varying routes. Nelson entered the opinion originally prepared for the seven majority justices, deciding the case on the authority of *Strader* v. *Graham*. Daniel merely restated Calhoun's doctrine of federal agency as prohibiting any interference with slavery. Campbell admitted the efficacy of the territories clause, but thought strict construction properly limited federal authority to mere administrative and conservatory acts, and to the enumerated powers of Congress. Catron thought the Louisiana Purchase treaty, which had guaranteed existing property rights in the territory, had made illegal any restriction on property rights in slaves within the confines of the original purchase. Wayne and Grier indicated more or less complete assent to Taney's opinion.

Justices Curtis and McLean dissented on Scott's status and on the validity of the Missouri Compromise. Denying the contention that because Scott was a Negro he was not a citizen, Curtis argued that free Negroes were citizens and had been accepted as such in 1787. Moreover, state citizenship was primary and automatically conferred national citizenship. As for Scott's personal status, it had been determined by his residence on free soil. And as for congressional power in the territories, it was supreme and plenary, and included power over slavery which had been exercised on numerous occasions. The minority concluded that the Missouri Compromise was valid and that Scott was a free man.

The legal effect of the *Dred Scott* decision was profound. Although the federal government had never claimed power over slavery in the states where it existed, Congress had prohibited slavery in national territory. By the same token, it had never established or recognized slavery by positive legislation. Although sanctioned by the Constitution, slavery had, therefore, always been considered a local institution, existing only by force of positive municipal law. Freedom was thought of as national. The *Dred Scott* decision altered this situation by asserting a positive constitutional right to take slave property into national territory, a right that Congress could not restrict. In a very real sense, therefore, it made slavery national and freedom local. Moreover, although restricted to the territories in the instant case, Taney's assertion of an expressly affirmed constitutional right to own slave property could conceivably be given national scope and effect, like the right of recaption in fugitive slave cases.

The *Dred Scott* case had important political as well as legal consequences. For several years the controversy over slavery in the territories had been conducted in two distinct forums. In the first, free-soilers upholding congressional power to restrict slavery had opposed Democrats insisting on congressional nonintervention. In the second arena of controversy, Democrats disagreed among themselves over the stage of territorial organization at which antislavery legislation might be adopted. The *Dred Scott* decision principally affected the former controversy. It struck at the Republican party's constitutional rationale, forcing antislavery men to denounce the opinion as obiter dictum or to question the authority of the Supreme Court as final arbiter of constitutional disputes. But the decision also exacerbated the conflict within the Democratic party over the meaning of popular sovereignty. It upheld the property right of slaveowners against the power of a territorial legislature to restrict slavery. In effect it endorsed the proslavery conception of popular sovereignty and repudiated the Douglas version.

The Lincoln-Douglas Debates

The legal and political effects of the *Dred Scott* decision were dramatically interjected into national politics in the Lincoln-Douglas debates of 1858, a brilliant episode in constitutional politics that explored the problem of slavery in the American republic. Abraham Lincoln and Stephen A. Douglas were competing for a senatorial seat from Illinois. They were also in effect vying for leadership of free soil opinion at the North. The outcome of the struggle to implement popular sovereignty in Kansas invested their contest with this broad significance.

After prolonged and violent conflict, antislavery forces prevailed in Kansas, and by the fall of 1858 the territory was a free soil area. The Buchanan administration had brought forward and had approved in the

Senate the fraudulent proslavery Lecompton constitution—fraudulent because it had been ratified in an election which allowed no genuine choice between slavery and freedom. The Lecompton constitution, however, was rejected by the House of Representatives. Congress then provided for another territorial election on the Lecompton constitution, and it was defeated by an overwhelming margin. As the dust settled, it became clear that destabilization of the party system had progressed ominously. For Douglas and the northern Democrats had strenuously opposed the Lecompton charter, in the process breaking with the Buchanan administration. Popular sovereignty, so long an effective means of intraparty compromise, turned out in this instance to be a free soil instrument. And it was this perception, however turbulent and costly the implementation of popular sovereignty had been, that made the contest between Lincoln and Douglas so critically important. Douglas's rejection of the Lecompton fraud brought him free soil favor, and if victorious in 1858 he stood a chance of leading a free soil popular front across the North. If, on the other hand, Lincoln won or made a strong showing, northern opinion would continue to be divided, yet also alienated against the South. The result would be a highly volatile, even dangerous situation.

Republicans and Democrats had together opposed the Lecompton constitution, but Lincoln, conceding nothing to Douglas, emphasized the differences of principle between the parties. In the debates he reaffirmed Republican opposition to slavery on both moral and political grounds. If slavery was not wrong, he said, nothing was wrong. At bottom the issue was "the right or wrong of slavery in this Union." Moreover, slavery contradicted the fundamental principle of equality, expressed in the Declaration of Independence. Lincoln did not insist on civil rights equality between Negroes and whites; he was in fact generally pessimistic about race relations in the United States. Yet he believed that all persons were equal in at least this respect: that they had the right not to be governed without their consent—the right, in other words, of personal liberty. The Republican party expressed this principle in opposing the expansion of slavery into the territories.

Stop the spread of slavery, Lincoln argued in 1858, and the people would believe once again—as at the founding of the nation—that slavery was in the course of ultimate extinction. Restore the country to its commitment to republican freedom, he reasoned, and slavery actually would be placed in the course of ultimate extinction. The Union would then endure. It could not continue to exist, however, half slave and half free: either the one condition or the other must be nationalized. Lincoln refused to say when or how slavery might be ended, but by focusing on the morality of slavery and speaking of its eventual elimination he took a radical position. At the same time, however, he presented a moderate aspect by arguing simply for a policy of slavery restriction, which he identified with the founding fathers, and by acknowledging the lack of federal power to interfere with slavery in the states where it existed.

Douglas defended popular sovereignty, unrestricted by any higher moral principle, as the touchstone of republican government and as the only basis of national unity. In his view majority rule was not a means to an end, but a self-justifying end in itself. In practical effect it meant that each political community, whether state or territorial, had the right to shape its domestic institutions, subject only to the requirements of the Constitution. And if slave labor was the choice of some communities, that choice was not inconsistent with republican government. Answering Lincoln's prediction that either slavery or freedom must be nationalized, Douglas said the government had been founded on such a division and could continue only on that basis. For this reason Douglas professed indifference to the moral aspect of slavery, saying he did not care whether it was voted up or down. To agitate the moral issue and try to settle it uniformly for the entire republic, he warned, would provoke conflict and disrupt the Union. In the final analysis, he declared on several occasions, the integrity of the Union was more important than the liberty of Negro slaves.

Douglas had always said that popular sovereignty was subject only to the Constitution, and it was in this context that Lincoln raised the issue of the legal effect of the *Dred Scott* decision. In Lincoln's view the case provided dramatic evidence of the legal tendency toward slavery expansion. The first step, he said, had been the Kansas-Nebraska Act removing the Missouri Compromise barrier against slavery extension. Moreover, although that act dealt with a territory, it stated that Congress had no intention of legislating slavery into any *state;* the purpose of the act was said to be to leave the people free to form local institutions subject only to the federal Constitution. Did this perhaps imply, asked Lincoln, that there were constitutional exceptions to the power of states to prohibit slavery? And did the disavowel of congressional intent to legislate on slavery in the states perhaps imply a power so to legislate?

Lincoln next pointed to Justice Nelson's statement, in his concurring opinion in the *Dred Scott* case, that "except in cases where the power is restrained by the Constitution of the United States, the law of the State is supreme over the subject of slavery within its jurisdiction." The fugitive slave clause, of course, constituted an exception to the states' absolute power over slavery, but did the *Dred Scott* decision create an additional and more threatening exception? What did it mean to say, as Chief Justice Taney had, that "the right of property in a slave is distinctly and expressly affirmed in the Constitution?" Perhaps, Lincoln suggested, it meant that the free states would be forced to recognize slave property generally. In his famous "house divided" speech in August 1858, he expressed this fear: "We shall all lie down pleasantly dreaming that the people of Missouri are on the verge of making their State free, and we shall awake to the reality instead that the Supreme Court has made Illinois a slave State."

In addition to posing this issue, Lincoln pointedly asked Douglas how he could reconcile popular sovereignty with the *Dred Scott* decision. Did not the right of constitutionally protected slave property supersede the right of a territorial community to exclude slavery? Douglas's answer, the famous Freeport doctrine, defended popular sovereignty as effective and legitimate, the *Dred Scott* decision notwithstanding. It did not matter what the Supreme Court said about the abstract question of property in slaves, Douglas explained, for slavery could not exist without the protection of local legislation. And if the people did not like slavery, they could pass "unfriendly legislation" preventing the adoption of the legal supports that slavery required.

Douglas had expressed the substance of the Freeport doctrine before; indeed, southerners themselves, before the split over the Lecompton constitution, in similar terms had reassured northern audiences with this argument. Now, however, Douglas's reiteration of the local sovereignty principle attracted national attention because of his break with the Buchanan administration. From Lincoln's standpoint there was little to be gained by placing Douglas at odds with the South and hence closer to free soil opinion. But intellectually and morally Lincoln put Douglas in an untenable position. Douglas had said local sovereignty was subject to the Constitution; like most politicians he took Supreme Court decisions as authoritative expositions of the Constitution, and stated that he accepted the *Dred Scott* decision. Yet he was now saying, in effect, that he would negate it. Lincoln captured the contradiction—and Douglas's flawed sense of constitutional morality—in charging that the Freeport doctrine amounted to saying that "a thing may be lawfully driven away from where it had a lawful right to be."

In the opinion of some historians, Lincoln was irresponsible in speaking of a "second *Dred Scott* decision" that would further nationalize slavery in the free states. Yet if southerners could be apprehensive about the effect of slavery restriction in "denationalizing" slavery and causing its eventual destruction, Republicans were warranted in pointing to the possibility of further slave advances, directed by the national judiciary, under the logic of the *Dred Scott* opinion. There were cases in northern state courts dealing with slaves in transit that the Supreme Court could have used to provide limited recognition of the right to hold slave property in the free states under the Fifth Amendment. Such a ruling, applying the Fifth Amendment to the states, would appear to run counter to the earlier decision in *Barron* v. *Baltimore* (1833), where the Court held that the first eight amendments were restrictions only on the federal government. The *Barron* case, however, was not unequivocally accepted as binding precedent in the antebellum period. In fact, arguments were frequently advanced in federal and state courts asserting the applicability of the Fifth Amendment and the Bill of Rights to the states. Thus if the Taney Court were to persist in its drive to destroy antislavery constitutionalism, another "Dred Scott" decision was by no means an impossibility. And that the Taney Court would so persist seemed apparent from its attack on northern personal liberty laws in the famous fugitive slave case of 1859, *Ableman* v. *Booth.*

State Sovereignty Vindicated: Ableman v. Booth

Despite a few highly publicized fugitive slave escapes, the Pierce and Buchanan administrations vigorously enforced the Fugitive Slave Act of 1850. Still, some slaves managed to escape, and of those who did only a small number was actually subjected to the rendition process. Southerners were dissatisfied with this circumstance, and their resentment was compounded by the adoption of new personal liberty laws in the northern states in the 1850s. Laws in Connecticut, Rhode Island, Massachusetts, Michigan, Maine, Ohio, and Wisconsin provided counsel for alleged fugitives, guaranteed them the writ of habeas corpus and trial by jury, denied the use of state jails for arrested fugitives, prohibited state officers from assisting in the return of fugitives, and punished kidnaping of free Negroes. *Ableman* v. *Booth* arose in this context.

The case began in 1854 when an abolitionist editor in Wisconsin, Sherman Booth, forcibly assisted in the escape of a fugitive slave. He was convicted in federal district court of violating the Fugitive Slave Law and was fined $1,000. The Wisconsin Supreme Court then issued a writ of habeas corpus, and on hearing, freed Booth, holding his conviction illegal and the Fugitive Slave Law void. The Wisconsin court insisted on its right to free its citizens from illegal confinement, even though examination into the constitutionality of federal law was involved. United States District Marshal Ableman then sought and obtained a writ of error in the federal Supreme Court, to review the Wisconsin court's finding. The Wisconsin Supreme Court refused to receive notice of the United States Supreme Court's writ, and in fact ignored the subsequent review completely.

In March 1859 Chief Justice Taney gave the opinion of the Supreme Court upholding Booth's conviction and denying the power of a state court to interpose its authority to prevent possibly illegal detention in federal hands. Using dual-federalist analysis, Taney said the federal and state governments were sovereign in their respective spheres, and the federal judiciary had an obligation to guard each in the exercise of the powers assigned it. In the instant case, said Taney, the state judiciary was interfering in the execution of federal law and asserting its supremacy over the courts of the United States. Denying the right of the state judiciary to intefere in federal cases, the chief justice upheld the supremacy of the federal Constitution and defended the role of the federal judiciary as the final tribunal to decide constitutional issues. He condemned the action of the Wisconsin court as unconstitutional, destructive of national sovereignty, and tantamount to "lawless violence."

Conventional wisdom has regarded *Ableman* v. *Booth* as a landmark decision in the development of constitutional nationalism, and the position of the Wisconsin Supreme Court as dangerously nullificationist in tendency. It is pertinent to note, however, that in the 1850s habeas corpus law concerning the powers of state courts in relation to federal authority was unsettled. According to one view, states could discharge persons illegally detained by the federal government, even when the constitutionality of federal actions was involved. It is significant, too, that Taney defended national judicial rather than legislative authority. He said nothing about congressional power, except to assert the constitutionality of the Fugitive Slave Act of 1850. His main concern was to exercise judicial power as the agent of the slave states. Despite the appearance of national centralization, therefore, *Ableman* v. *Booth* gave extrajurisdictional effect to the law of slavery, in accordance with the doctrine of state sovereignty and federal trusteeship. And by holding that the states could not inquire into confinement under federal authority, Taney effectively demolished the personal liberty laws of the free states.

Secession

The culmination of proslavery constitutionalism was the demand for enactment of a federal slave code in the territories. This was the ultimate expression of extrajurisdictional application of slave-state law through the agency of the federal government. A secondary demand was for repeal of the personal liberty laws. Douglas's Freeport doctrine spurred the former proposal, while free state attempts at interposition in fugitive slave cases, as in Wisconsin, provoked the latter. In the increasingly tense atmosphere that surrounded these demands, John Brown's raid on the federal arsenal at Harpers Ferry, Virginia, in November 1859 heightened southern fear of a free soil victory in the election of 1860.

In the campaign of 1860 four parties competed for control of the national government. The Democratic party, in reality split since the fight over the Lecompton constitution, now formally divided into two parties. Douglas ran for the northern Democracts on the basis of popular sovereignty and a promise to abide by Supreme Court decisions. Southern Democrats nominated John C. Breckinridge of Kentucky and insisted on federal protection of the rights of persons and property in the territories. The Republican nominee was Abraham Lincoln, who ran on a platform proclaiming that due process of law under the Fifth Amendment guaranteed freedom in the territories. The Republican platform also denounced popular sovereignty as a fraud and condemned the view that the Constitution of its own force carried slavery into the territories. Finally, a small body of Whigs from the upper South organized as the Constitutional Union party and ran John Bell of Tennessee for president. Fearful of what might happen if either Lincoln or Breckinridge were elected, the Constitutional Unionists deplored agitation of the slavery question. Advocating no policy, they simply appealed to patriotism, respect for the Constitution and the Union, and enforcement of the laws.

Lincoln carried every northern state but New Jersey, winning 180 electoral votes. Douglas won only Missouri and New Jersey, securing 12 votes. Breckinridge carried eleven southern states for 72 votes, while Bell won 39 votes in Kentucky, Tennessee, and Virginia. The vote thus resolved itself into a direct conflict between northern free soilers and southern proponents of slavery expansion for control of the electoral college. Although winning only a minority of the popular vote, Lincoln's electoral college majority won him the presidency.

Secession followed the election of 1860, but secession was not the main purpose of the doctrine of state sovereignty employed by the South from 1846 to 1860. It was, rather, a desperate final alternative in the face of impending disaster. For that was what Lincoln's election portended in southern eyes. However much Republicans might deny federal authority over slavery in the states where it existed, agree to enforce the Fugitive Slave Law, and support the repeal of personal liberty laws, southerners perceived a mortal threat to their way of life. They saw no distinction between direct and indirect attacks on slavery, between proposals to keep slavery out of the territories and demands for outright abolition. At some point the objective realities of slavery restriction symbolized the South's deepening sense of social and economic alienation from the North. By the same token, free soil opposition to slavery extension and to secession symbolized northern social fears and aspirations.

In retrospect it is easy to conclude that had southern members of Congress stayed where they were and remained calm, they could still have exercised considerable influence over national policy. Secession has, therefore, often seemed a great blunder—ill conceived, overreactive, irrational. Yet the triumph of a party committed to the ultimate extinction of slavery would probably have proven decisive in shaping national policy even without secession and war. Majority opinion, becoming increasingly antislavery and antisouthern, in time would have supported restrictions on the institution. In the short run the practical results of the election would have been evident in the appointment of Republican postmasters, customs collectors, and sundry government officials—a process that would have interfered with and possibly ended proslavery control of thought and behavior in the

South. The South was, therefore, justified in fearing the succession to national power of an exclusively sectional antislavery party.

Secession was now used to destroy the Union and the constitutional system. Yet years of theorizing about secession caused it to appear—or enabled southerners to regard it—as a legitimate constitutional instrument. Like Calhoun before them, the secession theorists of 1860 held that the several states retained complete sovereignty, and that the Union was a mere league, from which member states might withdraw at their pleasure. The Constitution was a compact between the states, not (as Lincoln was shortly to argue) between the people of the United States. Sovereignty was indivisible and could be neither divided nor delegated; therefore, the federal government had no sovereignty. The Constitution was thus a mere treaty, and the Union a mere league. From this it followed that secession was a self-evident right, since it could hardly be denied that a sovereign state could withdraw from a league at any time it chose to do so.

Jefferson Davis, perhaps the most brilliant secession theorist of the times, frequently adduced two additional historical arguments in support of secession. First, he pointed to the fact that the Constitutional Convention had rejected state coercion. If a state could not be coerced, Davis contended, then it was manifestly impossible to prevent it from withdrawing from the Union at will. Davis also pointed to the resolutions adopted by the various state conventions when ratifying the Constitution. The Virginia Convention, in particular, had resolved that "rights granted by the people may be resumed by the people at their pleasure," while New York and Massachusetts had enacted similar resolutions. Davis interpreted these resolutions as specifically reserving to the various states the right to withdraw from the compact should they desire to do so.

The South justified secession on the ground that actions of the northern states, as parties to the original constitutional compact, violated the commitment to protect slavery that was incorporated in the Constitution as the very basis of Union. According to the Mississippi legislature, "slavery existed prior to the formation of the Federal Constitution, and is recognized by its letter, and all efforts to impair its value or lessen its duration by Congress, or any of the free States, is a violation of the compact of Union." Specifically, the northern states had violated and obstructed the Fugitive Slave Law by passing personal liberty laws; made attacks on slavery in the South by permitting abolition societies to exist; tried to exclude slavery from the territories, thus denying the rights of the southern states there; opposed the *Dred Scott* decision and its guarantee of southern citizens' property rights; and launched a direct assault on the slave system of the South in the Harpers Ferry raid.

These arguments were by no means frivolous or patently inaccurate, for in some sense slavery *was* recognized in the constitutional settlement on which the republic was founded. The recognition, however, was nowhere so explicit and formal as southerners thought—were indeed required to think—as they undertook the radical expedient of secession. Opinion about slavery in 1787 was far more ambivalent, even among southerners themselves, than the secessionists could possibly have acknowledged. Furthermore, the constitutional settlement of 1787 included antislavery actions that northerners could point to as evidence of the framers' desire—in some instances a commitment—to see slavery ultimately abolished. Indeed, a strong argument could be made against secession on constitutional grounds. Weighing against secession as a legitimate constitutional action was the silence of the Constitution on the subject; the existence of federal powers not subject to state interference; the supremacy clause; the rejection of the Articles of Confederation in an election (i.e., the contest over ratification of the Constitution) which offered a choice between a league of sovereign states and a sovereign federal government; and the sanctity of majority rule in a republican system of government. In short, historical, constitutional, and moral right existed on both sides.

South Carolina seceded first. As soon as the result of the election became known, the state legislature called a constitutional convention which met at Charleston on December 17. Three days later, the convention by unanimous vote adopted an ordinance of secession. The ordinance purported to repeal the ordinance of 1787, whereby the state had ratified the Constitution. The convention also adopted a declaration of the causes of secession, which presented the southern theory of the Union and the various southern grievances of the hour. Alabama, Georgia, Florida, Mississippi, Louisiana, and Texas had also called conventions, all of which met in January and voted for secession by large majorities. Thus all seven states of the lower South had seceded by the end of January.

Attempts at Compromise

Meanwhile Buchanan's administration in Washington was involved in a paralyzing dilemma: if it did nothing to check the secessionist movement, the Union would most assuredly be dissolved; on the other hand, if the government used force against the seceding states, a terrible civil war might result. There was no assurance that the North was ready to support such a drastic policy. Moreover, the employment of force would probably precipitate secession in several of the remaining slave states of the upper South, then on the verge of leaving the Union.

Confronted by this quandary, President Buchanan stalled for time and awaited developments. In his annual message in December, he laid the responsibility for the current crisis at the door of the northern people's "intemperate interference" with slavery. He added, however, that Lincoln's election was not just cause for secession, and he also warned the South that no constitutional right of secession existed, since the Union had been intended to be permanent. He then nullified whatever force these last observations had with the statement that if a state chose to secede, there existed no constitutional remedy against its action, however illegal it might be. Buchanan's constitutionalism was thus the quintessence of futility. Seward ironically commented that "the message shows conclusively that it is the duty of the President to execute the law—unless someone opposes it; and that no state has the right to go out of the Union—unless it wants to." In justice to Buchanan, however, it must be observed that the political dilemma in which he found himself was a very real one, and that his policy of watchful waiting was basically the course that Lincoln adopted after his inauguration.

In reality, Buchanan hoped that Congress would again effect some sort of last-minute compromise. Moderate Democrats, both North and South, were working desperately to that end. The House on December 4, 1860, appointed a committee of thirty-three, one member from each state, to consider compromise proposals, and two days later the Senate created a committee of thirteen for the same purpose. The Republicans dominated the House committee, but the Senate group represented all factions, and included William H. Seward of New York and Ben Wade of Ohio for the Republicans, Stephen A. Douglas of Illinois and John J. Crittenden of Kentucky for the moderate Democrats, and Robert Toombs of Georgia and Jefferson Davis of Mississippi for the secessionists.

The most significant proposals presented were the Crittenden Resolutions, introduced to the Senate and the compromise committees by Senator Crittenden on December 18. These were recommendations for amendments to the Constitution that would extend the Missouri Compromise line to the Pacific, prohibiting slavery north and guaranteeing it south of 36°30′. This proposal, it should be noted, went beyond the 1820 Compromise by positively legislating slavery in national territory, something Congress had never before done. It was intended to apply, moreover, to existing territories and those "hereafter acquired." Other proposed amendments denied Congress power to abolish slavery in the District of Columbia or in places subject to federal jurisdiction where slavery existed in the surrounding state; denied Congress power to interfere with the domestic slave trade; and guaranteed federal compensation to slaveholders who were prevented from recovering fugitive slaves. Additional resolutions called for enforcement of the Fugitive Slave Law, repeal of the personal liberty laws, and, on the North's behalf, reinforcement of the laws against the African slave trade.

The compromise attempt failed mainly because the Republican party opposed it, although a large share of responsibility belongs to southern members of Congress who if they had stayed in Washington might have altered the outcome. Republicans believed Lincoln's election did not menace the South and that concessions to the southern states were, therefore, unnecessary. The party could not accept a solution that established slavery in the territories, for that would have contradicted its constitutional rationale, its election promises, and its very reason for being. It was especially important to reject any plan to legislate slavery into territories south of 36°30′ that might be acquired in the future, for the expansionist pressures that had affected American politics for two decades appeared likely to continue. Southerners had encouraged filibustering ventures into Nicaragua and Cuba in the 1850s, and anticipated Caribbean expansion as a means of maintaining their political power. Republicans were, therefore, categorically opposed to the dividing-line approach to the slavery question incorporated in the Crittenden Compromise. And if they needed any further reason for rejecting compromise, it could be found in the widespread belief that the Compromise of 1850 had been a grievous mistake because it only encouraged southern aggressiveness.

In February Congress did belatedly adopt a constitutional amendment guaranteeing slavery within the states in perpetuity against federal interference. "No amendment shall be made to the Constitution," the proposal read, "which will authorize or give to Congress the power to abolish or interfere, within any state, with the domestic institutions thereof, including that of persons held to labor or service by the laws of said state." Eventually, three states, Ohio, Maryland, and Illinois, ratified the amendment, but it came too late and conceded too little to influence the course of events.

The Unionist-dominated Virginia legislature also sponsored an unsuccessful peace conference. In response to Virginia's call, delegates from twenty-one states assembled at Washington on February 4, under the chairmanship of ex-President Tyler. The conference got nowhere. The seven seceded states refused to send delegates, while the northern delegations were for the most part controlled by Republicans determined to make no substantial concessions. Eventually, the conference adopted the substance of the Crittenden amendments, with some modifications, as well as a proposed amendment that the United States acquire no new territory except by a four-fifths vote of the Senate, with a majority of both free- and slave-state senators concurring. When presented in Congress, these proposals were overwhelmingly defeated. Almost all hope of compromise was now gone.

Formation of the Confederacy

On February 4, 1861, the very day when the futile peace conference met in Washington, delegates from the seven seceded states gathered in Montgomery, Alabama, for the purpose of forming a central government. They shortly adopted a temporary constitution converting themselves into a provisional congress and instructing the congress to elect a provisonal president and vice-president. On March 11, the congress adopted a permanent constitution and submitted it to the seceded states for ratification.

The Confederate constitution closely resembled that of the United States, although it contained a number of important differences. Certain provisions underscored state sovereignty. The preamble read, "We the people of the Confederate States, each state acting in its sovereign capacity . . . do ordain and establish this Constitution . . ." This implied that the resultant government arose out of a compact between sovereign states, and not between the people thereof. The right of secession might thereby be inferred. Interestingly enough, however, the constitution mentioned no such right, and in fact three different proposals guaranteeing the right were killed in convention without reaching the floor.

Other provisions grew directly out of the slavery controversy. Congress was forbidden to pass any law impairing the right of property in slaves. Citizens with their slaves were granted the right of transit and sojourn in other states, and such sojourn did not thereby impair ownership in such slaves. Negro slavery was specifically recognized in any territories the Confederacy might acquire. The foreign slave trade, however, except with slave-holding states of the United States, was forbidden. The South's long-standing grievance against the protective tariff was reflected in a clause forbidding import duties for the benefit of industry, while congressional appropriations for internal improvements, except those in navigational facilities, were also prohibited.

Substantial changes were made in the executive department. The president and vice-president were given six-year terms and made ineligible for re-election. The president was specifically granted a separate unconditional removal power over principal officers, and over minor officials for reasons of misconduct or incapacity. This provision evidently reflected the long quarrel over the removal power under the United States Constitution.

The president also had more effective control over money matters than did the president of the United States under the Constitution. He could veto separate items in appropriation bills, while Congress could appropriate money only by two-thirds vote of both houses unless the funds were requested by the executive. Another clause enabled Congress to grant cabinet officers a seat on the floor of either house to discuss matters pertaining to their departments. Such a provision might conceivably have led to the emergence of a parliamentary system of government, although no such tendency appeared during the Confederacy's brief history.

The new government also prepared to treat with the United States to effect a settlement with respect to "common property," the territories, debts, and the like. For this purpose the Confederate Congress accredited two commissioners to Washington. The new government also proceeded to take over certain forts, arsenals, and other United States property lying within the Confederacy. Apparently, it expected the government at Washington to offer little resistance to the erection of a new nation.

Lincoln's Policy toward Secession

On March 4, 1861, the Buchanan administration expired, and the tremendous responsibilities of the presidential office devolved upon Abraham Lincoln. Lincoln laid down the outlines of his policy toward slavery, secession, and the maintenance of national authority in his inaugural address of March 4. It was a reasoned and powerful address, lucid in its constitutional theorizing, but the president offered no compromise whatever to the South on the territorial question, as many southern Unionists desired him to do.

Lincoln first reminded the South that he had no constitutional authority to attack slavery within the southern states, and added that he was willing and even anxious to extend all the constitutional protection possible to the "prosperity, peace and security" of every section of the Union. He sanctioned the constitutional amendment specifically guaranteeing slavery in the states against congressional interference, adding that in any case this was already implied constitutional law.

On the subject of slavery in the territories, however, he suggested that the issue was a matter of policy not adequately covered by the provisions of the written Constitution. In what was obviously an oblique repudiation of the *Dred Scott* opinion, he added that he could not accept the proposition that opinions of the Supreme Court on constitutional questions bound finally the other two departments of government, who must decide constitutional issues for themselves. Matters of constitutional law not specifically covered by the written constitution, he implied, ought to be settled by the majority will, presumably by the mechanism of presidential and congressional elections. In other words, the constitutional status of slavery in the territories might ultimately be settled by Republican victories in national elections and the translation of party policy into law. The new president plainly intended to abide by the substance of his party's platform and to refuse to sanction any further extension of slavery in the territories.

There was in Lincoln's words the implication that the South could not secede in peace. The Union of 1789 was intended to be perpetual. Secession he denounced as the "essence of anarchy." It was "legally void," and acts of violence within any state or states "against the authority of the United States" were "insurrectionary or revolutionary, according to circumstances." He added that he would make no war upon the South, but that he would enforce federal law, collect taxes, and hold possession of federal property. Yet he also said that he would not do all that strict legal right entitled him to do in the way of upholding federal authority. Where hostility to the United States was so great as to prevent local citizens from holding office, for example, Lincoln stated that he would not appoint "obnoxious strangers." That would be "irritating" and impracticable, and he would rather "forego for the time being the uses of such offices." Similarly Lincoln said that the mails would be delivered, "unless repelled."

The new president thus took a position that was at once firm and conciliatory. Above all he saw clearly what Buchanan had not seen—that coercion of a seceding state was technically unnecessary and irrelevant, and that the proper answer to secession was the coercion of individuals resisting federal authority. Lincoln went on to warn the South to consider well the possible disadvantages involved in resorting to the undoubted right of revolution. Successful secession would solve none of the South's existing problems relating to the North and the Union; the same problems would exist after secession as before. He ended with an attempt to stir southern sentiment and loyalty for the Union. "The mystic chords of memory stretching from every battlefield and patriot grave to every living heart and hearthstone all over this broad land, will yet swell the chorus of the Union when again touched, as surely they will be, by the better angels of our nature."

Lincoln never wavered in the policy toward secession announced in his inaugural address. He did, however, proceed with great caution in its application. He desired above all else to avoid the charge of deliberately waging war upon the South. Moreover, he believed that a policy of caution might hold the states of the upper South in the Union, while the rash application of force would make their secession certain. The Virginia Unionists, in particular, were pleading with him to make no move, lest it precipitate their state's secession.

The issue of federal authority in the South very shortly focused upon Fort Sumter, in Charleston Harbor. Although the Confederates had taken over nearly all other federal properties, Buchanan had refused to surrender Sumter, and Lincoln continued this policy. When Lincoln notified the governor of South Carolina of his intention to replenish the fort's supplies, Confederate military officials replied, on April 12, 1861, with an attack on the fort. The bombardment ended the agonizing interim between secession and war. Four more states, Virginia, Tennessee, Arkansas and North Carolina, shortly seceded. Lincoln called for troops to suppress the "rebellion," and the Civil War had begun.

Lincoln's Responsibility for Secession and War

Lincoln's policy before and after his inaugural has been severely criticized by certain historians, who charge him with partial rsponsibility for the coming of secession and war. First, they assert, Lincoln's coldness toward the Crittenden compromise and his general unwillingness to extend to the

South any assurances on the territorial question inspired the remaining six states in the lower South to follow South Carolina out of the Union. Second, Lincoln's critics contend that the policy set forth in his inaugural address made war and further secession inevitable.

It is highly probable that the attitude of Lincoln and other Republican leaders toward the South after November 1860 strengthened the hand of the secessionists and thereby contributed to disunion. When the Republicans confined their assurances to a promise not to interfere with slavery in the southern states, the secessionists were enabled to argue that the forthcoming administration would ignore southern constitutional rights in the territories as enunciated in the *Dred Scott* case. Since the Republicans were willing to treat one set of constitutional rights in so cavalier a manner, the secessionists said, what assurance was there that a Republican administration might not ultimately attack slavery within the states themselves?

It is true that Lincoln's policy as laid down in his inaugural made war extremely likely. It was certain that the attempt to assert federal authority within the limits of the seceded states would lead to armed conflict, for the seceded states must of necessity resist such authority or their pretended status of independence would become absurd. Confederate defiance would, in turn, provoke military action, and war would follow automatically.

Behind the concern with Lincoln's responsibility for the war lies the more complex question of the North's reasons for resisting secession. Implicit in the criticism of Lincoln is the view that war is not justified, especially not a war for mere nationalism. But while northerners opposed secession out of a drive for national self-preservation, it was a particular kind of nationalism, possessing a distinct political character, that sustained them. From the founding of the nation, American nationality was defined with reference to republican self-government and citizenship. Moreover the Union government was not a unitary, centralized state, but a federal republic that permitted substantial local autonomy. In resisting secession, therefore, northerners defended republican self-government, identifying it with the Union as the basis of American nationality.

Northerners also resisted secession as a threat to constitutionalism. Here continuity is evident between antebellum struggles and the wartime crisis. For among the reasons for opposing slavery was its contradiction not only of the principles of equality and consent, but also of constitutionalism and the rule of law. Congressional gag rules, the mobbing of abolitionist speakers, interference with the mails and the denial of free speech in the South, fugitive slave recaptures that abrogated free states' due process of law—all were taken as illustrating in northern eyes the lawless, coercive, and anticonstitutional tendencies encouraged by the imperious rule of the slave power. Secession escalated this lawlessness into open repudiation of the rule of law. It was, as Lincoln said in his inaugural address, "the essence of anarchy" and an unjustified revolution against constitutional government. In opposing secession, therefore, Republicans were defending the peaceful methods of constitutional politics.

After secession and the assult on Fort Sumter, the pre-eminent issue in American politics shifted from the future of slavery in the American republic to the preservation of the Union and the Constitution. Ambiguous by design, combining elements both of a confederation expressing the size and diversity of the American people and a unitary government expressing their shared values, the federal republic would receive clearer constitutional definition in the trial of civil war.

SIXTEEN

The Civil War

――――――――――――――――― ✦ ✦ ✦ ―――――――――――――――――

A CONSTITUTIONAL CRISIS of the most profound sort, the Civil War called into question not only the existence of the Union, but also constitutionalism and the rule of law. Northern protest against the illegality of secession notwithstanding, the withdrawal of the southern states followed by the attack on Fort Sumter raised anew, after three-quarters of a century, the problem of continental political organization. The decentralized Union, part confederation and part unitary government, might be restored to its antebellum condition; a centralized, consolidated Union might emerge from the war; should the South prevail, two or more independent confederations of states might be the result. Equally uncertain was the continuation of constitutional politics. Although war was anticipated by the Constitution, fratricidal, civil war was not. Borne of deep-seated cultural and social differences, the conflict that began in 1861 generated enormous pressure to set aside the methods of constitutionalism in favor of arbitrary rule.

The first constitutional issue presented by the outbreak of hostilities was the adequacy of the Constitution in time of war. Many Unionists thought the war abrogated the Constitution in all matters related to the suppression of the rebellion, and made available the rules of warfare under international law. Most northerners believed, however, that although wartime adjustments would be necessary, constitutional law must continue to provide the institutional and legal setting in which the struggle should be carried on. No categorical shift to an all-war footing, requiring the suspension of constitutional procedures and rules, took place.

Believing the Constitution adequate, Americans throughout the Civil War and Reconstruction frequently clung to settled political and governmental habits. Yet one of the sources of strength in the constitutional system, and a principal reason why it was perceived as adequate, was the flexibility and responsiveness of existing constitutional institutions. Of these none was more important than the executive power, now wielded by a

Republican president committed to the preservation of the Union and willing to employ the resources of his office to defend the Constitution. The first clear evidence of the adequacy of the Constitution—startling for the contrast it offered to the Buchanan administration—was Lincoln's decisive direction of the government after the attack on Fort Sumter.

Lincoln's Constitutional Dictatorship

The period between November 1860 and April 1861 witnessed the rapid disintegration of national authority, the spectacular spread of secession, and the founding of the Confederate States of America. Never before nor since has the United States government under the Constitution been so near total collapse. Despite this grave situation Congress adjourned on March 4 and most members went home. Under such foreboding circumstances the awesome responsibility for saving the nation fell upon the new and inexperienced president, fresh from the prairies of Illinois. Lincoln surprised his enemies and detractors, and pleased his friends, by responding to the attack on Fort Sumter with imagination and vigor. Unlike many of his contemporaries, Lincoln believed that the Constitution was adequate to the supreme test of self-preservation, and he acted accordingly.

Neither the nature nor the location of the war power was established beyond debate by the Constitution. Although Unionists firmly believed that the national government possessed full powers to wage war successfully, they differed sharply among themselves over the relative authority of Congress and the president in the exercise of these powers. The Constitution specifically empowers Congress to declare war, to raise and support armies, to maintain a navy, and to provide for the government and the regulation of the land and naval forces, including militia employed in the United States service. On the other hand, the president is constituted the commander in chief of the national military forces and is vested with the full executive power of the government. Clashes between Congress and president during the War of 1812 and the Mexican War over the exercise of war powers had been neither serious nor conclusive in results. In this respect the Civil War was to be vastly different.

On April 15, immediately after the attack on Fort Sumter, Lincoln instituted his presidential quasi-dictatorship under which the powers of the executive were to be extended beyond their traditional limits. His first action was to call for 75,000 volunteers to suppress the insurrection. He also summoned Congress into extraordinary session but set the convening date far ahead to July 4. His failure to convene Congress immediately to provide additional legislation to cope with the grave national crisis defies conclusive explanation. His wish that members of Congress should acquaint themselves with the public temper before convening certainly did not justify the delay of eighty days. Undoubtedly Lincoln, like most northerners, failed to realize how effectively the secessionists had overpowered the Unionists in the lower South, and hence he seriously underestimated the task of restoring national authority. Perhaps he also thought the current states'-rights doctrines had so undermined Congress's power to cope with the emergency that the Union would have to be saved by some as yet largely untested source of national authority. This he found in the presidential oath and in the office of commander in chief.

Accordingly, Lincoln proceeded rapidly to prepare the nation for war without either aid or new authority from Congress. He not only determined the existence of rebellion and called forth the militia to suppress it, but he also proclaimed a blockade of the ports of the rebel states, an act equivalent legally to a declaration of war. Realizing soon that such steps were inadequate for the emergency, on May 3 he called for 42,034 United States volunteers to serve for three years, and he actually received a much larger number. He also directed that large additions be made to the regular army and to the navy. He had $2 million paid out of the federal Treasury, and he pledged the government's credit for the unprecedented sum of a quarter of a billion dollars, all without statutory authority. He had the privilege of the writ of habeas corpus suspended in certain places and ordered the arrest and military detention of citizens who were represented to him as being engaged in or contemplating "treasonable practices."

The overwhelming majority of northern people strongly endorsed the president's course, even when they were uncertain of his constitutional authority. In the nation's greatest crisis the people clamored for more action, not less—in order "to maintain the Union and to preserve the Constitution."

When Congress met in July 1861, Lincoln offered a twofold justification for his extraordinary course. He admitted that the calls for three-year volunteers and for additions to the regular army and navy were of doubtful legality, but he explained that those acts "were ventured upon under what appeared to be a popular demand and a public necessity, trusting then, as now, that Congress would readily ratify them." In other words, the president claimed the constitutional right in an emergency to take action which otherwise would be illegal, provided only that it was not "beyond the constitutional competency of Congress." This was indeed a new and remarkable doctrine to present to an American Congress, which could easily have been convened for previous authorization.

Lincoln's second and more significant justification was that the president possessed the war power and had been forced to use it in defense of the government. Thus he contended that his prescribed oath to "preserve, protect, and defend the Constitution" empowered and even obligated him in an emergency to resort to practically any action necessary to maintain the Union. This obligation stemming from the presidential oath was confirmed by a legal opinion of Attorney General Edward Bates, who held that it was the president's particular duty to suppress the rebellion, since the courts lacked the strength to do so. Lincoln, therefore, took the position that he might constitutionally disregard the guarantee of the habeas corpus privilege or any single law if he considered such a step necessary to preserve the government. Buttressing this contention was his fundamental concept of the nation as older than either the Constitution or the states and, therefore, superior to both. In short, he held that the president's oath and his position as commander in chief constituted him a virtual dictator, like those of the ancient Roman Republic, to save the life of the nation.

Congressional and Judicial Reactions

The great majority of the members of Congress—those from the Confederate states having withdrawn or having been expelled—approved the president's course, but they divided sharply over the constitutional justification of his actions. Intermittently throughout the special session of 1861 the Senate debated a proposed joint resolution which enumerated, approved, and validated the president's extraordinary acts, proclamations, and orders. The resolution had the support of the vast majority of Republicans, including some who assumed that certain of the president's acts were illegal when performed. Other Republicans, while approving the president's course, questioned the proposed method of validating his suspension of the writ of habeas corpus and his proclamation of a blockade. Owing to this disagreement the resolution never came to a vote. Instead a less specific and less comprehensive validating clause was attached as a rider to an act to increase the pay of privates and on the last two days of the session was rushed through both houses, with only five Democratic senators from border slave states recorded in opposition. By this law all of the president's acts, proclamations, and orders respecting the army, navy, militia, and volunteers were approved and "in all respects legalized and made valid, to the same intent and with the same effect as if they had been issued and done under the previous express authority and direction of the Congress." This congressional ratification of part of the president's extraordinary acts left the blockade and the suspension of the privilege of habeas corpus resting entirely upon presidential authority.

The measured congressional endorsement of Lincoln's crisis management reflected institutional jealousy more than political differences. By the winter of 1861 political disagreement over policy toward slavery was noticeable, but constitutional rivalry continued to provide the principal basis for congressional actions in relation to the conduct of the war. On numerous issues debate occurred over the relative authority of the president and Congress in the exercise of war powers under the Constitution. Conservative Republicans contended that the rights of war were executive, not legislative, and that questions of military necessity, by their very nature, must be decided by military commanders acting under the authority of the president as commander in chief. The majority of Republicans held in contrast that Congress's power to declare war encompassed full belligerent rights against an enemy, and hence that Congress possessed complete powers of sovereignty in the conduct of war. To buttress this position they invoked the principles of civilian control of the military and legislative regulation of executive power. And they rested these principles in turn on a theory of the separation of powers that gave Congress a decisive role in the constitutional system.

Constitutional orthodoxy since the founding of the government stipulated an admixture of separation of powers and checks and balances. The founding fathers believed that by separating the functions of government into three distinct branches, and by giving each branch a share of the power belonging to the others, consolidationist tendencies could be restrained. Civil War Republicans, however, returned to an earlier theory of the separation of powers that by ignoring or de-emphasizing checks and balances, made the lawmaking power the center of the government. In effect it denied a legislative role to the executive. Republican congressmen argued that the objects and duration of the war were proper subjects of legislation. Congress did not have tactical, battlefield authority, but it could, under the lawmaking authority that the Constitution entrusted to it, control the conduct of the war through military legislation as well as through confiscation and emancipation measures. "Only in the manner and in the mode we may prescribe by law," said Senator John Sherman of Ohio, could the president conduct the war. Senator Jacob Howard of Michigan declared: "It is idle to talk of a war-making power independent of the law-making power." In a prebureaucratic age when legislatures were ascendant, and when their authority was enhanced by close identification with the people, Congress presented a formidable challenge to executive power.

In December 1861 Congress created its own version of crisis government in the Joint Committee on the Conduct of the War. By no means the result of a radical cabal, the creation of the committee expressed a general legislative intention to restrain executive power and affirm civilian control of the military. Military defeat, resentment against the West Point officer class, and a desire to promote antislavery purposes spurred the formation of the committee. In conducting numerous investigations and publishing voluminous reports of its findings, the committee was severely critical of Democrats and conservative generals. Plainly, it tried to steer military policy in an antislavery direction, and occasionally its criticism was excessive and unwarranted. Yet considering that the subject of war powers lacked precise definition and that no model existed on which to pattern congressional-executive relations in an emergency of this sort, the committee was justified in following the well-established practice of legislative investigation of military campaigns. The Joint Committee played a less important role in military affairs after Lincoln reorganized the Union command in 1864. On the whole it facilitated executive-legislative cooperation and strengthened the Union's crisis government.

The Supreme Court, like Congress, was divided over the constitutionality of Lincoln's assumption of broad war powers, but a majority of the justices upheld his position. In the *Prize Cases* (1863) Justice Robert Grier declared for the majority that, although the President did not have power to initiate war, when it was begun by insurrection, he was "bound to accept the challenge without waiting for any special legislative authority." Grier concluded:

Whether the President in fulfilling his duties, as Commander-in-Chief, in suppressing an insurrection, has met with such armed hostile resistance, and a civil war of such alarming proportions as will compel him to accord to them the character of belligerents, is a question to be decided by him, and this court must be governed by the decisions and acts of the Political Department of the government to which this power was intrusted. "He must determine what degree of force the crisis demands." The proclamation of blockade is, itself, official and conclusive evidence to the court that a state of war existed which demanded and authorized a recourse to such a measure, under the circumstances peculiar to the case.

A minority of four justices insisted that the basic war power belonged to Congress and not to the president. Justice Samuel Nelson summarized the minority position when he declared:

The President does not possess the power under Constitution to declare war or recognize its existence within the meaning of the law of nations, which carries with it belligerent rights, and thus change the country and all its citizens from a state of peace to a state of war; that this power belongs exclusively to the Congress of the United States and, consequently, that the President had no power to set on foot a blockade under the law of nations.

Under these circumstances President Lincoln continued to formulate as well as to execute most of the essential war policies. In 1862 the War Department commissioned Professor Francis Lieber, a German immigrant and an authority on international law, to codify for the first time in America the rules and regulations for the conduct of armies in the field. The result, General Orders No. 100, was promulgated in April 1863 as the laws of war for the Union armies. All this was done without congressonal authorization, despite the fact that the Constitution specifically grants this power and responsibility to Congress. On the other hand, Congress on July 17, 1862, did make a thorough revision of the Articles for the Government of the Navy. Both sets of regulations, extensively revised, continued to be used through World War II.

In such other important fields as emancipation, reconstruction, and the impairment of civil rights, the president largely determined governmental policy, either in the absence of congressional action or in virtual disregard of it. In September 1862 he disregarded the emancipation section of the Second Confiscation Act and based his preliminary Emancipation Proclamation upon his power as commander in chief. In December 1863 he merely announced to the new Congress his own reconstruction program, and when Congress formulated a sterner plan in the Wade-Davis bill, he killed it with a pocket veto.[1]

For almost two years after the outbreak of hostilities Lincoln continued to suspend the habeas corpus privilege on his own authority. Both Republicans and Democrats repeatedly challenged his constitutional authority on the ground that the clause of the Constitution authorizing suspension was in Article I, Section 9, which deals with the powers of Congress and not those of the president. Nevertheless, in September 1862 he issued a proclamation subjecting broad categories of "disloyal" persons to martial law and suspending the privilege of habeas corpus in all cases involving such persons.

At its next session Congress, on March 3, 1863, finally passed the Habeas Corpus Act, by which the president, during the rebellion, was "authorized to suspend" the privilege of the writ in all cases in which he thought the public safety might require it. The phraseology was intentionally ambiguous, designed to win the support of those who believed that Congress was recognizing an existing presidential power as well as of those who believed that Congress was thereby conferring the power upon the president. Lincoln did not issue a fresh proclamation invoking this new authority until six months later, nor did the administration later materially alter its policy in making arbitrary arrests.

Although the Supreme Court never rendered a decision directly involving the location of the suspending powers, in the *Prize Cases* it did give indirect approval to the president's action in suspending the habeas corpus privilege. The suspension of the writ was not directly involved, but the Court held that when war was forced upon the United States, the president was obligated to take all appropriate steps to meet it "without waiting for any special legislative authority."

Lincoln continued his presidential domination to the end of his administration. The mounting success of Union arms, the favorable turn of international affairs, Lincoln's staunch adherence to his emancipation policy, all enhanced greatly the president's prestige and influence with Republican, independent, and even many Democratic citizens. Lincoln's remarkable ability to speak to and for the great mass of people through private conversations, public addresses, and open letters published in the newspapers tended to make him a grand tribune of the people.

1. See below, p. 331.

In nonmilitary matters Lincoln assumed a passive attitude of deference toward Congress that contributed to the postwar weakening of the presidency. Yet virtually singlehandedly at the beginning of the war he discovered within the confines of the Constitution, if he did not create, the power of emergency rule that permanently altered the presidential office. In an unprecedented situation he used the war power in unprecedented ways to affect not merely military but also civil and political affairs. Although the republican civic tradition recognized the need for emergency dictatorship, the founding fathers made no express provision for emergency government other than to anticipate the suspension of the writ of habeas corpus. Lincoln's lasting significance in constitutional history was to constitutionialize the doctrine of emergency prerogative that had arisen since the start of the government. The development is not one that can be viewed without irony or criticism, for in the twentieth century presidential appeals to national security to justify sometimes irresponsible exercises of executive power owe something to Lincoln's Civil War precedent. Whether for good or ill, Lincoln's exercise of the war power expanded the scope of executive authority.

The Legal Nature of the War

Although it was hardly an issue in the decision to meet the attack on Fort Sumter, once hostilities began it was necessary to deal with the constitutional question of the legal nature of the war. Was the conflict basically an insurrection, a rebellion, or an international war? This was an important question, since a variety of legal rights and responsibilities hinged upon the answer. An insurrection is legally construed to be an organized and armed uprising for public political purposes; it may seek to overthrow the government, or it may seek merely to suppress certain laws or to alter administrative practice. A rebellion in general is considered to have a much more highly developed political and military organization than an insurrection; in international law it conveys belligerent status. Generally, such belligerent status implies that the belligerent government is attempting by war to free itself from the jurisdiction of the parent state, that it has an organized *de facto* government, that it is in control of at least some territory, and that it has sufficient proportions to render the issue of the conflict in doubt. An international war, on the other hand, is one between two or more independent states who are recognized members of the family of nations.

In international law the rights of parties to an armed conflict vary greatly with their status. Insurgents have a very limited status; they are not mere pirates or bandits, but their activities do not constitute "war" in the *de jure* sense, and they cannot claim against neutrals the privileges of the laws of war. A full rebellion, on the other hand, is a "war" so far as international law is concerned and the rebel government possesses all the belligerent rights of a fully recognized international state, toward both neutrals and the parent state. Needless to say, a parent state may attempt by force to suppress either an insurrection or a rebellion. In domestic law rebels may be criminals in the eyes of the parent state, and answerable to its courts if their movement fails. Thus under the United States Constitution insurrection and rebellion constitute treason, for which the laws provide severe penalties.

The southern secessionists took the position that the armed conflict was an international war between the United States and the Confederate States of America. The Confederates believed that secession had been constitutional and that they had not only a *de facto* government entitled to full belligerent rights but also a *de jure* government whose independence and sovereignty should be recognized by foreign powers. In their hope of winning the war the southerners counted heavily upon the aid and the intervention of foreign nations and they were bitterly disappointed when little aid was forthcoming. Even after the collapse of the Confederacy all true southerners held that the struggle had been a "War between the States."

The official position of the Union government was that secession was a constitutional impossibility and nullity, and hence that the so-called Confederates were engaged in an insurrection against their lawful government. When the Confederates fired upon Fort Sumter, President Lincoln proclaimed on April 15, 1861, that the execution of federal laws was being obstructed "by combinations too powerful to be suppressed by the ordinary course of judicial proceedings." Therefore, he called for militia to suppress the insurrection, in much the same way that Washington had done in the Whisky rebellion of 1794. Both Congress and Supreme Court later supported Lincoln's theory of the war, even though the war attained enormous proportions.

In harmony with this insurrection theory the Union government throughout the war was meticulously careful to avoid any act that even suggested official recognition of the Confederacy as a *de jure* independent state. At first the United States attempted to deny that the Confederacy possessed even belligerent status. Thus in 1861 the State Department objected strongly to foreign powers granting belligerent rights to the Confederacy. Throughout the war the Lincoln administration maintained that no peace terms could be considered unless they were premised upon the legal nonexistence of the Confederacy and the complete submission of the "rebels" to Union authority. In theory Union spokesmen commonly insisted that they were dealing only with the "pretended government" of the "so-called Confederate States of America."

In practice, however, the Union government was very soon impelled to concede belligerent rights to the Confederates. The impotency of Buchanan's administration had permitted southern resistance to federal authority to become too extensive and powerful to be treated as mere insurrection. At the outbreak of hostilities Lincoln proclaimed a blockade of southern ports, an act that according to international law virtually recognized the belligerency of the Confederacy. Soon afterward the Lincoln administration abandoned its declared purpose of treating Confederate seamen as pirates. Threats of reprisal upon captured Unionists as well as humanitarian considerations induced the government to treat all captives as prisoners of war.

After initial protests the United States acquiesced in the recognition by foreign nations of the belligerent status of the Confederate government. In short, practical considerations led the Union government to treat the Confederates as belligerents, even though it still refused to recognize their belligerency in any direct, formal manner.

Congress agreed fully with the president that the United States could claim against the Confederates both sovereign rights and those rights arising out of the international law of war. This double status greatly influenced federal laws and policies. For example, Congress enacted a new treason law providing severe punishment for all those found guilty of supporting the rebellion, while other congressional acts held such persons to be public enemies.

The Supreme Court also sustained this dual status for the Confederates. In this connection the most important decision was in the *Prize Cases,* decided in March 1863, involving the legality of the capture of neutral ships and cargoes. These seizures occurred soon after Lincoln had issued his proclamations of blockade of Confederate ports on April 19 and 27, 1861, and before Congress had formally recognized the existence of war. In upholding the legality of the captures, Justice Robert Grier declared for the Court that it would and must accept the president's decision that the armed insurgents had become so formidable by April 19, 1861, that they must be accorded belligerent status. "A civil war," he asserted, "is never solemnly declared; it becomes such by its accidents—the number, power, and organization of the persons who originate and carry it on.... It is not the less a civil war, with belligerent parties in hostile array, because it may be called an 'insurrection' by one side, and the insurgents be considered as rebels and traitors." Therefore, the Court held that as far as foreign nationals were concerned the conflict was a civil war, fought according to the laws of nations, with both sides possessed of belligerent rights and responsibilities. In subsequent decisions the Court maintained the same position.

While the war from a military standpoint was between the belligerents, in constitutional theory the insurrection doctrine remained of great importance during both the war and the reconstruction period. Many war acts and words of the Unionists were based upon the assumption that they were fighting to suppress a gigantic insurrection, even though Union officials often spoke of the war as a rebellion. At the conclusion of the war no peace treaty was drawn up. Instead the subjugated Confederates threw themselves upon the mercy of the Union government, which thus was free to develop a reconstruction program premised upon the insurrection theory.

The Problem of Internal Security

The government's difficulty in determining the status of the Confederate foe had its parallel in the adoption of internal security measures to deal with opponents of the war. The constitutional issue raised here concerned the government's authority to impair civil liberties in wartime. This authority was problematic because of the prevailing Anglo-American concept of the rule of law—that the officers of government are always subject to the law and prohibited from exercising arbitrary authority over citizens. The peaceful conditions that had prevailed for a few brief periods since the adoption of the Constitution had accustomed the American people to a policy of noninterference with civil rights by the federal government. There had been very few occasions for suspension of the habeas corpus privilege, censorship of the press, or the establishment of martial law. There was in America no tradition or important precedent for military rule or summary procedure even for a war emergency.

At one level the internal security problem was simple and clear-cut: the Constitution defined and limited treason to levying war against the United States or adhering to its enemies and giving them aid and comfort. Thus any participation in insurrection or rebellion against the federal government constituted treason. Congress was authorized to declare the punishment of treason, but no attainder of treason should work corruption of blood or forfeiture except during the life of the person attainted. Therefore, the only constitutional method of procedure against traitors was by judicial conviction under treason statutes passed by Congress. Accordingly, in 1790 Congress had passed a law against treason, providing the death penalty for anyone convicted. Though no one had ever been executed for treason against the United States, this law was still operative in 1861.

The nature and scope of the Civil War soon demonstrated the practical impossibility of enforcing the existing treason law against Confederates. Several million southern people were adhering to the "rebellion," while hundreds of thousands of them were actually bearing arms against the United States. As explained above, for practical and humanitarian reasons the captured soldiers and sailors had to be treated as prisoners of war. Few civilian Confederates were captured during the early phases of the war, and with sympathetic witnesses and juries the possibilities of conviction for treason seemed remote even where the federal courts were open. Moreover, many persons in the border states and in the North were engaging in disloyal activities that did not amount to full treason. These activities were designed to bring about Union defeat and included spying, sabotage, recruiting for the enemy, stealing military supplies for potential Confederate invasions of the North, carrying on treasonable correspondence, plotting to split the remaining Union states, and otherwise aiding the enemy. Other persons professed loyalty to the Union but openly opposed the government's policy of suppressing the rebellion by complete subjugation of the Confederacy. Their activities were confined to discouraging enlistments, aiding desertion, circulating disloyal literature, and denouncing the Lincoln administration.

Recognizing the complex nature of the internal security problem, Congress enacted special legislation to adapt the punishment of treason to the emergency and to define as crimes disloyal acts that were less than treasonous. The Seditious Conspiracy Act of July 31, 1861, the first such law to be adopted since the Sedition Act of 1798, provided heavy fine and imprisonment for anyone convicted of conspiring to overthrow the United States government, or to levy war against the United States, or to oppose by force the authority of the government, or to interfere forcibly with the execution of federal laws, or to seize property of the United States. Technically, this act dealt with conspiracy and not with treason. Critics of the measure were partly right in contending that it nullified existing constitutional law prohibiting "constructive treason." However, they overlooked the fact that new emergencies often call for new statutes or new interpretation of laws.

In July 1862 Congress passed a more comprehensive war measure, the Second Confiscation Act. For reasons of political compromise the act brought together three distinct subjects—treason, confiscation, and emancipation—and proposed to deal with them in discrete ways. The treason sections were the work of conservative Republicans who, insisting on strict legal orthodoxy, proposed to punish leading rebels only after trial and conviction under criminal law procedures. This part of the 1862 law declared the penalty for treason to be either death or heavy fine and imprisonment at the discretion of a court. It also declared engaging in or aiding rebellion against the United States to be distinct from the crime of treason, with a separate penalty of fine and imprisonment. Finally, the act provided for freeing the slaves of anyone convicted of either treason or rebellion.

As federal judicial authority existed nowhere in the South, the act of July 1862 as a punishment for treason and rebellion was intended to serve a postwar rather than a wartime purpose. Accordingly, in its treason and rebellion sections it employed the ordinary legislative power of the government over individual citizens, rather than the war power under international law. The administration, therefore, did not contradict congressional purpose in pursuing, as it did, a cautious and lenient policy of enforcement. Grand juries brought numerous indictments for treason, especially in the border states, but few cases were prosecuted to completion. Instead, the district attorney usually continued the indictment from one term of court to another until eventually the case was dismissed. It is significant that despite the vast extent of rebellion, the government did not execute a single person for treason or even carry out completely a sentence of fine or imprisonment. This policy of leniency continued after the war, under a different president and in very different political circumstances. Even Jefferson Davis, former president of the Confederacy, escaped official punishment, although his treason case dragged through the federal courts for more than three years.

Unable to enforce treason and rebellion statutes in the South, the administration chose not to apply them rigorously in the North. Instead it adopted an internal security policy of dealing with suspected persons through military arrests and the suspension of the privilege of habeas corpus. In the early part of the war this policy was restricted to definite localities specified in presidential proclamations. Its operation was entrusted to the State Department, which directed arrests through an elaborate secret service as well as through federal marshals and military authorities. The national situation was very critical at the time, and hundreds of arrests were made. Prisoners were not told why they were arrested, and often the authorities acted without sufficient investigation or evidence to provide a reasonable basis for definite charges. With the habeas corpus privilege suspended, prisoners were held without legal action until the emergency which had led to their arrest had passed. Judges often sought to secure the release of such prisoners, but provost marshals and other military officers were usually under orders to disregard judicial mandates and to resist the execution of writs. This procedure resulted in numerous conflicts between civil and military authorities, with the latter necessarily prevailing.

In 1862 the administration both modified and extended its policy. In February the control of arbitrary arrests was transferred to the War Department, and the policy was mitigated by establishing a commission to provide for the examination and release of political prisoners. On September 24, however, the president issued a sweeping proclamation declaring that all persons discouraging enlistments, resisting the draft, or "guilty of any disloyal practice affording aid and comfort to rebels ... shall be subject to martial law, and liable to trial and punishment by courts-martial or military commissions." Further, the habeas corpus privilege was suspended for all persons arrested or already imprisoned on such charges. Thereafter thousands of citizens suspected of disloyalty were summarily arrested and imprisoned in all parts of the country.

In the actual use of such extraordinary powers the Lincoln administration generally manifested considerable circumspection and leniency. The broad prerogatives assumed and announced in proclamations were not always exercised. Since arrests were often precautionary, designed to prevent violence or interference with military or other governmental activities, many prisoners were released within a short time. Those detained were usually treated without undue harshness.

Nevertheless, Lincoln's policy of suspending the privilege of the writ of habeas corpus encountered bitter opposition among Democrats. Leading the attack was Chief Justice Taney, who in *Ex parte Merryman* (1861), a case involving a Maryland secessionist arrested for destroying railroad bridges, tried unsuccessfully to prevent the president from withholding the writ in military emergencies. After Union officers ignored Taney's writ of habeas corpus ordering the release of Merryman, the chief justice, in the federal circuit court at Baltimore, delivered an opinion stating that Lincoln acted without warrant in suspending the writ, since only Congress could do so. Taney argued for exclusive congressional control from the fact that the habeas corpus clause occurs in Article I, Section 9, which deals with the legislative power. The president's only power where the rights of citizens are involved, said Taney, is to take care that the laws "be faithfully carried into execution as they are expounded and adjudged by the co-ordinate branch of the government, to which that duty is assigned by the Constitution." Instead of performing his constitutional duty of assisting the judiciary in enforcing its judgments, Taney asserted, the chief executive in this case had actually thrust aside the judicial authorities and substituted military government.

Lincoln's reply to Taney came in his July 4, 1861, special message to Congress. He justified the arrest and detention of individuals "dangerous to the public safety" on the ground that courts were incapable of dealing adequately with organized rebellion. He also said it would be better for the president to violate a single law "to a very limited extent" than to have all laws go unexecuted and "the Government itself to go to pieces" through failure to suppress the rebellion. Lincoln denied, however, that he had violated any law, arguing that since the Constitution permits suspension of the writ of habeas corpus during a rebellion and does not specify which branch of the government is to exercise the suspending power, the president in an emergency must be allowed to use his discretion in the matter. Later Lincoln emphasized the precautionary or preventive purpose of the arbitrary arrests, which were made "not so much for what has been done, as for what probably would be done."

In a more elaborate opinion Attorney General Edward Bates refuted Taney's contention that the president had violated his constitutional duty of executing the laws. The executive, he insisted, was not subordinate to the judiciary, but was one of three coordinate departments of government. Moreover, the president's oath to "preserve, protect, and defend the Constitution" makes it particularly his duty to put down a rebellion since the courts are too weak to do so. Bates cited *Martin* v. *Mott* (1827) to support the president's discretionary power in the manner of discharging his duty.[2]

2. In this case, which arose out of the War of 1812, the Supreme Court upheld the president's right, under authority of Congress, to be the sole judge of the existence of those contingencies specified in the Constitution upon which the militia might be called out. The Court held further that the president's decision was binding upon state authorities and that the state militia in federal service was subject to the authority of officers appointed by the president.

Therefore, if the president in case of rebellion or insurrection considers the suspension of the habeas corpus privilege necessary for the public safety, he may order it on his own authority.

The Habeas Corpus Act of 1863

Unwilling categorically to defer to executive authority on this important war-related issue, Congress in the Habeas Corpus Act of March 3, 1863, attempted to regularize and modify the president's control of political prisoners so that the authority of the courts would be respected without restricting too seriously the executive and military authorities. The Habeas Corpus Act served the additional purpose, insofar as doubt persisted, of legitimizing the government's internal security program. Under the statute the president was "authorized to suspend" the habeas corpus privilege, and military officers were relieved from the obligation to answer the writ. On the other hand, the secretaries of state and war were required to furnish lists of political prisoners to the federal courts, and if grand juries found no indictments against them, they were to be released upon taking the oath of allegiance. Thus to some extent congressional authority and regulations were substituted for executive authority, and judicial procedure rather than executive discretion was made the basis for the detention of prisoners.

The Habeas Corpus Act also contained indemnity sections which granted broad immunity to federal enforcement officers and extended the jurisdiction of federal courts at the expense of state judiciaries. These provisions were necessary because federal officers carrying out conscription, internal security, revenue, and emancipation policies had in numerous instances been the object of suits in northern state courts charging them with violation of state laws and infringement of the civil rights of private individuals. This litigation, which specified unlawful seizure, false arrest, assault and battery, and the like, could seriously impede Union war policies. A bridge was needed within the federal system by which federal officers detained or charged by states could be protected, in accordance with well-established common law principles. Accordingly, the act of March 1863 provided that any order made by or under the authority of the president should be a defense in all courts to any action or prosecution for any search, seizure, arrest, or imprisonment. Provision was also made for the removal of suits of this type from state to federal courts and for imposing a two-year limitation upon the initiation of such suits.

The Habeas Corpus Act in practice did not greatly alter internal procedures already in operation. For some time commissions appointed by the secretary of war had been reviewing cases of civilians detained on suspicion of disloyal actions and releasing those against whom there was insufficient evidence for civil or military prosecution. For this reason executive authorities were slow in furnishing the courts with lists of prisoners. Furthermore, in implementing the Habeas Corpus Act Judge Advocate General Joseph

Holt ruled controversially that it did not apply to prisoners triable by military commissions. This ruling left the executive department without restraint in cases where martial law was instituted. But this was consistent with congressional policy as expresed in the Articles of War, which denied ordinary judicial process for civilians held for military offenses such as spying and sabotage. Thus, although release of political prisoners continued to be at the discretion of the War Department, the policy was in substantial accord with what members of Congress and the northern public regarded as procedurally fair and militarily effective.

The institution of martial law and the limited use of military tribunals for the trial of civilians in the loyal states represented the most serious departure from normal constitutional procedure in the government's internal security program. Since portions of all the border states were at various times during the war occupied by Confederate troops or hostile guerrillas, martial law was employed there as an essential means of military security. Moreover, disloyalty to the Union in these areas was so widespread and so violent that the president considered martial law necessary for the preservation of peace and order. Usually, martial law was applied in specified limited districts where the situation seemed most serious, but in July 1864 Lincoln put the whole state of Kentucky under martial law. At the time of Lee's invasion of Pennsylvania in 1863, the president, in response to the petitions of many citizens, proceeded to put that area under martial law.

In all these instances, however, actual interference with the civil authorities was generally held to a minimum, and the power over citizens entrusted to the military authorities was sparingly used. Political and judicial officers continued to function except as interruption was necessary for the military authorities to preserve order and punish military crimes. In short, the federal government made no effort to carry martial law beyond certain specified objectives considered necessary for the successful prosecution of the war.

More important to constitutional law was the actual trial and conviction of citizens before military tribunals. In regions under martial law military commissions could properly be used for the trial of civilians who had committed offenses of a military character, such as sniping or spying. The vast majority of cases brought before military commissions in the border states were of this general type, and many individuals were convicted and punished, sometimes severely, for such offenses. Little adverse criticism was made at that time, and little has been made since.

A great legal controversy arose, however, when citizens were subjected to military tribunals in regions remote from military operations and where the civil courts were unimpeded by the course of the war. This situation developed during 1863 and 1864, especially in Ohio, Indiana, and Illinois, where many Democrats were so opposed to the administration's new war policies that they were demanding a negotiated peace and obstructing the prosecution of the war.

The most famous wartime military tribunal case involved Clement L. Vallandigham, a former Democratic congressman from Ohio who in 1863 was placed under military arrest and tried by a military commission for a public speech bitterly denouncing the Lincoln administration. The commission found Vallandigham guilty of disloyal sentiments with the object of weakening the government. Subsequently, the case was carried to the Supreme Court, on the argument that the jurisdiction of a military commision did not extend to a citizen who was not a member of the military forces. In *Ex parte Vallandigham* (1864) the Supreme Court refused to review the case, declaring that its authority, derived from the Constitution and the Judiciary Act of 1789, did not extend to the proceedings of a military commission because the latter was not a court. The Supreme Court, said Justice James Wayne in the official opinion, "cannot without disregarding its frequent decisions and interpretation of the Constitution in respect to its judicial power, originate a writ of certiorari to review or pronounce any opinion upon the proceedings of a military commission." Neither in this case nor in any other during the war did the Court deny or even question officially the president's authority to establish military commissions for the trial of civilians in nonmilitary areas.

In very different political circumstances after the war the Supreme Court held in *Ex parte Milligan* (1866) that the military commission by which an Indiana citizen was tried and convicted for actual subversive activity was unlawful. The Court stated not only that the executive had violated the Habeas Corpus Act of 1863 by ignoring the requirement of indictment by a grand jury, but also that Congress lacked authority to institute military commissions to try civilians in areas remote from the theater of war where the courts were open. Politically, this case was important for reconstruction policy and will be discussed in that context.[3] Concerning its importance in the history of constitutional law, the judgment of the victors has prevailed. The Court's opinion in the *Milligan* case was not a realistic approach either in relation to the Civil War experience or in providing for a future contingency of a similar kind. There was ample ground for believing, as Lincoln did, that disloyalty in the North might become so violent, unless held in check by military authority, that it would materially bolster Confederate morale and thus jeopardize the Union cause, or at least prolong the war and bring about additional loss of life. Therefore, his policy of arbitrary arrests and military trials for suspected citizens was essentially precautionary and in case of civil war perhaps justifiable. Although as commander in chief he felt impelled in such a great crisis to employ military authority to curtail temporarily certain civil rights, he made no attempt to establish a despotic military regime. He did not believe that his policy would subvert the Constitution or permanently impair the rights of citizens, and his belief proved to be correct.

3. See below, p. 346.

Although Democratic war critics like Vallandigham have never been thought of in the popular imagination as champions of freedom, their opposition to the war cast them in the role of defenders of civil liberties. Regardless of motive, they argued for impartial protection of rights and contributed to the growth of a civil liberties legal tradition which in sweeping terms proclaimed that the constitutional rights of citizens would be guaranteed by the federal judiciary against arbitrary executive and legislative power.

Federal Centralization of Authority

Between 1801 and 1861 an irregular but considerable decentralization of constitutional and political authority had taken place in the United States. During these years population had increased rapidly and had spread over a vast area. The states had more than doubled in number, and their governments, rather than the federal government, had assumed most of the new governmental functions that had evolved. In general during this period all three branches of the federal government had interpreted federal powers somewhat narrowly, with the result that the people looked to the state governments rather than to Washington for the performance of many positive governmental services. Relatively little federal administrative machinery had been developed. States'-rights tendencies were strong in the free as well as the slave states. Consequently, in 1861 the loyal state governments assumed that they would play important roles in the prosecution of the war.

In 1861 and 1862 the governors and other state officials to a large degree took the lead in mobilizing the nation for war. They not only raised the militia called for initially by the president, but they also directed the recruiting of most of the regiments of federal volunteers. In addition the states often provided the troops with equipment, subsistence, and transportation. Such state governors as John A. Andrew of Massachusetts, Oliver P. Morton of Indiana, and Richard Yates of Illinois were more energetic and more efficient than Secretary of War Simon Cameron in mobilizing troops. Before Congress met in July 1861, more than a quarter of a million men had been mobilized, largely by state initiative.

Inevitably, friction and confusion arose between federal and state authority in these military matters. Federal recruiting officers sometimes clashed with governors over the raising of troops and the appointing of officers. Early in the war some states actually competed with the War Department in the purchase of arms and equipment. The president had the unpleasant task of trying to placate conflicting parties and to coordinate their activities. This task was made somewhat easier by the fact that at the time practically all free-state governors were Republicans, but it was also made more difficult by the fact that the governors under the federal system are not constitutional subordinates of the president, even in the raising and control of troops. It was conflicting authority of this kind as well as the decline of volunteering which caused Congress and the administration eventually to turn to a national conscription policy.

A different type of controversy arose in April 1861 between the federal government and the border slave states, especially Kentucky and Maryland. Many people, perhaps a majority, in those states accepted the doctrine of state sovereignty, yet they wanted neither secession nor war. In Kentucky the governor emphatically refused to supply troops to the federal government and the state senate formally declared that the state would maintain an armed neutrality, neither severing connection with the Union nor taking up arms for either side. This attempt to take a middle position was not only impractical but was also contrary to both the letter and the spirit of the Constitution. The power of neutrality is an integral part of the war-making power, which is specifically and necessarily assigned to the federal government.

At about the same time the state authorities of Maryland sought to prevent the passage of federal troops through the state on the way to the national capital. This action was flagrantly unconstitutional; for, as Marshall had pointed out in *McCulloch* v. *Maryland,* in matters which belong to the United States federal authority must be supreme and unimpeded by state interference. Within a brief time the Lincoln administration, by employing a waiting policy in Kentucky and a firm policy in Maryland, was able to maintain federal authority in both states and to secure a considerable degree of cooperation from state authorities.

Another case where national authority definitely won out over states' rights was in the partition of Virginia. The western portion of the state was geographically a part of the Ohio Valley, and for many years before 1861 the people there had disagreed politically and economically with the eastern Virginians. When the Virginia convention adopted an ordinance of secession, the westerners refused to be bound thereby, and in June 1861 organized a new Unionist or restored government for Virginia, which was recognized for most purposes by the federal government. This Unionist state government, meeting at Wheeling, authorized the western counties to frame a constitution for a new state of West Virginia; this, in turn, was ratified by the voters. Thus in an irregular manner the "state" of Virginia complied with the constitutional requirement of giving consent to the erection of a new state within its borders.

On December 31, 1862, Congress passed an act providing for the admission of West Virginia as a state as soon as it had provided for the gradual abolition of slavery. During the congressional debate on the subject the Republican majority took the position that the admission would aid in suppressing the rebellion, while conservative opponents contended that the real state of Virginia had not given its consent to partition. Although the cabinet also was divided over the constitutionality of the act, Lincoln reluctantly signed it, believing then, as he did throughout the war, that the determining consideration should be whether the measure aided or hampered the restoration of the Union. On June 20, 1863, West Virginia officially became a separate state.

The Supreme Court in *Virginia* v. *West Virginia* (1870) indirectly declared the process of separation to be constitutional by affirming the existence of "a valid agreement between the two States consented to by Congress." Thus did the federal government's policy of broad constitutional construction, in conjunction with what was virtually a revolution within a state, effect the partitioning of one of the oldest and largest states in the Union.

During 1862 Congress and the administration came to realize that more vigorous assertion of federal authority was necessary for the effective prosecution of the war. Two years of unwarranted decentralization and reliance upon state performance of certain war functions had proved unsatisfactory and may have prolonged the war. Gradually and reluctantly, therefore, the federal government adopted centralizing measures and policies. By 1863 it was exercising authority commensurate with that intended by the framers of the Constitution, having regained much that had been dissipated during two generations dominated by states'-rights doctrines and practices.

In order to finance the war the federal government had to resume definite control of the important fields of currency and banking, which had been left largely to the states since the 1830s. Between February 1862 and March 1863 Congress authorized the issuance of $450,000,000 in fiat money or greenbacks, which were made legal tender for both public and private debts. Even more significant was the enactment of the National Banking Act of February 25, 1863, with important modifications made by new laws in 1864 and 1865. Although these measures did not create a centralized national bank like those of 1791 and 1817, they did provide for an extensive system of national banking institutions, which under federal supervision could issue banknotes based largely upon United States bonds and guaranteed by the federal government. The 1865 law, which levied a 10-percent tax on all state banknotes, soon had the intended effect of driving these notes out of existence and leaving a uniform national currency based fundamentally upon the credit of the United States.

After a lapse of some thirty years the federal government once more assumed a prominent role in the field of internal improvements and transportation. In pursuance of an act of Congress, the president in May 1862 took official possession of all railroads and directed that all railroad companies and their employees hold themselves in readiness for the transportation of troops and munitions at the order of military authorities. Only in a very few instances did the government take more than nominal control of northern railroads, but through this act it did obtain effective cooperation from the roads. In the South the federal government, through the military authorities, actually repaired and operated many miles of railroads.

Congress took steps also to sponsor the construction of new railroad lines. In March 1863 a select committee of the House, in order to provide more adequately for the transportation of military forces and supplies, recommended that the federal government charter a special railroad line between Washington and New York to which the government would give its patronage and over which it would enjoy priorities and have extensive powers of regulation. Constitutional and political opposition to the federal government taking such a direct part in the railroad business, plus some effective lobbying by competing railroad lines, prevented the enactment of the measure. However, the Pacific Railroad Act of 1862, supplemented by another act in 1864, enabled the federal government to charter two corporations to build a railroad from Omaha to the Pacific and to grant them large tracts of land and extensive loans. This action proved to be only the beginning of the active part that the government was to play in rail transportation after the Civil War.

In general, however, the federal government attempted little or no regulation of private enterprise. Congress encouraged great industrial and agricultural expansion by the enactment of increasingly high protective tariff rates and by paying high prices for food, clothing, munitions, and other military supplies. But there were no price ceilings, no rationing, and practically no governmental controls over agriculture, commerce, industry, or labor.

Compulsory Military Service

The gigantic military task of conquering the Confederacy forced the federal government to re-examine the place of military forces under the Constitution. Practically no one seriously questioned the traditional American principle that the military authority is always subject to ultimate civilian control. The Constitution, in Article I, Section 8, gave Congress blanket power "to raise and support armies" and to provide for calling forth, organizing, arming, disciplining, and governing the militia when employed in federal service. By law and precedent three forms of military organization were available in 1861: the regular army, United States volunteers called into service during emergencies for limited periods, and the militia, which was in a degree both a state and a federal organization. In the War of 1812 and the Mexican War all troops had been raised by voluntary recruiting, although in the earlier struggle conscription had been seriously considered by Congress.

In April 1861 Lincoln called for 75,000 militia under the law of 1795, but the great bulk of the army raised in 1861, and in fact throughout the war, consisted of federal volunteers. When the supply of volunteers seemed inadequate, Congress, in July 1862, enacted a new Militia Act, which provided that the militia should include all male citizens between the ages of eighteen and forty-five and authorized the president to issue regulations to cover any defects in state laws for employment of the militia. With no more specific basis than this provision, the president in August 1862 assigned quotas to the states and ordered a draft through the state governors to fill any unfilled quotas. Under this curious mixture of federal and state authority the first men were conscripted in 1862. The chief constitutional significance of this entire procedure lies in the small amount of statutory law considered necessary to transform the old obligation for militia duty into compulsory federal military service.

The president and Congress soon realized that the militia could not be made into an effective national army and on March 3, 1863, enacted a comprehensive conscription law. All able-bodied male citizens between twenty and forty-five, and foreigners who had declared their intention to become citizens, were "to constitute the national forces" and were declared liable for military service upon call by the president. No reference was made to the militia, and a complete federal system of enrollment and administration was established. Any person failing to report after due service of notice was to be considered a deserter, and any person convicted of resisting the draft or of aiding or encouraging the same was subject to fine and imprisonment.

Such a drastic departure from previous American experience was bound to encounter serious opposition on constitutional as well as political grounds. In regions where prosouthern sentiment was strong, resistance to the draft took place in various forms, and federal troops were sometimes needed for enforcement. The Conscription Act was repeatedly denounced as un-American and unconstitutional in Congress, in the courts, in the press, in the public forums, and on the streets. From New York, where violent antidraft riots raged for four days in July 1863, Governor Horatio Seymour wrote to the president, declaring bluntly that conscription was unconstitutional and requesting its suspension. Except for minor interruptions, however, the draft was applied when necessary to meet quotas.

The constitutionality of the Conscription Act never came before the Supreme Court, but it was challenged in some of the lower courts without decisive results. Of all the constitutional arguments in support of conscription perhaps the most forceful was made by the president himself. In legal logic that was reminiscent of John Marshall at his best, Lincoln declared:

It is the first instance, I believe, in which the power of Congress to do a thing has ever been questioned in a case when the power is given by the Constitution in express terms. . . .

The case simply is, the Constitution provides that the Congress shall have power to raise and support armies; and by this act the Congress has exercised the power to raise and support armies. This is the whole of it. It is a law made in literal pursuance of this part of the United States Constitution.... The Constitution gives Congress the power, but it does not prescribe the mode, or expressly declare who shall prescribe it. In such case Congress must prescribe the mode, or relinquish the power. There is no alternative.... If the Constitution had prescribed a mode, Congress could and must follow that mode; but, as it is, the mode necessarily goes to Congress, with the power expressly given. The power is given fully, completely, unconditionally. It is not a power to raise armies if State authorities consent; nor if the men to compose the armies are entirely willing; but it is a power to raise and support armies given to Congress by the Constitution without an if.

Opponents of conscription usually resorted to states'-rights and strict-constructionist arguments and emphasized the distinction between the militia and the army. Many believed with Chief Justice Taney that although both federal and state governments exercised sovereign powers over the same territory and the same people at the same time, each was altogether independent of the other within its own sphere of action. They argued that the militia was primarily a state institution, and, therefore, the extent to which the Conscription Act interfered with this state institution by bringing state militiamen and state civil officials within the draft constituted a violation of the Constitution.

The preponderance of logic as well as legal public opinion supported the constitutionality of conscription. The power to raise armies as well as the power to declare war is expressly given to Congress without qualification as to means, and conscription may reasonably be considered a "necessary and proper" means to "carry into effect" these powers. To restrict federal powers within the narrow limits proposed by draft opponents would in effect have denied the United States the assured power to suppress the rebellion.

Union War Aims

Ultimately, the task of readying the machinery of war yielded in importance to the question of the uses to which it was put. At the outset the purpose of the war from the northern point of view was obvious: to restore the Union and preserve the Constitution. Thus Lincoln in his special message to Congress of July 4, 1861, said the issue was whether the republic could maintain its territorial integrity. Dwelling at length on the illegality of secession, he argued the perpetuity of the Union and the indestructibility of the states. And after some hesitation caused by Democratic demands for a concise and extremely restrictive expression of war aims, Congress agreed with him. In July 1861 it adopted the Crittenden-Johnson Resolutions declaring that the war was waged not for any purpose of conquest or subjugation, but to preserve the Union and the states with their rights and institutions unimpaired.

The means chosen to fight the war, however, as congressmen who passed the Crittenden-Johnson Resolutions well knew, might also affect its purpose and results. This was evident from the start in discussions of confiscation and emancipation. Each of these actions could be proposed as an expedient war measure, yet, if thoroughly and rigorously applied, each could also produce not merely a restored but a constitutionally changed Union.

Confiscation of enemy property was an ancient war usage, and most legal authorities had maintained that international law sanctioned a nation's right to confiscate. Yet by 1861 Western nations had largely abandoned the practice. Moreover, the United States Constitution provided safeguards for citizens' property by prohibiting such devices as bills of attainder and deprivation of property without due process of law. Nevertheless, under the dual-status theory of the nature of the war confiscation became a major issue in northern politics.

One view of confiscation intended it to weaken the Confederacy by seizing rebel property through military means. It would shorten the war and make the rebels pay much of the cost. A second view held that the property of leading Confederates should be confiscated as a punishment for rebellion and a guarantee of security for the future, but that this result could only ensue after trial and conviction of individual southerners for treason under the ordinary criminal law. As is apparent, this approach treated treason and confiscation together, as parts of the same legal process. A third view of confiscation, in the nature of a compromise between the first two, proposed to take enemy property under the war power, but to do so through the agency of federal courts. It was this approach that was embodied in the Confiscation Act of July 1862.

The act, as noted above, contained treason sections intended to punish individuals through *in personam* proceedings in national courts under federal criminal jurisdiction. The confiscation sections, based on international law and the "enemy" aspect of the dual-status doctrine, provided for *in rem* proceedings in federal courts against the property of southerners as enemies. In other words, property would not be taken as a punishment against individuals guilty of treason, but, in a borrowing from admiralty and revenue law, as a condemnation of things in themselves, independent of the guilt of the owner. The act directed the president to seize the property of officials of the Confederate government and, after sixty days' warning, the property of all other persons supporting the rebellion. The government could obtain title to the property only by instituting proceedings against the forfeited property of persons engaging in rebellion, in federal district courts where the property was located.

Conservatives had reason to complain about the method employed in the Confiscation Act, for in effect it punished rebels by taking away their property without the criminal trial that proper constitutional procedure required in matters of treason. It contrasted with the First Confiscation Act of August 1861, a measure important mainly for its emancipation content, which, ignoring treason, declared the forfeiture of all property used for insurrectionary purposes. The act of 1862 also had the effect of confiscating the property of persons guilty of treason beyond their lifetime, or permanently, in violation of the constitutional stipulation that limited forfeiture of property as a punishment for treason to the life of the guilty party. Lincoln objected to the Confiscation Act for both of these reasons. He prepared a veto message, whereupon Congress, in an unusual maneuver, passed an explanatory joint resolution removing part of the president's objections. The resolution stated that the law was not to be construed as working "a forfeiture of the real estate of the offender beyond his natural life." Satisfied by this restriction, Lincoln signed the bill.

Although the Confiscation Act expressed a radical desire for more forceful prosecution of the war, it also showed the persistence of constitutional restraint. Most important in this respect was the requirement of judicial procedure for the seizure of property. Despite congressional rhetoric that presented the act as a war measure, reliance on courts and judicial process marked it principally as a postwar instrument. What would come of it then, of course, could not be foretold. But despite the restriction on permanent forfeiture of property, it provided a framework for dealing with leading rebels and effecting potentially decisive changes in southern politics and society that would assure the future security of the Union. Meanwhile, because of the judicial requirement, wartime enforcement was limited to the northern and border states, where a small amount of rebel-owned property was located.

Emancipation

The confiscation act contained emancipation provisions that in an even more pointed way raised the question of war aims. If anything was clear in the prewar Republican platform, it was the constitutional inability of the federal government to interfere with slavery in the states. Moreover, most authorities on international law held that even during time of war a belligerent did not possess a legal right to emancipate the enemy's slaves except as they were used for military purposes. This was a major qualification, however, which figured in Republican thinking from the start of the war. In approving the Crittenden-Johnson Resolutions, for example, some Republican lawmakers said that while it was not the government's intention to abolish slavery, abolition might be a necessary result of the war. It did not take long for events to show the accuracy of this prediction. In August 1861

Congress passed a confiscation act that declared forfeit all claims to the labor of slaves employed in military efforts in support of the rebellion. Emancipation could thus be a means of conducting the war.

Nevertheless, although he signed the first Confiscation Act, Lincoln scrupulously placed preservation of the Union uppermost. Believing emancipation likely to alienate needed border state and southern Unionist allies, he repudiated an emancipation order issued by General John C. Frémont in September 1861. In December, however, Lincoln urged voluntary emancipation on the states, and in March 1862 proposed a formal plan of gradual, compensated emancipation. In his view this program recognized the constitutional rights of the states and the property rights of slaveholders. Congress accepted Lincoln's plan to the extent of passing a resolution offering cooperation and financial support to any state adopting gradual abolition. But when no positive results were forthcoming from the border area, both president and Congress turned to more straightforward emancipation measures.

Congress moved the more rapidly. In the first half of 1862 it forbade military officers to return fugitive slaves, prohibited slavery in the territories, and abolished slavery in the District of Columbia, with compensation for loyal owners. More important was the emancipation part of the Confiscation Act of 1862. This provided that all slaves of persons engaged in rebellion or in any way giving aid thereto, who should be captured or escape to Union lines, "shall be deemed captives of war, and shall be forever free of their servitude, and not again held as slaves." The legislation, however, provided no means of implementing the decree of emancipation, nor any guarantee of freed slaves' personal liberty.

The absence of legal machinery for effecting emancipation is evidence that members of Congress were primarily concerned with depriving the South of its labor supply and gathering resources for the Union war effort. (The act also authorized the use of Negroes for military labor.) Emancipation was more a military expedient than an expression of a consciously humanitarian liberation policy. The omission of legal devices for achieving freedom was also partly attributable to unwillingness to use *in rem* proceedings, appropriate to property, for the emancipation of slaves, whom Republicans viewed as *persons*. Moreover, legal uncertainties about national court jurisdiction in relation to slavery may help explain congressional reticence in regard to emancipation instruments. The main result of the confiscation act in any case was to confirm and legitimize the *de facto* emancipation that was occurring with the advance of Union armies.

Lincoln made no serious attempt to enforce the emancipation section of the act of July 1862 largely because he was himself shaping a more aggressive policy against slavery. In July 1862 he drafted for cabinet consideration an emancipation proclamation. Then, after the battle of Antietam in September, he issued a preliminary order stating that the war would continue to be prosecuted for the restoration of the Union, but that in all areas where the people were still in rebellion on January 1, 1863, all persons held as slaves would be free. On January 1, Lincoln announced the definitive proclamation. "As a fit and necessary war measure for suppressing the rebellion," he declared that in all the seceded states except Tennessee and parts of Louisiana and Virginia, all persons held as slaves "are, and henceforth shall be, free; and that the Executive Government of the United States, including the military and naval authorities thereof, will recognize and maintain the freedom of said persons."

The constitutional basis of the Emancipation Proclamation was the war power. It was the extraordinary military emergency alone that could justify departure from the constitutional rule against federal interference with slavery in the states. Opponents of the administration emphatically condemned Lincoln's proclamation as entirely unconstitutional and as a gross usurpation of power on the part of the executive. They argued that the federal government had no authority over slavery in the states under any circumstances, and that the laws of war did not warrant such a blanket destruction of private property.

More practically relevant was the question of the legal effect of the Emancipation Proclamation. Extreme conservatives argued that its utter unconstitutionality deprived it of any legal consequences. At the opposite pole, radicals held that the proclamation conferred a right of personal liberty on slaves regardless of their circumstances. Moderate Unionists, accepting the validity of the proclamation as a war measure, said that any legal effect it had would depend on its actual implementation by the advance of Union arms, and this was closest to the truth. There was agreement, moreover, that the Emancipation Proclamation did not abolish slavery as an institution recognized in the laws and constitutions of the southern states. Accordingly, constitutional amendments for the abolition of slavery were introduced into Congress in 1864. The Thirteenth Amendment, proposed by Congress in January 1865 and ratified by the states in December, completed the legal process begun by the Emancipation Proclamation.

Although in a constitutional and legal sense emancipation was an expedient military measure, its substantive moral and political content made it impossible to employ without at the same time altering the general understanding of the purpose of the war. Henceforth, the aim of the war was to preserve the Union and destroy slavery. Yet the military basis of emancipation ought not to obscure the historic antislavery purpose of the Republican party, nor the identity of constitutional and political principle between emancipation and defense of the Union. Both slavery and secession denied the republican principle of equality and government by consent, and both defense of the Union and wartime emancipation were intended to uphold this principle. In adopting military emancipation, therefore, the administration did not place the war effort on a higher moral and ideological plane than that on which defense of the Union rested. Rather it provided a solution to the problem of slavery in the American republic that was consistent with the principles on which resistance to secession was based.

Constitutional Significance of the Civil War

Amid change and upheaval, one of the most significant facts of wartime constitutional history was the continuous operation of political parties at the North. Elections were held and constitutional politics persisted. This fact testifies to the adequacy of the Constitution and the American people's commitment to constitutionalism. It also throws light on the Union's ultimate success. Party organization was a means by which federal authorities mobilized and sustained popular energies in support of the war. Moreover, party loyalties restrained states'-rights tendencies and brought federal and state governments into closer harmony, in contrast to the partyless South where states' rights impeded the Confederate war effort. Risky though elections were, especially with opponents of the war involved, they were important in focusing and reinforcing northern popular attitudes toward the war. A reciprocal effect was also evident. With the Union and the Constitution in the balance, wartime elections restored in the public mind an appreciation of the importance of party competition for republican government.

The most important constitutional result of the war was the repudiation of state sovereignty and the compact theory of the Union, with its corollary right of secession. For years ambiguity over the nature of the Union was not only tolerable, but useful as an ingredient in party competition. The federal Union was part confederation, part unitary government. Under the pressure of events concerning slavery this ambiguity eventually became intolerable, and on the eve of the war southerners denied categorically that the federal government possessed sovereignty. Sovereignty resided entirely in the states; to them rather than to the federal government citizens owed allegiance. Ambiguity over the nature of the Union was unacceptable for the additional reason that it was incompatible with the process of nationalization that occurred in the nineteenth century. Americans were becoming more unified and integrated in society, culture, and economy. Yet their government was weak and ineffectual. By 1860 there was doubt as to whether it was in any genuine sense a sovereign government.

The war settled this question unequivocally: the United States was indeed a sovereign nation, not a league of sovereign states. As a consequence of this sovereignty, much centralization took place during the war. Yet states' rights, as distinct from state sovereignty, were not extinguished.

Increased centralization produced not a unitary state, but a new and vigorous federalism in which both states and federal government gained power. Of course, by comparison with antebellum and wartime Democrats, Republicans were centralizers. But they retained a strong respect for states' rights. They were in fact states'-rights nationalists. The political theorist Francis Lieber expressed the party's point of view when he defended nationalism, yet warned against consolidation: "Centralism is the convergence of all the rays of power into one central point ... nationalization is the diffusion of the same life-blood through a system of arteries, throughout a body politic." The Supreme Court captured the twin concerns of Civil War Republicans in declaring, in *Texas* v. *White* (1869): "The Constitution, in all its provisions, looks to an indestructible Union, composed of indestructible States."

The second major constitutional result of the war was emancipation. The South's peculiar institution was irreparably shattered, yet in a constitutional sense the resolution of this issue had only begun in 1865. Emancipation raised a series of questions about the rights of the states and the federal government in relation to personal liberty and civil rights that would go far toward defining the balance of power in the reconstructed Union.

SEVENTEEN

Reconstruction: The Nationalization of Civil Rights

———————————— ✦ ✦ ✦ ————————————

RESTORING THE SECEDED STATES TO THE UNION was the central issue in American politics from 1865 to 1869. This was pre-eminently a constitutional question involving the distribution of power between the states and the federal government. Considered from a strictly legal standpoint reunification presented perplexing difficulties. Social and economic turmoil resulting from the destruction of slavery vastly complicated the problem, if it did not make a peaceful solution virtually impossible. Behind the rhetoric of states' rights and federal supremacy the core elements in the reconstruction problem were the status and rights of the former Confederates, on the one hand, and the status and rights of the emancipated slaves, on the other. The first group, if secession was the legal nullity it was proclaimed to be in official Union war policy, could ironically claim a right to participate in the reorganization of state governments in the South. The second group, if the promise of emancipation were to be made good by effective guarantees of civil rights, also had a legitimate claim to participate in reconstruction politics. The task of postwar Union policy was to reconcile the demands of these conflicting groups while restoring the federal system according to northern republican principles.

Wartime Reconstruction

Reconstruction as a problem in constitutional politics began with the disruption of the Union in the months before Sumter and continued throughout the war. The first ideas on the subject to be given practical expression were those advanced by President Lincoln at the beginning of the war. In his message to Congress in July 1861 and in a series of executive actions in subsequent months, Lincoln held that secession was null and void, and that the so-called seceded states were, therefore, still in the Union. He admitted that the southern states were out of their normal relationship to the other states and the federal government since they had no loyal governments and were controlled by persons in rebellion against federal authority. But the states, as political entities distinguished from their governments, still were in the Union. Hence all that was necessary for reconstruction was the suppression of actual military rebellion, the creation of loyal state governments by loyal citizens, and the resumption of normal relations with the federal government.

Lincoln assumed that it was the duty of the federal government to assist the states in reconstruction. The justification for this assumption he found in Article IV, Section 4, of the Constitution, by which the United States guaranteed every state a republican form of government. All subsequent reconstruction schemes drew upon this constitutional provision as justification for federal controls.

Finally, Lincoln assumed that the president had authority to carry through a competent reconstruction program with little congressional assistance. A principal step in the plan was the suppression of rebellion, already being accomplished under the president's war powers. Lincoln admitted that in practice Congress would have final authority to pass upon presidential reconstruction, since it could seat delegates from southern states at its discretion. President Andrew Johnson was later to claim that Congress could not lawfully refuse to seat delegates from reconstructed states, but Lincoln did not advance this argument.

Lincoln's plan had two great virtues. It was consistent, for it rested upon the same premise of the nullity of secession upon which the administration had prosecuted the war. And it was simple of execution and promised a rapid restoration of a normally functioning constitutional system. Its great practical weakness was that Congress could destroy it merely by refusing to seat delegates from the reconstructed states.

As long as the war was fought to restore "the Union as it was and the Constitution as it is," as conservatives described the government's aims, reconstruction was relatively unproblematic. Early in the war Congress began to consider a legislative solution to the essentially civil rather than military problem of governmental organization which lay at the heart of reconstruction. As in the conduct of the war, the separation of powers as a basic constitutional principle introduced into reconstruction politics an element of institutional rivalry between president and Congress. This rivalry was accentuated by military emancipation, which in an important sense altered the shape of reconstruction as a constitutional problem. If carried to its logical conclusion, emancipation would require changes in the laws and constitutions of the southern states when they re-entered the Union. No longer could personal liberty be the exclusive concern of state power. By the same token, the silence and disability of the federal government in matters of personal liberty and civil rights, so conspicuous a part of the prewar Constitution, would also end. If emancipation were to be made secure, the Constitution must in some form recognize the extension of federal power into an area of law and policy previously reserved to the states.

In the first two years of the war Lincoln tried with only limited success to stimulate Unionist sentiment in the occupied South by holding elections for members of Congress. In December 1863 he assumed more direct—though by no means exclusive—control of state restoration by issuing a Proclamation of Amnesty and Reconstruction. The proclamation committed the government to a reconstruction policy that confirmed emancipation and invited a small number of loyal white southerners to organize state governments with a minimum of federal supervision. With the exception of certain Confederate officials, it offered a pardon to anyone engaged in rebellion who agreed to take an oath of loyalty to the United States. It further declared that whenever the number of loyal persons qualified to vote within a state equaled 10 percent of the total qualified voters in 1860, they would be permitted to form a state government. Reconstructed governments were promised protection under the constitutional provision guaranteeing each state a republican form of government. Lincoln's amnesty proclamation also required participants in state reorganization to swear an oath supporting the Emancipation Proclamation and all acts of Congress dealing with slavery. To abandon emancipation, said Lincoln, would give up a vital lever of power and would be "a cruel and astounding breach of faith" toward Negroes. The president promised not to retract or modify the Emancipation Proclamation, nor to return any freed blacks to slavery.

Under this proclamation loyal state governments were organized before the end of the war in Tennessee, Arkansas, and Louisiana. The loyal voters in Union-occupied areas in these states first elected delegates to constitutional conventions. These conventions repudiated secession, abolished slavery, drafted new state constitutions, and provided for new state governments, which were set up in 1864. A loyal government in Virginia had been created under a similar arrangement in 1862. Thus four loyal state governments existed in the South before the war ended.

Congress endorsed Lincoln's policy of December 1863 because it satisfied the demand of virtually all Republicans that emancipation be made the basis of reconstruction. Yet Congress did not regard executive action alone as sufficient for effecting national reunification. Nor did Congress approve of the administration's policy on freedmen's rights which was adopted in occupied Louisiana, the centerpiece of presidential reconstruction. Lincoln's amnesty and reconstruction proclamation in effect allowed white southern Unionists to determine questions concerning the status, rights, labor conditions, and other circumstances of the freed people. Republicans in Congress, however, looking beyond emancipation to the general problem of civil liberty that blacks would face, proposed to establish under federal auspices legal guarantees of personal liberty and civil rights for the former slaves. Republican lawmakers articulated these concerns in the Wade-Davis reconstruction bill of July 1864.

Based on the guarantee-of-republican-government clause of the Constitution, the Wade-Davis bill required conventions in the seceded states, supported by a majority of the adult white male population, to draft new constitutions that would disenfranchise Confederate civil and military officers, repudiate the Confederate debt, and abolish slavery and guarantee the freedom of all persons. Furthermore, the bill prohibited the recognition or enforcement of state slavery laws, authorized federal courts to issue writs of habeas corpus for the release of freed slaves illegally detained on claims of labor, made kidnaping of former slaves a federal crime, and required that state laws for the trial and punishment of white persons should extend to all persons.

Lincoln pocket-vetoed the bill because it would have negated the steps taken to organize a loyal government in Louisiana and would have effectively postponed restoration of other states until after the war. Emphasizing their political value as governments-in-exile, Lincoln wanted to maintain the restored governments, however flimsy they seemed. In an attempt at compromise, congressional leaders in the winter of 1864–65 revived the Wade-Davis plan, with Louisiana exempted and limited Negro suffrage included.[1] The compromise failed, however, as the majority of Republicans were willing to entrust reconstruction policy—for the time being at least—to the president. In retaliation, congressional radicals blocked the readmission of the reconstructed government of Louisiana. Although other aspects of reconstruction were dealt with in the Thirteenth Amendment and the Freedmen's Bureau Act of March 3, 1865, at the end of the war no comprehensive policy existed for readmitting the seceded states to the Union.

Theories of Reconstruction

The Confederate surrender focused attention on constitutional issues of reconstruction which had long been discussed, but which now possessed an immediacy and importance previously denied them. Of these none was more perplexing than the status of the seceded states. This was the kind of legalistic question that was at once dismissed as theoretical, yet subjected to endless and highly emotional debate. Clearly, there was something real at stake, and although the issue was in a sense abstract—like all constitutional issues when they become the subject of political debate and action—its resolution had practical consequences. For the powers legally available to

1. The bill authorized blacks in Union military service to vote.

the government depended on the status that the states and their people occupied. The status of the states had symbolic value, moreover, as an issue through which lawmakers could identify themselves politically and appeal to public opinion.

With understandable inconsistency, southerners at the end of the war took up the official Union theory and argued that if secession was unconstitutional and without legal effect, then the states were still in the Union and qualified to resume their place in Congress with no strings attached. All that was necessary in this view was for state officers to take an oath to support the Constitution. A second view, endorsed by President Andrew Johnson, held that although the former Confederate states were still in the Union, they were temporarily disqualified from resuming their place in the federal system because of the treason in which their officers had engaged. Placed by events in a kind of constitutional limbo, the states could be revived and prepared for readmission through the exercise of the president's power of pardon and the war power.

At the opposite end of the political spectrum, radical theories of reconstruction aimed at establishing direct federal rule over the South for the purpose of achieving political and social revolution. One theory held that although secession was illegal, it was nevertheless an accomplished fact which placed the Confederate states in the status of enemies. Defeated as a belligerent, the states were conquered provinces with no internal political or constitutional rights whatever. Another radical theory, much discussed in the early stages of the war, was derived from constitutional rather than international law. It argued that although secession was unconstitutional, it had the legal effect of causing the states to revert to a territorial condition. This theory was careful to state that the former Confederate states were not out of the Union. But it insisted that lawful state governments, through the destructive actions of southerners themselves, had ceased to exist in the states. As a consequence the states became, in law and in fact, unorganized territory subject to the legislative power of Congress.

Identified with Thaddeus Stevens and Charles Sumner, these theories were more provocative than influential. They conceded too much to secession as the cause of constitutional change in the southern states and departed too drastically from traditional federalism. What was needed from the northern point of view was a theory of reconstruction that would regard the states as still in the Union and allow loyal citizens voluntarily to reorganize their government, but that would at the same time provide sufficient national power to assure that the reorganized states adhered to acceptable standards of republicanism for the future security of the Union.

The disorganized-states theory of reconstruction (also called the forfeited-rights theory) fulfilled these conflicting political and constitutional requirements. Taking as its point of departure the guarantee clause of the Constitution, the theory held that the seceded states were still in the Union.

Nevertheless, secession and war had deprived them of republican governments and left them in a disorganized condition. "The fact, as well as the
constitutional view of the condition of affairs in the States enveloped by the
rebellion," asserted Representative Henry Winter Davis of Maryland, "is
that a force has overthrown, or the people, in a moment of madness, have
abrogated the governments which existed in those States, under the Constitution." The seceded states, said Davis, were "by law . . . people forming a
State without a political organization, called State government." In this
disorganized condition the states were subject to federal jurisdiction, and, in
particular, to legislative authority to guarantee them a republican form of
government. The states were not, however, subject to absolute national
control; their existence as states constituted a limitation on the federal
government. As a reconstruction instrument under the disorganized-states
theory, therefore, the guarantee clause provided temporary federal control
that would be civil rather than military in nature, thus fulfilling a fundamental requirement of republicanism. It would also permit the people of
the seceded states voluntarily to exercise a degree of local self-government,
another requirement of republicanism. This moderate approach to the constitutional problem of reconstruction appealed to the majority of Republicans. It formed the basis for the Wade-Davis bill of 1864, and, with one
additional theoretical component, the Military Reconstruction Act of 1867.

The additional element sustaining the act of 1867 was the grasp-of-war
theory. This was a way of describing not the status of the states, but the
legitimacy of federal power over them for purposes of reconstruction.
Derived from the idea that the Confederacy was a belligerent under international law, it asserted that the federal government held the seceded states
temporarily under the war power and could demand changes in their constitution and laws necessary to guarantee the results of the war and the
future security of the Union. Like Lincoln's wartime crisis government, this
theory justified departure from normal constitutional requirements in the
name of ultimate restoration of the Constitution. In a situation where perfect consistency with the theory of rebellion on which the war was officially
fought presented intolerable political risks, the grasp-of-war theory set aside
the normal states'-rights limitations on the federal government in order to
re-establish federalism, with appropriate modifications.

Johnson's Policy of Reconstruction

Political circumstances favored Andrew Johnson on his accession to the
executive office in April 1865. Though a Democrat and a southerner, Johnson enjoyed a strong position in relation to the Republican party, whose
vice-presidential candidate he had been in 1864. Most Republicans were
moderates who wanted to secure the results of the war by guaranteeing

genuine freedom to emancipated slaves and by excluding leading Confederates from reconstruction politics. Convinced of the soundness and virtue
of their party's free-labor, free-speech, and equality-before-the-law principles, they wanted to extend these principles to the South. Their purposes
were to republicanize the region, unite the nation, and secure political control of federal and state governments for their party. But the main body of
Republicans was averse to political, social, and economic revolution in the
South, and was prepared to accept the leadership of the new president in
the initial stages of reconstruction.

After a period of uncertainty in which he gave the appearance of
having radical inclinations, Johnson formally initiated a reconstruction
policy that in broad outline was similar to Lincoln's. In a proclamation of
May 29, Johnson pardoned all persons lately engaged in rebellion, except
for high Confederate officials and Confederate supporters who possessed
more than $20,000 in property. Persons accepting amnesty were required to
take an oath of loyalty to the national government, which included a
promise to abide by and support all federal laws and proclamations
adopted during the war concerning the emancipation of slaves.

At the same time, Johnson issued a proclamation appointing W. W.
Holden provisional governor of North Carolina and outlining a plan of
presidential reconstruction for that state. The governor was to call a constitutional convention of delegates chosen by and from loyal voters accepting
the presidential amnesty. The convention was to "alter and amend" the
state constitution and to take the necessary steps to restore the state to its
normal constitutional status. Significantly, the proclamation said nothing of
Negro suffrage, although in subsequent statements the president advocated
extension of the franchise to Negro taxpayers and to literate Negroes. In the
course of the next six weeks Johnson issued similar proclamations for the
remaining southern states where Lincoln-sponsored governments had not
been erected. Meanwhile, he had extended full recognition to the four Lincoln governments.

Between August 1865 and March 1866, conventions met in all of the
seven unreconstructed states. These bodies, except in South Carolina,
passed resolutions declaring the various ordinances of secession to have
been null and void. South Carolina, clinging to discredited constitutional
theory, merely repealed the ordinance. All of the conventions formally
abolished slavery within their respective states. With the exception of South
Carolina and Mississippi, all repudiated the state debt incurred in rebellion.
The conventions also provided for elections of state legislative, executive,
and judicial officers.

The newly elected legislatures met shortly and, except in Mississippi,
ratified the Thirteenth Amendment. Johnson virtually insisted upon ratification, and it was by this device that the requisite three-fourths majority of

the states was secured for the adoption of the amendment. This requirement of ratification was altogether inconsistent with the theoretical sovereignty of the new governments; however, this technical consideration attracted little notice. The new legislatures also chose United States senators, and provided for the election of House members. Thus by the time Congress met in December 1865, the Johnson reconstruction program was approaching completion in every southern state. All that remained was for Congress to seat the southern delegates, and presidential reconstruction would be complete.

Though willing to accept the legitimacy of Johnson's policy, Republicans in Congress thought it far from conclusive. As under Lincoln, they believed that executive action was constitutionally insufficient and that national legislation was needed to reconstruct the Union. Politically, too, they had objections to Johnson's course of action. It was unsettling, to say the least, that many former Confederates were among the newly elected southern representatives and senators applying for seats in Congress. Republicans also had doubts about the wisdom of presidential policy as they observed the initial efforts of the reconstructed states to fix the status and rights of the freedmen in the so-called Black Codes. For these reasons, they blocked the admission of southern representatives and senators, by means of a Republican party caucus order instructing the clerks in each house to ignore the seceded states in the roll call. Congressional leaders then secured the appointment of a Joint Committee on Reconstruction, composed of nine representatives and six senators, carefully balanced between radical and moderate viewpoints, who were instructed to make a thorough study of the entire reconstruction problem and to report upon whether any of the southern states ought to be represented in Congress. Another resolution was passed pledging that neither house would seat representatives from the seceded states until the Joint Committee made its report.

Placed on the defensive by the swift restoration of state governments in the South, Congress undertook to review not only executive policy, but also measures dealing with emancipation and the freedmen that in effect formed a partial reconstruction policy. These measures were the Thirteenth Amendment and the Freedmen's Bureau Act.

Federal Freedmen's Policy in 1865

Approved for submission to the states in January 1865 and ratified in December with the support of eight southern states, the Thirteenth Amendment declared that neither slavery nor involuntary servitude, except as a punishment for crime, shall exist in the United States or its territories. The amendment further gave Congress power to enforce the prohibition by appropriate legislation.

The Thirteenth Amendment profoundly altered the federal system by curtailing previously exclusive state power over personal liberty. For the first time it gave the federal government authority in this sphere. Moreover the amendment authorized the federal government to enforce the prohibition of slavery against violation from whatever source, whether state government or private individual. For purposes of the amendment, in other words, the existence of the states was not to constitute a limitation on federal power.

Seemingly simple and straightforward, the Thirteenth Amendment nevertheless gave rise to vexing problems of interpretation that remained unresolved in December 1865. If it was obvious that the amendment placed 4 million black persons in a new condition of freedom, it was by no means clear precisely what additional civil rights it conferred upon them beyond personal liberty. For a moment's reflection suggested that the right of personal liberty needed to be amplified and supported with other rights in order to fulfill the promise of emancipation. Accordingly, Republican congressmen who framed the amendment asserted that it would confer fundamental civil rights on the freed slaves: the right to labor and enjoy the fruits thereof; to own property, make contracts, and exercise related economic rights; to bring suit and testify in courts of law; to enter into marriage and receive the protection of the private household; to speak and write freely and to be educated.

If it was hard to say what civil rights the prohibition of slavery impliedly bestowed, it was harder to say how—that is, under the jurisdiction of which government, state or federal—these rights would be enforced. It was plain that Congress could legislate to prevent the illegal detention or re-enslavement of freed persons or anyone else. But could it regulate and protect civil rights in general, as a corollary of its power to protect personal liberty? If so, it would replace the states in this sphere of public policy. In adopting the Thirteenth Amendment, however, Republicans made no claim for such a sweeping federal power. In fact, they rejected a proposed antislavery amendment introduced by Senator Charles Sumner declaring all persons equal before the law and authorizing Congress to enforce legal equality in a comprehensive way. Nor did Democratic opponents of the Thirteenth Amendment argue that under the enforcement section Congress would have power to legislate directly on civil rights, in derogation of the state police power. The main argument against the amendment was that it represented an unconstitutional exercise of the amending power.[2] As restored southern governments in late 1865 began to pass demeaning and discrimi-

2. Democrats argued that by interfering with the domestic institutions of the states, the Thirteenth Amendment revolutionized the federal system and was tantamount to the creation of a new constitution. If the amending power could be used to destroy slavery, Democrats contended, it could also be used to deprive states of power over other local institutions such as schools, property arrangements, and the like.

natory laws regulating the black population, however, and as the freedmen were victimized by violence, Republicans adopted a broader view of federal legislative power—or felt free to express ideas previously held but for political reasons not publicly revealed. By December 1865 this reconsideration or discovery of national legislative power under the Thirteenth Amendment was in process of formation.

A second aspect of federal freedmen's policy in December 1865 provided legal protection for emancipated slaves in the southern states. The origins of this policy lay in wartime efforts by the War and Treasury Departments to manage postemancipation problems among the large black refugee population of the South. Ending the long period of incapacity concerning slavery and personal liberty, the federal government, under the pressure of war, reached deep into local affairs. It recruited freedmen for the Union army, gathered them in refugee camps, and organized them under a free labor system on plantations in the occupied South. Early in the war it even undertook a few abortive overseas colonization ventures. Political controversy surrounded these various programs as many antislavery militants charged the Lincoln administration with failing adequately to protect the rights and well-being of the emancipated slaves. Often War and Treasury Department officials worked at cross-purposes in trying to gain control of freedmen's policy. In March 1865 Congress resolved this intragovernmental squabbling by passing the Freedmen's Bureau Act. The law created an agency in the War Department, to continue during the war and for one year thereafter, that was charged with extending welfare relief and protection to freedmen and white refugees and with establishing them in temporary occupancy of abandoned lands.

The Freedmen's Bureau began operations in May 1865. At once it became heavily involved in providing legal protection for freedmen through special military courts appointed by bureau head General Oliver Otis Howard. Responsible to the executive through the secretary of war, the Freedmen's Bureau found itself at odds with the civil governments restored by the president. It also clashed with the president himself, who encouraged the bureau to turn questions involving freedmen's rights over to state courts in return for the modification of state laws restricting and discriminating against blacks. To some extent General Howard complied with this request, but the agreement did not hold. Irrespective of state laws, local law enforcement officials continued to discriminate against blacks. By the time Congress assembled in December 1865, bureau officials were seeking stronger legislative authorization for protecting the liberty and rights of the freedmen.

Protection was mainly necessary against the Black Codes and the actions of state officials. Adopted by the reorganized state governments in 1865 and 1866, the Black Codes from the white southern point of view conferred new rights and a higher status on the mass of blacks. From a northern perspective, however, the laws bore a disturbing resemblance to the antebellum slave codes. They contained harsh vagrancy and apprenticeship provisions whose apparent purpose was to bind the ex-slaves to the soil and strip them of all the practical attributes of freedom. The penal sections provided for more severe and arbitrary punishment for Negroes than for whites, while several codes also called for racial segregation in schools and other public facilities. The Black Codes, in short, imposed an inferior citizenship upon the freedmen, along with a potential system of partial bondage. Many northern congressmen believed they violated the Thirteenth Amendment, unless the amendment's provisions against "involuntary servitude" were to be construed in the narrowest possible sense.

The Moderate Republican Policy of 1866

Responding to these varied influences and pressures, Congress in 1866 adopted a reconstruction policy aimed at protecting the liberty and rights of the freed blacks. This issue was the outstanding point of contention in the struggle between parties and sections that dominated postwar politics. Shaped by Republican moderates, the policy of 1866 proposed to accept the restored Johnson governments if they would agree to protect Negro civil rights. As states'-rights nationalists, the moderates desired the states to remain the principal centers of republicanism, protecting and regulating civil liberty under new national guarantees of equality before the law for American citizens.

The first step in this policy was the enactment of the second Freedmen's Bureau bill in February 1866. Introduced by Senator Lyman Trumbull of Illinois, the bill extended the life of the bureau indefinitely. More important, it placed Negro civil rights in the seceded states under federal military protection. Any person in any of the formerly seceded states charged with depriving a freedman of his civil rights was to be tried by a military tribunal or a Freedmen's Bureau agent in accordance with martial law. No presentment or indictment was required.

These provisions precipitated a serious constitutional debate in both houses of Congress. Democrats and more conservative Republicans, led by Senators Garrett Davis of Kentucky and Reverdy Johnson of Maryland, attacked the Trumbull bill as hopelessly unconstitutional, arguing that control of civil rights was not one of the enumerated or implied powers of Congress and, therefore, was exclusively reserved to the states. They argued also that the provisions for the military trial of civilians violated the procedural guarantees of the Fifth Amendment, which specifically enjoined presentment and indictment in federal criminal trials except in the armed forces and in the militia in time of war and which thus clearly implied a general immunity for civilians from peacetime military trial.

Republicans expressed the more capacious understanding of Thirteenth Amendment liberty and national power that events were forcing upon them. Lyman Trumbull argued that the constitutional amendment gave Congress a new power to legislate to protect civil rights, or at least those essential to the blacks' new status of freedom as opposed to slavery. But the clearer and more certain basis of the Freedmen's Bureau bill was the grasp-of-war theory. Accordingly, Trumbull defended the military-trial provisions on the ground that disturbed conditions persisted in the South and civil authority had not yet been completely restored. The bill's provisions were seen as temporary, however, for federal military power could not indefinitely govern local affairs in the manner now required. The task of providing permanent civil guarantees of Negro citizenship and rights remained.

Johnson vetoed the Freedmen's Bureau bill, calling the provisions for military trials a violation of the Fifth Amendment and questioning the capacity of the present Congress to function at all. A Congress that barred eleven states outright, the president said, was not legally capable of enacting any legislation, especially for the states it excluded. Congress sustained the veto by a narrow margin, but this was to be Johnson's last reconstruction victory of any consequence. In July, Congress was to pass another Freedmen's Bureau bill, very like the earlier measure, over Johnson's veto.

The second component in the moderate Republican policy was the Civil Rights Act of 1866. The purpose of this law was to provide a permanent guarantee of rights equality. The first question to be resolved concerned the citizenship of the freed people. To this end the bill declared that "all persons born or naturalized in the United States and not subject to any foreign power, except Indians not taxed," were citizens of the United States. The bill then stated that citizens of the United States, irrespective of race, color, or previous condition of servitude, should have the same right in every state "to make and enforce contracts, to sue, be parties, and give evidence, to inherit, purchase, lease, sell, hold, and convey real and personal property," and to enjoy the "full and equal benefit of all laws and proceedings for the security of person and property, as is enjoyed by white citizens." The rights thus enumerated were given sanction in Section 2, which declared that any person who under color of any law, statute, ordinance, regulation, or custom deprived any inhabitant of rights secured by the act, was guilty of a misdemeanor and upon conviction was subject to fine and imprisonment. The bill gave United States district courts exclusive jurisdiction over crimes committed against the act and concurrent jurisdiction to district and circuit courts over civil and criminal cases involving persons unable to enforce in state courts rights secured by the act.

In debate Republicans had little difficulty defending the attribution of citizenship to blacks. Chief Justice Taney himself in the *Dred Scott* opinion had insisted that control over citizenship was vested exclusively in Congress under the naturalization power. Executive and legislative actions during the Civil War had repudiated the Supreme Court's denial of Negro citizenship in the *Dred Scott* case. But as these actions were arguably not legally conclusive, and in view of the degraded status the Black Codes imposed on the freedmen, it was expedient formally to overrule Taney's exclusion of blacks from citizenship. This the Civil Rights Act did.

The Republican Congress accepted the idea of dual citizenship. But the citizenship which the Civil Rights Act conferred was dual and mutually reinforcing, in contrast to the strictly separate spheres of state and federal citizenship described by Taney in the *Dred Scott* case. Republicans viewed American citizenship as a single entity, in the nature of concentric circles of state and federal power. National citizenship encompassed state citizenship and consisted in general rights such as the Civil Rights Act enumerated. State citizenship was concerned with the specific entitlement of individuals to these categorical rights under state law. For example, every citizen had a right to make contracts, but the precise manner of exercising the right was determined and regulated by the states. National citizenship thus consisted of fundamental civil rights that were implemented in the sphere of state law, with the federal government acting as ultimate guarantor. In effect, the content of national citizenship was equality before states' laws as state citizens.

More problematic than the attribution of citizenship in the congressional debate was the prescription for civil rights. Especially alarming to conservatives was a clause in Trumbull's original bill which stated that "there shall be no discrimination in civil rights and immunities." This guarantee seemingly transferred the protection of all such rights from their historic lodgment with the states to the federal government. Democrats and several conservative Republicans objected that it would prevent the states from making any legal distinction whatever between Negroes and whites. Trumbull argued that the Thirteenth Amendment gave Congress power to legislate on civil rights in this plenary fashion, but most Republicans disagreed. Accordingly, they struck out the sweeping "no discrimination" clause.

More controversial still were the nature and scope of federal power employed in the Civil Rights Act. As the Black Codes indicated, the chief threat to freedmen's rights at this time came from the restored state governments, although private injury and discrimination were also widespread. Could Congress, and did the act, prohibit both official and private denial of civil rights, or only the former? Contemporary opinion was divided. Some Republicans held that the Thirteenth Amendment gave Congress plenary power to legislate against denials of rights from whatever source, as a necessary corollary of its power to prohibit slavery. Others held that Congress could not assume the power of local police and criminal law jurisdiction which this comprehensive and sweeping conception of rights protection implied. In this view Congress under the Thirteenth Amendment could legislate only in case of a denial of civil rights by state governments. There was, in other words, a state action limitation on congressional power, a stipulation that state action denying rights had to occur before Congress could legislate. Most Republicans appear to have supported this moderate view, believing—naïvely—that if state officers could be got to respect Negroes' rights and enforce state laws for the protection of person and property, private injury would cease. In a typical expression of this outlook, Representative James Wilson of Iowa said that the Civil Rights Act applied to state officers alone, rather than to all persons, because Congress was not legislating a general criminal code for the states.

Indeed, if the Civil Rights Act worked as its framers intended, it would itself prove to be a temporary measure. The expansion of federal jurisdiction contemplated by the act was potentially very considerable, as persons who were discriminated against in state courts through the application of unequal state laws could transfer their cases to the federal courts. Republican moderates believed that, facing this prospect, the states would drop their discriminatory laws in order to retain jurisdiction over the range of ordinary civil and criminal matters that had traditionally lain within their exclusive authority. The point was to get the states to treat their citizens equally. The act "will have no operation in any State where the laws are equal," said Trumbull, "where all persons have the same civil rights without regard to color or race."

Johnson vetoed the Civil Rights bill, advancing the same conservative state's-rights objections he had offered to the Freedmen's Bureau bill. However, on April 9 Congress passed the bill over his veto. Although the Democratic minority and a scattering of Republicans continued to support his administration, the Republican majority henceforth promptly passed all reconstruction measures of any consequence over his veto.

The Fourteenth Amendment

Plainly the Civil Rights Act of 1866 rested on the Thirteenth Amendment. Among several Republicans, however, doubt persisted about the sufficiency of this constitutional basis. This doubt critically influenced the drafting of another constitutional amendment authorizing national civil rights legislation in clear and unmistakable terms. This new measure was the work of the Joint Committee on Reconstruction, which for several months had been considering all aspects of the reconstruction question necessary for a comprehensive peace settlement.

In January 1866 the Joint Committee introduced a proposed constitutional amendment to exclude outright from the basis of congressional representation any person whose political rights were denied or abridged by the state on account of race or color. By implication this measure enjoined Negro suffrage under penalty of a reduction in the representation of any state not granting it. The amendment passed the House late in January, but the less radical Senate rejected it. After some further delay, the Joint Committee on April 30 reported out a far more comprehensive constitutional amendment, destined to emerge with some modifications as the Fourteenth Amendment.

The opening sentence of Section I of the proposed amendment provided that:

All persons born or naturalized in the United States, and subject to the jurisdiction thereof, are citizens of the United States and of the State wherein they reside.

Thus the lack of a citizenship clause in the original Constitution was formally remedied. National citizenship now became primary and state citizenship secondary; thereby the issue of the locus of citizenship, discussed in the Missouri Compromise and later debates and left in a confused condition by the *Dred Scott* decision, was finally put to rest. The clause also obviously conferred outright national and state citizenship upon Negroes, as was its intent.

Sections 2 and 3 dealt with the problem of southern representation. Section 2 as reported by the committee was a compromise. It based state representation in the House upon the whole number of people in each state and so abrogated the three-fifths clause, but it excluded from the basis of representation those persons denied the franchise for any reason other than "participation in rebellion, or other crime." This section in effect insured that the conservative white population should not be able to take advantage of increased state representation together with Negro disfranchisement to place the southern states and Democrats in control in Washington once more. At the same time, the section did not categorically bestow the vote upon Negroes.

As originally drafted by the Joint Committee, Section 3 unconditionally disfranchised all participants in the late rebellion until March 4, 1870. Many moderate Republicans thought this at once too severe and too temporary. It passed the House, but was then unanimously stricken out in both houses and a substitute provision by Senator Jacob Howard of Michigan put in its place. Howard's provision merely barred from state and federal offices all participants in rebellion who had formerly held political office and in that capacity taken an oath to support the Constitution. It further empowered Congress to remove this disability by a two-thirds vote.

Section 4 recited the obvious—it guaranteed the United States public debt and outlawed debts incurred in rebellion against the United States. Section 5 empowered Congress to enforce the amendment by appropriate legislation.

By far the most important part of the Fourteenth Amendment was the guarantee of civil rights contained in Section 1. Originally, the Joint Committee, using a formulation of Representative John Bingham of Ohio, proposed to give Congress power "to make all laws necessary and proper to secure to the citizens of each State all privileges and immunities of citizens in the several States, and to all persons in the several States equal protection in the rights of life, liberty, and property." Although Bingham later said this meant only that Congress could correct state laws that denied equal rights, the language seemed unequivocally to transfer legislative power over civil rights from the states to the federal government. It appeared to have the same revolutionary impact on the federal system as the "no discrimination" clause of the original civil rights bill. Sensitive to moderate and conservative objections, the Joint Committee, therefore, substituted an alternative civil rights section, also drawn by Bingham, which remained in the amendment as adopted: "No state shall make or enforce any law which shall abridge the privileges and immunities of citizens of the United States; nor shall any State deprive any person of life, liberty, or property, without due process of law; nor deny to any person within its jurisdiction equal protection of the laws."

These provisions expressed the state-action theory of federal legislative power over civil rights. For a few radicals with abolitionist backgrounds, the language of Section 1 had a clear and sweeping liberal humanitarian content that banned all forms of discrimination against blacks in law, politics, and society. Most Republican lawmakers, however, saw Section 1 as a restatement in broader terms of the Civil Rights Act, expressed in a form that prevented subsequent national legislative repeal. Most also saw it as removing all doubt about the constitutionality of the Civil Rights Act.

The Fourteenth Amendment nationalized civil rights, but it did so in a way that respected traditional federal values. The states had been the principal regulators of personal liberty and civil rights, and they would continue to perform that function. Now, however, they would do so under federal supervisory authority and national guarantees of rights protection, as expressed in the Thirteenth and Fourteenth Amendments and the Civil Rights Act. Nationalization of civil rights, in other words, was not to be accomplished by direct centralization and consolidation of legislative power in Congress. To be sure, by comparison with the prewar Constitution, the reconstruction amendments pointed in that direction, and there were Republicans who endorsed a centralist or unitary solution. They argued, for example, that if under the rule of slavery the right of recapturing fugitive slaves could be enforced as a national constitutional right against any interference whatever, whether from state government or private individuals, then surely under the rule of freedom the basic rights of citizenship could be protected by the federal government in the same direct and exclusive manner. Yet this view did not achieve majority support. The moderate center, when they considered the implications and ramifications of this more radical approach, rejected it. The revolution in federalism that began under wartime exigencies thus stopped at a halfway point.

The Fourteenth Amendment, passed by both houses of Congress on June 13, 1866, was part of a comprehensive reconstruction settlement submitted by the Joint Committee on Reconstruction. Eschewing the conquered provinces and territorialization theories, the committee adhered to the disorganized-governments–guarantee-clause conception of reconstruction. It declared that the states lacked legitimate civil governments and said the people must form and ratify new constitutions establishing republican government. The committee also took the position that while the federal government would determine the fundamental conditions, the people in the states should voluntarily accept the elements of a new republican order. Thus the guarantee clause offered a middle ground between exclusive federal control of reconstruction and virtually complete local autonomy or self-reconstruction, as under President Johnson's policy.

The Republican moderates in control of Congress were prepared to recognize the Johnson governments provided they agreed to protect the civil rights of all citizens, secure a "just equality of representation," and protect against rebel debt claims. These terms referred to the Fourteenth Amendment and to a bill introduced in April providing that any seceded state that ratified the amendment would be readmitted to Congress. Unwilling to make any formal commitment to receive the states, radicals blocked this bill. But the promise of readmission was clear. It was borne out when Tennessee was granted representation in Congress in July 1866 after ratifying the Fourteenth Amendment.

However, the other ten seceded states rejected the Fourteenth Amendment. Believing that time was on their side and that the northern public would not endorse the moderate program, let alone more radical proposals, southern political leaders denounced the amendment. They looked to the congressional elections of 1866 as a means of strengthening President Johnson's position. Should Johnson's supporters win control of Congress, the president could secure admission of the southern states on his own terms. Dubbed "masterly inactivity," this strategy in fact proved to be a grave mistake. For moderate and radical Republicans made heavy gains at Johnson's expense in the fall elections.

Meanwhile, as the northern public grew increasingly impatient with the failure of Congress to adopt a reconstruction plan, events were driving moderate and radical Republicans closer together. Johnson's unwillingness to accept any degree of federal civil rights protection, on the ground that it violated the rights of the states, strengthened Republican unity and resolve. The upshot of this political process was the adoption of a more radical congressional policy in the Military Reconstruction Act of 1867.

EIGHTEEN

Congressional Reconstruction

------------------------------ ✦ ✦ ✦ ------------------------------

WHEN CONGRESS CONVENED IN DECEMBER 1866, the need for a reconstruction policy had grown more imperative. Radicals might be willing to keep the former Confederate states waiting for a generation, but most northerners were disturbed by the constitutional anomaly of ten reconstructed state governments remaining unrepresented in the national legislature. Complicating the situation was the problem of protecting the liberty of the freed slaves, which most northerners regarded as necessary on both political and humanitarian grounds. The object of official state discrimination in the Black Codes, Negroes were increasingly the victims of private injury and denial of rights. Southern abuse of the freedmen was a major reason why the states were not yet readmitted to Congress. Yet, paradoxically, the condition of the freedmen was also a source of pressure to restore the states to the Union, on the theory that they would then be subject to the constraints of national civil rights guarantees. Still another issue demanding congressional attention was the challenge to national authority presented by civil and criminal suits in southern state courts against Union military personnel. These suits alleged violation of local citizens' civil rights through actions taken in the performance of military duties during and after the war. In short, a law-and-order problem existed in the South to add urgency to the task of adopting a reconstruction policy.

Long since alienated from the Republican party, President Johnson rejected the northern majority's perception of events. Intent on restoring the states with virtually all their antebellum rights intact, Johnson used his authority to frustrate federal protection of freedmen and Unionists. In April 1866, for example, he issued a proclamation declaring the insurrection ended and pronouncing the former rebellious states restored to the Union. In time of peace, Johnson observed, military tribunals and suspension of the writ of habeas corpus were a threat to civil liberty and individual rights. The president's message encouraged white southerners and alarmed the

Union military command, which in July 1866 authorized the use of military tribunals to try persons charged with crimes against federal officers and freedmen whom state officials failed to prosecute. In August Johnson issued another proclamation criticizing reliance on military government in place of civil authority, and in December 1866 the Supreme Court issued a similar warning. In its opinion in the *Milligan* case the Court held that in places remote from the theater of war, where the civil courts were open, military trial of civilians was unconstitutional. This dictum seemed to threaten existing operations of the army carried out under the provisions of the Freedmen's Bureau Act. It increased the uncertainty facing Congress as it turned once again to the problem of formulating a reconstruction policy.

The Military Reconstruction Acts of 1867

Although Republicans were united in opposition to Johnson's policy, moderate and radical factions continued to disagree in their approach to reconstruction. Radicals wanted to remove the Johnson governments, exclude all former rebels from citizenship, and force the states to write new constitutions and form new governments based on Negro suffrage. Seeking to revolutionize the South through confiscation, land redistribution, and public education programs, they would deny southerners representation indefinitely until they were genuinely penitent and republicanized. Moderates clung to the Fourteenth Amendment as a basic reconstruction policy. Averse to political and social revolution, they wanted to recognize the Johnson governments on condition that they accept the obligation to protect the civil rights of all citizens equally.

Anxious both to restore federalism and guarantee citizenship equality, moderates laid heavy stress on securing legislation that would expressly promise to readmit the states when they ratified the Fourteenth Amendment. As the southern states had already rejected this approach when they repudiated the Fourteenth Amendment, however, moderates could hardly regard it as a sufficient plan of reconstruction. Accordingly, they now accepted Negro suffrage as an essential additional step. Initially opposed to black voting out of a belief that the freedmen were unprepared for it and in deference to the constitutional rule that gave the states exclusive power to regulate voting, moderates now saw enfranchisement of Negroes as a way of solving both the civil rights and reconstruction questions. Armed with the vote, blacks would be able to protect themselves and demand recognition of their rights as citizens. Negro suffrage would also supply the political support needed in the southern states to get the Fourteenth Amendment adopted and the states readmitted. Perhaps most important, it would make continuing federal intervention in local affairs unnecessary.

Radical and moderate agendas aside, the most pressing need was to deal with the law-and-order problem. To this end the Joint Committee on Reconstruction in January 1867 introduced a military government bill authorizing the use of military tribunals for civil purposes. It was this bill, amended to accommodate the radical and moderate points of view on reconstruction, that became the Military Reconstruction Act of March 2, 1867.

The original bill divided the unrestored seceded states into five districts, under the command of military officers who were authorized to employ military tribunals to protect the person and property of all citizens and bring to trial disturbers of the peace and criminals. Any interference by state governments with the exercise of military power under the act was declared null and void. Based on the disorganized–states–republican–government theory of reconstruction, the act declared the existing civil governments in the South to be provisional only and subject to the paramount authority of the United States to abolish, modify, control, or supersede them. Thus Congress rejected the radical demand that the Johnson governments be removed, though it placed them on notice in that regard. Yet the radical point of view was satisfied in the requirement that the states form new constitutions guaranteeing Negro suffrage. On the other hand, while former rebels were excluded from the constitution-making process, the standard of exclusion was to be the Fourteenth Amendment, the moderates' lodestar. And the act further satisfied the moderates by providing that when the states ratified the Fourteenth Amendment, they would be readmitted to Congress.

The Military Reconstruction Act embodied more of the radical point of view than did the congressional policy of 1866. It was perceived in the South—and by most historians ever since—as a supremely radical measure that subjugated the states outright and imposed on them a political and social revolution. There is much truth in this assessment. It is equally important, however, to point out that within the range of reconstruction policies being contemplated, the act was a compromise that denied the radicals much of what they wanted—especially abolition of the Johnson governments, confiscation, and land redistribution. Moreover, it contained key moderate elements, including the all-important promise to readmit the states once they accepted the Fourteenth Amendment. This fact serves to remind us that the fundamental problem was how to restore the seceded states to the Union rather than how to govern them. Furthermore, in a reflection of the persistent faith in—or constitutional necessity of—local self-government, the act left the initiative in devising ways of proceeding to the Johnson governments themselves. It made no stipulation as to the steps to be taken in drafting new constitutions.

Johnson vetoed the military reconstruction bill, whereupon Congress overrode his veto. The states, however, refused to implement the act. Congress, therefore, adopted the Reconstruction Act of March 23, 1867. This measure gave the military commanders instructions for starting the constitution-making process and specified in detail the procedure to follow in holding elections for a constitutional convention. After a second veto and override by Congress, Johnson enforced the reconstruction acts as narrowly as possible in order to maintain the existing governments and minimize change. Attorney General Henry Stanbery, for example, sought to disfranchise as few white southerners as possible. He ruled that military-appointed registration boards, entrusted with the power to determine ineligibility for voting because of participation in the rebellion, could not exclude persons who wished to take the required oath denying disqualification, whether they were lying or not. Vigorous opposition promptly appeared in Congress and in the army against what Republicans regarded as the administration's obstructionist course. When additional conflicts arose over attempts of military commanders to remove state officers, Congress passed a Third Reconstruction Act in July 1867. This law set aside the attorney general's rulings on disqualification for rebellion and confirmed the authority of military commanders to remove state officers. From this point Johnson pursued his conservative objectives through use of the removal power, replacing the more radical military commanders and trying to drive Secretary of War Stanton out of the cabinet. Within a year his actions provoked the House of Representatives to impeach him.

Radical Reconstruction in the South

From the conservative point of view, the congressional policy of 1867 was hopelessly unconstitutional. It centralized power in the federal government and invaded states' rights. Furthermore, it imposed military government on states in disregard of the guarantee-of-republican-government clause, denied representation to states lawfully entitled to it, and imposed illegal conditions on those states before readmitting them to representation. From the Republican perspective, however, the policy was constitutional under the guarantee clause and the grasp-of-war theory, as the Supreme Court acknowledged in *Texas* v. *White* (1869). Yet even this radical plan of 1867, while stipulating conditions the states must meet in order to resume their place in the Union, left much to be carried out by the states themselves. Essentially, it was a policy of internal reconstruction by southerners. Congress intended no permanent centralization of power. On the contrary, the reconstruction act was a temporary expedient for restoring the states and making permanent federal control unnecessary.

Nevertheless, the congressional policy of 1867 portended a political revolution in the South. Reconstruction would in large part be accomplished by a new class of southerners created by congressional enfranchisement of the freedmen and formally organized as the Republican party. In the enrollment of eligible voters the proportion of Negroes was very large. In Alabama, for example, 104,000 out of 165,000 registered voters were Negroes. In only five states, however, were black voters a majority. Moreover, the white majority in the other states and in the South as a whole was not, as legend would have it, composed principally of carpetbagger immigrants from the North.

The new electorate was purified by the exclusion of former rebels, but the extent of this proscription was limited. The test employed—which applied only to election to and service in the state constitutional conventions—was the moderate Fourteenth Amendment one barring persons who had sworn an oath to uphold the Constitution as state or federal officers and then joined the rebellion. The number of southerners excluded under this test has been estimated at approximately 100,000, a number that may seem large or small depending on one's perspective. Plainly the policy did not proscribe a majority of white southerners, although quantitative evaluation is beside the point since the purpose was to exclude the key political leaders of the existing southern establishment. Nevertheless, the number proscribed was far fewer than the categorical elimination of former rebels that radicals had hoped for. Furthermore, although permanent disenfranchisement of persons excluded by the Fourteenth Amendment became an issue in state reconstruction politics, in only three states was it adopted. By and large, new state governments were formed in the South without a wholesale purge of the old political class or the removal of existing state governments.

In the fall of 1867, then, all ten unreconstructed southern states voted by large majorities to call constitutional conventions. Their principal purpose was to establish a new political order based on universal male suffrage and civil rights equality. But other significant changes also occurred. In general the new state charters strengthened state government against local autonomy, reorganized local government, made many offices elective that had been appointive, reapportioned legislative representation more equitably, and effected legal and penal reforms. Taxation and finance systems were modified, and in what was probably the most important single reform, free public education was introduced into the South. Drawn up by the new class of smaller farmers, business and industrial groups, and blacks, the reconstruction constitutions reflected typical mid-nineteenth-century progressive social and economic ideas.

Because the Reconstruction Act of March 23, 1867, required that a constitution must be ratified in an election in which a majority of all registered voters in the state participated, many enfranchised whites stayed away from the polls in an effort to prevent adoption of the new constitutions. In Alabama this device temporarily succeeded. In March 1868, however, Congress passed the Fourth Reconstruction Act providing that the new constitutions could be ratified by a simple majority of those voting. In all the remaining states except Mississippi the constitutions were ratified by large majorities. Accordingly, in June 1868 Congress voted to readmit Alabama, Arkansas, North Carolina, South Carolina, Georgia, Florida, and Louisiana. Texas, Mississippi, and Virginia were readmitted in 1870, after being required to ratify a new constitutional amendment protecting Negro suffrage.

The Impeachment of Johnson

As the reconstruction acts went into effect in 1867–68, a constitutional crisis unique in the history of the republic gripped the government at Washington. After months of backing and filling and two false starts, a frustrated, embittered, yet withal reluctant Congress impeached President Johnson out of a conviction that he had improperly obstructed the carrying out of congressional reconstruction policy.

Beginning in March 1867, Congress adopted a series of acts intended to restrict the president's authority as much as possible. The Army Appropriation Act of March 2, 1867, required that all army orders be issued through the general of the army, and that the general in command of the army should not be removed without the Senate's consent. The Third Reconstruction Act of July 19, 1867, vested the entire power to appoint and remove officials under the act in the general of the army, a direct transfer of the president's appointive power to a subordinate official. Of even greater significance was the Tenure of Office Act, also enacted on March 2, 1867. This law was intended to destroy the president's power to remove subordinate officials without the Senate's consent. It provided that all executive officials appointed with the Senate's consent should hold office until a successor was appointed and qualified in the same manner. Thus no presidential removal would be valid under the act until the Senate consented by ratifying the nomination of a successor. A partial exception was made for cabinet officers, who were to hold office only during the term of the president appointing them, and for one month thereafter.

Another section of the act provided for ad interim appointments. When the Senate was not in session, the president could remove an official for crime, misconduct, or incapacity and fill the vacancy so created with an ad interim appointment. But the president was obliged to report the removal to the Senate within twenty days after that chamber next convened. If the Senate then refused its consent to the removal, the office reverted to the former incumbent. Accepting or holding an office in violation of the statute was made a misdemeanor punishable by fine and imprisonment.

This statute reopened the old dispute over the president's removal power. As the reader is aware, the First Congress had decided that the president possessed a separate right of removal without the Senate's consent. Also, Jackson had successfully reaffirmed that right in 1833, and it had since been commonly exercised. Johnson's veto recalled these facts and denounced the bill as an unconstitutional usurpation of executive authority; however, Congress promptly passed the measure over his veto.

Meanwhile the radical leaders had been searching for plausible grounds upon which to impeach the president. In the spring of 1867 a House investigating committee had covered every possible charge thoroughly and had been forced to report in July that no adequate grounds for impeachment existed. The investigation continued, however, and in December the committee, under the direction of Representative George S. Boutwell of Massachusetts, recommended impeachment, although no specific grounds for such a step were presented.

In the debate that followed, the radical leaders contended that the phrase "high crimes and misdemeanors" was not to be construed narrowly, but that it embraced essentially political acts tending to undermine the government and the Constitution. This broad view was in part supported by the history of impeachment proceedings in Congress. Five times the House of Representatives had voted to impeach federal judges, but only once did it limit its charge to an indictable crime. On one occasion—the impeachment of demented Judge John Pickering in 1804—a nonindictable offense was the ground for conviction. Moreover, constitutional commentators throughout the nineteenth century agreed that impeachment was at bottom political rather than narrowly legalistic in character. It was intended to deal not with single offenses otherwise indictable under federal statute or common law, but with abuse of power and public trust. On the other hand, it was true that judgments by the Senate in impeachment trials supported the view that the power could be used only against defined, indictable offenses. For in all but one instance—that of Judge Pickering—nonindictable offenses had not led to conviction.

Boutwell drew the issue when, conceding that it might not be possible "by specific charge" to arraign Johnson for his "great crime," he nonetheless urged the president's impeachment on the ground that he had promoted the restoration of rebels to power. Representative James F. Wilson of Iowa, a Republican, answered that though Johnson was "the worst of the Presidents," "If we cannot arraign the President for a specific crime for what are we to proceed against him? . . . If we cannot state upon paper a specific crime how are we to carry this cause to the Senate for trial?" The House then rejected the committee report, 100 to 57.

At this point Johnson gave the Republican majority what they demanded: a flagrant violation of a federal statute, the Tenure of Office Act. The president had long been at odds with Secretary of War Edwin M. Stanton, who had openly aligned himself with the congressional radicals and had refused to resign. In August 1867 Johnson removed Stanton from office and appointed General Grant in his place. The removal and appointment were made ad interim (that is, while the Senate was not in session), and so did not constitute a violation of the Tenure of Office Act. In accordance with the act, Johnson gave the Senate reasons for removing Stanton, thereby implying that Stanton was covered by the statute. In December 1867 the Senate refused to confirm the appointment, whereupon Grant resigned and Stanton resumed office.

In February 1868 Johnson forced the issue by summarily removing Stanton as secretary of war and appointing Major General Lorenzo Thomas as his successor. Since the Senate was then in session, the president's act appeared to be a specific violation of the Tenure of Office Act. This was precisely what the radical leaders had been waiting for, since the president had now presumably committed the specific statutory offense that many hesitant Republicans considered necessary for impeachment. Two days later, on February 24, the House voted, 128 to 47, to impeach the president.

On March 2 and 3 the House voted eleven articles of impeachment against Johnson. The first three articles charged the president with deliberately violating the Tenure of Office Act in removing Stanton and appointing Thomas. Articles 4 to 8 charged the president with entering into a conspiracy with Thomas to violate the same law. Conspiracy to violate a federal statute was a punishable offense by a statute of July 31, 1861. Article 9 charged Johnson with having attempted to subvert the provision in the Army Appropriation Act of 1867, which made all orders issuable through the general of the army. Article 10, inserted at the insistence of the radicals, shifted the indictment to the broad political basis by charging Johnson with attempting to "bring into disgrace, ridicule, hatred, contempt, and reproach the Congress of the United States." Article 11 summarized the previous counts and also charged Johnson with obstructing the enforcement of the Reconstruction Act of March 2, 1867.

On March 30 the impeachment trial began before the Senate, with Chief Justice Salmon P. Chase presiding. The first important matter of contention was the Senate's judicial status. Was the Senate sitting as a court or as a political body? The issue was extremely important. If the Senate was a regular court, then it was bound by legal rules of evidence. Presumably, also, it could convict the president only if it found him guilty of a specific offense either at common law or as defined in a federal statute. It could not rightfully convict the president merely as a political enemy of Congress. On the other hand, if the Senate sat as a political body, not only could it hear evidence usually inadmissible in a regular court of justice, but also it might conceivably convict the president of a political offense.

Johnson's attorneys argued that the trial was strictly a judicial proceeding. The Constitution, they pointed out, adhered strictly to a common law terminology in describing impeachment. The Senate was empowered to "try" impeachments, make a conviction, and enter a judgment. With equal force they contended that if impeachment was a mere political proceeding, then the whole long-established constitutional relationship between executive and Congress would be threatened. Were the president removable merely because he was politically unacceptable to Congress, executive independence would be destroyed and parliamentary ascendancy would replace the American presidential system.

The prosecution, on the other hand, argued that the nature of impeachment made the Senate something more than a court. Offenses other than those known to the common law were impeachable. Impeachment, they said, could be pressed for improper motive, or even "action against the public interest." If not, what other method was there for getting rid of an incompetent officeholder? Here they cited the Pickering precedent.

The issue was technically settled in favor of the defense. Early in the trial the Senate voted 31 to 19 to permit the chief justice to settle all questions of law, evidence, and the like, unless the Senate overruled him. The implication was that the chief justice was the presiding officer in a regular court, the senators sitting as associate justices. In reality, however, this ruling hardly destroyed the political character of the proceedings—on the part of both the opponents of the president and his supporters. On each side senators were prepared to vote according to their political convictions regardless of the evidence. Nor should this be taken as a total constitutional irregularity or failing. Whether one employ the broadly political or narrowly legalistic definition of "high crimes and misdemeanors," impeachment could hardly be expected to occur except in highly charged political circumstances. Under such conditions political convictions and principles rightly exert influence. The paradox of impeachment was that it required the use of judicial standards and rules to resolve what was essentially a political-constitutional crisis.

The principal argument in the trial centered on Johnson's supposed violation of the Tenure of Office Act. The prosecution argued that Johnson had committed a deliberate violation of a constitutional statute, clearly an impeachable offense. Johnson's attorneys in reply argued that the Tenure of Office Act did not apply to Johnson's removal of Stanton at all. The act specified that cabinet officers were to hold office during the term of the president appointing them, and for one month thereafter. Stanton had been appointed by Lincoln, not Johnson, and Johnson had never reappointed him but had merely tacitly asserted to Stanton's continuance in office. The prosecution replied that Johnson was merely an "acting President" serving Lincoln's unexpired second term—a weak argument, for since Tyler's time vice-presidents succeeding to office had been considered as presidents-in-full.

The cornerstone of Johnson's defense, however, was the contention that the Tenure of Office Act was unconstitutional. Counsel for the president cited the debates in the First Congress on the removal power, Jackson's successful removal of Duane, and the established practice of eighty years, all of which supported the contention that the removal power was an executive prerogative separate and distinct from the power of appointment. Against the weight of these precedents the House managers retorted that the Tenure of Office Act was a formal declaration of the meaning of the Constitution, and, therefore, finally settled a long-mooted constitutional issue. This was tantamount to the assertion that Congress possessed a final right of constitutional interpretation even with regard to issues apparently settled by long-established practice.

Finally, the defense contended that Johnson's deliberate violation of law had not been subversive, but that the president had merely wished to test the act's constitutionality by bringing it before the courts. The president's action was, therefore, not a misdemeanor but an attempt to institute judicial proceedings. This argument the prosecution dealt with effectively. The president, they said, must like everyone else bear responsibility for his acts. If he violated a law on the grounds that it was unconstitutional, he must face the consequences if the proper tribunal, in this case the Senate, decided that the law was valid. If the Senate decided that the Tenure of Office Act was constitutional, then Johnson had committed a misdemeanor and must be punished regardless of intent.

On May 16 the Senate began balloting upon the impeachment articles. The Republican majority in the Senate, intent on securing a conviction, instructed the chief justice to poll the Senate first on Article 11, which included all possible charges and supposedly offered the greatest chance of conviction.

The final vote on Article 11 was 35 "guilty" and 19 "not guilty," one vote short of the two-thirds majority required by the Constitution for impeachment. After an adjournment to May 26, the Senate voted on Articles 2 and 3. On both Articles the vote was again 35 to 19, after which the Senate voted to adjourn as a tribunal *sine die.* Decisive votes were cast by seven Republican senators—Fessenden, Fowler, Grimes, Henderson, Ross, Trumbull, and Van Winkle—who joined with the Democratic minority in favor of acquittal. Historians have lauded these Republicans for selflessly rising above politics for the sake of constitutional principle, but in fact they had ample political reason to favor Johnson's acquittal. As conservative Republicans and hard-money men, they opposed the political and economic views of radical Senator Ben Wade of Ohio, president pro tempore of the Senate, who would become president if Johnson were removed. Furthermore, by mid-May Johnson's actions on reconstruction had allayed much of the apprehension that led to the vote for impeachment in February. At the urging of conservative Republicans, Johnson appointed General John M. Schofield, a conservative who had enforced the reconstruction acts in Virginia, as secretary of war. He also agreed to submit the constitutions of Arkansas and South Carolina to Congress instead of withholding them. These developments suggested an end of executive obstructionism toward congressional reconstruction policy and enabled conservative Republicans to follow their constitutional inclination and vote for acquittal.

Historians have usually condemned Congress for using the impeachment power improperly to punish Johnson for mere political disagreements, on the assumption that political convictions ought to have played no part in the process. It is hard to agree with this premise, however. The purpose of impeachment is to deal with fundamental political controversies. It was intended by the founding fathers as a means by which Congress, ordinarily prevented from interfering with the discretionary powers of the president, might restrain the chief executive when his actions threatened the safety of the republic or the integrity of the constitutional order. Necessarily, impeachment is employed in situations which require political evaluation and judgment, so that it misses the point to criticize Congress for letting politics enter into impeachment decisions. Of course, it can always be objected that if the legislature can impeach for other than a clearly defined crime, there is a danger that it will use the power irresponsibly to pursue petty political objectives and punish the executive for mere disagreements of policy. If constitutionalism has any reality, however, this is an unlikely danger.

The pertinent questions about impeachment are whether the political considerations involved are light, transient, and trivial, and whether they obliterate all other considerations and influences. In Johnson's case it seems clear that while political passions ran deep—on both sides of the question— they did not banish a concern for fair procedure. It seems clear, furthermore, that Republicans had genuine reason to object to Johnson's legally correct but nonetheless obstructionist enforcement of the reconstruction acts. It is well to remember also that no model existed to guide lawmakers in exercising the impeachment power; Congress necessarily had to interpret the Constitution as it went along. No one could say what was constitutionally correct in the impeachment of a president because it had never been done.

The decisive constitutional interpretation that Congress made in 1868 was to require evidence of an indictable offense, a clear violation of positive law, as warrant for impeaching a president. Once Congress committed itself to this position, the strength of its case depended on the nature and purpose of the law that Johnson violated. And the Tenure of Office Act proved to be a weak foundation for the undertaking. Not that the removal power belonged so unequivocally to the president that Congress had absolutely no business trying to regulate it in any way. The weight of constitutional history favored the president's position on removals, but it did not render all other approaches to the problem of removals patently unconstitutional.

What weakened the congressional position was that the Tenure of Office Act was passed with a view toward catching Johnson. His violation of the law was a pretext by which to reach his more substantively objectionable actions; it was symbolic of his overall obstructionist course. But once seized on and made the basis of impeachment proceedings, as the constitutional conservatism of the Republican majority required, violation of the Tenure of Office Act could not be dealt with merely as a symbol or legitimate pretext for Johnson's grave political offenses. It had to be considered on its merits, in isolation from the pattern of events that gave rise to it. Or at least the defense succeeded in presenting the lonely violation of law in this way. And from this perspective Johnson's disregard of the act assumed far less serious, not to say trivial, proportions, especially in light of the history of the removal power. When presidential impeachment next became an issue a century later, the lesson of the Johnson trial seemed to be that the impeachment power could be used only for indictable crimes, not political offenses no matter how serious they might be.

National Enforcement of Civil Rights

Johnson's acquittal was followed by the readmission of all but three ex-Confederate states in the summer of 1868. In November General Ulysses S. Grant was elected president on a platform that announced the restoration of peace. Reconstruction was not over yet, however, for though the new southern state constitutions provided for Negro suffrage, there was nothing to prevent revocation of the guarantee should conservatives regain control of state governments. In the northern states, moreover, attempts to enfranchise Negroes in several states and territories had met with defeat between 1865 and 1867, so that in all but a few states blacks were denied the suffrage. Republicans naturally wanted these votes, too, and, therefore, had political as well as ideological reasons for amending the Constitution to make Negroes voters throughout the nation.

Like civil rights, regulation of the suffrage before the war belonged exclusively to the states. The Constitution provided that members of the House of Representatives should be elected by those who were qualified to vote for the most numerous branch of the state legislature. This meant that while the right of suffrage in federal elections was lodged in the national Constitution, it did not actually arise until the franchise was conferred by the states. During the Civil War the disorganization of loyal state governments created a situation in which it was plausible, under the grasp-of-war and republican-government theories, to assert federal control over the suffrage. At the end of the war Negro suffrage was a leading radical reconstruction demand, but it was soon eclipsed by the more immediate problem of guaranteeing civil rights. Nevertheless, Negro suffrage was indirectly, though ineffectually, stipulated in the Fourteenth Amendment provision reducing the representation of states which denied blacks the right to vote. In January 1867 Congress enfranchised Negroes in the District of Columbia and the territories, and in March, as noted previously, the Military Reconstruction Act instituted black suffrage in the ten unreconstructed former rebel states.

The Fifteenth Amendment, framed in early 1869 and ratified in March 1870, authorized the federal government to regulate voting in limited respects without denying basic state control of the subject. It stated that "the right of citizens of the United States to vote shall not be denied or abridged by the United States or by any State on account of race, color, or previous condition of servitude." Section 2 gave Congress power to enforce the amendment by appropriate legislation. A moderate formulation, the Fifteenth Amendment not only embodied the state-action idea as a limitation on congressional power, but it also eschewed the radical demand for universal male suffrage. In other words, rather than confer the right to vote, it conferred the right not to be discriminated against in voting on racial grounds. Nor did the amendment, as radicals had proposed, protect blacks against exclusion from officeholding or prohibit states from employing literacy and property tests in regulating voting rights. As in other civil rights measures, Republican congressmen sought to achieve a balance between placing rights under national guarantees and maintaining traditional federalism.

Negro suffrage was the leading and by far the most bitter point of contention in the campaign waged by conservative white, ex-Confederate southerners to wrest control of the reconstructed state governments from southern Republicans. Whereas official state action was the chief threat to Negro rights in the early postwar period, the main danger after 1868 came from the private violence of individuals and terrorist groups attempting to keep blacks from the polls. In part aided by tactics of intimidation, conservatives regained control of Georgia, Tennessee, Virginia, and North Carolina in 1870, and threatened to drive Republicans from power elsewhere in the South. To meet the political crisis presented by this movement, Congress passed additional civil rights laws known as the Enforcement Acts.

The purpose of the new laws was to enforce the Fourteenth and Fifteenth Amendments. The first measure, adopted in May 1870, prohibited state election officials from discriminating among voters on the basis of color in the application of local election laws. It also made bribery and intimidation of voters by individuals a federal crime and, in a section directed at terrorist groups, outlawed conspiracies to prevent citizens from exercising federal constitutional rights. The second Enforcement Act of February 1871 placed congressional elections in cities of over 20,000 population under direct federal supervision. The most important of the new civil rights laws, however, was the Ku Klux Act of April 1871.

Adopted in response to President Grant's request for action to stem southern violence directed against blacks, the Ku Klux Act represented the most far-reaching assertion of federal legislative power to enforce civil rights in the reconstruction era. In an attempt to stop private violence,

Congress stretched the state-action theory to its outer limit. As initially drafted, the bill proposed to punish violations of civil rights resulting from specific crimes of murder, assault, arson, etc., as carried out by individuals. Moderate and conservative Republicans thought the bill extended federal power too far into local affairs, however. Accordingly, they modified it to punish only the general crime of denying equal protection of the law and privileges and immunities of citizens. Reference to specific crimes was thus dropped. The act was directed at individuals on the theory that the failure of the states to punish private violence against blacks was a form of state action justifying congressional legislation. Where conspiracies and violence deprived persons of constitutional rights, the measure declared, "such facts will be deemed a denial by such State of the equal protection of the laws." The act also prohibited acts of individuals that prevented state officers from giving citizens equal protection of the law. Finally, it authorized the president to suspend the writ of habeas corpus and employ military power to deal with conspiracies against civil rights.

Enormous obstacles impeded federal civil rights enforcement, the largest of which was the overwhelming opposition of the vast majority of whites in the South. In the context of the country's deep-seated commitment to federalism, this fact in the long run was sufficient to cause the failure of the national enforcement effort. Nevertheless, in the crisis atmosphere of 1870–71 federal officials applied the civil rights law with vigor. In October 1871 Grant suspended the writ of habeas corpus and imposed martial law in South Carolina. Elsewhere federal officers initiated prosecutions, and by 1872 the Ku Klux Klan had been disbanded. The gain was merely temporary, however, for southern conservatives, who were opposed to the Klan now that it had outlived its usefulness, resorted to more sophisticated legal or quasi-legal forms of intimidation and coercion to deny black civil rights. At the same time, President Grant and the main body of Republicans, expressing northern opinion, desired reconciliation. In short, the next few years revealed that the task of enforcing Negro civil and political rights in the South was beyond the constitutional capacity of the federal government and the moral and ideological commitment of the Republican party.

Party moderates known as Liberal Republicans led the movement for reconciliation and an end to federal interference in southern affairs. In 1872 Congress took action under Section 3 of the Fourteenth Amendment, passing a broad amnesty act restoring the right of officeholding to nearly all ex-Confederates. This measure was adopted shortly after Liberal Republicans and Democrats met in Cincinnati and nominated Horace Greeley for president on a platform that called for "the immediate and absolute removal of all disabilities on account of the rebellion." Grant and the regular Republicans, benefiting from the sense of outrage that accounts of southern terrorism produced at the North, easily defeated the Liberal Republican-

Democratic ticket in the election of 1872. But they failed to persist in civil rights enforcement. Costs were high, appropriations from Congress for civil rights enforcement were low, federal district judges in the South were unsympathetic, and federal officers often lacked competence. And always, of course, there was the profound and enduring white hostility. By 1873 government attorneys dropped most of the charges against former Klansmen. Altogether between 1870 and 1877 the government had a 34 percent success rate in prosecuting violations of the enforcement acts in the South.

As the northern desire to secure justice for the freedmen waned, the expedient political purpose that had also motivated the policy of civil rights enforcement remained. It was true that if justice were to be done, the Republican party must do it and must, therefore, be maintained in power. Yet after it became clear that justice could not be done, the quest for power naturally persisted and contributed to a further discrediting of the entire rights-enforcement enterprise. Recognizing the impossibility of sustaining Republican regimes in the South without permanent federal intervention, Republicans concentrated on keeping their hold on the North. Accordingly, more than half the money appropriated for federal supervision of elections under the Enforcement Act of 1871 was spent in northern and border states (where were located 63 of 68 cities of over 20,000 population affected by the act).

Under these circumstances Republicans refused to pass legislation interfering in the internal affairs of the southern states. Southern conservatives now had virtually a free hand. By 1875, operating mainly through the Democratic party, they had recovered control in eight of the eleven former Confederate states. Only in South Carolina, Florida, and Louisiana did Republican regimes still exist.

Meanwhile, in the election of 1874 the Republicans lost control of the House of Representatives. The effect on them, perhaps paradoxically, was to spur one final civil rights effort. Partly in an attempt to retain the loyalty of southern blacks and partly as a sentimental tribute to exhausted idealism and the recently deceased Senator Charles Sumner, the lame-duck Congress passed the Civil Rights Act of 1875. Originally introduced by Sumner in 1870, the bill declared that all persons were entitled to the full and equal enjoyment of public accommodations in inns, transportation facilities, and places of public amusement. It punished any person who denied others equal access in these places. While its focus on social as opposed to political and legal discrimination gave the bill a radical appearance, significantly it had been stripped of its school desegregation features. It was generally thought to be practically unenforceable. Constitutionally, the act expressed a moderate interpretation of congressional power under the Fourteenth Amendment. Although it dealt with private denials of rights, Republicans upheld the act on the theory that the prohibited discrimination was in effect carried on under state authority—by businesses or institutions created or regulated by state law or in which the state had a substantial interest. Thus it did not depart from, though it went to the verge of, the state-action theory of the Fourteenth Amendment.

The Election of 1876

The presidential election of 1876, which resulted in a bitter political and constitutional controversy, greatly hastened the disintegration of congressional reconstruction.

The election at first appeared to have resulted in a victory for Samuel J. Tilden, the Democratic candidate. An early tabulation gave him 184 undisputed electoral votes, with but 185 votes necessary for election. Rutherford B. Hayes, the Republican candidate, had 165 undisputed votes. However, it soon appeared that Hayes had a chance to win. South Carolina, Florida, and Louisiana, with nineteen electoral votes, emerged as disputed states. Conflict also developed in Oregon, where one Republican elector was ineligible because he was a federal officeholder. Eventually all four states submitted dual electoral returns to Congress. If the disputed electoral votes of all four were added to the Republican column, Hayes would win.

Unfortunately, there was no constitutional provision governing such a situation, nor was there any clear precedent for solving the problem. The Constitution stipulated merely that electoral returns were to be opened by the president of the Senate in the presence of both houses, and should then be counted. Did this mean that the president of the Senate had the right to count the votes and to decide between conflicting returns? If this contention, immediately advanced by the Republicans, was correct, it would presumably place Hayes in the White House, for Thomas W. Ferry, president of the Senate pro tem, was a Republican. However, the argument had little weight, for the president of the Senate had never in the past assumed to exercise any discretionary authority in counting the vote.

After some initial confusion, a joint Senate-House committee on January 18 reported a bill creating an Electoral Commission of Fifteen to decide all disputed returns. The commission was to be composed of five representatives (three Democrats and two Republicans), five senators (three Republicans and two Democrats), and four justices of the Supreme Court, who were to name a fifth justice. The four justices designated were those assigned to the first, third, eighth, and ninth circuits, which in reality meant Nathan Clifford, Stephen J. Field, William Strong, and Samuel Miller—two Democrats and two Republicans. It was generally understood that the fifth justice would probably be David Davis of Illinois, who was nominally a Republican but very moderate in his viewpoint. The bill provided that the commission's decision on all disputed returns should be final unless an objection were sustained by the separate vote of both houses.

Nearly all Democrats and most Republicans supported this proposal. The Democrats believed that the commission would settle at least one disputed return in their favor and so elect Tilden. This expectation was badly shaken when the Illinois legislature elected Davis to the Senate. As a result the fifth justice named was Joseph Bradley, who was a staunch Republican, and thus the Republicans controlled the commission by a count of eight votes to seven.

When the electoral votes were counted in joint session, the returns from the four states were all disputed and were, therefore, referred to the commission. The commission settled the dispute by refusing "to go behind the election returns." It held that it had power merely to decide what electors had been certified in the proper manner by the correct returning board, in accordance with the state law; and that it could not investigate the actual popular vote to determine whether the returning board had correctly counted that vote. The commission based this conclusion on the argument that each state under the Constitution was entitled to choose its electors as it saw fit. The federal government, the commission held, had no constitutional power to control this process, for to do so would be an intrusion upon the sovereign sphere of state authority. In accordance with this rule, the commission decided, by a vote of eight to seven in each instance, that the Republican electors in South Carolina, Florida, and Louisiana had been properly certified and that their vote was valid.

The Oregon case was more difficult, but the commission resolved it by deciding that under Oregon law the secretary of state alone was the properly constituted returning board and that he had originally certified the election of the three Republican electors. Thus the commission by a partisan vote of eight to seven decided every disputed return in favor of the Republicans. The House dissented from the commission's report in every instance, but the Senate concurred, and, therefore, the commission's decisions stood. Hayes was accordingly declared elected, 185 votes to 184, the final decision being formally reached on March 3, the day before the scheduled inauguration.

With some merit Democrats contended that the Republicans stole the election. Hayes electors were evidently "counted in" in Florida and Louisiana under heavy Republican pressure. The commission also made all its decisions by a straight partisan majority; plainly, the eight Republican members were concerned mainly with placing Hayes in the White House. But the charges of fraud were so difficult to sort out that there really was not time for a thorough investigation. Furthermore the commission's decision had a certain consistency in constitutional theory. The contention that federal authority over state choice was limited to fixing the identity of the electors lawfully certified by the legal state agency for this purpose had a great deal of force. Electors are technically state officials, and the Constitution does indeed give each state the right to choose its electors as it wishes.

To "go behind the returns" and subject a state election to scrutiny and analysis might well be considered an act of doubtful constitutionality.

Hayes's election marked the practical end of congressional reconstruction and federal control of the South. The Republicans had already lost control of the House, and the new president was a moderate who did not approve of continued federal interference in state affairs. Hayes at once withdrew federal troops from the three Republican-controlled southern states. The Democrats shortly assumed control in all of them, thereby bringing the Republican era in the South to a close.

Reconstruction and the Judiciary

If from the congressional and executive perspectives reconstruction policy effectively ended with the election of 1876, it persisted in constitutional law. Congress first shaped the public law of civil rights through constitutional amendment and legislation, but the Supreme Court had the last word as it confirmed and clarified changes emanating from the legislature.

The judicial history of reconstruction involves two separate considerations: the decisions of the Supreme Court in reconstruction-related cases, and the jurisdiction of the national courts as a critical feature in federalism. Decisionally, the Court recognized reconstruction as an essentially political question in which judicial intervention would be inappropriate. Maintaining a neutrality that was sympathetic to the congressional reconstruction program, the Court in its interpretation of the reconstruction amendments on the whole confirmed the moderate states'-rights nationalist outlook evinced in Congress. Jurisdictionally a similar nationalist pattern of change emerged. Although Congress was careful to guard its reconstruction policies against possible judicial obstruction, it relied heavily on judicial power in its southern program and significantly enlarged federal court jurisdiction.

The announcement of the Court's decision in *Ex parte Milligan* in April 1866 had given pause to congressional Republicans, and the publication of the opinion in the case in December provoked further apprehension. By ruling against military trial of civilians where civil courts were open, the Court appeared to jeopardize the protection of freedmen's rights by existing Freedmen's Bureau courts, and by military tribunals that Congress might create in the future. In January 1867, in *Cummings* v. *Missouri,* the Court again acted adversely to Republican interests. It struck down, as a bill of attainder and ex post facto law, a provision in the Missouri constitution of 1865 requiring voters, ministers, attorneys, and candidates for public office to swear that they had never engaged in rebellion against the United States, or given aid to rebels, or even expressed any sympathy for their cause. The same day, by an identical 5–4 margin, the Court in *Ex parte Garland* held the Federal Test Act of 1865, imposing a similar oath upon federal attorneys, unconstitutional on the same grounds. These decisions prompted sharp criticism of the Supreme Court, and in January 1868 the House passed a bill requiring a two-thirds vote of the Court in order to declare an act of Congress unconstitutional. The Senate, however, allowed the bill to die.

Meanwhile the Court, in *Mississippi* v. *Johnson* (1867), refrained from seizing upon a dubious opportunity to rule upon the constitutionality of the Congressional Reconstruction Acts of March 1867. In April attorneys for the Johnson government in Mississippi, then about to be replaced by a federal military administration, asked the Court to issue an injunction restraining the president from enforcing the two acts in question, on the ground that they were unconstitutional. This request was, to say the least, extraordinary, for although the Court, beginning with *Marbury* v. *Madison,* had several times held the executive to be amenable to judicial writ, the present petition was utterly unprecedented in that it asked the justices to interpose their authority directly against that of the president in his execution of an act of Congress. Attorney General Stanbery, appearing before the Court in response to the petition, called the request "scandalous" and in derogation of the president's properly constituted authority.

In a unanimous decision, the Court rejected Mississippi's plea. In an opinion that followed Stanbery's argument almost precisely, Chief Justice Chase drew a distinction between mere ministerial acts involving no discretion and large executive acts such as those carrying into effect a statute of Congress. The former, he said, could be enjoined; the latter involved political discretion and could not be. Such an injunction would amount to interference with the political acts of the legislative and executive branches of the government; defiance of it, Chase pointed out, would create an absurd situation.

In February 1868, in *Georgia* v. *Stanton,* the Court dismissed a similar suit in which the states of Georgia and Mississippi asked injunctions restraining the secretary of war and General Grant from enforcing the Reconstruction Acts. The suits, said the Court, involved proposed adjudication of political questions over which the Court had no jurisdiction. In February 1868, however, the Court consented to hear argument in *Ex parte McCardle,* a case arising in a Mississippi military tribunal, and carried on appeal under the authority of the Habeas Corpus Act of 1867. The case by implication involved the constitutionality of the Reconstruction Acts, since the appellant McCardle contended that the military tribunal which existed by virtue of the acts had no lawful authority.

When it thus became apparent that the Court might dare to declare the Reconstruction Acts invalid, the Republican majority immediately moved to end the possibility. In March, Congress passed a bill dealing with appeals in customs and revenue cases. Attached was a rider repealing the Supreme Court's jurisdiction in all cases arising under the Habeas Corpus Act of

1867. The rider was admittedly designed to kill the *McCardle* case. Johnson gave the bill a blistering veto, but Congress immediately overrode the veto. In April 1869, accordingly, the Court dismissed McCardle's plea on the ground that the new act had destroyed its jurisdiction in the case. Whether or not the justices had acted in part out of a sense of caution is uncertain; however, their constitutional position was entirely sound. As Chief Justice Chase pointed out in his opinion, the Court holds its appellate jurisdiction entirely at the discretion of Congress, so that it was no longer empowered to act.

That the Court had not in any undue sense capitulated to Congress became clear in October 1869 when it accepted jurisdiction in a similar case. Edward M. Yerger, arrested and tried by a military commission for killing an army officer, sought release from an army prison in Mississippi on a writ of habeas corpus. In light of congressional repeal of part of the Habeas Corpus Act of 1867, the question was whether the Court had jurisdiction. Chief Justice Chase held in the affirmative, on the ground that the repeal of the sections of the 1867 law under which McCardle's suit was brought left intact the still very substantial habeas corpus jurisdiction of the Supreme Court under the Judiciary Act of 1789. Although in the *Yerger* case the Court did not examine the validity of the detention, its response to the jurisdictional question showed a distinct sense of judicial independence.

Not because it was cowed, but because reconstruction was fundamentally a political question, the Supreme Court steered clear of pronouncements concerning the constitutionality of the Reconstruction Acts of 1867. In *Texas* v. *White* (1869), it expressed this point of view while endorsing the congressional theory of reconstruction. The case involved an action by the Johnson government of Texas to recover title to certain United States bonds formerly the property of the state but sold by the Confederate state government during the war. It offered an opportunity to pass on the status of both the Confederate and Johnson state governments, and hence to analyze theories of secession and reconstruction.

Chief Justice Chase first presented the orthodox Lincoln theory of secession. The United States, said Chase, was an indissoluble Union of indissoluble states. Hence secession did not destroy the state of Texas, nor the obligations of Texans as citizens of the United States. The pretended Confederate state government, though for some purposes a *de facto* government, was in its relations to the United States a mere illegal combination. Nevertheless, Chase reasoned, the war altered the relationship of the state to the Union. Its government refused to recognize its constitutional obligations, assumed the character of an enemy, and after the war ceased to exist. In consequence, Chase declared, "the rights of the State as a member, and of her people as citizens of the Union, were suspended." It had no government. Under the circumstances the national government—and Congress in particular—had to assume the responsibility for re-establishing the state's relationship with the Union. As congressional reconstruction theorists had done, Chase cited the opinion of the Supreme Court in *Luther* v. *Borden* that Congress had power under Article IV, Section 4, to guarantee republican governments in the states and to recognize the correct government in any state. Chase specifically refrained from expressing any opinion on the constitutionality of the Reconstruction Acts.

If it was proper for the judiciary to avoid pre-eminently political questions, it was necessary to settle conflicts concerning individual rights that involved the nature and scope of federal power under the new civil rights laws and constitutional amendments. In resolving questions of this sort, the Supreme Court played a major role in determining the long-range impact of reconstruction on the Constitution, as well as the lasting legal benefits of congressional reconstruction policy.

The earliest judicial interpretation of reconstruction civil rights legislation supported a broad view of national power. In 1867, for example, Chief Justice Chase, in the circuit court case *In re Turner* (1867), upheld the Civil Rights Act of 1866 under the Thirteenth Amendment in the course of striking down a Maryland apprenticeship law for blacks. In another circuit decision, *U.S.* v. *Rhodes* (1866), Justice Noah Swayne held the Civil Rights Act constitutional and interpreted the Thirteenth Amendment in sweeping fashion as a guarantee of free institutions, not merely a prohibition of chattel slavery. In litigation arising a few years later under the enforcement acts, federal judges exhibited a similarly extensive view of federal power. Thus in circuit court decisions Supreme Court Justices William B. Woods and William Strong upheld congressional power to legislate directly against private civil rights offenders when states, through inaction, denied Negro citizens equal protection of the laws.

By 1873 civil rights enforcement zeal was flagging, however, and judicial decisions reflected the changing northern outlook. The *Slaughterhouse Cases,* the occasion for the Supreme Court's first interpretation of the Fourteenth Amendment, revealed the moderate nationalist position that would characterize the Court's reconstruction decisions for the next decade. Asserting that the Fourteenth Amendment was intended to protect Negro rights, Justice Samuel F. Miller, for a 5–4 majority, dismissed the contention of a group of white butchers from New Orleans that a Louisiana law creating a monopoly in the slaughtering trade deprived them of rights of United States citizenship under the Fourteenth Amendment. Blacks were thus not directly involved in the case, but they would be affected by the Court's subsequent definition of Fourteenth Amendment rights. They would not be encouraged by what they heard.

Reviving the old dual-federalist point of view, Justice Miller described state and federal citizenship as basically separate. He said that national citizenship comprehended the relatively few rights arising from an individual's direct relationship with the federal government (e.g., the right to receive protection abroad, to engage in interstate and foreign commerce, to petition the national government). The other innumerable rights belonging to Americans as citizens in a free society were, in contrast, attributes of state citizenship. Explaining the principal ground of the decision, Miller said that acceptance of the argument against the Louisiana law would make the Supreme Court "a perpetual censor upon all legislation of the States, on the civil rights of their own citizens." Furthermore, if the Court could regulate the states in this manner, Congress could, too. The result would then be a revolution in federalism. Yet it was manifestly not the intention of Congress and the states in adopting the Fourteenth Amendment, Miller observed, "to transfer the security and protection of all the civil rights . . . from the States to the federal government." Rejecting the idea of a reciprocally reinforcing relationship between national and state citizenship, which had informed the congressional civil rights policy of 1866, Miller thus regarded state and national citizenship as fundamentally distinct.

In the next several years a series of decisions interpreted the reconstruction amendments and civil rights laws from the moderate states'-rights nationalist perspective. The Supreme Court's central purpose in these decisions was to vindicate federal power to protect civil rights, while maintaining the states' primary jurisdiction in regulating civil rights. In *United States v. Cruikshank,* for example, a circuit court case in which scores of Louisiana whites were indicted under the Enforcement Act of 1870 for conspiracy to deprive Negroes of their rights as United States citizens, Justice Joseph P. Bradley held that the Fourteenth Amendment authorized federal legislation only against state action denying rights. Under the Thirteenth and Fifteenth Amendments Congress could prohibit private denial of rights, Bradley reasoned, but only where the denial was motivated by racial hostility rather than ordinary criminal intent. Because the government's indictment of the Colfax rioters failed to specify their intention to deprive blacks of civil rights on account of race, Bradley found it invalid.

The Supreme Court affirmed this decision in 1876. Reiterating the state-action theory of the Fourteenth Amendment, Chief Justice Morrison R. Waite held that the amendment "adds nothing to the rights of one citizen as against another. It simply furnishes a federal guaranty against any encroachment by the States upon the fundamental rights which belong to every citizen as a member of society." Waite did not deny that Congress could punish private discrimination under the Thirteenth and Fifteenth Amendments. But he ruled the indictment invalid under the Thirteenth Amendment (and also the Civil Rights Act of 1866) because it did not expressly aver racial hostility as the basis for the denial of rights. In *United States* v. *Harris* (1883) the Supreme Court invalidated an indictment of whites for denial of Negro rights on the ground that the Ku Klux Act of 1871, the basis of the indictment, failed to respect the state-action limitation of the Fourteenth Amendment. The act was not framed, explained Justice

William B. Woods, so as to take effect only after it was established that states had denied civil rights. Rather, it punished private wrongs irrespective of state efforts in enforcing civil rights.

Similarly, in the *Civil Rights Cases* of 1883 the Supreme Court struck down the Civil Rights Act of 1875 because it was directed against private discrimination, not state action. Yet, though it was small consolation to blacks, the Court again recognized the possibility of federal legislation punishing private individuals under the Fourteenth Amendment on a showing of state failure to protect citizens against private wrongs. Justice Bradley also held in the *Civil Rights Cases* that under the Thirteenth Amendment Congress could legislate to protect the fundamental rights inherent in freedom, to abolish the "badges and incidents" of slavery. Yet regard for federalism required placing a limit even on this power to abolish slavery, in the sense of drawing a distinction between essential civil rights and social rights. Like his moderate Republican colleagues, Bradley rejected the contention that denial of equal access to public accommodations was a "badge" of slavery that Congress could prohibit.

In voting rights cases the Supreme Court also accommodated the retreat from reconstruction without surrendering to the conservative demand for a complete denial of federal power and restoration of antebellum federalism. Indeed, in this sphere the Court upheld extensions of national power more firmly than in the civil rights field generally. In *United States* v. *Reese* (1876), the leading case, the Court pointed out the obvious but important fact, clearly understood by its framers, that the Fifteenth Amendment did not confer the right of suffrage on anyone. It merely prohibited the states or the United States from excluding a person from the franchise because of race, color, or previous condition of servitude. The primary control of suffrage remained with the states. Accordingly, the Court threw out an indictment of a Kentucky voting official for refusing to count a Negro's vote, on the ground that the law on which the indictment was based, the Enforcement Act of 1870, did not in express terms restrict itself to racially motivated offenses. It unconstitutionally provided penalties for obstructing or hindering any person from voting in any election. With respect to state elections, Congress could only legislate against discrimination based on race, but it could direct its sanction against both state and private individual action.

The Waite Court affirmed more extensive federal power to protect voting rights in national elections. Initially in the early 1870s lower federal courts held that the right to vote in federal elections derived from state constitutions and laws. In *Ex parte Yarbrough* (1884), however, the Supreme Court declared that voters in national elections owed their right of suffrage to the federal Constitution, although it was necessary to consult state constitutions and laws to find out the qualifications for voting. The *Yarbrough* case was significant also for establishing federal power to protect the right to vote in national elections against private discrimination, whether racially motivated or not. In *Ex parte Siebold* (1880), *Ex parte Clark* (1880), and *United States* v. *Gale* (1883), the Court upheld convictions of state officers for fraudulent interference with national elections. Thus the Court in general affirmed federal power to guard the right to vote in state elections against racially inspired denial by either state officers or private individuals, and in federal elections against denial from any source and for any reason whatever.

Formal state discrimination against blacks, the reason for adopting civil rights laws and amendments in the first place, also came under the Court's ban. Thus in *Strauder* v. *West Virginia* (1880) the Court found a law limiting jury duty to whites to be in violation of the equal protection clause of the Fourteenth Amendment. In *Ex parte Virginia* (1880) it declared the action of a state judge in excluding blacks from jury service a violation of the Civil Rights Act of 1875. And in *Neal* v. *Delaware* (1880) it held that although a state's constitution and laws did not exclude blacks, the exclusion of Negroes from jury service in actual practice denied equal protection. Yet the Court undercut the force of these decisions when it ruled in *Virginia* v. *Rives* (1880) that the absence of Negroes from a jury did not necessarily mean a denial of right. By the cautious exercise of discretionary authority local officials could practically exclude Negroes.

The Court in the 1870s and early 1880s was hardly inclined to stop the retreat from reconstruction undertaken by the political branches and the northern public. Nevertheless, the Court generally confirmed the moderate nationalist view of the changes in federalism intended by the framers of the reconstruction amendments. And though most of the short-run consequences of the Court's decisions were practically debilitating for civil rights enforcement, the confirmation of national power, even if in doctrines and dicta that would not be employed for decades, prevented the adoption of the extreme conservative view that denied virtually any change in federal-state relations. The Court, like Congress, tried to fashion instruments for national protection of civil rights while, in deference to federalism, allowing the states to retain primary responsibility for the administration of justice in ordinary civil and criminal matters. As between these conflicting purposes, compromise was necessary.

The ultimate abandonment of the reconstruction equal-rights purpose came in the 1890s with the acceptance of the "separate but equal" doctrine by a very different Supreme Court. In *Plessy* v. *Ferguson* (1896) the Court found no constitutional objection to a Louisiana law requiring separate railway coaches for whites and blacks, provided that Negroes were furnished accommodations equal to whites. Formal racial classification, which the Court had earlier condemned, was thus legitimized, and was rapidly extended to schools and most other social institutions. In respect of political rights, too, the Court at this time acquiesced in southern disenfranchisement devices. In *Williams* v. *Mississippi* (1898) it approved a law authorizing literacy tests by which blacks could effectively be excluded from elections. In the same case the Court endorsed the poll tax as a valid prerequisite for the franchise. Yet even in the militantly racist atmosphere of the early twentieth-century reconstruction did not quite end. In 1915 the Supreme Court, in *Guinn* v. *United States,* struck down "grandfather laws" which disenfranchised Negroes by extending the franchise only to those whose ancestors had had the right to vote in 1866. And in 1917, in *Buchanan* v. *Warley,* the Court ruled unconstitutional municipal ordinances prohibiting blacks from moving into white neighborhoods. With this rejection of an official apartheid policy the equal rights story pointed ahead to the "Second Reconstruction" of the mid-twentieth century.

National Court Jurisdiction

If Supreme Court opinions during reconstruction frequently revealed an assertive independence, the legislation by which Congress marked out the scope of judicial power also expressed confidence in the national judiciary. In this technical and often pedestrian sphere of policy Republican lawmakers enlarged national power to overcome prewar incapacities borne of excessive concern with states' rights.

Removal of cases from state to federal courts was a major source of expanded national judicial power. As noted previously, this process began in the Habeas Corpus Act of 1863, which permitted removal from states to federal courts of civil and criminal cases involving all acts performed under orders by national officials. This bridge in the federal system was widened in the Civil Rights Act of 1866, the Internal Revenue Act of 1866, and the voting rights Enforcement Act of 1871. In these statutes removal was intended to facilitate the carrying out of substantive policies; in others expansion of federal court jurisdiction was the chief object. The most important of these measures was the Jurisdiction and Removal Act of 1875, which permitted removal in all suits arising under the Constitution, laws, and treaties of the United States; suits in which the United States was a plaintiff; suits between citizens of different states; and suits between citizens and aliens. The act also gave the lower federal courts original jurisdiction in all cases arising under the Constitution, laws, and treaties. Thus the old Federalist party objective of giving the national courts jurisdiction as broad as the Constitution permitted, expressed in the short-lived Judiciary Act of 1801, was finally achieved.

Another extremely important change in federalism was accomplished by legislation enlarging the habeas corpus jurisdiction of federal courts. The decisive statute for this purpose was the Habeas Corpus Act of February 5, 1867. Under the Judiciary Act of 1789 the writ of habeas corpus had application only to persons held under federal authority, in executive confinement. It could not, in other words, be used to secure release from state detention. The Habeas Corpus Act of 1867, however, broke down this barrier of state power. It made the writ available "in all cases where any person may be restricted of his or her liberty in violation of the Constitution, or of any treaty or law of the United States." Although in 1867 Congress repealed the part of the law that allowed the Supreme Court to review a lower federal court's disposition of a habeas corpus petition, federal courts retained the power under the act to review even the highest state court decisions.

Both for political and technical-professional reasons Congress altered the organization of the federal court system in the 1860s. Before the war five of nine judicial circuits comprised slave states exclusively. In order to reduce southern influence in the judicial system Congress in 1862 redrew the lines to put the slave states into three circuits. It also added a tenth circuit for the West Coast and increased the number of Supreme Court judges to ten. In 1866, principally on the advice of the Court itself, Congress reduced the size of the Court from ten to seven, effective with the next two vacancies (Justice Catron had died in 1865). It further changed circuit lines so that only one circuit, the Fifth, would consist exclusively of former slave states, and it reduced the number of circuits to nine. Additional reform occurred in 1869 when, with the Court numbering eight justices, Congress increased its size to nine and added nine circuit court judges to relieve Supreme Court justices of some of the burden of riding circuit. Shortly after passage of this act a Supreme Court vacancy occurred, and President Grant had two appointments to make. He named Republicans Bradley and Strong, and the augmented Court, reversing the decision in *Hepburn* v. *Griswold* (1870), upheld the Legal Tender Act of 1862 as constitutional in the *Second Legal Tender Cases* (1872). Democrats cried "court packing," but the charge was groundless, for Congress enlarged the Court mainly to give it an odd number of justices and eliminate tie votes.

The Constitutional Significance of Reconstruction

The enormous expansion of federal power since the New Deal, as well as the acceptance of the idea of racial equality in the mid-twentieth century, have made it difficult to appreciate the constitutional significance of reconstruction as it appeared to the Civil War generation. From their perspective reconstruction restored the states to a properly balanced federal Union, under rules and principles of equal rights that brought republican government to the former slave states and secured the liberty and basic civil rights of the freed blacks. From a late twentieth-century perspective, the restoration of federalism occurred at the expense of genuine black freedom and equal rights. If this difference in perception is inevitable and perhaps irrec-oncilable, it is nevertheless remarkable that in a society so strongly com-mitted to the idea of Negro inferiority the doctrine of equal rights found expression as fully as it did in the constitutional amendments and laws of the day.

The most significant constitutional change occurring between 1860 and 1880 was the extension of national power over personal liberty and civil rights through the Thirteenth, Fourteenth, and Fifteenth Amendments, the Civil Rights Act of 1866, and the Enforcement Acts of the 1870s. The corollary of this expansion of federal power was the destruction of state sovereignty and the curtailment of states' rights. No longer were the states autonomous in matters of individual rights. Civil rights were thus nation-alized. But only in limited ways did this nationalization employ the consti-tutional technique of centralization. States retained their primary responsibility and power to regulate civil rights. They did so, however, under national equal rights guarantees that gave the federal government a qualified but potentially effective power to protect the rights of American citizens. The twentieth-century liberal correlation of centralized national power and individual liberty owes much of its appeal to the accomplish-ments of the Union government in abolishing slavery and introducing equal rights principles into American constitutional law.

Nevertheless, by 1880 nationalizing civil rights energies were all but exhausted as northerners acquiesced in the restoration of conservative white rule and the end of federal intervention in the South. Changes in economy and society had, of course, continued to take place throughout the recon-struction period. These changes now became central issues in constitutional politics as Americans tried to adjust their still largely decentralized govern-mental system to the new social environment created by the industrial rev-olution of the late nineteenth century.

NINETEEN

Constitutional Change in the Era of the Industrial Revolution

♦ ♦ ♦

WITH THE END OF RECONSTRUCTION national economic development, a process that included the completion of continental expansion and the start of overseas imperialism, provided the central issues in constitutional politics. Although temporarily subordinated, questions of commercial and industrial policy had, of course, not ceased during the Civil War. Congress adopted banking, tariff, and internal improvements legislation in the 1860s, and the Supreme Court, in the important municipal bond case of *Gelpcke* v. *Dubuque* (1864), in effect announced that the national policy of publicly guaranteed promotional investment would be protected against state repudiation. Whether the Civil War itself stimulated or retarded economic growth, in the years after 1870 the United States was transformed from an agrarian republic into an industrialized and urbanized nation. Encouraged and sanctioned by laissez-faire ideas and conceptions of private property deeply embedded in the legal system, this transformation, in turn, had an enduring impact on the constitutional order.

In the first phase of the era of the industrial revolution, from 1860 to approximately 1880, constitutional institutions in many respects seemed inadquate to the demands placed upon them. "Spoilsmen" and "robber barons" sought payoffs and special privileges, causing corruption at all levels of government. Party leaders and operatives regarded politics as an opportunity for material gain, just like any other enterprise. Administrative competence and integrity often appeared nonexistent.

In the two decades after 1880, however, lawmakers, executive officers, judges, and party officials started to fill the void in governance caused by the staggering social transformations of the day. Although still deeply attached to localism and minimal government, they created new constitutional forms in an attempt to adjust the structure of government to the new environment. Party organizations became more disciplined and systematic at the national level as Congress, the bailiwick of top party leaders, re-formed itself internally. Under pressure from gentleman reformers and an aroused public opinion, Congress legislated reform in the federal civil service, reducing its own power over patronage and weakening its position in relation to the executive. Congress also adopted regulatory legislation aimed at railroads and large corporations, the key units in the nation's increasingly integrated economy. The constitutional system was still basically decentralized, but the Interstate Commerce Act of 1887 and the Sherman Antitrust Act of 1890 were decisive, if modest, exercises of sovereign national authority which anticipated the regulatory state of the twentieth century.

Americans thus tried to impose order on turbulent social conditions in ways that would preserve individual liberty and responsible constitutional government. In dealing with foreign-policy questions arising out of national expansion they attempted to apply liberal ideals under the old Jeffersonian notion of an empire of liberty. In pursuit of national interests the government imposed its sovereignty on, then tried to integrate into the polity, the nation's indigenous native American population. Simultaneously, it conquered overseas territories and proposed, at least in part, to extend to them the benefits of republican government. In each instance, however, serious internal contradictions resulted which transgressed the spirit of American constitutionalism.

Congressional Government

In 1885 the political scientist Woodrow Wilson pointed to the discrepancy between the theory of the separation of powers and checks and balances, and the actual constitution of government in which, he argued, Congress reigned supreme. Wilson, a southerner, exaggerated somewhat, but basically his description of the operative Constitution in *Congressional Government* was accurate. To begin with, at both ends of Pennsylvania Avenue a Whig theory of the presidency prevailed which denied the chief executive virtually all legislative influence. Presidents might continue to mention topics of potential legislation in their annual messages, but that was as far as their efforts were likely to go. Grant, Hayes, Garfield, Arthur, Cleveland, Harrison—all regarded the presidency as narrowly administrative. Accordingly, policy making belonged exclusively to Congress, whence originated the major legislation of the day.

Congress furthermore exercised broad administrative powers through its control of patronage and the fiscal process. Senators and representatives held dominant positions in the national party organizations and distributed thousands of federal jobs. And although presidents won a few spectacular battles over the patronage, lawmakers by and large retained control of it.

Congress also influenced administration by establishing close relationships between its committees and the executive departments. Congressional committees used their powers of investigation, legislation, and appropriation to curb executive discretion. Department heads had little leeway in managing agencies under their charge, and were forced to go to Congress for legislation to permit them to do even the smallest things. It would not be too much to say that the executive at this time functionally became a multiple rather than a unitary institution. Although a bill introduced in 1881 to allow department heads to hold seats in Congress was not adopted, it expressed the post–Civil War tendency toward congressional domination of the executive.

The most important congressional lever on administration was control over the Treasury. No federal budget existed as a tool of presidential power; not until 1921, after executive influence had grown considerably, would that administrative instrument be created. Federal budgetary policy in the Gilded Age, if it can be called that, consisted in Congress raising money where it could—principally through the tariff, internal revenue duties, and land sales—and spending it as the political process determined. Congress made item-by-item appropriations that kept the executive departments on a strict leash, and in particular prohibited the transfer of funds from one purpose to another and from one fiscal year to the next. In using its power over appropriations to influence administration, Congress was reacting to the broad executive discretion that had existed during the Civil War. But it was also demonstrating institutional tendencies characteristic throughout the nineteenth century. From the standpoint of twentieth-century public administration, Congress failed to recognize the distinction between legislative policy making and control of administration through legislation and fiscal oversight. Yet judged according to traditional values, especially those of decentralization and popular sovereignty, congressional government was constitutionally sound.

In a few dramatic contests presidents fought rear-guard actions to maintain the independence of the executive branch. When the Democrats controlled the House of Representatives in the late 1870s, they tried, through the device known as coercion by riders, to force President Hayes to abandon all forms of federal voting rights protection in the South. To routine appropriations bills they attached substantive measures, or riders, preventing the use of federal force to guard the polls. The tactic had been used before, but never so blatantly as to bring about a substantive change in policy. Hayes steadfastly opposed the practice, rejecting half a dozen such attempts over two Congresses until the Democrats gave up.

Hayes and his successor, James A. Garfield, also defended executive prerogative in administrative appointments. The decisive showdown involved members of the Republican party on the question of staffing the New York Customs House, perhaps the most important patronage assignment in the country. Stalwart Republican senators Orville H. Platt and Roscoe C. Conkling of New York figured to control the key post, as they had for years. But after losing out to an adamant Hayes, they resigned their Senate seats in an attempt to force the acquiescence of the next president, Garfield. Determined not to be what he called "the registering clerk of the Senate," Garfield refused to compromise and eventually prevailed in his choice of the New York customs collector. Finally, in less conspicuous holding actions, Democratic president Grover Cleveland vindicated executive power in the matter of removals. He forced Congress to repeal the Tenure of Office Act in 1887, and exercised the veto on hundreds of occasions to curtail the congressional practice of influencing administration by passing private bills.

The Nature and Tendency of Federal Governance

Congress not only dominated the executive branch, but it also, despite retrenchment after the war, continued an activist policy-making course. The nationalization of civil rights was the outstanding illustration of this tendency, but it had important parallels in government promotion of the economy. The creation of a national banking system, the Homestead Act, the Land Grant Act to promote education, upward tariff revision, and vast internal improvement projects including waterways, rivers and harbors, and railways—all reflected a neomercantilist federal policy of encouraging private economic development. Yet government in the Gilded Age was also administratively incompetent, irresolute, and ineffectual. Indeed, it was government weakness as much as capitalist greed that produced the excesses of corruption and exploitation that characterized public life at this time.

The corruption that afflicted American government in the Gilded Age is well known. It was no doubt caused in part by the social demoralization that occurred as wartime idealism turned into postwar cynicism. Constitutionally, however, the problem was rooted in the strategic place which political parties occupied in the governmental system. As they had since their inception, parties performed a constitutional function. They mediated between the people in the electorate and the formal institutions of government and coordinated the separate branches of government. During the Jacksonian era parties acquired greater significance as numerous appointive offices were made elective, rotation in office was instituted as a principle of administration, and government generally was brought closer to the people. Instead of becoming more deeply involved in government, however, the people ceded control to a special class of political professionals—the party managers and bosses. And this new class, acting like an economic interest group, routinely sought material advantage for itself. Politics was a way of

getting ahead in the society, and the principal commodity on which politicians traded was the privileges that government could make available for
economic development.

In the 1860s and 1870s party bosses more often clashed than cooperated with businessmen in an unstable and debilitating relationship. The
pursuit of narrow self-interest, in virtually every sphere, overwhelmed
whatever tradition of administrative and civil-service integrity was handed
down from the Federalist-Jeffersonian period. The federal role in the construction of the transcontinental railroads illustrates what has aptly been
described as "the weakened spring of government" in the Gilded Age.

In the 1860s Congress incorporated the Union Pacific Railroad Company and granted millions of acres of land to it and other railroads. In the
first place, the laws for promoting a national transportation system were
loosely drawn. They did not define the standards to be employed in supervising construction of the railroad nor clearly specify the rights and duties
of the corporations or the government. Government inspectors charged
with examining the progress of construction were irresponsible, turning in
reports prepared by company workers, for example, and hardly making a
pretense at criticism of defects. Lobbyist activity was nothing new in state
and national politics, but in relation to the railroad business it assumed a
new level of importance as a way of dealing with a capricious Congress.
What Congress gave with one hand it often took away with the other,
forcing rival corporations to pay dearly for needed subsidies and tax exemptions. The distribution of economic resources is always easier to accomplish politically than regulation of economic units or redistribution of
wealth. But in the Gilded Age Congress and the executive branch failed to
govern even in the limited sense of providing stable laws and even-handed
administration. For example, Congress created no territorial government
before it authorized the building of the Union Pacific Railroad. It only
organized Wyoming Territory in 1868 at the urging of the corporation. In
effect the territorial government became the property of the railroad company, with the U.S. Army on loan to it for its own private purposes.

Federal administrative weakness was apparent also in the enormous
task of transferring public lands to private corporations. Congress granted
millions of acres without establishing definite policies to control the process
by which railroad corporations claimed lands. Moreover, there were numerous laws under which land could be acquired, and these often worked at
cross-purposes and led to conflict. The General Land Office in the Interior
Department was equally remiss and incompetent in administering the
grants, with political partisanship counting more than administrative skill.
Usually, it took years for the government to give—or for the railroads to
secure—land patents. This was because both the government and the corporations had reasons to delay the patenting process, the former as a means
of bringing pressure to bear on the railroads to force compliance with con-

struction requirements, the latter as a way of avoiding state and local taxation on their lands. In a sense the genius of economic development in America had always lain in government-business cooperation, in the use of private interest and ambition to promote public purposes. But in the Gilded Age public administration, overwhelmed by the magnitude of the tasks assigned it, was so infirm and variable that both businessmen and the public at large demanded constitutional changes that would strengthen and stabilize government.

Political Parties in the Gilded Age

Among the institutions that to some extent filled the void in government in the late nineteenth century were political parties. A historically justified if not a theoretically necessary part of the constitutional order, the parties in the Civil War and early reconstruction era performed a programmatic as well as a constitutional function. Clear-cut differences in ideology between Democrats and Republicans led to bitterly contested policies on race relations and civil rights. In the 1870s, however, ideological politics gave way to a politics based on organization and discipline. Sharp policy differences faded as Republicans conceded home rule to the South and Democrats, at least in a formal sense, accepted the new national canon of Negro citizenship and set aside the race issue. The parties continued to differ on national questions such as the tariff and currency, with the Republicans in general favoring protective trade barriers and the gold standard and Democrats opposing them. But within each party there was considerable blurring of ideological lines and an unwillingness to make correct positions on these issues tests of party loyalty. Instead, party leaders shifted to a nonideological mode of party behavior and made loyalty to the organization itself the standard of good political conduct.

In the view of many critics, this devotion to party regularity lay at the root of governmental corruption in the Gilded Age. Considered within the republican civic tradition, the critique was not without merit. But party politics based on organizational discipline was not the purposeless and irrelevant activity that civil service reformers and many subsequent historians have made it out to be. The parties acted most constructively at the state and local level, where they expressed a wide range of ethnic and cultural concerns. Here significant differences between the parties appeared as issues such as prohibition, sabbatarianism, public support of religious schools, and English-language instruction in religious schools were dealt with.

The party of native American Protestant morality and pietism, Republicans were generally inclined to impose middle-class norms on people for their own and society's good through legislation and legal coercion.

Democrats were the dissenting party of liturgically oriented ethnic groups, most typically Roman Catholic and Lutheran. They resisted conformity to mainstream cultural standards and proclaimed individual liberty and opposition to government control as fundamental political values. National politicians avoided these volatile issues, which were local in nature, preferring to campaign on safer though hardly irrelevant economic issues such as the money question. By the same token, the tariff and currency were discussed in state and local elections, in which context, however, they carried cultural-symbolic meaning as much as practical economic significance.

Beyond their ethnocultural content, the oft-maligned "issueless" politics and party organizations of the late nineteenth century served the function of political socialization and education. The parties introduced both immigrants and native citizens to American political institutions and inculcated in them republican values. Sharing in the work of the party gave people a sense of belonging in both the local and national community. Moreover, participation in elections was extremely high, indicating a popular sense of effective representation through the party organization. The dense network of associations that made this representation effective provided opportunities for—or exacted a definite cost in terms of—financial peculation and corruption for the benefit of the party bosses. Yet it is possible, without romanticizing the work of party machines, to recognize the important function they performed in helping to meet the employment and welfare needs of immigrant and transplanted native workers in the hostile urban setting. Furthermore, parties played a mediating role in adjusting relations between government and new economic interests.

Parties not only provided a needed element of responsibility in a decentralized constitutional system, but they also encouraged order and stability in a society experiencing disruptive change in its economic and class relations. Parties oriented toward ethnocultural issues at the local level, and maintaining nonideological standards of party regularity at the national level, helped American society avoid destructive class conflict and the sacrifice of political liberty as it underwent industrialization. The development of disciplined party organization eased and anticipated the transition of the United States from a small-scale individualistic society to a more centralized and integrated social order.

Civil Service Reform

If parties served important governmental and social functions, they did not do so without costs and liabilities. Since the beginning of the republic, fear of corruption caused by the illicit interaction of government and private economic interests had been a staple of political rhetoric. The political scandals of the Gilded Age reactivated this fear and stimulated efforts to curtail the influence of parties by instituting reform of the civil service.

Civil service reform sought to improve public administration by making merit rather than political partisanship the criterion for government service. As articulated in the late 1860s, the goals of civil service reformers were to make government more efficient by eliminating waste and to elevate the moral quality of public life. From their position outside government, reformers saw the creation of a professional civil servant class as a means of breaking the parties' hold on government, maintained through their control of the patronage. It was believed that reform would also strengthen the presidency against the party-dominated legislative branch. Admiring of the British civil service, reformers regarded professionalization of government service as a means of restoring republican virtue against the corrupt alliance of spoilsmen and businessmen.

In an expression of good-government idealism and the postwar desire for retrenchment, Congress in 1871 authorized the president to alter the patronage system by making rules governing entrance into the federal civil service. President Grant, a supporter of reform, appointed a Civil Service Commission which drafted rules establishing competitive examinations for government workers at the lowest level and requiring promotion based on merit. Predictably, the commission's actions antagonized congressional and party leaders, who by cutting off its meager appropriation effectively killed it in 1874. Nevertheless, civil service reform continued to be a major source of controversy. Identifying their position with the republican tradition, opponents of reform attacked it as aristocratic and antirepublican. They also argued that it was unconstitutional, on the ground that it gave effective power over government appointments to a board of examiners rather than to the president. Defenders of civil service reform also claimed to be upholding republicanism, stressing its public-virtue rather than its populistic aspect.

By 1881 a National Civil Service Reform League existed, and public opinion was more favorably disposed toward the merit system. An important asset was the support of many businessmen. Grown weary of the costly struggles made necessary by the demands of political spoilsmen, businessmen regarded civil service reform as a way of curbing the power of the politicos and forming more stable business-government relationships. The decisive impetus for reform, however, came from the assassination of President Garfield in 1881 by a rejected office seeker. This event provoked a strong public demand for reform and led Congress, by large majorities and in a bipartisan manner, to pass the Pendleton Civil Service Act in 1883.

The Pendleton Act provided for the creation of a bipartisan three-member Civil Service Commission, to be appointed by the president with the advice and consent of the Senate for an indefinite period of time, subject to executive removal. The commission was authorized to make rules for competitive examinations to determine qualified candidates for appointment to the federal service. The act required the departments to classify a certain number of jobs, protected these positions against political interference, prohibited campaign assessments from federal employees, and established a nonpartisan system of advancement based on merit. Constitutionally, the act strengthened the president vis-à-vis the legislature by giving him authority to extend the classified civil service by executive order and by taking some patronage away from the party managers in Congress.

The act of 1883 classified about 14,000 of 100,000 federal jobs. In the next decade defenders of the patronage system tried to negate the effect of the reform while civil service reformers pressed for its extension. Presidents generally dealt with these cross-pressures by adding a number of jobs to the classified list at the end of their term, thus protecting the positions against replacement by the other party and enlarging the number of nonpolitical appointments. By 1900 about 86,000 jobs, approximately half the federal work force, were covered by civil service regulations.

The key constitutional idea behind the Pendleton Act was the belief that public administration was a separate and distinct phase of government that could be divorced from politics. In a modest and indirect way it represented an attempt to adjust government to the new social and economic environment by taking a controversial political problem and subjecting it to a bureaucratic solution outside the political arena. Improved methods of appointment to government service, Woodrow Wilson subsequently observed, were significant as a prelude to more extensive and substantive political reforms. By "establishing the sanctity of public office as a public trust," Wilson wrote, civil service reform started the process of making government more "businesslike" and capable of performing the complex functions required of it by commercial expansion and the growth of powerful corporations.

Toward National Economic Regulation

Despite the fact that it served constructive purposes, postreconstruction politics, in the opinion of increasing numbers of groups and individuals in the society, failed adequately to meet the demands of the new industrial age. Businessmen were among those who desired reform in government and politics. To be sure, businessmen in the Gilded Age received subsidies and other privileges, but politicians made them pay dearly through bribes and other corrupt schemes. Dissatisfied with the situation, many businessmen in the 1870s and 1880s attempted to stabilize and rationalize their segment of the economy by forming voluntary associations outside the formal governmental and party structure. Pooling arrangements among railroads, the organization of trusts in manufacturing and marketing enterprises, and other trade and commercial associations were intended to regulate market conditions.

Despite their difficulties, businessmen in their dealings with government were well off compared to groups that had almost no access to public policy makers. The most visible of these virtually unrepresented groups were workingmen and farmers. The 1880s was a period of intense struggle in the labor movement as the Knights of Labor and later the American Federation of Labor tried to organize workers for self-protective and market-regulatory purposes. Eschewing conventional political organization and action, labor groups utilized the economic instruments of strikes and boycotts in pursuit of protective, prolabor legislation and collective bargaining with employers. Meanwhile, farmers pursued political action outside the established party structure. The Granger, Greenback, and Antimonopoly third-party movements of the 1870s illustrated this tendency and anticipated the Populist party of 1890–96. The Populist attempt to reform government for the benefit of agriculture in turn rested on a broad base of private voluntary associations, the Farmers' Alliances of the 1880s.

As these and other groups (e.g., prohibitionists) organized themselves for regulatory and reform purposes, the nation's political institutions began to change in ways that eventually facilitated the establishment of a more stable and cooperative relationship between government and the functional units of the national economy. One indication of this change was the substantial decrease, after about 1880, in bribes and payoffs from businessmen to politicians. Another was the introduction of the practice whereby corporations made regular contributions to the parties and corporate leaders themselves increasingly entered politics. A more constructive, less adversarial relationship between political parties and the business community was the result.

Moreover, the parties, instead of remaining loose coalitions of state and local machines, became more highly centralized, efficient, and influential at the national level. After 1885, for example, the party caucus became a decisive force in the conduct of business in the Senate. The caucus determined membership of the committees that shaped legislation, controlled the order of legislative business, achieved compromises in bill drafting, and enforced discipline in voting. In the House of Representatives a similar centralization of power occurred, chiefly through the strengthening of the Speakership. Under the regime of Republican Thomas B. Reed of Maine as Speaker, party discipline and regularity acquired decisive influence. Reed ended the tactic of refusing to answer a roll call and then raising the plea of "no quorum" as a device for blocking House business. In 1895 he was responsible for the adoption of a permanent rule against filibustering. The Rules Committee, including the Speaker and the chairmen of the powerful Ways and Means and Appropriations Committees, acted as a steering committee and established the order of business that often determined the fate of legislation. By 1900 these internal reforms made Congress more nearly a national forum to which interest groups in the society could appeal.

Furthermore, by the mid-1880s government regulation of the economy, at least in certain critical respects, was coming to be recognized as necessary. Nor did it require a radical sensibility to reach this conclusion. In calling for the study of public administration to meet "new conceptions of state duty," Woodrow Wilson wrote in 1887: "Even if our government is not to follow the lead of the governments of Europe in buying or building telegraph and railroad lines, no one can doubt that in some way it must make itself master of masterful corporations." In the early nineteenth century the requisite control of business enterprise had been achieved through the use of public-purpose corporations created by state legislatures. After general incorporation laws were adopted in the 1840s, private corporations proliferated and regulation by specific charter modification was no longer feasible. More systematic regulation—by general statute prohibiting certain business practices or by creation of an administrative commission—became the means of asserting the necessary degree of public control over the economy.

In a constitutional order committed to private property, entrepreneurial freedom, minimal government, and localism, it was difficult to create and employ coercive instruments of national economic regulation. To do so was to revive mercantilist forms of governance, with potentially consolidating, centralizing effects. Moreover, to do so while retaining the ideal of laissez faire and limited government created a distinct paradox. Yet this was what Americans did in the late nineteenth century.

Although national economic regulation objectively ran counter to classical liberal ideology, its purpose paradoxically was to restore the self-regulating, nonpolitical mechanisms of the free market. Demanded by an aroused public opinion, government regulation was intended to promote the public interest by keeping corporations from gaining excessive power through unfair business practices. At the same time, however, regulation was often intended to benefit businessmen. Clearly, the movement for government regulation of the economy was not anticapitalistic in spirit. In fact, throughout the history of national economic regulation, key business groups have supported government regulation, usually as a means of rationalizing and stabilizing market conditions. Government regulation has often been an adjunct of, and has provided a sanction for, industrial self-government.

Inherent in government regulation, therefore, was a tension between the "public interest" that has dominated the politics and rhetoric of the regulatory movement and the needs of private interests that have often been the object of government intervention in the economy. No objective calculus has ever existed for measuring the extent to which these possibly conflicting interests are served. The judgment is inevitably a subjective political one, with public and private needs sometimes seeming to be compatible and at other times contradictory. In any event, consistent with the American tradition of employing private means to accomplish public ends. government regulation was intended to combine both restrictive and promotional purposes in relation to capitalist enterprise. These dual purposes, appropriate to a people wedded to laissez-faire norms yet prepared to use government power, were evident in the earliest federal regulatory measures, the Interstate Commerce Act of 1887 and the Sherman Antitrust Act of 1890.

Railroad Regulation: The Interstate Commerce Act of 1887

Railroads and manufacturing corporations were the principal concern in the first era of national economic regulation, but they presented different problems and were dealt with in different ways. In the railroad industry the problem was excessive competition. The generally desired solution was to stabilize pooling or market-sharing and rate-setting arrangements. The problem with large corporations was monopolistic power, and here the desired solution was to revive competition by breaking up the combinations that corporations formed.

Railroad companies were capable of wielding monopoly power, and often did so to the detriment of farmers, businessmen, and others whose shipping needs depended on them. When this happened, excessively high rates were the result. Aggrieved interests accordingly demanded regulation in the form of government determination of maximum fair rates, either by administrative fiat or action of the state legislature itself. In the 1860s and 1870s these conditions led to the formation of so-called "strong" railroad commissions with rate-setting powers in ten midwestern states. At the same time in other states, mainly in the East where railroads were an older and more established part of the economy, legislatures created railroad commissions that had investigatory and publicity powers but no rate-setting ability. Referred to as "weak" commissions, these were advisory bodies which sought to restrict railroads when appropriate. In the main, however, they existed to promote the interests of the railroads by encouraging a stable and predictable relationship with the public and its government. This was also considered to be in the public interest.

A direct result of the new economic forces, the railroad question became a national political issue in the 1880s. It ceased to be a state-defined matter because state regulation was incapable of dealing with it. Under existing constitutional law, states could regulate commercial activity within their jurisdiction through the police power, and under certain circumstances could impose restrictions of an incidental or minor nature on interstate commerce. Plainly, however, with railroads crossing several states, intrastate regulation would mean dozens of different rate structures with no rational organization on a nationwide basis. By the mid-1880s the inadequacy of state regulation was evident. Several states, therefore, abolished their rate-setting commissions, in part because of an adverse effect on new rail development. In 1886 the Supreme Court made national legislative action constitutionally imperative when, in *Wabash, St. Louis, and Pacific Railway Company* v. *Illinois,* it struck down an Illinois law prohibiting long-short haul rate discrimination as an intrusion on the federal commerce power.

Railroad legislation had for several years been introduced into Congress, and political support from a variety of sources existed for the adoption of some form of regulation. In 1886, however, the main problem was not high rates but rather excessive competition that led to rate wars and generally unstable conditions damaging to the railroads and to the public. Railroad corporations tried unsuccessfully to regulate themselves through pooling arrangements, whereby in competitive situations traffic and earnings were shared. What many of the railroads wanted was a government commission to assist in organizing a system of industrial cooperation that would eliminate destructive competition and stabilize market conditions and rates. In other words, government should sanction pooling, or railroad cartels.

Public opinion was on the whole willing to accept cartelization. Yet there were aspects of the railroads' operations that complicated the picture and pointed in a different direction. The most important of these was the practice of charging different rates for long and short hauls, so that it was sometimes as expensive to ship freight 100 miles as 1,000 miles. This was outright discrimination, and although the practice was the key to the railroads' ability to charge lower rates generally, it imposed unfairly high rates on shippers in certain cities and regions. Discrimination of this sort seemed to flow directly from the railroads' great power, and it stimulated in the public mind the familiar fear of monopoly. Related to it were other abuses such as rebates. This was the practice of secretly refunding to a shipper a portion of the established rate for a given haul. From the "public interest" or popular standpoint, then, shaped as it was by antimonopoly zeal, what was needed was prohibition of pooling and long-short haul discrimination. This position was strengthened by the existence in several states of a certain amount of case and statutory law prohibiting collusive pooling agreements as a restraint of trade.

The Interstate Commerce Act of 1887 combined these conflicting purposes. For some time the House of Representatives, under the leadership of Texas Democrat John H. Reagan, favored a law that would prohibit pooling and long-short haul discrimination. The Senate, led by Republican Senator Shelby Moore Cullom of Illinois, preferred a bill that would create a commission and, by ignoring pooling and long-short haul rate making, implicitly approve these practices. The act that Congress passed in 1887 was a compromise between these two approaches. It provided at the outset that all charges for rail transportation in interstate commerce should be reasonable and just, and declared unjust charges illegal. It did not attempt to define a reasonable and just rate. In its antimonopoly features the law prohibited pooling of traffic or earnings, rate-fixing agreements, rebates and other forms of preferential treatment, discriminatory rate agreements, and long-short haul discrimination. On the other hand, the act implicitly invited collusion among the railroads by requiring the announcement of uniform rates from which it was illegal to deviate, and by not prohibiting the railroads from setting rates.

Moreover, the act did not really ban long-short haul rate-making. Section 4, dealing with this issue, stated that under substantially similar conditions it was unlawful to charge more for a shorter than a longer haul. But then it declared that in special cases railroads could apply to the Interstate Commerce Commission and receive authority to discriminate in this manner. This was obviously a major exception, and although the law did not say so explicitly, it was intended to allow railroads to retain long-short haul rate setting for discriminatory purposes while eliminating it when it led to undue competition. The Senate demanded this concession before it would approve the bill. Also expressing the cartelizing purpose of the railroads and their supporters in the Senate was the five-member advisory commission created by the act. The Interstate Commerce Commission was given powers to hear complaints, inquire into the records and accounts of railroads, compel attendance of witnesses, and issue cease and desist orders against practices or actions violating the law. The commission was not given rate-setting powers, either originally or after declaring an existing rate unjust and illegal.

Its inconsistency of purpose notwithstanding, the Interstate Commerce Act was constitutionally significant for creating the first permanent federal administrative agency with a combination of functional powers. The commission had certain functions similar to those of a court—namely, the holding of hearings, the taking of evidence, and the handing down of decisions which had the effect of court orders. Its administrative orders had the effect of law and were quasi-legislative in character. In the main, however, the quasi-executive nature of the ICC stood out. Members of the commission were appointed by the president, and their duty was to enforce the law. The commission had no final authority to enforce its orders, which were reviewable and enforceable in federal courts, and it had no rate-setting power, pre-eminently a legislative power. The ICC was looked on chiefly as an advisory, information-gathering body intended to mediate between the government, especially Congress, and the railroads.

Under the leadership of its first chairman, the noted jurist Thomas M. Cooley, the Interstate Commerce Commission tried within the limits of the act to promote coordination of the railroads and mediate between the industry and the public. In an important early decision it allowed railroads to suspend Section 4—the prohibition of long-short haul discrimination—when in their opinion market circumstances warranted it. The railroads thus retained the key rate-making power on which the ability to avoid destabilizing competition depended. The Supreme Court confirmed this policy in 1897 in its interpretation of Section 4 in the case of *I.C.C.* v. *Alabama Midland Railway Company.*

In other respects the Supreme Court impaired the powers of the ICC, though not in ways that defeated the congressional purpose in passing the 1887 law. After a few years the commission concluded that it had an implicit power to fix rates, derived from its power to declare existing rates unreasonable. In *Cincinnati, New Orleans, and Texas Pacific Railway Co.* v. *Interstate Commerce Commission* (1896) and *Interstate Commerce Commission* v. *Cincinnati, New Orleans, and Texas Pacific Railway Co.* (1897), the Court denied this contention. It held that exercise of the rate-fixing power, essentially a legislative power, by an executive-administrative body violated the separation of powers. This ruling was consistent with existing constitutional theory, which prohibited delegation of legislative power to the executive, and with the congressional decision not to give the ICC rate-setting power. In *Interstate Commerce Commission* v. *Alabama Midland Railway Co.* (1897), the Court weakened the fact-finding power of the ICC by holding that circuit courts, as courts of equity hearing appeals from the orders of the commission, could investigate anew all facts in every case.

The Supreme Court frustrated the purposes of the Interstate Commerce Commission more seriously in its antitrust decisions under the Sherman Act of 1890 than in its interpretation of the Interstate Commerce Act. Owing to their character as quasi–public utilities with heavy fixed capitalization costs, railroads were pretty much forced by economic realities to form cartels. Accordingly, in the 1890s, with ICC approval, they continued to enter into pooling agreements (called rate bureaus) in an attempt to stabilize and coordinate their operations. In *United States* v. *Trans-Missouri Freight Association* (1897), however, the Supreme Court declared these arrangements restraints of interstate commerce in violation of the Sherman Antitrust Act. The Supreme Court was more inclined to a laissez-faire perspective than to the cartelizing outlook of the ICC, and its decisions ended the legal limbo in which pooling and other forms of voluntary self-regulation had existed for years. When railroad legislation appeared on the progressive agenda a few years later, Congress moved to strengthen the powers of the ICC so that it could more effectively promote railroad cartelization.

The Sherman Antitrust Act of 1890

If antimonopoly attitudes received partial expression in the Interstate Commerce Act, they were more clearly evident in the regulation of business enterprise in general. For here the problem was domination of the market by a small number of powerful corporations which by various methods of combination eliminated competition. Sometimes the combination took the form of price- or rate-fixing agreements, or allocation of production and pooling and prorating of profits. In the 1880s, moreover, businessmen devised new legal instruments for promoting economic consolidation and national market control. The first of these, the trust, was an organization to which participating corporations in an industry turned over their stock, in turn receiving trust certificates. This scheme was designed to avoid state laws prohibiting corporations from holding the stock of other companies or owning property outside the state. The holding company, the second instrument of corporate combination, was a corporation authorized by a state to gain control of out-of-state (i.e., foreign) corporations by acquiring their stock or purchasing their assets with stock issued for that purpose.

The holding company was invented and first sanctioned by the state of New Jersey in the late 1880s as a way of averting successful legal action such as had been undertaken against the trust form of organization in several states. Although the trusts were unprecedentedly large, legal precedents were available for dealing with them. Trusts were made up of corporations, in law artificial persons created by the states. Under existing constitutional law, state legislatures had undisputed authority to regulate them by means of the police power. Corporation charters defined the structure of the corporation and the nature and scope of the activities it was permitted to engage in. If a corporation exceeded its powers, states could take legal action against it under the doctrine of *ultra vires*. States could also exclude foreign corporations seeking to do an exclusively intrastate business within their borders. In all of this exercise of the police power, however, states were concerned with production or manufacturing, not marketing in other states. The latter subject legally formed a part of interstate commerce and was beyond the competence of the individual states. To put it another way, the federal commerce power pertained only to marketing arrangements involving the transport of goods in interstate commerce, not to the structure of a corporation as a productive enterprise. That was a matter for the states to regulate.

In general, states did not choose vigorously to exercise their regulatory powers to restrict corporations in the post–Civil War era because they wanted to encourage economic development. In the 1880s, however, the creation of a handful of powerful trusts able to control the entire national market in a given industry produced a strong public reaction and spurred a series of antitrust legal actions in several states. Louisiana, New York, California, Nebraska, Illinois, and Ohio successfully prosecuted the sugar, whiskey, oil, and other trusts on the ground that constituent firms had violated state laws prohibiting corporations from restructuring themselves and abdicating control of their operations. The Supreme Court, moreover, had long upheld state power to regulate corporations by means of the *ultra vires* doctrine. It confirmed this power in *Central Transportation Co.* v. *Pullman's Palace Car Co.* (1890), where it negated a monopolistic contractual agreement by which one corporation acquired the business of another. In this political and legal setting Congress took up the problem of trust regulation in 1888.

The initial approach favored in Congress, expressed in a bill of Republican Senator John Sherman of Ohio, was federal regulation of both manufacturing and marketing activities of corporations producing goods for interstate commerce. The underlying rationale of this proposal was that the trusts, not incorporated in any state and hence beyond the ability of the states to regulate, were ipso facto obstacles to interstate commerce which only Congress was competent to control. There were constitutional objections to this point of view, however, for it disregarded the distinction long recognized in constitutional law between commerce, or the transport and marketing of goods in the national economy, and manufacturing. It also ignored recent efforts in the states to attack the trusts under the *ultra vires* doctrine. For both of these reasons the Senate Judiciary Committee amended Sherman's bill to make it apply only to marketing activities in the sphere of interstate commerce.

As adopted on July 2, 1890, the Sherman Antitrust Act was expressly intended to protect trade and commerce against unlawful restraints and monopolies. It declared illegal "every contract, combination in the form of trust or otherwise, or conspiracy, in restraint of trade or commerce among the several States, or with foreign nations." Combining or conspiring to monopolize interstate or foreign commerce was declared a misdemeanor, punishable by $5,000 fine and one year imprisonment. The act was to be enforced by the Justice Department under the equity jurisdiction of federal courts, and persons with grievances against corporations could also bring suit to enforce the law.

The decision to restrict the scope of the Sherman Act to restraint of trade in marketing activities was not, as has sometimes been suggested, a pro-business maneuver intended to render the law ineffectual. On the contrary, there were numerous abuses carried on by the trusts in the marketing or interstate sphere—including exclusive dealing contracts, price discrimination, and agreements to divide markets—which serious reform would eliminate. Another frequently misunderstood issue is whether the framers of the Sherman Act intended categorically to prohibit all combinations in restraint of trade. Although the language of the law suggested as much, the intent of Congress was to adopt the antimonopoly definitions and rules of the common law, and these did not absolutely condemn all combinations. Instead, under a standard of reasonableness (later called the rule of reason), the common law prohibited mergers and combinations that resulted in substantial control of a market and that depended on unfair trade practices.

Because large corporations were economically and socially productive in providing goods and services that people desired, Congress did not intend to outlaw them per se. Indeed, viewed historically, corporate integration appears as an inevitable stage in the development of large-scale industries in all capitalistic economies. Hence the antitrust law would not apply against combinations that were the result of superior efficiency in an open and competitive market.

Congress chose the traditional method of statutory restriction and judicial enforcement to regulate corporations, in contrast to the bureaucratic commission method employed in railroad regulation. Because railroads were viewed as a kind of public utility, their market activities seemed to warrant exceptional treatment in the form of more direct administrative supervision. Corporate enterprise on the other hand, though assuming vast proportions, was dealt with in a more legally orthodox fashion. The intention was to eliminate the distorting forces impinging on the market so that it could again become self-regulating.

In the famous sugar trust case, *United States* v. *E. C. Knight Co.* (1895), the Supreme Court implemented antitrust policy by upholding the congressional distinction between manufacturing and commerce. It did so on the theory that the states would move against the trusts, or at least that their power to do so ought to be preserved. The case involved a suit brought by the government for dissolution of the American Sugar Refining Company, on the ground that contracts that it made with constituent corporations to control more than 90 percent of all refined sugar in the United States constituted a substantial restraint on commerce among the states. The government's case was weak, however, because it was directed not at the kind of unfair marketing activities that the Sherman Act was concerned with, but rather at the structure of the company as a productive enterprise.

The opinion of the Supreme Court, given by Chief Justice Melville W. Fuller, rejected the government's claim. Fuller admitted that the combination constituted a trust to monopolize the manufacture of sugar, but held that it was not on that account illegal. For the trust was in manufacturing, not interstate commerce, and the Sherman law was aimed only at combinations in the latter field. Fuller drew a further distinction between direct and indirect effects on commerce. If a trust or monopoly had a direct effect on commerce, then presumably it was subject to federal regulation. Combinations in manufacturing might tend to restrain interstate commerce, but the restraint would be an indirect result. "Slight reflection will show," Fuller said, "that if the national power extends to all contracts and combinations in manufacture, agriculture, mining and other productive industries, whose ultimate result may affect external commerce, comparatively little of business operations and affairs would be left for state control."

The Supreme Court's decision in the *Knight* case has often been criticized for introducing what later appeared to be an artificial distinction between manufacturing and commerce. It was true, however, that a broad interpretation of the Sherman Act would have expanded federal power at the expense of the states' ability to control the trusts by regulating corporate structure. If the Court had accepted the argument that manufacturing and commerce were as one under federal jurisdiction, the trusts would be protected against state laws prohibiting foreign manufacturing companies from exercising franchises within their borders. Although it is not generally understood and was not everywhere perceived at the time, the holding companies that proliferated in the 1890s as an alternative to the trusts were subject to legal attack in the form of state prosecution of their constituent corporations for exceeding their chartered powers. The Supreme Court decision in the *Knight* case preserved this power at a time when it appeared likely still to be used by the states for reform purposes.

The conjoint federal-state antitrust strategy that underlay the Sherman Act failed not because of the Supreme Court's decision in the sugar trust case, but because the states chose not to break up the trusts and holding companies. The decisive factor was the relationship between economic conditions and public policy. The states might proceed against the trusts, as several had in the years 1887 to 1890. But while this was politically satisfying in promoting the republican ideal of dispersal of power, it did not solve the economic problems states faced in regard to tax revenues, employment, and industrial productivity. New Jersey was the first state to embrace the new monopolistic entities, permitting holding companies to organize in the state under its law of 1889. A decade later other states were imitating New Jersey in an attempt to lure revenue-producing corporations within their jurisdictions. Economically and politically, it proved impossible to destroy the large concentrations of economic power that the trusts represented, and they acquired *de facto* legitimacy in the period 1895 to 1905 as the basis of an integrated national economy. In the future, national economic regulation would increasingly, though not exclusively, take the form of federal administrative supervision of giant corporations as quasi-independent states or private governments.

Imperialism and Federal Indian Policy

Industrialization not only enlarged the role of the federal government in domestic affairs, but it also contributed to foreign-policy developments that raised significant constitutional questions about the nature of the United States as a national community. Although it no longer involved foreign nations, continental expansion continued to present the intractable problem of the status of the nation's indigenous Indian population. Irresistibly advancing since the seventeenth century, the westward movement culminated in the 1890s in the destruction of tribal sovereignty among the

Indians, who two generations earlier had been driven from the eastern states and forcibly settled on the Great Plains. Expansionism took a more explicitly colonial form after the Spanish-American War when the United States acquired overseas territories and faced the problem of assimilating foreign populations in the republic. Given the consensual, noncoercive basis of republican government, could the nation incorporate subject peoples to whom it denied the rights of citizenship and political equality? The imperial impulse of the late nineteenth century, as seen in federal Indian policy and the decision to annex foreign territory, made this a pertinent issue in constitutional politics and pointed to an internal contradiction in the traditional idea of republican expansionism.

Since the seventeenth century the status of the Indian tribes of North America and their relationship to white society had been a vexing problem. To the English settlers the Indians were a heathen and alien people to be dealt with by war, conquest, and treaty negotiations. After the Revolution the United States government continued the British practice of regarding the Indian tribes in a legal sense as foreign nations with whom treaties could be made. By the 1830s, however, the clash of cultures between Indians and whites was so one-sided, due to the latter's superior numbers and technology, that the notion of the tribes as autonomous foreign nations could no longer be sustained. Accordingly, the Supreme Court, in *Cherokee Nation* v. *Georgia* (1831), modified the traditional doctrine by declaring that the Indian tribes in the United States were "domestic dependent nations." Chief Justice Marshall further stated that the Indians were "in a state of pupilage" and occupied a relationship to the federal government like that of "a ward to his guardian." The tribes enjoyed a right of possession of the land, but the United States asserted a title to the territory independent of the Indians' will. In a political and diplomatic sense, Marshall concluded, the Indians were "under the sovereignty and dominion of the United States."

Although the treaty-making fiction persisted, starting in 1830 the federal government exercised its sovereignty over the eastern tribes by removing them to the interior of the continent, to a vast area on the Great Plains known as the Indian Country. The removal policy was intended to preserve Indian civilization by eliminating all contact with whites. White encroachment on and aggrandizement of Indian lands were irresistible, however, and eventually destroyed the internal or local sovereignty which the government had always permitted the tribes to exercise. This process of internal subjugation occurred in stages. In 1871 Congress weakened tribal authority by declaring that henceforth the government would make no further treaties with the tribes, but would instead enter into agreements. For a number of years thereafter Congress made no attempt to substitute any external authority for the declining authority of the tribal chiefs. As a result, serious problems of law and order emerged among the Indians. At length, under pressure from critics and reformers, Congress adopted an assimilation policy in which the government exercised the power of local sovereignty. At the same time, on the model of freedmen's rights, the government attempted to integrate the Indians into the civil order on the basis of equal citizenship.

As members of tribes legally defined as domestic dependent nations, Indians, like slaves in the antebellum period, were regarded neither as aliens nor citizens, but rather as subjects of the United States. Despite the fact that American citizenship was birthright citizenship, and that Indians had been born in the United States, they were not regarded as citizens under the Fourteenth Amendment. As tribal authority disintegrated and pressure increased on Congress to deal with the problem of internal governance, a corresponding movement developed to confer citizenship on the Indians. The Supreme Court made congressional action on both of these questions imperative when it held that the United States had no jurisdiction over crimes committed by Indians against each other, and that Indians who voluntarily left their tribe were not citizens of the United States.[1]

In response to the Court's decisions, Congress in 1885 extended over Indian tribes living on reservations federal criminal jurisdiction with respect to major crimes such as murder, larceny, rape, arson, etc. In 1887 Congress dealt with both the law-and-order problem and the question of Indian citizenship in the Dawes Act. The key measure in the new integration policy, the Dawes Act provided for the allotment of tribal land to Indians in severalty—that is, on an individualistic basis—with a view toward destroying the tribes and transforming Indians into private-property owners. Indians who took allotments were to be subject to the civil and criminal law of the state or territory in which they resided, and were to be guaranteed equal protection of the law. The Dawes Act also granted citizenship to Indians who received land allotments, and to those who had voluntarily left their tribe. Indians remaining in tribes were still excluded from citizenship.

The policy of integration reached a climax in the 1890s with the destruction of the Indian territory, the unorganized land west of Arkansas where the Five Civilized Tribes had dwelt since the removal of the 1830s. Congress extended federal civil and criminal jurisdiction to this area, displacing tribal authority; it also introduced the land-allotment system provided for in the Dawes Act. In 1890 Oklahoma Territory was organized in that part of the Indian land where white settlement was heaviest. In 1907, expanded to include all of the former Indian Country, Oklahoma entered the Union. Meanwhile, Congress completed the process of Indian enfranchisement. In 1901 it conferred citizenship on Indians living in the Indian territory; in 1919, on those who served in the armed forces during World War I; and in 1924, on all other Indians who had not yet been accorded the status.

1. *Ex parte Crow Dog* (1883); *Elk* v. *Wilkins* (1884).

Long before 1924, however, it was clear that the policy of Indian as-similation was a failure. Mulcted of their lands by whites, most Indians remained resistant to cultural assimilation. Furthermore, the promise of citizenship and equal protection of the law, for all the good intentions that went into it, proved equally misconceived. Indians who left the reservation became a nearly helpless minority in the larger society, while those who stayed came under the often corrupt and arbitrary rule of the government's Indian agents. Humanitarian friends of the Indian believed at the time that the allotment and integration policy proceeded too slowly, but in actuality it appears to have been implemented too rapidly: the cultural conflict was far more profound than policy planners realized. At any rate, by the 1920s the failure of assimilation caused the pendulum to swing back toward the no-tion of tribal autonomy and local self-government. This became the focal point of federal Indian policy in the New Deal period.[2]

Overseas Imperialism

Simultaneously with its attempt to assimilate native Americans, the United States acquired a colonial empire. Between 1898 and 1900, Puerto Rico, the Philippines, Guam, and Hawaii became territorial possessions of the United States. In its practical effects this imperialistic undertaking, like late nineteenth-century Indian policy, posed the question of whether a re-public could legitimately govern alien peoples against their will.

The acquisition of overseas territories stimulated an intense public de-bate between imperialists and anti-imperialists which had a strong consti-tutional component. Supporters of colonialism argued that the United States as a sovereign nation possessed the power to acquire new territory by purchase, treaty, or war. They reasoned further that the United States could govern its territories as it saw fit, without the promise of statehood or guar-antees of constitutional protection. These benefits might be granted, but they were not constitutionally required. The anti-imperialists contended on the other hand that to govern alien peoples without their consent violated the spirit of American constitutionalism. Reflecting the dominant racial assumptions of the day, opponents of colonial annexation insisted that the inclusion of alien colored peoples in the national community—which in their view the Constitution would require should colonies be obtained—would destroy the cultural unity on which the republic rested. The anti-im-perialists made much of the slogan "the Constitution follows the flag." Their main concern, however, was to keep both Constitution and flag from being deployed abroad.

In 1899 the Senate ratified the peace treaty with Spain that concluded

2. See below, p. 633.

the Spanish-American War. It thereby committed the nation to a colonial policy and resolved the constitutional dispute about the acquisition of foreign territory in favor of the imperialists. A few years later litigation arising out of the specific provisions made by Congress for governing the nation's overseas possessions led to a more precise definition of their constitutional status.

The first of the so-called insular cases, *DeLima* v. *Bidwell* (1901), dealt with the collection of import duties on sugar coming from Puerto Rico. The owners of the sugar sued for recovery of the duties on the ground that Puerto Rico was no longer a foreign country, but part of the United States. The Supreme Court agreed, holding that as a result of the treaty with Spain the island was not a foreign country within the meaning of the tariff laws. The duties in question had, therefore, been collected unlawfully. In *Downes* v. *Bidwell* (1901), however, the Supreme Court reversed itself—or refined its position. It decided that special duties on other imports from Puerto Rico, collected in accordance with the Foraker Act of 1900 for the government of the island, were constitutional.

The Supreme Court defined a middle position on the question of whether, in the rhetoric of the imperialist versus anti-imperialist debate, the Constitution followed the flag. In essence the justices held that the Constitution protected the inhabitants of colonial possessions in their basic civil rights, but did not confer citizenship or political rights on them. Justice Brown for the majority and Chief Justice White in a concurring opinion both acknowledged the power of Congress to acquire territory, determine its status, and govern it. The inhabitants of annexed territories could claim no right of American citizenship. Yet colonial peoples, said Justice Brown, were not completely subject to the unrestrained power of Congress; they were not totally beyond the protection of the Constitution. There were "natural rights enforced in the Constitution," Brown explained, such as the right to personal liberty, property, religious freedom, and freedom of speech. These rights were indispensable to free government and beyond the power of Congress to deny anywhere. Chief Justice White similarly noted general prohibitions in the Constitution favoring liberty and property that imposed an absolute limitation on Congress under any circumstances. The Constitution thus applied to annexed territory. But the *extent* to which it applied, said White, depended on whether the territory had been incorporated in the United States.

White derived his doctrine of incorporation from debate over territorial annexation at the time of the Louisiana Purchase. In the manner of most judicial formulas that are intended to provide a basis for compromise, it was imprecise or ambiguous on crucial points. White did not specify, for example, in what incorporation consisted or how it occurred. Fundamentally, however, it meant extending to aliens the privileges and immunities of citizenship, in effect admitting them to the national political community. If a territory was incorporated, it enjoyed the full range of constitutional protection; if it was not, then only the basic guarantees of personal liberty and civil rights were available.

With respect to Puerto Rico, the treaty with Spain expressly stated that Congress would determine the political status of its inhabitants. The island was, therefore, not incorporated, and the constitutional requirements concerning uniform duties throughout the United States did not apply. Deferring to the congressional view of the constitutionality of annexation, the Supreme Court thus confirmed overseas imperialism.[3] Nevertheless, the justices tried to reconcile colonialism with republican principle by describing a sphere of minimal rights belonging to persons in the territories. The status which the Court accorded territorial inhabitants—an anomalous intermediate position between citizenship and alienage—appears similar to the status assigned to Negroes by Chief Justice Taney in the *Dred Scott* case.[4] Yet the Court believed its resolution of the imperialist question was far more liberal and humane than its predecessor's resolution of the question of Negro rights. In words that paraphrased Taney's famous dictum in the *Dred Scott* case denying Negroes any rights, Justice Brown said the Court rejected "the theory that they [i.e., inhabitants of annexed territories] have no rights which [the government] is bound to respect."

In subjugating the Indian tribes and creating an overseas colonial empire the United States pursued its national interest in the manner of a great power, without impediment from constitutional limitations. The Supreme Court confirmed the judgment of contemporary politics that it was legal for the government to acquire and govern colonies. Whether colonial rule was constitutionally legitimate, however, was another matter which admitted of no easy answer. Critics of imperialism denied that it was, arguing that a republic, by definition, could not govern others without their willing consent. The supporters of overseas expansion believed colonial rule to be consistent with the Constitution. Yet in some degree they seemed to acknowledge the force of the critics' argument in their assertions of civil rights and promises of equal protection of the law for colonial inhabitants.

Events showed these promises to be empty gestures, the tribute that political expediency paid to constitutional virtue. Yet in view of the enormous cultural differences between the United States and its territorial possessions, and considering also the pronounced racism of the age, what is

3. In subsequent cases the Court applied or refused to apply provisions of the Bill of Rights to territorial possessions according to its judgment of whether the territory had been incorporated. It held that grand-jury indictment and trial by a twelve-man petit jury were not constitutionally required in Hawaii or the Philippines, which were found not to be incorporated, but were required in Alaska, which had been incorporated. Cf. *Hawaii* v. *Mankichi* (1903); *Dorr* v. *United States* (1904); *Rasmussen* v. *United States* (1905); *Dowdell* v. *United States* (1911).

4. Cf. above, p. 279.

perhaps most surprising is the imperialists' optimistic assumption that the benefits of constitutionalism could be extended to alien peoples. As the imperialist burden increased, the United States withdrew from direct colonial rule and permitted greater degrees of self-government in its territorial possessions. Eventually most of them secured national independence or statehood. In other areas of American foreign policy, however, belief in the exportability of constitutional liberty continued to play a significant role in the twentieth century.

TWENTY

The Supreme Court and Entrepreneurial Liberty

—————————— ✦✦✦ ——————————

TOWARD THE END OF THE NINETEENTH CENTURY the federal judiciary assumed an increasingly important role in American government, adopting an activist, interventionist posture that has generally continued to the present day. Since the time of John Marshall, federal and state courts had in varying degree been involved in political controversy and had participated in the making of public policy. Although the Supreme Court on only two occasions declared acts of Congress unconstitutional, the legitimacy of judicial review was well established. Except in times of political crisis, judicial resolution of constitutional questions was accepted as authoritative and conclusive. Still, the courts did not possess a monopoly over constitutional interpretation. During the Civil War and reconstruction, moreover, the Supreme Court, though by no means passive, yielded to the president and Congress in the settlement of major constitutional controversies. As economic issues became more prominent in the 1870s, the Court persisted in its traditional role. Mainly concerned with federal-state relations, it balanced state regulation of business enterprise against federal protection of an increasingly integrated national economy.

In the late 1880s, however, the Supreme Court began to respond more directly to the social and political pressures of the emerging industrial order. In doing so it helped to fill the void in governance that the new economic forces created. Fearing social upheaval, the federal courts accepted a broad conception of property rights and a forthright responsibility to prevent radical change. Employing Jacksonian Democratic ideas of equal rights and entrepreneurial liberty for conservative purposes, the Supreme Court boldly exercised the power of judicial review against state and federal regulatory legislation. More specifically, it gave a substantive economic interpretation to the due process clause of the Fourteenth Amendment which differed sharply from its original equal rights purpose. The upshot was the fashioning of what was in effect a new and more potent instrument of judicial review. In a series of key cases in the 1890s the Supreme Court wrote into constitutional law doctrines of property rights and entrepreneurial liberty that would be used for a generation to organize and protect the new system of industrial and finance capitalism.

States' Rights and Economic Regulation

During reconstruction, as previously noted, federal courts mediated between the states and the federal government in matters of civil rights. Much the same concern for federal-state balance was evident as well in questions unrelated to reconstruction. In the case of *Collector* v. *Day* (1871), for example, the Supreme Court held that the salary of a state official was protected against federal income tax assessment. Invoking dual federalism, the Court declared that the states and the federal government were separate and distinct sovereignties, and that in their reserved powers the states were as sovereign and independent as the federal government.

Under the broad latitude allowed them by the Supreme Court, many states actively used the police power to regulate corporate behavior and commercial activity in general in the 1870s. Although corporations were a useful means of stimulating capital investment which had long benefited from state promotional policies, they represented potentially dangerous concentrations of economic and political power. By the 1870s the railroads in particular provoked old republican antimonopoly fears and were the object of regulatory legislation in several midwestern states. Yet there were limits to the states' regulatory power. The doctrine of natural rights was axiomatic in American political theory, and under it private property was inextricably linked with individual liberty and protected against governmental interference. In the late eighteenth century, as noted earlier, the doctrine of vested rights was absorbed into constitutional law as an alternative expression of natural law liberty and property rights. The vested rights doctrine limited government in the form of the contract clause of the Constitution, when it was not interpreted simply as an inherent characteristic of republican government.

In the mid-nineteenth century the vested rights idea began to be associated with the guarantee of due process of law in state and federal constitutions. Historically, in Anglo-American law the guarantee of due process referred, as the term itself suggested, to procedures that protected persons against arbitrary punishment. It secured the right to be protected against arrest without a warrant, the right to counsel, the requirement of indictment by a grand jury before trial, the right of the accused to hear the nature of the evidence against him, and so forth. In other words, it was significant primarily in criminal cases, and meant that if the government was going to deprive a person of liberty or property for committing a crime, it had to follow certain steps in doing so. In a few instances in the Civil War era, however, courts gave what came to be called—however contradictorily—a substantive interpretation to the due process clause as an absolute limitation on legislative action for the defense of property. In this view due process meant, as the doctrine of vested rights before it had meant, that there were certain things that government—especially the legislative power—could not do, no matter what process or procedure it followed. And in the three cases in which substantive due process was broached—*Wynehamer* v. *New York* (1856), involving a state prohibition law; *Dred Scott* v. *Sandford* (1857), involving the Missouri Compromise Act; and *Hepburn* v. *Griswold* (1870), involving federal legal tender legislation—what the government was prevented from doing was to deprive persons of property. During reconstruction the due process clause of the Fifth Amendment was written into the Fourteenth Amendment, and in the early 1870s legal arguments began to be heard interpreting the Fourteenth Amendment as a safeguard of property and economic liberty against state interference.

When this point of view was first presented, and for many years thereafter, the Supreme Court rejected it and expressed basic approval of state regulatory legislation. The landmark decision on this question was the *Slaughterhouse Cases* of 1873. At issue was a law of Louisiana that in effect conferred a monopoly of the slaughtering business in New Orleans and banned all other slaughterhouses already established in the city. Some of the businesses affected brought suit in the Louisiana courts, asserting among other things that the law in question was a violation of the Fourteenth Amendment. The Supreme Court of Louisiana, however, held that the law constituted a legitimate exercise of the police power of the state and thus upheld the constitutionality of the act. An appeal was then taken to the Supreme Court of the United States.

The chief claim of the appellants was that the legislation abridged the privileges and immunities of United States citizens, as protected by Section 1 of the Fourteenth Amendment. As previously noted, the Court rejected this claim on the ground that the rights in question were attributes of state rather than national citizenship. The Fourteenth Amendment, said Justice Miller, did not change the fact that the fundamental rights of civil liberty that citizens possessed under republican government remained within the jurisdiction of the states. More to the point in the present context, the New Orleans butchers had argued that the right to labor and pursue a trade was an aspect of property as well as liberty. They contended that the state law deprived them of liberty and property without due process of law as guaranteed in the Fourteenth Amendment. The Court simply dismissed this contention with the observation that "under no construction of that provision that we have ever seen, or that we deem admissible, can the restraint imposed by the state of Louisiana ... be held to be a deprivation of property within the meaning of that provision." In other words, the Court accepted without debate the procedural interpretation of due process.

To accept the interpretation of the Fourteenth Amendment advanced against the Louisiana law would have produced a revolutionary shift in the federal-state balance which the Court was plainly unwilling to permit. Rejecting the argument that the Louisiana statute denied equal protection of the laws to the butchers, Justice Miller for the Court presented the Negro-rights theory of the purpose of the Fourteenth Amendment. By implication, the amendment had done nothing to disturb or restrict the power of the states to regulate private-property interests within their boundaries. Four justices dissented, however, and three of them approved the substantive application of the Fourteenth Amendment—especially the due process clause—to economic issues. Justice Bradley wrote: "A law which prohibits a large class of citizens from adopting a lawful employment . . . does deprive them of liberty as well as property without due process of law." Yet it is important to note that the dissenters Bradley and Justice Stephen J. Field, who also adopted the more comprehensive view of the Fourteenth Amendment, were not seeking to promote a policy of big-business expansion. On the contrary, they objected to the state law as class (i.e., special) legislation intended to benefit a single corporation. Theirs was an equal rights, antimonopoly attitude, sympathetic with the three hundred butchers who were in effect denied the right to practice their trade.

Four years later the Supreme Court handed down another major decision upholding state regulatory power in *Munn* v. *Illinois* and the related *Granger Cases*. The *Munn* case arose out of an act passed in 1873 by the Granger-controlled legislature of Illinois fixing the rates for the storage of grain in warehouses located in cities of 100,000 population or more. The only city in Illinois of that size was Chicago, and the law was in reality aimed at preventing abuse of the monopoly which the elevator operators had succeeded in establishing over the grain elevator business at the mouth of the Chicago River. Some nine different elevator firms were engaged in business in this vicinity; yet the uniformity and exorbitancy of their rates indicated clearly that the various firms constituted a near-monopoly.

The elevator operators shortly attacked the constitutionality of the statute in the Illinois courts, asserting that the act constituted an infringement upon the power of Congress to regulate interstate commerce and that it violated the due process clause of the Fourteenth Amendment. The decision of the Illinois Supreme Court was favorable to the constitutionality of the act, and an appeal was then taken to the Supreme Court of the United States.

The *Granger Cases* had a similar origin. A number of Granger-controlled western legislatures, among them those of Wisconsin, Iowa, and Minnesota, had enacted statutes fixing rail rates within the states. The railroads had attacked the constitutionality of these statutes in the courts of the several states. The issue here was the same as that in *Munn* v. *Illinois,* and the Court, therefore, settled these cases by direct reference to the former decision.

The Supreme Court in the *Munn* case, in an opinion of Chief Justice Morrison R. Waite, upheld the Illinois law as a legitimate exercise of the police power, even though it had an incidental effect on interstate commerce. Waite began with an analysis of the police power, which the courts since Taney's time had defined as the inherent sovereign capacity of the several states to legislate for the health, safety, morals, and welfare of the community. He rested his argument both upon the nature of constitutional government and upon an appeal to history. He quoted the constitution of Massachusetts, which describes the body politic as "a social compact by which the whole people covenants with each citizen, and each citizen with the whole people." From this it followed that the social compact authorized "the establishment of laws requiring each citizen to ... so use his own property as not unnecessarily to injure another." This was an old common law doctrine which Waite now invoked to support police power.

Chief Justice Waite defined the extent of the state's regulatory authority by asserting that private property devoted to a public use was subject to public regulation. "When, therefore," he said, "one devotes his property to a use in which the public has an interest, he, in effect, grants to the public an interest in that use, and must submit to be controlled by the public for the common good." Waite quoted the seventeenth-century English jurist Lord Chief Justice Hale as authority for the public interest doctrine. But his decision was solidly built on a large body of nineteenth-century American case law in which state courts had held that bridges, ferries, railroads, navigable streams, and riparian property were regarded as having a public interest, and hence were subject to regulation under the power of eminent domain as well as the police power.

Waite's opinion also illustrated the traditional conception of judicial review that prevailed in the nineteenth century. Having explained the public-interest doctrine, Waite asked whether the facts concerning the grain elevators justified the state legislation. Accepting the evidence presented in the case describing the businesses in question, Waite declared: "For our purposes we must assume that if a state of facts could exist that would justify such legislation, it actually did exist when the statute under consideration was passed." Waite continued: "For us the question is one of power, not of expediency.... Of the proprietary of legislative interference within the scope of legislative power, the legislature is the exclusive judge." It was the proper function of the judiciary, in other words, to determine whether the power in question was a legitimate constitutional power. If it was, the manner or extent of its exercise was a political question beyond the competence of the judiciary. The Court thus presumed the constitutionality of the legislation.

In a further expression of judicial restraint, Waite said that while property clothed with a public interest was entitled to a reasonable compensation, it was for the legislature to decide what was reasonable. Waite acknowledged that this power was subject to abuse. But he asserted that for protection against legislative abuse the people must turn to the polls, rather than the courts. Finally, Waite said that while the Illinois law had an incidental effect on interstate commerce, it was principally a local regulation and was valid until Congress should act in regard to the interstate commerce aspect of the situation.

Justice Field, dissenting, argued for a substantive conception of the due process clause. Field opposed the Illinois law, but not because he was categorically opposed to governmental restrictions on business. Seeking to draw a fixed line between private rights and public power, he based his dissent on the fact that the grain elevator firms were not corporations but strictly private enterprises. Had they been corporations, acting under legislative charter with special privileges, they would have acquired a public character making them subject to government regulation. If the legislature wished to regulate unincorporated ordinary trades and businesses, Field reasoned, it must do so by means of the power of eminent domain, in which case, however, it must provide compensation for the injury to or the taking of property. Undoubtedly, Field looked less favorably on government regulation of business than his fellow justices. He tried to prevent the application of the police power, which did not require compensation if it caused injury to property, for regulatory purposes dealt with previously under the power of eminent domain, which did. But he was no apologist for the new corporate giants. Although dissenting from the majority opinion in the *Granger Cases,* for example, Field agreed that railroads as chartered corporations possessed a public interest that rendered them subject to legislative control. He rejected the majority view in this case that railroads were merely agents of the state. The difference between Field and the Waite Court majority concerned where the line should be drawn between the public and private sectors. According to Field, the logic of the *Munn* decision would permit the legislature to bring every business enterprise under its regulatory supervision, a course that he believed dangerous to liberty.

Judicial Protection of the National Market

At the same time that the Supreme Court sanctioned intrastate economic regulation, it took steps to bring an increasingly integrated national market under the protection of federal authority. In a few instances decisions were based on conflict between a state law and superior national legislation, but most of the time the Court held that the commerce power of its own force precluded state regulation. These decisions, spanning the period 1873 to 1890, worked a serious alteration in federal-state relations by restricting the previously unquestioned ability of the states to tax and inspect goods passing in interstate commerce.

In *Philadelphia and Reading Railroad Company* v. *Pennsylvania* (1873) the Court struck down a tonnage tax on freight originating out of state as an unconstitutional regulation of interstate commerce.[1] Especially important in removing obstacles to the national marketing structure that emerged after the Civil War was the case of *Welton* v. *Missouri* (1875). Using its taxing power to protect local manufacturers, Missouri had imposed a license tax on persons selling products manufactured out of state, but not on those selling locally produced goods. The Supreme Court ruled this tax unconstitutional as a restraint on interstate commerce. Justice Field explained for the Court that the federal commerce power protected articles of commerce until they ceased to be the subject of discriminatory legislation directed at their foreign origin.

The *Welton* case protected new marketing techniques that depended on direct dealing between manufacturers and local retailers. States responded by imposing a license fee on sales agents representing out-of-state manufacturers who did not have a regularly licensed local business. In *Robbins* v. *Shelby County Taxing District* (1887) the Court invalidated this kind of tax, too, as a burden on interstate commerce. State power to pass inspection laws meanwhile seemed unassailable. Yet when used to exclude out-of-state shipments of meat prepared by the new national packing companies, inspection laws were also declared unconstitutional. The Court so held in *Minnesota* v. *Barber* (1890), as it struck down a state law that prohibited the sale of meat that had not been inspected by state officials within twenty-four hours before slaughter. While these decisions supported economic expansion, in eliminating unfair discrimination between local and out-of-state businessmen they also promoted equal rights values. Moreover, the decisions reflected the willingness of the Court to adapt constitutional law to changing social and economic circumstances in a flexible, pragmatic way.

Related to the Court's protection of the national market was its concern for national transportation and communication facilities. *Pensacola Telegraph Company* v. *Western Union Telegraph Company* (1877) illustrated this concern. The case involved a conflict between the Pensacola Company, claiming exclusive state-granted privileges of operating a telegraph business in the northern part of Florida, and the Western Union Company, claiming to operate under an act of Congress. The federal law, adopted in 1866, gave any company the right to construct and maintain telegraph lines through any portion of the public domain of the United States, under conditions prescribed by Congress. The Supreme Court upheld the Western Union Company on the basis of this statute, which it said prohibited all state monopolies in this new field of interstate commerce. A decade later, as noted in a previous chapter, the Court in the *Wabash* case struck down

---

1. However, when Pennsylvania taxed the gross receipts of railroads, the Court approved the tax even though part of the railroads' revenues came from interstate commerce.

legislation setting rates between Illinois and points outside the state as a
violation of the commerce clause.[2] Yet the Court was by no means doctrinaire in upholding national authority and a broad conception of commerce.
This was apparent in the distinction it maintained between commerce and
manufacturing. Thus in *Kidd* v. *Pearson* (1888) it permitted a state to prohibit the manufacture of liquor for shipment outside the state as not inconsistent with the federal commerce power.

Toward a Conservative Jurisprudence

Starting in the late 1880s, the changes that were transforming American social and economic life found clearer and more prominent expression
in constitutional law. By the end of the century the federal judiciary
emerged as a key defender of corporate property interests, negating or
counteracting state and federal regulatory legislation through the use of an
expanded power of judicial review. The Court's new outlook was not immanent in its earlier doctrines and attitudes, but rather was shaped by
political events and changes in the Court's membership that reflected
changes in American society.

New justices were appointed who by social background and professional experience in the law were familiar with and sympathetic to the
needs of railroads, corporations, and the entrepreneurial class in general. By
1890 seven of the justices who had participated in *Munn* v. *Illinois* had left
the Court: Nathan Clifford, Ward Hunt, William Strong, Morrison R.
Waite, Noah H. Swayne, David Davis, and Samuel F. Miller. They were
replaced, after 1877, by John Marshall Harlan, Horace Gray, Samuel
Blatchford, David J. Brewer, and Henry B. Brown—all property-minded
Republicans—and conservative Democrats Melville W. Fuller, who was appointed chief justice by Cleveland in 1888, and Lucius Quintus Cincinnatus
Lamar. In 1894 Cleveland appointed Edward D. White, a Louisiana sugar
planter, and in 1895 Rufus W. Peckham, a conservative New York attorney,
as associate justices.

Major outbursts of industrial violence and agrarian protest occurred in
the late 1880s and 1890s which alarmed large numbers of Americans and
raised the specter of social revolution. In this situation the new justices were
concerned with the stability of the existing order in ways that their predecessors had not been. They were receptive to doctrines long advanced by
corporation lawyers to prevent government economic regulation—doctrines
limiting the scope of the police power, for example, and enlarging the
sphere of entrepreneurial liberty protected under the concept of due process
of law. These doctrines were extensions or elaborations of traditional con-

2. See above, p. 384.

cepts of liberty, property, and negative or limited government which were fundamental in American political thought, and which throughout most of the nineteenth century, in the environment of material abundance that Americans enjoyed, promoted republican liberty and equality for most people. In the rapidly changing social order produced by industrialization, however, these laissez-faire doctrines protected inequalities of wealth and power that in the view of an increasing number of people undermined republican values. The American political and social order was beset with serious internal contradictions which it became the task of twentieth-century reform to eliminate.

Fundamental constitutional changes occur slowly, and it is possible to discern a gradual acquiescence to conservative, probusiness constitutional doctrines in the years after reconstruction. In the interpretation of the due process clause of the Fourteenth Amendment, for example, the dissents of Justices Field and Bradley in the *Slaughterhouse Cases* may be seen as auguring the inevitable triumph of laissez-faire constitutionalism. Other decisions of the Supreme Court seem to point in the same direction. Thus in *Loan Association* v. *Topeka* (1875), in striking down a state law authorizing municipalities to issue bonds to support a private bridge company, the Supreme Court said there were limitations on the legislative power: a law that took property from A and gave it to B would be void. A few years later, upholding a city ordinance levying an assessment on landholders to pay for the drainage of swampland, the Court in *Davidson* v. *New Orleans* (1878) stated that under extreme circumstances a law transferring property from one party to another would be a violation of the Fourteenth Amendment. Commentators have seen ominous portent also in Chief Justice Waite's admission, in the Mississippi rate case of *Stone* v. *Farmers Loan and Trust Co.* (1886), that a state could not require a railroad to carry passengers or freight without reward, or take private property for public use without just compensation or due process of law.

Yet in each of these decisions the Court upheld the state regulation, or, as in the *Topeka* case, struck down a state law that was favorable to private economic interests. In the 1880s the results of most cases challenging state regulatory legislation gave little encouragement to businessmen. What appear to be doctrinal concessions to lawyers' continued iteration of substantive due process arguments were unexceptionable expressions of limits on legislative power lying at the core of American constitutionalism. Nor was there special significance in the fact that in 1886 the Supreme Court accepted the idea that the corporation was a person in the sense of the Fourteenth Amendment. Corporations had enjoyed standing to sue under federal diversity jurisdiction since the 1840s,[3] and the Court had been hearing cases involving corporations under the Fourteenth Amendment for

3. See above, p. 237.

several years. Thus the Waite Court offered slight comfort to economic interests seeking national protection under the Fourteenth Amendment against state regulation.

Nevertheless, there were signs in the late 1880s, especially at the state level, of changing judicial attitudes toward government-business relations. In 1885 the New York Court of Appeals, in the case *In re Jacobs,* struck down a New York law restricting the manufacture of cigars in tenement houses on the ground that though purporting to be an exercise of the police power, in reality it arbitrarily deprived a cigar maker of liberty and property in violation of the New York constitution. While the decision did not involve the Fourteenth Amendment, the New York court's reasoning was similar to the argument for an economic interpretation of the due process clause as a protection of liberty and property. The next year the Pennsylvania Supreme Court invalidated a state law prohibiting mining and manufacturing companies from paying workers in other than lawful money or scrip. According to the Pennsylvania court, the law interfered with employers' and employees' liberty of contract. Here was further hostility toward legislative controls on business that might also be expressed through the language of the Fourteenth Amendment.

In a case of 1887, *Mugler* v. *Kansas,* the U.S. Supreme Court gave notice of a less trusting and more scrutinizing attitude toward state regulatory legislation. While rejecting the contention that a Kansas prohibition law was a deprivation of property without due process of law as required by the Fourteenth Amendment, Justice John Marshall Harlan for the Court majority declared that exercises of the police power would not automatically be accepted at face value as constitutional. "The courts are not bound by mere forms," Harlan said. "They are at liberty—indeed are under a solemn duty—to look at the substance of things, whenever they enter upon the inquiry whether the legislature has transcended the limits of its authority." If a law based on the police power and purporting to protect the health, welfare, safety, and morals of the community had no real or substantial relation to those objects, Harlan stated, but instead invaded constitutional rights, the Court would declare it unconstitutional. In the *Mugler* case the Court upheld the state legislation, yet the decision was in actuality consistent with the jurisprudential outlook described by Harlan. For rather than presume the constitutionality of the Kansas statute, Harlan took cognizance of the fact, "within the knowledge of all, that the public health, the public morals, and the public safety may be endangered by the general use of intoxicating drinks."

In 1890 the Supreme Court assumed a more critical posture toward state regulatory legislation. In *Chicago, Milwaukee, and St. Paul Railway Co.* v. *Minnesota* the Court for the first time declared a state rail law to be in violation of the due process clause of the Fourteenth Amendment. The case involved a Minnesota law of 1887 that set up a rail and warehouse commission with power to examine rail rates and to revise those which it found to be unreasonable or unequal. Justice Samuel Blatchford, author of the majority opinion, based his argument principally on the fact that the law did not require notice and hearing before the commission set rates. Moreover, the law gave the commission final rate-fixing authority; its decisions were not subject to review by the courts as to their equality or reasonableness. According to Blatchford, the statute "deprives the company of its right to a judicial investigation, by due process of law, under the forms and with the machinery provided by the wisdom of successive ages for the investigation judicially of the truth of a matter in controversy." The question of whether a rate was reasonable, he continued, "involving as it does the element of reasonableness both as regards the company and as regards the public, is eminently a question for judicial investigation, requiring due process of law for its determination. If the company is deprived of the power of charging reasonable rates for the use of its property, and such deprivation takes place in the absence of an investigation by judicial machinery, it is deprived of the lawful use of its property, and thus, in substance and effect, of the property itself, without due process of law and in violation of the Constitution of the United States."

At one level, Blatchford was concerned with procedural regularity in the conduct of administrative agencies. He found procedural defects in the commission's prescribed method of rate fixing—namely, the lack of notice and hearing and the failure to provide the right of appeal. This procedural concern has usually been viewed as a subterfuge concealing the Court's determination to halt the regulatory movement and arrogate to itself the power to evaluate rates. But there is evidence that the concern for administrative procedure was genuine. For in other cases the Court refused to review legislatively determined public utility rates and upheld rates set by commissions where utility companies had been given notice and hearing.

Nevertheless, at another level the Court in the *Chicago, Milwaukee* case was concerned with the substantive threat of regulatory legislation and unequivocally claimed the power to judge the reasonableness of public utility rates. The Minnesota commission was really an arm of the legislature, and the implication of the decision was that even if the legislature itself had set the rate, it would have been a violation of due process of law. Justice Bradley pursued this line of reasoning in a cogent dissent in which he asserted that the majority decision practically overruled *Munn* v. *Illinois*. In that case the Court had apparently established the rule that the rates charged by a business affected with a public interest were subject to public regulation. Now the Court was in effect saying that public regulation must be reasonable, and that the definition of reasonableness was a judicial question. Bradley disagreed. "On the contrary," he declared, the question of reasonableness "is pre-eminently a legislative one, involving considerations of policy as well as of remuneration." Bradley thus regarded the Court's decision as a usurpation of legislative authority to determine public policy.

Following the logical implications of the *Chicago, Milwaukee* decision, the Supreme Court in the next several years wrote substantive due process squarely into constitutional law. In *Reagan* v. *Farmers' Loan and Trust Co.* (1894), it invalidated rates set by a Texas railroad commission as a deprivation of property without due process of law. Moreover, the Court's opinion stated that the judiciary had the power to judge the reasonableness of rates set directly by the legislature. The justices took this step in *Smyth* v. *Ames* (1898), striking down a Nebraska statute setting intrastate freight rates. After protracted inquiry into the earning power of the railroads affected, the opinion concluded that the law imposed rates so low as to be unreasonable, amounting to a deprivation of property without due process of law.

In reviewing the reasonableness of railroad and other public utility rates the Supreme Court assumed a key policy-making role in the new national economy. Basing rate evaluation on such factors as the original cost of construction, the cost of improvements, the market value of a company's stocks and bonds, and operating expenses, the justices inaugurated a line of decisions stretching over the next forty years that involved them in abstruse and highly technical questions of economics. Reformers were quick to condemn the Court for exceeding the proper limits of judicial authority and usurping legislative power. But it is clear in retrospect that the justices were trying to regulate—as well as foster and protect—a key sector of the national economy which the political branches effectively ignored. This was the securities market for public utilities. In the absence of any other national policy, the Supreme Court's attempt to encourage public utilities investment while protecting the public interest filled a public policy need. Furthermore, the Court's sympathies were by no means entirely on the side of the corporations in public utilities regulation. In several cases it denied claims for damages brought by utility companies protesting franchise revocation by municipalities which built and operated their own utility plants.

Conservative Constitutionalism: The Courts and Labor

It was not, of course, logic alone nor the necessity of filling a policy-making void that led the Supreme Court to assume a legislative function in the rate cases of the 1890s. Turbulent political and social events also pushed the judiciary into a more straightforward defense of property rights. The Haymarket Square riot of 1886 provoked fears of labor militance that spread throughout middle-class society and multiplied in the 1890s as strikes and industrial violence proliferated. Working-class unrest had its agrarian counterpart in the Populist movement, a third-party reform effort that sprang into prominence in 1892 and within a few years appeared capable of exerting a decisive influence on national politics. Meanwhile antitrust sentiment, a powerful current of opinion in the late 1880s, was exacerbated by the depression of 1893. Amid growing dissatisfaction with the existing political and economic power structure, reformist tendencies began to appear among mainstream politicians.

Expressing this reformist outlook, Congress in 1894 passed an income-tax law. In the opinion of many conservatives the measure showed the danger to established property interests inherent in the power of organized legislative majorities. At the same time conflict between capital and labor erupted with significant constitutional consequences in the Pullman strike, which saw the federal executive and judiciary boldly exercise national power to maintain stability and order. The triumph of the Republican party in the election of 1896 contained the forces of protest and radical change and concluded a decade of political and social upheaval.

The defense of propertied interests by the judiciary produced numerous changes in constitutional interpretation, but in no area of public policy was innovation more dramatic than in labor law. Since the landmark state case of *Commonwealth* v. *Hunt* in 1842 labor unions were not illegal, but by the 1890s they might as well have been for all the restraints that courts had placed upon them. Strikes to secure higher wages and better working conditions were legal, but boycotts and strikes to force an employer to recognize a union were not. State courts declared these actions to be unlawful interferences with an employer's liberty or property, public nuisances, or conspiracies in restraint of trade. Federal courts were less directly involved in labor problems, although they were able to control the activities of some railway workers when bankrupt railroad corporations passed into federal receivership and their operations came under the supervision of the judiciary. It was difficult to regulate militant labor tactics through the traditional common law methods available to state and federal courts, however, for prosecution and trial often took place after irreparable damage had occurred. Moreover, local juries were often sympathetic to labor militants, making convictions difficult to obtain.

In order to restrict union activities, courts improvised new uses of injunctions under their equity powers. Under equity jurisdiction American courts could act expeditiously to do justice or prevent injury in matters where reliance on common law remedies was likely to result in permanent harm. The relief available in equity was in the form of an injunction—an order to refrain from a certain action or to perform particular acts that was issued by a court without a jury trial. Typically, in labor disputes an injunction was issued to stop members of a union, allegedly in the context of a criminal conspiracy, from carrying out tortious acts such as a strike or boycott interfering with an employer's property. At the same time, property was significantly redefined to include the expectation of doing business rather than simply tangible or real property. In the early 1890s state and federal courts frequently used injunctions to prevent labor unions from injuring business interests. They were aided in doing so by the broadened scope of federal criminal jurisdiction resulting from enactment of the Interstate Commerce Commission and Sherman Antitrust laws. Thus in 1893 a federal district court issued an injunction forcing members of a railway union to handle the freight of a struck railroad under the requirement of the Interstate Commerce Act that common carriers accept the freight of all connecting railroads without discrimination.[4]

In July 1894 the Cleveland administration used the labor injunction to help break the Pullman strike, one of the most important labor actions in American history. In May 1894, the Pullman Car Company, because of the prevailing business depression, imposed a 20-percent wage cut on its employees. At the same time it maintained the existing level of executive salaries and company dividends. Several thousand Pullman workers, organized within the American Railway Union, thereupon went out on strike. Under the leadership of Eugene V. Debs, the union presently resorted to a secondary boycott by refusing to move trains hauling Pullman cars. The strikers and their sympathizers shortly engaged in mob violence to block rail traffic. The result was the physical obstruction of interstate commerce and blockage of the mails in Chicago and elsewhere in the nation.

To deal with this crisis the Cleveland administration employed an anti-strike strategy. The basis of it was injunctions issued by federal courts which provided a justification for executive intervention in support of judicial authority. At the first serious signs of disorder interrupting rail service, Attorney General Richard Olney sought an injunction in the United States District Court in Chicago to restrain the strikers. Known as the "omnibus injunction" because of its extremely broad sweep, the court order asserted jurisdiction under the Sherman Act and the constitutional authority of the federal government to deliver the mails. The injunction directed Debs, the officers of the American Railway Union, and all others combining and conspiring with them to stop interfering with the business of twenty-two named railroads, interfering with any mail trains or other trains engaged in interstate commerce, compelling or inducing by threats, intimidation, persuasion, force, or violence any employees of the named railroads from performing their duties, and from doing any act whatsoever in furtherance of any conspiracy to interfere with the transportation of interstate commerce.

The day after the injunction was issued further rioting occurred, at which point President Cleveland decided to interfere in the strike. Over the protest of Illinois governor John P. Altgeld, he despatched federal troops to

4. *Toledo, Ann Arbor and Northern Michigan Railway Co. v. Pennsylvania Co.,* 54 Fed. 730 and 54 Fed. 746 (N.D. Ohio, 1893).

Chicago and assigned 5,000 deputy marshals sworn in for the occasion. In the next few days rioting and violence spread, but within a week the injunction and the presence of federal troops, along with new workers brought in from other regions, broke the strike. Meanwhile Debs and his fellow leaders, ignoring the court order, were arrested for conspiring to obstruct the mails and interfere with interstate commerce.

In December 1894 Debs was tried and convicted in the Federal Circuit Court for northern Illinois. In sentencing Debs the court invoked the Sherman Act as authority for the injunction and for the convictions, on the ground that the strikers had engaged in a conspiracy in restraint of trade within the meaning of the law. The court disregarded the objection that in enacting the antitrust law Congress had presumably been aiming at corporate trusts and not at labor union activities.

When Debs and his associates sought a writ of habeas corpus from the United States Supreme Court, the Court denied the writ. Justice Brewer made his opinion in *In re Debs* the occasion for a forceful exposition of national supremacy and the commerce power. The federal government, he said, had "all the attributes of sovereignty," and federal authority within its proper sphere was necessarily supreme over that of the states when the two came in conflict. "The strong arm of the national government," he said, "may be put forth to brush away all obstructions to the freedom of interstate commerce or the transportation of the mails." Resort to injunction, he added, was a proper remedy for securing the protection of commerce and the mails. He did not mention the Sherman law, as the circuit court had done, but instead he rested his opinion on the broadest possible grounds of national sovereignty and supremacy.

In the words of President Cleveland, the Court had established "in an absolutely authoritative manner and for all time, the power of the national government to protect itself in the exercise of its functions." Legitimate as this purpose was, the federal intervention also had a distinct class character. The administration's decisive action, backed by the federal judiciary, reflected the propertied classes' fear of social revolution. Constitutionally, the Pullman strike demonstrated in dramatic fashion the strategic potential of the injunction as a political weapon. Traditionally, injunctions were used to protect individual rights at private law. Now they were used to deal with social and economic problems of major political import. With good reason the Pullman strike came to be seen as the first forceful example of government by injunction.

Conservative Constitutionalism: The Income Tax Cases

While dealing with labor agitation from below, property interests faced perhaps a more serious threat in the income tax law adopted by Congress in

1894. The tax law was objectionable from the standpoint of laissez-faire theory because its burden fell on a particular segment of the population and violated the principle of equality. But businessmen's opposition to the law was in a practical sense based largely on the fear that it portended further attacks on wealth by the power of organized legislative majorities. Although opposition to the income tax lacked the broad social appeal that resistance to labor militance evoked during the Pullman strike, it aroused judicial concern. The Supreme Court seized the opportunity to do something about it in the famous income tax cases of 1895.

As a federal revenue measure, the income tax was not new. An income tax had been levied by Congress during the Civil War and had remained in effect until 1872. In *Springer* v. *United States* (1881) the Court in a unanimous decision had held this tax to be constitutional as applied to lawyers' professional earnings. Thus the new income tax seemed to involve no novel issue of federal power.

The income tax recognized important shifts in the nature of taxable wealth that were occurring in the country. The older forms of wealth had been principally realty and personal property. Since the Constitution required that direct taxes be apportioned among the states, it was impracticable for the national government to tax realty. Congress, therefore, had hitherto depended primarily upon import duties and excises in raising federal revenue. The assets of the new industry, however, were primarily in the earning power of its capital investments, the visible symbols of which were stocks and bonds, the intangible property of banks, corporations, and private individuals scattered over the nation.

For twenty years agrarian radicals and reformers of various sorts had introduced income tax bills into Congress. In 1892 the Populists placed great emphasis on the issue, and after the depression of 1893 western and southern Democrats were able to push an income tax proposal through Congress. They attached provisions to the Wilson-Gorman Tariff Act of 1894 which levied a 2-percent tax upon all kinds of income—rent, interests, dividends, salaries, profits, and the like—over $4,000. The tax, in other words, was not graduated but imposed a flat rate. The $4,000 exemption was considered fairly high and excluded most working-class persons. It was on the whole a popular measure.

A few months after passage of the Wilson-Gorman Act, *Pollock* v. *Farmers' Loan and Trust Company* (1895), a case challenging the income tax provisions of the law, reached the Supreme Court. Although the suit was clearly collusive, the Court agreed to hear the case. A brilliant array of legal learning, headed by Joseph Choate of New York and former senator George Edmunds of Vermont, argued against the constitutionality of the income tax. They made three points. The first was that the law, by levying a tax on income from realty, was in effect a land tax. Land taxes had always been classified as direct taxes, and according to the Constitution direct taxes must be levied among the states according to population. Since the income tax was not apportioned in that way, Choate and Edmunds reasoned, it was unconstitutional. The second argument against the law was that since it exempted all persons and corporations earning less than $4,000 yearly and certain other persons and corporations, it violated Article I, Section 8, of the Constitution, which required that all taxes must be uniform throughout the United States. The third point against the law was that it was invalid insofar as it was levied upon the income of state and municipal bonds.

Chief Justice Fuller's majority opinion dealt chiefly with the question of whether a tax on the income from land was a direct tax. Two precedents appeared pertinent. The first was *Hylton* v. *United States* (1796), in which the Supreme Court had held that a tax on carriages was not a direct tax but an excise. The second and even stronger precedent was *Springer* v. *United States,* upholding the Civil War income tax. Yet Chief Justice Fuller refused to be guided by these precedents. He asserted that direct taxes included taxes on real estate, personal property, or the rents or income thereof. Accordingly, those portions of the income tax law that taxed income from land were a direct tax and were unconstitutional. On the basis of precedents which prohibited the federal government from taxing state bonds, Fuller held that the parts of the law that taxed income from state and municipal bonds were also unconstitutional. Five justices concurred with Fuller on these two points, while only two dissented.

But did the unconstitutionality of two parts of the law make the entire statute void, and was the entire law a violation of the principle of uniformity and, therefore, unconstitutional? Fuller did not answer these questions, but simply said the Court was divided upon them 4 to 4. This made the decision inconclusive and led Choate to ask for a rehearing. The Court granted the petition, since Justice Jackson was expected to return to the bench shortly. The case was subsequently reargued and a second decision handed down in May 1895.

In the second *Pollock* decision the Supreme Court struck down all the income tax sections of the Wilson-Gorman Act as unconstitutional. Chief Justice Fuller reiterated the main point of his first opinion—namely, that income taxes on land were direct taxes and, therefore, unconstitutional. He then argued—contrary to what he had said in the first case—that there was no essential difference between a tax on income from land and taxes on income from other property. Following a rule of statutory construction according to which an entire law must be invalidated if integral portions of it are unconstitutional, Fuller declared all the income tax sections of the law unconstitutional.

The two *Pollock* cases were egregious decisions, to say the least. They disregarded one hundred years of decisions by the Court itself in which the meaning of a direct tax had been narrowly and definitely established. Plainly the justices, apparently responding to the fear of majoritarian attacks on wealth, assumed an essentially legislative function by questioning the wisdom of congressional policy. It was the use of the taxing power for what the Court considered unreasonable and even illegitimate social and political purposes that seemed to lie at the heart of the decisions. Chief Justice Fuller indicated as much when he said that the purpose of the requirement that direct taxes be apportioned among the states was "to prevent an attack upon accumulated property by mere force of numbers."

It is important to bear in mind, however, that Fuller did not speak for a united Court. Indeed, the decision invalidating the entire income tax law in the second case was the result of one justice changing his mind. Justice Jackson missed the first case but took part in the second and stood with Harlan, White, and Brown in the minority. But in the first case, four justices, names unknown, had also been in favor of the constitutionality of the law in its larger aspects. Had all four men in favor of the law in the first case again voted in favor of the law five weeks later, it is clear that, except for the provisions for taxes on income from land and income from state bonds, the law would have been declared constitutional by a vote of 5 to 4. Thus it is obvious that one of the original four men who favored the law in the first case shifted his vote in the second case and voted against the law's constitutionality.

By a process of elimination one can narrow the identity of the "vacillating judge" to Shiras, Gray, or Brewer. The most persuasive theories point to either Shiras or Gray, although at present no conclusive answer can be given. The significant fact, however, is that both Shiras and Gray were known as legal traditionalists unsympathetic to the more overtly legislative, activist judicial review evident in the rate regulation cases since 1890. Yet so great was their fear for the existing order that both Shiras and Gray were willing in the final analysis to repudiate a century of tax law precedent and oppose the entire income tax law.

Judicial Supremacy

In addition to striking down the income tax law, the Supreme Court in 1895 approved the government's intervention in the Pullman strike and denied the application of the Sherman Antitrust Act to manufacturing in the unpopular sugar trust decision. Two years later, in *Allgeyer* v. *Louisiana,* it added liberty of contract to the cluster of laissez-faire doctrines used to defend inequality of wealth rather than serve their original equal-rights purposes.

Drawn from laissez-faire economics, the doctrine of liberty of contract held that when two parties reached an agreement that was not contrary to public policy, the legislature had no right to interfere and dictate the terms of that agreement or the conditions under which it would be carried out.

The liberty protected by the due process clause of the Fourteenth Amendment, said the Court in *Allgeyer,* included "not only the right of the citizen to be free from the mere physical restraint of his person . . . but the right . . . to be free in the enjoyment of all his faculties; to be free to use them in all lawful ways; to live and work where he will; to earn his livelihood by any lawful calling; to pursue any livelihood or avocation, and for that purpose to enter into all contracts which may be proper, necessary, and essential to his carrying out to a successful conclusion the purposes above mentioned." This resounding defense of contractual freedom, of course, meant little to workers whose bargaining position in relation to their employers was anything but equal. Nevertheless, it became the law of the land.

Critics attacked the Court's defense of property rights in the 1890s and condemned "judicial supremacy" and "government by judiciary." Echoing their point of view, historians have argued that by writing into constitutional law substantive due process, liberty of contract, the distinction between commerce and manufacturing, the labor injunction, and limitations on the police power, the Supreme Court effectively blocked reform for a generation. To some extent this criticism is justified. Unquestionably, the Court at critical junctures defended existing class relations and property arrangements, and many of its decisions reflected the social and economic predilections of the judges themselves rather than simply the conclusions of legal logic. Yet there were important considerations transcending the personal outlook of the justices that led them to adopt an activist, policy-making role at this time.

The condition of the party system was a principal reason for the emergence of judicial activism in the late nineteenth century. Throughout the postreconstruction period the two major parties were evenly balanced at the national level. As a result, neither of them was able to gain decisive control over national policy making. Although the parties by 1900 were organizationally more disciplined and legislatively more productive, for almost two decades a condition of stasis existed in which the Democrats controlled the House of Representatives and the Republicans the presidency. This created a vacuum of power which the judiciary to some extent filled. The power of judicial review had always given the courts a political role. When after reconstruction the pace of social and economic change outstripped the ability of president, Congress, and the political parties to deal with it, the courts necessarily assumed a larger governmental role.

A new kind of judicial review took shape under the pressure of events in the 1890s. Instead of confining itself to the question of whether a legislative power was constitutional, the Supreme Court increasingly concerned itself with the wisdom of legislation. Formerly, the Court had assumed that the decision of the legislature was conclusive as to the limits of the police power. Now, however, it reserved for itself the right to consider the whole question of whether the statute under review constituted a valid exercise of that power. Theoretically, the will of the legislature was still held in high respect. But in fact the Court was often openly disapproving of the reasons that had impelled legislatures to pass the legislation in question.

Due process under the Fourteenth Amendment provided the chief doctrinal instrument by which the judiciary filled an essentially legislative role. Due process was, broadly speaking, a general substantive limitation upon the police power of the state. Any state statute, ordinance, or administrative act which imposed any kind of limitation upon the right of private property or free contract immediately raised the question of due process of law. And since a majority of statutes of a general public character imposed some limitations upon private property or contractual right, the ramifications of due process were endless.

To be accepted as within the bounds of due process a statute must in the opinion of the Court be "reasonable." This was the general and all-inclusive test that a law under review had to meet and pass. If the purpose for which the statute had been enacted was a reasonable one, if the act employed reasonable means to achieve its ends, if the means employed bore a reasonable and substantial relationship to the purposes of the act, and if the law imposed no unreasonable limitations upon freedom of contract or private vested right, then the Court would accept the law as a legitimate exercise of the police power. Closely associated with the concept of reasonableness was the requirement that a statute should not be "arbitrary." On most occasions where a law was found to be unreasonable, it was also found to be arbitrary, an arbitrary statute being one "which restricts individual liberty or property right more severely than advantage to the community can possibly justify."

Formidable as the new judicial power was, it did not give the courts a plenary power to govern or make them the dominant institution in the constitutional system. "Judicial supremacy" was a political rallying cry rather than an accurate description of constitutional reality. Before 1890, as we have seen, the federal judiciary adopted a tolerant attitude toward state regulatory legislation. After the emergence of the new judicial review it continued to uphold most state laws that came before it. In 558 cases presenting state legislation challenged under the due process clause between 1887 and 1910, the Supreme Court sustained the states 83 percent of the time. Critics have pointed out that the Court, while approving most state regulation, nevertheless insisted on its right to review the reasonableness of legislation. If that is true, then the Court was far less conservative than has been supposed and on substantive grounds supported most social and economic regulation.

A more likely explanation is that the Supreme Court justices in most instances did not have complete discretion to decide things according to their own political and social values. Most cases could be disposed of under established precedents and rules of law. It was the strongly political and sociological character of critical interventions such as the income tax cases that suggested otherwise. Later the teaching of the legal realists—that judicial decision making followed no set rules and was thoroughly capricious—reinforced and gave a scholarly cast to the conclusion that judges, especially conservative ones, decided all cases according to their personal values and policy preferences. To be sure, this was sometimes the Court's method. But alongside the new activist style of review the traditional restraint model existed as an alternative. This fact was exceedingly important. The Supreme Court could presume legislation to be constitutional and, leaving the question of reasonableness to the legislature, consider only whether the power in question existed. Alternatively, it could assume a law to be unconstitutional because on its face it dealt with property and contractual relationships. In that situation it would reserve the question of reasonableness for itself. The existence of these options greatly increased the policy-making capability of the judiciary without making it supreme.

It has become clear in the later twentieth century that judicial activism and substantive due process are not inherently conservative in a socioeconomic sense, although they are subject to the charge of being antidemocratic. They are instruments of power that can be used for different political purposes. This fact was made apparent when the Supreme Court under Chief Justice Earl Warren invoked substantive due process in order to rid the statute books of restrictive legislation that could not meet the standards of a new generation's liberal values.

Evaluating recent judicial history, Charles A. Beard in 1914 insisted on the distinction between power and the manner of its exercise. Arguing that the crucial fact since the end of reconstruction was the emergence of a national economic system, Beard wrote: "It is possible to hold that the Court has been too tender of corporate rights in assuming the power of judicial review, and at the same time recognize the fact that such a power, vested somewhere in the national government, is essential to the continuance of industries and commerce on a national scale." Not that Beard, a nationalist, was necessarily right in his assessment; there was plenty of room to dispute his view from a reformist, states'-rights perspective. Nevertheless, Beard accurately identified the objective economic development that was a principal foundation of the judiciary's enhanced power in the late nineteenth century.

The Election of 1896

Although the Supreme Court played an important part in containing the social turbulence of the 1890s, more decisive events occurred in the political arena. By the 1890s it was clear that in the opinion of ever-increasing numbers of Americans, neither of the major parties was dealing satisfactorily with the problems of the new economic era. Under the impact of the depression of 1893, however, the parties began to change their general outlook.

For a generation both parties had shaped their identity for electoral purposes largely in relation to local issues. Democrats represented ethnocultural immigrant diversity, personal liberty, and resistance to official, government-imposed cultural and moral standards. Republicans stood for pietistic Protestant and bourgeois moral and cultural orthodoxy. In the 1890s, however, the Republicans adopted a more tolerant, flexible, non-doctrinaire approach to politics that emphasized both cultural and interest-group pluralism within a framework of national unity and social harmony. Large corporations were a prominent force in the Republican party, but industrial workers and immigrants also provided essential support. These groups believed that their interest lay in the protective economic policies symbolized by the gold standard and the tariff—the key elements in the Republican platform. Seeking an accommodation with labor, which was prepared to shift its support from the Democrats after Cleveland's handling of the Pullman strike, the party broadened its appeal to include many former Democrats, including reform-minded leaders who in the next two decades would give direction to the Progressive movement. The Democrats on the other hand, running William Jennings Bryan as a fusion candidate with the Populist party, adopted a narrow, crusading, ideological outlook symbolized in the campaign for the free coinage of silver. Badly divided between a conservative, business-minded eastern wing and a triumphant wing of radical westerners, the Democrats became the party of moralistic, self-righteous reform.

A massive shift in voter alignment to the Republican party had started in the congressional elections of 1894. This realigning trend continued in 1896 as McKinley won a resounding victory, especially in large urban centers that had previously been Democratic strongholds. The result showed the weakness of the Democrats' doctrinaire, ideological style of politics compared to the Republicans' strategy of pragmatic, pluralistic accommodation. Along with the new judicial review exercised by the Supreme Court in the 1890s, this pluralistic, interest-group approach to politics would have a profound impact on American constitutionalism in the twentieth century. Even more than the new judicialism, the transforming effects of interest-group pluralism appeared in the broad-based reform movement that revitalized constitutional politics in the first two decades of the twentieth century.

TWENTY-ONE

Progressive Constitutionalism

————————————— ✦✦✦ —————————————

LESS THAN A DECADE after agrarian radicalism and working-class militance
sent shock waves through American society, a broadly popular reform impulse began to transform American politics. Known reassuringly if somewhat cryptically as progressivism, this reform movement was directed at
many of the grievances that the Populists had attacked in the 1890s. In
general the object of progressive reform was to redress the imbalances and
inequalities of political and economic power caused by the new system of
industrial capitalism. Reformers sought to restrain the power that the great
national corporations exercised as virtually private governments, to constitutionalize them by making them accountable and subject to public control.
Yet in its social constituency and general political outlook progressivism
differed from reform in the 1890s. Instead of narrow agrarian and working-class aims expressed in the rhetoric of class conflict, progressive reform
emphasized shared community and public interests. It rested on a broad
spectrum of middle-class support that included consumer groups, businessmen, white-collar workers, and professionals, in addition to farmers and
trade unionists.

Without abandoning the traditional American attachment to laissez
faire and minimal government, progressive reformers established the competing constitutional legitimacy of government regulation of the economy.
Government played an active economic role throughout the nineteenth
century in the United States, but its chief task was the politically congenial
one of granting corporate privileges and distributing natural resources. In
the 1880s groups and classes that had been excluded from this public-policy
process demanded that government not only promote, but also regulate
economic development. In the early twentieth century broad segments of
middle-class society reaffirmed this demand, with a view toward preserving
the traditional values of a competitive market and dispersed political and
economic power. Initially, the progressive regulatory movement reflected a
unified sense of republican citizenship that sought to prevent businessmen

from corrupting and dominating government and politics. Yet the reform movement was not simply a struggle between "the people" and "the interests." Progressive reform was basically an attempt to reintegrate the social order following the dislocations and upheaval of the industrial revolution. This reintegration required political and constitutional changes that affected and enlisted the active support of key sectors of the business community, as well as organized middle-class professional and civic groups.

Although the politics of the regulatory movement was usually hostile toward business, its deeper purpose was protective as well as restrictive of capitalistic enterprise. For while Americans frequently protested the power of the trusts and giant corporations, they desired the goods and services that modern economic organization made possible. Public opinion, in short, was ambivalent toward large-scale corporate enterprise. Intended to serve the needs of businessmen as well as the community at large, the regulatory movement was similarly ambiguous in nature. This ambiguity was evident in the tension that existed between the public-interest demands that supported the creation of regulatory agencies, and the friendly client-adviser relationship with business that usually resulted from the regulatory experience. Nor was this protective function apparent only in retrospect. In certain industries corporate leaders actively sought federal regulation or, sensing its inevitability, tried to make it compatible with their own purposes. By the end of the progressive era a growing network of regulatory agencies existed that was capable of representing organized economic interest groups, yet capable also of upholding the public interest.

In addition to restricting the economic marketplace, progressive reform aimed at regulating the political marketplace and the institutions that controlled it—the organized political parties. Despite their important constitutional functions, the parties were widely regarded as a corrupting force in political life. Accordingly, political machines and bosses became the object of reforms intended to make government more responsive to the people as well as more honest and efficient. Here, too, however, reform was ambiguous. For the introduction of democratizing devices, such as the referendum, was accompanied by a decline in popular participation in government. If the test of democracy is merely voter turnout, then progressive reform encouraged antidemocratic tendencies. In fact, however, by checking party power and ambition reformers created opportunities for pluralistic participation in the political system. As in the economy, political competition among regulated interest groups was the constitutional achievement and legacy of progressivism.

Toward the Modern Presidency

Earlier reform movements typically aimed to promote individual liberty by restricting government, in accordance with the decentralist and laissez-faire bias of the political culture. Progressivism, in contrast, signaled a shift toward a progovernment attitude on the part of reformers, a belief that the protection of individual liberty required the positive exercise of government power rather than its inhibition. Furthermore, whereas the nineteenth century was an age of legislative dominance, progressivism foreshadowed the ascendancy of executive and administrative institutions in the twentieth century. With legislatures discredited for their involvement with corrupt party machines, reformers eagerly, if naïvely, turned to executive action. Henry Jones Ford, a prominent reformer, wrote in 1898: "The only power which can end party duplicity and define issues in such a way that public opinion can pass upon them decisively, is that which emanates from presidential authority." In a similar vein the political scientist Woodrow Wilson admonished: "We must find or make somewhere in our system a group of men to lead us, who represent the nation in the origin and responsibility of their power; who shall draw the Executive . . . into cordial cooperation with the legislature." Wilson expressed the new reformist outlook in adding: "There is no danger in power if only it be not irresponsible."

President Cleveland's intervention in the Pullman strike demonstrated the strategic importance of executive power and the potency of the office in the new industrial era. With far more popular support, William McKinley, the first president in a generation to have the benefit of party majorities in both houses of Congress, proved a capable legislative leader in the conduct of foreign and domestic policies. However, it was Theodore Roosevelt, succeeding the assassinated McKinley in 1901, who first wielded executive power in a distinctly modern way. Through speeches and messages, and by virtue of his ability to dramatize any cause he adopted, Roosevelt made the presidency the center of the constitutional system.

Roosevelt conceived of the presidency as a "stewardship," in whose care the common welfare and destiny of the American people were entrusted. Any matter concerning national welfare Roosevelt assumed to be his affair. He felt himself to be personally responsible for the safety, prosperity, and happiness of the entire United States. This theory of presidential duties took him far afield of the constitutionally prescribed functions of the presidency. Thus in the great coal strike of 1902, Roosevelt interfered and used the prestige of his office to force a settlement. So also, in the panic of 1907, Roosevelt stepped in to prevent the spread of a financial crisis in Wall Street. In this instance, he took upon himself the responsibility for suspending the operation of the Sherman law in order to make possible a financial combination deemed desirable to check the panic.

Roosevelt revived the old Hamiltonian doctrine of inherent executive prerogative power which held that the president was not limited in authority by the enumeration of executive functions in the Constitution. To put it differently, the president could do anything that the Constitution or some act of Congress did not forbid him to do. Acting according to this concept,

Roosevelt felt himself justified in settling a coal strike, quieting a financial panic, or arranging the finances of the Dominican Republic.

Roosevelt appointed numerous unsalaried information-gathering commissions, and occasionally interpreted legislation in a very latitudinarian way to pursue administration policies. In promoting federal railroad legislation in 1906 he successfully organized and directed congressional opinion through party leaders, although toward the end of his second term lawmakers' resentment, principally against his conservation policies, caused a decline in executive-legislative relations. William Howard Taft, Republican successor to Roosevelt, lacked his predecessor's gift for effective public relations and rhetoric. Nevertheless, he represented a continuation of the activist progressive presidency rather than a revival of the negative nineteenth-century presidential style. Responding to Roosevelt's politically motivated assertion of the stewardship theory in the 1912 campaign, Taft criticized the notion of an undefined executive power. Yet his conduct of the office revealed his belief in a strong executive. Taft was the first president actually to have bills drafted and sent to Congress, and later as chief justice he delivered an important opinion in the *Myers* case that defended broad executive removal power.[1]

Woodrow Wilson, who had described the presidency as "the vital link of connection with the thinking nation," was even more significant than Roosevelt in strengthening the executive office. Elected when the Republican party split in the election of 1912, Wilson was a political science professor turned politician whose practical experience in government was confined to a two-year term as reform governor of New Jersey. Critical of legislative hegemony in his 1885 work, *Congressional Government,* Wilson had long since concluded that Congress had failed in its task of public leadership and had shown itself incapable of coping with the complex problems of modern society. Wilson had also expressed the belief that an effective program of legislation would require presidential formulation and leadership. He had condemned the doctrine of the separation of powers as inhibiting strong presidential leadership in legislation and had expressed admiration for the British parliamentary system with its automatic cooperation between executive and legislature. Parliament, he had observed, did not really originate legislation; it merely ratified or rejected the cabinet's recommendations, seldom refusing its assent. This resulted, Wilson had concluded, in strong concerted leadership in government and in an absence of the paralysis so frequently present in relations between the American president and Congress.

Once in the White House, Wilson undertook to model his relations with Congress upon the British principle of executive ascendancy in legislation. He believed that this involved no unconstitutional usurpation of power. On the contrary, he found his authority to control legislation in

1. See below, p. 512.

Article II, Section 3, of the Constitution, which instructs the president to recommend to Congress such measures as the president judges necessary. Obviously, Wilson's capacity to imitate the British parliamentary system was limited by the fact that he could not prorogue Congress or "go to the country" if it failed to do his bidding. He believed, however, that his own prestige and the Democratic party's eagerness to achieve a successful reform program would compensate for the constitutional limits upon his coercive power.

In accordance with these ideas, Wilson presented Congress with a series of legislative proposals, framed in cooperation with his intimate associates, various experts, and Democratic leaders in the House and Senate. When an important bill was ready for action, Wilson customarily appeared in person before Congress, delivered a message dealing solely with the measure in question, and urged its immediate passage. In thus appearing before Congress, Wilson revived a practice in disuse for over a hundred years.

Immediately following such a message, administration supporters introduced the bill into both houses of Congress. Although the president technically could not introduce legislation into Congress, all concerned knew that the measure in question was largely Wilson's own. It was given the right of way by steering committees in both houses, and unless the Democratic members of Congress wished to break openly with their own president, they were obliged to support the proposal. In the early days of his administration Wilson went frequently to the President's Room, off the Senate chamber, to confer with Democratic leaders. It was plainly understood that he would not tolerate unreasonable delay or any substantial alteration in the text of a proposed law. When occasionally rebellion threatened an administration bill, Wilson did not hesitate to take the strongest measures to whip Congress into line. When, for example, he became convinced that various lobbyists were delaying the passage of the Underwood tariff bill, he went over the head of Congress to the people. In a dramatic message to the press, he attacked the "sinister interests" interfering with enactment of the law. Opposition to the measure thereupon collapsed, and the bill became law without further delay.

Wilson never formally enunciated Roosevelt's stewardship theory, but it is clear that he accepted the idea completely. He had the same understanding of the manner in which the common man now looked to the president for leadership, and he, too, had remarkable abilities as a popular leader. Further, he did what Roosevelt had failed to do—he presented Congress with a well-defined reform program, with the full understanding that his own prestige as a national leader was so great that the men on Capitol Hill could not refuse his demands.

To many Americans the unprecedented position that Wilson exercised in the initiation and passage of legislation seemed at variance with the soundest traditions of the American constitutional system. Presidential control of legislation, they held, violated the principle of the separation of powers and usurped the functions of Congress. The ancient fear of executive prerogative and dictatorship was still very much alive in many minds, and a president who openly made his office more powerful than Congress seemed headed straight for dictatorship and despotism. From Wilson's time to the present, many a politician has declaimed against the new tyranny of the presidential office. Even those who recognized the necessity of strong executive leadership at times had the uneasy thought that a republic ought not to permit the concentration of so much power in the hands of one person.

The Growth of Executive Ordinance Power

While Wilson successfully asserted the new technique of presidential leadership in legislation, other forces were at work to break down the doctrine of the separation of powers and to make the president a lawmaker in his own right. In theory, the execution of laws was a function entirely distinct from their enactment, and the legislature could not delegate any part of its lawmaking powers to the president. Actually, however, the line between lawmaking and administration had never been rigidly drawn. It was impossible for Congress to draft a law in such detail as to cover every possible contingency arising under it. Congress had early recognized this fact by delegating a certain amount of minor "administrative discretion" to the president. After 1890, however, there developed a trend toward the enactment of measures granting a much broader delegation of discretionary power to the executive. In addition, many of the new statutes carried with them a certain amount of authority to formulate policy.

In a series of important decisions between 1892 and 1911 the Supreme Court recognized this situation and substantially enlarged the doctrine of administrative discretion. *Field* v. *Clark* (1892), the first case of this kind, arose out of a provision in the Tariff Act of 1890. The statute authorized the president to suspend free import and to levy a prescribed schedule of duties against the goods of any nation whenever in his opinion he was satisfied that the country in question was imposing "reciprocally unequal or unreasonable" duties on imports from the United States. A number of importers presently attacked this last provision as unconstitutional, contending that the law delegated legislative power to the president and was, therefore, invalid because it was in conflict with Article I, Section 1, of the Constitution.

Justice Harlan's opinion rejected this plea. He admitted that the outright delegation of legislative power was unconstitutional, but said the act in question did not violate this rule, for it left nothing "involving the expediency or the just operation" of the law to the president. The suspension of existing duties was absolutely required when the executive "ascertained the existence of a particular fact." Thus the Court gave formal recognition to a distinction long existing in practice—that between the mere ascertainment of fact and actual policy making. This distinction became a fundamental one in the Court's subsequent attempts to distinguish between lawful and unlawful delegations of authority to the executive.

In *Buttfield* v. *Stranahan* (1904) the Court recognized that Congress might lawfully delegate to the executive certain minor policy-making decisions. The Tea Inspection Act of 1897 had given the secretary of the treasury the power to appoint a Board of Tea Inspectors, who were authorized to recommend certain standards in tea grading and to inspect and grade all imported tea. The act went beyond the delegation considered in *Field* v. *Clark,* for the executive was here empowered to fix standards that could be enforced as law. Yet the Court did not judge this to involve policy making and an unlawful delegation of legislative power. Congress, said Justice White, had fixed the "primary standard" and policy for the tea board to follow, and this was sufficient to insure the law's constitutionality.

In 1911, in the case of *United States* v. *Grimaud,* the Supreme Court extended the doctrine of administrative discretion to recognize that administrative rulings had the force of law and that violations of them might be punished as infractions of a criminal statute, if Congress should so provide. An act of 1891 had authorized the president to set aside public lands in any state or territory as forest reservations. In 1905, another statute transferred the administration of such lands to the secretary of agriculture and empowered him to make rules and regulations for their occupancy and use. The act further made violations of the secretary's rules subject to a fine of not more than $500 and imprisonment for not more than a year, or both. Under the authority of the 1905 act, the Department of Agriculture had issued certain regulations to limit grazing on such reserves. It was the constitutionality of these regulations which now came before the Court. Justice Joseph R. Lamar in a brief opinion cited *Field* v. *Clark* and *Buttfield* v. *Stranahan,* and then concluded that "the authority to make administrative rules is not a delegation of legislative power, nor are such rules raised from an administrative level to a legislative character because the violation thereof is punishable as a public offense."

Thus by 1911 the Court had accepted as constitutional the delegation of a large element of administrative discretion to the executive. In theory, to be sure, the doctrine of the separation of powers remained unimpaired, and in each case that thereafter came before the Court, it carefully distinguished between "administrative discretion" and outright delegation of legislative power, the latter still being pronounced unconstitutional. In fact, however, this carefully drawn distinction was weakened by the Court's willingness to accept as constitutional delegations of authority far broader than those in the early constitutional period.

Bureaucratic Administration: The Fourth Branch of Government

Although progressives criticized the separation of powers and called for realistic recognition of the lawmaking function of the executive, they did not abandon the essential insight that separation of the functions of government was the key to preserving responsible constitutional government. Indeed, they gave the idea new expression in asserting a fundamental distinction between politics and administration. Policy making and legislation belonged to the popularly elected branches of government, the executive proposing policies and the legislature disposing of them and providing the element of accountability. Between them the two branches expressed public opinion, or what progressive theorists called the will of the state. Once the sovereign will was expressed in law, however, its implementation depended on administration. And the task of administration, as Woodrow Wilson had earlier written, was believed to lie outside the sphere of politics.

According to reform political scientist Frank J. Goodnow, administrators would become in effect a fourth branch of government. They would, said Goodnow, be "free from the influence of politics because of the fact that their mission is the exercise of foresight and discretion, the pursuit of truth, the gathering of information, the maintenance of a strictly impartial attitude ... and the provision of the most efficient possible administrative organization." Nonpolitical, objective, technically skilled and expertly informed, administrators occupied in progressive constitutional thought the position that courts did in traditional constitutionalism. Ironically, considering that their descriptions of the judiciary would acknowledge the political nature of judicial decision making, reformers transferred to administration the constitutionalist's faith in the possibility of transcending politics. Herbert Croly, author of the progressive treatise *The Promise of American Life,* wrote that administrators, "lifted out of the realm of partisan and factious political controversy," would "need and be entitled to the same kind of independence and authority in respect to public opinion as that which has traditionally been granted to a common law judge."

In progressive governance the legislature, guided by the executive, would make a general declaration of policy to be carried out by administrators in flexible, discretionary, nonpolitical ways. Administrators would not, wrote Croly, enforce rigid prohibitions as though policemen, but would be free to work out "flexible and articulate human adjustments." Progressive regulation, especially at the federal level, tended to assume this character as it became increasingly general and abstract.

The first national regulatory statute, the Interstate Commerce Act of 1887, professed the general purpose of assuring fair and reasonable rail rates, but it also specified numerous railroad practices to be prohibited. The Sherman Antitrust Act similarly was intended to prohibit specific business practices of the trusts. Later progressive legislation, however, was concerned with abstract qualities of articles of commerce—their inferior quality or outright harmful or immoral nature—rather than with specific practices of commerce and industry. Although the method of regulation was still proscriptive, the Pure Food and Drug Act of 1906 and the Mann White Slave Traffic Act of 1910 were but two of numerous measures that set standards of quality or behavior to guide administrators. Still other regulatory measures were general, abstract, and discretionary. The Federal Trade Commission Act of 1914, for example, created a government agency to prohibit unfair methods of competition and unfair or deceptive practices, but left the definition of unfair methods or "fair competition" to the agency. A shift thus occurred from regulation as a legislatively determined prohibition of specific practices to regulation as a discretionary adjustment of economic relationships by independent commissions, under abstract standards proclaimed by the legislature.

The progressive interest in administration was evident in the creation of several new regulatory agencies. As part of a new Department of Commerce and Labor, Congress in 1903 created a Bureau of Corporations to assist the executive in shaping government-business relations. A major result of President Wilson's reform program was the creation of the Federal Reserve Board with extensive discretionary powers to control banking and credit. The board exercised control over twelve district Federal Reserve Banks, which through their relationship with national banks (required to become members of the federal reserve system) were to regulate the amount of commercial credit and thus exercise some control over the business cycle. The Federal Trade Commission, as noted, was to supervise fair market practices. Other agencies created in the Wilson period were the Federal Farm Loan Board, with control over rural credits; the U.S. Shipping Board, with authority to construct and operate a merchant marine; the Railway Labor Board, empowered with mediating labor disputes; and the comptroller general of the United States, established by the Budget Act of 1921, a kind of one-man commission supervising budgetary matters.

Independent regulatory agencies exercising the functions of all three branches of government were anomalous from the standpoint of orthodox constitutional theory, especially in their relationship to the executive. Some commissions were appointed by the president simply with the consent of the Senate and presumably were removable at his discretion. Others, appointed for a set term, could be removed only for malfeasance in office and were meant to be basically independent of the president. The larger constitutional issue raised by the technical question of removal concerned the responsibility of the president for overall national policy planning. Starting in the New Deal era, when the policy-making functions of regulatory agencies were more clearly perceived, executives would feel the need to gain control over an ever-growing structure of regulatory agencies. This has been the purpose of executive reorganization plans since the 1930s.

A related issue has been the accountability of administrators to public opinion. Where legislation spelled out prohibitions or set definite standards for administrative implementation, no conflict between agency and popular majority appeared. Where legislation allowed wide discretion to administrators, however, in effect delegating lawmaking power to them, the question of democratic accountability arose. Naïve as they appear in their faith that politics and administration are separate, progressive reformers perceived the danger of an unrepresentative, irresponsible bureaucracy. Using the term in this sense, Woodrow Wilson warned against "an offensive official class—a distinct, semi-corporate body with sympathies divorced from those of a progressive, free-spirited people, and with hearts narrowed to the meanness of a bigoted officialism." The inevitably subjective nature of evaluations of the representative character of bureaucracy detracted nothing from the importance of this issue in later years.

National Regulation and Constitutional Law

The expansion of governmental authority for regulatory purposes required the formulation of new doctrines of constitutional power, especially at the federal level. And although the executive now tended to become the center of policy making, in constitutional law the crucial development was the expansion of congressional power. In a cooperative development Congress and the Supreme Court in the progressive era boldly fashioned a federal police power useful for a wide variety of reform purposes.

No constitutional principle was more fundamental than that which gave the federal government specific powers to deal with matters of general national import, while reserving to the states the general power to govern the social and economic affairs of the people in their local communities. The power to legislate for the health, safety, welfare, and morals of the community was called the police power, and it belonged principally to the states. The federal government was not completely excluded from police power considerations, but its chief involvement was negative insofar as it placed restrictions on state legislation. Federal ability to affect the internal welfare of the people by positive legislation consisted mainly in the power over foreign and interstate commerce. But from the beginning of the government to the late nineteenth century little legislation was adopted on this basis.

In the early twentieth century Congress began to use its commerce and taxing powers to legislate for the general welfare as though it possessed a federal police power. An objective basis for this constitutional development existed in the national economy and increasingly integrated society resulting from industrialization. National events and conditions were more important to citizens' everyday lives than ever before. Nevertheless, local interests were still of great importance, if not paramount, and states still obviously needed to determine public policy. More than in most industrialized nations, the idea of local self-government would persist as a constitutional ideal in the United States, despite the continuous expansion of federal authority. Accordingly, there were valid reasons for the states to insist on retaining the police power in opposition to the doctrine of a federal police power. Until the New Deal temporarily resolved the issue, the old antagonism between federal centralization and states' rights found renewed expression in struggles to adopt reform legislation.

Matters of real consequence were involved, therefore, in the laws and litigation, much of it unheralded and pedestrian, that supplied the content of national regulation and laid the foundation for the doctrine of a federal police power. In 1895, for example, Congress passed an act forbidding the shipment of lottery tickets in interstate commerce. In 1902 it enacted a law raising the excise on artificially colored oleomargarine to ten cents a pound, but at the same time taxing oleomargarine that was free from artificial coloring only one-fourth cent per pound. The obvious intent of the statute was not to raise revenue but to suppress the manufacture and sale of artificially colored margarine, then being widely sold as butter. When approved and rationalized by the Supreme Court, these laws, adopted more out of response to special interests than unified national opinion, became doctrinal landmarks in the constitutional law of the federal police power.

In upholding the lottery act in *Champion* v. *Ames* (1903), Justice Harlan for a 5–4 Court majority asserted that the commerce power was vested in Congress as absolutely as in a unitary government, and could be used to prohibit commerce as well as promote it. There was no novelty in defining the commerce power in this broad manner; the innovation lay in permitting its application in a manifestly noncommercial, social issue. The Court acted similarly in upholding the oleo tax in *McCray* v. *U.S.* (1904). Defending the use of the taxing power, Justice White said that if on the surface Congress had power to levy the tax in question, the Court could not inquire into the motive behind the law. Aware of the threat to state power that these decisions represented, a minority led by Chief Justice Fuller dissented in both cases. In the lottery case Fuller gave a minority opinion stating that the law was not really a regulation of commerce but a suppression of lotteries and thus an invasion of the police power of the states. Carried to its logical conclusion, said Fuller, the doctrine of a federal police power would break down all distinction between state and national authority.

Between 1906 and 1916 Congress adopted a series of social reform laws based on the commerce and taxing powers. Usually the legislation followed dramatic revelations of corruption and immorality by muckraking mass-circulation magazines. The Pure Food and Drug Act of 1906 barred adulterated and misbranded foods from interstate commerce, and rested on information provided by Dr. Harvey Wiley, a chemist in the Department of

Agriculture. The Meat Inspection Act of the same year, passed rapidly after publication of Upton Sinclair's novel *The Jungle,* provided for local inspection services by the Department of Agriculture and banned from interstate commerce uninspected and rejected meat. Prostitution was the object of the Mann Act of 1910, prohibiting the transportation of women for immoral purposes in interstate or foreign commerce.

A long-standing effort to prevent the use of child labor came to fruition in the Keating-Owen Act of 1916. Based on the commerce power, the act was plainly intended to alter the employment practices of local manufacturing establishments and eliminate a crying social evil. The act made it a misdemeanor for any manufacturer to ship in interstate commerce the product of any factory, cannery, or similar workshop in which children under fourteen had been employed or children from fourteen to sixteen had worked more than eight hours a day or more than forty-eight hours in any week. Seemingly irrefutable authority for the act existed in Supreme Court pronouncements. For example, in *Hoke* v. *U.S.* (1913), upholding the Mann Act, Justice McKenna declared that "The power of Congress under the commerce clause of the Constitution is the ultimate determining question. . . . If the statute be a valid exercise of that power, how it may affect persons or States is not material to be considered. It is the supreme law of the land and persons and States are subject to it." The commerce power lent itself to reform purposes more clearly than the taxing power, which was used in the Harrison Act of 1914 to set up a system of federal antinarcotic controls.

Congress also used the commerce power to regulate labor relations between interstate carriers and railway workers. In 1898 it adopted the Erdman Act, prohibiting "yellow dog" contracts by which employees promised as a condition of employment not to join a labor union. The act also forbade discrimination against employees because of membership in any labor organization. In 1906 Congress passed the Employer's Liability Act, making common carriers engaged in interstate commerce liable for the injury or death of any employee sustained in the carrier's employ. The law specifically abrogated the old "fellow-servant rule" of the common law, which held an employer not liable for injuries to an employee suffered through the negligence of a fellow workman. It also modified the common law rule of "contributory negligence," according to which the employer was not liable for injuries to an employee suffered through the negligence or carelessness of the injured person. When the Supreme Court ruled this law unconstitutional as an invasion of intrastate commerce, Congress in 1908 passed a second Employer's Liability Act, applying in unequivocal terms to workers engaged in interstate commerce. In 1917 Congress adopted the Adamson Act, providing an eight-hour day for workers on railroads operating in interstate commerce.

The expansion of federal power in these statutes was too great to pass without challenge. Although the Supreme Court upheld most federal police power legislation, in two notable instances it said no. The first was *Adair* v. *U.S.* (1908), in which it ruled the Erdman Act a violation of liberty of contract under the due process clause of the Fifth Amendment. Ten years later, in *Hammer* v. *Dagenhart,* the Court stunned the nation by invalidating the Child Labor Act as an invasion of the state police power. For several years opponents of the federal police power had asked where its application would stop. The Court responded to this concern by negating a law that was transparently intended to challenge the fundamental distinction in constitutional law between commerce and manufacturing. When Congress then turned to the taxing power to accomplish the same reform, the Court nullified that effort, too. Nevertheless, the reform legislation approved by the Court formed an impressive line of precedents for the exercise of a federal police power in the 1920s and 1930s.

Progressive Regulation: The Trust Question

Although in many respects progressivism was an episodic series of reform efforts, two issues were of sufficient importance to require continuing governmental attention after the indignation aroused by muckraking revelations had subsided. These issues were the trusts and the railroads. The manner in which they were dealt with between 1901 and 1917 illustrates the ambiguous nature of federal regulation in the progressive era.

In 1900, after a decade of not very fruitful experience, antitrust regulation occupied an uncertain position in constitutional politics. Politically, the trust question retained its popularity. But public policy had done almost nothing to restrain the economic forces operating in this sphere. Indeed, from 1895 to 1905 an unprecedented number of mergers and consolidations took place as businessmen tried to impose order in competitive circumstances that were frequently chaotic. Yet new businesses continued to spring up, throwing plans to rationalize market conditions into disarray and leading many corporate heads to consider the possibility of a federal role in stabilizing industrial conditions. The states meanwhile were contributing little to public policy on the trust question. They were clearly capable in a legal sense of regulating the internal structure and market power of corporations, but the political and economic obstacles to effective state regulation were insuperable. Rather than break up the trusts, the states welcomed them for the economic benefits they could provide.

The federal government was marking time on the trust problem. Under heavy public pressure, the Cleveland administration had brought the *Sugar Trust* case and lost; the McKinley administration did even less, initiating only three antitrust suits. The Supreme Court was not to be looked to for leadership in a campaign against corporate power, though it could not be blamed for the failure of the states or the federal government to impose restraints on the trusts. Actually, the Court was not hostile to the Sherman Act, as it showed by upholding antitrust restrictions against a combination of pipe manufacturers whose marketing practices restrained interstate commerce, and against railroads' pooling agreements.[2]

Excluding outright prohibition, which though legally possible under the state police power or the federal taxing power was neither politically nor economically feasible, there were two ways of regulating corporate power. The first, represented by the Sherman Act, consisted in legislative prohibition of specific business practices with judicial enforcement. Yet by 1900 many reformers doubted that the trust question could or should be dealt with in this way. The alternative, which increasingly seemed preferable to the vagaries and uncertainties of litigation, was regulation by means of an administrative commission, staffed by experts and capable of adjusting the relations between business and government.

Employing the first of these techniques, the administration of Theodore Roosevelt inaugurated a highly publicized campaign to enforce the Sherman Act which decisively institutionalized and legitimated antitrust litigation as an instrument of public policy. The Roosevelt administration also proposed and to some extent experimented with bureaucratic regulation of corporate activity that would avoid reliance on the judiciary.

Regarding the trusts as virtually autonomous states over which the federal government must assert its authority, Roosevelt initiated several antitrust suits and won dramatic victories in two cases, *Northern Securities Co.* v. *United States* (1904) and *Swift and Co.* v. *United States* (1905). In the former case the government brought a suit in equity to dissolve the Northern Securities Company, a railroad holding company organized by James J. Hill and E. H. Harriman. The Supreme Court in a 5–4 decision held that the company was an unlawful combination within the meaning of the Sherman Act. The Court's opinion, delivered by Justice Harlan, rejected the argument that the company was the result of a stock transaction that was not commerce and hence was beyond the scope of the antitrust law. While agreeing that the antitrust law had no reference to the manufacturing or production of goods, Harlan said it applied to all contracts or combinations that directly or necessarily operated in restraint of interstate trade. In other words, a combination did not have to be in commerce to be brought under the act (although no combination could more obviously be in interstate commerce than the railroad merger in question). In the *Swift* case the Court held unanimously that the activities of meat packing houses in controlling sales at several stages of market operations were clearly interstate commerce. Justice Holmes for the Court described the separate local transactions as "a current of commerce among the states," thus enunciating the

---

2. *Addystone Pipe and Steel Co.* v. *United States* (1899) and *United States* v. *Trans-Missouri Freight Association* (1897).

"stream of commerce" doctrine that was later used to justify applications of the commerce power.

Despite these victories, Roosevelt preferred an administrative rather than a juridical approach to the corporation question. The attempt "to provide in sweeping terms against all combinations of whatever character, if technically in restraint of trade," he said, "must necessarily be either futile or mischievous, or both." Regarding economic combinations as inevitable and on the whole beneficial, Roosevelt would evaluate corporate behavior not in economic but moral terms, distinguishing between good and bad trusts, or reasonable and unreasonable ones. It is easy to ridicule this approach as amounting in practice merely to the operation of Roosevelt's prejudices. But it reflected a widespread public attitude that certain business methods were fair, while others were predatory and collusive.

In any event, with these ideas in mind Roosevelt approved the creation of a Bureau of Corporations in the Department of Commerce and Labor in 1903. The bureau would publicize corporate activity not in the public interest, gather information useful for possible legislation, and advise corporations about actions that might be in violation of the antitrust law. At the start of his administration Roosevelt favored a law requiring federal incorporation as a means of regulating interstate businesses. Toward the end of his second term he supported amendments to the Sherman Act that would have empowered the Bureau of Corporations to act as a regulatory and advisory commission to the trusts. It was proposed, for example, that corporations register with the bureau and submit merger and consolidation plans for approval; if the bureau did not disapprove within thirty days, the plans would be legal and the corporations would be immune from antitrust prosecution. Though not adopted, these proposals reflected the thinking of many progressive Republicans and key corporate leaders. They also gave formal expression to practices employed by the Roosevelt administration whereby the government made agreements with corporations not to apply the antitrust law if the corporation would cooperate in investigations carried out by the Bureau of Corporations. From the administration's point of view, the purpose of these "gentleman's agreements" was to assert the authority of the national government over great financial and industrial empires. The corporations saw them as a way of avoiding antitrust entanglements in the federal courts.

The Taft administration preferred the legalistic method of federal regulation. Discontinuing the practice of making gentleman's agreements with the corporations, it initiated numerous antitrust suits. The result of these trust-busting efforts, however, was judicial modification of the Sherman Act along the lines of Roosevelt's distinction between reasonable and unreasonable combinations.

Although in adopting the Sherman law most members of Congress believed that it prohibited not all combinations but only those that were unreasonable or against public interest, the language of the act did not affirm this intention. Moreover, in the *Trans-Missouri* case of 1897 the Supreme Court stressed that the law applied to *all* combinations in restraint of trade, including railroads. From the time he arrived on the Court in 1894, however, Justice Edward D. White objected to a literalistic interpretation of the Sherman Act as illogical and unreasonable—every contract was in some sense a restraint of trade, he pointed out—and gradually his point of view gained adherents. Justice Holmes, for example, dissenting in the *Northern Securities* case, scouted the idea that the Sherman Act prohibited all combinations that restrained trade. By 1911 the Court's collective view comported with the outlook evolving in public opinion at large, as reflected in Theodore Roosevelt's recommendations on the trust question. The next step was to announce the "rule of reason" for applying the Sherman Act. This the Court did in *Standard Oil* v. *United States* (1911).

In an opinion by Chief Justice White, the Supreme Court affirmed a lower court decision holding the Standard Oil Company in violation of the Sherman Act. But White took the occasion to review the law of monopoly and concluded that the correct interpretation of the Sherman Act was that it forbade only unreasonable combinations or contracts in restraint of trade. "Reasonable" monopolies, he held, were legal. In the same session the Court decided a second major antitrust case in favor of the government, ordering the American Tobacco Company to reorganize in a manner consistent with the Sherman Act. Chief Justice White refused to impose absolute dissolution, but instead sought a remedy that would uphold the prohibitions of the law without injuring the interests of the public or of private property. In its own way, therefore, the Supreme Court tried to fashion a pragmatic, flexible approach to trust policy that would curtail publicly disapproved business practices without altering the basic structure of the economy.

Despite its antimonopoly heritage, the new Democratic administration of Woodrow Wilson accepted the Supreme Court's rule of reason in antitrust law. Wilson had no greater desire than any other American politician to break up the modern corporate economy, but to distinguish himself from Roosevelt in the 1912 campaign he had argued for a legalistic approach that would force corporations to behave by prohibiting specific business practices. He proposed this in contrast to Roosevelt's preferred method of regulating corporations by administrative commission. In practice, however, Wilson quickly adapted to the new bureaucratic rationale. His administration resumed the practice of entering into gentleman's agreements with corporations, securing their pledge to reform their business methods in return for immunity from antitrust prosecution. These agreements were now formally drawn up by the Justice Department and filed in federal courts as "consent decrees." The central features of Wilson's antitrust policy, however, were set forth in the Clayton Antitrust Act and the Federal Trade Commission Act of 1914.

Initially Wilson urged legislation enumerating and outlawing unwholesome corporate practices in a rigorous, straightforward way. In 1913 the House of Representatives passed a bill to this effect, but a year later, persuaded that a more flexible administrative approach was desirable, Wilson strongly supported the creation of a regulatory commission and allowed significant modifications in the antitrust proposal. Consequently, the Clayton Act, while it singled out practices such as price discrimination between different purchasers, exclusive selling arrangements, holding companies, and interlocking corporate directorates, forbade these practices only where their effect was "to substantially lessen competition or tend to create monopoly." To more militant foes of the trusts this vague guideline seriously qualified and weakened the force of the prohibition. Also unsatisfactory to many reformers were sections of the act intended to remove labor unions from the reach of antitrust law. Instead of simply stating that antitrust did not apply to labor, the act said that nothing in the antitrust laws was to be construed as forbidding the existence of labor unions or the lawful activities thereof.

The Federal Trade Commission Act of 1914, supported by business leaders as well as bureaucratic-minded progressives, declared unfair trade practices unlawful and created a five-man agency to prevent their use. Patterned after the Interstate Commerce Commission, the FTC could receive complaints, hold hearings, gather evidence, compel the attendance of witnesses, and issue cease and desist orders where it found unfair trade practices to exist. By a combination of formal and informal rulings, the commission in the next decade carried out Wilson's intention of providing information and guidance so that businessmen could know the meaning of the antitrust laws and plan accordingly. The purpose of government regulation carried on in this form was to keep business honest yet productive. In the view of progressive reformer Thurman Arnold, it enabled Americans to enjoy the benefits of large-scale economic organization while maintaining the ideal of free and fair competition among individuals. Behavior evaluated in moral terms, rather than for its economic effects, was the essence of the rule of reason that guided progressive regulation.

Progressive Regulation: The Railroads

The general problem in railroad regulation at the turn of the century was to promote a stable national transportation system at rates fair both to the carriers and their customers. As with regulation of business in general, however, political and economic realities had conflicting effects that confused the task of defining public policy. In political terms, railroads were monopolistic villains responsible for high rates and discriminatory practices that placed small shippers at a commercial disadvantage and worked hardship on the public. Economically, however, the railroads themselves operated under disadvantages imposed by powerful producer-shipper interests. They suffered from rate cutting and rebating tactics of competing lines. Facing higher costs in a generally inflationary economy, they needed higher rates for increased revenues. To deal with these circumstances the railroads formed communities of interest, or cartels, under ICC approval. Yet the commission, to whom critics of the railroads also turned for relief, could do little because it had very little power. Between the provisions of the Interstate Commerce Act of 1887 and restrictions added by the Supreme Court, the ICC was indeed virtually powerless, lacking above all the authority to set rates. Accordingly, reform involved first the strengthening of the commission. How the ICC should use its powers was a second and more problematic question.

Seeking to end practices that disrupted the communities of interest they were trying to form, the railroads supported federal legislation against rebating. Their backing was the major force in the passage of the Elkins Act of 1903, which made the published rate the legal rate and declared any deviation from it a crime. Approved with overwhelming support, the law left the broader aspects of the railroad structure untouched.

More controversial was legislation strengthening the ICC. The railroads wanted federal assistance in raising rates and defending against costly state regulation, while retaining themselves the power initially to set rates. When legislation affecting rates appeared inevitable, the railroads supported it. As a kind of insurance, they pressed for broad judicial review that would allow federal courts to examine new evidence not considered by the ICC and thus in effect to set rates. Reform-minded antirailroad lawmakers wanted to empower the ICC to set rates originally, or at least after hearing shippers' complaints against excessively high rates. Proponents of this approach urged narrow judicial review that would confine courts to examination of the method by which the commission made its rate judgments rather than the reasonableness of the judgment itself.

The House in 1906 passed a bill giving the ICC power to set rates on complaint and provided for judicial review of whether a commission order had been "regularly made"—that is, according to procedures prescribed by law. The bill was attacked in the Senate by opponents of ICC rate setting who favored broad judicial review. A compromise amendment was then agreed on which avoided the whole question of the limits of judicial review of ICC orders, in effect giving the matter to the courts for future definition. The amendment provided further that the orders of the commission should take effect within a reasonable time and should run for two years. For the first time, too, the burden of appeals rested on the railroads rather than the ICC. The House agreed to this amendment, and the result was the Hepburn Act of 1906.

Congress further strengthened the ICC by giving it original rate-setting powers in the Mann-Elkins Act of 1910. Although the railroads were still permitted to set rates, the commission on its own initiative (rather than on complaint) could suspend rates and conduct an investigation. In a move apparently intended to satisfy conservatives, Congress also created a Commerce Court with power to hear appeals from the ICC, thereby presumably restraining it. The Commerce Court proved ineffectual, however. More nearly resembling an administrative agency than an Article III judicial body—its members, for example, served five-year terms—the Commerce Court lacked the institutional protection needed to enable it to challenge the regulatory role of the ICC. The railroads, moreover, preferred the administrative management of the ICC against rapidly proliferating state regulatory laws. After a member of the Commerce Court was impeached for financial peculation, Congress abolished it in 1913.

In the next few years the ICC vindicated its authority as the dominant regulatory agency for the railroad industry. The Supreme Court, accepting the unmistakable congressional intention, showed no inclination to challenge the revitalization of the commission. Allowed to define the scope of its review, the Court chose a narrow approach in *ICC* v. *Illinois Central Railroad Company* (1910). Disavowing any policy-making intention, the Court said it could consider only the question of whether the ICC had power to make an order, not whether the power was wisely exercised. The Supreme Court also upheld the commission's rate-fixing powers, both original and on complaint, and rejected the notion that for Congress to delegate rate-setting power to the commission was an unconstitutional delegation of legislative authority to the executive branch.

ICC efforts to control intrastate commerce when it directly affected interstate commerce also received judicial approval. Although upholding a state commission's intrastate rate order, the Court in the *Minnesota Rate Cases* (1913) noted the interrelated nature of national and local commerce and said that the federal government had some authority to regulate strictly internal commerce. In the *Shreveport Rate Cases* in 1914 the Court sustained an ICC order that regulated intrastate rates by disallowing rates between Houston and Dallas to east Texas that were lower than from Shreveport (Louisiana) to east Texas. The local Texas rate was found by the commission to have an adverse effect on interstate commerce and, therefore, could be superseded by a higher rate.

Although these decisions clearly recognized the legal authority of the ICC and its superiorty over state regulatory commissions, the commission did not use its power to modify or improve the national transportation system in any significant way. State regulation, in the form of taxation and legislation dealing with hours of service, safety requirements, employers' liability, and the like, continued to proliferate and had a major effect on the operating expenses of the railroads. Together with higher labor, material, and capital charges, the cost of meeting state requirements led the railroads to seek rate increases from the ICC.

The commission's response to this situation showed the difficulty of deciding what the public interest required and the ambiguous nature of federal regulation. From one perspective the ICC served the public interest by keeping rail rates low, on the theory that the railroads' monopolistic powers needed to be held severely in restraint. If railroad revenues were lower than costs, the solution was more careful management and increased productivity. This was a politically popular approach, and it was the course pursued by the ICC between 1906 and 1917. Most of the time the commission rejected requests for rate increases or, as in a series of celebrated rate cases in 1914, granted a 5-percent increase to midwestern and eastern lines that was substantially less than requested. Whether this policy was best calculated in the long run to promote the public interest, however, was a legitimate question raised by a minority of ICC members who favored higher rates. In their view rate increases were needed to enable the railroads to improve and increase their services and strengthen their financial position. In this conception of federal regulation, which, of course, the railroads supported, the ICC was concerned with the relationship of the railroads to the economy as a whole. Specifically, the ICC should seek to rationalize the system by allowing railroads to form cartels and by protecting them against conflicting and burdensome state regulations.

Resisting pressure from President Wilson, the ICC persisted in its narrow and negative conception of regulation until World War I. In December 1917 wartime exigencies led the Wilson administration to entrust regulation of the railroads to an executive-created agency. Subsequently, Congress suspended antitrust and antipooling laws to permit coordination of the railroads into an integrated national system. Instructed by this wartime experience, Congress in the Transportation Act of 1920 restored the ICC to its dominant regulatory position, giving it express powers to coordinate railroad operations into a limited number of cartels.

Government Regulation of Politics: Restoring Government to the People

At the heart of reform ideology lay the perception that powerful economic interests, through graft, corruption, and the like, had perverted the political process and undermined republican civic virtue. As it was necessary in economic life to restore democracy by regulating the great private corporations, so it was necessary to restore government to the people by restricting the activities of political parties.

By the time of the Civil War political parties were recognized as an essential part of the constitutional system. Their principal functions were to represent and organize public opinion and inculcate republican values. Their importance increased in the late nineteenth century as they fulfilled a variety of social and cultural purposes and became more disciplined in their management of public life. Yet parties bore a heavy onus of scandal. Party activity was continually marred by venality and corruption, especially in the elaborate schemes of plunder carried on by political machines in the great industrial cities. By the start of the progressive era civil service reform was a generation old, but it had done little to break the grip of party on the institutions of government. State legislatures were especially beholden to party machines and were widely discredited as a result.

Around 1905, however, muckraking reports in mass-circulation magazines enabled political corruption to be seen as a national phenomenon and gave decisive impetus to efforts to regulate party activity. Although a few reformers argued that parties should be made responsible by means of a centralized leadership that would enable them to perform their constitutional functions more effectively, most opinion desired to subject the parties to greater government control. Originally intended to represent the people, parties had become a barrier between the people and their government. Reformers concluded that their powers must be limited so that the people themselves could rule.

At the national level the antiparty tendency was earliest expressed in the famous revolt against "Cannonism," or the power of the Speaker of the House. In the 1890s Democrats for their own partisan reasons institutionalized the rules originally conceived by Republican Thomas B. Reed to strengthen the Speaker and through him the role of the party in the conduct of legislative business. From 1903 to 1909 Republican Joseph Cannon of Illinois, trained in the Reed tradition, wielded the gavel with all the arbitrary power of his preceptor. In 1909 a coalition of progressive Republicans and Democrats struck at Cannon's power by securing an amendment to the House rules setting aside one day a week on which the Speaker would be obliged to "call the calendar"—that is, to take up the business of the House in order, without regard to priorities fixed by the Rules Committee. Subsequent reforms, by making the Rules Committee elective and denying the Speaker a seat on it, deprived the Speaker of his power to appoint committees and to control legislation on the floor. These reforms had a narrow political motivation in the desire of insurgent Republicans to minimize the electoral liability that "Cannonism" had become in the Republican party. Yet their actions confirmed the larger public belief that identified "Cannonism" with machine politics.

A second antiparty reform at the federal level was the direct election of senators. For years many people asserted that election of senators by the state legislatures was inconsistent with the principles of democratic government. The defeat of state sovereignty during the Civil War weakened the idea that the states as such were represented in the Senate, and the identification of many late nineteenth-century senators with party machines provoked demands for the popular election of senators. The Populists first agitated this issue, and in 1893, 1894, 1898, 1900, and 1902 the House approved a constitutional amendment for this purpose. Each time, however, it was defeated in the Senate. Meanwhile, the states began to hold senatorial primary elections, the results being automatically approved by the state legislatures. By 1912 twenty-nine states employed this method of choosing senators. When in 1911 an Illinois senator was found to have been fraudulently elected, the Senate agreed to the amendment for direct election of senators. In 1913 it became the Seventeenth Amendment.

Women's suffrage, insofar as it was motivated by a belief that it would have a stabilizing and purifying effect on public life, may also be seen as reflecting an antiparty impulse. Party bosses long opposed women's suffrage, in part because it was associated with the general cause of political reform but also because of uncertainty as to the effects of suddenly doubling the size of the electorate. Principally, the women's suffrage movement was an extension of the drive to improve the legal and general social status of women in the second half of the nineteenth century. Colorado in 1897 was the first state to enfranchise women, and by 1914 twelve states, all of them western, had adopted the reform. Instead of continuing their efforts at the state level, women's suffrage strategists now pressed for a national constitutional amendment. Sensing the inevitability of the reform, national party leaders began to change their minds about it, and the Republican party endorsed the enfranchisement of women in the presidential campaign of 1916.

The main obstacle to women's suffrage in Congress was the South. Fearing that any increase in federal power over voting would threaten their recent disenfranchisement of the Negro, southern members of Congress, all Democrats, consistently opposed a women's suffrage amendment. With increasing numbers of women engaged in business and industry during World War I, however, the reform became irresistible. At last in 1919, under Republican leadership, Congress approved the women's suffrage amendment for submission to the states. The Nineteenth Amendment became part of the Constitution in August 1920.

The states rather than the federal government were the main focus of reforms aimed at regulating political parties. This was because parties were local voluntary associations whose principal functions concerned elections, which it was still primarily the states' responsibility to regulate. Starting in 1888 in Massachusetts, a movement caught on to institute the Australian or secret ballot, replacing party-distributed, colored ballots that made possible identification of a voter's choice. By 1900 the change was generally adopted as an antiparty reform. To stop corrupt business-party interaction, states also passed laws restricting campaign contributions and regulating lobbying. States further struck at the power of political parties by introducing direct primary elections to reform the nominating process. Instituted by Wisconsin in 1903, direct primaries replaced party-controlled conventions as a means of selecting candidates. By 1915, thirty-two states had adopted this change, setting qualifications for voters, fixing the date, and paying costs as in a general election.

Still another antiparty reform was direct legislation through the initiative and referendum, enabling the people to circumvent the state legislature. These instruments were first advocated by the Populists in 1896. In 1898, South Dakota wrote the initiative into its constitution by an amendment which permitted the people to present legislation to the assembly by petition. The legislature was permitted either to enact the law or to present an alternative proposal to the people. Oregon followed with a more famous reform in 1902, by which both constitutional amendments and ordinary legislation might be proposed by petition. These, in turn, were required to be submitted to the voters of the state for acceptance or rejection in a general election. This provision became a model for most states subsequently adopting the initiative and referendum. By 1914, eighteen states had adopted the initiative and referendum for ordinary legislation, and twelve of these permitted the device to be used for constitutional amendment as well.

Another device, the recall, was intended to place popular controls upon executive officers. A small percentage of the voters, usually about 8 percent in statewide elections, could petition for a special election, in which the electorate could decide whether or not a specified official was to be removed from office. Oregon pioneered in this reform also, with a constitutional amendment adopted in 1908. By 1915, some eleven states had followed Oregon's lead, and seven of these permitted the recall of judges.

Related to the antiparty tendency was the effort to check legislative dishonesty. After 1900 the states adopted a growing number of amendments which imposed restrictions upon the scope of legislative authority, competence, and discretion, and which specified legislative procedure and function in great detail. Large areas of special legislation were withdrawn from the control of the assembly entirely. In general, the power to fix rates for public utilities was handed to special commissions. Other amendments fixed tax schedules and specified permissible kinds of taxation, while still others forbade the enactment of special legislation for private interest groups. There were new provisions which established county seats, drew the boundaries of assembly districts, or fixed the salaries of public officials. Other provisions set up state factory inspection systems, limited the length of the working day for women, or set up workmen's compensation systems. Thus the typical state constitution came to resemble a statute book, mainly because the people no longer trusted the legislature to protect their interests or to exercise the degree of discretion which had once been accorded it.

The struggle against corrupt party politics was carried on with special fervor in the movement for municipal reform. One aspect of the movement was the demand for home rule. As an outgrowth of nineteenth-century state sovereignty, orthodox constitutional theory gave states control over local government. Usually the state legislature delegated particular powers to municipal corporations or passed special laws directed to local needs. Reformers attacked this system, arguing that state legislatures, typically under the control of party bosses, were unfit to govern autonomous local communities. Some reformers defended home rule as true popular sovereignty, but more often the justification was honesty and efficiency in government.

Part of the home-rule question was the further issue of the type of government that ought to exist at the local level. Here reformers were especially critical of the decentralized, mayor-and-council form of government that prevailed in the late nineteenth century. It gave lower-class ethnic ward leaders a strong voice, but one which was often indistinguishable from that of the party machine. The system was corrupt, wasteful, and inefficient, and in its place reformers proposed either the commission or the commission-plus-city manager form of government. Instead of being chosen by ward elections, these governments would be selected by city-wide, at-large elections. While reformers viewed these changes as restoring government to the people, they were also justified on the basis of common-sense business intelligence. Merchants, manufacturers, and professional men formed the chief sources of support for municipal transportation facilities and public services which it was believed more honest, efficient, and technically competent government could provide.

Reforms that imposed public control on the political parties were ambiguous in relation to democratic theory. Frequently defended as democratic, they had the observable effect, especially in municipal government, of reducing the power of lower-class groups and giving a political advantage to middle-class professionals and businessmen. Moreover reforms such as the initiative and referendum, or primary elections, did not stimulate wider popular involvement in government. On the contrary, voter participation declined during the progressive era, initiating a trend that continued throughout the twentieth century. Some historians have discerned a middle-class quest for power in these reforms, but in fact reformers acted on the belief—probably correct—that the lower classes would receive more benefit from public services provided by an honest government than from occasional favors of corrupt, machine-dominated government. If municipal reform decreased the power of lower-class ethnic groups, the party- and ward-dominated local government that it replaced possessed no inherent constitutional or democratic legitimacy. Indeed, from another perspective these changes in state and local government were democratic, for they adapted the constitutional order more readily to the pluralistic, interest-group structure that was coming to characterize American society in the early twentieth century. Organized and conscious of their interests, businessmen supported and utilized progressive governmental reforms. In time, however, other interests, including minority groups, would gain access to the political arena through these changes.

Despite its emphasis on the need to expand federal power, progressive constitutionalism maintained a strong orientation toward state and local government. It is significant, for example, that until 1913 the movement to abolish child labor foreswore a federal solution as constitutionally improper and pursued its objective through state legislation. Indeed on many issues—workmen's compensation, hours of labor, industrial safety, and so on—uniform state legislation rather than centralized federal law was the objective of reformers. Success was considerable in some spheres, but overall it was limited, mainly because of economic rivalries between states and regions. Nevertheless, the conscious pursuit of reform through uniform state legislation is a reminder that federalism continued to be a basic value in the constitutional system and a valid means of dealing with national social and economic problems.

The Income Tax Amendment

In the long run, however, the momentum of progressive reform was centralizing, despite the persistence of states'-rights sentiment. The federal income tax amendment, one of the most important foundations of federal sovereignty in the twentieth century, provides apt illustration.

As part of their campaign against the special interests, reformers during the Roosevelt and Taft administrations introduced income tax legislation. Although the two *Pollock* decisions of 1895 apparently blocked such a measure, the Supreme Court had recently ruled that an excise tax on corporations, calculated as a percentage of corporate income, was not a direct tax within the meaning of the Constitution. This decision suggested that a tax law might be devised that could meet the Court's approval. The alternative was a constitutional amendment enabling Congress to levy a tax on income without the necessity of apportionment among the states according to population. But as this constitutional change would notably expand federal power, it was thought to have no realistic chance of adoption by the states.

In 1909 midwestern Republicans and Democrats, allied in opposition to higher tariff rates, joined in support of an income tax proposal to be added to the tariff bill. When it appeared likely that the measure, virtually a reenactment of the old 1894 income tax law, would be approved, conservative Republican leaders took the extraordinary step of presenting a constitutional amendment to legalize the income tax. The proposal was conceived solely as a device to defeat the income tax provision in the tariff bill. President Taft, who had earlier supported a corporation excise tax, sent a message to Congress recommending passage of the amendment, and the strategy worked. In the belief that the amendment would fail to get ratification, Congress sent it to the states, while enacting a corporation excise tax as a substitute for the income tax proposal in the tariff bill. Reformers voted for the amendment despite its conservative support.

Contrary to expectation, however, the states ratified the Sixteenth Amendment and it became part of the Constitution in 1913. The amendment inaugurated a new era in federal finance, within a few years becoming the principal source of federal revenue. Of greatest immediate importance, it enabled the government to finance the country's participation in World War I. Yet the full centralizing effect of the income tax amendment and its redistributionist social and economic consequences lay in the future. Neither its framers nor its ratifiers intended it to revolutionize the federal system, but rather to provide a more equitable means of distributing the costs of government, especially in times of crisis. The Supreme Court confirmed the limited character of the amendment in relation to federalism when it held in 1916 that although the amendment stated that Congress might tax income from whatever source derived, it could not tax income from state bonds or the income of state employees. This decision symbolized the tension between centralization and states' rights that characterized constitutional politics in the progressive era.

TWENTY-TWO

The Constitution and World War I

———————————— ✦✦✦ ————————————

THE ENTRY OF THE UNITED STATES into war in 1917 brought into sharp relief two important constitutional problems, neither of which was altogether new. These were the conflict between a decentralized constitutional system and the requirements of wartime centralization, and the conflict between executive war powers and congressional legislative power.

Federal Power in Wartime

In 1917 the United States experienced for the first time the full impact of war upon the modern social order. War, the nation soon learned, was no longer an isolated state activity divorced from civil affairs and of little interest to the common citizen. Instead it involved every part of the nation's social and economic life. Both the Allies and the Central Powers had had this lesson driven home to them well before 1917, and the United States soon grasped the same reality. The imperative necessities of modern war posed a difficult constitutional issue: How could a total effort be reconciled with the limited extent of federal sovereignty? Did the war power suspend the federal system in wartime and so make constitutional the economic and social controls necessary to victory?

The extent of federal power in wartime became a major issue in Congress in June 1917, when the administration introduced the Lever Food Control bill giving the federal government authority to deal with the impending food shortage and rising food prices. The preamble of this measure announced that for reasons of national defense it was necessary to secure an adequate supply and distribution of food and fuel. The food and fuel industries were, therefore, declared to be affected with a public interest and subject to federal regulation. It was made unlawful to waste, monopolize, fix prices, or limit production in foodstuffs. Whenever necessary, the executive was authorized to license the manufacture and distribution of foodstuffs, to take over and operate factories and mines, and to subject markets and exchanges to executive regulation. In "extreme emergencies" the president could impose schedules of prices upon any industry. The Lever bill was designed primarily to control food and fuel production, but its terms were so broad as to subject virtually the entire economic life of the nation to whatever regulation the president thought necessary for victory.

The bill at once precipitated a bitter debate in Congress, where much of the discussion hinged upon the federal war power. The bill's supporters contended that the war power could not be narrowly construed. Senator Frank B. Kellogg of Minnesota, for example, argued that in wartime the national government could "in fact do anything necessary to the support of the people during the war and to lend strength to the cause," an opinion concurred in by Senator Paul O. Husting of Wisconsin. More moderate was the position taken in the House by Representative Sidney Anderson of Minnesota, who contended simply that the federal government in wartime could do anything having a reasonable relationship to the war effort. This theory of the war power, it presently appeared, was accepted by a large majority in both houses of Congress.

The bill nevertheless drew fire from a vociferous minority in both houses. Senator James Reed of Missouri, an intransigent Democratic opponent of Wilson, attacked federal price and production controls as a violation of the Tenth Amendment, which he contended threw the burden of proof upon the proponents of any particular federal right in question. No federal right, he said, could be established by broad interpretation. Senator Thomas W. Hardwick of Georgia, also a Democratic enemy of Wilson, advanced a more moderate claim. He admitted that Congress could do anything immediately and directly connected with the prosecution of the war, but he insisted that the outbreak of war did not immediately break down all the reserved powers of the states. The difficulty with this position was that a large majority in and out of Congress recognized how necessary federal food control was to the successful prosecution of the war. The House reflected this attitude when it passed the Lever bill late in June after only a week of debate. The measure was delayed in the Senate through an attempt to establish a congressional committee to direct the war effort, but the bill eventually passed the upper house and became law on August 10, 1917.

While the Lever Act was the most dramatic instance in the First World War in which the federal government used the war power to invade a sphere of sovereignty ordinarily reserved to the states, there were numerous other measures of a similar character. Thus by various statutes, Congress authorized the president to force preferential compliance with government war contracts, to take over and operate factories needed for war industries, and to regulate the foreign-language press of the country. In the War Prohibition Act, passed on November 21, 1918, Congress forbade the manufacture and sale of alcoholic liquors for the duration of the war. Other statutes, such as those for the wartime operation of the railroads, the censorship of the mails, the control of cable and radio communications, and the regulation of exports, were in part justified by the war emergency; but they could also be adjudged constitutional by other specific powers of Congress, notably that over interstate commerce. The Selective Service Act of May 18, 1917, establishing a wartime military draft, rested in part upon the constitutional provision empowering Congress to raise and support armies as well as upon the war power.

The important decisions bearing upon the extent of the federal war power were made by Congress and the president without guidance of the Supreme Court. Most of the critical war measures never came before the Court; and with one exception, the few that did reached the Court well after the armistice, when the constitutional issues involved were no longer of immediate significance. As in Civil War days, it would have been difficult or impossible for the Court to challenge successfully the constitutionality of a federal war activity while the war was in progress. One may assume that had the Court passed unfavorably upon vital war legislation while the war was still going on, ways and means probably would have been discovered to ignore or to circumvent the decision.

In the *Selective Draft Law Cases,* decided in January 1918, the Court unanimously upheld the constitutionality of the Selective Service Act of 1917. Chief Justice White found the constitutional authorization to impose compulsory military service in the clause empowering Congress to declare war and "to raise and support armies." He held that the power was derived also from the very character of "just government," whose "duty to the citizen includes the reciprocal obligation of the citizen to render military service in case of need and the right to compel it." He then pointed to the long historical record of compulsory military service in English and colonial law and in the American Civil War, to bolster his assertion that the power to draft men into military service was a necessary incidence both of the federal war power and of federal sovereignty. The Court's decision was obvious and inevitable, since it was evident that an adverse ruling upon the constitutionality of the draft would have interposed the Court's will directly athwart the national war effort.

Later decisions also sustained a broad interpretation of federal war powers. In the *War Prohibition Cases,* decided in December 1919, the Court upheld the validity of the War Prohibition Act, although the law had been passed after the signing of the armistice. Justice Brandeis in his opinion simply assumed the validity of the act under the federal war power and held further that the signing of the armistice did not make the statute inoperative or void, since the war power was not limited merely to insuring victories in the field but extended to the power to guard against renewal of the conflict. A few months later, in *Rupert* v. *Caffey* (1920), the Court again upheld the law. Brandeis's opinion rejected the plea that the act was an invasion of the states' police powers with the observation that "when the United States exerts any of the powers conferred upon it by the Constitution, no valid objection can be based upon the fact that such exercise may be attended by the same incidents which attend the exercise by a state of its police power."

In *Northern Pacific Ry. Co.* v. *North Dakota* (1919) the Court passed favorably upon the provision in the Army Appropriation Act of August 19, 1916, authorizing presidential seizure and operation of the railroads in wartime. Speaking for a unanimous Court, Chief Justice White observed that "the complete and undivided character of the war power of the United States is not disputable." He added that wartime federal operation could lawfully brush aside intrastate rate controls normally binding upon the roads in time of peace, since to interpret the exercise of the federal war power "by a presumption of the continuance of a state power limiting and controlling the national authority was but to deny its existence." In other words, the federal war power here broke in upon state authority and set aside the normal division between state and national power.

In *United States* v. *L. Cohen Grocery Co.* (1921) the Court invalidated Section 4 of the Lever Act (as re-enacted October 22, 1919), which had made it illegal to impose any unreasonable charge for food. But the Court's reason for taking this step was not that it thought the federal government could not fix prices in wartime. Instead, Chief Justice White's opinion held the law unconstitutional on the ground that the statute had failed to fix any standards for what constituted unjust prices, had fixed no specific standards for guilt, and had forbidden no specific act, and so violated the Fifth and Sixth Amendments, which prohibited the delegation of legislative power to the courts, the punishment of vague and inadequately defined offenses, and deprivation of the citizen's right to be informed of the nature of the accusation against him. In short, the law was unconstitutional not because it fixed prices, but because it failed to do so with any clarity. White's opinion said nothing of the larger constitutional issues implicit in the Lever Act, the Court presumably accepting as constitutional the main principle of the statute.

Thus the Court in several opinions recognized that the requirements of modern war left little of federalism in wartime. This was indeed little more than a judicial recognition of a condition already existing and of a truth so imperative that it would have been futile for the Court to deny its existence.

Wilson's War Dictatorship

Wilson has often been compared to Lincoln on the ground that both men were elevated to dictatorships by the exigencies of war. Yet the comparison must be made with some caution. Lincoln was faced with an internal war, for which there was no constitutional precedent, as well as a confusing constitutional problem growing out of the whole issue of secession. He solved the difficulties of his position by assuming certain arbitary powers by virtue of his constitutional authority as commander in chief of the armed forces, and for several months he carried on a war against the secessionists by presidential fiat and without benefit of congressional authorization. Even after Congress had formally recognized the war, Lincoln took certain important steps—notably the Emancipation Proclamation and certain preliminary reconstruction decisions—without congressional authorization.

Wilson's position was somewhat different. The war was formally declared by Congress, and Wilson acted from the beginning by virtue of certain large grants of authority delegated to him by Congress. While he made frequent use of his authority as commander in chief, he was never obliged to take any fundamental step without the authorization of Congress.

If Wilson was in any sense a dictator, it was because Congress in certain spheres came close to a virtual delegation of its entire legislative power to the president for the duration of the war. Many federal war statutes merely described the objectives of the act in broad terms and then delegated to the president authority to enforce the law. Delegation of this kind went far beyond that considered in *Field* v. *Clark,* or *United States* v. *Grimaud,* for the war statutes in question erected no standards for executive guidance other than the general objectives of the law. Legislative delegation on this scale was unprecedented and little short of revolutionary.

This issue arose several times during the war, but was extensively discussed for the first time in the debates on the Lever Act. As already noted, the bill gave the president extraordinarily broad discretionary powers. He could license the manufacture and distribution of food and related commodities, take over and operate mines and factories, regulate exchanges, and fix commodity prices. No limits whatever were fixed upon his action in pursuance of any of these provisions so long as he deemed a particular step essential to secure the purposes of the act.

Administration supporters in both houses tried to defend delegation on this scale on the ground that adequate standards were erected by the announced purposes of the act. But as Senator Thomas W. Hardwick of Georgia pointed out in a discussion of the bill's price-fixing provisions, no standards whatever were provided except the general welfare and the successful conduct of the war. Most of the Republicans and a generous sprinkling of Democrats thought such delegation utterly unconstitutional. Representative George M. Young of North Dakota voiced this position when he denounced the bill as an attempt to create a presidential dictatorship by law, an opinion echoed in the Senate by James Reed of Missouri.

This attitude led to a Senate attempt to establish a Joint Congressional Committee on the Conduct of the War, with the intent to effect a general congressional dictorship over all war operations. While the Lever bill was in the upper house, Senator John Wingate Weeks of Massachusetts introduced an amendment providing for a congressional war committee, to be composed of ten men, three Democrats and two Republicans from each house. It was to study all problems arising out of the war, and to confer and cooperate with the president and other executive heads. It was also to possess extensive powers of investigation into all phases of war activity.

The proposed committee was modeled after a similar body established by Congress in 1861. It will be recalled that the Civil War committee had been inspired by Republican dissatisfaction with Lincoln's war efforts and the president's extraordinary assumption of power. Under Ben Wade's leadership the committee had attempted to exercise powers of executive supervision and control and had been a constant source of annoyance to Lincoln. Presumably, then, Weeks intended to place heavy shackles upon Wilson's war leadership. Ex-President Roosevelt, who bitterly distrusted Wilson and was now loud in his denunciation of the president, was in fact the principal inspiration for the Weeks amendment, but many congressmen of both parties, more than a little fearful of executive ascendancy, also supported the measure.

In the discussions on the Senate floor, both friends and enemies of the administration appealed to the authority of history to prove or disprove the wisdom of establishing another such committee. In an attempt to demonstrate that the Civil War committee had worked well, Republican senators Joseph I. France of Maryland, Boies Penrose of Pennsylvania, and Laurence Y. Sherman of Illinois and Democratic senators Reed and Hardwick quoted contemporary writers, the historians James Ford Rhodes and William H. Dunning, and even Wilson's historical works. In turn, Senator Lee Overman of North Carolina and Wilson's other supporters quoted John Hay, Gideon Welles, and Lincoln in an effort to show that the committee had worked badly and had embarrassed Lincoln's war effort. In the end, the Senate adopted a slight variant of the Weeks amendment by a vote of 51 to 31.

When the House took up the Senate amendments to the Lever bill, Wilson immediately made it clear that he regarded the proposed committee as an attempt to deprive him of executive leadership in the war. The committee would involve, he said, "nothing less than an assumption on the part of the legislative body of the executive work of the administration." He concluded with the warning that he would interpret the final adoption of the committee measure by Congress as a vote of lack of confidence in himself. Wilson's message killed the proposal, for the House eliminated it from the bill.

After the passage of the Lever Act on August 10, 1917, there was for the moment little further effective resistance to the delegation of broad legislative authority to the president. The Selective Service Act of May 18,

1917, had given the executive almost complete discretion to conscript an army as he saw fit. The Trading with the Enemy Act, which became law on October 6, 1917, gave the president discretionary authority to license trade with Germany, and to censor mail, cable, and radio communications with foreign states. A provision in the Army Appropriation Act of August 29, 1916, had already conferred upon the president the right to take over and operate common carriers in time of war. A joint resolution of Congress enacted July 16, 1918, authorized him to seize and operate telephone and telegraph lines.

Not until the Overman bill came before Congress in the spring of 1918 did Congress make any further show of resistance to presidential ascendancy. This bill, an administration measure introduced on February 6 by Senator Lee Overman of North Carolina, was inspired by a desire to introduce some order and flexibility into the chaotic welter of wartime bureaus, commissions, and other special agencies. The bill authorized the president to "make such redistribution of functions among executive agencies as he may deem necessary, including any functions, duties, and powers hitherto by law conferred upon any executive department." The act was to remain in force until a year after the close of the war, when all executive offices were to revert to their prewar status. Thus the reorganization projected was not permanent, but merely a wartime emergency measure.

The Overman bill proposed to delegate an extraordinary measure of legislative discretion to the president. So broad and sweeping was its phraseology that the president could, for example, have transferred all the functions of the State Department to the War Department, or the functions of the Federal Reserve Board to the Treasury Department. Since those and similar executive units had been created and their functions defined by acts of Congress, the bill thus empowered the president to suspend during the war all past congressional statutes organizing the executive. No limits on executive discretion were specified, and no standards were erected, other than the president's decision that any given step was necessary to the efficient prosecution of the war.

The Overman bill reached the Senate floor in March 1918, and there the principal discussion centered on the constitutionality of the measure. Overman and other administration supporters contended that the bill made no actual substantive grant of legislative authority to the president, since he could create no new functions but could merely transfer those already in existence. The bill was justified also, argued Senator James Hamilton Lewis of Illinois, by the extraordinary powers which the president could lawfully exercise as wartime commander in chief. Oddly enough, Republican Senator Henry Cabot Lodge of Massachusetts admitted that in his opinion the president already possessed the powers delegated by the bill, since presidential war power existed by virtue of the Constitution, and not by act of Congress.

Some Democrats as well as Republicans joined in the attack on the constitutionality of the bill. Reed and Hardwick insisted that the bill could not be justified by the war power, since many departments and functions not related to the war could be affected by its terms. Republican Senator Frank B. Brandegee of Connecticut denounced the bill as an attempt to force Congress to "abdicate completely its legislative power and confer it upon the executive branch of the government," a sentiment concurred in by Senator Albert Cummins of Iowa. As in the debate on the Lever Act, the opposition emphasized the absence of adequate standards for executive guidance.

The Overman Act nevertheless passed the Senate on April 29, by a vote of 63 to 13, the size of the vote indicating that the great majority of senators were impressed with the need for the law and refused to allow constitutional doubts to interfere with the passage of the bill. But Senator Brandegee expressed the minority attitude in the Senate just before the voting began, when he offered an ironical amendment providing that "if any power, constitutional or not, has been inadvertently omitted from this bill, it is hereby granted in full." A few days later the House concurred in the passage of the bill, and it became law on May 20, 1918. Like the Lever Act, the Overman Act demonstrated that all ordinary restraints upon the delegation of legislative power to the president were largely put aside for the duration of the war.

Wilson did not personally exercise all the tremendous authority delegated by Congress to the president. Instead he used his ordinance-making powers to establish a whole series of commissions, boards, bureaus, and government-owned corporations to carry on the multifarious wartime executive functions. Six major boards, each responsible to the president, exercised most of the vitally important functions incident to the conduct of the war. The Office of Food Administration, which in turn controlled the United States Food Administration and the Sugar Equalization Board, carried out the provisions of the Lever Act in managing the production and consumption of foodstuffs by price controls, licensing, and carrying out food conservation campaigns. The Office of Fuel Administration, which also derived its authority from the Lever Act, administered public and private consumption of coal during the war. The War Industries Board had complete authority over all war purchases and eventually came to exercise something like a complete dictatorship over all industry. The War Industries Board rested upon no statute whatsoever; it was created solely by virtue of the president's authority as commander in chief.

Carrier operation was eventually put under a Director General of the Railroads. The United States Shipping Board, created by Congress in 1916, acting through the Emergency Fleet Corporation, constructed and operated the necessary wartime merchant marine. The Export Trade Board, which derived its authority from the Trading with the Enemy Act, imposed general controls upon export and import trade. The Committee on Public Information, also created by the president solely by virtue of his war powers, exercised an informal censorship accepted voluntarily by the press, and it acted also as an information and propaganda bureau. In addition to these bodies there were a host of lesser committees, offices, and agencies, some authorized by law, some created by presidential fiat, some voluntary and informal, but all performing some wartime executive function.

Perhaps the principal significance of this extraordinary executive structure lay in the example it offered for later national emergencies. The First World War did much to accustom the American people to an enlarged conception of federal authority; and thus when the great economic crisis of the 1930s beset the nation, the country more readily accepted legislation that delegated various measures of legislative authority to the president and that invaded the traditional sphere of state authority. Still later, the president's power to erect emergency offices, commissions, and bureaus based upon his constitutional authority as commander in chief was again prominently exercised in World War II.

TWENTY-THREE

The Constitution in Transition: 1900–1933

———————————— ✦ ✦ ✦ ————————————

ALTHOUGH BUREAUCRATIC CENTRALIZATION was relied on heavily during World War I, laissez-faire constitutionalism was by no means extinct. It had been persistently evident throughout the prewar reform period in a series of unpopular Supreme Court decisions upholding property rights and curtailing state and federal regulation of the economy. The postwar desire for a return to "normalcy" encouraged the revival of laissez-faire ideas, which were most clearly expressed in the judiciary's reassertion of the doctrines of substantive due process, liberty of contract, and dual federalism. Yet the postwar period was by no means a time of unreconstructed entrepreneurial constitutionalism. Regulatory measures based on the progressive concept of positive government, reflecting especially the outlook of Secretary of Commerce and then President Herbert Hoover, were adopted by the Republican administrations of the 1920s. Despite the dismantling of wartime controls, the federal government significantly expanded the scope of its activities to accommodate the ever more numerous interest groups in American society. Throughout the postwar decade, moreover, the enforcement of national prohibition, a progressive reform adopted in 1919, led the federal government to intervene in local affairs and in the lives of its citizens in an unprecedented way.

Thus in the first third of the twentieth century two separate streams of constitutional precedent and public policy existed. One pointed to increasing government regulation of social and economic life, principally under federal but also involving state authority. The other promised to maintain traditional limitations on government in the interest of personal liberty and entrepreneurial freedom. During the prewar years the regulatory movement made significant advances, frequently prevailing in public-policy controversies at both the state and national level. With the Republican party controlling the executive and judicial branches of the federal government in the 1920s, the two traditions could satisfactorily coexist, despite the greater political appeal of laissez-faire ideology. Ultimately, however, the two lines of constitutional development were irreconcilable. This fact became clear during the depression, when decentralized laissez-faire constitutionalism was superseded by the theory and practice of the regulatory state.

Conflicting Tendencies in Constitutional Law

The development of constitutional law from 1900 to about 1930 reflected the tension between old and new governmental tendencies as Americans tried to adapt their institutions to modern conditions, while preserving the values of individual liberty and local self-government. As a result of events in the 1890s, the Supreme Court, far more than ever before, was capable of performing an essentially legislative, policy-making function. In effect it had authority to consider the reasonableness of legislation, traditionally a political task. Decisive as the new judicial review often was, however, the Supreme Court used it only sporadically. Most of the time the justices presumed legislation to be constitutional, accepting the lawmakers' judgment of its reasonableness and inquiring only into whether the power in question existed in the Constitution.

The availability of two methods or approaches to judicial review broadened the scope of judicial action considerably. Yet the Court's discretionary power, like any constitutional instrument, lent itself to multiple purposes. If active judicial review was first used in the 1890s to defend property rights, in the early twentieth century it was frequently employed to restrict property and promote reform purposes. To be sure, the Supreme Court relied on laissez-faire constitutional doctrines when it thought regulatory proposals threatened the fundamental structure of the existing order. At no time, however, did the justices assume a categorically negative attitude toward the regulatory movement. On the contrary, they often approved laws that interjected government into economic affairs.

As noted previously, the Supreme Court in a series of decisions in the early twentieth century confirmed the existence of a federal police power under the commerce and taxing powers of Congress.[1] In doing so the Court adhered to the traditional concept of judicial review, refraining from a consideration of congressional motive and accepting the lawmakers' judgment of the reasonableness of public policy. In a number of instances, however, the Court showed that the new activist judicial review could also be used to promote reform purposes. In *Holden* v. *Hardy* (1898), for example, the Court upheld as a reasonable exercise of the police power a Utah law prohibiting the employment of workingmen in mines, smelters, or ore

1. See above, pp. 429-30.

refineries for more than eight hours in any one day. Justice Henry B. Brown's opinion for the Court emphasized factual information concerning unhealthful conditions in mines as a justification for the law. Brown also noted, contrary to the theory of worker-employer equality and liberty of contract, that mine owners and their employees were not in fact equal and that their interests conflicted. While eschewing a categorical judgment, Brown concluded that "there are reasonable grounds for believing that such determination [i.e., limiting the hours of labor in mines] is supported by the facts."

In 1908, after hearing an elaborate argument by Louis D. Brandeis that introduced a vast array of social facts and statistics, the Court ruled in *Muller* v. *Oregon* than an Oregon law limiting the employment of women in factories and laundries to ten hours per day was constitutional. The logic behind the famous "Brandeis brief" was to accept the legislative character of the new judicial review and seek to persuade the Court of the reasonableness of the legislation. Brandeis's main point was that women were different from men and should be recognized as such in industrial regulatory legislation. His argument, unusual because of its exclusive concern with the soundness of the law as public policy in the light of social conditions, was a spectacular success. Justice Brown alluded to the Brandeis materials, stating that although constitutional questions were not settled by public opinion, "when a question of fact is debated and debatable, and the extent to which a special constitutional limitation goes is affected by the truth in respect to that fact, a widespread and continued belief concerning it is worthy of consideration." In effect admitting that social policy concerns and not simply constitutional precedent were decisive in the Court's action, Brown said: "We take judicial cognizance of all matters of general knowledge."

In *Bunting* v. *Oregon* (1917) the Court approved an Oregon ten-hour statute applying to both men and women, even though it had a time-and-a-half requirement for overtime pay that arguably made it a wage regulation. Again, a survey of similar legislation in other states provided a factual basis for finding the law reasonable. In *New York Central R.R. Co.* v. *White* (1917) the Court upheld a New York Workmen's Compensation Act because it approved of the social purpose behind the law, though the fact that thirty-five states had adopted laws of this sort also influenced the decision. The Court furthermore accepted a workmen's compensation law that required contributions by the employer to a state compensation fund whether or not any injuries had befallen the employer's own workers. Speaking for a 5–4 majority, Justice Mahlon Pitney said the statute had a reasonable relationship to a matter of great importance to the public welfare.[2]

Other proregulatory decisions rested on an older conception of judicial review in which the Court deferred to the legislative judgment of the

2. *Cf. Mountain Timber Co.* v. *Washington* (1917).

reasonableness of legislation. For example, it upheld state tax levies that conceivably could have been invalidated as unconstitutional because they were not directed toward a public purpose. In *Fallbrook Irrigation District* v. *Bradley* (1896) the Court accepted the constitutionality of a California statute permitting groups of landowners by vote to organize themselves into irrigation districts with authority to levy assessments on all landowners within the district. In *Jones* v. *Portland* (1917) it accepted a Maine law authorizing any city or town to establish a fuel yard to sell wood and coal to the inhabitants. And in *Green* v. *Frazier* (1920) the Court approved North Dakota legislation that allowed a state industrial commission to engage in a variety of business enterprises, to issue bonds to capitalize the enterprises, and to pay for the bonds by taxation.

In yet another series of decisions approving government intervention in the economy the Supreme Court accepted the manifest intention of Congress to make the Interstate Commerce Commission the dominant regulatory authority for the transportation system as a whole. As noted previously, after passage of the Hepburn Act of 1906 the Court ceased to exercise broad review over the actions of the ICC. The Minnesota and Shreveport rate cases, moreover, sustained commission regulation of intrastate rates that affected the interstate structure of railroad tariffs.[3] Judicial endorsement of this phase of the regulatory movement continued after Congress passed the Transportation Act of 1920. This measure strengthened the positive rate-setting powers of the commission and gave it power to restrict the earnings of the railroads through a recapture clause that interfered with their character as private property. In *Railroad Commission of Wisconsin* v. *C.B. and Q.* (1922) the Court upheld the 1920 law and the power of the ICC to revise intrastate rates upward to secure the railroads a fair income. In *Dayton-Goose Creek Railway Company* v. *United States* (1924) the Court approved the recapture clause in particular, Chief Justice William Howard Taft declaring that a carrier was "not entitled, as a constitutional right, to more than a fair operating income upon the value of its properties" devoted to transportation. In *Stafford* v. *Wallace* (1922) the Court sustained another national regulatory measure, the Packers and Stockyards Act of 1921, which attempted to eliminate discriminatory and monopolistic trade practices in the meat industry. Basing his opinion on the *Swift* precedent, Chief Justice Taft gave new emphasis to the stream-of-commerce doctrine as a source of federal regulatory power.

Preserving the Fundamentals

If there were relatively few proregulatory or progressive decisions in the later 1920s, it is nevertheless inaccurate to draw a sharp distinction

3. See above, p. 437.

between the Supreme Court in the pre- and postwar eras. For throughout the period 1900 to 1930 the Court drew the line against social and economic legislation that seemed to alter market and property relationships too drastically. Often the Court's nay-saying was unexpected, disregarding what appeared to be controlling precedents in support of regulatory legislation. Yet in a deeper sense there was a defensible rationale in the fitfulness of the Court's response to social legislation, for it expressed the reluctance of the society as a whole to move too rapidly toward positive government and the regulatory state.

Although the Court allowed numerous interventions by state governments that could have been regarded as interfering with property rights, the doctrines of substantive due process and liberty of contract remained valid propositions in constitutional law.[4] Their hold on the judicial mind appeared clearly in *Lochner* v. *New York* (1905), a case decided at approximately the same time that the Court upheld the antitrust law and discovered a federal police power for reform purposes.

The *Lochner* case concerned a New York law that regulated conditions of labor in the baking industry. The statute dealt with the construction and maintenance of bakeries, including drainage, plumbing, safety and sanitary conditions, and hours of labor. Sixty hours of labor were permitted per week, or ten in any one day. The law was intended to protect the health of workers against such hazards, for example, as excessive inhalation of flour dust. The Supreme Court, however, refused to accept this justification of the law. Speaking for a 5–4 majority, Justice Rufus W. Peckham declared that although the police power might on occasion limit freedom of contract, there were necessary restrictions on it. Peckham said there was "no reasonable foundation" in the instant case for holding the law to be necessary or appropriate as a health law to safeguard the public health or that of bakers. On the contrary, Peckham asserted, "the real object and purpose were simply to regulate the hours of labor between the master and his employees . . . in a private business." Peckham, therefore, concluded that the New York law was an unconstitutional interference with liberty of contract as protected by the Fourteenth Amendment.

In one of the most famous dissenting opinions in Supreme Court history, Justice Oliver Wendell Holmes impugned the majority for deciding the case on the basis of the theory of laissez faire—a theory, he declared, "which a large part of the country does not entertain." "The Fourteenth Amendment," Holmes reprovingly observed, "does not enact Mr. Herbert Spencer's Social Statics." Yet if the Court followed laissez-faire doctrine, it

4. The Supreme Court approved the exercise of the state police power in 369 of 422 cases in which it was challenged between 1889 and 1918. Furthermore, two-thirds of the cases in which the police power was found unconstitutional dealt with rates of public utility corporations. Charles Warren, *The Supreme Court in United States History*, 2 vols. (Boston, 1922), II, p. 741.

did so only after hearing—and rejecting as unpersuasive—a large body of statistical and social evidence introduced by the state to prove the reasonableness of the legislation. In other words, the Court's approach in this case was similar to that which it employed earlier in *Holden* v. *Hardy* (1898) and which it would use subsequently in *Muller* v. *Oregon* (1908). The difference was that in *Lochner* the justices rejected the facts intended to show social injustice and supported instead a contrasting social perception—the belief that baking was a wholesome and harmless occupation.

Three years later, in the same session in which it upheld the Oregon ten-hour law for women, the Court reaffirmed entrepreneurial liberty in *Adair* v. *U.S.* (1908). It declared the Erdman Act of 1898, which made it a crime for an interstate carrier to dismiss an employee for membership in a labor union, an unconstitutional interference with the employer's and employees' liberty of contract under the due process clause of the Fifth Amendment. Justice Harlan stated flatly that the act of Congress had no reasonable public character, adding that it was "not within the functions of government to compel any person, in the course of his business and against his will, to accept or retain the personal services of another, or to compel any person, against his will, to perform personal services for another." Thus the attempt to ban yellow-dog contracts in federal jurisdiction failed. In *Coppage* v. *Kansas* (1915) the Court held a state law forbidding yellow-dog contracts unconstitutional under the Fourteenth Amendment. Again the Court's evident hostility to the social purpose of the law—to assist the trade-union movement—led it to conclude that the state law had no reasonable relationship to the health, morals, and welfare of the community such as would justify interference with liberty of contract.

The ambivalent attitude of the judiciary toward the regulatory movement was evident also in decisions concerning the federal police power. On the basis of precedents upholding a federal police power, Congress in 1916 enacted the Owen-Keating law prohibiting the passage in interstate commerce of goods produced by child labor. In *Hammer* v. *Dagenhart* (1918), however, the Supreme Court declared the act unconstitutional. Calling the measure an outright prohibition rather than a regulation of commerce, Justice William R. Day distinguished it from earlier laws that the Court had approved prohibiting the movement in interstate commerce of things said to be harmful in themselves, such as impure food. This part of the opinion, an unconvincing exercise in judicial ingenuity, revived a distinction apparently long since discredited. More realistic and substantive was Day's discussion of local and national authority over child labor in the federal system. Questioning congressional motivation in passing the law, Day said its transparent purpose was to regulate child labor rather than protect commerce. But, he explained, the nature and conditions of labor were part of production or manufacturing, and under the doctrine of the *Knight* case production was distinct from commerce and came under the jurisdiction of the states. Accordingly, the act was unconstitutional as an invasion of the state police power under the Tenth Amendment. This argument was also unconvincing to many people, and Day's misquoting of the Tenth Amendment—he inserted "expressly" into it, as in "the powers not expressly delegated to the national government are reserved to the states"—did not help his cause. The decision, which ranks with *Lochner* as among the most politically notorious in Supreme Court history, reflected the Court's belief that fundamental changes in the economic order must be stopped at almost any cost.

Less than nine months after the *Dagenhart* decision, Congress passed a second child labor act based on the taxing power, the second of the two constitutional instruments through which a federal police power could be exercised. Defining child labor in the same terms as the 1916 law, the act imposed a tax of 10 percent on the net profits of any firm employing child labor. In *Bailey* v. *Drexel Furniture Co.* (1922) the Supreme Court declared this law unconstitutional also, on the ground that it invaded the reserved powers of the states under the Tenth Amendment. Chief Justice Taft's opinion rested in large part on the distinction between a tax and a penalty, the former being intended to raise revenue while the latter was a regulation aimed at accomplishing some ulterior social purpose. Although this distinction had long been recognized in constitutional law, Taft ignored the fact that the Court had often accepted regulatory federal taxes as constitutional. Yet the attempt by Congress to circumvent the first child labor decision was transparent, and it contradicted Taft's belief that Supreme Court settlement of constitutional questions could only be reversed by constitutional amendment. Taft concluded that what Congress could not do under the commerce power, neither could it achieve under the taxing power.

While the Supreme Court was willing to accept hours-of-labor legislation, it regarded prices and wages in a more direct sense as the foundation of the free enterprise system and hence in need of protection against government interference. *Adkins* v. *Children's Hospital* (1923), in which the Court struck down a District of Columbia minimum-wage law for women passed by Congress in 1918, forcefully demonstrated this concern. Speaking for a 5-3 majority, Justice George Sutherland declared the law a violation of liberty of contract under the due process clause of the Fifth Amendment. Counsel had presented an extensive survey of social conditions intended to justify the act. But Sutherland said it could not be shown that minimum wage legislation actually raised wages, or that higher-paid women guarded their morals more carefully than those who were poorly paid. Even more than *Adair*, the *Adkins* decision became the classic expression of the identification of laissez-faire economics with constitutional right. During the next few years the case was repeatedly cited as precedent for a broad interpretation of the scope of freedom of contract. Under its authority several state minimum wage laws became inoperative on the plausible assumption that the Fourteenth Amendment imposed restraints on the police power of the states similar to those imposed by the Fifth Amendment on the federal government.

Labor and the Supreme Court

As if the Court's decisions upholding liberty of contract were not a sufficient deterrent to trade unionism, a line of decisions specifically restricted the political and economic actions of labor unions. One of the most potent judicial instruments for this purpose was the labor injunction. Courts used the injunction to protect employers from labor violence, secondary boycotts, and similar practices that could be seen as imposing unlawful restraints on interstate commerce or interfering with property rights. In 1908 the Supreme Court ruled in *Loewe* v. *Lawlor* that secondary boycotts—wherein a union tried to coerce third parties not concerned with the labor dispute in question to sever business relations with the offending employer—might constitute an unlawful interference with interstate commerce. The Court held that persons resorting to such practices were liable under the Sherman Act. Resort to the Sherman Act to defeat labor union tactics had in turn inspired Congress to incorporate a number of provisions in the Clayton Antitrust Act of 1914 which were intended to protect labor unions from the limitations and penalties imposed in the federal antitrust laws. Thus Section 6 of the Clayton Act had provided that labor was "not a commodity or article of commerce," and that the antitrust laws should not be construed to forbid labor organizations as such nor their lawful pursuit of legitimate objectives. Section 20 had provided that "no restraining order or injunction shall be granted by any court of the United States ... in any case between an employer and employees ... unless necessary to prevent irreparable injury to property, or to a property right." This section also prohibited injunctions against peaceful persuasion of others to strike and injunctions against primary boycotts. All of these provisions were phrased somewhat vaguely and were somewhat general in character, and, accordingly, there remained some doubt as to the exact status of labor-union activities under the antitrust laws.

Although the new legislation was not formally at issue, the Court's decision in *Hitchman Coal and Coke Co.* v. *Mitchell* (1917) suggested that it had not changed its mind about the utility of the injunction as an antilabor weapon. Several years earlier the company, alleging violation of the antitrust act and breach of contract, got an injunction against the United Mine Workers prohibiting its attempts to unionize workers who signed yellow-dog contracts as a condition of employment. The Supreme Court upheld the injunction on the ground that the company could require yellow-dog contracts of its employees. Unions were legitimate, said Justice Pitney for the Court, but inducing workers to break their contracts—even though the contract stipulated that joining a union would lead to dismissal—was not a legitimate activity for a union to engage in.

In *Duplex Printing Press Co.* v. *Deering* (1921) the Court first interpreted the provisions of the Clayton Act concerning injunctions and labor-union activities. The case involved a secondary boycott, and since this practice had long been held an illegal interference with interstate commerce, it did not come under the protection of Section 6 of the Clayton law. Justice Pitney noted furthermore that the boycott was enjoinable, notwithstanding the provisions against labor injunctions in Section 20 of the Clayton Act, because that restriction applied only to the immediate parties in a dispute. Since the boycotting union was not an immediate party to the dispute, its illegal activities were subject to judicial control.

But it was not just secondary boycotts that came under the judicial ban. In *American Steel Foundries* v. *Tri-City Central Trades Council* (1921) the Court ruled that an injunction against picketing by striking workers was not prohibited by the Clayton Act. The workers claimed that their actions were peaceful and, therefore, protected by the law. But Chief Justice Taft held that under the circumstances the picketing was intimidating and inconsistent with peaceful persuasion. In *Bedford Cut Stone Company* v. *Journeymen Stone Cutters Association* (1927) the Court upheld an injunction against a union that refused to work on stone that had been cut by nonunion labor. In order to reach this result the Court tendentiously interpreted the union action as a secondary boycott interfering with interstate commerce, even though the refusal to work was directed against building enterprises and was strictly local. The practical upshot of these decisions was to minimize the protection that the Clayton Act gave labor unions in industrial disputes. In taking the stance it did the Court did not distort or disregard congressional intention, but rather interpreted an ambiguous law according to its perception of sound public policy.

In other cases concerning labor the Supreme Court assumed a similarly unsympathetic attitude. In *Truax* v. *Corrigan* (1921) it declared unconstitutional an Arizona statute forbidding state courts to grant injunctions against picketing. Under the statute the Arizona judiciary had refused to intervene in a dispute between a restaurant owner and striking employees. Chief Justice Taft said the law violated the due process requirements of the Fourteenth Amendment by protecting palpable wrongful injuries to property rights. In *United Mine Workers* v. *Coronado Coal Co.* (1922) the Court held that a trade union was suable and liable to damages under the Sherman Act. This decision was considered antilabor, although the progressive Justice Brandeis supported it on the theory that if unions were legally responsible they would be less likely to be the object of injunctive action by the courts.

Substantive Due Process and State Social Legislation

The judiciary's concern for maintaining the existing economic order was evident also in numerous decisions striking down state regulatory legislation under the doctrine of substantive due process. The public interest concept, for example, according to which business affected with a public interest was subject to regulation, was originally used to uphold state legislation, as in *Munn* v. *Illinois* (1877). In the 1920s, however, the Supreme Court adapted this concept to conservative, antiregulatory purposes. The specific question in constitutional law was whether states could regulate only legal monopolies and public utilities, which by definition possessed a public interest, or whether they could make a finding that any business was subject to regulation on this ground. After tending toward the latter view in the early years of the twentieth century, the Court shifted to a legal-monopoly or public-utility concept of public interest regulation.

In *Wolff Packing Company* v. *Kansas Court of Industrial Relations* (1923) the Court ruled that a state law vesting power in a commission to settle wage disputes and fix wages in the food, clothing, fuel, and other industries said to be affected with a public interest was a violation of freedom of contract and due process of law. Speaking for a unanimous Court, Chief Justice Taft said that the state could not endow a business with a public interest merely by declaring that a public interest existed. Taft acknowledged that besides public utilities, businesses not public at their inception could become so and would then warrant government regulation. But the criterion for determining this condition, said Taft, was "the indispensable nature of the service and the exorbitant charges and arbitrary control to which the public might be subjected without regulation." Under this narrow view of public interest the Court in subsequent cases struck down a New York law restricting ticket scalping (*Tyson and Bros.* v. *Banton,* 1927), a New Jersey law regulating employment agencies (*Ribnik* v. *McBride,* 1928), a Tennessee statute authorizing a commissioner to fix gasoline prices within the state (*Williams* v. *Standard Oil Co.,* 1929), and an Oklahoma law declaring the manufacture and sale of ice to be affected with a public interest and requiring a license for engaging in the business (*New State Ice Co.* v. *Liebmann,* 1932). It also invalidated several state laws that imposed restrictions on private property or business enterprise which the justices deemed arbitrary or unreasonable.[5]

Throughout the period 1900 to 1930 a series of unpopular decisions, as in the New York bakeshop and child labor cases, laid the Court open to the charge of usurping legislative power. Reformers argued that the judiciary

---

5. *Pennsylvania Coal Co.* v. *Mahon* (1922); *Jay Burns Baking Co.* v. *Burns* (1924); *Weaver* v. *Palmer Bros. Co.* (1926).

followed no rules or precedents, but simply decided cases on the basis of the justices' own social and political attitudes. Examining history, critics contended that judicial review was not intended by the founding fathers. To restrict courts many progressives proposed the recall of judges or the recall of judicial decisions.[6] The latter idea, supported by Theodore Roosevelt, aroused major controversy at the Republican convention in 1912 and was a factor in the split that created the Progressive party. In 1924 a new Progressive party ran Senator Robert M. La Follette on a platform that included proposals to limit judicial review.

Little came, however, of the progressive attack on the judiciary. The historical research stimulated by the attack showed that judicial review was part of the original constitutional system. Moreover the Supreme Court's occasional reactionary holdings in the prewar period were balanced by numerous liberal decisions. While the Court in the 1920s invalidated state legislation half again as often as in the previous two decades, most of the time it accepted state legislation as constitutional regardless of its social implications. Furthermore, if the courts acquired a greater political role under the new activist judicial review, they did so with the approval of progressives as well as conservatives. That was the special significance of the Brandeis brief in *Muller* v. *Oregon:* it showed that progressives accepted the idea that courts should consider the wisdom and reasonableness of legislation. Indeed, the Brandeis brief became the model for litigation involving state social legislation as liberals demonstrated their intention to use the expanded power of judicial review for reform purposes.

Decisive as judicial review could occasionally be, the courts by no means controlled the political destiny of the country between 1900 and 1930. Nor were they responsible for the failure of the regulatory movement to gain full political acceptance. Rather, as at most times, the judiciary followed the main outlines of public policy as determined by the political branches of government. The Supreme Court's handling of the trust question illustrates this pattern of adaptation.

After confirming the legitimacy of antitrust prosecution during the Roosevelt administration, the Court evolved the rule of reason as a gloss on the Sherman Act expressing the widespread belief that bigness itself ought not to be judged a violation of the antitrust law. In *United States* v. *U.S. Steel* (1920) the Court followed this rule in refusing to order the dissolution of the country's largest steel manufacturer. At the same time, however, the Court applied the Sherman Act to the trade-association movement. Trade associations were a means by which businessmen, rather than seeking to control production and prices directly through mergers, tried to reduce

6. In 1911 Arizona sought to gain admission to the Union with a provision for the recall of judges in its constitution. Congress and the president forced the removal of this provision before the territory became a state, but Arizona, after entering the Union, adopted it as a constitutional amendment.

competition and stabilize their industry by exchanging information on prices, cost of production, advertising, etc. The Harding administration invoked the antitrust laws against this new form of business cooperation, and the Court, in *American Column and Lumber Co.* v. *United States* (1921), supported the administration's position. The exchange of information that trade associations engaged in, reasoned the Court, was aimed at restraining trade. The Court's conservative wing, ordinarily probusiness in outlook, ironically formed the majority while the liberals Holmes and Brandeis dissented.

There was disagreement within the federal government between the Justice Department, which favored antitrust prosecution, and the Commerce Department, which supported the trade-association movement as a means of avoiding destructive competition and economic instability. The Commerce Department, led by Secretary Herbert Hoover, gained the upper hand and successfully promoted the trade association movement. And within a few years the Supreme Court changed its mind and approved the new cooperative business technique. In *Maple Flooring Association* v. *United States* (1925) the Court found trade associations to be a means of stabilizing economic conditions and avoiding waste and, hence, not a violation of the antitrust laws. Only Justice James C. McReynolds, known for his hard-line defense of property interests, opposed the ruling, while the liberals Holmes, Brandeis, and Stone supported it.

Conflicting Theories of Jurisprudence

The conflict between the older entrepreneurial and the newer regulatory mode of constitutionalism had its parallel in the dominant conceptions of jurisprudence that prevailed in the period 1900 to 1930. At the very moment when courts were assuming a larger political role under the new judicial review, leading voices in the legal establishment were reasserting the declaratory theory of law. This theory, pejoratively described by critics as mechanical jurisprudence or the "slot machine" theory of law, held that law consisted in a body of objective rules and principles impartially applied by courts in the resolution of disputes. Its advocates contended that courts did not make law—a legislative function—but rather discovered or declared it. Although judicial decisions might have political consequences, courts were bound by the requirements of legal reasoning to accept the results marked out by the rule of precedent; they were not free to seek what individual judges might personally regard as a desirable or sound result. Implicitly if not explicitly, the declarative theory of law recognized that judges, as nonelective officers possessing political influence, were under an obligation to act in accordance with—and to justify their decisions by reference to—legal doctrines and rules that transcended narrow political considerations.

According to the theory of declarative jurisprudence, the Constitution was fundamental, fixed, and absolute. Containing by implication the answer to every constitutional question that might be raised by a state or federal statute, it was a written expression of basic principles of natural right, justice, and individual liberty. In the actual conduct of constitutional politics judges who professed this theory of law sometimes seemed to disregard it in the most egregious manner. In the *Lochner* case, for example, Justice Peckham said that in every case that comes before the Court the question necessarily arises: "Is this a fair, reasonable, and appropriate exercise of the police power of the State...?" Here was an apparently candid admission of the essentially legislative function of the Court under the new judicial review, a statement seemingly at odds with the belief that courts merely declare what the Constitution is after holding a statute against it for analysis. Yet Peckham went on to say, obviously guided by the requirements of the declarative theory of law: "This is not a question of substituting the judgment of the court for that of the legislature. If the act be within the power of the State it is valid, although the judgment of the court might be totally opposed to the enactment of such a law."

It is, of course, easy to ridicule the theory of declarative jurisprudence and regard its invocation, as in the *Lochner* opinion, as mere hypocrisy. The important point, however, is that the theory served as a social myth essential to maintaining judicial legitimacy at a time of rapid political and social change. Reformers argued that the ideas of declarative jurisprudence were but a rationalization for judicial legislation that reflected the judges' social and economic attitudes. To some extent this was no doubt true, but the dominance of the declarative theory involved more than personal or class interest. Roscoe Pound, perhaps the most influential critic of declarative jurisprudence, denied that it appealed simply as a rationalizing device. On the contrary, Pound observed, the theory was held as an article of faith that aroused genuine conviction. Indeed, he added, it was ideological commitment to declarative jurisprudence that made legal and constitutional reform so hard to achieve.

The idea of an objective law impartially applied by the courts was fundamental to American constitutionalism in its formative stages, and in a somewhat different form it has continued to occupy a central place in the constitutional thought and practice of our own time. In the early twentieth century, however, the declarative theory of law was so closely identified with the conservative defense of property rights that it was widely discredited, especially in intellectual and reform circles. In its place, or alongside it, there emerged a theory of law that its proponents regarded as more realistic, democratic, and humane. This was the theory of sociological jurisprudence.

According to sociological jurisprudence, law was not a body of immutable principles and rules, but rather an institution shaped by social pressures that was constantly changing. It was valid not in any universal sense, but only in relation to a particular time and place. Sociological jurisprudence taught that law developed through experience rather than logic; its essence lay in considerations of expediency rather than timeless justice. And legal change occurred not through the operation of abstract principles, but by the agency of judges who as political actors shaped specific social policies. In a real sense, therefore, judges made law rather than discovered or declared it, pragmatically adapting it to changing social conditions. Yet so strong was the traditional notion of law as a body of impartial rules that proponents of sociological jurisprudence felt obliged to explain that pragmatic judicial decision making would not degenerate into mere subjectivism. Courts would preserve their objectivity by taking their bearings from society. In the words of the noted jurist and later Supreme Court justice Benjamin N. Cardozo, they would enforce in their decisions not their own ideas and values, but the "customary morality, the *mores* of the times."

From sociological jurisprudence there emerged in the 1920s a more radical and reform-oriented theory of law, legal realism. In part a response to the apparent subjectivism of the Supreme Court's most reactionary decisions in the postwar years, legal realism was a form of positivism that rejected the idea of law as a body of rules existing apart from the judges who decided specific controversies. Emphasizing personal psychological factors in the mind of the judge rather than adjustment of the law to social change, legal realists all but abandoned the traditional idea of the rule of law as the basis of the constitutional state. Instead of a body of fixed rules and controlling precedents, law for the legal realists became a kind of *ad hoc* method of arbitration.

Legal realism was too radical to attract more than a tiny following even in the law schools, but sociological jurisprudence gained a considerable measure of acceptance as the legal philosophy of progressivism. As it became harder to defend laissez-faire individualism because of the social inequities that it produced, the state assumed greater importance as a source of social values. Social justice, though still defined with reference to equal opportunities for individuals, became in progressive or liberal theory a conscious concern and obligation of government. Sociological jurisprudence provided an explanation and justification of this development, for it taught that law, so far from being an immutable expression of absolute right and justice, was an instrument by which conservative, property-minded classes had promoted their own narrow interests in contradiction to those of society as a whole. By the same token sociological jurisprudence pointed the way by which groups and classes not included in the ruling establishment, or forced to assume a subordinate place in it, could reform public policy to make it serve their own interests.

Justices Holmes and Brandeis expressed the judicial liberalism that derived from sociological jurisprudence and that became a factor in constitutional politics in the postwar period. In his *The Common Law* (1880) Holmes had written that the life of the law was not logic, but experience and pragmatic social invention. His reputation as a liberal was based on this theoretical contribution rather than on any personal interest in reform or on the belief that judges should shape the law according to their personal view of sound public policy. Holmes in fact held to the traditional narrow conception of judicial review which required deference to the legislative judgment of the reasonableness of legislation. When lawmakers enacted social reform measures that passed judicial scrutiny under the traditional view of the judicial function, however, Holmes's theory of judicial self-restraint caused him to be counted a judicial liberal. He expressed his position most clearly in his dissent in *Lochner* v. *New York*. Dominant social opinions, he said, should be permitted to be expressed in legislation, "unless it can be said that a rational and fair man necessarily would admit that the statute proposed would infringe fundamental principles as they have been understood by the traditions of our people and our law."

Judicial liberalism also referred to the use of the new power of judicial review to achieve progressive social and economic change. It was this more substantive liberalism (in contrast to Holmes's procedural liberalism) that Brandeis represented. As a reform lawyer, Brandeis accepted the quasi-legislative nature of the new judicial review. His method was to prove the reasonableness of social legislation by presenting a mountain of social facts, as in *Muller* v. *Oregon*. As a judge Brandeis made lengthy analyses of the social background of the case at hand, often writing his own views of the reasonableness of legislation into his opinions. Zealous, self-righteous, and concerned with improving politics and society, Brandeis, far more than Holmes, gave the progressive reform impulse tangible expression in constitutional law and anticipated the judicial liberalism of the mid-twentieth century.

Toward Positive Government and the Regulatory State

The political history of the 1920s—the return to "normalcy" under Harding, the "new era" business prosperity, the Republican ascendancy lasting until the election of Franklin D. Roosevelt—has obscured the continuity of constitutional development throughout the period 1900 to 1933. As laissez-faire constitutionalism did not disappear from constitutional law only to reappear in the Taft Court in the 1920s, so the imperative carrying the country toward positive government and the regulatory state continued after the politics of progressivism ended during the world war. Under Republican auspices the bureaucratization of government-business relations assumed a more cooperative, less adversarial form than under the Wilson government or the subsequent Roosevelt administration, both of which were influenced by the antibusiness tone of progressive or liberal politics. Yet the transformation of the federal government into a centralized, modern service state, responsive to a variety of special interests, continued nonetheless.

To be sure, classical laissez-faire attitudes persisted in branches of government other than the judiciary. Throughout the 1920s Secretary of the Treasury Andrew W. Mellon, for example, who served under all three Republican presidents, favored tax cuts, government retrenchment, stern antilabor measures, the removal of restraints on business—in short, the minimal-government constitutional program characteristic of late nineteenth-century industrialization. An important influence also was President Calvin Coolidge, a Republican of the old school whose vetoes of interventionist, regulatory measures rang the changes on the virtues of laissez-faire individualism. In significant respects, moreover, public policy followed the model of entrepreneurial freedom and limited government. The federal government turned the railroads back to private management after the war, got out of the nitrogen-production and electric power business that it had carried on during the emergency, sold merchant ships, reduced taxes, and used the injunction against striking workers in the West Virginia coal fields in 1922.

At the same time, however, though in less politically conspicuous ways, the federal government expanded its role in the economy and society. As private groups increasingly looked to it for assistance in advancing their occupational, professional, or social goals, the federal government became a huge service institution performing countless informational, educational, and research activities. There were, for example, significant increases in federal expenditures for services to business, for federal conservation of natural resources, for direct aids to agriculture, and for grants-in-aid to the states for roads, maternity welfare, educational and vocational services, rural sanitation, and agricultural extension services. The number of regulatory agencies also increased as science and technology continued to transform the society. Government programs of this kind, once established, tended to expand rather than to contract. Not only were they convenient and useful to large numbers of citizens, but also they became vested interests of the bureaus that administered them and hence worked for their continuance.

In the broadest sense the development of a federal service state reflected the trend in all modern states toward enlargement of the sphere of government and centralization of administration. Specifically, it was promoted by a number of bureaucratic-administrative progressives in business, government, and the professions. The most important of these figures in the 1920s was Herbert Hoover. Vilified during the New Deal era as an uncompassionate laissez-faire individualist, Hoover in fact tried to adapt the drive toward positive government to the traditional liberal values of individual liberty, community responsibility, and local self-government. Recognizing the necessity of stronger, more active government under the conditions of modern industrial society, he nevertheless feared the stifling, illiberal effects that he believed would follow should the regulatory movement create a centralized bureaucracy. But Hoover feared not only concentrated government power. In the private sector he saw the danger that could ensue from the concentrated, organized power of the great corporations on the one hand, and trade unions on the other. The result in the one case would be fascism, in the other socialism. To guard against these dangers Hoover proposed what he called a "new individualism." This term conjured up the image of voluntary associations carrying on their business or professional activity with the assistance of government in a cooperative way, for their own benefit as well as that of the community as a whole.

An engineer by training with a strong faith in the application of scientific knowledge to the organization of social affairs, Hoover believed that cooperation among the functional units of the economy, and between them and the government, would reduce waste and inefficiency, promote productivity, and improve both individual and collective well-being. As secretary of commerce under Harding and Coolidge, Hoover made his department a kind of comprehensive agency for economic planning and development. Trade associations, a form of cooperation which aimed at stabilizing market conditions, were in Hoover's view the key to achieving economic progress and a higher standard of living for all classes and groups without the ruinous social costs and instability that marred nineteenth-century capitalism. Accordingly, he encouraged the formation of trade associations. Through the Bureau of the Census, Hoover facilitated the exchange of statistical and other information about materials, production, marketing, and advertising that permitted corporations within a given industry to maintain prices at a satisfactory profit level while eliminating costly, destructive, and wasteful competition. Although this associative, cooperative approach did not suspend or revoke the antitrust laws, it subordinated them in the interest of industrial self-government under the sponsorship of the federal government. At the urging of the Commerce Department, trade associations in many industries set up codes of fair competition and business ethics that eliminated some of the illegal trade practices that were the object of the antitrust laws. Furthermore, through the Bureau of Standards, the department assisted businessmen in simplifying and rationalizing the production of industrial goods.

The Commerce Department, whose new office building was the largest in Washington and literally formed the base of the monumental "Federal Triangle" of government buildings begun in the 1920s, acquired under Hoover a great deal of power through administrative fiat. For example, Hoover annexed the mines and patents sections of the Interior Department; poached on the area of the State Department by interjecting the Department of Commerce into international trade relations; and created agencies in the department to supervise aviation safety and coordinate the allocation of frequencies in the new radio industry. Hoover also persuaded the Justice Department to relax its antitrust efforts and encouraged the Federal Trade Commission to act in a more friendly and advisory fashion toward corporations and trade associations.

There were other manifestations of bureaucratic-regulatory activity besides Hoover's administration of the Commerce Department. At the start of the decade Congress passed special interest, regulatory legislation concerning railroads and agriculture. The Transportation Act of 1920 returned the railroads to the control of private management and confirmed all the rate-setting powers of the ICC, which was now authorized to initiate, modify, and adjust rates so that the carriers might earn a fair return under efficient management. Emphasizing cooperation rather than competition, the act contained a recapture clause enabling the commission to recover one-half of all profits in excess of 6 percent earned by any road. Out of this fund roads earning less than 4.5 percent were to receive additional compensation. Most important, the act instructed the ICC to plan the consolidation of the railroads into a limited number of national systems.

In 1921 Congress passed the Packers and Stockyards Act, placing the meat packers' interstate business under strict federal control. Adopted after a congressional inquiry into monopolistic conditions in the meat industry, it forbade packers to engage in unfair, discriminatory, or deceptive market practices. It also required all rates for handling livestock in the yards to be fair and nondiscriminatory. The secretary of agriculture was given authority to enforce the law through cease and desist orders, subject to appeal to the courts. In subsequent years Congress authorized the formation of agricultural producers associations for marketing purposes and exempted them from the antitrust laws; established federal credit banks for farmers; and passed grain futures legislation intended to prevent fluctuations in the price of grain that were injurious to farmers.

A favorite device for promoting and regulating special interests was the federal grant-in-aid. This was an instrument through which the federal government extended many important social services in its new capacity as a service state. The grant-in-aid was an appropriation by the federal government to the states for some special purpose, certain stipulations being attached to the grant. These were, first, the formal acceptance of the grant by the legislature of any state accepting the grant; second, federal supervision and approval of state activities under the appropriation; third, state appropriation of a sum of money at least equal to that advanced by the federal government; and fourth, federal right to withhold the grant from any state violating the stipulated agreement.

Federal appropriations to the states were not altogether new. Notable early examples were the distribution of the federal surplus in 1837, various land grants, and the Morrill Act of 1862 granting federal lands to the states for agricultural colleges. Grants to the states increased in frequency after 1880, but before 1911 they lacked the provisions for systematic federal control characteristic of the modern grant-in-aid.

The Weeks Act, passed in 1911, established perhaps the first modern grant-in-aid. The statute appropriated money to the states for forest-fire prevention programs. A participating state was required to accept the grant by legislative act, to establish a satisfactory fire protection system of its own, and to appropriate to it a sum of money at least equal to the federal grant in prospect. State officials were to supervise the fire protection system, which was nonetheless subject to federal inspection and approval. The total congressional appropriation in the Weeks Act was but $200,000, but the law was the prototype of all subsequent grants-in-aid.

Several similar statutes were enacted during the next few years. These included the Smith-Lever Act of 1914, providing for state-federal agricultural extension work; the Federal Road Act of 1916, appropriating money for state highway programs; and the Smith-Hughes Act of 1917, granting money to the states for vocational education. In 1920 Congress enacted the Fess-Kenyon Act appropriating money for disabled veteran rehabilitation by the states, and in 1921 it passed the Sheppard-Towner Act subsidizing state infant and maternity welfare activities. After 1921 no important grant acts were passed for several years, although the annual appropriations under existing statutes of this type were greatly increased. In 1925 grants-in-aid to the states totaled some $93 million, compared with approximately $11 million in 1915. Nearly all of the increase went to highway construction and educational projects.

Opponents of the grant-in-aid argued that it was a method of extending federal power that usurped functions properly belonging to the states and thus undermined state sovereignty. To the rebuttal that state acceptance of a grant was voluntary, critics said this was not really true, since the financial penalty for noncooperation was so great as to force the states to accept the federal offer. In *Massachusetts* v. *Mellon* (1923) the Supreme Court reviewed and rejected this argument. The case involved a challenge by the state of Massachusetts of the constitutionality of the Sheppard-Towner Maternity Aid Act. Justice Sutherland's opinion dismissed the suit for want of jurisdiction, but, in a series of obiter dicta, implied that grants-in-aid were not coercive and were constitutional. Taking the legislation at face value, the Court said it imposed no obligation but simply extended an option which the state was free to accept or reject.

Federal authority was also extended by the creation of two new regulatory agencies. The Water Power Act of 1920 established a Federal Power Commission with authority to license and regulate power plants on the navigable streams of public lands. During the next decade, however, the board functioned so weakly that it was of little practical value or significance. Radio broadcasting was another field into which the federal government extended its controls. Since 1912, radio transmission had been subject to extensive regulation and restriction, but the great growth of broadcasting after 1920 produced chaotic conditions that required additional controls. The Radio Act of 1927 accordingly created a Federal Radio Commission, composed of five men appointed by the president for six-year terms. The commission was given extensive powers over radio transmission, including the right to classify radio stations, prescribe services, assign frequency bands, and regulate chain broadcasting. The act also gave the secretary of commerce a general right of inspection and regulation over radio operators and apparatus.

Of the older regulatory agencies, the ICC, as noted, was called upon by Congress to play a more active role in planning a national transportation system. The Supreme Court continued to uphold the powers granted to the commission, but on the whole the agency did not use its powers in the manner that Congress contemplated in the Transportation Act of 1920. It maintained the status quo in rates, allowed the railroads broad latitude in setting financial policies, and instead of taking the initiative in planning a series of national systems let the railroads control the question. Entering into its mature phase, the ICC provided a sanction for a form of industrial self-government by the railroads that was compatible with Hoover's noncoercive, associative conception of regulation and government-business relations.

Like the ICC in the early years of its existence, the more recently created Federal Trade Commission was the object of careful judicial supervision that severely qualified its regulatory powers. Although the FTC Act of 1914 gave the agency power to define unfair trade practices, the Supreme Court in *Federal Trade Commission* v. *Gratz* (1920) held this to be a matter for judicial determination. Unsympathetic to the broad discretionary power that Congress had given the FTC, the Court reasoned that since the judiciary had final power to interpret the law, it also had the power to decide what constituted an unfair trade practice. In *Federal Trade Commission* v. *Curtis Publishing Co.* (1923) the Court undercut the fact-finding powers of the commission. It held that because Congress gave the judiciary power to make and enter a decree affirming, modifying, or setting aside an order, it must also have power to examine the whole record and ascertain for itself the issues presented, including whether there were material facts not presented by the commission. Moreover, after 1925 new appointments to the commission inclined it toward a more sympathetic view of business. It confined its investigations to specific trade practices rather than study the broad economic impact of corporate activity, settled cases by informal agreement, and sponsored conferences to identify and secure pledges to stop unfair trade practices. The commission approved approximately fifty codes of fair practice voluntarily drawn up by businessmen, thereby anticipating the pattern of government-business relations entered into by the National Recovery Administration under Franklin D. Roosevelt in 1933.

There was always the possibility that the regulatory movement and the drive toward positive government would go too far and obtrude unconstitutionally on individual and local liberty. Each group had its threshold on this issue. For Hoover and the Republicans in the 1920s the limit was reached in the attempt to extend federal authority over agricultural production in the McNary-Haugen bill of 1927. Adopted under heavy pressure from agricultural interests, the measure provided for a series of equalization fees to be paid by the growers of certain staple crops to a Federal Farm Board. The board was empowered to use this money to dump crop surpluses abroad, to buy and sell agricultural products, and to make crop loans to farm cooperatives. President Coolidge vetoed the bill on the ground that it exceeded federal authority over interstate commerce by attempting to fix commodity prices. He also said that it unconstitutionally put the federal government into the buying and selling of agricultural commodities. The heart of Coolidge's objection to the bill, however, concerned its bureaucratic character. It created an agency with the power to fix prices, but established no standards, imposed no restrictions, and required no regulation of any kind. The act, said Coolidge, jeopardized the agricultural industry "by subjecting it to the tyranny of bureaucratic regulation and control." Moreover, by permitting farmers to determine when controls should be put into effect, the bill unconstitutionally delegated legislative authority to private individuals. It was, said Coolidge, class legislation that used the coercive power of government to aid special groups of farmers and processors at the expense of other farmers and the society as a whole.

The Muscle Shoals electric power project was a second congressional proposal which in the opinion of Republicans exceeded the proper limits of government intervention for regulatory purposes. During the war the government built electric power and nitrogen plants at Muscle Shoals on the Tennessee River in Alabama. After the war it was unable to dispose of the facilities, and in 1927 a bloc of agrarian progressives succeeded in getting a bill through Congress creating a government corporation to produce electric power and fertilizer at Muscle Shoals for the purpose of sale to the public at inexpensive rates. Coolidge vetoed the bill, however, because it placed the government in competition with private companies. When Congress passed a second Muscle Shoals bill in 1931 President Hoover rejected it for the same reason. The proper function of government, Hoover said in his veto message, was to promote justice and equal opportunity by regulation for the protection of all the people, rather than engage in competition against them. Despite these vetoes, Republicans were not averse to interventionist, positive government, provided it remained within proper constitutional limits. Thus, while blocking the Muscle Shoals bill, Coolidge approved legislation for Boulder Dam that authorized the construction of a federally operated power plant and water delivery system for the Southwest. However, the dam would not compete against private-sector utility companies.

National Prohibition

The most extreme exercise of federal authority in the 1920s was prohibition. Adopted as a constitutional amendment in 1919, prohibition interjected the federal government into the private lives of American citizens in an unprecedented way. It was a costly constitutional innovation which brought discredit on federal authority and led to wholesale disrespect for national law.

Although a staple of nineteenth-century reform, prohibition made little progress nationally until it was associated with the reform movement of the early twentieth century. Humanitarianism, a desire for greater social order, industrial efficiency, and the progressive belief in the possibility of creating a more wholesome social environment combined to make prohibition a potent political force within a short period of time. Only five states had adopted statewide prohibition acts before 1900; by 1916 nineteen states had done so, and large portions of the remainder were dry under local option laws. In 1913 Congress responded to the growing prohibition sentiment by adopting the Webb-Kenyon Act forbidding the shipment of liquor in interstate commerce into dry states. In 1917 Congress adopted prohibition by statute in the Lever Act as a wartime food-control measure. And in December 1917 it submitted a constitutional amendment to the states prohibiting the manufacture, transportation, and sale of intoxicating liquors within the United States. The amendment gave the states and the federal government concurrent authority to enforce it. The Eighteenth Amendment was ratified in January 1919, and in December 1919 Congress passed the Volstead Act to enforce national prohibition. Drafted by the Anti-Saloon League, the nonpartisan interest group that had lobbied so effectively for prohibition, the Volstead Act set the very strict standard of .5 percent as the maximum permissible alcoholic content of beer, wine, and other spirituous beverages.

The Eighteenth Amendment was legislation dealing with a very sensitive aspect of personal liberty, presented in the form of a constitutional amendment. In a country as vast and varied as the United States, the task of enforcing such sumptuary legislation would appear practically impossible. Yet at the time of its adoption supporters of the Eighteenth Amendment did not anticipate any special difficulty in enforcing it. Congress created a Prohibition Bureau in the Treasury Department with 1,500 agents and a modest budget of $5 million. The states meanwhile adopted or revised their prohibition laws in accordance with the national law. The task of enforcement, however, proved to be monumental. The amendment was widely disregarded, prosecutions under the Volstead Act overloaded the federal courts, and by 1926 a growing number of people, many of them former drys, objected to prohibition as an unwarranted intrusion of federal authority in local affairs and encroachment on personal liberty.

National prohibition involved several constitutional innovations. In submitting the Eighteenth Amendment to the states Congress for the first time imposed a time limit of seven years on the ratification process. In Ohio the state legislature ratified the Eighteenth Amendment, but a popular referendum, held in accordance with a wet-sponsored state constitutional amendment, rejected it. The Supreme Court settled the question of whether Ohio had ratified the Eighteenth Amendment. In *Hawke* v. *Smith* (1920) the Court upheld the legislative ratification as consistent with congressional purpose, for the first time interpreting Congress's power to submit amendments under Article V of the Constitution. In the *National Prohibition Cases* (1920) the Court for the first time heard a challenge to the constitutionality of a constitutional amendment. Asserting that the prohibition amendment invaded state sovereignty, Rhode Island, a nonratifying state, argued that if the amending power could be used to undermine state power over a subject of internal legislation like prohibition, it could be used to remove all restrictions on federal authority. Rhode Island contended further that the amendment was an act of legislation rather than a constitutional measure dealing with the organization and distribution of governmental power. The Supreme Court rejected this argument and upheld the Eighteenth Amendment as constitutional. In a number of other cases presenting civil liberties challenges to federal authority to enforce prohibition the Supreme Court also sustained national power.[7]

Prohibition became a partisan issue in the 1928 election campaign. The Democratic candidate, Al Smith, was a wet, and the Republican party, obliged to enforce the Eighteenth Amendment throughout the 1920s, became identified with support of prohibition. Despite the Democratic defeat, the movement for repeal of the prohibition amendment was strengthened by the onset of the depression. The economic crisis created a demand for federal revenues which the legalization of the liquor business could help supply. Accordingly, when the Democrats returned to power in 1933, they promptly submitted a constitutional amendment repealing prohibition. It

---

7. The Court rejected a claim that state and federal prosecution for violating prohibition laws was unconstitutional under the Fifth Amendment guarantee against double jeopardy (*United States* v. *Lanza* [1922]); sustained prohibition agents' seizure of liquor concealed in an automobile against a claim that it violated the Fourth Amendment's search and seizure requirements (*Carroll* v. *United States* [1925]); approved the use of evidence in a federal prohibition case gained by wiretapping (*Olmstead* v. *United States* [1925]); and upheld an act of Congress restricting the amount of alcohol that could be dispensed for medical purposes against a physician's claim that it interfered with his constitutional right to practice his profession (*Lambert* v. *Yellowley* [1924]).

was ratified as the Twenty-first Amendment in 1933, marking the first time a constitutional amendment had ever been repealed. Still another innovation was the ratification of the Twenty-first Amendment by popularly elected state constitutional conventions, the only time this method of ratification has been employed.

Although prohibition reduced the consumption of alcoholic beverages in the United States, the Eighteenth Amendment was more harmful than beneficial in its constitutional effects. The enforcement experience served to discredit moralistic progressive legislation aimed at modifying people's personal living habits. The difficulties encountered in enforcing prohibition also cast the federal government in an unfavorable light and strengthened states'-rights sentiment. While revealing the responsiveness of the constitutional system to pressure from well organized interest groups backed by mass opinion, prohibition showed the limitations of centralized reform in a nation as diverse as the United States.

The Hoover Administration and the Depression

If the depression marked the end of the experiment in national sumptuary legislation, it was to prove the cause of major federal interventions in the economy which established the regulatory state as a constitutional norm. These interventions began during the Republican administration of Herbert Hoover. Even before the stock market crash Hoover attempted to implement his theory of business-government cooperation under supportive federal auspices. In 1929 he called a special session of Congress to deal with the farm problem, and approved the Agricultural Marketing Act aimed at supporting farm prices and influencing agricultural production by indirect, noncoercive means. The law set up a Federal Farm Board and gave it authority to administer a $500-million fund to lend to agricultural marketing associations and state-chartered commodity stabilization corporations for the purchase and storage of surplus agricultural commodities. The purpose of this program was essentially the same as the McNary-Haugen bill—that is, to adjust and control market conditions for the benefit of farmers. The difference was that its method of operation was noncoercive. It aptly illustrated Hoover's conviction that government should play a positive role in providing scientific expertise and advice, protection against adverse outside forces, and even capital to foster agriculture, industry, and foreign commerce. In trying to achieve social and economic goals, however, government should refrain from legal compulsion or direct rule, trusting instead to the spirit of self-interested voluntary cooperation.

The stock market crash of October 1929 triggered a catastrophic economic collapse which brought suffering and distress to millions of Americans. Within three years industrial production had declined by 50 percent, and more than 12 million persons were unemployed. In the face of this crisis Hoover persisted in his belief that voluntary cooperation among businessmen, encouraged and directed by the federal government, would solve the nation's economic problems, which in any case were thought to be the result of external factors and cyclical tendencies in the capitalist system. Although Hoover stopped far short of what the New Deal would attempt to do, he did not, as his New Deal detractors charged, adopt a passive role or cling to laissez-faire individualism and states'-rights conservatism.

In formal White House conferences Hoover called on business, labor, and agricultural leaders to cooperate in adopting economic measures to revive production, sustain employment, and maintain prices and wages. Furthermore he proposed public works appropriations, tax reduction, and expansion of credit facilities to promote economic activity. When these policies failed, in part because the separate functional units and special interest groups in the economy persisted in placing their own goals uppermost, Hoover accepted more direct government intervention. The chief expression of this more coercive outlook was the Reconstruction Finance Corporation. Chartered and owned by the federal government, the RFC was given $2 billion by Congress to lend to banks, trust companies, insurance companies, and railroads to sustain the basic financial structure of the country.

Fearful of bureaucratic centralization, Hoover resisted tremendous political pressure for federal appropriations for the relief of the unemployed, to be administered through the states. He insisted that such a step, though depending on federal-state cooperation, would erode the personal initiative of individuals and undermine local governmental responsibility. In regard to welfare and relief, the Hoover administration confined itself to coordinating efforts by local authorities, both public and private. This policy was politically disastrous, causing Hoover to appear insensitive to the needy while willing to provide assistance to businessmen and financiers. Yet Hoover also resisted strong pressure from corporate interests to abrogate the antitrust laws and establish legalized cartels under federal authority. Such a scheme, he said, would create a fascist corporate state dominated by the most powerful business interests. Thus Hoover feared both excessive government power and concentrated private economic power, which under the sanction of government would seek to promote its own narrow interests.

Considered against the tradition of laissez-faire government that was the constitutional norm through most of the nation's history, Hoover significantly extended positive government and administrative management. The first modern chief executive in his attempt to apply the methods of social science and data gathering to the tasks of government, he went further than previous presidents in using federal authority to encourage the participation of interest groups in the management of the economy and the formulation of public policy. Yet, a traditionalist in his commitment to the paradoxical idea of noncoercive government, Hoover disliked legal compulsion as a means of administrative regulatory action. Unwilling formally to delegate legislative or governmental power to private corporations, trade associations, or special interest groups, he remained devoted to individual personal and local community initiative and responsibility. In combination with his abhorrence of centralized bureaucracy, this devotion kept him from embracing the statist and quasi-corporatist economic recovery policies later adopted by Franklin Roosevelt's New Deal.

Because he held out against formal interest-group representation and special-interest or class legislation, Hoover ultimately was the last laissez-faire president. It was nonetheless true, however, as Walter Lippmann perceptively observed in 1935, that in meeting the depression in an activist manner Hoover irreversibly committed the government to using its powers to regulate the economy. "The business cycle has been placed within the orbit of government," wrote Lippmann, "and for laissez faire and individual adjustment and liquidation there has been substituted conscious management by the political state." Although for political and ideological reasons his role has seldom been properly acknowledged, Hoover helped lay the foundation of the modern regulatory state.

TWENTY-FOUR

The New Deal

————————————— ✦✦✦ —————————————

LOCKED IN THE GRIP of near-paralyzing economic depression, the country in 1932 repudiated Hoover and the Republicans in favor of the Democratic candidate, the genial patrician governor of New York, Franklin D. Roosevelt. Although Hoover had taken unprecedented steps to revive the economy, his political ineptness obscured his executive activism and caused him to be condemned for failing to deal adequately with the economic crisis. Moreover, although business depressions had never won the incumbent party any votes, the emphatic rejection of Hoover's cooperative individualism after his one-sided victory in 1928 reflected the extent to which the electorate had come to hold the president and the federal government responsible for the nation's economic welfare.

For a generation the course of public policy and constitutional development had alternated between the laissez-faire, self-regulating market approach to the political economy and the interventionist, regulatory approach. Exercising power boldly and energetically as in a wartime emergency, the Roosevelt administration repudiated the laissez-faire ideal and established the regulatory welfare state as the dominant constitutional orthodoxy. Based on the commerce, taxing, and general welfare powers of the federal government, New Deal legislation created an American-style centralized bureaucracy that in effect revolutionized the federal system.

At the center of these developments, presiding over the rapidly expanding federal bureaucracy and acting like a broker among economic interest groups competing for federal protection, was President Roosevelt. Roosevelt was concerned in an essentially conservative way with reintegration of the social order on the basis of a reformed, more socially responsible capitalism. Nevertheless, whether out of instinct or circumstance, in a constitutional sense he was an agent of significant change. Sustained by an almost continual sense of national crisis, adept in the use of communications media that enhanced his political skills and enabled him to summon broad popular support, Roosevelt fashioned the presidency into a kind of elective kingship and went far toward making it the sovereign center of the constitutional system.

New Deal Constitutional Politics: The Analogue of War

In the perspective of modern liberalism the New Deal stands in the long line of reform movements that since the time of Jefferson and Jackson have sought to restrict the power of the business community in the interest of enlarging the liberty and opportunity of other groups in the society. While there is much to be said for this view, its emphasis on pluralistic group conflict is misplaced in an analysis of the politico-constitutional strategy of the New Deal in its beginning phase. Whatever else it signified, Roosevelt's election at the very least meant that Americans demanded that the federal government do more than it had done under the Hoover administration to combat the depression. The rejection of laissez-faire did not, however, answer the question of how and to what ends the power of government should be employed. The nature of positive government within the American constitutional framework, the method by which government should intervene, was the fundamental unresolved issue.

Two choices, both rooted in the history of the preceding three decades, existed. One was regulation of the economy through the rules of antitrust and fair competition, applied in a juridical way by courts or independent regulatory agencies with a view toward restoring the market as an autonomous means of regulation. In this view, which essentially defines modern pluralism or interest-group liberalism, government actively intervenes in discrete, particularistic ways. It assists interest groups to compete more effectively in the shaping of public policy, much as in the era of laissez faire government promoted individual liberty and opportunity. The second conception of the positive state, less favored in progressive rhetoric and ideology though perhaps more earnestly pursued in public policy, was business-government cooperation for the accomplishment of national and corporate economic goals through executive-bureaucratic means. This approach was premised on the rejection of market competition and maximum profit seeking, and was similar in a general way to the idea of the corporate state popular in Europe in the 1920s. It drew on Theodore Roosevelt's new nationalism and Hoover's cooperative individualism in accepting the inevitability of large-scale corporate organization, while seeking to adapt the corporate structure to a collective social purpose through centralized administrative planning and management.

At its inception in 1933 the New Deal embodied the second of these approaches to positive government far more than the first. It did not adopt a theory of pluralistic group conflict and hostility toward business. On the contrary, national unity, class harmony, and the coordination of interest-group economic activity under the auspices of, if not directly through, the agency of the federal government provided the rationale of early New Deal measures. FDR's outlook was thus essentially similar to his predecessor's. Like Hoover, he sought to preserve the system of private-enterprise capitalism, maximize the production and distribution of goods, and promote social unity. To accomplish the task of social reconstruction and restoration, specific instruments of constitutional authority lay ready to hand in the form of the federal police power and the general welfare power. So profound was the sense of national crisis, however, that the administration went beyond these orthodox doctrines of constitutional law and invoked the analogue of war to support its strategy of national revitalization. Most extraordinarily in time of peace, with constitutional consequences that few could perceive and even fewer could feel apprehensive about, the government in formal and informal ways relied on the war power.

Asserting the purpose of "national consecration" and restoration, Roosevelt, who along with many other New Dealers had served in the wartime Wilson administration, urged the application of values "more noble than mere monetary profit." In his inaugural address he outlined his intention to stimulate the country's productive capacity, raise the value of agricultural products, and provide an adequate and sound currency. He also stressed the interdependence of "the various elements in, and parts of, the United States." Roosevelt's most compelling theme, however, was that the crisis must be dealt with as though it were war. "If we are to go forward we must move as a trained and loyal army willing to sacrifice for the good of a common discipline," he declared. Announcing his willingness to assume "the leadership of this great army of our people," he pledged himself to larger purposes that "will bind upon us all ... with a unity of duty hitherto evoked only in time of armed strife." To deal with the emergency the Constitution was available: "so simple and practical," said Roosevelt, "that it can always meet extraordinary needs." The president warned, however, that it might be necessary to set aside the normal balance of executive and legislative authority. He added that if Congress failed to enact needed measures he would "ask ... for the one remaining instrument to meet the crisis—broad executive power to wage a war against the emergency as great as the power that would be given me if we were in fact invaded by a foreign foe."

In the warlike atmosphere thus evoked, amid pledges of cooperation from leaders in business, labor, and agriculture, Roosevelt created an emergency or crisis government through unilateral executive action and executive leadership of Congress. Backed by large Democratic majorities, he called Congress into special session and all but formally set aside the separation of powers as he virtually became the nation's lawmaker. The administration sent numerous bills to Congress, which restricted its usual procedures for debate and amendment of legislation and approved them mainly because they came from the White House. Constitutionally, the measures Roosevelt requested were significant for delegating legislative power to the executive and for increasing—in an almost geometric ratio—the size of the federal bureaucracy.

The only group that Roosevelt in any way singled out for criticism in his inaugural address was bankers and investment financiers. Yet like Hoover before him, he placed the highest priority on preserving the nation's banking structure. In the winter of 1933 a wave of bank failures was sweeping the nation, while abnormal gold exports and panicky currency hoarding were undermining the stability of the monetary system. To meet this situation, the president immediately declared a temporary "bank holiday" closing all banks in the nation. He also suspended gold exports and foreign-exchange operations. He took these steps under the dubious legal authority of the Trading with the Enemy Act of 1917. However, the Emergency Banking Act of March 1933 ratified the president's action and made provision for reopening banks under executive direction. The act also required the surrender of all gold and gold certificates to the Treasury Department as a preparatory step for an inflationary devaluation of the currency. Under congressional authorization, Roosevelt further lowered the gold content of the dollar. This action and the retirement of gold from circulation made necessary the Joint Resolution of June 1933 by which Congress canceled the gold clause in private contracts and government bonds.

Many of the laws intended to stimulate production or employment posed no serious constitutional issues. The acts creating the Civilian Conservation Corps, which established reforestation camps for unemployed direct relief appropriations to the states, and the Home Owners Loan Corporation, which provided for the refinancing of home mortgages through federal savings and loan associations, could all be justified under the federal power to appropriate money for the general welfare. Since they involved no coercive controls, it was difficult to attack them in the courts, and the judiciary thus had no opportunity to pass upon their constitutionality.

More controversial, however, was the act of May 18, 1933, creating the Tennessee Valley Authority. The TVA was organized as a government corporation, whose three-man board of directors was to be appointed by the president. The corporation was authorized to construct dams, reservoirs, power lines, and the like; to manufacture fertilizer and explosives for the War Department; and to sell all surplus power not used in its operations. The law in reality projected a gigantic rehabilitation and development program in the Tennessee Valley region, embracing flood control, power development, reforestation, and agricultural and industrial development.

Coordinating the National Economy

Major constitutional significance attached to the New Deal policies adopted for the revival of agriculture and industry. The Agricultural Adjustment Act of May 12, 1933, declared that the prevailing economic crisis was in part the consequence of a disparity between agricultural prices and the prices of other commodities, a disparity that had broken down farm purchasing power for industrial products. This provision advanced, by implication, three different constitutional arguments to justify federal regulation of agriculture: the theory of emergency powers, the general welfare, and the effect of agriculture upon interstate commerce.

The announced purpose of the law was the restoration of agricultural prices to a prewar parity level. This was to be accomplished by agreements between farmers and the federal government for reduction of acreage of production in seven basic agricultural commodities—wheat, cotton, corn, rice, tobacco, hogs, and milk—in return for federal benefit payments. Funds for benefit payments were to be secured by an excise tax to be levied upon processors of the commodity in question. The tax was to be at such a rate as to equal the difference between the current average farm price of the commodity and its "fair exchange" value, the latter being defined as that price that would give the commodity the same purchasing power as it had in the 1909–14 base period. Thus the act made use of the federal taxing power and the right to appropriate for the general welfare as the constitutional basis of agricultural control.

Although New Deal agricultural policy had the same inflationary, market-regulation purpose as the Agricultural Marketing Act of 1929, it operated by legal compulsion rather than voluntary cooperation. The processing tax, much objected to as not really a tax but simply a money transfer from one group to another, was the backbone of the measure and an obviously coercive device. The secretary of agriculture had a wide range of discretionary power over production, and the whole idea of the federal governnent paying farmers to reduce their acreage smacked of centralized regimentation. Under the circumstances farmers had little choice but to accept the government's program.

Yet from another perspective the farm policy of the New Deal can be seen as respecting the traditional values of individual liberty and free enterprise within the framework of federal coordination. Spokesmen for farm organizations played a major role in formulating the legislation, and agents of the Agriculture Adjustment Administration went directly to the local level to persuade farmers voluntarily to sign contracts. Moreover, the majority of farmers in a commodity program had to agree by referendum before it could go into effect, while at the state and county levels farmers sat on the committees that assigned production quotas. Critics might dismiss these features as insignificant, but there is no reason to doubt that they reflected a serious attempt to reconcile the need for federal control of a major sector of the economy with individual and local liberty.

The most innovative and constitutionally experimental New Deal measure of 1933 was the National Industrial Recovery Act. Drafted by national economic planners in the executive branch, in collaboration with representatives from business and labor, the bill provided for government coordination of the economy with a view toward stimulating production, restoring employment, maintaining just prices and wages, achieving reforms in industrial working conditions, and establishing efficient and fair business practices in commerce and industry. The introductory section declared that "a national emergency productive of widespread unemployment and disorganization of industry, which burdens interstate commerce, affects the public welfare, and undermines the standards of living of the American people, is hereby declared to exist." Thus the law cited the economic emergency, the relation between the economic crisis and interstate commerce, and the federal welfare power in an attempt to provide a constitutional foundation for federal regulation of industry.

The substance of Title I of the National Industrial Recovery Act, astonishing in its breadth, concerned the adoption of codes of fair competition for the government of virtually all economic enterprise in the United States. The act authorized "trade or industrial associations or groups" to formulate and place before the president for his approval codes of fair competition, subject only to the requirements that they not promote monopoly or eliminate or oppress small enterprises, and that they recognize the right of employees to organize and bargain collectively. Not competition, however, but industrial coordination was the purpose of the act, and to this end it exempted the codes of fair competition from the antitrust laws. The president was authorized to approve the codes thus drawn up, and to cause codes to be drafted where none was forthcoming from private groups. He was also empowered, without any guidelines or criteria, to enter into agreements with business groups or approve agreements among them. Finally, the president was given the power to license business enterprises as a means of forcing them to desist from unfair price, wage, and trade practices. In effect a means of driving a business out of existence, the licensing power was limited to one year, while the other features of the law operated under a two-year limitation. Violation of the codes was declared an unfair method of competition in the sense of the Federal Trade Commission Act of 1914. The act also contained a title providing for public-works construction.

The NIRA, described by historian Henry Steele Commager as perhaps the most extraordinary law ever passed by an American Congress, possessed twofold constitutional significance. First, it delegated vast legislative power to the president, in effect giving him plenary authority to regulate the economic life of the nation. On other occasions Congress had delegated legislative authority to the executive, most notably during World War I.

Now, however, Congress made an even more extensive delegation of its legislative power, one which was accompanied by no standards, guidelines, or criteria to be employed in code writing except for the collective-bargaining stipulation. In many ways the law, under which Roosevelt created the National Recovery Administration as a bureaucratic enforcement mechanism, was like an enabling act in a formal constitutional dictatorship. But if the NIRA granted exceptional powers to the president, it also had the paradoxical effect of weakening the government by delegating legislative power in turn to private interest groups. This was the second notable constitutional feature of the measure. The provision for code drafting by corporations and trade associations gave them what they had long sought: the power of industrial self-government under federal sanction—and with practically no strings attached.

The NRA was not entirely anomalous in the American constitutional tradition, for since the colonial period government had often relied on private groups to accomplish public purposes. Nineteenth-century internal improvement policy depended largely on the blending of public purpose and private interest, and most recently the Hoover administration had tried to involve trade associations in mutually rewarding efforts for the attainment of national economic goals. The NRA carried the tendency to such an extreme, however, assuming the form of centralized bureaucratic control, that it provoked what eventually proved to be insuperable constitutional objections.

Paradoxically, however, coercive as the NRA was in theory, it was weak and ineffectual in actual operation. The irony is that this most far-reaching federal intervention really depended for its implementation on the voluntary cooperation of private groups, persuaded if need be by the force of public opinion. The government's purpose, said NRA head General Hugh S. Johnson, was to "put the enforcement of this law into the hands of the whole people." Amid the hoopla of parades, speeches, poster campaigns, radio advertisements, and other propaganda techniques, the recovery program was launched with a great show of public enthusiasm. What enforcement ultimately came to was the posting of the famous Blue Eagle decal—stating "We do our part"—in the offices and windows of businesses that cooperated, and the withholding of it from those that did not.

This is not to deny the potentially oppressive nature of mass opinion or the legitimate apprehension that could arise over the concentration of power in the executive branch. In fact, however, public opinion was not oppressive, the codes proved difficult to enforce, and within a year the NRA was a serious political liability for the Roosevelt administration. Small businessmen complained of monopolistic control by big corporations. Reformers and nonbusiness groups saw the NRA as unrestrained industrial self-government aimed at keeping prices up and wages down. And once they got a little economic breathing room, corporation leaders themselves recalled their laissez-faire roots and denounced the NRA as collectivism. In truth it was preposterous to think that the federal government could, on its own authority and through its own agency, enforce the vast system of codes covering the whole of the country's economic life. The constitutional tradition of minimal government, the high value placed on individual and local liberty, and the irrepressible nature of interest-group conflict militated against central economic planning and control in the overtly corporatist form of the NRA.

The Supreme Court and the New Deal

The weakness of centralized authority under the New Deal is, of course, far clearer in retrospect than it was at the time. What stood out was the constitutional novelty of the AAA, NRA, and other New Deal measures, and the severe challenge they posed to traditional political and governmental values. In previous periods of crisis government during the Civil War and World War I, executive action that strained or exceeded constitutional limits met no serious resistance from the legislative or executive branches. In the 1930s, however, New Deal constitutional experimentation enjoyed no such immunity. Given the nature of constitutional policies in the United States, it was only a matter of time before the judiciary would be in a position to pass judgment on the constitutional legitimacy of the Roosevelt administration's recovery programs. After some initial hesitation, the Supreme Court reasserted the politically discredited doctrines of laissez-faire constitutionalism against the regulatory movement in general and against centralized bureaucratic control of the economy in particular. By doing so the judiciary provoked the constitutional crisis of 1937 centering on President Roosevelt's plan to increase the size of the Supreme Court.

The political outlook of the Supreme Court in the 1930s was basically conservative. Four justices—Willis Van Devanter, Pierce Butler, George Sutherland, and James McReynolds—were strongly identified with entrepreneurial liberty and were opponents of the regulatory movement. Louis D. Brandeis and Harlan F. Stone on the other hand were liberals. Named to the Court in the early 1930s were Charles Evans Hughes, replacing Taft as chief justice, and Owen Roberts and Benjamin N. Cardozo. Cardozo was a liberal who had served on the New York Court of Appeals and had made a significant contribution through scholarly writings to the theory of sociological jurisprudence. Roberts, a Republican from Pennsylvania, was a conservative attorney, while Hughes was returning to the Court after a distinguished career as a Republican statesman. Hughes served as governor of New York, associate justice of the Supreme Court from 1911 to 1916,

Republican presidential candidate in 1916, and secretary of state from 1921 to 1925. A progressive Republican early in his career, he was now regarded as a conservative.

Two opinions of 1934, neither of which directly involved federal legislation, suggested that a majority of the Supreme Court might view the New Deal with some sympathy. In *Home Bldg. and Loan Association* v. *Blaisdell,* decided in January 1934, a majority of five justices held the Minnesota moratorium law constitutional. The decision was significant, for the statute declared a limited moratorium on mortgage payments, and the Court might easily have decided that it violated the obligation-of-contracts clause. Instead, Hughes's opinion skirted close to the proposition that an emergency might empower government to do things which in ordinary times would be unconstitutional. An emergency, said the chief justice, could not create power, but it could furnish the occasion for the exercise of latent power.

In *Nebbia* v. *New York* (1934) the Court sustained the validity of a New York statute setting up a state milk control board authorized to fix maximum and minimum milk prices. This was precisely the kind of legislation that the Court had struck down in the 1920s as a violation of due process, on the ground that the business regulated did not fall within the narrow conception of public interest then entertained by the justices. Yet Justice Roberts now asserted that "there is no closed class or category of businesses affected with a public interest." Roberts said a state was in general free to adopt toward any business "whatever economic policy may reasonably be deemed to promote public welfare."

Contrary to liberals' hopes, however, the Supreme Court took no such favorable view of federal power when used to combat the depression. Over a sixteen-month period, starting in January 1935, it decided ten major cases involving New Deal statutes. In eight instances the decision went against the government. Stricken down in succession were Section 9 (c) of the National Industrial Recovery Act, the NIRA itself, the Railroad Pension Act, the Farm Mortgage law, the Agricultural Adjustment Act, the AAA amendments, the Bituminous Coal Act, and the Municipal Bankruptcy Act. Only two measures, the emergency monetary enactments of 1933 and the Tennessee Valley Authority Act, were given approval in carefully circumscribed and conditional terms.

The Court's first invalidation of a New Deal law came in January 1935, in *Panama Refining Co.* v. *Ryan,* a case involving the so-called "hot oil" provisions of the NIRA. Section 9 (c) of the law authorized the president to prohibit the transportation in interstate commerce of oil produced or stored in excess of the limitations imposed by states to bolster faltering oil prices and to conserve oil resources. Chief Justice Hughes, speaking for eight of the nine justices, held Section 9 (c) unconstitutional as an invalid delegation of legislative power, on the ground that it did not set adequate standards for executive guidance. The Court thus for the first time held unconstitutional a statute that delegated legislative authority to the executive.

Offsetting this decision, the Court upheld the government in the Gold Cases. At issue was the power of Congress to nullify the gold clauses in private and public contracts, as it had done in the Joint Resolution of June 1933. The specific question was whether the government could impair the obligation of contracts, public and private, in pursuance of the monetary power. Chief Justice Hughes held in the affirmative. He stated that contracts for payment in gold were not commodity contracts but were in reality contracts for payment in money and hence, by implication, fell within the federal monetary power. As for government bonds as distinct from private obligations, Hughes held them to be contractual obligations which Congress had unconstitutionally broken in its resolution of June 1933. Hughes ruled, however, that the plaintiff had suffered no more than nominal damages and was not entitled to sue in the Court of Claims. The invalidation of the Joint Resolution was thus without practical meaning.

It appears probable that the majority in the Gold Cases was impressed by practical considerations. The government's emergency monetary policy was, in theory at least, a gigantic breach of obligation of contract. But the gold policy had failed in its intended result, and acceptance of its constitutionality would have no practical effects, whereas enforcement of gold contracts in devalued dollars would have had a catastrophic effect on the national economy. The government's victory may also be explained in part by the fact that the Gold Cases did not involve the most controversial issue of the regulatory movement—the exercise of federal control over various aspects of production. In a general way the broad and comprehensive character of the federal monetary power was already well established, and the emergency measures under review contemplated the creation of no new sphere of federal activity.

But if the government could claim this victory, a string of stinging defeats lay just ahead. In May 1935 the full weight of judicial disapproval of Roosevelt's program was released, as the Court struck down New Deal statutes in three cases. On May 6 the Court, in *Retirement Board* v. *Alton Railroad Co.,* voted 5 to 4 to invalidate the Railroad Retirement Pension Act. Justice Roberts in the majority opinion held that certain mechanical details of the pension law were arbitrary and unreasonable and so violated due process and the Fifth Amendment. More significantly, however, Roberts was of the opinion that the whole subject of old-age pensions had no real relationship to the safety or efficiency of rail transportation and so lay outside the federal commerce power.

Three weeks later, in a unaminous opinion in *Schechter* v. *United States,* the Supreme Court held the National Industrial Recovery Act to be unconstitutional. The case involved an appeal from a conviction for violation of the code of fair competition for the live poultry industry of New York City. In his opinion for the Court, Chief Justice Hughes took up three questions: whether the law was justified "in the light of the grave national crisis with which Congress was confronted," whether the law illegally delegated legislative power, and whether the act exceeded the limits of the interstate commerce power.

Hughes settled the first question by observing that "extraordinary conditions do not create or enlarge constitutional power." He then passed to the issue of legislative delegation. Had Congress in authorizing the codes of fair competition fixed adequate "standards of legal obligation, thus performing its essential legislative function . . .?" The chief justice thought not. In reality, he said, the codes embraced whatever "the formulators would propose, and what the President would approve, or prescribe, as wise and beneficent measures for the government of trades and industries." In short, trade groups had been given a blanket power to enact into law whatever provisions for their business they happened to think wise. With some feeling, Hughes asserted that such a delegation "is unknown to our law and is utterly inconsistent with the constitutional prerogatives and duties of Congress." If the codes had any validity, he continued, it must have been because they were promulgated by the president. Yet the act also fixed no real limits upon the president's code-making power, so long as he sought the vague objectives set forth in the statute's preamble. It, therefore, illegally delegated legislative power to the executive, and was void.

Behind Hughes's argument one senses two additional powerful objections to the NRA's code-making features, although these objections were nowhere clearly stated. First, the Court was appalled by the unprecedented magnitude of the delegation of legislative authority projected in the law. Previously, delegation had been on a comparatively small scale; in this case Congress had given the president authority to draft regulations governing the whole vast sweep of the nation's economic life. Cardozo expressed this difficulty more specifically in his concurring opinion, when he said that "this is delegation run riot."

Second, the Court viewed with evident distaste the fact that code making was in the first instance carried out not by the president but by private business groups, the president merely putting his stamp of approval upon the codes. The law thus came close to a delegation to private individuals. Technically, perhaps, there was no ground for objection since the president promulgated the codes, but the break with traditional methods of quasi-legislative delegation was plain enough.

Finally, Hughes found that the poultry code under review attempted to regulate intrastate commercial transactions and hence exceeded the federal commerce power. He rejected the stream-of-commerce doctrine as not applicable, on the ground that there was no "flow" in the Schechters' business, their transactions being conducted on a purely local basis. Hughes held also that the Schechters' business had only an indirect effect upon interstate commerce and so was beyond federal control.

The administration, while discouraged by the outcome of the *Schechter* case, did not abandon its attempts to regulate industry. The summer of 1935 saw the passage of two landmarks in New Deal legislative policy, the National Labor Relations Act of July 5, 1935, and the National Bituminous Coal Conservation Act of August 30, 1935. Both of these acts imposed regulations upon industry in apparent defiance of the *Schechter* opinion and thus flung the issue of federal economic controls back at the Court. Roosevelt's position became even clearer when he wrote a letter to Representative J. Buell Snyder of Pennsylvania asking Congress to pass the coal bill regardless of any doubts, "however reasonable," that it might have about the bill's constitutionality. On the basis of this letter the president was widely represented as urging Congress to disregard the Constitution. However, the Pension and NRA decisions were not necessarily binding upon the Coal Act, whose constitutionality was at least open to question. Undoubtedly, however, the president was in part challenging the finality of the Court's interpretation of the Constitution.

In *Louisville Bank* v. *Radford,* another opinion handed down on May 27, the Court declared the so-called Frazier-Lemke Act void. Justice Brandeis, speaking for a unanimous Court, first pointed out that unlike earlier federal and state laws, the Frazier-Lemke Act compelled the mortgagee to surrender the property in question free of any lien without full payment of the debt. While the federal government could lawfully impair the obligation of contracts, it could not take private property, even for a public purpose, without just compensation. Since the act destroyed pre-existing creditor property rights under state law, it violated the Fifth Amendment and was, therefore, void.

In January 1936, in *United States* v. *Butler,* the Court invalidated the Agricultural Adjustment Act by a 6–3 vote. The decision revealed how bitterly divided the justices were on certain crucial constitutional issues involved in the New Deal. The case arose out of a district-court order directing the receiver for a bankrupt cotton-milling corporation to pay the processing taxes required under the AAA. Justice Roberts for the majority first argued that the processing tax was not a tax at all, but in reality part of a system for the regulation of agricultural production. This did not necessarily mean the system of regulation was unconstitutional, only that it could not be held valid under the taxing power. Roberts next considered whether crop benefits could be justified under the general welfare clause, which authorizes Congress to "provide for the common defense and general welfare of the United States." He concluded that Congress could, apart from its other enumerated powers, appropriate for the general welfare. But he then held the crop benefits unconstitutional as a system for regulating agricultural production in violation of the Tenth Amendment. The design for regulation, Roberts contended, was no less real for being disguised under supposedly voluntary crop controls. In fact, the farmer had no real choice but to accept benefits and submit to regulation. Ambivalent about the basic issue of positive government, Roberts thus admitted a power to appropriate for the general welfare, yet denied that the government could impose conditions on those who accepted its grants. This conclusion ignored the fact that in land grants and grants-in-aid the federal government had been "purchasing compliance," as Roberts termed it, since 1802. Moreover the Court itself, in *Massachusetts* v. *Mellon* (1923), had said with respect to grants-in-aid that a state could avoid submission to federal requirements by refusing the grant.

In a sharp dissenting opinion Justice Stone defended the agricultural regulatory program under the power to appropriate for the general welfare. Stone also gave comfort to New Dealers by attacking the Court's tendency to legislate through the judicial power. Denying that it was the business of the courts to sit in judgment upon the wisdom of legislative action, he said: "Courts are not the only agencies of government that must be assumed to have the capacity to govern." The administration took heart from the fact that Stone, Brandeis, and Cardozo, generally considered to be the most learned and intelligent men on the Court, had set their stamp of approval on a New Deal reform of even more long-run importance than the Recovery Act.

Congress did not accept *United States* v. *Butler* as the final word in agricultural regulation. Seven weeks later it enacted a new agricultural relief measure, the Soil Conservation Act. The new law sought to avoid the charge of coercion by payments of benefits for soil conservaton programs. Also, the act levied no taxes, and thus avoided the charge of regulatory taxation. But crop control was still the obvious purpose underlying the law, and the Court might well have taken warning, for here was evidence of a strong congressional determination to resist judicial fiat, an intention to force through the major New Deal objectives even at the risk of a head-on collision with the judiciary.

In February 1936 the New Deal won a limited judicial victory, when, in *Ashwander* v. *Tennessee Valley Authority,* the Court upheld the validity of a contract between the Tennessee Valley Authority and the Alabama Power Company for the sale of "surplus power" generated by Wilson Dam. Hughes's opinion pointed out that the dam in question had been built for national defense and for the improvement of navigation, both objects specifically lying within the scope of federal power. The federal government's right to dispose of property legally acquired, he added, could not be denied.

In May 1936, however, the Court struck at another New Deal attempt to regulate production when it invalidated the Bituminous Coal Act of 1935. Drawn up to replace the NRA with a new code, the act declared that the coal industry was "affected with a national public interest," and that the production and distribution of coal directly affected interstate commerce and so made federal regulation necessary. The law created a National Bituminous Coal Commission and gave it authority to formulate a Bituminous Coal Code, regulating coal prices through district boards in various coal-producing areas. It also levied a tax of 15 percent on all coal sold at the mine head, nine-tenths of which was to be remitted to producers who accepted the code provisions. A separate section, Part III, guaranteed collective bargaining and provided that wage contracts negotiated between operators producing two-thirds of the tonnage and half or more of the workers should be binding upon the entire industry. The act specifically provided that the constitutionality of the labor and price-fixing sections should be considered separately and that neither should necessarily be invalidated should the other be declared void.

In *Carter* v. *Carter Coal Company* (1936) the Supreme Court in a 6-to-3 decision declared the entire act unconstitutional. Justice Sutherland, citing the precedent of the *Knight* case, held the labor provisions void on the ground that they regulated an aspect of production having only an indirect effect on interstate commerce. Despite the express intention of Congress to separate the labor and price-fixing sections of the law, Sutherland contended that the legislature would not have enacted the other sections of the law without the labor provisions. The bone and sinew of the law were, therefore, gone, and the price-fixing provisions were hence also unconstitutional. Reduced to simplest terms, Sutherland's argument was that price fixing was unconstitutional because it was too closely bound up with matters directly reserved to the states. Reviving the doctrine of dual federalism, Sutherland came close to denying the supremacy of national powers over the states.

Analysis of the judicial reaction to the New Deal reveals that the justices had three principal objections to the legislation they reviewed. First, the Court firmly rejected all attempts to extend federal authority over production. It denied in succession that interstate commerce, appropriations for the general welfare, or taxation could be used to this end. Second, the Court denied the constitutionality of legislative delegation to the executive on the scale attempted in the NRA or the Guffey Act. Third, and more broadly, the Court refused to accept the concept of constitutional growth, either by evolution or through economic emergency. The most important of these attitudes was the Court's stand on federal control over production; this issue evidently divided the justices most sharply. Even the myth of a static constitutional system might have been preserved, and most of the New Deal still validated, had the justices admitted that production "directly" affected interstate commerce and that the welfare and taxing powers were positive instruments of federal authority.

Undoubtedly, the conservatives who struck down New Deal measures saw them as an assault on private property, contractual rights, and the laissez-faire market. Yet it is evident that the New Deal involved a tremendous extension of federal authority, much of it at the expense of the states. Although precedents for national economic regulation existed, the new laws constituted a substantial alteration in the scope of federal powers—an alteration that the majority believed violated the fundamental nature of the Union. Brandeis, Cardozo, and Stone were more willing to accept federal control over production, as their dissents in the *AAA* and *Carter* decisions showed. But they, too, objected when federal controls over production were carried to an extreme under the NRA. It is important to remember, moreover, that the three liberals stood with their conservative brethren in questioning the expansion of executive power through legislative delegation.

The Court-Packing Crisis of 1937

The Court's decisions striking down New Deal legislation provoked an intense outpouring of antijudicial criticism. As in 1896, 1912, and 1924, when "government by judiciary" was a campaign issue, liberals condemned both the reactionary results of Supreme Court decision making and the quasi-legislative conception of judicial review on which they rested. Particularly offensive to reformers was the discrepancy between the conservative majority's profession of declaratory jurisprudence, with its emphasis on the politically neutral, law-discovering function of the judiciary, and the socio-economic conservatism that the Court's decisions so plainly embodied. The more liberals criticized "mechanical jurisprudence," however, the more the conservative justices on the Supreme Court denied the idea of a changing, socially responsive law and insisted that the Constitution was a fixed body of principles. A high point in the conservative profession of faith came in *United States* v. *Butler,* when Justice Roberts, denying the courts acted in a legislative manner, asserted: "When an act of Congress is appropriately challenged in the courts as not conforming to the constitutional mandate, the judicial branch of the Government has only one duty,—to lay the article of the Constitution which is invoked beside the statute which is challenged and to decide whether the latter squares with the former."

The controversy that thus took shape in 1935–36 over the Supreme Court concerned both substantive interpretation of the Constitution, especially in regard to federal power to regulate production, and the role of the judiciary in the constitutional system. Defenders of the Supreme Court—businessmen, lawyers, editors, and other professional groups—held to the traditional declaratory theory of law as illustrated in Roberts's *Butler* opinion. Liberal critics of the Court, generally of the same social and professional class standing, defended the extension of federal regulatory power on the basis of a theory of constitutional change derived from sociological jurisprudence and legal realism.

Rejecting the static formalism of declaratory jurisprudence, reformers promised a more politically oriented and socially relevant constitutionalism that would develop through legislative and executive action rather than judicial explication of the constitutional text. Rather than an inflexible, mechanistic structure valued chiefly for its usefulness in maintaining the status quo, the Constitution in this view was a living and growing complex of institutions shaped by human agency in accordance with social needs. The noted constitutional commentator Edward S. Corwin argued, for example, that the NRA reflected the growth of federal executive power and the decline of the judicial role in national policy making. The old constitutional order, said Corwin, was marked by tension and competition between the branches of government under the doctrine of the separation of powers, and between the states and the nation. The new order, Corwin predicted, in contrast would be characterized by fusion of powers and cooperation between government and business, state and nation, president and Congress. Revolutionary governmental changes were fostering a more political and less legalistic view of the Constitution. "We shall value it," Corwin wrote, "for the aid it lends to considered social purpose, not as a lawyers' document." Columbia law professor Karl Lewellyn carried the politicist theme even further, asserting that the actions and practices of government officials, rather than the formal written Constitution, determined the nation's real constitution or fundamental law. The public in general was loyal to the empty symbol of the documentary Constitution, said Llewellyn, leaving "specialists in governing" "free to shape and reshape the working Constitution in *almost* any way they please."

As the constitutional controversy deepened, the Roosevelt administration in 1935 began to explore possible means of counteracting judicial obstruction of New Deal policies. A constitutional amendment clarifying federal legislative power was contemplated, but was rejected as impractical and also as conceding the weakness of New Deal constitutional theory. Solutions dealing directly with judicial power were more feasible, and scores of them were introduced into Congress in 1936. They included proposed constitutional amendments abolishing the Court's power to declare acts of Congress unconstitutional; requiring a two-thirds vote of the Court whenever it declared an act of Congress unconstitutional; and permitting Congress to validate laws previously declared unconstitutional by repassing them with a two-thirds vote of both houses. Congressmen also proposed legislation restricting the Court's appellate power in cases involving certain kinds of constitutional issues and formally depriving the Court of the power to invalidate federal legislation.

Meanwhile, the president for the most part remained silent about the Supreme Court and let the situation ripen. In the spring of 1935, after the *Schechter* decision, he complained of the Court's "horse-and-buggy definition of interstate commerce" and said it was necessary to decide "whether in some way we are going to . . . restore to the Federal Government the powers which exist in the national governments of every other nation in the world." In succeeding months, however, Roosevelt refrained from comment in the belief that the conservative majority's unpopular decisions constituted a sufficient indictment of the Court. The president's studied reticence continued into the 1936 election campaign. Avoiding any reference to the Supreme Court, the Democratic platform stated merely that the party would deal with national problems "through legislation within the Constitution." Vindicated by his overwhelming triumph, however, Roosevelt in late 1936 decided to submit a proposal for judicial reform to Congress.

Historically, the most feasible and expeditious way of influencing judicial interpretation of the Constitution had been to change the composition of the Supreme Court by altering its size. Congress had the undisputed power to fix the size of all federal courts, and on several occasions had changed the number of justices on the Supreme Court—from six in 1789 to five in 1801, six in 1802, nine in 1837, ten in 1863, seven in 1866, and nine in 1869. After considering the alternatives, the Roosevelt administration chose this method of constitutional reform, but with a peculiarly modern twist. Justice Department lawyers came up with the idea of adding a new member to the Court whenever a sitting justice reached the age of seventy and chose not to retire. The proposal acquired irresistible and ironic appeal when Attorney General Homer Cummings discovered that Justice McReynolds, perhaps the most hidebound of the conservative majority, had in 1913 as attorney general recommended a plan providing for the retirement of federal judges at age seventy with full pay, with the appointment of a younger judge for each one choosing to remain on the bench beyond that age. Thus after months of deliberation, all of it kept secret from members of Congress, the administration settled on a plan for judicial and constitutional reform that seemed legitimate, expeditious, and, in view of the president's strengthened political position after his re-election, almost certain of success.

On February 5, 1937, the president broke a long silence on the Court question by presenting Congress with a bill to reorganize the federal judiciary. The bill provided that whenever any federal judge who had served ten years or more failed to retire within six months after reaching his seventieth birthday, the president might appoint an additional judge to the court upon which the septuagenarian was serving. No more than fifty additional judges in all might be appointed under the act, and the maximum size of the Supreme Court was fixed at fifteen. The bill also gave the chief justice power to shift district and circuit judges to accommodate the work load of the federal courts, prohibited federal courts from issuing injunctions on constitutional questions without notice to the attorney general, and provided for direct appeal to the Supreme Court of any decision against an act of Congress by a court of first instance.

Roosevelt accompanied his proposal with a message to Congress arguing the need for new blood in the judiciary to meet the complexities of
modern society. Asserting that courts were handicapped by insufficient
personnel and by the presence of too many superannuated judges, Roosevelt said that most old judges were physically unable to perform their
duties and were antiquated in outlook. "Little by little," be observed, "new
facts become blurred through old glasses fitted, as it were, for the needs of
another generation." In terms that were more familiar to proponents of
judicial reform, the president further criticized conflicting opinions on constitutionality that made the law unequal and uncertain, and excessive use of
the injunction that brought government to a standstill. The central focus of
the message, nevertheless, was the problem of a "static" judiciary. In conclusion Roosevelt urged his proposal as one that would eliminate the need
for "fundamental change in the powers of the courts or the Constitution of
our government."

The reception given the proposal for judicial reform, which was in-
stantly and permanently dubbed Roosevelt's Court-packing plan, showed
the old-age strategy to be an egregious blunder. Republicans could be expected to oppose it and they did, denouncing it as an attempt to destroy the
independence of the judiciary. What was not expected was the hostile reaction within the president's own party. Walking out of the Capitol after
hearing the plan announced, Representative Hatton Sumners of Texas,
chairman of the House Judiciary Committee, declared his opposition to it
and let it be known that he would not even bring it up in committee.
Tactically this was an important move which for all practical purposes
killed the measure. The administration had more solid support in the House
than in the Senate, and had the Court reform plan been promptly reported
out of committee and adopted in the lower chamber—a likely outcome
considering the size of the Democratic majority—its chances of passage in
the Senate would have been greatly enhanced. With the House Judiciary
Committee refusing to consider the bill, however, it was necessary to take it
up first in the Senate, where it ran into heavy opposition.

In a stinging report a few months later, the Senate Judiciary Committee, under Democratic leadership, called the bill a devious, indirect, and
unconstitutional attempt to force the judiciary to change its interpretation
of the Constitution. Charging that the bill contained the seed of centralized,
executive-controlled administration of law, the Senate committee said "its
practical operation would be to make the Constitution what the executive
or legislative branches of the Government choose to say it is—an interpretation to be changed with each change of administration." Many Democrats
supported the proposal without enthusiasm simply because it came from
the White House. Still others believed Roosevelt erred by failing to address
what they considered the real issue—the wrong-headed, out-of-date interpretation of the Constitution persisted in by the Court's conservative ma-

jority. Indeed, most liberals who supported the plan at bottom did not object to the quasi-legislative power of judicial review that the Court had so long exercised. "What we demanded for our generation," wrote Robert H. Jackson, assistant attorney general, "was the right consciously to influence the evolutionary pattern of constitutional law, as other generations had done."

The hostility to the plan that emerged in Congress was reinforced by the course that the Supreme Court now pursued. Between March and June the Court dramatically reversed itself on several outstanding constitutional issues. In succession, the Court validated a state minimum-wage law, the Farm Mortgage Act of 1935, the amended Railway Labor Act of 1934, the National Labor Relations Act of 1935, and the Social Security Act of 1935. It thus appeared that there was now no necessity for coercing the judiciary in order to push through the New Deal program, and that the Court bill could, therefore, be dropped.

The administration, however, refused to back off. The fact that the justices—and in particular Justice Roberts—had changed their minds was taken as evidence of the need for the bill; they could, it was argued, just as easily switch back again to a conservative position in the future! Oblivious to criticism and confident of success, Roosevelt accordingly refused to compromise. The situation changed further in May when Justice Van Devanter announced his resignation, clearing the way for a Roosevelt appointment and further weakening the case for the bill. By June the critics' message was beginning to sink in and the administration let it be known that it was prepared to accept a compromise by which one Supreme Court justice would be appointed per year for each justice over the age of seventy-five. It was too late, however, for compromise. Critics of the bill were in the majority, and when Senator Robinson, the Democratic floor leader in the Senate, died in July all hope of passing the measure ended. As a sop to the president, Congress passed the Judiciary Reform Act in August 1937. This act made the government a party to any action in the federal courts involving the constitutionality of an act of Congress and provided for direct appeal to the Supreme Court whenever a lower federal court declared an act of Congress unconstitutional.

Considering Roosevelt's reputation for political acumen, his colossal miscalculation on the issue of judicial reform wants explanation. To begin with, the plan was principally a Court-packing scheme rather than a genuine proposal for the reorganization and reform of the judiciary. Moreover, it was presented in such a way as to avoid the real issue in the controversy. This, of course, appeared differently to different groups. Most liberals and New Deal supporters believed the crux of the matter was the Supreme Court's tortured, unrealistic, socially reactionary interpretation of the Constitution. Others, including many congressmen with solidly pro–New Deal voting records, thought the real issue was the independence of the judiciary and the nature and function of judicial review. It is significant that despite the long-standing criticism of post-1890s judicial review as a usurpation of legislative authority, when the chips were down very few liberals saw the main issue as the institutional power of the judiciary. In any event, Roosevelt's proximate purpose seems to have been to bring about change in constitutional interpretation. In seizing on the apparently neutral factor of age, however, he raised a false issue, obscuring his immediate aim and laying himself open to the charge of deviousness and sophistry. Supporters came to his defense with explanations of the need to bring constitutional interpretation into line with the views of the democratic majority in the legislature. But critics could equate this otherwise reasonable demand and expectation with an attack on the independence of the judiciary and the whole idea of the separation of powers.

The press and public in general sprang to the Court's defense, affirming the need for impartial judicial declaration of the meaning of the Constitution. As never before in the history of the Court, the people's deep attachment to the idea of the judiciary as the inviolable guardian of the Constitution, transcending politics, became apparent. Roosevelt did not anticipate this reaction, yet implicitly perhaps it was his recognition of the secure place that the myth of an impartial judiciary and a fixed Constitution had in the public mind that kept him from an overt attack on the Court's constitutional interpretations. For an open attack on the Court's doctrines would have been to admit that the Constitution is open-ended and its interpretation a subjective process influenced by the social and political outlook of individual judges.

At one level, then, Roosevelt desired to maintain the traditional belief in an impartial judiciary, along with the institution of judical review as it had developed since the 1890s. Not the least of his reasons for approaching the matter in this way was the expectation that the existing structure of judicial power could be made to serve the purposes of the New Deal. Roosevelt's emphasis on the justices' age, however, at another level betrayed a legal-realist conception of the nature of constitutional adjudication that gravely weakened the proposal. The point appeared to be to get new members on the Court who would support the New Deal, on the legal-realist assumption that judges act strictly on the basis of subjective personal outlook. Looking at the question from this perspective, the administration could not be reassured when the Supreme Court started to approve New Deal measures, for if willful and subjective judges changed their minds once, they could change them back again. Hence the administration persisted with its original proposal and dug itself into an even deeper hole.

Throughout American history presidents have, of course, appointed members of the Supreme Court with awareness of the fact that their general political outlook would have a bearing on their interpretation of the Constitution. So, too, alteration of the size of the Supreme Court by Congress has sometimes expressed a desire to influence judicial interpretation of the Constitution. Roosevelt's age-based Court appointment plan, however, so obvious in its indirection and sophistry, struck most members of Congress and the general public as a blatant and improper expression of this familiar intention and expectation.

Roosevelt's intentions aside, it seems reasonable to conclude that in the political and constitutional setting that existed in 1937 the effect of the Court-packing plan, had it been approved, would have been to weaken the independence and integrity of the judiciary. In a very real sense the basic constitutional issue was not the scope of federal power over production or the place of the judiciary in the governmental structure, but rather the nature and scope of executive power. Although the executive domination that characterized the early New Deal had ended and Congress was more legislatively assertive in 1935–36, the president's power remained enormous. Especially important for understanding the reaction produced by Roosevelt's Court-packing plan was his concurrent proposal, to be discussed in the next chapter, for reorganization of the executive branch that would give the president greater control over the federal bureaucracy. The Supreme Court problem developed independently of this question, but by the end of 1937 Roosevelt's proposals for judicial and executive reform both seemed to express his desire to aggrandize executive power.

It is usually said that in the Court-packing controversy President Roosevelt lost the battle but won the war, in the sense that the Supreme Court went on to approve New Deal policies and constitutional doctrines. From another perspective, however, Roosevelt lost the war. For the Court fight split the Democratic party and destroyed the widespread support that New Deal measures had previously received. Complex political forces underlay this development, but it is doubtful that Roosevelt's reform coalition fell apart simply because key middle-class elements, suddenly finding their interests satisfied, became defenders of the status quo. A more plausible explanation is that for legitimate reasons many people became apprehensive about the concentration of power in the executive branch.

TWENTY-FIVE

The New Deal and the Emergence of a Centralized Bureaucratic State

$\diamond\,\diamond\,\diamond$

THE SUPREME COURT'S abrupt reversal of outlook in the spring of 1937 signaled the start of momentous changes in constitutional law that laid to rest the doctrines of substantive due process, liberty of contract, and dual federalism. In their place the Court established the legitimacy of economic controls and social welfare policies under federal authority. By the end of the decade, moreover, despite a considerable backlash against executive power, the institution of the presidency had been significantly strengthened by the adoption of the Executive Reorganization Act of 1939. These developments in turn produced a decisive centralization of power that revolutionized the federal system and placed the states in a distinctly subordinate relationship to the federal government.

The Court Accepts the New Deal

The first clear indication of the Supreme Court's new position came on March 29, 1937, in *West Coast Hotel Co.* v. *Parrish,* when it sustained a Washington minimum wage law. Only the year before, in *Morehead* v. *New York ex rel. Tipaldo* (1936), the justices had held unconstitutional a similar New York statute, on the authority of *Adkins* v. *Children's Hospital.* But now Chief Justice Hughes, speaking for the 5-4 majority, said the *Adkins* decision was wrong and should be overruled. He thrust aside the embarrassing *Tipaldo* precedent with the assertion that the Court had not reexamined the constitutionality of minimum wage legislation in that case because it had not been asked to do so.

The stunning series of reversals that started with this decision were long viewed as a shrewd political maneuver designed to defeat Roosevelt's Court-packing plan—"the switch in time that saved nine." In actuality, however, Justice Roberts, the "swing man" in the *Parrish* decision, had earlier decided that the Court's position on minimum wage legislation, maintained since the *Adkins* decision of 1923, was wrong and ought to be abandoned. In December 1936, after the *Parrish* case had been argued, Roberts announced his change of position to his fellow justices. However, Justice Stone's illness left the justices divided four to four on the decision and so prevented publication at that time of an opinion holding minimum wage legislation constitutional well before the president's court plan became known. Not that Roberts and Hughes, whose votes sustained New Deal measures in 1937, were unaware of the political implications of the Court's shift. The change, however, involved a genuine reassessment of the constitutional issues at stake as well as judicial forbearance and prudence.

In April the New Deal scored a further victory, as Hughes and Roberts joined the liberals in several decisions sustaining the National Labor Relations Act. This law imposed extensive and detailed controls upon labor-management relations in industry. Although it thus plainly attempted to regulate a phase of production, Chief Justice Hughes, in *N.L.R.B.* v. *Jones and Laughlin Steel Corporation* (1937), thrust aside the *Schechter* and *Carter* precedents as "inapplicable." Resting his opinion mainly upon the "stream of commerce" doctrine, Hughes pointed out that the respondent steel firm drew its raw materials from interstate commerce and shipped its products back into that commerce. He bluntly rejected the old categorical distinction between direct and indirect effects upon commerce.

The Court's holding in an accompanying case, *N.L.R.B.* v. *Friedman–Harry Marks Clothing Company* (1937), was even more significant. Here the respondent clothing firm was a small manufacturer whose production could not have had more than a negligible effect upon interstate commerce. Yet Hughes's opinion emphasized the interstate character of the clothing industry at large, and ignored the question of the actual effect production in the case at hand had upon commerce.

At the same time the Court held in *Associated Press* v. *N.L.R.B.* (1937) that the labor relations of newspapers and press associations were also subject to regulation under the Labor Relations Act. Petitioners had attacked the law as a violation of the First Amendment on the ground that the statute permitted the federal government to dictate to the press the persons to be employed in preparing news and editorials and thus to control editorial policy, thereby curtailing freedom of the press. Justice Roberts's opinion rejected this contention as unsound and without relevance to the case at hand. The law, he said, did not regulate the press but only its labor relationships.

In May the Court reaffirmed its new-found nationalism in two opinions validating the Social Security Act. In *Stewart Machine Company* v. *Davis* (1937), it accepted the unemployment excise tax upon employers and the provisions for unemployment grants to states enacting satisfactory unemployment compensation laws. Cardozo's majority opinion contained an exceedingly nationalistic defense of the federal taxing power, which he held to be as comprehensive, except for specific constitutional limitations, as that of the states. And credits to the states, said Cardozo, were not an attempt to coerce the states, but were rather an instance of federal-state cooperation for a national purpose. In the second Social Security Act case, *Helvering* v. *Davis* (1937), Cardozo upheld the statute's old-age tax and benefit provisions. The old-age tax, he said, was a valid exercise of the taxing power, while of the benefit provisions he observed merely that "Congress may spend money in aid of the general welfare." Cardozo's two opinions went far to repudiate the entire theory of dual federalism, which had reached its apogee in the *Butler* case.

The administration's somewhat precarious majority on the Court was presently confirmed and strengthened by a series of resignations and new appointments, beginning with Justice Van Devanter's retirement in May 1937. President Roosevelt nominated Senator Hugo Black of Alabama, a liberal whose previous membership in the Ku Klux Klan was briefly a source of embarrassment to the administration. In 1938 Justice Sutherland resigned and Justice Cardozo died. Roosevelt replaced them with Stanley Reed, former solicitor general who had argued for New Deal legislation before the Court, and Felix Frankfurter, a Harvard Law School professor who as a protégé of Brandeis and informal advisor to FDR was perhaps the best-known liberal reformer of the time. Justice Brandeis resigned in 1939, and his place was taken by William O. Douglas, also a noted liberal and a member of the Securities and Exchange Commission. When Justice Butler died in 1939 Roosevelt appointed Frank Murphy, former Philippine high commissioner and governor of Michigan. In 1941 Justice McReynolds, the last remaining conservative opponent of the New Deal, resigned. The president filled the vacancy with Attorney General Robert H. Jackson, a staunch New Dealer. Chief Justice Hughes resigned in 1941, whereupon Roosevelt appointed Stone to the chief justiceship and Senator James Byrnes of South Carolina to the vacancy. Byrnes left the Court a year later to take an administrative post, and the president appointed Wiley Rutledge of Iowa to the vacancy in 1943. Thus the Court was now firmly in the hands of New Deal liberals.

The New Constitutional Law: The Federal Regulatory State

While these changes in personnel were occurring, the Supreme Court reshaped the contours of constitutional law. In one group of cases it fully confirmed the implications of the initial Labor Board opinions with respect to federal controls over labor and production. In *Santa Cruz Fruit Packing Co.* v. *N.L.R.B.* (1938) the Court upheld the validity of a Labor Board order directed to a fruit-packing concern, only 37 percent of whose products moved in interstate commerce. Chief Justice Hughes, observing that the stream-of-commerce doctrine was not exactly applicable to the case, held that federal control was nonetheless valid, since labor disturbances at the plant had a substantial disruptive effect upon interstate commerce.

In *Consolidated Edison Co.* v. *N.L.R.B.* (1938) the Court sustained federal control over the labor relations of a power company selling its output entirely within one state. Chief Justice Hughes pointed out that the company sold power to radio stations, airports, and railroads, which were in turn directly engaged in interstate commerce, and that the concern's relationship to interstate commerce was, therefore, sufficient to warrant federal control. Of like import was *N.L.R.B.* v. *Fainblatt* (1939), in which the Court sustained application of the National Labor Relations Act to a small-scale garment processor who delivered his entire output within the state. These cases meant that it was no longer necessary to show either an immediate stream of commerce or a large volume of business in order to establish federal authority. As long as a potential labor disturbance in the business in question would have a disruptive effect, however slight, upon interstate commerce, the labor relations of the business in question were subject to regulation.

The Court shortly employed the constitutional conceptions devoloped in the Labor Board Cases to validate the Fair Labor Standards Act of June 25, 1938. This law prescribed an original minimum wage of twenty-five cents an hour and maximum hours of forty-four a week, subject to time and a half for overtime, for all employees engaged in interstate commerce or in the production of goods for interstate commerce. In addition to those sections of the statute regulating wages directly, other provisions made it unlawful to ship in interstate commerce goods manufactured in violation of the minimum wage requirements of the statute. The act also prohibited the shipment in interstate commerce of the products of any establishment where child labor had been used in the previous thirty days. This provision constituted virtual re-enactment of the Child Labor Act of 1916. The statute thus plainly defied the dictum in the first Child Labor Case, as well as that in the *Schechter* and *Carter* opinions.

In *United States* v. *Darby* (1941) the Supreme Court upheld the Fair Labor Standards Act as constitutional. The case involved a federal prosecution to enforce minimum wage standards upon an operator in the southern lumber industry. Justice Stone's opinion for a unanimous Court analyzed and upheld the provisions prohibiting the movement of proscribed goods in interstate commerce. Formally overruling *Hammer* v. *Dagenhart,* Stone said the commerce power was complete, that Congress could lawfully employ absolute prohibition, and that the Court could not inquire into the motives behind an act of Congress. The sections of the law imposing direct federal regulation of wages were also valid, since Congress could "regulate intrastate activities where they have a substantial effect on inter-state commerce." In subsequent Fair Labor Standards Act cases the Court interpreted the concept of "production of goods for commerce" broadly to include employees engaged in plant maintenance rather than actual pro-duction for commerce. Only employees of certain purely local activities remained beyond the protection of the Fair Labor Standards law.

In another line of decisions the Court sustained the Norris–La Guardia Anti-Injunction Act of 1932. This statute prohibited the issuance by any federal court of injunctions in labor disputes, except where unlawful acts had been threatened or committed, and where substantial and irreparable injury would result were relief not granted. It will be recalled that Section 20 of the Clayton Act had prohibited the issuance of federal injunctions in labor disputes unless necessary to prevent irreparable injury to property. However, in *Duplex Printing Press Co.* v. *Deering* (1921), the Court had virtually thrust aside Section 20 of the Clayton Act, with the opinion that the limitation upon injunctions must be interpreted very narrowly to forbid injunctions only against the actual employees involved in the dispute, so that the activities of the employees' union might in fact be enjoined. The Norris–La Guardia Act represented an attempt by Congress to undo the effect of the Duplex opinion.

In *Lauf* v. *Shinner and Co.* (1938) the Court held briefly that the Norris–La Guardia Act was constitutional. There could be no question, said Justice Roberts, of the power of Congress to define the jurisdiction of the lower federal courts. In *United States* v. *Hutcheson* (1941) the Court held that the Norris–La Guardia Act had in effect altered the status of criminal prosecutions against labor unions under the Sherman Antitrust law. The case involved a criminal action under the Sherman Act against a carpenters' union which by a jurisdictional strike, picketing and boycotting a construc-tion company, had allegedly interfered with interstate commerce. Justice Frankfurter's opinion infused the spirit of the Norris–La Guardia Act into Section 20 of the Clayton Act. He noted that under the Norris–La Guardia Act the union's activities would not be enjoinable in equity proceedings. It was absurd, he thought, to conclude that such action could still "become the road to prison" through criminal proceedings under the Sherman Act when it could not even be enjoined in equity proceedings.

Far-reaching federal controls on agricultural production also received prompt judicial approval. In 1938 Congress adopted a new Agricultural Adjustment Act aimed at price maintenance for cotton, wheat, corn, to-bacco, and rice. Constitutionally justified by the effect of agricultural pro-duction on interstate commerce, the law provided for a system of marketing quotas to be imposed by the secretary of agriculture, subject to approval by referendum of two-thirds of the producers concerned. The secretary was authorized to assign individual quotas to each farm and to assess heavy penalties for marketing quantities in excess of the quotas.

In *Mulford* v. *Smith* (1939) the Court sustained the constitutionality of the new Agricultural Adjustment Act against an attack by several tobacco growers who sought to have their quotas set aside on the ground that the new law in effect regulated production and so invaded the reserved powers of the states in violation of the Tenth Amendment. But Justice Roberts, who had written the opinion in *United States* v. *Butler* invalidating the earlier Agricultural Adjustment Act, declared for the majority of the Court that the 1938 statute did not regulate production, but instead merely imposed market regulations at the "throat" of interstate commerce. Congress, he added, could lawfully limit the amount of any commodity to be transported in interstate commerce, even through the imposition of an absolute prohibition if it so desired.

The Agricultural Marketing Agreement Act of 1937 empowered the secretary of agriculture to maintain parity prices for a variety of commodities through the imposition of marketing quotas and price schedules. In *United States* v. *Rock Royal Cooperative* (1939) and in *Hood* v. *United States* (1939) the Supreme Court upheld this law, approving orders of the secretary of agriculture fixing the price of milk paid to farmers in New York and Boston interstate milksheds. Justice Reed said that since most of the milk sold eventually crossed state lines, the local sales transactions were the beginning of interstate commerce and hence subject to federal control. *United States* v. *Wrightwood Dairy* (1942) further sustained the marketing agreement law by holding that the federal government might regulate the price of milk sold exclusively within state lines and not commingled with interstate milk but merely sold in competition with it.

In *Wickard* v. *Filburn* (1942) the Court sustained the validity of the wheat-marketing quota provisions of the Agricultural Adjustment Act of 1938, even though Congress in 1941 had amended the statute to authorize the secretary of agriculture to fix marketing quotas for wheat which would include wheat consumed on the premises as poultry and livestock feed, as seed, and as household food, as well as for wheat sold into interstate commerce. Only wheat insulated by storage was exempt from the calculation of the total amount marketed and thus from the penalties imposed for marketing in excess of quotas. In a forceful opinion, Justice Jackson not only repudiated the old distinction between direct and indirect effects but also proceeded virtually to discard entirely the distinction between commerce and production as a constitutional touchstone. The test of the power to regulate any local activity must hereafter, he said, be a practical economic one of the extent of economic effect the activity in question had upon interstate commerce. Applying this test, he found that wheat locally consumed did have an appreciable practical effect upon the price of wheat moving in interstate commerce; therefore, wheat locally consumed was subject to federal regulation although it did not itself ever move in commerce at all.

In *Sunshine Anthracite Coal Company* v. *Adkins* (1940) the Supreme Court accepted the Bituminous Coal Act of 1937, a statute containing substantially the same provisions for price fixing and the regulation of competition as in the law invalidated in the *Carter* decision. Under the commerce power, the Court declared, Congress could fix coal prices and establish market rules. In a series of cases between 1938 and 1946 the justices also upheld regulation of the utility industry under the commerce power. This involved approval of the Public Utility Holding Company Act of 1935, which required gas and electric companies to register with the Securities and Exchange Commission under penalty of losing their right to use the mails or to engage in interstate commerce. The statute also authorized the SEC to break up holding companies into their integral parts in order to limit each to the operation and control of a single public utility system.[1]

On its own cognizance rather than in confirmance of an act of Congress, the judiciary brought the insurance business within the scope of federal regulation. Under a nineteenth-century decision, *Paul* v. *Virginia* (1869), the business of insurance was defined as subject to regulation by the state police power and not as part of interstate commerce. In *Polish National Alliance* v. *National Labor Relations Board* (1944), however, the Court held that the activities of insurance companies affected interstate commerce and hence were subject to regulation under the National Labor Relations Act. In *United States* v. *Southeastern Underwriters Association* (1944) the Court held further that the insurance business itself was interstate commerce and, therefore, subject to the provisions of the Sherman Antitrust Act. These decisions cast doubt on the validity of state laws regulating insurance companies. Congress accordingly passed an act in effect providing that the states could regulate the insurance business until the federal government saw fit to supersede them. This legislation made the various states federal agents in the exercise of a federal power, and allowed them to retain effective control of policy making in this sector of the economy.

Extensive federal control over navigable streams formed another aspect of the new constitutional law based on the commerce power. Previous decisions upholding federal authority over waterways were based on the proposition that the waterways in question were navigable in interstate commerce; the implication was that federal authority did not extend to nonnavigable waters. In *United States* v. *Appalachian Electric Power Company* (1940), however, the Supreme Court affirmed federal control over the nonnavigable portion of an interstate stream, on the theory that the stream might become navigable in the future. More far-reaching was the decision in *Oklahoma ex rel. Phillips* v. *Atkinson* (1941), which confirmed federal

1. *Electric Bond and Share Company* v. *S.E.C.* (1938); *North American Co.* v. *S.E.C.* (1946); *American Power and Light Co.* v. *S.E.C.* (1946).

dam-building authority not only for navigational purposes, but also to promote flood control and waterway development.

In addition to the commerce power, the New Deal regulatory state rested on the constitutional basis of the federal spending power. As noted previously, in 1937 the Supreme Court sustained congressional exercise of the taxing and spending powers in the Social Security Act.2 Subsequently, the justices placed federal spending and public works projects beyond constitutional attack. In *Alabama Power Col.* v. *Ickes* (1938) the Court denied the plea of several state-chartered power companies that it enjoin federal loans to municipalities for power projects. The power companies had no right to be free of competition, said the Court; and because they could not show any impairment of legal right, they had no standing in court to attack the government's funding of local projects. The Court used the same reasoning to reject an attempt by state-chartered power companies to put the TVA out of business as an encroachment on the state police power.3 These two decisions meant that in practical effect the federal spending power and federal public works projects were beyond judicial control.

State Regulation and the Commerce Power

In broadening the scope of the commerce power for regulatory purposes the Supreme Court reviewed a great variety of state laws affecting interstate commerce. Most of them involved the imposition of state taxes on interstate commerce or out-of-state business. Often these measures represented genuine attempts of local and state governments to find new sources of revenue to compensate for the decline in real and personal property taxes since 1929 and to pay for unemployment and poor relief. The Supreme Court generally approved such legislation after 1937, in part apparently on the principle of imposing as few limits on governmental sovereignty as possible.

Many state tax laws, however, were really attempts to discriminate against interstate commerce or out-of-state business in favor of local commerce and industry. These laws contradicted the goal of creating a national free trade area that the Court had more or less systematically pursued since the late nineteenth century. The New Deal Court was similarly concerned with protecting the national market. Thus in *Hale* v. *Bimco Trading Co.* (1939) it struck down a Florida inspection fee on cement imported from outside the state that was really a tax intended to benefit local industry. Retail sales taxes, which became an important source of revenue for most state governments during the depression, were also invalidated when states used them to reach beyond their own jurisdiction. On the other hand, "user

2. *Stewart Machine Co.* v. *Davis; Helvering* v. *Davis.*
3. *Tennessee Electric Power Co.* v. *T.V.A.* (1939).

taxes," although apparently a device for evading the limitations on taxing interstate commerce, generally met with the Court's approval. Thus the judiciary balanced the revenue needs of the states against the requirements of the national economy.

In dealing with social problems during the depression states passed local police regulations that sometimes affected interstate commerce. Only in those instances in which state legislation interposed an obviously discriminatory barrier to commerce or in which state legislation intruded upon a sphere of commerce essentially national in character or that had been pre-empted by Congress did the Supreme Court refuse to accept state social legislation affecting interstate commerce. The best known such case was *Edwards* v. *California* (1941), in which the Court unanimously held unconstitutional a California law making it a misdemeanor to transport an indigent person or pauper into the state. The obvious purpose of the statute, known as the "Okie law," was to hold down the cost of the state's relief rolls. Social policy was the real issue, but constitutionally the matter was dealt with under the commerce power. Declaring that the transportation of persons across state lines was interstate commerce, the Court held that the California law plainly erected "an unconstitutional barrier" to such commerce. Notable concurring opinions were filed by Justices Black, Douglas, Murphy, and Jackson, who argued that the California law violated the privileges and immunities of national citizenship under the Fourteenth Amendment.

In most instances, however, the Court accepted as constitutional state police statutes whose evident purpose was to protect the health and welfare of the community, despite an incidental effect on interstate commerce. In *Milk Board* v. *Eisenburg* (1939), for example, it approved a Pennsylvania law authorizing a state milk board to license milk dealers and to fix prices. In *California* v. *Thompson* (1941) the Court upheld a statute requiring the licensing of agents who sold or negotiated for public transportation over state highways. And in *Parker* v. *Brown* (1943) the justices sustained a California law establishing a marketing control program for the raisin industry.

The Rejection of Economic Due Process

The corollary of the Supreme Court's acceptance of far-reaching federal regulation under the commerce and taxing powers was its abandonment of substantive due process, liberty of contract, and the other elements of laissez-faire constitutionalism. Far more than is usually the case in matters of constitutional law, this change approached being revolutionary in nature. A body of apparently sound precedents, rooted not only in the assumptions of late nineteenth-century entrepreneurial liberty but also in the nation's republican political tradition, was suddenly discarded. Only once in the decade afer 1937 was state legislation imposing restrictions on property rights struck down as a violation of the due process or equal protection clauses of the Fourteenth Amendment.[4] By the same token, an attempt to revive the privileges-and-immunities clause of the Fourteenth Amendment and give it an economic content was quickly repudiated after the liberal New Deal appointees gained control of the Court.[5]

In fashioning a body of constitutional law for the regulatory state the Supreme Court did not formally disavow the rationality test that had been employed in substantive due process litigation—the requirement, that is, that legislation rest upon a provably rational basis in order to be found constitutional. Yet the test became purely nominal; in practical effect the Court did abandon it. It thus returned, at least in one sphere of public-policy questions, to a pre-1890s presumption of the constitutionality of legislation. Occasionally, this fact was recognized. In *Olsen* v. *Nebraska* (1941), an employment-agency rate-regulation case, Justice William O. Douglas declared that the state did not have to show the existence of evils that it sought to eliminate for its legislation to be accepted as constitutional. Where social and economic legislation was involved, the reasonableness of legislation would be assumed.

For some members of the Court deference to legislative judgment was a matter of principle to be maintained almost categorically. Felix Frankfurter was the outstanding representative of this point of view. For a majority of the New Deal justices, however, the virtually complete tolerance of state regulatory legislation reflected the liberal belief that property rights could and should be separated from and regarded as inferior to civil, political, or human rights. A paradoxical situation thus resulted in which the New Deal in political and economic terms sought to preserve and reform private enterprise capitalism, while in constitutional law the Supreme Court abandoned long established guarantees of economic rights in the course of legitimating the regulatory state.

Reforming the Bureaucracy: Executive Reorganization

While the Supreme Court shaped doctrines of constitutional law affirming the legitimacy of positive government, president and Congress

---

4. *Connecticut General Life Insurance Co.* v. *Johnson* (1938).

5. In *Colgate* v. *Harvey* (1936) the Court held that the right to contract, to transact any lawful business, or to make a loan of money in another state was an attribute of national citizenship protected by the privileges-and-immunities clause of the Fourteenth Amendment. The New Deal justices overturned this decision in *Madden* v. *Kentucky* (1940), upholding a Kentucky law that imposed a tax on citizens' bank deposits outside the state five times as high as that imposed on deposits within the state. In the *Colgate* case the Court had declared unconstitutional a Vermont income tax law involving a similar principle.

clashed over the question of rationalizing the vast array of administrative agencies that had come into existence to carry out national regulatory and welfare policies. Although it only now became a major political issue, administrative reform was by no means a new problem. As the federal government gradually assumed a more interventionist role after 1900, the questions of coordinating and systematizing a growing number of administrative boards and commissions frequently arose. Though functionally similar to the executive departments in being responsible for the implementation and enforcement of law, a large portion of the federal bureaucracy had an independent status that could be described as in, but not of, the executive branch. Presidents, in any case, because of the bureaucracy's policy-making potential, had an interest in making government administration more orderly, economical, and efficient. Their efforts to do so were described as executive reorganization, and the struggle that occurred in 1937 over Franklin D. Roosevelt's plan to reform the bureaucracy culminated almost two decades of skirmishing between the political branches over this issue.

Throughout the nineteenth century Congress had exercised close oversight over administrative activity in the executive department, largely through its control of appropriations. As the increase in regulatory functions made government administration more complex and costly, Congress was pleased to blame the executive for mismanagement, but refused to give him the authority needed to reorganize and reform executive agencies in the interest of more efficient and economical administration. Theodore Roosevelt tried to define administrative reform as an executive responsibility, but he offended Congress when he appointed a presidential investigative commission that reached this conclusion. President Taft, more solicitous of legislative opinion, invited Congress to share in the investigation of the need for administrative reform. He focused efforts on the establishment of a federal budget as a means of efficiency and economy in government, and thus prepared the way for the Budget and Accounting Act of 1921. This measure created a Bureau of the Budget in the Treasury Department, under a comptroller general appointed by the president who was charged with preparing estimated executive and administrative expenses for submission to the president and then to Congress.[6]

In the 1920s it became apparent that the initiative for executive reorganization would never come from the legislature because congressional committees, engaged in mutually supportive relationships with administrative agencies and interest groups, had an interest in maintaining the status quo. Administrative reform, therefore, came to be seen as an executive

6. Congress passed a budget bill in 1920, but Wilson vetoed it because it provided for appointment of the comptroller general by Congress. The act of 1921, signed by Harding, gave the president the power to appoint the comptroller general, but not to remove him.

responsibility. Accordingly, the Coolidge administration adopted the strategy of asking Congress for a grant of power to reorganize the bureaucracy, the changes to go into effect unless rejected by Congress within a specified period of time. In 1932, as an economy measure, President Hoover persuaded Congress to pass an act authorizing him to consolidate government agencies. Congress rejected the changes that Hoover subsequently submitted, however, and enacted a measure giving the incoming president even greater authority to abolish and consolidate agencies, subject to legislative disapproval by joint resolution which the president could veto.

With economic recovery the overriding concern, Roosevelt in 1933 was in no position to pursue the question of executive reorganization. A few years later, however, after scores of new laws led to a dramatic proliferation of administrative agencies, the president recognized the need to rationalize the resulting bureaucratic hodgepodge with a view toward strengthening executive control over it. In part outside forces brought Roosevelt to this awareness. The *Schechter* decision in May 1935, expressing the unanimous judgment of the Supreme Court, served as a warning signal that the expansion of government by the delegation of legislative authority to the president had gotten out of hand. Even more provocative was a second unanimous Supreme Court decision, in *Humphrey's Executor* v. *United States,* handed down the same day as the *Schechter* opinion.

On the basis of the *Myers* case of 1926, in which the Supreme Court upheld the presidential removal power in exceedingly broad terms, Roosevelt had tried to fire conservative Republican William E. Humphrey from the Federal Trade Commission.[7] He gave as his reason that the purposes of the administration so far as the FTC was concerned could be carried out more effectively by the appointment of someone of the president's own choosing. The Supreme Court, however, invalidated Humphrey's dismissal. Pointing out that under the FTC Act members could be removed only for inefficiency, neglect of duty, or malfeasance in office, the Court said the commission was a quasi-legislative and quasi-judicial body rather than an extension of the executive branch. Far more than *Schechter,* this decision threatened presidential control of the bureaucracy outside the executive branch.

Seeking greater coherence in administrative policy making, Roosevelt

---

7. The *Myers* case involved a suit for back salary by a former postmaster who had been summarily removed from office by Woodrow Wilson. The Supreme Court denied the appeal and confirmed the removal, in an opinion by Chief Justice Taft which defined the scope of the removal power to include minor executive officials as well as policy-making officers. Theoretically Taft's sweeping opinion might have been taken to mean that civil service legislation guaranteeing tenure to minor executive officials was unconstitutional. In practice, however, no such application of the case was made. Another implication of the opinion was that members of independent regulatory agencies could be removed by the president—the question tested by the *Humphrey* case.

in 1936 appointed the President's Committee on Administrative Management, also known as the Brownlow committee. Up to this time efficiency and economy were the watchwords of executive reorganization, the ultimate purpose being to reduce the size and expense of government in accordance with the traditional notion of minimal government. The Brownlow committee, however, approached reorganization from the standpoint of strengthening the executive with respect to overall policy planning and management of national resources. Accepting the positive state as a necessity, the committee proposed reforms that would enable the president more effectively to meet the policy-making responsibilities imposed on him by the requirements of modern government.

In January 1937 the recommendations of the Brownlow committee were presented to Congress in a bill for executive reorganization. The bill provided for the expansion of the White House staff; created the Executive Office of the President; transferred the Bureau of the Budget from the Treasury to this new Executive Office; authorized the president to reorganize more than one hundred agencies, boards, and commissions under twelve departments; created two new executive departments (public works and social welfare); replaced the Civil Service Commission with a single administrator appointed by the president; and revised the fiscal system to give the president control of accounts, and Congress a postaudit over government transactions. Besides the direct accretions of power to the presidency, the chief effect of the plan was to place the independent regulatory agencies under the line departments of the executive branch and thus subject them to direct presidential control.

Introduced with little notice in January 1937, the reorganization bill passed the House of Representatives in August. By the time it was taken up in the Senate, however, in January 1938, the meaning of the Supreme Court fight of the previous year had had a chance to sink in and opponents of the reorganization plan were legion. According to critics, the reorganization proposal was of a piece with the Court-packing plan in seeking to aggrandize power in the executive branch, in this instance at the expense of the independent regulatory agencies. Yet the sweeping power to reorder the administrative structure was not really at issue in the bill before the Senate, because the interest-group clientele of key bureaucratic units had succeeded in having those units placed on a protected list that the president could not touch. Nevertheless, the transfer of the Budget Bureau, the replacement of the Civil Service Commission, and the provision for presidential veto of the means by which Congress could defeat reorganization orders seemed sufficiently dangerous extensions of executive power to provoke strong opposition.

Despite the growth of antiexecutive, anti–New Deal opinion, the reorganization bill narrowly passed the Senate. It did so amid talk of dictatorship that was serious enough to prompt Roosevelt to make the extraordinary announcement that he had no dictatorial inclinations or ambitions. The House was now solidly against the reorganization measure, however, and sent it back to committee and to defeat in April 1938.

New reorganization bills were introduced, and in 1939 Congress approved a much revised and far narrower version of the original plan. Although passage of the Executive Reorganization Act marked a political setback for the Roosevelt administration, it is clear in retrospect that it laid the institutional foundation for the creation of the modern presidency. The act gave the president power to consolidate and shift administrative agencies, although not to abolish any department, to create new departments, or to interfere with any of a great many regulatory agencies to which Congress had given immunity. Most significantly, the act created the Executive Office of the President, transferred the Bureau of the Budget out of the Treasury Department to this new office, and enlarged the White House staff. Because of constitutional objections to executive lawmaking, the measure authorized the president to submit "plans" rather than issue "orders" for administrative reorganization, the plans to become law in the event that Congress did not reject them by concurrent resolution within sixty days. The statute terminated after two years. In 1941 and on several subsequent occasions, however, Congress passed similar statutes. With the relentless expansion of federal regulatory functions, the ability of the president to influence the bureaucracy through administrative reorganization would become a key point of conflict in the struggle between the executive and legislative branches for the control of national economic and social policy.

A further expression of the antiexecutive temper that swept through Congress in the late 1930s was the Hatch Act of 1939, restricting political activity by employees in the executive branch. From the beginning of the government the republican fear of executive power and corruption had led to sporadic efforts to limit partisan activities of officeholders. Nothing came of this reform impulse until the progressive era, when the Civil Service Commission imposed a restriction on employees in the classified service. Bills were introduced into Congress to extend the rule in the 1920s as the nonclassified federal work force grew to outnumber the classified. With the enormous expansion of the federal bureaucracy during the depression the issue became even more timely, and in 1935 the House of Representatives passed a bill restricting partisan activity by government employees. Evidence of federal relief officers' widespread efforts to use their official position to promote the cause of the Democratic party in the elections of 1938 gave the issue national prominence and led to the adoption of the Hatch Act in 1939.

Using the idiom of early republicanism, the Hatch Act aimed at preventing "pernicious political activities." The act prohibited any officer or employee in the executive branch, with the exception of the president, vice-president, department heads, and policy-making officers, from taking "any active part in political management or in political campaigns." Politically, the Hatch Act was a bipartisan measure reflecting hostility toward Roosevelt and the New Deal among conservative Democrats and Republicans who had defeated the Court-packing and executive reorganization plans. Constitutionally, the legislation raised the question of the need to protect the integrity of the electoral system against improper executive influence on the one hand, and to uphold the civil rights of government employees on the other. Out of concern for civil rights, the act, unlike previous Civil Service Commission rules, guaranteed executive-department officials the right to vote and express their opinions on all political subjects. The Supreme Court affirmed the constitutionality of the Hatch Act in 1947 and again in 1973, though by the latter date considerable pressure existed to amend the law to permit voluntary party activity by federal employees.

Federalism and the New Deal

A major effect of the Supreme Court's reinterpretation of constitutional law and the strengthening of executive authority was the centralization of power in the federal government. There was nothing novel about this issue; since the Civil War, the federal-state balance had gradually been shifting in the direction of centralization. The change that occurred in the 1930s as a result of New Deal legislation, however, noticeably accelerated the trend and left the states in the paradoxical position of having expanded their sphere of governmental activity while having lost most of their policy-making autonomy to the federal government.

Federalism is the division of sovereignty among governments sharing the same area and constituent basis, and throughout the nineteenth century the principal characteristic of the system in the United States was competition and conflict. The federal government and the states were usually rivals, at best coexisting and only rarely cooperating in joint ventures. A pre-eminent question in public policy considerations was whether a subject or power was assigned to the federal government or to the states. Although the Constitution gave the federal government distinct powers of sovereignty, the tendency of the system in the first half of the nineteenth century was toward decentralization. Despite increasing nationalization in culture and society, power devolved on the states, which were for all practical purposes autonomous.

The Civil War reversed this trend and vindicated federal sovereignty. A significant degree of centralization occurred as a result of the civil rights constitutional amendments and legislation of the reconstruction period. Centralization proceeded a good deal further in the late nineteenth century as the federal government formulated policies concerning money and banking, transportation, labor relations, corporate expansion, and interstate commerce, often in ways that conflicted with state policies in these matters. Occasionally, the federal government gave money or land to the states to promote certain objectives, such as public education, but this assistance did not significantly reduce the policy-making autonomy of the states.

In the progressive era centralization of policy making paralleled the increasing integration of the national economy. A significant innovation was the promotion of federal ascendancy through programs that involved the states in shared governmental responsibilities, but that reduced their policy-making discretion. This intergovernmental approach, usually termed cooperative federalism, depended on grants-in-aid that required the states to adopt certain measures in order to qualify for federal funds. The principal focus of cooperative federalism in the 1910s and 1920s was education, highway construction, and land conservation projects. Cooperation also took the form of federal legislation supporting state police measures regulating such matters as the liquor traffic or the "white slave" market. This pattern of persistent though modest centralization in regard to economic regulation, accompanied by limited intergovernmental cooperation, continued until the New Deal.

The impact of the New Deal on federalism was threefold. First and most conspicuously, the federal government asserted its sovereignty in whole areas of public policy that left the states with little room for significant policy initiative. Agricultural production and marketing, labor-management relations, the sale of securities, public works, relief and social welfare, and flood control were the outstanding new spheres of federal sovereignty. While none of them was entirely withdrawn from state control, federal policy for each of them became of far more importance than the regulatory measures of any of the states. Federal control was undertaken on a grand scale in industrial production and business enterprise generally under the NRA. Although this attempt failed, national economic policy making continued in a less integrated fashion through the actions of separate departments and the independent regulatory agencies.

It is probable that the New Deal worked a permanent alteration in the American people's conception of the federal government's responsibility for the operation of the national economic system. Earlier administrations had on occasion asserted the necessity for federal control over certain phases of the national economy. Theodore Roosevelt had preached conservation of natural resources, railroad regulation, and administrative management of the corporate economy. Woodrow Wilson had emphasized regulation of the banking and financial system, tariff adjustment, and tightening of the anti-trust laws. The Hoover adminisration committed the federal government to an active if limited role in national economic policy making, preparing the way for the New Deal. Roosevelt's administration, however, was the first to assume that the federal government was responsible for virtually every important phase of the national economy—production, labor, unemployment, social security, money and banking, housing, public works, flood control, and the conservation of natural resources. The fact that this momentous shift occurred in a time of unprecedented economic crisis is testimony to the deeply rooted nature of traditional constitutional values: other than through war, this was probably the only way that the country's attachment to states' rights and the laissez-faire market could have been loosened to the extent needed to permit the federal government to play such an expanded role. It appears, moreover, that the centralizing trend was irreversible. Emergency actions in time gave way to permanent changes in the governmental structure, and subsequent crises in the 1940s and 1950s justified still further federal interventions. Federal responsibility for the solution of problems in both the internal economy and foreign affairs is something that most Americans now more or less take for granted.

A second effect of the New Deal on federal-state relations was the apparently permanent extinction of dual federalism as a constitutional philosophy. This doctrine, it will be recalled, held that the federal government and the separate states constituted two mutually exclusive systems of sovereignty, that both were supreme within their respective spheres, and that neither could exercise its authority in such a way as to intrude, even incidentally, upon the sphere of sovereignty reserved to the other. The Court in *United States* v. *Darby* specifically repudiated this doctrine in favor of the doctrine of national supremacy—which points out that the Constitution makes federal law superior to state law and which holds accordingly that Congress may not be prevented from exercising any of its delegated powers merely because the performance of those powers may break in upon an area of sovereignty hitherto reserved to the states.

The third consequence of the New Deal in relation to federalism was a great increase in programs of intergovernmental cooperation between state and national authority. Intergovernmental cooperation through the instrumentality of grants-in-aid was the favored method of dealing with numerous public issues, including health care, housing, relief of the indigent, highway construction, and conservation. Perhaps the most notable example of the cooperative federalist approach was the social security program. The Social Security Act of 1935 created an old-age insurance program administered directly by the federal government for individuals. But it provided that assistance to blind persons, the elderly, and dependent and crippled children, as well as maternal and child welfare and unemployment compensation, should be administered by the states. The act authorized grants to the states for these purposes under rules requiring the states to contribute certain sums and manage the program in specific ways.

The term "cooperative federalism" implies a larger degree of spontaneous, voluntary support by the states for federal programs, and less political conflict in their administration, than was actually the case in the 1930s. Liberals wanted welfare policy and other matters to be the exclusive concern of the federal government. But the states were too powerful and the ideology of states' rights too deeply entrenched to permit their circumvention in matters that had traditionally been left to local liberty. On the other hand, although conservatives in the states resisted as best they could, the demand for positive government could not be gainsaid and was a force drawing the states to take up new duties. Motivated by the incentive of federal money as well as institutional and political rivalry, the states became agents of national policy.

States thus shared in the general expansion of government produced by the economic crisis of the 1930s. The decline of substantive due process opened up new areas of state social legislation which had hitherto been closed. Interstate treaties, permissible under the Constitution where the contracting parties obtained the consent of Congress, created another sphere of state activity. They were used to solve a number of regional problems, particularly in the field of water-power projects and flood control. Nevertheless, if the scope of state activity broadened, the states experienced a loss of power as their policy-making autonomy was sharply circumscribed by cooperative federalism and by outright federal centralization, as in controls over production. There is little likelihood that proposals to abandon existing state lines in favor of regional units, popular during the depression and occasionally still heard, will be adopted; the tradition of local and state government is far too strong to permit that. Yet the states have undoubtedly lost much of the sovereign policy-making power they once possessed and have increasingly become subordinate administrative units in a centralized national system.

Constitutional Significance of the New Deal

The substantive effect of the New Deal was nothing less than the creation of an American version of the centralized bureaucratic state. After the failure of the NRA, with its proposal for a basically new constitutional direction, the Roosevelt administration returned to the idea of government-regulated free market competition as its politico-constitutional strategy. Accordingly, whereas in the early New Deal only the securities legislation represented this competitive regulatory approach, in later years it was manifested in measures such as the Public Utilities Holding Company Act, the creation of the National Labor Relations Board as a regulatory agency under the Wagner Act, the Banking Act of 1935, and the revival of antitrust prosecution. Though not in the highly centralized, coordinated way envisioned in 1933, federal intervention proceeded *pari passu*, with national policy being made by independent regulatory agencies and administrative bodies, under delegations of legislative power more circumscribed than those of the National Industrial Recovery Act.

More clearly than ever before, the American political economy assumed the form of interest-group pluralism. At its head was the president, in brokerlike fashion promoting the interest of different private groups in an attempt to create a stable yet productive equilibrium between the major functional units of the economy. Compared to the corporatist and collectivist systems of Europe, the pluralist or interest-group liberal approach allowed for considerable fragmentation and decentralization of government authority. Catering to special interest groups, the executive departments and regulatory agencies often seemed to work at cross-purposes. Indeed, political scientists formulated a theory of public administration to describe the reality of New Deal government—the competitive theory of administration. Nevertheless, as never before, policy-making power was centralized in the federal government and was exercised through bureaucratic institutions.

A second major result of the New Deal was the transformation of the presidency into an instrument of virtually permanent emergency government. Roosevelt's reliance on a World War I statute as the basis for the bank holiday in 1933 was followed in the next six years by thirty-five instances in which he referred to emergency, crisis, or national peril as justification for legislative or executive action. Without questioning the gravity of the situation when Roosevelt took office, it would not be too much to say that in time emergencies and crises became routine events, and crisis management a standard New Deal governing technique. When as part of the reaction against the executive the Senate in 1939 requested the attorney general to enumerate the president's powers, it learned of over one hundred statutes, many of them dating from the world war, that gave special powers to the president upon the proclamation of a national emergency. Equally significant was the tendency for emergency measures to be assimilated into the regular structure of government. Perhaps the outstanding illustration of this tendency was the development of state welfare systems and the federal Works Progress Administration out of the Federal Emergency Relief Administration.

A cynic might say that only in time of national emergency could Congress and the people be stirred from their lethargy to make needed social reforms. Yet government by crisis does not always result in reform, and it exacts a high constitutional cost, not least in the blurring of the distinction between peace and war that formerly limited executive power. As presidents in the era of the cold war increasingly invoked national security as a justification for their actions, sometimes carrying it past the point of constitutional legitimacy, the consequences of Roosevelt's pathbreaking use of emergency powers in peacetime came more clearly into focus.

A third constitutional result of the New Deal was the confirmation of judicial power as it had developed since the 1890s and its adaptation to liberal reform purposes. This result was to become clear, however, only in light of events after World War II; in the late 1930s judicial power seemed weakened and likely to be eclipsed. There was genuine cause for apprehension in Roosevelt's Court-packing plan; and when the fight it provoked was over, the judiciary appeared to have suffered a real setback. Contemporaries used the concept of judicial self-restraint to describe the post-1937 situation of the judiciary.

Judicial restraint meant above all that courts ought not to usurp legislative power. They should respect the people's judgment of what constituted sound social and economic policy, as expressed in the legislative output of their elected representatives. When the Supreme Court reversed its course and approved New Deal legislation, this point of view was widely regarded as having gained acceptance on the high bench. Ten years later a constitutional law scholar looked back on "the decline of the so-called 'mechanical theory' of constitutional interpretation, and its gradual replacement by the concept of 'judicial self-restraint' as the principle by which the judiciary will in fact allow all possible constitutional discretion to the political branches in coping with increasingly complex economic and social problems."[8]

Under this new judicial attitude the Supreme Court stopped declaring unconstitutional acts of Congress and the state legislatures that created positive government and the regulatory state. Courts also relaxed their grip on the independent regulatory agencies, allowing them more discretion in the policy-making function assigned to them by Congress. Courts now held, for example, that an administrative agency need not have the preponderance of evidence on its side to have a decision upheld; "substantial" evidence was sufficient. It also appeared likely that, deprived of its ability to choose between the federal police power and the dual federalist streams of precedent, the judiciary would lose its critical role as the arbiter of federal-state relations.

An extraordinary expression of the Supreme Court's new posture of judicial restraint was its decision in *Erie Railroad Co.* v. *Tompkins* (1938). It will be recalled that under the doctrine of *Swift* v. *Tyson* (1842), federal courts disregarded state court rules of decision in diversity cases and created a federal common law dealing with commercial and corporate enterprise in regard to private-law questions such as tort, contract, negligence, agency, and so on. The development of a federal commercial common law under the *Tyson* precedent had not, however, as was intended, produced legal uniformity in commercial matters, for the states had continued to go their own way. In fact, two sets of common law rules for the settlement of commercial controversies came into existence. Moreover, the federal common law shaped by the United States courts generally favored interstate corporations, which could evade restrictive state legislation by "forum shopping" in federal jurisdiction. Accordingly, liberal critics of the judiciary in

---

8. Vincent M. Barnett, Jr., "The Supreme Court and the Capacity to Govern," *Political Science Quarterly* (1948).

the early twentieth century, in addition to attacking substantive due process, mounted a campaign against the exercise of judicial power derived from the *Tyson* case. They argued that this power denied the rightful authority of state courts in diversity cases.

In *Erie* v. *Tompkins* a chastened Supreme Court overruled *Swift* v. *Tyson,* thus depriving the federal judiciary of authority it had exercised for nearly a century. What is more, Justice Brandeis's majority opinion stated that the 1842 decision was unconstitutional—the only time in its history that the Supreme Court has ever reversed itself by declaring one of its own decisions unconstitutional. Recalling the Jeffersonian dogma of the early nineteenth century in regard to the common law, Brandeis announced: "There is no federal common law.... Congress has no power to declare substantive rules of common law applicable in a State whether they be local in their nature or general.... And no clause in the Constitution purports to confer such a power upon the federal courts." The *Tyson* decision, Brandeis asserted, contradicted "the constitution of the United States, which recognizes and preserves the autonomy and independence of the states—independence in their legislative and independence in their judicial departments." In diversity cases, therefore, where the federal Constitution, statutes, and treaties were not controlling, federal courts must follow state law, including the substantive rules of decision of state courts.[9]

The self-denying ordinance announced in the *Erie* decision was more expressive than decisive, however. Even in the technical field of diversity jurisdiction no significant redistribution of judicial power from national to state courts occurred. In time it became clear that the power of the federal judiciary had not been diminished, but merely translated into new spheres of public policy. For one thing, statutory interpretation, especially in relation to the broad delegations of legislative authority to administrative bodies that increasingly characterized congressional legislation, gave the courts plenty of leverage in policy making and the actual conduct of government. Second, even as reformers applauded "laissez faire for legislators" in the social and economic realm, they argued for judicial scrutiny of legis-

9. The *Erie* case involved an injury sustained by a man walking along the tracks of the Erie Railroad in Pennsylvania. In the Pennsylvania courts the injured man would have been regarded as negligent under the pertinent case law and would not have been entitled to recover damages. He, therefore, filed suit in federal court on diversity-of-citizenship grounds and won a $30,000 judgment against the railroad under federal common law rules. The Supreme Court, however, remanded the case for reconsideration under the relevant Pennsylvania case law. The Court stated that *Swift* v. *Tyson,* the source of authority for the federal rule followed in the lower court, had wrongly excluded state court decisions as a guide to decision in diversity cases. Section 34 of the Judiciary Act of 1789 states that, except where the Constitution, laws, and treaties of the United States provide, "the laws of the several states" shall be regarded as the rules of decision in trials at common law in federal courts in diversity cases. Justice Story in *Tyson* had held that state court decisions were not part of "the laws" of the states referred to in Section 34. Justice Brandeis now declared that they were.

lation dealing with political and civil liberties. For a long time defenders of
property rights had praised the Supreme Court for protecting minority
rights against the potential tyranny of the majority; liberals now appropriated this theme as the judiciary, even before the about-face of 1937,
began to uphold individual rights against legislative restriction.

"Released from suspicion of political or partisan entanglement," Edward S. Corwin wrote in 1940, the Supreme Court "will be free as it has not
been in many years to support the humane values of free thought, free
utterance and fair play." With the pall of totalitarianism and war hanging
over the Western democracies, the alteration in outlook that Corwin described seemed timely and salubrious. For in the age of positive government and centralized bureaucracy, even in its American version, a concern
for civil liberties was a necessary makeweight to government repression and
control. In subsequent decades this newly emerging concern for individual
liberty and civil rights was to provide a principal focus of constitutional
development.

TWENTY-SIX

The Development of Modern Civil Liberties Law: 1919–1950

♦ ♦ ♦

ALTHOUGH POLITICAL FREEDOM was the informing idea of American constitutionalism from the outset, the shaping of an intricate and far-reaching body of public law protecting civil liberties has been a modern development. In the course of the twentieth century the idea of liberty has been transformed from a majoritarian political attitude concerned with maintaining republican government into a set of judicially prescribed legal rules guaranteeing individual rights. In the preindustrial era liberty was but one of several values deemed essential to a well-ordered society. In the twentieth century it has become the particular concern of special-interest constituencies seeking either protection against economic and social injury and discrimination or access to social and economic benefits. To put the matter another way, whereas the idea of liberty was once embodied in classical laissez-faire liberalism, it is now principally expressed in the doctrine of civil libertarianism.

Needless to say, the founders of the republic were deeply concerned with liberty. Framing written constitutions to establish it on a permanent basis, they sought to achieve government by the consent of the governed. Political liberty, by which they meant the absence of arbitrary rule by one man or a group of men, was the ultimate goal, and this in turn comprehended civil liberty—the condition in which one exercised specific civil rights such as the right to own property, enter into contracts, bring suit and testify at law, and speak, write, assemble, and worship freely.[1] Neither po-

---

1. In contemporary constitutional analysis "civil rights" refers to the legal protection that individuals enjoy against injury, discrimination, and denial of rights by other private individuals as well as by government, especially respecting the social and economic pursuits that constitute the affairs of everyday life. "Civil liberties" has a more distinctly political connotation, referring to legal guarantees, pre-eminently under the First Amendment, by which individuals are protected against governmental interference with their ability to speak, write, express their opinions, and associate for the purpose of political action.

litical freedom, however, in the sense of participation in government through the suffrage, nor civil liberty as just described was universally available. Not only did women, children, paupers, and criminals live under legal disabilities, but also persons belonging to particular ethnic and religious groups suffered discrimination in civil rights. In the federal system states had constitutional power—exclusive before the Civil War, primary and still preponderant after it—to regulate the sphere of civil liberty. Local communities in turn had effective power to maintain a consensus based on the values of the majority and to impose sanctions on dissenting individuals and groups. Liberty in a decentralized constitutional system was primarily corporate and local in nature, and civil liberty qua individual civil rights was often qualified by majoritarian attitudes. Members of minority groups often could acquire civil liberty only by moving to a more congenial community.

Civil liberties and civil rights law has evolved in twentieth-century America as an aspect of the tendency toward political centralization and social integration that characterizes the modern nation-state. As observed in previous chapters, the creation of urban industrial society in the late nineteenth century led to a significant expansion of federal authority. With respect to personal liberty and civil rights, the augmentation of national authority began during the Civil War with slave emancipation and the enfranchisement of the freedmen. Although national enforcement of civil rights beyond personal liberty availed little against continuing states'-rights-sanctioned community bias, the formal constitutional changes that authorized federal intervention in local civil liberty matters made possible national protection of economic rights under laissez-faire doctrines in the late nineteenth century. Once this pattern of intervention on behalf of property rights was established, it was but a short step to national protection of civil liberties against state infringement by means of the Fourteenth Amendment.

The most conspicuous fact about civil liberties and civil rights law in the twentieth century is that it has developed principally under the auspices of the federal government. During this same time a centralized bureaucratic state has emerged, regulating the social and economic life of the nation directly through its sovereign power over individual citizens, or indirectly through its power over the states. Although classical liberalism taught that government power and individual liberty were eternally opposed, so that nationalization of civil liberties and centralization of power might appear contradictory developments, there was a historical relationship between them.

The modern centralized nation-state, including the version that emerged in the United States, has based its claim to sovereignty on a direct and exclusive relationship with the individual. In this relationship the state grants citizenship to and promises to protect the individual in the basic rights of civil liberty, while in return demanding allegiance and support. It was by means of this social contract that the nation-state in the early modern era sundered the ties that for centuries had bound the individual to kinship group, church, local nobility, private association, and local community—competing centers of authority that had previously engaged the loyalties of the individual. The authority of the state in the Western political tradition thus came to rest on the loyalty of the individual citizen, who reciprocally, in his peculiar or paradoxical position of isolation within mass society, depended on the state for protection of his civil liberties. In recent years this dependency on the state has been extended to basic human needs such as housing, sustenance, employment, and medical care. The historical logic of civil rights and civil liberties guarantees thus has been to legitimize the power of the centralized nation-state.

Civil Liberties Law before World War I

To argue for the historical connection between civil liberties and centralized authority does not mean that in specific historical situations power has never conflicted with liberty, or that in civil liberties struggles in the United States the federal government has consistently upheld the liberty of the individual. Often the reverse has been true. During World War I, for example, federal authorities restricted acts of speech and publication in the name of national security. The government's internal security measures gave rise to conflicts that made civil liberties a political issue and began to produce a body of constitutional law on the subject.

Federal involvement in civil liberties questions, aside from the problem of slavery, had been limited to the Alien and Sedition Act of 1798 and Lincoln's suspension of the writ of habeas corpus and other emergency actions during the Civil War. Accordingly, the wartime status of the first nine amendments was, in 1917, still vague and confused. Two things, however, could be said with certainty. First, the state of war did not suspend operation of the Bill of Rights; in fact, the Third and Fifth Amendments specifically mentioned wartime conditions. Further, the efficacy of the Bill of Rights in wartime had been confirmed in *Ex parte Milligan* (1866). With this precedent in mind, the Wilson administration in 1917 immediately renounced any intention of suspending the Bill of Rights for the duration of the war. Second, it was equally clear from Civil War practice that the guarantees in the Bill of Rights were not necessarily the same under wartime conditions as in peacetime. Between these two extreme positions there was a broad area of conflict between civil rights and the federal war power.

To an even greater extent than in Civil War days, it was the First Amendment, with its guarantees of free speech, free press, free assembly, and petition that caused most difficulty. Certain restrictions on freedom of speech and of the press were recognized by military and governmental officials as essential, both because of military necessity and because of the requirements of public morale. Furthermore, controls were demanded by an overwhelming proportion of the people, who were in no mood to listen to those opposing war with Germany.

Besides the wartime precedent of *Ex parte Milligan,* very little constitutional law pertained to civil liberties in 1917, and that which did gave broad discretionary authority to the states. Still valid from John Marshall's days was the decision of the Supreme Court in *Barron* v. *Baltimore* (1833) that the Fifth Amendment, and by extension the Bill of Rights, applied only against the federal government. The Fourteenth Amendment restricted the states, but in practice its principal effect was to protect property rights against state interference. The amendment did not comprehend or incorporate the First Amendment or other parts of the Bill of Rights so as to make them limitations on state power. The Supreme Court had clarified this point in *Hurtado* v. *California* (1884), when it held that the due process clause of the Fourteenth Amendment did not require the states to indict by grand jury in capital crimes or, by implication, to follow other Fifth Amendment rules governing criminal procedure under federal jurisdiction. In another Bill of Rights decision, *Twining* v. *New Jersey* (1908), the Court said that the Fifth Amendment rule against self-incrimination pertained only to the federal government. A state could thus regard refusal to testify as tantamount to an admission of guilt.

Guidance in resolving wartime conflicts over free speech was also available in the common law. The pertinent rule that emerged from this source, both in England and the American states, was that freedom of speech and of the press meant that the government could not censor or stop publication—that is, the rule of no prior restraint. After publication, however, a writer or speaker was subject to prosecution if what he said did injury to others or to the government. At this point the rule of proximate causation was employed to judge the intent of the speaker or writer, since proof of intent was an essential part of criminal prosecution under the law of seditious libel.

In establishing criminal intent common law courts inquired into the degree of proximity between the spoken or written word and the illegal act supposed to have resulted. The rule of proximate causation as a test of intent required the showing of a direct and immediate relationship between the spoken word and the illicit act. Printed or spoken statements of a general character remote from a particular illicit act were not illegal and did not make the speaker or writer an accessory. Mere "bad tendency" or "constructive intent" was not sufficient to constitute a breach of the immunities of free speech. In practice, however, more often than not the rule that obtained was the bad-tendency test. Publication and speech were held to be punishable if they evinced a reasonable tendency, at some future point, to undermine the government. In other words, the content, rather than the circumstances in which an act of speaking or writing occurred, became the critical consideration.

In a case in 1907, *Patterson* v. *Colorado,* the United States Supreme Court affirmed the traditional common law interpretation of freedom of speech under the First Amendment. Upholding the contempt conviction of a newspaper publisher who had printed articles and cartoons critical of the Colorado Supreme Court and claimed protection under the First Amendment, Justice Oliver Wendell Holmes declared that freedom of the press consisted in the absence of prior restraint. The First Amendment, explained Holmes, did not prevent the subsequent punishment of material deemed contrary to the public welfare.

At the local level, however, new currents of thought on civil liberties questions were appearing. In several states civil liberties conflicts arose in the late nineteenth and early twentieth centuries as radicals and unorthodox religious groups sought First Amendment protection to hold rallies, parades, and meetings in conflict with restrictions imposed by local governments under the police power. State courts generally upheld antiradical police actions, while rejecting efforts to curtail religious groups provided they refrained from creating civil disturbances. In the course of these struggles a civil libertarian point of view began to emerge among a small number of lawyers who argued that speech and writing, no matter how disagreeable to local majority opinion, were constitutionally protected and could be stopped only at the point where they produced unlawful actions or material injury.

The War and the Bill of Rights

American entry into the European war in 1917 renewed the old conflict between the Bill of Rights and military necessity. While Congress adopted no general censorhip law during the war, it did enact two statutes which, among other matters, imposed certain limitations upon press and speech. The Espionage Act adopted on June 15, 1917, included certain provisions for military and postal censorship. The amendment to the Espionage Act, which became law on May 16, 1918, and was often referred to as the Sedition Act of 1918, was more comprehensive and general in character.

The Espionage Act carried two principal censorship provisions. One section made it a felony to attempt to cause insubordination in the armed forces of the United States, to attempt to obstruct the enlistment and recruiting services of the United States, or to convey false statements with intent to interfere with military operations. The other established a postal censorship, under which treasonable or seditious material could be banned from the mails at the discretion of the postmaster general. A great many publications, including the *Saturday Evening Post* and the *New York Times,* as well as many radical and dissident periodicals and newspapers, were banned temporarily from the mails under this provision.

The Sedition Law of 1918 was enacted at the insistence of military men and a general public alarmed at the activities of pacifist groups, certain labor leaders, and a few overpublicized "Bolsheviks" and radicals. The law made it a felony to "incite mutiny or insubordination in the ranks of the armed forces," to "disrupt or discourage recruiting or enlistment service, or utter, print, or publish disloyal, profane, scurrilous, or abusive language about the form of government, the Constitution, soldiers and sailors, flag, or uniform of the armed forces, or by word or act support or favor the cause of the German Empire or its allies in the present war, or by word or act oppose the cause of the United States."

The Supreme Court first passed upon the military censorship provisions of the Espionage Act in *Schenck* v. *United States* (1919). The case involved an appeal from a conviction in the lower federal courts on a charge of circulating antidraft leaflets among members of the United States armed forces. Schenck, the secretary of the Socialist party, contended that the Espionage Act violated the First Amendment and was unconstitutional.

In reply Justice Holmes wrote an opinion, unanimously concurred in by the Court, upholding the constitutionality of the Espionage Act. The right of free speech, he said, had never been an absolute one at any time, in peace or in war. "Free speech would not protect a man in falsely shouting fire in a theatre, and causing a panic." When a nation was at war, he added, "many things that might be said in time of peace are such a hindrance to its [war] effort that their utterance will not be endured so long as men fight," and "no court could regard them as protected by any constitutional right." Holmes then described an approach to resolving free speech conflicts, in the nature of an adaptation of the rule of proximate causation, that became the "clear and present danger" rule. "The question in each case," he said, "is whether the words used are used in such circumstances and are of such a nature as to create a clear and present danger that they will bring about the substantive evils that Congress has a right to prevent. It is a question of proximity and degree."

Although the clear-and-present-danger test later became a key civil libertarian doctrine, Holmes's use of it in *Schenck* was no different from the use he might have made of the bad-tendency test. His main concern was with the intended effect of the antidraft writings, not the specific circumstances in which they were disseminated. "Of course the document would not have been sent," he said, "unless it had been intended to have some effect, and we do not see what effect it could be expected to have upon persons subject to the draft except to influence them to obstruct the carrying of it out." He concluded: "If the act, its tendency and the intent with which it is done are the same, we perceive no ground for saying that success alone warrants making the act a crime."

The *Schenck* decision indicated a favorable Supreme Court response to the government's wartime security measures. At the same session, with Holmes again rendering the opinions, the Court in *Frohwerk* v. *United States* and *Debs* v. *United States* (1919) upheld convictions under the Espionage Act directed at speeches and publications critical of the war. Making no reference to the clear-and-present-danger idea, Holmes dwelt on the speakers' intent and the probable effect of their communications on the government's military efforts. *Pierce* v. *United States* (1920) was yet another case in which the Court used the bad-tendency test to uphold the conviction of a socialist for publishing a pamphlet attacking conscription and the war, although it could not be shown that there was intent to interfere with the draft or that circulation of the document had any proximate effect on the war effort. In the lower federal courts about 2,000 cases involving the Espionage Act arose, and in nearly all of them vague statements criticizing the war, the administration, or the American form of government were usually accepted as having a bad tendency or constituting intent to bring about insubordination in the armed forces.

The Court also upheld the Sedition Act. In *Abrams* v. *United States* (1919) it reviewed a conviction of appellants charged with violating the act by the publication of pamphlets attacking the government's expeditionary force to Russia and calling for a general strike. The majority opinion, written by Justice John H. Clarke, upheld the conviction and the statute. The purpose of the pamphlet, Clarke said, was to "excite, at the supreme crisis of the war, disaffection, sedition, riots, and ... revolution." No such right could be protected by the First Amendment. Justice Holmes, joined by Justice Brandeis, dissented from the majority opinion on the ground that it had not been shown that the pamphlet had any immediate effect upon the government's war effort. In what is usually regarded by civil libertarians as the first genuine application of the clear-and-present-danger doctrine, Holmes wrote: "Nobody can suppose that the surreptitious publishing of a silly leaflet by an unknown man, without more, would present any immediate danger that its opinions would hinder the success of the government arms or have any appreciable tendency to do so."

The courts were only the most prominent of a wide array of public and private institutions that restrained political speech and action during the war. Headed by agents of the Bureau of Investigation in the Justice Department, federal officials in several departments enforced the Espionage and Sedition Acts. The postmaster general actively employed the power of censorship entrusted to him under the Sedition Act to exclude antiwar material from the mails. The Immigration Bureau in the Labor Department moved administratively against large numbers of aliens whose radical political ideas were said to violate the Immigrant Acts of 1917 and 1918, providing for deportation of aliens advocating or teaching the overthrow of the government by force or violence. The Committee on Public Information, created by the president under his wartime emergency powers, disseminated propaganda to encourage prowar attitudes. Following the federal example, many states passed their own sedition acts and criminal syndicalism laws. And scores of private organizations and quasi-official bodies created under government auspices, such as the American Protective League, enforced conformity to a prowar point of view through vigilante tactics at the local level.

By the standards and law of a later generation the government's civil liberties record during World War I was exceedingly poor, and its security program an unconstitutional denial of freedom of speech and of the press. The program did not violate constitutional law as it then existed, however, nor as it was interpreted by the Supreme Court in the cases already discussed. The people overwhelmingly supported the administration and accepted the imposition of restrictions on political speech and action as legitimate because they were adopted by their representatives through democratic means.

There were, however, a number of dissenters who argued that the government's security measures violated not only the nation's central idea of political liberty but also the Constitution properly understood in relation to individual civil liberties. Expressing this view was the Civil Liberties Bureau, an emanation of the left-wing American Union against Militarism, which in 1917 was organized to protect conscientious objectors, socialists, and labor radicals against government repression. The Civil Liberties Bureau acted as a civil liberties interest group and advanced a libertarian philosophy based on the declared purpose of preserving "constitutional rights on general principle in the interest of democratic institutions." In 1920 the bureau was reorganized as the American Civil Liberties Union.

By 1920 a libertarian point of view existed which evolved more fully in the next two decades. Ironically, considering that his original statement of the clear-and-present-danger idea served to uphold the government and send Schenck to jail, the views of Justice Holmes came to be seen as an authoritative expression of the libertarian philosophy. In a series of opinions Holmes asserted that all political ideas and opinions should be given the broadest possible scope for expression, and should be restricted only if they created an immediate danger of unlawful action or material injury. If one could be absolutely certain that one's opinions were true, Holmes said in his *Abrams* dissent, persecution of other erroneous opinions would be logical. In fact, however, he observed, "men have realized that time has upset many fighting faiths" and hence "may come to believe ... that the ultimate good desired is better reached by free trade in ideas." Borrowing a metaphor from laissez-faire economic theory, Holmes argued that "the best test of truth is the power of the thought to get itself accepted in the competition of the market.... That ... is the theory of our Constitution."

In his dissent in *Gitlow* v. *New York* (1925), in which the Supreme Court upheld the conviction of a Communist party leader under the New York criminal anarchy law, Holmes expressed the libertarian conception of free speech even more pointedly. Noting that Gitlow's "Left Wing Manifesto" created no present danger of the overthrow of the state government, he said that even proponents of subversive ideas must be allowed to compete in the political marketplace. "If, in the long run," he averred, "the beliefs expressed in proletarian dictatorship are destined to be accepted by the dominant forces of the community, the only meaning of free speech is that they should be given their chance and have their way." In the *Gitlow* case the majority reasoned that advocacy of overthrow of the government was inherently unlawful and, therefore, constitutionally unprotected; the clear-and-present-danger test did not apply. Holmes, however, regarding all political ideas as equal, denied that any category of speech could be denied protection and proscribed. Only if speech immediately threatened the overthrow of the government or some equally serious catastrophe could it be curtailed.

Civil Liberties in the 1920s

Although the Supreme Court did not subscribe to the emerging libertarian philosophy, the justices' laissez-faire bias toward individual freedom produced occasional decisions in the 1920s expanding the sphere of civil liberty. In *Meyer* v. *Nebraska* (1923), for example, the Court held void a Nebraska statute prohibiting the teaching of modern foreign languages to children in elementary schools. The liberty guaranteed by the Fourteenth Amendment, said Justice McReynolds, included the right to bring up one's children according to the dictates of individual conscience. The statute, he declared, invaded that right and, therefore, violated the Fourteenth Amendment's due process clause. In the same vein, the Court in *Pierce* v. *Society of Sisters* (1925) struck down an Oregon law requiring children between the ages of eight and sixteen to attend public school. The statute, said Justice McReynolds, destroyed property rights in private schools and violated the right of parents to educate their children as they saw fit.

Of greater importance for the subsequent triumph of libertarianism was the beginning in the 1920s of the nationalization of the Bill of Rights. At first almost casually, then with greater theoretical acuity and awareness, the Supreme Court inaugurated a line of decisions that would eventually make the guarantees of virtually the entire Bill of Rights effective against the states through the due process clause of the Fourteenth Amendment. In order to understand this development it is necessary to consider briefly the relationship between the Fourteenth Amendment and the Bill of Rights.

In *Hurtado* v. *California* (1884) the Supreme Court had pointed out the logical difficulty that stood in the way of any attempt to apply the Bill of Rights to the states by means of the due process clause of the Fourteenth Amendment. The Fifth Amendment refers to a series of procedural requirements, such as indictment by a grand jury in capital cases, the right not to be tried twice for the same offense, the right against self-incrimination, and so on. Separate from these procedural guarantees is the right not to be deprived of life, liberty, or property without due process of law. Under the rule of statutory construction which states that no part of a document is superfluous, the Supreme Court in the *Hurtado* case reasoned that due process meant something different from the other guarantees and rights mentioned in the Fifth Amendment. On the further assumption that words possess the same meaning throughout a document, the Court concluded that due process in the Fourteenth Amendment meant the same thing as in the Fifth Amendment. Therefore, due process in the Fourteenth Amendment could not logically include the other procedural guarantees of the Fifth Amendment nor, by extension, those in the rest of the Bill of Rights.

Events soon showed that logic alone, or the rule of nonsuperfluousness, would not govern the resolution of controversies arising from attempts to enlarge the meaning of the due process clause. In *Chicago, Burlington, and Quincy Railroad Co.* v. *Chicago* (1897), for example, the Supreme Court held that the due process clause of the Fourteenth Amendment prohibited the states from taking private property for a public use without just compensation—the same limitation that was imposed on the federal government by the Fifth Amendment. As previously noted, in *Twining* v. *New Jersey* (1908) the Court refused to interpret the Fourteenth Amendment as requiring the states to acknowledge a right against self-incrimination, as provided in the Fifth Amendment. But the Court also declared in *Twining* that some rights protected by the due process clause were similar to rights enumerated in the first eight amendments to the Constitution. Though denying an express textual identity, the justices thus suggested a practical correspondence between the Fourteenth Amendment and the Bill of Rights.

Conflicts over civil liberties during World War I turned attention to the relationship between the Fourteenth Amendment and the First Amendment. In *Gilbert* v. *Minnesota* (1920), for example, the Supreme Court affirmed a state law punishing speech aimed at discouraging enlistment in the armed forces. In dissent, Justice Brandeis said the law interfered with the right of a United States citizen to discuss a federal function—namely, the war power. Brandeis implied that the law violated the Fourteenth Amendment. Justice McKenna's majority opinion, while upholding the state law, seemed tacitly to concede that liberty under the Fourteenth Amendment might comprehend freedom of speech. McKenna, at any rate, did not deny this proposition, nor did he reiterate the orthodox view that the First Amendment restricted only the federal government. To have insisted on this point would have precluded any discussion of the limits states could impose on freedom of speech, which was the Court's chief practical concern.

In *Gitlow* v. *New York* (1925) the Supreme Court took the decisive initial step toward incorporating the First Amendment in the due process clause of the Fourteenth Amendment. Justice Sanford declared in his majority opinion: "For the present purposes, we may and do assume that freedom of speech and of the press—which are protected by the First Amendment from abridgement by Congress—are among the fundamental personal rights and 'liberties' protected by the due process clause of the Fourteenth Amendment from impairment by the states." This assertion, so significant in retrospect, was considered of very little importance at the time. No one, including the state of New York, which accepted the proposition that the First Amendment was incorporated in the Fourteenth Amendment, perceived the practical consequences for federalism of a decision that could potentially subject state legislation to more exacting federal standards. This was because the Court's main purpose was to uphold the New York criminal syndicalism law, and it would have had no warrant for doing this if it had taken the position that the First Amendment applied only to the federal government. Logically, it would then have been required to dismiss the case for want of jurisdiction.

The Court cannot be said to have actually incorporated the First Amendment in the due process clause of the Fourteenth Amendment until *Stromberg* v. *California* (1931). In that case for the first time it struck down a state law as a violation of free speech guarantees of the First Amendment applied against the states under the Fourteenth Amendment.[2] The legislation declared invalid was a California statute that prohibited the display of the red flag as an emblem of anarchism or of opposition to organized government. "It has been determined," said Chief Justice Charles Evans Hughes, "that the conception of liberty under the due process clause of the Fourteenth Amendment embraces the right of free speech." The California law, Hughes observed, was worded so broadly as conceivably to impose penalties on peaceful and orderly opposition to government. It, therefore, violated due process of law. At the same session, in *Near* v. *Minnesota* (1931), the Court held unconstitutional a Minnesota statute providing for the suppression of any malicious, scandalous, or defamatory newspaper. Pointing out that the law went well beyond existing standards of responsibility under libel laws, Chief Justice Hughes said the measure violated freedom of the press and hence the due process clause of the Fourteenth Amendment.

2. In *Whitney* v. *California* (1927), although it did not reiterate its assumption about the First Amendment being part of the Fourteenth Amendment, the Court upheld the constitutionality of a criminal conviction under the California criminal syndicalism act on the same theoretical premise as in *Gitlow*.

In *Powell* v. *Alabama* (1932) the Supreme Court first included one of the criminal procedure guarantees of the Bill of Rights in the due process clause. The case arose out of the famous Scottsboro incident, in which nine Negro boys were convicted of raping two white girls. The Court held that the refusal of the state of Alabama to grant the Negroes accused of rape the right of access to counsel—a right specified in the Sixth Amendment—violated the due process clause of the Fourteenth Amendment. Although this decision did not specifically overrule *Hurtado* v. *California,* it seriously weakened the authority of that precedent. Moreover, the Court consciously departed from the rationale of *Hurtado* as it dealt with the theoretical issues raised by its incipient nationalization of the Bill of Rights. Citing the *Chicago, Burlington, and Quincy* decision, Justice Sutherland stated that the doctrine of nonsuperfluousness was not absolutely dispositive of questions concerning the relationship between the Fourteenth Amendment and the Bill of Rights. Some rights, said Sutherland—those that constituted "fundamental principles of liberty and justice which lie at the base of all our civil and political institutions"—were protected by both the Bill of Rights and the Fourteenth Amendment.

Civil Liberties in the New Deal Era

As modern liberalism began during the New Deal, so civil libertarianism first achieved substantial results in constitutional law in the 1930s. The two developments were connected. Liberalism aimed at coordinating the nation's major functional interest groups into a more rationalized and centrally directed political economy, first through the abortive NRA corporatist method, then by means of the group-conflict strategy of federal regulation. In either case, both in a substantive and procedural sense, the purpose of federal policy was to give previously excluded groups, especially labor and agriculture, representation in the politico-constitutional system. Libertarian legal developments had much the same integrative, representational purpose. Individuals and groups previously denied access to the political system frequently were the beneficiaries of judicial decisions that broadened the sphere of civil liberty protected against public and private interference.

Liberal political strategy and civil libertarian legal theory came together in the labor question. Before the New Deal labor had effectively been excluded from national policy making, often by the use of the labor injunction to enforce rules of constitutional law that severely restricted labor union activity. Through the 1920s and 1930s a major concern of the American Civil Liberties Union and libertarian reformers was to secure labor the right to strike, picket, organize, and assemble. To be prevented from engaging in these actions, libertarians argued, was to be denied fundamental civil liberties under the First Amendment.

The Wagner Act of 1935 signified the inclusion of labor in the governmental system of interest-group liberalism and the guarantee of civil liberties to organized labor under federal auspices. The National Labor Relations Board was the key agency of representation and protection, entrusted with upholding the legal right of labor to organize and bargain collectively. The NLRB faced obstacles in the first few years of its existence as businessmen challenged the new labor rights law as an unconstitutional interference with liberty of contract and economic due process. The Supreme Court's decision in the *Jones and Laughlin* case in 1937 eliminated this obstacle by upholding the Wagner Act. The Senate Committee on Education and Labor, under the chairmanship of Senator Robert M. La Follette, Jr., also enforced labor's "Magna Charta" by hearing testimony and publicizing business violations of the Wagner Act and other antilabor practices.

In areas other than labor, protection of civil liberties occurred mainly through the exercise of judicial power. The Supreme Court had demonstrated concern with civil liberties and private rights from the early 1930s, Justices Brandeis, Cardozo, and Stone consistently taking a liberal position in cases of his kind. After the advent of Justices Black and Douglas, a libertarian outlook was even more clearly dominant on the Court, and the addition of Justices Murphy and Rutledge reinforced the tendency. Justice Frankfurter, whose theory of judicial self-restraint and respect for legislative prerogative were later to lead him to a conservative position on civil liberties quesions, in this period also voted generally with the libertarian majority.

In effect the Supreme Court modernized the Bill of Rights, formulating new constitutional guarantees to protect labor unions in strikes and picketing and upholding the rights of racial and religious minorities. Constitutionally, the result was to strengthen the tendency toward centralization encouraged by New Deal legislation generally. By restricting the scope of the state police power in the civil liberties field, the national government, as it extended its sovereignty in social and economic affairs, increasingly protected the liberty of the individual. A second consequence of the libertarian movement was the reaffirmation of judicial power following the Court-packing fight of 1937. Steadfastly adhering to judicial restraint in regard to social and economic regulation, the Court for the next decade or so employed quasi-legislative judicial activism to restrain legislatures from interfering with civil liberties.

During the 1930s the nationalization of the Bill of Rights emerged with further clarity as a central issue in constitutional law. In the space of a decade the Supreme Court had made the free speech and free press guarantees of the First Amendment, as well as the right of counsel in the Sixth Amendment, effective elements of due process under the Fourteenth Amendment. The question arose whether the other rights specified in the first eight amendments were also requirements of due process. If they were not part of due process, what distinguished them from the rights that were included as limitations on the states under the Fourteenth Amendment?

In *Palko* v. *Connecticut* (1937) the Supreme Court addressed these issues. The case concerned a Connecticut law that permitted the state to appeal the outcome of a criminal trial, and that had been used to reverse a second-degree murder conviction and secure a first-degree conviction instead. The question was whether this law violated the due process clause of the Fourteenth Amendment, construed to include the Fifth Amendment right not to be tried twice for the same offense. Denying the contention, the Supreme Court offered a theory of liberty, explaining the relationship between the Fourteenth Amendment and the Bill of Rights.

Justice Cardozo's opinion for the Court rejected the view, asserted by counsel for the convicted felon, that the due process clause in the Fourteenth Amendment incorporated all of the Bill of Rights. Yet, as the Court had on several occasions indicated, some of the rights guaranteed in the federal Bill of Rights, through what Cardozo called "a process of absorption," had become part of Fourteenth Amendment due process of law. The basis of this distinction was the fact that some rights were more important than others. Those rights that had been absorbed or incorporated, said Cardozo, had been found to be "implicit in the concept of ordered liberty." They were the "fundamental principles of liberty and justice which lie at the base of all our civil and political institutions." These rights, Cardozo continued, existed on a "different plane of social and moral values." Freedom of speech and of the press in particular formed the "matrix, the indisputable condition, for nearly every other freedom." Using this criterion, Cardozo concluded that the right against double jeopardy was not essential to the scheme of ordered liberty.

Cardozo's *Palko* opinion proved seminal. Over the next thirty years it provided the theoretical framework within which the nationalization of the Bill of Rights would proceed. Given the libertarian outlook of a majority of the post-1937 Court, there was an irresistible tendency to increase the number of rights regarded as "implicit in the concept of ordered liberty." In the vanguard of this development was Justice Black, who satisfied himself on the basis of historical evidence that the framers of the Fourteenth Amendment incorporated the entire Bill of Rights in the due process clause. Black's total-incorporation doctrine, which he expressed most fully in *Adamson* v. *California* (1948), insisted on a direct identification of the due-process clause with the express language of the first eight amendments. Black's fellow libertarians—Douglas, Murphy, and Rutledge—agreed with him on the issue of total incorporation, but went further in contending that due process was not limited to the Bill of Rights. In their view due process included any right deemed to be fundamental, whether enumerated in the Bill of Rights or not.

At the opposite end of the spectrum of judicial ideology was Justice Frankfurter. More sensitive to the value of federalism, he argued that the rights absorbed in the Fourteenth Amendment were merely similar, not identical, to those listed in the Bill of Rights. As limitations on the states, these guarantees could accordingly differ in scope and meaning from those that restricted the federal government. Frankfurter rejected Black's total incorporation theory as unsound, and various scholars attacked it as historically inaccurate. Yet, although the Court would never in a formal sense accept Black's thesis, through a case-by-case process of selective incorporation it gradually brought more and more of the substance of the Bill of Rights within the scope of the Fourteenth Amendment due process clause.

Within the incorporationist framework the preferred-freedoms doctrine became a key civil libertarian issue in the late 1930s. With totalitarianism spreading across Europe, it seemed reasonable to conclude that the personal liberties that distinguished democratic government deserved special protection by the judiciary. A continuing criticism of judicial review as practiced by property-minded judges before 1937 had been that it usurped the power of democratic majorities. If judicial review could be made to promote democracy, however, its legitimacy could not be questioned. Accordingly, libertarian-minded reformers held that judicial decisions upholding First Amendment liberties that enabled minority interests to transform themselves into a majority were democratic, even if they overturned the majority's legislative judgment. Furthermore, judicial defense of minority groups' civil liberties and civil rights was politically expedient for it promoted the interests of key elements of the New Deal's political constituency.

Justice Cardozo anticipated the preferred-freedoms doctrine in his *Palko* opinion when he said that the rights absorbed in the due process clause possessed a higher moral standing. Justice Stone, however, gave the doctrine its most notable expression in his opinion in *United States* v. *Carolene Products Co.* (1938). Stone wrote in a now famous footnote: "There may be narrower scope for the operation of the presumption of constitutionality where legislation appears on its face to be within a specific prohibition of the Constitution, such as those of the first ten amendments, which are deemed equally specific when held to be embraced within the Fourteenth." That is, while under ordinary circumstances, the burden of legal proof was against those attacking the constitutionality of a statute, in First Amendment cases the burden of proof was to be reversed, and it became the obligation of the state to demonstrate that notwithstanding the prohibition on regulation in the First Amendment, the regulation in question was constitutional.

The particular focus of judicial concern as Stone saw it was the democratic political process and the representation of minorities. "It is unnecessary to consider now," he wrote, "whether legislation which restricts those political processes which can ordinarily be expected to bring about repeal of undesirable legislation, is to be subjected to more exacting judicial scrutiny under the general prohibitions of the Fourteenth Amendment than are most other types of legislation." Similarly, "statutes directed at particular religious ... or national ... or racial minorities" may call for a "more searching judicial inquiry." The tentative quality of these suggestions expressed Stone's hesitation in laying judicial claim to a quasi-legislative role in the civil liberties field. Others asserted the preferred-freedoms doctrine more vigorously, especially Justices Murphy, Rutledge, Black, and Douglas. Indeed, the latter two judges came close to holding that the First Amendment categorically prohibited all legislation restricting in any fashion the rights it guaranteed.

Libertarian though the Supreme Court often was after 1937, it by no means identified itself exclusively with this position. A theoretical alternative to the preferred-freedoms doctrine was available in the idea that the interest of the individual in free speech must be weighed against the interest of society in maintaining public order and civility. Referred to as the "balancing test," this was a restatement of the traditional notion that liberty and authority must be kept in equilibrium. More specifically, it held that as liberty depends on order, in certain situations it is permissible and even necessary to restrict individual liberty for the general good. As the preferred-freedoms doctrine was associated with judicial activism, so the balancing test was identified with judicial restraint.

The clear-and-present-danger doctrine also formed a key part of the civil liberties question. Although often considered synonymous with civil libertarianism, the doctrine was originally intended to provide a means of protecting individual speech while preserving the government against instability and possible subversion in national-security cases. Accordingly, it was a kind of balancing device that could be and was used both by activist- and restraint-minded judges. The difficulty, of course, was that it was hard to tell when a threat to the state became clear and immediate. In the late 1930s this problem was obviated somewhat when the clear-and-present-danger rule was revived and used frequently in nonnational security cases, where by definition the speech or activity in question did not present an ultimate threat to society. In national security cases, however, as became clear during the cold war, proponents of balancing used the clear-and-present-danger concept to justify restrictions on speaking and writing.

The New Meaning of Freedom of Speech: Picketing

A notable example of the legal and philosophic difficulty the justices encountered in resolving civil liberties conflicts appeared in the development of the doctrine that picketing during the course of a labor dispute was a form of free speech protected by the First Amendment. For one thing, this approach involved a precipitous shift from the values of the "old" constitutional law with its primary concern for property rights. In *Truax* v. *Corrigan* (1921) the Court had struck down a state statute forbidding injunctions against picketing on the ground that the law in question wrongfully exposed private property rights to possible injury. By contrast, the "free speech" approach to picketing, when carried to an extreme, minimized or even disregarded potential damage to private property rights and focused instead almost entirely on a right of free communication.

Complicating the matter was the fact that picketing involved other elements than mere freedom of expression. Picketing, many analysts pointed out, might indeed carry a "message" properly protected as free speech, but as a rule it was also intimately associated with a labor dispute or strike, which even conducted peacefully was in fact a form of industrial warfare, however legitimate. Moreover, picketing all too often did not confine itself to peaceful communication. Even when overtly abstaining from violence, it generally involved threats and intimidation aimed at both employers and nonstriking workers. Mass picketing went further; it often blocked plant entrances to employers and employees alike, while at worst it spilled over into rioting, violence, and even sabotage.

The Court took its first step toward the doctrine that picketing was a form of free speech protected by the First Amendment in *Senn* v. *Tile Layers Union* (1937). Here the majority justices upheld the constitutionality of a Wisconsin statute legalizing peaceful picketing. "Clearly," said Brandeis for the majority of five justices, "the means which the state authorizes—picketing and publicity—are not prohibited by the Fourteenth Amendment. Members of a union might, without special statutory authorization by a State, make known the facts of a labor dispute, for freedom of speech is guaranteed by the Federal Constitution." This language not only affirmed the constitutionality of the Wisconsin law; it also carried the implication that peaceful picketing was a form of free speech with which a state could not legally interfere.

Justice Brandeis's suggestion that picketing was a form of free speech was confirmed in *Thornhill* v. *Alabama* (1940), where the Court held "invalid on its face" an Alabama law prohibiting peaceful picketing. "In the circumstances of our time," said Justice Murphy, "the dissemination of information concerning the facts of a labor dispute must be regarded as within that area of free discussion that is guaranteed by the Constitution." In *American Federation of Labor* v. *Swing* (1941) the Court strengthened its identification of picketing with free speech by holding that a state might not lawfully enjoin picketing merely because those doing it were not parties to an immediate labor dispute.

It soon became evident, however, that picketing as a constitutional right was subject to certain limitations. In *Milk Wagon Drivers Union* v.

Meadowmoor Dairies (1941) the Court held that a state court might lawfully enjoin picketing marked by violence and destruction of property. In *Carpenters and Joiners Union* v. *Ritter's Cafe* (1942) the justices found that a state could lawfully prohibit the picketing of an employer not involved in a labor dispute in order to bring pressure upon another employer who was so involved. Freedom of speech, said Justice Frankfurter for the majority, did not become completely inviolable merely by the circumstances of its occurring in the course of a labor dispute. He went on to balance the general police power of the state against the constitutional right of free speech precisely as the Court before 1937 had balanced vested rights against state police power in substantive due process cases. Black, Douglas, Murphy, and Reed dissented, contending that peaceful picketing, even against a neutral, was simple communication and ought not lawfully to be enjoined.

Quite plainly there was a serious difference of constitutional philosophy separating the majority and minority positions. The majority justices evidently believed that picketing, on occasion at least, involved elements other than mere communication—coercion, violence, intimidation, or conspiracy to accomplish unlawful ends. They believed also that the Court ought to recognize a discretionary right of the states to subject these elements to regulation and control. The minority, on the other hand, wished to treat picketing as mere free expression and as such entitled to a preferred position under the First Amendment, thereby making it very nearly immune from state attempts at regulation.

A few years later, in the more conservative postwar political climate, the Court moved consistently toward the position that picketing was so bound up with elements of economic coercion, restraint of trade, labor relations, and other social and economic problems that a large measure of discretion in regulating it must be restored to the states. In *Giboney* v. *Empire Storage and Ice Co.* (1949), speaking through Justice Black, the Court unanimously sustained a Missouri injunction prohibiting picketing that had been intended to force an employer into an agreement in violation of the state's antitrust laws. "It is clear," said Black, "that appellants were doing more than exercising a right of free speech or press.... They were exercising their economic power to compel Empire [Storage] to abide by union rather than state regulation of trade."

A possible implication of the *Giboney* decision was that a state might regulate or prohibit picketing whenever it was directed toward ends the state considered socially undesirable. The following year, in *International Brotherhood of Teamsters* v. *Hanke* (1950), the Court gave overt expression to this doctrine. The case involved an injunction prohibiting picketing intended to compel the self-employed proprietor of a small auto shop to adopt the union shop. Labeling picketing a "hybrid" of free speech and "other elements," Frankfurter emphasized the Court's "growing awareness that these cases involved not so much questions of free speech as review of the balance struck by a state between picketing that involved more than 'publicity' and competing interests of public policy." Black, Minton, and Reed dissented, pointing out that the Court now had virtually abandoned the position that peaceful picketing for lawful purposes was a form of free speech protected by the First Amendment.

Any remaining doubt concerning the Court's new position vanished in *International Brotherhood of Teamsters, Local 695* v. *Vogt* (1957), in which the justices sustained a Wisconsin injunction issued in pursuance of a state statute prohibiting peaceful picketing directed against an employer in the absence of a labor dispute. While Frankfurter admitted that a state could not "enact blanket regulations against picketing," it was nonetheless entitled to exercise virtually unlimited discretion in controlling the social objectives for which picketing was conducted.

Freedom of Speech: Public Meetings, Parades, Pamphlet Peddling

In another series of cases the Court used the guarantees of the First Amendment to erect new safeguards around individuals speaking at public meetings, staging parades, and the like. For some years the Court adhered closely to the doctrine that communication of this kind, even more than picketing, had a preferred constitutional position, giving it at least partial immunity from state controls. The justices were especially quick to strike down statutes that imposed restrictive license requirements of "prior restraint" upon First Amendment activities as well as state or local ordinances that vested arbitrary discretion in local police officers in granting permits for meetings, parades, and the like.

The problem of state attempts to control public meetings first came before the Court in *Hague* v. *C.I.O.* (1939), a case involving the constitutionality of a Jersey City municipal ordinance requiring permits from a "director of public safety" for the conduct of public meetings. In the background of the case was a history of police violence in which labor-union meetings had been broken up, the dissemination of printed material forcibly stopped, and union organizers run out of town. The Court found the ordinance in question unconstitutional, on the ground that it violated the right of United States citizens "peaceably to assemble" as guaranteed by the Fourteenth Amendment, or the due process clause of the Fourteenth Amendment.

However, the Court soon made it clear that the rights of free speech and assembly were not absolutely immune to reasonable regulation under the state police power. The most significant case for this purpose was *Chaplinsky* v. *New Hampshire* (1942). Here the Court upheld a conviction under a New Hampshire statute making it unlawful for any person to "address any offensive, derisive or annoying word to any other person who is lawfully in any street or public place." The defendant had addressed an impromptu street meeting with a denunciation of all organized religion as a "racket." Later he had cursed a complaining officer as a "God-damned racketeer" and the "whole government of Rochester" as "Fascists or agents of Fascists." Justice Murphy, speaking for a unanimous Court, observed that "there are certain well-defined and narrowly limited classes of speech, the prevention of which has never been thought to raise any constitutional problem. These include the lewd and obscene, the profane, the libelous, and the insulting or 'fighting' words—those which by their very utterance inflict injury or tend to incite an immediate breach of the peace." Utterances of this kind, Murphy thought, were "of such slight social value as a step to truth" that they were not entitled to any constitutional protection. The statute in question, construed to punish only this kind of speech, was therefore constitutional.

However, the justices continued to deal sternly with attempts on the part of the state to use the licensing of public meetings as a restrictive device. Thus in *Thomas* v. *Collins* (1945) the Court threw out a contempt conviction imposed by the Texas courts in pursuance of a statute requiring labor organizers to register with state officials and procure an organizer's card before soliciting membership in labor unions. The appellant had addressed an open mass meeting of oil workers, and in his speech he had deliberately solicited members for the CIO oil union, in direct defiance of an anticipatory restraining order issued by the local courts. Justice Rutledge, who delivered the majority opinion, held that the Texas statute, as applied in the present case, was unconstitutional. The great "indispensable democratic freedoms secured by the First Amendment," he asserted, had a constitutional priority which "gives these liberties a sanctity and a sanction not permitting dubious intrusions." Any attempt to restrict them "must be justified by clear public interest, threatened not doubtfully or remotely, but by clear and present danger."

The Supreme Court also attempted to define the area of constitutional liberty involved in pamphlet peddling. The question was difficult because, in addition to elements of free speech, press, and religion, cases of this kind often involved commercial activity. The right of local communities to regulate peddling was well established at law; moreover after 1937 the Court gave virtually carte blanche to states in their regulation of economic activity. Nevertheless rights of free speech were involved in commercial enterprise, and some of the justices believed these rights ought to be protected. As with public meetings, it was the presence of prior restraint or of capricious or arbitrary licensing authority on the part of local officials that aroused the Court's hostility.

The Court took its departure of this problem in *Lovell* v. *Griffin* (1938), when it unanimously invalidated a city ordinance of Griffin, Georgia, prohibiting the distribution of pamphlets and literature without written permission from the city manager. The case was among the first of many involving the religious sect of Jehovah's Witnesses, who acknowledge allegiance to divine law alone—not to any political or temporal government or its statutes. Their difficulties with local and state police ordinances were to furnish much of the raw material for the Court's development of civil liberties doctrine in the next few years. The ordinance, said Chief Justice Hughes, "is such that it strikes at the very foundation of freedom of the press by subjecting it to license and censorship."

The *Lovell* decision served as the basis for the Court's finding a year later in *Schneider* v. *Irvington* (1939), in which it struck down four city ordinances that attempted to control the distribution of circulars, flyers, and the like in the interest of preventing littering. This was an insufficient objective to sustain what amounted to a censorship through license in violation of the First Amendment, said the Court. Similarly, in *Cantwell* v. *Connecticut* (1940) the Court invalidated as a denial of religious liberty in violation of the due process clause of the Fourteenth Amendment a Connecticut law prohibiting solicitation of money for any religious or charitable purpose without prior approval by the secretary of the public welfare council.

Subsequently, the Court found some difficulty in adhering to the position taken in the *Lovell* and *Cantwell* cases. In *Jones* v. *Opelika* (1942) a majority of five justices upheld the constitutionality of a city ordinance of Opelika, Alabama, which required book peddlers to procure a ten-dollar city license before doing business. Justice Reed's majority opinion emphasized that the constitutional rights guaranteed by the Fourteenth Amendment were "not absolute" but that instead it was necessary to balance them against the general right of the states "to insure orderly living, without which constitutional guarantees of civil liberties would be a mockery."

In *Murdock* v. *Pennsylvania* (1943), however, the Court ruled that an ordinance licensing door-to-door sale and dissemination of religious tracts was unconstitutional. At the same time, in *Martin* v. *Struthers* (1943), it struck down an ordinance prohibiting doorbell ringing, knocking on doors, and the like for the purpose of distributing religious tracts and advertisements. Justice Black's opinion admitted that some police regulation of the right to distribute literature might on occasion be legal, but he insisted that the right in question was so "clearly vital to the preservation of a free society that, putting aside reasonable police and health regulations of time and manner of distribution, it must be fully preserved." Despite warnings from Justice Frankfurter against substituting judicial for legislative discretion, the Court for the time being continued to protect the peddling of religious books as essentially a religious occupation that could not be taxed.[3]

As with picketing, however, the Supreme Court in the early 1950s

3. *Cf. Follett* v. *McCormick* (1944), *Marsh* v. *Alabama* (1946), *Tucker* v. *Texas* (1946).

adopted a more conservative view of controversies over assembly, pamphlet peddling, and other forms of expression of opinion. It emphasized very heavily the balancing argument—that First Amendment rights were not absolute or even preferred, but must be weighed against the right of the state to protect the public welfare.

In *Terminiello* v. *Chicago* (1949) the Court considered the conflict between First Amendment rights and the interest of the community in protecting law and order. Terminiello was an unfrocked priest who had been convicted of disorderly conduct following a scurrilous anti-Semitic speech in Chicago. The disturbance that led to his arrest and trial had been precipitated not by him or his followers but by persons in the audience who were outraged by what he had to say. In a 5–4 decision the Supreme Court, applying the clear-and-present-danger rule, overturned the conviction. The trial judge, interpreting the law under which Terminiello had been convicted, said it made punishable "speech which stirs the public to anger, invites dispute, brings about a condition of unrest or creates a disturbance." So construed, declared Justice Douglas in his majority opinion, the Illinois law was unconstitutional. Although not absolute, the right of free speech, Douglas asserted, could be suppressed only in the face of a "clear and present danger of a serious and substantive evil that rises far above public inconvenience, annoyance, or unrest." In dissent Vinson, Frankfurter, Jackson, and Burton attacked the majority decision for showing a doctrinaire disregard for the rights of the states in free speech matters.

In *Feiner* v. *New York* (1950) the conservative Terminiello minority became a majority. The case involved a conviction of a street orator under a New York law forbidding speaking on the streets "with intent to provoke a breach of the peace." As in the Chicago case, the disturbance was caused by those who resented the speaker's remarks. Chief Justice Vinson's majority opinion affirming the conviction pointed out that the lower courts had found evidence of a "genuine attempt to arouse Negro people against the whites." There was no evidence, he said, that the police had interfered merely because of the opinions Feiner had expressed.

Meanwhile, in a series of pamphlet-peddling cases, the Court moved back very close to the position taken in *Jones* v. *Opelika* (1942)—that the commercial element in door-to-door solicitation was sufficiently prominent to justify a city license requirement even when elements of freedom of religion or freedom of speech were involved. Thus in *Breard* v. *Alexandria* (1951) the Court sustained a municipal ordinance forbidding canvassers from calling upon private residences except when invited to do so.

The following year, in *Beauharnais* v. *Illinois* (1952), the Court moved still further toward a recognition of state police power discretion in pamphlet peddling, when it accepted the constitutionality of an Illinois criminal libel law. The law in question forbade the distribution of printed material that "exposes the citizens of any race, color, creed, or religion to contempt, derision, or obloquy, or which is productive of breach of the peace or riots." The defendant, head of a so-called "White Circle League," had been convicted under the law after distributing inflammatory pamphlets calling for "one million self-respecting white people to unite to prevent the white race from being mongrelized by the Negro."

By a 5–4 vote, the Court upheld the conviction. Justice Frankfurter's opinion for the majority developed the novel idea of "group libel" in defense of the statute. He first quoted with approval the *Cantwell* and *Chaplinsky* opinions upholding the right of the state to punish expressions of "the lewd and obscene, the profane, the libelous and the insulting or 'fighting' words." If the state properly could punish language of this kind when aimed at an individual, Frankfurter observed, then the Court could not "deny the state power to punish the same utterances directed at a defined group."

Obviously, the concept of "group libel" greatly broadened state police power at the expense of First Amendment rights, and Black, Douglas, Reed, and Jackson all entered strenuous dissents. Black and Douglas protested that the Court's new dictum "degrades the First Amendment to a 'rational basis' level," by which they meant that instead of applying the preferred-position doctrine, the majority now balanced First Amendment rights against the state police power. Jackson's criticism was different and more conservative: he thought the Court should apply the "clear and present danger" test in cases of this kind.

In *Burstyn* v. *Wilson* (1952), however, the Court refused to apply the group-libel principle to validate censorship of a movie offensive to Roman Catholics. The case arose under a New York statute that made it unlawful to treat any religion with contempt, mockery, or ridicule. Justice Clark for the Court resorted to the now all-but-abandoned preferred-freedoms doctrine to assert that a state could not ban a film merely as "sacrilegious." The decision gave films a very broad immunity under the First Amendment that lasted until the Warren Court modified it a decade later.

"Captive audience" cases involved the Court in still another phase of the attempt to balance state police power and First Amendment rights. At issue was the constitutionality of state laws or city ordinances attempting to regulate or forbid sound trucks, street amplifying devices, and advertising broadcasts on public vehicles. Cases of this kind were especially perplexing in that they involved conflict between two sets of First Amendment rights—that of freedom of expression as against a contrary right of individuals not to be compelled to listen against their will to the utterances of others.

The question first reached the Court in *Saia* v. *New York* (1948), in which the justices voted 5 to 4 to strike down a city ordinance giving the chief of police discretionary power to license sound trucks and amplifying equipment in the public parks. Justice Douglas's opinion treated the law as a simple instance of "prior license" and studiously ignored any question of a contrary right of the listener to privacy. Frankfurter, with whom Reed and Burton joined in dissent, protested that "surely there is not a constitutional right to force other people to listen."

A year later, in *Kovacs* v. *Cooper* (1949), the Court overturned the *Saia* precedent almost completely, holding constitutional a Trenton ordinance that prohibited outright the operation of sound trucks emitting "loud and raucous noises." Justice Reed's opinion made it evident that he thought it a perversion of the right of free speech to guarantee sound trucks a captive audience. However, the new majority was not quite willing to defend a categorical right of privacy in the absence of regulatory legislation. This became clear in *Public Utilities Commission* v. *Pollak* (1952), in which the Court reversed a District of Columbia Court of Appeals decision which had held that the practice of Washington bus companies in playing radio programs on their vehicles violated a Fifth Amendment–guaranteed right of privacy.

Dissident Minorities: Revival of the Clear-and-Present-Danger Doctrine

National security concerns increased in the late 1930s as totalitarian movements spread throughout Europe and threatened the outbreak of war. Numerous states enacted statutes punishing seditious activity directed against the state or the United States, and there was a wave of laws providing for loyalty oaths by teachers and other government employees. In spite of concerted public pressure of this kind, the Roosevelt Court with fair consistency invoked the clear-and-present-danger doctrine to protect dissident political minorities.

DeJonge v. *Oregon* (1937), in which the Court invalidated conviction of a Communist under the Oregon criminal syndicalist law, was a notable example of the Court's attitude. Chief Justice Hughes's unanimous opinion pointed out that the sole charge against the defendant was that he had participated in a Communist political meeting. There was no record that he had advocated violence, sabotage, revolution, or criminal behavior at the meeting or elsewhere, nor was he charged with having done so. "Peaceable assembly for lawful discussion," said Hughes, "cannot be made a crime." The conviction, therefore, was in violation of the defendant's constitutional right to freedom of speech and assembly.

Hughes had drawn upon a general philosophy of constitutional liberty rather than any specific legal doctrine. However, in *Herndon* v. *Lowry* (1937) the Court invoked the clear-and-present-danger doctrine to invalidate the Georgia conviction of a Communist party organizer charged with violating a state statute against inciting to insurrection. Justice Roberts's majority opinion cited with approval the proposition that the defendant's conduct, to be punishable, must show some immediate incitement to violence or insurrection. The evidence, he pointed out, wholly failed to show any such tendency.

The Court temporarily abandoned the clear-and-present-danger doctrine in *Minersville School District* v. *Gobitis* (1940), in which it upheld the action of a Pennsylvania district school board in expelling two children from the public schools for refusal to salute the flag as part of a daily school exercise. The ritual in question was highly offensive to the members of Jehovah's Witnesses, who had attacked the requirement in the courts as an infringement of religious liberty.

Justice Frankfurter's majority opinion admitted that the case posed a dilemma between majority power and minority rights. But in this instance he thought the interests of the state more fundamental. The flag salute was intended to build up a sentiment of national unity, and "national unity is the basis of national security," since "the ultimate foundation of a free society is the binding tie of cohesive sentiment." The legislative judgment that the flag salute was a necessary means to this end, therefore, ought to be respected by the courts. Justice Stone alone dissented.

The *Gobitis* opinion was clearly at variance with the prevailing tendency of the Court to protect dissident minorities against punishment or coercion by the state. It is probable that the justices were deeply affected by the wave of patriotism then sweeping the nation as the threat of war grew nearer. At any rate, three years later, in *West Virginia State Board of Education* v. *Barnette* (1943), the Court invoked the clear-and-present-danger doctrine once more, to overrule the *Gobitis* precedent and declare unconstitutional a West Virginia flag-salute statute similar in all essentials to the earlier Pennsylvania board rule. Justice Jackson, speaking for the new majority, pointed out that the refusal to salute did not at all interfere with the rights of other individuals. Emphasizing that censorship of expression was permissible "only when the expression presents a clear and present danger of action of a kind the State is empowered to prevent and punish," he argued that the present law went even beyond ordinary censorship to require the affirmance of positive belief. "To sustain the compulsory flag salute," he said, "we are required to say that a Bill of Rights which guards the individual's right to speak his own mind, left it open to the public authorities to compel him to utter what is not in his mind." Here was an argument for a "right of silence" equivalent in constitutional force to the other guarantees of the First Amendment.

In *Taylor* v. *Mississippi* (1943) the Court held unconstitutional the conviction of a Jehovah's Witness under a Mississippi sedition statute which made it a felony to encourage disloyalty to the United States. The defendant was freed on the ground that the statute as construed made it a criminal offense to communicate to others views and opinions respecting governmental policies and prophecies concerning the future of the government.

Yet the evidence, said Justice Roberts, showed no incitement to subversive action or any clear and present danger to American institutions or government. This was the only free speech case in the New Deal era even remotely involving national security in which speech was protected under the clear-and-present-danger test.

In nonnational security cases, however, as the *Herndon* and *Barnette* decisions showed, the clear-and-present-danger doctrine was often an effective instrument for defending civil liberties. In *Bridges* v. *California* (1941), for example, the Court reversed a conviction for contempt of court imposed upon radical labor leader Harry Bridges and the editors of the *Los Angeles Times* because of their published comments on litigation pending before the California courts. Citing the clear-and-present-danger rule, Justice Black added the requirement that the evils in prospect must be both substantial and serious. The supposed substantive evils inherent in criticism of the courts, he observed, were two: disrespect for the judiciary, and disorderly and unfair administration of justice. As for the first, Black thought that the "assumption that respect for the judiciary can be won by shielding judges from published criticism wrongly appraises the character of American public opinion." As for disorderly administration of justice, Black thought that to imply that mere adverse editorial criticism would "have a substantial influence upon the course of justice would be to impute to judges a lack of firmness, wisdom, or honor—which we cannot accept as a majority premise."

The Court reached a like decision in *Pennekamp* v. *Florida* (1946). This case involved the conviction for contempt of court of a newspaper editor who had printed several editorials attacking the Florida courts for obstructing the process of criminal justice. Justice Reed's opinion, holding the conviction in violation of the Fourteenth Amendment, admitted that it was not possible to define categorically what constituted a clear and present danger to the impartial administration of justice, but he held that editorial attempts to destroy faith in the integrity of judges and the efficiency of the courts did not constitute such a danger, since "we have no doubt that Floridians in general would react to these editorials in substantially the same way as citizens of other parts of our common country"—that is, they would weigh them and disregard them if found unfair.

The New Deal Court's strong concern for the protection of civil liberties against attack by the state also appeared in *United States* v. *Lovett* (1946), in which the justices invoked the seldom-used constitutional prohibition against bills of attainder in order to defend three federal employees who had been made the victims of an attack by the Committee on Un-American Activities. The Committee had denounced Goodwin B. Watson, William E. Dodd, Jr., and Robert Morss Lovett as guilty of subversive activities against the United States, and Congress had adopted a rider to a 1943 appropriations act providing that no funds available under any act of

Congress should be paid out as salary or other compensation for government service to the three men in question, unless the president should appoint them to office before November 15, 1943, with the advice and consent of the Senate. In effect, this forced the removal of the men from the federal payroll, and they presently sued in the Court of Claims to recover unpaid portions of their salaries. The Court of Claims ruled in their favor, and the case was then certified to the Supreme Court.

Speaking through Justice Black, a majority of the Court held that the congressional provision was in effect a bill of attainder and, therefore, unconstitutional. "What is involved here," said Black, "is a congressional proscription of Lovett, Watson, and Dodd, prohibiting their ever holding a government job." Recalling the definition of a bill of attainder in *Cummings* v. *Missouri* as "a legislative act which inflicts punishment without a judicial trial," Black held that Congress plainly had intended to inflict punishment upon the three men in the form of a ban of their holding federal office, although they had not been subjected to any judicial proceedings. The section in question, therefore, violated Article I, Section 9, of the Constitution and was void.

Thus by 1950 civil liberties questions had superseded conflicts over social and economic regulation as the most problematic and controversial area of constitutional law. From the protest of a beleaguered minority during World War I, civil libertarianism had evolved into the dominant constitutional philosophy of the liberal majority in the New Deal era. Yet in the post–World War II period the principal doctrines of libertarianism—the clear-and-present-danger test and the preferred-freedoms idea—did not go unchallenged. Conservatives, professing concern for the right of local communities to maintain civility and order and the right of the federal government to protect national security, proposed to balance the interest of the individual in the free expression of ideas against the well-being of society as a whole. The stage was set for even more dramatic liberal-conservative confrontations over civil liberties during the cold war of the 1950s.

TWENTY-SEVEN

The Constitution and World War II

———————————————— ✦✦✦ ————————————————

In September 1939 Hitler's legions plunged Europe into the chaos of World War II. This event virtually terminated the already diminished concern of the Roosevelt administration and the American people with the internal political and constitutional issues incident to the New Deal; thereafter, national interest focused on the European war and the equally ominous program of Japanese imperialist expansion in eastern Asia. The United States managed to preserve an uneasy and increasingly dubious neutrality for more than two years, but after the fall of France in June 1940, President Roosevelt's program of aid to the Allies and frantic preparations for national defense absorbed public attention almost completely. The era of "neutrality" precipitated a severe crisis in foreign policy, which in turn raised constitutional issues of the utmost importance for American democracy.

Presidential Prerogative and the Crisis in Foreign Policy, 1939–1941

The crisis in foreign policy arose from the fact that the prospect of an unlimited German victory in Europe and the march of Japanese imperialism in East Asia both constituted major threats to the national interest of the United States. President Roosevelt very soon made it clear that he was aware of the menace and that he deemed it of vital importance for the United States to take steps to assist the enemies of Hitler and to balk Japanese expansion.

Conceivably, the president could have asked Congress for a declaration of war, as other chief executives confronted with major assaults upon American national interest from abroad had done in the past. However, at the moment, such a solution was not politically possible, nor did the Roosevelt administration deem it wise policy. The United States was not under immediate threat of attack, and Congress would not have consented to embark on a "preventive" war. Moreover, the mood of the American people as they contemplated the conflict in Europe was a curiously bifurcated one. On the one hand, an overwhelming number of people sympathized with the Allied cause and agreed with President Roosevelt's estimate of the seriousness of the German threat. On the other hand, an equally large portion of the people believed that the United States ought to stay out of the war at almost any cost. This situation ruled out any open declaration of war on Germany, but it also made a program of aid to the Allies "short of war" politically feasible.

Accordingly, Roosevelt instituted a vigorous program of aid to the Allies and resistance to the Axis powers, in support of which he resorted to a variety of constitutional and legal devices. First and most important, he invoked to an extraordinary degree the executive prerogative in foreign policy. Second, he asserted the concept of an expanded presidential prerogative in a national emergency. Third, he sought and obtained legislation from Congress in support of his policy. Fourth, he issued a long series of executive decrees resting either on specific statutory authority or on his general constitutional powers. Fifth, he made extensive use of his authority as commander in chief of the Army and Navy to dispose of American armed forces in a fashion favorable to the Allies and ultimately to institute a "shooting war" against German submarines in the Atlantic.

Roosevelt carried the president's prerogative power in foreign policy to greater lengths than had any previous chief executive. However, this was not mere constitutional usurpation. The conception of a very broad executive prerogative in foreign policy had received extended support in both theory and practice ever since Alexander Hamilton had first set forth the idea in his *Pacificus* essays. Moreover, the Supreme Court, in *United States v. Curtiss-Wright Export Corporation* (1936), had expounded with approval the same doctrine. Justice Sutherland's opinion had observed that "the very plenary and exclusive power of the President as the sole organ of the federal government in foreign relations" was "a power which does not require as a basis for its exercise an act of Congress, but which, of course, like every other governmental power, must be exercised in subordination to the applicable provisions of the Constitution."

Roosevelt used his foreign-policy prerogative to conduct extended negotiations both in person and through the State Department with various belligerent governments, with the object of strengthening the Allied cause and diverting the course of German, Italian, and Japanese high policy. It also provided the constitutional support for a number of extraordinary executive agreements with foreign governments which Roosevelt effected in support of his program. The most significant of these, perhaps, were the Declaration of Panama, signed in October 1939, whereby the United States and nineteen Latin American republics established the so-called "neutrality belt" around the Western Hemisphere and provided for a "neutrality patrol" of hemisphere waters; the Destroyer-Base Deal, concluded with Great Britain in September 1940; and the so-called Atlantic Charter, which Roosevelt and Prime Minister Churchill promulgated in August 1941.

The constitutionality of the executive agreement as an instrument of the president's prerogative in foreign policy had long been recognized in constitutional law. However, the foregoing agreements went far beyond the usual scope of such arrangements. Under ordinary circumstances, they would either have been submitted to the Senate for ratification as treaties or made the basis for enabling legislation in Congress. In part, the president was able to avoid either recourse because he had the means at his disposal to execute them on his own authority. Thus, Roosevelt established the neutrality patrol simply by issuing the requisite order as commander in chief of the Navy. And the Atlantic Charter, while it appeared on its surface to set up something like a military alliance and define the war aims of the "United Nations," was ultimately only a propaganda document requiring no specific implementation of a legislative kind.

However, the Destroyer-Base Deal presented far more serious constitutional difficulties. By this agreement, the president transferred fifty "overage" destroyers from the United States Navy to the British fleet. In return, the United States received ninety-nine-year leases to seven naval bases on British soil at strategic points in the Caribbean, West Indies, and North Atlantic. Roosevelt entered into this extraordinary arrangement on the basis of an official opinion from Attorney General Robert H. Jackson, who advised him that the transaction would be altogether constitutional and had adequate statutory authority.

Jackson's opinion rested on a provision in an old statute of 1883 for the disposal of worn-out naval vessels and a section in a recently enacted statute of June 1940 which authorized the president to dispose of naval materials only when the chief of naval operations "shall first certify that such material is not essential to the defense of the United States." The first of these laws had obviously been drafted for a purpose altogether different from the one at hand; the second had been written by the Senate in a specific attempt to guarantee against the transfer or disposal of war materials still useful to the United States. Jackson was obliged to argue that the 1940 law properly should be interpreted so that "not essential to the defense of the United States" would mean merely that it would serve the national interest to make the transfer, an interpretation which evidently nullified congressional intent in passing the law.

Moreover, the destroyer transfer was in apparently direct violation of an act of Congress of June 1917 which made it unlawful in any foreign war in which the United States was a neutral "to send out of the jurisdiction of the United States any vessel built, armed, or equipped as a vessel of war . . . with any intent or any agreement or contract, written or oral, that such vessel shall be delivered to a belligerent nation." This language stated a generally accepted principle of international law which Great Britain and the United States had originated in the Treaty of Washington in 1871 and which had been written into the Hague Convention of 1907. But Jackson interpreted the act as not applying in the present instance, since the vessels, he said, had not originally been built with any intent to deliver them to a foreign belligerent. Unhappily for this interpretation, a reading of the law makes it clear that the intent expressed in the statute relates to the delivery of the vessels to a foreign belligerent, not to their construction. A better argument was that of Professor Quincy Wright of the University of Chicago, who pointed out that the 1917 law was a criminal statute intended to control the acts of private persons; conceivably, it was not applicable to acts of the United States government.

It is difficult to escape the conclusion that President Roosevelt, in executing the Destroyer-Base Deal, acted on the basis of dubious statutory authority. It is obvious, also, that the whole stuff of the agreement was such as would ordinarily have been made the subject of a treaty or an act of Congress. In effect, the president gave away a considerable portion of the United States Navy without adequate authority of law. Professor Edward S. Corwin, in a letter to the *New York Times* characterized the agreement as "an endorsement of unrestrained autocracy in the field of our foreign relations," and scouted Jackson's legalisms with the assertion that "no such dangerous opinion was ever before penned by an Attorney-General of the United States." Indeed, President Roosevelt himself had earlier expressed the opinion that the legal and constitutional difficulties in the way of the transfer were insurmountable.

Nonetheless, the president escaped any severe condemnation in Congress or at the bar of public opinion. The country at large was prepared to accede to the law of necessity rather than to cogent constitutional analysis, for the president's action appeared to benefit American national interest.

To some extent, Roosevelt rested his foreign policy on the theory of an expanded presidential prerogative in a national emergency. On September 8, 1939, the president formally declared a limited state of national emergency to exist. This was done, he said, "solely to make wholly constitutional and legal certain necessary measures." And in May 1941 he proclaimed an "unlimited national emergency" for the purpose of repelling potential acts of aggression against the Western Hemisphere.

There was substantial uncertainty concerning the constitutional status of these proclamations and the constitutional and legal situation that resulted from them. Neither cited any specific constitutional or statutory authority upon which they might be based. Congress itself was evidently in considerable doubt about the constitutional meaning of the "state of emergency," for on September 28, 1939, the Senate addressed a resolution to Attorney General Frank Murphy requesting him to report on "what executive powers are made available to the President under his proclamation of national emergency." Murphy refused to give the Senate any formal legal opinion on the matter, but he nonetheless told the Senate that "it is universally recognized that the constitutional duties of the Executive carry with them the constitutional powers necessary for their proper performance."

One consequence of the emergency proclamations was clear enough, however: they activated an impressive list of presidential powers which Congress by statute had stipulated could be exercised only in time of national emergency or state of war. Murphy accompanied his reply to the Senate with a long list of such statutes, clear evidence that Congress itself had repeatedly recognized that it might grant the president certain powers which were to be exercised only in time of national emergency. Modern delegation of this kind began with the National Defense Act of 1916, which had authorized the president, among other things, to make seizures of plants and communication facilities in time of national emergency or state of war. Other statutes gave the president emergency control of radio stations, the right to seize powerhouses and dams, to increase the size of the Army and Navy beyond authorized strength, to regulate and prohibit all Federal Reserve transactions, to seize any plant refusing to give preference to government contracts, and to take control of all communication facilities in the United States.

A more difficult constitutional question remained: Did the proclamation of a national emergency expand the presidential prerogative in some general fashion without regard to any specific statutory authority? There was no doubt that various presidents, from Lincoln on, had acted upon the assumption that executive prerogative somehow increased greatly under the pressure of war or grave national emergency. The reader is already aware of Lincoln's extraordinary assumption of emergency power in the spring of 1861. Theodore Roosevelt's "Stewardship Theory," it will be recalled, had assumed that the president possessed a "mighty reservoir of crisis authority."[1] And Wilson's assumption of a broad executive prerogative in World War I, when he had acted to set up a variety of executive boards without any specific statutory authority, constituted another impressive precedent which influenced Franklin Roosevelt very heavily. The truth of the matter was that the president's emergency prerogative, within extremely broad limits, was subject principally to the political control of public opinion.[2]

The most notable legislative measures that Roosevelt sought in support

---

1. Clinton Rossiter, *Constitutional Dictatorship: Crisis Government in the Modern Democracies* (Ithaca, 1948), p. 219.

2. In the Steel Seizure Case, in 1952, the Supreme Court was to frown officially upon the idea of an expanded executive prerogative in time of emergency. However, President Truman's seizure of the steel industry was to be carried out in apparent direct defiance of a congressional statutory mandate, a situation somewhat different from that which Roosevelt faced during World War II. See below, pp. 575–78.

of his foreign policy during the prewar crisis were the Neutrality Act of November 1939, repealing the embargo on private arms shipment to belligerents; the Lend-Lease Act of March 1941; and the Joint Resolution of November 1941, repealing the prohibition against American merchant vessels entering war-zone waters.

The most interesting constitutional element in these enactments was the large delegation of quasi-legislative authority to the executive which they involved. Most extraordinary in this respect was the Lend-Lease Act, which in sweeping terms authorized the president to manufacture or procure any defense article for the government of any country "whose defense the President deems vital to the defense of the United States," and to sell, exchange, lease, lend, and otherwise dispose of such articles to the government in question as he saw fit. This was the kind of unlimited legislative delegation which the Supreme Court had struck down in the *Schechter* and *Carter* cases. But the Curtiss-Wright opinion had held that congressional delegation of legislative authority properly might be much broader in the area of foreign affairs than in domestic matters, and conceivably this distinction rescued the constitutionality of the Lend-Lease Law.

Roosevelt's executive orders were a critically important aspect of his larger foreign policy. They poured forth in a steady stream, all being calculated to influence in some fashion the course of the world crisis. Characteristic were those terminating on six months' notice the United States–Japanese commercial treaty of 1911 (July 1939), placing an embargo on the export of aviation gasoline to Japan (July 1940), banning the sale of scrap iron and steel to Japan (October 1940), freezing Japanese financial assets in the United States (July 1941), establishing war zones under the Neutrality Law (November 1939), and declaring the Red Sea no longer a war zone (April 1941). Some of these had direct statutory authority; most of them did not and rested instead merely on the prerogative power in foreign policy.

There were numerous constitutional precedents for Roosevelt's use of his powers as commander in chief of the Army and Navy to influence foreign policy. President Adams had waged naval war with France in 1798 without formal authorization from Congress, and Wilson had used both the Army and Navy in punitive military expeditions against Mexico. There had been numerous small military expeditions against the Caribbean republics, all staged on presidential order, and there had been similar expeditions in China, notably the American participation in the suppression of the Boxer Rebellion in 1899. In particular, presidents have felt free to order the Navy about in support of foreign policy, and it was this tradition to which Roosevelt now resorted. His order to the Navy of October 1939 establishing the Neutrality Patrol in the western Atlantic was of this kind.

More controversial constitutionally was the process whereby Roosevelt instituted convoys for British merchant vessels carrying lend-lease supplies and subsequently commenced a shooting war against German submarines. The Lend-Lease Act itself had contained an ambiguous disclaimer that "nothing in this act shall be construed to authorize or to permit the authorization of convoying vessels by naval vessels of the United States." But in July 1941 the president ordered American armed forces to occupy Iceland, a step he took by virtue of an executive agreement with the newly independent Republic of Iceland and under his authority as commander in chief. The occupation of Iceland made convoying for the protection of American military supply ships an imperative necessity.

Accordingly, in August the president ordered the Navy to begin convoying American and British ships as far east as Iceland, although it was obvious that "convoys mean shooting and shooting means war." In defense of the president's action, it may be pointed out that this action was in a general way taken in support of a policy ratified by Congress, that of furnishing military supplies to the Allied powers, and that from a standpoint of international law the United States was hardly any longer a neutral in the European war.

In September 1941 the president on his own authority began an actual "shooting war" against German submarines in the Atlantic. The occasion was a supposed submarine attack against the destroyer *Greer,* then on convoy duty in the Greenland Straits. In retaliation, Roosevelt ordered the Navy to hunt down and destroy on sight the "rattlesnakes of the Atlantic." Here was a *de facto* war against a great power waged on presidential fiat and without the consent of Congress. John Adams had done much the same thing against France in 1798; however, it is probable that Adams had a far clearer congressional mandate than Roosevelt could have inferred from the Lend-Lease Law.

When Roosevelt's conduct in the international crisis between 1939 and 1941 is examined in the large, it appears to be closely analogous constitutionally to that of Lincoln in the Civil War crisis of April–July 1861. Each president confronted what he firmly believed to be a paramount threat to national security. In order to deal with the crisis, each assumed that the emergency endowed the executive with prerogative powers of a large and indefinite kind adequate to meet the emergency. Each took critically important steps without adequate statutory authority or in actual disregard of pertinent acts of Congress. Each believed that his conduct was justified by the necessity of saving the nation from disaster. And in each case, ultimately it was public and congressional recognition of the extraordinary character of the crisis that gave a kind of political sanction to the president's conduct.

It is conceivable that had the state of affairs existing in the fall of 1941 lasted any great length of time, Roosevelt's continued use of the executive prerogative in foreign policy and his powers as commander in chief might have precipitated a major constitutional crisis. However, the attack on Pearl

Harbor on December 7, 1941, and the declarations of war on Japan, Germany, and Italy which followed, averted a potential confrontation between the president and Congress over executive power.

The Federal Government in World War II

The task of organizing the federal government for the prosecution of World War II gave rise to much less constitutional controversy than had been the case in 1917. This was true mainly because the constitutional practices of World War I had pretty thoroughly broken down prior inhibitions about the scope of federal war power. As a consequence, the limitations inherent in the American constitutional system which in theory made it a poor instrument for waging total war had almost entirely been overcome.

The Supreme Court itself had recognized the force of this argument in the World War I era; later it had paid homage to an expansive theory of the federal war power. Thus in the *Minnesota Moratorium* case, Chief Justice Hughes had asserted that "the war *power* of the Federal Government ... is a *power* to wage war successfully, and thus ... permits the harnessing of the entire energies of the people in a supreme co-operative effort to save the nation." In the *Curtiss-Wright* case, the Court had taken an even more extreme position. Justice Sutherland had asserted that the power to wage war was inherent in national sovereignty, antedated the Constitution itself, and was not dependent upon the enumeration of federal powers in Article I, Section 8. This notion of the right to wage war as an "inherent power" was far more expansive than any enumerated power; as Professor Corwin has pointed out, it "logically guarantees the constitutional adequacy of the war power by equating it with the full actual power of the nation in waging war."[3]

This is not to say that the United States entered upon World War II with the doctrine established that there were absolutely no restraints either on the scope of federal sovereignty in war or on the means of exercising federal power in wartime. It was generally recognized that the specific prohibitions of the written Constitution remained in force, that national power, while vastly enlarged, was not without constitutional limits, and that private rights were still valid, although they were admittedly subject to certain limitations not ordinarily applicable in peacetime. These various limitations on federal power proved in practice to be by no means clear, however, and it remained for the progress of the war to mark them out by actual practice and occasional judicial decisions.

Both before and after Pearl Harbor, Congress enacted a series of criti-

3. E. S. Corwin, *Total War and the Constitution* (New York, 1947), p. 37.

cal statutes, all of which asserted vast federal powers for the prosecution of the war. These statutes were alike also in that they made tremendous grants of authority to the executive for the exercise of the powers over which Congress asserted its sovereignty.

Most important, perhaps, were the Selective Service Act of September 1940, and Lend-Lease Act of March 1941, the First War Powers Act of December 1941, the Second War Powers Act of March 1942, the Emergency Price Control Act of January 1942, and the War Labor Disputes Act of June 1943.

The Selective Service Act authorized the executive to inaugurate a comprehensive system of military conscription, although the United States was still technically at peace. The Lend-Lease Act, renewed repeatedly after Pearl Harbor, provided the president with *carte blanche* executive authority whereby some $50 billion of war supplies were delivered to America's allies. The First War Powers Act, essentially a re-enactment of the Overman Act of World War I days, gave the president authority to reorganize all executive departments and independent commissions at his discretion for the effective prosecution of the war. The Second War Powers Act was a hodge-podge dealing with all manner of emergency grants of power to the executive; among other things, it gave the president comprehensive plant-requisitioning power, and control of overseas communications, alien property, the allocation of war-related materials and all defense contracts. The Emergency Price Control Act created an Office of Price Administration and a price administrator appointed by the president, and granted the administrator a general power to regulate both rents and commodity prices. And the War Labor Disputes Act authorized executive seizure of plants closed by strikes or other labor disputes.

This body of legislation, creating as it did a vast and ramified federal dictatorship over the national economy, went far beyond the reaches of the Lever Act of World War I days. Yet the entire legislative program went through Congress with hardly a constitutional ripple. In part, this was because there was now a general acceptance of the all-inclusive scope of the federal war power. Also, Congress was far less disposed to quarrel with executive authority than it had been in 1861 or 1917; Congress and the president as a rule now constituted something like a working partnership for the prosecution of the war.

Roosevelt's Wartime "Dictatorship"

The foregoing legislation in reality assumed the creation of a wartime executive mechanism modeled on Wilson's presidential "dictatorship" of 1917–18. It was to this World War I precedent that Roosevelt now turned.

Roosevelt's notion of his war powers and emergency powers was at least as expansive as that of Lincoln and Wilson before him. Like Wilson, he created a vast executive mechanism for the conduct of the war, most of which rested originally upon no other direct authority than an executive order, "letter," or "directive." A bewildering succession of such decrees brought into being by the end of 1942 more than one hundred wartime offices, boards, commissions, autonomous corporations, and other agencies. So rapidly did the president create, reorganize, and reshuffle offices and functions that the result was a bureaucratic nightmare of multiple agencies and overlapping jurisdictions verging on utter chaos.

A great many of the wartime agencies were technically subordinate branches of the Office of Emergency Management. Established in May 1940 by an "Administrative Order" of the president, the Office of Emergency Management drew its authority specifically from the Reorganization Act of 1939. It thus served as a kind of legal cover for executive agencies which the president could not conveniently assign elsewhere. The OEM speedily became a kind of White House management agency coordinating in some degree at least the wartime executive structure.

Principal OEM agencies were the Office of Production Management (January 1941), the War Production Board (January 1942), the Office of Defense Transportation (December 1941), the War Shipping Administration (February 1942), the War Manpower Commission (April 1942), the War Labor Board (January 1942), the Office of War Information (June 1942), and the Office of Civilian Defense (June 1942).

The Office of Production Management was Roosevelt's first attempt at an agency to coordinate production for war. When it failed to function effectively, the president created the War Production Board, which soon established a virtual dictatorship over the mobilization of American industry. The Office of Defense Transportation coordinated land and coastal transportation, while the War Shipping Administration coordinated overseas shipping facilities. The War Manpower Commission had charge of the mobilization of the nation's manpower for war purposes, including the recruitment, training, and placement of workers in industry and agriculture. In December 1942, the president also put the Selective Service System under the War Manpower Commission's jurisdiction. However, the War Labor Board had general jurisdiction over collective bargaining. The Office of War Information was essentially a public-information and propaganda bureau, performing the same functions as the Creel Committee had exercised in 1918. And the Office of Civilian Defense was concerned primarily with protecting civilian communities against the threat of enemy bombing attack. This hardly exhausts the list of OEM agencies, some twenty-nine of which were functioning at the end of the war.

Outside the OEM, there existed a complex, sprawling bureaucracy of boards, commissions, offices, authorities, and autonomous corporations. Very important was the office that Harry Hopkins occupied as special assistant to the president. His functions, necessarily confidential in nature, were essentially those of an interdepartmental expediter and trouble shooter. The most important independent administrative agency was the Office of Price Administration, first set up in April 1941 without benefit of any statutory authority, to study plans for rationing and price fixing. However, the Emergency Price Control Act of 1942, as already observed, established the OPA as an independent executive agency headed by an administrator appointed by the president with the advice and consent of the Senate.

The Board of Economic Warfare, another separate agency with some statutory powers, exercised control over exports and imports of strategic significance for war. The Office of War Censorship exercised a censorship over foreign communications, as authorized by the First War Powers Act. Beyond these, there were more than a hundred other independent war corporations, many of them virtually autonomous. The Rubber Reserve Corporation, the Defense Plant Corporation, and the Defense Supplies Corporation were but a few.

The precise constitutional status of most of these agencies was a matter of some uncertainty. The great majority of them had come into existence merely through a presidential order or directive and without the specific authority of any statute. Yet the fact was that in one fashion or another the president possessed almost unlimited authority to delegate his wartime authority virtually as he saw fit. In the first place, several of the emergency wartime statutes gave the president unlimited discretion to delegate the powers granted him by the law in question. The First War Powers Act was written in language so sweeping as to give the president the authority not only to shuffle functions among old agencies but also to create new agencies for war purposes. The Second War Powers Act stipulated that "the President may exercise any power, authority, or discretion conferred on him by this section, through such department, agency, or officer of the Government as he may direct, and in conformity with any rules and regulations which he may procure." In addition, Congress repeatedly gave a belated statutory sanction to presidential agencies by appropriating money for their continued operations. Finally, the lower federal courts several times during the war rejected the argument that the president had improperly delegated his powers to an authorized agency; significantly, the Supreme Court itself consistently refused to review such decisions.

Many of the independent agencies technically had only advisory powers; yet in the tense atmosphere of wartime Washington, "advisory" directives were often in fact coercive in character. It proved impossible to develop a successful constitutional challenge in the courts against "advisory" instructions of this kind. Thus an attempt to secure judicial review of certain War Labor Board orders failed when the District of Columbia Court of Appeals held that the board's "directives" technically were only advisory, imposed no sanctions, constituted only a moral obligation upon employers and workers, and hence were not subject to judicial review.

In *Steuart and Bros.* v. *Bowles* (1944) the system of "indirect sanctions," whereby the OPA imposed its controls upon the economy without formal resort to the judicial process, came under judicial scrutiny. The case involved the right of the OPA to suspend fuel-oil deliveries to a retail oil dealer who had sold oil in violation of the coupon-ration system. The suspension obviously had some of the earmarks of an arbitrary administrative penalty imposed without benefit of any judicial process. But the Court refused to see the matter in this light. Speaking through Justice Douglas, it held that the suspension order was not "designed to punish petitioner" but only to promote the efficient distribution of fuel oil in accordance with the purposes of the law.

This was another way of saying that the Court refused to interfere with the principal coercive device whereby the various executive agencies gave practical force to their directives. Some indication of how important indirect sanctions were to the operation of the wartime executive machine may be gained from the fact that the War Production Board alone issued more than five thousand "penalty" orders of this sort during the war. When a congressional committee in 1944 took under consideration a measure to forbid executive agencies to impose penalty sanctions except where they were specifically authorized by an act of Congress, a spokesman for the War Production Board protested in some dismay that the proposed law "would destroy our control completely." Significantly, Congress did not enact the proposal.

Actual seizure of industrial establishments was perhaps the most drastic sanction resorted to by the president in support of his "dictatorship." In June 1941, Roosevelt seized the North American Aviation plant at Inglewood, California, mainly as a means of breaking up a strike which threatened to paralyze vitally needed plane production. The executive proclamation announced merely that the president was acting pursuant to the powers vested in him by "the Constitution and laws of the United States, as President of the United States, and as Commander in Chief of the Army and Navy of the United States." How these conferred the right of seizure no one explained in any detail. Roosevelt made some six other seizures of this kind before the passage of the War Labor Disputes Act in 1943, all of them without citing any specific statutory authority. The War Labor Disputes Act, as already observed, belatedly gave the president general powers of plant seizure in support of the war effort. Thereafter, most of the forty-odd wartime seizures took place under the statutory authority of this law.

Perhaps the most extraordinary assertion of wartime executive power by President Roosevelt came when he threatened to nullify an act of Congress unless it were forthwith repealed. In a message to Congress on September 7, 1942, the president warned that he would set aside a section of the Emergency Price Control Act dealing with ceiling prices on farm products unless Congress forthwith repealed the provision. "In the event that the Congress should fail to act, and act adequately," he warned, "I shall accept the responsibility and I will act."

Here was a presidential claim of a right of executive nullification of a portion of a constitutional statute, solely on the ground that the law in question did not conform with the president's notion of what constituted intelligent national policy. No more extraordinary claim to executive prerogative has ever been advanced in the history of the American constitutional system. Only a theory of virtually unlimited wartime executive power could sustain the constitutional validity of the president's position. No test of the president's claim occurred, however, for Congress promptly complied with Roosevelt's request.

The War Dictatorship and the Japanese Minority

The unhappiest aspect of the presidential "dictatorship" during World War II was the government's segregation and confinement of the Japanese-American minority. Some 112,000 persons of Japanese descent, more than 70,000 of whom were American citizens, were removed from their homes, separated from their jobs and property, and transferred to detention camps, where they were forcibly detained for periods of up to four years. The official excuse for this program was that it was made necessary by the exigencies of war. Seemingly, it violated in a flagrant fashion the fundamentals of due process of law, although the Supreme Court was to accept it in part as constitutional.

Segregation and confinement of the Japanese-American minority had its origin on February 19, 1942, when President Roosevelt promulgated Executive Order No. 9066. This order authorized the secretary of war and appropriate military commanders to prescribe military areas from which any or all persons might be excluded; and the right of other persons to enter, leave, or remain might be subjected to whatever restrictions the secretary of war or appropriate military commanders might think necessary. The president issued this order solely upon his authority as commander in chief of the Army and Navy. However, Congress on March 21 enacted a statute embodying substantially the provisions of the original order, so that the segregation program also received legislative approval.

Meanwhile, on March 2, 1942, General J. L. DeWitt, commanding general of the Western Defense Command, designated by proclamation the entire Pacific coastal area as particularly subject to military attack and established Military Areas No. 1 and No. 2, comprising the entire region. The proclamation warned that subsequent notices would exclude certain classes of persons from the designated areas, or would permit them to remain only under suitable restrictions. On March 24, 1942, General DeWitt declared a curfew between the hours of 8:00 P.M. and 6:00 A.M. for German and Italian nationals and all persons of Japanese ancestry resident within Military Area No. 1, the coastal region.

A series of military orders directed against Japanese-Americans now followed. A proclamation of March 27 prohibited Japanese nationals and Americans of Japanese ancestry from leaving the coastal area except under future orders. Another order of May 9 formally decreed the exclusion of all persons of Japanese origin from the area. Thus Japanese-Americans were now under two contradictory orders—one prohibiting their departure except under future orders, and another excluding them from the same area. Compliance was possible only by reporting to one of a number of designated Civil Control Stations, where Japanese-Americans were gathered together and shipped out of the area to a number of so-called "Relocation Centers."

The "Relocation Centers" were in fact detention camps. They were operated by the War Relocation Authority, an executive agency created for this purpose by presidential order on March 18, 1942. In them, Japanese-Americans were detained for periods up to four years and then resettled outside the Pacific coastal area. In effect, therefore, the relocation program tore thousands of American citizens from their homes and subjected them to forcible confinement, although they had been convicted of no offense whatsoever.

The relocation program—astounding in its constitutional implications—first came before the Supreme Court in June 1943 in *Hirabayashi* v. *United States*. The case concerned the conviction of an American citizen of Japanese descent who had been charged with violating the military curfew and with failure to report to a designated Civil Control Station. For technical reasons, however, the Court confined itself to a consideration of the constitutionality of the curfew order; thus it escaped the much larger issue of the constitutional validity of the segregation program in general.

Chief Justice Stone's opinion for a unanimous Court held that the Act of Congress of March 21, 1942, had clearly authorized the curfew order, and that the order lay within the combined congressional and presidential war powers and was constitutional. He emphasized the grave character of the national emergency that had confronted the nation in 1942, and the possible disloyalty of portions of the Japanese-American minority. The Court, he thought, ought not to challenge the conclusion of the military authorities that the federal war power be interpreted as broadly as possible. The curfew, Stone added, did not violate the Fifth Amendment, which, he pointed out, contained no equal protection clause. Discrimination based solely upon race was, he admitted, "odious to a free people whose institutions are founded upon the doctrine of equality"; for this reason, discrimination based upon race alone had in the past sometimes been held to violate due process. But in earlier cases, Stone pointed out, discrimination based upon race had been irrelevant to the national welfare; in the present case, race was not irrelevant, and Congress, therefore, had a right to take it into account.

The validity of the West Coast exclusion orders finally came before the Court in December 1944, in *Korematsu* v. *United States,* a case involving the conviction of a Japanese-American who had remained in the region contrary to the military orders in question. Justice Black's majority opinion ruled briefly that the exclusion program, consideration of which he carefully separated from the detention program, had been within the combined federal war powers of Congress and the executive. The crux of his argument was bare military necessity. It was imperative, he implied, to allow the Army to make decisions of this kind in wartime. Admittedly, the exclusion order worked hardship on the Japanese-American population. "But hardships are a part of war and war is an aggregation of hardships." Moreover, the exclusion program did not constitute racial discrimination as such; Korematsu had not been excluded because of his race but because of the requirements of military security. However, the opinion specifically refrained from passing upon the constitutionality of the relocation and confinement portions of the program, which Black said posed separate constitutional questions.

Justices Roberts, Murphy, and Jackson all entered vigorous dissents. Roberts thought it a plain "case of convicting a citizen as punishment for not submitting to imprisonment in a concentration camp, solely because of his ancestry," without evidence concerning his loyalty to the United States. He refused to accept Black's separation of the exclusion orders from the relocation and detention program. The appellant, he pointed out, had been under contradictory orders, which in reality "were nothing but a cleverly devised trap to accomplish the real purpose of the military authority, which was to lock him up in a concentration camp."

In *Ex parte Endo,* decided the same day as the *Korematsu* case, the Court upheld the right of a Japanese-American girl, whose loyalty to the United States had been clearly established, to a writ of habeas corpus freeing her from the custody of the Tule Lake War Relocation Camp. Justice Douglas's opinion avoided any ruling upon the constitutionality of the confinement program in its entirety, but instead held merely that the War Relocation Authority had no right to subject persons of undoubted loyalty to confinement or conditional parole. "The authority to detain a citizen or to grant him a conditional release as protection against espionage or sabotage is exhausted," he said, "at least when his loyalty is conceded."

Douglas dodged the embarrassing question of whether the president's order and the Act of Congress behind it were not thereby at least in part unconstitutional by pointing out that neither statute nor executive order anywhere specifically authorized detention. Illegal detention, in other words, had technically resulted from the abuse of presidential orders by the War Relocation Authority. The larger constitutional issue—whether a citizen charged with no crime could be forcibly detained under orders of military authority in other than an immediate combat area—Douglas did not discuss at all.

The Court refused to examine the relocation program in the light of military necessity. There was little or no evidence that any substantial portion of the Japanese-American population was disloyal. There appeared to be no reason whatever why the few potentially disloyal and seditious individuals in the larger group, practically all of whom were known to the Federal Bureau of Investigation and military intelligence, could not have been weeded out and subjected to whatever special controls were necessary. This was in fact what was done with the German-American and Italo-American minorities, the great majority of whose members were permitted their unconditional liberty.

The Court's refusal to examine these considerations put a stamp of approval upon a new relativism of "military necessity" in wartime civil liberties cases. In future wars, no person belonging to a racial, religious, cultural, or political minority can be assured that community prejudice and bigotry will not express itself in a program of suppression justified as "military necessity," with resulting destruction of his basic rights as a member of a free society.

Military Government in Hawaii: Duncan v. Kahanamoku

A second major instance of the wartime suppression of civil liberties by military authority occurred in Hawaii, where the Army erected a military government and for a time suspended all civilian governmental functions, including the writ of habeas corpus and the operation of the regular civil courts. Ultimately, the Supreme Court held that military government in Hawaii had been illegal although it did not so rule until after the war ended.

On December 7, 1941, immediately following the attack on Pearl Harbor, the governor of Hawaii by proclamation suspended the writ of habeas corpus, placed the territory of Hawaii under martial law, and delegated to the commanding general, Hawaiian Department, his own authority as governor as well as all judicial authority in the territory. He took these steps under the Hawaiian Organic Act, adopted by Congress on April 30, 1900, which authorized such action "in case of rebellion or invasion, or imminent danger thereof, when the public safety requires it."

General Short at once proclaimed himself military governor of Hawaii and set up a military regime superseding the civil government. Order No. 4 of December 7 established military courts to try civilians in cases involving offenses against the laws of the United States or the territory of Hawaii, or the rules and orders of the military authorities. Sentences imposed by these tribunals were not subject to review by the regular federal courts, and all regular civil and criminal courts were closed. Civil courts were shortly permitted to reopen as "agents of the commanding general," but they were prohibited from exercising jurisdiction in criminal cases and from empaneling juries. In February 1943 the president partially restored the independent functions of the civil governor and the regular courts. However, the writ of habeas corpus remained suspended, and military courts were still empowered to try civilians for violations of existing military orders. Military government was not terminated entirely until October 1944, at which time all threat of invasion had long since passed.

After much delay, the Supreme Court in February 1946 held in *Duncan* v. *Kahanamoku*, 6 to 2, that the establishment of military tribunals in Hawaii to try civilians had been illegal. The opinion avoided passing on the constitutionality of the suspension of the writ of habeas corpus on the ground that the present appeal had been taken after the restoration of the writ in October 1944.

Black's opinion for the majority argued that the Hawaiian Organic Act of 1900 had not authorized military authorities to declare martial law except under conditions of actual invasion or rebellion. On the contrary, he pointed out, the act had specifically extended the Constitution to the territory so that civilians in Hawaii were entitled to the same guarantees of a fair trial as persons in other parts of the United States. Moreover, military trial of civilians was altogether contrary to American constitutional tradition. Congress had authorized it but once, in the Reconstruction Acts; and President Johnson had challenged that system with a series of vetoes "as vigorous as any in the country's history."

The most surprising aspect of *Duncan* v. *Kahanamoku* was the Court's reluctance to rely more heavily upon *Ex parte Milligan* as a leading precedent. No doubt the explanation lies in the extent to which the *Milligan* decision had been criticized in recent years. Various commentators had pointed out that the exigencies of war on occasion may leave little room for so large a play of civilian authority in a possible field of military operations as the *Milligan* case insisted upon. Put differently, they argued that the "open court" rule may endanger national security. Also, the *Milligan* case had been said to lack realism in that it came after the close of the Civil War and was, therefore, in a sense an indulgence in a "peacetime luxury." Apparently, similar considerations motivated the Court in the *Kahanamoku* case.

Military Trial of Enemy War Criminals

A similar determination not to interfere with the conduct of the war undoubtedly was a large factor in the Court's refusal to extend the protection of the Bill of Rights to enemy military personnel charged with violations of the laws of war.

The question of whether enemy military personnel could claim the protection of the Constitution and the Bill of Rights first arose in *Ex parte Quirin* (1942), a case growing out of the arrest of eight members of the German military forces who had entered the United States in disguise with intent to commit acts of sabotage against American war industry. Following their capture in June 1942, the president ordered the saboteurs tried before a specially constituted military tribunal, on charges of violating the laws of war. While their trial was still in progress, seven of the prisoners sought writs of habeas corpus before federal district courts and the Supreme Court. Late in July the Court denied the appeal without publishing a full opinion explaining why it did so. In October the Court published a unanimous opinion written by Chief Justice Stone, setting forth at some length the reasons for its decision three months earlier.

Stone's opinion held that the saboteurs were not entitled to other than summary military trial. The chief justice first examined and rejected the contention that the offenses for which the petitioners were being tried—violations of the laws of war—were defined neither in the Constitution nor in any federal statute and were, therefore, unknown to the law of the United States. In reply, Stone held that the Fifteenth Article of War, which authorized trial by military commissions of offenses under the laws of war, was sufficient statutory authorization for the present charge. The chief justice also denied the contention of counsel that the president was without adequate authority to establish the military commission, since he had departed slightly from the specifications of the Articles of War. Stone said merely that the national war power was sufficient to establish the commission, and he refused to separate congressional war power from the president's powers as commander in chief. Finally, Stone denied that summary military trial of the saboteurs violated the guarantees of jury trial set forth in Article III, Section 2, of the Constitution and the procedural guarantees of civil trial extended by the Fifth and Sixth Amendments. Military tribunals, he pointed out, had long been held not to be courts within the meaning of the Constitution. It would be absurd, he concluded, to hold that the Constitution, which specifically withheld trial by jury from members of the American armed forces, nonetheless extended that right to enemy military personnel.

A possible implication of the Court's willingness to hear an appeal in the saboteurs' case was that the Constitution somehow protected all persons who in any fashion came under the authority of the United States. However, *In re Yamashita* (1946) refuted this idea. The case involved an appeal by a captured Japanese general from his summary military conviction for violating the laws of war. As in the *Quirin* case, Yamashita's counsel in effect argued that he had been deprived of a fair trial in violation of the guarantees of the Fifth Amendment. But Chief Justice Stone's opinion in substance denied that the Japanese general had any constitutional rights at all. His conviction, said Stone, was subject to review only by higher military authority; he had no standing whatever in the civil courts under the Constitution. Justices Rutledge and Murphy dissented, arguing that the guarantees of the Constitution applied whenever and wherever the authority of the United States was exercised. This decision, which was consistent with past American practice, made possible subsequent trials of enemy military and political personnel by summary military procedure and without the interference of American civil courts.

The Cramer and Haupt Treason Cases: What Is an Overt Act?

An interesting sequel to the saboteurs' case was a pair of treason trials which gave the Supreme Court its first opportunity in history to expound the meaning of Article III, Section 3, of the Constitution, which defines the offense of treason against the United States. The critical question in both cases was the meaning of the phrase "overt act" as set forth in the Constitution.[4] In the first case, the Court defined the meaning of "overt act" so narrowly as to make convictions for treason extremely difficult if not impossible except where the defendant formally enlisted himself in the service of an enemy power. In the second case, however, the Court substantially modified its stand.

The first case, *Cramer* v. *United States* (1945), came to the Court on appeal from the conviction of a naturalized American citizen of German background who had befriended two of the Nazi saboteurs during the brief time they had remained at large in New York City. Cramer had voluntarily met with the saboteurs, had eaten with them and had conversed with them at some length. The prosecution had argued that these activities constituted overt acts within the meaning of the constitutional requirement, and that the testimony of the FBI agents met the constitutional requirement that there be two witnesses to the acts in question. The trial judge had adhered to this interpretation in his charge to the jury, which had accordingly returned a verdict of "guilty."

By a vote of 5 to 4 the Supreme Court reversed the conviction and set Cramer free. The critical legal issue, Justice Jackson's majority opinion made clear, was whether the Constitution required that the overt act in question must manifest virtually on its face an obvious intent to commit treason or whether the treasonous character of an act innocent in itself might be demonstrated by surrounding testimony and evidence. Jackson

4. Article III, Section 3, provides that "no person shall be convicted of Treason unless on the Testimony of two Witnesses to the same overt Act, or on Confession in open Court."

adopted the first point of view almost unconditionally. While he admitted that an overt act might in itself be innocent and gain its traitorous character from the intent involved, he held that the evidence of two or more witnesses to the act in question must establish its traitorous intent beyond a reasonable doubt.

The majority justices in the *Cramer* case were undoubtedly motivated by a high-minded conviction that in a constitutional democracy the offense of treason ought to be defined as narrowly as possible. The difficulty with the Court's position, as Justice Douglas pointed out for the minority, was that it made subsequent convictions for treason all but impossible, primarily because it was now necessary to establish the intent of the overt act itself through the testimony of two witnesses. This requirement, Douglas contended, was at odds with both history and the intent of the framers of the Constitution.

However, in *Haupt* v. *United States* (1947), another case growing out of the saboteurs' activities, the Court modified substantially the force of its restrictive interpretation of what constituted an overt act. Hans Haupt, the father of one of the saboteurs, had given shelter to his son, attempted to secure him a job in a factory manufacturing the Norden bombsight, and helped him to purchase an automobile. On the strength of testimony by the required two witnesses to these acts, the trial court had convicted the elder Haupt of treason. As in Cramer's case, the overt acts in question were admittedly innocent in themselves. Indeed they conceivably could be interpreted as evidence of nothing more than the natural concern of a father for his son and not of intent to aid the enemy. The Court nonetheless voted 8 to 1 to sustain Haupt's conviction. Justice Jackson, who again wrote the majority opinion, argued that the present case differed fundamentally from Cramer's in that there could be no question that Haupt's acts were "helpful to an enemy agent" and had "the unmistakable quality which was found lacking in the Cramer case of forwarding the saboteur in his mission."

The Haupt conviction opened the way for a number of treason prosecutions of American nationals who had lent assistance to the Nazis or Japanese during the war. In several of these cases the defendant had committed his alleged act of treason while in the enemy country. For example, Douglas Chandler, an American "Lord Haw-Haw," was convicted of treason in 1948 on the strength of his Berlin radio broadcasts for Germany during the war. This raised the interesting question of whether an American could commit treason while in a foreign country, or whether on the contrary treason, like most other felonies, had territorial limits and must be committed within the jurisdiction of the United States. In *Kawakita* v. *United States* (1952) the Court put this question to rest, ruling that treason was an offense without territorial limits and might be committed by an American national while in a foreign country.

Other Wartime Civil Liberties Issues: Denaturalization and Espionage Cases

It is notable that during World War II, in spite of the disgraceful treatment of the Japanese minority, the political atmosphere in the country was far more open and free from repression than it had been during World War I. There was no counterpart in 1941–45 to the semihysterical suppression of German culture which had occurred in 1917. The Supreme Court both reflected and contributed to this libertarian spirit. Thus in *Schneiderman* v. *United States* (1943) the Court reversed, 6 to 3, a lower federal court decision revoking a certificate of naturalization obtained by a petitioner who at the time of his original naturalization proceedings had been a member of the Communist party. The government had argued that party membership was decisive evidence that petitioner had not been "attached to the principles of the Constitution and well disposed to the good order and happiness of the United States," as the law required. His certificate of naturalization hence had been fraudulently obtained.

Murphy's opinion rejected this argument. He first declared firmly that while naturalization admittedly was a privilege controlled by Congress and not a constitutional right, the Court would refuse to construe "general phrases" in the naturalization statutes in such a way as to "circumscribe liberty of political thought." Communist party membership, he pointed out, had not been illegal as of 1927. Moreover, an examination of the principles of the Communist party led him to the conclusion that membership in that organization was "not absolutely incompatible" with loyalty to the Constitution. Hence, he concluded, the government had not rested its case upon the "clear, unequivocal, and convincing evidence" which successful denaturalization proceedings properly required. Chief Justice Stone, whom Frankfurter and Jackson joined in dissent, protested that membership in the Communist party, contrary to Murphy's conclusion, was in fact "utterly incompatible" with loyalty to the Constitution.

A year later, in *Baumgartner* v. *United States* (1944), the Court again reversed a denaturalization finding, aimed this time at a professed Nazi sympathizer. Frankfurter's opinion drew back slightly from the "clear, unequivocal, and convincing" formula Murphy had invoked in the the *Schneiderman* case. The evidence in a denaturalization proceeding, he held, must be "clear and unequivocal" and of such a character as to "leave no troubling doubt in deciding a question of such gravity."

In *Hartzel* v. *United States* (1944) the majority justices applied the *Schneiderman* formula to reverse a conviction under Section 3 of the Espionage Act of 1917, which made punishable wartime attempts to cause insubordination, disloyalty, mutiny or refusal of duty in the armed forces, or willfully to obstruct the recruiting or enlistment services of the United States. The petitioner had circulated articles vilifying Jews, the English, and the president of the United States and had in effect called for both an alliance with Germany and conversion of the war into a racial conflict. Recipients had included high military personnel. But Murphy's opinion held that the government had not succeeded in estabishing by "clear, convincing, and unequivocal evidence" the petitioner's intent to violate the law. Since intent was an essential ingredient in the statute, the conviction must be overturned. Reed, dissenting along with Frankfurter, Douglas, and Jackson, protested that it had been altogether reasonable for the trial jury to conclude from the evidence that the petitioner's purpose had been "to undermine the will of our soldiers to fight the enemy."

The Significance of World War II for Constitutional Government

It is evident that American constitutional government met the challenge of total war between 1941 and 1945 as it had in 1861 and 1917. There was, in fact, a striking similarity between the nature of the constitutional problems that arose in all three eras. In each instance the war crisis exposed something of the inconsistency between the nature of constitutional government and the requirements of national security and military policy. In each instance the executive solved the problem of the effective conduct of the war by establishing a kind of quasi-constitutional dictatorship, erected in part on a statutory basis and in part merely on the presidential prerogative as commander in chief in wartime. In each instance, also, there was some interference with civil liberties in the name of the larger war effort. In World War II, however, this interference was limited largely to forced segregation of the Japanese minority and the imposition of military government on Hawaii.

Most important, the spirit of constitutional government survived the exigencies of war. Once more the remarkable flexibility of the American constitutional system had been demonstrated; it could adjust rapidly to the requirements of war and then return as rapidly to the institutions of peace. As the United States entered upon a new postwar era, however, an even more difficult test of constitutional government emerged. The Constitution had met the test of total war; could it also meet the test of survival in a world that lived in a perpetual state of international crisis and half war lasting not for two or four years but for decades and perhaps generations? Not long after 1945 this appeared to be the gravest constitutional question of the twentieth century.

TWENTY-EIGHT

The Constitution and the Cold War: Collective Security and Individual Rights

———— ✦✦✦ ————

THE CONTINUING CONFLICT between the United States and the Soviet Union known as the cold war began after World War II. Immediately after the Allied victory the United States demobilized. In 1948, however, spurred by Soviet expansion into eastern Europe, the United States rebuilt its military establishment and returned virtually to a wartime economy. The Soviet Union did likewise, and both countries, despite being members of the United Nations collective security organization, proceeded to create elaborate systems of military alliances.

The pressures generated by the cold war were responsible in considerable part for a series of internal constitutional problems, many of them fraught with grave implications for American constitutionalism. Principal among them was the growth of presidential power, an inevitable consequence of the fact that for a decade or more the United States lived in an almost continuous state of proclaimed national emergency. The impact of collective security agreements on the federal system was a second issue of great moment, while a third concerned the conflict between internal security measures and constitutionally protected civil liberties.

American membership in the United Nations and the new alliances affected the constitutional balance of power between the president and Congress. American consent to participation in the application of military sanctions against an aggressor state was at the discretion of the United States delegate to the Security Council, who in turn was under the control of the president and the secretary of state. Technically, a U.N. "police action" would not be war, but it was probable that in practice this would prove to be a distinction without a difference.

Congress itself presently recognized the practical force of this situation with the passage of the United Nations Participation Act of 1945. Section 6 of this law authorized the president to negotiate military agreements with the Security Council to earmark American military contingents for the council, subject to congressional approval of the agreements negotiated. The act further provided that the president "shall not be deemed to require the authorization of Congress" to make such forces available to the council in any specific collective security action. In short, Congress here recognized that the President could now commit the United States to a venture in military sanctions under the Charter without congressional consent. Technically, agreements of the kind provided for in the act were not subsequently negotiated. In fact, this mattered little, as the Korean war presently demonstrated.

Similarly, the North Atlantic Treaty of 1949 stipulated that in the event of an attack against any signatory state, each of the NATO countries was to lend assistance "by taking such action as it deems necessary, including the use of armed force, to restore and maintain the security of the Atlantic area." Although this provision was carefully drafted to avoid any specific obligation on the part of the United States to go to war, it was obvious that the president might deploy American armed forces in such a fashion as virtually to commit the country to war. Senate rejection of a proposal requiring congressional approval of NATO military assistance was evidence that lawmakers understood and endorsed this enlargement of executive power.

The Korean war provided a dramatic illustration of the president's war-making powers under collective security. Following the attack by North Korea on the South Korean Republic, the Security Council on June 25, 1950, adopted a resolution calling upon the North Korean forces to withdraw and asking United Nations member-states to "render every assistance in the execution of this resolution." On June 27, President Truman announced that in accordance with the council's request he had ordered American military forces into the fighting in Korea. The president took this action in spite of the fact that the United States had never signed any specific agreement with the United Nations assigning American forces to the council for police purposes.

Thus presidential discretion alone took the United States into a large-scale *de facto* war. Technically, the Korean "police action" was not war in a formal constitutional sense, for war was never declared by Congress. However, Congress was perforce constrained to underwrite the president's policy, which it did through the passage of comprehensive war legislation and military appropriations for the war's prosecution. The Korean "police action" ultimately proved to be the fourth largest war up to that time in American history; it cost some 30,000 lives and scores of billions of dollars and placed the nation on a partial war footing for some three years.

The events of the next two decades did little to weaken the executive prerogative in war making. In 1951 President Truman's decision to send four divisions to Germany in support of the NATO treaty touched off a debate in which constitutional conservatives charged the executive with usurpation of power, and the president defended his power to move troops anywhere without the consent of Congress. At most he conceded that he might on occasion consult with individual members of the two houses as a "practical matter." Passage of a weak Senate resolution approving the president's move and expressing the wish that in the future he obtain congressional approval of troop movements abroad ended the debate and marked a victory for the executive branch.

To all intents and purposes the issues surrounding the question of presidential war-making prerogative now were very nearly settled. President Eisenhower, notably careful in his recognition of congressional war-making prerogative, in 1955 obtained the support of a joint resolution of Congress authorizing him to use armed force to defend the offshore Nationalist Chinese Islands, should he see fit to do so. But when in 1958 Eisenhower, confronted with a sudden crisis in the Middle East, abruptly moved troops into Lebanon, his action caused scarcely a ripple in Congress. In 1962 President Kennedy took the same step without serious congressional objection, both in Thailand and in Vietnam. And in October of that year, in response to the Soviet emplacement of missiles in Cuba, Kennedy upon his own authority proclaimed a naval "quarantine" of Cuba, a move that lacked the formal character of an act of war under international law only because he avoided use of the word "blockade." In short, presidential control of the war power now appeared to have become primary and that of Congress secondary, and there appeared to be very little that aroused senators, the Court, or anyone else could do about it. The massive presidential military intervention that took place in Vietnam after 1964 heavily reinforced this conclusion.

The Continued Exercise of Federal War Powers

Hostilities in World War II had ended in August 1945, but the speedy development of the cold war, the consequent delay in the negotiation of peace treaties with Germany and Japan, and the onset of the Korean war kept the United States technically at war for the next several years and resulted in maintaining indefinitely large portions of the wartime emergency government. On December 31, 1946, the president issued a proclamation officially terminating hostilities, and in July 1947, Congress enacted a joint resolution which repealed a great variety of wartime statutes and set termination dates upon others. However, some 103 wartime statutory provisions still remained active. And in signing the joint resolution the president noted that the emergencies declared in 1939 and 1941 continued to exist and that it was "not possible at this time to provide for terminating all war and emergency powers."

Thereafter, Congress, the president, and the courts continued to assume the existence of a state of wartime emergency. In June 1947, Congress enacted a new Housing and Rent Act which continued the rent-control system established in the Emergency Price Control Act of 1942. A new Rent Control Act passed in 1949 continued rent controls in defense areas but provided for decontrol at the option of state and local governments. In 1948, Congress enacted a new Selective Service Law; thereby it put the draft on a regular "peacetime" basis, although there was no imminent prospect of hostilities, as had been the case in 1940. And with the outbreak of the Korean war, Congress in 1950 passed the Defense Production Act, which established once more general presidential control over the economy for war purposes. A new executive proclamation of war emergency followed in December. Thereafter, the president by executive order created the Office of Defense Mobilization and the Office of Price Stabilization for executive regulation of the war economy.

The dangers for constitutional government in all this were evident enough. If the state of emergency became a permanent affair the constitutional barriers upon the scope of peacetime federal power and upon the executive power of the president in time might crumble away.

The Steel Seizure Case: A Check to Presidential Emergency Power

After upholding presidential power with certain misgivings in a few cases involving the Housing and Rent Act of 1947 and the deportation of aliens, the Supreme Court met President Truman's seizure of the steel industry in 1952 with a full-scale condemnation of emergency government. The Steel Seizure Case grew out of President Truman's efforts to avert a long-threatened strike which promised to have a catastrophic effect on the prosecution of the Korean war. Efforts at compromise through the Wage Stabilization Board ended in failure, and early in April 1952 the United Steel Workers of America called a nationwide strike to begin on April 9.

On the eve of the walkout, the president issued an executive order to Secretary of Commerce Charles Sawyer, instructing him to take possession of the steel mills and operate them in the name of the United States government. The order cited the national emergency proclaimed on December 16, 1950, and the necessity of maintaining uninterrupted steel production for the Korean war and the atomic energy program. The president issued the order by virtue of his authority "under the Constitution and laws of the United States" and as commander in chief, but did not cite any specific statutory authority. Secretary Sawyer immediately issued a seizure order to the companies. The president reported the seizure to Congress in a special message in which he invited legislative action should that body think it necessary. However, Congress took no action, although a great many members subjected the president's seizure to severe criticism.

From a constitutional point of view, the most extraordinary fact about the seizure order was its total lack of statutory authority. The Selective Service Act of 1948 and the Defense Production Act of 1950 both authorized the seizure of industrial plants which failed to give priority to defense orders, but neither mentioned seizure to resolve labor disputes. Moreover, Congress in enacting the Taft-Hartley Act in 1947 had considered and rejected just such a proposal, and had instead incorporated in the law a provision permitting the president to obtain an injunction postponing for eighty days any strike threatening the national welfare. However, President Truman had chosen to ignore this procedure, in part because the strike already had been delayed more than eighty days by the Wage Stabilization Board, and had instead fallen back upon his general executive prerogative. In short, here was an assertion of executive prerogative power rivaling those of Lincoln, Wilson, and Franklin Roosevelt.

The steel companies immediately attacked the constitutionality of the seizure in the federal courts. Judge Pine of the United States District Court for the District of Columbia presently issued a preliminary injunction restraining the secretary of commerce from continuing in possession of the mills. The District of Columbia Court of Appeals thereafter stayed the injunction; further legal maneuvering brought the case to the Supreme Court.

By a 6-to-3 vote the Court in *Youngstown Sheet and Tube Co.* v. *Sawyer* (1952) held that the president's steel seizure was an unconstitutional usurpation of legislative power. Justice Black's brief and rather summary majority opinion avoided the more complex constitutional aspects of the case and rested instead squarely upon the separation of powers and a summary rejection of the theory of executive prerogative. After observing that there was "no statute that expressly authorizes the President to take possession of property as he did here," Black rejected in succession the propositions that the president's powers as commander in chief authorized the seizure or that some inherent executive prerogative flowing from the Constitution itself supplied the necessary authority. Although the president's order "resembled a statute in form" it was nonetheless invalid, for the Constitution limited the president's role in lawmaking "to the recommending of laws he thinks wise and the vetoing of laws he thinks bad." The seizure, it followed, was unconstitutional and void. Significantly, Black avoided any discussion whatever of expanded executive prerogative in times of emergency.

There were lengthy concurring opinions by the other five majority justices. Frankfurter placed special weight upon the fact that the president had ignored "the clear will of Congress" on plant seizures as expressed in

the Taft-Hartley Act. He did not totally reject the notion of executive prerogative, but he thought the history of plant seizures during World War I
and World War II showed no such sweeping pretensions to emergency
prerogative power as did the present action. Douglas, like Black, was
shocked by "the legislative nature of the action taken by the President."
Jackson, on the other hand, attempted to distinguish three circumstances of
executive prerogative: first, when the president acted in pursuance of a
specific statute or constitutional provision; second, when he acted in the
absence "either of a congressional grant or denial of authority," and third,
when he took "measures incompatible with the expressed or implied will of
Congress." In the last instance, he thought, presidential prerogative power
was at its lowest ebb. Burton, like Frankfurter, found decisive the president's violation of the strike settlement procedures set forth in the Taft-
Hartley Act. Clark alone of all the majority specifically subscribed to the
theory of an expanded executive prerogative "in times of grave and imperative national emergency." Such a grant, he thought, "may well be necessary to the very existence of the Constitution itself." Nonetheless, the president's violation of the procedures for strike settlement laid down by law
obliged him to agree that the present seizure was unconstitutional.

Chief Justice Vinson wrote a lengthy and spirited dissent, in which
Reed and Minton joined. The main weight of his argument was that in a
grave national crisis the president must necessarily exercise a very large
degree of discretionary prerogative power. "Those who suggest that this is a
case involving extraordinary powers should be mindful that these are extraordinary times." He made much of the fact that the president's seizure in
a general way had been in support of declared congressional policy as set
forth in the Mutual Security Program and appropriations for the Korean
war. He offered a very broad construction of the provision in Article II of
the Constitution that the president "shall take care that the laws be faithfully executed." He cited Lincoln's extraordinary actions at the outbreak of
the Civil War, Cleveland's use of the army to protect the mails and interstate commerce, Wilson's creation of wartime agencies without statutory
authority, and Franklin Roosevelt's seizure of the North American plant
before Pearl Harbor, again without statutory authority. He concluded that
President Truman's seizure of the steel industry was altogether within this
tradition.

After twenty years of dramatic expansion of executive power, the Supreme Court's willingness to say no to the president, even more than the
doctrines of constitutional law that it expounded, stood as the chief constitutional significance of the Steel Seizure Case. Plainly the justices did not
agree that a real emergency existed, a judgment corroborated by contemporary reports that the nation's steel supplies were adequate. Doctrinally,
the restrictions imposed on executive power were harder to evaluate. Further national crises requiring emergency presidential action could be ex-

pected to occur, and seven of the nine justices accepted the idea of an inherent, discretionary executive power. Nevertheless there was enormous constitutional value in the Court's reiteration of the fundamental principle that the president is not above the law.

The United Nations and Federal-State Relations

A constitutional issue that commanded considerable public attention in the postwar era was that arising out of the potential impact of the United Nations Charter and the U.N. Covenant on Human Rights upon federal-state relations. The problem first attracted notice when Justices Black, Murphy, Douglas, and Rutledge, in a concurring opinion, argued that a California law denying aliens ineligible to become citizens the right to own land was void because it conflicted with Article 55 of the United Nations Charter. Under Article 55 the United States pledged itself to "promote ... universal respect for, and observance of, human rights and fundamental freedoms for all without distinction as to race, sex, language, or religion."[1] Subsequently, a California court ruled the law invalid on this ground. Over the next few years discussion ensued over whether the U.N. Charter was a self-executing treaty and capable, as the supreme law of the land, of setting aside state and federal statutes in areas of civil rights and vested interests. One view held the Charter to be a vague declaration of national intent, effective as internal law only to the extent that Congress implemented it by statute. Others insisted it was indeed a self-executing treaty and supreme law. The International Covenant on Human Rights, then in process of preparation, raised the same question. This document would have bound signatory states to an elaborate series of legal guarantees of the kind found in the first eight amendments to the Constitution and in the various state bills of rights.

In response to widespread agitation, Senator John Bricker of Ohio in 1952 introduced a constitutional amendment to limit the scope of the federal treaty power. The Bricker amendment read as follows:

Section 1. A provision of a treaty which conflicts with this Constitution shall not be of any force and effect.
Section 2. A treaty shall become effective as internal law only through legislation which would be valid in the absence of a treaty.
Section 3. Congress shall have the power to regulate all Executive and other agreements with any foreign power or international organization. All such agreements shall be subject to the limitations imposed on treaties by this article.

Thus Senator Bricker and his supporters sought to negate the possibil-

1. *Oyama* v. *California* (1948).

ity, implicit in the Supreme Court opinion in *Missouri* v. *Holland* (1920), that a treaty could enlarge federal power at the expense of the states, and equally that a treaty might be internally self-enforcing without the consent of Congress.[2] The provision seeking to bring executive agreements under congressional control was an afterthought, growing out of the partisan controversy then being pursued over the late President Franklin Roosevelt's extensive resort to this device in his conduct of foreign relations. Opponents of the Bricker admendment asserted that it constituted a very serious assault upon both the doctrine of national ascendancy and upon executive control of foreign relations. They centered their fire on the so-called "which clause" in Section 2, stipulating that treaties were to become effective as internal law only through legislation which would be valid in the absence of a treaty. This language, they pointed out, constituted a serious impairment of the treaty provision in Article VI, Section 2, of the Constitution, which had been written specifically to enable the national government to make treaties upon matters that ordinarily lay within the province of the states. As for the provision calling for congressional regulation of executive agreements, critics added, it would not even have reached such arrangements as those entered into at Cairo, Yalta, and Potsdam, which had been negotiated under the president's powers as commander in chief rather than by virtue of his prerogative in foreign affairs. But the greatest concern expressed by the Bricker amendment's opponents was that if adopted, it would interfere with the president's conduct of foreign affairs so decisively as to make an effective foreign policy impossible.

Although at one point it appeared that Bricker had the votes needed to pass the amendment, this support dwindled when President Eisenhower and Secretary of State Dulles announced their opposition to the proposal. In February 1954 the Senate voted 60 to 31, one vote short of the required two-thirds constitutional majority, for a modified version of the Bricker amendment that omitted the "which clause" and toned down somewhat the language on executive agreements. With this defeat the amendment rapidly lost its political force, and by the late 1950s it had become a dead issue.

---

2. *Missouri* v. *Holland* involved the validity of the Migratory Bird Act of 1918, enacted in pursuance of a treaty between Great Britain and the United States which established closed seasons on several species of birds migrating annually between Canada and the United States. Missouri attacked the statute as an unconstitutional invasion of the powers of the states, and argued that a treaty could not convey powers to the national government that it did not already possess by virtue of the powers of Congress. Rejecting the argument, Justice Holmes for the Supreme Court said the treaty power was broader than the enumerated powers of Congress. "Acts of Congress are the supreme law of the land only when made in pursuance of the Constitution," he observed, "while treaties are declared to be so when made under the authority of the United States." The implication of the decision was that a treaty could accomplish anything of a national character so long as its subject matter were plausibly related to the general welfare.

Internal Security and Civil Liberties

By far the most politically explosive constitutional issue arising out of the cold war was the clash between internal security requirements and civil liberties guarantees. That an internal security problem existed was owing not simply to Soviet-American hostility, but to the nature of the Communist party of the USA as a conspiratorial organization committed to and controlled by the USSR. Communist activity in the United States took two forms: underground espionage work carried on directly with the Soviet apparatus, and open advocacy of political causes through the CPUSA. In the 1930s and 1940s a small number of Communists acting in the former capacity held positions in the federal government. The discovery after World War II of several Soviet spies in England, Canada, and the United States stunned the American people into awareness of the possibility of domestic espionage and signified the existence of a Communist problem. Subsequently, the Soviet domination of eastern Europe, the outbreak of the Korean war, the Communist revolution in China, and the Soviet acquisition of an atomic capability produced a crisis in American foreign policy. Out of this crisis came a powerful anti-Communist movement in domestic politics.

For several years a bitter debate raged over policy to be adopted toward the Communist party in particular and toward totalitarian political groups in general. Civil libertarians held that any individual or group had a constitutional right to the guarantees of the First Amendment and the Bill of Rights, no matter how outrageous, unorthodox, or revolutionary its point of view and purpose. In essence the libertarian argument rested on Holmes's marketplace-of-ideas metaphor and his contention that all ideas—even the most odious which we believe to be utterly wrong—should be protected and given a chance of acceptance by public opinion. Libertarians regarded free speech and other civil liberties as the essence of the American democratic ideal, to be maintained as ends in themselves, if not quite as absolutes. Only if speech, writing, or political action created a clear and present danger of imminent physical harm to the government or society could the government legitimately suppress it. Contending that the Communist problem, if it existed at all, was wildly exaggerated, libertarian critics charged that the real purpose of internal security programs was not to find Communists, but to harrass and suppress liberal and radical opinion in the United States.

Conservatives, anti-Communist liberals, and probably a majority of the American people held that the proper policy toward subversive totalitarian organizations such as the Communist party was to deny them a constitutional right to civil liberties, while tolerating their overt political activity on a prudential basis as circumstances permitted. Denying that all political ideas were equally deserving of protection, proponents of this view reasoned that some political purposes—subversion of constitutional government, for example—ought not to be accorded the legitimacy that recognition of a constitutional right to promulgate them would imply. Supporters of internal security measures made a distinction, moreover, between the expression of ideas through speech and writing, and expression through other means including political association and action. The former ought to be permitted without hindrance, they argued, while the latter might be restricted, depending on the purpose of the political association, its size and strength, and its method of operation. Advocates of internal security measures said that in the case of the Communists it was not their ideas that needed guarding against, but their conspiratorial tactics. The nature of Communist tactics made the small size of the Communist party in the United States—fewer than 54,000 in 1954—more or less irrelevant. Finally, the clear-and-present-danger doctrine was pertinent to the internal security question as a test to determine when the actions of a political association, short of the actual application of force and violence, warranted restriction.

American national policy on the Communist problem throughout the most intense period of the cold war in the late 1940s and 1950s was a compromise between these two positions. At first Communists or suspected Communists were ostracized and restricted, the restriction being based on the clear-and-present-danger doctrine as expounded by the Supreme Court in the *Dennis* case. At the same time some procedural safeguards were extended to Communists on an expedient basis. Subsequently, as anti-Communist fears waned in the later 1950s, Communists were recognized as having constitutionally protected rights like any other dissident group.

Internal security concerns first assumed legislative form during World War II. In the Hatch Act of 1939 Congress prohibited federal employee membership in organizations advocating the overthrow of the government. A more far-reaching measure was the Alien Registration Act, known as the Smith Act, adopted by Congress in 1940. The most significant part of the law was the "advocacy" section. This made it unlawful to "advocate, abet, advise, or teach . . . overthrowing any government of the United States by force or violence," forbade publication of printed matter "advising or teaching" such overthrow, prohibited the organization of groups so to teach or to advocate, and forbade conspiracy to commit any of the foregoing acts. Another provision, the so-called "membership clause," forbade "knowing" membership in any group advocating forcible overthrow of the government. The act did not mention the Communist party as such, but it was obvious that the measure had been inspired principally by alarm at Communist activities. For a number of years the act was little used, although the government in 1941 procured the conviction under the law of several obscure Minneapolis Trotskyites. In 1943 the government resorted to the act in an indictment and unsuccessful prosecution in a mass trial of some twenty-eight American Fascists.

The Federal Loyalty Program

Although antisubversive legislation such as the famous McCarran Act attracted the greatest amount of public attention at the height of the cold war, the importance of such legislation was more symbolic than practical. In actual impact the mainstay of the government's internal security policy was the federal employees loyalty program established by President Truman in 1947. Internal security had first become a serious concern of the federal government in 1940, at which time President Roosevelt instituted a limited loyalty review process through a series of executive orders. In 1943 Roosevelt created an Interdepartmental Committee on Loyalty Investigations that handled federal loyalty checks for the next several years. In the immediate postwar period the *Amerasia* scandal threw serious doubts on the loyalty of several federal officials, and the discovery of a widespread Communist spy network in North America suddenly made "Communists in government" an important issue in American politics.

Accordingly, in November 1946, President Truman established a Temporary Commission on Employee Loyalty to investigate the problem and to recommend more effective federal security measures. In March 1947, in accordance with the commission's findings, the president issued Executive Order 9835, setting up a comprehensive new federal loyalty program. The order directed the FBI to conduct loyalty checks of all federal employees and to forward any derogatory information to the loyalty boards herewith established in all principal federal bureaus. When any person was accused of disloyalty, the board in question was to conduct hearings to determine whether "reasonable grounds exist for belief that the person involved is disloyal to the United States." Membership in any organization designated by the attorney general as "totalitarian, Fascist, Communist, or subversive" was to be the principal ground for establishing such belief. An accused person was entitled to a hearing before his board, in which he might be represented by counsel, and to present counterevidence on his behalf. However, he could not examine the FBI files in question, nor was he entitled to learn the name of his accusers. He did have a right of appeal to his agency head and ultimately to a Loyalty Review Board, whose findings, although technically only advisory, were, in fact, final.

The Truman loyalty program was immediately put into general operation. Between 1947 and 1953 the loyalty of some 4,750,000 federal employees was scrutinized, some 26,000 "cases" created thereby being referred to various loyalty boards for further investigation. Of these, some 16,000 were ultimately given loyalty clearance, some 7,000 resigned or withdrew applications while under investigation, and 560 persons were actually removed or denied employment on loyalty charges. Meanwhile, several "sensitive" departments and agencies, among them the State, Defense, Army, Navy, Air Force, Commerce, and Justice Departments, the Economic Cooperation

Administration, the National Security Resources Board, and the Atomic Energy Commission, each developed its own programs under various special statutory authorizations, while the attorney general's office by 1953 had designated some 200 organizations as subversive.

Meanwhile spectacular revelations of Communist espionage within the government emerged from the trials of Alger Hiss and Julius and Ethel Rosenberg in 1949–50. Public opinion became alarmed, creating a situation in which the irresponsible anticommunism of Senator Joseph R. McCarthy of Wisconsin could become a dominant force in American politics. Thrown on the defensive, President Truman in April 1951 issued Executive Order 10241, inaugurating a new and more strenuous loyalty program. The new procedures provided that an employee could be discharged after a hearing that found that there was a "reasonable doubt as to the loyalty of the person involved to the Government of the United States." In other words, the government now did not have to prove disloyalty; it merely had to find "reasonable doubt" of an employee's loyalty, a far easier task. In the next two years 179 additional federal employees were discharged under the "reasonable doubt" formula.

In spite of these measures, the Republicans made communism in government a major issue in the 1952 election, and President Dwight D. Eisenhower came into office pledged to clean up the Communist "conspiracy" in Washington. On April 27, 1953, accordingly, Eisenhower promulgated Executive Order 10450, setting up still another executive loyalty program. The criterion for discharge after hearing now became simply a finding that the individual's employment "may not be clearly consistent with the interests of national security." Seven categories of "security criteria" were set up. These included sexual immorality and perversion; drug addiction; conspiracy or acts of sabotage, treason or unauthorized disclosure of classified information; and refusal to testify before authorized government bodies on grounds of possible self-incrimination. Obviously, these offenses involved much more than mere disloyalty or possible Communist affiliation; instead, they covered virtually every possible ground on which an employee might be released as unsatisfactory. In October 1954 the Eisenhower administration announced that there had been more than 8,000 security program releases under the president's order, but it soon became clear that only 315 persons had actually been discharged for loyalty reasons.

Both the Truman and Eisenhower loyalty programs provoked serious constitutional controversy. Critics charged that the programs violated procedural due process in that persons were too often discharged for "a state of mind" rather than for an overt act; that "evidence" of disloyalty often consisted of nothing more than "guilt by association"; that the accused was often the victim of "faceless informers" whom he could neither confront nor cross-examine; and that the programs in the large amounted to a form of virulent censorship seriously at odds with the First Amendment. They also argued that the attorney general's List of Subversive Organizations constituted virtually an executive bill of attainder.

Defenders of the loyalty program, insisting that it protected civil liberties, pointed out that by setting up a regular procedure with provision for appeal it improved on existing administrative law and practice. They also observed that the Supreme Court itself had repeatedly held that there was no constitutional right of federal employment and that the government had an undoubted right to assure itself of the loyalty of its public servants. Opponents of loyalty programs, they said, had confused the hearings with criminal proceedings, which they were not, for they made no finding of guilt and inflicted no punishment. Supporters of the loyalty program argued further that the FBI could not investigate disloyalty effectively if it were obliged to reveal its sources of information. And as for guilt by association, they said its use amounted to no more than recognition of the old adages that "birds of a feather flock together" and "a man is known by the company he keeps."

Congressional Investigations

Congressional investigations formed an even more controversial part of internal security policy during the cold war. As with the loyalty program, legislative concern with Communist subversion began several years earlier with the creation of the Dies Committee in 1938. Charged with investigating subversion and un-American propaganda in the United States, the committee acquired permanent standing as the House Un-American Activities Committee in 1945. In 1947 it won notoriety for its investigation of Communists in the film industry, and it played a major role in the early stages of the Hiss case in 1948. The Senate counterparts of the HUAC were the permanent Senate Investigating Subcommittee, created in 1946, and the Internal Security Subcommittee of the Judiciary Committee, appointed in 1950.

The chief purpose of congressional investigations has always been to assist in the formulation of legislation, but throughout its history the committees of Congress have frequently exceeded this purpose. Instead of or in addition to preparing legislation, they have used their fact-finding power to restrain executive authority, shape public opinion, and in general exert influence on the course of government policy. The internal security committees during the cold war were no exception to this pattern. Nor did they depart from the method of fact finding and publicity used by earlier committees to achieve substantive policy results. What made them so controversial was the vastly greater power of the instrument of publicity in an age of mass communication, the profound hostility generated in the debate on the Communist problem, and the ruthless and demagogic tactics of some congressional investigators.

Although some legislation was eventually proposed, the purpose of congressional internal security investigations was not primarily to draft legislation, but to expose, publicize, and destroy the Communist party and communism as an influence in American life. The House Committee on Un-American Activities acknowledged this purpose in 1948 when it said that its function was "to permit American public opinion ... an ... opportunity to render a continuing verdict on all of its public officials and to evaluate the merit of many in public life who either openly associate with and assist disloyal groups or covertly operate as members or fellow-travelers of such organizations." In the view of the committee and its defenders, this approach, which has been termed "prescriptive publicity," was justified by the conspiratorial, subversive nature of the Communist party. Without formally proscribing the party, congressional internal security committees sought to fix a rule of conformity—no membership in Communist organizations—that it would enforce through its legitimate fact-finding and publicity powers. The object was to invoke the sanction of public opinion against Communists, ostracizing and injuring them in a political and social sense.

While this approach effectively subjected communism to damaging vilification, it uncovered few actual Communists. Most Communists refused to cooperate with the committees. The method of prescriptive publicity also lent itself to serious abuse by conservative politicians eager to attack liberals, radicals, and reformers. Casting a wide net, the internal security committees injured many people innocent of any association with Communists, let alone guilty of membership in the Communist party or subversive activity. The committees harrassed witnesses, denied them the right to counsel, refused to let them examine evidence or cross-examine their accusers. Should a witness invoke the Fifth Amendment right against self-incrimination, he or she would frequently be dubbed a "Fifth Amendment Communist." Critics contended that the committees tried, convicted, and punished individuals with the practical effect of an official criminal verdict, yet without the procedural requirements of due process found in any court of law.

Defenders of the committees replied that they were not courts of law and were not, therefore, required to follow judicial due process. The limited amount of constitutional law dealing with congressional investigating powers tended to support the committee point of view in this controversy.[3]

---

3. In *Kilbourn* v. *Thompson* (1881) the Supreme Court held that the House of Representatives had exceeded its jurisdiction in investigating the losses suffered by the United States as a creditor of Jay Cooke and Company. In 1927, however, the Court approved in broad terms the power of investigation. In *McGrain* v. *Daugherty,* a case arising out of the scandals of the Harding administration, it stated that Congress has not only powers expressly delegated, but also "such auxiliary powers as are necessary and appropriate to make the express powers effective." The Court said there was no general power to inquire into private affairs, but "rightly applied," the rule about auxiliary powers permitted limited inquiry into and disclosure of private matters.

Nevertheless, criticism of internal security investigations in Congress raised the question of whether constitutional law should be changed to impose more stringent limits on the investigating power.

Internal Security Legislation

A third phase of the government's internal security program, made all but inevitable by the excited condition of public opinion after the start of the Korean war, was legislation directed against the Communist party. The first-explicitly anti-Communist measure had in fact been adopted in 1947, when Congress included in the Taft-Hartley amendments to the National Labor Relations Act a section requiring union officials to file affidavits disavowing membership in the Communist party. In 1948 the House of Representatives passed the Mundt-Nixon bill requiring the registration of the Communist party and Communist organizations. This proposal formed the basis of the Internal Security Act, popularly known as the McCarran Act, which Congress passed in September 1950.

The express purpose of the Internal Security Act was to force the Communist party to register with the government and submit to a rule of disclosure concerning its officers, membership, sources of financial support, and activities. The act first declared that there existed "a world Communist movement," the object of which was to establish "a Communist totalitarian dictatorship" throughout the world by deceit, infiltration, espionage, and terrorism. It stated further that "the Communist movement in the United States, . . . the recent success of Communist methods in other countries, and the nature and control of the world Communist movement itself, present a clear and present danger to the security of the United States and to the existence of free American institutions." In accordance with this finding, the law then provided for the registration of "Communist-action" and "Communist-front" organizations with a Subversive Activities Control Board. Should a suspected front organization fail to register, the attorney general was empowered to petition the board for a registration order, which could then hold hearings and issue such an order if it found that the group in question was indeed an "action" or "front" organization. Board orders, however, were subject to a right of appeal to the courts. Other provisions of the law made it illegal to conspire to establish a "totalitarian dictatorship" in the United States, imposed virtually prohibitive limitations upon the entry into the United States of aliens with Communist connections, and permitted the compulsory detention, after presidential proclamation of an "internal security emergency" and hearing and appeal, of any person who "probably will conspire with others to engage in acts of espionage and sabotage."

Coming as it did amid Senator McCarthy's reckless hunt for Communists in the government, the McCarran Act provoked bitter controversy. Its critics assailed it as an unconstitutional infringement of First Amendment rights. Vetoing the bill, President Truman said it was "the greatest danger of freedom of speech, press, and assembly since the Sedition Act of 1798." Significantly, Truman did not object to the registration requirement for the Communist party. He argued, however, that in providing for the designation of organizations that failed to register as Communist-front organizations, the act would allow organizations whose opinions happened to coincide with those of the Soviet Union to be officially condemned. The act, said Truman, attempted to restrict and punish "the simple expression of opinion." Libertarian critics also argued that by requiring Communists, or persons committed to the overthrow of the government, to register, the act opened them to prosecution under the provisions of the Smith Act that made it a crime to advocate the overthrow of the government. The act thus violated the Fifth Amendment privilege against self-incrimination.

The Internal Security Act did not outlaw the Communist party but rather, in a legal sense, assumed its continued existence and operation. In this respect it differed from the Smith Act, which by making teaching and advocacy of the overthrow of the government illegal presumably aimed at the dissolution of the party. In actual effect, of course, the sponsors of the McCarran Act intended to destroy the Communist party, on the theory that the First Amendment did not require the government to recognize as having constitutional rights groups professing the avowed purpose of overthrowing constitutional government. Revolutionary groups might be tolerated on an expedient basis, but they forfeited their right to constitutional guarantees by adopting subversive purposes. Nevertheless, although it imposed numerous disabilities on Communists, such as declaring them ineligible for employment in the government or in defense plants, the McCarran Act did not formally proscribe Communist organizations.

Defenders of the McCarran Act emphasized that the rule of disclosure now applied to Communist organizations had long been employed in American politics and in congressional legislation. In support of their position they pointed to the Supreme Court decision in *New York ex rel. Bryant v. Zimmerman* (1928), where the Court upheld a New York law requiring the registration of the Ku Klux Klan and disclosure of its membership and finances. Moreover, many civil libertarians had argued that disclosure rather than suppression was the preferable and constitutional method for dealing with the Communist problem. Supporters of the McCarran Act could, therefore, make a plausible case for its constitutionality. So far from denying Communists the freedom of speech and press with which to carry on their propaganda activity, asserted Republican Senator Karl Mundt, the act "simply forces them to do those things in the open, exactly as we require the Democratic and Republican parties to act in the open."

Passed by huge majorities over the president's veto, the McCarran Act was ineffectual in operation. The Subversive Activities Control Board in 1953 duly found that the Communist party was a Communist-action organization, but the party refused to register. A fifteen-year legal battle ensued which ended in the federal judiciary declaring the registration provisions of the law unconstitutional. Yet as the expression of a powerful national feeling of apprehension about the spread of communism, the act had symbolic importance. It reaffirmed the nation's political orthodoxy by attaching the stigma of moral and political illegitimacy to Communist organizations, while legally tolerating their existence.

Four years after passage of the McCarran Act a group of Senate liberals, apparently hoping to kill off campaign charges that their party was soft on communism, introduced a bill to make membership in the Communist party a crime. They contended that this approach to the Communist problem improved on the 1950 act by giving the task of determining membership in the Communist party to the courts, which would protect the civil liberties of accused persons. The Eisenhower administration strongly opposed the measure, however, largely because it feared that it would present individual Communists with a plausible pretext for not registering under the McCarran Act, on the ground that registration now would amount to self-incrimination in violation of the Fifth Amendment. Accordingly, the bill was amended to outlaw the Communist party but not to make party membership itself a crime. In this form the bill was enacted into law by an overwhelming vote of both houses.

The Communist Control Act of 1954, like the act of 1950, was premised on the idea that the Communist party, the agency of a hostile foreign power and the instrumentality of a conspiracy to overthrow the United States government, was "a clear and present danger to the security of the United States" and "should be outlawed." It proposed to accomplish this end by terminating whatever rights, privileges, and immunities had been granted to the party by any laws of the United States or the states. Although the act did not legally abolish the party and confiscate its property, as the laws of some other nations did at this time, it looked to the dissolution of the party. In this sense it resembled the Smith Act rather than the Internal Security Act of 1950. It enacted a partial proscription of the Communist party rather than rely simply on publicity and ostracism. Technically, the act raised First and Fifth Amendment questions, but these were never resolved because the measure was never implemented so as to present a test of the constitutional issues.

A fourth phase of the country's internal security policy was state loyalty programs. Such programs generally had as their starting point a loyalty oath whereby the government employee, under pain of discharge, was obliged formally to swear to a denial of membership in the Communist party and other subversive organizations, and to repudiate belief in any doctrine of the revolutionary overthrow of the government by force and violence. Quite generally, also, state loyalty programs provided for the discharge of employees who, as witnesses before legislative investigating committees, refused to answer questions about Communist party affiliation. Needless to say, such programs required the discharge of persons exposed as having Communist party or other affiliations.

The Judicial Reaction to Internal Security Policy

At each stage the internal security program raised vexing and important constitutional questions which lawmakers and executive officers in the first instance had to resolve. Conclusive judgment about the constitutionality of their actions and of the program, however, belonged to the Supreme Court. Generally the Court found internal security policy to be within the framework of existing constitutional law, especially in its earlier years. Yet certain aspects of the program violated national standards of due process, and in these matters the Court fashioned new doctrines of constitutional law. The effect was to constitutionalize legislative and administrative procedures that previously operated virtually without restraint and with adverse effect on civil liberties. A further effect was to recognize the constitutional rights of Communists, thus removing the stigma of illegitimacy that attached to the profession of Communist purpose in the early years of the cold war.

The country's postwar conservative mood combined with changing judicial personnel to produce a less libertarian-minded Supreme Court majority in the late 1940s and early 1950s. The intellectual leader of the Court was Felix Frankfurter. An ardent reformer in his earlier career as a Harvard Law School professor and adviser to FDR, Frankfurter now demonstrated an increasing respect for legislative discretion, state police power, and society's concern for stability, security, and continuity. Justice Jackson, formerly a staunch liberal, took on something of the same conservative shading, as did Justice Reed, who earlier had been a moderate New Dealer. Meanwhile, President Truman named Harold H. Burton, a former Republican senator from Ohio, as associate justice in 1945 and Fred M. Vinson, a conservative Democrat from Kentucky, as chief justice in 1946. In 1949 Truman appointed Tom Clark, a conservative Texas Democrat who had been attorney general since 1945, and Sherman Minton of Indiana, a former Democratic senator and a U.S. Circuit Court judge. When Vinson died in 1953 President Eisenhower appointed Earl Warren of California as chief justice. Warren later became a liberal activist judge, but at the time he was appointed he was regarded as a mildly liberal Republican who had been governor of California and vice-presidential candidate in 1948. John Marshall Harlan, grandson of the nineteenth-century associate justice of the same name, joined the Court in 1955 and became a distinguished proponent of judicial restraint. Eisenhower also appointed William J. Brennan, a moderate Democrat from New Jersey and a former state Supreme Court justice, in 1956. A year later he named Charles E. Whittaker, a moderate Republican from Missouri, as associate justice.

The Court approached internal security questions in an attitude of judicial restraint. This meant deferring to the legislative view of the reasonableness of public policy, refraining from judicial legislation, and avoiding, whenever possible, the holding of either state or federal legislation unconstitutional. The specific constitutional strategy most frequently employed by the Court at this time was the balancing test. Refusing to treat First Amendment liberties as having any absolute or near-absolute character, the majority balanced the liberty of the individual against the need of society for order, security, and stability. Justices Black and Douglas, on the other hand, now the dissenting minority, still adhered firmly to preferred-freedoms libertarianism. With respect to free speech cases in particular, the Court relied on the clear-and-present-danger doctrine, although there was little agreement as to its exact meaning.

The Court first dealt with the Communist problem in *American Communication Association* v. *Douds* (1950), a case arising out of the registration provisions of the Taft-Hartley Act. Under the act union officers were required to swear an affidavit that they were not members of the Communist party and did not believe in, nor were members of any organization that believed in, overthrow of the government by force or by any illegal or unconstitutional methods. The Communications union, which had a record of rather serious Communist infiltration, had refused to comply with this provision of the law. Instead, it attacked the law in the courts, claiming that it violated freedom of speech, assembly, and thought as guaranteed by the First Amendment.

The Supreme Court upheld the affidavit requirement as a constitutional exercise of the federal commerce power, used now to protect national security as it had been used in the New Deal to promote social reform. Chief Justice Vinson's majority opinion presented the case as one that required weighing the effects of the non-Communist oath on the exercise of First Amendment rights, against the congressional judgment that political strikes, which had frequently been caused by Communist-controlled unions, burdened interstate commerce. Vinson acknowledged that the affidavit discouraged the lawful exercise of political freedom inasmuch as unions would henceforth not elect Communists to leadership positions. For that reason the union argued that free speech was involved and that the clear-and-present-danger test should apply. Vinson said, however, that the restriction of political freedom was slight, and he denied that the requirement was in reality a restriction of speech. Congress did not fear, and, therefore, try to restrict, beliefs and their free expression—even Communist belief and expression; nor did it restrict conduct and actions—i.e., political strikes—that resulted from the assertion of political opinions in the marketplace of ideas. Rather, said Vinson, Congress prevented union leaders who were Communists from using their official position and power to achieve ends that it could rightfully prevent.

The Court was split in the *Douds* case, with Black in dissent objecting that the act violated the First Amendment, and Frankfurter and Jackson concurring but criticizing that portion of the affidavit that went beyond Communist party membership and was concerned with beliefs about unconstitutional methods of overthrowing the government. Significantly, however, all but Black agreed that Congress could exclude Communists from the federal labor-management regulatory structure. "I cannot believe," said Justice Jackson, "that Congress has less power to protect a labor union from Communist Party domination than it has from employer domination." There was significance, too, in the distinction Vinson drew between free speech, protected by the First Amendment, and freedom of political association, a form of action the purpose of which was a legitimate concern of Congress and which enjoyed less protection than speech and writing. Most civil libertarians rejected this distinction, regarding free speech and the right of political association as identical and constitutionally protected in equal measure.

The Dennis Case

Concerned more directly with the problem of totalitarian groups, and thus broader and more controversial in its implications, was *Dennis* v. *United States* (1951). In 1948 the Department of Justice moved against the leadership of the Communist party, procuring Smith Act indictments against twelve principal party officers. The indictments alleged a conspiracy to form groups advocating the overthrow of the government by force and violence, and to teach and advocate such ideas. The issue, in other words, was not revolutionary acts by the individual defendants, but the nature and tendency of the Communist party as a political association. In 1949, at a spectacular trial in New York that was thoroughly permeated with cold war political overtones, the Communist leaders were found guilty. The court of appeals sustained the conviction, and the case went to the Supreme Court. The high bench, too, affirmed the lower court judgment, upholding the constitutionality of the "advocacy" section of the Smith Act.

There were two approaches available to the Court for dealing with the *Dennis* case. One followed the precedent of *Gitlow* v. *New York* (1925), wherein the Court upheld, as a reasonable exercise of the police power, a criminal anarchy law that declared a certain category of speech—that advocating the overthrow of the government—constitutionally unprotected and "inherently unlawful." Under the *Gitlow* approach the question was not whether speech occurred in circumstances that created a clear and present danger, but whether it fell within a proscribed category. The second approach rejected the notion of proscribed categories and assumed the protected status of all speech, sanctioning restriction only when it occurred under conditions that created a clear and present danger of a substantive evil or was accompanied by unlawful acts of violence. In tone and attitude Chief Justice Vinson's majority opinion leaned toward the former approach. Yet so strong was the hold of the libertarian clear-and-present-danger doctrine on the judicial mind at this time that Vinson evidently felt obliged to employ it to give the decision legitimacy.

When an offense is specified by a statute in nonspeech terms, said Vinson, such as the Smith Act specifying the crime of conspiracy to form a subversive association, a conviction based on speech or writing as evidence of a violation is constitutional only if the speech creates a clear and present danger. Yet what does the clear-and-present-danger doctrine mean, Vinson asked with some perplexity? To some extent Vinson had explored this question in his *Douds* opinion. Suggesting that the doctrine, like any other constitutional provision, must be treated not as a rigid mathematical formula but must be understood in relation to its origin and line of growth as an organic, living institution, he there stated that it was intended to measure the substantiality, rather than the immediacy and certainty, of the evil in prospect.

In his *Dennis* opinion Vinson developed this idea further by reference to the appellate court opinion of Judge Learned Hand, who had also defined the clear-and-present-danger rule. In each case, Hand had said, "courts must ask whether the gravity of the 'evil,' discounted by its improbability, justifies such invasion of free speech as is necessary to avoid the danger." Vinson now employed this "sliding scale" conception of the clear-and-present-danger doctrine. The rule did not mean, Vinson reasoned, that before the government could suppress speech "it must wait until the putsch is about to be executed, the plans have been laid, and the signal is awaited." An attempt to overthrow the government by force, even if undertaken by so few as to make its failure certain, could be prevented. Quoting verbatim Hand's version of the clear-and-present-danger doctrine, he said courts must consider whether the seriousness of a potential evil, though relatively remote, did not justify suppressing speech that communicated the threat. He stated further that the Communist party, an apparatus designed to overthrow the government and ready to do so at the earliest opportunity, constituted under existing circumstances a clear and present danger. Therefore, the conspiracy to organize the party for the purpose of advocating overthrow of the government, though it included elements of speech, presented a danger sufficiently grave to warrant suppression.

In vigorous dissenting opinions Justices Black and Douglas called the Smith Act a "virulent form of prior censorship of speech and press" and unconstitutional on its face. Douglas did not deny that the nature of communism in world politics was pertinent in assessing the danger of the advocacy in question. But he thought the strength of the Communist party in the United States was a far more relevant question, and it was plain to him that as a political party the Communist party was of little consequence. There was simply no basis for concluding that the party presented the kind of instant threat that the clear-and-present-danger rule required in order to suppress speech. The party was not teaching terror or advocating sedition, which Douglas said under no conditions would receive First Amendment protection. It was merely organizing people to teach Marxism-Leninism. It was engaging in speech alone without any "overt acts."

Although many civil libertarians condemned the *Dennis* decision, in political effect it struck a compromise between the conservative and liberal approaches to the Communist problem. Conservatives, apparently reflecting public opinion, wanted to proscribe Communists without any recognition of their right to constitutional protection. Liberals would protect Communist speech and subject it to restraint only under circumstances in which it presented an imminent danger to national security. The Supreme Court's ruling satisfied the conservative demand that the Communist party be stopped, but it justified this result under the liberal clear-and-present-danger doctrine. After being employed in the preceding decade and a half to resolve a variety of conflicts between unpopular individuals and society, the clear-and-present-danger doctrine functioned in the *Dennis* case as it had originally been used in the *Schenck* decision: to uphold the government in a national security crisis.

In the next six years the Department of Justice procured Smith Act conspiracy indictments of some one hundred twenty-eight "second-string" Communist party officers. There were "little" Smith Act trials in Seattle, Detroit, Los Angeles, Pittsburgh, New York, Cleveland, Philadelphia, Baltimore, Honolulu, Denver, New Haven, and St. Louis. Nearly one hundred convictions resulted, the government obtaining guilty verdicts in practically every instance where the defendant had not already renounced party membership. The government also procured indictments of nine Communists under the membership clause of the Smith Act, and obtained convictions against five of them.

Judicial Approval of Internal Security Measures

In less politically freighted matters of internal security the Supreme Court accepted the government's policy, though not uncritically or without regard for libertarian standards. In *Bailey* v. *Richardson* (1951), for example, the Court by a 4–4 vote without opinion upheld a loyalty review board dismissal of an employee. In effect it confirmed the principle cited by the appeals court that there was no constitutional right to federal employment and that due process in removal was, therefore, not necessary. In *Joint*

Anti-Fascist Committee v. *McGrath* (1951), however, the Court imposed strictures on the government. The plaintiff organization had sued to remove its name from the attorney general's list of Subversive Organizations, and the Supreme Court sustained the plea on the ground that the attorney general had denied due process of law by designating the group subversive without a hearing where it could deny allegations against it.

In subsequent cases the Court found against the government on narrow technical grounds, without questioning the constitutionality of internal security measures. In *Peters* v. *Hobby* (1956), for example, it held that a medical school professor's discharge as a security risk was without authorization. In *Cole* v. *Young* (1956) it ruled the dismissal of a Food and Drug Administration official unlawful because the position he held was "nonsensitive." Similarly, in *Greene* v. *McElroy* (1959) the Court found that the denial of clearance that had caused an official of a private firm to lose his job lacked adequate statutory authority. Chief Justice Warren's opinion expressed open shock at the government's resort to "faceless informers," and observed sternly that the Court would be unwilling to accept a security program "which is in conflict with our long accepted notions of fair procedures" without explicit authority from either the president or Congress. Thereafter President Eisenhower issued an executive order setting up a new industrial security program with improved procedural safeguards, including hearings and the right of confrontation under all circumstances.

In the early 1950s the Court worked out a fairly consistent body of constitutional law with respect to state loyalty programs. Holding that there was no inherent right to state employment, it said states had a constitutional right, through oath, affidavit, and the like, to obtain adequate assurance that an employee was not engaged in subversive activity and did not subscribe to the overthrow of the federal or state government by force or violence. Only one constitutional limitation restricted such affidavits: they must require the disavowal only of knowing membership in subversive organizations, as contrasted with membership innocent of any understanding of subversive purpose. On occasion, also, the Court viewed with suspicion oaths requiring retroactive disavowal of subversive affiliations, although this was not enough to condemn a loyalty statute out of hand. In any event, the Court as a rule held discharges for refusal to testify as to party affiliation to be constitutional, if accompanied by adequate procedural safeguards.[4] Only when a statute imposed retroactive disavowal which at the same time failed to distinguish between innocent and knowing subversive membership did the justices unite to strike down the offensive enactment.[5]

---

4. *Cf. Gerende* v. *Election Board* (1951); *Garner* v. *Board of Public Works* (1951); *Adler* v. *Board of Education* (1952).
   5. *Cf. Wieman* v. *Updegraff* (1952).

Under Chief Justice Warren the Court for a number of years vacillated with respect to state loyalty programs. At first the liberals prevailed. Thus the Court invalidated the arbitrary discharge of a college professor who, in testifying before the Senate Internal Security Subcommittee, had invoked the Fifth Amendment in response to questions concerning former possible Communist party affiliations.[6] The Court also protected two lawyers with alleged Communist backgrounds against exclusion from the state bar.[7] These controversial decisions, which spurred legislation in Congress to deny the Court jurisdiction in cases of this kind, were followed by a series of conservative judgments affirming state dismissals of employees as consistent with the requirements of due process of law.[8]

The Triumph of Libertarianism in Internal Security Matters

In the liberal climate of the 1960s the Supreme Court rewrote constitutional law in the field of internal security from a staunchly libertarian perspective. A major influence on the Court was the fact that by the late 1950s anxiety about the Communist problem had abated among mainstream political groups. In the changing political atmosphere the resignations of Justices Frankfurter and Whittaker in 1962 removed from the Court two of the bloc of conservative justices who since 1958 had maintained a precarious ascendancy in the field of political dissidence. The appointment of Justices Goldberg (1962) and Fortas (1965) gave the libertarian bloc of Warren, Black, Douglas, and Brennan a decisive voice.

The first politically significant decision anticipating the ultimate libertarian triumph in internal security law occurred in the case of *Yates* v. *United States* in 1957. Without formally repudiating the "sliding scale" standard of the *Dennis* opinion or ruling the Smith Act unconstitutional, the Court overturned the conviction of several second-level Communists for conspiracy to advocate the overthrow of the government. Justice Harlan for the Court first held that the organization of subversive groups prohibited by the Smith Act referred to the original act of forming the group, not the continuous recruitment and proselytising of members. Because the three-year statute of limitations had elapsed in relation to the reorganization of the Communist party in 1945, the party leaders were immune from prosecution under the organization section of the Smith Act.

The crux of Harlan's opinion was his distinction between advocacy of subversive action and advocacy of doctrine. The trial court, he said, had

6. *Slochower* v. *Board of Education of the City of New York* (1956).
7. *Schware* v. *New Mexico Board of Bar Examiners* (1957); *Konigsberg* v. *California* (1957).
8. *Beilan* v. *Board of Education* (1958); *Lerner* v. *Casey* (1958); *Nelson and Globe* v. *City of Los Angeles* (1960).

improperly charged the jury by failing to point out that the Smith Act prohibited not advocacy of "a mere abstract doctrine of forcible overthrow," but "action to that end, by the use of language reasonably and ordinarily calculated to incite persons to such action." Asserting that the trial court in the *Dennis* case had attended to this distinction, Harlan concluded that the kind of advocacy for which the Communist leaders were indicted in *Yates* was "too remote from concrete action to be regarded as the kind of indoctrination preparatory to action which was condemned in Dennis." Accordingly, the Court cleared five of the defendants completely, holding the evidence in their cases insufficient for conviction, and remanded the cases of nine others for retrial.

The requirement of the *Yates* opinion that the government show a nexus of specific acts of advocacy of revolution brought an abrupt end to the main body of Smith Act prosecutions then under way. After some delay, the Department of Justice quashed the indictments against the nine Communists whose cases the Court had remanded for retrial, on the ground that it could not meet the new evidentiary requirements for conviction.

There remained the question of prosecution under the Smith Act provision forbidding "knowing" membership in a group advocating forcible overthrow of the government. In *Scales* v. *United States* (1961) the Court approved the membership clause of the Smith Act, although it attached to it the evidentiary requirements of the *Yates* opinion. It thereby made conviction by this route as unlikely as under the advocacy section. Harlan's opinion distinguished between "knowing" membership and mere passive membership in a subversive organization. To prove the former it was necessary to show an understanding of the group's revolutionary purposes and deliberate participation in activities directed toward that end. In the *Scales* case the evidence met that criterion. In a companion case, however, *Noto* v. *United States* (1961), the Court reversed a membership-clause conviction on the ground of insufficient evidence.

Meantime, in *Pennsylvania* v. *Nelson* (1956), the Court banned state prosecutions for sedition against the United States simply by ruling that Congress already had decisively pre-empted the field of sovereignty in question. The *Nelson* case involved an appeal from a conviction in the Pennsylvania courts of a leading Communist party member who had been indicted for conspiracy to overthrow the government of the United States by force and violence. Chief Justice Warren asserted that the Smith Act, McCarran Act, and Communist Control Act of 1954 established a scheme of federal regulation "so pervasive" as to make reasonable the inference that Congress had left no room for the states to supplement it.

Since forty-two states had laws on their books punishing sedition, criminal anarchism, or criminal syndicalism which would presumably be invalid, the Nelson decision aroused strong opposition. Twice in 1958 and 1959 the House of Representatives passed bills declaring that only if an act of Congress expressly said that it excluded the states could it be construed as doing so. The Senate, however, refused to act on the bill. Under the *Nelson* ruling the states were permitted to prosecute for sedition against themselves, but in *Dombrowski* v. *Pfister* (1965) the Supreme Court put such legislation under a further constitutional cloud when it ruled the Louisiana Subversive Activities Criminal Control Act unconstitutional for vagueness. Then in *Brandenburg* v. *Ohio* (1969), a case involving a member of the Ku Klux Klan, the Court voided the Ohio Criminal Syndicalism Act of 1919. "The constitutional guarantees of free speech," the Court said, "do not permit a state to proscribe advocacy of the use of force . . . except where such advocacy is directed to inciting or producing imminent lawless action." In so declaring, the Court specifically overruled *Whitney* v. *California* (1927), in which an almost identical state law had been found valid. These decisions left no room for prosecution under state versions of the Smith Act generally. Even "knowing" Communist party membership by this time was immune from prosecution, while "advocacy" now would have to be tied to immediate acts of revolution or criminal violence.

The Warren Court also rendered virtually unenforceable the registration provisions of the McCarran Act. The initial attempt of the Subversive Activities Control Board to get the Communist party to register failed when the Supreme Court in 1956 threw out the board's case against the party as tainted by the testimony of professional informers.[9] In 1961 the Court upheld a board registration order on the precedent of numerous federal statutes that required registration and disclosure of lobbyists, businessmen, and others.[10] When the Communist party refused to register, the SACB ordered several of its officers personally to do so. They refused also, and in *Albertson* v. *S.A.C.B.* (1965) the Court upheld their refusal. Registration, said the Court, would require them to give information that made them liable to prosecution under the Smith Act and was, therefore, self-incriminatory under the Fifth Amendment. In 1967 the United States Court of Appeals for the District of Columbia, reversing a criminal conviction of the Communist party for failing to register, held that the registration provision of the McCarran Act itself violated the Fifth Amendment right against self-incrimination. The McCarran Act having long since been all but formally repealed through judicial interpretation, the SACB was terminated in 1973 for lack of appropriations.

The Supreme Court also stopped the State Department from denying passports to Communists. In *Kent* v. *Dulles* (1958) the Court ruled that such a policy was an unconstitutional violation of the "right to travel" guaranteed by the Fifth Amendment. In 1961 the State Department renewed the ban under a section of the McCarran Act prohibiting Communists who

9. *Communist Party* v. *Subversive Activities Control Board* (1956).
10. *Communist Party* v. *Subversive Activities Control Board* (1961).

were under an order to register from applying for a passport. In *Aptheker* v. *Secretary of State* (1964) the Court declared the passport section of the McCarran Act unconstitutional on its face as a restriction of the Fifth Amendment right to travel.

One of the most significant constitutional results of the Supreme Court's libertarian attack on internal security policy was limitation of the congressional power of investigation. The process of restriction began in 1957 in *Watkins* v. *United States,* where the Court reversed the contempt conviction of a witness who invoked the First Amendment in refusing to answer questions of the House Committee on Un-American Activities. The resolution creating the committee and the committee's definition of the subject matter under investigation, declared Chief Justice Warren, suffered from the "vice of vagueness" and thus violated the due process clause of the Fifth Amendment. Moreover, Warren sternly admonished the committee that the congressional investigative power was not unlimited, that it was not a general authority to expose individuals' private affairs in a manner unrelated to a specific function of Congress, and that Congress was not a law-enforcement or adjudicative agency. At the same time, in *Sweezy* v. *New Hampshire* (1957), the Court held a state legislative investigation in violation of the plaintiff's First Amendment rights under the Fourteenth Amendment.

In the late 1950s and early 1960s the Court temporarily retreated from this position by sanctioning HUAC and state legislative investigations in a series of cases. Perhaps most notable was Justice Harlan's opinion upholding a contempt conviction in *Barenblatt* v. *United States* (1959), on the ground that the right of congressional inquiry touched upon the nation's "ultimate right of self-preservation itself." "The balance between the individual and the governmental interests here at stake," Harlan stated, "must here be struck in favor of the latter."[11]

Presently, however, the libertarian point of view prevailed. In *Russell* v. *United States* (1962) the Court reversed contempt convictions stemming from HUAC and Senate Internal Security Sub-Committee investigations because the indictments had not identified the subject under congressional subcommittee inquiry. *Gibson* v. *Florida Legislative Investigating Committee* (1963) saw the Court rule a state contempt conviction invalid on the ground that the committee failed to establish the "adequate foundation for inquiry" necessary before it could intrude on First Amendment rights. And in *Gojack* v. *United States* (1966) the Court found no HUAC resolution authorizing the subcommittee inquiry in question, nor any record defining the jurisdiction of the subcommittee. By the end of the 1960s, the Court's strictures against private exposure unrelated to legislative needs, against vague-

---

11. *Cf.* also *Wilkinson* v. *United States* (1961); *Braden* v. *United States* (1961); *Hutcheson* v. *United States* (1962).

ness of committee charge, upon the necessity of pertinency in a line of questioning, and in favor of First Amendment rights stood as the principal judicial guideposts in a strongly libertarian approach to legislative inquiries generally.

Libertarian views prevailed finally in conflicts over state loyalty oaths. As noted previously, the Court cautiously approved most of the loyalty programs it reviewed in the 1950s. Foreshadowing its attitude of unfavorable scrutiny was the case of *Cramp* v. *Board of Public Instruction of Orange County* (1961). Here the Court invalidated a Florida law requiring each state employee to subscribe to an oath that he had never lent "aid, support, advice, counsel, or influence to the Communist Party." Justice Stewart said the law forbade nothing specific, such as advocacy of party membership, and hence was "afflicted with the vice of unconstitutional vagueness." A few years later the Court struck down on the same ground Washington state loyalty statutes that obliged state employees to "promote respect for the flag and institutions" of the United States and required them to disavow being "a subversive person."[12] The Court also invalidated an Arizona law requiring an oath to support and defend the Constitution of the United States and the state.[13] Justice Douglas said the law was so broad and uncertain in application as to threaten the "freedom of association" protected by the First Amendment. Notable also was the Court's condemnation of New York laws that made seditious utterances, advocacy of the overthrow of the government, and membership in the Communist party grounds for dismissal from state employment.[14]

The Historical Significance of Libertarianism

Long before the legal conflicts over internal security had been finally resolved, the Communist problem had receded into political insignificance. With the rise of the new left movement and the anti-Vietnam protest of the 1960s, public opinion ceased to distinguish between constitutional-democratic and "un-American" political ideas, or to regard the refusal to sanction totalitarian philosophies as a matter of common sense. With this restraint removed the libertarian impulse of the Warren Court prevailed. The result was the writing into constitutional law of the idea, originally expressed in Holmes's *Gitlow* dissent, that all political opinions are equal and ought to be given equal protection of the law.

The Supreme Court's libertarian outlook was widely regarded in the media and in academic circles as evidence of a new maturity and sophisti-

12. *Baggett* v. *Bullitt* (1964).
13. *Elfbrandt* v. *Russell* (1966).
14. *Keyishian* v. *Board of Regents of the University of the State of New York* (1967).

cation on the part of the American people. No longer, it was said, did Americans harbor the irrational fear that equal recognition of Communist or other totalitarian ideas would have any practical effect on their political existence. For years the notion of un-American political ideas was treated in educated and intellectual circles as the last refuge of reactionaries unwilling to accept liberal social reforms and modern positive government. Now this view became the law of the land. It replaced the belief, rooted in the revolutionary origins of the United States, that republican institutions were so essential to the definition of American nationality that antirepublican ideas and purposes could legitimately be regarded as un-American and a threat to the nation.

In any event, although the Smith Act remained on the books, it was for all practical purposes unenforceable in relation to Communists or any other potentially subversive group. The McCarran Act, more of a symbolic measure to begin with, was, if possible, even more irrelevant. The states could not require disavowal of "knowing" Communist party membership, nor exclude persons from employment because of Communist party membership. First Amendment rights thus acquired an exceedingly broad scope. Indeed, they went so far beyond speech, writing, and assembly as to be transformed into a new right of political association that was subject to no restriction, and that carried with it a sanction that would have been incomprehensible to the American people as recently as World War II.

In 1974, for example, the Supreme Court held that the refusal of the Communist party of Indiana to file an affidavit that it did not advocate the overthrow of the government by force and violence was not a sufficient ground for the state to exclude it from the ballot.[15] A long line of precedents since the *Yates* decision protected advocacy of subversive doctrine in contrast to advocacy of action, but the decisive consideration, explained Justice Brennan, was the Communists' "First and Fourteenth Amendment rights to associate with others for the advancement of political beliefs and ideas." Critics of libertarian decisions feared less the strength of the Communist party as a subversive association than the indifference toward republican institutions signified by the recognition of the equal status—and presumably equal legitimacy and validity—of Communist ideas. Critics wondered whether measures such as the Indiana affidavit, though ineffective in persuading people with subversive intentions to give them up, did not serve the useful purpose of instructing and educating public opinion on the difference between republican and antirepublican political values and methods.

Libertarians on the other hand believed that a truly democratic government permitted the expression of any and all political ideas by individuals or associations irrespective of their size and strength. First Amendment speech, expression, and association could be suppressed only when they

15. *Communist Party of Indiana* v. *Whitcomb* (1974).

were translated into or became one with violence, force, and unlawful action. "The line between what is permissible and not subject to control, and what may be made impermissible and subject to regulation," said Justice Douglas in his concurring opinion in *Brandenburg*, "is the line between ideas and overt acts." Only "where speech is brigaded with action," Douglas asserted, could it be stopped. In this view organizing a political association, recruiting members, raising money, advocating certain principles, and so forth were not overt acts but simply forms of speech or expression.

The distance traveled on the libertarian road by the 1970s appeared clearly in Douglas's repudiation, in his *Brandenburg* opinion, of the clear-and-present-danger doctrine as a test of the permissibility of speech. Reviewing with disillusionment and consternation the application of the doctrine from *Schenck* to *Dennis*, Douglas concluded: "I see no place in the regime of the First Amendment for any 'clear and present danger' test, whether strict or tight as some would make it, or free-wheeling as the Court in Dennis rephrased it." "Action," said Douglas, "is often a method of expression and within the protection of the First Amendment." Douglas's was not the final word on the subject, but it provided insight into a kind of direct-action libertarianism that in the late 1960s and early 1970s generated new controversies in civil liberties law.

TWENTY-NINE

Civil Rights and the Constitution

❖❖❖

THE ACHIEVEMENT OF CIVIL RIGHTS EQUALITY for black Americans in the twentieth century did not require change in the Constitution so much as fulfillment of the original intention of the framers of the Thirteenth, Fourteenth, and Fifteenth Amendments. The purpose of these amendments was to integrate the freed slaves into the political and social order on the basis of legal equality. Reconstruction fell woefully short of this goal, and in the late nineteenth and early twentieth century patterns of discrimination and physical separation between the races that had begun to take shape in the South after emancipation were transformed into legally sanctioned segregation and disfranchisement. From the tacit introduction of segregation in the federal civil service under President Wilson to the dramatic increase in the number of lynchings and attacks on Negroes that occurred throughout the country, appalling evidence mounted that, amid the ferment of progressive reform, the Negro's dream of first-class citizenship had sunk to a cruel nadir.

Nevertheless, though it had been reduced to a mere flicker, the flame of equal-rights law was not completely extinguished. Through the quiet but persistent efforts of black leaders, a few legal victories were won when the Supreme Court, between 1910 and 1917, invalidated debt-labor or peonage laws as a form of involuntary servitude in violation of the Thirteenth Amendment; struck down the "grandfather laws" as an infringement of Fifteenth Amendment rights; and ruled that an ordinance requiring residential segregation was a denial of property rights under the due process clause of the Fourteenth Amendment.[1] The formation of the National Association for the Advancement of Colored People in 1910 signified the appearance of a Negro professional and white-collar class, and in the 1920s the black population in many northern cities, its ranks augmented by the heavy migration out of the South incident to World War I, was substantial

---

1. *Bailey* v. *Alabama* (1910); *Guinn* v. *United States* (1915); *Buchanan* v. *Warley* (1917).

enough to wield some political power. Bargaining with urban political machines, black politicians traded Negro votes in return for jobs in the police department and city bureaucracy, a lax policy toward rent evictions, equal access to certain bathing beaches and parks, and a primitive system of poor relief.

Although politically and ideologically the New Deal placed no serious emphasis on equality, let alone racial equality, blacks to some extent benefited from the liberal politics of the 1930s. Suffering frightfully in the depression, they broke their historic allegiance to the Republican party and joined Roosevelt's New Deal coalition. Support for FDR yielded Negroes positions in the lower ranks of the federal bureaucracy, access to WPA jobs and welfare rolls, and admission to public housing projects. Perhaps more important for blacks in the long run was the shift in political and constitutional outlook to positive government. For once it was established that the government was responsible for social and economic security, it was easier to hold it responsible for protecting civil rights against public and private infringement.

The nation's profession of democratic ideals during World War II and the cold war gave Negroes an irrefutable moral claim to equality in American life. To begin with, severe labor shortages during the war increased the demand for black workers and thereby served to break down at least some of the barriers to the entry of Negroes into trade unions and the professions. It was impossible, moreover, to ignore the stark contrast between the condemnation of Nazi racism in American wartime propaganda and the shocking reality of racial injustice in the United States. President Roosevelt, forced to acknowledge the discrepancy by a threatened mass march of Negroes in Washington, in June 1941 established a Fair Employment Practices Commission and prohibited discrimination by race in defense industries and the government. Subsequently, the government expanded the employment of blacks in the federal bureaucracy and wrote "no discrimination" clauses into war contracts.

The adoption of the United Nations charter, with its profession of respect for human rights without regard to race, sex, language, or religion, enabled American Negroes to make further claims on their government for equal rights. To be sure, nothing came of black organizations' petitions to the U.N. seeking assistance in the struggle against discrimination in the United States. But for the first time since the end of reconstruction civil rights received mainstream political attention. In 1945 New York created a state fair employment practices commission, the first of more than a score of such agencies established in the next two decades. In 1946 President Truman appointed a Committee on Civil Rights and two years later submitted legislation to Congress proposing to enforce civil rights. Truman also issued executive orders creating a fair employment board in the Civil Service Commission and mandating equal treatment irrespective of race in the armed forces. The civil rights question even had some political impact in 1948 when many southern Democrats, objecting to civil rights recommendations in the party platform, formed the states'-rights Dixiecrat party. When a few years later military exigencies during the Korean war forced the army to integrate, the stage was set for major public policy changes establishing black civil rights equality in the 1950s and 1960s.

The civil rights struggle proceeded on many fronts over a long period of time. Its fundamental purpose was to establish the principle, asserted by Justice Harlan in his dissent in the *Civil Rights Cases* in 1883, that "the Constitution is color-blind." This meant first of all preventing the states from discriminating against persons on the basis of race or, more technically, using race as a reasonable classification in legislation and public policy. A second civil rights objective—to prevent private discrimination against Negroes—was far more difficult to accomplish because under existing consitutional law federal power under the Fourteenth Amendment could be exercised only against state denials of rights. The same limitation applied to the Fifteenth Amendment, while the Thirteenth Amendment, though containing no state action restriction, had been interpreted narrowly as applying only to slavery and peonage and was of limited utility. The commerce power and the spending power could also be used to protect civil rights but had not been applied to that end.

The earliest organized civil rights legal efforts in the 1930s attacked discrimination against Negroes in jury selection, denial of voting rights, and exclusion from state-supported professional and graduate education. In the 1940s legal challenges were undertaken against segregation in housing, transportation, public accommodations, and public school education. Although the general purpose of these efforts was to remove the disqualification of race, the specific nature of the constitutional problems encountered varied from issue to issue. A topical rather than a strict chronological analysis, therefore, provides a clearer understanding of the civil rights revolution of the twentieth century.

Desegregation in Housing and Transportation

The most important constitutional battle for equal rights was to be that fought over segregated school systems in the South. Well before the 1954 decision in *Brown* v. *Board of Education,* however, the Supreme Court made it clear that not all was well with the *Plessy* v. *Ferguson* dictum of "separate but equal," which had so long reconciled racial classification with the Fourteenth Amendment. This was most evident in the successful attack conducted by the NAACP on restrictive racial covenants in housing and upon segregated interstate transportation.

After legalized apartheid was constitutionally condemned by the Supreme Court in the Louisville residential zoning case of 1917,[2] restrictive racial covenants served the purpose of maintaining residential segregation. Perhaps even more common in the North than in the South, racial covenants bound the property owners in a particular neighborhood to sell only to other "members of the Caucasian race." In *Corrigan* v. *Buckly* (1926) the Court had ruled that such covenants constituted mere private agreements and were not state action within the meaning of the Fourteenth Amendment. The Court also had refused to apply the Fifth Amendment to the outlawing of restrictive covenants in the District of Columbia.

In *Shelley* v. *Kraemer* (1948), however, the Court, in a unanimous five-justice opinion, ruled that judicial enforcement of restrictive covenants constituted state action and so violated the Fourteenth Amendment. Adhering very carefully to the distinction drawn in the *Civil Rights Cases,* Chief Justice Vinson agreed that restrictive covenants in themselves did not constitute state action. But judicial enforcement, he asserted, involved the powers of the state and so ran afoul of the equal protection clause. In a companion case, *Hurd* v. *Hodge* (1948), the Court held that judicial enforcement of restrictive covenants in the District of Columbia not only violated the Civil Rights Act of 1866 but was also inconsistent with the public policy of the United States when such action in state courts had been ruled illegal.

Destruction of segregation in interstate transportation facilities began on the eve of World War II, when the Court, in *Mitchell* v. *United States* (1941), held that denial of a Pullman berth to a Negro when such facilities were available to whites was a violation of the Interstate Commerce Act. Chief Justice Hughes's opinion took its stand upon congressional implementation of the commerce power and not upon the Fourteenth Amendment. However, Hughes implied broadly that discrimination in Pullman facilities, if practiced by a state, would violate the equal protection clause. Five years later, in *Morgan* v. *Virginia* (1946), the Court again used the interstate-commerce approach to invalidate a Virginia statute requiring racial segregation on public buses moving across state lines.

The Court was not aiming at absolute legal consistency but rather at the destruction of segregation in transportation. This became evident in *Bob-Lo Excursion Co.* v. *Michigan* (1948), a case involving the constitutionality of a provision in the Michigan Civil Rights Act guaranteeing full and equal accommodations on public carriers. A local steamship line, following a whites-only policy, had refused a ticket to a Negro girl for transportation to a nearby Canadian resort island; criminal prosecution of the company had followed. Here the state obviously was involved in the regulation of foreign commerce, and the logic of the *Morgan* case implied that the law in question was invalid. However, Justice Rutledge's majority opin-

---

2. *Buchanan* v. *Warley* (1917). See above, p. 369.

ion emphasized the purely local character of the foreign transportation in question and so found the Michigan law constitutional under the Court's dictum in *Cooley* v. *Pennsylvania Board of Wardens.*

The Court struck another judicial blow at segregation in transportation in *Henderson* v. *United States* (1950), invalidating racial discrimination in railroad dining-car facilities. At stake was the practice, then common in several southern states, of setting up a curtained-off section of the dining car for Negroes. Justice Burton found this to be a violation of the Interstate Commerce Act of 1887, which forbade railroads "to subject any particular person to any undue or unreasonable prejudice or disadvantage." The *Morgan* and *Henderson* opinions undoubtedly lay behind an order of the Interstate Commerce Commission, announced in 1955, terminating all racial segregation in trains and buses crossing state lines. The order also banned discrimination in auxiliary rail and bus facilities, waiting rooms, rest rooms, restaurants, and the like.

The Constitutional Battle over School Segregation

At the center of the battle for equal rights was the NAACP's attack upon school segregation in the South. In 1945 legalized school segregation prevailed virtually everywhere in the South and border states, extending to some communities in Indiana, Illinois, and Kansas. Eighteen states had statutes making mandatory the segregation of white and Negro children, while six others permitted segregation at the discretion of local school boards. The constitutionality of these laws rested on two Supreme Court decisions that extended the *Plessy* doctrine of separate but equal to public schools.[3]

The first crack in the wall of segregation that had been erected in public education occurred at the postgraduate level before World War II. *Missouri ex rel. Gaines* v. *Canada* (1938) arose out of the refusal of the University of Missouri to admit a black applicant to its law school. Although Missouri had no law school for Negroes, it offered to pay the student's expenses at any of the law schools in neighboring states that admitted blacks. The Supreme Court, however, held that Missouri's refusal to admit the applicant to the state law school violated the equal protection clause of the Fourteenth Amendment. This decision did not imply that there was anything legally wrong with the separate-but-equal doctrine; the Court merely found that Negro students had a right of access to a white educational institution where no separate but equal facility existed for blacks. Under the decision, however, the South's entire system of segregated schools might be in serious trouble, for separate facilities for Negroes

3. *Cumming* v. *Richmond Co. Board of Education* (1899); *Gong Lum* v. *Rice* (1927).

throughout the region—in buildings, libraries, trained teacher personnel, and academic standards—were notoriously unequal to those for whites. This fact might lead to the conclusion that equality and segregation were intrinsically incompatible. Throughout the South, accordingly, a concerted movement to improve Negro schools began.

After World War II the NAACP selected higher education in the South as the most promising sector for its attack on school segregation. In retrospect desegregation appears to have proceeded with a sense of historic inevitability, providing a remarkable example of the ability of the modern Supreme Court to influence public policy. At the time, however, the only certainty was that the task facing the opponents of segregation—and the Supreme Court, if it chose to take up the challenge—was monumental. In fact the Court accepted the challenge, aware of the political risk involved in intervening into local affairs in an attempt to reform a basic institution of American society. The Court's awareness of the political risk it was undertaking affected the constitutional strategy it employed in the desegregation campaign for the next decade. The justices placed a premium on unanimity, in the belief that only a united Court could speak with the authority needed to make desegregation decisions politically legitimate and effective. Unanimity came at a certain price, however, for opinions that could meet the approval of all the justices, who were by no means agreed on how to proceed against segregation, often lacked the legal persuasiveness that the political magnitude of the task demanded.

The first victory in the desegregation campaign came in *Sipuel* v. *Board of Regents* (1948), another case involving a state's refusal to admit a qualified student to the state law school. The *Gaines* case, now for the first time cited as a precedent, provided authority for preventing the state of Oklahoma from discriminating against its Negro citizens. It is notable, however, that the Court decided the case *per curiam,* cautiously refraining from discussing segregation or offering any substantive rationale for its action.

Two years later, again acting with unanimity, the Court in *Sweatt* v. *Painter* (1950) refused to admit that a Texas state law school, established specifically to meet the requirement of equality for Negroes in legal education, could satisfy the demands of the equal protection clause. Now undertaking a more extensive analysis of the issues involved, Chief Justice Vinson showed how the Negro law school did not in fact furnish blacks with true equality in their professional training. He pointed out the obvious advantages of the regular university law school in library, buildings, faculty, prestige, and the like. Sweatt's exclusion from this institution, therefore, violated the equal protection clause of the Fourteenth Amendment. At the same time, in *McLaurin* v. *Oklahoma State Regents* (1950), the Court held that a scheme by which the state university admitted blacks to its graduate school but segregated them within classrooms, library, dining hall, etc., was also unconstitutional.

It was now apparent that while the separate-but-equal rule was still valid law, the trend of the Court's decisions raised numerous questions about the legitimacy of segregation as a general principle forming the basis of state legislation and public policy. The three graduate school decisions were all narrowly drawn. Yet they had obvious implications for other segregated institutions, and these implications increasingly commanded attention. Pressure thus developed both outside the Court and within it to broaden the desegregation campaign. In agreeing to adjudicate five school segregation cases in 1952 the Supreme Court brought these larger questions into the constitutional forum.

Four of the school segregation cases involved state segregation laws; a fifth concerned school segregation in the District of Columbia. The cases quickly became a *cause célèbre* as a battery of well-known lawyers, led by John W. Davis for the southern states and Thurgood Marshall for the NAACP, prepared the briefs. Following initial argument by counsel, the Supreme Court ordered the cases reargued with special attention to the question of whether Congress and the states in adopting the Fourteenth Amendment had intended to ban segregated schools. The justices were also troubled about the means and consequences of a sweeping desegregation order throughout the South, for they asked counsel to discuss how a finding that segregated schools were unconstitutional might be put into effect.

After a long silence, the Court in *Brown* v. *Board of Education* (1954) and *Bolling* v. *Sharpe* (1954) decided unanimously that school segregation, both in the states and in the District of Columbia, violated the Constitution. There appeared to be three strategies available to the Court for reaching this conclusion. One was to apply the separate-but-equal rule and examine the condition of Negro schools in comparison to white. A second strategy was to consider whether state segregation policies, obviously unfavorable to blacks, violated the original intention of the equal protection clause of the Fourteenth Amendment. A third possibility was to review the *Plessy* decision in the light of Supreme Court decisions prior to 1896 that clearly regarded official state racial classification as unconstitutional under the Fourteenth Amendment.

Chief Justice Warren's opinion for the Court rejected all of these approaches in favor of a fourth that focused on contemporary sociological and psychological perceptions of the nature and effect of segregation in American society. Warren first established the importance of education, describing it as the basis of citizenship and the key to success in modern life. He then asked whether segregation deprived children of minority groups of equal educational opportunity. Citing psychological studies that showed low self-esteem among black students in northern all-Negro schools, Warren said segregation imposed an inferior status on Negro children. It generated "a feeling of inferiority as to their status in the community that may affect their hearts and minds in a way unlikely ever to be undone." Asserting that the doctrine of separate but equal had no place in the field of public education, Warren declared: "Separate educational facilities are inherently unequal." He, therefore, concluded that school segregation violated the equal protection clause of the Fourteenth Amendment.

The District of Columbia case presented a peculiar problem. The Fourteenth Amendment equal protection clause did not restrict the federal government, and the Bill of Rights contained no comparable equal rights injunction. Counsel for the Negro school children had offered a substantive due process argument, insisting that segregation denied "fundamental liberty" under the Fifth Amendment. Although initially attracted to this line of reasoning in a draft opinion, Chief Justice Warren retreated from it. His final opinion in *Bolling* v. *Sharpe* stated instead that segregation was not "reasonably related to any proper governmental objective." He said further that segregation was an improper restriction of "liberty under law" as protected by the Fifth Amendment. And for good measure he advanced a moral argument. It was absurd, Warren declared, to suppose that the Constitution permitted the national government to maintain segregated schools when it forbade the practice to the states. Hence segregation in the District of Columbia was also unconstitutional.

Earlier in a private memorandum the chief justice had said his objective was to write an opinion that would be "short, readable by the lay public, non-rhetorical, unemotional, and, above all, non-accusatory." Clearly, he achieved his purpose. In a case so fraught with momentous political and social significance Warren's opinion was conspicuously and deliberately understated. In part the volatile mix of personalities on the Court at this time—especially Frankfurter, Douglas, Jackson, and Black—gave Warren reason to say as little as possible lest he provoke internal controversy. Fear of offending southern white sensibilities was perhaps a stronger influence on the chief justice, causing him to refrain from calling attention to the universally understood nature of segregation as injurious to Negroes, and from striking it down as a prima facie contradiction of the Fourteenth Amendment. Warren evidently believed the safest strategy was to rest the decision on contemporary social-science findings. Yet in doing so, and eschewing a more logically compelling argument from constitutional law, he laid the Court open to attack from hostile southerners who disliked the result and from many legal scholars who, though sympathetic with the purpose of desegregation, criticized the decision as judicial legislation.

The major question raised by the *Brown* decision concerned the constitutional status of racial classification. At the time, the principal theoretical aim of the civil rights movement was to repudiate the idea, given sanction in *Plessy* v. *Ferguson,* that race was a reasonable classification for legislatures to employ. Although Warren, consistent with the nonlegalistic logic on which he relied, specifically rejected only that part of *Plessy* which contradicted the finding that segregation was psychologically harmful, in effect the *Brown* decision overruled the doctrine of separate but equal, at least in education. It was not entirely clear, however, whether Warren was saying that the harmful effects of segregation outweighed its reasonableness, thus making racial classification unacceptable under existing circumstances, or whether he regarded racial classification per se as unconstitutional. Warren's reliance on psychological evidence seemed to suggest the former approach, yet in stating that separate schools were "inherently unequal" he appeared to endorse the latter position. Given the prevailing conception of equal opportunity as the removal of racial disability, however, the *Brown* decision was widely perceived as placing all racial classification under a constitutional ban. It was not until many years later that the question was reopened, under pressure for compensatory programs to assist blacks.

The Court, in deciding the case, significantly had issued no enforcement order; instead it asked counsel to reargue once more the means of implementing the decision. It thus separated its enunciation of the constitutional ban on segregation from the question of how southern society was to adjust to the new standard. The Court's answer came in 1955 in *Brown* v. *Board* (second case).

Invoking the principles of equity law, the Supreme Court in the second *Brown* opinion remanded the cases to the several lower courts concerned and ordered them to work out equitable solutions to eliminate the obstacles involved. Gradualism was the dominant theme of the Court's advice to the lower federal courts. Chief Justice Warren said the states that had discriminated must make "a prompt and reasonable start toward full compliance" with the desegregation order. Once a start was made, however, the lower federal courts could, if necessary, take additional time to carry out the decision, taking into account such problems as transportation, personnel transfers, revision of school district boundaries, etc. Moreover, instead of a class action decree, which at one point the Court had contemplated as more appropriate for the desegregation problem, the remedy in the second *Brown* opinion was directed solely to the parties in the suit. The essence of the Court's gradualistic, cautious approach was summed up in its instruction to the lower federal courts to admit the parties of the cases "to the public schools on a racially non-discriminatory basis with all deliberate speed."[4]

Enforcement of School Desegregation

Although the border states generally complied with the decision, the rest of the South undertook a policy of "massive resistance" to school desegregation. And while dubious from a constitutional point of view, the

---

4. The expression "all deliberate speed" came from Justice Frankfurter, who had used it in five previous opinions, none of which involved race relations.

strategy was comparatively successful. Ten years after the Court's order, in the school year 1964–65, only a little more than 2 percent of the black students in the eleven former Confederate states were in attendance at integrated schools.

Anachronistic and discredited though it was from a national point of view, the nineteenth-century doctrine of state interposition provided the theoretical basis of massive resistance. Virginia, South Carolina, Georgia, Alabama, Mississippi, Louisiana, and Arkansas all adopted interposition resolutions condemning the *Brown* decision as unconstitutional and purporting to interpose their authority to block it. More formidable in an immediate sense were the various school laws adopted by the southern states as a part of their massive resistance programs. These included pupil-placement laws intended to enable local school boards to shift children among school districts so as to maintain segregation, repeal of compulsory school attendance acts to permit parents to withdraw children from integrated public schools, acts providing for indirect support of segregated private schools through tuition payments to parents, statutes threatening to withdraw tax support from any school system that submitted to integration, "freedom of choice" plans that allowed a pupil to select his own school, and laws providing for the outright closure of the public schools as a last resort if all other evasive devices failed.

The NAACP met massive resistance with a systematic program of litigation in the southern states that often spilled over into political conflict and occasionally civic violence. The most important such instance occurred in Little Rock, Arkansas, in September 1957, when Governor Orval Faubus called out the Arkansas National Guard to block federal judicial enforcement of a desegregation plan drawn up by the city school board. After a federal injunction secured the removal of state troops, mob action prevented Negro students from entering the high school. At length President Eisenhower intervened by sending in U.S. troops and placing the city under martial law. Subsequent attempts by the school board to gain a thirty-month stay against desegregation led the following year to a Supreme Court ruling affirming a lower federal court desegregation order.

The Court's opinion in *Cooper* v. *Aaron,* published in late September and signed personally by every one of the justices, constituted a solemn admonition to the state of Arkansas on the folly and futility of attempting to frustrate the sovereign will of the Supreme Court and the national government. Admitting that the Little Rock School Board had acted in good faith, the Court pointed out that the recent disturbances were "directly traceable" to action by Arkansas officials "which reflect their own determination to resist this Court's decision in the Brown case." The constitutional rights of Negro children, the Court warned, "can neither be nullified openly and directly by state legislators or state executive officials nor nullified indirectly by them by evasive schemes for segregation."

Notable federal-state conflicts over school desegregation also occurred in Louisiana and Mississippi. In Louisiana federal judge Skelly Wright, supported by large numbers of U.S. marshals, blocked the legislature's seizure of the schools with an injunction and secured the token integration of two New Orleans schools. In *United States* v. *Louisiana* (1960) the Supreme Court affirmed the lower court's opinion declaring void a Louisiana interposition law and eighteen segregation statutes. Two years later, when Governor Ross Barnett's forceful exclusion of a Negro student, James Meredith, from the University of Mississippi was sustained by massive rioting, President Kennedy sent in several thousand U.S. troops and federalized Mississippi National Guardsmen to restore peace and protect Meredith's matriculation at the school.

Elsewhere massive resistance was on the wane. In Virginia, where it began, it was reduced to a series of efforts by school boards to prevent desegregation by closing their schools. Federal court orders forced the opening of desegregated schools where this occurred, with the exception of Prince Edward County. Here the county, though a state tuition grant program and tax credits, subsidized a private school system for white children, while Negro children, whose parents rejected an invitation to form a separate system for blacks, remained without any schools. The Supreme Court, however, in *Griffin* v. *County Board of Prince Edward County* (1964), held that county authorities in closing the public schools and at the same time subsidizing private white schools had denied black students the equal protection of the laws. Stating that "The time for mere 'deliberate speed' has run out," Justice Black for the Court informed the district court that it had the power, at its discretion, to order the county to levy school taxes and to command the Board of Education to reopen the public schools.

Notwithstanding this stern admonition, the great majority of local school boards continued to operate dual school systems in the South. Not until the late 1960s, with the emergence of black power militancy and widespread Negro rioting and disorder, would federal authorities transform school desegregation into a systematic policy of racial integration.

The Collapse of Segregation in Southern Society

Civil rights progress was most rapid in the 1950s with respect to state-operated or -regulated facilities other than schools. The desegregation decision was the signal for a general attack by civil rights organizations on the state laws providing for mandatory racial segregation in public parks, swimming pools, theaters, athletic contests, and the like. Almost invariably the federal district court where the suit had been commenced held that the *Brown* decision had outlawed the old *Plessy* separate-but-equal rule, not only for schools but for all public facilities of whatever kind, so that the statute under review violated the equal protection clause. The Supreme Court in turn without exception confirmed decisions of this kind without opinion. In those few cases where the lower court had managed to rationalize the statute in question as constitutional, the Court invariably remanded the case *per curiam* to the lower court for further proceedings "not inconsistent with *Brown* v. *Board.*" This pattern of summary extension of the desegregation decision, undertaken without any legal explanation, showed that the school case was thought to have rendered all racial classification unconstitutional.

In extending the *Brown* ruling the Court from the beginning demanded immediate integration. And since the integration of parks, theaters, and the like apparently offered less challenge to southern mores than did school integration, and since such facilities also were peculiarly vulnerable to the boycotts and crusades that Martin Luther King and other Negro leaders were to wage within the next few years, the Court's orders ultimately commanded a substantially larger element of compliance in the South than was the case with segregated southern school systems.

As a problem in constitutional law, desegregation proceeded within the framework of the state-action theory of the Fourteenth Amendment. It will be recalled that according to this theory, civil rights were protected against state infringement but not private discrimination. Sometimes a state law directly commanding segregation either in a state or private facility was at issue; here the Court had no difficulty in finding that the statute violated the equal protection clause. Typical of such decisions were those abolishing racial segregation in municipal bathing beach facilities, on city-owned golf courses in public parks, at public athletic events, on city bus lines, and in state and county courthouses and courtrooms.[5] Significantly, the Court consistently refused to allow the application of the "all deliberate speed" rule to the desegregation of state and municipal facilities or to state laws imposing racial segregation on private facilities, or to accept legal evasions or delays of other kinds.

In a second group of cases the Court struck down racial segregation or discrimination which in the immediate instance was practiced by private parties, but where the authority of the state loomed in the background. Thus the Court invalidated the exclusion of Negroes from a private theater located in a public park, and from a private restaurant operating in a county courthouse.[6]

---

5. *Baltimore* v. *City of Dawson* (1955); *Holmes* v. *City of Atlanta* (1955); *Watson* v. *Memphis* (1963); *State Athletic Commission* v. *Dorsey* (1959); *Gayle* v. *Browder* (1956); *Evers* v. *Dwyer* (1958); *Johnson* v. *Virginia* (1963).

6. *Muir* v. *Louisiana Park Theatrical Association* (1955); *Derrington* v. *Plummer* (1957). The Court held that racial segregation in a private restaurant operating in an interstate bus terminal was in violation of the Interstate Commerce Act. *Boynton* v. *Virginia* (1960).

Cases of this kind early raised the question of whether or not the Court was in effect engaged in subtly destroying the distinction between state and private action, as originally set forth in the *Civil Rights Cases* of 1883. However, in *Burton* v. *Wilmington Parking Authority* (1961) the Court went on record officially to the contrary. The case involved the constitutionality of segregation in a private restaurant located on the premises of a municipal parking authority. Clark's opinion took pains specifically to reaffirm the principle of the *Civil Rights Cases* as "embedded in our constitutional law." But the Court nonetheless held that the connection between the restaurant and the municipality was intimate enough to categorize the former's policies as "state action" within the meaning of the Fourteenth Amendment.

Perhaps the ultimate in the Court's determintion to break down state-imposed racial segregation came with its invalidation of southern statutes forbidding sexual relations or intermarriage between the white and black races. The Court long manifested great reluctance to interfere with laws of this kind, in all probability because it recognized the extreme sensitivity of southern whites in matters of miscegenation. But at length, in *McLaughlin* v. *Florida* (1964), the Court struck down as unconstitutional under the equal protection clause a Florida law that prohibited cohabitation between unmarried whites and blacks. Three years later, in *Loving et ux.* v. *Virginia* (1967), the Court voided Virginia's miscegenation statute.

In the early 1960s the sit-in movement seriously challenged the validity of the state-action concept. Sit-ins represented a new and more radical technique developed by black leaders and their supporters, as the civil rights movement passed from its earlier legalistically oriented phase to involvement in civil disobedience and other forms of direct action. The sit-in pattern was a fairly standard one. A group of young Negroes "invaded" a restaurant serving only whites and demanded service, refusing to leave when ordered to do so by management or the police. Arrest and prosecution for trespass, disturbing the peace, or the like then followed. Occasionally, also, sit-ins took place in hotels, libraries, courthouses, and even in jails.

The Court found itself exceedingly perplexed in deciding various sit-in cases to find some rule under which it might reasonably classify the racial discrimination imposed as state rather than private action. The difficulty was that by traditional standards the refusal to serve a customer in a private restaurant—one not located in a state facility and where no state law commanded the discrimination in question—was mere private discrimination and so fell outside the aegis of the Fourteenth Amendment. The Court might have solved this dilemma by wiping out entirely the old distinction between state and private action, as Justice Douglas on occasion apparently was prepared to do. But in a pluralistic society where the right of private discrimination was a widely recognized fact of daily life, this solution promised to open a veritable Pandora's box of constitutional difficulties. (What of the right of a church, for example, to exclude members not of its faith, or of a private club to limit its membership to whites or blacks, Catholics, Protestants, or Jews?)

The Court also flirted with a second possible rule, derived from *Shelley* v. *Kraemer,* where the Court had held that privately negotiated restrictive covenants were in themselves not illegal but that any attempt to enforce them in the courts automatically became state action invalid under the equal protection clause. By this theory a private restaurant operator had a right to engage in discrimination, but the state had no right to arrest or prosecute sit-in offenders. Close to this idea was the further legal theory that when a restaurant owner discriminated in accordance with current local custom enforceable by police and the courts, he was in fact taking action required by state policy whether or not any specific segregation law was involved. Finally, Justice Douglas on occasion argued that restaurants, hotels, and the like were engaged in a form of public activity closely akin to the services extended by the state in operating swimming pools, parks, libraries, and other state-owned facilities and that discrimination in such places hence might be said to involve state action.

But no one of these theories captured a consistent majority of the justices, so that the Court very often settled sit-in cases upon somewhat narrow technical grounds. Almost invariably it ruled in favor of the Negro petitioners, but it did so without creating any broad new rule of what constituted state action. Thus in *Garner* v. *Louisiana* (1961), the first sit-in case to reach the Court, the justices reversed the conviction of a group of Baton Rouge sit-in demonstrators who had been arrested and convicted for disturbing the peace. The convictions, Warren's opinion held, were "totally devoid of evidentiary support" for such a charge. Douglas, concurring, thought that the Court should have held that Louisiana was itself enforcing a policy of racial segregation, while Harlan would have ruled the convictions unconstitutional for vagueness under the Louisiana statute as applied.

On the other hand, in *Peterson* v. *Greenville* (1963) and *Lombard* v. *Louisiana* (1963), the Court moved close to the theory that arrests for sit-ins meant in effect that the state was supporting a segregation policy and that the convictions were, therefore, illegal under the equal protection clause. In the *Peterson* case, where the defendants had been arrested for a lunch-counter sit-in after the management had excluded them under a local segregation ordinance, Chief Justice Warren's opinion found that the restaurant management in excluding Negroes had done "precisely what the law requires," so that the state "to a significant extent" had become involved in the segregation practice in question, thereby removing it from the sphere of private action. The subsequent convictions for trespass, therefore, violated the equal protection clause. In the *Lombard* case, where arrests for trespass had followed a New Orleans lunch-counter sit-in, there had been no local segregation law. But Warren's opinion emphasized that the restaurant had acted in accordance with a policy announced by the mayor, and that its management, in asking petitioners to leave, had asserted that "we *have* to sell to you at the rear of the store," and had "called the police as a matter of routine procedure." Therefore, said Warren, it was "the voice of the state directing segregated service," and the convictions could not stand.

In *Bell* v. *Maryland* (1964) the Court's inability to resolve the theoretical problems inherent in the state-action concept became apparent. Here the Court confronted an appeal from the conviction of twelve Baltimore sit-in demonstrators who had been tried for violating a Maryland criminal trespass law. Justice Brennan for a 6–3 majority disposed of the case by remanding it to the state court of appeals for reconsideration in light of a new state law, enacted subsequent to the convictions, forbidding restaurant owners and operators to deny any person service because of race. In concurring and dissenting opinions, however, six justices chose to examine the state-action question.

Douglas insisted that the basic issue was the right of equal access to public accommodations for all persons regardless of race or class. This right he found to be inherent in the historic purposes of the Thirteenth, Fourteenth, and Fifteenth Amendments; it was also an attribute of national citizenship. Goldberg, holding that the Fourteenth Amendment was intended to bind the states to enforce common law guarantees of equal access to public facilities, argued that state enforcement of private segregation violated the equal protection clause. In dissent, Black, Harlan, and White contended that the Fourteenth Amendment did not prohibit private discrimination, that the Maryland trespass law was constitutional, and that persons practicing discrimination in their conduct of a private business had a right to call upon the state for the defense of their property.

The Supreme Court eventually abrogated the state-action limitation on federal power. But before this happened Congress settled the matter in a practical way by adopting comprehensive civil rights legislation that guaranteed equal access to public accommodations under the commerce power. The Civil Rights Act of 1964, followed by the Voting Rights Act of 1965, marked the high point of a long drive for civil rights legislation that paralleled the juridical struggle against racial discrimination. Coinciding with the eruption of black protest and civil disorder, the legislation of the mid-1960s culminated a historic and distinct phase of the civil rights movement.

The Drive for Federal Civil Rights Legislation

The early campaign for civil rights legislation concentrated upon three issues: protection of voting rights, enactment of an antilynch law, and adoption of a federal fair employment practices statute. Of these measures, proposals for federal legislation to protect Negro voting rights seemingly offered the most promise of success and the least constitutional difficulty.

A number of judicial decisions over many years had negated state legislation which by one device or another sought to nullify the Fifteenth Amendment. In *Nixon* v. *Herndon* (1927), for example, the Court held unconstitutional the Texas white primary law barring Negroes from participation in the Democratic party primary. When this favorite device for excluding blacks was invalidated, the southern states allowed political parties to organize as "private clubs" and hence to fix their own qualifications for membership. Thereafter, various state Democratic party organizations, acting under such laws, barred blacks from participation in their "private" primary election. This technique proved temporarily successful, when the Court in *Grovey* v. *Townsend* (1935) held that under such legislation state conventions could lawfully restrict party membership to whites, since by law the party now was a private organization and, therefore, not subject to the limitations imposed on state action under the Fourteenth and Fifteenth Amendments.

The *Townsend* decision was presently repudiated, however. In *United States* v. *Classic* (1941), a case dealing with ballot-box tampering by state officials in a primary election, the Court held that the federal government could lawfully regulate a state primary, where such an election was an integral part of the machinery for choosing candidates for federal office. A possible implication of this decision was that the guarantees of the Fifteenth Amendment extended to state primary elections. Finally, in *Smith* v. *Allwright* (1944) the Court specifically reversed the *Townsend* decision. Justice Reed's opinion pointed out that since the state of Texas had delegated to the Democratic party the right to fix the qualifications for party membership, the party convention in barring Negroes constituted "state action" within the meaning of the Fifteenth Amendment. The exclusion of Negroes by the party was, therefore, unconstitutional.

From time to time thereafter the Court disposed of other state devices designed to evade the force of the Fifteenth Amendment. Thus in *Schnell* v. *Davis* (1949) the Court refused to review the decision of a lower federal court declaring void Alabama's so-called Boswell Amendment, which provided that voters in order to register must be able to "understand and explain" any article in the state constitution. In *Terry* v. *Adams* (1953) the Court extended the principles of the Allwright decision to cover private primaries held by the altogether unofficial but highly influential "Jaybird Party," whose nominees in a Texas county thereafter invariably received local Democratic nominations. The Court held simply that the "Jaybird Party" had in fact become a part of the state's election machinery, so that its elections were covered by the Fifteenth Amendment. And in *Gomillion* v. *Lightfoot* (1960) the Court unanimously declared invalid an Alabama law that had carefully redrawn the boundaries of the city of Tuskegee in such a way as to exclude from the city all but a small fraction of that municipality's former Negro residents and thus had excluded them from participating in the city's elections. The law, said the Court in a unanimous opinion, constituted an obvious attempt to subvert the Fifteenth Amendment.

One device that remained beyond the reach of federal authority was the poll tax, whereby a state required the payment of a small head tax as a prerequisite to voting. Civil rights activists condemned the tax as a means of disenfranchising Negroes. But the Supreme Court, in *Breedlove* v. *Suttles* (1937), held that the tax, properly administered, did not violate either the equal protection clause of the Fourteenth Amendment, or the Fifteenth Amendment. Continual efforts to abolish the poll tax by congressional legislation could not overcome the obvious fact that the Constitution made both federal and state elections primarily a matter of state responsibility. Only by amending the Constitution (Twenty-fourth Amendment) was it finally possible in 1964 to eliminate this relic of nineteeth-century election law in relation to the election of federal officials.

The campaign to enact a federal antilynching law encountered a far more formidable constitutional obstacle than the drive for suffrage did. This obstacle was the division of sovereignty that gave the states, and denied to the federal government, a comprehensive police power with respect to the private rights of one individual as against another.

As of 1940 there were but two federal statutes, both of them products of the reconstruction era, which could conceivably be construed as of some value in protecting Negroes against lynching, violence, or intimidation. Section 51, Title 18, of the United States Code, derived from the Enforcement Act of 1870, forbade conspiracies to deny any person the rights "secured to him by the Constitution and laws of the United States." Section 52, Title 18, a remnant of the Civil Rights Act of 1866, made it a misdemeanor willfully to deprive any person under color of state law of rights "secured or protected by the Constitution or laws of the United States or to subject any person to different pains or penalties on account of race."[7]

These measures in reality were of very limited efficacy. Section 51 had repeatedly been interpreted by the Supreme Court—for example, in *Logan* v. *United States* (1892) and in *United States* v. *Powell* (1909)—to mean little more than the right of a person to be free from violence by officials while in federal or state custody. Until 1941, Section 52 had never been subjected to scrutiny by the Supreme Court, but the provision quite evidently applied only to the misuse of power against individuals by state officials. In *United States* v. *Classic* (1941), the Court confirmed this restrictive interpretation of Section 52. And in *Screws* v. *United States* (1945), the Court, speaking through Justice Douglas, held that Section 52 could be construed as consti-

7. Section 51 has since become 18 U.S.C. 241; Section 52 is now 18 U.S.C. 242.

tutional only if applied to state officials who acted "under color of law" to deprive a person of a specific right secured to him by the Constitution or laws of the United States. Thus Sections 51 and 52, far from proving themselves in practice to be effective federal antilynch laws, ultimately served only to emphasize the constitutional difficulties involved in such legislation. In the face of these obstacles, bills defining the right not to be lynched as an incident of national citizenship, regularly introduced by liberals starting in 1946, got nowhere.

Federal fair employment practices legislation met fewer constitutional obstacles than the antilynching effort. In 1941, as already noted, President Roosevelt established a Fair Employment Practices Commission, essentially as a wartime measure. Congress appropriated money for this agency annually until 1945. Nearly all northern leaders of both major parties were at least nominally in favor of a federal FEPC statute, and numerous bills were introduced for this purpose after the war. None, however, was enacted in the 1940s.

Despite President Truman's support of civil rights measures, it was not until the later 1950s that political circumstances were favorable for any kind of legislative success in the civil rights field. In these years Republican politicans seized on the civil rights issue as a means of drawing the northern black vote away from its traditional New Deal political allegiance. The Republican platforms of 1952 and 1956 strongly demanded comprehensive civil rights legislation, giving northern Democrats, who were aware of the negative effect that the southern opposition to civil rights had on the party, little alternative but to meet the Republican initiative.

In 1957 Congress passed a modest civil rights act devoted largely to strengthening judicial enforcement of voting rights in the South. The act established a temporary six-man Commission on Civil Rights, charged with investigating alleged franchise discrimintions based upon race, and instructed it to make its final report within two years. (Subsequent special acts extended the commission's life indefinitely.) Other provisions empowered the attorney general to seek injunctions to prevent interference with the right to vote, made it a federal offense to intimidate or coerce anyone in order to interfere with the exercise of the franchise, and empowered federal courts to try criminal contempt cases without juries, where the punishment to be imposed was a fine of not more than $300 and imprisonment for not more than forty-five days. The law also fixed for the first time the qualifi-ations of federal jurors, making eligible all citizens over twenty-one who could read and write, who had been a resident for one year of the judicial district in question, and who had not been convicted of a crime.

Three years later, after the Civil Rights Commission reported almost no progress in registering black voters, Congress adopted a second measure to eliminate discrimination in voting. The Civil Rights Act of 1960 made mandatory the preservation of state records of federal elections for at least twenty-two months, and provided for the appointment by federal courts of voter-referees empowered to receive applications from any person allegedly denied the right to vote, which might result ultimately in a court order declaring the person qualified to vote. Other provisions made arson and bombing federal crimes, where the offenders crossed state lines, authorized the establishment of schools for members of the armed forces when local state facilities were not made available for such persons, and provided for a $1,000 fine and a year's imprisonment for anyone convicted of obstructing the orders of a federal court. (In its original form, this last provision had been aimed only at defiance of school integration orders, but at the insistence of southern senators it had been broadened to include all court orders.)

The Civil Rights Act of 1964

In the early 1960s the rapid spread of sit-ins and freedom marches, the rise to prominence of new civil rights leaders such as James Farmer and Martin Luther King, and the burgeoning of the Black Muslims whose most charismatic leader, Malcolm X, was openly advocating black revolution and the establishment of a Negro republic, all testified to the growing sense of outrage in the Negro community. The civil rights revolution was moving into a new stage, characterized by civil disobedience, direct action, and even the resort to violence. In the lower South, also, there was an ominous rise in white violence, as reactionaries countered sit-downs and freedom marches with mass arrests, intimidation, and, on occasion, even with bombings and the murder of civil rights workers.

These developments convinced the Kennedy administration and the liberal bloc in Congress that further federal legislation was imperative. Their first move was against the poll tax. In August 1962 Congress passed and sent to the states a constitutional amendment abolishing the poll tax in federal elections. Ratification took place rapidly, the Twenty-fourth Amendment becoming part of the Constitution in February 1964.

In June 1963 President Kennedy submitted to Congress proposals for a new civil rights act. The president asked for a prohibition upon the denial of equal facilities to any person in restaurants, hotels, and the like; authorization for school-desegration suits to be instituted by the attorney general; a ban on job discrimination because of race; statutory creation of an Equal Employment Opportunity Commission; a prohibition on racial discrimination in all federally funded programs; the establishment of a Community Relations Service to advise on the adjustment of racial conflicts; and a new and more comprehensive system of federal voter registration. Furthermore, responding to persistent liberal complaints about a lack of presidential commitment to the cause, Kennedy for the first time called civil rights a moral issue. His message expressed a sense of urgency as he warned that the price of inaction might be that leadership in the civil rights crisis would "pass from the hands of reasonable and responsible men to the purveyors of hate and violence."

A House Judiciary subcommittee subsequently drafted a very strong bill that prohibited discrimination in all facilities affecting interstate commerce and in all state-licensed enterprises. The measure was so strong that the administration became alarmed. At its insistence Title II was amended to exempt certain small enterprises—"Mrs. Murphy's boarding house"—and the compromise bill was agreed to in committee. At this point the political situation changed drastically with the assassination of President Kennedy in November 1963. Whatever difficulties the bill appeared to face before, there was now irresistible pressure to enact the measure as a kind of memorial to the slain president, and it was at length adopted in June 1964.

The heart of the Civil Rights Act of 1964 was Title II. In language reminiscent of the repudiated Civil Rights Act of 1875 nearly a century earlier, it declared all persons to be entitled to "the full and equal enjoyment" of the facilities of inns, hotels, motels, restaurants, motion picture houses, theaters, concert halls, sports arenas, and the like, "without discrimination or segregation" because of "race, color, religion or national origin." These guarantees were applicable to any establishment if it "affects commerce or if discrimination is supported by state action." This last was said to be present if discrimination was carried on under color of law, was required by local custom or usage enforced by state officials, or was required by the state itself.

Other provisions of the new law ranged over a wide variety of civil rights problems. Title III authorized the attorney general to file suits for the desegregation of public facilities other than public schools. Title IV required the commissioner of education to conduct a survey of the lack of availability of equal educational facilities because of race, color, religion, or national origin, and also authorized him to "render school boards technical assistance" in preparing desegregation plans. It also authorized the attorney general on complaint to institute suits for the desegregation of public schools.

Title V empowered the Civil Rights Commission to investigate all situations where citizens were deprived of the equal protection of the laws because of race, color, religion, or national origin. Title VI prohibited discrimination on account of race, color, religion, or national origin in any program receiving federal financial assistance. Title VII created a five-man Equal Employment Opportunity Commission, banned discrimination in employment on account of race, color, religion, or national origin by employers, labor unions, and employment agencies, and gave the new commission the power through investigations, hearings, and civil actions to enforce the law. Title X established the new Community Relations Service, and instructed it to assist communities in resolving "disputes, disagreements, or difficulties" relating to discriminatory practices based upon race, color, religion, or national origin.

Title I, virtually a separate statute, incorporated a variety of measures intended to promote effective federal enforcement of the right to vote. It prohibited any person acting under color of law from applying any discriminatory standard to a prospective voter different from those applicable to other voters in the same district, and it also forbade any denial of the right to vote because of any error in the registration proceedings. The law also put state literacy tests for the franchise under very restrictive controls. It forbade outright the employment of any such test in federal elections unless it was administered in writing and required of all prospective registrants, and it stipulated also that there was to be a "rebuttable presumption" that any person who had completed the sixth grade in a public school possessed sufficient "literacy, comprehension and intelligence to vote in a federal election."

Title II of the new act, embodying its public-accommodations provisions, was not long in meeting and passing a crucial test of constitutionality. In December 1964, less than six months after the act's passage, the Court unanimously sustained Title II as a legitimate exercise of the commerce power.

In *Heart of Atlanta Motel* v. *United States* (1964), Justice Clark, who delivered the opinion of the Court, declared that Congress possessed "ample power" under its authority to regulate interstate commerce to forbid racial discrimination in motels and hotels serving interstate travelers and thus "affecting commerce." The crucial constitutional test, Clark said, was whether the activity to be regulated concerned "commerce which affects more than one state" and bore a "real and substantial relationship" to the national interest. Significantly, Clark refrained from invoking the equal protection clause. This enabled him to dismiss as not "apposite" the embarrassing precedent of the *Civil Rights Cases,* where an earlier Court had invalidated the public-accommodations provisions of the Civil Rights Act of 1875.

Clark followed essentially the same line of reasoning in a companion case, *Katzenbach* v. *McClung* (1964), to hold that the prohibition in Title II upon racial discrimination in restaurants was a constitutional exercise of the commerce power. The case presented the Court with a particularly sharp test of the applicability of the law, since "Ollie's Barbeque," the Birmingham eating place whose discriminatory practices were at issue, did not serve out-of-state customers, and the only possible basis for bringing it under the aegis of the law was that it drew from out of the state "a substantial portion of the food served."

In spite of the fact that service to interstate travelers technically was not at issue, however, Clark's opinion emphasized nonetheless that the congressional inquiry prior to passage of the law had been "replete with testimony of the burden placed on interstate commerce by discrimination in restaurants." In any event, Clark held, Ollie's place came within the purview of the law because a substantial portion of the food it served came from outside the state.

Though concurring with the result, Justices Douglas and Goldberg expressed a widespread liberal preference for upholding the Civil Rights Act of 1964 under the equal protection clause of the Fourteenth Amendment. The concern of the law, after all, said Goldberg, was with "the vindication of human dignities and not mere economics." Nevertheless, liberals could hardly quarrel with the fact that the Court had rendered meaningless the time-honored distinction between state and private action in respect of civil rights. Two years later, six members of the Court further demolished the state-action limitation on federal power by declaring that Congress under the Fourteenth Amendment could "enact laws punishing all conspiracies—with or without state action—that interfere with Fourteenth Amendment rights."[8] Finally, in *Jones* v. *Mayer* (1968) the Court simply ignored the problem of state action under the Fourteenth Amendment in holding that private racial discrimination in the sale of housing was prohibited by the Civil Rights Act of 1866, authority for which was the Thirteenth Amendment.

The Civil Rights Act of 1964 provided impetus for yet another profoundly important measure, the Voting Rights Act of 1965. Previous statutes intended to prevent disenfranchisement of Negroes had been of negligible effect and were likely to remain so as long as the remedy relied on was case-by-case adjudication or administrative action against prejudiced southern registrars. In 1963, for example, the Civil Rights Commission pointed out 100 counties in the lower South where Negro voter registration was less than 10 percent of the eligible black population. Early in 1965, however, a series of dramatic protest marches to Selma and Montgomery, Alabama, led by Martin Luther King, spurred the passage in Congress of a drastic new federal statute designed to force even the most recalcitrant portion of the South to yield to the black American's demand for the franchise.

The Voting Rights Act of 1965 was designed specifically to eliminate franchise discrimination against Negroes in the South, in particular that achieved through resort to literacy devices, educational tests, and the like. The law automatically suspended the use of such devices in any state or subdivision thereof where the attorney general found them to be in use and where the director of the Census determined that less than 50 percent of the persons of voting age were registered or had voted in the presidential elec-

8. *United States* v. *Guest* (1966).

tion of 1964. Such suspension, once in effect, was not reviewable by any court and was to remain in force for five years.

The law also provided for the appointment of federal "examiners" to supervise elections in states practicing discrimination in violation of the Fifteenth Amendment. Whenever the attorney general instituted legal proceedings against any state to enforce the guarantees of the Fifteenth Amendment the court was to authorize the appointment of such officers by the Civil Service Commission. Examiners were authorized to prepare lists of eligible voters regardless of any existing registration list, and were to enforce the right of such persons to vote by inspection of polling places on Election Day. Furthermore, the act required states covered by it to obtain from the attorney general or the District Court of the District of Columbia approval of any new voting practice, procedure, or standard.

The act also prohibited any state from qualifying the right to vote of persons educated in "American-flag schools," where a language other than English was used. Suffrage thus could not be conditional upon the ability to read and write English. In effect, this set aside New York's law requiring literacy in English as a prerequisite for the franchise. Still another provision of the law declared that the poll tax had been used in some states to deny the rights of citizens to vote and directed the attorney general to institute suits against such taxes—in effect to test their constitutionality.

Immediately after passage, the attorney general by proclamation extended coverage under the new law to South Carolina, Alabama, Alaska, Louisiana, Mississippi, Virginia, twenty-six counties in North Carolina, and one county in Arizona. Subsequently, coverage was extended to two more counties in Arizona, one county in Hawaii, and one in Idaho. A great many suits and countersuits intended to block or affect operation of the law followed within the next few months.

After some delay, the Supreme Court agreed to hear arguments in *South Carolina* v. *Katzenbach* (1966). South Carolina challenged those sections of the Voting Rights Act dealing with literacy devices and with the appointment and functions of federal examiners. At bottom the state's argument was that Congress in passing the act had exceeded its legislative powers under the Fifteenth Amendment, thereby encroaching on the reserved powers of the states. Chief Justice Warren's opinion for the Court rejected this argument almost out of hand. Congress, Warren emphasized, possessed broad legislative powers under the Fifteenth Amendment, and might "use any rational means to effectuate the constitutional prohibition of racial discrimination in voting." Accordingly, he concluded that the portions of the act under review were "a valid means for carrying out the commands of the Fifteenth Amendment."

A few weeks later, in *Katzenbach* v. *Morgan* (1966), the Court passed favorably upon the portion of the law which in effect outlawed New York's English literacy requirement in order to guarantee the franchise to the state's Spanish-speaking population. A three-man federal district court had held the provision unconstitutional, on the ground that it invaded the reserved powers of the states in violation of the Tenth Amendment. On appeal, the Court now reversed. Justice Brennan's opinion emphasized once more the broad sweep of congressional legislative authority in the implementation of its delegated powers—in this instance in enforcement of the equal protection clause of the Fourteenth Amendment. Brennan also dismissed as "inapposite" several earlier decisions holding state literacy tests constitutional, notably that in *Lassiter* v. *Northampton Election Board* (1959), since these cases had been decided in the absence of federal legislation.

Meanwhile in March, the Court had completed the destruction of the poll tax, by ruling in *Harper* v. *Virginia Board of Elections* (1966) that such taxes introduced "wealth or payment of a fee as a measure of a voter's qualifications" and so imposed "an invidious discrimination . . . that runs afoul of the equal protection clause." Accordingly, said Justice Douglas for the majority, the decision in *Breedlove* v. *Suttles,* in which the Court had held to the contrary, now stood overruled.

Toward the New Equality: Affirmative Action

Passage of the Voting Rights Act occurred at the very moment when militant appeals to black power, combined with the explosion of ghetto violence in scores of cities throughout the country, threatened to destroy the civil rights movement as a peaceful force for political and social change. Violent black protest continued to erupt in the next few years, reaching a climax in the wave of civic disorders that followed the assassination of Martin Luther King in April 1968. Whatever the motivation of the thousands of individual rioters, taken as a whole the outbreak of collective violence had a profound political effect.

One consequence, reinforced by the hostile public reaction to the simultaneously unfolding anti-Vietnam and new left student protest movements, was the desire of a majority of Americans to re-establish stability and order. In relation to the civil rights question in particular, this conservative attitude, described as a white backlash, resisted the intervention of the federal government into local affairs (just as it resisted the concurrent judicial imposition of national standards in matters of criminal procedure, freedom of expression, and the like). A second consequence of the radicalization of Negro opinion was a change in the ideology of the civil rights movement. For over a generation the basic aim of the movement had been to secure equality before the law by eliminating racial classification and discrimination in the operation of American institutions. With this goal largely attained, at least in a formal sense, many black leaders began to redefine equal rights with reference to the distribution of social and economic benefits in the society. Backed by the federal judiciary and the bureaucracy of the Department of Health, Education, and Welfare, civil rights organizations continued to use the rhetoric of equality of opportunity and equal access. But they contended that the elimination of racial barriers was no longer sufficient to achieve equal rights, and that the historical effects of discrimination required remedial programs based on a conception of compensatory justice. Black leaders and white liberals argued further that equality should be measured not by the presence or absence of racial barriers, or even the intention to discriminate, but by quantitative evidence showing actual black participation or inclusion in the social and economic activities of mainstream society. The upshot was the formulation of new public policies—referred to as affirmative action programs—aimed at achieving substantial racial integration in public schools, increased Negro enrollment in higher education and employment in business and industry, and black political power through the exercise of the suffrage.

An old issue that received a traditional civil rights solution in the period of upheaval and transition from 1965 to 1968 was the housing question. For decades, as blacks in unprecedented numbers moved into northern and western cities, whites fled to the suburbs. Here, in spite of the fact that restrictive covenants were illegal, a cautious network of understandings among home owners, realtors, and local officials kept these communities all white. Angry Negroes, seeking to escape the inner city, fought for, and with the aid of white liberals often succeeded in obtaining, open housing legislation in some seventeen states and sixty cities. Resentful and apprehensive whites in turn passed various laws confirming the old common law rule that a property owner might lawfully restrict the sale of his property to buyers of his own choice—a polite euphemism for a right to refuse to sell to Negroes or other "undesirables."

In California the issue came to a head in 1964 when voters by referendum approved Proposition 14, a constitutional amendment providing that the state could not interfere with the right of any person to sell or rent or "to decline to sell or rent" his property to "such persons as he in his absolute discretion chooses." Proposition 14 had the effect of repealing a variety of California statutes and constitutional guarantees against racial discrimination in housing, notably the Rumford Fair Housing Act of 1963, and as such precipitated a long legal battle in the courts.

At length, in *Reitman* v. *Mulkey* (1967) the Supreme Court upheld the decision of the California Supreme Court, which had ruled Proposition 14 to be a violation of the Fourteenth Amendment. The California Court, Justice White's majority opinion pointed out, had treated Proposition 14 as one in which the state had "expressly authorized and constitutionalized the right to discriminate." Agreeing with this analysis, White concluded that "the right to discriminate is now one of the basic policies of the state," and thus significantly involved the state in private racial discrimination. Proposition 14 hence violated the equal protection clause.

Meanwhile, fair housing legislation made its way through Congress. In 1968 a bill that had languished since passing the House two years earlier was promoted by liberals as a response to the worsening racial crisis. The inclusion of an antiriot provision, making it a federal crime to cross state lines to incite a riot, enabled supporters of the bill to break a seven-week southern filibuster and push it through the Senate. After the assassination of Martin Luther King, against the backdrop of burning cities, a shocked House of Representatives approved the measure.

The central feature of the Civil Rights Act of 1968, as the new law was known, was to be found in Title VIII, in effect a federal fair housing law. This provided for a general ban on racial and religious discrimination in the sale and rental of housing, to be imposed in three time stages, culminating in December 1969. Only dwellings of four units or fewer sold without the services of a broker were exempted from the law. A separate provision of the statute, Title I, incorporated the new antiriot measure. Other provisions of the act extended the Bill of Rights to Indians living on reservations under tribal self-government.[9]

Within weeks of the enactment of the new law the Supreme Court took matters into its own hands by ruling, in *Jones* v. *Mayer* (1968), that private discrimination in the sale or rental of housing was prohibited by the century-old Civil Rights Act of 1866. Section 1982 of the federal code, originally a section of the 1866 law, provided that "all citizens of the United States shall have the same right . . . as is enjoyed by white citizens thereof to inherit, purchase, lease, sell, hold, and convey real and personal property." Examining the early history of reconstruction, Justice Stewart for the Court concluded that the act was intended to wipe out both government-supported and purely private racial discrimination as "badges and incidents of slavery." Passed before the Fourteenth Amendment was approved by Congress, the Civil Rights Act of 1866 was constitutional under the Thirteenth Amendment. Theoretically, the Court's decision had vast potential as an instrument of equality, since the Thirteenth Amendment contained no state-action distinction and since almost any form of discrimination or unfavorable treatment of Negroes could be viewed as a badge or incident of slavery.

Nevertheless, the Court's opinion in *Jones* v. *Mayer* was more interesting for the historical interpretation it presented of reconstruction than for its impact on constitutional politics. The effects of the decision were negligible, for if the battle for open housing was not completely won, considerable progress had been made. This could not be said, however, of the problem which had been the original focus of civil rights activism—school desegre-

9. See below, p. 647.

gation. Massive resistance had been defeated, but little substantial progress had been made in dismantling separate school systems for black and white. Accordingly, it was in this sphere that administrative and judicial policy makers began to redefine the concept of equal rights.

School Integration

Up to this time desegregation meant the assignment of students to schools without regard to race. That was the definition employed in the Civil Rights Act of 1964, which had also stated, at the insistence of apprehensive southerners, that school desegregation was not to mean the assignment of students to schools in order to overcome racial imbalance. Logically, however, and to some extent, of course, in a practical sense, desegregation produced integration. In the mid-1960s there were tremendous political and social pressures leading federal officials, employing this logic, to regard desegregation and integration as interchangeable concepts, and to transform the prohibition of racial discrimination into a requirement of racial integration. This tendency was strengthened by years of watching southerners try to avoid, if not evade, the requirement of the *Brown* ruling, through freedom-of-choice plans and other devices that often seemed mere subterfuges. Ten years after the historic *Brown* decision only 2.3 percent of the Negro school age population was enrolled in schools with white children. Somehow school desegregation had to mean more than this, in the view of northern liberal policy makers.

The Department of Health, Education, and Welfare in 1966 laid the groundwork for a policy of racial integration by issuing desegregation "guidelines." Retaining the notion of desegregation planning, rather than simply requiring the immediate assignment of students to the nearest school on a nonracial basis, the Office of Education in the department stated that no single plan was suitable for every school. The guidelines, which were carefully distinguished from the "rules, regulations, and orders" referred to in the Civil Rights Act of 1964, pointed out further that nonracial attendance zones might not be sufficient to achieve desegregation. The guidelines suggested other means by which that goal might be accomplished. These alternative means included closing certain schools, reorganizing grade structure and pairing schools, permitting students to transfer to a school where they would be in the racial minority, and permitting a school system to assign students to such a school. The HEW guidelines also adopted a quantitative approach toward evaluating compliance with the desegregation requirement: the actual shift of black students into white schools and vice versa was to be the test of the legitimacy of a desegregation plan.

The federal judiciary welcomed the HEW guidelines and quickly transformed them into effective policy. For this purpose a key case was

United States v. *Jefferson County Board of Education,* decided by the Fifth Circuit Court of Appeals in 1966. Rejecting a local desegregation proposal, the Court held on the basis of the HEW rules that school officials had a positive duty to integrate, rather than merely to refrain from segregating. "The only adequate redress for a previously overt system-wide policy of segregation directed against Negroes as a collective entity," wrote Judge John Minor Wisdom, "is a system-wide policy of integration." In a manner that foreshadowed the practices of federal judges in the years to come, the Circuit Court specified the steps local officials must take to integrate their schools.

The Supreme Court let the Jefferson County decision stand, and in 1968 handed down an opinion of its own promoting the new policy of integration. In *Green* v. *County Board of New Kent County* (1968) the Court reviewed a freedom-of-choice plan that had resulted in the transfer of 115 blacks to a previously all-white school, where they attended with 550 whites. The former black school remained all-black. The school board, contending that the Fourteenth Amendment could not be read as requiring compulsory school integration, argued that it had complied with the desegregation mandate of *Brown.* The Court rejected the argument, holding that the county was still operating a segregated system.

Justice Brennan's opinion for the Court stated that so far from satisfying the desegregation requirement, the decision to open the previously all-white school to Negroes "merely begins, not ends, our inquiry whether the Board has taken steps adequate to abolish its dual segregated system." Without categorically condemning freedom-of-choice plans, Brennan said they would be acceptable only if they promised substantial integration. Although he did not specify any figure, Brennan implied that some numerical ratio between black and white students must be obtained before desegregation could be said to be achieved. The 15 percent degree of integration in the instant case was obviously unacceptable. Brennan in any event said that school districts had "an affirmative duty to take whatever steps might be necessary to convert to a unitary system in which racial discrimination would be eliminated root and branch."

In a unanimous *per curiam* decision in *Alexander* v. *Holmes* (1969) the Court reiterated its demand that school boards take immediate steps to end racially identifiable schools. Significantly, Chief Justice Warren E. Burger, recently appointed by President Richard Nixon, joined the decision. By 1970 HEW threats to cut off federal financial assistance to discriminatory schools led school boards to develop affirmative action integration plans as required in *Green* v. *New Kent County.* Some 30 percent of the black school-age population now attended at least nominally integrated schools.

Significant as this increase was from the 2.3 percent level of 1964, public policy required yet more vigorous measures. Of numerous expedients designed by educational technicians to achieve integration, the most efficient was cross-district busing. In the 1970s busing became an explosive issue in northern cities under pressure to end *de facto* segregation, or segregation caused by residential housing trends and the ecology of urban growth. Busing was first sanctioned, however, not for the nation as a whole, but as a regional policy to achieve integration in southern school districts marked with the stigma of *de jure* (or state sanctioned) segregation.

The Supreme Court took this step in *Swann* v. *Charlotte-Mecklenburg Board of Education* (1971). A federal district court had ordered an affirmative action plan for the schools of Charlotte, North Carolina, which not only restructured attendance zones but also employed a school pairing technique that necessitated extensive intracity busing. In a unanimous opinion the Court upheld the district court's order. Chief Justice Burger's opinion, which deliberately undertook to provide guidelines for affirmative action, emphasized very heavily the broad equity powers of the lower federal courts in such programs. School pairings and grouping and interschool busing, he declared, were all legitimate instruments of the Court's equity power. Thus the Court began a new phase of its bold foray into local school management in an attempt to achieve racial integration.

Affirmative Action in Voting and Employment

Where blacks had for years been the victims of state-sponsored discrimination, there was an understandably strong tendency, in order to compensate for past injustices, to insist on remedial action that would temporarily take into account racial considerations. That this was the case in regard to school segregation in the South was only too apparent. It was perhaps less true in other spheres, where differences between the races were less clearly the result of government-decreed discrimination. Nevertheless, political pressures generated by the ghetto riots and a widespread sense of white responsibility and guilt for historic injustices against Negroes led federal officials to apply the result-oriented, affirmative action approach to other civil rights issues. Of these, equality in voting and in employment opportunities was the most important.

The Voting Rights Act of 1965 was remarkably successful in its original purpose of giving blacks access to the ballot box. In 1964 1,500,000 blacks were registered to vote in the eleven states of the former Confederacy; by 1969 the number was 3,100,000. Whereas in 1963 there were fewer than 100 elected Negro officials in the entire South, a decade later there were 191 in Mississippi alone. Yet access to the ballot did not produce as much social and economic change in the conditions of black life as perhaps had been expected. That perception, in combination with the humanitarian and professional bureaucratic instincts of government officials, led the Department of Justice and the federal judiciary to redefine voting rights as maximum political effectiveness, rather than as equal opportunity to participate without discrimination.

Gaston County v. *United States* (1969) pointed to a result-orientation in voting-rights cases. A North Carolina county's literacy test was found to be discriminatory by the District Court of the District of Columbia, mainly on the ground that the county's operation of a segregated school system until 1965 prevented Negroes from acquiring an equal ability to pass the test. The Supreme Court upheld the lower court decision, declaring the literacy test discriminatory in its effect, though not in intention. Indeed, impartial (i.e., nonracial) administration of the test, said Justice Harlan for the Court, "would serve only to perpetuate these inequities in a different form."

Even more important for redefining voting rights was *Allen* v. *State Board of Elections* (1968). Here the Court considered whether a Mississippi law changing the election of county supervisors from a single-member district to an at-large system had to be submitted for approval to the attorney general under the Voting Rights Act of 1965. Section 5 of the act required that in states covered by the law "any voting qualification or prerequisite to voting, or standard, practice, or procedure with respect to voting," must be cleared by the attorney general. This was intended to reinforce the ban on literacy tests by preventing states from devising additional subterfuges to bar black voting. The Court held that the change in Mississippi election law was covered by Section 5, however, and required federal approval because it could be used to disfranchise Negroes. "The right to vote," said Chief Justice Warren, "can be affected by a dilution of voting power as well as by an absolute prohibition on casting a ballot." Warren added that voters who were members of a racial minority might form the majority in a single district, but only a minority in the county as a whole. Hence they would be disfranchised. Although this was not necessarily the case, the important constitutional point was Warren's redefinition of the right to vote as the possession of a seemingly measurable share of political power or influence.

In adopting a broad interpretation of Section 5 of the Voting Rights Act, the Supreme Court brought under federal supervision numerous substantive changes in state election law, such as annexation proposals and laws requiring the appointment rather than the election of officers. These were not the sort of procedures and devices that Congress appeared to have in mind in adopting Section 5 in 1965. Nevertheless, the Department of Justice accepted the Court's broad view of the statute and from 1969 to 1975 reviewed 5,000 voting law changes in the states. From 1965 to 1969 it had passed on but 323 election law changes.

Employment equality was a third area in which federal judges and administrators applied a result-oriented conception of equal rights. Nondiscrimination in employment was the subject of Title VII of the Civil Rights Act of 1964, which created an Equal Employment Opportunity Commission. By requiring plans for increasing the number of minority employees, and by investigating individual complaints, the EEOC put pressure on employers to eliminate discriminatory practices. Simultaneously, the Office of Contract Compliance in the Department of Labor required businesses receiving federal contracts to submit affirmative action plans showing the proportion of minority employees and establishing goals and timetables for increasing their number. Affirmative action was here defined as remedial practices going beyond passive nondiscrimination to the inclusion, through positive action, of previously excluded minorities. Now measured statistically, equal opportunity in employment came to mean the actual hiring of minorities in proportion to their percent of the population.

Federal courts confirmed and extended the new public law and policy of employment equality. Dealing with recruitment, screening, promotion, dismissal, seniority, and pensions, the judiciary established the basic point that the requirement of desegregation or nondiscrimination was not satisfied by the use of impartial, nonracial procedures. In fact, considered in the context of the historic injustices done to blacks, the use of formally impartial procedures was itself held to be discriminatory. Moreover, where past discrimination could be proved, courts generally ordered employers to take remedial action.

A landmark case in the emerging law of equal employment opportunity was *Griggs* v. *Duke Power Company* (1971). Here the company's use of a high school diploma and general intelligence tests to screen job applicants was attacked as discriminatory against blacks on the ground that school segregation had denied blacks the opportunity to acquire skills equal to those of whites. The Supreme Court ruled against the company, finding the test discriminatory not in its purpose but in its effect. Interpreting the Civil Rights Act of 1964, Chief Justice Burger said that only tests and evaluative devices that accurately predicted job performance were constitutionally permissible. "Good intent or absence of discriminatory intent," Burger asserted, "does not redeem employment procedures or testing mechanisms that operate as 'built-in headwinds' for minority groups and are unrelated to measuring job capability."

Constitutional Significance of the New Equality

Thus by 1971 the basis of a new conception of civil rights existed. Its historical origins were rooted ultimately in the language of the Fourteenth Amendment equal protection clause and more immediately in the stark choice between equality and inequality that Americans faced after World War II. The choice of equality carried in its train the expectation of significant social and economic change, and unquestionably significant change occurred. Yet in another twist of the spiral, the considerable success of the civil rights movement in knocking down the barriers to legal and political equality renewed the demand for economic improvement which had alternated with political and civil rights as the major focus of black aspirations since the Civil War. The constitutional expression of this shift in outlook, in the nature of a conflation of these two traditional goals of blacks, was the result-oriented concept of affirmative action.

The purpose of removing racial qualification and disability was to give blacks equal access to the goods of the society under the traditional liberal goal of equality of opportunity and careers open to talents. In the face of the enormous obstacles that a century of discrimination had produced, however, civil rights organizations and government officials shaped policies that looked to actual results as a definition of equality. In their statutes and court decisions policy makers continued to talk of desegregation and equal opportunity, for these terms described the aspiration to live in a society in which racial considerations would play no part. In reality, however, civil rights policy in the late 1960s and early 1970s aimed at equality of outcome, or at least less disparity in the circumstances of blacks compared to whites. Affirmative action programs, moreover, as in school integration and employment, utilized racial classification.

The constitutional implications of this new approach to civil rights were profound. Perhaps most important, civil rights strategy now looked to group action and departed from the traditional individual rights orientation of American constitutionalism. To be sure, there was ample justification for this approach to civil rights in the conditions of Negro life in the United States, as well as in the group orientation of American politics. Moreover, there was a precedent for a racially defined affirmative action program in the federal government's Indian policy since the 1930s.[10] Nevertheless, the formal introduction into constitutional law of a collective, racial group rationale marked a significant change.

10. Although in the late 1960s and early 1970s the Negro civil rights movement helped stimulate a protest movement and heightened rights consciousness among native Americans, the theory of affirmative action formed the basis of federal Indian policy long before the civil rights movement began, and long before the term "affirmative action" was coined. It will be recalled that the assimilation policy introduced late in the nineteenth century by the Dawes Act was an acknowledged failure by the 1920s. Accordingly, the pendulum of federal policy swung back toward tribal sovereignty. The Indian Reorganization Act of 1934 was intended to restore tribal authority and ethnic consciousness among Indians. It repealed the land allotment programs, restored unsold lands to the tribes, authorized tribal constitutions and representative councils for the purpose of local self-government, and provided for the organization of the tribes as business corporations for the management and commercial development of land and water resources. Under this new separation policy the government also poured a great deal of money into educational and health-care facilities for Indians, encouraged the preservation of Indian civilization and racial consciousness, and took steps to bring Indians into the administration of Indian affairs in the Interior Department bureaucracy. During the 1950s Indian policy reverted once again to assimilation or integration (called, in an unfortunate phrase, "termination"), the intention being to transfer responsibility for the Indians to the states, which would oversee their entrance into mainstream society. In the 1960s policy shifted back to separation, although the express goal of federal policy was now said to be self-determination. Indians were to be given a choice between remaining in their tribe or integrating into white society. Under the Great Society programs of the Johnson administration Indians were designated a minority group eligible for a wide variety of welfare benefits. The result was a greater dependence on the federal government.

A second consequence of the new equality was to reinforce bureau-cratic centralization, already well advanced as a result of the New Deal and World War II. The vindication of Fourteenth and Fifteenth Amendment rights under the older conception of equal opportunity required the impo-sition of national standards on localities in a single region—the South. The vindication of equal rights as redefined in affirmative action law and policy would require the imposition of national standards on localities all over the country. Such an undertaking not only promised to revive the old conflict between centralization and localism, but it also raised the question of the nature of the United States as a national community. Constitutional politics in the 1970s would in considerable measure be concerned with resolving these issues arising out of the new civil rights equality.

THIRTY

The Warren Court and the
Culmination of New Deal Liberalism

— ✦✦✦ —

CONFORMING TO THE JUDICIARY's historic pattern of supporting the dominant political coalition, the Supreme Court in the 1960s played a major role in the resurgence and transformation of modern liberalism. Although the momentous school desegregation decision prophetically marked the start of the Warren era, for several years the Court generally adopted a politically cautious attitude. The revival of liberal politics in the early 1960s, however—a revival that owed much to the Court's initiative in the sphere of civil rights—created a political climate that encouraged the activist tendencies of a majority of the justices. Acting with breathtaking boldness, and for the most part independently of Congress and the executive, the Court undertook sweeping reforms of the electoral system and the nature of political representation, the administration of criminal justice in the states, school desegregation and race relations, the law of freedom of speech including the local regulation of obscenity, and the status of religion in public life.

These reforms were so portentous as to seem almost revolutionary. In fact their constitutional content—principally the imposition of national standards on the states—was familiar, if still in many circles deeply objectionable. Nor was there novelty in the Warren Court's jurisprudential method. As conservative, property-minded judges from 1890 to 1937 relied on substantive due process to make policy in an essentially legislative way, so the civil-rights-minded justices of the Warren Court used the tool of substantive equal protection to promote liberal policies that they deemed essential to the public good. In the realm of ideology, however, there was significant change, as the Supreme Court helped to transform New Deal liberalism into a public policy of egalitarianism.

Throughout most of American history equality of opportunity had served to reconcile the values of liberty and equality. Even when regulatory and redistributionist purposes entered into public policy in the twentieth century, Americans remained attached to the idea of equality before the law as the basic meaning of equal opportunity. Yet in meeting the economic crisis of the 1930s the New Deal to some extent made equality of condition as well as opportunity an effective if unacknowledged aim of modern liberalism. Similarly, the civil rights movement, though formally dedicated to eliminating racial discrimination, was expected to alleviate black economic inequality. In the early 1960s the "discovery" of poverty caused liberals to include economic democracy in their Great Society programs, and when the achievement of formal equality before the law in the mid-1960s failed significantly to alter the socioeconomic status of the great majority of Negroes, many black leaders added their voices to the demand for a new equality of economic condition. Politically, liberals could not afford to abandon the rhetoric of equal opportunity. But by the end of the decade their "war on poverty" attempted to lessen the inequalities of wealth that the older liberal principle of equal opportunity had permitted to exist.

Within the limits of the judicial process the Warren Court—at times with almost doctrinaire zeal—pursued the egalitarian goal of abolishing distinctions of class and wealth in American society. To some extent the Court's activism was influenced by the liberal climate of opinion. Equality, it was said, was "an idea whose time has come." Undoubtedly, too, the personal humanitarianism of the justices played a large part in shaping their reformist course. Moreover, like other Courts at other times, the Warren justices sought to promote the political and economic interests of the governing groups with which they were in sympathy—namely, the New Deal–New Frontier liberal coalition.

The outstanding feature of constitutional law after 1937 was the judicial abandonment of property rights to legislative-executive regulation on the one hand and the defense of civil liberties and civil rights on the other. Justice Stone's Carolene Products footnote of 1938, suggesting deference to legislative policy making in social and economic affairs and active review of legislation touching on political and civil liberties, proved prophetic. Except for an embattled remnant of laissez-faire conservatives, post–New Deal politics has adhered to the distinction between property rights and human or civil rights that was implicit in Stone's proposed strategy. The distinction surely had a plausible basis in the history of late nineteenth and early twentieth century capitalism. What was not immediately apparent, however, was the extent to which the Supreme Court's double-standard defense of civil liberties, culminating in the Warren era, served the economic interests of the New Deal–New Frontier coalition.

Judicial self-restraint, the more prevalent judicial style in the late 1940s and early 1950s, was premised on the assumption that legislative and executive policy making satisfactorily represented the dominant political forces of the community. Judicial activism, on the other hand, less trusting of the political branches, encouraged judges to shape their own distinctive policies to protect liberal interests. In the immediate aftermath of the constitutional revolution of 1937, for example, the Supreme Court protected picketing and other labor activities as free speech, thereby defending the economic position of the most important single New Deal interest group. The Court's civil liberties stance in the 1940s and 1950s, although only occasionally satisfying to radical libertarians, had symbolic value as an expression of support for society's underdogs. It had practical importance, too, as a form of representation of religious and cultural minorities not otherwise available in the political system. At the same time the Court's increasing tendency in internal security questions to regard government employment as a right rather than a privilege had the effect of protecting the economic interest of an increasingly large federal bureaucracy whose political loyalty was generally to the Democratic party.

The Court's desegregation campaign in the 1960s also had a distinct economic dimension. Unquestionably, justice was served, but so were the interests of a key element in the liberal governing coalition. Similarly, the Warren Court's reform of criminal procedure benefited lower-class groups, a disproportionate share of whom were blacks, while the reapportionment revolution was intended to redress the imbalance that had grown up between conservative rural and liberal urban constituencies. Finally, in an age of mass communications the Court's defense of First Amendment rights has protected the economic interests of a journalistic community whose political sympathies are recognizably liberal, as well as strengthening the economic position of the great corporations that control the media.

This is not to say that the Warren Court's egalitarianism lacked a basis in social reality. On the contrary, the creation of a homogeneous consumer society, based on an all-encompassing commercialism, has had profoundly democratizing effects. Moreover the productivity of the economic system, continually on display to even the poorest elements in the society through the medium of television, encouraged a sense of envy and entitlement that stimulated the egalitarian impulse in politics. In the highly volatile social setting created by these circumstances, the Warren Court, disposed by temperament, judicial philosophy, and political orientation toward activist intervention, undertook to promote the new liberalism.

The Apportionment Revolution

Apart from its leadership in the black revolution, the most significant egalitarian reformist activism in which the Warren Court engaged was its imposition of the "one man, one vote" principle upon representation in state legislatures and in Congress. The Court's interference in state legislative and congressional apportionment had its inception in the gross malapportionment both of the great majority of American state legislatures and of state delegations to the House of Representatives in Congress. This situation had come about over the years because rural-dominated state legislatures had persisted in ignoring the vast shifts in population produced by the growth of cities in the twentieth century. They deliberately flouted provisions in their own constitutions requiring periodic redistricting, both of their own houses and of their state congressional delegations. As of 1960, thirty-six states had constitutional requirements for redistricting, but twelve state senates and twelve state houses of representation had not been reapportioned for thirty years or more.

There had been fairly extensive state legislative reapportionment in the 1950s, twenty-eight senates and thirty-one lower houses being restructured during the decade. However, this generally had involved resort of some sort to the federal principle, whereby each electoral district received at least one vote regardless of population, so that the original requirement of the state constitution for districting according to population alone underwent substantial modification. The result was a distortion of anything like equitable representation. In California, for example, the population of the state senate's county districts varied from 6,000,000 for Los Angeles down to a mere 14,000 for the least populous rural district in the state. In Florida, senate districts ranged in population from a maximum of 900,000 to a minimum of 9,500, a difference that apportionment experts expressed as a "variance ratio" of 98 to 1. In Vermont, the population differential for districts in the lower house extended from a maximum of 33,000 to a minimum of 238, a variance ratio of about 140. Population disparities in congressional apportionment were as a rule less striking, ranging from variance ratios of 6.9 in Michigan and 4.4 in Texas, down to 1.3 in Iowa and 1.1 in Maine.

For more than a generation, political reformers had attempted to get the Supreme Court to interfere in apportionment, but that tribunal had consistently refused to do so on the ground that apportionment involved a political question and hence was not subject to adjudication by the courts. The most pertinent precedent was *Colegrove* v. *Green* (1946), in which the Court by a 4-to-3 vote had refused to invalidate the Illinois Apportionment Act of 1901. Plaintiffs had contended that the statute in question violated both the equal protection clause and the federal Congressional Apportionment Acts of 1911 and 1929. "Appellants," Frankfurter declared for the majority justices, "ask of this Court what is beyond its power to grant." Legislative apportionment, he explained, fell in the category of cases having "a peculiarly political nature and therefore not meet for judicial determination." Black, Douglas, and Murphy had dissented, the former protesting that the "complaint presented a justiciable case and controversy," in which "appellants had standing to sue." Although the decision dealt with congressional apportionment and not with that of state legislatures, the principle the Court enunciated obviously covered both types of cases. In the next few years the Court several times turned back apportionment cases without opinion, on the basis of the *Colegrove* precedent.

That the Court might at last be moving toward a change in its position, however, became apparent in *Gomillion* v. *Lightfoot* (1960), where, it will be recalled, the Court had struck down an Alabama law redrawing the boundaries of Tuskegee, Alabama, so as to exclude Negroes from the city franchise. In the *Gomillion* case the Court acted under the aegis of the Fifteenth Amendment, but it was apparent that it would be only a very short step to a finding that the boundaries of state and congressional legislative districts were also subject to judicial scrutiny.

Baker v. *Carr* (1962), in which the Court at length abandoned its long-standing self-imposed prohibition upon judicial interference in apportionment matters, began with a suit in a federal district court in Tennessee attacking the constitutionality of that state's 1901 law apportioning the general assembly, on the ground that it violated the equal protection clause. When that court, acting on the basis of *Colegrove* v. *Green,* refused to interfere, the suit went on appeal to the Supreme Court.

This time the Court threw both precedent and the political-questions doctrine overboard. It held by a 6–2 vote that state legislative apportionment properly was subject to judicial scrutiny and possible remedy under the equal protection clause. The Court's opinion, delivered by Justice Brennan, decided three principal points—that the federal courts properly possessed jurisdiction of the subject matter of the case; that the case presented a "justiciable cause of action"; and that appellants had "standing to challenge" the Tennessee statute in question.

The crucial issue, Brennan made clear, was whether or not the case presented a "justiciable cause of action"—that is, whether or not legislative apportionment was a political question and hence not subject to judicial scrutiny. Brennan reviewed at length the various categories of political questions that the Court had recognized in the past—foreign relations, the duration of hostilities in war, the ratification of constitutional amendments, the status of Indian tribes, and the guarantee to the states of a republican form of government—and concluded that each of these possessed one or the other of two essential elements. In certain instances, the Constitution committed the matter at hand to "a coordinate political department," so that it was ascendantly one for control by Congress or the president. In other instances, the controversy before the Court was characterized by "a lack of judicially discoverable and manageable standards for resolving it."

State legislative apportionment, Brennan now found, involved neither of these elements. In reaching this conclusion, Brennan rejected respondent's claim that the present case properly arose under the Constitution's guarantee to the states of a republican form of government, and hence was controlled by the application of the political questions doctrine thereto in *Luther* v. *Borden* (1849). The present case, Brennan held, was not such, but was simply one of "arbitrary and capricious" state action. Nor was *Cole-grove* v. *Green* a barrier to the present decision, Brennan held, since even there, four justices actually had treated apportionment as a justiciable matter. Far more significant as a precedent, Brennan thought, was the recent decision in *Gomillion* v. *Lightfoot,* where the Court had deliberately rejected the claim that redefinition of district boundaries by a state legislature lay beyond judicial control.

Second, Brennan concluded that for dealing with the apportionment controversy, in contrast to the situation where political questions were concerned, "Judicial standards under the Equal Protection Clause are well developed and familiar." Presumably, Brennan had these standards in mind when he called the Tennessee system of representation arbitrary and capricious, but he refused to say what they were. Instead, deciding that the case presented a justiciable cause of action, he remanded it to the lower federal court to arrive at a decision and hand down orders that would be subject to review on appeal.

Frankfurter and Harlan both dissented at length. Frankfurter denounced the Court's decision as "a massive repudiation of the experience of our whole past in asserting destructively novel judicial power," insisting that the case at hand, despite the majority opinion, indeed involved a "republican form of government" question and so was controlled by *Luther* v. *Borden.* Harlan thought that there was "nothing in the Federal Constitution to prevent a state, acting not irrationally, from choosing any electoral structure it thinks best suited to the interests, temper, and customs of its people." He also examined at some length the apportionment system in Tennessee, in order to refute to his own satisfaction the argument that it was "so unreasonable as to amount to a capricious classification of voting strength."

The Court's decision in *Baker* v. *Carr* provoked a great deal of apportionment litigation in the several states, along with a general legislative scramble to adjust to the Court's ruling. By the end of 1963, federal suits attacking apportionment of the legislature had been instituted in thirty-one states, while like suits had been commenced in the state courts of nineteen other states.

This litigation took place amidst vast legal confusion, for the Court, in refusing to pass on the merits of the Tennessee situation, had failed thereby to furnish any standards by which either state legislatures or the lower state and federal judiciary could proceed. Such questions as how large a variance ratio the Court would find acceptable; whether or not federal plans employing some kind of area representation were constitutional; whether or not a state in apportioning itself might recognize sectional, party, class, geographic, historical, and class factors as well as population; and whether or not an apportionment plan, otherwise dubious, might receive some additional constitutional sanction if the people by formal referendum gave it their approval, were matters upon which both legislatures and the lower courts alike remained altogether in the dark.

The first clear intimation of what the Court's new apportionment standard might be came in March 1963 in *Gray* v. *Sanders,* in which the majority justices struck down Georgia's so-called "county unit" rule. This system of representation assigned each county in the state a number of so-called "votes," or "units," determined only in part by population, and required all successful candidates for nomination to state offices in primary elections to poll a majority of such unit votes. The plan discriminated heavily against the votes of citizens in the more populous counties, and a three-man federal district court had issued an injunction against it, forbidding the state thereafter to employ any unit scheme that resulted in greater disparities among voters than those that existed between voters of different states through the operation of the electoral college in national presidential elections.

On appeal, the Supreme Court held the entire county unit rule plan unconstitutional as a violation of the equal protection clause. Justice Douglas, who spoke for a majority of eight, further condemned as "inapposite" the attempt of the lower court to fix guidelines by analogy with the federal electoral college system. "The conception of political equality from the Declaration of Independence to Lincoln's Gettysburg Address, to the Fifteenth, Seventeenth, and Nineteenth Amendments," he said, "can mean only one thing—one person, one vote." Justice Harlan in a lone dissent protested that the "one man, one vote" rule "flies in the face of history" and "is constitutionally untenable."

Gray v. *Sanders* technically was a voting-rights case and not one having to do with legislative apportionment, so that, as Justices Stewart and Clark pointed out in a concurring opinion, it could not properly be read as dealing with "the basic ground rules implementing *Baker* v. *Carr*." Nevertheless, Douglas's sweeping assertion, though quite inaccurate historically, had a seeming logic and fairness about it that gave it irresistible appeal. As long as the Court insisted on regarding problems of political representation as questions of individual voting rights, it was impossible to argue with Douglas's proposed standard.

This was borne out in *Wesberry* v. *Sanders* (1964), in which the Court employed the one man, one vote principle to declare void a 1931 Georgia congressional apportionment law. Justice Black, who wrote the majority opinion, delved deeply into early American history to determine to his own satisfaction that the provision in Article I, Section 2, of the Constitution, which directed the apportionment of representatives among the states according to population, had been intended by the Philadelphia convention to assure that "as nearly as is practicable one man's vote in a congressional election is to be worth as much as another's." In an embittered dissent, Justice Harlan pointed out, correctly enough, that Black's historical analysis had confused the debate in the 1787 convention over the apportionment of representatives *between* the states with the present matter of apportionment of representatives *within* the states.

Despite Harlan's dissent, the Court now was firmly embarked upon its campaign to apply simple majoritarianism to all legislative apportionment. Four months later, in *Reynolds* v. *Sims* (1964), the Court applied the one man, one vote principle to strike down both the existing apportionment of the Alabama state legislature and a complex proposal for reform that combined representation by population with a federal plan. Restrictions on the right to vote, declared Chief Justice Warren sternly for the majority of eight, "strike at the heart of representative government." The *Wesberry* decision, he added, had "clearly established that the fundamental principle of representative government in this country is one of equal representation for equal numbers of people, without regard to race, sex, economic status, or place of residence within the state." The "federal analogy" he dismissed as "inapposite and irrelevant to state legislative redistricting schemes." Warren conceded that on occasion "some deviation from the equal population principle" might be permissible to achieve "some flexibility" and to avoid gerrymandering, but he warned that "neither history alone nor economic or other sorts of group interests are permissible factors in attempting to justify disparities from population-based representation." "One man, one vote," in other words, was virtually a pure and intractable rule.

In five other cases, decided the same day as *Reynolds* v. *Sims,* the Court struck down legislative apportionment schemes in New York, Maryland, Virginia, Delaware, and Colorado, in each instance simply by applying the "one man, one vote" rule. The last of these, *Lucas* v. *Forty-Fourth General Assembly of Colorado* (1964), was of particular significance, for the plan in question not only came fairly close to establishing a straight population ratio (the variance ratio in the Colorado House of Representatives was only 1.7 to 1), but it also had been approved as a constitutional amendment in a popular election. However, the plan did take account of the division of the state into certain "natural" geographic districts, and the chief justice, who spoke for a majority of six, observed simply that the apportionment of the state senate, where a variance ratio of about 3.6 to 1 was involved, incorporated "departures from population-based representation too extreme to be acceptable."

The reapportionment decisions aroused strong opposition among state legislators and members of Congress whose power was threatened by reform of the system of representation. From 1962 to 1967 many of these opponents proposed by legislation, constitutional amendment, and even a constitutional convention of the states to restrict the power of the federal judiciary over representation. The most serious such measure was a constitutional amendment introduced by Senator Everett Dirksen of Illinois in 1965 permitting the people of a state to apportion one house of a bicameral legislature on the basis of population, geography, and political subdivisions as they saw fit. The amendment was defeated in the Senate, however, 57 to

37. Critics of the reapportionment decisions continued to point out that simple majoritarianism in representation was seriously at odds with the tradition of American representative government, which historically had attempted to recognize pluralistic interest groups. They also observed that the one man, one vote rule created opportunities for gerrymandering, so that legislative bodies might prove no more representative of that elusive thing called majority will than they had been before the apportionment upheaval. Nevertheless, the general public accepted the reapportionment decisions, apparently in part because of the theoretical appeal of the one man, one vote rule as a democratic principle.

In the late 1960s, after allowing lower federal courts to manage the reapportionment revolution for a few years, the Warren Court affirmed in even more doctrinaire fashion its belief that equal numbers would result in equal representation. In *Swann* v. *Adams* (1967) the Court held unconstitutional a Florida apportionment statute that involved a variance ratio for the state senate of only 1.3 to 1 and, for the house, of only 1.4 to 1. Although Justice White said that under the *Sims* precedent absolute mathematical exactness was not required, two years later the Court declared that it was. In *Kirkpatrick* v. *Preisler* and *Wells* v. *Rockefeller* (1969) the Court rejected Missouri and New York congressional redistricting plans that allowed deviations from the statistical ideal of only 3.1 percent and 6.6 percent. For the 5-to-4 majority, Justice Brennan asserted that the one man, one vote principle "requires that the state make a good faith effort to achieve precise mathematical equality." The usual factors that might conceivably enter into legislative apportionment, such as economic and social interests or traditional political subdivisions, Brennan dismissed as irrelevant.

In *Avery* v. *Midland County* (1968) the Court brought county and city government under the one man, one vote rule for their legislative bodies. In applying the rule to the last of the more obvious units of American government, the Court had gone about as far as it could without extending the principle of strict representational equality to matters such as the internal operation of a legislative body organized on a seniority system. Contrary to the expectations of those who inaugurated the reapportionment revolution, however, the Court's intervention did not strengthen urban liberals so much as moderate and conservative politicians in predominantly Republican suburban areas. Undoubtedly, this was an additional major reason for the popular acceptance of the Court's activism in this sphere.

The Reform of Criminal Procedure: The Nationalization of the Bill of Rights

One of the most ambitious projects of the Warren Court was its attempt to reform criminal procedure by requiring the states to conduct criminal trials under the guarantees of fair procedure that applied in federal courts. This involved the extension of the guarantees of the Fourth, Fifth, and Sixth Amendments as limitations upon the states through the due process clause of the Fourteenth Amendment. By the close of the Warren era the Supreme Court had effectively nationalized the Bill of Rights, effecting a major revolution in federal-state relations.

As noted previously, the First Amendment was subsumed under the Fourteenth Amendment in the 1920s and 1930s. The provisions of the Bill of Rights dealing with criminal procedure, however, had for the most part remained effective only against the federal government.[1] The administration of criminal justice had always been one of the central responsibilities of state government under the federal system. Accordingly, the Supreme Court in the 1930s and 1940s permitted the states broad latitude in this sphere, and no further incorporation of the Bill of Rights occurred. Such were the pressures for national uniformity in American society, however, that the nationalization of civil liberties continued nonetheless, albeit on a modest scale. This took place under the "fair trial" method of monitoring the states' administration of criminal justice.

The basic criterion in the fair-trial test was not whether state criminal justice procedures recognized the guarantees of the Bill of Rights, as the incorporation theory insisted, but whether state procedures were fundamentally fair. Like the ideas of selective and total incorporation, this rule derived from Justice Cardozo's statement in *Palko* v. *Connecticut* (1937) that some of the rights in the Bill of Rights were absorbed in the Fourteenth Amendment because they were implicit in the concept of ordered liberty.[2] In evaluating state practices under this rule the Court professed to be guided, in Justice Frankfurter's words, by the community's "accepted notions of justice." The Court used this approach in declaring aspects of Michigan's one-man grand jury system to be a violation of the due process

---

1. In a strict legal sense none of the criminal procedure guarantees of the Bill of Rights had been applied to the states, but in a practical sense the Supreme Court had twice asserted federal limitations on state authority in criminal justice matters. In *Powell* v. *Alabama* (1932) the Court held that due process in the Fourteenth Amendment required granting the right of counsel to the accused in a capital crime, as provided in the Sixth Amendment. In *Brown* v. *Mississippi* (1936) the Court held that due process prohibited the use of forced confessions in state criminal trials, thus in effect validating against the states the Fifth Amendment right not to be forced to be a witness against oneself in a criminal trial. In neither of these cases did the Supreme Court declare that the due process right in question was identical to that specified in the Bill of Rights. At most there was a correspondence or similarity between the right or guarantee which was applicable against state power and that which applied to the federal government under the Bill of Rights.

2. The difference between selective and total incorporation and the fair-trial test was that under the former approach the Fourteenth Amendment was seen as containing rights *identical* to those specified in the Bill of Rights, while under the latter the rights protected by the Fourteenth Amendment were merely *similar* to those in the Bill of Rights. Having their source in the concept of "ordered liberty," these rights could differ in scope and meaning from rights enumerated in the Bill of Rights.

clause of the Fourteenth Amendment.[3] The Supreme Court also used the fair-trial criterion in an important search-and-seizure case, *Wolf* v. *Colorado* (1949), where it functioned as a method of supervising state criminal procedure.

At issue in the *Wolf* case was the validity of a criminal conviction based on evidence obtained by an unlawful search. In a federal court such evidence would have been inadmissible under the exclusionary rule, adopted by the Supreme Court in *Weeks* v. *United States* (1912) with the intention of preventing illegal searches. If the exclusionary rule applied to the states as part of the Fourth Amendment, the Colorado conviction was unconstitutional. The Supreme Court affirmed the conviction, however, refusing to extend the federal rule on the ground that it was not essential to a scheme of ordered liberty. The due process clause of the Fourteenth Amendment, said Justice Frankfurter, did not incorporate the Bill of Rights. The most that could be said about the Fourth Amendment in relation to the Fourteenth, he reasoned, was that the core of the amendment—protection against arbitrary intrusion by the police—was part of due process of law. But Frankfurter contended that this was not because the Fourth Amendment was incorporated in the Fourteenth and hence binding on the states in the same form it applied to the federal government. It was because basic fairness demanded its inclusion in the concept of due process.

Using the fair-trial concept, the Supreme Court invalidated some state criminal justice procedures and approved others. In *Rochin* v. *California* (1952), for example, it held that the medically supervised use of a stomach pump to obtain evidence used to prosecute a person was so shocking and offensive as to render the state action a violation of due process. On the other hand, the use of a blood sample taken from an unconscious person was compatible with due process.[4] The apparent subjectivity of these decisions—a subjectivity, to be sure, inherent in the original *Palko* concept of "ordered liberty" and present as well in the technique of selective incorporation—opened the fair-trial rule to serious criticism. By 1960 four libertarian justices—Warren, Black, Brennan, and Douglas—could argue persuasively for an explicit identification of the due process clause with the guarantees of the Fourth, Fifth, and Sixth Amendments.

Between 1961 and 1969 the Warren Court incorporated virtually all of the criminal procedure guarantees of the Bill of Rights into the due process clause of the Fourteenth Amendment. The first key breakthrough came in *Mapp* v. *Ohio* (1961), where the Court applied the federal exclusionary rule to state criminal procedure. Citing *Wolf* v. *Colorado*—in actuality reinterpreting that decision—Justice Clark in his majority opinion said the Court had already decided that the Fourth Amendment applied to the states. In

3. *In re Oliver* (1948).
4. *Breithaupt* v. *Abram* (1957).

order to enforce this earlier promise the Court would now require the states to adhere to the exclusionary rule. Tellingly, Clark observed that more than half the states had adopted the more stringent federal requirement on illegally seized evidence.

The Warren Court next brought the Sixth Amendment right to counsel in criminal cases within the Fourteenth Amendment. It will be recalled that *Powell* v. *Alabama* (1932) had established that a right to counsel in capital cases was necessary for a fair trial and hence was a requirement of due process under the Fourteenth Amendment. In *Betts* v. *Brady* (1942), however, the Court refused to define the right of counsel as essential for a fair trial in all criminal cases. During the next twenty years, under the fair-trial rule for evaluating state procedures, the Court modified this holding; it required the appointment of counsel when special circumstances (mental capacity of the accused, nature of the crime, etc.) seemed to warrant it. The result was a great deal of uncertainty in the rules governing the appointment of counsel, an unsatisfactory situation which led twenty-three states to urge the abandonment of *Betts* v. *Brady*. This the Court did in *Gideon* v. *Wainwright* (1963).

For a unanimous Court, Justice Black declared that the Sixth Amendment right to counsel in criminal cases was applicable to the states under the due process clause of the Fourteenth Amendment. Black, the great advocate of total incorporation, did not employ this theory as the basis of his opinion. His main contention, rather, was that the right to counsel was "fundamental and essential to a fair trial." This was sound judicial strategy, for under the fair-trial standard conservatives like Justice Harlan could reach the conclusion that *Betts* should be overruled. In practical result, however, the *Gideon* decision was a major victory for the incorporationists.

The next element in federal criminal procedure to be included in the Fourteenth Amendment due process clause was the Fifth Amendment right against self-incrimination. In *Malloy* v. *Hogan* (1964) the Supreme Court achieved this result, overruling *Twining* v. *New Jersey* (1908). Moreover, the Court explicitly based its decision on the theory of selective incorporation. The "Fifth Amendment's exception from compulsory self-incrimination," said Justice Brennan, "is also protected by the Fourteenth Amendment against abridgment by the states." The right guaranteed against state infringement, in other words, was not merely similar to that recognized in the Bill of Rights, it was identical to it.

Linking the newly nationalized Fifth Amendment right against self-incrimination and the Sixth Amendment right to counsel, the Supreme Court undertook the politically controversial task of reforming the states' pretrial procedures for dealing with accused persons. Coerced confessions formed the crux of the matter. An early relevant precedent was *Brown* v. *Mississippi* (1936), in which the Court had held that a confession elicited by police torture violated the due process clause of the Fourteenth Amendment. More recently, in *Escobedo* v. *Illinois* (1964), the Court declared that a confession obtained after a police investigation in which the accused had not been permitted to consult his lawyer nor informed of his right to remain silent, violated the Sixth Amendment as incorporated in the due process clause.

In *Miranda* v. *Arizona* (1966) the Court attempted to establish uniform station-house procedures for states to follow. At issue was the admissibility of confessions resulting from interrogations in which police failed to advise suspects of their right to consult an attorney and to remain silent. The Court threw the confessions out as a violation of the Fifth Amendment right against self-incrimination, applicable against the states under the Fourteenth Amendment. Chief Justice Warren reasoned that when a person was taken into custody, the privilege against self-incrimination was jeopardized. Therefore, the guarantees protecting an accused person during a trial must be applied in the period of pretrial custody. Warren specified several procedural safeguards to protect the right against self-incrimination, including informing the suspect of his right to remain silent, warning him that any statement he made might be used as evidence against him, and advising him of his right to have an attorney present during the interrogation.

In less controversial cases the Supreme Court also incorporated into the Fourteenth Amendment the Sixth Amendment right to be confronted with the witnesses against a person, and the right to have compulsory process for obtaining witnesses in his favor.[5] Conflict over civil rights provided the occasion for declaring the Sixth Amendment right to a speedy trial and the right to a jury trial to be requirements of due process under the Fourteenth Amendment.[6] Still another part of the Bill of Rights, the Eighth Amendment prohibition of cruel and unusual punishment, had been included in the due process clause in the early 1960s.[7] Aptly enough, the judicial phase of the nationalization of the Bill of Rights culminated in a reversal of *Palko* v. *Connecticut* (1937), in which the Court had first expounded the theory of selective incorporation. This reversal came in *Benton* v. *Maryland* (1969), where the Court held that the double jeopardy prohibition of the Fifth Amendment restricted the states through the Fourteenth Amendment. The final step in nationalizing the Bill of Rights was taken by Congress. In the Civil Rights Act of 1968 it extended the guarantees of the first eight amendments to Indians living under tribal authority on reservations. Thus all governments in the United States—federal, state, local, and Indian tribal—were restricted by the Bill of Rights.

The criminal procedure decisions, although technically involving the due process clause of the Fourteenth Amendment, were aimed at promot-

5. *Pointer* v. *Texas* (1965); *Washington* v. *Texas* (1967).
6. *Klopfer* v. *North Carolina* (1967); *Duncan* v. *Louisiana* (1968).
7. *Robinson* v. *California* (1962).

ing equal protection of the law in a substantive sense by removing distinctions of class and wealth in the administration of justice. Like the reapportionment cases, they stirred controversy among state and local officials who predicted that they would undermine law and order. No widespread popular opposition to the reforms emerged, however, probably because most people thought the Bill of Rights already did apply to the states, and because the decisions seemed to embody a fundamental fairness. It was hard to deny, for example, that a person accused of a crime ought to have a lawyer. Whether the decisions had a practical effect on the criminal justice system at all proportional to the excitement they generated among opponents and supporters, however, was doubtful. Subsequent studies showed that the number of confessions given by criminal suspects, the reformers' chief concern, remained about the same. Nevertheless, constitutional law had changed considerably. Whereas in 1961 only eight of twenty-six provisions in the Bill of Rights were effective against the states, by 1969 there were only seven provisions that had not been incorporated in the Fourteenth Amendment. If the Warren Court was in fact unable to impose uniformity in the administration of justice at the local level, it was not for want of trying.

Freedom of Expression: The Law of Libel

The Warren Court's campaign to impose national standards on local communities extended also to the sphere of social and cultural expression. Here the tendency of decisions was to broaden the degree of personal freedom that was beyond state control. The basis for this liberalization was the continuing revolution of modernity that, through the influence of the mass media, spread secular and cosmopolitan values throughout the society. The very notion of "free expression," amorphous and vague by comparison with the older categories of speech and writing, reflected this modern sensibility. In any event the Court's efforts on behalf of freedom of expression, while principally to be seen as part of its pursuit of libertarianism, appealed to much the same liberal constituency that supported social egalitarianism. The Court's decisions in this field had the effect, moreover, of furthering the economic interests of the large number of journalists and communications professionals who formed part of the liberal governing coalition.

These concerns came together in the Supreme Court's nationalization of the law of libel, which it now brought within the aegis of the First Amendment. Historically, the law of private, or tort, libel held that certain classes of defamatory statements rendered the publisher liable for damages. The classic defense in a libel suit for damages was the actual truth of the allegedly false utterance. The burden for such proof fell upon the defendant, but if offered successfully, it rendered the libel "justified" and the publisher immune to damages therefor.

All defamatory statements were customarily said to be actuated by malice. When a defamatory utterance had been published through simple error or in good faith it was said to carry "simple malice." But a deliberately false or defamatory statement or a statement published with reckless disregard for its truth or falsity was said to carry "special malice" or "actual malice." Important also was the concept of privilege, which held that certain classes of utterances were immune to damage suits, either because of their character or because of the status of the person who uttered them. Privilege, the law held, was of two kinds: absolute and qualified. The utterances of public officials in their official capacity—the official reports of legislative bodies, executive offices, and the like—carried absolute privilege. On the other hand, the utterances of certain classes of persons in a professional capacity—among them lawyers and physicians—carried qualified privilege, which protected their utterer under most circumstances.

The most controversial aspect of tort libel law was the threat to free and open criticism of public officials and other personages in the public eye. Newspapers, rival politicians, and other commentators who were guilty even of simple error in criticizing such persons very often laid themselves open to heavy suits for damages. Nor was the fact that truth was a defense an adequate safeguard for newspapers and others engaged in responsible public political discussion. For defamatory statements, even when uttered in good faith or as a result of obvious error, constituted "simple malice" and could bring on a potentially devastating damage suit. Libel law thus involved a dilemma for intelligent public policy. To wipe out entirely the right of the victims of defamatory statements to sue for damages would have allowed the vicious and irresponsible free rein to damage the innocent without remedy. On the other hand, the threat of private libel actions was a serious limitation on open and free discussion.

By the opening of the twentieth century, the courts in many states were solving this conflict of values by recognizing the necessity for a very great degree of freedom to criticize public officials free from the threat of actions for damages of even simple and innocent error. It was in this spirit that the Supreme Court of Kansas in 1908, in Coleman v. McLennan, formulated the rule that the Supreme Court of the United States was to adopt nearly a half century later. Political criticism of public officials, the Kansas court held, should carry qualified privilege and be free from damage suits, except where the publisher resorted to "deliberate falsehood and malice." The whole area of public criticism of political officials, in short, was to be treated as very nearly outside the law of libel, except where deliberate, malicious falsehood was concerned.

Historically, the law of defamation had been almost entirely a matter for the state courts; the Supreme Court consistently refused to recognize that it involved any federal question or constitutional issue, except under a few special circumstances.[8] In *New York Times* v. *Sullivan* (1964), however, a case that bore the influence of the civil rights struggle, the court reversed this pattern and adopted the *McLennan* rule.

The *New York Times* case had its origin in an advertisement in the paper, signed by sixty-four clergymen and other persons of some prominence, charging the police and city commissioners of Montgomery, Alabama, with instituting an "unprecedented wave of terror" in their attempts to suppress various desegregation activities of Negro college students, Martin Luther King, and their white supporters. Significantly, several of the statements in the advertisement were erroneous, at least in detail, and a Montgomery city commissioner had promptly sued the *Times* for libel. The Alabama trial court had found the disputed statements to be libelous per se, and had refused to instruct the jury that for the defendant to be liable he must have published the statements with "actual malice"—that is, as deliberate or reckless falsehood. The result had been a $5-million judgment against the *Times,* which the Alabama Supreme Court had affirmed.

In a unanimous decision, the United States Supreme Court overturned the Alabama judgment for "failure to provide the safeguards for freedom of speech and of the press that are required by the First and Fourteenth Amendments." The First Amendment, said Justice Brennan's opinion, required that public criticism of governmental officials be invested with qualified privilege. Citing *Coleman* v. *McLennan* as his major precedent, Brennan ruled that henceforth a public official, in order to recover damages for a publication criticizing his official conduct, would be obliged to show "actual malice" on the part of the publisher. This Brennan now defined as publication of a false defamatory statement "with knowledge that it was false or with reckless disregard of whether it was false or not."

It soon became clear that a majority of the justices were not prepared to make the *New York Times* "actual malice" rule applicable to political discussion of all "public personages," in or out of office. Thus in *Rosenblatt* v. *Baer* (1966) the Court, in another opinion written by Justice Brennan, declared carefully that the new rule ought to apply to those "among the actual hierarchy of government employees who have, or appear to have, substantial responsibility for the control of public affairs." The *New York Times* formula, in other words, presumably was to be limited in its scope to policy-making governmental officers.

In *Curtis Publishing Co.* v. *Butts* (1967) and *Associated Press* v. *Walker* (1967), a pair of cases disposed of with a single opinion, the Court formulated a new libertarian standard by which to judge libel suits for public

8. For exceptions, see *Near* v. *Minnesota* (1931) and *Beauharnais* v. *Illinois* (1952), discussed above, pp. 533, 544.

personages other than governmental officials. The *Curtis* case arose out of an article in the *Saturday Evening Post* that accused "Wally" Butts, the athletic director at the University of Georgia, of conspiring to "fix" a football game with the University of Alabama. General Edwin Walker's suit against the Associated Press had its origins in his activities on the campus of the University of Mississippi during the Meredith riots in 1962. An Associated Press dispatch described the former army general as having led a charge against the federal marshals who had been sent to the campus to preserve order. Neither Butts nor Walker was a government officer of any kind; thus the two cases afforded the Court a clear opportunity to decide whether the *Times* actual malice rule ought to be extended to anyone other than public officials.

The Court majority refused to do so. Instead, Justice Harlan's opinion laid down a new formula, intended to "strike a balance between the interests of the community in free circulation of information and those individuals seeking damages for harm done by the circulation of defamatory falsehood." "A 'public figure' who is not a public official," Harlan held, may recover damages for defamation "on a showing of highly unreasonable conduct" on the part of the publisher, "constituting an extreme departure from the standards of investigation and reporting ordinarily adhered to by responsible publishers." Applying this formula, the Court confirmed the state court's award of damages in the *Butts* case and reversed the Texas court decision granting damages to Walker.

The Court now found itself split several different ways on the precise reach of the newly nationalized law of libel. A majority of the justices, excepting perhaps only Harlan and Stewart, were willing to apply the *Times* formula to all policy-making government officials and perhaps to lower governmental officials as well. But there agreement ended. Black and Douglas were close to holding that the whole concept of civil as well as criminal libel law ought to be outlawed entirely under the First Amendment for all public political discussion. Warren, Brennan, and White thought the *Times* rule should extend at least to all public personages, such as Butts and Walker. And Harlan and Stewart apparently wanted the *Times* rule limited to impersonal suits against private persons—that is, when such suits came close to prosecutions for seditious libel. The situation, in short, had become one of considerable confusion.

The Right of Privacy

In fashioning a constitutional right of privacy virtually out of whole cloth, the Warren Court gave apt expression to its libertarian, and to a lesser extent its egalitarian, outlook. The notion of privacy as a legal right was not altogether new. No such right had existed in older common law, but a variety of courts since the 1890s had recognized it in one fashion or another, on occasion relating it to the law of libel in the sense of an individual's right to be free from exposure through irresponsible utterance. Hitherto, however, the right of privacy had been without any formal constitutional foundation. But now from time to time the justices, as they expounded upon the right of immunity from illegal search and the right to remain silent in the face of police interrogation, asserted that the right in question was an aspect of a larger right—the right of the individual to protect certain sacred precincts of his private life from intrusion by others or by the state.

In *Griswold* v. *Connecticut* (1965), in which the Court outlawed state legislation prohibiting the use of contraceptives and the dispensing of birth-control information to married couples, the justices gave even more specific recognition to a constitutional right of privacy. In an opinion that has come to be regarded as a classic illustration of judicial activist constitutional interpretation, Justice Douglas for the majority asserted that the "specific guarantees in the Bill of Rights have penumbras formed by emanations from those guarantees that give life and substance." Such "penumbras," guaranteeing "zones of privacy" for the individual, Douglas found to lie around the guarantees of the First, Fourth, and Fifth Amendments as "protection against all governmental invasions of the sanctity of a man's home." Applying the concept of a constitutional right of privacy to the Connecticut law, he concluded that its provisions, particularly the one prohibiting the use of contraceptives by married persons, violated a "marital right of privacy" and were unconstitutional.

Griswold v. *Connecticut* also demonstrated the difficulty the Court sometimes had in identifying the sources of rights that it wished to recognize in order to adjust the law to changing social mores. Four justices, concurring in the result, offered different reasons for invalidating the law. These ranged from Harlan's use of the incorporation doctrine, to Goldberg's reliance on the Ninth Amendment (protecting rights of the people not specifically enumerated in the first eight amendments), to White's assertion that the prohibitions of the statute bore no reasonable relationship to the state's avowed purpose of discouraging illicit sexual intercourse. Black and Stewart dissented, and it is hard not to agree with Black's criticism that the majority engaged in a piece of activist judicial legislation no different from the "natural law–due process philosophy" of *Lochner* v. *New York*. Moreover, while the decision obviously reflected the society's more relaxed attitude toward sex, it also had the effect of equalizing conditions between middle-class persons who had easy access to birth-control information and devices, and lower-class persons who did not.

A privacy decision that went the other way, to the benefit of the mass media, was *Time* v. *Hill* (1967). *Life* magazine published a story about a fictionalized play based on the Hill family's captivity by escaped convicts, without making clear the fictionalized nature of the play. A New York court awarded damages to Hill under a provision of the state's civil code forbidding invasions of privacy for commercial purposes. The Supreme Court, speaking through Justice Brennan, set aside the judgment on the ground that the trial judge should have instructed the jury that it could return a verdict of liability only if the statements in the article were made "with knowledge of their falsity or in reckless disregard of the truth." In other words, the Court borrowed the *New York Times* "actual malice" libel formula and applied it to a privacy suit.

Plainly, a libertarian-inspired right of privacy here ran up against the libertarian power of the press. Not surprisingly, unallied with any special social cause, privacy lost out. What Brennan and the majority did essentially was to define any "newsworthy" story as constitutionally protected except where the publisher had resorted to "deliberate falsity or a reckless disregard for the truth." And what constituted a "newsworthy" story, Brennan made clear, was to be determined, after all, by a news medium's decision that the matter at hand was worth publishing. Thus the sphere of constitutional protection the majority had accorded the press in its potential invasions of privacy appeared to be extremely broad.

Freedom of Expression: Obscenity

In promoting cultural libertarianism the Warren Court made further inroads on state power by imposing national standards on the local regulation of obscenity. Perhaps it would be more accurate to say that the Court abandoned standards in this area, since under the rule it fashioned nothing was ever found to be obscene.

In *Chaplinsky* v. *New Hampshire* (1942) Justice Murphy had expressed the long accepted view that "the lewd and obscene" lay outside the protection of the First Amendment. Although it would at no point ever formally deny this proposition, the Court in 1957 entered upon the tortuous task of defining obscenity. In *Roth* v. *United States* (1957), a decision upholding postal censorship of obscene materials, Justice Brennan employed this test: "Whether to the average person, applying contemporary community standards, the dominant theme of the material as a whole appeals to prurient interests." In *Manuel Enterprises* v. *Day* (1962) Justice Harlan refined the test in striking down postal censorship of three homosexual magazines. Obscene material, he stated, not only appealed to prurient interest, but also was characterized by "patent offensiveness and indecency." Moreover Harlan said that national rather than local standards of decency were to be consulted, since federal law must reconcile a great diversity of community and cultural backgrounds.

With the libertarians Black and Douglas contending that the very idea

of censorship of obscenity violated the First Amendment, the Court subsequently went further in narrowing its definition of material that could be
constitutionally proscribed. In *Jacobellis* v. *Ohio* (1964) Justice Brennan
said that to be judged obscene the material in question must be " 'utterly'
without social importance." In *Ginzburg* v. *United States* and *Mishkin* v.
New York (1966) the Court broke the pattern that had prevailed since *Roth*
by sustaining convictions for violating federal postal censorship laws and
the obscenity laws of New York. Yet the Court did not find the publications
in these cases obscene; rather the manner in which they were advertised
and marketed, said Justice Brennan, amounted to the "sordid business of
pandering." In another decision the same term, *Memoirs* v. *Massachusetts*
(1966), the Court regained its libertarian stride by reversing a Massachusetts ruling that *Fanny Hill,* the ribald eighteenth-century novel, was obscene and thus subject to suppression. Further redefining *Roth,* Brennan
added to the previous standards for judging obscenity the requirement that
the material be "utterly without redeeming social value."

By 1969 the Warren Court was under attack from libertarians who
objected to categorizing obscenity as constitutionally unprotected and conservatives who believed the Court's rulings had contributed to the vulgar-
ization of the culture. The pertinent fact seemed to be that under the test
announced in the *Fanny Hill* case, anything could be found to have a social
value, so nothing was obscene.[9] It is hard to discern the Court's policy goal
in the obscenity cases, but it seems clear that the effect was to eliminate
censorship and give free rein to the spirit of raw commercialism and exploitation in this part of the culture. Perhaps the Court saw this result as the
necessary price of libertarianism. It may also have acted on the egalitarian
idea that pornography ought to be made publicly available to everyone, not
merely to the wealthy, who could indulge their tastes privately.

The Establishment and the Free Exercise of Religion

Scarcely less controversial than the obscenity rulings among large segments of the public were the Warren Court's decisions concerning the separation of church and state. Almost everyone accepted the idea that church
and state should be separated, but there was disagreement about where to
draw the line between them. To the framers of the Constitution the First
Amendment prohibition of any federal law "respecting an establishment of
religion" meant that the government could not favor one religious denomi-
nation over another; it did not preclude encouragement of religion in general as a source of public virtue. The wall of separation, in other words, was
not intended to be complete. Accordingly, church and state historically had

9. The Court did, however, permit states to prohibit the sale of harmful materials to
minors. See *Ginsberg* v. *New York* (1968).

rubbed shoulders in a variety of ways. There were chaplains in Congress, in the armed forces, and in state legislatures; the states often granted tax exemption to church property and gave some support, direct or indirect, to parochial schools; and in public ceremonies the mandatory invocation of divine providence was evidence of an amorphous but nonetheless real civil religion.

After World War II conflict grew intense between conservative groups who desired stronger state support of religion and liberals who tried to make the wall of separation higher. The conservatives had the better of it, securing numerous state laws recognizing or permitting Bible reading and prayer in public schools, released-time programs for religious instruction, and subsidies for transportation, school lunches, free textbooks, and so on. Religious groups achieved major victories when the Supreme Court approved state funding of transportation to parochial schools and released-time religious education schemes.[10] Affirming the principle of separation of church and state, the Court, in the words of Justice Douglas, nevertheless declared in 1952: "We are a religious people whose institutions presuppose a Supreme Being.... When the state encourages religious instruction or cooperates with religious authorities ..., it follows the best of our traditions."

A decade later under Earl Warren the Court steered a very different if somewhat confused course in church-state relations. In a series of cases dealing with Sunday closing or blue laws, it upheld state legislation even though a strict interpretation of the separation principle would seem to have required negating the laws. Chief Justice Warren's opinion in *McGowan* v. *Maryland* (1961) met the secular challenge to the state policy, however, by explaining that whereas the laws had religious origins, they now served the secular purpose of rest and relaxation. The retail businesses that brought the cases also claimed denial of equal protection of the law, on the ground that entertainment and resort businesses had been permitted to operate on Sunday. Yet the Court dismissed this claim out of hand. It also rejected the contention of Jewish businessmen, who had to close on Saturday for religious reasons and on Sunday because of the blue laws, that the state policy interfered with their free exercise of religion under the First Amendment. That the decisions reflected more hostility toward retail businessmen than sympathy for religion was suggested by a decision two years later in which the Court held that the state of South Carolina interfered with a Seventh Day Adventist woman's free exercise of religion. The state did so, the Court ruled, by cutting off unemployment compensation to her when she refused to take a job because it would have required her to work on Saturday, contrary to the rules of her religion.[11]

10. *Cf. Everson* v. *Board of Education* (1947), and *Zorach* v. *Clausen* (1952).
11. *Sherbert* v. *Verner* (1963).

Shortly afterward the Court kicked off a terrific controversy between conservative religious groups and civil libertarians by prohibiting prayers and Bible reading in public schools. In *Engel* v. *Vitale* (1962) it found a nonsectarian prayer, adopted by various local New York school boards in pursuance of a recommendation by the State Board of Regents, to be an unconstitutional violation of the establishment clause of the First Amendment. Then in *School District of Abington Township* v. *Schempp* (1963) the Court struck down a Pennsylvania statute that required that "at least ten verses from the Holy Bible" be read daily in all public schools. The First Amendment, said Justice Clark, forbade not only preference for one religion over another, but also aid for religion in general.

Far more than the reapportionment and criminal procedure decisions, the school prayer rulings aroused popular opposition. A campaign was begun in Congress to adopt a constitutional amendment affirming a right to voluntary school prayers and religious services. Liberals prevailed, however, and no school prayer amendment was recommended by Congress. Nevertheless, the Court's policy on religion in the schools was by no means uniformly accepted. Though in the minority nationally, a large number of local communities refused to comply with it.

Probably because the question could be seen more as a matter of economic benefits, the Court was more receptive to federal and state appropriations for private sectarian schools that raised the establishment of religion issue. In the "Great Society" spirit Congress in 1965 passed the Elementary and Secondary Education Act, a $1.5-billion grant-in-aid measure for assistance to primary and secondary education that was specifically worded to provide for grants both to public and private sectarian and secular schools. Critics desiring to challenge the law as a violation of the First Amendment establishment clause faced an apparently insurmountable obstacle in the 1923 decision in *Frothingham* v. *Mellon,* which denied standing to sue to taxpayers attacking the constitutionality of a congressional spending statute. Without deciding the church-state question, the Supreme Court in *Flast* v. *Cohen* (1968) threw out this precedent as inconsistent with modern conditions. Shortly afterward, however, in deciding the church-state question on its merits, the Court approved state aid to religion. This was the upshot of *Board of Education* v. *Allen* (1968), in which the Court sustained a New York law requiring local public schools to furnish free textbooks to all children enrolled in grades seven through twelve both in public and in private schools.

In free-exercise-of-religion cases the Court liberalized the traditional definition of religion so as to remove some of the distinctions between mainstream churches and nontraditional or secular faiths. In *Torcaso* v. *Watkins* (1961), in the course of upholding the refusal of a notary public under the First Amendment to swear a belief in God as required by the state of Maryland, the Court said that nontheistic moral codes were religions protected by the free-exercise clause. Justice Black mentioned Buddhism, Taoism, secular humanism, and ethical culture as examples of nontheistic religions. Then in *United States* v. *Seeger* (1965) the Court interpreted the conscientious-objector provisions of the Selective Service Act to include nontheistic religions. The act exempted from combat training anyone who by reason of religious training and belief was conscientiously opposed to war. In the statute Congress defined religious belief as belief "in a Supreme Being," not including political or philosophical views or personal moral codes. Nevertheless, the Court interpreted "Supreme Being" as referring to all religions, including those that did not teach a belief in God. The test to be applied, said Justice Clark, was "whether a given belief that is sincere and meaningful occupies a place in the life of its possessor parallel to that filled by the orthodox belief in God."

The Warren Court and Substantive Equal Protection

In its pursuit of egalitarianism the Warren Court employed a flexible, double-standard method of judicial review in essentially the same quasi-legislative way that the pre-1937 Court used substantive due process to protect property rights. In the spirit of Justice Stone's preferred-freedoms doctrine, with its presumption of the constitutionality of social and economic legislation and the unconstitutionality of statutes dealing with civil rights and liberties, the Court held that legislation raising equal-protection questions might be considered in either of two ways. If the legislation contained a suspect classification such as race or touched on fundamental rights or interests such as the right to fair criminal procedure, the Court would review it with special scrutiny, and the state would have to show a compelling interest in the policy in order to justify it. If neither a suspect classification nor a fundamental right was involved, the Court would apply ordinary review and require only that the legislation have a rational basis or be reasonably related to a legitimate state purpose.

Shapiro v. *Thompson* (1969) illustrated the Warren Court's double-standard method of equal-protection review. The case involved the constitutionality of Connecticut and Pennsylvania laws requiring one year's residence in the state in order to be eligible for public assistance. The states argued that the one-year rule served the rational purpose of maintaining early entry into the labor market. The Supreme Court, however, by a 6-to-3 majority, held the laws unconstitutional.

Justice Brennan for the majority said that by creating two classes of families indistinguishable from each other except for the length of residence in the state, the laws created a classification that constituted an invidious discrimination and denied equal protection of the laws. Formally concerned with residence but in reality based on wealth, the classification was in

Brennan's view suspect, and was justified by no compelling governmental interest. Furthermore, Brennan continued, the standard of a "compelling interest" was required because the legislation, intended to discourage an influx of indigents into the state, interfered with a fundamental civil right—the right of interstate travel.[12] Moreover, the state laws denied a whole class of citizens "the ability to obtain the means to subsist—food, shelter, and other necessities of life." The pertinent jurisprudential rule, explained Brennan, was that "any classification which serves to penalize the exercise of [a fundamental] right, unless shown to be necessary to promote a *compelling* governmental interest, is unconstitutional."

Brennan's opinion expressed as a formal rule, and extended in an exceedingly broad way, the policy-making function that was evident in the Supreme Court's earlier disposition of racial classification cases. Applied to the more general purpose of promoting social egalitarianism, however, the new double-standard equal protection rule smacked of purely legislative discretion. Thus Justice Harlan, while agreeing that the original intention of the framers of the equal protection clause was to make race a suspect classification, objected to the Court's startling extension of the idea. Calling the "compelling interest" doctrine a prescription for judicial legislation, Harlan said it invited the Court "to pick out particular human activities, characterize them as 'fundamental,' and give them added protection under an unusually stringent equal protection test."

The *Shapiro* decision also epitomized the Warren Court's concern for promoting the economic interests of liberal Democratic interest groups under the concept of civil rights. In earlier racial discrimination questions the equal rights struggle had had economic overtones. But here was an outright economic interest of an important liberal constituency—the poor—which the Court deemed worthy of protection. In his opinion Brennan noted that public assistance was a right, not a privilege, thus accepting a key tenet in the new equality argument. Yet consistent with the liberal activist judicial strategy derived from Stone's Carolene Products footnote, he regarded the economic interest in a formal sense as a civil right—in this instance, the right of interstate travel.

By the 1960s there was nothing new about the charge of judicial legislation which the Court's egalitarian policy making provoked. What was new was the way in which the Warren Court expressed its legislative activism. Though not widely appreciated by the public, the Court's most significant innovation concerned the technical question of the retrospective effect of judicial decisions.

12. The existence of a right of interstate travel as an attribute of national citizenship had previously been asserted in *Crandall* v. *Nevada* (1868), *Crutcher* v. *Kentucky* (1891), and *Twining* v. *New Jersey* (1908). In a manner analogous to the *Shapiro* case, it formed the basis for concurring opinions in *Edwards* v. *California* (1941), where the Court struck down the California "Okie law."

The Nature of Activist Decision Making

Judicial decisions are ordinarily retrospective since they are intended to rectify a previous situation or alter a past judgment. Legislation, by contrast, deals with future situations and is prospective. In the implementation of the Court's decisions in the field of criminal procedure, however, strict adherence to the rule of retrospectivity presented serious practical difficulties. Taking *Mapp* v. *Ohio* and the exclusionary rule as an example, it meant that if Mapp was to be released from prison because she had been wrongly convicted on the basis of illegally seized evidence, all others similarly convicted should be released, too. Sound public policy argued against such a course. But instead of allowing the retrospective principle to inhibit its reform ardor, the Warren Court abandoned the rule and, in true legislative fashion, applied its new criminal procedure rules prospectively.

The Court held first that new rules dealing with criminal justice would be employed in all cases that had not been finally decided as of the promulgation of the rule. This was established in *Linkletter* v. *Walker* (1965), in which Justice Clark said the exclusionary rule in Fourth Amendment cases would be given only limited retroactive effect. The purpose of the new rule was to improve police performance, said Clark, and it was impractical to do otherwise. When this approach appeared to have too broad a retrospective effect, the Court 'shifted to new ground. In implementing the *Miranda* and *Escobedo* decisions, it said it would apply the new rules on interrogation only to persons whose trial began after the announcement of the rules. Finally, in *Stovall* v. *Denno* (1967), concerning a rule requiring counsel at police line-ups, the Court said it would be applied only to future violations.

The problem of retroactivity had theoretical implications about the nature of law and the judicial function. Underlying the traditional rule of retroactivity was the declarative theory of law. This held that when a court decided a case, it said what the law was and had always been, thereby revealing previous actions in conflict with it to have been wrong and in need of rectification. The prospective approach, by contrast, rested on the theory that courts, like legislatures, make law. Despite the apparent wisdom of the prospective method in the matter of criminal procedure, critics contended that it would ultimately weaken the authority of the Supreme Court by removing the functional distinction between courts and legislatures. The effect, critics feared, would be to undermine the idea of law as an objective body of rules impartially applied by judges.

In reaction to the Warren Court's activist policy making, the old idea of judicial impartiality, long the object of intellectual ridicule in the country's leading law schools, experienced a revival. It figured prominently in controversy that persisted throughout the Warren era over the proper role of the judiciary in the constitutional system. Originating in the conflict be-

tween judicial activism and judicial restraint that began after the Court-
packing crisis, the controversy simmered through the 1950s and emerged in
the 1960s as a major issue in constitutional politics. With a lamentable
disregard for history but with shrewd political insight, presidential candidate Richard M. Nixon in 1968 translated the debate about the judiciary
into the issue of appointing "strict constructionist" judges to the Supreme
Court.

Judicial activists accepted the policy-making, quasi-legislative function
of judicial review as it had developed between 1890 and 1937, but were
determined to use this power for "good" liberal purposes rather than "bad"
conservative ones. Justice Stone's double-standard preferred-freedoms doctrine provided an appropriate rationale for the new outlook. The Court
would actively uphold civil and political liberties against legislative encroachment, while giving prima facie approval to legislative regulation of
property. Judicial activism usually took the form of declaring legislative acts
unconstitutional under "strict scrutiny" judicial review. It could, however,
also operate very effectively by means of statutory interpretation, especially
in view of the broad, open-ended nature of modern congressional legislation.

Judicial power not accountable in any direct way to the electorate had
always presented something of a problem from the standpoint of democratic theory in the United States. To defenders of judicial activism, however, it was plain that judicial interference with the will of the majority
where political and civil rights were concerned was democratic. The necessity of preventing a possible tyranny of the majority, an axiom of American
constitutionalism, provided the first line of judicial activist defense. Indeed,
by the 1960s activist policy-making review was so well established that its
proponents, obscuring the difference between it and pre-1890 judicial review, could draw on the classic republican government justification of the
judicial function to defend it. Thus J. Skelly Wright, a leading activist
federal judge, asserted that judicial review was a means of keeping the
community true to its fundamental principles. In this view the adoption of
the Constitution was a democratic act, and protection of the Constitution
against executive and legislative violation through the institution of judicial
review was also democratic.

Looked at in this formal structural way, judicial activism was the response to a constitutional command—especially to protect the freedoms of
the Bill of Rights—that allowed no judicial discretion. Justice Black, for
example, long regarded as a leading activist, approached constitutional adjudication from this perspective. Taking a literalistic view of the Constitution, Black said the framers of the First Amendment had done all the
balancing between liberty and security that was required; it only remained
for the justices of the Supreme Court to follow their instructions. Yet inevitably it appeared to outside observers that an element of choice or creativity

entered into the activist application of the Bill of Rights, even where Justice Black was concerned. And sometimes interpretive creativity became sheer inventiveness, as in Justice Douglas's identification of a right of privacy out of the "penumbras" of the First Amendment in the *Griswold* case. More often, commentators and judges concealed or glossed over such inventiveness by describing the Court's policy-making actions as evidence of the fact that the United States had a "living Constitution."

Political scientists intent on providing a realistic rather than merely formalistic analysis of the constitutional system also defended judicial activism against the antidemocratic charge. They pointed out that the other branches and institutions of government also failed in a variety of ways to fulfill the criteria of pure democracy. Defenders of an activist judiciary further argued that in its libertarian and egalitarian policy making the Supreme Court represented interests—racial and religious minorities, the indigent, criminals, and so on—that were otherwise ignored by the system of interest-group liberalism. So far from being undemocratic, the Court was a representative institution which, by tapping fundamental values in the polity, was able to effect necessary changes in national policy. Still other defenders of activist intervention frankly argued for decisions based on expediency rather than legal principle, as part of a conscious effort to promote social justice and human dignity. In their view the Supreme Court was essentially an agency of positive government, the legitimacy of whose decisions depended on their social utility and adequacy.

Epitomizing modern liberal activism, the Warren Court stimulated a revival of judicial restraint theory among scholarly critics and public lawyers. Restraint advocates agreed that the judiciary had a special responsibility to uphold the Constitution and to protect minorities against the potential tyranny of the majority. More than their activist colleagues, however, they were impressed in a formal sense with the undemocratic character of judicial review, and were concerned that the Supreme Court avoid the policy-making excesses of the pre-1937 Court. Theorists of judicial restraint understood the political dimension of the judicial process and the impossibility of complete detachment. Nevertheless, they thought that to guard against usurpation and legitimize its power, the Court should as much as possible base its decisions on the reasoned elaboration of neutral principles of constitutional law rather than on the justices' subjective policy preferences. In general, restraint theorists advised, the Court should defer to legislative and executive policy making and use its power sparingly so as to employ it more effectively in situations where it was needed to defend constitutional rights.

Critics writing from a judicial restraint standpoint charged the Warren Court with basing its decisions on expedient social considerations while ignoring precedent and long-standing rules of law. They contended further that the Court showed insufficient regard for the exposition of rational legal principles on which the maintenance of judicial authority rested. And by promoting reforms outside the normal channels of political and social change, often through decisions that failed to receive compliance in the society at large, critics said the Court diminished the rule of law.

Defenders of the Warren Court answered that the reforms undertaken in apportionment, criminal procedure, racial discrimination, and so on could have been achieved in no other way, given the conservative nature of the political system of interest-group pluralism. The substantive justice of the reforms, liberals insisted, justified the sometimes extraordinary exercise of judicial power that the Court engaged in. The Court had always been a political institution, and so it continued to be. But under Chief Justice Warren, wrote historian Leonard Levy in a typical liberal evaluation, "Freedom of expression and association, and ... racial justice, criminal justice, and political justice became the Court's preoccupation." Liberals thus saw the Court as responsive to the nation as a whole rather than to any single interest.

During periods of political change and realignment, when one governing coalition yields to another, the Supreme Court has often been the focus of intense controversy. In the political crisis of the late 1960s it appeared possible that the Warren Court might usher in a new liberalism based on affirmative action, equality of results, and a sweeping commitment to egalitarianism. On the other hand, the wave of popular criticism that greeted several of its decisions, especially in the cultural and social sphere, suggested that the new equality contradicted the outlook of a possibly emerging conservative consensus. Subsequent events, starting with Republican victories in the elections of 1968 and 1972, seemed to show the latter to be the more accurate view. The discrediting of New Deal liberalism and the failure of the radical new egalitarianism to command a national majority were to involve far more than the problems raised by judicial power. The reform activism of the Warren Court, however, formed an integral theme in the larger crisis of liberalism that occurred in the 1960s and early 1970s.

THIRTY-ONE

Liberal Constitutionalism in a Bureaucratic Age: The Post–New Deal American Polity

—————————— ✦✦✦ ——————————

ALTHOUGH CONFLICT between the regulatory movement and laissez faire persisted in political rhetoric, the New Deal resolved the struggle with apparent finality at the level of public policy and constitutional law. The American version of the regulatory welfare state, henceforth identified as liberal despite its rejection of classical liberalism, rested on the constitutional bases of emergency executive power and the commerce and spending powers of Congress. Its political foundation was a mass electorate reduced to economic hardship and suffering. Deeply nationalistic in its formative stages, the New Deal polity emerged from World War II even more strongly committed to the institutions of pluralistic democracy and publicly regulated capitalism that lay at the heart of the constitutional settlement of the 1930s.

In the postwar era constitutional politics proceeded on the assumptions laid down during the depression. Despite some erosion resulting from war-induced prosperity, the New Deal coalition of organized labor, Negroes, the urban lower class including white ethnic groups, government workers, intellectuals, and the South remained solidly in place. Moreover, although the practical question now was not whether but how much the government ought to interfere in the market, the central issue in domestic politics continued to be government intervention for social and economic security. After a Republican hiatus which questioned neither the regulatory function of the federal government nor the dominant role of the presidency, a renewal of Democratic rule in the 1960s extended the logic of New Deal interest-group liberalism to new issues produced by two decades of social change.

The explosive result, exacerbated if not caused by the Vietnam war and the inner logic of the civil rights movement, was a radical challenge to the post–New Deal liberal constitutional state. In an atmosphere resembling that of civil war, a crisis of public authority occurred in the late 1960s and early 1970s in which violence and civil disorder on the left provoked lawless reaction on the right. In a proximate sense the culmination of the crisis, though hardly its resolution, was the Watergate affair, the crisis of the presidency that came to a head during the Nixon administration.[1] Meanwhile, the governmental system absorbed the kicks and screams and non-negotiable demands of the protest movements, even as the society insisted on a restoration of order. A modified but still thoroughly reformist regime of interest- and issue-group pluralism, under both Democratic and Republican auspices, attempted throughout the 1970s to adapt the bureaucratic regulatory state to contemporary social realities.

Positive Government: Confirming the Modern Presidency

Expanded executive power was the central fact of New Deal government, and although it was not immune to alteration, the presidency continued to identify the central focus of constitutional politics in the next forty years. Irresistible as this development may seem in retrospect, especially in view of the persistent international crises that have been its chief justification, it was by no means inevitable. No constitutional office, to begin with, depends so heavily on the accidents of contingency and personality to define its operational impact as the presidency. Moreover, despite changes that translated some of President Franklin D. Roosevelt's power into institutional reality, his influence extended so far beyond the formal dimensions of the office that his death could have left the institution paradoxically weakened. Constitutionally, therefore, much depended on the aptitude and ambition for executive leadership of Roosevelt's successor, Harry S. Truman.

Truman never encouraged the illusion that the presidency and the government were equivalent terms, as Roosevelt on occasion did. But his actions expressed and reinforced the growing tendency to regard the president as chiefly responsible for the security and well-being of the nation. Using the colloquial expression "the buck stops here" to express his willingness to assume decisive responsibility, Truman acted boldly in utilizing the atomic bomb to end World War II and in resisting Soviet expansion. In domestic affairs Truman pursued a set of legislative aims in the spirit of the New Deal regulatory-welfare state, and added to it proposals for federal civil rights protection. Secure in his standing with other elites in the gov-

1. See below, Chapter 32.

erning establishment, Truman took risky and at times unpopular actions in leading the country into the Korean war, ending segregation in the armed forces, removing General MacArthur from military command, and seizing the steel mills as a war-related measure in 1951.

Less conspicuous though not less important, Truman also presided over enhancement of the formal attributes of executive power. In the Employment Act of 1946 Congress provided a Council of Economic Advisers to assist the president in long-range economic planning. In general the act gave institutional expression to the idea of federal—and especially executive—responsibility for maintaining the nation's economic well-being through the management of fiscal and monetary policy. Further reflecting the country's willingness to rely on executive power was the creation by Congress of the National Security Council to assist the president in defense and foreign-policy planning. In addition to using these new instruments, Truman employed the Bureau of the Budget, since 1939 formally part of the Executive Office of the President, to help shape domestic policy. Through review of departmental appropriations requests and the fiscal requirements of proposed legislation, the BOB became the president's principal means of formulating a coherent legislative program. The president also exercised greater power as a result of the Administrative Reform Act of 1950, which permitted him to name the chairmen of the independent regulatory agencies.

Truman was generally unsuccessful in his efforts to secure "Fair Deal" legislation, and his successor, General Dwight D. Eisenhower, brought to the office no mandate for legislative activism such as had been associated with previous strong presidents in the twentieth century. Moreover, Eisenhower in taking office spoke in Whiggish terms of restoring the balance between the legislative and executive branches. Nevertheless, during the Republican interlude of the 1950s the presidency suffered no decline of power. Presently the Eisenhower administration offered a legislative program, thus confirming the policy-making responsibility of the president. Eisenhower utilized the Bureau of the Budget to coordinate a legislative program, relied more heavily on an enlarged White House office—the infrastructure of aides and assistants directly and exclusively responsible to the president in a personal sense—and made greater use of the National Security Council in foreign and defense policy. Perhaps most important, despite being held in disdain by many liberal intellectuals, Eisenhower enjoyed enormous popularity and respect that contributed to the "presidentialization" of American politics and government. Although executive power was subject to real restraints depending on political circumstances, by 1960 the responsibilities and expectations associated with the office had assumed the almost limitless proportions that would continue to characterize the contemporary presidency.

The Regulatory State: Interest-Group Liberalism

The administrative machinery of the regulatory state, to some extent subject to executive direction but principally and designedly independent of the presidency, formed the policy-making substance of the post–New Deal polity. After the abortive NRA experiment in American-style corporatism, the New Deal adopted a regulatory strategy of countervailing power more consistent with the decentralized nature of American politics. Derived from the Wilsonian strand of progressivism, this version of the regulatory state theoretically operated on the judicial model of impartial rule application by nonpolitical administrators settling conflicts between private interests. In the sphere of public law its characteristic expression was the antitrust tradition, which regarded government intervention as exceptional. In accordance with the persistent myth of laissez faire, antitrust action was intended to restore the regulatory mechanism of the free market.

In the post–World War II political economy judicial policy making under the antitrust laws continued to be part of the regulatory apparatus of the positive state. Antitrust became institutionalized in a complex body of highly technical law, the main point of which was to focus on market power rather than morally bad behavior. It existed alongside, however, and was less important in a policy-making sense than, regulation by the federal bureaucracy, both in the executive departments and the independent administrative agencies. Moreover, despite the failure of the NRA and the judicial disapproval of the legal doctrine on which it rested—namely, the delegation of legislative power to the executive—this governing technique became the outstanding characteristic of the postwar positive state. Adapted to the interest-group structure of the economy, it developed into interest-group liberalism, the politico-constitutional expression of democratic capitalism in the mid-twentieth century.

If individualism has always dominated American political thought, conflict between interest groups has dominated American politics. Madison gave faction a prominent place in his theory of republicanism, and as the economy developed in the nineteenth century, merchants, producers, workingmen, farmers, professionals, and businessmen of all sorts organized themselves in order to promote their interests in public policy. As the corporation, the most highly developed and powerful form of private association, threatened to overwhelm all other private interests in the early twentieth century, the notion of competing organized interest groups began to supersede laissez-faire individualism as the key idea in politico-economic analysis.

At about the same time, students of American politics began to assimilate from English sources the political doctrine of pluralism. In the American context pluralism historically referred to the multiplicity of religious and cultural groups in American society. In the 1930s and 1940s, however, the term acquired a specifically political meaning, derived from the attack on unitary sovereignty carried out by the English philosophical pluralists of the early twentieth century. These writers, such as Harold Laski and G. D. H. Cole, argued that power did not inhere in government, but rather in the churches, trade unions, and other private groups and associations that were the focus of ordinary social life and to which people gave their deepest loyalty. Americans had no need to learn the decentralizing, antigovernmental content of this message since their whole political experience had made it part of the constitutional culture. Ideologically, however, they found it a useful substitute for traditional individualism, which was increasingly discredited by identification with laissez-faire conservatism.

In the context of the nation's basic commitment to capitalism, reaffirmed by the New Deal at its very outset, interest-group liberalism signified the conjunction of the regulatory movement and philosophical pluralism. In the years after World War II it became a full-fledged constitutional theory that hypostatized and elevated to the level of principle the conflict between social and economic groups that formed so important a part of American political history. Perceived as America's alternative to Communist and fascist totalitarianism on the one hand, and reactionary laissez-faire individualism on the other, interest-group liberalism posited a dynamic and open democratic conflict in the legislative arena, where basic national policy was formed.

According to interest-group liberal theory, heterogeneous groups rather than atomistic individuals formed majority coalitions from one issue to the next. Public policy as expressed in statutes represented the balance of competing forces resulting from the pluralistic struggle. It was the responsibility, in turn, of impartial administrators and judges to carry into effect the public policies agreed on by the competing groups in the legislature. If imbalance occurred and certain interests were consistently placed at a disadvantage, the theory of interest-group liberalism required government intervention to build up countervailing power on the part of less favored groups. Accepting the decentralized bias of the political culture, theorists of the new liberalism held that no single power or interest, either public or private, ruled in the United States. The process of government, explained a writer in the *American Political Science Review* in 1952, amounted to a "never-ending march and countermarch, thrust and parry, among economic groups, enforcement agencies, legislators, and executive functionaries," in which "today's losers may be tomorrow's winners."

Government under Interest-Group Liberalism

In the 1930s and 1940s interest-group liberalism provided a means of including labor and agriculture along with business in national policy making. And under the exigencies of the depression and later the international diplomatic crisis, in the opinion of most Americans it satisfactorily reconciled public and private interests. In time, however, the governmental realities of interest-group liberalism so far diverged from pluralist theory as to create severe political problems.

One difficulty concerned the regulatory agencies, the most visible governmental manifestation of the interest-group liberal state. In the late nineteenth century, administrative bodies combining legislative, executive, and judicial functions were a constitutional novelty of doubtful legitimacy because they contradicted the doctrine of the separation of powers. By the 1930s the regulatory agencies had existed long enough to satisfy doubts on this score. Moreover, they had overcome the limitations that rigorous judicial review had imposed on them. Yet an antibureaucratic bias persisted which was greatly exacerbated by the expansion of the administrative structure during the New Deal. Considered in light of the minimal-government–laissez-faire ideal, the regulatory agencies again faced a problem of legitimacy.

The solution to the problem was to constitutionalize the bureaucracy. This was the purpose of the Administrative Procedure Act of 1946. Concerned with the way in which the federal bureaucracy reached decisions, Congress imposed a judicial model on the administrative process. It prescribed a minimum set of procedures for agencies to follow in gathering information, prosecuting violations of public law, and issuing administrative orders and rules. The act recognized that administrative regulation depended on combining the ordinarily separate functions of government. But it placed limits on the extent to which the powers of government could be fused, as in prohibiting a member of a commission from discussing the facts of a case with the commission's staff lest the impartiality of the decision-making process be compromised. The point was to legitimize the administrative process by following the judicial model. Accordingly, the act of 1946 went far toward protecting individual rights and requiring administrators to approach regulation in a case-by-case adjudicatory manner, rather than from a broader policy-making perspective.

Pressure to judicialize the administrative process reinforced the chief characteristic of interest-group liberalism as a system of government— namely, the practice by which regulatory agencies shared power with private groups. Disregarding the *Schecter* rule, Congress in the postwar era generally passed laws announcing sweeping national goals but imposing no standards of administrative action. In other words, it delegated discretionary power to administrators, who in turn delegated it to or shared it with economic interest groups in a complex process of bargaining over policies and rules.

Looked at from the outside, the regulatory state in the postwar era appeared as a centralized bureaucracy capable of encroaching upon individual liberty. Looked at from the inside, however, it appeared much less powerful, if not actually too weak to govern. One manifestation of this weakness was the tendency of regulatory agencies over a period of time to identify with, and hence open themselves to the charge of being captured by, the interest groups they were supposed to regulate. Although this criticism overlooked the fact that one of the purposes of federal regulation was to promote private as well as public interests, the ties between agency and interest group often seemed too close for the public good. Yet whether they were or not was at bottom a political judgment. What seemed clear in any case was that interest-group liberal government consisted in what political scientists called "iron triangles," comprising an administrative agency, a private interest group, and a congressional committee. Within these structures, power and influence flowed reciprocally as agencies looked to the interest groups for technological expertise in rule making, the latter looked to the former for favorable resolution of conflicts, and both looked to Congress for protection against outside interference, including interference from the executive.

Sustained by the general economic expansion of the postwar period, interest-group liberalism as a governing system was reinforced by tendencies in the electoral system. After the political realignment of the 1930s, the two-party system operated in its usual manner to discourage ideological extremes of either left or right. Disagreeing mainly over the extent to which government should intervene in the economy, the major parties occupied the broad middle ground, each attempting to win support from the other side. The result, despite ostensibly sharp liberal-conservative differences in campaign rhetoric, was centrist policies that maintained the New Deal welfare state without significant retrenchment or extension. Another moderating influence was the tendency of voters, on the basis of identifications formed at an early age through family and culture, to remain loyal to a single party over a long period of time. Voting behavior appeared to rest more on emotional than rational, issue-related considerations. Thus the electoral system, by placing more value on stability and continuity than on citizen participation, gave ample scope for elite decision makers in Congress, the judiciary, and the executive-administrative agencies to shape national policy.

The New Frontier and Interest-Group Liberalism

In the context of international crisis that existed in the postwar era, interest-group liberalism proved a stable, effective, and broadly satisfactory governing system. Around 1960, however, strains began to appear within the political system, originating especially in the civil rights movement and the mood of national doubt created by Soviet advances in space technology in the late 1950s. The New Frontier of President John F. Kennedy was the liberal Democratic response to this situation. Politically, the New Frontier was based on the familiar New Deal coalition of labor, agriculture, minorities, intellectuals, and the South. Constitutionally, it raised the question of whether the system of interest-group pluralism would be reinforced and extended, or whether a shift toward a more centralized, state-controlled political economy might occur.

Many liberals were dissatisfied with the decentralizing tendency of pluralism, which they said fragmented governmental authority and allowed private corporations to exercise vast and undemocratic control over American society and politics. Echoing reformers' time-honored charges, they condemned "special interests," lamented the capture of the regulatory agencies by interest groups, and scored the failure of the federal government to adopt a national economic policy. And as in previous reform eras, liberals looked to centralized executive power as a remedy. Congress, they argued, should delegate more legislative power to the president. Party discipline and regularity should be more stringently enforced under presidential control. The independent regulatory agencies should be brought under executive policy management. Some critics even suggested, on the model used in executive reorganization, that the president's legislative proposals should automatically become law unless Congress vetoed them within a specific period of time! Insisting that only the president could represent the interest of the entire nation, liberals, like their progressive forebears, argued for a concentration of power in the executive branch. Constitutional government could meanwhile be maintained, they reasoned, by assuring popular controls over the purposes to which executive power was employed.

John F. Kennedy strengthened the presidency enormously, for a short while at least fulfilling the aspirations of liberal intellectuals and reformers. At the same time Kennedy—and even more his successor, Lyndon B. Johnson—applied the governing technique of interest-group liberalism to the egalitarian social concerns that emerged from the civil rights movement. In doing so Kennedy and Johnson carried public policy beyond the limits of the New Deal. Both in the exercise of presidential power and in the shaping of new social and economic policies, however, liberal Democratic governance provoked strong opposition.

Without abandoning the "old politics" methods of patronage distribution and party manipulation, Kennedy, in part through skillful use of the mass media, created a "new politics" style of presidential leadership. His bold actions in the Bay of Pigs invasion, the Berlin crisis, the Cuban missile crisis, and the Vietnam war were in considerable measure shaped by cold war strategic requirements. Yet they also reflected his evident tendency to take advantage of the public's willingness, under the tutelage of the mass media, to support the president in periods of national crisis. Whether or not this tendency led Kennedy to delay action until a crisis existed, as some critics suggested, the clearest result of his campaign promise to "get the country moving again" was an exaggerated sense of public expectation about the ability of the president, not merely to solve specific problems, but also to provide a kind of secular salvation by determining the nation's basic direction and purpose. Unfortunately, Kennedy's assassination in 1963, by preventing a conventional reckoning of his accomplishments, only accentuated the attitude of expectation with which people regarded the modern presidency.

The Vietnam war, which Kennedy supported in its critical initial stages, became so unpopular during Lyndon Johnson's administration that it provoked a major reaction against executive power. In time this reaction led to the crisis of the presidency under Richard Nixon. Meanwhile, the domestic policies of the New Frontier–Great Society tried to accommodate the turbulent social forces of the 1960s.

Although Kennedy at times used statist rhetoric (as in urging Americans, in his inaugural, to "ask not what your country can do for you—ask what you can do for your country"), his administration consistently applied the logic of interest-group liberalism in delegating power to private groups. Unwilling to confine factional maneuvering and bargaining to the legislative arena, liberal Democratic social programs encouraged policy making as a joint public-private undertaking in the administrative-executive branch of government. The approach could be seen in such pedestrian matters as farm price supports and profit and wage guidelines, where the president or department heads brought representatives of the major economic interests directly into the policy-making process. The same technique was evident in the new space communications venture known as COMSAT, a public corporation created by Congress comprising the American Telephone & Telegraph Company, the National Aeronautics and Space Administration, and the Federal Communications Commission. In this mixed public and private organization the government and private corporations shared start-up costs, while the corporations received whatever profits might accrue.

The method of interest-group delegation of power was also used to deal with the problems of social justice and equality that grew out of the successful struggle for civil rights in the 1960s. To fight what the Johnson administration dramatically presented as a "war on poverty," for example, the Economic Opportunity Act of 1964, in addition to funding job training, adult education, and other social services programs, authorized "maximum feasible participation" by the urban poor. Organized in Community Action Programs, welfare recipients and others in the poverty class were asked to help decide how federal funds should be spent to eliminate poverty. Providing no standards for administrative action, the law in effect recognized the poor as an official interest group, gave them a subsidy, and invited them to exercise discretionary lawmaking power just like more traditional interest groups.

Similar in their functional representational effect were New Frontier–Great Society social programs employing federal-state cooperation. Categorical grants-in-aid, the traditional form of intergovernmental cooperation since the New Deal, were the means of channeling federal money through state governments to support programs in vocational training, mental health, education, transportation, and so on in an endless enumeration of social problems. Private interests benefited from these policies of cooperative federalism, but more characteristic of the pluralist spirit of the 1960s was "creative federalism." This was the name given to programs based on what were called "block grants." In contrast to categorical grants-in-aid for strictly defined matters, block grants by-passed the states and gave money directly to local governments according to formulas involving population, unemployment, and other social indicators. They allowed local authorities wide discretion in spending federal money for broad policy objectives such as housing, community development, social services, and the like. Moreover, in awarding block grants the federal government explicitly urged local governments to include private groups, whether profit- or social-issue-minded, in the policy-making process. Thus liberal Democratic lawmakers and executives tried to adapt the functional representation of group pluralism to new social forces.

The Crisis of Public Authority in the 1960s

Even as liberals extended the pluralist system, however, radical student groups and militant blacks attacked it as politically illegitimate and morally corrupt. Black protest, rooted in centuries of racial discrimination at the hands of the white majority, had its proximate source in the expectations of equality raised by the civil rights movement. It also fed on the desire for material possessions stimulated by the prosperous consumer society evident all about the urban slums, where so many Negroes lived. For a time black nationalism became an effective rallying cry, but only a small number of Negroes rejected the values of American nationalism and democratic capitalism. Most of the rioters in the ghetto upheavals that occurred from 1964 to 1968 desired access to the politico-economic system that full-fledged citizenship was thought to provide. Whatever their motivation, however, the black riots posed a challenge to lawful authority that signified serious political and constitutional disorder.

The student and new left protest movement, beginning among small numbers of students at prestigious universities, arose from less easily understandable social origins but offered a clearer and more negative political message. The students who founded SDS in 1962 urged civil rights equality and economic democracy within the liberal pluralist framework. By 1968 the protest movement rejected not only interest-group liberalism, but also the conception of constitutionalism to which it had been assimilated since the New Deal. Guided by a number of radical political scientists, the student activists condemned pluralism as a class-biased system of privilege that enabled a power elite of military, industrial, political, academic, and media leaders—the despised establishment—to control the economic and political system to the exclusion of blacks, the poor, women, ethnic minority groups, and students.

With the exception of civil liberties guarantees that protected them, radical activists also expressed scorn for liberal constitutionalism. Their principal charge was that constitutionalism failed to provide for and encourage authentic political action by the people. From the founding of the republic, radicals argued, constitutionalism fragmented and trivialized public life by relying on mechanistic devices that served merely to promote economic interests. While revulsion against bourgeois capitalism was evident in the protest movement, proposals for changing "the system" usually focused on political rather than economic means. These included the use of civil disobedience as an instrument of representation, and worker controls that would democratize the corporations. The radical activists' favorite notion, however, drawn directly from the tradition of popular sovereignty, was that of a revitalized citizenry extruding the power elite and governing the nation through institutions of "participatory democracy." "Nothing less than a society all of whose members are active participants in an interminable process," enthused one political scientist, was the goal of regenerative democratic citizenship.

Although no one mistook the civil disorders of the late 1960s for a revolutionary situation in the classic sense, the black and new left protest movements created a genuine crisis of authority in the constitutional system. And while the deeply controversial Vietnam war provided a focus for the challenge, it was clear that student radicals and black-power advocates were not the first groups in the postwar era to attack the legitimacy of liberal pluralist law and policy. McCarthyite anti-Communists, white-supremacist defenders of segregation, and the neopopulist movement led by Alabama governor George C. Wallace in the 1960s had all questioned the legitimacy of the post–New Deal liberal polity. This fact suggested that flaws within the system were now being exacerbated.

In part the upheavals that occurred in American society, as in countries from eastern Europe to England, resulted from a relaxation of tension in international affairs which allowed societies to look inward and deal with social changes that had accumulated during the cold war of the 1950s. Moreover, because of the postwar baby boom, young people now constituted a larger proportion of the American population—a fact that was bound to focus attention on the problems of youth and give them a large public voice and visibility. Nevertheless, coming as it did from the previously sympathetic left instead of the predictably hostile right, the attack on the liberal pluralist state in the late 1960s was a stunning political development. When in 1969–71 a small number of radicals turned to terrorist violence, the prospect of a severe rightist reaction began to seem possible.

The Liberal Response to the Crisis of Public Authority

A reaction to the civil disorders occurred, but it was not severe or extreme, and it did not preclude substantial acceptance of many of the black and student activist demands in a new wave of regulatory legislation in the 1970s. Moreover, although the Democratic party was more receptive to the protest movement, to a remarkable extent the Republican administrations of Richard M. Nixon and Gerald R. Ford also sought to accommodate the new social forces represented in proposals for environmental protection, affirmative action, welfare rights, consumer protection, and the like. A decade after the governmental system seemed to be coming apart, the interest-group liberal state, modified to include new social-issue and minority groups and "purified" by injections of participatory democracy, continued to provide the governing infrastructure of the American polity.

Although officials condemned the ghetto riots, they did not suppress them in a reactionary way. In most instances local police and federal troops let the rioting take its course, implicitly regarding it as the result of a kind of spontaneous social combustion caused by poor living conditions. Subsequently, a number of official commissions investigating the disorders adopted this view. They described the riots as directed at abuses in the politico-economic system rather than at the system itself, and hence nonrevolutionary. In effect the liberal governing establishment took the position that some rioting was occasionally permissible within a democratic polity, provided it was selective and restrained and did not lead to terrorist violence of a political nature. Though denying that the riots had a revolutionary or an anticolonial content, officials nevertheless placed a large burden of blame on white racism and proposed more social programs to alleviate the conditions of relative deprivation that were seen as causing the upheaval.

Government officials and political leaders met the protests of student radicals with a more forthright insistence on restoring law and order. And although Republicans gained the most politically from this law-and-order appeal in the election of 1968, Democrats endorsed it, too. It was they who passed antiriot and crime control laws in 1967–68, for example, creating the Law Enforcement Assistance Administration and giving money to local authorities to help deal with civic disorders. In the face of the public's disapproval of militant and often violent protest, even the Supreme Court retreated somewhat from its advanced libertarian position. In 1966–67 the Court upheld convictions of Negro demonstrators in cases like those which had previously ended in reversal of conviction.[2] Justice Black's warning delivered in an earlier dissent, that "the crowd moved by noble ideals today can become the mob ruled by hate and ... violence tomorrow," seemed to have an effect. The Court furthermore upheld a recent amendment to the Selective Service Act that made it a crime to destroy or mutilate draft cards, as antiwar protesters were wont to do.[3] The law-and-order reaction was apparent also in Justice Department suits against antiwar activists. The government brought charges against Benjamin Spock and other prominent opponents of the war for conspiring to obstruct the draft, and it indicted a group of radicals—the Chicago Seven—for violating the antiriot act of 1968 in disturbances surrounding the Democratic convention in 1968.

Yet the law-and-order reaction was not reactionary, either in the legal efforts undertaken against protesters or with respect to subsequent public policy. In the case of the Chicago Seven, for example, a federal district court jury decision that found five defendants guilty of crossing state lines with intent to riot was overturned in 1972 by the Seventh Circuit Court of Appeals. The government chose not to appeal the decision. The Chicago defendants had also been found guilty of contempt of court in this most political of the Vietnam war era trials, but in 1973 the contempt convictions were reversed at the circuit court level. On remand the district court dismissed the defendants. Trial court convictions in the Spock conspiracy case were also overturned at the circuit level. To be sure, the government was not supine when confronted by direct-action protesters. Heads were cracked and arrests made, and in a few instances the confrontation between police and protesters turned violent and some students were killed. On the whole, however, authorities used force with restraint.

The government's response to the May Day protest in Washington in 1971, the final major surge of antiwar activity, illustrates this restraint. When upward of 40,000 protesters started to "shut the city down," federal and city officials arrested over 13,000 people in a five-day period. After legal maneuvering between the government, defense lawyers, and the courts that lasted several days, almost all the persons detained were released without incurring arrest records, the main subject of concern in the emergency litigation. Several years later a suit for damages resulted in the award of compensation, varying from $120 to $1,800, depending on the time detained, to protesters who had been improperly arrested. Improper arrest meant that protesters were detained without the "field arrest form," which police were required to use but which authorities at a certain point decided not to use even though they knew they could not get convictions without it. Although it was dispensed with, the very idea of using a bureaucratic field arrest form—complete with a Polaroid photograph!—in

2. Cf. *Adderley* v. *Florida* (1966) and *Walker* v. *Birmingham* (1967).
3. *United States* v. *O'Brien* (1968).

emergency situations, showed the extent to which the liberal state sought to act with constitutional restraint.

Republican victories in the elections of 1968 and 1972 reflected conservative popular attitudes on the questions of civil disobedience and social permissiveness raised by the protest movements. To a remarkable extent, however, politico-constitutional institutions absorbed and integrated the reform demands of radical critics. The principal manifestations of this responsiveness in public policy were changes to encourage greater citizen participation in politics, reforms in election campaign financing, a new wave of federal regulatory legislation, and a proliferation of activist issue groups whose rights claims and public-interest demands contributed to an increasing politicization of the society. At the end of the 1970s the polity retained its pluralist and in many respects decentralized structure. But the operative rules were not so much those of the "old politics" system of interest-group aggregation and coalition building, as a progressive, media-dominated "new politics" rationale.

Changes in the electoral system, though paradoxically accompanied by declining voter turnout in presidential elections, reflected the heavy emphasis placed on political participation in the wake of the protest movements of the 1960s. Begun in the voting rights struggle in the South, a bipartisan effort to facilitate political participation resulted in the adoption of the Voting Rights Act of 1970. Most significantly, the act lowered the minimum voting age in national and state elections to eighteen. It also fixed residential requirements in presidential elections at thirty days, thereby nullifying existing state requirements that ranged from six months to one year. In 1971 the Supreme Court held the law constitutional in relation to federal elections, although it was unconstitutional as applied to the states.[4] This decision was in turn superseded by the Twenty-sixth Amendment, ratified in June 1971, which declared that the right of citizens of the United States, who are eighteen years of age or older, to vote "shall not be denied or abridged by the United States or any state on account of age."

The assimilation of participatory democracy by the mainstream political culture was evident also in the decisive importance that primary elections came to assume in presidential politics. In 1960 sixteen states held primaries, but in only a handful did presidential aspirants compete against each other. In 1980 the number of primaries was thirty-seven, and presidential contenders were all but obliged to enter them because on the outcome depended the selection of delegates to the national party conventions who were legally required to support designated candidates. In 1968, 11 million persons participated in presidential primaries; in 1976, 30 million.

Changes in party organization, especially in the Democratic party, also reflected the high value placed on political participation in the 1970s. In

4. *Oregon* v. *Mitchell* (1971).

order to take power from old-style political bosses, Democratic reformers adopted new rules for the national party convention. The most important effect of the rules was to require the inclusion on a proportional basis of women, minority groups, and young people. These changes, plus numerous others intended to transfer power to citizen activists, were implemented by a centralized party organization that not only altered the nature of the party as a confederation of state organizations, but also claimed legal superiority over state laws governing the conduct of elections. In 1975 the Supreme Court upheld the party's rules as superior to state law under the First and Fourteenth Amendment's guarantee of freedom of association.[5]

New federal election laws were passed in 1971, 1974, and 1976 limiting financial contributions to election campaigns by individuals and groups. These measures further revealed the purpose of restricting the power of "the interests" and facilitating the participation of ordinary citizens in the political process. The laws permitted individuals to contribute up to $1,000 for primary elections and another $1,000 for the general election; organizations could give $5,000 per candidate. Candidates were limited to $20 million for the general election, and, as an endorsement of the participatory rationale, the federal government agreed to pay on a matching fund basis up to half the campaign expenses of all candidates who qualified. Initiated by liberal reformers, the campaign financing laws had the desired effect of reducing the role of parties in presidential elections. They did this by encouraging contributions directly to candidates who, relying increasingly on television advertising, ran independently of party organizations. These changes stimulated participation by new political action groups, especially among educated, well-to-do, middle-class professionals interested in promoting social reform.

The New Wave of Federal Regulation

Perhaps the most significant expression of the responsiveness of the political system to the protest movements was the wave of regulatory legislation adopted in the 1970s. President Nixon began it in 1969 with an executive order creating the Environmental Protection Agency out of several existing programs, and charging it with protecting the environment by abating pollution. In 1970 Congress dealt with the problems of inflation and recession in the Economic Stabilization Act, giving the president power to set prices and wages through the instrumentalities of a Cost of Living Council, Price Commission, and Wage Board. The latter two bodies included representatives of business and labor, much in the manner of the New Deal NRA. Indeed, in a nice bit of irony, the act delegated to the

---

5. *Cousins* v. *Wigoda* (1975).

Republican president the same vast legislative authority that Franklin D. Roosevelt had received in 1933. This time, however, no constitutional controversy arose, testimony to the legitimacy that the regulatory state based on delegation of legislative power had acquired in the intervening period.

In the next several years a flood of regulatory legislation poured out of Congress. It would be tedious to enumerate the measures adopted—approximately forty statutes were passed in seven years. But in general they concerned employment and civil rights equality, environmental protection, energy conservation, consumer protection, and industrial health and safety. With respect to each of these matters Congress created a federal regulatory agency if one did not already exist; charged it in abstract, universal terms with accomplishing a good purpose, such as—in the example of the Occupational Safety and Health Administration—"to assure so far as possible every working man and woman in the nation safe and healthful working conditions"; and gave it discretion to set standards of behavior for private individuals and businesses through written rules and case-by-case adjudication. The quantum increase in the amount of regulation resulting from this legislation was staggering. Yet the number of federal employees did not expand proportionally. This was because Congress did not attempt formally to create within the federal service the truly mammoth bureaucracy that would have been needed to implement the new regulatory programs. Such an expression of federal sovereignty was still, in the 1970s, politically unacceptable. What the government did instead, adhering to the rationale of interest-group liberalism, was to invite private groups into the policy and law-making process.

Yet the regulatory state of the 1970s differed from the older pluralistic structure in this respect: whereas the New Deal brought into the government economic interest groups, the new liberal state, without extruding interest groups, comprehended the new phenomenon of "issue groups." These were organizations concerned with worthy public purposes like a clean environment, rather than capitalistic profit. By the end of the decade there were more than 1,500 such organizations, most of them formed by highly educated professionals with a considerable expertise and deep moral concern about a particular issue. This is not to say that members of issue organizations had no economic interests; frequently as consultants to government agencies they received large fees, giving some truth to the old saw that reformers come to do good and end up doing well. Indeed, conservatives regarded the regulatory programs of the 1970s as a form of government largesse to lawyers, social scientists, and assorted upper-middle-class professionals. Whatever the sociology of the matter, however, issue groups assumed an important function in the administrative policy-making structure.

The Environmental Protection Agency, for example, in setting standards for clean air and water routinely consulted organizations such as the

Sierra Club. The Department of Transportation might rely on studies prepared by safety experts in the private sector in formulating safety standards for automobiles. The result was the creation of a kind of modern putting-out system, based on federal contracts, that provided a technical information base to guide federal policy makers. And given the likelihood of an increase in the scientific study of social problems in the future, it appeared probable that the nexus between issue groups and government would continue to be constitutionally important.

Resting on the modern tendency to assume that all problems have solutions and the corollary belief that the federal government must find them, issue-group bureaucratic management was an adaptation of interest-group liberalism that absorbed, at the same time that it met, many of the reform demands of the 1960s. Yet like the older pluralism, the new approach raised a number of constitutional questions. One of them concerned the legitimacy of public policy made not only by government officials, but also by private groups and individuals not accountable to the people. Government by nameless and faceless bureaucrats, it has been said, is government by nobody. After the protests of the 1960s, the underlying legitimacy of such a system appeared increasingly tenuous.

A second issue was the politicization of society that occurred as more and more aspects of everyday life came under regulatory scrutiny. Government administrators' reliance on scientific research findings to shape policies dealing with such long-range and recondite matters as the proper ecological balance were subject to dispute in the light of other research findings. They became as politically controversial as any conflict over pedestrian economic interests in the "old politics" of interest-group liberalism. Moreover, many issue-oriented policy makers, in the government as well as in the issue organizations, were so committed to a particular position based on moral or scientific grounds that controversies over policy making assumed pronounced ideological overtones. Often they became matters of principle difficult to resolve through traditional methods of compromise. Was compromise morally acceptable when the question was whether handicapped persons ought to be given equal access to public transportation by requiring all buses to be equipped with special lift devices? Should the Occupational Safety and Health Administration consider the costs to industry resulting from regulations protecting workers' health? Should or could human life be given a monetary value to be weighed against the costs required to enforce new industrial safety regulations? These questions were not easily dealt with by the traditional method of interest aggregation and compromise, as in interest-group pluralism.

In almost any big-city newspaper in the late 1970s it was possible to read bureaucratic horror stories that reinforced a persistent and growing popular hostility toward government regulation. Thus a microbiologist in the Food and Drug Administration issues new regulations banning from the market an inexpensive salt-tablet treatment for cleaning contact lenses and in effect requiring the use of a much more costly product. As a result of the decision one manufacturer suffers considerably while another reaps enormous profits. A man unwilling to pay $2,500 to equip his imported automobile with the required antipollution devices sees the vehicle turned into scrap metal by order of the Environmental Protection Agency. A federal court rules that in regulating the industrial environment, OSHA is limited only by the requirement that its standards be technologically and economically feasible for the regulated industry. If specific firms within the industry are driven out of business, so be it.

As these examples illustrate, the issue at stake in much contemporary public policy is not only the public interest, but also property rights. In this sense the situation is as it was in the age of enterprise, when many businessmen opposed economic regulation on the ground that it was destructive of property, and the general public and other businessmen supported it in the name of the general welfare. Regulators are still genuinely concerned with serving the public interest, and they are often supported by commercial firms and professional and academic consultants who have an economic interest in new regulatory programs. And just as it was difficult in 1910 to say exactly what amount of government intervention optimally served the joint public and private purposes of the regulatory movement, so the question remained unresolved in 1980. There is a key difference, however, between the early regulatory movement and the situation in the late twentieth century. Contemporary regulators, committed to a particular issue, may be less sympathetic to the purpose of private business enterprise than their predecessors.

In the late 1970s attacking the bureaucracy was politically popular. President Carter in 1976 and President Reagan in 1980 both appeared to benefit from stances that criticized the Washington governing establishment for being out of touch with the people and hence in some sense lacking legitimacy. In public policy, criticism of "captured" regulatory agencies led to limited "deregulation" efforts—for example, in the airline and trucking industries. The antibureaucracy refrain expressed the traditional distrust of government as well as the deep ideological attachment to the free-enterprise ideal. Whether it would seriously challenge the modern belief that government can and should solve society's problems was perhaps doubtful, but the criticism of administrative overload reasserted the value of the self-governing ideal that has been central to American constitutionalism throughout its history.

Reassertion of the self-government ideal was present also in the encouragement of grass-roots political action and in the participation of issue groups in public policy. The consequence of this spreading politicization, ironically, was a severe discrediting of political parties, as evidenced in their growing inability to retain voter identification and loyalty. The significance of this development for constitutional government remained to be seen, but parties, like economic interest groups, appeared to lose much of their legitimacy. The prospect appeared of American politics being conducted by ideologically committed and elite-directed issue organizations, appealing directly to the electorate by means of television and the other media and governing the country through their connections with the federal bureaucracy. Such a polity would probably be described as a constitutional democracy, yet its substance would be very different from the kind of constitutional politics based on pluralistic interest groups that has prevailed through most of American history.

THIRTY-TWO

The Watergate Scandal and the Crisis of the Modern Presidency

———————————— ✦ ✦ ✦ ————————————

PRESIDENT RICHARD M. NIXON'S overwhelming victory in the election of 1972 signified the response of the existing order to the radical protest movements of the late 1960s. Within months of the election, however, evidence came to light implicating the White House in the burglary and electronic bugging of the Democratic National Committee offices in the Watergate apartment in Washington in June 1972. Throughout 1973 investigations by courts, congressional committees, and the press produced astonishing revelations not merely about the president's involvement in the Watergate break-in, but also about a whole series of executive actions of questionable legality and constitutional propriety dating from the start of the Nixon administration. The extent and magnitude of presidential wrongdoing provoked an impeachment inquiry by the House of Representatives, and when it appeared certain in August 1974 that the House would vote to impeach him, Richard Nixon became the first president in United States history to resign from office.

Politics and personality surely played a part in the Watergate scandal. For a generation Nixon had been the bête noire of the Democratic party, and it is difficult to believe that this political enmity did not supply an extra incentive for the liberals in Congress and the press who conducted the investigations that proved so damning to him. Nor is it likely that events would have taken the course they did but for Nixon's distinctive personality. From the outset of the Watergate investigations the president dug himself in deeper and deeper, denying any involvement in the matter even as the evidence piled up, until his ruin was complete. Ultimately, however, Watergate was a constitutional crisis that transcended politics and personality and threatened to create an unprecedented executive sovereignty within the federal government. Moreover it was rooted not in the character traits of Richard Nixon, important as these were to the outcome of the drama, but in aggrandizements, distortions, and excesses of presidential power dating from the time of Franklin D. Roosevelt.

Growth of the Imperial Presidency

The expansion of presidential power from World War II to the Vietnam war, though it did not go unchallenged, was clearly accepted as politically and constitutionally legitimate. Nevertheless, it had the effect of removing restraints on executive power, eventually with untoward constitutional consequences. President Roosevelt's decision to engage in undeclared naval warfare against Germany in 1941 was the most conspicuous of a series of actions which at best, in the words of sympathetic historian Arthur M. Schlesinger, Jr., revealed only "a lurking sensitivity to constitutional issues." Truman went further in creating an executive power to commence war by taking the country into the Korean war and moving several divisions to Germany in 1951. John F. Kennedy's naval "quarantine" of Cuba in the 1962 missile crisis, his commitment of combat troops to Vietnam as "advisers," and President Johnson's action in landing U.S. marines in the Dominican Republic in 1965 further damaged the constitutional prerogative of Congress to declare war. Furthermore, in usurping congressional power in this sphere presidents utilized the Central Intelligence Agency for secret military operations, in apparent conflict with its statutory charter.

In domestic affairs executive power was less considerable because other branches and agencies of government had clearer and more substantial constitutional roles to play. Yet this circumstance was itself the source of constitutional instability as the political demands on the presidency grew tremendously in the postwar era and became discrepant with the actual capabilities of the office. By 1960, as noted previously, the president was generally expected to initiate a legislative program, manage the national economy, and give focus to the nation's long-range aspirations and purpose as its ultimate leader. To accomplish these tasks presidents had at their disposal formal institutional powers of command, and also informal powers of persuasion arising from personality, circumstance, and political skill.

An additional asset of executive power in the postwar period was the academic and intellectual consensus that existed in favor of a strong presidency. As though legitimizing and confirming Franklin Roosevelt's exertions of power, a large number of political scientists, liberal in outlook, regarded the presidency as the nation's only truly representative institution. Because of his unique vantage point, they reasoned, the president was able to overcome the parochial concerns that prevailed in Congress and act in the national interest. Scholars urged further strengthening of the office by giving the president greater control over the regulatory agencies, and a larger role in a more disciplined and programmatic party system. Meanwhile, liberal historians discerned a kind of historical law of constitutional development which supposedly led strong presidents to support progressive reforms and weak ones to defer to conservative policy making in Congress. And in situations where presidents had seemed to exceed their constitutional powers, as in Roosevelt's conduct of diplomacy on the eve of World War II, historians explained the actions as necessary in order to make the people aware of the nation's true interests and needs.

Appeals for a stronger presidency were a response to the increasingly heavy political demands that were made on the office in the age of the national security state. Regarded as responsible for the safety and well-being of the nation, the president, though presiding over a continually growing executive establishment, often seemed to lack the powers necessary for accomplishing what was expected of him. Usually the chief impediment was Congress, a congeries of parochial power centers loosely coordinated by an undisciplined party system and, since the late 1930s, frequently controlled by a Republican-southern Democrat alliance. Problematic, too, was the president's relationship with the administrative agencies. Despite the fact that since 1950 the president could name the chairmen of the independent regulatory agencies, these institutions remained substantially impervious to executive direction and influence. The president's leverage was slight even in relation to administrative boards and commissions within the regular executive departments, which were securely located in the "iron triangles" of interest-group pluralism. Another uncertain element in the political environment surrounding the executive was the media. Skill in utilizing public relations techniques was virtually a prerequisite for governmental success in the era of mass communications. Yet increasingly the media formed a distinct interest group that could seriously affect the exercise of presidential power.

In the hostile environment that often confronted them in the postwar era, presidents not only employed the powers of constitutional command and political persuasion inherent in the office, but they also had recourse to covert and illegal exercises of executive power. From Franklin Roosevelt through Lyndon Johnson, presidents authorized the FBI to use wiretaps and other forms of electronic surveillance to gather information theoretically for national security purposes, but in reality for the purpose of White House political intelligence and espionage. The uniquely powerful position that the FBI occupied during the internal security crises of World War II and the cold war was perhaps the essential element in the situation. Led by the shrewd bureaucratic tactician and empire builder J. Edgar Hoover, the bureau became a power unto itself which had the overwhelming support of public opinion. This fact was itself symptomatic of the executive's inability to manage his political environment. Yet president after president accepted

Hoover, not only because they feared his political power but also because they benefited from the FBI's covert intelligence operations.

In the late 1960s, principally as a consequence of the Vietnam war, a reaction against what was now called the imperial presidency began to set in. Lyndon B. Johnson first bore the brunt of critical attack for his actions in escalating the war in Vietnam. In August 1964, amid reports of unprovoked North Vietnamese attacks on U.S. Navy ships in the Gulf of Tonkin, Johnson went to Congress with a resolution authorizing the president to "repel any armed attack against the forces of the United States and to prevent further aggression" in Southeast Asia. Congress quickly adopted the resolution, thus providing a plausible constitutional and political basis for the military action that the government undertook in the next four years. Yet even as Congress approved the Tonkin Gulf resolution, critics contended that the United States had created the incident, a view given support in subsequent congressional investigation. The president, it appeared, had deceived Congress and the public in order to gain endorsement of actions that he considered necessary for national security.

By the late 1960s the national security argument had been so frequently invoked as a justification for executive action that it was beginning to lose its persuasiveness and legitimacy. Often it seemed to be used to conceal duplicity if not illegality in the exercise of executive power. In Congress and the courts, meanwhile, efforts were undertaken to restrict the presidential war-making power. Arising from diverse political sources and reflecting mainly revulsion against the Vietnam war, these efforts also served as a vehicle for the new left and student radical challenge to the legitimacy of the nation's basic political institutions. It was in these straitened circumstances that Richard M. Nixon assumed the presidency in 1969.

Nixon and the Culmination of the Liberal Activist Presidency

The chief tasks facing Nixon required action, albeit action of a negative sort. After several years of urban riots, student strikes, and protest marches, public opinion clearly demanded a restoration of order. It also demanded an end to the Vietnam war that would allow the United States to withdraw from the fighting without suffering complete national humiliation and disgrace. Pursuing these objectives was a president with activist or aggressive personality traits who proposed not only to employ the powers of the presidency which statute and usage since the New Deal had sanctioned, but also to centralize national policy making in ways long advocated by liberal advocates of a more powerful presidency.

Nixon's war policy, called "Vietnamization," at once widened the scope of the conflict in Indochina while bringing about a withdrawal of

American troops. The constitutional status of the war now altered substantially. In the spring of 1970, the president ordered a tactical invasion of Cambodia, thereby extending the war into a foreign state at least nominally neutral. Relying solely on his constitutional powers as commander in chief, Nixon took this step without any consultation with Congress. Thereafter disillusioned lawmakers sought to bring hostilities to a close. In January 1971 they repealed the Tonkin Gulf Resolution, an action that conceivably withdrew from the president further constitutional authority to conduct hostilities in Southeast Asia. In fact, however, repeal had no visible impact on the conduct of the war. In January 1973 the president finally terminated American military operations in Vietnam by means of an armistice negotiated with North Vietnam and the South Vietnamese Communists (Viet Cong). But the air war against the Cambodian "rebels" continued until Congress, in June 1973, voted to cut off all supplies for its support.

Meanwhile, the Supreme Court rejected all attempts to involve it in the constitutional controversy over the president's prosecution of an undeclared war. In 1967 it twice refused to grant certiorari from lower court decisions upholding plenary executive war powers. Again in 1970 the Court let stand a Court of Appeals decision in *Massachusetts* v. *Laird,* holding that since the president in carrying on the Vietnam war had acted with congressional support, the Constitution had not been breached. Finally, in August 1973 a district court ruled the war in Cambodia unconstitutional and issued an injunction against its continuance. But an Appellate Court stayed the injunction, a decision endorsed by the Supreme Court. Thereupon the Appellate Court, in *Holtzman* v. *Schlesinger* (1973), invoked the doctrine of political questions to hold that the federal courts could not intervene against a presidential war.

In domestic politics Nixon insisted on a restoration of social order. Yet he also supported reform measures dealing with environmental protection and the welfare system. Ironically, because of the liberals' own shift to the left in the late 1960s, Nixon took positions closer to New Deal liberalism than liberal Democrats did. Affirming traditional social values, he upheld equality of opportunity, competition, and the work ethic when Democrats supported affirmative action in the sense of equality of result. When radicals expressed scorn for "bourgeois liberties" and spoke of "repressive tolerance," Nixon argued for the free exchange of opinion under traditional doctrines of freedom of speech. And when the left condemned the electoral system as fraudulent, Nixon defended it as legitimate, invoking the sanction of the "silent majority."

Using conventional Republican rhetoric, Nixon's campaign in 1968 stressed decentralization and local self-government. In fact, however, his administration promoted the very concentration of executive power that liberals had urged for a generation. At the start of his first term Nixon tackled an issue that had plagued every president from Roosevelt to Johnson: the resistance of the bureaucracy to executive policy control. For Nixon the problem was exacerbated by the fact that recently adopted Great Society legislation had created major new social programs staffed and managed by liberal bureaucrats whose political differences with the administration would encourage even stronger resistance to executive influence. Nixon's answer to the problem was to strengthen and expand the White House staff.

The major centralizing move was to bring the Bureau of the Budget under closer presidential control and make it more political. Through an executive reorganization plan in 1970, which renamed the bureau the Office of Management and Budget, Nixon added new positions below the office of director to coordinate policy planning with the White House. He strengthened the agency in relation to the executive departments. Furthermore, he created a Domestic Council to replace the departments as the principal source of policy formulation, just as the National Security Council superseded the State Department in foreign policy planning. Nixon also appointed to undersecretaryships in the departments persons of no particular distinction whose chief task was to represent the White House point of view and inhibit independent policy initiatives.

The increase in the size of the White House staff from about 1,700 to over 3,500 reflected the unprecedented concentration of power under the president's personal command that occurred during Nixon's first term. Previously, White House assistants, first authorized in the Executive Reorganization Act of 1939, were hardly more than highly competent executive secretaries possessing no real influence or power. Nixon's principal administrative assistants—H. R. Haldeman, John Ehrlichman, and others—were in fact powerful ministers of state who shaped the internal policies of the administration.

If Nixon antagonized the bureaucracy, he acted even more provocatively toward Congress. Perhaps most egregious was his impoundment of monies appropriated for purposes of which he did not approve. The result was not only to give him what amounted to a line-item veto over the provisions of congressional appropriation acts, but also to arrogate to the executive a virtually uncontrollable power to block any federal program whatever involving the expenditure of money.

Nixon's impoundment program was by no means without some precedent. Jefferson in 1803 had held up a $50,000 gunboat appropriation for a short time (though merely to ascertain what model was most advisable), while Grant in 1876 had interpreted a congressional appropriation for public works as not "obligatory" in view of the current economic depression. And Franklin Roosevelt in 1941, anticipating the will of Congress, had suspended expenditures on public works not related to the war effort. Even as he acted, however, Roosevelt had assured Congress that impoundment could not constitutionally be used to "nullify the express will of Congress."

More to the point were the impoundments by Presidents Truman, Kennedy, and Johnson between 1949 and 1969 of funds for military appropriations of one sort or another. But in virtually every one of these instances, impoundment could be justified either by the permissive language of the appropriation act itself or by the president's action in obtaining the unofficial consent of Congress. Military impoundment, it also could be argued, was a special case which conceivably fell within the president's powers as commander in chief.

President Nixon's impoundments, the first of which occurred in 1969, were without precedent in frequency, in the amount of money involved, and in purpose. By the end of 1973, the president had impounded monies from more than one hundred different programs, involving expenditures of more than $15 billion. Many of these actions had to do with federal programs for pollution control, housing, assistance to public education, and the like. For the first time, impoundment represented the imposition of public policy contrary to that upon which Congress had acted. The president, in other words, was doing what FDR in 1941 had warned he could not properly do: substituting his legislative will for that of Congress.

Nixon and his subordinates defended impoundment as a necessary policy to stop inflation. But they also argued that it had statutory and constitutional bases. The statutory authority claimed was the antideficiency acts of 1905 and 1906, which permitted the president to withhold the appropriations of an agency in order to prevent it from spending all its money before the end of the fiscal year. The purported constitutional authority for impoundment was the requirement that the president faithfully execute the laws. How this could possibly justify simple refusal to enforce duly enacted statutes was mystifying to most people, including Assistant Attorney General William Rehnquist, who in a memorandum wrote: "It seems an anomalous proposition that because the Executive is bound to execute the laws, it is free to decline to execute them." Nevertheless, Nixon in January 1973 insisted that his constitutional power to make national policy through impoundment was "absolutely clear." Evidently, he believed that popular dissatisfaction with inflation, and with the government spending that was widely believed to be the cause of it, would sustain this extraordinary exercise of power.

Impoundment was in effect a kind of selective law enforcement; by it, the president decided upon his own authority which appropriation acts he would recognize and which he would nullify. Closely related to this form of executive nullification was Nixon's decision from time to time not to enforce one statute or another of whose policy implications he disapproved. His procedure here was reminiscent of Roosevelt's warning to Congress in 1942 that he would refuse to enforce certain provisions of the Emergency Price Control Act unless Congress repealed them forthwith. But there was one important difference: FDR had asked Congress for repeal; Nixon on two notable occasions imposed executive nullification without bothering to ask Congress for repeal.

In July 1969, the Nixon administration announced formally that the Department of Justice and the Department of Health, Education, and Welfare would no longer enforce Title VI of the Civil Rights Act of 1964. This was the provision which prohibited discrimination based upon race, color, religion, or national origin in programs receiving federal financial assistance, and which required a fund cutoff in those instances in which HEW ascertained that such discrimination existed. A federal district court pronounced the administration's action to be illegal, but no change in administrative practice resulted. The implications were clear: the Nixon administration was pursuing a policy toward racial discrimination inconsistent with the intent of the law.

Another dramatic step was taken in January 1973 when the administration decided to dismantle the Office of Economic Opportunity, an agency created by statute as a part of Lyndon Johnson's campaign to end poverty. The Nixon-appointed OEO director, acting under presidential order, thereupon set to work to liquidate the agency's personnel and to terminate its activities. The legal excuse offered for this action was simply that the president had decided not to include an appropriation for OEO in his forthcoming budget message to Congress. A federal district court ruling partially checked the formal process of dismantling, but the OEO nonetheless headed for innocuous obscurity.

Still another "legislative" device adopted by President Nixon was his unprecedented and highly unorthodox use of the "pocket veto." Article I, Section 7, of the Constitution allows the president to kill a bill enacted by Congress within ten days of an adjournment simply by failing to sign it into law. The language of the Constitution poses a constitutional question of some importance: what is an "adjournment?"

In 1928, in the Pocket Veto Case, the Supreme Court had ruled that the president could constitutionally impose a pocket veto at the end of a session of Congress, as well as at the adjournment incident to the ending of a Congressional term. The president's right to resort to a pocket veto during an even shorter adjournment—a holiday recess of a few days—remained uncertain. But in *Wright* v. *United States* (1938) the Court ruled that during a short recess (in this instance one of three days), the secretary of the Senate had the constitutional power to receive a veto message. The plain implication of Chief Justice Hughes's opinion was that the pocket veto could not properly be applied to an adjournment of only a few days.

But in December 1970 President Nixon nonetheless imposed a pocket veto on a bill adopted by Congress during its Christmas recess. The bill, the Family Practice of Medicine Act, involved appropriations of some $225 million for hospital and medical school support, and had been adopted by the two houses by overwhelming majorities eight days before the recess.

Two days after the recess commenced, however, President Nixon announced that he was refusing to sign the law, and that because of the pocket-veto provision he would also refuse to return it to Congress. The president's strategy was evident: instead of a two-thirds majority veto, which he would exercise were he to return the measure to Congress with a veto message, he had in effect endowed himself in this instance with an absolute veto. Senator Jacob Javits of New York declared in indignation that the president's pocket veto was "illegal." In 1972 and again in 1973 Congress appropriated monies intended to give the "vetoed" law force and effect; however, Nixon, in turn, ignored the appropriation acts.

Toward the Plebiscitary Presidency

Looked at through the prism of the Watergate investigations, President Nixon's use of executive power from the outset of his administration seemed high-handed in the extreme. It is important to remember, however, that no widespread public outcry arose against Nixon's actions in the period before 1973, however offensive those actions were to members of the Washington governing establishment. Indeed, that offensiveness may have been to Nixon's advantage, since hostility toward the liberal bureaucracy was one of the sources of his political support. Certainly, the result of the 1972 election—an unprecedented landslide victory—must have confirmed in Nixon's mind the correctness of his course. In any case, as Nixon cut himself off from other governing elites in Congress and the bureaucracy, not to mention the press, with whom his relationship had always been testy and problematic, he cultivated a direct relationship with the people that pointed toward a new conception of executive power. This was the idea of the plebiscitary presidency.

European in origin, the term "plebiscitary" refers to arrangements that permit executive officials to wield broad authority, subject only to the restraint of periodic approval from the people in elections that serve to judge past conduct rather than provide specific direction for future policy. The conception was alien to the founders of the republic, but the history of the presidency since FDR gave more than a plausible basis for Nixon's tendency in this direction. The key idea in the plebiscitary conception was the relationship between the executive and the electorate. Jefferson and Jackson in the nineteenth century, and Wilson, Franklin Roosevelt, and the other liberal Democratic presidents in the twentieth century, clearly regarded the president as uniquely qualified to act for the nation. A long line of reformers since the progressive era had argued that there was nothing to fear in a generous exercise of executive power, provided only that it was kept accountable to the people in free elections.

Accordingly, the way was well prepared for Nixon's venture into plebiscitarian presidential government. In a general sense the actions of his first term, frequently justified by reference to the views of the "silent majority" which he professed to represent, expressed the idea of the president exercising a general prerogative power with little regard for the limitations that the Constitution imposed on him. More specifically illustrative was Nixon's 1972 re-election campaign. He cut himself off from the Republican National Committee and formed his own personal election organization, the Committee to Re-elect the President. Known by the unfortunate acronym CREEP, this was strictly a White House operation that ignored other Republican candidates and concentrated on getting Nixon the largest possible majority. Thanks to the Democrats' decision to run George McGovern, the effort was overwhelmingly successful, whereupon the president and his supporters laid claim to a mandate that in their view justified uncompromising insistence on administration policies. Of course, all of this owed much to Nixon's penchant for solitary political combat and the deep sense of social and class resentment he felt toward liberals. It seems equally clear, however, that the isolation of Nixon and the White House from the pluralistic mainstream of American politics was an accentuation of the progressive estrangement of the presidency that occurred as the office became at once more powerful and burdened with ever greater responsibility in the post–New Deal period.

Convinced that the antiwar movement presented a national security problem, Nixon even before his re-election created a White House–controlled security and espionage system intended to protect the country against subversives. Its purpose was also to protect the Executive Office against disclosure of confidential materials either to Congress or the nation generally. Here, again, Nixon followed the example of earlier presidents who had used the FBI for purposes of political intelligence. Yet Nixon carried the national security idea to such lengths as virtually to discredit it as a legitimate issue in constitutional politics.

Early in his administration, President Nixon expressed dissatisfaction with the system of security against subversive activity established by the Federal Bureau of Investigation under J. Edgar Hoover. In its place he sought to develop a system of his own. In July 1970 the president endorsed and promulgated secretly a memorandum prepared by Tom Huston, a youthful White House staff member, which authorized a comprehensive program for surveillance of those Americans who "pose a major threat to our internal security." The memorandum called for the warrantless search of domestic mails, infiltration by government agents into radical student organizations on university campuses, the monitoring of all overseas mail, cable, and phone communications by American citizens, and outright burglary of both offices and private homes where surveillance authorities thought it necessary. The president at the same time ordered warrantless wiretaps placed on thirteen members of the National Security Council as well as on several newspapermen. None of this rested on any statutory authority.

The Huston security program was blatantly unconstitutional on its face. Ironically, J. Edgar Hoover, who hitherto had hardly established a reputation as a defender of constitutional liberty, forthwith denounced the program as illegal and unacceptable. The president ordered the plan abandoned, but executive-authorized domestic espionage, mail searches, and the like continued. Early in 1971 the president set up an Intelligence Evaluation Committee to coordinate undercover White House espionage activities. In July following the controversy over publication of the so-called *Pentagon Papers,* the president also established a special White House espionage unit—shortly dubbed the "Plumbers"—and placed Egil Krogh in charge. In effect, Nixon gave Krogh and the "Plumbers" carte blanche authority to engage in whatever forms of espionage they thought necessary in the interests of national security.

The "Plumbers" immediately embarked upon a program of nation-wide espionage altogether unauthorized by any statutory or constitutional authority. It was a "Plumbers" task force which in late August burglarized the office of the psychiatrist who had treated Daniel Ellsberg, the dissident Defense Department employee who had stolen the *Pentagon Papers* for the *New York Times.* So outrageous were the "Plumbers'" antics that John Ehrlichman, astonished and indignant, dissolved the unit in December 1971. But the "Plumbers'" personnel, still available, were presently reassigned to the White House–controlled Committee to Re-elect the President. It was a CREEP task force that, in June 1972, staged the bungled burglary of the Democratic National Committee in the Watergate apartment complex.

The Watergate Affair

Nixon's re-election by the largest popular and electoral majority in American history placed him in a seemingly impregnable position. The concentration of power in the executive branch that within a few months would appear nothing short of revolutionary was by way of being accepted, despite evidence of constitutionally questionable activities. Presidential war making, the new use of the White House staff to supersede the departments in policy making, impoundment, the pocket veto, and increased reliance on the national security idea were all apparent. It was known that the administration had tried to impose prior restraint on the *New York Times* and *Washington Post* in the matter of the *Pentagon Papers,* and that it employed wiretapping for domestic security surveillance without warrants. Moreover, administration officials had broached the possibility of revoking the licenses of radio stations considered guilty of liberal bias, and of initiating antitrust

action against media corporations. Against the background of social upheaval and instability caused by the protest movements, however, people
were willing to accept Nixon, given the alternative of McGovern.

In this regard the legitimating effect of the 1972 election was profound.
It restored to the constitutional system much of the legitimacy that radicals
had tried to deny it, conferring on the administration seemingly authoritative approval. Had the Watergate incident not occurred, the concept of the
plebiscitary presidency would undoubtedly have been greatly strengthened
by the close of Nixon's second term in office.

The Watergate burglary and bugging incident occurred in June 1972.
It aroused limited interest at best, as did investigations by the General
Accounting Office and the FBI in the fall of 1972 into campaign finance
tactics of the Committee to Re-elect the President. In January 1973, however, the trial of the seven Watergate burglars, probingly conducted by
Federal District Court Judge John Sirica, produced evidence suggesting
White House involvement in the break-in. Spurred by the court's findings
and by newspaper reports of alleged administration wrongdoing, the Senate
in February 1973 appointed a Select Committee to inquire into illegal and
unethical activities in connection with the 1972 election.

Through the spring and summer the Select Committee turned up astonishing information about the Nixon White House. It now became known
that the president had created a secret security and political intelligence and
espionage system; used the Internal Revenue Service as a weapon to attack
political enemies; falsely backdated a gift of presidential papers to the
National Archives in order to get a tax credit; was inexplicably careless in
preparing his tax returns; and spent large amounts of government money to
improve his private estates at San Clemente and Key Biscayne—to name
only the most conspicuous acts of administrative lawlessness and malfeasance. Even more damning was the discovery of a tape-recording system in
the White House which appeared to provide evidence of President Nixon's
participation in a plan to cover up the bugging incident.

In May 1973 the Senate established the Office of Special Prosecutor
and gave the prosecutor sweeping powers to investigate the Watergate incident. The House of Representatives began an impeachment inquiry in
October, and in March 1974 President Nixon was named as an unindicted
co-conspirator by a grand jury that charged John Mitchell, John Ehrlichman, H. R. Haldeman, and other White House aides with conspiracy to
defraud the United States and to obstruct justice. Four months later the
House Judiciary Committee voted to impeach the president, and in early
August Nixon resigned.

Two specific constitutional issues provided the focus of the Watergate
crisis: executive privilege and the scope of the impeachment power. Executive privilege had to do with the alleged constitutional right of the president
to withhold documents from Congress and from the courts. The issue was

not a new one in American history. President Washington in 1792 had insisted upon his right to withhold certain papers from the House of Representatives in connection with General St. Clair's defeat by the Ohio Indians. Again, in 1795, he had refused a request from the House of Representatives for executive papers having to do with the negotiation of the Jay Treaty. And in 1807 Jefferson had successfully defied a *subpoena duces tecum* directed to him by John Marshall, presiding as a United States Circuit Judge in the Burr treason trial.

Thereafter other presidents, when it suited their interest to do so, had refused congressional requests for executive documents. In a notable modern case, President Truman in 1948 had successfully defied a House resolution directing him to turn over whatever executive papers its committees found necessary "to properly perform their duties." The president, said Truman in a general order to all executive departments, would determine on the basis of "the public interest in each case" when papers were to be handed over to Congress or its committees. The Eisenhower, Kennedy, and Johnson administrations subsequently adopted much the same position. In general it was recognized that Congress needed information, and the president confidentiality. No categorical claim was made for executive privilege, a term first used in the Eisenhower period, nor had the judiciary ever adjudicated the question. Conflicts were resolved by political means, in a spirit of comity and common sense.

In the first Nixon administration the president claimed executive privilege four times himself, and his assistants did so on twenty-three occasions. During the Watergate investigations, however, executive privilege became a litany ceaselessly invoked by the president as he fought to conceal his involvement in the cover-up conspiracy. The question first arose when the Senate Select Committee, under Senator Ervin, sought to obtain by subpoena five critically important tapes, only to encounter a firm presidential refusal. The committee then appealed to the courts, but federal district Judge Sirica rejected the committee's plea for a *subpoena duces tecum* directed to the president. The long-standing tradition of executive privilege with respect to congressional demands for executive documents had been decisive.

Presidential defiance of a subpoena addressed to the executive by the federal courts proved to be a different matter. In July the special prosecutor, Archibald Cox, addressed a *subpoena duces tecum* to the president, ordering him to produce a series of tapes before a grand jury of the District of Columbia. Nixon refused. And when Judge Sirica directed him to comply, the president's lawyers appealed to the Circuit Court of the District of Columbia, claiming that the order of the district court "threatened the continued existence of the presidency as a functioning institution."

In mid-October, the Circuit Court ruled, 5 to 2, in *Nixon* v. *Sirica* (1973), that the president's claim of executive privilege was in this instance invalid, and that the president must comply with the subpoena. The majority judges conceded that presidential conversations are "presumptively privileged." But it was for the courts to determine whether "a mere assertion of privilege" was sufficient to overcome the need of the party subpoenaing the document in question. In the present instance, the opinion concluded, the president's invocation of executive privilege "must fail in the face of the uniquely powerful showing made by the special prosecutor."

The president now attempted to arrange a compromise with Cox, whereby the prosecutor would agree to accept an authenticated summary of the nine contested tapes in place of the tapes themselves. As might have been expected, Cox refused. Nixon thereupon invoked his authority as chief executive: he ordered Cox "as an employee of the Executive Branch to make no further attempt by judicial process" to obtain the tapes in question. But, in a defiant press conference, Cox pointed out that Nixon in reality was refusing outright to obey a direct order of the appellate court. The president thereupon directed Richardson to remove Cox from office. However, both Richardson and Assistant Attorney General William Ruckelshaus in turn refused to obey Nixon's order and forthwith resigned. Ultimately Assistant Attorney General Robert Bork, who was now precipitated suddenly into the attorney general's office, executed the president's order.

In discharging Cox, Nixon was upon firm constitutional ground. Cox was technically an employee of the executive department, and the president's right to remove subordinate executive officers, which Presidents Jackson and Andrew Johnson had heatedly defended, had been undisputed since the Supreme Court's decision in the Myers case. Politically, however, "The Saturday Night Massacre," as the press dubbed Nixon's action, was disastrous. All across the nation, an outraged people, including party leaders, newspaper editors, students, university professors, and businessmen, attacked Cox's discharge as an outrageous violation of elementary public morality.

The Cox "firestorm," as presidential aide Alexander Haig called it, led to the first serious consideration by congressional leaders of the possiblity of Nixon's impeachment. The idea of the president's impeachment also had been rendered more palatable by the forced resignation of vice-president Spiro Agnew in early October and his subsequent replacement by Representative Gerald Ford of Michigan.

In late September it had become apparent that there was a strong likelihood that Agnew would be indicted by a federal court in Maryland on a charge of income tax evasion. In an effort to avoid such a development, Agnew had asked the leaders of both parties in the House of Representatives to move for his impeachment, arguing that as vice-president he was immune to the criminal processes of the courts and that impeachment was the only appropriate mode of procedure against him. But House leaders, after consultation, had refused to accept Agnew's contention and had declined to intervene. Thereafter Attorney General Richardson had worked out an arrangement in accordance with which Agnew had agreed to plead *nolo contendere*[1] to a single count of income tax evasion but had been allowed to resign as vice-president without the imposition of any further punishment by the court.

Agnew's resignation, the first such since that of Calhoun in 1832, brought the provisions of the Twenty-fifth Amendment into play. Section 2 of that amendment stipulated that "whenever a vacancy occurs in the office of Vice President, the President shall nominate a Vice President who shall take office upon confirmation by a majority vote of both Houses of Congress." With Agnew's resignation, accordingly, President Nixon submitted Ford's name to the two houses for the vacated office. Ford was a conservative Republican and political ally of the administration, but he enjoyed a high reputation for personal integrity, and his confirmation by Congress came a few weeks later without serious opposition.

Meanwhile, the House Judiciary Committee started an impeachment inquiry. It began by considering the meaning of the constitutional provision in Article II, Section 4, which stated that the president, vice-president, and other civil officers of the United States were impeachable for "Treason, Bribery, or other high Crimes and Misdemeanors." Did this refer to serious common law felonies or specific statutory crimes, or to abuse of power and gross disregard of constitutional duties? To put the matter another way, was impeachment a quasi-judicial process for removing an official charged with a crime, or was it a quasi-political process for removing an officer whose main offense lay in a breach of public trust?

The lesson of Andrew Johnson's impeachment trial, as it had been interpreted by most students of the presidency in the twentieth century, was that impeachment was essentially a judicial procedure that required an indictable offense. Most scholars who now renewed study of the matter, however, held that impeachment was intended to deal with serious politico-constitutional offenses, not mere criminal acts. The House Judiciary Committee staff adopted this view, contending that impeachment was a "remedial measure" and "constitutional safety valve" whereby a president might be removed for "substantial misconduct" not necessarily of a specifically criminal nature. Not the intrinsic quality of a particular action, the committee staff argued, but the effect of a series of substantial actions on the constitutional system was the crucial consideration. On the other hand, the president's lawyers insisted that "high crimes and misdemeanors" must be read to require the commission of a specific criminal offense. In the forceful vernacular of the moment, this became the "smoking gun" theory of impeachment.

For a time, lacking hard evidence of a specific Nixon criminal offense,

1. Literally, "I do not wish to contest"—i.e., in effect, an admission of guilt.

the Judiciary Committee stalled. But evidence was soon forthcoming. In March 1974, after Nixon had been named as an unindicted co-conspirator by the grand jury that indicted Mitchell, Ehrlichman, *et al.,* Special Prosecutor Leon Jaworski issued a new *subpoena duces tecum* directed to the president and requiring the surrender of certain additional tapes needed for the impending trial. Again Nixon refused, on the ground that the dispute with the special prosecutor was intraexecutive and hence nonjusticiable. When Judge Sirica denied the president's motion to quash the Jaworski subpoena, the controversy over the tapes went to the Supreme Court.

In *United States* v. *Nixon,* in July 1974, the Supreme Court unanimously decided that the president must obey the special prosecutor's subpoena. Chief Justice Burger's opinion declared that the intraexecutive character of the dispute was no bar to its justiciability. The attorney general, Burger pointed out, had, by regulations possessing the force of law, vested in the special prosecutor authority to sue in the name of the United States, as well as explicit authority to contest the invocation of executive privilege. In this instance the regulations had given rise to a "traditionally justiciable controversy." Burger then sharply rejected the president's claim that he possessed an "absolutely unqualified privilege" against any judicial process. The need for presidential privacy, Burger conceded, did indeed justify a "presumptive privilege" for executive communications. At the same time, however, both the rule of law and respect for the integrity of the judicial process made it imperative for the courts to weigh any such claim against the importance of assuring the production in court of relevant evidence and ultimately of protecting the system of criminal justice itself.

Even as the Supreme Court spoke, the House Judiciary Committee was moving swiftly to bring in a bill of impeachment. After yet another unsuccessful attempt to subpoena White House tapes, the committee in late July reviewed the evidence assembled by its staff. In hearings that were carried on national television, several Republicans, led by Albert Wiggins of California, advanced the "smoking gun" theory of impeachment. There was no hard evidence, they argued, that the president had been guilty of a specific criminal offense; therefore, he could not properly be impeached. In reply Democrats asserted the "abuse of power" theory of impeachment. Emphasizing the seriousness and substantiality of Nixon's breach of public trust, they argued for impeachment as a means of maintaining the integrity of the executive office, without regard for hard evidence. Significantly, several Republicans, led by Tom Railsback of Illinois, Hamilton Fish of New York, and William Cohen of Maine, broke away from their Republican colleagues and supported the abuse-of-power conception of impeachment.

The committee concluded by voting three articles of impeachment against the president. Article I, a carefully constructed bipartisan compromise, charged that Nixon had "prevented, obstructed, and impeded the administration of justice," in "violation of his constitutional duty to take care that the laws be faithfully executed." The bill of particulars made it clear that this had to do with the Watergate break-in.

Article II charged the president with conduct "violating the Constitutional rights of citizens, impairing the due and proper administration of justice," and "contravening the laws governing agencies of the executive branch." Here the bill of particulars dealt, among other things, with Nixon's attempted manipulation of the Internal Revenue Service, with his "misuse" of the FBI, and with his maintenance of a secret White House investigative unit with its unlawful utilization of the CIA.

Article III charged the president with ignoring the subpoenas of the House Judiciary Committee itself, by which the committee had attempted to obtain materials relevant to the impeachment process. Two additional articles, ultimately rejected, would have charged Nixon with illicitly bombing Cambodia and with corruptive manipulation of his personal and partisan finances.

The committee tried to establish that Nixon's actions, more than being a mere indictable offense, posed a serious threat to the constitutional order. It is doubtful that the committee succeeded in this effort, however, for in the final analysis Nixon's criminal behavior was so obvious as virtually to compel adoption of the indictable-offense view of impeachment. After the Supreme Court ruled that the president must surrender the tapes, his lawyers reviewed the tape of June 23, 1972. In it Nixon had ordered his staff to use the CIA to abort the Watergate investigation—unequivocal evidence of the crime of obstruction of justice. Facing almost certain impeachment by the House of Representatives and possible conviction in the Senate, Nixon resigned on August 8, 1974. Notwithstanding Nixon's usurpation of power and abuse of constitutional trust, it was revulsion against his criminal acts that drove him from office. With respect to constitutional law, therefore, the Watergate scandal will probably be taken as supporting the indictable-offense theory of impeachment.

The Significance of Watergate

Watergate—the bugging incident and the broader pattern of executive usurpation of which it was a part—signified the introduction into domestic politics of attitudes and techniques long evident and employed in American cold war policy. The techniques were those of political espionage and secret intelligence gathering by electronic surveillance and other means. The attitude was that of fundamental ideological conflict between enemies committed to a strategy of mutual destruction. Such an outlook was abundantly evident in the White House enemies list and in Nixon's strategy sessions preserved on the White House tapes. Once the affair was ended, these things seemed somewhat amusing, but they suggested that a lawless, European-style seizure of power could possibly occur in the United States.

In the aftermath of Nixon's resignation there seemed to be agreement that the Watergate affair differed from earlier American political scandals in which power was abused for purposes of economic gain. Vice-President Agnew's misdeeds belonged to this more familiar tradition of scandal and hence could more readily be comprehended. Agnew acted the way a crooked politician was supposed to act. In contrast Nixon acted mainly for ideological reasons. The end he sought in aggrandizing and usurping power was to preserve the social and political order and eliminate the enemy on the left—especially the violent protest movements. It is far too early to essay a conclusive judgment, but it appears that Nixon and his followers—along with millions of other Americans—believed a genuine social and political crisis existed in the late 1960s that threatened American institutions.

Of course, it can be argued that Nixon *et al.* believed no such thing, but merely used "national security" in a cynical way to justify lawless actions aimed at maintaining their own personal power. From the standpoint of constitutional history, however, the question of motivation is less important than the fact that repeated aggrandizement of power, and reliance on national security as an all-encompassing rationale by previous chief executives, made possible Nixon's concentration of power in the White House. Equally significant in creating the circumstances in which Watergate could occur was the tendency toward ideological politics earlier manifested in the white-supremacist reaction against school desegregation, the neopopulist Wallace movement, and the new left and anti-Vietnam protest movements.

Watergate gave rise to conflicting evaluations of the condition of American constitutionalism. One widely held view was that the country had come dangerously close to having executive tyranny imposed upon it. According to this theory, the basic flaw lay in an electoral system that allowed a man like Nixon to become president. Only by accident—the bungling of the break-in, the discovery of the secret White House tapes—was tyranny prevented. In the opinion of others, however, the outcome of the Watergate affair showed that the constitutional system worked satisfactorily. According to this view, courageous journalists dug out evidence of White House wrongdoing, and Congress and the judiciary, representing an outraged public opinion, took the appropriate steps to stop Nixon's assault on free institutions.

Keeping in mind the obviously important effects of sheer contingency, including Nixon's personality, Watergate ended as it did because the governing elites whom Nixon had offended retaliated against him. The journalistic reporting that did so much to reveal the administration's cover-up plan and other illegalities depended heavily on leaks from within the government by persons hostile to Nixon. Once the facts started to come out,

members of Congress, who had ample reason to oppose Nixon's centralization of power, pursued the case enthusiastically. No doubt Nixon's arro-
gance in the exercise of power made it easier for his opponents to join in
what eventually became a bipartisan undertaking. Ultimately, however, the
attack was not *ad hominem,* but was aimed at defending the established
pluralistic executive-administrative governing system that Nixon's plebiscitary presidency threatened. In the pluralistic system, elites in the various
departments, agencies, and committees of Congress formulated public policy and maintained accountability by mutual checks and restraints. Disregarding the elites and appealing directly to the electorate, Nixon challenged
this method of government. Rather than concluding that the Constitution
worked, it would be more accurate to say that the outcome of Watergate
restored for the time being this pluralistic system of administrative management.

In a more specific and technical sense the Watergate scandal had a
significant effect on constitutional law. The claim of executive privilege
suffered a clear setback when the Supreme Court ordered President Nixon
to hand over the tapes. Yet the result was not all one-sided, for executive
privilege was now formally recognized as a doctrine of constitutional law.
Presidential communications, the Court declared, enjoyed a "presumptive
privilege." A second major result concerned the revitalization of the presidential impeachment power. The near certainty of Nixon's impeachment
showed the procedure to be both usable and useful, if still cumbersome and
time-consuming. Moreover the first resignation by a president in American
history may have established a precedent, making resignation an alternative consitutional procedure for restraining executive power.

The Post-Watergate Presidency

The most obvious constitutional reaction to the Watergate affair was a
series of judicial and legislative restrictions on presidential power. Judicial
curtailment of the executive had occurred before the scandal was revealed.
In 1971, as noted previously, the Supreme Court denied the administration's attempt to impose prior restraint on the publication of the *Pentagon
Papers,* the Defense Department's inside history of the war in Southeast
Asia. The government argued that publication of the papers would cause
"grave and irreparable" injury to the United States and was also in violation of the Espionage Act of 1917 forbidding the communication of defense
information harmful to the security of the United States. The Supreme
Court, however, in a *per curiam* opinion in *New York Times Co.* v. *United
States,* rejected the argument and removed all restraints on publication.
Although several justices took the view that publication might be stopped in
a national security crisis involving something as serious as actual war plans,

the Court said that any system of prior restraint bore a heavy presumption against its constitutionality.

In *United States* v. *United States District Court* (1972) the Supreme Court placed restrictions on the administration's system of wiretapping for domestic security surveillance purposes. At issue was the constitutionality of warrantless security surveillance, conducted by the attorney general's office on the authority of the president as a reasonable exercise of his power to protect the national security. Denying an inherent presidential power to conduct electronic surveillance for domestic security purposes without judicial approval, the Court said that such cases involved First and Fourth Amendment values which required the employment of proper constitutional procedures.

Congress was the principal source of antiexecutive measures in the 1970s. A limited initial step was the Case Act of 1972, requiring the secretary of state to submit to Congress within six days the text of any international agreement made by the executive branch. In 1973, over President Nixon's veto, Congress attempted to rein in presidential war making by passing the War Powers Act. Sponsored by Senator Jacob Javits of New York, the act provided that in the absense of a formal declaration of war by Congress, the president could initiate hostilities only under four conditions: to repel an attack on the United States; to protect American forces overseas; to protect the lives of Americans abroad; or to fulfill the specific statutory military obligations of the United States. The act required consultation with Congress whenever possible prior to the commitment of U.S. troops abroad; the submission of a written report to Congress within forty-eight hours of a troop commitment; and termination of the commitment within sixty days unless Congress approved continuation.

In domestic affairs Congress struck at Nixon's exertions of power in the Budget and Impoundment Control Act of 1974. This law required the president to recommend to Congress in a special message any proposal to impound funds, either by a recision permanently eliminating the appropriation, or by a deferral postponing it. The former required approval by both houses within forty-five days, the latter by one house within the same period of time. The act also created a Congressional Budget Office to help lawmakers deal with departmental appropriations requests. In 1975 the Supreme Court supplemented the congressional action when it in effect condemned the Nixon impoundment program as illegal. In *Train* v. *City of New York,* the Court ruled that the president had no power under the Federal Water Pollution Control Act of 1972 to refuse to allot to the states for expenditure a total of $6 million appropriated by Congress. The Court concluded that executive impoundment, except where authorized by permissive statutory language, was illegal.

In 1976 Congress tried to restrict the power lying at the root of the imperial presidency by passing the National Emergencies Act. This law terminated states of national emergency that had been declared on March 4, 1933 (the depression), December 16, 1950 (Chinese entry into the Korean war), March 23, 1970 (postal strike), and August 15, 1971 (international monetary crisis). It also provided a procedure for declaring national emergencies. The president must inform Congress of the emergency, specify the powers he plans to use in dealing with it, and every six months Congress must determine whether the emergency still exists. Moreover, Congress might terminate the emergency at any time by concurrent resolution.

In the National Emergency, War Powers, Impoundment Control, and numerous other acts Congress employed what was called the legislative veto. This permitted Congress to prohibit presidential actions pursuant to existing authority by concurrent resolution, or resolution of either house, within a specified period. Resting on the theory that if Congress could delegate power to the president it could withdraw it, the legislative veto in 1978 was approved by the Supreme Court as compatible with the separation of powers.[2]

After the Watergate scandal, the political environment in which executive power operated became more hostile than at any time in the twentieth century. Congressional legislation reflected this hostility and in many respects operated as an effective restraint. The Budget and Impoundment Act successfully limited the executive and enhanced congressional power. The War Powers Act was less clearly effective, despite the submission of four reports by President Ford in accordance with the statute in 1975. Nevertheless, widespread revulsion against the use of military force in the aftermath of the Vietnam war effectively restricted the executive war-making power. The National Emergencies Act was not used at all, though its symbolic importance as an antiexecutive device was clear.

Notwithstanding these increased restrictions on executive power, the political demands on the presidency remained enormous. Watergate as the culmination of the liberal presidency taught Americans that the executive branch was not tantamount to the entire government. But the constitutional system still provided for—indeed, required—the exercise of a vast degree of executive authority. Whether the elite managerial bureaucracy that blocked Nixon's concentration of power could continue to be effective depended on whether the larger pluralist polity of which it was a part could maintain its legitimacy. At the same time, at the end of the 1970s tendencies toward a plebiscitarian presidency, though temporarily arrested, were still present. Indeed, this possibility appeared inherent in the existence of a mass electorate subject to manipulation by the media in an age of continuing international crisis.

2. *Adkins* v. *United States* (1978). This decision by no means settled the constitutional dispute over the legislative veto, however, which was included in over two hundred recent statutes delegating authority to administrative agencies. In January 1982 the U.S. Circuit Court of Appeals for the District of Columbia declared unconstitutional the legislative veto in the Natural Gas Policy Act of 1978.

THIRTY-THREE

The Burger Court and Contemporary Constitutional Law

--- ◆ ◆ ◆ ---

MORE SO THAN AT ANY TIME since the 1930s, the Supreme Court in the late 1960s became an issue in presidential politics. Attacking the Warren Court, Republican candidate Richard Nixon in 1968 charged it with "seriously hamstringing the peace forces in our society and strengthening the criminal forces." To redress the balance Nixon promised to appoint to the high bench judges of a "strict constructionist" point of view. This term, which historically referred to a narrow interpretation of national legislative power, was Nixon's way of expressing the idea of judicial restraint, the central theme in criticism of the Warren Court in the 1960s. In a practical sense, however, strict-construction judges were those presumably who would give greater scope to the conservative attitudes that Nixon's election represented.

Nixon's attack on the Supreme Court both reflected and contributed to the heightened politicization of constitutional law that occurred in the 1960s. The actions of Chief Justice Earl Warren had a similar effect. In June 1968, Warren, now seventy-seven years old, submitted his resignation to President Lyndon Johnson, to take effect upon Senate confirmation of his successor. Johnson, however, who had announced that he would not seek re-election, was a lame duck president, and the maneuver seemed intended to install a suitably liberal replacement for Warren in order to prevent Nixon, should he win the election, from controlling the Court. The stratagem did not succeed. Johnson nominated Associate Justice Abe Fortas, a close personal and political friend and a libertarian activist. But an unprecedented Senate filibuster sent the Fortas nomination down to defeat, amid cries of "cronyism" and charges of an unethical attempt to steal the chief justiceship from the incoming president. With Nixon's election, Warren bowed to the inevitable, announcing his retirement to take effect the following June.

The stakes in the struggle for control of the Court increased when in May 1969, on the eve of Chief Justice Warren's departure, a scandal forced

Justice Fortas to resign. A story in *Life* magazine revealed that Fortas had accepted a $20,000 retainer fee from a foundation created by financier Louis Wolfson, who was then under investigation by the Securities and Exchange Commission. Fortas had in fact signed a contract with Wolfson that would guarantee Fortas and his wife each $20,000 annually for the rest of their lives. Though Fortas broke no law, the impropriety was evident; rather than fight, he chose to resign, the first Supreme Court justice to do so under public criticism. The situation was rendered even more damaging to liberals by the fact that Fortas's decision to resign was in part intended to allay attacks on Justice William O. Douglas for extrajudicial financial arrangements with another private foundation which had produced talk of Douglas's impeachment. Thus Nixon now had two Court nominations in hand.

In June, President Nixon nominated Judge Warren E. Burger of the Federal Court of Appeals for the Eighth Circuit, a former prominent Eisenhower Republican, to be chief justice. Burger had a reputation as a fairly hard-line "law and order" judge, but the Senate liberals had been demoralized by the Fortas resignation and he won confirmation, 74 to 3, with scarcely a murmur of dissent. However, Nixon's attempt to choose Fortas's successor ran into difficulties. The president first nominated Judge Clement Haynesworth, a conservative southerner with a distinctly segregationist reputation in civil rights matters. The Senate liberal bloc, thoroughly aroused, rallied to defeat the nomination, 45 to 55. Refusing to learn, Nixon then nominated an even more vulnerable candidate, G. Harrold Carswell. A judge of the Court of Appeals for the Fifth Circuit, Carswell not only had a segregationist background, but he was also thoroughly undistinguished professionally and intellectually. In April 1970 his nomination was defeated in the Senate, 45 to 51.

Abandoning his southern strategy, the president turned next to Judge Harry A. Blackmun of the United States Court of Appeals for the Eighth Circuit. Blackmun, a tax specialist, provoked no opposition and was confirmed in the Senate 94 to 0. A year later two more vacancies opened up when Justices Black and Harlan retired. To replace them Nixon in October 1971 nominated Lewis F. Powell, a distinguished Virginia lawyer who had been severely critical of the Warren Court's stance in civil liberties, and William H. Rehnquist, a conservative Republican from Arizona. In December the Senate approved both names by lopsided majorities. By the end of 1971, therefore, President Nixon had placed four of his nominees on the Supreme Court.

In the ensuing decade the Court under Chief Justice Burger shifted to a more conservative position on several issues, most notably criminal law procedure and non-race-related equal protection matters. The effect of this shift was to permit the states greater latitude, a result that was also encouraged by a renewal of interest in federalism as a general constitutional value. The Burger Court furthermore abjured the Warren Court's doctrinaire libertarianism in First Amendment questions, especially with respect to claims of freedom of the press. Yet the Court did not turn back the clock by reversing landmark Warren era decisions—not in criminal justice, reapportionment, or civil liberties. Moreover in race-related civil rights matters, so far from reversing the direction established by the Warren Court, the Supreme Court under Chief Justice Burger extended the logic of result-oriented affirmative action to the point of accepting racial classification as constitutional.

The Burger Court also demonstrated continuity in its exercise of judicial power and its decision-making method. Although occasionally professing deference to legislatures in accordance with judicial restraint theory, the Court on numerous occasions fashioned constitutional rights out of whole cloth in the best judicial activist style. Indeed, despite its rightward shift in a policy sense—and to some extent perhaps because of it—the Court and the federal judiciary in general came to be described unfavorably as the "imperial judiciary." Changes in society and in the political culture, of course, created the circumstances in which the judiciary was asked to play a larger governing role. But as issue groups pressed a wide range of rights claims and public policy demands, courts were increasingly responsive. To some extent perhaps even in spite of themselves, federal judges in the 1970s continued the judicial and legal aggrandizement that had characterized the Warren era.

The Judicial Resistance to Social Egalitarianism

At the end of the 1960s the quest for civil rights equality gave promise of becoming a movement for social egalitarianism that would condemn poverty as a suspect category under the equal protection clause, even as race had been condemned. The Warren Court's decision in *Shapiro* v. *Thompson* (1969), upholding welfare recipients' entitlement to public assistance in the guise of a right of interstate travel, pointed in this direction and possibly augured acceptance by the Court of the "new property" theory popular at the time among radicals and reformers. This was the argument that poor people, forced by the requirements of modern corporate society to occupy inferior social and economic positions, were entitled to welfare assistance, employment, housing, medical care, legal services, and so on as a form of property protected by the Constitution. In 1970 the Court's decision in *Goldberg* v. *Kelly,* another welfare rights case, moved closer toward acceptance of the new property theory.

The *Goldberg* case arose when New York welfare officials, in accordance with state law, cut off public assistance to a person whose eligibility was in question, guaranteeing him a posttermination hearing. In a 5–4 decision the Supreme Court ruled the state action unconstitutional because the hearing did not precede termination. Justice Brennan stated that to cut off welfare without a prior hearing, thus depriving someone who might be eligible of the means of livelihood, was "unconscionable" unless overwhelming considerations justified it. Brennan could find none that did. Technically, the decision held the state action to be a violation of procedural due process under the Fourteenth Amendment; in reality it promoted the substantive equal protection doctrine that reformers hoped to use to declare distinctions of wealth constitutionally suspect. Citing law review articles propounding the new property theory, Brennan wrote: "Welfare, by meeting the basic demands of subsistence, can help bring within the reach of the poor the same opportunities that are available to others to participate meaningfully in the life of the community."

Even before President Nixon made further appointments, however, the Court stopped the trend toward a broader egalitarianism. The key case was *Dandridge* v. *Williams* (1970). The Court here considered whether Maryland's $250-per-month maximum payment under the federal AFDC program was a denial of equal protection of the law to children of large families (defined as having more than five children), each of whom received less than children in smaller families. Ironically employing the double-standard, special scrutiny mode of equal-protection analysis previously employed by liberals to promote egalitarianism, Justice Stewart for a 6–3 majority upheld the state law. The case, Stewart reasoned, dealt not with civil liberties or civil rights, but with "state regulation in the social and economic field." Under the double-standard approach originally advanced in the Carolene Products footnote, Stewart explained that in assessing the constitutionality of social and economic regulation it was necessary only that the Court find a reasonable basis for the state action in question. Maryland's desire to encourage gainful employment and maintain an equitable balance between welfare families and families not on welfare satisfied this rationality test. Hence the classification embodied in the state program—categories of families differentiated by degrees of wealth—did not violate the equal protection clause and was not constitutionally suspect.

In *James* v. *Valtierra* (1971) the Court reaffirmed its opposition to substantive equal protection beyond the sphere of racial discrimination. Here it reviewed a provision of the California constitution that required low-income housing proposals adopted by state officials to be approved by a popular referendum of voters in the city, town, or county affected. The provision was challenged as a denial of equal protection of the law to low-income persons, a view accepted by a lower federal court. The Supreme Court, however, by a 5–3 vote upheld the referendum requirement as constitutional because it did not on its face contain any racial classification, the only classification regarded as suspect under the equal protection clause. Rejecting the contention that the provision discriminated against the poor by creating obstacles to their efforts to influence public policy which did not exist for other groups, Justice Black asserted: "A lawmaking procedure that 'disadvantages' a particular group does not always deny equal protection."

The Burger Court's most important decision in the new field of nonracial equal protection concerned the traditional American system of public school financing based on local property taxes. In every state wealthier communities, with their larger tax base, spent more money on schools than lower-income communities. Reformers argued that as a result, poor children were given inferior education in violation of the equal protection clause of the Fourteenth Amendment. In several states class action suits were brought as test cases, and in 1971 the California Supreme Court ruled that local property tax financing rested on a suspect classification—wealth—and encroached upon a fundamental right—education. Also in 1971 a federal district court in Texas found the Texas school system a denial of equal protection under the Fourteenth Amendment.

In *San Antonio School District* v. *Rodriguez* (1973) the Supreme Court, in a 5–4 decision, reversed the lower court's ruling in the Texas case. While recognizing the principle that wealth discrimination was not a suspect classification requiring strict scrutiny of a state action employing it, Justice Powell in a complex factual analysis concentrated on showing that the Texas school financing system did not discriminate against any social class. Furthermore, Powell contended that education was not a fundamental right—that is, a right explicitly or implicitly guaranteed by the Constitution. Accordingly, strict scrutiny of the challenged state action was not required. What was at issue, said Powell, was social and economic legislation that warranted simply the rationality test. He concluded that the Texas system, which he described as a reasonable attempt to provide education for each child within the context of substantial community control of schools, was constitutional.

The irony of these conservative decisions was that in reaching its conclusions the Burger Court used the double-standard, strict-scrutiny doctrine that had been forged by the liberal activists to expand minority rights. The Burger justices, however, applied the doctrine in order to limit fundamental rights. If welfare and the various entitlements of poor people were in effect to be regarded as a form of property, then under the modern liberal distinction between property rights and civil or human rights they could be viewed as within the sphere of social and economic legislation and regulated under the less rigorous criterion of reasonableness.

Similarly conservative were decisions in which the Supreme Court narrowed the meaning of liberty and property under the Fourteenth Amendment due process clause, thereby giving broader scope to the state police power. During the Warren era the trend of decisions in this field had been just the opposite: virtually any interest a person could define in the public sector, such as possession of a driver's license used in employment, was regarded as a basis for challenging any state restriction or modification of the interest on procedural due process grounds. In *Board of Education* v. *Roth* (1972), however, the Burger Court stopped the trend toward recognizing any status in the public sector as a form of property protected by the Fourteenth Amendment. The Court held that the failure of a state university to renew the employment of a teacher who had been hired on a one-year contract did not violate the due process clause. No hearing was necessary before the university's decision not to rehire. Similarly, in *Bishop* v. *Wood* (1976) the Burger Court approved the dismissal of a policeman who had achieved the status of a permanent employee. Denying that the policeman had a property interest in the expectation of continued employment, the Court declared that he held his job at the will and pleasure of the city. This decision suggested the possible revival of the long-discredited notion that public employment was a privilege, rather than a right, which the state could restrict as it saw fit.

In rejecting a broader application of the equal protection and due process clauses of the Fourteenth Amendment as instruments of social reform, the Burger Court showed its willingness to defer to the states in key areas of social policy. This implicit or indirect recognition of a wider role for the states coincided in the 1970s with a renewal of interest in state autonomy provoked by an increased demand for state services. The Supreme Court gave expression to this concern for federalism in a notable decision in which, for the first time in forty years, it struck down a congressional statute based on the commerce power.

The case, *National League of Cities* v. *Usery* (1976), arose out of amendments to the Fair Labor Standards Act, adopted by Congress in 1974, which applied federal minimum wage and maximum hours requirements to virtually all employees of state governments. Some years earlier Congress had extended the wage and hour provisions of the labor standards law to employees in state schools and hospitals; the Supreme Court had approved the extension in *Maryland* v. *Wirtz* (1968). In *National League of Cities* v. *Usery,* however, the Burger Court by a 5–4 margin held the 1974 amendments unconstitutional.

Taking his bearings from the Tenth Amendment, Justice Rehnquist in his majority opinion declared that the sovereignty of the states operated as a limitation on the powers of Congress. In the present instance the element of state sovereignty at issue was the power of the states to determine the wages paid to employees carrying out state functions. In language reminiscent of nineteenth century dual federalism, Rehnquist contended that if Congress could withdraw from the states the authority to control their employment policy, "we think there would be little left of the States' 'separate and independent existence.' " "This exercise of congressional authority," Rehnquist concluded, "does not comport with the federal system of government embodied in the Constitution."

It remained to be seen whether *National League of Cities,* as many critics of the decision feared, would lead to further attempts to restrict federal welfare and spending programs under the doctrine of state sovereignty and the idea of preserving the integrity of the state governments in the areas of their traditional functions. In theory at least the potential for a far-reaching counterrevolution in federalism was there. Meanwhile, in less conspicuous ways the Burger Court shifted the federal-state balance toward the states, or, as some thought, redressed the imbalance created by the centralizing reforms of the Warren Court. For the most part this shift concerned the relationship between the federal judiciary and the states. Thus the Burger Court showed less willingness to see the equity powers of the federal courts used to intervene in and supervise the performance of state and local governments.[1] The Court also curtailed lower federal courts' monitoring and modification of state courts' administration of criminal justice through injunctive relief and the use of federal habeas corpus authority.

Affirmative Action and Substantive Equal Protection

While the Burger Court resisted the drive for egalitarian social reforms and encouraged state autonomy in the general sphere of social and economic policy, it supported and extended the rationale of federal affirmative action developed by the Warren Court to deal with race-related civil rights questions. In school desegregation, employment practices, and university admission cases the Court took the extremely significant step of adopting a racially qualified view of the Fourteenth Amendment equal protection clause.

As noted previously, in *Swann* v. *Charlotte-Mecklenburg Board of Education* (1971) the Supreme Court unanimously approved a variety of means, including busing, for achieving a proper racial mixture in public schools.[2] Busing for the purpose of racial balance was highly unpopular, however, so Chief Justice Burger's opinion struck certain cautionary notes. The courts, he declared, could act only upon the basis of "a finding of constitutional violation"—that is, that *de jure* segregation existed. He asserted, moreover, that the imposition of rigid racial quotas in a school system was not constitutionally acceptable. Nor did the continued existence of some one-race schools within a school system necessarily mean that it was still legally segregated. Finally, the chief justice warned that although busing was a legitimate affirmative-action tool, it must not be employed so as to risk children's health or disrupt the educational process.

1. *Rizzo* v. *Goode* (1976).
2. See above, p. 630.

In the early 1970s the focus of school desegregation efforts shifted to the North, and to the heavily black school systems that existed there as a result of residential and demographic trends. If taken seriously, the limitations spelled out in the *Swann* decision would make it difficult to attack northern segregation, which had always been regarded as *de facto* rather than *de jure* in nature. Gradually, however, the Court in effect set this distinction aside and required integration based on specific racial balance outside the South.

In *Keyes* v. *School District No. 1, Denver, Colorado* (1973), for example, the Court held that the Denver school board practiced a policy of segregation by its choice of school construction sites, attendance zones, pupil transfer plans, and so on. Maintaining the *de jure–de facto* distinction, the Court stated that a finding of *de jure* segregation in one part of a school system established a primary case of intentional segregation in all of Denver's core city schools. Absent evidence of a contrary intention, said Justice Brennan, the school board had "an affirmative duty to desegregate the entire system, 'root and branch.'" Remanding the case to the district court, the Supreme Court all but formally required busing as an integration technique for the first time in a northern city.

Reflecting the widespread opposition to busing among the general public, the Court in the next few years hesitated on the question of northern integration. In *Milliken* v. *Bradley* (1974) it rejected, 5–4, a comprehensive interdistrict plan to integrate the school systems of metropolitan Detroit. Based on a district court ruling that *de jure* segregation existed in Detroit's schools, the plan sought to integrate the schools of the city, now nearly three-quarters black, with those of fifty-three outlying suburban school districts that were overwhelmingly white. No finding of *de jure* segregation existed in the latter; they were included simply because integration of the Detroit schools had ceased to have any great meaning. The Supreme Court turned back the plan, however, on the ground that no interdistrict violation had occurred to justify an interdistrict remedy—at least not one as sweeping as that projected, involving almost 800,000 students. Observing that under such a plan the federal courts might become in effect a legislative authority, Chief Justice Burger warned against depriving the people of local control over their schools. Two years later the Court rejected a federal district court desegregation plan for Pasadena, California, that prohibited any school from having a majority of black students, and that required yearly adjustments to maintain a specific racial balance.[3]

Hesitation on the part of the Supreme Court, however, by no means signaled the decline of court-ordered integration in public schools. Despite the manifest hostility of public opinion to busing, federal judges continued to draw up desegregation plans, and integration occurred in several cities,

---

3. *Pasadena Board of Education* v. *Spangler* (1976).

often amid violent white protest. In Wilmington, Delaware, and Louisville, Kentucky, for example, city and suburb were combined in integration plans that the Supreme Court approved. The caution with which the Court approached the volatile issue of busing could be seen in its handling of the situation in Dayton, Ohio. In 1977 the Court rejected a system-wide integration plan for Dayton on the ground that it exceeded the degree of segregation attributable to city officials. Racial imbalance alone, said the Court, was not evidence of deliberate discrimination. After the case was remanded for further study, however, evidence was produced of more widespread segregation practices, and in 1979 the Court approved an integration plan requiring the busing of 15,000 students.[4] In accepting the plan, moreover, the Court appeared to abandon the distinction between *de jure* and *de facto* segregation, at least as it had been commonly understood; for since the late nineteenth century Ohio law had not commanded racial separation in public schools. Although in places like south Boston white opposition to busing attracted national attention, for the most part school integration carried out according to racial formulas by the end of the 1970s had been institutionalized in the federal judiciary at a relatively low level of public visibility.

Paralleling, if not exceeding, its liberal record on school integration, the Supreme Court furthermore accepted a concept of affirmative action in employment practices and higher education admissions that provided preferential, or compensatory, treatment for blacks. After prohibiting non-job-related tests and criteria for employment in the important *Griggs* case of 1971,[5] the Court retreated somewhat in *Washington* v. *Davis* (1976). It held that a screening test for policemen in the District of Columbia that excluded a larger proportion of blacks than whites was not unlawful if intention to discriminate could not be proved. In the late 1970s, however, the Court resumed its pursuit of result-oriented affirmative action by approving racial classification when employed for benign purposes.

The Court achieved this important change in three distinct stages. First, it established race as a legitimate consideration in public policy, apart from demonstrated denial of individual rights. This was the significance of *University of California Regents* v. *Bakke* (1978), the celebrated reverse discrimination case. Bakke, a thirty-eight-year-old white man, was rejected by the University of California medical school at Davis in a year when the school set aside 16 of 100 places in its entering class for minority applicants. Bakke, whose test scores were higher than those of some of the blacks admitted to the program, claimed that the school's policy denied his right to equal protection of the law under the Civil Rights Act of 1964 and the Fourteenth Amendment. At the heart of the controversy produced by the

4. *Dayton Board of Education* v. *Brinkman* (1979).
5. See above, p. 632.

case was a conflict between the right of an individual not to be discriminated against on account of race and the power of the state to redress the effects of past social discrimination by legislating in favor of certain groups on the basis of a racial classification. The traditional conception of equal protection thus clashed with the group-disadvantage interpretation of the equal-protection principle advanced by egalitarian reformers.

As best it could, the Burger Court compromised this fundamental conflict. In a 5–4 decision it struck down the medical school admission policy as a denial of Bakke's right to equal protection of the law under the Civil Rights Acts and the Fourteenth Amendment. But the Court also held that race was a reasonable and legitimate basis for state action. In upholding Bakke's right to equal protection and hence admission to the medical school, Justice Powell for the majority dwelt at length on the unconstitutionality and injustice of racial and ethnic classifications. This part of his opinion affirmed the individual-rights view of the Fourteenth Amendment, and received the assent of Justices Stewart, Rehnquist, Stevens, and Chief Justice Burger. Powell went on to hold, however, that in operating its universities and professional schools the state could legitimately take race into account. And in arguing this point he was supported by Justices Brennan, Blackmun, Marshall, and White.

Powell justified a concern with race under what might be called the pluralistic approach to equal educational opportunity, with help from the First Amendment. He reasoned that a university, in order to encourage intellectual vitality and creativity, had a compelling interest, based largely on First Amendment guarantees, in forming a diverse student body. One element of such a student body was racial and ethnic heterogeneity. But the key point was the formal recognition of race. Previously, race had been considered only in respect of remedial action ordered by courts to redress specific proved discrimination, as in school desegregation or denial of voting rights. Now it was pronounced valid for general legislative purposes. Justice Brennan, in a partially concurring opinion, called attention to this fact in observing that the "central meaning" of the Court's opinion was that "Government may take race into account when it acts not to demean or insult any racial group, but to remedy disadvantages cast on minorities by past racial prejudice."

In 1979 the Supreme Court took race-conscious affirmative action a step further by approving a preferential employment plan in private industry. In *United Steelworkers of America* v. *Weber,* a white employee of the Kaiser Aluminum and Chemical Corporation, who had been rejected for a training program in which half the places were reserved for blacks, claimed that the program violated Title VII of the Civil Rights Act of 1964 prohibiting discrimination in employment against any individual on the ground of race. Federal district and circuit courts sustained the claim, but the Supreme Court rejected it.

In a 5–2 opinion, Justice Brennan held that Title VII did not apply to private affirmative action programs. Brennan conceded that a literalistic reading of the language of Title VII so as to prevent operation of the Kaiser program was possible. But he said that such an interpretation would violate the spirit of the Civil Rights Act. To forbid "all race-conscious affirmative action" would defeat Congress's purpose of improving the economic conditions of Negroes, Brennan explained. A section of the act stated further that nothing in the law "shall be interpreted to require any employer . . . to grant preferential treatment . . . to any group" for the purpose of correcting a statistical racial imbalance in the work force. According to Brennan, the failure of this language to state that preferential treatment was to be neither required *nor permitted* expressed Congress's intention to allow private companies to institute voluntary race-conscious employment programs.

While it was true that Congress in 1964 was concerned with ameliorating economic conditions for blacks, Brennan's was a strained interpretation of the Civil Rights Act which ignored the manifest congressional opposition to race-conscious preferential treatment. Presumably, that opposition led Congress to adopt language categorically prohibiting racial discrimination, no matter what its purpose. Brennan also ignored the fact that the private voluntary plan at issue in the *Weber* case was initiated under affirmative-action pressure from the federal government. Yet undoubtedly opinion had changed a great deal since 1964, and the disadvantaged-group conception of equal protection that in a substantive sense underlay the *Weber* opinion had gained widespread acceptance.

Indicative of such acceptance, the Burger Court in 1980 sanctioned a racially preferential policy for awarding federal contracts. The case, *Fullilove* v. *Klutznick,* concerned the constitutionality of the Public Works Employment Act of 1977, which required at least 10 percent of federal funds for public works projects to be spent on services or supplies from minority business enterprises. Nonminority contractors challenged the act on its face as a violation of the equal protection clause of the Fourteenth Amendment, but in a 6–3 decision the Supreme Court sustained the measure.

Chief Justice Burger's majority opinion declared that it was a legitimate objective for Congress, under its commerce and spending powers, to eliminate practices in the construction business that in the past had prevented minority businesses from enjoying equal opportunity in the award of contracts. Moreover, for Congress to act in a remedial fashion, as in the 1977 law, it was not necessary that there be evidence of deliberate discrimination by individual contractors; the existence of obvious discriminatory barriers, as seen in the disparity between contract awards to minority and nonminority businesses, was sufficient. Furthermore, Burger said, the remedial means chosen by Congress—a race-conscious quota system—was acceptable because in a remedial context Congress need not act in a wholly color-blind manner. Burger cited the school desegregation cases to support this point. Justice Powell, concurring, argued even more broadly that the Thirteenth and Fourteenth Amendments gave Congress power to remedy the effects of past racial discrimination through temporary race-conscious policies. Justice Marshall, quoting a statement made by Justice Blackmun in the *Bakke* case, more bluntly concluded: "In order to get beyond racism, we must first take account of race. There is no other way."

The affirmative action decisions of the late 1970s can hardly be re-garded as the work of a conservative Court. Although the Burger justices ratified policies introduced elsewhere in the constitutional system, those policies were guided by earlier judicial decisions pointing toward race-conscious remedial action. In any event, the constitutional significance of *Bakke, Weber,* and *Fullilove* was profound. Previously, despite the group orientation of American politics, constitutional rights had always been in-terpreted in an individualistic framework. Now, however, the Supreme Court recognized a conception of constitutional liberty and rights that de-pended on racial and ethnic identity.

Race and ethnicity, needless to say, have been enormously important forces in American history. And if the purpose of constitutional law is to embody and reflect social and political realities, then the affirmative-action decisions were philosophically and intellectually sound. This was the view of defenders of the decisions. Asserting the constitutionally novel idea that there were "natural classes" or social groups in American society, they argued for a group rather than individualistic interpretation of the concept of equal protection of the law. Regarding this approach as morally right as well as historically valid in view of the pro-Negro purpose of the Civil War amendments, supporters of race-conscious affirmative action saw it as nothing more than an expression of the traditional principle of compensa-tion for damages. A more apt description perhaps was reparations, a term drawn from international law which in the affirmative action context im-plied that blacks, as the recipients of compensatory awards, were a separate national group.

Although defenders of racial classification said it would be temporary as well as benign, critics argued that the Court's decisions seriously weak-ened the principle of individual personal right that lay at the heart of American constitutionalism. In their view, race-conscious affirmative action policies raised questions that were not only exceedingly difficult to resolve in a practical sense, but also possibly pernicious in their political effect—questions such as defining membership in a racial group or determining the point at which one could say that appropriate compensation for historic wrongs had been made. To be sure, class legislation was by no means a novelty in twentieth century American politics; based on economic and occupational considerations, it was introduced into public policy in a major way in the New Deal period. The 1977 affirmative action statute that was approved in the *Fullilove* decision could be viewed in this perspective. It was, moreover, a small program relatively insignificant in the larger picture of social and economic disadvantage that characterized the lives of most blacks in the United States. Nevertheless, insofar as pronouncements of constitutional law do not merely reflect social reality but also shape public opinion, the Court's affirmative action decisions suggested a reorientation of American constitutionalism away from its traditional individual rights bias toward a group or class conception of equality and justice.

Equal Protection and Women's Rights

In controversies over women's rights, which gained prominence in the atmosphere of rights consciousness created by the civil rights movement, the Burger Court generally adhered to a traditional conception of equality before the law. Responding to changes in public attitudes and to legislative initiatives against sex discrimination, the Court seriously weakened, if it did not decisively undermine, the principle of classification by gender that formed the legal basis for long-standing federal and state-sanctioned denial of equal rights to women. To grasp the dimensions of this development a brief consideration of the constitutional status of women before this time will be helpful.

Despite significant steps toward the emancipation of women resulting from such measures as the married women's property acts, nineteenth-century state law, reflecting the male-dominated social consensus, consigned women to an inferior status in public life and in the world of the private household and domestic relations. Women were generally excluded from voting, officeholding, and jury service, denied educational and professional opportunities available to men, and in numerous ways defined as the subordinate partner in the marriage relationship. Nor did the Fourteenth Amendment, which temporarily raised feminist hopes of a major advance toward legal and political equality, alter this pattern of discrimination. Two notable constitutional cases of the reconstruction era made this fact clear.

In *Bradwell* v. *Illinois* (1873) the Supreme Court rejected the claim of a Chicago woman that the right to practice law was an attribute of U.S. citizenship protected by the privileges and immunities clause of the Fourteenth Amendment. The states, declared the Court, could regulate admission to the bar as they saw fit. In an equally important holding the Supreme Court declared, in *Minor* v. *Happersett* (1875), that states could restrict the suffrage to men, the right to vote not having been conferred on women by the Fourteenth Amendment. Although the Nineteenth Amendment at length guaranteed women the right not to be discriminated against in voting on account of sex, and although states gradually adopted reforms recognizing a greater degree of legal autonomy and equality for women, before the 1960s numerous legal disabilities and forms of discrimination continued to restrict women in American society.

In the context of the civil rights movement, however, women activists' long-frustrated demands for full equality before the law began to receive mainstream political recognition. In 1963 Congress amended the Fair Labor Standards Act to require equal pay for equal work as between men and women. In Title VII of the Civil Rights Act of 1964 Congress declared unlawful employment practices that discriminated on the basis of sex, and in 1967 President Johnson, under Executive Order 11375, prohibited sex discrimination by employers under federal contracts. The women's rights movement made further gains in the 1970s as Congress submitted the Equal Rights Amendment to the states for ratification and enacted a series of laws barring discrimination on account of sex in federally supported educational programs, in the extension of credit opportunities, and in the administration of social security programs. Congress also strengthened the authority of the Equal Employment Opportunity Commission to enforce the ban on sex discrimination in employment contained in Title VII of the 1964 Civil Rights Act.

The Burger Court consistently upheld these antidiscrimination statutes. In *Phillips* v. *Martin Marietta Corporation* (1971), for example, it found that a company's refusal to hire women with preschool-age children—a policy not applied to men—violated the Civil Rights Acts of 1964. The Court affirmed the Equal Pay Act of 1963 against the practice of paying women day workers less as a base wage than men night-shift workers where performance of the same task was involved.[6] In still another typical case the Burger Court invalidated an Alabama law that effectively excluded women from employment in state prisons by stipulating minimum height and weight requirements for prison guards. This law also violated the Civil Rights Act of 1964.[7]

Going beyond statutory interpretation, the Supreme Court in other cases applied the due process and equal protection clauses of the Fourteenth Amendment and the due process clause of the Fifth Amendment, respectively, to strike down state and federal laws that rested on gender classifications found to be injurious to women. The leading case in this line of decisions was *Reed* v. *Reed* (1971). Here the Court upheld the claim of an Idaho woman that a state court's appointment of her estranged husband as the administrator of their deceased child's estate, in accordance with an Idaho law that categorically favored men over women in matters of this sort, was a denial of equal protection of the law under the Fourteenth Amendment. In *Frontiero* v. *Richardson* (1973), the Burger justices declared a federal law unconstitutional as a violation of the equal protection requirement considered to be implicit in the due process clause of the Fifth Amendment. The law in question regarded the dependents of male military personnel as automatically entitled to a basic subsistence allowance, but required the dependents of female military personnel to prove their actual

---

6. *Corning Glass Works* v. *Brennan* (1974).
7. *Dothard* v. *Rawlinson* (1977).

dependency before they could qualify for an allowance. The Court further struck down a Utah statute that required divorced fathers to support their sons until age twenty-one but their daughters only until age eighteen; an Oklahoma law that permitted the sale of beer to women at age eighteen while prohibiting it to men until age twenty-one; and a Louisiana law that excluded women from jury duty unless they volunteered for it.[8]

In employment matters the Court held that states could not force pregnant women to take maternity sick leave at a specified time on the ground that such a policy violated the due process clause of the Fourteenth Amendment.[9] Although states and private employers could deny disability insurance benefits to women undergoing normal pregnancy and childbirth, they could not deny women employees unemployment compensation benefits when they stopped working because of pregnancy, nor deny them accrued seniority.[10] In other actions the Supreme Court found unconstitutional federal social security programs that provided benefits to widows but not to widowers. Such programs, said the Court, discriminated against working women by giving them fewer financial benefits for their social security tax contribution than were given to male workers.[11]

In venturing into the field of sex discrimination the Supreme Court initially employed the conventional rational-basis test, used in ordinary review of state social and economic legislation, to decide whether legislation containing gender classification was constitutional. Thus in *Reed* v. *Reed,* Chief Justice Burger explained that legislation differentiating between the sexes, in order to be constitutional, "must be reasonable, not arbitrary, and must rest upon some ground of difference having a fair and substantial relation to the object of the legislation." Liberals like Justice Brennan pressed for adoption of a more rigorous test that would regard gender classification, like racial classification, as inherently suspect, and justifiable only if it served a compelling state interest. The Court did not adopt such a stringent test. Nevertheless, in *Craig* v. *Boren,* the Ohio drinking-age case, Brennan's majority opinion stated that gender classifications "must serve important governmental objectives and must be substantially related to the achievement of those objectives." This language appeared to go somewhat beyond the rational-basis test while stopping short of the "inherently suspect" test.

The Court's unwillingness to regard sex distinctions as inherently suspect allowed it to accept a series of affirmative action or reverse discrimination laws based on gender classification that favored women. Thus it upheld a state law exempting widows from a special property tax and a federal law that gave women naval officers a longer period in which to seek

8. *Stanton* v. *Stanton* (1975); *Craig* v. *Boren* (1976); *Taylor* v. *Louisiana* (1975).
9. *Cleveland Board of Education* v. *LeFleur* (1974).
10. *Geduldig* v. *Aiello* (1974); *General Electric Co.* v. *Gilbert* (1976); *Turner* v. *Department of Employment* (1975); *Nashville Gas* v. *Satty* (1978).
11. *Weinberger* v. *Wiesenfeld* (1975); *Califano* v. *Goldfarb* (1977).

promotion than was given to male officers.[12] In 1981 the Court again accepted legislation containing gender distinctions. It approved an act of Congress requiring men but not women to register for the draft, and a state law charging a male with statutory rape for having sex with a female under eighteen, but not a woman who had sex with a male under eighteen.[13] Like society in general, the justices appeared willing to recognize certain functional distinctions between the sexes, while generally disapproving gender classifications that served no apparent rational purpose or that did not compensate women for past discrimination.

The Burger Court and Criminal Procedure

The Supreme Court's actions in the area of women's rights on the whole met broad public acceptance. Public support was also forthcoming in decisions concerning the rights of criminal defendants—the law-and-order problem that formed an important part of the conservative reaction of the late 1960s and early 1970s. The Fourth Amendment exclusionary rule and the Fifth Amendment *Miranda* doctrine were the key instruments fashioned by the Warren Court in this field, and while the Burger justices did not repudiate either of them, they gave the doctrines a distinctly nonlibertarian application.

The exclusionary rule, adopted for the states by the Supreme Court in the *Mapp* decision in 1961, prohibited the use in criminal prosecution of evidence obtained in violation of the Fourth Amendment ban on unreasonable searches and seizures. Defenders of the rule said it preserved the integrity of the criminal justice system by preventing the courts from becoming accomplices in police lawlessness. Critics contended that mere technical violations of the rule, often resulting from police actions taken in good faith, ought not to defeat the successful prosecution of known criminals. After a transition period in which the Warren holdover justice generally maintained the defendant-oriented libertarian position, the Burger Court, sympathizing with critics of the exclusionary rule, applied it cautiously and with circumspection.

United States v. *Harris* (1971) pointed the new direction. At issue was the validity of a search warrant resting on an anonymous informer's tip, a question possibly to be regarded as settled by previous decisions. Instead, Chief Justice Burger's opinion attacked "mere hypertechnicality" in warrant affidavits and said that a policeman's knowledge of a suspect's reputation, "a practical consideration of everyday life," was sufficient to support a warrant application. Subsequently, the Court took a broader view of the

---

12. *Kahn* v. *Shevin* (1974); *Schlesinger* v. *Ballard* (1975).
13. *Rostker* v. *Goldberg* (1981); *Michael M.* v. *Superior Court of Sonoma County* (1981).

"probable cause" that was required for the granting of a search warrant; accepted a warrantless search as voluntary on the basis of the totality of circumstances in a given situation rather than on whether a person knowingly gave his consent; and decided that illegally seized evidence might be presented to a grand jury, in distinction to a jury trial.[14] Furthermore in 1976 the Court ruled that as long as states provided opportunity for full and fair litigation of Fourth Amendment claims, federal habeas corpus relief could not be granted on the ground that illegally obtained evidence was used at a defendant's trial.[15] The Burger Court also approved "stop and frisk" practices by state police and upheld an arrest under a "stop and identify" law which permitted police to question persons whom they had reason to believe warranted investigation.[16]

Yet the Burger Court by no means adopted an exclusively law-and-order approach to Fourth Amendment questions. Border searches by U.S. authorities, which Congress had always authorized without warrants, were to some extent brought within the scope of the Fourth Amendment.[17] Furthermore, the Court struck down a New York law that authorized police to conduct a warrantless search, by force if necessary, of a private home in order to make a felony arrest.[18] While the justices gave state police broad latitude to conduct auto searches, they prohibited warrantless interrogation of motorists to check driver's licenses and registrations without probable cause suggesting possible criminal activity. If the Burger Court permitted police to search the passenger compartment of a car stopped for a traffic violation and to seize evidence subsequently used to prosecute for violation of narcotics laws, it also prohibited the search of a vehicle's luggage compartment.[19] Continuing an earlier line of decisions, the Court prohibited federal health and safety inspectors from making warrantless searches of working areas in private businesses against the owner's objection.[20] And in the politically sensitive matter of electronic surveillance, which had been brought within the scope of the Fourth Amendment and subjected to judicial regulation by Congress in 1968, the Burger justices took an antigovernmental stand by denying the claims of the Nixon administration to conduct warrantless wiretaps in situations where national security was involved.[21]

Concerning the self-incrimination question, the Burger Court, while maintaining the *Miranda* doctrine for suspects in police custody, refused to

---

14. *Cady* v. *Dombrowski* (1973); *Schneckleth* v. *Bustamente* (1973); *United States* v. *Calandra* (1973).

15. *Stone* v. *Powell* (1976).

16. *Adams* v. *Williams* (1972), and *Michigan* v. *DeFillippo* (1979).

17. *Almeida-Sanchez* v. *United States* (1973); *United States* v. *Brignoni-Ponce* (1975).

18. *Payton* v. *New York* (1980).

19. *New York* v. *Belton* (1981); *Robbins* v. *California* (1981).

20. *Marshall* v. *Barlow's, Inc.*, (1978).

21. *United States* v. *United States District Court* (1972).

extend it to new situations. In *Harris* v. *New York* (1971) the Court ruled that a confession obtained without the *Miranda* warnings, though it could not be directly made a part of the prosecution case, could be used to impeach a defendant's credibility if he contradicted it in testifying in his own behalf. The Court also permitted the use against a defendant of testimony provided by a witness who was discovered as a result of statements made by the defendant before he was told of his right to consult a lawyer.[22] In still other nonextensions of *Miranda* the Court held that grand-jury witnesses need not be apprised of their rights even though they might later be defendants, and it ruled that Internal Revenue Service questioning of a person in a private home did not require issuing *Miranda* warnings.[23]

In Sixth Amendment right-to-counsel cases the Burger justices made the guarantee of a right of counsel, first assured for felony prosecutions in *Gideon* v. *Wainwright* (1963), applicable in all trials for criminal offenses that possibly could lead to imprisonment.[24] Simultaneously, the Court refrained from applying the guarantee to persons in police line-ups who had not yet been indicted. Here the Court departed from the logic of a Warren precedent that had excluded police line-up identifications from the trials of persons who were indicted at the time of the line-up.[25] Yet in doing so it followed the lead of Congress, which in the Crime Control and Safe Streets Act of 1968 authorized the use in federal trials of line-up evidence obtained in the absence of counsel.

The Burger Court showed similar mixed tendencies in Sixth Amendment jury trial questions. In *Duncan* v. *Louisiana* (1968) the Warren justices had applied the jury trial guarantee to the states, limiting it to felony prosecutions. *Baldwin* v. *New York* (1970) extended the right to include all petty misdemeanors punishable by six months' imprisonment or more. At the same time the Court did not insist that the states follow the federal practice of having twelve-man juries, ruling in *Williams* v. *Florida* (1970) that six-man jury trials were constitutional in noncapital cases. However, it refused to allow the states to conduct five-man juries.[26] Furthermore, the Court decided that unanimity was not required on twelve-man juries, holding that state laws that permitted 9-to-3 and 10-to-2 verdicts were constitutional.[27] The Court did demand unanimity, however, when a state used a jury of six in a criminal trial for a nonpetty offense.[28]

Continuity with Warren era tendencies, tempered by respect for public opinion, was evident in the Burger Court's decisions on capital punishment

22. *Michigan* v. *Tucker* (1974).
23. *United States* v. *Mandujano* (1976); *Beckwith* v. *United States* (1976).
24. *Argersinger* v. *Hamlin* (1972).
25. *Kirby* v. *Illinois* (1972). The Warren precedent was *United States* v. *Wade* (1967).
26. *Ballew* v. *Georgia* (1978).
27. *Johnson* v. *Louisiana, Apodaca* v. *Oregon* (1972).
28. *Burch* v. *Louisiana* (1979).

in the 1970s. In 1968 the Court had prohibited the states from excluding from juries in capital cases all persons who opposed the death penalty.[29] In *Furman* v. *Georgia* (1972) the Warren holdover justices, in a 5–4 decision, found unconstitutional state laws imposing the death penalty in murder and rape convictions. Although Justices Brennan and Marshall thought the death penalty was unconstitutional under all circumstances, the other majority justices (Douglas, Stewart, White) objected on the more limited ground that the manner in which the penalty was applied was arbitrary. The apparently random pattern of punishment following conviction, in the view of these justices, violated the prohibition against cruel and unusual punishment in the Eighth Amendment.

Guided by this reasoning, ten states adopted mandatory death sentences for certain crimes, thus removing the objection of arbitrariness; twenty-five other states provided for a special posttrial sentencing hearing for the purpose of deciding whether to impose the death penalty. In 1976, in *Gregg* v. *Georgia,* the Supreme Court refused to declare the death penalty unconstitutional in all circumstances and approved laws providing a two-stage procedure for employing capital punishment. Stage one was to determine guilt or innocence; stage two, the nature of the punishment. On the other hand, the Burger Court struck down laws imposing mandatory capital punishment for first-degree murder and requiring the death penalty for the crimes of rape and killing a police officer.[30] In 1978 the Court struck down a law that took an unduly narrow view of the factors to be considered in deciding on the applications of capital punishment.[31]

The Abortion Cases

As in the death penalty cases, the Burger Court manifested moderate reform tendencies on the abortion question, a controversial social issue throughout the 1970s. In *Roe* v. *Wade* (1973) it struck down a Texas law that made abortion a criminal offense, on the ground that the law violated a woman's constitutional right of privacy under the Fourteenth Amendment. Justice Blackmun's majority opinion stipulated that in the first and second trimesters of pregnancy the state's power to regulate abortion was either nonexistent or subordinate to the woman's right to decide the question of birth or abortion. Only in the third trimester might the state prohibit abortion outright, and even then it could not prohibit abortion to save the life or health of the mother. In *Doe* v. *Bolton* (1973), relying on the same ground of invasion of privacy, the Court invalidated the recent Georgia law that

29. *Witherspoon* v. *Illinois* (1968).

30. *Roberts* v. *Louisiana, Woodson* v. *North Carolina* (1976); *Roberts* v. *Louisiana, Coker* v. *Georgia* (1977).

31. *Lockett* v. *Ohio, Bell* v. *Ohio* (1978).

made abortion a crime but excepted operations performed for medical reasons under certain circumstances.

The abortion decisions aroused strong opposition among political and religious conservatives. Numerous state legislatures and courts virtually ignored the *Roe* and *Doe* decisions; others adopted laws restricting abortions to medically approved purposes in accordance with the Supreme Court's rulings, and in addition refusing to pay the cost of nontherapeutic abortions under their welfare programs. In 1976 Congress passed similar legislation, known as the Hyde Amendment, excluding from coverage under the Medicaid program abortions that were not medically necessary to protect the life of the mother. These efforts superseded an attempt in Congress to approve a constitutional amendment to restore to the states the power to regulate and prohibit abortions.

Although the Supreme Court did not repudiate its original position, it upheld these legislative attempts to prevent the right to have an abortion from being transformed into an entitlement thereof at public expense. In *Maher* v. *Roe* (1977) it considered a Connecticut statute, challenged as a denial of equal protection of the law, that denied public funding for Medicaid recipients having abortions, but that paid for medical care connected with child birth. Employing equal protection analysis, the Court found no suspect classification in the distinction between Medicaid recipients seeking abortion and women not covered by Medicaid, who were unrestricted in their ability to have an abortion. Nor did the law, which placed no governmental restriction on access to abortion, in the view of the Court encroach on a fundamental right. Accordingly, under the minimal reasonableness test, the Court held that the Connecticut law bore a rational relationship to the legitimate state objective of protecting life and was, therefore, constitutional.

By a similar course of reasoning the Court subsequently upheld the comparable federal restriction in the Hyde Amendment. *Harris* v. *McRae* (1980) centered on the contention that the restriction of federal funding of abortions for women on Medicaid was a denial of liberty under the due process clause of the Fifth Amendment. The Court rejected the argument, explaining that the existence of a right against government interference did not confer an entitlement to financial subsidies necessary to realize all the possible advantages of the right. Thus while the Court approved the apparent judgment of society that abortion was permissible, it placed limits on the practical consequences of that toleration for public policy.

First Amendment Free-Speech Problems

In dealing with First Amendment questions the Burger Court displayed a moderate attitude similar to that which it evinced on the abortion issue. In many respects it protected or enlarged freedom of speech and of the press. In Warrenlike fashion it defended "freedom of expression," an exceedingly broad category going well beyond speaking and writing to include symbolic speech. *California* v. *Cohen* (1971), for example, reversed the conviction of a young man found guilty of violating an "offensive conduct" statute for entering a California courthouse wearing a sweater bearing the slogan "F— the draft." In numerous subsequent cases the Court overturned convictions for using foul and offensive language in public, leaving the old Chaplinsky "fighting words" doctrine technically valid but practically meaningless.[32] The Burger justices furthermore protected "expressive activity," such as wearing a flag on the seat of one's pants or displaying a peace symbol on a flag, that state authorities had prosecuted.[33]

More innovative was the Court's extension of free speech guarantees to commercial advertising, previously unprotected under the First Amendment. It accomplished this by negating a Virginia law prohibiting pharmacists from advertising the prices of prescription drugs.[34] Without denying that some government regulation of advertising was necessary to protect consumers against fraud, the Court defended the open communication of commercial information as essential to a free market economy. In the political campaign field, however, the Court invalidated on First Amendment grounds sections of the Federal Election Campaign Act of 1974 that restricted the amount of money that could be spent in a campaign.[35] To limit the money spent on a campaign, reasoned the Court, was to curb political expression by restricting the number of issues dealt with, the depth of their discussion, and the scope of the audience made aware of them. In a related decision the Court broke new free-speech ground by declaring unconstitutional a Massachusetts law that prohibited business corporations from contributing money to influence elections except on questions that materially affected them in a specific way. Allowing a Boston bank to contribute to a campaign against a state income tax, the Court held that corporations had a First Amendment right to spend money on political campaigns involving popular referendums.[36]

Extending First Amendment guarantees to businessmen was hardly the kind of libertarianism practiced in the Warren era. But the major difference between the Burger and Warren Courts in the area of free speech was the frequent denial of First Amendment claims by the Burger justices.

---

32. *Gooding, Warding,* v. *Wilson* (1972); *Rosenfeld v.* New Jersey (1972); *Lewis* v. *City of New Orleans* (1972); *Hess* v. *Indiana* (1973).

33. *Smith* v. *Goguen* (1974); *Spence* v. *Washington* (1974).

34. *Virginia State Board of Pharmacy* v. *Virginia Citizens Consumer Council* (1976).

35. *Buckley* v. *Valeo* (1976). However, the Court upheld limits on individual contributions to political campaigns, despite an inhibiting effect on freedom of speech. It considered these limits justified by the government's interest in preventing political corruption.

36. *First National Bank* v. *Bellotti* (1978).

On the pornography question, for example, they deliberately departed from the "anything goes" approach adopted by the Warren Court. In *Miller* v. *California* (1973) the Court by a 5–4 vote in effect sustained a conviction under a California statute that prohibited the knowing sale of obscene matter. Chief Justice Burger's majority opinion rejected the Warren Court's *Jacobellis* definition of obscenity—that the materials in question be "utterly without redeeming social value"—and postulated another formula which asked whether, under contemporary community standards, a work appealed to a prurient interest, depicted sexual conduct in a patently offensive way, and lacked "serious artistic, political or scientific value." Burger furthermore rejected the idea of a national community standard for pornography and said trial courts should measure obscenity by local community standards. The Court's decision, however, appeared to produce no noticeable decline in the cultural sleaziness that was part of the national urban scene.

In a series of shopping center free speech cases, the Court narrowed the public forum governed by the guarantees of the First Amendment. The relevant precedent from the Warren period denied the owner of a shopping mall the right to prohibit picketing of a store in the mall, on the theory that the area was the functional equivalent of a town's business district and, therefore, public.[37] In 1972 the Burger Court qualified this holding by forbidding distribution of antiwar handbills unrelated to commercial enterprises within the plaza.[38] Emphasizing the private character of the commercial property, the Court said it was not available to the public for any and all purposes. Subsequently, the Court restricted free speech on private property even further by prohibiting striking employees of a company from picketing one of its stores in a shopping center.[39]

Freedom of the Press in the 1970s

The Burger Court dealt with a number of questions concerning the media that raised freedom-of-the-press claims under the First Amendment. That such cases arose in the 1970s was testimony not only to the litigious spirit of the day, but also to the powerful position the media had come to occupy in American life. The press naturally resented outside interference with its business. Editors and reporters automatically and with virtual unanimity condemned any denial of a First Amendment claim made by the media as an attack on American liberty. Observers not connected with the media reasoned that if, as the media insisted, the public interest ordinarily

37. *Amalgamated Food Employees Union Local 590* v. *Logan Valley Plaza* (1968).
38. *Lloyd Corporation, Ltd.* v. *Tanner* (1972).
39. *Hudgens* v. *National Labor Relations Board* (1976).

demanded broad scope for freedom of the press, there were nevertheless times when the public interest required restrictions on the press. These restrictions took the form not of prior restraint, but rather the obligation to give evidence in criminal trials, submit to searches, and so on, just like the rest of the society. Characteristically, the Burger Court tried to mediate these conflicting views.

The basic purpose of the First Amendment is to protect the right of the individual to speak and write freely, without prior restraint or subsequent punishment by the government. In the most celebrated and politically important free speech case of the decade, the *Pentagon Papers* case, the Burger court blocked the government's attempt to impose prior restraint on the publication of the Defense Department history of the Indochina war.[40] In a more complicated case occurring several years later, however, the Court approved an instance of prior restraint. The case, *Snepp* v. *United States* (1980), arose when Snepp, an employee of the CIA, signed a contract agreeing not to publish anything about the agency during or after his period of service without its prior approval. Subsequently, Snepp published a book about the agency without approval. The government thereupon brought suit to take away his profits from the work and to require him to clear any future writings with the CIA. The Supreme Court upheld the government on the ground that Snepp had waived his First Amendment rights by signing the contract.

With respect to punishment for publication, or libel, the Burger Court rejected claims for freedom of the press that would have extended the *New York Times* actual malice rule to private individuals. This rule, it will be recalled, held that public figures claiming damages for false and defamatory statements must prove actual malice on the part of the publisher—i.e., that the material was published with knowledge of its falseness or with reckless disregard for the truth. When the question of applying this rule in the case of an ostensibly private individual arose in 1971, the Court followed the *New York Times* precedent. It denied the request of a nudist magazine distributor, who had been arrested in a pornography raid, for damages against a radio station that announced that he had been arrested for possession of obscene literature.[41]

In 1974, however, the Burger Court decided that private individuals defamed by false published accounts need not prove actual malice in order to recover damages. The pertinent case, *Gertz* v. *Robert Welch, Inc.*, arose when Gertz, a lawyer who had shot a policeman, sought damages from the John Birch Society magazine *American Opinion*, which had called him a "Leninist" and accused him of conspiracy to discredit the Chicago police. The Supreme Court sustained Gertz's claim, declaring that the actual-

40. See above, pp. 700–1.
41. *Rosenboom* v. *Metromedia Inc.* (1971).

malice rule did not apply to the publication of defamatory material about private individuals. The effect of the decision was to restrict the scope of the public-figure concept and hence the latitude available to the press. The Court confirmed this modification of the law of libel in subsequent cases, holding that a member of a socially prominent family involved in a divorce contest, a Russian émigré alleged to have been a Soviet spy, and a scientist who received a mock award from a U.S. senator for wasting public money were not public figures and did not have to prove actual malice to collect damages for false statements published about them.[42] At the same time, however, the Burger Court followed a Warren precedent in striking down a state law that prohibited the publication of the names of rape victims. In other words, the actual-malice rule protected the publication of nondefamatory material about persons whom events happened to make newsworthy. Thus the Court in general tried to balance the rights of individuals against the institutional power of the media.

With investigative journalism becoming a glamorous profession and the press receiving credit for breaking open the Watergate cover-up, the media tried to extend freedom of the press into a comprehensive sanction protecting all phases of the news business. As a result, numerous conflicts arose over the claim of the media to special privilege concerning not only access to information and confidentiality of sources, but also immunity from searches, depositions relating to criminal justice, and other responsibilities of citizenship that affected the public in general. Again, the Burger Court sought a middle position.

On the question of whether, in order to assure a fair trial, courts might exclude or otherwise restrict the press, the Court vacillated. Although a precedent for doing so existed from the Warren era, in *Nebraska Press Association* v. *Stuart* (1976), the Burger justices issued an emphatic no. They held that a state judge's order prohibiting the press from reporting about the trial of a mass murderer violated the First Amendment ban on prior restraint. In another case, however, in which it was asked to decide whether a judge could bar the press from a pretrial hearing to consider the question of admissible evidence in a murder case, the Court gave a different answer. In *Gannett Co.* v. *DePasquale* (1979) it denied the claim of journalists to a constitutional right under the Sixth and First Amendments to attend the hearing in question. Yet a year later, in *Richmond Newspapers, Inc.* v. *Virginia* (1980), the Court refused to allow a criminal trial to be closed to the press, as a lower court had ordered. The rationale offered by Chief Justice Burger was not, as libertarians argued, that journalists possessed a special constitutional right of access, but that in the absence of compelling circumstances suggesting otherwise, the public had a right to attend the kind of criminal trials that had historically been open to it.

42. *Time Inc.* v. *Firestone* (1976); *Wolston* v. *Readers' Digest Association, Inc.* (1979); *Hutchinson* v. *Proxmire* (1979).

The press further claimed a constitutional right to withhold the identity of their sources, on the theory that their revelation would discourage anonymous informants from providing information vital to democratic government. In the landmark case of *Branzburg* v. *Hayes* (1972), the Supreme Court rejected this claim to journalistic privilege. Branzburg, a reporter for a Louisville newspaper, had written a series of articles about the drug traffic, based on observations he was permitted to make by drug users on condition that he not reveal their identity. For a 5–4 Court majority, Justice White, declaring that the Constitution gave no testimonial privilege to reporters not enjoyed by other citizens, held that Branzburg must testify before a grand jury investigating violations of drug laws. The public interest in the administration of justice, said White, outweighed any possible burden that answering questions before a grand jury or court might impose on the news business, which in any case he thought would be slight.

Subsequent decisions confirmed this denial of special privilege to the media. In *Herbert* v. *Lando* (1979), the Court held that a public figure charging a television corporation with actual malice in a libel suit may cause an inquiry to be made into the state of mind and editorial process producing the alleged libel. In a controversial state case a reporter was found guilty of criminal and civil contempt by the New Jersey Supreme Court for refusing to surrender material in his files thought to be pertinent to a defendant in a murder trial.[43] The United States Supreme Court refused to grant certiorari, thus allowing the conviction to stand. And in the *Stanford Daily* case (1978) the Burger justices decided that police armed with a court-issued warrant could search the offices of a newspaper for evidence related to a crime. Denying the newspaper's contention that a subpoena for specific materials was the proper course for the police to take, the Court asserted that freedom of the press was adequately protected by the Fourth Amendment.

The Burger Court and the Judicial Function

Notwithstanding the "strict construction" political background of their appointments and their conservative position on several issues, the Burger justices yielded little to the Warren Court in the way of judicial policy making. After years of criticism of activist, result-oriented jurisprudence, many legal scholars were dismayed to see the Burger Court engaging in judicial lawmaking of its own. Among many choices, the abortion decisions of 1973 came in for the heaviest criticism. One respected commentator declared, for example, that as the decisions rested on no text of the Constitution nor any principle or value contained therein, they were not truly

43. *New Jersey and Dr. Mario Jascalevich* v. *Myron Farber and the New York Times Company* (1978).

constitutional law.[44] Indeed, the Burger Court's resort to judicial legislation, as well as its penchant for discretionary case-by-case balancing of competing interests, provoked yet another round in the continuing debate over the nature of the judicial function. Several scholars insisted that it was entirely legitimate for courts, as they had always done, to rely in their decisions on extraconstitutional sources of authority, such as the fundamental values and norms of the society. Others, critical of the notion of a "living constitution" that was used to justify judicial activism, called for decisions based on fidelity to the Constitution—that is, the constitutional text, the original intention of the framers, or structures and principles plainly evident in the Constitution.

By no means merely academic, the controversy reached the level of the Supreme Court. In the late 1970s Justice Lewis F. Powell in off-the-bench remarks tried to explain the nature and role of the judicial power in the American system of government. On the one hand Powell spoke like a legal realist in stating that the Constitution was "a sort of living political organism," and in observing that the Court often could not rely on the original intent of the framers. Powell also said the Court must make decisions necessary for the society that the legislature was reluctant to make. If that sounded uncharacteristically activist for a conservative southern judge, Powell on another occasion described the work of the Court in the language of judicial restraint. In a speech a year later he criticized those who urged the Court to "take every opportunity to advance some preferred moral, philosophic, or political viewpoint." "That would not be a court of law," said Powell. "It would be a supreme legislature." Powell's seemingly contradictory statements reflected the tension between two conceptions of the role of the judiciary, each deeply rooted in the history of the Supreme Court. Though at the expense of theoretical consistency, the Court's tendency to alternate between policy-making activism and policy-approving restraint assured a balance between change and continuity in American constitutionalism.

The controversy over the Supreme Court formed part of the larger picture of judicial power in the contemporary constitutional system. Despite the rise of the administrative state, the judiciary continued to occupy an important—indeed an increasingly important—place in American government. Judicial review in the traditional sense—that is, determination of the constitutionality of legislation—was but a small part of the juridical task. Of greater consequence was the policy-making role that the courts enjoyed through statutory interpretation and as the preferred forum for those seeking changes in public policy. Eschewing legislatures and expressing a seemingly pervasive attitude of litigiousness throughout the society, reform

44. John Hart Ely, "The Wages of Crying Wolf: A Comment on *Roe* v. *Wade*," *Yale Law Journal* 82 (April 1973): 947.

groups and individuals asserted rights claims and public-policy demands that became requests for the courts to take action in matters ranging from discipline in the public schools to international diplomacy.

Considering that the post–New Deal judiciary defined its modern role mainly in the field of civil liberties and civil rights, it was fitting that a major source of the federal courts' expanded case load in the 1970s was a reconstruction-era civil rights law. The pertinent statute, Section 1983 of the U.S. Code, gave a federal right of action against any state law or executive or administrative action that deprived a person of "any rights, privileges, or immunities secured by the Constitution and laws" of the United States. Intended to protect Negro civil rights in the 1870s, this provision in the 1970s became an all-purpose instrument for pursuing grievances against state and local governments that went far beyond the sphere of civil rights as traditionally understood. It was the basis, for example, of a $200,000 damage award to a concert promoter for lost ticket sales resulting from actions taken by the local government that caused a public controversy and discouraged attendance at a concert. The number of suits filed under Section 1983 increased from 300 in the mid-1960s to 9,000 in 1980.

The sheer volume of litigation in federal and state courts meant that some of these claims would be accepted no matter what the jurisprudential outlook of the judges. The probability of acceptance, and thus of circumvention of the legislature, was greater among activist-minded judges, who had encouraged litigation by liberalizing access to the courts. In the 1960s, while lawmakers and executives created legal services units that urged poor people and others to make rights claims against government, courts broadened the concept of standing so that almost anyone affected by a particular policy could bring suit.[45] Class action suits aimed at affecting public policy were a major consequence of this change. The ripeness doctrine—the idea that an issue as presented was not ready for resolution because it lacked concreteness—was another technique of judicial restraint that fell into disuse in the 1960s. And, of course, the doctrine of political questions had long since been all but abandoned as courts recognized few, if any, matters as peculiarly within the competence of the political branches.

The upshot was "government by judiciary," a term originally used by progressive reformers to criticize conservative courts, but now applied to equal protection-minded liberal activist judges. Perhaps more aptly, the term "imperial judiciary" came into use to capture the sense of comprehensive policy-making power that courts were asked and often agreed to assume. In any event, as public opinion was divided on the issue of group-oriented egalitarianism versus traditional liberal individualism, so it was split over the proper judicial role. Some observers approved the court's far-flung power and proposed new concepts of public law litigation in which

45. *Cf. Flast* v. *Cohen,* discussed above, p. 656.

judges would frankly shape public policy as an extension of the political process. In this view law would be assimilated to politics, and the results of judicial decisions justified by the social justice they embodied. Other students of public law, however, including some who had spoken for liberal activism in the 1960s, advised judicial moderation. Unless the American people were prepared to convert courts into organs of general government, wrote Professor Charles Black in 1976, a line had to be drawn somewhere between law and politics.[46] Where the line should be drawn was by no means clear. But of its necessity there seemed little doubt if American constitutionalism in the 1980s was to continue to rest on the principles and values set forth at the beginning of the republic.

---

46. Charles L. Black, Jr. and Bob Eckhardt, *The Tides of Power: Conversation on the American Constitution* (New Haven, 1976).

Epilogue:
American Constitutionalism in the
1980s

AS THE NATION looked to the bicentennial of the Constitution in 1987, conflicting tendencies made predictions about the future course of American constitutionalism problematic at best. Paradoxical as it appeared, there was evidence that American government might become either too strong or too weak for the preservation of constitutional liberty. In a proximate sense this divided assessment reflected the familiar conflict of pluralistic politics. As in the past, competing groups sought to use government—or prevent it from being used—to serve particular ends. More fundamentally, the paradox was rooted in the conflict between power and liberty that has been intrinsic to American constitutionalism throughout its history. This conflict is most clearly evident in the dual traditions of negative and positive liberty that have defined the character of constitutional government in the United States.

In the classic constitutionalist expression, negative liberty is liberty against government. It rests on the assumption that the purpose of politics and the basic goal of government is to free the individual for the uninhibited pursuit of his or her interests. In the struggle against English rule in the eighteenth century, liberty against government formed the principal—though by no means the exclusive—theme of nascent American constitutionalism. In the nineteenth century, especially as seen in the policies of the Democratic party from Andrew Jackson to Grover Cleveland, negative liberty achieved an ideological ascendancy that established it as higher law both in a philosophical and constitutional sense. Most conspicuously apparent in the demand for entrepreneurial freedom, it was evident also in social and cultural matters such as the opposition to prohibition and the desire for parochial schools.

In the late nineteenth century the dominance of the corporation, based to a very great extent on laissez-faire law and policy, served to discredit the idea of negative liberty. Henceforth reformers, instead of urging restraints on government to enlarge the sphere of individual liberty, would demand that government intervene in society to protect the individual against the private power of overmastering business interests. Accordingly, liberty against government acquired a predominantly conservative connotation. It became the major theoretical basis for opposing the interventionist policies of progressivism, the New Deal, and post–World War II liberalism. Nevertheless, although reduced to minority status in an intellectual and constitutional sense, negative liberty remained deeply embedded in American political culture. The frustrations and discontents of modern liberalism, reflected especially in resentment against big government and bureaucracy, enabled negative liberty once again to become a vital political force in the 1970s. The election of a conservative Republican president in 1980 showed the considerable appeal that laissez-faire liberty still possessed in American politics.

The theory of positive liberty, on the other hand, holds that genuine freedom consists not in the absence of restraint, but in the ability of citizens to achieve their goals and aspirations, either individually or as members of groups. In the eighteenth century the ideal of positive liberty was embodied in the republican belief that citizens' participation in the political life of the community was the essence of civic virtue and the source of true happiness. Implicit in this formulation, and central to the theory of positive liberty, is the notion of positive government. For typically the inclusion of citizens in the political community—the pre-eminent expression of positive liberty from the suffrage reforms of the American Revolution to the civil rights movement of the 1960s—has depended on government intervention into the political process.

The tradition of positive liberty derived from the ancient Greek theory of the polis by way of Italian Renaissance civic humanism and the classical republicanism of seventeenth-century England. In the United States positive liberty formed an important, if ultimately subordinate, element in revolutionary republican constitutionalism. It was expressed more systematically in the elitist republicanism of the Federalist party and the mercantilist policies of Alexander Hamilton, aimed at encouraging economic development. In the nineteenth-century setting of political egalitarianism Henry Clay's American system, followed by the emancipationist and civil rights policies of Lincoln and the Republican party in the Civil War era, carried on the ideal of positive liberty.

In the twentieth century war and economic crisis established positive government as a permanent constitutional reality. In the course of this development liberalism, previously conceived of in negative, antigovernmental terms, was redefined as the positive guarantee of political and civil rights and the assurance of economic security. Departing from its traditional laissez-faire outlook, the Democratic party under Woodrow Wilson and Franklin D. Roosevelt identified itself with activist governmental intervention as the means of achieving positive liberty. Since the New Deal, successive versions of modern liberalism have supported ever more far-reaching government intervention to remedy social evils and provide the material resources needed to enable citizens to fulfill their potential, either as individuals or as members of economic and ethnic groups.

These rival theories of liberty form the basis for conflicting approaches to contemporary constitutional politics. Modern liberals and the left in general endorse an ideal of constitutional liberty that seeks to establish a greater degree of social and economic equality, and that depends for its implementation on judicial and bureaucratic policy making in particular. There appears to be little doubt, moreover, that the relationship between positive liberty and the positive state that has been forged by events in the twentieth century will continue into the foreseeable future. This relationship, an almost symbiotic identification supported by the logic of mass politics, rests on the acceptance of social justice as a basic constitutional value.

At the same time, the tradition of negative liberty persists as a political force. Conservatives and the right in general cling to this ideal, especially in economic affairs. While acknowledging the seeming permanence of the regulatory-welfare state, they try to restrict its growth in the interest of individual liberty. Yet conservatives themselves stand ready to use government on a selective basis to deal with social problems that they regard as especially important, such as drug abuse and abortion. Balancing this inconsistency, liberals change their philosophical complexion and support the negative-liberty ideal in their efforts to expand First Amendment liberties and provide procedural safeguards for criminal defendants. Thus, in part because neither left nor right subscribes completely to either conception, both negative and positive theories of liberty retain their constitutional vitality.

If this fact helps explain why American government can at once appear possibly either too strong or weak for the preservation of constitutional liberty, another is to be found in the traditional pluralistic structure of American politics. Interest groups and issue groups on both left and right desire government to be strong enough to assist them in attaining their goals, yet not so strong as to be able to control them. When public policy pursues ends with which certain groups disagree, those groups tend to decry the destruction of constitutional liberty. When policy goals are agreeable to them, the same groups hail the upholding of the Constitution and the maintenance of democratic liberties. This use of constitutional rhetoric, disingenuous though it may appear, is not cynical in any vulgar sense, but rather illustrates the normal operation of constitutional politics. Nevertheless, in assessing the state of constitutionalism, the rhetoric of constitutional politics must be taken at a certain discount and its instrumental and pragmatic nature understood. When this is done, one can fairly conclude that since the constitutional crisis of the 1930s and the rise of the positive state, constitutional government—government that is effective yet responsible and limited—has been satisfactorily maintained in the United States. Furthermore, despite some uncertainty about its future direction, there was much evidence of the vitality of constitutionalism at the start of the 1980s.

One indication of constitutional vitality was the movement in the states to require Congress to call a constitutional convention. Never before successfully invoked, Article V of the Constitution declares that on the application of the legislatures of two-thirds of the states, Congress shall call a convention for amending the Constitution. At the end of 1980 thirty states of the requisite thirty-four had petitioned Congress for a convention. Perplexing questions loomed over how a convention should be called and whether it could be restricted to a single issue, such as a balanced federal budget, as proponents contended. There was concern, too, that to deal with a policy matter as complex as the federal budget through the amending power was to misconceive the nature and purpose of the Constitution. According to critics of the convention proposal, the fiscal problems it was intended to address were essentially legislative and regulatory. The legitimacy of an Article V convention was undeniable, however, and the strong support it received reflected an attitude of genuine constitutional seriousness. The budget balancers' resort to the amendment process showed how important they considered the issue to be.

Two constitutional amendments approved by Congress and submitted to the states offered additional evidence that constitutionalism remained a vital force in American politics. One amendment proposed to give voting representation to the District of Columbia, "as though it were a state." The amendment would permit citizens of the District of Columbia to elect two senators and one representative to Congress. A precedent existed for regarding the District in some respects as a state, for in 1961 the Twenty-third Amendment gave it the right to appoint electors of president and vice-president who "shall be considered ... appointed by a State." Supporters of the District of Columbia voting representation amendment invoked the principle of "no taxation without representation," while opponents, perhaps fearing the political consequences of giving the largely Democratic federal city voting in Congress, insisted that only states could send voting representatives to the national legislature. By the end of 1980, two years after Congress had approved the amendment, only nine states had ratified it.

Far more controversial was the Equal Rights Amendment, a product of the social ferment of the late 1960s. Adopted by Congress in 1972, the amendment declared that "Equality of rights under the law shall not be abridged by the United States or by any State on account of sex." Within three years of its passage, thirty-five of the required thirty-eight states had ratified the ERA. By 1979, however, at the end of the seven-year ratification period set by Congress, no additional states had approved it. Congress thereupon extended the time limit to 1982, the first time since it began placing restrictions on ratification in 1917 that it had prolonged the period for approving a constitutional amendment. This action provoked legal and ethical questions, which were compounded by two states' recision of their earlier ratification of ERA. These issues were obviated, however, by the failure of the Equal Rights Amendment to gain the three additional state ratifications needed to make it part of the Constitution by June 30, 1982, the expiration of the extended ratification period.

Significant constitutional change continued to occur outside the formal amendment process. Although scarcely novel, one of the most perplexing issues in contemporary constitutionalism concerned the role of the judiciary. As the above account has shown, the end of the Warren era by no means marked the end of judicial activism. Interpreting the broad and imprecise standards of regulatory legislation, and impelled by the belief that the purpose of government is to redress injury and promote the communal good, courts in the 1970s acquired an ever-broader policy-making function. It was in the Burger era, which ironically began with President Nixon's pledge to appoint "strict construction" judges, that critics began to employ the term "imperial judiciary" to describe the scope of judicial power.

Much of the controversy over the place of the judiciary in American government was, of course, familiar. Adhering to the theory of judicial restraint, critics of the imperial judiciary insisted that by constitutional design public policy should be determined by elected legislatures rather than by unelected courts. It could be argued with equal cogency, however, that restrictions on legislative power—restrictions that were typically imposed by the judiciary with policy-making consequences—formed perhaps the most basic principle of American constitutionalism. While formal democratic theory might support the model of judicial restraint, history clearly vindicated judicial activism—including its most recent manifestations in the Burger period. Critics of judicial activism were forced to concede, moreover, that some constitutional problems—reapportionment, for example—were impervious to any but a judicial solution.

There was perhaps a certain reassurance to be gained in observing the persistence of judicial policy making in the post–New Deal era, despite the very different political complexion it assumed. At the start of the twentieth century courts protected entrepreneurial freedom and corporate power under guarantees of due process and liberty of contract. In the late twentieth century they promoted social justice and civil and political liberties under the equal protection clause and the Bill of Rights. And while critics of the imperial judiciary warned that a persistent activist course would erode judicial authority, no evidence of increasing noncompliance with Supreme Court decisions appeared. The political impact of judicial review, contrary to the theory of judicial restraint, remained one of its basic sources of legitimacy.

The question arose, however, whether the continuous expansion of judicial power had not after all transformed the judicial function, with potentially serious consequences for American constitutionalism. Some degree of judicial involvement in politics was a fact from the beginning of the government and had long been accepted as salutary and legitimate. In the early twentieth century the extent of the courts' political involvement appeared more considerable as observers pointed out the distinctive lawmaking function of the judiciary, which enabled it to shape public policy. At first criticized by reformers who opposed "government by judiciary," this policy-making role was widely accepted as legitimate by the end of the 1930s. What appeared to be happening in the 1980s, however, in yet another phase of the assimilation of the judiciary into the political system, was the bureaucratization of judicial power.

Indeed, a reciprocal transformation could be discerned between courts and administrative agencies. In theory administrative bodies, employing lawmaking power delegated by the legislature, made general and prospective rules; they did not adjudicate disputes concerning the application of law. In fact, however, there was increasing pressure on administrative agencies to act like courts. Under what is called "due process in rule making," the agencies have been required—sometimes by the courts, more often by Congress—to give notice of proposed rules, hold hearings for the presentation of facts and arguments, record evidence, maintain at least some degree of impartiality, offer reasons for their decisions, and in general operate in a spirit of judiciousness and fair play.

Courts on the other hand have taken on many of the institutional attributes of bureaucracy. In the first place, their number has increasd significantly to meet the vast increase in litigation that occurred in the 1960s and 1970s. In 1978 Congress created 35 additional appellate judgeships (for a total of 132) and 115 district court judgeships (raising the number to 516). The number of law clerks and staff attorneys assigned to federal judges also rose. In the face of staggering case loads, these support personnel began to perform functions previously regarded as judicial. They screened cases, decided which ones merited oral argument, and wrote opinions. Like other faceless officials in the bureaucracy, they also took up the practice of leaking confidential information about the Supreme Court's decision-making process to journalists. Within the legal profession concern spread that the bureaucratic production of opinions, when perceived as such, would undermine public and professional confidence in the judiciary. It was feared that courts, too often engaging in legislative rule making, were abandoning the unique adjudicative function that had always been the principal basis of their authority and the source of their legitimacy.

The underlying cause of judicial bureaucratization was the relentless expansion of the sphere of law, and especially of federal court jurisdiction. Responding to the demands of litigants, courts intervened in an ever-wider array of public policy questions. Employing the techniques of administrative rule making, at the urging of reform organizations the judiciary undertook the management of public institutions such as schools, hospitals, and prisons. Encouraging this development was the belief dominant in most of the major law schools that judicial decision making was in essence no different from political and administrative rule making. Judges, it was said, like other political actors in government were concerned mainly with promoting specific policy goals.

The problem of judicial bureaucratization came more fully into view with the passage of the Judicial Conduct and Disability Act of 1980. For over forty years bills had ben introduced into Congress to provide a means other than impeachment for dealing with disabled or otherwise irresponsible federal judges. Out of regard for the principle of judicial independence, none was ever adopted. In the 1970s, however, rising dissatisfaction with the imperial judiciary made the issue of judicial discipline politically relevant and finally enabled a reform measure to pass. The Judicial Conduct and Disability Act of 1980 provided that any person might file a complaint with the circuit judicial council (the administrative organ of federal judges in each circuit), charging a circuit or district court judge with disability or with conduct prejudicial to the effective administration of the business of the court. The circuit council was authorized to dismiss the complaint if it concerned the merits of a decision or was "frivolous." If the complaint had substance, however, the council could request the offending judge to retire, withhold his caseload, censure him, or recommend impeachment by Congress.

Opponents of the Judicial Conduct and Disability Act declared it an unconstitutional interference with judicial independence. They argued that impeachment was the only constitutional means of dealing with the problem of irresponsible or arbitrary judicial behavior. Supporters of the act, insisting that judges, like all other government officers, must be held accountable, said it was necessary because impeachment was useless as a check on judicial conduct. Whatever its actual impact might prove to be, the measure imposed a new bureaucratic restraint on federal judges. And although the matter was defined in strictly procedural terms, the possibility existed that the new bureaucratic arrangement would inhibit the substantive policy-making function of the judiciary.

If the new judicial bureaucracy aroused suspicion, the older executive-administrative bureaucracy was often the object of outright hostility. It was easy to find examples of bureaucratic bungling and stupidity to justify the increasingly popular demand for relaxation of government regulations. To some extent, moreover, the call for deregulation of the economy expressed the antigovernmental animus present in American constitutionalism from the outset. Yet there were distinct limits to any practical efforts to reduce the size of the federal bureaucracy. Although complaints against big government might even gain majority appeal at times, the decisive fact was that an increasing number of people were becoming dependent on government for employment, education, medical care, and other social services. Less obviously but no less significantly, businessmen, professional groups, and private institutions of almost every description had in one way or another become dependent upon government. For these reasons positive government was certain to continue, and with it, presumably, reliance on bureaucratic organization. Nevertheless, a nagging question persisted: bureaucracy could make discrete policies, but could it actually govern in a coherent and authoritative manner, fragmented as it was by alliance with literally thousands of interest and issue groups?

For almost two hundred years American constitutionalism had succeeded in maintaining a constructive tension between law and politics in the conduct of government. As the society was transformed from an agrarian republic to an industrial empire, public policy and public law in fundamental ways conformed to the demands of successive political generations, within an established framework of constitutional values and procedures. This creative tension between the demands of political expediency and the requirements of constitutional principle formed the essence of the rule of law—the imprecise but still politically potent symbol that in the popular mind continued to express the real meaning of American constitutionalism.

In many respects the rule of law appeared to have been not only confirmed but also extended into new spheres by recent tendencies and events in constitutional history. This was the inference to be drawn from facts such as the judicialization of administrative agencies, the spread of "due process" throughout the society, and the intervention of the law into matters once regarded as exclusively private. Yet again the evidence was contradictory, for there were also trends that pointed to a weakening of the rule of law. Of these the most important was the tendency toward an ever greater politicization of society and the institutions of government.

Politicization refers to the process by which all aspects of social and economic life are drawn into the vortex of politics, becoming subject to the dictates of expedient policy making. More specifically politicization occurs when private groups effectively exercise governmental power through formal and informal relationships with bureaucratic and judicial rule makers. To some extent, of course, governmental power in America has always been shared with private groups; in a sense that has been the meaning of self-government in a pluralistic society. In the 1960s and 1970s, however, the cultural homogeneity and national community consensus that made it possible in the past to limit the power of special interest groups were seriously eroded. This fact was reflected in the declining influence of the mainstream political parties and the corresponding rise of single-issue politics.

At any rate, as society fragments into discrete groups unchecked by any overarching consensus—or at least any consensus that can be translated into a coherent public policy—there is likely to be increased reliance on the forms and institutions of law. The litigation explosion of the 1970s appears to bear this out. In the absence of shared community values, however, the motive force behind the proliferating legal action—and behind the continuing judicial and administrative lawmaking which it engenders—is political expediency and ideology. A legal realist might argue that it has ever been thus, that politics has always been the decisive factor in constitutional change. There appears to be no danger, moreover, of European-style politicization on the totalitarian model of the 1930s. Nevertheless, if the trend toward ideologically based single-issue politics continues, it will threaten the balance between law and politics that has been the essential condition of constitutional government in the United States.

APPENDIX
ONE

Articles of Confederation

To ALL to whom these Presents shall come, we the undersigned Delegates of the States affixed to our Names send greeting.

Whereas the Delegates of the United States of America in Congress assembled did on the fifteenth day of November in the Year of our Lord One Thousand Seven Hundred and Seventy-seven, and in the Second Year of the Independence of America agree to certain articles of Confederation and perpetual Union between the States of Newhampshire, Massachusetts-bay, Rhodeisland and Providence Plantations, Connnecticut, New York, New Jersey, Pennsylvania, Delaware, Maryland, Virginia, North-Carolina, South-Carolina and Georgia in the Words following, viz.

"Articles of Confederation and perpetual Union between the States of New-hampshire, Massachusetts-bay, Rhodeisland and Providence Plantations, Connecticut, New-York, New-Jersey, Pennsylvania, Delaware, Maryland, Virginia, North-Carolina, South-Carolina and Georgia.

ARTICLE I. The stile of this confederacy shall be "The United States of America."

ARTICLE II. Each State retains its sovereignty, freedom and independence, and every power, jurisdiction and right, which is not by this confederation expressly delegated to the United States, in Congress assembled.

ARTICLE III. The said States hereby severally enter into a firm league of friendship with each other, for their common defence, the security of their liberties, and their mutual and general welfare, binding themselves to assist each other, against all force offered to, or attacks made upon them, or any of them, on account of religion, sovereignty, trade or any other pretence whatever.

ARTICLE IV. The better to secure and perpetuate mutual friendship and intercourse among the people of the different States in this Union, the free inhabitants of each of these States, paupers, vagabonds and fugitives from justice excepted, shall be entitled to all privileges and immunities of free citizens in the several States; and the people of each State shall have free ingress and regress to and from any other State, and shall enjoy therein all the privileges of trade and commerce, subject to the same duties, impositions and restrictions as the inhabitants thereof respectively, provided that such restrictions shall not extend so far as to prevent the removal of property imported into any State, to any other State of which the owner is an inhabitant; provided also that no imposition, duties or restriction shall be laid by any State, on the property of the United States, or either of them.

If any person guilty of, or charged with treason, felony, or other high misdemeanor in any State, shall flee from justice, and be found in any of the United States, he shall upon demand of the Governor or Executive power, of the State from which he fled, be delivered up and removed to the State having jurisdiction of his offence.

Full faith and credit shall be given in each of these States to the records, acts and judicial proceedings of the courts and magistrates of every other State.

ARTICLE V. For the more convenient management of the general interests of the United States, delegates shall be annually appointed in such manner as the legislature of each State shall direct, to meet in Congress on the first Monday in November, in every year, with a power reserved to each State, to recall its delegates, or any of them, at any time within the year, and to send others in their stead, for the remainder of the year.

No State shall be represented in Congress by less than two, nor by more than seven members; and no person shall be capable of being a delegate for more than three years in any term of six years; nor shall any person, being a delegate, be capable of holding any office under the United States, for which he, or another for his benefit receives any salary, fees or emolument of any kind.

Each State shall maintain its own delegates in a meeting of the States, and while they act as members of the committee of the States.

In determining questions in the United States, in Congress assembled, each State shall have one vote.

Freedom of speech and debate in Congress shall not be impeached or questioned in any court, or place out of Congress, and the members of Congress shall be protected in their persons from arrests and imprisonments, during the time of their going to and from, and attendance on Congress, except for treason, felony, or breach of the peace.

ARTICLE VI. No State without the consent of the United States in Congress assembled, shall send any embassy to, or receive any embassy from, or enter into any conference, agreement, alliance or treaty with any king, prince or state; nor shall any person holding any office of profit or trust under the United States, or any of them, accept of any present, emolument, office or title of any kind whatever from any king, prince or foreign state; nor shall the United States in Congress assembled, or any of them, grant any title of nobility.

No two or more States shall enter into any treaty, confederation or alliance whatever between them, without the consent of the United States in Congress assembled, specifying accurately the purposes for which the same is to be entered into, and how long it shall continue.

No State shall lay any imposts or duties, which may interfere with any stipulations in treaties, entered into by the United States in Congress assembled, with any king, prince or state, in pursuance of any treaties already proposed by Congress, to the courts of France and Spain.

No vessels of war shall be kept up in time of peace by any State, except such number only, as shall be deemed necessary by the United States in Congress assembled, for the defence of such State, or its trade; nor shall any body of forces be kept up by any State, in time of peace, except such number only, as in the judgment of the United States, in Congress assembled, shall be deemed requisite to garrison the forts necessary for the defence of such State; but every State shall always keep up a well regulated and disciplined militia, sufficiently armed and accoutred, and shall provide and constantly have ready for use, in public stores, a due number of field pieces and tents, and a proper quantity of arms, ammunition and camp equipage.

No State shall engage in any war without the consent of the United States in Congress assembled, unless such State be actually invaded by enemies, or shall have received certain advice of a resolution being formed by some nation of Indians to invade such State, and the danger is so imminent as not to admit of a delay, till the United States in Congress assembled can be consulted: nor shall any State grant commissions to any ships or vessels of war, nor letters of marque or reprisal, except it be after a declaration of war by the United States in Congress assembled, and then only against the kingdom or state and the subjects thereof, against which war has been so declared, and under such regulations as shall be established by the United States in Congress assembled, unless such State be infested by pirates, in which case vessels of war may be fitted out for that occasion, and kept so long as the danger shall continue, or until the United States in Congress assembled shall determine otherwise.

ARTICLE VII. When land-forces are raised by any State for the common defence, all officers of or under the rank of colonel, shall be appointed by the Legislature of each State respectively by whom such forces shall be raised, or in such manner as such State shall direct, and all vacancies shall be filled up by the State which first made the appointment.

ARTICLE VIII. All charges of war, and all other expenses that shall be incurred for the common defence or general welfare, and allowed by the United States in Congress assembled, shall be defrayed out of a common treasury, which shall be supplied by the several States, in proportion to the value of all land within each State, granted to or surveyed for any person, as such land and the buildings and improvements thereon shall be estimated according to such mode as the United States in Congress assembled, shall from time to time direct and appoint.

The taxes for paying that proportion shall be laid and levied by the authority and direction of the Legislatures of the several States within the time agreed upon by the United States in Congress assembled.

ARTICLE IX. The United States in Congress assembled, shall have the sole and exclusive right and power of determining on peace and war, except in the cases mentioned in the sixth article—of sending and receiving ambassadors—entering into treaties and alliances, provided that no treaty of commerce shall be made whereby the legislative power of the respective States shall be restrained from imposing such imposts and duties on foreigners, as their own people are subjected to, or from prohibiting the exportation or importation of and species of goods or commodities whatsoever—of establishing rules for deciding in all cases, what captures on land or water shall be legal, and in what manner prizes taken by land or naval forces in the service of the United States shall be divided or appropriated—of granting letters of marque and reprisal in times of peace—appointing courts for the trial of piracies and felonies committed on the high seas and establishing courts for receiving and determining finally appeals in all cases of captures, provided that no member of Congress shall be appointed a judge of any of the said courts.

The United States in Congress assembled shall also be the last resort on appeal in all disputes and differences now subsisting or that hereafter may arise between two or more States concerning boundary, jurisdiction or any other cause whatever; which authority shall always be exercised in the manner following. Whenever the legislative or executive authority or lawful agent of any State in controversy with another shall present a petition to Congress, stating the matter in question and praying for a hearing, notice thereof shall be given by order of Congress to the legislative or executive authority of the other State in controversy, and a day assigned for the appearance of the parties by their lawful agents, who shall then be directed to appoint by joint consent, commissioners or judges to constitute a court for hearing and determining the matter in question: but if they cannot agree, Congress shall name three persons out of each of the United States, and from the list of such persons each party shall alternately strike out one, the petitioners beginning, until the number shall be reduced to thirteen; and from that number not less than seven, nor more than nine names as Congress shall direct, shall in the presence of Congress be drawn out by lot, and the persons whose names shall be so drawn or any five of them, shall be commissioners or judges, to hear and finally determine the controversy, so always as a major part of the judges who shall hear the cause shall agree in the determination: and if either party shall neglect to attend at the day appointed, without reasons, which Congress shall judge sufficient, or being present shall refuse to strike, the Congress shall proceed to nominate three persons out of each State, and the Secretary of Congress shall strike in behalf of such party absent or refusing; and the judgment and sentence of the court to be appointed, in the manner before prescribed, shall be final and conclusive; and if any of the parties shall refuse to submit to the authority of such court, or to appear or defend their claim or cause, the court shall nevertheless proceed to pronounce sentence, or judgment, which shall in like manner be final and decisive, the judgment or sentence and other procedings being in either case transmitted to Congress, and lodged among the acts of Congress for the security of the parties concerned: provided that every commissioner, before he sits in judgment, shall take an oath to be administered by one of the judges of the supreme or superior court of the State where the cause shall be tried, "well and truly to hear and determine the matter in question, according to the best of his judgment, without favour, affection or hope of reward:" provided also that no State shall be deprived of territory for the benefit of the United States.

All controversies concerning the private right of soil claimed under different grants of two or more States, whose jurisdiction as they may respect such lands, and the states which passed such grants are adjusted, the said grants or either of them being at the same time claimed to have originated antecedent to such settlement of jurisdiction, shall on the petition of either party to the Congress of the United States, be finally determined as near as may be in the same manner as is before prescribed for deciding disputes respecting territorial jurisdiction between different States.

The United States in Congress assembled shall also have the sole and exclusive right and power of regulating the alloy and value of coin struck by their own authority, or by that of the respective States—fixing the standard of weights and measures throughout the United States—regulating the trade and managing all affairs with the Indians, not members of any of the States, provided that the legislative right of any State within its own limits be not infringed or violated—establishing and regulating post-offices from one State to another, throughout all the United States, and exacting such postage on the papers passing thro' the same as may be requisite to defray the expenses of the said office—appointing all officers of the land forces, in the service of the United States, excepting regimental officers—appointing all the officers of the naval forces, and commissioning all officers whatever in the service of the United States—making rules for the government and regulation of the said land and naval forces, and directing their operations.

The United States in Congress assembled shall have authority to appoint a committee, to sit in the recess of Congress, to be denominated "a Committee of the States," and to consist of one delegate from each State; and to appoint such other committees and civil officers as may be necessary for managing the general affairs of the United States under their direction—to appoint one of their number to preside, provided that no person be allowed to serve in the office of president more than one year in any term of three years; to ascertain the necessary sums of money to be raised for the service of the United States, and to appropriate and apply the same for defraying the public expenses—to borrow money, or emit bills on the credit of the United States, transmitting every half year to the respective States an account of the sums of money so borrowed or emitted,—to build and equip a navy—to agree upon the number of land forces, and to make requisitions from each State for its quota, in proportion to the number of white inhabitants in such State; which requisition shall be binding, and thereupon the Legislature of each State shall appoint the regimental officers, raise the men and cloath, arm and equip them in a soldier like manner, at the expense of the United States; and the officers and men so cloathed, armed and equipped shall march to the place appointed, and within the time agreed on by the United States in Congress assembled: but if the United States in Congress assembled shall, on consideration of circumstances judge proper that any State should not raise men, or should raise a smaller number of men than the quota thereof, such extra number shall be raised, officered, cloathed, armed and equipped in the same manner as the quota of such State, unless the legislature of such State shall judge that such extra number cannot be safely spared out of the same, in which case they shall raise officer, cloath, arm and equip as many of such extra number as they judge can be safely spared. And the officers and men so cloathed, armed and equipped, shall march to the place appointed, and within the time agreed on by the United States in Congress assembled.

The United States in Congress assembled shall never engage in a war, nor grant letters of marque and reprisal in time of peace, nor enter into any treaties or alliances, nor coin money, nor regulate the value thereof, nor ascertain the sums and expenses necessary for the defence and welfare of the United States, or any of them, nor emit bills, nor borrow money on the credit of the United States, nor appropriate money, nor agree upon the number of vessels of war, to be built or purchased, or the number of land or sea forces to be raised, nor appoint a commander in chief of the army or navy, unless nine States assent to the same: nor shall a question on any other point, except for adjourning from day to day be determined, unless by the votes of a majority of the United States in Congress assembled.

The Congress of the United States shall have power to adjourn to any time within the year, and to any place within the United States, so that no period of adjournment be for a longer duration than the space of six months, and shall publish the journal of their proceedings monthly, except such parts thereof relating to treaties, alliances or military operations, as in their judgment require secresy; and the yeas and nays of the delegates of each State on any question shall be entered on the Journal, when it is desired by any delegate; and the delegates of a State, or any of them, at his or their request shall be furnished with a transcript of the said journal, except such parts as are above excepted, to lay before the Legislatures of the several States.

ARTICLE X. The committee of the States, or any nine of them, shall be authorized to execute, in the recess of Congress, such of the powers of Congress as the United States in Congress assembled, by the consent of nine States, shall from time to time think expedient to vest them with; provided that no power be delegated to the said committee, for the exercise of which, by the articles of confederation, the voice of nine States in the Congress of the United States assembled is requisite.

ARTICLE XI. Canada acceding to this confederation, and joining in the measures of the United States, shall be admitted into, and entitled to all the advantages of this Union: but no other colony shall be admitted into the same, unless such admission be agreed to by nine States.

ARTICLE XII. All bills of credit emitted, monies borrowed and debts contracted by, or under the authority of Congress, before the assembling of the United States, in pursuance of the present confederation, shall be deemed and considered as a charge against the United States, for payment and satisfaction whereof the said United States, and the public faith are hereby solemnly pledged.

ARTICLE XIII. Every State shall abide by the determinations of the United States in Congress assembled, on all questions which by this confederation are submitted to them. And the articles of this confederation shall be inviolably observed by every State, and the Union shall be perpetual; nor shall any alteration at any time hereafter be made in any of them; unless such alteration be agreed to in a Congress of the United States, and be afterwards confirmed by the Legislatures of every State.

And whereas it has pleased the Great Governor of the world to incline the hearts of the Legislatures we respectively represent in Congress, to approve of, and to authorize us to ratify the said articles of confederation and perpetual union. Know ye that we the undersigned delegates, by virtue of the power and authority to us given for that purpose, do by these presents, in the name and in behalf of our respective constituents, fully and entirely ratify and confirm each and every of the said articles of confederation and perpetual union, and all and singular the matters and things therein contained: and we do further solemnly plight and engage the faith of our respective constituents, that they shall abide by the determinations of the United States in Congress assembled, on all questions, which by the said confederation are submitted to them. And that the articles thereof shall be inviolably observed by the States we respectively represent, and that the Union shall be perpetual.

In witness whereof we have hereunto set our hands in Congress. Done at Philadelphia in the State of Pennsylvania the ninth day of July in the year of our Lord one thousand seven hundred and seventy-eight, and in the third year of the independence of America.

APPENDIX TWO

The Constitution of the United States

WE THE PEOPLE OF THE UNITED STATES, in order to form a more perfect Union, establish Justice, insure domestic Tranquility, provide for the common defence, promote the general Welfare, and secure the Blessings of Liberty to ourselves and our Posterity, do ordain and establish this Constitution for the United States of America.

ARTICLE. I

Section. 1. All legislative Powers herein granted shall be vested in a Congress of the United States, which shall consist of a Senate and House of Representatives.

Section. 2. The House of Representatives shall be composed of Members chosen every second Year by the People of the several States, and the Electors in each State shall have the Qualifications requisite for Electors of the most numerous Branch of the State Legislature.

No Person shall be a Representative who shall not have attained to the Age of twenty five Years, and been seven Years a Citizen of the United States, and who shall not, when elected, be an Inhabitant of that State in which he shall be chosen.

Representatives and direct Taxes shall be apportioned among the several States which may be included within this Union, according to their respective Numbers, which shall be determined by adding to the whole Number of free Persons, including those bound to Service for a Term of Years, and excluding Indians not taxed, three fifths of all other Persons. The actual Enumeration shall be made within three Years after the first Meeting of the Congress of the United States, and within every subsequent Term of ten Years, in such Manner as they shall by Law direct. The Number of Representatives shall not exceed one for every thirty Thousand, but each State shall have at Least one Representative; and until such enumeration shall be made, the State of New Hampshire shall be entitled to chuse three, Massachusetts eight, Rhode-Island and Providence Plantations one, Connecticut five, New-York six, New Jersey four, Pennsylvania eight, Delaware one, Maryland six, Virginia ten, North Carolina five, South Carolina five, and Georgia three.

When vacancies happen in the Representation from any State, the Executive Authority thereof shall issue Writs of Election to fill such Vacancies.

The House of Representatives shall chuse their Speaker and other Officers; and shall have the sole Power of Impeachment.

Section. 3. The Senate of the United States shall be composed of two Senators from each State, chosen by the Legislature thereof, for six Years; and each Senator shall have one Vote.

Immediately after they shall be assembled in Consequence of the first Election, they shall be divided as equally as may be into three Classes. The Seats of the Senators of the first Class shall be vacated at the Expiration of the second Year, of the second Class at the Expiration of the fourth Year, and of the third Class at the Expiration of the sixth Year, so that one third may be chosen every second Year; and if Vacancies happen by Resignation, or otherwise, during the Recess of the Legislature of any State, the Executive thereof may make temporary Appointments until the next Meeting of the Legislature, which shall then fill such Vacancies.

No Person shall be a Senator who shall not have attained to the Age of thirty Years, and been nine Years a Citizen of the United States, and who shall not, when elected, be an Inhabitant of that State for which he shall be chosen.

The Vice President of the United States shall be President of the Senate, but shall have no Vote, unless they be equally divided.

The Senate shall chuse their other Officers, and also a President pro tempore, in the Absence of the Vice President, or when he shall exercise the Office of President of the United States.

The Senate shall have the sole Power to try all Impeachments. When sitting for that Purpose, they shall be on Oath or Affirmation. When the President of the United States is tried, the Chief Justice shall preside: And no Person shall be convicted without the Concurrence of two thirds of the Members present.

Judgment in Cases of Impeachment shall not extend further than to removal from Office, and disqualification to hold and enjoy any Office of honor, Trust or Profit under the United States: but the Party convicted shall nevertheless be liable and subject to Indictment, Trial, Judgment and Punishment, according to Law.

Section 4. The Times, Places and Manner of holding Elections for Senators and Representatives, shall be prescribed in each State by the Legislature thereof, but the Congress may at any time by Law make or alter such Regulations, except as to the Places of chusing Senators.

The Congress shall assemble at least once in every Year, and such Meeting shall be on the first Monday in December, unless they shall by Law appoint a different Day.

Section. 5. Each House shall be the Judge of the Elections, Returns and Qualifications of its own Members, and a Majority of each shall constitute a Quorum to do Business; but a smaller Number may adjourn from day to day, and may be authorized to compel the Attendance of absent Members, in such Manner, and under such Penalties as each House may provide.

Each House may determine the Rules of its Proceedings, punish its Members for disorderly Behaviour, and, with the Concurrence of two thirds, expel a Member.

Each House shall keep a Journal of its Proceedings, and from time to time publish the same, excepting such Parts as may in their Judgment require Secrecy; and the Yeas and Nays of the Members of either House on any question shall, at the Desire of one fifth of those Present, be entered on the Journal.

Neither House, during the Session of Congress, shall, without the Consent of the other, adjourn for more than three days, nor to any other Place than that in which the two Houses shall be sitting.

Section. 6. The Senators and Representatives shall receive a Compensation for their Services, to be ascertained by Law, and paid out of the Treasury of the United States. They shall in all Cases, except Treason, Felony and Breach of the Peace, be privileged from Arrest during their Attendance at the Session of their respective Houses, and in going to and returning from the same; and for any Speech or Debate in either House, they shall not be questioned in any other Place.

No Senator or Repreentative shall, during the Time for which he was elected, be appointed to any civil Office under the Authority of the United States, which shall have been created, or the Emoluments whereof shall have been encreased during such time; and no Person holding any Office under the United States, shall be a Member of either House during his Continuance in Office.

Section. 7. All Bills for raising Revenue shall originate in the House of Representatives; but the Senate may propose or concur with Amendments as on other Bills.

Every Bill which shall have passed the House of Representatives and the Senate shall, before it become a Law, be presented to the President of the United States; If he approve he shall sign it, but if not he shall return it, with his Objections to that House in which it shall have originated, who shall enter the Objections at large on their Journal, and proceed to reconsider it. If after such Reconsideration two thirds of that House shall agree to pass the Bill, it shall be sent, together with the Objections, to the other House, by which it shall likewise be reconsidered, and if approved by two thirds of that House, it shall become a Law. But in all such Cases the Votes of both Houses shall be determined by yeas and Nays, and the Names of the Persons voting for and against the Bill shall be entered on the Journal of each House respectively. If any Bill shall not be returned by the President within ten Days (Sundays excepted) after it shall have been presented to him, the Same shall be a Law, in like Manner as if he had signed it, unless the Congress by their Adjournment prevent its Return, in which Case it shall not be a Law.

Every Order, Resolution, or Vote to which the Concurrence of the Senate and House of Representatives may be necessary (except on a question of Adjournment) shall be presented to the President of the United States; and before the Same shall take Effect, shall be approved by him, or being disapproved by him, shall be repassed by two thirds of the Senate and House or Representatives, according to the Rules and Limitations prescribed in the Case of a Bill.

Section. 8. The Congress shall have Power To lay and collect Taxes, Duties, Imposts and Excises, to pay the Debts and provide for the common Defence and general Welfare of the United States; but all Duties, Imposts and Excises shall be uniform throughout the United States.

To borrow Money on the credit of the United States;

To regulate Commerce with foreign Nations, and among the several States, and with the Indian Tribes;

To establish an uniform Rule of Naturalization, and uniform Laws on the subject of Bankruptcies throughout the United States;

To coin Money, regulate the Value thereof, and of foreign Coin, and fix the Standard of Weights and Measures;

To provide for the Punishment of counterfeiting the Securities and current Coin of the United States;

To establish Post Offices and Post Roads;

To promote the Progress of Science and useful Arts, by securing for limited Times to Authors and Inventors the exclusive Right to their respective Writings and Discoveries;

To constitute Tribunals inferior to the supreme Court;

To define and punish Piracies and Felonies committed on the high Seas, and Offences against the Law of Nations;

To declare War, grant Letters of Marque and Reprisal, and make Rules concerning Captures on Land and Water;

To raise and support Armies, but no Appropriation of Money to that Use shall be for a longer Term than two Years;

To provide and maintain a Navy;

To make Rules for the Government and Regulation of the land and naval Forces;

To provide for calling forth the Militia to execute the Laws of the Union, suppress Insurrections and repel Invasions;

To provide for organizing, arming, and disciplining, the Militia, and for governing such Part of them as may be employed in the Service of the United States, reserving to the States respectively, the Appointment of the Officers, and the Authority of training the Militia according to the discipline prescribed by Congress;

To exercise exclusive Legislation in all Cases whatsoever, over such District (not exceeding ten Miles square) as may, by Cession of particular States, and the Acceptance of Congress, become the Seat of the Government of the United States, and to exercise like Authority over all Places purchased by the Consent of the Legislature of the State in which the Same shall be, for the Erection of Forts, Magazines, Arsenals, dock-Yards, and other needful Buildings;—And

To make all Laws which shall be necessary and proper for carrying into Execution the foregoing Powers, and all other Powers vested by this Constitution in the Government of the United States, or in any Department or Officer thereof.

Section. 9. The Migration or Importation of such Persons as any of the States now existing shall think proper to admit, shall not be prohibited by the Congress prior to the Year one thousand eight hundred and eight, but a Tax or duty may be imposed on such Importation, not exceeding ten dollars for each Person.

The Privilege of the Writ of Habeas Corpus shall not be suspended, unless when in Cases of Rebellion or Invasion the public Safety may require it.

No Bill of Attainder or ex post facto Law shall be passsed.

No Capitation, or other direct, Tax shall be laid, unless in Proportion to the Census or Enumeration herein before directed to be taken.

No Tax or Duty shall be laid on Articles exported from any State.

No Preference shall be given by any Regulation of Commerce or Revenue to the Ports of one State over those of another: nor shall Vessels bound to, or from, one State, be obliged to enter, clear, or pay Duties in another.

No Money shall be drawn from the Treasury, but in Consequence of Appropriations made by Law, and a regular Statement and Account of the Receipts and Expenditures of all public Money shall be published from time to time.

No Title of Nobility shall be granted by the United States: And no Person holding any Office of Profit or trust under them, shall, without the Consent of the Congress, accept of any present, Emolument, Office, or Title, of any kind whatever, from any King, Prince, or foreign State.

Section. 10. No State shall enter into any Treaty, Alliance, or Confederation; grant Letters of Marque and Reprisal; coin Money; emit Bills of Credit; make any Thing but gold and silver Coin a Tender in Payment of Debts; pass any Bill of Attainder, ex post facto Law, or Law impairing the Obligation of Contracts, or grant any Title of Nobility.

No State shall, without the Consent of the Congress, lay any Imposts or Duties on Imports or Exports, except what may be absolutely necessary for executing it's inspection Laws: and the net Produce of all Duties and Imposts, laid by any State on Imports or Exports, shall be for the Use of the Treasury of the United States; and all such Laws shall be subject to the Revision and Controul of the Congress.

No State shall, without the Consent of Congress, lay any Duty of Tonnage, keep Troops, or Ships of War in time of Peace, enter into any Agreement or Compact with another State, or with a foreign Power, or engage in War, unless actually invaded, or in such imminent Danger as will not admit of delay.

ARTICLE. II.

Section. 1. The executive Power shall be vested in a President of the United States of America. He shall hold his Office during the term of four Years, and, together with the Vice President, chosen for the same Term, be elected, as follows

Each State shall appoint, in such Manner as the Legislature thereof may direct, a Number of Electors, equal to the whole Number of Senators and Representatives to which the State may be entitled in the Congress: but no Senator or Representative, or Person holding an Office of Trust or Profit under the United States, shall be appointed an Elector.

The Electors shall meet in their respective States, and vote by Ballot for two Persons, of whom one at least shall not be an Inhabitant of the same State with themselves. And they shall make a List of all the Persons voted for, and of the Number of Votes for each; which List they shall sign and certify, and transmit sealed to the Seat of the Government of the United States, directed to the President of the Senate. The President of the Senate shall, in the Presence of the Senate and House of Representatives, open all the Certificates, and the Votes shall then be counted. The Person having the greatest Number of Votes shall be the President, if such Number be a Majority of the whole Number of Electors appointed; and if there be more than one who have such Majority, and have an equal Number of Votes, then the House of Representatives shall immmediately chuse by Ballot one of them for President; and if no Person have a Majority, then from the five highest on the List the said House shall in like Manner chuse the President. But in chusing the President, the Votes shall be taken by States, the Representation from each State having one Vote; A quorum for this Purpose shall consist of a Member or Members from two thirds of the States, and a Majority all the States shall be necessary to a Choice. In every Case, after the Choice of the President, the Person having the greatest Number of Votes of the Electors shall be the Vice President. But if there should remain two or more who have equal Votes, the Senate shall chuse from them by Ballot the Vice President.

The Congress may determine the Time of chusing the Electors, and the Day on which they shall give their Votes; which Day shall be the same throughout the United States.

No Person except a natural born Citizen, or a Citizen of the United States, at the time of the Adoption of this Constitution, shall be eligible to the Office of President, neither shall any Person be eligible to that Office who shall not have attained to the Age of thirty five Years, and been fourteen Years a Resident within the United States.

In Case of the Removal of the President from Office, or of his Death, Resignation, or Inability to discharge the Powers and Duties of the said Office, the Same shall devolve on the Vice President, and the Congress may by Law provide for the Case of Removal, Death, Resignation or Inability, both of the President and Vice President, declaring what Officer shall then act as President, and such Officer shall act accordingly, until the Disability be removed, or a President shall be elected.

The President shall, at stated Times, receive for his Services, a Compensation, which shall neither be encreased or diminished during the Period for which he shall have been elected, and he shall not receive within that Period any other Emolument from the United States, or any of them.

Before he enters on the Execution of his Office, he shall take the following Oath or Affirmation:—"I do solemnly swear (or affirm) that I will faithfully execute the Office of President of the United States, and will to the best of my Ability, preserve, protect and defend the Constitution of the United States."

Section. 2. The President shall be Commander in Chief of the Army and Navy of the United States, and of the Militia of the several States, when called into the actual Service of the United States; he may require the Opinion, in writing, of the principal Officer in each of the executive Departments, upon any Subject relating to the Duties of their respective Offices, and he shall have Power to grant Reprieves and Pardons for Offences against the United States, except in Cases of Impeachment.

He shall have Power, by and with the Advice and Consent of the Senate, to make Treaties, provided two thirds of the Senators present concur; and he shall nominate, and by and with the Advice and Consent of the Senate, shall appoint Ambassadors, other public Ministers and Consuls, Judges of the supreme Court, and all other Officers of the United States, whose Appointments are not herein otherwise provided for, and which shall be established by Law; but the Congress may by Law vest the Appointment of such inferior Officers, as they think proper, in the President alone, in the Courts of Law, or in the Heads of Departments.

The President shall have Power to fill up all Vacancies that may happen during the Recess of the Senate, by granting Commissions which shall expire at the End of their next Session.

Section. 3. He shall from time to time give to the Congress Information of the State of the Union, and recommend to their Consideration such Measures as he shall judge necessary and expedient; he may, on extraordinary Occasions, convene both Houses, or either of them, and in Case of Disagreement between them, with Respect to the Time of Adjournment, he may adjourn them to such Time as he shall think proper; he shall receive Ambassadors and other public Ministers; he shall take Care that the Laws be faithfully executed, and shall Commission all the Officers of the United States.

Section. 4. The President, Vice President and all civil Officers of the United States, shall be removed from Office on Impeachment for, and Conviction of, Treason, Bribery, or other high Crimes and Misdemeanors.

ARTICLE. III.

Section. 1. The judicial Power of the United States, shall be vested in one supreme Court, and in such inferior Courts as the Congress may from time to time ordain and establish. The Judges, both of the supreme and inferior Courts, shall hold their Offices during good Behaviour, and shall, at stated Times, receive for their Services, a Compensation, which shall not be diminished during their Continuance in Office.

Section. 2. The judicial Power shall extend to all Cases, in Law and Equity, arising under this Constitution, the Laws of the United States, and Treaties made, or which shall be made, under their Authority;—to all Cases affecting Ambassadors, other public Ministers and Consuls;—to all Cases of admiralty and maritime Jurisdiction;—to Controversies to which the United States shall be a Party;—to Controversies between two or more States;—between a State and Citizens of another State;—between Citizens of different States,—between Citizens of the same State claiming Lands under Grants of different States, and between a State, or the Citizens thereof, and foreign States, Citizens or Subjects.

In all cases affecting Ambassadors, other public Ministers and Consuls, and those in which a State shall be Party, the supreme Court shall have original Jurisdiction. In all the other Cases before mentioned, the supreme Court shall have appellate Jurisdiction, both as to Law and Fact, with such Exceptions, and under such Regulations as the Congress shall make.

The Trial of all Crimes, except in Cases of Impeachment, shall be by Jury; and such Trial shall be held in the State where the said Crimes shall have been committed; but when not committed within any State, the Trial shall be at such Place or Places as the Congress may by Law have directed.

Section. 3. Treason against the United States, shall consist only in levying War against them, or in adhering to their Enemies, giving them Aid and Comfort. No Person shall be convicted of Treason unless on the Testimony of two Witnesses to the same overt Act, or on Confession in open Court.

The Congress shall have Power to declare the Punishment of Treason, but no Attainder of Treason shall work Corruption of Blood, or Forfeiture except during the Life of the Person attainted.

ARTICLE. IV.

Section. 1. Full Faith and Credit shall be given in each State to the public Acts, Records, and judicial Proceedings of every other State. And the Congress may by general Laws prescribe the Manner in which such Acts, Records and Proceedings shall be proved, and the Effect thereof.

Section. 2. The Citizens of each State shall be entitled to all Privileges and Immunities of Citizens in the several States.

A Person charged in any State with Treason, Felony, or other Crime, who shall flee from Justice, and be found in another State, shall on Demand of the executive Authority of the State from which he fled, be delivered up, to be removed to the State having Jurisdiction of the Crime.

No Person held to Service or Labour in one State, under the Laws thereof, escaping into another, shall, in Consequence of any Law or Regulation therein, be discharged from such Service or Labour, but shall be delivered up on Claim of the Party to whom such Service or Labour may be due.

Section. 3. New States may be admitted by the Congress into this Union; but no new State shall be formed or erected within the Jurisdiction of any other State; nor any State be formed by the Junction of two or more States, or Parts of States, without the consent of the Legislatures of the States concerned as well as of the Congress.

The Congress shall have Power to dispose of and make all needful Rules and Regulations respecting the Territory or other Property belonging to the United States; and nothing in this Constitution shall be so construed as to Prejudice any Claims of the United States, or of any particular States.

Section. 4. The United States shall guarantee to every State in this Union a Republican Form of Government, and shall protect each of them against

Invasion; and on Application of the Legislature, or of the Executive (when the Legislature cannot be convened) against domestic Violence.

ARTICLE. V.

The Congress, whenever two thirds of both Houses shall deem it necessary, shall propose Amendments to this Constitution, or, on the Application of the Legislatures of two thirds of the several States shall call a Convention for proposing Amendments, which, in either Case, shall be valid to all Intents and Purposes, as Part of this Constitution, when ratified by the Legislatures of three fourths of the several States, or by Conventions in three fourths thereof, as the one or the other Mode of Ratification may be proposed by the Congress; Provided that no Amendment which may be made prior to the Year One thousand eight hundred and eight shall in any Manner affect the first and fourth Clauses in the Ninth Section of the first Article; and that no State, without its Consent, shall be deprived of it's equal Suffrage in the Senate.

ARTICLE. VI.

All Debts contracted and Engagements entered into, before the Adoption of this Constitution, shall be as valid against the United States under this Constitution, as under the Confederation.

This Constitution, and the Laws of the United States which shall be made in Pursuance thereof; and all Treaties made, or which shall be made, under the Authority of the United States, shall be the supreme Law of the Land; and the Judges in every State shall be bound thereby, any Thing in the Constitution or Laws of any State to the Contrary notwithstanding.

The Senators and Representatives before mentioned, and the Members of the several State Legislatures, and all executive and judicial Officers, both of the United States and of the several States, shall be bound by Oath or Affirmation, to support this Constitution; but no religious Test shall ever be required as a Qualification to any Office or public Trust under the United States.

ARTICLE. VII.

The Ratification of the Conventions of nine States, shall be sufficient for the Establishment of this Constitution between the States so ratifying the Same.

Done in Convention by the Unanimous Consent of the States present the Seventeenth Day of September in the Year of our Lord one thousand seven hundred and Eighty seven and of the Independence of the United States of America the Twelfth. In witness thereof We have hereunto subscribed our Names,

G°: WASHINGTON—Presid^t
and deputy from Virginia

New Hampshire	{ John Langdon Nicholas Gilman	Delaware	Geo: Read Gunning Bed- ford jun John Dickinson Richard Bassett Jaco: Broom
Massachusetts	{ Nathaniel Gorham Rufus King		
Connecticut	{ Wm Saml Johnson Roger Sherman	Maryland	James McHenry Dan of St Thos Jenifer Danl Carroll
New York	{ Alexander Hamilton		
New Jersey	Wil: Livingston David A. Brearley. Wm Paterson. Jona: Dayton	Virginia	{ John Blair— James Madison Jr.
Pennsylvania	B. Franklin Thomas Mifflin Robt Morris Geo. Clymer Thos. FitzSimons Jared Ingersoll James Wilson Gouv Morris	North Carolina	W^m. Blount Richd Dobbs Spaight. Hu Williamson
		South Carolina	J. Rutledge Charles Cotesworth Pinckney Charles Pinckney Pierce Butler.
		Georgia	{ William Few Abr Baldwin

Amendments to the Constitution

ARTICLES IN ADDITION TO, and Amendment of the Constitution of the United States of America, proposed by Congress, and ratified by the Legislatures of the several States, pursuant to the fifth Article of the original Constitution.

ARTICLE I.

Congress shall make no law respecting an establishment of religion, or prohibiting the free exercise thereof; or abridging the freedom of speech, or of the press; or the right of the people peaceably to assemble, and to petition the Government for a redress of grievances.

ARTICLE II.

A well regulated Militia, being necessary to the security of a free State, the right of the people to keep and bear Arms, shall not be infringed.

ARTICLE III.

No Soldier shall, in time of peace be quartered in any house, without the consent of the Owner, nor in time of war, but in a manner to be prescribed by law.

ARTICLE IV.

The right of the people to be secure in their persons, houses, papers, and effects, against unreasonable searches and seizures, shall not be violated, and no Warrants shall issue, but upon probable cause, supported by Oath or affirmation, and particularly describing the place to be searched, and the persons or things to be seized.

ARTICLE V.

No person shall be held to answer for a capital, or otherwise infamous crime, unless on a presentment or indictment of a Grand Jury, except in cases arising in the land or naval forces, or in the Militia, when in actual service in time of War or public danger; nor shall any person be subject for the same offence to be twice put in jeopardy of life or limb; nor shall be compelled in any criminal case to be a witness against himself, nor be deprived of life, liberty, or property, without due process of law; nor shall private property be taken for public use, without just compensation.

ARTICLE VI.

In all criminal prosecutions, the accused shall enjoy the right to a speedy and public trial, by an impartial jury of the State and district wherein the crime shall have been committed, which district shall have been previously ascertained by law, and to be informed of the nature and cause of the accusation; to be confronted with the witnesses against him; to have compulsory process for obtaining witnesses in his favor, and to have the Assistance of Counsel for his defence.

ARTICLE VII.

In Suits at common law, where the value in controversy shall exceed twenty dollars, the right of trial by jury shall be preserved, and no fact tried by a jury, shall be otherwise re-examined in any Court of the United States, than according to the rules of the common law.

ARTICLE VIII.

Excessive bail shall not be required, nor excessive fines imposed, nor cruel and unusual punishments inflicted.

ARTICLE IX.

The enumeration in the Constitution, of certain rights, shall not be construed to deny or disparage others retained by the people.

ARTICLE X.

The powers not delegated to the United States by the Constitution, nor prohibited by it to the States, are reserved to the States respectively, or to the people. [The first ten amendments went into effect December 15, 1791.]

ARTICLE XI.

The Judicial power of the United States shall not be construed to extend to any suit in law or equity, commenced or prosecuted against one of the United States by Citizens of another State, or by Citizens or Subjects of any Foreign State. [January 8, 1798.]

ARTICLE XII.

The Electors shall meet in their respective states, and vote by ballot for President and Vice-President, one of whom, at least, shall not be an inhabitant of the same state with themselves; they shall name in their ballots the person voted for as President, and in distinct ballots the person voted for as Vice-President, and they shall make distinct lists of all persons voted for as President, and of all persons voted for as Vice-President, and of the number of votes for each, which lists they shall sign and certify, and transmit sealed to the seat of the government of the United States, directed to the President of the Senate;—The President of the Senate shall, in the presence of the Senate and House of Representatives, open all the certificates and the votes shall then be counted;—The person having the greatest number of votes for President, shall be the President, if such number be a majority of the whole number of Electors appointed; and if no person have such majority, then from the persons having the highest numbers not exceeding three on the list of those voted for as President, the House of Representatives shall choose immediately, by ballot, the President. But in choosing the President, the votes shall be taken by states, the representation from each state having one vote; a quorum for this purpose shall consist of a member or members from two-thirds of the states, and a majority of all the states shall be necessary to a choice. And if the House of Representatives shall not choose a President whenever the right of choice shall devolve upon them, before the fourth day of March next following, then the Vice-President shall act as President, as in the case of the death or other constitutional disability of the President.—The person having the greatest number of votes as Vice-President, shall be the Vice-President, if such number be a majority of the whole number of Electors appointed, and if no person have a majority, then from the two highest numbers on the list, the Senate shall choose the Vice-President; a quorum for the purpose shall consist of two-thirds of the whole number of Senators, and a majority of the whole number shall be necessary to a choice. But no person constitutionally ineligible to the office of President shall be eligible to that of Vice-President of the United States. [September 25, 1804.]

ARTICLE XIII.

Section 1. Neither slavery nor involuntary servitude, except as a punishment for crime whereof the party shall have been duly convicted, shall exist within the United States, or any place subject to their jurisdiction.

Section 2. Congress shall have power to enforce this article by appropriate legislation. [December 18, 1865.]

ARTICLE XIV.

Section 1. All persons born or naturalized in the United States, and subject to the jurisdiction thereof, are citizens of the United States and of the State wherein they reside. No State shall make or enforce any law which shall abridge the privileges or immunities of citizens of the United States; nor shall any State deprive any person of life, liberty, or property, without due process of law; nor deny to any person within its jurisdiction the equal protection of the laws.

Section 2. Representatives shall be apportioned among the several States according to their respective numbers, counting the whole number of persons in each State, excluding Indians not taxed. But when the right to vote at any election for the choice of electors for President and Vice President of the United States, Representatives in Congress, the Executive and Judicial officers of a State, or the members of the Legislature thereof, is denied to any of the male inhabitants of such State, being twenty-one years of age, and citizens of the United States, or in any way abridged, except for participation in rebellion, or other crime, the basis of representation therein shall be reduced in the proportion which the number of such male citizens shall bear to the whole number of male citizens twenty-one years of age in such State.

Section 3. No person shall be a Senator or Representative in Congress, or elector of President and Vice President, or hold any office, civil or military, under the United States, or under any State, who, having previously taken an oath, as a member of Congress, or as an officer of the United States, or as a member of any State legislature, or as an executive or judicial officer of any State, to support the Constitution of the United States, shall have engaged in insurrection or rebellion against the same, or given aid or comfort to the enemies thereof. But Congress may by a vote of two-thirds of each House, remove such disability.

Section 4. The validity of the public debt of the United States, authorized by law, including debts incurred for payment of pensions and bounties for services in suppressing insurrection or rebellion, shall not be questioned. But neither the United States nor any State shall assume or pay any debt or obligation incurred in aid of insurrection or rebellion against the United States, or any claim for the loss or emancipation of any slave; but all such debts, obligations and claims shall be held illegal and void.

Section 5. The Congress shall have power to enforce, by appropriate legislation, the provisions of this article. [July 28, 1868.]

ARTICLE XV.

Section 1. The right of citizens of the United States to vote shall not be denied or abridged by the United States or by any State on account of race, color, or previous condition of servitude——

Section 2. The Congress shall have power to enforce this article by appropriate legislation.——[March 30, 1870.]

ARTICLE XVI.

The Congress shall have power to lay and collect taxes on incomes, from whatever source derived, without apportionment among the several States, and without regard to any census or enumeration. [February 25, 1913.]

ARTICLE XVII.

The Senate of the United States shall be composed of two senators from each State, elected by the people thereof, for six years; and each Senator shall have one vote. The electors in each State shall have the qualifications requisite for electors of the most numerous branch of the State legislature.

When vacancies happen in the representation of any State in the Senate, the executive authority of such State shall issue writs of election to fill such vacancies: *Provided,* That the legislature of any State may empower the executive thereof to make temporary appointments until the people fill the vacancies by election as the legislature may direct.

This amendment shall not be so construed as to affect the election or term of any senator chosen before it becomes valid as part of the Constitution. [May 31, 1913.]

ARTICLE XVIII.

After one year from the ratification of this article, the manufacture, sale, or transportation of intoxicating liquors within, the importation thereof into, or the exportation thereof from the United States and all territory subject to the jurisdiction thereof for beverage purposes is hereby prohibited.

The Congress and the several States shall have concurrent power to enforce this article by appropriate legislation.

This article shall be inoperative unless it shall have been ratified as an amendment to the Constitution by the legislatures of the several States, as provided in the Constitution, within seven years from the date of the submission thereof to the States by Congress. [January 29, 1919.]

ARTICLE XIX.

The right of citizens of the United States to vote shall not be denied or abridged by the United States or by any State on account of sex.

The Congress shall have power by appropriate legislation to enforce the provisions of this article. [August 26, 1920.]

ARTICLE XX.

Section 1. The terms of the President and Vice-President shall end at noon on the twentieth day of January, and the terms of Senators and Representatives at noon on the third day of January, of the years in which such terms would have ended if this article had not been ratified; and the terms of their successors shall then begin.

Section 2. The Congress shall assemble at least once in every year, and such meeting shall begin at noon on the third day of January, unless they shall by law appoint a different day.

Section 3. If, at the time fixed for the beginning of the term of the President, the President-elect shall have died, the Vice-President-elect shall become President. If a President shall not have been chosen before the time fixed for the beginning of his term, or if the President-elect shall have failed to qualify, then the Vice-President-elect shall act as President until a President shall have qualified; and the Congress may by law provide for the case wherein neither a President-elect nor a Vice-President-elect shall have qualified, declaring who shall then act as President, or the manner in which one who is to act shall be selected, and such person shall act accordingly until a President or Vice-President shall have qualified.

Section 4. The Congress may by law provide for the case of the death of any of the persons from whom the House of Representatives may choose a President whenever the right of choice shall have devolved upon them, and for the case of the death of any of the persons from whom the Senate may choose a Vice-President whenever the right of choice shall have devolved upon them.

Section 5. Sections 1 and 2 shall take effect on the 15th day of October following the ratification of this article.

Section 6. This article shall be inoperative unless it shall have been ratified as an amendment to the Constitution by the legislatures of three-fourths of the several States within seven years from the date of its submission. [February 6, 1933.]

ARTICLE XXI.

Section 1. The eighteenth article of amendment to the Constitution of the United States is hereby repealed.

Section 2. The transportation or importation into any State, Territory or possession of the United States for delivery or use therein of intoxicating liquors, in violation of the laws thereof, is hereby prohibited.

Section 3. This article shall be inoperative unless it shall have been ratified as an amendment to the Constitution by convention in the several States, as provided in the Constitution, within seven years from the date of the submission thereof to the States by the Congress. [December 5, 1933.]

ARTICLE XXII.

Section 1. No person shall be elected to the office of the President more than twice, and no person who has held the office of President, or acted as President, for more than two years of a term to which some other person was elected President shall be elected to the office of the President more than once. But this Article shall not apply to any person holding the office of President when this Article was proposed by the Congress, and shall not prevent any person who may be holding the office of President, or acting as President, during the term within which this Article becomes operative from holding the office of President or acting as President during the remainder of such term.

Section 2. This article shall be inoperative unless it shall have been ratified as an amendment to the Constitution by the legislatures of three-fourths of the several States within seven years from the date of its submission to the States by the Congress. [February 27, 1951.]

ARTICLE XXIII.

Section 1. The District constituting the seat of government of the United States shall appoint in such manner as the Congress may direct:

A number of electors of President and Vice-President equal to the whole number of Senators and Representatives in Congress to which the District would be entitled if it were a State, but in no event more than the least populous State; they shall be in addition to those appointed by the States, but they shall be considered, for the purposes of the election of President and Vice-President, to be electors appointed by a State; and they shall meet in the District and perform such duties as provided by the twelfth article of amendment.

Section 2. The Congress shall have the power to enforce this article by appropriate legislation. [March 29, 1961.]

ARTICLE XXIV.

Section 1. The right of citizens of the United States to vote in any primary or other election for President or Vice President, for electors for President or Vice President, or for Senator or Representative in Congress, shall not be denied or abridged by the United States or any State by reason of failure to pay any poll tax or other tax.

Section 2. The Congress shall have power to enforce this article by appropriate legislation. [January 23, 1964.]

ARTICLE XXV.

Section 1. In case of the removal of the President from office or of his death or resignation, the Vice President shall become President.

Section 2. Whenever there is a vacancy in the office of Vice President, the President shall nominate a Vice President who shall take office upon confirmation by a majority vote of both Houses of Congress.

Section 3. Whenever the President transmits to the President pro tempore of the Senate and the Speaker of the House of Representatives his written declaration that he is unable to discharge the powers and duties of his office, and until he transmits to them a written declaration to the contrary, such powers and duties shall be discharged by the Vice President as Acting President.

Section 4. Whenever the Vice President and a majority of either the principal officers of the executive departments or of such other body as Congress may by law provide, transmit to the President pro tempore of the Senate and the Speaker of the House of Representatives their written declaration that the President is unable to discharge the powers and duties of his office, the Vice President shall immediately assume the powers and duties of the office as Acting President.

Thereafter, when the President transmits to the President pro tempore of the Senate and the Speaker of the House of Representatives his written declaration that no inability exists, he shall resume the powers and duties of his office unless the Vice President and a majority of either the principal officers of the executive departments or of such other body as Congress may by law provide, transmit within four days to the President pro tempore of the Senate and the Speaker of the House of Representatives their written declaration that the President is unable to discharge the powers and duties of his office. Thereupon Congress shall decide the issue, assembling within forty-eight hours for that purpose if not in session. If the Congress, within twenty-one days after receipt of the latter written declaration, or, if Congress is not in session, within twenty-one days after Congress is required to assemble, determines by two-thirds vote of both Houses that the President is unable to discharge the powers and duties of his office, the Vice President shall continue to discharge the same as Acting President; otherwise, the President shall resume the powers and duties of his office. [February 10, 1967.]

ARTICLE XXVI.

Section 1. The right of citizens of the United States, who are eighteen years of age or older, to vote shall not be denied or abridged by the United States or by any State on account of age.

Section 2. The Congress shall have power to enforce this article by appropriate legislation [June 30, 1971.]

Bibliography

Abbreviations used: *AHR (American Historical Review); AJLH (American Journal of Legal History); Annals (Annals of the American Academy of Political and Social Science); APSR (American Political Science Review); CWH (Civil War History); JAH (Journal of American History); JP (Journal of Politics); JSH (Journal of Southern History); MVHR (Mississippi Valley Historical Review); Pres. Studies Q. (Presidential Studies Quarterly); PSQ (Political Science Quarterly); WMQ (William and Mary Quarterly); Western Pol. Q. (Western Political Quarterly).*

I. *American Constitutional History and Constitutionalism: Primary Sources and General Works*

Edward S. Corwin *et al.*, eds., *The Constitution of the United States: Analysis and Interpretation* (1952, 1964, 1973 eds., 1976 and 1978 suppl.), is an annotation of the constitutional text on the basis of Supreme Court decisions. Corwin, *The Constitution and What It Means Today*, 14th ed., rev. Harold W. Chase and Craig R. Ducat (1978), is a similar work of briefer scope. Francis Newton Thorpe, ed., *The Federal and State Constitutions, Colonial Charters and Other Organic Laws*, 7 vols. (1909), and William F. Swindler, comp., *Sources and Documents of United States Constitutions*, 10 vols. (1973–79), are basic documentary collections. Primary sources for constitutional development as seen through the national legislature are *Statutes at Large of the United States of America 1789–1873*, 17 vols. (1850–73; *United States Statutes at Large* (1874–   ); *United States Code*, 16 vols. (1977; 4 vols., 1979 suppl.); *Annals of Congress*, 1789–1824; *Register of Debates in Congress, 1825–1837; Congressional Globe*, 1833–73; *Congressional Record, 1873–   ; American State Papers: Documents, Legislative and Executive*, 38 vols. (1832–61), covering the First through the Fourteenth Congress. Reports, Executive Documents, and Miscellaneous Papers of the House of Representatives and the Senate, referred to as the Congressional Serials Set, start with the Fifteenth Congress. Executive documents are presented in *Compilation of the Messages and Papers of the Presidents*, 20 vols. to 1929; *Public Papers of the Presidents of the United States* (1958–   ), beginning with the Truman administration; *Code of Federal Regulations* (1938–   ), an annual codification of administrative rules; *Federal Register* (1936–   ), a daily listing of administrative rules and agency decisions; *Official Opinions of the Attorneys-General.* Decisions of the Supreme Court are found in *United States Reports* (1970-   ). Before 1875 reports of decisions were published under the names of the official court reporters: Dallas, Cranch, Wheaton, Peters, Howard, Black, Wallace. The decisions of the Supreme Court are also published in *United States Supreme Court Reports: Lawyers' Edition,* and *The Supreme Court Reporter.* Lower federal court decisions are found in *Federal Cases, 1789-1879; Federal Reporter, 1880-1924; Federal Reporter, 1924-* 2d ser.; *Federal Supplement, 1932-   ; American Law Reports—Federal, 1969-   .*

Documentary collections of materials in constitutional history include Henry Steele Commager, ed., *Documents of American History,* 9th ed. (1973); Donald O. Dewey, ed., *Union and Liberty: A Documentary History of American Constitutionalism* (1969); James M. Smith and Paul L. Murphy, eds., *Liberty and Justice, Forging the Federal Union: American Constitutional Development to 1869* (1965); Smith and Murphy, eds., *Liberty and Justice—The Modern Constitution: American Constitutional Development since 1865* (1968); Allen Johnson, ed., *Readings in American Constitutional History, 1776-1876* (1912); Allen Johnson and William T. Robinson, eds., *Readings in Recent American Constitutional History, 1876-1926* (1927). Among the better constitutional law casebooks and treatises are Gerald Gunther, *Cases and Materials on Constitutional Law* (1975); Paul A. Freund *et al., Constitutional Law: Cases and Other Problems,* 4th ed. (1977); Paul Brest, *Processes of Constitutional Decision Making: Cases and Materials* (1975); Lawrence H. Tribe, *American Constitutional Law* (1978); C. Herman Pritchett, *The American Constitution,* 2d ed. (1968). Stanley I. Kutler, ed., *The Supreme Court and the Constitution: Readings in American Constitutional History,* 2d ed. (1977), is a collection of Supreme Court opinions.

The intellectual roots of constitutional government in the United States may be explored in a variety of works dealing with European and English constitutionalism. Especially relevant are Charles H. McIlwain, *Constitutionalism, Ancient and Modern* (1940; 1947); Edward S. Corwin, *The "Higher Law" Background of American Constitutional Law* (1955); J. W. Gough, *Fundamental Law in English Constitutional History* (1955); Francis D. Wormuth, *The Origins of Modern Constitutionalism* (1949); M. J. C. Vile, *Constitutionalism and the Separation of Powers* (1967); J. G. A. Pocock, *The Ancient Constitution and Feudal Law: A Study of English Historical Thought in the Seventeenth Century* (1957). Pocock, *The Machiavellian Moment: Florentine Political Thought and the Atlantic Republican Tradition* (1975), emphasizes positive liberty defined as participation in the political life of the community, rather than negative liberty or restraints upon government. On this distinction, see Isaiah Berlin, "Two Concepts of Liberty," in *Four Essays on Liberty* (1969).

Carl J. Friedrich, *Constitutional Government and Democracy: Theory and Practice in Europe and America,* 4th ed. (1968), is magisterial in scope and enlightening in its insights into the nature of constitutionism. An excellent recent analysis of the roots of American constitutionalism is Harvey Wheeler, "Constitutionalism," in Fred I. Greenstein and Nelson W. Polsby, eds., *Handbook of Political Science, vol. 5: Governmental Institutions and Processes* (1975). Pertinent also is J. Roland Pennock and John W. Chapman, eds., *Constitutionalism: Nomos,* vol. 20 (1979), a collection of essays dealing with philosophical and historical aspects of the subject in Europe and America. Other important works on constitutionalism are Giovanni Sartori, "Constitutionalism: A Preliminary Discussion," *APSR* 56 (1962); W. H. Morris-Jones, "On Constitutionalism," *APSR* 59 (1965); K. C. Wheare, *Modern Constitutions* (1958); William Yandell Elliott, *The Pragmatic Revolt in Politics: Syndicalism, Fascism and the Constitutional State* (1928); Judith Shklar, *Legalism* (1964); Stanley Diamond, "The Rule of Law and the Order of Custom," *Social Research* 38 (1971); John Henry Merryman, *The Civil Law Tradition: An Introduction to the Legal Systems of Western Europe and Latin America* (1969); Harro Höpfl and Martyn P. Thompson, "The History of Contract as a Motif in Political Thought," *AHR* 84 (1979); Kirk Thompson, "Constitutionalism and Political Action," *JP* 31 (1969).

Martin E. Spencer, "Politics and Rhetorics," *Social Research,* 37 (1970), is a perceptive analysis of the way in which constitutional rules and principles shape the conduct of American government and politics. A similar point is made in Arthur E. Bestor, "The American Civil War as a Constitutional Crisis," *AHR* 69 (1964). The nature of constitutional politics in the United States is illuminated in Edward S. Corwin, "The Constitution as Instrument and as Symbol," *APSR* 30 (1936); Corwin, "Constitution v. Constitutional Theory," *APSR* 19 (1925); Karl Llewellyn, "The Constitution as an Institution," *Columbia Law Review* 34 (1934); Gerald Garvey, *Constitutional Bricolage* (1971); Glendon Schubert, "The Rhetoric of Constitutional Change," *Journal of Public Law* 16 (1967); Daniel J. Boorstin, "The Perils of Indwelling Law," in *The Decline of American Radicalism: Reflections on America Today* (1970); John Brigham, *Constitutional Language: An Interpretation of Judicial Decision* (1978); Charles L. Black, Jr., *Structure and Relationship in Constitutional Law* (1969); William F. Harris II, "Bonding Word and Polity: The Logic of American Constitutionalism," *APSR* 76 (1982).

Commentaries on the Constitution have always to some extent provided a record of constitutional development. The most important works in this genre for the early national period and nineteenth century are James Madison, Alexander Hamilton, John Jay, *The Federalist;* James Wilson and Thomas McKean, *Commentaries on the Constitution of the United States of America* (1792); St. George Tucker, *Blackstone's Commentaries, with Notes of Reference to the Constitution and Laws of the Federal Government of the United States, and of the Commonwealth of Virginia* (1797); John Taylor, *An Inquiry into the Principles and Policy of the Government of the United States* (1814); Taylor, *New Views of the Constitution of the United States* (1823); William Rawle, *A View of the Constitution of the United States of America* (1825); Nathaniel Chipman, *Principles of Government, a Treatise on Free Government, Including the Constitution of the United States* (1833); Joseph Story, *Commentaries on the Constitution of the United States,* 3 vols. (1833); James Kent, *Commentaries on American Law,* 4 vols. (1826–30); John Alexander Jameson, *A Treatise on Constitutional Conventions, Their History, Power, and Modes of Proceeding* (1867); Thomas M. Cooley, *A Treatise on Constitutional Limitations Which Rest upon the Legislative Power of the States of the American Union* (1868); Christopher G. Tiedeman, *A Treatise on the Limitations of the Police Power in the United States* (1886). Notable commentaries in the twentieth century are Westel Woodbury Willoughby, *The Constitutional Law of the United States,* 3 vols. (1924), and, most recently, Bernard Schwartz, *A Commentary on the Constitution of the United States,* 5 vols. (1963–68).

Early constitutional histories that retain scholarly value are Herman Eduard von Holst, *The Constitutional and Political History of the United States*, 7 vols. (1877–92); George Ticknor Curtis, *Constitutional History of the United States*, 2 vols. (1889); James Shouler, *Constitutional Studies, State and Federal* (1897); James Bryce, *The American Commonwealth*, 2 vols. (1888); Henry Jones Ford, *The Rise and Growth of American Politics: A Sketch of Constitutional Development* (1898); Francis Newton Thorpe, *The Constitutional History of the United States*, 3 vols. (1901). There is much solid constitutional history in Andrew C. McLaughlin and Albert Bushnell Hart, eds., *Cyclopedia of American Government*, 3 vols. (1914). Twentieth-century works include William Seal Carpenter, *The Development of American Political Thought* (1930); Andrew C. McLaughlin, *The Foundations of American Constitutionalism* (1932); McLaughlin, *A Constitutional History of the United States* (1935); Erik M. Eriksson and David N. Rowe, *American Constitutional History* (1933); Homer C. Hockett, *The Constitutional History of the United States, 1776–1876*, 2 vols. (1939); Carl B. Swisher, *American Constitutional Development* (1943, 1954); Arthur E. Sutherland, *Constitutionalism in America: Origins and Evolution of Its Fundamental Ideas* (1965). The contribution of Edward S. Corwin, perhaps the pre-eminent constitutional historian of the twentieth century, is well represented in Alpheus T. Mason and Gerald Garvey, eds., *American Constitutional History: Essays by Edward S. Corwin* (1964); Richard Loss, ed., *Presidential Power and the Constitution: Essays by Edward S. Corwin* (1976); and Corwin's "Introduction" to *The Constitution of the United States: Analysis and Interpretation* (1952).

More specialized works that cover a broad sweep of constitutional history include Charles Warren, *The Supreme Court in United States History*, 2 vols. (1922); Charles Grove Haines, *The American Doctrine of Judicial Supremacy* (1911, 1932); Louis B. Boudin, *Government by Judiciary*, 2 vols. (1932); Conyers Read, ed., *The Constitution Reconsidered* (1938); Benjamin F. Wright, *The Growth of American Constitutional Law* (1942); G. Edward White, *The American Judicial Tradition: Profiles of Leading American Judges* (1976); Robert J. Steamer, *The Supreme Court in Crisis: A History of Conflict* (1971); Leon Friedman and Fred L. Israel, eds., *The Justices of the United States Supreme Court 1789–1969*, 4 vols. (1969); John R. Schmidhauser, *The Supreme Court as Final Arbiter in Federal-State Relations, 1789–1957* (1958). William M. Wiecek, *The Guarantee Clause of the U.S. Constitution* (1972), is concerned with controversy over the nature of republican constitutionalism.

The formal amendment process, usually considered less worthy of study than methods of informal constitutional change, receives illuminating treatment in Alan P. Grimes, *Democracy and the Amendments to the Constitution* (1978), and Clement E. Vose, *Constitutional Change: Amendment Politics and Supreme Court Litigation since 1900* (1972). Herbert W. Horwill, *The Usages of the American Constitution* (1925), employs an English mode of analysis to describe what Americans sometimes refer to as extraconstitutional practices and institutions. M. Judd Harmon, ed., *Essays on the Constitution of the United States* (1978), provides broad analysis of constitutional development based on current scholarship, while recent constitutional tendencies are described in American Academy of Political and Social Science, *The Revolution, the Constitution, and America's Third Century: The Bicentennial Conference on the United States Constitution*, 2 vols. (1980), and

Charles L. Black, Jr., and Bob Eckhardt, *The Tides of Power: Conversations on the American Constitution* (1976).

On the writing of constitutional history, see Paul L. Murphy, "Time to Reclaim: The Current Challenge of American Constitutional History," *AHR* 69 (1963); Herman Belz, "The Realist Critique of Constitutionalism in the Era of Reform," *AJLH* 15 (1971); Glendon A. Schubert, "The Future of Public Law," *George Washington Law Review* 34 (1966); James G. Randall, "The Interrelation of Social and Constitutional History," *AHR* 35 (1929). Harry N. Scheiber, "American Constitutional History and the New Legal History: Complementary Themes in Two Modes," *JAH* 68 (1981), discusses the relationship between public law and private law. This relationship is illustrated in Lawrence M. Friedman, *A History of American Law* (1973); James W. Hurst, *Law and Social Process in United States History* (1960); Hurst, "Legal Elements in United States History," *Perspectives in American History*, vol. 5 (1971); Harry N. Scheiber and Lawrence M. Friedman, eds., *American Law and the Constitutional Order: Historical Perspectives* (1978); Wythe Holt, ed., *Essays in Nineteenth-Century American Legal History* (1976); Stephen B. Presser and Jamil S. Zainaldin, eds., *Law and American History: Cases and Materials* (1980). The use of history in constitutional adjudication is examined in Charles A. Miller, *The Supreme Court and the Uses of History* (1969); Alfred H. Kelly, "Clio and the Court: An Illicit Love Affair," *Supreme Court Review 1965* (1966); Julius Goebel, Jr., "Constitutional History and Constitutional Law," *Columbia Law Review* 38 (1938).

Four good bibliographical aids are Alpheus T. Mason and D. Grier Stephenson, Jr., comps., *American Constitutional Development* (1977); Earlean M. McCarrick, *U.S. Constitution: A Guide to Information Sources* (1980); Stephen M. Millett, comp., *A Selected Bibliography of American Constitutional History* (1975); Kermit L. Hall, comp., *A Comprehensive Bibliography of American Constitutional and Legal History, 1896–1979* (1982).

II. *The Founding of the Colonies and Constitutional Development in the Seventeenth Century*

The best general works dealing with constitutional aspects of colonization are John E. Pomfret, *Founding the American Colonies, 1583–1660* (1970); Wesley Frank Craven, *The Southern Colonies in the Seventeenth Century* (1949); Craven, *The Colonies in Transition 1660–1713* (1968). Of lasting importance for the study of early American constitutional development are Herbert L. Osgood, *The American Colonies in the Seventeenth Century*, 3 vols. (1904–7), and Charles M. Andrews, *The Colonial Period of American History*, 4 vols. (1935–39). Andrew C. McLaughlin, *The Foundations of American Constitutionalism* (1932) is a classic statement of the significance of the corporation and covenant in the formation of American government. William Robert Scott, *The Constitution and Finance of English, Scottish and Irish Joint-Stock Companies to 1720*, 3 vols. (1912), provides detailed information about the colonizing activities of English merchant-adventurers. John P. Davis, *Corporations: A Study of the Origin and Development of Great Business Combinations and Their Relation to the Authority of the State*, 2 vols. (1905), is a superior analysis of the influence of the corporation on the colonial constitution. Still worthwhile are a series of seminal articles by Herbert L. Osgood: "The Corporation as a Form of Colonial Government," *PSQ* 11 (1896); "The Proprietary Province as a Form of Colonial Government," *AHR* 2 (1897); "The Political Ideas of the Puritans," *PSQ* 6 (1891).

On the development of government in Virginia, see Sigmund Diamond, "From Organization to Society: Virginia in the Seventeenth Century," *American Journal of Sociology* 63 (1958); Wesley Frank Craven, "And So the Form of Government Became Perfect," *Virginia Magazine of History and Biography* 77 (1969); Warren Billings, "The Growth of Political Institutions in Virginia, 1634 to 1676," *WMQ* 31 (1974).

Valuable works on Massachusetts include Samuel Eliot Morison, *Builders of the Bay Colony* (1930); Frances Rose-Troup, *The Massachusetts Bay Company and Its Predecessors* (1930); Perry Miller, *Orthodoxy in Massachusetts, 1630–1650* (1933); Charles H. McIlwain, "The Transfer of the Charter to New England and Its Significance in American Constitutional History," *Massachusetts Historical Society Proceedings* 63 (1929), reprinted in McIlwain *Constitutionalism and the Changing World* (1939); T. H. Breen, *The Character of the Good Ruler: A Study of Puritan Political Ideas in New England, 1630–1730* (1970); Robert E. Wall, Jr., *Massachusetts Bay: The Crucial Decade, 1640–1650* (1972); Richard P. Gildrie, *Salem, Massachusetts, 1626–1683: A Covenant Community* (1972); Richard S. Dunn, *Puritans and Yankees: The Winthrop Dynasty of New England, 1630–1717* (1962). George Langdon, Jr., *Pilgrim Colony: A History of New Plymouth, 1620–1691* (1966), is a standard account, while Mary Jeane Anderson Jones, *Congregational Commonwealth: Connecticut 1636–1662* (1968), relates developments in that New England colony.

The early constitutional history of Maryland is described in Newton D. Mereness, *Maryland as a Proprietary Province* (1901), and Matthew P. Andrews, *The Founding of Maryland: Province and State* (1933). Studies of the later proprietary colonies include John E. Pomfret, *The Province of East New Jersey, 1609–1702: The Rebellious Proprietary* (1962); Pomfret, *The Province of West New Jersey 1609–1702: A History of Organization of an American Colony* (1956); Wesley Frank Craven, *New Jersey and the English Colonization of North America* (1964); J. S. Bassett, *The Constitutional Beginnings of North Carolina* (1894); Hugh T. Lefler and Albert R. Newsome, *The History of a Southern State: North Carolina* (1954); Edwin R. Bronner, *William Penn's 'Holy Experiment': The Founding of Pennsylvania 1681–1701* (1962); Mary Maples Dunn, *William Penn: Politics and Conscience* (1967); Gary B. Nash, "The Framing of Government in Pennsylvania: Ideas in Contact with Reality," *WMQ* 23 (1966); Robert C. Ritchie, *The Duke's Province: A Study of New York Politics and Society, 1664–1691* (1977).

On the political and constitutional changes of the later seventeenth century, see David S. Lovejoy, *The Glorious Revolution in America* (1972); Lois G. Carr and David W. Jordan, *Maryland's Revolution in Government 1689–1692* (1974); Wilcomb E. Washburn, *The Government and the Rebel: A History of Bacon's Rebellion in Virginia* (1957); Bernard Bailyn, "Politics and Social Structure in Seventeenth Century Virginia," in James M. Smith, ed., *Seventeenth Century America: Essays in Colonial History* (1959); Michael G. Hall, *Edward Randolph and the American Colonies, 1676–1703* (1960); Philip S. Haffenden, *New England in the English Na-*

tion, 1689–1713 (1974); Lawrence H. Leder, *Robert Livingston, 1654–1728, and the Politics of Colonial New York* (1961); Jerome R. Reich, *Leisler's Rebellion: A Study of Democracy in New York, 1664–1720* (1953). Wesley Frank Craven, *The Colonies in Transition* (1968), and Clarence L. VerSteeg, *The Formative Years, 1607–1763* (1964), are good on this period. Michael Kammen, *Deputyes and Libertyes: the Origins of Representative Government in Colonial America* (1969), sees decisive acquisitions of power by the colonial assemblies in the seventeenth century. Stephen Saunders Webb, *The Governors-General: The English Army and the Definition of the Empire, 1569–1681* (1979), contends that centralized military rule characterized the British empire from the outset. This interpretation is disputed in J. M. Sosin, *English America and the Restoration Monarchy of Charles II: Transatlantic Politics, Commerce, and Kinship* (1980). Viola F. Barnes, *The Dominion of New England: A Study in British Colonial Policy* (1923), and Louise P. Kellogg, "The American Colonial Charter," American Historical Association *Annual Report, 1903,* vol. I, are worthwhile accounts of the early British imperial system.

III. *The Colonial Constitution in the Eighteenth Century*

The growth of assembly power as the basis of effective local autonomy forms the central theme in accounts of eighteenth-century constitutional development. Influential among recent works have been Bernard Bailyn, *The Origin of American Politics* (1968) and *The Ideological Origins of the American Revolution* (1967), both of which identify English republican writers as the chief source of American constitutional thought. Other valuable studies include Jack P. Greene, *The Quest for Power: The Lower Houses of Assembly in the Southern Royal Colonies, 1689–1776* (1963); Green, "Political Mimesis: A Consideration of the Historical and Cultural Roots of Legislative Behavior in the British Colonies in the Eighteenth Century," *AHR* 75 (1969); Lawrence Leder, *Liberty and Authority: Early American Political Ideology, 1689–1763* (1968); J. R. Pole, *Political Representation in England and the Origins of the American Republic* (1966); Stanley N. Katz, "The Origins of American Constitutional Thought," *Perspectives in American History,* III (1969); Alfred de Grazia, *Public and Republic: Political Representation in America* (1951); George N. Dargo, *Roots of the Republic: A New Perspective on Early American Constitutionalism* (1974); Patricia Bonomi, *Politics and Society in Colonial New York* (1971); George Edward Frakes, *Laboratory for Liberty: The South Carolina Legislative Committee System, 1719–1776* (1970); Lucille Griffith, *The Virginia House of Burgesses, 1750–1774* (1963); Raymond C. Bailey, *Popular Influence upon Public Policy: Petitioning in Eighteenth Century Virginia* (1979); James Henretta, "*Salutary Neglect": Colonial Administration under the Duke of Newcastle* (1972); Stanley N. Katz, *Newcastle's New York: Anglo-American Politics, 1732–1753* (1968); M. Eugene Sirmans, *Colonial South Carolina: A Political History 1663–1763* (1967). Important older accounts are Mary P. Clarke, *Parliamentary Privilege in the American Colonies* (1943); Evarts B. Green, *The Provincial Governor in the English Colonies of North America* (1898); Leonard W. Labaree, *Royal Government in America: A Study of the British Colonial System before 1783* (1930); Labaree, *Conservatism in Early American History* (1948); Beverly W. Bond, Jr., *The Quit-Rent System in the American Colonies* (1919).

The Lockean, liberal individualist view of colonial constitutional thought is found in William Seal Carpenter, *The Development of American Political Thought* (1930); Benjamin F. Wright, Jr., *American Interpretations of Natural Law* (1931); Max Savelle, *Seeds of Liberty: The Genesis of the American Mind* (1948); Clinton L. Rossiter, *Seedtime of the Republic* (1953). The problem of democracy in early America has received intensive study, especially the question of suffrage requirements. Key works examining this issue are B. Katherine Brown, "Freemanship in Puritan Massachusetts," *AHR* 50 (1954); Brown, "Puritan Democracy: A Case Study," *MVHR* 50 (1963); Robert F. and Katherine Brown, *Virginia: 1705–1788: Democracy or Aristocracy?* (1964); Robert F. Brown, *Middle Class Democracy and the Revolution in Massachusetts, 1691–1780* (1955), all of which argue that democracy existed in colonial America. This view is disputed in Timothy H. Breen, "Who Governs: The Town Franchise in Seventeenth Century Massachusetts," *WMQ* 27 (1970), and Robert E. Wall, Jr., "The Decline of the Massachusetts Franchise, 1647–1666," *JAH* 69 (1972). A rewarding treatment of the subject is J. R. Pole, "Historians and the Problem of Early American Democracy," *AHR* 67 (1962). See also John C. Rainbolt, "The Alteration in the Relationship between Leadership and Constituents in Virginia, 1660 to 1720," *WMQ* 27 (1970); Richard V. Buel, "Democracy and the American Revolution: A Frame of Reference," *WMQ* 22 (1965); Roy N. Lokken, "The Concept of Democracy in Colonial Political Thought," *WMQ* 16 (1959); John B. Kirby, "Early American Politics—the Search for Ideology: An Historiographical Analysis and Critique of the Concept of Deference," *JP* 32 (1970). Albert E. McKinley, *The Suffrage Franchise in the Thirteen English Colonies in America* (1905), and Chilton Williamson, *American Suffrage from Property to Democracy, 1760–1860* (1960), provide essential data concerning suffrage laws and practices.

The reception of the common law and the development of colonial legal and judicial institutions are discussed in Lawrence M. Friedman, *A History of American Law* (1973); George L. Haskins, *Law and Authority in Early Massachusetts: A Study in Tradition and Design* (1960); Herbert A. Johnson, "American Colonial Legal History: A Historiographical Interpretation," in *Perspectives in Early American History,* ed. Alden T. Vaughn and George A. Billias (1973); David H. Flaherty, ed., *Essays in the History of Early American Law* (1969); Stanley N. Katz, "The Politics of Law in Colonial America: Controversies over Chancery Courts and Equity Law in the Eighteenth Century," *Perspectives in American History,* vol. 5 (1971); Julius Goebel, Jr., *History of the Supreme Court of the United States,* vol. 1: *Antecedents and Beginnings* (1971); Erwin C. Surrency, "The Courts in the American Colonies," *AJLH* 11 (1967); George A. Billias, ed., *Law and Authority in Colonial America* (1965); Stanley N. Katz, "Looking Backward: The Early History of American Law," *University of Chicago Law Review* 33 (1966); Herbert A. Johnson, "The Prerogative Court of New York, 1686–1776," *AJLH* 18 (1973); Milton M. Klein, *The Politics of Diversity: Essays in the History of Colonial New York* (1974); Richard B. Morris, *Studies in the History of American Law, with Special Reference to the Seventeenth and Eighteenth Century* (1930); Paul S. Reinsch, *English Common Law in Early American Colonies* (1899); Francis R. Aumann, *The Changing American Legal System: Some Selected Phases* (1940).

There are numerous recent studies examining oligarchical control of local government and the relationship between town government and provincial authority. See, in particular, Michael Zuckerman, *Peaceable Kingdoms: New England Towns in the Eighteenth Century* (1970); David G. Allen, "The Zuckerman Thesis and the Process of Legal Rationalization in Provincial Massachusetts," *WMQ* 29 (1972); L. Kinvin Wroth, "Peaceable Kingdoms: The New England Town from the Perspective of Legal History," *AJLH* 15 (1971); Bruce C. Daniels, *The Connecticut Town: Growth and Development, 1635–1790* (1979); Bruce C. Daniels, ed., *Town and County: Essays on the Structure of Local Government in the American Colonies* (1978); Kenneth A. Lockridge and Alan Kreider, "The Evolution of Massachusetts Town Government, 1640 to 1740," *WMQ* 23 (1966); Hendrik Hartog, "The Public Law of a County Court: Judicial Government in Eighteenth Century Massachusetts," *AJLH* 20 (1976). Roy H. Akagi, *The Town Proprietors of the New England Colonies: A Study of their Development, Organization, Activities, and Controversies, 1620–1770* (1924) is a superior older work.

IV. *The American Revolution, the State Constitutions and the Articles of Confederation*

Works describing the nature and development of the British imperial system include: Lawrence Henry Gipson, *The British Empire before the Revolution*, 14 vols. (1936–68); Dora Mae Clarke, *The Rise of the British Treasury: Colonial Administration in the Eighteenth Century* (1960); Michael Kammen, *A Rope of Sand: The Colonial Agents, British Politics, and the American Revolution* (1968); Alison G. Olson, "Parliament, Empire, and Parliamentary Law, 1776," in *Three British Revolutions: 1641, 1688, 1776,* ed. J. G. A. Pocock (1980); Thomas C. Barrow, *Trade and Empire: The British Customs Service in America, 1660–1775* (1967); Lawrence Harper, *The English Navigation Laws: A Seventeenth Century Experiment in Social Engineering* (1939); O. M. Dickerson, *The Navigation Acts and the American Revolution* (1951); F. P. Wickwire, *British Subministers and Colonial America, 1766–1783* (1966); George Louis Beer, *Origins of the British Colonial System* (1908) and *The Old Colonial System* (1912).

The debate about parliamentary power and the status of the colonies in the empire has produced some of the classic works in constitutional history. These include Charles H. McIlwain, *The American Revolution: A Constitutional Interpretation* (1923); Randolph G. Adams, *The Political Ideas of the American Revolution* (1922); Robert L. Schuyler, *Parliament and the British Empire* (1929); Carl L. Becker, *The Declaration of Independence* (1922); Herbert L. Osgood, "England and the Colonies," *PSQ* 2 (1887); Claude H. Van Tyne, *The Causes of the War of Independence* (1922); Andrew C. McLaughlin, "The Background of American Federalism," *APSR* 12 (1918); Charles F. Mullett, *Fundamental Law and the American Revolution, 1760–1776* (1933); Julian P. Boyd, *Anglo-American Union: Joseph Galloway's Plans to Preserve the British Empire* (1941). More recent works that should be consulted are James H. Kettner, *The Development of American Citizenship, 1608–1870* (1978); Edmund S. Morgan, "Colonial Ideas of Parliamentary Power, 1764–1776," *WMQ* 5 (1948); Harvey Wheeler, "Calvin's Case and the McIlwain-Schuyler Debate," *AHR* 61 (1955–56); Walter F. Bennett, *American Theories of Federalism* (1964); Barbara A. Black, "The Constitution of the Empire: The Case for the Colonists," *University of Pennsylvania Law Review* 124 (1976); David Ammerman, "The British Constitution and the American Revolution: A

Failure of Precedent," *William and Mary Law Review* 17 (1976); John Phillip Reid, "In the First Line of Defense: The Colonial Charters, the Stamp Act Debate and the Coming of the American Revolution," *New York University Law Review* 51 (1976); Reid, "In an Inherited Way: English Constitutional Rights, the Stamp Act Debate, and the Coming of the American Revolution," *Southern California Law Review* 45 (1976).

Charles M. Andrews, "The American Revolution: An Interpretation," *AHR* 31 (1926), is a classic statement of the thesis that the movement for independence was essentially constitutional in nature. See also R. A. Humphreys, "The Rule of Law and the American Revolution," *Law Quarterly Review* 53 (1937). More recent studies that advance this view are Daniel J. Boorstin, *The Genius of American Politics* (1953); Edmund S. Morgan and Helen M. Morgan, *The Stamp Act Crisis: Prologue to Revolution* (1953); Edmund S. Morgan, *The Birth of the Republic, 1763-1789* (1956); David S. Lovejoy, "Rights Imply Equality: The Case against Admiralty Jurisdiction in America, 1764-1776," *WMQ* 16 (1959). A more sophisticated version of this thesis is developed by Bernard Bailyn, *The Ideologial Origins of the American Revolution* (1967), and Bailyn, "Political Experience and Enlightenment Ideas in Eighteenth Century America," *AHR* 67 (1962). Works which emphasize the importance of English republican and eighteenth-century Enlightenment ideas in the American Revolution include Edmund S. Morgan, "The American Revolution Considered as an Intellectual Movement," in Morton White and Arthur Schlesinger, Jr., eds., *Paths of American Thought* (1973); Gordon Wood, *The Creation of the American Republic, 1776-1787* (1969); Hannah Arendt, *On Revolution* (1963); J. G. A. Pocock, "1776: The Revolution against Parliament," in Pocock, ed., *Three British Revolutions: 1641, 1688, 1776* (1980); William H. Nelson, "The Revolutionary Character of the American Revolution," *AHR* 70 (1965); William D. Liddle, " 'A Patriot King, or None': Lord Bolingbroke and the American Renunciation of George III," *JAH* 65 (1979); Garry Wills, *Inventing America: Jefferson's Declaration of Independence* (1978); Morton White, *The Philosophy of the American Revolution* (1978); Pauline Maier, *From Resistance to Revolution: Colonial Radicals and the Development of American Opposition to Britain, 1765-1776* (1972); Alan Rogers, *Empire and Liberty: American Resistance to British Authority, 1755-1763* (1974); Stanley N. Katz, "Republicanism and the Law of Inheritance in the American Revolutionary Era," *Michigan Law Review* 76 (1977); Library of Congress Symposia on the American Revolution: *The Development of a Revolutionary Mentality* (1972); Willi Paul Adams, "Republicanism in Political Rhetoric before 1776," *PSQ* 85 (1970). An interesting older work on this subject is George M. Dutcher, "The Rise of Republican Government in the United States," *PSQ* 55 (1940).

The problem of fundamental law and the new American conception of constitutionalism that emerged during the Revolution are analyzed in Edward S. Corwin, "The 'Higher Law' Background of American Constitutional Law," *Harvard Law Review* 42 (1928-29), reprinted under the same title in book form in 1955; Charles H. McIlwain, "The Fundamental Law behind the Constitution of the United States," in *Constitutionalism in a Changing World* (1939); Charles F. Mullett, "Coke and the American Revolution," *Economica* 12 (1932); Bailyn, *The Ideological Origins of the American Revolution;* Thomas C. Grey, "Origins of the Unwritten Constitution: Fundamental Law in American Revolutionary Thought," *Stanford Law Review* 30 (1978). Donald S. Lutz, "From Covenant to Constitution in American Political Thought," *Publius* 10 (1980), surpasses previous studies in the thoroughness and precision with which it traces the development of American thinking on constitutions.

For detailed description of the first state constitutions the following works are worth consulting: Donald S. Lutz, *Popular Consent and Popular Control: Whig Political Theory in the Early State Constitutions* (1980); Willi Paul Adams, *The First American Constitutions: Republican Ideology and the Making of the State Constitutions in the Revolutionary Era* (1980); Allan Nevins, *The American States during and after the Revolution, 1775–1789* (1924); Benjamin F. Wright, "The Early History of Written Constitutions in America," in *Essays in History and Political Theory in Honor of Charles Howard McIlwain,* ed. Carl Wittke (1936); Wright, *Consensus and Continuity, 1776–1787* (1958); W. F. Dodd, "The First State Constitutional Conventions, 1776–1783," *APSR* 2 (1908); W. C. Morey, "The First State Constitutions," *Annals* 4 (1893); W. C. Webster, "A Comparative Study of the State Constitutions of the American Revolution," *Annals* 9 (1897); Thad W. Tate, "The Social Contract in America, 1774–1787: Revolutionary Theory as a Conservative Instrument," *WMQ* 22 (1965); Fletcher Green, *Constitutional Development of the South Atlantic States, 1776–1860* (1930); John N. Shaeffer, "Public Consideration of the 1776 Pennsylvania Constitution," *Pennsylvania Magazine of History and Biography* 98 (1974); Ronald M. Peters, *The Massachusetts Constitution of 1780: A Social Compact* (1974); Jere N. Daniell, *Experiment in Republicanism: New Hampshire Politics and the American Revolution 1741–1794* (1970); Peter S. Onuf, "State-Making in Revolutionary America: Independent Vermont as a Case Study," *JAH* 67 (1981).

The relationship between the separation-of-powers doctrine and the theory of mixed government has been one of the more perplexing questions in colonial and revolutionary constitutional history. The best analysis of the problem is M. J. C. Vile, *Constitutionalism and the Separation of Powers* (1967). Other pertinent works are W. B. Gwyn, *The Meaning of the Separation of Powers* (1965); Murray Dry, "The Separation of Powers and Republican Government," *Political Science Reviewer* 3 (1973); Martin Diamond, "The Separation of Powers and the Mixed Regime," *Publius* 8 (1978); William Seal Carpenter, "The Separation of Powers in the Eighteenth Century," *APSR* 22 (1928); Francis G. Wilson, "The Mixed Constitution and the Separation of Powers," *Southwestern Social Science Quarterly* 15 (1934); Benjamin F. Wright, "The Origin of the Separation of Powers in America," *Economica* 13 (1933); Malcom P. Sharpe, "The Classical American Doctrine of the Separation of Powers," *University of Chicago Law Review* 2 (1935).

The progressive interpretation of revolutionary constitution making, concerned more with social and economic interests than constitutional principles and ideas, is well illustrated in Merrill Jensen, *The Founding of a Nation* (1968); Jensen, *The American Revolution within America* (1974); Jensen, "Democracy and the American Revolution," *Huntington Library Quarterly* 20 (1957); Elisha P. Douglass, *Rebels and Democrats: The Struggle for Equal Political Rights and Majority Rule during the American Revolution* (1955); Jackson Turner Main, *The Upper House in Revolutionary America, 1763–1788* (1967); Main, *The Sovereign States 1775–1783* (1973).

The development of a distinctive national outlook and loyalty in the colonial and revolutionary period is discussed in Harry M. Ward, *"Unite or Die": Intercolony Relations, 1690–1763* (1971); J. M. Bumsted, " 'Things in the Womb of

Time': Ideas of American Independence, 1633 to 1763," *WMQ* 31 (1974); Edwin G. Burrows and Michael Wallace, "The American Revolution: The Ideology and Psychology of National Liberation," *Perspectives in American History* 6 (1972); Max Savelle, "Nationalism and Other Loyalties in the American Revolution," *AHR* 67 (1962); John Blassingame, "American Nationalism and Other Loyalties in the Southern Colonies, 1763-1775," *JSH* 34 (1968); Thomas C. Barrow, "The American Revolution as a Colonial War for Independence," *WMQ* 25 (1968). The central importance of political and constitutional ideas in defining American nationality is perceptively analyzed in Yehoshua Arieli, *Individualism and Nationalism in American Ideology* (1964).

The Articles of Confederation are interpreted as expressing the democratic spirit of the Revolution in various works of Merrill Jensen. See his *The Articles of Confederation: An Interpretation of the Social-Constitutional History of the American Revolution, 1774-1781* (1940), and *The New Nation: A History of the United States during the Confederation 1781-1789* (1950). Andrew C. McLaughlin, *The Confederation and the Constitution, 1781-1789* (1905) is the classic nationalist interpretation of the Confederation era. It is complemented by the more recent accounts of Morgan, *The Birth of the Republic;* Wright, *Consensus and Continuity;* Forrest McDonald, *E Pluribus Unum: The Formation of the American Republic 1776-1790* (1965). There is an excellent analysis of the problem of sovereignty in the Confederation period in Claude H. Van Tyne, "Sovereignty in the American Revolution: An Historical Study," *AHR* 12 (1907).

Recent general accounts of the Confederation are H. James Henderson, *Party Politics in the Continental Congress* (1974); Joseph L. Davis, *Sectionalism in American Politics, 1774-1787* (1977); Jack N. Rakove, *The Beginnings of National Politics: An Interpretive History of the Continental Congress* (1979). Studies of institutional development in the Confederation era include Herbert A. Johnson, "Toward a Reappraisal of the Federal Government: 1783-1789," *AJLH* 8 (1964); Edmund C. Burnett, *The Continental Congress* (1941); Jennings B. Sanders, *The Presidency of the Continental Congress 1774-1789: A Study in American Institutional History* (1930); Sanders, *Evolution of the Executive Departments of the Continental Congress, 1774-1789* (1935); Charles C. Thach, *The Creation of the Presidency, 1775-1789* (1922); Jay Caesar Guggenheimer, "The Development of the Executive Departments, 1775-1789," in J. Franklin Jameson, ed., *Essays in the Constitutional History of the United States in the Formative Period, 1775-1789* (1889). Peter Onuf, "Toward Federalism: Virginia, Congress, and the Western Lands," *WMQ* 34 (1977), is an illuminating discussion of the territorial character of governmental sovereignty in American federalism. Arthur Bestor, "Constitutionalism and the Settlement of the West: The Attainment of Consensus, 1754-1784," in John Porter Bloom, ed., *The American Territorial System,* and Robert F. Berkhofer, Jr., "Jefferson, the Ordinance of 1784, and the Origins of the American Territorial System," *WMQ* 29 (1972), analyze an important aspect of Confederation policy making.

V. *The Federal Constitution of 1787*

Key studies of the movement for constitutional reform that led to the federal convention are Edward S. Corwin, "The Progress of Constitutional Theory between the Declaration of Independence and the Meeting of the Philadelphia Convention," *AHR* 30 (1925); Merrill Jensen, "The Idea of a National Government during the American Revolution," *PSQ* 58 (1943); E. J. Ferguson, "The Nationalists of 1781–1783 and the Economic Interpretation of the Constitution," *JAH* 56 (1969); Wood, *The Creation of the American Republic.*

Max Farrand, ed., *The Records of the Federal Convention of 1787,* 4 vols. (1911–37), provides the basic documentary foundation for study of the convention. The following works offer good narrative accounts of the convention: Andrew C. McLaughlin, *A Constitutional History of the United States* (1935); McLaughlin, *The Confederation and the Constitution, 1781–1789* (1905); Max Farrand, *The Fathers of the Constitution* (1913); Charles Warren, *The Making of the Constitution* (1929); David G. Smith, *The Convention and the Constitution* (1965); Clinton L. Rossiter, *1787: The Grand Convention* (1966). Among the more useful of numerous biographical studies are Irving Brant, *James Madison: Father of the Constitution* (1950) and Charles P. Smith, *James Wilson, Founding Father, 1742–1798* (1956).

The best study of the politics of the convention is Calvin C. Jillson, "Constitution-Making; Alignment and Realignment in the Federal Convention of 1787," *APSR* 75 (1981). Other valuable analyses are John P. Roche, "The Founding Fathers: A Reform Caucus in Action," *APSR* 55 (1961); Stanley Elkins and Eric McKitrick, "The Founding Fathers: Young Men of the Revolution," *PSQ* 76 (1961); Arnold A. Rogow, "The Federal Convention: Madison and Yates," *AHR* 60 (1955); Staughton Lynd, "The Compromise of 1787," *PSQ* 81 (1966); Calvin Jillson and Thornton Anderson, "Realignments in the Convention of 1787: The Slave Trade Compromise," *JP* 39 (1977); Howard A. Ohline, "Republicanism and Slavery: Origins of the Three Fifths Clause in the United States Constitution," *WMQ* 28 (1971); William Cuddihy and B. Carmon Hardy, "A Man's House Was Not His Castle: Origins of the Fourth Amendment to the United States Constitution," *WMQ* 37 (1980); Robert H. Birkby, "The Politics of Accommodation: The Origin of the Supremacy Clause," *Western Pol. Q.* 19 (1966); Bernard Donahoe and Marshall Smelser, "The Congressional Power to Raise Armies: The Constitutional and Ratifying Conventions 1787–1788," *Review of Politics* 33 (1971); Frederick W. Marks III, *Independence on Trial: Foreign Affairs and the Making of the Constitution* (1973).

Numerous works analyze the achievement of the Constitutional Convention from the standpoint of political and constitutional theory. Among the more helpful in understanding the nature of the Constitution and the ideas of the framers are Rozann Rothman, *Acts and Enactments: The Constitutional Convention of 1787* (1974), written from a Kenneth Burkean symbolic perspective; Rothman, "The Impact of Covenant and Contract Theories on Conceptions of the U.S. Constitution," *Publius* 10 (1980); Martin Diamond, "Democracy and the Federalist: A Reconsideration of the Framers' Intent," *APSR* 53 (1959); Diamond, "The Declaration and the Constitution: Liberty, Democracy, and the Founders," *The Public Interest* 41 (1975); Alpheus T. Mason, "The Federalist—a Split Personality," *AHR* 58 (1952); Mason, "Our Federal Union Reconsidered," *PSQ* 65 (1950); George W. Carey and James McClellan, "Towards the Restoration of the American Political Tradition," *JP* 38 (1976); Ralph A. Rossum and Gary L. McDowell, eds., *The American Founding: Politics, Statesmanship, and the Constitution* (1981).

More specialized studies focusing on republicanism are Charles F. Hobson, "The Negative on State Laws: James Madison, the Constitution, and the Crisis of

Republican Government," *WMQ* 36 (1979); Robert J. Morgan, "Madison's Analysis of the Sources of Political Authority," *APSR* 75 (1981); George W. Carey, "Separation of Powers and the Madisonian Model: A Reply to the Critics," *APSR* 72 (1978); Douglass Adair, " 'That Politics May Be Reduced to a Science': David Hume, James Madison, and the Tenth *Federalist,*" *Huntington Library Quarterly* 20 (1957); Neal Riemer, "The Republicanism of James Madison," *PSQ* 69 (1954); James Conniff, "The Enlightenment in American Political Thought: A Study of the Origins of Madison's *Federalist* Number 10," *Political Theory* 8 (1980); Edward J. Erler, "The Problem of the Public Good in *The Federalist,*" *Polity* 13 (1981); Jean Yarbrough, "Representation and Republicanism: Two Views," *Publius* 9 (1979); Yarbrough, "Thoughts on *The Federalist's* View of Representation," *Polity* 12 (1980); Paul Peterson, "The Meaning of Republicanism in *The Federalist,*" *Publius* 9 (1979); Robert G. McCloskey, ed. *The Works of James Wilson* (1967), Introduction; George M. Dennison, "The 'Revolutionary Principle': Ideology and the Constitution in the Thought of James Wilson," *Review of Politics* 39 (1977).

Federalism is analyzed philosophically in S. Rufus Davis, *The Federal Principle: A Journey through Time in Quest of Meaning* (1978), and Rozann Rothman, 'The Ambiguity of American Federal Theory," *Publius* 8 (1978). William T. Hutchinson, "Unite to Divide; Divide to Unite: The Shaping of American Federalism," *MVHR* 46 (1959), and McLaughlin, "The Background of American Federalism," *APSR* 12 (1918), approach the subject historically.

Charles A. Beard's, *An Economic Interpretation of the Constitution of the United States* (1913), arguing that the framers created a strong central government to restrain democracy and protect property interests, has become a field of study unto itself that bears directly on the question of the ratification of the Constitution. Beard's views were anticipated in part by Orin G. Libby, *The Geographical Distribution of the Vote by the Thirteen States on the Federal Constitution, 1787–8* (1894), and J. Allen Smith, *The Spirit of American Government, a Study of the Constitution: Its Origin, Influence and Relation to Democracy* (1907). After a long period of intellectual hegemony, the Beard thesis was attacked by scholars who perceived an underlying consensus in American politics and who asserted the primacy of constitutional principles over class interests. See especially Morgan, *Birth of the Republic* (1956); Forrest McDonald, *We the People: The Economic Origins of the Constitution* (1958); McDonald, *E Pluribus Unum: The Formation of the American Republic, 1776–1790* (1965); Wright, *Consensus and Continuity* (1958); Robert E. Brown, *Charles Beard and the Constitution* (1956); Brown, *Reinterpretation of the Formation of the American Constitution* (1963); Henry Steele Commager, "The Constitution: Was It an Economic Document?" *American Heritage* 9 (1958); Lee Benson, *Turner and Beard* (1960); Richard Hofstadter, *The Progressive Historians* (1968); Douglass Adair, "The Tenth Federalist Revisited," *WMQ* 8 (1951).

More sophisticated and empirically sound versions of the Beardian social-conflict interpretation of the Constitution appear in Jackson Turner Main, *The Antifederalists: Critics of the Constitution, 1781–1788* (1961); E. James Ferguson, *The Power of the Purse: A History of American Public Finance 1776–1790* (1961); Staughton Lynd, "Capitalism, Democracy, and the U.S. Constitution," *Science and Society* 27 (1963); Merrill Jensen, *The American Revolution within America* (1974); John P. Diggins, "Power and Authority in American History: The Case of Charles A. Beard and His Critics," *AHR* 86 (1981).

Jonathan Elliot, ed., *The Debates in the Several State Conventions on the*

Adoption of the Federal Constitution, 5 vols. (1936), is the basic documentary source for the study of ratification. Herbert J. Storing, ed., *The Complete Anti-Federalist,* 7 vols. (1982), supplements this record. Storing, *What the Anti-Federalists Were For,* vol. I of this collection, presents a sympathetic analysis of Antifederalist constitutional ideas. Stimulating analyses of the ratification controversy blending the insights of both the neo-Beardian and the consensus-ideological points of view on the Constitution, appear in John M. Murrin, "The Great Inversion, or Court versus Country: A Comparison of the Revolutionary Settlements in England (1688–1721) and America (1776–1816)," in Pocock, ed., *Three British Revolutions: 1641, 1688, 1776* (1980), and James H. Hutson, "Country, Court, and Constitution: Antifederalism and the Historians," *WMQ* 38 (1981). Other important works are Cecelia Kenyon, "Men of Little Faith: The Anti-Federalists on the Nature of Representative Government," *WMQ* 12 (1955); Kenyon, "Republicanism and Radicalism in the American Revolution: An Old-fashioned Interpretation," *WMQ* 19 (1962); Wood, *The Creation of the American Republic;* Charles W. Roll, Jr., "We Some of the People: Apportionment in the Thirteen State Conventions Ratifying the Constitution," *JAH* 56 (1969); Linda Grant DePauw, *The Eleventh Pillar: New York State and the Federal Constitution* (1966); Stephen R. Boyd, *The Politics of Opposition: Antifederalists and the Acceptance of the Constitution* (1979); Alpheus T. Mason, *The States Rights Debate: Antifederalism and the Constitution* (1964). The relationship between the Declaration of Independence and the Constitution is considered in Edmund S. Morgan, "The Great Political Fiction," *New York Review of Books,* March 9, 1978; Gary J. Schmitt and Robert H. Webking, "Revolutionaries, Antifederalists, and Federalists: Comments on Gordon Wood's Understanding of the American Founding," *Political Science Reviewer* 9 (1979); Martin Diamond, "The American Idea of Equality: The View from the Founding," *Review of Politics* 38 (1976).

VI. *Constitutional Development in the Early National Period*

The rapid acceptance of the Constitution as the legitimate basis for the conduct of government and politics is dealt with in Lance Banning, "Republican Ideology and the Triumph of the Constitution, 1789 to 1793," *WMQ* 31 (1974); Michael Lienesch, "The Constitutional Tradition: History, Political Action, and Progress in American Political Thought, 1787–1793," *JP* 42 (1980); Frank I. Schecter, "The Early History of the Tradition of the Constitution," *APSR* 9 (1915). Arendt, *On Revolution* (1963), contains an illuminating analysis of the nature of constitutional legitimacy as derived from the act of foundation.

On the problem of establishing the legitimacy of the new federal government, see Seymour Martin Lipset, *The First New Nation* (1963). The statecraft and policies of Alexander Hamilton in relation to the problem of legitimacy are treated in Forrest McDonald, "The Fourth Phase: The Completion of the Continental Union, 1789–1792," in E. P. Willis, ed., *Fame and the Founding Fathers* (1967); Cecelia M. Kenyon, "Alexander Hamilton: Rousseau of the Right," *PSQ* 73 (1958); Gerald Stourzh, *Alexander Hamilton and the Idea of Republican Government* (1970); Clinton L. Rossiter, *Alexander Hamilton and the Constitution* (1964); John C. Koritansky, "Alexander Hamilton's Philosophy of Government and Administration,"

Publius 9 (1979); L. K. Caldwell, "Alexander Hamilton: Advocate of Executive Leadership," *Public Administration Review* 4 (1944). Also pertinent is Louise Burnham Dunbar, *A Study of "Monarchical" Tendencies in the United States, from 1776 to 1801* (1922).

Concerning the executive branch, Congress, and administration, see James Hart, *The American Presidency in Action, 1789: A Study in Constitutional History* (1948); Edward S. Corwin, *The President: Office and Powers* (1957); Leonard D. White, *The Federalists: A Study in Administration* (1948); Raoul Berger, *Executive Privilege: A Constitutional Myth* (1974); Forrest McDonald, *The Presidency of George Washington* (1974); Lloyd M. Short, *The Development of National Administrative Organization in the United States* (1923); Carl E. Prince, *The Federalists and the Origins of the U.S. Civil Service* (1977); Ralph V. Harlow, *History of Legislative Methods before 1825* (1917); Joseph Cooper, *The Origins of the Standing Committees and the Development of the Modern House* (1971); George B. Galloway, *History of the House of Representatives* (1961); Nelson Polsby, "The Institutionalization of the U.S. House of Representatives," *APSR* 62 (1968). On the constitutional ideas and presidency of John Adams, see John R. Howe, Jr., *The Changing Political Thought of John Adams* (1966); Manning J. Dauer, *The Adams Federalists* (1953); Joseph Dorfman, "The Regal Republic of John Adams," *PSQ* 59 (1944); Correa M. Walsh, *The Political Science of John Adams* (1915); Stephen G. Kurtz, "The Political Science of John Adams, a Guide to His Statecraft," *WMQ* 25 (1968).

Jefferson's exercise of presidential power is the subject of numerous studies. Among the more useful are Dumas Malone, *Jefferson and His Time*, vols. 4 and 5 (1970–74); Merrill D. Peterson, *Thomas Jefferson and the New Nation: A Biography* (1970); Forrest McDonald, *The Presidency of Thomas Jefferson* (1976); Robert M. Johnstone, Jr., *Jefferson and the Presidency: Leadership in the Young Republic* (1978); Noble E. Cunningham, Jr., *The Process of Government under Jefferson* (1978); Leonard D. White, *The Jeffersonians: A Study in Administrative History* (1951); James MacGregor Burns, *The Deadlock of Democracy: Four-Party Politics in America* (1963). Jefferson's constitutional legacy is defined in terms of negative government and laissez faire in Dumas Malone, "Jefferson, Hamilton, and the Constitution," in W. H. Nelson, ed., *Theory and Practice in American Politics* (1964), and Caleb Perry Patterson, *The Constitutional Principles of Thomas Jefferson* (1953). In contrast, Julian P. Boyd, "Thomas Jefferson's Empire of Liberty," *Virginia Quarterly Review* 24 (1948), and Charles M. Wiltse, *The Jeffersonian Tradition in American Democracy* (1935), regard Jefferson as a national-minded governmental activist.

Jefferson's immediate successors in the White House are described in Irving Brant, *James Madison: The President, 1809–1812;* Brant, *Commander in Chief, 1812–1836* (1961); Ralph Ketcham, *James Madison: A Biography* (1971); Edward M. Burns, *James Madison: Philosopher of the Constitution* (1938); Abbot Smith, "Mr. Madison's War: An Unsuccessful Experiment in the Conduct of National Policy," *PSQ* 57 (1942); Harry Ammon, *James Monroe: The Quest for National Identity* (1971); George A. Lipsky, *John Quincy Adams: His Theory and Ideas* (1950).

Helpful for an understanding of the conflict between Federalist and Republican constitutionalism are the following studies of political thought and ideology: Lance Banning, *The Jeffersonian Persuasion: Evolution of a Party Ideology* (1978);

Richard V. Buel, *Securing the Revolution: Ideology in American Politics 1789–1815* (1972); Linda K. Kerber, *Federalists in Dissent: Imagery and Ideology in Jeffersonian America* (1970); Drew R. McCoy, *The Elusive Republic: Political Economy in Jeffersonian America* (1980); Burton Spivak, *Jefferson's English Crisis: Commerce, Embargo, and the Republican Revolution* (1979); Daniel Sisson, *The American Revolution of 1800* (1974); Robert E. Shalhope, *John Taylor of Caroline: Pastoral Republican* (1980); Benjamin F. Wright, "The Philosopher of Jeffersonian Democracy," *APSR* 22 (1928); Manning J. Dauer and Hans Hammond, "John Taylor: Aristocrat or Democrat?" *JP* 6 (1944); Charles E. Merriam, "The Political Theory of Jefferson," *PSQ* 17 (1902); William Seal Carpenter, *The Development of American Political Thought* (1930).

The Sedition Act crisis is dealt with in James M. Smith, *Freedom's Fetters: The Alien and Sedition Laws and American Civil Liberties* (1956); John C. Miller, *Crisis in Freedom: The Alien and Sedition Acts* (1951); Adrienne Koch and Harry Ammon, "The Virginia and Kentucky Resolutions: An Episode in Jefferson's and Madison's Defense of Civil Liberties," *WMQ* 5 (1948); Frank M. Anderson, "The Enforcement of the Alien and Sedition Laws," American Historical Association *Annual Report, 1912* (1914). For analysis of the free-speech problem in relation to the Sedition Act, see Leonard W. Levy, "Liberty and the First Amendment," *AHR* 67 (1962); James M. Smith, "The Sedition Law, Free Speech, and the American Political Process," *WMQ* 9 (1952); Walter Berns, "Freedom of the Press and the Alien and Sedition Laws: A Reappraisal," *Supreme Court Review 1970* (1971). The nature of freedom of speech and press generally in the eighteenth century is the subject of Leonard W. Levy, *Legacy of Suppression: Freedom of Speech and Press in Early American History* (1960), and Levy, ed., *Freedom of the Press from Zenger to Jefferson;* Lawrence H. Leder, *Liberty and Authority; Early American Political Ideology 1689–1763* (1968); Leder, "The Role of Newspapers in Early America: 'In Defense of Their Own Liberty,' " *Huntington Library Quarterly* 30 (1966); George N. Dargo, *Roots of the Republic: A New Perspective on Early American Constitutionalism* (1974). Civil liberties problems during Jefferson's presidency are analyzed in Leonard W. Levy, *Jefferson and Civil Liberties: The Darker Side* (1963).

The formation of political parties has attracted the interest of many historians and political scientists. An excellent introduction to the constitutional significance of parties is Theodore J. Lowi, "Party, Policy, and Constitution in America," in William N. Chambers and Walter Dean Burnham, eds., *The American Party Systems: Stages of Political Development* (1967). For parties in the early national period see Ronald P. Formisano, "Deferential-Participant Politics: The Early Republic's Political Culture, 1789–1840," *APSR* 68 (1974); William N. Chambers, *Political Parties in a New Nation: The American Experience, 1776–1809* (1963); Paul Goodman, "The First American Party System," in Chambers and Burnham, eds., *The American Party Systems;* Richard Hofstadter, *The Idea of a Party System: The Rise of Legitimate Opposition in the United States, 1780–1840* (1969); Michael Wallace, "Changing Concepts of Party in the United States: New York, 1815–1828," *AHR* 74 (1968); John F. Hoadley, "The Emergence of Political Parties in Congress, 1789–1803," *APSR* 74 (1980); John Zvesper, *Political Philosophy and Rhetoric: A Case Study of the Origins of American Party Politics* (1977); James Stirling Young, *The Washington Community, 1800–1828* (1966); Roy F. Nichols, *The Invention of the American Political Parties* (1967); Rudolph M. Bell, *Party and*

Faction in American Politics: The House of Representatives, 1789–1801 (1973); Joseph Charles, *The Origins of the American Party System* (1961); Noble E. Cunningham, Jr., *The Jeffersonian Republicans: The Formation of Party Organization, 1789–1801* (1957); Cunningham, *The Jeffersonian Republicans in Power: Party Operations, 1801–1809* (1963); James H. Broussard, "Regional Pride and Republican Politics: The Fatal Weakness of Southern Federalism, 1800–1815," *South Atlantic Quarterly* 73 (1974); David Hackett Fischer, *The Revolution of American Conservatism: The Federalist Party in the Era of Jeffersonian Republicanism* (1965); James M. Banner, *To the Hartford Convention: The Federalists and the Origins of Party Politics in Massachusetts, 1789–1815* (1969); Charles S. Syndor, "The One-Party Period in American History," *AHR* 51 (1946).

The impact of party development on the formal constitutional system is perceptively shown in John J. Turner, Jr., "The Twelfth Amendment and the First American Party System," *Historian* 35 (1973). See also Lucius Wilmerding, Jr., *The Electoral College* (1958). Worthwhile older works on party development are Charles A. Beard, *Economic Origins of Jeffersonian Democracy* (1915); Andrew C. McLaughlin, *The Courts, the Constitution, and Parties* (1912); Henry Jones Ford, *The Rise and Growth of American Politics: A Sketch of Constitutional Development* (1898); M. Ostrogorski, *Democracy and the Party System in the United States: A Study in Extra-Constitutional Government* (1910); Lolabel House, *A Study of the Twelfth Amendment to the Constitution of the United States* (1901).

VII. *Judicial Power and Constitutional Law in the Marshall Era*

The most thorough accounts of the establishment of the federal judicial system are Julius Goebel, *History of the Supreme Court of the United States*, vol. 1: *Antecedents and Beginnings to 1801* (1971); William W. Crosskey, *Politics and the Constitution in the History of the United States*, 2 vols. (1953); Charles Warren, "New Light on the Judiciary Act of 1789," *Harvard Law Review* 37 (1923). An illuminating analysis of the politics of judicial reform in the 1790s is Kathryn Turner, "Federalist Policy in the Judiciary Act of 1801," *WMQ* 22 (1965). The best recent study of the early federal judiciary, focusing on the problem of federal common law, is Stephen B. Presser, "A Tale of Two Judges: Richard Peters, Samuel Chase, and the Broken Promise of Federalist Jurisprudence," *Northwestern University Law Review* 73 (1978). Other valuable works are Mary K. B. Tachau, *Federal Courts in the Early Republic: Kentucky, 1789–1816* (1978); Richard E. Ellis, *The Jeffersonian Crisis: Courts and Politics in the Young Republic* (1971); Joseph H. Smith, "An Independent Judiciary: The Colonial Background," *University of Pennsylvania Law Review* 124 (1976); William F. Swindler, "Seedtime of an American Judiciary: From Independence to the Constitution," *William and Mary Law Review* 17 (1976); Henry J. Bourguignon, *The First Federal Court: The Federal Appellate Prize Court of the American Revolution, 1775–1787* (1977); Dwight F. Henderson, *Courts for a New Nation* (1971); Kathryn Turner, "The Mid-night Judges," *University of Pennsylvania Law Review* 109 (1961); Turner, "The Appointment of John Marshall," *WMQ* 17 (1960); Erwin C. Surrency, "The Judiciary Act of 1801," *AJLH* 2 (1958); Richard B. Morris, *John Jay: The Nation and the Court* (1967); J. Franklin Jameson, "The Predecessor of the Supreme Court," in

Essays in the Constitutional History of the United States in the Formative Period,
1775–1789 (1889).

Studies of judicial review have focused on the question of whether review was
intended by the framers or was a usurpation by the courts. Pioneering works include Brinton Coxe, *Judicial Power and Unconstitutional Legislation* (1893); James
Bradley Thayer, "The Origin and Scope of the American Doctrine of Constitutional Law," *Harvard Law Review* 7 (1893); Charles Grove Haines, *The American
Doctrine of Judicial Supremacy* (1911, 1932); Charles A. Beard, *The Supreme Court
and the Constitution* (1912); Edward S. Corwin, *The Doctrine of Judicial Review*
(1914); Andrew C. McLaughlin, *The Courts, the Constitution, and Parties: Studies
in Constitutional History and Politics* (1912); Horace A. Davis, *The Judicial Veto*
(1914); Charles Warren, *Congress, the Constitution, and the Supreme Court* (1925);
Louis Boudin, *Government by Judiciary,* 2 vols. (1932). More recent are Crosskey,
Politics and the Constitution, denying that judicial review was part of the original
constitutional system, and Raoul Berger, *Congress v. the Supreme Court* (1969),
arguing that it was. Donald G. Morgan, *Congress and the Constitution: A Study in
Responsibility* (1966), is an important work which examines orthodox judicial review in relation to the departmental approach to resolving constitutional controversies. William E. Nelson, "Changing Conceptions of Judicial Review: The
Evolution of Constitutional Theory in the States, 1790–1860," *University of Pennsylvania Law Review* 120 (1972), relates judicial review to an emergent interest-
group approach to public-policy formation. A useful account of the judicial-review
debate is provided by Alan Westin's introductory essay in Beard, *The Supreme
Court and the Constitution* (1962).

The attitude of Jefferson and the Republican party toward the judiciary is
dealt with in Henry Steele Commager, "Judicial Review and Democracy," *Virginia
Quarterly Review* 19 (1943); Samuel Krislov, "Jefferson and Judicial Review: Ref-
ereeing Cahn, Commager, and Mendelson," *Journal of Public Law* 9 (1960); Donald O. Dewey, *Marshall versus Jefferson: The Political Background of Marbury v.
Madison* (1970); Ellis, *The Jeffersonian Crisis;* Richard B. Lillich, "The Chase
Impeachment," *AJLH* 4 (1960); Kenneth Treacy, "The Olmstead Case, 1778–
1809," *Western Pol. Q.* 10 (1957); Jerry W. Knudson, "The Jeffersonian Assault on
the Federalist Judiciary, 1802–1805: Political Forces and Press Reaction," *AJLH* 14
(1970); Curtis Nettels, "The Mississippi Valley and the Federal Judiciary 1807–
1837," *MVHR* 12 (1925).

Recent studies which refute the simplistic progressive view of John Marshall
as a conservative defender of vested rights include George L. Haskins and Herbert
A. Johnson, *History of the Supreme Court of the United States,* vol. 2: *Foundations
of Power: John Marshall, 1801–15* (1981); Haskins, "Law Versus Politics in the
Early Years of the Marshall Court," *University of Pennsylvania Law Review* 130
(1981); William Nelson, "The Eighteenth Century Background of John Marshall's
Jurisprudence," *Michigan Law Review* 76 (1978); Robert K. Faulkner, *The Jurisprudence of John Marshall* (1968); Morton J. Frisch, "John Marshall's Philosophy
of Constitutional Republicanism," *Review of Politics* 20 (1958); C. Umbamhowar,
"Marshall on Judging," *AJLH* 7 (1963); Gerald Gunther, ed., *John Marshall's
Defense of McCulloch v. Maryland* (1969); Bruce A. Campbell, "John Marshall, the
Virginia Political Economy, and the Dartmouth College Decision," *AJLH* 19
(1975); William W. Crosskey, "John Marshall and the Constitution," *University of*

Chicago Law Review 23 (1956). R. Kent Newmyer, *The Supreme Court under Marshall and Taney* (1968), is a fine work of synthesis, and Francis N. Stites, *John Marshall: Defender of the Constitution* (1981), is a capable brief biography.

The modern institutional development of the Supreme Court under Marshall is described in Donald M. Roper, "Judicial Unanimity and the Marshall Court—a Road to Reappraisal," *AJLH* 9 (1965); Donald G. Morgan, *Justice William Johnson, the First Dissenter* (1954), and Morgan, "The Origin of Supreme Court Dissent," *WMQ* 10 (1953). Specialized studies of aspects of constitutional law under Marshall include C. Peter Magrath, *Yazoo: Law and Politics in the New Republic: The Case of Fletcher v. Peck* (1966); Maurice G. Baxter, *The Steamboat Monopoly: Gibbons v. Ogden, 1824* (1972); Francis N. Stites, *Private Interest and Public Gain: The Dartmouth College Case, 1819* (1972); Albert S. Abel, "Commerce Regulation before Gibbons v. Ogden: Interstate Transportation Facilities," *North Carolina Law Review* 25 (1946). For Marshall's role in the controversy between Aaron Burr and Jefferson, see Robert K. Faulkner, "John Marshall and the Burr Trial," *JAH* 53 (1966), and Bradley Chapin, *The American Law of Treason: Revolutionary and Early National Origins* (1964). The Marshall Court's involvement in the problem of Indian policy is examined in Joseph Burke, "The Cherokee Cases: A Study in Law, Politics, and Morality," *Stanford Law Review* 21 (1969).

Older works that interpret Marshall as a conservative nationalist are Albert J. Beveridge, *The Life of John Marshall,* 4 vols. (1916–19), still the best biography; Edward S. Corwin, *John Marshall and the Constitution* (1919); Charles Warren, *The Supreme Court in United States History,* 3 vols. (1922). For the progressive reaction to the nationalist interpretation, see Charles Grove Haines, "Histories of the Supreme Court of the United States written from the Federalist Point of View," *Southwestern Social Science Quarterly* 4 (1923); Haines, *The Role of the Supreme Court in American Government and Politics 1789–1835* (1944); Max Lerner, "John Marshall and the Campaign of History," *Columbia Law Review* 34 (1939); Wallace Mendelson, "New Light on Fletcher v. Peck and Gibbon v. Ogden," *Yale Law Journal* 58 (1949). More sympathetic assessments of Marshall, reflecting the use of his centralizing principles in New Deal liberalism, are found in W. Melville Jones, ed., *Chief Justice Marshall: A Reappraisal* (1956); George L. Haskins, "John Marshall and the Commerce Clause," *University of Pennsylvania Law Review* 104 (1955); and Edward S. Corwin, "John Marshall, Revolutionist Malgré Lui," *University of Pennsylvania Law Review* 104 (1955); Samuel J. Konefsky, *John Marshall and Alexander Hamilton: Architects of the Constitution* (1964). Standard works tracing Marshall's handling of two key problems in constitutional law are Felix Frankfurter, *The Commerce Clause under Marshall, Taney, and Waite* (1937), and Benjamin F. Wright, *The Contract Clause of the Constitution* (1938).

VIII. *Constitutional Change in the Jacksonian Era*

Studies of executive and administrative aspects of constitutional change in the middle period include Leonard D. White, *The Jacksonians: A Study in Administrative History, 1829–1860* (1954); Richard B. Latner, *The Presidency of Andrew Jackson: White House Politics, 1829–1837* (1979); Latner, "The Kitchen Cabinet and Andrew Jackson's Advisory Cabinet," *JAH* 65 (1978); Richard P. Longaker,

"Was Jackson's Kitchen Cabinet a Cabinet?" *MVHR* 44 (1957); Matthew A. Crenson, *The Federal Machine: Beginnings of Bureaucracy in Jacksonian America* (1975); Sidney H. Aronson, *Status and Kinship in the Higher Civil Service: Standards of Selection in the Administrations of John Adams, Thomas Jefferson, and Andrew Jackson* (1964); Carlton Jackson, *Presidential Vetoes, 1792–1945* (1967); Richard P. Longaker, "Andrew Jackson and the Judiciary," *PSQ* 71 (1956); Albert Somit, "Andrew Jackson as Administrator," *Public Administration Review* 8 (1948). Robert V. Remini, *Andrew Jackson and the Bank War: A Study in the Growth of Presidential Power* (1967). Executive developments after Jackson are recounted in James C. Curtis, *The Fox at Bay: Martin Van Buren and the Presidency, 1837–1841* (1970); R. J. Morgan, *A Whig Embattled: The Presidency under John Tyler* (1954); Charles G. Sellers, *James K. Polk, Continentalist, 1843–1846* (1968).

Political party development is analyzed in Richard P. McCormick, *The Second American Party System: Party Formation in the Jacksonian Era* (1966); McCormick, "Political Development and the Second Party System," in W. N. Chambers and W. D. Burnham, eds., *The American Party Systems: Stages of Political Development* (1967); Perry M. Goldman, "Political Virtue in the Age of Jackson," *PSQ* 87 (1972); Lynn L. Marshall, "The Strange Stillbirth of the Whig Party," *AHR* 72 (1967); Ronald P. Formisano, "Deferential-Participant Politics: The Early Republic's Political Culture, 1789–1840," *APSR* 68 (1974); Formisano, "Political Character, Antipartyism and the Second Party System," *American Quarterly* 21 (1969); Hofstadter, *The Idea of a Party System* (1968); Henry Jones Ford, *The Rise and Growth of American Politics* (1898); M. Ostrogorski, *Democracy and the Organization of Political Parties,* 2 vols. (1902); James S. Chase, *Emergence of the Presidential Nominating Convention, 1789–1832* (1973).

Studies of political thought and ideology that contribute to an understanding of constitutional politics in the Jacksonian era include Clinton Rossiter, *The American Quest, 1790–1860: An Emerging Nation in Search of Identity, Unity, and Modernity* (1971); Major L. Wilson, *Space, Time and Freedom: The Quest for Nationality and the Irrepressible Conflict, 1815–1861* (1974); Daniel Walker Howe, *The Political Culture of the American Whigs* (1979); Herbert Ershkowitz and William G. Shade, "Consensus or Conflict? Political Behavior in the State Legislatures during the Jacksonian Era," *JAH* 58 (1971). Richard H. Brown, "The Missouri Crisis, Slavery, and the Politics of Jacksonianism," *South Atlantic Quarterly* 65 (1966), emphasizes the proslavery outlook of the Jacksonians, while John M. McFaul, "Expediency vs. Morality: Jacksonian Politics and Slavery," *JAH* 62 (1975), criticizes this interpretation and stresses Jacksonian nationalism.

Concerned with class and group conflict in Jacksonian-Whig constitutional politics are Lee Benson, *The Concept of Jacksonian Democracy: New York as a Test Case* (1961); Glyndon G. Van Deusen, *The Jacksonian Era, 1828–1848* (1959); Van Deusen, "Some Aspects of Whig Thought and Theory in the Jacksonian Period," *AHR* 63 (1958); Arthur M. Schlesinger, Jr., *The Age of Jackson* (1945).

The nullification crisis is capably analyzed in James B. Stewart, " 'A Great Talking and Eating Machine': Patriarchy, Mobilization and the Dynamics of Nullification in South Carolina," *CWH* 27 (1981); Richard B. Latner, "The Nullification Crisis and Republican Subversion," *JSH* 43 (1977); Edwin A. Miles, "After John Marshall's Decision: Worcester v. Georgia and the Nullification Crisis," *JSH*

39 (1973); William H. Freehling, *Prelude to Civil War: The Nullification Contro-versy in South Carolina, 1816–1836* (1966); C. S. Boucher, *The Nullification Con-troversy in South Carolina* (1916). Two excellent articles on political ideology in South Carolina are Kenneth S. Greenberg, "Revolutionary Ideology and the Pro-slavery Argument: The Abolition of Slavery in Antebellum South Carolina," *JSH* 42 (1976), and Greenberg, "Representation and the Isolation of South Carolina, 1776–1860," *JAH* 64 (1977).

Among numerous works on the constitutional thought of John C. Calhoun, see especially George Kateb, "The Majority Principle: Calhoun and His Anteced-ents," *PSQ* 84 (1969); Ralph Lerner, "Calhoun's New Science of Politics," *APSR* 57 (1963); William H. Freehling, "Spoilsmen and Interests in the Thought and Career of John C. Calhoun," *JAH* 52 (1965); Charles M. Wiltse, "Calhoun's De-mocracy," *JP* 3 (1941); Gunnar Heckscher, "Calhoun's Idea of the Concurrent Majority and the Constitutional Theory of Hegel," *APSR* 33 (1939); Darryl Baskin, "The Pluralist Vision of Calhoun," *Polity* 2 (1969); Peter J. Steinberger, "Calhoun's Concept of the Public Interest: A Clarification," *Polity* 13 (1981); August O. Spain, *The Political Theory of John C. Calhoun* (1950); Jesse Carpenter, *The South as a Conscious Minority* (1930). Andrew C. McLaughlin, "Social Compact and Consti-tutional Construction," *AHR* 5 (1900), is a judicious analysis of the relationship between Calhoun's theory of union and that of Jefferson and Madison in the Kentucky and Virginia Resolutions.

Valuable studies of theories of the Union in the Jacksonian period are Ken-neth M. Stampp, "The Concept of a Perpetual Union," *JAH* 65 (1978); Major L. Wilson, " 'Liberty and Union': An Analysis of Three Concepts Involved in the Nullification Controversy," *JSH* 33 (1967); Charles M. Wiltse, "From Compact to National State in American Political Thought," in M. Konvitz and A. Murphy, eds., *Essays in Political Theory, Presented to George H. Sabine* (1948); Yehoshua Arieli, *Individualism and Nationalism in American Ideology* (1964); Edward S. Corwin, "National Power and State Interposition, 1787–1861," *Michigan Law Review* 10 (1912); Elizabeth C. Bauer, *Commentaries on the Constitution, 1790–1860* (1952); Paul C. Nagel, *One Nation Indivisible: The Union in American Thought* (1964).

Constitutional change at the state level is dealt with in Merrill Peterson, ed., *Democracy, Liberty and Property: The State Constitutional Convention of the 1820s* (1966), a documentary collection; Bayrd Still, "An Interpretation of the Statehood Process, 1800 to 1850," *MVHR* 23 (1936); Benjamin F. Wright, "Political Institu-tions and the Frontier," in Dixon Ryan Fox, ed., *Sources of Culture in the Middle West* (1934); Fletcher Green, *Constitutional Development in the South Atlantic States, 1776–1860* (1930); Robert M. Ireland, *The County Courts in Antebellum Kentucky* (1972); James Q. Dealey, *Growth of American State Constitutions, 1776–1914* (1915). The best studies of the Dorr War and its resolution in the case of *Luther* v. *Borden* are George M. Dennison, *The Dorr War: Republicanism on Trial, 1831–1861* (1976); Dennison, "Martial Law: The Development of a Theory of Emergency Powers, 1776–1861," *AJLH* 18 (1974); William M. Wiecek, *The Guar-antee Clause of the U.S. Constitution* (1972); Wiecek, " 'A Peculiar Conservatism' and the Dorr Rebellion: Constitutional Clash in Jacksonian America," *AJLH* 22 (1978); C. Peter Magrath, "Optimistic Democrat: Thomas W. Dorr and the Case of *Luther* v. *Borden*," *Rhode Island History* 29 (1970); Michael Conron, "Law, Politics, and Chief Justice Taney: A Reconsideration of the *Luther v. Borden* Decision," *AJLH* 11 (1967); John S. Schuchman, "The Political Background of the Political-Question Doctrine: The Judges and the Dorr War," *AJLH* 16 (1972).

IX. *Constitutional Law in the Taney Era*

Harold M. Hyman and William M. Wiecek, *Equal Justice under Law: Constitutional Development, 1835–1875* (1982), is an outstanding survey of the period based on the most recent scholarship. Carl B. Swisher, *History of the Supreme Court of the United States,* vol. 5: *The Taney Period, 1836–1864* (1974), at once magisterial and encyclopedic, provides an excellent general account of the Jacksonian judiciary. Other valuable general treatments are R. Kent Newmyer, *The Supreme Court under Marshall and Taney* (1968); Robert J. Harris, "Chief Justice Taney: Prophet of Reform and Reaction," *Vanderbilt Law Review* 10 (1957); Wallace Mendelson, "Chief Justice Taney—Jacksonian Judge," *University of Pittsburgh Law Review* 12 (1951); Mendelson, *Capitalism, Democracy and the Supreme Court* (1960); Charles Grove Haines and Foster H. Sherwood, *The Role of the Supreme Court in American Government and Politics* (1957); Charles Warren, *The Supreme Court in United States History,* 3 vols. (1922).

Two excellent interpretations of the Taney Court dealing with the problem of law and economic change are Stanley I. Kutler, *Privilege and Creative Destruction: The Charles River Bridge Case* (1971), and R. Kent Newmyer, "Justice Joseph Story, the Charles River Bridge Case and the Crisis of Republicanism," *AJLH* 17 (1973). Gerald Garvey, *Constitutional Bricolage* (1971), and Garvey, "The Constitutional Revolution of 1837 and the Myth of Marshall's Monolith," *Western Pol. Q.* 18 (1965), emphasize doctrinal continuity between the Marshall and Taney courts. Comparison of Marshall and Taney is also the focus of Edward S. Corwin, *The Commerce Power versus States Rights* (1936); Benjamin F. Wright, *The Contract Clause of the Constitution* (1938); Felix Frankfurter, *The Commerce Clause under Marshall, Taney and Waite* (1937); Louis B. Boudin, "John Marshall and Roger B. Taney," *Georgetown Law Journal* 24 (1936).

Biographical studies which throw light on constitutional law in the Taney era include Carl B. Swisher, *Roger B. Taney* (1935); Swisher, "Mr. Chief Justice Taney," in Allison Dunham and Philip Kurland, eds., *Mr. Justice* (1964); Charles W. Smith, Jr., *Roger B. Taney: Jacksonian Jurist* (1936); Albert Grant Mallison, "The Political Theories of Roger B. Taney," *Southwestern Political Science Quarterly* 1 (1920); James McClellan, *Joseph Story and the American Constitution: A Study in Political and Legal Thought* (1971); Gerald T. Dunne, *Justice Joseph Story and the Rise of the Supreme Court* (1970); Henry Steele Commager, "Joseph Story," in *The Gaspar G. Bacon Lectures on the Constitution of the United States* (1953); William R. Leslie, "Similarities in Lord Mansfield's and Joseph Story's View of Fundamental Law," *AJLH* 1 (1957); John P. Frank, *Justice Daniel Dissenting: A Biography of Peter V. Daniel* (1964); Alexander A. Lawrence, *James Moore Wayne: Southern Unionist* (1943); Francis P. Weisenburger, *The Life of John McLean: A Politician on the United States Supreme Court* (1937); Henry G. Connor, *John Archibald Campbell, Associate Justice of the U.S. Supreme Court, 1853–1861* (1920); Maurice G. Baxter, *Daniel Webster and the Supreme Court* (1966).

The relationship between law and economic development in the Jacksonian era forms the subject of numerous studies. Edward S. Corwin, "The Basic Doctrine of American Constitutional Law," *Michigan Law Review* 12 (1914), and Corwin, "The Doctrine of Due Process of Law before the Civil War," *Harvard Law Review* 24 (1910), are seminal articles describing judicial protection of private property against legislative interference, especially at the state level. Max Lerner, "The Supreme Court and American Capitalism," *Yale Law Journal* 42 (1933), analyzes the same phenomenon from the liberal-reform perspective. The legal history of the corporation is recounted in E. M. Dodd, *American Business Corporations until 1860* (1954), and G. C. Henderson, *The Position of Foreign Corporations in American Constitutional Law* (1918).

Accounts of state mercantilism showing how law and public policy, contrary to the myth of laissez faire, were used to promote economic development include James Willard Hurst, *Law and the Conditions of Freedom in the Nineteenth Century United States* (1956); Lawrence M. Friedman, *A History of American Law* (1973); Harry N. Scheiber, *Ohio Canal Era: A Case Study of Government and the Economy, 1820–1861* (1969); Scheiber, "Public Economic Policy and the American Legal System: Historical Perspectives," *Wisconsin Law Review* (1980); Scheiber, "Federalism and the American Economic Order, 1789–1910," *Law and Society Review* 10 (1975); Scheiber, "The Road to Munn: Eminent Domain and the Concept of Public Purpose in the State Courts," *Perspectives in American History* 5 (1971); Charles W. McCurdy, "Stephen J. Field and Public Land Law Development in California, 1850–1866," *Law and Society Review* 10 (1976); Carter Goodrich, *Governmental Promotion of American Canals and Railroads, 1800–1890* (1960); Louis Hartz, *Economic Policy and Democratic Thought: Pennsylvania, 1776–1860* (1948); Oscar Handlin and Mary F. Handlin, *Commonwealth: A Study of the Role of Government in the American Economy: Massachusetts, 1774–1861* (1947). Theodore J. Lowi, "American Business, Public Policy, Case-Studies, and Political Theory," *World Politics* 16 (1964), presents a valuable theoretical framework for analyzing government's relationship to the economy. J. R. Pole, "Property and Law in the American Republic," in *Paths to the American Present* (1979), and Harry N. Scheiber, "At the Borderland of Law and Economic History: The Contributions of Willard Hurst," *AHR* 75 (1970), contain perceptive historiographical commentary. Homer C. Hockett, *The Constitutional History of the United States, 1776–1876*, 2 vols. (1939), has a thorough discussion of the constitutional controversy over internal improvements. Daniel J. Elazar, *The American Partnership: Intergovernmental Cooperation in the Nineteenth Century United States* (1962), argues that federal-state sharing of power dates from the early national period.

Morton J. Horwitz, *The Transformation of American Law, 1780–1860* (1977), dealing with tort and contract law in the state courts, asserts a schematic class interpretation which contends that states in effect subsidized the process of industrialization at the expense of the public. For criticism of this thesis, see Gary T. Schwartz, "Tort Law and the Economy in Nineteenth-Century America: A Reinterpretation," *Yale Law Review* 90 (1981); A. W. B. Simpson, "The Horwitz Thesis and the History of Contracts," *University of Chicago Law Review* 46 (1979); Harry N. Scheiber, "Back to 'The Legal Mind'? Doctrinal Analysis and the History of Law," *Reviews in American History* 5 (1977); Randolph Bridwell and Ralph W. Whitten, *The Constitution and the Common Law: The Decline of the Doctrines of*

Separation of Powers and Federalism (1977). The development of federal commercial common law after *Swift* v. *Tyson* is dealt with in Tony Freyer, *Harmony and Dissonance: The Swift and Erie Cases in American Federalism* (1981), and Freyer, *Forums of Order: The Federal Courts and Business in American History* (1979); Charles A. Heckman, "The Relationship of Swift v. Tyson to the Status of Commercial Law in the Nineteenth Century and the Federal System," *AJLH* 17 (1973); Heckman, "Uniform Commercial Law in the Nineteenth Century Federal Courts: The Decline and Abuse of the *Swift* Doctrine," *Emory Law Journal* 27 (1978).

Diverse aspects of federal and state constitutional change involving the judiciary in the first half of the nineteenth century are examined in Kermit L. Hall, *The Politics of Justice: Lower Federal Court Selection and the Second Party System, 1829–61* (1979); Hall, "The Children of the Cabins: The Lower Federal Judiciary, Modernization, and the Political Culture, 1789–1899," *Northwestern University Law Review* 75 (1980); Maxwell Bloomfield, *American Lawyers in a Changing Society, 1776–1876* (1976); William E. Nelson, *The Americanization of the Common Law: The Impact of Legal Change on Massachusetts Society, 1760–1830* (1975); Leonard W. Levy, *The Law of the Commonwealth and Chief Justice Shaw: The Evolution of American Law, 1830–1860* (1957); Stanley I. Kutler, "John Bannister Gibson: Judicial Restraint and the 'Positive State,' " *Journal of Public Law* 14 (1965); Jean V. Matthews, *Rufus Choate: The Law and Civic Virtue* (1980); Charles M. Cook, *The American Codification Movement: A Study of Antebellum Legal Reform* (1981); John T. Horton, *James Kent: A Study in Conservatism, 1763–1844* (1939).

Jurisprudential tendencies are traced in Perry Miller, *The Life of the Mind in America: From the Revolution to the Civil War* (1965); Roscoe Pound, *The Formative Era of American Law* (1938); Grant Gilmore, *The Ages of American Law* (1977); William E. Nelson, "The Impact of the Antislavery Movement upon Styles of Judicial Reasoning in Nineteenth Century America," *Harvard Law Review* 87 (1974); Morton J. Horwitz, "The Rise of Legal Formalism," *AJLH* 19 (1975); Horwitz, "The Emergence of an Instrumental Conception of American Law, 1780–1820," *Perspectives in American History* 5 (1971); Karl N. Llewellyn, *The Common Law Tradition: Deciding Appeals* (1960); Harry N. Scheiber, "Instrumentalism and Property Rights: A Reconsideration of American 'Styles of Judicial Reasoning' in the 19th Century," *Wisconsin Law Review* (1975).

X. *Slavery, the Constitution and the Crisis of the Union*

The constitutional status of slavery at the beginning of the government and in the early national period is described in William M. Wiecek, *The Sources of Antislavery Constitutionalism in America, 1760–1848* (1977); Wiecek, "*Somerset:* Lord Mansfield and the Legitimacy of Slavery in the Anglo-American World," *University of Chicago Law Review* 42 (1974); David Brion Davis, *The Problem of Slavery in the Age of Revolution, 1770–1823* (1975); Donald L. Robinson, *Slavery in the Structure of American Politics, 1765–1820* (1971); William W. Freehling, "The Founding Fathers and Slavery," *AHR* 77 (1972); Arthur Zilversmit, *The First Emancipation: The Abolition of Slavery in the North* (1967); Howard A. Ohline, "Slavery, Economics, and Congressional Politics, 1790," *JSH* 46 (1980); Walter Berns, "The Constitution and the Migration of Slaves," *Yale Law Journal* 78

(1968). The colonial background for the constitutional acceptance of slavery is discussed in William M. Wiecek, "The Statutory Law of Slavery and Race in the Thirteen Mainland Colonies of British America," *WMQ* 34 (1977), and A. Leon Higginbotham, *In the Matter of Color: Race and the American Legal Process: The Colonial Period* (1978).

Two outstanding accounts of the emergence of slavery as an issue in constitutional politics are Harold M. Hyman and William M. Wiecek, *Equal Justice under Law: Constitutional Development, 1835–1875* (1982), and Don E. Fehrenbacher, *The Dred Scott Case: Its Significance in American Law and Politics* (1978), a far broader work than its title implies. Other valuable accounts are Wiecek, *The Sources of Antislavery Constitutionalism;* Wiecek, "Slavery and Abolition before the United States Supreme Court, 1820–1860," *JAH* 65 (1978); Robert Cover, *Justice Accused: Antislavery and the Judicial Process* (1975); Donald M. Roper, "In Quest of Judicial Objectivity: The Marshall Court and the Legitimation of Slavery," *Stanford Law Review* 21 (1969); John T. Noonan, Jr., *The Antelope: The Ordeal of the Recaptured Africans in the Administration of James Monroe and John Quincy Adams* (1977); Glover Moore, *The Missouri Controversy, 1819–1821* (1953). The constitutional ideas of the abolitionists are described in the book by Wiecek cited above, and in Dwight L. Dumond, *Antislavery: The Crusade for Freedom in America* (1961); Howard Jay Graham, *Everyman's Constitution: Historical Essays on the Fourteenth Amendment, the "Conspiracy Theory," and American Constitutionalism* (1968); Jacobus ten Broek, *The Anti-Slavery Origins of the Fourteenth Amendment* (1951; reprinted as *Equal under Law,* 1965). William S. Jenkins, *Pro-Slavery Thought in the Old South* (1935), and Jesse T. Carpenter, *The South as a Conscious Minority* (1930), perform a similar function for the defenders of slavery.

Among more specialized studies of constitutional controversies over slavery, Thomas D. Morris, *Free Men All: The Personal Liberty Laws of the North, 1780–1861* (1974), is an excellent account of northern attempts to protect free blacks under state law. Paul Finkelman, *An Imperfect Union: Slavery, Federalism, and Comity* (1981), is definitive on interstate conflicts arising over the transit of slaves in free society. On the fugitive slave question, see Joseph C. Burke, "What Did the Prigg Decision Really Decide?" *Pennsylvania Magazine of History and Biography* 93 (1969); Paul Finkelman, "Prigg v. Pennsylvania and Northern State Courts: Anti-Slavery Uses of a Pro-Slavery Decision," *CWH* 25 (1979); Stanley W. Campbell, *The Slave Catchers: Enforcement of the Fugitive Slave Law, 1850–1860* (1968); Levy, *The Law of the Commonwealth and Chief Justice Shaw* (1957); William R. Leslie, "The Influence of Joseph Story's Theory of the Conflict of Laws on Constitutional Nationalism," *MVHR* 35 (1948); Larry Gara, "The Fugitive Slave Law: A Double Paradox," *CWH* 10 (1964); Allen Johnson, "The Constitutionality of the Fugitive Slave Acts," *Yale Law Journal* 31 (1920). Other slavery-related constitutional disputes are discussed in Russell B. Nye, *Fettered Freedoms: Civil Liberties and the Slavery Crisis, 1836–1860* (1949), and Clement Eaton, "Censorship of the Southern Mails," *AHR* 48 (1943).

Studies of politics and ideology in the antebellum era pertinent to an understanding of constitutional struggles over slavery include Eric Foner, *Free Soil, Free Labor, Free Men: The Ideology of the Republican Party before the Civil War* (1970); Richard H. Sewell, *Ballots for Freedom: Antislavery Politics in the United States, 1837–1860* (1976); Chaplain Morrison, *Democratic Politics and Sectionalism: The*

Wilmot Proviso Controversy (1967); Eric Foner, "The Wilmot Proviso Revisited," *JAH* 56 (1969); Michael F. Holt, *The Political Crisis of the 1850s* (1978); J. Mills Thornton, *Politics and Power in a Slave Society: Alabama, 1800–1860* (1978); William R. Brock, *Parties and Political Conscience: American Dilemmas, 1840–1850* (1979); Roy F. Nichols, *The Disruption of the American Democracy* (1948); James B. Stewart, "The Aims and Impact of Garrisonian Abolitionism, 1840–1860," *CWH* 15 (1969).

Allan Nevins, *The Ordeal of the Union*, 2 vols. (1947), Nevins, *The Emergence of Lincoln*, 2 vols. (1952), and David M. Potter, *The Impending Crisis, 1848–1861* (1979), are superior general accounts of the coming of the Civil War. The most perceptive analysis of the problem of slavery expansion into the territories is Arthur Bestor, "State Sovereignty and Slavery: A Reinterpretation of Proslavery Constitutional Doctrine, 1846–1861," *Journal of the Illinois State Historical Society* 54 (1961). See also Allan Nevins, "The Constitution, Slavery, and the Territories," *The Gaspar G. Bacon Lectures on the Constitution of the United States, 1940–1953* (1953).

Popular sovereignty as the solution to the territorial question is sympathetically presented in Robert Johannsen, *Stephen A. Douglas* (1972); Allen Johnson, "The Genesis of Popular Sovereignty," *Iowa Journal of History and Politics* 2 (1905); George Fort Milton, *The Eve of Conflict: Stephen A. Douglas and the Needless War* (1934). Johannsen, "Stephen A. Douglas and the Territories in the Senate," in John Porter Bloom, ed., *The American Territorial System* (1973), reviews the larger issue of territorial policy. Robert R. Russel, "What Was the Compromise of 1850?" *JSH* 22 (1956), is a cogent analysis of the legislative history of popular sovereignty in the Compromise of 1850, while Holman Hamilton, *Prelude to Conflict: The Crisis and Compromise of 1850* (1964), explains the voting alignments which supported the compromise. On the Kansas-Nebraska Act, see Roy F. Nichols, "The Kansas-Nebraska Act: A Century of Historiography," *MVHR* 43 (1956); Robert R. Russell, "The Issues in the Congressional Struggle over the Kansas-Nebraska Bill, 1854," *JSH* 29 (1963); Russell, "Constitutional Doctrines with Regard to Slavery in the Territories," *JSH* 32 (1966); Milo M. Quaife, *The Doctrine of Non-Intervention with Slavery in the Territories* (1910). Events in Kansas are analyzed in James C. Malin, *The Nebraska Question, 1852–1854* (1953), a trenchant and original work; James H. Rawley, *Race and Politics: Bleeding Kansas and the Coming of the Civil War* (1969); David C. Meerse, "Presidential Leadership, Suffrage Qualifications, and Kansas: 1857," *CWH* 24 (1978).

Fehrenbacher, *The Dred Scott Case*, is the most thorough and penetrating account of the Supreme Court's attempt to resolve the question of slavery in the territories. Other studies include Walter Ehrlich, *They Have No Rights: Dred Scott's Struggle for Freedom* (1979), a chronicle tracing the development of the case in minute detail; Vincent Hopkins, *Dred Scott's Case* (1951); Wallace Mendelson, "Dred Scott's Case—Reconsidered," *Minnesota Law Review* 38 (1953); Edward S. Corwin, "The Dred Scott Decision in the Light of Contemporary Legal Doctrines," *AHR* 17 (1911). Frederick S. Allis, Jr., "The Dred Scott Labyrinth," in H. Stuart Hughes, ed., *Teachers of History: Essays in Honor of Lawrence Bradford Packard* (1954), is an able historiographical account. The question of Negro citizenship under state and federal law in the antebellum period is treated in James H. Kettner, *The Development of American Citizenship, 1608–1870* (1978). Although peripheral to the constitutional struggles that dominated national politics in the 1850s, slave law in the states has received careful study by scholars. See, in particular, A. E. Keir Nash, "Reason of Slavery: Understanding the Judicial Role in the Peculiar Institution," *Vanderbilt Law Review* 32 (1979), a book-length monograph that also surveys recent writings in the field. Also useful are Mark Tushnet, "Approaches to the Study of the Law of Slavery," *CWH* 25 (1979), and Tushnet, *The American Law of Slavery 1810–1860: Considerations of Humanity and Interest* (1981). Helen T. Catterall, ed., *Judicial Cases Concerning American Slavery and the Negro,* 5 vols. (1926–37), provides the basic documentary record.

The best analysis of the political and constitutional issues involved in the struggle between Lincoln and Douglas is Harry V. Jaffa, *Crisis of the House Divided: An Interpretation of the Lincoln-Douglas Debates* (1959). Of great value for understanding Lincoln's handling of the territorial question is Don E. Fehrenbacher, *Prelude to Greatness: Lincoln in the 1850s* (1962). Other worthwhile studies of Lincoln and the Republican party are G. S. Boritt, "Was Lincoln a Vulnerable Candidate in 1860?" *CWH* 27 (1981); Donald Reitveld, "Lincoln and the Politics of Morality," *Journal of the Illinois State Historical Society* 68 (1975); William E. Gienapp, "The Crime against Sumner: The Caning of Charles Sumner and the Rise of the Republican Party," *CWH* 25 (1979). Douglas's devotion to popular sovereignty is discussed in Robert W. Johannsen, "Stephen A. Douglas, 'Harpers Magazine,' and Popular Sovereignty," *MVHR* 45 (1959). Able accounts of the disruption of the union after the election of Lincoln are Ralph A. Wooster, *The Secession Conventions of the South* (1962); Dwight L. Dumond, *The Secession Movement, 1860–1861* (1931); Philip S. Klein, *President James Buchanan* (1962); Charles R. Lee, *The Confederate Constitutions* (1963). Among numerous works on the secession crisis the following make significant contributions: David M. Potter, *Lincoln and His Party in the Secession Crisis* (1942); Kenneth M. Stampp, *And the War Came: The North and the Secession Crisis, 1860–1861* (1950); Richard N. Current, *Lincoln and the First Shot* (1963); Harold M. Hyman, "The Narrow Escape from a 'Compromise of 1860': Secession and the Constitution," in Hyman and Leonard W. Levy, eds., *Freedom and Reform: Essays in Honor of Henry Steele Commager* (1967); Robert W. Johannsen, "The Douglas Democracy and the Crisis of Disunion," *CWH* 9 (1963); George H. Knoles, ed., *The Crisis of the Union, 1860–1861* (1965). A. C. Cole, "Lincoln's Election an Immediate Menace to Slavery in the States," *AHR* 36 (1931), and J. G. de R. Hamilton in an article of the same title, *AHR* 37 (1932), debate the impact of the election from northern and southern points of view. Final and futile peace efforts are described in R. G. Gunderson, *Old Gentlemen's Convention: The Washington Peace Conference of 1861* (1961).

XI. *The Civil War and Reconstruction*

There are three excellent general accounts of Civil War constitutional history: Harold M. Hyman and William M. Wiecek, *Equal Justice under Law: Constitutional Development, 1835–1875* (1982); Harold M. Hyman, *A More Perfect Union: The Impact of the Civil War and Reconstruction on the Constitution* (1973); James G. Randall, *Constitutional Problems under Lincoln* (1926; rev. ed., 1951). Arthur Bestor, "The Civil War as a Constitutional Crisis," *AHR* 69 (1964), illuminates the configurative effect of the Constitution in shaping the crisis of the Union. An incisive analysis of northern reasons for resisting secession is Phillip S. Paludan, "The American Civil War Considered as a Crisis in Law and Order," *AHR* 77 (1972).

On the constitutional issues involved in the war, see also Roy F. Nichols, "Federalism *versus* Democracy: The Significance of the Civil War in the History of United States Federalism," in *Federalism as a Democratic Process: Essays by Roscoe Pound, Charles H. McIlwain, and Roy F. Nichols* (1942); Allan Nevins, *The War for the Union*, 4 vols. (1959–71); Carl Russell Fish, *The American Civil War* (1937); William A. Dunning, *Essays on the Civil War and Reconstruction* (1904); John W. Burgess, *The Civil War and the Constitution*, 2 vols. (1901); Peter J. Parish, *The American Civil War* (1975). Eric McKitrick, "Party Politics and the Union and Confederate War Efforts," in W. D. Burnham and W. N. Chambers, eds., *The American Party System: Stages of Political Development* (1967), shows the persistence of organized party activity in northern constitutional politics. Confederate constitutional problems are discussed in Frank L. Owsley, *State Rights in the Confederacy* (1925); Clement Eaton, *A History of the Confederacy* (1954); Emory Thomas, *The Confederate Nation, 1861–1865* (1979).

Lincoln's exercise of presidential power and constitutional outlook are analyzed in James G. Randall, *Lincoln the President*, 4 vols. (1945–55); Randall, "The Rule of Law under Lincoln," in *Lincoln the Liberal Statesman* (1947); Don E. Fehrenbacher, "Lincoln and the Constitution," in Cullom Davis, ed., *The Public and Private Lincoln: Contemporary Perspectives* (1979); Glen E. Thurow, *Abraham Lincoln and American Political Religion* (1976); Clinton L. Rossiter, *Constitutional Dictatorship: Crisis Government in the Modern Democracies* (1948); Dunning, *Essays on the Civil War and Reconstruction;* Andrew C. McLaughlin, "Lincoln, the Constitution, and Democracy," *International Journal of Ethics* 47 (1936); Morgan D. Dowd, "Lincoln, the Rule of Law and Crisis Government: A Study of His Constitutional Law Theories," *University of Detroit Law Journal* 39 (1962); David Donald, "Abraham Lincoln: A Whig in the White House," in *Lincoln Reconsidered: Essays on the Civil War Era* (1961). Lincoln's political thought is dealt with in James A. Rawley, "The Nationalism of Abraham Lincoln," *CWH* 9 (1963); T. Harry Williams, "Abraham Lincoln—Principle and Pragmatism in Politics: A Review Article," *MVHR* 40 (1953); Thomas J. Pressly, "Bullets and Ballots: Lincoln and the 'Right of Revolution,' " *AHR* 67 (1962). William B. Hesseltine, *Lincoln and The War Governors* (1948), and Robert M. Spector, "Lincoln and Taney: A Study in Constitutional Polarization," *AJLH* 15 (1971), describe Lincoln's concentration of power in the federal executive. Gottfried Dietze, *America's Political Dilemma: From Limited to Unlimited Democracy* (1968), is severely critical of Lincoln's exercise of executive power, while Ludwell H. Johnson, "Jefferson Davis and Abraham Lincoln as War Presidents: Nothing Succeeds Like Success," *CWH* 27 (1981), rates Lincoln's presidential performance lower than that of the Confederate president.

Congress during the Civil War is examined in Allan G. Bogue, *The Earnest Men: Republicans of the Civil War Senate* (1981); Hyman, *A More Perfect Union;* Hyman, "Lincoln and Congress: Why Not Congress and Lincoln?" *Journal of the Illinois State Historical Society* 68 (1975); Leonard Curry, *Blueprint for Modern America: Nonmilitary Legislation of the First Civil War Congress* (1968); Wilfrid E. Binkley, *President and Congress* (1962); T. Harry Williams, "Lincoln and the Radicals: An Essay in Civil War History and Historiography," in Grady McWhiney, ed., *Grant, Lee, Lincoln and the Radicals: Essays on Civil War Leadership* (1964); Williams, *Lincoln and the Radicals* (1941); Roy F. Nichols, *Blueprints for Leviathan: American Style* (1963). Emergency government in the legislative branch is dealt with in W. W. Pierson, Jr., "The Committee on the Conduct of the War," *AHR* 22 (1918); T. Harry Williams, "The Committee on the Conduct of the War: An Experiment in Civilian Control," *Journal of the American Military Institute* 3 (1939); Hans L. Trefousse, "The Joint Committee on the Conduct of the War: A Reassessment," *CWH* 10 (1964).

Union internal security policies are dealt with in Hyman, *A More Perfect Union;* Hyman, *Era of the Oath: Northern Loyalty Tests during the Civil War and Reconstruction* (1954); Hyman and Benjamin P. Thomas, *Stanton: The Life and Times of Lincoln's Secretary of War* (1962); Charles Fairman, *The Law of Martial Rule* (1930); William F. Dukes, *A Constitutional History of Habeas Corpus* (1980). On conscription and army organization, see Eugene C. Murdock, *One Million Men: The Civil War Draft in the North* (1971); J. F. Leach, *Conscription in the United States: Historical Background* (1953); Fred A. Shannon, *The Organization and Administration of the Union Army, 1861–1865,* 2 vols. (1928); William B. Weedon, *War Government: Federal and State, 1861–1865* (1906). James F. Childress, "Francis Lieber's Interpretation of the Laws of War: General Orders No. 100 in the Context of His Life and Thought," *American Journal of Jurisprudence* 21 (1976), and Frank Freidel, "General Orders 100 and Military Government," *MVHR* 32 (1946), deal with the problem of restraining military power. Patricia L. M. Lucie, "Confiscation: Constitutional Crossroads," *CWH* 23 (1977), is particularly good on that subject, while William Whiting, *War Powers under the Constitution of the United States* (1871), is a legal treatise dealing with most aspects of wartime constitutionalism. The constitutional results of the war are considered in Harold M. Hyman, "Law and the Impact of the Civil War," *CWH* 14 (1968), and Erwin W. Surrency, "The Legal Effects of the Civil War," *AJLH* 5 (1961).

Emancipation as a constitutional problem and federal policy toward freedmen are described in Randall, *Constitutional Problems under Lincoln;* Herman Belz, *A New Birth of Freedom: The Republican Party and Freedmen's Rights 1861–1866* (1976); Belz, *Emancipation and Equal Rights: Politics and Constitutionalism in the Civil War Era* (1978); Harry V. Jaffa, "The Emancipation Proclamation," in Robert A. Goldwin, ed., *100 Years of Emancipation* (1964); V. Jacque Voegeli, *Free but Not Equal: The Midwest and the Negro during the Civil War* (1967); Louis S. Gerteis, *From Contraband to Freedman: Federal Policy toward Southern Blacks, 1861–1865* (1973); Mary F. Berry, *Military Necessity and Civil Rights Policy: Black Citizenship and the Constitution, 1861–1868* (1977). Lincoln's attitude and actions on the question of freedmen's rights are explored in La Wanda Cox, *Lincoln and Black Freedom: A Study in Presidential Leadership* (1981); Don E. Fehrenbacher, "Only His Stepchildren: Lincoln and the Negro," *CWH* 22 (1974); George M. Fredrickson, "A Man but Not a Brother: Abraham Lincoln and Racial Equality," *JSH* 41 (1975).

The origins of reconstruction as a constitutional problem during the Civil War are discussed in Herman Belz, *Reconstructing the Union: Theory and Policy during the Civil War* (1969). Works dealing with constitutional issues in reconstruction generally are Hyman and Wiecek, *Equal Justice under Law;* Hyman, *A More Per-*

fect Union; Hyman, "Reconstruction and Political-Constitutional Institutions: The Popular Expression," in *New Frontiers of the American Reconstruction* (1966); Michael Les Benedict, *A Compromise of Principle: Congressional Republicans and Reconstruction, 1863–1869* (1974); Dunning, *Essays on the Civil War and Reconstruction.* A special focus on the civil rights question in reconstruction policy is found in Patricia Lucie, "On Being a Free Person and a Citizen by Constitutional Amendment," *Journal of American Studies* 12 (1978); Belz, *Emancipation and Equal Rights;* Belz, "The New Orthodoxy in Reconstruction Historiography," *Reviews in American History* I (1973); Phillip S. Paludan, *A Covenant with Death: The Constitution, Law, and Equality in the Civil War Era* (1975); C. Vann Woodward, "Seeds of Failure in Radical Race Policy," in Hyman, ed., *New Frontiers of the American Reconstruction.* The best general accounts of reconstruction politics are La Wanda Cox and John H. Cox, *Politics, Principle, and Prejudice, 1865–1866: Dilemma of Reconstruction America* (1963); W. R. Brock, *An American Crisis: Congress and Reconstruction, 1865–1867* (1963); David Donald, *The Politics of Reconstruction, 1863–1867* (1965); Eric L. McKitrick, *Andrew Johnson and Reconstruction* (1960); Michael Perman, *Reunion without Compromise: The South and Reconstruction, 1865–1868* (1973); William A. Dunning, *Reconstruction, Political and Economic, 1865–1877* (1907).

The problems of maintaining order and organizing politically acceptable governments in the southern states through the use of military power are dealt with in Harold M. Hyman, "Johnson, Stanton, and Grant: A Reconsideration of the Army's Role in the Events Leading to Impeachment," *AHR* 66 (1960), and James E. Sefton, *The United States Army and Reconstruction, 1865–1877* (1967). The best analyses of the Military Reconstruction Act of 1867 are found in Benedict, *A Compromise of Principle,* and Brock, *An American Crisis.* For the constitutional theories supporting congressional reconstruction policy, see William M. Wiecek, *The Guarantee Clause of the U.S. Constitution* (1972); Benedict, "Preserving the Constitution: The Conservative Basis of Radical Reconstruction," *JAH* 61 (1974); Belz, *Emancipation and Equal Rights;* Phillip S. Paludan, "John Norton Pomeroy: State Rights Nationalist," *AJLH* 12 (1968); Charles Larsen, "Nationalism and States' Rights in Commentaries on the Constitution after the Civil War," *AJLH* 3 (1959). James E. Sefton, *Andrew Johnson and the Uses of Constitutional Power* (1980), and Albert Castel, *The Presidency of Andrew Johnson* (1979), show greater regard for Johnson's constitutional views than most recent historians have. Jonathan T. Dorris, *Pardon and Amnesty under Lincoln and Johnson: The Restoration of the Confederates to Their Rights and Privileges* (1953), discusses that subject in exhaustive detail.

The best accounts of Johnson's impeachment with emphasis on the constitutional dimension are John R. Labovitz, *Presidential Impeachment* (1978); Raoul Berger, *Impeachment: The Constitutional Problem* (1973); Michael Les Benedict, *The Impeachment and Trial of Andrew Johnson* (1973). Worth consulting also are David Miller De Witt, *The Impeachment and Trial of Andrew Johnson* (1903); James E. Sefton, "The Impeachment of Andrew Johnson: A Century of Writing," *CWH* 14 (1968); Hans L. Trefousse, *Impeachment of a President: Andrew Johnson, the Blacks, and Reconstruction* (1975); Martin E. Mantell, *Johnson, Grant, and the Politics of Reconstruction* (1973). Peter C. Hoffer and N. E. H. Hull, "Power and Precedent in the Creation of an American Impeachment Tradition: The Eighteenth

Century Colonial Record," *WMQ* 36 (1979), provides background information.

An extensive literature has developed on the civil rights question in reconstruction. The efforts of the Freedmen's Bureau to deal with the problem are discussed in Donald G. Nieman, *To Set the Law in Motion: The Freedmen's Bureau and the Legal Rights of Blacks, 1865–1868* (1979); James Oakes, "Failure of Vision: The Collapse of the Freedmen's Bureau Courts," *CWH* 25 (1979); Thomas D. Morris, "Equality, 'Extraordinary Law,' and Criminal Justice: The South Carolina Experience, 1865–1866," *South Carolina Historical Magazine* 83 (1982); George R. Bentley, *A History of the Freedmen's Bureau* (1955). The southern states' legislation defining the status of the freedmen is described in Theodore B. Wilson, *The Black Codes of the South* (1965), and Gilbert T. Stephenson, *Race Distinctions in American Law* (1910).

Special attention is accorded the original intention of the framers of the Thirteenth Amendment in Ten Broek, *Equal under Law;* Belz, *A New Birth of Freedom;* G. Sidney Buchanan, *The Quest for Freedom: A Legal History of the Thirteenth Amendment,* reprinted from *Houston Law Review* 12 (1976); Howard Devon Hamilton, "The Legislative History of the Thirteenth Amendment," *National Bar Journal* 9 (1951). The relationship between the Thirteenth Amendment, the Civil Rights Act of 1866, and the Fourteenth Amendment is the focus of Mark De Wolfe Howe, "Federalism and Civil Rights," *Massachusetts Historical Society Proceedings* 77 (1965), and Hyman and Wiecek, *Equal Justice under Law.* Among Fourteenth Amendment studies the following possess special merit: Alfred H. Kelly, "The Fourteenth Amendment Reconsidered: The Segregation Question," *Michigan Law Review* 54 (1956); Alexander M. Bickel, "The Original Understanding and the Segregation Decision," *Harvard Law Review* 69 (1955); Laurent B. Frantz, "Congressional Power to Enforce the Fourteenth Amendment against Private Acts," *Yale Law Journal* 73 (1964); Charles Fairman, "Does the Fourteenth Amendment Incorporate the Bill of Rights?" *Stanford Law Review* 2 (1949); W. W. Crosskey, "Charles Fairman, 'Legislative History,' and the Constitutional Limitations on State Authority," *University of Chicago Law Review* 22 (1954); John P. Frank and Robert F. Munroe, "The Original Understanding of 'Equal Protection of the Law,'" *Columbia Law Review* 50 (1950); Joseph B. James, *The Framing of the Fourteenth Amendment* (1956); Horace E. Flack, *The Adoption of the Fourteenth Amendment* (1908). Howard J. Graham inaugurated the modern study of the Fourteenth Amendment in two path-breaking articles: "The 'Conspiracy Theory' of the Fourteenth Amendment," *Yale Law Journal* 37–38 (1938), which demolished the argument that the framers of the amendment intended to protect corporations, and "The Early Anti-Slavery Backgrounds of the Fourteenth Amendment," *Wisconsin Law Review* 23 (1950), which identified prewar abolitionism as the source of the civil rights prescriptions written into Section 1 of the amendment. These articles are reprinted in Graham, *Everyman's Constitution* (1968). On the economic interpretation of the Fourteenth Amendment, see also Andrew C. McLaughlin, "The Court, the Corporation, and Conkling," *AHR* 46 (1940); Louis B. Boudin, "Truth and Fiction about the Fourteenth Amendment," *New York University Law Quarterly Review* 16 (1938); James F. S. Russell, "The Railroads and the 'Conspiracy Theory' of the Fourteenth Amendment," *MVHR* 41 (1955). Raoul Berger, *Government by Judiciary* (1977), adopts a narrow view of the purpose of the Fourteenth Amendment in a tendentious work attacking contemporary judicial activism.

The relevant modern study of the framing of the Fifteenth Amendment is William Gillette, *The Right to Vote: Politics and the Passage of the Fifteenth Amendment* (1965). Its emphasis on political expediency is challenged in La Wanda Cox and John H. Cox, "Negro Suffrage and Republican Politics: The Problem of Motivation in Reconstruction Historiography," *JSH* 33 (1967). Federal enforcement of civil and political rights in the 1870s is dealt with in Alfred Avins, "The Ku Klux Act of 1871: Some Reflected Light on State Action and the Fourteenth Amendment," *St. Louis University Law Journal* 11 (1967); William Gillette, "Anatomy of a Failure: Federal Enforcement of the Right to Vote in the Border States during Reconstruction," in Richard L. Curry, ed., *Radicalism, Racism, and Party Realignment: The Border States during Reconstruction* (1969); Everette Swinney, "Enforcing the Fifteenth Amendment, 1870–1877," *JSH* 28 (1962); Albie Burke, "Federal Regulation of Congressional Elections in Northern Cities, 1871–1894," *AJLH* 14 (1970); Richard L. Claude, *The Supreme Court and the Electoral Process* (1970); J. M. Mathew, *Legislative and Judicial History of the Fifteenth Amendment* (1909); Bertram Wyatt-Brown, "The Civil Rights Act of 1875," *Western Pol. Q.* 18 (1965); Alfred H. Kelly, "The Congressional Controversy over School Segregation, 1867–1875," *AHR* 64 (1959); Alfred Avins, "The Civil Rights Act of 1875: Some Reflected Light on the Fourteenth Amendment and Public Accommodations," *Columbia Law Review* 66 (1966); John Hope Franklin, "Enforcement of the Civil Rights Act of 1875," *Prologue* 6 (1974).

On the judiciary generally during the Civil War and reconstruction, see Stanley I. Kutler, *Judicial Power and Reconstruction Politics* (1958); Charles Fairman, *History of the Supreme Court of the United States*, vol. 6: *Reconstruction and Reunion, 1864–88: Part One* (1971); David M. Silver, *Lincoln's Supreme Court* (1956); William M. Wiecek, "The Reconstruction of Federal Judicial Power: 1863–1875," *AJLH* 13 (1969); Wiecek, "The Great Writ and Reconstruction: The Habeas Corpus Act of 1867," *JSH* 36 (1970); J. David Hoeveler, Jr., "Reconstruction and the Federal Courts: The Civil Rights Act of 1875," *Historian* 31 (1969); John V. Orth, "The Eleventh Amendment and the North Carolina State Debt," *North Carolina Law Review* 59 (1981); C. Peter Magrath, *Morrison R. Waite: The Triumph of Character* (1963); Warren, *The Supreme Court in United States History;* Boudin, *Government by Judiciary.* Judicial interpretation of civil rights is the focus of Robert J. Harris, *The Quest for Equality: The Constitution, Congress and the Supreme Court* (1960); John Anthony Scott, "Justice Bradley's Evolving Concept of the Fourteenth Amendment from the Slaughterhouse Cases to the Civil Rights Cases," *Rutgers Law Review* 25 (1971); Ira Nerken, "A New Deal for the Protection of Fourteenth Amendment Rights: Challenging the Doctrinal Basis of the Civil Rights Cases and State Action Theory," *Harvard Civil Rights–Civil Liberties Law Review* 12 (1977); Milton R. Konvitz, *A Century of Civil Rights* (1961); M. L. Benedict, "Preserving Federalism: Reconstruction and the Waite Court," *Supreme Court Review 1978* (1979).

Constitutional change in the former Confederate states is treated in Jack B. Scroggs, "Carpetbagger Constitutional Reform in the South Atlantic States, 1867–1868," *JSH* 27 (1961), and Richard L. Hume, "Carpetbaggers in the Reconstruction South: A Group Portrait of Outside Whites in the 'Black and Tan' Constitutional Conventions," *JAH* 64 (1977). Valuable studies of reconstruction politics in the South are William Gillette, *Retreat from Reconstruction, 1869–1879* (1979); William

R. Brock, "Reconstruction and the American Party System," and Otto H. Olsen, "Southern Reconstruction and the Question of Self-Determination," in George M. Fredrickson, ed., *A Nation Divided: Problems and Issues of the Civil War and Reconstruction* (1975). C. Vann Woodward, *Reunion and Reaction: The Compromise of 1877 and the End of Reconstruction* (1951), has long been the standard account of that subject but it is challenged in Allen Peskin, "Was There a Compromise of 1877?" *JAH* 60 (1973); Keith Polakoff, *The Politics of Inertia: The Election of 1876 and the End of Reconstruction* (1973); Michael Les Benedict, "Southern Democrats in the Crisis of 1876–1877: A Reconsideration of *Reunion and Reaction*," *JSH* 46 (1980). See also the older work of Paul L. Haworth, *The Hayes-Tilden Disputed Presidential Election of 1876* (1906). The condition of Negro civil liberty in the aftermath of reconstruction is discussed in William Cohen, "Negro Involuntary Servitude in the South, 1865–1940: A Preliminary Analysis," *JSH* 42 (1976); Howard N. Rabinowitz, "From Exclusion to Segregation: Southern Race Relations, 1865–1890," *JAH* 63 (1976); Pete Daniel, "The Metamorphosis of Slavery, 1865–1900," *JAH* 66 (1979). Judicious assessments of reconstruction are provided in Eric McKitrick, "Reconstruction: Ultraconservative Revolution," in C. Vann Woodward, ed., *The Comparative Approach to American History* (1968); Phillip S. Paludan, "The American Civil War: Triumph through Tragedy," *CWH* 20 (1974); Cox, "Reflections on the Limits of the Possible," in *Lincoln and Black Freedom.*

XII. *The Constitutional System in the Late Nineteenth Century*

Morton Keller, *Affairs of State: Public Life in Late Nineteenth Century America* (1977), is a comprehensive account of law, politics, and administration at the federal and state levels. Its magisterial scope recalls James Bryce's classic work *The American Commonwealth*, 3 vols. (1888). An important study of the role of state government is Ballard C. Campbell, *Representative Democracy: Public Policy and Midwestern Legislatures in the Late Nineteenth Century* (1980). Worthwhile also for a general overview of the period are Loren Beth, *The Development of the American Constitution 1877–1917* (1971); Charles E. Merriam, *American Political Ideas: Studies in the Development of American Political Thought, 1865–1917* (1920); Edward R. Lewis, *A History of American Political Thought from the Civil War to the World War* (1937). Concerned especially with the emergence of a critical realistic attitude in the constitutional thought of the period are Herman Belz, "The Constitution in the Gilded Age: The Beginnings of Constitutional Realism in American Scholarship," *ALJH* 13 (1969); Martin Landau, "The Myth of Hyperfactionalism in the Study of American Politics," *PSQ* 83 (1968); Christopher Wolfe, "Woodrow Wilson: Interpreting the Constitution," *Review of Politics* 41 (1979).

The standard work on the interactions between president, Congress, and administration in this period is Leonard D. White, *The Republican Era: A Study in Administrative History, 1869–1901* (1958). Other works dealing generally with this subject include Corwin, *The President: Office and Powers:* Binkley, *President and Congress;* Stephen Horn, *The Cabinet and Congress* (1960); Paul P. Van Riper, *A History of the United States Civil Service* (1958); Woodrow Wilson, *Congressional Government* (1885); Dorothy G. Fowler, *The Cabinet Politician: The Postmasters*

General, 1829–1909 (1943); Henry Jones Ford, *The Rise and Growth of American Politics* (1898); Homer Cummings and Carl McFarland, *Federal Justice: Chapters in the History of Justice and the Federal Executive* (1937).

David Rothman, *Politics and Power: The U.S. Senate, 1869–1901* (1966), describes the more disciplined organizational politics that superseded the ideological conflict of the Civil War era. Additional studies of Congress are Nelson Polsby, "The Institutionalization of the House of Representatives," *APSR* 62 (1968); Neil McNeil, *Forge of Democracy: The House of Representatives* (1963); George B. Galloway, *History of the House of Representatives* (1961); George H. Haynes, *The Senate of the United States: Its History and Practice,* 2 vols. (1938); W. A. Robinson, *Thomas B. Reed: Parliamentarian* (1930); De Alva Stanwood Alexander, *History and Procedure of the House of Representatives* (1916); Oscar Kraines, "The Cockrell Committee 1887–1889; The First Comprehensive Congressional Investigation into Administration," *Western Pol. Q.* 4 (1951).

A thorough reassessment of political parties in the late nineteenth century has occurred in the past two decades as historians have rejected the older economic interpretation of American history. Outstanding examples of the revisionist view, which stresses ethnocultural as well as economic group conflict, are Paul Kleppner, *The Third Electoral System, 1853–1892: Parties, Voters, and Political Cultures* (1979); Kleppner, *The Cross of Culture: A Social Analysis of Midwestern Politics, 1850–1900* (1970); Richard Jensen, *The Winning of the Midwest: Social and Economic Conflict, 1888–1896* (1971); Samuel T. McSeveney, *The Politics of Depression: Political Behavior in the Northeast, 1893–1896* (1972); Richard L. McCormick, "Ethno-cultural Interpretations of Nineteenth Century American Voting Behavior," *PSQ* 89 (1974). The concept of critical elections and electoral realignment has also been a dominant motif in recent accounts of party history. See Walter Dean Burnham, "The Changing Shape of the American Political Universe," *APSR* 59 (1965); Burnham, "Party Systems and the Political Process," in Burnham and W. N. Chambers, eds., *The American Party Systems: Stages of Political Development* (1967); Burnham, *Critical Elections and the Mainsprings of American Politics* (1970); James L. Sundquist, *Dynamics of the Party System: Alignment and Realignment of Political Parties in the United States* (1973); V. O. Key, "A Theory of Critical Elections," *JP* 17 (1955); Key, "Secular Realignment and the Party System," *JP* 21 (1959).

Also of value for understanding parties in the late nineteenth century are Samuel P. Hays, "Political Parties and the Community–Society Continuum," in Burnham and Chambers, eds., *The American Party Systems;* Robert D. Marcus, *Grand Old Party: Political Structure in the Gilded Age, 1880–1896* (1971); J. Morgan Kousser, *The Shaping of Southern Politics: Suffrage Restriction and the Establishment of the One-Party South, 1880–1910* (1974); Stephen L. Hansen, *The Making of the Third Party System: Voters and Parties in Illinois 1850–1876* (1980); Jerome L. Sternstein, "The Problem of Corruption in the Gilded Age: The Case of Nelson W. Aldrich and the Sugar Trust," in A. S. Eisenstadt *et al.,* eds., *Before Watergate: Problems of Corruption in American Society* (1978); Peter H. Argersinger, " 'A Place on the Ballot': Fusion Politics and Antifusion Laws," *AHR* 85 (1980); Morton Keller, "The Politicos Reconsidered," *Perspectives in American History* 1 (1967). The older progressive view of late nineteenth-century politics can be found in Matthew Josephson, *The Politicos, 1865–1896* (1938), and John D. Hicks, *The Pop-*

ulist Revolt (1930). It is updated in Lawrence Goodwyn, *Democratic Promise: The Populist Moment in America* (1976).

Richard L. McCormick, "The Party Period and Public Policy: An Exploratory Hypothesis, *JAH* 66 (1979), evaluates the programmatic function of parties in relation to their constituent and cultural function. The activist role of government in economic affairs in the late nineteenth century is discussed in Campbell, *Representative Democracy;* Harry N. Scheiber, "Regulation, Property Rights, and Definition of 'The Market': Law and the American Economy," *Journal of Economic History* 41 (1981); Scheiber, "Property Law, Expropriations, and Resource Allocation by Government: The United States, 1789–1910," *Journal of Economic History* 33 (1973); Lance E. Davis and John Legler, "The Government in the American Economy, 1815–1902: A Quantitative Study," *Journal of Economic History* 26 (1966); Robert A. Lively, "The American System: A Review Article," *Business History Review* 29 (1955). See also the works by Lowi and Hurst cited in Section IX.

The growing importance of public administration in the late nineteenth century can be seen in Woodrow Wilson's classic essay, "The Study of Administration," *PSQ* 2 (1887). Accounts of the implementation of governmental policy showing the problematic nature of public administration include Wallace D. Farnham, " 'The Weakened Spring of Government': A Study in Nineteenth-Century American History," *AHR* 68 (1963); Leslie E. Decker, "The Railroads and the Land Office: Administrative Policy and the Land Patent Controversy, 1864–1896," *MVHR* 46 (1960); Decker, *Railroads, Lands, and Politics: The Taxation of the Railroad Land Grants, 1864–1897* (1964); Harold H. Dunham, *Government Handout: A Study in the Administration of the Public Lands 1875–1891* (1941). Corruption and reform in politics and administration are treated in Ari Hoogenboom, *Outlawing the Spoils: A History of the Civil Service Reform Movement 1865–1883* (1961); Hoogenboom, "Did the Gilded Age Scandals Bring Reform?" in Eisenstadt *et al.*, eds., *Before Watergate;* Eric McKitrick, "The Study of Corruption," *PSQ* 72 (1957).

A general examination of the movement for national regulation of the economy is Stephen Skowronek, *Building a New American State: The Expansion of National Administrative Capacities, 1877–1920* (1982). Much study has been devoted to the politics, social sources, and economic rationale of railroad regulation. The best accounts dealing with these issues are Albro Martin, "The Troubled Subject of Railroad Regulation in the Gilded Age—A Reappraisal," *JAH* 61 (1974); George W. Hilton, "The Consistency of the Interstate Commerce Act," *Journal of Law and Economics* 9 (1966); Robert W. Harbeson, "Railroads and Regulation, 1877–1916: Conspiracy or Public Interest?" *Journal of Economic History* 27 (1967); George H. Miller, *Railroads and the Granger Laws* (1973); Edward A. Purcell, Jr., "Ideas and Interests: Businessmen and the Interstate Commerce Act, *JAH* 54 (1967); Gabriel Kolko, *Railroads and Regulation, 1877–1916* (1965); Edwin R. A. Seligman, "Railway Tariffs and the Interstate Commerce Law," *PSQ* 2 (1887); Lee Benson, *Merchants, Farmers and Railroads: Railroad Regulation and New York Politics: 1850–1887* (1955); Robert B. Carson, "Railroads and Regulation Revisited: A Note on Problems of Historiography and Ideology," *Historian* 34 (1972). The difficulties faced by the ICC in its early years are analyzed in Ari Hoogenboom and Olive Hoogenboom, *A History of the Interstate Commerce Commission: From Panacea to Palliative* (1976); Robert E. Cushman, *The Independent*

Regulatory Commissions (1941); I. W. Sharfman, *The Interstate Commerce Commission,* 5 vols. (1931–37); Alan Jones, "Thomas M. Cooley and the Interstate Commerce Commission: Continuity and Change in the Doctrine of Equal Rights," *PSQ* 81 (1966).

Charles L. McCurdy, "The Knight Sugar Decision of 1895 and the Modernization of American Corporation Law, 1869–1903," *Business History Review* 53 (1979), analyzes the purpose of the Sherman Antitrust Act in relation to state efforts to regulate corporations. More comprehensive treatments of this subject are Robert H. Bork, *The Antitrust Paradox: A Policy at War with Itself* (1978); William Letwin, *Law and Economic Policy in America: The Evolution of the Sherman Anti-trust Act* (1965); Hans Thorelli, *The Federal Anti-Trust Policy: Origination of an American Tradition* (1955). For discussion of the context of social and political thought in which the antitrust law was adopted, see Sidney Fine, *Laissez Faire and the General Welfare State* (1956); Richard Hofstadter, "What Happened to the Antitrust Movement?" in *The Paranoid Style in Politics and Other Essays* (1965); Sanford D. Gordon, "Attitudes toward Trusts Prior to the Sherman Act," *Southern Economic Journal* 30 (1960).

Territorial administration after the Civil War is the subject of Jack E. Eblen, *The First and Second United States Empires: Governors and Territorial Government, 1784–1912* (1968), and Earl S. Pomeroy, *The Territories and the United States, 1861–1890: Studies in Colonial Administration* (1947).

The following works provide an introduction to constitutional problems in federal Indian policy in the nineteenth century: Wilcomb E. Washburn, *Red Man's Land/White Man's Law: A Study of the Past and Present Status of the American Indian* (1971); Washburn, "The Historical Context of American Indian Legal Problems," *Law and Contemporary Problems* 40 (1976); Howard R. Berman, "The Concept of Aboriginal Rights in the Early Legal History of the United States," *Buffalo Law Review* 27 (1978); Frederick J. Martone, "American Indian Tribal Self-Government in the Federal System: Inherent Right or Congressional License?" *Notre Dame Lawyer* 51 (1976); Bernard W. Sheehan, *Seeds of Extinction: Jeffersonian Philanthrophy and the American Indian* (1973); Ronald N. Satz, *American Indian Policy in the Jacksonian Era* (1975); Francis Paul Prucha, *American Indian Policy in the Formative Years: The Indian Trade and Intercourse Acts, 1780–1834* (1962); Grant Foreman, *Indian Removal: The Emigration of the Five Civilized Tribes of Indians* (1953); Robert A. Trennert, Jr., *Alternative to Extinction: Federal Indian Policy and the Beginning of the Reservation System, 1846–51* (1975); Henry E. Fritz, *The Movement for Indian Assimilation, 1860–1890* (1963); Loring Benson Priest, *Uncle Sam's Stepchildren: The Reformation of United States Indian Policy, 1865–1887* (1942); Francis Paul Prucha, *American Indian Policy in Crisis: Christian Reformers and the Indians, 1865–1900* (1975); Paul Stuart, *The Indian Office: Growth and Development of an American Institution* (1979); William T. Hagan, *Indian Police and Courts: Experiments in Acculturation and Control* (1966); D. S. Otis, *The Dawes Act and the Allotment of Indian Lands* (1934, 1972). Indian policy in the twentieth century is described in Hagan, *American Indians* (1961). Russell L. Barsh and James Y. Henderson, *The Road: Indian Tribes and Political Liberty* (1980), is an impassioned argument for tribal political rights within the federal system that contains useful information about the recent history of Indian policy.

Constitutional aspects of territorial annexation and colonial administration after the Spanish-American War are treated in Jose A. Cabranes, *Citizenship and the American Empire: Notes on the Legislative History of the United States Citizenship of Puerto Ricans* (1979; orig. published in *University of Pennsylvania Law Review* 127 [1978]); Whitney T. Perkins, *Denial of Empire: The United States and Its Dependencies* (1962); Julius W. Pratt, *America's Colonial Experiment: How the United States Gained, Governed, and in Part Gave Away a Colonial Empire* (1950); W. F. Willoughby, *Territories and Dependencies of the United States: Their Government and Administration* (1905); David Y. Thomas, *A History of Military Government in Newly Acquired Territory of the United States* (1904). Four excellent contemporary legal analyses of the insular problem remain pertinent: C. C. Langdell, "The Status of Our New Territories," *Harvard Law Review* 12 (1899); Simeon E. Baldwin, "The Constitutional Questions Incident to the Acquisition by the United States of Island Territory," *Harvard Law Review* 12 (1899); A Lawrence Lowell, "The Status of Our New Possessions— a Third View," *Harvard Law Review* 13 (1899); Frederick R. Coudert, "The Evolution of the Doctrine of Territorial Incorporation," *Columbia Law Review* 26 (1926). The relationship between Indian policy and colonialism is pointed out in Walter L. Williams, "United States Indian Policy and the Debate over Philippine Annexation: Implications for the Origins of American Imperialism," *JAH* 66 (1980).

XIII. *Constitutional Law in the Late Nineteenth Century*

A number of recent works refute the long-entrenched progressive view of the late nineteenth-century judiciary as apologists for and defenders of laissez-faire capitalism. The best of the revisionist accounts are Charles W. McCurdy, "Justice Field and the Jurisprudence of Government-Business Relations: Some Parameters of Laissez-Faire Constitutionalism, 1863–1897," *JAH* 61 (1975); Mary Cornelia Porter, "That Commerce Shall Be Free: A New Look at the Old Laissez-Faire Court," *Supreme Court Review 1976* (1977); Alan Jones, "Thomas M. Cooley and Laissez Faire Constitutionalism: A Reconsideration," *JAH* 53 (1967). Other works in a revisionist vein are Robert Goedecke, "Justice Field and Inherent Rights," *Review of Politics* 27 (1965); Robert E. Garner, "Justice Brewer and Substantive Due Process: A Conservative Court Revisited," *Vanderbilt Law Review* 18 (1965); Walter F. Pratt, "Rhetorical Styles on the Fuller Court," *AJLH* 24 (1980), refuting the assumption that legal formalism adequately describes the outlook of the Supreme Court in the late nineteenth century; Charles C. Goetsch, "The Future of Legal Formalism," *AJLH* 24 (1980), an appraisal of the conservative jurist Simeon E. Baldwin.

Arnold M. Paul, *Conservative Crisis and the Rule of Law: Attitudes of Bar and Bench, 1887–1895* (1960), is a fine study in the progressive tradition which explains the judicial acceptance of laissez-faire constitutionalism by reference to threats to the established order in the 1890s. Written from the same perspective are John P. Roche, "Entrepreneurial Liberty and the Commerce Power: Expansion, Contraction, and Casuistry in the Age of Enterprise," *University of Chicago Law Review* 30 (1963); Loren P. Beth, *The Development of the American Constitution, 1877–1917* (1971), chapters dealing with the judiciary; William F. Swindler, *Court and Constitution in the Twentieth Century: The Old Legality, 1889–1932* (1969). Many of the standards works of progressive historiography deal with this period, including Charles Grove Haines, *The Doctrine of Judicial Supremacy* (1911; rev. ed., 1932); Edward S. Corwin, *Liberty against Government: The Rise, Flowering, and Decline of a Famous Juridical Concept* (1948); Corwin, *Court over Constitution* (1938); Corwin, *Twilight of the Supreme Court* (1934); Corwin, *The Commerce Power versus States Rights* (1936); Benjamin R. Twiss, *Lawyers and the Constitution: How Laissez Faire Came to the Supreme Court* (1942); Clyde E. Jacobs, *Law Writers and the Courts: The Influence of Thomas M. Cooley, Christopher M. Tiedeman, and John E. Dillon upon American Constitutional Law* (1954); Carl B. Swisher, *Stephen J. Field: Craftsman of the Law* (1930).

Worthwhile biographical accounts of late nineteenth-century justices are Charles Fairman, *Mr. Justice Miller and the Supreme Court, 1862–1890* (1939); C. Peter Magrath, *Morrison R. Waite: The Triumph of Character* (1963); Willard L. King, *Melville Weston Fuller* (1950); Bruce R. Trimble, *Chief Justice Waite: Defender of the Public Interest* (1938); Fairman, "What Makes a Great Justice? Mr. Justice Bradley and the Supreme Court, 1870–1892," *Boston University Law Review* 30 (1950); Alan F. Westin, "John Marshall Harlan and the Constitutional Rights of Negroes: The Transformation of a Southerner," *Yale Law Journal* 66 (1957); Loren P. Beth, "Justice Harlan and the Uses of Dissent," *APSR* 49 (1955); Henry J. Abraham, "John Marshall Harlan: A Justice Neglected," *Virginia Law Review* 41 (1955); Floyd B. Clark, *Constitutional Doctrines of Justice Harlan* (1915); D. Grier Stephenson, Jr., "The Chief Justice as Leader: The Case of Morrison R. Waite," *William and Mary Law Review* 14 (1973); Robert B. Highsaw, *Edward Douglas White: Defender of the Conservative Faith* (1981); Howard J. Graham, "Justice Field and the Fourteenth Amendment," *Yale Law Journal* 52 (1943); Wallace Mendelson, "Mr. Justice Field and Laissez-faire," *Virginia Law Review* 36 (1950); Alan F. Westin, "Stephen J. Field and the Headnote to O'Neill v. Vermont: A Snapshot of the Fuller Court at Work," *Yale Law Journal* 67 (1958); F. Bergan, "Mr. Justice Brewer: Perspective of a Century," *Albany Law Review* 25 (1961).

The development of substantive due process under the Fourteenth Amendment is the subject of several classic articles: Edward S. Corwin, "The Supreme Court and the Fourteenth Amendment," *Michigan Law Review* 7 (1909); Robert E. Cushman, "The Social and Economic Development of the Fourteenth Amendment," *Michigan Law Review* 20 (1922); Charles Grove Haines, "Judicial Review of Legislation in the United States and the Doctrine of Vested Rights," *Texas Law Review* 2–3 (1924); Walton H. Hamilton, "The Path of Due Process of Law," *Ethics* 48 (1938), reprinted in Conyers Read, ed., *The Constitution Reconsidered* (1938); Roscoe Pound, "Liberty of Contract," *Yale Law Journal* 18 (1909). Pertinent also are Rodney L. Mott, *Due Process of Law* (1926); Loren P. Beth, "The Slaughterhouse Cases," *Louisiana Law Review* 23 (1963); Keith Jurow, "Untimely Thoughts: A Reconsideration of the Origins of Due Process of Law," *AJLH* 19 (1975); L. A. Powe, Jr., "Rehearsal for Substantive Due Process: The Municipal Bond Cases," *Texas Law Review* 58 (1975). The contrast between property rights and women's rights in the interpretation of the Fourteenth Amendment is underscored in Charles E. Corker, "*Bradwell v. State:* Some Reflections Prompted by Myra Bradwell's Hard Case That Made 'Bad Law,'" *Washington Law Review* 53 (1978).

There are rewarding discussions of judicial regulation of commerce and industry in Harry N. Scheiber, "The Road to Munn: Eminent Domain and the

Concept of Public Purpose in the State Courts," *Perspectives in American History* 5 (1971); Charles Fairman, "The So-Called Granger Cases, Lord Hale, and Justice Bradley," *Stanford Law Review* 5 (1953); Breck P. McAllister, "Lord Hale and Business Affected with a Public Interest," *Harvard Law Review* 43 (1930); Charles W. McCurdy, "American Law and the Marketing Structure of the Large Corporation, 1875–1890," *Journal of Economic History* 38 (1978). On the Sherman Act and its application in the 1890s, see Charles W. McCurdy, "The Knight Sugar Decision of 1895 and the Modernization of American Corporation Law, 1869–1903," *Business History Review* 53 (1979), a perspective and illuminating study, and Joe A. Fisher, "The Knight Case Revisited," *Historian* 35 (1973).

Important insights concerning the nature and extent of judicial power following the acceptance of substantive due process are provided in Morton Keller, *Affairs of State: Public Life in Late Nineteenth Century America* (1977); Christopher Wolfe, "A Theory of U.S. Constitutional History," *JP* 43 (1981); Wallace Mendelson, "The Politics of Judicial Supremacy," *Journal of Law and Economics* 4 (1961); Stuart S. Nagel, "Political Parties and Judicial Review in American History," *Journal of Public Law* 11 (1962); G. Edward White, *The American Judicial Tradition: Profiles of Leading American Judges* (1976); Robert G. McCloskey, *The American Supreme Court* (1960); McCloskey, *American Conservatism in the Age of Enterprise, 1865–1910* (1951); Alan Westin, "The Supreme Court, the Populist Movement and the Campaign of 1896," *JP* 15 (1953). Two contemporary essays of great value for understanding the new judicial review of the 1890s are James Bradley Thayer, "The Origin and Scope of the American Doctrine of Constitutional Law," *Harvard Law Review* 7 (1893), and Charles E. Shattuck, "The True Meaning of the Term 'Liberty' in Those Clauses in the Federal and State Constitutions Which Protect Life, Liberty, and Property," *Harvard Law Review* 4 (1891).

XIV. *The Constitution in an Age of Transition, 1900–1930*

The best introduction to progressive constitutional thought, emphasizing reformers' quest for positive government and reliance on new techniques of public administration, is M. J. C. Vile, "Progressivism and Political Science in America," in *Constitutionalism and the Separation of Powers* (1967). Richard L. McCormick, "The Discovery That 'Business Corrupts Politics': A Reappraisal of the Origins of Progressivism," *AHR* 86 (1981), effectively reasserts and links the older liberal democratic interpretation of progressive reform with the newer view which regards bureaucratic-administrative management as the essential purpose of progressivism. Good examples of the older view are Edward R. Lewis, *A History of American Political thought from the Civil War to the World War* (1937); Charles E. Merriam, *American Political Ideas: Studies in the Development of American Political Thought, 1865–1917* (1920); Charles McKinley, "The Constitution and the Tasks Ahead," *APSR* 49 (1955); J. Allen Smith, *The Spirit of American Government; A Study of the Constitution: Its Origin, Influence, and Relation to Democracy* (1907; Herbert Croly, *The Promise of American Life* (1909); Croly, *Progressive Democracy* (1914); Frank J. Goodnow, *Social Reform and the Constitution* (1911). The bureaucratic-managerial interpretation of progressivism is best represented by Robert L. Wiebe, *The Search for Order, 1877–1920* (1967), a general survey which contains valuable dis-

cussions of government and administration, and Louis Galambos, "The Emerging
Organizational Synthesis in Modern American History," *Business History Review*
44 (1970). The managerial thesis is given a Marxian application in Gabriel Kolko,
The Triumph of Conservatism 1900–1916 (1963).

David P. Thelen, *The New Citizenship: Origins of Progressivism in Wisconsin,*
1885–1900 (1972), stresses popular sovereignty and opposition to special privilege
as the central themes of the reform movement. There are thoughtful interpretations
also in Thomas K. McCraw, "The Progressive Legacy," in Lewis L. Gould, ed., *The*
Progressive Era (1974), and Otis A. Pease, "Urban Reformers in the Progressive
Era," *Pacific Northwest Quarterly* 62 (1971). Theoretical tendencies in reform constitutionalism are described in Bernard Crick, *The American Science of Politics*
(1959); Herman Belz, "The Realist Critique of Constitutionalism in the Era of
Reform," *AJLH* 15 (1971); Paul F. Bourke, "The Pluralist Reading of Madison's
Tenth *Federalist,*" *Perspectives in American History* 9 (1975). Austin Ranney, *The*
Doctrine of Responsible Party Government: Its Origins and Present State (1954),
analyzes the thought of leading progressives on political parties. Calvin Woodard,
"Reality and Social Reform: The Transition from Laissez-Faire to the Welfare
State," *Yale Law Journal* 72 (1962), is a penetrating examination of key changes in
the meaning of basic political and constitutional concepts in the early twentieth
century.

Students of the regulatory movement and government-business relations have
debated the extent to which regulation served the needs of corporations and other
economic groups or promoted the public interest. An excellent guide to this controversy is Thomas K. McCraw, "Regulation in America: A Review Article," *Busi-*
ness History Review 49 (1975). The issues and evidence considered in the debate can
be traced in Thomas K. McCraw, ed., *Regulation in Perspective* (1982); Robert L.
Wiebe, *Businessmen and Reform: A Study of the Progressive Movement* (1962);
Jonathan Lurie, "Private Associations, Internal Regulation and Progressivism: The
Chicago Board of Trade as a Case Study," *AJLH* 16 (1972); Stanley P. Caine, *The*
Myth of Progressive Reform: Railroad Regulation in Wisconsin 1903–1910 (1970);
John H. Garvey, "Judicial Consideration of the Delegation of Legislative Power to
Regulatory Agencies in the Progressive Era," *Indiana Law Journal* 54 (1978);
Marver H. Bernstein, *Regulating Business by Independent Commission* (1955);
Oscar E. Anderson, Jr., "The Pure-Food Issue: A Republican Dilemma 1906–
1912," *AHR* 61 (1956); Bruce W. Dearstyne, "Regulation in the Progressive Era:
The New York Public Service Commission," *New York History* 58 (1977); Melvin
I. Urofsky, *Big Steel and the Wilson Administration: A Study in Business-Govern-*
ment Relations (1969); Arthur M. Johnson, *Government-Business Relations: A Prag-*
matic Approach to the American Experience (1965); Johnson, "Anti-trust Policy in
Transition, 1908: Ideal and Reality," *MVHR* 48 (1961); Johnson, "Theodore Roosevelt and the Bureau of Corporations," *MVHR* 45 (1959). On the two agencies
which have received the closest study in relation to this issue, see Douglas Walter
Jaenicke, "Herbert Croly, Progressive Ideology, and the FTC Act," *PSQ* 93 (1978);
G. Cullom Davis, "The Transformation of the Federal Trade Commission, 1914–
1929," *MVHR* 49 (1962); Gabriel Kolko, *Railroads and Regulation, 1877–1916*
(1965); Richard H. K. Vietor, "Businessmen and the Political Economy: The Railroad Rate Controversy of 1905," *JAH* 64 (1977); Albro Martin, *Enterprise Denied:*
Origins of the Decline of American Railroads, 1897–1917 (1971); Ari Hoogenboom

and Olive Hoogenboom, *A History of the ICC: From Panacea to Palliative* (1976); George E. Dix, "The Death of the Commerce Court: A Study in Institutional Weakness," *AJLH* 8 (1964). Also pertinent are older administrative histories: Carl McFarland, *Judicial Control of the Federal Trade Commission and the Interstate Commerce Commission 1920–1930* (1933); Thomas C. Blaisdell, *The Federal Trade Commission* (1932), I. L. Sharfman, *The Interstate Commerce Commission,* 5 vols. (1931–37); Robert E. Cushman, *The Independent Regulatory Commissions* (1941); W. O. Weymouth, *The Federal Reserve Board* (1933). The judicial reaction to the emerging regulatory state is the subject of John Dickinson, *Administrative Justice and the Supremacy of Law in the United States* (1927).

Important developments in the history of the presidency during the progressive era are analyzed in John Morton Blum, *The Republican Roosevelt* (1954); William Harbaugh, *Power and Responsibility: The Life and Times of Theodore Roosevelt* (1961); Robert L. Wiebe, "The House of Morgan and the Executive, 1905–1913," *AHR* 65 (1959). Woodrow Wilson's contribution to the modern presidency is treated in Earl Latham, ed., *The Philosophy and Policies of Woodrow Wilson* (1958), a collection of essays; Arthur Link, *Woodrow Wilson: The New Freedom* (1956); Arthur W. MacMahon, "Woodrow Wilson as Legislative Leader and Administrator," *APSR* 50 (1956). Wilson's own works, *Congressional Government* (1885), and *Constitutional Government in the United States* (1908), should be consulted, as well as several contemporary accounts: Henry Jones Ford, "The Growth of Dictatorship," *Atlantic Monthly* 121 (1918); Henry Campbell Black, *The Relation of the Executive Power to Legislation* (1919); John W. Burgess, *Recent Changes in American Constitutional Theory* (1923); William Bennett Munro, "Woodrow Wilson and the Accentuation of Presidential Leadership," in *The Makers of the Unwritten Constitution* (1930). Donald F. Anderson, *William Howard Taft: A Conservative's Conception of the Presidency* (1973), emphasizes the persistence of traditional rule-of-law values in the era of reform.

Robert D. Cuff, *The War Industries Board: Business-Government Relations during World War I* (1973), shows how the war presented opportunities to realize bureaucratic-managerial reforms. Standard accounts of wartime government are Carl B. Swisher, *American Constitutional Development* (1954); Swisher, "The Control of War Preparations in the United States," *APSR* 34 (1940); William F. Willoughby, *Government Organization in War Time and After* (1919); Harold A. Van Dorn, *Government-Owned Corporations* (1926); Charles R. Van Hise, *Conservation and Regulation in the United States during the World War* (1917).

The bureaucratic-managerial aspect of progressivism as reflected in the career of Herbert Hoover is discussed in Ellis Hawley, *The Great War and the Search for a Modern Order: A History of the American People and Their Institutions, 1917–1933* (1979); Hawley, "Herbert Hoover, the Commerce Secretariat, and the Vision of the 'Associative State,' 1921–1928," *JAH* 61 (1974); Robert D. Cuff, "Herbert Hoover, the Ideology of Voluntarism and War Organization during the Great War," *JAH* 64 (1977); Peri E. Arnold, "The 'Great Engineer' as Administrator: Herbert Hoover and Modern Bureaucracy," *Review of Politics* 42 (1980). Concerned more broadly with the development of executive power over the bureaucracy are Oscar Kraines, "The President versus Congress: The Keep Commission, 1905–09," *Western Pol. Q.* 23 (1970); Harold T. Pinkett, "The Keep Commission, 1905–1909: A Rooseveltian Effort for Administrative Reform," *JAH* 52 (1965); Peri E. Arnold, "Executive

Reorganization and the Origins of the Managerial Presidency," Polity 13 (1981); Barry Dean Karl, *Executive Reorganization and Reform in the New Deal: The Genesis of Administrative Management, 1900–1939* (1963); Karl, "Presidential Planning and Social Science Research: Mr. Hoover's Experts," *Perspectives in American History* 3 (1969). Larry Berman, *The Office of Management and Budget and the Presidency 1921–1979* (1979), describes the Budget Act of 1921 and its enhancement of executive power. Thomas B. Silver, "Coolidge and the Historians," *American Scholar* 50 (1981), is a refreshing analysis of the liberal biases that have colored accounts of that president. The *Myers* case and the controversy over the removal power are dealt with in James Hart, *Tenure of Office under the Constitution* (1930), and Edward S. Corwin, "Tenure of Office and the Removal Power under the Constitution," *Columbia Law Review* vol. 27 (1927).

Awareness of the growth of big government in the 1920s is documented in a number of contemporary works: Charles A. Beard and William Beard, *The American Leviathan: The Republic in the Machine Age* (1931); Carroll H. Woody, *The Growth of the Federal Government, 1915–1932* (1934); Walter Thompson, *Federal Centralization* (1923); President's Research Committee, *Recent Social Trends in the United States* (1933). Changes in federalism in this period are examined in Harry Scheiber, "The Condition of American Federalism: An Historian's View," in Frank Smallwood, ed., *The New Federalism* (1967), and William Graebner, "Federalism in the Progressive Era: A Structural Interpretation of Reform," *JAH* 64 (1977). Two contemporary accounts are A. F. MacDonald, *Federal Aid: A Study of the American Subsidy System* (1928), and A. N. Holcombe, "The States as Agents of the Nation," *Southwestern Political Science Quarterly* 1 (1921). Charles Warren, *Congress as Santa Claus, or National Donations and the General Welfare Clause* (1932, 1978), traces the emergence of special interest and class legislation and its effect in eroding states' rights.

Several works describe federal policy toward labor union militance, among them Jerry M. Cooper, *The Army and Civil Disorder: Federal Military Intervention in Labor Disputes* (1980); Gerald C. Eggert, *Railroad Labor Disputes: The Beginnings of Federal Strike Policy* (1967); Edwin E. Witte, *The Government in Labor Disputes* (1932); Felix Frankfurter and Nathan V. Green, *The Labor Injunction* (1930); Edward Berman, *Labor Disputes and the President* (1924). The problem of child labor is examined in Stephen B. Wood, *Constitutional Politics in the Progressive Era: Child Labor and the Law* (1968), and R. G. Fuller, *Child Labor and the Constitution* (1929).

The evolution of a federal police power on the one hand and the persistence of laissez-faire constitutionalism on the other form the central themes in the history of constitutional law in the progressive era. In addition to the general works on the Supreme Court by Warren, Boudin, Wright, and McCloskey, there are two valuable studies that focus on this period: John E. Semonche, *Charting the Future: The Supreme Court Responds to a Changing Society, 1890–1920* (1978), and William F. Swindler, *Court and Constitution in the Twentieth Century: The Old Legality, 1889–1932* (1969). Ernst Freund, *The Police Power* (1904), is a standard treatise which illuminates the nature of the federal police power. See also John Braeman, "The Square Deal in Action: A Case Study in the Growth of the National Police Power," in Braeman *et al.*, eds., *Change and Continuity in Twentieth Century America* (1966). Conservative tendencies in the judiciary are underscored in John P.

Roche, "Entrepreneurial Liberty and the Fourteenth Amendment," *Labor History* 4 (1963); Thomas Reed Powell, "The Supreme Court and State Police Power, 1922-1930," *Virginia Law Review* 17-18 (1931-32); Powell, "The Judiciality of Minimum Wage Legislation," *Harvard Law Review* 37 (1924); Walton H. Hamilton, "Affectation with a Public Interest," *Yale Law Journal* 39 (1930); Maurice Finkelstein "From Munn v. Illinois to Tyson v. Banton: A Study in the Judicial Process," *Columbia Law Review* 26 (1927); Felix Frankfurter, "Hours of Labor and Realism in Constitutional Law," *Harvard Law Review* 29 (1916). Ray A. Brown, "Due Process of Law, Police Power, and the Supreme Court," *Harvard Law Review* 40 (1927), and Brown, "Police Power—Legislation for Health and Personal Safety," *Harvard Law Review* 42 (1929), present a favorable assessment of the Supreme Court's handling of social and economic legislation. Revisionist views of a famous conservative decision appear in Frank Strong, "The Economic Philosophy of Lochner: Emergence, Embrasure and Emasculation," *Arizona Law Review* 15 (1973); Sidney G. Tarrow, "Lochner versus New York: A Political Analysis," *Labor History* 5 (1964); Albert Mavrinac, "From Lochner to Brown v. Topeka: The Court and Conflicting Concepts of the Judicial Process," *APSR* 52 (1958).

Worthwhile studies of individual judges include G. Edward White, "The Rise and Fall of Justice Holmes," *University of Chicago Law Review* 39 (1971); Samuel J. Konefsky, *The Legacy of Holmes and Brandeis: A Study in the Influence of Ideas* (1956); Mark De Wolfe Howe, *Justice Oliver Wendell Holmes,* 2 vols. (1957-63); Francis Biddle, *Justice Holmes, Natural Law, and the Supreme Court* (1961); Felix Frankfurter, *Mr. Justice Holmes and the Supreme Court* (1938); Mark Tushnet, "The Logic of Experience: Oliver Wendell Holmes on the Supreme Judicial Court," *Virginia Law Review* 63 (1977); Samuel Krislov, "Oliver Wendell Holmes: The Ebb and Flow of Judicial Legendry," *Northwestern University Law Review* 52 (1957); Symposium, "Mr. Justice Holmes: Some Modern Views," *University of Chicago Law Review* 31 (1964); Francis E. Lucey, "Holmes—Liberal—Humanitarian—Believer in Democracy?" *Georgetown Law Journal* 39 (1951); Melvin I. Urofsky, *Louis D. Brandeis and the Progressive Tradition* (1981); Allon Gal, *Brandeis of Boston* (1980); Alpheus T. Mason, *Brandeis: A Free Man's Life* (1946); Mason, *William Howard Taft: Chief Justice* (1965); J. F. Paschal, *Mr. Justice Sutherland: A Man against the State* (1951); Sister Marie Carolyn Klinkhamer, "The Legal Philosophy of Edward Douglas White," *University of Detroit Law Journal* 35 (1957); Hoyt L. Warner, *Life of Mr. Justice Clarke: A Testament to the Power of Liberal Dissent in America* (1959); J. E. McLean, *William Rufus Day: Supreme Court Justice from Ohio* (1946); Vernon W. Roelofs, "Justice William R. Day and Federal Regulation," *MVHR* 37 (1950); David J. Danelski, *A Supreme Court Justice Is Appointed* (1964), concerning the Pierce Butler appointment.

The progressive attack on the judiciary is discussed in Stephen Stagner, "The Recall of Judicial Decisions and the Due Process Debate," *AJLH* 24 (1980). Representative contemporary writings on this theme include W. F. Dodd, "The Growth of Judicial Power," *PSQ* 24 (1909); Louis B. Boudin, "Government by Judiciary," *PSQ* 26 (1911); Gilbert E. Roe, *Our Judicial Oligarchy* (1912). The political involvement of two renowned progressive jurists is revealed in Bruce Allen Murphy, *The Brandeis/Frankfurter Connection: The Secret Political Activities of Two Supreme Court Justices* (1982), and David W. Levy and Bruce Allen Murphy, "Preserving the Progressive Spirit in a Conservative Time: The Joint Reform Efforts of

Justice Brandeis and Professor Frankfurter, 1916–1933," *Michigan Law Review* 74 (1980).

Progressive trends in jurisprudence are explained in David Wigdor, *Roscoe Pound: Philosopher of Law* (1973); Fred V. Cahill, *Judicial Legislation* (1952); Morton White, *Social Thought in America: The Revolt against Formalism* (1949); Benjamin N. Cardozo, *The Nature of the Judicial Process* (1921); Cardozo, *The Growth of the Law* (1924); Thomas Reed Powell, "The Logic and Rhetoric of Constitutional Law," *Journal of Philosophy* 15 (1918); John W. Johnson, *American Legal Culture, 1908–1940* (1981). Sundry problems in constitutional law are dealt with in Bruce Bringhurst, *Antitrust and the Oil Monopoly: The Standard Oil Cases, 1890–1911* (1979); M. Browning Carrott, "The Supreme Court and American Trade Associations, 1921–1925," *Business History Review* 44 (1970); Stanley I. Kutler, "Labor, the Clayton Act, and the Supreme Court," *Labor History* 3 (1962); Kutler, "Chief Justice Taft, National Regulation and the Comemerce Clause," *JAH* 51 (1965); Morton Keller, "The Judicial System and the Law of Life Insurance, 1888–1910," *Business History Review* 35 (1961).

Scholarly attention has also been directed toward the reform movement as seen in state and local governmental changes. Able surveys of the constitutional problems involved in municipal government are Jon C. Teaford, *City and Suburb: The Political Fragmentation of Metropolitan America, 1850–1970* (1979); Teaford, *The Municipal Revolution in America: Origins of Modern Urban Government, 1650–1825* (1975); Teaford, "Special Legislation and the Cities, 1865–1900," *AJLH* 23 (1979); Anwar H. Syed, *The Political Theory of American Local Government* (1966). The argument that municipal reformers were antidemocratic elitists is made in Samuel P. Hays, "The Politics of Reform in Municipal Government in the Progressive Era," *Pacific Northwest Quarterly* 55 (1964); James Weinstein, "Organized Business and the City Commission and Manager Movements," *JSH* 38 (1962). On local government, see also David Nord, "The Experts versus the Experts: Conflicting Philosophies of Municipal Utility Regulation in the Progressive Era," *Wisconsin Magazine of History* 58 (1975); Clifford W. Patton, *The Battle for Municipal Reform: Mobilization and Attack, 1875 to 1900* (1940); Ernest S. Griffith, *The Modern Development of City Government in the United Kingdom and the United States*, 2 vols. (1927); Howard Lee McBain, *The Law and Practice of Municipal Home Rule* (1916); Delos Wilcox, *Municipal Franchises* (1910); John F. Dillon, *Treatise on the Law of Municipal Corporations* (1872).

Electoral reforms at the state level are treated in Jerrold G. Rusk, "The Effect of the Australian Ballot Reform on Split Ticket Voting: 1876–1908," *APSR* 64 (1970), and Jack L. Walker, "The Diffusion of Innovations among the American States," *APSR* 63 (1969). William B. Munro, ed., *Initiative, Referendum, and Recall* (1912), and Ellis P. Oberholtzer, *The Referendum in America* (1911), provide a record of the contemporary interest in creating instruments of direct popular rule.

Federal taxation and the politics of the Seventeenth Amendment are covered in John D. Buenker, "Urban Liberalism and the Federal Income Tax Amendment," *Pennsylvania History* 36 (1969); Buenker, "The Urban Political Machine and the Seventeenth Amendment," *JAH* 56 (1969); Sidney Ratner, *American Taxation* (1942); R. Alton Lee, *A History of Regulatory Taxation* (1973); Robert E. Cushman, "Social and Economic Controls through Federal Taxation," *Minnesota Law Review* 18 (1934). For constitutional and legal aspects of the women's suffrage and prohibition amendments, see David Morgan, *Suffragists and Democrats: The Politics of Woman Suffrage in America* (1972), and David E. Kyvig, *Repealing National Prohibition* (1979).

XV. *The New Deal Era in American Constitutionalism*

In recent years scholars have pointed out elements of political and constitutional continuity between the efforts of the Hoover administration to combat the depression and those of the New Deal administration of Franklin D. Roosevelt. Hoover's policies and governmental attitudes are examined in Jordan A. Schwarz, *The Interregnum of Despair: Hoover, Congress, and the Depression* (1970); Alfred U. Romasco, *The Poverty of Abundance: Hoover, the Nation, the Depression* (1965); James Stuart Olson, *Herbert Hoover and the Reconstruction Finance Corporation, 1931–1933* (1977); Harris G. Warren, *Herbert Hoover and the Great Depression* (1967); Martin L. Fausold and George T. Mazuzan, eds., *The Hoover Presidency: A Reappraisal* (1974); Craig Lloyd, *Aggressive Introvert: A Study of Herbert Hoover and Public Relations Management, 1912–1932* (1972); Carl N. Degler, "The Ordeal of Herbert Hoover," *Yale Review* 52 (1963); Walter Lippmann, *The New Imperative* (1935).

A cogent interpretation of the political-constitutional strategy of the early New Deal is provided in William E. Leuchtenburg, "The New Deal and the Analogue of War," in John Braeman, *et al.,* eds., *Continuity and Change in Twentieth Century America* (1965). Clinton Rossiter, *Constitutional Dictatorship: Crisis Government in the Modern Democracies* (1948), contains a good account of Roosevelt's expansion of executive power. General works on the New Deal which cast light on constitutional issues include Paul K. Conkin, *FDR and the Origins of the Welfare State* (1967); Arthur M. Schlesinger, Jr., *The Coming of the New Deal* (1958); Schlesinger, *The Politics of Upheaval* (1960); Edgar E. Robinson, *The Roosevelt Leadership, 1933–1945* (1955); Charles A. Beard and Mary Beard, *America in Mid-Passage* (1939); James MacGregor Burns, *Roosevelt: The Lion and the Fox* (1956); Mario Einaudi, *The Roosevelt Revolution* (1959); William E. Leuchtenburg, *Franklin D. Roosevelt and the New Deal: 1932–1940* (1963); Jewel Bellush, "Old and New Left Reappraisals of the New Deal and Roosevelt's Presidency," *Pres. Studies Q.* 9 (1979); Gerald D. Nash, *The Great Depression and World War II: Organizing America, 1933–1945* (1979); Elliot A. Rosen, *Hoover, Roosevelt, and the Brains Trust: From Depression to New Deal* (1977), a refutation of the revisionist thesis that Hoover anticipated the New Deal's commitment to federal intervention.

More specialized considerations of New Deal constitutionalism include Morton J. Frisch, "Franklin D. Roosevelt and the Problem of Democratic Liberty," *Ethics* 72 (1962); Frisch, "Roosevelt the Conservator: A Rejoinder to Hofstadter," *JP* 25 (1963); Rexford G. Tugwell, "Design for Government," *PSQ* 48 (1933); Tugwell, "The New Deal: Available Instruments of Governmental Power," *Western Pol. Q.* 2 (1949); Francis G. Wilson, "The Revival of Organic Theory," *APSR* 36 (1942); Walton Hamilton and Douglass Adair, *The Power to Govern: The Constitution—Then and Now* (1937); Luther Gulick, "Politics, Administration, and the 'New Deal,'" *Annals* 169 (1933); John Dickinson, "Political Aspects of the New Deal," *APSR* 28 (1934); Jane Perry Clark, "Emergencies and the Law," *PSQ* 49

(1934); Edward S. Corwin, "Some Probable Consequencs of 'Nira' on Our Constitutional System," *Annals* 172 (1934); William Yandell Elliott, *The Need for Constitutional Reform: A Program for National Security* (1935); Harold Laski, "The Constitution under Strain," *Political Quarterly* 8 (1937); Norton E. Long, "Party and Constitution," *JP* 3 (1941).

The relationship between groups and regulatory agencies in constitutional politics in the New Deal era is discussed in Grant McConnell, *Private Power and American Democracy* (1966); Louis L. Jaffe, "Law Making by Private Groups," *Harvard Law Review* 51 (1937); James J. Robbins and Gunnar Heckscher, "The Constitutional Theory of Autonomous Groups," *JP* 3 (1941); Charles M. Wiltse, "The Representative Function of Bureaucracy," *APSR* 35 (1941); E. Pendleton Herring, *Group Representation before Congress* (1929); Reinhard Bendix, "Bureaucracy and the Problem of Power," *Public Administration Review* 5 (1945); Vincent M. Barnett, Jr., "Modern Constitutional Development: A Challenge to Administration," *Public Administration Review* 4 (1944).

Roosevelt's attempt to gain greater executive control over the structure of influence created by interest groups and bureaucratic agencies is recounted in studies of executive reorganization. See especially Barry D. Karl, *Executive Reorganization and Reform in the New Deal: The Genesis of Administrative Management 1900–1939* (1963); Clinton L. Rossiter, "The Constitutional Significance of the Executive Office of the President," *APSR* 43 (1949); Richard Polenberg, *Reorganizing Roosevelt's Government* (1966); Polenberg, "Roosevelt, Carter, and Executive Reorganization: Lessons of the 1930s," *Pres. Studies Q.* 9 (1979); A. J. Wann, *The President as Chief Administrator: A Study of Franklin D. Roosevelt* (1968). Roosevelt's relations with Congress can be traced in James T. Patterson, *Congressional Conservatism and the New Deal: The Growth of the Conservative Coalition in Congress, 1933–1935* (1967); J. Joseph Huthmacher, *Robert A. Wagner and the Rise of Urban Liberalism* (1968); Lawrence H. Chamberlain, *The President, Congress and Legislation* (1946), containing the legislative history of many New Deal measures. Roosevelt's attempt to impose greater executive control on the Democratic party is analyzed in Charles M. Price and Joseph Boskin, "The Roosevelt 'Purge': A Reappraisal," *JP* 28 (1966).

The establishment of federal regulatory and social welfare structures is described in numerous works. The best accounts of industrial recovery and reform are Ellis W. Hawley, *The New Deal and the Problem of Monopoly: A Study in Economic Ambivalence* (1966), and Bernard Bellush, *The Failure of the NRA* (1975). Paul L. Murphy, "The New Deal Agricultural Program and the Constitution," *Agricultural History* 29 (1955), is a solid analysis, while Merle Fainsod, Lincoln Gordon, and Joseph C. Palamountain, *Government and the American Economy* (1959), is a comprehensive survey of the regulatory state. On the subjects indicated the following studies are reliable guides: Thomas K. McCraw, *TVA and the Power Fight, 1933–1939* (1971); C. Herman Pritchett, *The Tennessee Valley Authority: A Study in Public Administration* (1943); Irving Bernstein, *The New Deal Collective Bargaining Policy* (1950); Bernstein, *Turbulent Years: A History of the American Worker 1933–1941* (1969), discussing the National Labor Relations Act; Susan Estabrook Kennedy, *The Banking Crisis of 1933* (1973); Michael E. Parrish, *Securities Regulation and the New Deal* (1970); Sidney Fine, *The Automobile Industry under the Blue Eagle: Labor, Management, and the Automobile Manufacturing Code* (1963);

Daniel Nelson, *Unemployment Insurance: The American Experience, 1915–1935* (1969); William Graebner, *A History of Retirement: The Meaning and Function of an American Institution, 1885–1978* (1980), containing an account of the Social Security Act; Roy Lubove, *The Struggle for Social Security: 1900–1935* (1968); Paul A. Kurzman, *Harry Hopkins and the New Deal* (1974), concerning administration of the federal relief program; Searle F. Charles, *Minister of Relief: Harry Hopkins and the Depression* (1963).

Samuel P. Huntington, "The Marasmus of the ICC: The Commission, the Railroads, and the Public Interest," *Yale Law Journal* 61 (1952), covers problems in transportation regulation in the 1930s and 1940s. Otis L. Graham, *Toward a Planned Society: From Roosevelt to Nixon* (1976), is a survey of the concept of national economic planning. Charles E. Merriam, "The National Resources Planning Board: A Chapter in American Experience," *APSR* 38 (1944), and John D. Lewis, "Democratic Planning in Agriculture," *APSR* 35 (1941), are contemporary arguments for national planning. Donald A. Ritchie, *James M. Landis: Dean of the Regulators* (1980), provides an able survey of New Deal administrative history. Corwin D. Edwards, "Thurman Arnold and the Antitrust Laws," *PSQ* 58 (1943), argues for the effectiveness of New Deal regulation of corporations.

Changes in federalism produced by the New Deal are considered in Harry N. Scheiber, "The Condition of American Federalism: An Historian's View," in Frank Smallwood, ed., *The New Federalism* (1967); James T. Patterson, *The New Deal and the States* (1969); Jane Perry Clark, *The Rise of a New Federalism* (1938); V. O. Key, Jr., *Administration of Federal Grants to States* (1937); H. J. Bitterman, *State and Federal Grants in Aid* (1938).

The hostility of the Supreme Court toward the New Deal before 1937 is well described in Paul L. Murphy, *The Constitution in Crisis Times, 1919–1969* (1972); William F. Swindler, *Court and Constitution in the Twentieth Century: The New Legality, 1932–1968* (1970); Alpheus T. Mason, *The Supreme Court: Vehicle of Revealed Truth or Power Group, 1930–1937* (1953); Robert H. Jackson, *The Struggle for Judicial Supremacy* (1941); Dean Alfange, *The Supreme Court and the National Will* (1937); Merlo J. Pusey, *Charles Evans Hughes,* 2 vols. (1951); Samuel Hendel, *Charles Evans Hughes and the Supreme Court* (1951); William Harbaugh, *Lawyer's Lawyer: The Life of John W. Davis* (1973). Several of Edward S. Corwin's works written in the 1930s illuminate the Court's anti–New Deal outlook. See especially *The Twilight of the Supreme Court* (1934) and *The Commerce Power versus States Rights* (1936). Gerald Garvey, "Edward S. Corwin in the Campaign of History: The Struggle for National Power in the 1930s," *George Washington Law Review* 34 (1965), is pertinent in this regard. Corwin's "Curbing the Court," *Annals* 185 (1936), is a valuable analysis of the problem of constitutional reform created by the Court's negative course. A provocative anti–New Deal decision that added to liberal dissatisfaction with the Court is discussed in William E. Leuchtenburg, "The Case of the Contentious Commissioner: Humphrey's Executor v. U.S.," in Harold M. Hyman and Leonard W. Levy, eds., *Freedom and Reform: Essays in Honor of Henry Steele Commager* (1967).

The best accounts of the court-packing crisis are William E. Leuchtenburg, "The Origins of Franklin D. Roosevelt's 'Court-Packing' Plan," *Supreme Court Review 1966* (1967); Leuchtenburg, "Franklin D. Roosevelt's Supreme Court 'Packing' Plan," in George Wolfskill *et al., Essays on the New Deal* (1969); Lionel

V. Patenaude, "Garner, Sumners, and Connally: The Defeat of the Roosevelt Court Bill in 1937," *Southwestern Historical Quarterly* 74 (1970); Gene M. Gressley, "Joseph C. O'Mahoney, FDR and the Supreme Court," *Pacific Historical Review* 40 (1971). See also Charles A. Leonard, *A Search for a Judicial Philosophy: Mr. Justice Roberts and the Constitutional Revolution of 1937* (1971); John W. Chambers, "The Big Switch: Justice Roberts and the Minimum Wage Cases," *Labor History* 10 (1969); Leonard Baker, *Back to Back: The Duel between F.D.R. and the Supreme Court* (1967); Barry A. Crouch, "Dennis Chavez and Roosevelt's 'Court Packing' Plan," *New Mexico Historical Review* 42 (1967); Karl A. Lamb, "The Opposition Party as Secret Agent: Republicans and the Court Fight, 1937," *Papers of the Michigan Academy of Science, Arts, and Letters* 46 (1961). Joseph Alsop and Turner Catledge, *The 168 Days* (1938), and Merlo J. Pusey, *The Supreme Court Crisis* (1937), are vivid journalistic accounts of the crisis.

The changes in constitutional law inaugurated in 1937 are analyzed in Richard C. Cortner, *The Jones and Laughlin Case* (1970); Cortner, *The Wagner Act Cases* (1964); C. Herman Pritchett, *The Roosevelt Court: A Study in Judicial Politics and Values, 1937-1947* (1948); Alpheus T. Mason, *Harlan Fiske Stone: Pillar of the Law* (1956); Robert L. Stern, "The Commerce Clause and the National Economy, 1933-1946," *Harvard Law Review* 59 (1946); Virginia Wood, *Due Process of Law, 1932-1949* (1951); Robert G. McCloskey, "Economic Due Process and the Supreme Court: An Exhumation and Reburial," *Supreme Court Review 1962* (1963); J. Woodford Howard, Jr., *Mr. Justice Murphy: A Political Biography* (1968); Carl B. Swisher, *The Growth of Constitutional Power in the United States* (1946); John P. Frank, *Mr. Justice Black: The Man and His Opinions* (1949); Bernard Schwartz, *The Supreme Court: Constitutional Revolution in Retrospect* (1957). The liberal commitment to maintaining pro–New Deal tendencies on the Court is vividly depicted in William E. Leuchtenburg, "A Klansman Joins the Court: The Appointment of Hugo L. Black," *University of Chicago Law Review* 41 (1973).

Broad assessments of the constitutional impact of the New Deal and the role of the Supreme Court after 1937 are found in Vincent M. Barnett, Jr., "The Political Philosophy of the New Supreme Court," *Journal of Social Philosophy and Jurisprudence* 7 (1942); Barnett, "The Supreme Court and the Capacity to Govern," *PSQ* 63 (1948); Walton H. Hamilton and George D. Braden, "The Special Competence of the Supreme Court," *Yale Law Journal* 50 (1941); Max Lerner, "The Great Constitutional War," *Virginia Quarterly Review* 18 (1942); Kenneth Culp Davis, "Revolution in the Supreme Court," *Atlantic Monthly* 166 (1940); Henry Steele Commager, *Majority Rule and Minority Rights* (1943); Edward S. Corwin, *Constitutional Revolution, Ltd.* (1941); Corwin, "The Dissolving Structure of Our Constitutional Law," *New Jersey Law Journal* 69 (1946); Corwin, "The Passing of Dual Federalism" *Virginia Law Review* 37 (1950); E. F. Albertsworth, "Streamlining the Constitution," *New York University Law Quarterly Review* 16 (1938); Thomas Reed Powell, *Vagaries and Varieties in Constitutional Interpretation* (1956); Henry Rottschaefer, *The Constitution and Socio-Economic Change* (1948). Improvement in federal judicial organization as a partial response to the Court-packing crisis is described in Peter G. Fish, "Crises, Politics, and Federal Judicial Reform: The Administrative Office Act of 1939," *JP* 32 (1970). The *Erie* case is the subject of a large body of technical legal literature, the scope of which can be seen in John Hart Ely, "The Irrepressible Myth of Erie," *Harvard Law Review* 87 (1974).

An interesting narrative of the case is provided in Irving Younger, "What Happened in *Erie,*" *Texas Law Review* 56 (1978).

The philosophy of legal realism that influenced the Court-packing plan and New Deal liberalism in general is well represented in Karl Llewellyn, "The Constitution as an Institution," *Columbia Law Review* 34 (1934); Charles A. Beard, "The Living Constitution," *Annals* 185 (1936); Thurman Arnold, *The Symbols of Government* (1935); Max Lerner, "Constitution and Court as Symbols," *Yale Law Journal* 46 (1937). See the analyses of these and other constitutional critics in Herman Belz, "Changing Conceptions of Constitutionalism in the Era of World War II and the Cold War," *JAH* 59 (1972); Edward A. Purcell, Jr., *The Crisis of Democratic Theory: Scientific Naturalism and the Problem of Values* (1973); Douglas Ayer, "In Quest of Efficiency: The Ideological Journey of Thurman Arnold in the Interwar Period," *Stanford Law Review* 23 (1971); Edward N. Kearney, *Thurman Arnold, Social Critic: The Satirical Challenge to Orthodoxy* (1970).

Concerning constitutional problems during World War II, see Edward S. Corwin, *Total War and the Constitution* (1947); Bernard Schwartz, "The War Power in Britain and America," *New York University Law Quarterly Review* 20 (1945); Clinton Rossiter, *The Supreme Court and the Commander-in-Chief* (1951); Eliot Janeway, *The Struggle for Survival: A Chronicle of Economic Mobilization in World War II* (1951); Nathan Grundstein, "Presidential Subdelegation of Administrative Authority in War-time," *George Washington Law Review* 16 (1948); Louis Smith, *American Democracy and Military Power: A Study of Civil Control of the Military Power in the United States* (1951); Charles Fairman, "The Supreme Court on Military Jurisdiction: Martial Rule in Hawaii and the Yamashita Case," *Harvard Law Review* 59 (1946); Jacobus ten Broek *et al., Prejudice, War and the Constitution: Japanese-American Evacuation and Resettlement* (1954); Roger Daniels, *Concentration Camps U.S.A.: Japanese Americans and World War II* (1971); E. V. Rostow, "The Japanese American Cases—A Disaster," *Yale Law Journal* 54 (1945); Willard Hurst, *The Law of Treason in the United States* (1971). Roosevelt's wartime leadership is the subject of James MacGregor Burns, *Roosevelt: The Soldier of Freedom* (1970).

XVI. *Civil Liberties and Modern Constitutionalism*

An excellent introduction to modern problems of civil liberties, distinguishing between pluralistic, community-oriented civil liberty in the nineteenth century and centralized, judicially maintained civil liberties in the twentieth century, is John P. Roche, "American Liberty: An Examination of the 'Tradition' of Freedom," in Milton R. Konvitz and Clinton Rossiter, eds., *Aspects of Liberty: Essays Presented to Robert E. Cushman* (1958). Good examples of the libertarian position are provided by Zechariah Chafee, Jr., *Free Speech in the United States* (1941); Alexander Meiklejohn, *Political Freedom: The Constitutional Powers of the People* (1965); O. K. Frankel, *The Supreme Court and Civil Liberties* (1960); Thomas I. Emerson, *Toward a General Theory of the First Amendment* (1966); Emerson, *The System of Freedom of Expression* (1970).

Civil liberties issues are viewed from a conservative perspective in Walter F.

Berns, *Freedom, Virtue and the First Amendment* (1957); Berns, *The First Amendment and the Future of American Democracy* (1976); Robert Nisbet, *The Twilight of Authority* (1975); George Anastaplo, *The Constitutionalist: Notes on the First Amendment* (1971). Reliable general accounts reflecting the high value placed on civil liberties protection since the New Deal are Milton R. Konvitz, *Expanding Liberties: Freedom's Gains in Post-War America* (1966); Konvitz, *Fundamental Liberties of a Free People: Religion, Speech, Press, Assembly* (1957); Henry J. Abraham, *Freedom and the Court: Civil Rights and Liberties in the United States* (1967); William Spinrad, *Civil Liberties* (1970); Samuel Krislov, *The Supreme Court and Political Freedom* (1968); Irving Brant, *the Bill of Rights: Its Origin and Meaning* (1965); Paul G. Kauper, *Civil Liberties and the Constitution* (1966); Martin Shapiro, *Freedom of Speech: The Supreme Court and Judicial Review* (1966).

The emergence of rights consciousness and the assertion of civil liberties claims in the late nineteenth and early twentieth centuries is described in Alexis J. Anderson, "The Formative Period of First Amendment Theory, 1870–1915," *AJLH* 24 (1980), and David M. Rabban, "The First Amendment and Its Forgotton Years," *Yale Law Journal* 90 (1981). Developments during World War I are examined in Paul L. Murphy, *World War I and the Origins of Civil Liberties in the United States* (1979); Stephen Vaughn, "First Amendment Liberties and the Committee on Public Information," *AJLH* 23 (1979); Fred D. Ragan, "Justice Oliver Wendell Holmes, Jr., Zechariah Chafee, Jr., and the Clear and Present Danger Test for Free Speech: The First Year, 1919," *JAH* 58 (1971); Gerald Gunther, "Learned Hand and the Origins of Modern First Amendment Theory: Some Fragments of History," *Stanford Law Review* 27 (1975); Harry N. Scheiber, *The Wilson Administration and Civil Liberties, 1917–1921* (1960); James R. Monk, *Censorship 1917* (1941); Carl B. Swisher, "Civil Liberties in War Time," *PSQ* 55 (1940). William Preston, Jr., *Aliens and Dissenters: Federal Suppression of Radicals, 1900–1933* (1963), and H. C. Peterson and Gilbert C. Fite, *Opponents of War 1917–1918* (1957), are chronicles of wartime government restrictions. Contemporary evaluations of wartime civil liberties policies are found in Zechariah Chafee, Jr., *Freedom of Speech* (1920), critical of the government, and Edward S. Corwin, "Freedom of Speech and Press under the First Amendment: A Résumé," *Yale Law Journal* 30 (1920), supportive of the government.

Paul L. Murphy, *The Meaning of Freedom of Speech: First Amendment Freedoms from Wilson to FDR* (1972), is a thorough examination of civil liberties claims raised principally by radicals, labor protestors, and aliens in the 1920s. Other pertinent accounts are Donald Johnson, *The Challenge to American Freedom: World War I and the Rise of the American Civil Liberties Union* (1963); David B. Tyack, "The Perils of Pluralism: The Background of the Pierce Case," *AHR* 74 (1968); Kenneth B. O'Brien, Jr., "Education, Americanization and the Supreme Court in the 1920s," *American Quarterly* 13 (1961); David Williams, "The Bureau of Investigation and Its Critics: The Origins of Federal Political Surveillance," *JAH* 68 (1981); Robert K. Murray, *Red Scare: A Study in National Hysteria 1919–1920* (1955); Paul L. Murphy, "Communities in Conflict 1919–1930," in Alan Reitman, ed., *The Pulse of Freedom: American Liberties 1920–1970s* (1975). Ernest Sutherland Bates, *This Land of Liberty* (1930), is a liberal lament about the neglect of liberty, while Roger N. Baldwin and Clarence B. Randall, *Civil Liberties and In-*

dustrial Conflict (1938), describes contemporary libertarian concerns. For developments in the 1930s, see Jerold S. Auerbach, "The Depression Decade," in Reitman, ed., *The Pulse of Freedom;* Auerbach, *Labor and Liberty: The LaFollette Committee and the New Deal* (1966); John P. Roche, *The Quest for the Dream: The Development of Civil Rights and Human Relations in Modern America* (1963); Charles H. Martin, *The Angelo Herndon Case and Southern Justice* (1976); David M. Bixby, "The Roosevelt Court, Democratic Ideology, and Minority Rights: Another Look at *United States v. Classic,*" *Yale Law Journal* 90 (1981); John E. Hartmann, "The Minnesota Gag Law and the Fourteenth Amendment," *Minnesota History* 27 (1960), dealing with *Near* v. *Minnesota.* Contemporary accounts are Harry Shulman, "The Supreme Court's Attitude Toward Liberty of Contract and Freedom of Speech," *Yale Law Review* 40 (1931); Edwin Borchard, "The Supreme Court and Private Rights," *Yale Law Journal* 47 (1938); Louis B. Boudin, "The Supreme Court and Civil Rights," *Science and Society* 1 (1937).

The incorporation of the Bill of Rights into the Fourteenth Amendment is treated in an excellent work by Richard C. Cortner, *The Supreme Court and the Second Bill of Rights* (1981). Other valuable studies of this problem are Klaus H. Heberle, "From Gitlow to Near: Judicial 'Amendment' by Absent-Minded Incrementalism," *JP* 34 (1972); Charles Warren, "The New Liberty under the Fourteenth Amendment," *Harvard Law Review* 39 (1926), unique among contemporary reactions for its understanding of the centralizing potential of the incorporation of the First Amendment into the Fourteenth; Charles Fairman, "Does the Fourteenth Amendment Incorporate the Bill of Rights? The Original Understanding," *Stanford Law Review* 2 (1949); Stanley Morrison, "The Judicial Interpretation," *Stanford Law Review* 2 (1949); W. W. Crosskey, "Legislative History and the Constitutional Limitations on State Authority," *University of Chicago Law Review* 22 (1954); Norman Redlich, "Are There 'Certain Rights Retained by the People?'" *New York University Law Review* 37 (1962); Louis Henkin, "Selective Incorporation in the Fourteenth Amendment," *Yale Law Journal* 73 (1963); Felix Frankfurter, "Memorandum on 'Incorporation' of the Bill of Rights into the Due Process Clause of the Fourteenth Amendment," *Harvard Law Review* 78 (1965); Robert E. Cushman, "Incorporation: Due Process and the Bill of Rights," *Cornell Law Quarterly* 51 (1966).

The preferred-freedoms doctrine as a key instrument of modern judicial liberalism and civil libertarianism is discussed in general accounts of the post-1937 judiciary and in numerous specialized studies. Alpheus T. Mason, "The Core of Free Government, 1938–40: Mr. Justice Stone and 'Preferred Freedoms,'" *Yale Law Journal* 65 (1956), is a good introduction to the problem. The author of the famous Carolene Products footnote, Louis Lusky, law clerk to Justice Stone, comments on its significance in "Minority Rights and the Public Interest," *Yale Law Journal* 52 (1942), and in *By What Right? A Commentary on the Supreme Court's Power to Revise the Constitution* (1975). See also Robert B. McKay, "The Preference for Freedom," *New York University Law Review* 34 (1959).

The development of libertarian trends in the 1940s and 1950s can be traced in the following works: Charles L. Black, Jr., "Mr. Justice Black, the Supreme Court, and the Bill of Rights," *Harper's Magazine* 222 (1961); Clyde E. Jacobs, *Justice Frankfurter and Civil Liberties* (1961); John P. Frank, "Hugo L. Black: Free Speech and the Declaration of Independence," *University of Illinois Law Forum* (1977); Philip B. Kurland, "Justice Robert H. Jackson—Impact on Civil Rights and Civil Liberties," *University of Illinois Law Forum* 1977 (1977); L. A. Powe, Jr., "Evolution to Absolutism: Justice Douglas and the First Amendment," *Columbia Law Review* 74 (1974); Vern Countryman, "Justice Douglas and Freedom of Expression," *University of Illinois Law Forum* 1978 (1978); S. Sidney Ulmer, "Parabolic Support of Civil Liberty Claims: The Case of William O. Douglas," *JP* 41 (1979); Hugo L. Black, "The Bill of Rights," *New York University Law Review* 35 (1960); "Justice Black and First Amendment 'Absolutes': A Public Interview," *New York University Law Review* 37 (1962); William J. Brennan, "The Supreme Court and the Meiklejohn Interpretation of the First Amendment," *Harvard Law Review* 79 (1965). Learned Hand, *The Bill of Rights* (1958), is a classic critique of preferred-freedoms and clear-and-present-danger libertarianism.

The controversy between liberals and conservatives over balancing in civil liberties cases is well illustrated in Laurent B. Frantz, "The First Amendment in the Balance," *Yale Law Journal* 71 (1962), attacking the balancing test, and Wallace Mendelson, "On the Meaning of the First Amendment: Absolutes in the Balance," *California Law Review* 50 (1962), criticizing the preferred-freedoms idea. Two useful accounts of this problem are C. Herman Pritchett, *Civil Liberties and the Vinson Court* (1954), and Pritchett, *The Political Offender and the Warren Court* (1958). Robert E. Cushman, *Civil Liberties in the United States: A Guide to Current Problems and Experience* (1956), and Walter Gellhorn, *American Rights: The Constitution in Action* (1960), provide a good description of civil liberties law and practice in the 1950s. John P. Roche, "We've Never Had More Freedom," *New Republic* 134 (1956), is a provocative analysis that contradicts the perceptions of many other writers during the McCarthy era.

Two thoughtful studies of cold war civil liberties issues are Earl Latham, *The Communist Controversy in Washington: From the New Deal to McCarthy* (1966), and Robert A. Horn, *Groups and the Constitution* (1956). Cogent statements of the conservative position on internal security matters are Harry V. Jaffa, "On the Nature of Civil and Religious Liberty," in *Equality and Liberty: Theory and Practice in American Politics* (1965); Willmoore Kendall, *The Conservative Affirmation* (1963); Sidney Hook, *Common Sense and the Fifth Amendment* (1957). The libertarian approach receives forceful expression in Carey McWilliams, *Witch Hunt: The Revival of Heresy* (1950, 1975); Alan Barth, *The Loyalty of Free Man* (1951); Henry Steele Commager, *Freedom, Loyalty, Dissent* (1954); Thomas I. Emerson and David M. Helfeld, "Loyalty among Government Employees," *Yale Law Journal* 58 (1948). Worthwhile discussions of the loyalty issue also appear in Harold W. Chase, *Security and Liberty: The Problem of Native Communists, 1947–1955* (1955); Thomas I. Cook, *Democratic Rights versus Communist Activity* (1954); Morton Grodzins, *The Loyal and the Disloyal* (1956); Harold M. Hyman, *To Try Men's Souls: Loyalty Tests in American History* (1959).

On the government's internal security regulations, see Eleanor Bontecou, *The Federal Loyalty-Security Program* (1953), containing sober criticism of the policy; Seth W. Richardson, "The Federal Employee Loyalty Program," *Columbia Law Review* 51 (1951), a defense of the government; Roger S. Abbott, "The Federal Loyalty Program," *APSR* 42 (1948). Anti-Communist legislation is described in

Arthur E. Sutherland, "Freedom and National Security," *Harvard Law Review* 64 (1951); John P. Sullivan and David N. Webster, "Some Constitutional and Practical Problems of the Subversive Activities Control Act," *Georgetown Law Journal* 45 (1957); Carl A. Auerbach, "The Communist Control Act of 1954: A Proposed Legal-Political Theory of Free Speech," *University of Chicago Law Review* 30 (1956). Latham, *The Communist Controversy in Washington,* is excellent on congressional investigations. Also pertinent are Walter Goodman, *The Committee: The Extraordinary Career of the House Committee on Un-American Activities* (1968); Carl Beck, *Contempt of Congress: A Study of the Prosecutions Initiated by the Committee on Un-American Activities, 1945–1957* (1955); M. Nelson McGeary, *The Development of Congressional Investigating Power* (1940); Marshall Dimock, *Congressional Investigating Committees* (1929). State internal security efforts are covered in Walter Gellhorn, ed., *The States and Subversion* (1952), and Lawrence Chamberlain, *Loyalty and Legislative Action: A Survey of Activity by the New York Legislature 1919–1949* (1951).

The *Dennis* case provoked numerous analyses, notable among which are Edward S. Corwin, "Bowing Out 'Clear and Present Danger,' " *Notre Dame Lawyer* 27 (1952); Wallace Mendelson, "Clear and Present Danger: From Schenck to Dennis," *Columbia Law Review* 52 (1952); J. A. Gorfunkel and J. W. Mack, II, "Dennis v. United States and the Clear and Present Danger Rule," *California Law Review* 39 (1951). Later Smith Act and McCarran Act prosecutions are reviewed in Robert Mollan, "Smith Act Prosecutions: The Effect of the Dennis and Yates Decisions," *University of Pittsburgh Law Review* 26 (1965); Kathleen L. Barber, "The Legal Status of the Communist Party: 1965," *Journal of Public Law* 15 (1966); Frank E. Strong, "Fifty Years of Clear and Present Danger: From Schenck to Brandenburg—and Beyond," *Supreme Court Review 1969* (1970). Two broader accounts of the internal security question are Michael R. Belknap, *Cold War Political Justice: The Smith Act, the Communist Party, and American Civil Liberties* (1977), and Alan D. Harper, *The Politics of Loyalty: The White House and the Communist Issue, 1946–1952* (1969).

The following provide good introductions to diverse aspects of civil liberties problems in the 1940s and 1950s: Edgar A. Jones, Jr., "The Right to Picket: Twilight Zone of the Constitution," *University of Pennsylvania Law Review* 102 (1954); Charles L. Black, Jr., "He Cannot But Choose to Hear: The Plight of the Captive Auditor," *Columbia Law Review* 53 (1953); Loren P. Beth, "Group Libel and Free Speech," *Minnesota Law Review* 39 (1955); Leo Pfeffer, *Church, State and Freedom,* rev. ed. (1967); Loren P. Beth, *The American Theory of Church and State* (1958); David Manwaring, *Render unto Caesar: The Flag Salute Controversy* (1962); John Hart Ely, "*United States v. Lovett:* Litigating the Separation of Powers," *Harvard Civil Rights–Civil Liberties Law Review* 10 (1975).

Constitutional questions raised by cold war collective security agreements are studied in Jacob D. Hyman, "Constitutional Aspects of the Covenant," *Law and Contemporary Problems* 14 (1949); M. G. Pausen, "Charter and Constitution: The Human Rights Provisions in American Law," *Vanderbilt Law Review* 4 (1951); Glendon Schubert, "Politics and the Constitution: The Bricker Amendment during 1953," *JP* 16 (1954); Arthur E. Sutherland, "Restricting the Treaty Power," *Harvard Law Review* 65 (1952); Sutherland, "The Flag, the Constitution, and International

Agreements," *Harvard Law Review* 68 (1955). Samuel P. Huntington, *The Soldier and the State: The Theory and Politics of Civil–Military Relations* (1957), is pertinent for the study of cold war constitutionalism.

XVII. *The Constitution and Civil Rights*

J. R. Pole, *The Pursuit of Equality in American History* (1978), and Terry Eastland and William J. Bennett, *Counting by Race: Equality from the Founding Fathers to Bakke and Weber* (1979), are good general historical accounts of civil rights problems. Other useful surveys are Charles Redenius, *The American Ideal of Equality: From Jefferson's Declaration to the Burger Court* (1981); Milton R. Konvitz, *A Century of Civil Rights* (1961); Robert J. Harris, *The Quest for Equality: The Constitution, Congress, and the Supreme Court* (1960); Duane Lockard, *Toward Equal Opportunity: A Study of State and Local Anti-Discrimination Laws* (1968); Morroe Berger, *Equality by Statute: The Revolution in Civil Rights,* rev. ed. (1968); Jack Greenberg, *Race Relations and American Law* (1959). Derrick A. Bell, Jr., ed. *Race, Racism, and American Law* (1973), is a case book.

The two late nineteenth-century cases that mark the base point for studies of the modern civil rights movement are analyzed in Richard A. Maidment, "Plessy v. Ferguson Re-examined," *Journal of American Studies* 7 (1973) and J. Morgan Kousser, "Separate but *Not* Equal: The Supreme Court's First Decision on Racial Discrimination in Schools," *JSH* 46 (1980), a study of the *Cumming* case. The following works treat civil rights issues in the first half of the twentieth century: Roger L. Rice, "Residential Segregation by Law, 1910–1917," *JSH* 34 (1968); Daniel T. Kelleher, "The Case of Lloyd Lionel Gaines: The Demise of the 'Separate-but-Equal' Doctrine," *JNH* 56 (1971); Augustus M. Burns III, "Graduate Education for Blacks in North Carolina, 1930–1951," *JSH* 46 (1980); Edward J. Knebler, "The Desegregation of the University of Maryland," *Maryland History Magazine* 71 (1976); Genna Rae McNeil, "Justiciable Cause: Howard University Law School and the Struggle for Civil Rights," *Howard Law Journal* 22 (1979); Daniel A. Novak, *The Wheel of Servitude: Black Forced Labor after Slavery* (1978); Pete Daniel, *The Shadow of Slavery: Peonage in the South, 1901–1969* (1972); William H. Hastie, "Toward an Equalitarian Legal Order, 1930–1950," *Annals* 407 (1973); Robert L. Zangrando, *The NAACP Crusade against Lynching, 1909–1950* (1980); Loren Miller, *The Petitioners: The Story of the Supreme Court of the United States and the Negro* (1966); Clement E. Vose, *Caucasians Only: The Supreme Court, the N.A.A.C.P. and the Restrictive Covenant Cases* (1959); Donald R. McCoy and Richard T. Ruetten, *Quest and Response: Minority Rights and the Truman Administration* (1973); Irving F. Lefberg, "Chief Justice Vinson and the Politics of Desegregation," *Emory Law Journal* 24 (1975); Richard Dalfiume, *Desegregation of the U.S. Armed Forces: Fighting on Two Fronts, 1939–1953* (1969); Robert K. Carr, *Federal Protection of Civil Rights: Quest for a Sword* (1947); Charles F. Kellogg, *NAACP: A History of the National Association for the Advancement of Colored People* (1967); Randall W. Bland, *Private Pressure on Public Law: The Legal Career of Justice Thurgood Marshall* (1973); Mary F. Berry, *Black Resistance/White Law: A History of Constitutional Racism in America* (1971).

A good contemporary account of the school desegregation problem on the eve of *Brown* v. *Board of Education* is John P. Roche, "Education, Segregation and the Supreme Court—A Political Analysis," *University of Pennsylvania Law Review* 99 (1951). Richard Kluger, *Simple Justice: The History of Brown* v. *Board of Education and Black America's Struggle for Equality* (1975), is an exhaustive narrative of the *Brown* case. The best analysis of the actual shaping of the decision is Dennis Hutchinson, "Unanimity and Desegregation: Decision-making in the Supreme Court, 1948–1958," *Georgetown Law Journal* 68 (1979). See also S. Sidney Ulmer, "Earl Warren and the Brown Decision," *JP* 33 (1971), and Alfred H. Kelly, "The School Desegregation Case," in John Garraty, ed., *Quarrels That Have Shaped the Constitution* (1964), providing an inside view of the preparation of the argument against segregation.

A number of works have analyzed Chief Justice Warren's opinion from a jurisprudential standpoint. See in particular Charles L. Black, Jr., "The Lawfulness of the Segregation Decisions," *Yale Law Journal* 69 (1960); Ira M. Heyman, "The Chief Justice, Racial Segregation and Friendly Critics," *California Law Review* 49 (1961); Morris D. Forposch, "The Desegregation Opinion Revisited: Legal or Sociological," *Vanderbilt Law Review* 21 (1967); Morton J. Horwitz, "The Jurisprudence of *Brown* and the Dilemmas of Liberalism," *Harvard Civil Rights–Civil Liberties Law Review* 14 (1979). The southern reaction to the *Brown* decision is described in Numan V. Bartley, *The Rise of Massive Resistance: Race and Politics in the South during the 1950s* (1969); Neil R. McMillen, *The Citizens Council: Organized Resistance to the Second Reconstruction, 1954–1964* (1971); Arthur S. Miller, *Racial Discrimination and Private Education: A Legal Analysis* (1957); Charles Fairman, "Attack on Segregation Cases," *Harvard Law Review* 70 (1956); Walter F. Murphy, "The South Counterattacks: The Anti-N.A.A.C.P. Laws," *Western Pol. Q.* 12 (1959). Albert P. Blaustein and C. C. Ferguson, Jr., *Desegregation and the Law: The Meaning and Effect of the School Segregation Cases,* rev. ed. (1962), is an early study of the implications of the decision.

Surveys of the progress of school desegregation reveal the shift to integration and affirmative action as a legal remedy. Pertinent works include Alexander M. Bickel, "The Decade of School Desegregation: Progress and Prospects," *Columbia Law Review* 64 (1964); John Kaplan, "Segregation Litigation and the Schools," *Northwestern University Law Review* 58–59 (1963–64); James R. Dunn, "Title VI, the Guidelines and School Desegregation in the South," *Virginia Law Review* 53 (1967); Harrell R. Rodgers, Jr., "The Supreme Court and School Desegregation: Twenty Years Later," *PSQ* 89 (1975); Charles S. Bullock III and Harrell R. Rodgers, Jr., "Coercion to Compliance: Southern School Districts and School Desegregation Guidelines," *JP* 38 (1976); Symposium, "School Desegregation: Lessons of the First Twenty-five Years," *Law and Contemporary Problems* 42 (1978); Tyll Van Geel, "Racial Discrimination from Little Rock to Harvard," *University of Cincinnati Law Review* 49 (1980).

J. Harvie Wilkinson III, *From Brown to Bakke: The Supreme Court and School Integration, 1954–1978* (1979), and Lino Graglio, *Disaster by Decree: The Supreme Court Decisions on Race and the Schools* (1976), are detailed accounts which criticize the judicial shift to result-oriented integration and affirmative-action policies based on racial considerations. Also critical are Richard A. Posner, "The De Funis Case and the Constitutionality of Preferential Treatment of Racial Minorities," *Supreme Court Review 1974* (1975); Robert G. Dixon, "The Supreme Court and

Equality: Legislative Classifications, Desegregation, and Reverse Discrimination," *Cornell Law Review* 62 (1977); Edmund W. Kitch, "The Return of Color-Consciousness to the Constitution: Weber, Dayton, and Columbus," *Supreme Court Review 1979* (1980); Iredell Jenkins, "The Impact and Implications of *De Funis* and *Bakke*," *American Journal of Jurisprudence* 24 (1979); David M. White, "Pride, Prejudice and Prediction: From *Brown* to *Bakke* and Beyond," *Howard Law Journal* 22 (1979); William Van Alstyne, "Rites of Passage: Race, the Supreme Court, and the Constitution," *University of Chicago Law Review* 46 (1978); Ralph A. Rossum, "Ameliorative Racial Reference and the Fourteenth Amendment: Some Constitutional Problems," *JP* 38 (1976).

The case for result-oriented affirmative-action policies based on racial group classification is made in Owen Fiss, "Racial Imbalance in the Public Schools: The Constitutional Concepts," *Harvard Law Review* 78 (1965); Fiss, "The Fate of an Idea Whose Time Has Come: Anti-Discrimination Law in the Second Decade after *Brown* v. *Board of Education*," *University of Chicago Law Review* 41 (1974); Fiss, "Groups and the Equal Protection Clause," *Philosophy and Public Affairs* 5 (1976); John Hart Ely, "The Constitutionality of Reverse Racial Discrimination," *University of Chicago Law Review* 41 (1974); Norman Vieira, "Racial Imbalance, Black Separatism, and Permissible Classification by Race," *Michigan Law Review* 67, (1969); William H. Hastie, "Affirmative Action in Vindicating Civil Rights," *University of Illinois Law Forum* 1975 (1975); J. Skelly Wright, "Color-Blind Theories and Color-Conscious Remedies," *University of Chicago Law Review* 47 (1980); Lawrence B. Joseph, "Some Ways of Thinking about Equality of Opportunity," *Western Pol. Q.* 33 (1980); Timothy J. O'Neill, "The Language of Equality in a Constitutional Order," *APSR* 75 (1981); Boris I. Bittker, *The Case for Black Reparations* (1973).

The busing problem in school desegregation is treated in Gary Orfield, *Must We Bus? Segregated Schools and National Policy* (1978), and James Bolner and Robert Shanley, *Busing: The Political and Judicial Process* (1974). On the preferential admissions cases, see Symposium, "Regents of the University of California v. Bakke," *California Law Review* 67 (1979); Lawrence H. Tribe, "Perspectives on Bakke: Equal Protection, Procedural Fairness, or Structural Justice?" *Harvard Law Review* 92 (1979); Guido Calabresi, "Bakke as Pseudo-Tragedy," *Catholic University Law Review* 28 (1979); Allen P. Sindler, *Bakke, De Funis, and Minority Admissions: The Quest for Equal Opportunity* (1978); Robert M. O'Neil, *Discriminating against Discrimination: Preferential Admissions and the De Funis Case* (1975).

Several works describe the expansion of civil rights efforts in the 1960s: William H. Chafe, *Civilities and Civil Rights: Greensboro, North Carolina, and the Black Struggle for Freedom* (1980), an account of the sit-in movement; M. G. Paulsen, "The Sit-In Cases of 1964: 'But Answer There Came None,' " *Supreme Court Review 1964* (1965); Benjamin Muse, *Ten Years of Prelude: The Story of Integration since the Supreme Court's 1954 Decision* (1964); C. C. Ferguson, Jr., "Civil Rights Legislation 1964: A Study of Constitutional Resources," *Federal Bar Journal* 24 (1964); Louis Lusky, "Racial Discrimination and the Federal Law: A Problem in Nullification," *Columbia Law Review* 63 (1963); Robert G. Dixon, Jr., "Civil Rights in Transportation and the I.C.C.," *George Washington Law Review* 31 (1962); Leon Friedman, ed., *Southern Justice* (1967); Arnold M. Rose, ed., "The Negro Protest," *Annals* 357 (1965). Donald B. King and Charles W. Quick, eds.,

Legal Aspects of the Civil Rights Movement (1965), is a useful survey of civil rights law in the mid-1960s.

Questions concerning voting and other political rights are examined in Philip L. Martin, "The Quest for Racial Representation in Legislative Apportionment," *Howard Law Journal* 21 (1978); Abigail M. Thernstrom, "The Odd Evolution of the Voting Rights Act," *Public Interest* no. 55 (1979); Joseph F. Zimmerman, "The Federal Voting Rights Act and Alternative Election Systems," *William and Mary Law Review* 19 (1978); Ward Y. Elliott, *The Rise of Guardian Democracy: The Supreme Court's Role in Voting Rights Disputes, 1845-1969* (1974); Charles V. Hamilton, *The Bench and the Ballot: Southern Federal Judges and Black Voters* (1973); Donald S. Strong, *Negroes, Ballots, and Judges: National Voting Rights Legislation in the Federal Courts* (1968); Warren Christopher, "The Constitutionality of the Voting Rights Act of 1965," *Stanford Law Review* 18 (1965); Frederick D. Ogden, *The Poll Tax in the South* (1958); Darlene Clark Hine, *Black Victory: The Rise and Fall of the White Primary in Texas* (1979); L. Thorne McCarty and Russell B. Stevenson, Jr., "The Voting Rights Act of 1965: An Evaluation," *Harvard Civil Rights-Civil Liberties Law Review* 3 (1968); Richard Claude, *The Supreme Court and the Electoral Process* (1970).

Employment discrimination against blacks is discussed in Herbert Hill, *Black Labor and the American Legal System,* 2 vols. (1977); Michael I. Sovern, *Legal Restraints on Racial Discrimination in Employment* (1966); Harry T. Edwards, "Race Discrimination in Employment: What Price Equality?" *University of Illinois Law Forum* 1976 (1976); Joe R. Feagin and Clairece B. Feagin, *Discrimination American Style: Institutional Racism and Sexism* (1978); Joel William Friedman, "The Burger Court and the Prima Facie Case in Employment Discrimination Litigation: A Critique," *Cornell Law Review* 65 (1979); Andrea H. Beller, "The Economics of Enforcement of an Antidiscrimination Law: Title VII of the Civil Rights Act of 1964," *Journal of Law and Economics* 21 (1978). The problem of affirmative action is analyzed in Bernard D. Meltzer, "The *Weber* Case: The Judicial Abrogation of the Antidiscrimination Standard in Employment," *University of Chicago Law Review* 47 (1980); William E. Boyd, "Affirmative Action in Employment—The *Weber* Decision," *Iowa Law Review* 66 (1980).

The state action–private action distinction in civil rights litigation is analyzed in Charles L. Black, Jr., "The Constitution and Public Power," *Yale Review* 52 (1962); Laurent B. Frantz, "Congressional Power to Enforce the Fourteenth Amendment against Private Acts," *Yale Law Journal* 73 (1964); Donald M. Cohen, "The Impact of Shelley v. Kraemer on the State Action Concept," *California Law Review* 44 (1956); Louis Henkin, "Shelley v. Kraemer, Notes for a Revised Opinion," *University of Pennsylvania Law Review* 110 (1962); Thomas P. Lewis, "The Meaning of State Action," *Columbia Law Review* 60 (1960); John Silard, "A Constitutional Forecast: Demise of the 'State Action' Limit on the Equal Protection Guarantee," *Columbia Law Review* 66 (1966); Charles L. Black, Jr., "Foreword: State Action, Equal Protection, and California's Proposition 14," *Harvard Law Review* 81 (1967). A recent survey of the problem is Thomas D. Rowe, Jr., "The Emerging Threshold Approach to State Action Determinations: Trying to Make Sense of *Flagg Brothers, Inc.* v. *Brooks,*" *Georgetown Law Journal* 69 (1980).

The use of reconstruction-era statutes in modern civil rights litigation is considered in Roy L. Brooks, "Use of the Civil Rights Act of 1866 and 1871 to Redress

Employment Discrimination," *Cornell Law Review* 62 (1977); Judith Olans Brown
et al., "Treating Blacks As If They Were White: Problems of Definition and Proof
in Section 1982 Cases," *University of Pennsylvania Law Review* 124 (1975); Gerhard
Casper, "Jones v. Mayer: Clio, Bemused and Confused Muse," *Supreme Court
Review 1968* (1969); Irving A. Gordon, "The Nature and Uses of Congressional
Power under Section Five of the Fourteenth Amendment to Overcome Decisions
of the Supreme Court," *Northwestern University Law Review* 72 (1978); G. Sidney
Buchanan, *The Quest for Freedom: A Legal History of the Thirteenth Amendment,*
reprinted from *Houston Law Review* 12 (1976).

There are thoughtful discussions of civil rights law in Derrick A. Bell, Jr.,
"Brown v. Board of Education and the Interests-Convergence Dilemma," *Harvard
Law Review* 93 (1980); Earleen M. McCarrick, "Equality v. Liberty: An Unresolved
Constitutional Conflict," *Polity* 10 (1978); Charles L. Black, Jr., "Civil Rights in
Times of Economic Stress—Jurisprudential and Philosophic Aspects," *University of
Illinois Law Forum* (1976); Frank P. Samford, III, "Toward a Constitutional Defini-
tion of Racial Discrimination," *Emory Law Journal* 25 (1976); Petra T. Shattuck
and Jill Norgren, "Political Use of the Legal Process by Black and American Indian
Minorities," *Howard Law Journal* 22 (1979); Walter Berns, "Racial Discrimination
and the Limits of Judicial Remedy," in Robert Goldwin, ed., *100 Years of Emancipation* (1963).

XVIII. *Constitutional Law and Modern Liberalism: The Warren Era*

There has been controversy since the Court-packing fight of 1937 over the
nature and function of judicial review. In the 1950s and 1960s the activist position
was represented in a number of works, chief among them Eugene V. Rostow, "The
Democratic Character of Judicial Review," *Harvard Law Review* 66 (1952); Alpheus T. Mason, "The Supreme Court, Temple and Forum," *Yale Law Review* 58
(1959); Mason, *The Supreme Court: Palladium of Freedom* (1963); Charles L.
Black, Jr., *The People and the Court: Judicial Review in a Democracy* (1960); Arthur
S. Miller and Ronald F. Howell, "The Myth of Neutrality in Constitutional Adjudication," *University of Chicago Law Review* 27 (1960); J. Skelly Wright, "The
Role of the Supreme Court in a Democratic Society—Judicial Activism or Restraint?" *Cornell Law Quarterly* 53 (1968). The judicial restraint model is described
in Felix Frankfurter, "Some Reflections on the Reading of Statutes," *Columbia
Law Review* 47 (1947); Learned Hand, *The Bill of Rights* (1958); Herbert Wechsler,
"Toward Neutral Principles of Constitutional Law," *Harvard Law Review* 73
(1959); Alexander M. Bickel, *The Least Dangerous Branch: The Supreme Court at
the Bar of Politics* (1962); Wallace Mendelson, *Black and Frankfurter: Conflict in
the Court* (1961). Howard E. Dean, *Judicial Review and Democracy* (1966), and
Robert J. Steamer, *The Supreme Court in Crisis: A History of Conflict* (1971), are
able surveys of the problem of judicial review. Sam J. Ervin, Jr. and Ramsey Clark,
Role of the Supreme Court: Policymaker or Adjudicator? (1970), presents a debate
over the judicial function.

The neorealist approach to judicial review is seen in Martin Shapiro, *Law and
Politics in the Supreme Court: New Approaches to Political Jurisprudence* (1964);
Shapiro, *Freedom of Speech: The Supreme Court and Judicial Review* (1966); Glen-

don A. Schubert, *Judicial Policy Making* (1965, 1974); Schubert, *The Judicial Mind: The Attitudes and Ideologies of Supreme Court Justices, 1946–1963* (1965). George Braden, "The Search for Objectivity in Constitutional Law," *Yale Law Journal* 57 (1948), anticipates this point of view in a perceptive commentary on Justices Black, Frankfurter, and Stone.

The best historical analysis of the post–New Deal judiciary through the Warren era is Martin M. Shapiro, "The Supreme Court from Warren to Burger," in Anthony King, ed., *The New American Political System* (1978). See also Shapiro, "The Court and Economic Rights," in M. J. Harmon, ed., *Essays on the Constitution of the United States* (1978). There are perceptive accounts in Sanford B. Gabin, *Judicial Review and the Reasonable Doubt Test* (1980); Karl E. Klare, "Judicial Deradicalization of the Wagner Act and the Origins of Modern Legal Consciousness, 1937–1941," *Minnesota Law Review* 62 (1978); Alexander M. Bickel, *The Supreme Court and the Idea of Progress* (1970); Bickel, *Politics and the Warren Court* (1965); Philip B. Kurland, *Politics, the Constitution and The Warren Court* (1970); Robert G. McCloskey, *The Modern Supreme Court* (1972); Archibald Cox, *The Warren Court: Constitutional Decision as an Instrument of Social Reform* (1968); Richard A. Maidment, "Policy in Search of Law: The Warren Court from *Brown* to *Miranda*," *Journal of American Studies* 9 (1975). Paul A. Freund, *On Law and Justice* (1968), offers temperate and judicious reflections on major constitutional problems in the Warren era, while Leonard W. Levy, ed., *The Supreme Court under Earl Warren* (1972), and Arthur J. Goldberg, *Equal Justice: The Supreme Court in the Warren Era* (1971), describe events from a libertarian perspective. Useful studies of judicial liberalism are found in Richard H. Sayler *et al.*, eds., *The Warren Court: A Critical Analysis* (1969); "Symposium: The Warren Court," *Michigan Law Review* 67 (1968); Clifford M. Lytle, *The Warren Court and Its Critics* (1968).

Justices Black and Frankfurter have been the most popular subjects of study among individual justices. The best works on Black are James J. Magee, *Mr. Justice Black: Absolutist on the Court* (1980); Gerald T. Dunne, *Hugo Black and the Judicial Revolution* (1977); Howard Ball, *The Vision and the Dream of Justice Hugo L. Black: An Examination of a Judicial Philosophy* (1975); Sylvia Snowiss, "The Legacy of Justice Black," *Supreme Court Review 1973* (1974); Virginia Van der Veer Hamilton, *Hugo Black: The Alabama Years* (1972); Tinsley Yarbrough, "Mr. Justice Black and Legal Positivism," *Virginia Law Review* 57 (1971); Charles A. Reich, "Mr. Justice Black and the Living Constitution," *Harvard Law Review* 76 (1963). Frankfurter's career is analyzed in Michael E. Parrish, *Felix Frankfurter and His Times: The Reform Years* (1982); H. N. Hirsch, *The Enigma of Felix Frankfurter* (1981); Gary Jacobsohn, "Felix Frankfurter and the Ambiguities of Judicial Statesmanship," *New York University Law Review* 49 (1974); Helen Thomas, *Felix Frankfurter: Scholar on the Bench* (1960); Joel B. Grossman, "Role-Playing and the Analysis of Judicial Behavior: The Case of Mr. Justice Frankfurter," *Journal of Public Law* 11 (1962); Louis L. Jaffe, "The Judicial Universe of Mr. Justice Frankfurter," *Harvard Law Review* 62 (1949); Samuel J. Konefsky, *The Constitutional World of Mr. Justice Frankfurter* (1949).

Other worthwhile accounts dealing with the post-1937 judiciary include James F. Simon, *Independent Journey: The Life of William O. Douglas* (1980); G. Edward White, *Earl Warren: Paradoxes of a Public Life* (1982); Jack Harrison Pollack, *Earl*

Warren: The Judge Who Changed America (1979), a journalistic treatment; Donald Roper, "The Jurisprudence of Arthur Goldberg: A Commentary," *Harvard Civil Rights–Civil Liberties Law Review* 8 (1973); Norman Redlich, "A Black-Harlan Dialogue on Due Process and Equal Protection: Overheard in Heaven and Dedicated to Robert M. McKay," *New York University Law Review* 50 (1975); J. Harvie Wilkinson III, "Justice John M. Harlan and the Values of Federalism," *Virginia Law Review* 57 (1971); Norman Dorsen, "The Second Mr. Justice Harlan: A Constitutional Conservative," *New York University Law Review* 44 (1969); Fowler B. Harper, *Justice Rutledge and the Bright Constellation* (1965); John P. Frank, "Fred Vinson and the Chief Justiceship," *University of Chicago Law Review* 21 (1954); Glendon Schubert, *Dispassionate Justice: A Synthesis of the Judicial Opinions of Robert H. Jackson* (1969); Symposium, "Mr. Justice Jackson–a Symposium," *Stanford Law Review* 8 (1955).

Two significant assessments of judicial power in the post–New Deal period are Robert A. Dahl, "Decision-Making in a Democracy: The Supreme Court as a National Policy-Maker," *Journal of Public Law* 6 (1958), and Willard Hurst, "Review and the Distribution of National Power," in Edmond Cahn, ed., *Supreme Court and Supreme Law* (1954). As the Supreme Court attempted to alter local institutions in the 1960s, a number of compliance studies were undertaken that cast light on judicial power. See, for example, Theodore L. Becker and Malcolm M. Feeley, eds., *The Impact of Supreme Court Decisions* (1973); Stephen L. Wasby, *The Impact of the United States Supreme Court: Some Perspectives* (1970); Richard M. Johnson, *The Dynamics of Compliance: Supreme Court Decision-Making from a New Perspective* (1967). The power of the federal judiciary in the post–New Deal era is viewed from the standpoint of federal-state relations in Ruth Locke Roettinger, *The Supreme Court and State Police Power: A Study in Federalism* (1957) and Paul R. Benson, *The Supreme Court and the Commerce Clause 1937–1970* (1970).

The legal literature on specific constitutional problems in the 1950s and 1960s is voluminous, but the key developments can be explored in a number of seminal studies. Jonathan D. Casper, *The Politics of Civil Liberties* (1972), and Milton R. Konvitz, "The Flower and the Thorn," in Alan Reitman, ed., *The Pulse of Freedom: American Liberties: 1920–1970s* (1972), survey civil liberties developments in the 1960s. On reapportionment see Gordon E. Baker, *The Reapportionment Revolution* (1967); Robert G. Dixon, Jr., "The Warren Court Crusade for the Holy Grail of 'One Man–*One Vote*,' " *Supreme Court Review 1969* (1970); Dixon, *Democratic Representation: Reapportionment in Law and Politics* (1968); Richard C. Cortner, *The Apportionment Cases* (1970); Robert McKay, *Reapportionment: The Law and Politics of Equal Representation* (1964); Anthony Lewis, "Legislative Apportionment and the Federal Courts," *Harvard Law Review* 71 (1958).

The school-prayer decisions are dealt with in John Herbert Laubach, *School Prayers: Congress, the Courts, and the Public* (1969); Charles E. Rice, *The Supreme Court and Public Prayer: The Need for Restraint* (1964); Paul G. Kauper, "Prayer, Public Schools and the Supreme Court," *Michigan Law Review* 61 (1963); Leo Pfeffer, "Court, Constitution, and Prayer," *Rutgers Law Review* 16 (1962). Earlier establishment-of-religion questions are examined in Wilbur Katz, "Freedom of Religion and State Neutrality," *University of Chicago Law Review* 20 (1953), and Edward S. Corwin, "The Supreme Court as a National School Board," *Law and*

Contemporary Problems 14 (1949). William K. Muir, Jr., *Prayer in the Public Schools: Law and Attitude Change* (1967), and Kenneth M. Dolbeare and Phillip E. Hammond, *The School Prayer Decisions: From Court Policy to Local Practice* (1971), are impact studies of Supreme Court decisions in this area.

In the field of criminal procedure, Richard C. Cortner, *The Supreme Court and the Second Bill of Rights* (1981), is an excellent account of the application of federal constitutional requirements to the states under the due process clause of the Fourteenth Amendment. Also valuable on this question are Adam C. Breckenridge, *Congress against the Court* (1970), a study of the legislative reaction to judicial decisions in criminal procedure; Fred P. Graham, *The Due Process Revolution: The Warren Court's Impact on Criminal Law* (1970); A. Kenneth Pye, "The Warren Court and Criminal Procedure," *Michigan Law Review* 67 (1968); Walter V. Schaefer, "Police Interrogation and the Privilege against Self-Incrimination," *Northwestern University Law Review* 61 (1966); Henry J. Friendly, "The Bill of Rights as a Code of Criminal Procedure," *California Law Review* 53 (1965); Jay Sigler, *Double Jeopardy: The Development of a Legal and Social Policy* (1969); Phillip Johnson, "Retroactivity in Retrospect," *California Law Review* 56 (1968).

Alfred H. Kelly, "Constitutional Liberty and the Law of Libel: A Historian's View," *AHR* 74 (1968), is a good summary of the civil libel question in its historical and contemporary aspects. Other worthwhile discussions of free-speech issues are Harry Kalven, Jr., " 'Uninhibited, Robust, and Wide-Open'—a Note on Free Speech and the Warren Court," *Michigan Law Review* 67 (1968); Donald Meiklejohn, "Public Speech and the First Amendment," *Georgetown Law Journal* 55 (1966); Arthur L. Barney, "Libel and the First Amendment—a New Constitutional Privilege," *Virginia Law Review* 51 (1965). Control of pornography is intelligently discussed in Harry M. Clor, *Obscenity and Public Morality: Censorship in a Liberal Society* (1969); Richard H. Kuh, *Foolish Figleaves? Pornography in—and out of—Court* (1969); C. Peter Magrath, "The Obscenity Cases: The Grapes of Roth," *Supreme Court Review 1966* (1967); Louis Henkin, "Morals and the Constitution: The Sin of Obscenity," *Columbia Law Review* 63 (1963); William B. Lockhart and Robert C. McClure, "Literature, the Law of Obscenity, and the Constitution," *Minnesota Law Review* 38 (1954); Richard Funston, "Pornography and Politics: The Court, the Constitution, and the Commission," *Western Pol. Q.* 24 (1971).

The right to privacy receives broad examination in Alan F. Westin, *Privacy and Freedom* (1967); Adam C. Breckenridge, *The Right to Privacy* (1970); Edward V. Long, *The Intruders: The Invasion of Privacy by Government and Industry* (1967); William M. Beaney, "The Constitutional Right to Privacy in the Supreme Court," *Supreme Court Review 1962* (1963). The birth-control decision is analyzed in Robert G. Dixon, "The Griswold Penumbra: Constitutional Charter for an Expanded Law of Privacy?" *Michigan Law Review* 64 (1965); Thomas I. Emerson, "Nine Justices in Search of a Doctrine," *Michigan Law Review* 64 (1965); William M. Beaney, "The Griswold Case and the Expanded Right to Privacy," *Wisconsin Law Review* 1966.

The expansion of equal-protection law as a basic corollary of positive government is forecast in a seminal article by Joseph Tussman and Jacobus ten Broek, "The Equal Protection of the Laws," *California Law Review* 37 (1949). For later development of the equal-protection idea, see Gerald Gunther, "Foreword: In Search of Evolving Doctrine on a Changing Court: A Model for a Newer Equal

Protection," *Harvard Law Review* 86 (1972); Note, "The Evolution of Equal Protection: Education, Municipal Services, and Wealth," *Harvard Civil Rights–Civil Liberties Law Review* 7 (1972); Philip B. Kurland, "Egalitarianism and the Warren Court," *Michigan Law Review* 68 (1970); Frank I. Michelman, "Foreword: On Protecting the Poor through the Fourteenth Amendment," *Harvard Law Review* 83 (1969). Charles Reich, "The New Property," *Yale Law Journal* 73 (1964), is an important argument for a redefinition of welfare-state benefits as constitutionally protected property. See also "Symposium: Law of the Poor," *California Law Review* 54 (1966). Robert M. O'Neil, *The Price of Dependency: Civil Liberties in the Welfare State* (1970), is a comprehensive study of this new area of constitutional law. The expanded rights of government employees in the 1960s are described in David H. Rosenbloom, *Federal Service and the Constitution: The Development of the Public Employment Relationship* (1971), and William W. Van Alstyne, "The Demise of the Right-Privilege Distinction in Constitutional Law," *Harvard Law Review* 81 (1968).

XIX. *The Liberal Regulatory State and the Modern Presidency: 1945–1980*

Roland Young, *American Law and Politics: The Creation of Public Order* (1967), offers a good description of the post–New Deal polity. M. J. C. Vile, *Politics in the U.S.A.* (1970), and H. G. Nicholas, *The Nature of American Politics* (1980), are analyses of the constitutional order from a British perspective which take into account the changes resulting from radical protest movements of the 1960s, while Samuel P. Huntington, *American Politics: The Promise of Disharmony* (1981), is a penetrating analysis of recent constitutional politics that emphasizes the conflict between ideals and institutions in American political culture. Theodore J. Lowi, *The End of Liberalism: Ideology, Policy, and the Crisis of Public Authority* (1969; rev. ed., 1979), describes the delegation of governmental power to private interest groups and offers a sharp critique of this liberal-pluralist method of government. James L. Sundquist, *Politics and Policy: The Eisenhower, Kennedy, and Johnson Years* (1968), and A. James Reichley, *Conservatives in an Age of Change: The Nixon and Ford Administrations* (1981), provide historical accounts of the major public-policy questions that have dominated constitutional politics in the past three decades. Changes in the electorate are described in Everett Carll Ladd, Jr., with Charles D. Hadley, *Transformations of the American Party System: Political Conditions from the New Deal to the 1970s* (1975).

The relationship between private groups and regulatory agencies that forms the basis of the liberal-pluralist political economy is discussed in Earl Latham, "The Group Basis of Politics: Notes for a Theory," *APSR* 46 (1952); Peter H. Odegard, "A Group Basis of Politics: A New Name for an Ancient Myth," *Western Pol. Q.* 20 (1958); Norton E. Long, "Bureaucracy and Constitutionalism," *APSR* 46 (1952); Wolfgang G. Friedmann, "Corporate Power, Government by Private Groups, and the Law," *Columbia Law Review* 57 (1957); Grant McConnell, *Private Power and American Democracy* (1966); Robert L. Hale, *Freedom through Law: Public Control of Private Governing Power* (1952). Arthur F. Bentley, *The Process of Government: A Study of Social Pressures* (1908), is a classic source of pluralist theory. Andrew Shonfield, *Modern Capitalism* (1965), Michael D. Regan, *The Managed Economy* (1963), and Eugene V. Rostow, *Planning for Freedom: The Public Law of American Capitalism* (1959), focus on the problem of public and private power in the post–New Deal political economy.

In criticizing the delegation of power to private groups through the process of administrative rule making, Lowi, *The End of Liberalism,* stimulated a reconsideration of the principle of nondelegation of legislative power. See in this connection Sotirios A. Barber, *The Constitution and the Delegation of Congressional Power* (1975); James O. Freedman, "Delegation of Power and Institutional Competence," *University of Chicago Law Review* 43 (1975); Carl McGowan, "Congress, Court, and Control of Delegated Power," *Columbia Law Review* 77 (1977); Bernard Schwartz, "Of Administrators and Philosopher-Kings: The *Republic,* the *Laws,* and Delegations of Power," *Northwestern University Law Review* 72 (1978). Lowi's recommendation for a return to the *Schechter* rule provides the focus for Richard F. Bensel, "Creating the Statutory State: The Implications of a Rule of Law Standard in American Politics," *APSR* 74 (1980); Robert C. Grady, "Interest-Group Liberalism and Juridical Democracy: Two Theses in Search of Legitimacy," *American Politics Quarterly* 6 (1978); Lyle Downing and Robert B. Thigpen, "A Liberal Dilemma: The Application of Unger's Critique of Formalism to Lowi's Concept of Juridical Democracy," *JP* 44 (1982).

There are perceptive observations about the modern regulatory state in James O. Freedman, *Crisis and Legitimacy: The Administrative Process and American Government* (1978); James Q. Wilson, "The Rise of the Bureaucratic State," *Public Interest* no. 41 (1975); David Vogel, "The Corporation as Government Challenge and Dilemmas," *Polity* 8 (1975–76); Hugh Heclo, "Issue Networks and the Executive Establishment," in Anthony King, ed., *The New American Political System* (1978); Richard B. Stewart, "The Reformation of American Administrative Law," *Harvard Law Review* 88 (1975); Vincent Ostrum, *The Intellectual Crisis in American Public Administration* (1974). Ernest Gellhorn and Glen O. Robinson, "Rulemaking 'Due Process': An Inconclusive Dialogue," *University of Chicago Law Review* 48 (1981), considers the ways in which administrative agencies have adapted to judicial standards and methods of operation. Antitrust as a regulatory instrument is covered in Robert H. Bork, *The Antitrust Paradox: A Policy at War with Itself* (1978). Kenneth W. Clarkson and Timothy J. Muris, eds., *The Federal Trade Commission since 1970* (1981), reviews the revitalization of one of the more controversial regulatory agencies in recent years. The position of trade unions in the liberal pluralist state is the subject of Katherine Van Wezel Stone, "The Post-War Paradigm in American Labor Law," *Yale Law Journal* 90 (1981).

The best recent historical surveys of the presidential office are Arthur M. Schlesinger, Jr., *The Imperial Presidency* (1973), and Fred I. Greenstein, "The Modern Presidency," in Anthony King, ed., *The New American Political System* (1978). Scholarly views toward the presidency have changed significantly in the past decade and a half. Liberal approval of a powerful presidency is seen in the classic works of Harold Laski, *The American Presidency: An Interpretation* (1940); Pendleton Herring, *Presidential Leadership* (1940); Clinton Rossiter, *Constitutional Dictatorship: Crisis Government in the Modern Democracies* (1948); Rossiter, *The American Presidency* (1956); Walter Lippmann, *Essays in the Public Philosophy* (1955); Richard Neustadt, *Presidential Power: The Politics of Leadership* (1956);

Neustadt, "The Presidency at Mid-Century," *Law and Contemporary Problems* 21 (1956); Rexford G. Tugwell, *The Enlargement of the Presidency* (1960); Louis W. Koenig, *The Chief Executive* (1964); James MacGregor Burns, *Presidential Government: The Crucible of Leadership* (1965).

There were dissenters to the liberal theory of presidential power, notably Caleb Perry Patterson, *Presidential Government in the United States: The Unwritten Constitution* (1947); Edward S. Corwin, *The President: Office and Powers* (1940, 1957); and Herman Finer, *The Presidency: Crisis and Regeneration* (1960), who argued that far too much was demanded of the chief executive. In reaction to the Vietnam war and the Watergate affair, criticism of presidential power and emphasis on the limitations of the office dominated scholarly analyses. See Aaron Wildavsky, "The Past and Future Presidency," *Public Interest* no. 41 (1975); Norton Long, "Reflections on Presidential Power," *Public Administrative Review* 29 (1969); James David Barber, *The Presidential Character* (1972); Charles M. Hardin, *Presidential Power and Accountability* (1974); Thomas E. Cronin, *The State of the Presidency* (1975); Richard M. Pious, *The American Presidency* (1979); Hugh Heclo and Lester M. Salamon, eds., *The Illusion of Presidential Government* (1981).

The president's relationship with the bureaucracy and the problem of executive management are discussed in Larry Berman, *The Office of Management and Budget and the Presidency, 1921–1979* (1979); Louis Fisher and Ronald C. Moe, "Presidential Reorganization Authority: Is It Worth the Cost?" *PSQ* 96 (1981); Harold H. Bruff, "Presidential Power and Administrative Rulemaking," *Yale Law Journal* 88 (1979); Barry Dean Karl, "Executive Reorganization and Presidential Power," *Supreme Court Review 1977* (1978); Harvey C. Mansfield, "Federal Executive Reorganization: Thirty Years Experience," *Public Administrative Review* 29 (1969). Peri E. Arnold, "The First Hoover Commission and the Managerial Presidency," *JP* 38 (1976), shows how conservative critics of FDR were reconciled to a modern conception of executive control in the Truman period. Diverse aspects of recent presidential history are covered in "Symposium: The Presidency in Transition," *JP* 11 (1949); Richard Fenno, *The President's Cabinet* (1959); Clinton Rossiter, *The Supreme Court and the Commander-in-Chief* (1951); Glendon Schubert, *The Presidency in the Courts* (1957); Richard P. Longaker, *The Presidency and Individual Liberties* (1961); Donald L. Robinson, "The Routinization of Crisis Government," *Yale Review* 63 (1973).

Among works dealing with individual presidents, the following have value for constitutional history: Maeva Marcus, *Truman and the Steel Seizure Case: The Limits of Presidential Power* (1977); Francis H. Heller, ed., *The Truman White House: The Administration of the Presidency 1945–1953* (1980); Fred I. Greenstein, "Eisenhower as an Activist President: A Look at New Evidence," *PSQ* 94 (1979–80); Robert Griffith, "Dwight D. Eisenhower and the Corporate Commonwealth," *AHR* 87 (1982); Arthur M. Schlesinger, Jr., *A Thousand Days: John F. Kennedy in the White House* (1965); Henry Fairlie, *The Kennedy Promise: The Politics of Expectation* (1973); Doris Kearns, *Lyndon Johnson and the American Dream* (1976); Garry Wills, *Nixon Agonistes: The Crisis of the Self-Made Man* (1970).

A number of works illustrate the disenchantment with modern liberal constitutionalism that occurred in the 1960s. See, for example, C. Wright Mills, *The Power Elite* (1956); Jack L. Walker, "A Critique of the Elitist Theory of Democracy," *APSR* 60 (1966); Kirk Thompson, "Constitutional Theory and Political Action," *JP* 31 (1969); William E. Connolly, ed., *The Bias of Pluralism* (1969); Henry S. Kariel, "Expanding the Political Present," *APSR* 63 (1969). Herman Belz, "New Left Reverberations in the Academy: The Anti-Pluralist Critique of Constitution-alism," *Review of Politics* 36 (1974), assesses this body of literature. Still the best general analysis of radical attitudes is Ronald Berman, *America in the Sixties: An Intellectual History* (1968), while Anthony M. Platt, *The Politics of the Riot Com-missions, 1917–1970* (1971), provides a good view of the public disorders of the late 1960s and the government's response to them. There are perceptive observations on the riots and protest movements in David Potter, "Changing Patterns of Social Cohesion and the Crisis of Law under a System of Government by Consent," in Eugene V. Rostow, ed., *Is Law Dead?* (1971); Walter Dean Burnham, "Crisis of American Political Legitimacy," *Society* 10 (1972); Samuel P. Huntington, "Para-digms of American Politics: Beyond the One, the Two, and the Many," *PSQ* 89 (1974); Gerald Garvey, *Constitutional Bricolage* (1971); Samuel Beer, "In Search of a New Public Philosophy," in A. King, ed., *The New American Political System* (1978); Lowi, *The End of Liberalism;* Lowi, *The Politics of Disorder* (1971). Jerold S. Auerbach, *Unequal Justice: Lawyers and Social Change in Modern America* (1976), argues that the crisis of the 1960s resulted from the deliberate divorce of the legal order and the legal profession from social justice.

Rostow, ed., *Is Law Dead?,* contains essays on civil disobedience and the protest movements, for which see also Wilson Carey McWilliams, "Civil Disobe-dience and Contemporary Constitutionalism: The American Case," *Comparative Politics* 1 (1969); Hannah Arendt, "Civil Disobedience," in *Crises of the Republic* (1972); Paul F. Power, "On Civil Disobedience in Recent American Democratic Thought," *APSR* 64 (1970); Power, "Civil Disobedience as Functional Opposi-tion," *JP* 34 (1972). John T. Elliff, *Crime, Dissent, and the Attorney General: The Justice Department in the 1960s* (1971), is a narrative of the riots and protests, and Isaac D. Balbus, *The Dialectics of Legal Repression: Black Rebels before the Ameri-can Criminal Courts* (1973), analyzes the riots from a Marxist point of view.

The most pertinent background for the Watergate affair from a constitutional standpoint is the expansion of presidential power in foreign affairs and for national security purposes. On these matters, see W. Taylor Reveley III, *War Powers of the President and Congress: Who Holds the Arrows and Olive Branch?* (1981); Francis O. Wilcox and Richard A. Frank, eds., *The Constitution and the Conduct of Foreign Policy* (1976); Louis Henkin, *Foreign Affairs and the Constitution* (1972); Francis Wormuth, *The Vietnam War: The President vs. the Constitution* (1974); John Nor-ton Moore, *Law and the Indo-China War* (1972); Raoul Berger, "War Making by the President," *University of Pennsylvania Law Review* 121 (1972); Charles A. Lof-gren, "*United States* v. *Curtiss-Wright Export Corporation:* An Historical Assess-ment," *Yale Law Journal* 83 (1973); Richard F. Haynes, *The Awesome Power: Harry S. Truman as Commander in Chief* (1973). Domestic political intelligence operations preceding President Nixon are the focus of Richard W. Steele, "Frank-lin D. Roosevelt and His Foreign Policy Critics," *PSQ* 94 (1979); Barton J. Bern-stein, "The Road to Watergate and Beyond: The Growth and Abuse of Executive Power since 1940," *Law and Contemporary Problems* 40 (1976); Athan Theoharis, *Spying on Americans: Political Surveillance from Hoover to the Huston Plan* (1978); David Wise, *The American Police State: The Government against the People* (1976); Victor Lasky, *It Didn't Start with Watergate* (1977).

Concerning the impoundment question, see Louis Fisher, *Presidential Spending Power* (1975); Abner J. Mikva and Michael Hertz, "Impoundment of Funds—the Courts, the Congress and the President: A Constitutional Triangle," *Northwestern University Law Review* 69 (1974); Warren Archer, "Presidential Impoundment of Funds," *University of Chicago Law Review* 40 (1973). John W. Dumbrell and John D. Lees, "Presidential Pocket-Veto Power: A Constitutional Anachronism?" *Political Studies* 28 (1980), is a good analysis of that issue. Valuable studies of executive privilege are Raoul Berger, *Executive Privilege: A Constitutional Myth* (1974); Archibald Cox, "Executive Privilege," *University of Pennsylvania Law Review* 122 (1974); Paul Freund, "Foreword: On Presidential Privilege," *Harvard Law Review* 88 (1974); Adam C. Breckenridge, *The Executive Privilege: Presidential Control over Information* (1974); "Symposium: United States v. Nixon," *UCLA Law Review* 22 (1974).

There are perceptive analyses of the Watergate affair and its constitutional significance in Nelson W. Polsby, *Political Promises: Essays and Commentary on American Politics* (1974); Josiah Lee Auspitz and Clifford W. Brown, Jr., "What's Wrong with Politics?" *Harper's Magazine* 248 (1974); Alexander M. Bickel, "Watergate and the Legal Order," *Commentary* 57 (1974); Philip S. Kurland, *Watergate and the Constitution* (1978); The Ripon Society and Clifford W. Brown, Jr., *Jaws of Victory: The Game-Plan Politics of 1972, the Crisis of the Republican Party, and the Future of the Constitution* (1974); James David Barber, "Nixon's Brush with Tyranny," *PSQ* 92 (1977–78); Paul F. Kress, "Of Action and Virtue: Notes on the Presidency, Watergate, and Liberal Society," *Polity* 10 (1978); Arthur J. Vidrich, "Political Legitimacy in Bureaucratic Society: An Analysis of Watergate," *Social Research* 42 (1975); Sanford Levinson, "The Specious Morality of the Law," *Harper's Magazine* 254 (1977). Ronald E. Pynn, ed., *Watergate and the American Political Process* (1975), is a good collection of essays, while contemporary assessments of Watergate include David Saffell, ed., *Watergate: Its Effects on the American Political System* (1974); Frederick C. Mosher *et al.*, *Watergate: Implications for Responsible Government* (1974); Ralph K. Winter, *Watergate and the Law: Political Campaigns and Presidential Power* (1974); Symposium, "American Political Institutions after Watergate—a Discussion," *PSQ* 89 (1974–75).

Several able works on impeachment predated the inquiry directed at President Nixon. They include Raoul Berger, *Impeachment: The Constitutional Problems* (1973); Irving Brant, *Impeachment: Trials and Errors* (1972); Charles L. Black, Jr., *Impeachment: A Handbook* (1974); Arthur Bestor, "Impeachment," *Washington Law Review* 49 (1973), a review of Berger's book. Materials dealing with the proposed Nixon impeachment are found in *U.S. House of Representatives, Committee on the Judiciary, President Richard M. Nixon: Report by the Committee on H. Res. 803, 93rd Cong., 2nd sess., 1974.* John R. Labovitz, *Presidential Impeachment* (1978), is an excellent recent study. Other worthwhile observations on impeachment and Watergate are found in Bernard Schwartz, "Bad Presidents Make Hard Law: Richard M. Nixon in the Supreme Court," *Rutgers Law Review* 31 (1977); David W. Dennis, "Impeachment Revisited," *Indiana Law Review* 9 (1976), the reflections of a Republican Congressman; Louis H. Pollak, "The Constitution as an Experiment," *University of Pennsylvania Law Review* 123 (1975); Philip S. Kurland, "The Power and the Glory: Passing Thoughts on Reading Judge Sirica's Watergate Expose," *Stanford Law Review* 32 (1979); Leon Jaworski, *The Right and the Power: The Prosecution of Watergate* (1976).

The reaction against the imperial presidency can be seen in the general works on the presidency cited previously, and in Howard J. Silver, "Presidential Power and the Post-Watergate Presidency," *Pres. Studies Q.* 8 (1978) and Norman C. Thomas, "Presidential Accountability since Watergate," *Pres. Studies Q.* 8 (1978). The restoration of congressional power as a direct consequence of Watergate is examined in James L. Sundquist, *The Decline and Resurgence of Congress* (1981); Thomas E. Cronin, "A Resurgent Congress and the Imperial Presidency," *PSQ* 95 (1980); Harvey G. Zeldenstein, "The Reassertion of Congressional Power: New Curbs on the President," *PSQ* 93 (1978); Morris P. Fiorina, *Congress: Keystone of the Washington Establishment* (1977); Harvey Mansfield, ed., *Congress against the President* (1976). James MacGregor Burns, *Congress on Trial: The Legislative Process and the Administrative State* (1949), is an older critique of Congress. More positive evaluations of Congress forming a basis for the reassessment of the institution in the 1970s are found in Nelson W. Polsby, "Strengthening Congress in National Policy-Making," *Yale Review* 59 (1970); Polsby, *Congress and the Presidency* (1964); Ronald C. Moe and S. C. Teel, "Congress as Policy-Maker: A Necessary Reappraisal," *PSQ* 85 (1970); Joseph Harris, *Congressional Control of Administration* (1964); Alfred deGrazia, *Republic in Crisis: Congress against the Executive Force* (1965); Roland Young, *The American Congress* (1958); James Burnham, *Congress and the American Tradition* (1959); Lawrence H. Chamberlain, *The President, Congress, and Legislation* (1946).

In the 1970s the legislative veto became the focal point of conflict between Congress and the executive and administrative departments and agencies. See John B. Henry II, "The Legislative Veto: In Search of Constitutional Limits," *Harvard Journal on Legislation* 16 (1979); Robert G. Dixon, Jr., "The Congressional Veto and Separation of Powers: The Executive on a Leash?" *North Carolina Law Review* 56 (1978); Arthur S. Miller and George M. Knapp, "The Congressional Veto: Preserving the Constitutional Framework," *Indiana Law Journal* 52 (1977); Harold H. Bruff and Ernest Gellhorn, "Congressional Control of Administrative Regulation: A Study of Legislative Vetoes," *Harvard Law Review* 90 (1977).

Significant changes in election campaign laws and political party organization as a reaction to Watergate are surveyed in Austin Ranney, "The Political Parties: Reform and Decline," in King, ed., *The New American Political System;* Michael J. Malbin, ed., *Parties, Interest Groups, and Campaign Finance Laws* (1980); Symposium, "Federal Election Laws," *Emory Law Journal* 29 (1980); Thomas B. Curtis, "Reflections on Voluntary Compliance under the Federal Election Campaign Act," *Case Western Reserve Law Review* 29 (1979); Harold Leventhal, "Courts and Political Thickets," *Columbia Law Review* 77 (1977). Benjamin R. Civiletti, "Post-Watergate Legislation in Retrospect," *Southwestern Law Journal* 34 (1981), reviews the operation of a variety of reform measures in the 1970s.

XX. *Constitutional Law and the Burger Court*

Richard Y. Funston, *Constitutional Counterrevolution? The Warren Court and the Burger Court: Judicial Policy Making in Modern America* (1977), is an excellent general account which emphasizes continuity in the development of constitutional law in the 1970s. Archibald Cox, *The Role of the Supreme Court in American Government* (1976), adopts a similar perspective in analyzing the policy-making activity of the Burger Court. There are good general analyses of the Burger period in Walter Berns, *The First Amendment and the Future of American Democracy* (1976); Robert J. Steamer, "Contemporary Supreme Court Directions in Civil Liberties," *PSQ* 92 (1977); Symposium, "The Burger Court: Reflections of the First Decade," *Law and Contemporary Problems* 43 (1980); William W. Van Alstyne, "The Recrudescence of Property Rights as the Foremost Principle of Civil Liberties: The First Decade of the Burger Court," *Law and Contemporary Problems* 43 (1980).

Arguing that the Burger Court has departed significantly from Warren Court precedents are Edward V. Heck, "Civil Liberties Voting Patterns in the Burger Court 1975–1978," *Western Pol. Q.* 34 (1981); Robert D. Goldstein, "A *Swann* Song for Remedies: Equitable Relief in the Burger Court," *Harvard Civil Rights–Civil Liberties Law Review* 13 (1978); Alan B. Morrison, "Rights without Remedies: The Burger Court Takes the Federal Courts Out of the Business of Protecting Federal Rights," *Rutgers Law Review* 30 (1977); Tinsley E. Yarbrough, "Litigant Access Doctrine and the Burger Court," *Vanderbilt Law Review* 31 (1978). Earlier assessments of the Burger justices are similarly mixed. See, for example, Leonard W. Levy, *Against the Law: The Nixon Court and Criminal Justice* (1974); William F. Swindler, "The Court, the Constitution, and Chief Justice Burger," *Vanderbilt Law Review* 27 (1974); Alpheus T. Mason, "The Burger Court in Historical Perspective," *PSQ* 89 (1974); Symposium, "The Burger Court: New Directions in Judicial Policy-Making," *Emory Law Journal* 23 (1974).

There are able general discussions of Burger Court decisions concerning federalism in A. E. Dick Howard, "The Supreme Court and Federalism," in *The Courts: The Pendulum of Federalism* (1979); Henry P. Monaghan, "The Burger Court and 'Our Federalism,' " *Law and Contemporary Problems* 43 (1980); Neil D. McFeeley, "The Supreme Court and the Federal System: Federalism from Warren to Burger," *Publius* 8 (1978); Louise Weinberg, "A New Judicial Federalism?" *Daedalus* 107 (1978); Lewis B. Kaden, "Politics, Money, and State Sovereignty: The Judicial Role," *Columbia Law Review* 79 (1979). On federal-state relations under the commerce power, see Bernard Schwartz, "Commerce, the States, and the Burger Court," *Northwestern University Law Review* 74 (1979), and Earl M. Maltz, "The Burger Court, the Commerce Clause, and the Problem of Differential Treatment," *Indiana Law Journal* 54 (1978–79).

The attitude of the Supreme Court toward state courts and local governments is considered in Richard A. Michael, "The 'New' Federalism and the Burger Court's Deference to the States in Federal Habeas Proceedings," *Iowa Law Review* 64 (1979), and Archibald Cox, "Federalism and Individual Rights," *Northwestern University Law Review* 73 (1978). Worthwhile analyses of the *Usury* case, the federalism decision that attracted the most attention in the Burger era, are Richard E. Johnston and John T. Thompson, "The Burger Court and Federalism: A Revolution in 1976?" *Western Pol. Q.* 33 (1980); Lawrence H. Tribe, "Unraveling National League of Cities: The New Federalism and Affirmative Rights to Essential Government Services," *Harvard Law Review* 90 (1977); Kenneth F. Ripple and Douglas W. Kenyon, "State Sovereignty—a Polished but Slippery Crown," *Notre Dame Lawyer* 54 (1979). The Burger Court's attitude toward litigation under Section 1983 of the U.S. Code, claiming violations of civil rights by state and local governments, is analyzed in Melvyn R. Durchslag, "Federalism and Constitutional Liberties:

Varying the Remedy to Save the Right," *Michigan Law Review* 54 (1979), and Eric Schnapper, "Civil Rights Litigation after *Monell,*" *Columbia Law Review* 79 (1979). Federal-state relations as affected by the Eleventh Amendment are examined in Martha A. Field, "The Eleventh Amendment and Other Sovereign Immunity Doctrines: Congressional Imposition of Suit upon the States," *University of Pennsylvania Law Review* 126 (1978); Clyde E. Jacobs, *The Eleventh Amendment and Sovereign Immunity* (1972).

Decisions of the Burger Court concerning criminal procedure in general are discussed in Louis M. Seidman, "Factual Guilt and the Burger Court: An Examination of Continuity and Change in Criminal Procedure," *Columbia Law Review* 80 (1980); Stephen A. Saltzburg, "Foreword: The Flow and Ebb of Constitutional Criminal Procedure in the Warren and Burger Courts," *Georgetown Law Journal* 69 (1980); Robert Popper, "De-Nationalizing the Bill of Rights," in *The Courts: The Pendulum of Federalism* (1979); Jerold H. Israel, "Criminal Procedure, the Burger Court, and the Legacy of the Warren Court," *Michigan Law Review* 75 (1977). The fate of a key Warren Court ruling is explored in Geoffrey R. Stone, "The Miranda Doctrine in the Burger Court," *Supreme Court Review 1977* (1978), and Thomas S. Schrock *et al.,* "Interrogational Rights: Reflections on *Miranda v. Arizona,*" *Southern California Law Review* 52 (1978).

Fourth Amendment problems are treated in William A. Schroeder, "Deterring Fourth Amendment Violations: Alternatives to the Exclusionary Rule," *Georgetown Law Review* 69 (1981); Lane Y. Sunderland, "Liberals, Conservatives, and the Exclusionary Rule," *Journal of Criminal Law and Criminology* 71 (1980); Tinsley E. Yarbrough, "The Flexible Exclusionary Rule and the Crime Rate," *American Journal of Criminal Law* 6 (1978); Ronald J. Bacigal, "Some Observations and Proposals on the Nature of the Fourth Amendment," *George Washington Law Review* 46 (1978).

On recent developments concerning the death penalty and the Eighth Amendment, see Margaret Jane Radin, "Cruel Punishment and Respect for Persons: Super Due Process for Death," *Southern California Law Review* 53 (1980), and Kenneth M. Murchison, "Toward a Perspective on the Death Penalty Cases," *Emory Law Journal* 27 (1978). Also pertinent are Charles L. Black, Jr., *Capital Punishment: The Inevitability of Caprice and Mistake* (1974); Arthur J. Goldberg and Nan M. Dershowitz, "Declaring the Death Penalty Unconstitutional," *Harvard Law Review* 83 (1970); Malcolm E. Wheeler, "Toward a Theory of Limited Punishment: An Examination of the Eighth Amendment," *Stanford Law Review* 24 (1972).

"Symposium on the Law and Politics of Abortion," *Michigan Law Review* 77 (1979), covers recent developments on that controversial subject. Earlier reactions to the abortion question are found in Richard E. Epstein, "Substantive Due Process by Any Other Name: The Abortion Cases," *Supreme Court Review 1973* (1974); John Hart Ely, "The Wages of Crying Wolf: A Comment on Roe v. Wade," *Yale Law Review* 82 (1973); Laurence H. Tribe, "Foreword: Toward a Model of Roles in the Due Process of Life and Law," *Harvard Law Review* 87 (1973).

Two good accounts of the Burger Court's blunting of Warren Court egalitarianism are Richard Y. Funston, "The Double Standard of Constitutional Protection in the Era of the Welfare State," *PSQ* 90 (1975), and Wallace Mendelson, "From Warren to Burger: The Rise and Decline of Substantive Equal Protection,"

APSR 66 (1972). Subsequent equal protection developments are analyzed in Scott H. Bice, "Standards of Judicial Review under the Equal Protection and Due Process Clauses," *Southern California Law Review* 50 (1977); Richard Van Alstyne, "Cracks in 'the New Property,'" *Cornell Law Review* 62 (1977); Tinsley E. Yarbrough, "The Burger Court and Unspecified Rights: On Protecting Fundamental and Not-So-Fundamental 'Rights' or 'Interests' through a Flexible Conception of Equal Protection," *Duke Law Journal* 1977; Edward L. Barrett, "The Rational Basis Standard for Equal Protection Review of Ordinary Legislative Classifications," *Kentucky Law Journal* 68 (1979–80). The use of the due process clause to promote egalitarian goals is examined in Ira C. Lupu, "Untangling the Strands of the Fourteenth Amendment," *Michigan Law Review* 77 (1979), and Richard B. Saphire, "Specifying Due Process Values: Toward a More Responsive Approach to Procedural Protection," *University of Pennsylvania Law Review* 127 (1978).

For general description of free-speech decisions in the Burger era, see Archibald Cox, "Foreword: Freedom of Expression in the Burger Court," *Harvard Law Review* 94 (1980); Thomas I. Emerson, "First Amendment Doctrine and the Burger Court," *California Law Review* 68 (1980); David A. Farber, "Content Regulation and the First Amendment: A Revisionist View," *Georgetown Law Journal* 69 (1981). Commercial speech under First Amendment protection is discussed in Daniel A. Farber, "Commercial Speech and First Amendment Theory," *Northwestern University Law Review* 74 (1979); Thomas H. Jackson and John C. Jeffries, Jr., "Commercial Speech: Economic Due Process and the First Amendment," *Virginia Law Review* 65 (1979); R. H. Coase, "Advertising and Free Speech," *Journal of Legal Studies* 6 (1977). The free-speech rights of corporations are considered in David B. Keto, "The Corporation and the Constitution: Economic Due Process and Corporate Speech," *Yale Law Journal* 90 (1981). The contrasting treatments accorded print and broadcast media are the subject of Lee C. Bollinger, Jr., "Freedom of the Press and Public Access: Toward a Theory of Partial Regulation of the Mass Media," *Michigan Law Review* 75 (1976).

On the law of libel, see "Symposium: Toward a Resolution of the Expanding Conflict between the Press and Privacy Interests," *Iowa Law Review* 64 (1979). Other pertinent studies of the First Amendment include Daniel A. Farber, "Civilizing Public Discourse: An Essay on Professor Bickel, Justice Harlan, and the Enduring Significance of *Cohen v. California,*" *Duke Law Journal* (1980); Steven Shiffrin, "Government Speech," *UCLA Law Review* 27 (1980); David E. Landau, "Public Disclosure of Lobbying: Congress and Associational Privacy after *Buckley v. Valeo,*" *Howard Law Journal* 22 (1979); Harry W. Wellington, "On Freedom of Expression," *Yale Law Journal* 88 (1979). The obscenity problem receives analysis in Frederick Schauer, "Speech and 'Speech'—Obscenity and 'Obscenity': An Exercise in the Interpretation of Constitutional Language," *Georgetown Law Journal* 67 (1979), and Stephen Daniels, "The Supreme Court and Obscenity: An Exercise in Empirical Constitutional Policy-Making," *San Diego Law Review* 17 (1980).

First Amendment establishment and free exercise of religion issues are examined in Leo Pfeffer, "Freedom and/or Separation: The Constitutional Dilemma of the First Amendment," *Minnesota Law Review* 64 (1980); Kenneth F. Ripple, "The Entanglement Test of the Religion Clauses—a Ten Year Assessment," *UCLA Law Review* 27 (1980); Nancy H. Fink, "The Establishment Clause According to the Supreme Court: The Mysterious Eclipse of Free Exercise Values," *Catholic Uni-*

versity Law Review 27 (1978); Gail Merel, "The Protection of Individual Choice: A Consistent Understanding of Religion under the First Amendment," *University of Chicago Law Review* 45 (1978); David W. Louisell, "Does the Constitution Require a Purely Secular Society?" *Catholic University Law Review* 26 (1976). Reapportionment law is reviewed in Bruce Adams, "A Model State Reapportionment Process: The Continuing Quest for 'Fair and Effective Representation,'" *Harvard Journal of Legislation* 14 (1977); Gerhard Casper, "Apportionment and the Right to Vote: Standards of Judicial Scrutiny," *Supreme Court Review 1973* (1974); Robert G. Dixon, Jr., "The Court, the People, and 'One Man, One Vote,'" in Nelson W. Polsby, ed., *Reapportionment in the 1970s* (1971).

XXI. *American Constitutionalism in the 1980s*

Thoughtful analyses of present tendencies in American politics and constitutionalism appear in James L. Sundquist, "The Crisis of Competence in Our National Government," *PSQ* 95 (1980); Samuel P. Huntington, *American Politics: The Promise of Disharmony* (1981); Theodore J. Lowi, *The End of Liberalism: Ideology, Policy, and the Crisis of Public Authority,* rev. ed. (1979); Robert A. Dahl, "On Removing Certain Impediments to Democracy in the United States," *PSQ* 92 (1977); Charles Frankel, "The Moral Environment of the Law," *Minnesota Law Review* 61 (1977); Walter Dean Burnham, "Revitalization and Decay: Looking toward the Third Century of American Electoral Politics," *JP* 38 (1976); Alexander M. Bickel, *The Morality of Consent* (1975). Arthur Selwyn Miller, *Democratic Dictatorship: The Emergent Constitution of Control* (1981), presents a pessimistic view of the future of constitutional liberty, while Morris P. Fiorina, "The Decline of Collective Responsibility in American Politics," *Daedalus* 109 (1980), discusses the weakened condition of political parties. Lawrence B. Joseph, "Democratic Revisionism Revisited," *American Journal of Political Science* 25 (1981), questions the relationship between constitutional democracy and capitalism. David Vogel, "The Public Interest Movement and the American Reform Tradition," *PSQ* 95 (1980–81), explains how attempts to involve citizens in public policy formation lead to more federal regulation.

The role of the judiciary in American government and the nature of constitutional adjudication continue to be problematic and controversial. Two recent interpretations of the role of the Supreme Court are Richard Funston, "The Supreme Court and Critical Elections," *APSR* 69 (1975), arguing that the Court's antimajoritarian potential is significant only during times of electoral realignment, and Jonathan D. Casper, "The Supreme Court and National Policy Making," *APSR* 70 (1976), asserting that the Court has a more consequential policy role than was recognized in Robert Dahl's influential study, "Decision-Making in a Democracy: The Supreme Court as a National Policy-Maker," *Journal of Public Law* 6 (1958). Other worthwhile general studies of the judiciary in the constitutional order are Christopher Wolfe, "A Theory of U.S. Constitutional History," *JP* 43 (1981); Sanford Byron Gabin, *Judicial Review and the Reasonable Double Test* (1980); Charles L. Black Jr., "Toward a Judicial Role for the Twenty-First Century," *Washington Law Review* 52 (1977); Archibald Cox, "The New Dimensions of Constitutional Adjudication," *Washington Law Review* 51 (1976); Wallace Mendelson, "Separation, Politics, and Judicial Activism," *Indiana Law Journal* 52 (1977); David Adamany, "Legitimacy, Realigning Elections, and the Supreme Court," *Wisconsin Law Review* (1973).

Less detached in argument is the criticism of judicial activism in Raoul Berger, *Government by Judiciary: The Transformation of the Fourteenth Amendment* (1977); Louis Lusky, *By What Right? A Commentary on the Supreme Court's Power to Revise the Constitution* (1975); Nathan Glazer, "Toward an Imperial Judiciary?" *Public Interest* no. 41 (1975); William H. Rehnquist, "The Notion of a Living Constitution," *Texas Law Review* 54 (1976); Rehnquist, "The Adversary Society," *University of Miami Law Review* 33 (1978). Judicial activism is vigorously defended by four federal judges in Frank M. Johnson, Jr., "In Defense of Judicial Activism," *Emory Law Journal* 28 (1980); James L. Oakes, "The Proper Role of the Federal Courts in Enforcing the Bill of Rights," *New York University Law Review* 54 (1979); David L. Bazelon, "Civil Liberties—Protecting Old Values in the New Century," *New York University Law Review* 51 (1976); Marvin E. Frankel, "From Private Fights toward Public Justice," *New York University Law Review* 51 (1976).

At a more sophisticated jurisprudential level several theoretical defenses of judicial activism have appeared, among them Abram Chayes, "The Role of the Judge in Public Law Litigation," *Harvard Law Review* 89 (1976); Laurence H. Tribe, "Structural Due Process," *Harvard Civil Rights–Civil Liberties Law Review* 10 (1975); Owen M. Fiss, "Foreword: The Forms of Justice," *Harvard Law Review* 93 (1979). More restrained is the conception of judicial power advanced in John Hart Ely, *A Theory of Judicial Review* (1980); Ely, "Foreword: On Discovering Fundamental Values," *Harvard Law Review* 92 (1978); Jesse H. Choper, *The Supreme Court and the Political Branches: Judicial Review in the National Political Process: A Functional Reconsideration of the Role of the Supreme Court* (1980). See also the discussions of constitutional adjudication in Stephen R. Munzer and James W. Nickel, "Does the Constitution Mean What It Always Meant?" *Columbia Law Review* 77 (1977); Walter F. Murphy, "An Ordering of Constitutional Values," *Southern California Law Review* 53 (1980); Murphy, "The Art of Constitutional Interpretation," in M. Judd Harmon, ed., *Essays on the Constitution of the United States* (1978); Thomas C. Grey, "Do We Have an Unwritten Constitution?" *Stanford Law Review* 27 (1975); Kent Greenawalt, "The Enduring Significance of Neutral Principles," *Columbia Law Review* 78 (1978); Gary J. Jacobsohn, "Constitutional Adjudication and Judicial Statesmanship: Principle, Fact, and Doctrine," *Emory Law Journal* 23 (1974). Alexander Bickel, one of the most important constitutional commentators of the post–New Deal era, is the subject of two studies which throw light on the nature and tendency of recent judicial power: Robert K. Faulkner, "Bickel's Constitution: The Problem of Moderate Liberalism," *APSR* 72 (1978); Edward A. Purcell, Jr., "Alexander M. Bickel and the Post-Realist Constitution," *Harvard Civil Rights–Civil Liberties Law Review* 11 (1976).

Karen Orren, "Standing to Sue: Interest Group Conflict in the Federal Courts," *APSR* 70 (1976), argues that excessive judicial political involvement resulting from the relaxation of rules governing access to the courts threatens the rule of law. Of related interest is Louis Henkin, "Is There a 'Political Question' Doctrine?" *Yale Law Journal* 85 (1976). Wade H. McCree, Jr., "Bureaucratic Justice: An Early Warning," *University of Pennsylvania Law Review* 129 (1981), criticizes the tendency toward bureaucratization in the judicial system, while Jethro K. Lieberman, *The Litigious Society* (1981), and Richard Neely, *How Courts Govern America* (1981), offer an explanation and justification for the recent expansion of the judicial policy-making role. Tinsley E. Yarbrough, *Judge Frank Johnson and Human Rights in Alabama* (1981), recounts the career of an activist judge.

The balance between state and federal power has regained some of its former importance as criticism of centralized federal bureaucracy has increased. Good analyses of federalism are found in Leon D. Epstein, "The Old States in a New System," in Anthony King, ed., *The New American Political System* (1978); Symposium, "The State of American Federalism: 1979," *Publius* 10 (1980); Vincent Ostrum, "The Contemporary Debate over Centralization and Decentralization," *Publius* 6 (1976); George D. Brown, "Beyond the New Federalism—Revenue Sharing in Perspective," *Harvard Journal of Legislation* 15 (1977); Daniel J. Elazar, "The New Federalism: Can the States Be Trusted?" *Public Interest* no. 35 (1974); Michael D. Reagan, *The New Federalism* (1972). Mary Cornelia Porter, "State Supreme Courts and the Legacy of the Warren Court: Some Old Inquiries for a New Situation," *Publius* 8 (1978), describes increased state court activism.

The states have also been conspicuous in proposals for an Article V convention to revise the Constitution. See the discussion of this issue in Wilbur Edel, *A Constitutional Convention: Threat or Challenge?* (1981); Walter E. Dellinger, "The Recurring Question of the 'Limited' Constitutional Convention," *Yale Law Journal* 88 (1979); William W. Van Alstyne, "The Limited Constitutional Convention—the Recurring Answer," *Duke Law Journal* 1979; P. Brannan *et al.*, "Critical Details: Amending the United States Constitution," *Harvard Journal of Legislation* 16 (1979); Paul Bator *et al.*, *A Constitutional Convention: How Well Would It Work?* (1979); Charles L. Black, Jr., "Amending the Constitution: A Letter to a Congressman," *Yale Law Journal* 82 (1972); Philip L. Martin, "The Application Clause of Article V," *PSQ* 85 (1970); Paul G. Kauper, ed., *The Article V Convention Process: A Symposium* (1971), reprinted from *Michigan Law Review* 66 (1968); Lester B. Orfield, *The Amending of the Federal Constitution* (1942). Historical and political background is provided in Kermit L. Hall *et al.*, eds., *The Constitutional Convention as an Amending Device* (1981). Related to apprehension about a "runaway" constitutional convention is criticism of instruments of direct democracy, as in Derrick A. Bell, Jr., "The Referendum: Democracy's Barrier to Racial Equity," *Washington Law Review* 54 (1978); David James Jordan, "Constitutional Constraints in Initiative and Referendum," *Vanderbilt Law Review* 32 (1979); Louis J. Sirico, Jr., "The Constitutionality of the Initiative and Referendum," *Iowa Law Review* 65 (1980).

On the District of Columbia representation amendment, see Clement E. Vose, "When District of Columbia Representation Collides with the Constitutional Amendment Institution," *Publius* 9 (1979); Peter Raven-Hansen, "Congressional Representation for the District of Columbia: A Constitutional Analysis," *Harvard Journal on Legislation* 12 (1975). Constitutional problems concerning the equal rights amendment are discussed in Ruth Bader Ginsburg, "Ratification of the Equal Rights Amendment: A Question of Time," *Texas Law Review* 57 (1979); Grover Rees III, "Throwing Away the Key: The Unconstitutionality of the Equal Rights Amendment," *Texas Law Review* 58 (1980); Samuel S. Freedman and Pamela J. Naughton, *ERA: May a State Change Its Vote?* (1978); A. Diane Baker, "ERA: The Effect of Extending the Time for Ratification on Attempts to Rescind

Prior Ratifications," *Emory Law Journal* 28 (1979). For analysis of the equal rights amendment and constitutional law on women's rights, see O. John Rogge, "Equal Rights for Women," *Howard Law Journal* 21 (1977); Ruth Bader Ginsburg, "Sex Equality and the Constitution," *Texas Law Review* 52 (1978); "Equal Rights for Women: A Symposium on the Proposed Constitutional Amendment," *Harvard Civil Rights–Civil Liberties Law Review* 6 (1971); Janet K. Boles, *The Politics of the Equal Rights Amendment: Conflict and the Decision Process* (1979).

The constitutional amendment dealing with presidential succession is treated in John D. Feerick, *The Twenty-fifth Amendment: Its Complete History and Earliest Application* (1976). The possibility of "new-modeling" the Constitution is considered in Rexford G. Tugwell, *The Emerging Constitution* (1974), and Leland D. Baldwin, *Reframing the Constitution: An Imperative for Modern America* (1972).

Table of Cases

Index

1890	MORRISON R. WAITE ★ 1874-1888	SAMUEL BLATCHFORD 1882-1893			WILLIAM B. WOO... 1880-1887
			HORACE GRAY 1881-1902		LUCIUS Q. C. LAM... 1888-1893
					HOWELL E. JACKS... 1893-1895
1900	MELVILLE W. FULLER ★ 1888-1910	EDWARD D. WHITE 1894-1910			RUFUS W. PECKHA... 1895-1909
1910	EDWARD D. WHITE ★ 1910-1921		OLIVER WENDELL HOLMES 1902-1932		HORACE H. LURTO... 1909-1914
1920		WILLIS VAN DEVANTER 1910-1937			JAMES C. McREYNOLDS 1914-1941
	WILLIAM H. TAFT ★ 1921-1930				
1930	CHARLES E. HUGHES ★ 1930-1941		BENJAMIN N. CARDOZO 1932-1938		
1940	HARLAN F. STONE ★ 1941-1946				JAMES F. BYRNES 1941-1942
			FELIX FRANKFURTER 1939-1962		WILEY B. RUTLEDG... 1943-1949
1950	FRED M. VINSON ★ 1946-1953	HUGO L. BLACK 1937-1971			SHERMAN MINTO... 1949-1956
1960	EARL WARREN ★ 1953-1969				WILLIAM J. BRENNAN, JR. 1956-
			ARTHUR J. GOLDBERG 1962-1965		
			ABE FORTAS 1965-1969		
1970	WARREN E. BURGER ★ 1969-		HARRY A. BLACKMUN 1970-		
		LEWIS F. POWELL, JR. 1972-			
1980					